THE BIBLICAL CANONS

BIBLIOTHECA EPHEMERIDUM THEOLOGICARUM LOVANIENSIUM

CLXIII

THE BIBLICAL CANONS

EDITED BY

J.-M. AUWERS & H.J. DE JONGE

LEUVEN
UNIVERSITY PRESS

UITGEVERIJ PEETERS
LEUVEN

2003

ISBN 90 5867 309 x (Leuven University Press)
D/2003/1869/35
ISBN 90-429-1154-9 (Peeters Leuven)
ISBN 2-87723-651-x (Peeters France)
D/2002/0602/75

Leuven University Press / Presses Universitaires de Louvain
Universitaire Pers Leuven
Blijde-Inkomststraat 5, B-3000 Leuven (Belgium)

© 2003 – Peeters, Bondgenotenlaan 153, B-3000 Leuven (Belgium)

PREFACE

These volumes contain papers dealing with "the biblical canons", the topic of the fiftieth Colloquium Biblicum Lovaniense (Journées Bibliques de Louvain / Bijbelse Studiedagen) which took place from July 25 to 27, 2001. These papers have all been read at the colloquium; they have all been extensively revised and annotated for publication.

The fiftieth Colloquium Biblicum seemed to be an ideal occasion to bring together students of both the Old and the New Testament (as used to be the case from 1949, the first meeting, to 1954 and again in 1974). Consequently, the jubilee called for a theme that concerned both the Old and the New Testament. Hence the choice of the theme "the biblical canons". The plural "canons" intends to take account of the different shapes the Bible has taken in different traditions, different periods and different regions.

The presidential addresses, by the two presidents of the colloquium, Jean-Marie Auwers and Henk Jan de Jonge, as well as CBL Secretary Frans Neirynck's jubilee address, were given in plenary sessions[1]. The same applies to the opening lecture by Thomas Söding. All other main papers were given in two series of parallel sessions, one centering around the Old Testament, the other around the New. The programme was so scheduled as to allow participants to switch from one series to the other and *vice versa*. Short papers were also read in parallel sessions. Six seminars, two in English, two in German, one in French and one in Dutch, met each twice on successive days. All main papers, a number of short papers, and the working papers submitted to the seminars have been edited and included in these volumes.

The papers deal, *inter alia*, with the history of (parts of) the biblical canon, the relevance of the canon for the exegesis of particular (passages of) books included in the Bible, and the consequences of reading the Bible as canon. Historical, hermeneutical and theological aspects of the biblical canons competed for the participants' attention.

During this fiftieth meeting of the Colloquium Biblicum Lovaniense, Frans Neirynck resigned his office of Secretary to the standing CBL committee. Since 1979 he was the driving force of the Colloquium. He

---

1. These three addresses were published separately in *Colloquium Biblicum Lovaniense 1-50. Jubilee Session, July 25, 2001. The Biblical Canons*, Leuven: Katholieke Universiteit Leuven, Faculteit Godgeleerdheid, 2001, 39 p. They have been revised for inclusion in the present volumes.

assisted at the preparation of the 30th up to the 50th meeting (1979-2001)[2]. The participants in these meetings, and especially the presidents, are grateful to him for his efforts to make the Leuven Colloquium an annual success. At this occasion the CBL statutes were revised and Joseph Verheyden was appointed as Secretary of the Colloquium.

The 2001 colloquium was sponsored by the National Fund for Scientific Research (FWO/FNRS, Brussels), the Katholieke Universiteit Leuven and the Université Catholique de Louvain. The colloquium met in the Maria-Theresia College. Lodging was provided in the adjacent Paus Adrianus VI College. Thanks are due to its president, L. Leijssen, and his staff for their extraordinary hospitality. Finally, the signatories of this preface wish to thank Joseph Verheyden for his aid in the preparation of these volumes.

Jean-Marie AUWERS
Henk Jan DE JONGE

---

2. See *Colloquium Biblicum Lovaniense. Journées Bibliques de Louvain/Bijbelse Studiedagen te Leuven, 1-50, 1949-2001*. Edited by F. NEIRYNCK (SNTA, 19), Leuven, University Press – Peeters, 2001, 116 p. 000.

CONTENTS

OLD TESTAMENT

MAIN PAPERS

OFFERED PAPERS

INDEXES

INTRODUCTION

I. Les canons de l'Ancien Testament

La question du canon du Premier Testament présente des aspects complexes, historiques, méthodologiques et herméneutiques, que les contributions rassemblées dans ce volume envisagent tour à tour. Dans le texte liminaire, Jean-Marie Auwers (Louvain-la-Neuve) montre, à partir du cas particulier du Psautier, les effets de sens que produit une exégèse qui prend au sérieux le canon des Écritures, en envisageant successivement la forme massorétique du livre des psaumes, le canon hébreu des Écritures, et la Bible judéo-chrétienne prise comme un tout. On voit ici comment la prise en compte de la forme canonique d'un écrit biblique et l'inscription de celui-ci dans un canon induisent des lectures particulières et concernent donc l'exégèse.

Les quatre textes suivants abordent la question de la clôture de l'Ancien Testament. Arie van der Kooij (Leyde) s'intéresse plus particulièrement à la phase du processus de canonisation des livres hébreux qui se situe vers 150 av. J.-C. Cette étape apparaît comme décisive et s'éclaire à la lumière du projet de restauration religieuse des Hasmonéens visant à assurer la publicité du patrimoine littéraire ancestral conservé dans les archives du Temple. On peut déjà parler d'un «canon» de structure tripartite à cette époque, au sens d'une collection non encore close d'écrits reconnus comme faisant autorité. Van der Kooij ouvre ici une voie nouvelle en s'intéressant aux raisons fonctionnelles du processus qui a abouti à la fixation du canon.

Johan Lust (Leuven) fait le point sur la question du prétendu «canon alexandrin» avant d'envisager la reconstitution d'un canon prémassorétique, plus large que le canon dit «palestinien», sur base de la Septante et des données qumrâniennes. Les copies hébraïques sélectionnées en vue de la traduction grecque étaient déjà considérées comme faisant autorité, même si, pour certains livres, leur contenu diffère du texte massorétique qui sera ultérieurement reconnu comme canonique. Dans le cas particulier du livre d'Ézéchiel, le texte court de la Septante conservé par le papyrus 967 (IIIe s. ap. J.-C.) offre un bel exemple d'un texte hébreu «canonique» plus ancien que le TM; il présente des accents théologiques propres, notamment des tendances apocalyptiques et eschatologiques qui sont estompées dans la recension longue du TM.

Eugene Ulrich (Notre Dame, IN) réserve le mot «canon» pour désigner la liste définitive des livres qui sont reconnus comme inspirés et normatifs par une confession religieuse, indépendamment de la forme textuelle spécifique de ces livres. Les documents découverts dans le désert de Juda n'attestent pas encore l'existence d'un «canon» entendu en ce sens précis. Simplement, dans la bibliothèque de Qumrân, certains livres étaient reconnus comme contenant la parole de Dieu et, à ce titre, comme faisant autorité. Plusieurs critères permettent de l'affirmer (nombre de copies, formules d'introduction, mode de citation, existence de commentaires et de traductions de ces livres), mais le contenu de la collection que la communauté reconnaissait comme Écriture ne peut être déterminé avec précision. Par ailleurs, les rouleaux bibliques retrouvés à Qumrân ne représentent pas une forme textuelle des livres bibliques propre à la secte, mais reflètent l'état des Écritures telles que le judaïsme palestinien en général les recevait à la fin de la période du Second Temple.

Enfin, Gilles Dorival (Université de Provence, Aix – Marseille) dégage la contribution que les Pères de l'Église apportent à l'histoire du canon juif, et, en particulier, aux questions suivantes: la division (bipartite, tripartite ou quadripartite) du canon des Hébreux, le nombre des livres canoniques (de vingt-deux à quarante-quatre), le déclassement des livres prophétiques (Ruth, Lamentations et Daniel) parmi les Écrits, la clôture des Écrits, et les livres deutérocanoniques. À ce propos, deux hypothèses sont émises: les deutérocanoniques sont peut-être ce que la tradition rabbinique appelle les «livres extérieurs» (ספרים חיצונים), appellation qui aurait été étendue a posteriori aux livres des hérétiques chrétiens; selon la deuxième hypothèse, les deutérocanoniques chrétiens seraient un groupe de livres juifs qui avaient en commun d'être lus, mais non étudiés; Esther aurait fait partie de cette catégorie de livres avant de passer de cette catégorie à celle des Ketûbîm, tandis que le Siracide aurait effectué le mouvement inverse.

Les deux contributions suivantes cherchent à faire se rencontrer les questions historiques et les questions herméneutiques, et font voir l'intérêt que présente la confrontation des différentes formes canoniques d'un même livre biblique, en même temps qu'une lecture croisée des textes bibliques dans l'enceinte canonique. Erich Zenger (Münster) montre l'incidence qu'ont eue sur la lecture des livres du premier Testament les questions de nomenclature, de délimitation, d'ordonnancement et de structuration du canon. Ensuite, il fait voir quelles sont les implications herméneutiques de la prise en compte du canon, en abordant «le Psautier dans l'horizon de la Torah et de la prophétie». La rédaction finale du

Psautier (en cinq livres) peut être qualifiée de «mosaïcisante» dans la mesure où elle réfère le recueil à la Torah de Moïse que, d'emblée, elle invite à méditer (Ps 1,2). Mais, d'un autre côté, une perspective prophétique y est également bien marquée, notamment à travers l'espérance messianique que la mise en évidence du personnage de David diffuse dans les trois premiers livres des psaumes, et à travers la forte charge eschatologique du Hallel final.

Johann Cook (Stellenbosch) envisage le problème de la diversité textuelle et de l'uniformité canonique à la fois au niveau des lexèmes et des unités littéraires individuelles et au niveau global de l'ensemble d'un livre. Ainsi, la traduction grecque des Proverbes prend des libertés tant à l'égard des sentences isolées qu'à l'égard de l'organisation même du livre; le profil de la collection s'en trouve considérablement modifié. Une exégèse attentive aux différences entre le TM et la LXX permet de mieux comprendre le propos du traducteur. D'autre part, l'examen des textes bibliques attestés à Qumrân (par exemple, Gn 1,9 en 4QGen[h]; Jer 50 [= 43 LXX] en 4QJer[b]) confirme l'existence de formes textuelles prémassorétiques. Le phénomène de la diversité textuelle ne doit pas pour autant être majoré (la *Vorlage* de la Septante des Proverbes correspond largement au TM), et la part de créativité qui se manifeste dans le processus d'uniformisation ne peut être niée. Cela dit, la diversité textuelle n'affecte pas la canonicité des livres, puisque ni les traducteurs grecs ni les membres de la communauté de Qumrân ne semblent avoir été gênés par les formes textuelles différentes.

De son côté, Pierre-Maurice Bogaert (Maredsous – Louvain-la-Neuve) dévoile la face cachée du processus canonique, en mettant en lumière ses aspects matériels, non moins contraignants que les critères théologiques. Il étudie les implications matérielles des démarches successives et progressives qui ont abouti à la fixation du canon biblique dans les Églises chrétiennes. Avant que la Bible puisse être copiée en un seul codex, le canon n'avait pas eu vraiment d'existence palpable, et les listes jouaient un rôle décisif. Parmi les plus anciennes listes dans le monde latin, certaines avaient un but avant tout utilitaire. Ainsi, la Stichométrie de Mommsen, datable de 359, est une liste à l'usage des *scriptoria*, destinée à déterminer le prix de la copie des livres bibliques en fonction de leur longueur. Les ressemblances et les différences entre le *Vaticanus* et le «canon» d'Athanase (*Lettre Festale* 39) s'expliquent en fonction de la mesure du texte copié, qui suppose un *scriptorium* aguerri. Comme le *Vaticanus*, la Stichométrie de Mommsen se trouve au carrefour de plusieurs facteurs: le *scriptorium* (avec ses copistes) et la librairie (avec ses clients) d'abord, une liste agréée de livres ensuite, qui suppose que l'on s'entende sur les titres et leur contenu, enfin des *codices* ou même des rouleaux qui ont servi comme modèles immédiats ou lointains et dont l'homogénéité est a priori incertaine ou improbable. Chez les Latins, un consensus sur le canon est acquis autour de 400, sans que pour autant ait pu être évité tout risque d'équivoque sur le contenu des livres. C'est ainsi que Baruch a disparu de la plupart des bibles latines pendant cinq siècles, de 700 (*Amiatinus*) à 1200 environ (*Biblia Parisiensia*). Quant aux divergences entre les listes des livres canoniques, elles peuvent s'expliquer par le fait que les Églises chrétiennes ont reçu pour leur Ancien Testament les livres que les communautés juives voisines tenaient pour Écriture et que la liste des Ketûbîm pouvait varier de l'une à l'autre, non seulement pour des raisons de principe, mais aussi pour des raisons pratiques de possession effective de tous les livres reconnus.

Les deux contributions suivantes portent spécifiquement sur l'exégèse canonique initiée par Brevard S. Childs. Georg Steins (Osnabrück) présente et commente quatorze thèses, dont la première est que le caractère canonique d'un texte biblique n'est pas un phénomène négligeable ou un aspect secondaire, mais une qualité intrinsèque qui doit guider l'exégèse dès le début. Les thèses 2 à 9 portent sur le canon biblique comme texte, c.-à-d. comme littérature, et sur certaines prémisses de l'exégèse moderne qui, depuis Spinoza, pose l'univocité du sens du texte et la non-pertinence d'un contexte comme celui du canon. Au contraire, note G. Steins, les théories littéraires post-modernes insistent sur la pluralité du sens et sur l'importance du contexte dans lequel le lecteur fait activement œuvre de compréhension. Quant aux cinq dernières thèses, elles se proposent de définir la place de l'exégèse canonique au sein des méthodes exégétiques, qui ont pour but à la fois de reconstituer les connaissances encyclopédiques qui sont une condition préalable à la compréhension des textes, mais aussi d'ouvrir les potentialités de signification d'un écrit biblique dans le contexte du canon. La fixation normative de cette signification incombe aux communautés croyantes, non à l'exégèse elle-même. On voit ici que la lecture canonique de la Bible n'est ni un aspect particulier de l'exégèse historico-critique, ni une alternative.

John Barton (Oxford) offre une description critique du «canonical approach», tel que l'entend Childs, et en identifie les racines. Barton montre l'équivoque de la notion de «forme finale» chez Childs (pour désigner, dans une perspective barthienne, la communication de la parole divine), l'ambiguïté du terme «canon» et le rapport problématique de l'approche canonique vis-à-vis des diverses méthodes critiques d'exégèse (par rapport auxquelles elle se présente comme asymétrique,

tout en prétendant poser la seule question pertinente). L'approche canonique opère un retour à l'exégèse pré-critique, non pas au sens où elle
aurait recours à l'allégorie ou à d'autres méthodes patristiques ou médié-
vales, mais en ce sens que, comme l'exégèse des Pères et celle des Réformateurs, elle s'intéresse à la Bible en tant que corpus achevé et recherche avant tout l'édification spirituelle des lecteurs. À ce titre, elle
ressortit davantage à la théologie systématique qu'à l'exégèse; c'est une
théorie relative à la manière d'utiliser la Bible pour approfondir la foi.

Les communications brèves abordent des aspects particuliers de la
problématique du canon de l'Ancien Testament: l'œuvre deutéronomiste
comme canon avant la lettre (J. Vermeylen, Bruxelles), l'histoire de
Samson et la finale du livre des Juges dans une perspective d'exégèse
canonique (M. Millard, Dortmund), la Septante du livre de Jérémie
et son Épître (E. Dafni, Athènes – Göttingen), les titres des Psaumes
(S. Gillmayr-Bucher, Erfurt), le statut canonique du Siracide (V. Koperski, Miami; J. Leemans, Leuven), la question du salut dans la perspective du canon (B. Gosse, Antony), le canon chrétien comme «pa-
limpseste» (I. Spangenberg, Pretoria), et la structure symétrique de la
Bible chrétienne (W. Vogels, Ottawa).

Ce volume fait le point sur les questions débattues. La théorie classique envisageait le canon rabbinique comme le produit d'un développement historique en trois étapes: un premier corpus, la Torah, aurait été
fixé à l'époque d'Esdras, soit vers 450 ou vers 400; le corpus des Prophètes (entendus au sens large) aurait été fixé peu avant la révolte des
Maccabées; enfin, la clôture des Écrits, concomitante de celle de l'ensemble du canon de la Bible hébraïque, serait le résultat des décisions du
soi-disant «Concile de Jamnia» qui est à situer entre 90 et 105 ap. J.-C.
La théorie classique expliquait également la différence de contenu entre
la Bible des Massorètes et la Bible grecque (soit la présence, dans celle-
ci, de ce que les catholiques appellent les Deutérocanoniques) par l'op-
position entre un canon palestinien et un canon alexandrin, plus large[1].
Cette théorie fait aujourd'hui l'objet de remises en cause fondamentales.
D. Barthélemy a montré que les décisions prises par les rabbins réunis à
Jamnia ne portaient que sur la détermination de certaines incertitudes[2].
Ainsi, cette assemblée s'est prononcée en faveur du statut canonique du

---

1. H.E. RYLE, *The Canon of the Old Testament. An Essay on the Gradual Growth and Formation of the Hebrew Canon of Scripture*, London, 1892.
2. D. BARTHÉLEMY, *L'état de la Bible juive depuis le début de notre ère jusqu'à la deuxième révolte contre Rome (131-135)*, in J.-D. KAESTLI & O. WERMELINGER (eds.), *Le canon de l'Ancien Testament. Sa formation et son histoire* (Le Monde de la Bible), Genève, 1984, pp. 9-45; = ID., *Découvrir l'Écriture* (LD), Paris, 2000, pp. 19-55.

Cantique et de Qohèlèt, et a rejeté d'autres livres comme le Siracide. D'autre part, la théorie d'un canon alexandrin est aujourd'hui abandonnée. Dans ce volume, J. Lust indique les principales raisons de ce revirement: tout d'abord, cette hypothèse suppose qu'Alexandrie soit devenue le centre religieux référentiel de la Diaspora juive, ce qui est contredit par les sources historiques, y compris alexandrines; ensuite, le nombre des livres cités comme Écriture par les auteurs du Nouveau Testament et par les Pères apostoliques ne correspond ni au canon rabbinique ni au soi-disant canon alexandrin, mais les excède l'un et l'autre; enfin, l'hypothèse de l'origine gréco-égyptienne des Deutérocanoniques a dû être abandonnée dès lors qu'il s'est avéré que certains de ces livres avaient été écrits originellement en hébreu et que la plupart étaient reçus au moins dans une frange du judaïsme palestinien.

Aucune nouvelle théorie n'a pour autant réussi à s'imposer. En fait, depuis une vingtaine d'années, plusieurs hypothèses se font concurrence: selon la première, le processus de canonisation de la Bible hébraïque (au moins pour la Torah et les Prophètes) était déjà bien avancé à l'époque perse[3]; selon la deuxième théorie, la collection des livres de la Bible hébraïque, telle que nous la connaissons, était établie dès 150 av. J.-C.[4]; selon la dernière hypothèse, le judaïsme ancien n'a pas fixé la liste définitive de ses Écritures avant le IIe s. ap. J.-C.[5]. À vrai dire, l'opposition entre ces diverses hypothèses est plus formelle que réelle, dans la mesure où, depuis que B. Childs et surtout J.A. Sanders ont pris l'initiative d'élargir l'emploi du mot «canon», le sens du substantif et de l'adjectif correspondant sont devenus flous. Il est donc désormais de-

---

3. J. BLENKINSOPP, *Prophecy and Canon: A Contribution to the Study of the Jewish Origins*, Notre Dame, IN, 1977; O.H. STECK, *Der Abschluss der Prophetie im Alten Testament. Ein Versuch zur Frage der Vorgeschichte des Kanons* (Biblisch-theologische Studien, 17), Neukirchen, 1991; S. DEMPSTER, *An "Extraordinary Fact": Torah and Temple and the Contours of the Hebrew Canon*, in *Tyndale Bulletin* 48 (1997) 23-56 et 191-218; S.B. CHAPMAN, *The Law and the Prophets. A Study in Old Testament Canon Formation* (FAT, 27), Tübingen, 2000.

4. R. BECKWITH, *The Old Testament Canon of the New Testament Church and Its Background in Early Judaism*, Grand Rapids, MI, 1985; ID., *Formation of the Hebrew Bible*, in A.J. MULDER (ed.), *Mikra*, Assen – Maastricht – Philadelphia, PA, 1988, pp. 39-86; S.Z. LEIMAN, *The Canonization of Hebrew Scripture: The Talmudic and Midrashic Evidence*, Hamden, CT, 1976; A. VAN DER KOOIJ, *The Canonization of Ancient Books Kept in the Temple of Jerusalem*, in ID. & K. VAN DER TOORN (eds.), *Canonization and Decanonization* (Studies in the History of Religions, 82), Leiden, 1998, pp. 17-40.

5. E. ULRICH, *The Canonical Process, Textual Criticism, and Latter Stages in the Composition of the Bible*, in M. FISHBANE & E. TOV (eds.), *"Sha'arei Talmon": Studies in the Bible, Qumran, and the Ancient Near East Presented to S. Talmon*, Winona Lake, IN, 1992, pp. 267-291; = ID., *The Dead Sea Scrolls and the Origins of the Bible*, Grand Rapids, MI, 1999, pp. 51-78; M. PERANI, *Il processo di canonizzazione della Bibbia ebraica. Nuove prospettive metodologiche*, in *RivBib* 48 (2000) 385-400.

venu indispensable d'indiquer en quel sens – strict ou élargi – on entend
le mot et ses dérivés: selon l'acception dans laquelle on prend le substantif, on refusera de parler d'un canon des Écritures à Qumrân (avec
E. Ulrich) ou on parlera d'un canon *de facto*, au sens d'une liste non encore close d'écrits reconnus comme faisant autorité (avec A. van der
Kooij[6]). Pour le fond, chacune des hypothèses qui viennent d'être évoquées est lourde d'implications dogmatiques. Ainsi, si on situe la clôture
du canon hébreu à la fin du Ier s. ap. J.-C. ou au début du siècle suivant,
soit à l'époque où les chrétiens commençaient à lire comme saints les
évangiles et les écrits apostoliques, on en vient à se demander, avec des
auteurs comme S.W. Baron, J. Bloch et D. Barthélemy[7], si un des motifs
de la volonté de clore définitivement le canon ne fut pas d'éviter que
certains juifs ne fussent eux aussi tentés de traiter comme saintes ces
nouvelles Écritures. En d'autre termes, la reconstitution de la genèse du
canon hébreu est certes un travail d'érudition, mais elle va de pair avec
la production d'une certaine image du judaïsme ancien.

La division tripartite est-elle attestée dans la documentation qumrânienne? La réponse à cette question dépend de la manière dont on re-
constitue et dont on interprète un passage de 4QMMT, et E. Ulrich fait
voir que le débat est loin d'être clos. Comme le montre A. van der
Kooij, le Prologue du Siracide, qui distingue «la Loi, les prophètes et les
autres livres de nos Pères» constitue le noyau dur de l'hypothèse d'un
développement du canon de l'Ancien Testament en trois étapes. Mais,
d'un autre côté, une série de témoignages patristiques convergents, rassemblés par G. Dorival, donne à penser que la tripartition du canon hébreu est apparue peu de temps avant Jérôme et qu'elle était encore sujette à discussion à son époque. Comme on le voit, le débat reste ouvert.

Pour E. Ulrich, «c'est le livre qui est canonique, et non la forme textuelle spécifique du livre»[8]. Le concept de «forme canonique», forgé
analogiquement, peut malgré tout se révéler opératoire, dès lors que les
découvertes archéologiques nous mettent en présence d'états textuels
qui n'ont été avalisés par aucune confession religieuse soucieuse de se
donner un canon des Écritures, et dès lors que la méthode historico-critique aboutit à la reconstitution de formes textuelles hypothétiques. L'ad-

---

6. Dans le même sens: P.R. Davies, *Scribes and Schools. The Canonization of the Hebrew Scriptures*, Louisville, KE, 1998, pp. 71-73.

7. Cf. Barthélemy, *L'état de la Bible juive* (n. 2), pp. 30-34, qui renvoie à S.W. Baron, *A Social and Religious History of the Jews*, t. 2, New York, ²1952, pp. 144-145 et J. Bloch, *Outside Books*, in S.Z. Leiman (ed.), *The Canon and Masorah of the Hebrew Bible*, New York, 1974, p. 205.

8. E. Ulrich, *Qumran and the Canon of the Old Testament*, ci-dessous, p. 59.

jectif «canonique» sert à distinguer, par exemple, le Psautier massorétique (canonique) et le grand rouleau des psaumes de grotte 11 de
Qumrân (non canonique), ou le Pentateuque et les textes-sources que
postule la théorie documentaire, ou encore les évangiles canoniques et la
Quelle. Le fait que le décret *De canonicis Scripturis* (1546) déclare canoniques les livres de la Bible *prout in Ecclesia catholica legi
consueverunt et in veteri vulgata latina editione habentur*[9] montre que
les Pères du Concile de Trente avaient en vue des formes textuelles traditionnelles dans l'Église catholique: ils ont déclaré canoniques le livre
de Jérémie et celui de Baruch dans une forme qui inclut respectivement
les Lamentations et la Lettre de Jérémie, ce qui explique que, à la différence, par exemple, du concile de Laodicée et du «canon» d'Athanase[10],
le Décret de 1546 ne mentionne pas explicitement ces derniers livres. Ils
ont déclaré canoniques les livres d'Esdras dans une forme qui correspond au deuxième Esdras du grec (Εσδρας Β′) et non au premier, bien
qu'il lui soit largement parallèle (Εσδρας Α′ = III Esdras)[11]. Quand les
Pères du Concile de Trente déclarent canonique le livre de Daniel, ils
désignent le livre avec ses suppléments, puisque ceux-ci figurent dans la
Vulgate.

La forme canonique d'un livre biblique doit-elle nécessairement être
unique? Il ne semble pas. L'histoire nous apprend que, pour certains livres, plusieurs formes ont été reçues dans l'Église. Ainsi, avant que la
version hiéronymienne ne s'impose en Occident, circulait une «forme
longue» du livre de Tobie, attestée par la *Vetus Latina* et déjà citée par
Cyprien, tandis qu'en Orient circulait un «texte court», massivement représenté par les manuscrits grecs[12]. Il ne serait pas facile, au regard de la

9. Pour le commentaire, voir E. MANGENOT, Art. *Canon des livres saints*, in *DTC* 2
(1923), cc. 1550-1605, spéc. 1593-1604; P.G. DUNCKER, *De singulis S. Scripturae libris
controversis in Concilio Tridentino*, in *Miscellanea Biblica et Orientalia A. Miller...
oblata* (Studia Anselmiana, 27-28), Rome, 1951, pp. 66-93; ID., *The Canon of the Old
Testament at the Council of Trent*, in *CBQ* 15 (1953) 277-299. Quoi qu'ait pu affirmer
É. REUSS, *Histoire du canon des Saintes Écritures dans l'Église chrétienne*, Strasbourg,
1863², pp. 296-299, la référence à la Vulgate, dans le décret du Concile, ne vise pas une
langue, mais un contenu; cf. E. MANGENOT, Art. *Vulgate*, in *DB* 5 (1912), cc. 2456-2500,
spéc. 2484-2490.

10. Cf. P.P. JOANNOU (ed.), *Discipline générale antique (IVᵉ-IXᵉ siècles)*, t. 1/2 *Les canons des Synodes particuliers*, Grottaferrata (Rome), 1962, p. 155, l. 2-3 (Canon 59 du
Concile de Laodicée); t. 2 *Les canons des Pères grecs*, Grottaferrata (Rome), 1963, p. 73,
l. 26 (Lettre Festale 39 d'Athanase, datée de 391).

11. Cf. P.-M. BOGAERT, *Les livres d'Esdras et leur numérotation dans l'histoire du
canon de la Bible latine*, in *RBén* 110 (2000) 5-26.

12. Le modèle grec du texte long est fourni par le *Sinaiticus* (= 𝕲¹). L'histoire des formes textuelles anciennes du livre de Tobie a été étudiée par R. HANHART, *Text und
Textgeschichte des Buches Tobit* (MSU, 17), Göttingen, 1984, qui distingue également

tradition de l'Église catholique, de refuser le label «canonique» à ces trois formes textuelles: les livres liturgiques catholiques suivent la version hiéronymienne de Tobie, mais la Néo-Vulgate revient à la forme longue du livre, en révisant le texte vieux-latin du *codex Vercellensis*[13]; les Pères grecs, à partir d'Origène, citent le texte court (= $\mathfrak{G}^{II}$), et c'est le texte court qui est reproduit dans les éditions de la Septante réalisées au XVIe siècle, non seulement la *Complutensis* et l'Aldine, mais aussi l'édition Sixtine que les Pères du Concile de Trente avaient appelée de leurs vœux. De même, les deux formes – longue et courte – du Siracide peuvent être tenues pour canoniques, dans la mesure où l'Église ancienne a admis l'une et l'autre, ce qui est encore le cas des traducteurs catholiques modernes[14]. Le décret *De canonicis Scripturis*, lorsqu'il mentionne «le Psautier davidique de cent cinquante psaumes», semble exclure le Ps 151[15]. Cependant ce dernier figure dans bon nombre de manuscrits bibliques latins (y compris de la Vulgate)[16] et est mentionné dans la stichométrie de Mommsen qui, si elle n'est pas l'expression d'une autorité ecclésiastique, est malgré tout le reflet d'un usage ancien[17]. Il figure dans la *Traduction Œcuménique de la Bible* (1975), qui, si elle n'engage que les responsables impliqués et non les Églises elle-mêmes, jouit néanmoins d'une large diffusion dans les milieux catholiques et protestants[18]. La question, ici, n'est pas seulement de savoir si le Ps 151 est ou non canonique, mais si un Psautier incluant le Ps 151 est une forme canonique du livre. En effet, la présence d'une «signature davidique» (Ps

---

une forme intermédiaire (= $\mathfrak{G}^{III}$), qui est une contamination des deux autres types de texte grec.

13. Verceil, Archivio capitolare Eusebiano XXII = VL 123.

14. Voir à ce propos M. GILBERT, *L'Ecclésiastique: quel texte? quelle autorité?*, in *RB* 94 (1987) 233-250.

15. Cf. S.M. ZARB, *De historia canonis utriusque Testamenti* (Opuscula Biblica Pontificii Instituti Angelici), Rome, 1934, p. 262.

16. Cf. *Le Psautier Romain et les autres anciens Psautiers latins*, éd. critique par R. WEBER (Collectanea Biblica Latina, 10), Rome, 1953, pp. 357-358; *Biblia Sacra iuxta Latinam Vulgatam Versionem*, cura et studio Monachorum Abbatiae Pontificiae sancti Hieronymi in Urbe O.S.B., X. *Liber Psalmorum*, Rome, 1953, p. 299 (Appendix).

17. Cf. P.-M. BOGAERT, *Aux origines de la fixation du canon*, ci-dessous, p. 166 et n. 34. — Le fichier du Vetus Latina Institut de Beuron, depuis peu disponible sur CD-ROM, signale plusieurs citations et réminiscences du Ps 151 chez les Pères latins.

18. P. VALLIN, *La Bible, objet culturel ou livre chrétien?*, in C. THEOBALD (ed.), *Le canon des Écritures. Études historiques, exégétiques et systématiques* (LD 140), Paris, 1990, pp. 541-558: «Aujourd'hui, il semble opportun d'inclure au psautier, à l'exemple de la LXX byzantine, le psaume de David vainqueur sur Goliath que cette version grecque classe comme "hors du nombre", en 151e position, et dont l'original hébreu a été retrouvé à Qumrân. On peut aussi considérer comme canonique, au sens de la règle d'immanence culturelle, les diverses finales de Marc, ou les deux versions du livre des Actes» (p. 542). Pour les finales de Marc, voir C. FOCANT, *La canonicité de la finale longue (Mc 16,9-20)*, ci-dessous, pp. 587-597.

151) à la fin du recueil n'est pas sans incidence sur la lecture des pièces qui précèdent, où David n'apparaît que peu[19].

Cela étant, la notion de «forme canonique» ne peut être opératoire que si on désigne par là les contours généraux d'un type de texte, et non une «édition» précise dans l'acception que ce mot a pris depuis l'invention de l'imprimerie, ou même une recension particulière[20]. Il n'y a pas de sens à se demander si la leçon de tel manuscrit est, ou non, canonique, et ce serait un grave anachronisme que d'identifier le texte reçu comme canonique par l'Église ancienne de langue grecque avec, pour l'Ancien Testament, celui qui est reconstitué par la *Septuaginta* de Göttingen – ou même le texte publié par A. Rahlfs d'après les grands onciaux –, et, pour le Nouveau, la dernière édition de Nestle-Aland. Du reste, même à l'époque où les Pères du Concile de Trente ont affirmé «l'authenticité» de la Vulgate, il n'y avait pas encore d'édition qui fît autorité.

Ce n'est pas un mince paradoxe que le canon des Écritures, loi fondamentale pour la vie des communautés chrétiennes, n'a jamais cessé, au cours de l'histoire, d'être interrogé, contesté et soumis à de nouvelles légitimations, toujours historiquement situées.

II. The Canons of the New Testament

The second section of these proceedings includes several papers that deal with the canonization of groups of New Testament writings such as the Pauline correspondence, the four gospels, and the Johannine literature. Other papers focus on the process that led to the canonization of some separate writings such as the Acts of the Apostles and the Apocalypse of John. Further contributions go into such themes as the acceptance of an Old Testament canon in the early Church and the rise of a canon of New Testament writings in the second century. Several papers

19. Cf. J.-M. Auwers, *Les voies de l'exégèse canonique du Psautier*, ci-dessous, p. 5, n. 3.

20. M. Gilbert, *L'Ecclésiastique* (n. 14) tient le texte long du Siracide pour canonique, tout en reconnaissant que «nous ne savons pas de façon absolument certaine où il se trouve» (p. 248), étant donné que ce texte nous est parvenu en de multiples recensions. Si on voulait préciser laquelle de ces recensions est canonique, on en viendrait soit à trancher de manière plus ou moins arbitraire entre les divers états textuels qui ont circulé dans l'Église ancienne, soit à multiplier indéfiniment les recensions qui ont quelque titre à prétendre au label «canonique». Pour le livre de Tobie, il faudrait sans doute tenir pour canonique la recension très paraphrasée dans laquelle la première Bible d'Alcalá (ou *Complutensis* I: Madrid, Bibl. de la Universidad Central, 31 = VL 109) présente le texte long. En effet, c'est ce texte que cite le *Liber de divinis scripuris* pseudo-augustinien, qui témoigne de la diffusion de cette réécriture; cf. F. Vattioni, *Tobia nello Speculum e nella prima Bibbia di Alcalá*, in *Augustinianum* 15 (1975) 169-200.

pursue the question of the relevance or necessity of interpreting New Testament writings in the context of the New Testament canon or the canon of the Christian Bible as a whole.

In an introductory note H.J. de Jonge (Leiden) argues that in confirming or rejecting the authority of early Christian writings, ecclesiastical authors often tended to adduce other grounds than the one they actually had in mind, namely orthodoxy. The criterion of orthodoxy played a more dominant part than our sources allow us to see *prima facie*. Orthodoxy was a fundamental, but often tacit criterion. This criterion implied that in order to be accepted as authoritative, a writing, had to reflect the recognition of the real humanity of Jesus Christ, the expectation of his second coming and, accordingly, the conviction that there is no salvation without incarnation and eschatological judgement. De Jonge points out that if this criterion of orthodoxy influenced the selection and preservation of Jesus traditions from 30 to 70 CE as strongly as it did the acceptance and rejection of gospels and other writings in the second and third centuries, the best sources for recovering the historical Jesus are now contained in the canonical New Testament.

In a wide-ranging opening paper Thomas Söding (Wuppertal) lays the hermeneutical foundations for the interpretation of the Bible as canon[21]. He argues that the Jewish and the Christian canons of the Bible result from Israel's and the Church's will to preserve, as the communities' collective memory, the revelation imparted to them. The presupposition of both canons is God's revelation. It is this revelation which makes canonical writings canonical. Consequently, the task of the biblical exegetes is to explain what precisely in canonical writings makes them canonical. Exegetes should clarify the canon's claim to canonicity by explaining what is canonical within each of the Old and New Testament writings, that is to say, what is revealed in them.

Söding goes on to specify these views with regard to each of the two canons, the Jewish Bible and the Christian Bible. Ultimately, the former's claim to authority goes back to God's own claim to authority, the latter's to that of Christ. The Jewish and Christian canons of the Bible are each the result of the believers' endorsement and acceptance of the claims to authority contained in the biblical writings themselves. Ultimately, the canons are based on the believers' recognition of the authority of God and Christ respectively.

These considerations lead to a comprehensive canonical hermeneutics. First of all, the individual character of each canon, Jewish and

---

21. T. SÖDING, *Der Kanon des Alten und Neuen Testaments. Zur Frage nach seinem theologischen Anspruch*, in this volume, pp. XLVII-LXXXVIII.

Christian, should be recognized. Only after this has been achieved can efforts be made to delineate their mutual theological relationship. The New Testament should not be read without reference to the Old Testament. The Old Testament as Jewish Scripture should be read without reference to the New Testament. The Old Testament, as the first part of the Christian Bible, should first be read as a witness of the faith before the coming of Christ. The New Testament should then be interpreted as witnessing to the Christian faith after Christ's coming. Finally, the latter interpretation may entail a new understanding of the Old Testament.

The biblical canons are the believers' responses to God's revelation and thus claim to derive from that revelation. Consequently, canonical hermeneutics demands that biblical exegesis speak out explicitly with regard to what is, or is not, theologically true.

Subsequently, three papers discuss the way in which certain groups of early Christian writings attained recognition as canon: Paul's letters, the four gospels and the Johannine corpus.

First, Andreas Lindemann (Bethel) scrutinizes the literary evidence for the rise of collections of Paul's letters from 50 CE to 150 CE. Originally, Paul's authentic letters were addressed to specific, individual Christian communities, not to a general audience. Paul never had the intention to bring them together in one body, nor did he take any initiative to collect them (contra D. Trobisch[22]). The pseudo-Pauline letters to the Colossians and Ephesians, however, already reflect the rise of combinations of Pauline letters. The earliest indirect evidence that a collection of some Pauline letters existed is the fact that the Pastoral Epistles originated as a threefold composition; this presupposes the existence of a collection of at least some Pauline letters. Somewhat later, Ignatius of Antioch (ca 130 CE?), Polycarp and 2 Peter provide direct evidence that collections of Pauline letters existed. Polycarp, for instance, knew at least Philippians, 1 Corinthians and Ephesians and seems to have regarded Paul's letters as belonging to the Scriptures. Marcion finally knew a collection of ten Pauline letters (not the Pastorals). This collection must have corresponded to a rival collection that was current in main stream Christianity, but the precise extent of that rival collection cannot be ascertained. This is how the collection of Paul's letters developed until the middle of the second century. This process was not controlled by any specific authority. Like the "canonisation" of Christian writings in a later period, this first and second-century prelude to the canonisation of Paul was nothing but the confirmation of what had pre-

---

22. D. TROBISCH, *Die Paulusbriefe und die Anfänge der christlichen Publizistik* (KT, 135), Gütersloh, Kaiser, 1994.

viously been decided and become practice in the Church. It should be noticed anyway that there has never been a time in which Paul's letters were *not* recognized as of apostolic authority. In a way they never needed to be canonized; they were "canonical" from the outset.

The very fact that Paul's letters were collected had as a consequence that they had to be interpreted for other and later audiences than their original addressees and to be applied to new situations. Yet second-century Christians remained aware of the historical context in which each letter of Paul originated. Moreover, Paul's letters were included in the New Testament canon without being revised or edited for that purpose. There is no compelling reason for contemporary exegetes, therefore, to take the Pauline corpus, let alone the entire New Testament, as the hermeneutical horizon for the interpretation of Paul's letters.

Second, Graham Stanton (Cambridge) investigates the growth in status of the four gospels in the second century. Distinguishing between quoted sayings, respected traditions, authoritative texts, Scripture, and the New Testament canon, Stanton tries to establish where on this ascending scale Justin (ca 155 CE) and Irenaeus (ca 180 CE) placed the Jesus traditions known to them. In Justin's view the sayings of Jesus had the same standing as the words of the Old Testament prophets; the written gospels had the same level of authority as the prophets' books. Clearly, Justin's regard for written gospels (he knew Matthew, Luke and Mark and in all probability also John) was already very high, although he does not yet refer to them with the term Scripture or with the phrase "it is written". Irenaeus in his turn not only accepted the four gospels mentioned, giving them the same status as he did to the Old Testament writings, but also called them "Scripture" once or twice and sometimes referred to them with "it is written: … ". Irenaeus also went further than Justin in stressing that the number of gospels is complete: according to Irenaeus, there are four gospels, no more, no less.

Thus, Justin and Irenaeus have the same high regard for the gospels. Both of them put them on the same level of authority as the Old Testament. Both of them look upon the gospels primarily as written books, not merely as traditions. But for Irenaeus the gospels are nearer to acceptance as a fixed and closed "canon" of four books than for Justin. There is reason to suppose that the gradual emergence of the four gospel canon which we witness in Justin and Irenaeus was related to the dissemination of the four gospel codex.

Third, Jean Zumstein (Zürich) examines the rise of the notion of Scripture in the Johannine literature. Zumstein remarks that the main criteria used to assess canonicity in the second to fourth centuries (apostolicity, orthodoxy, wide acceptance among believers), were already in the minds of the authors of John's gospel and letters at the moment of composing these writings. These documents claim that their message is of the highest possible authority, incontestable orthodoxy and widely accepted among believers.

In the gospel, the Paraclete and the beloved disciple serve to warrant the truth of the gospel's teaching in the post-Easter situation of the Johannine community. As a result, the author claims absolute authority, an authority amounting to what is later called apostolicity. Furthermore, the evangelist aims to present his views as the only truth. The gospel contrasts this truth with convictions outside the Church; the Letters defend the truth against views held within the Church. Finally, the authors of both the gospel and the Letters present their message as credible owing to the fact that it rests on authorities already recognized and accepted by the addressees: the beloved disciple, Peter, and the gospel itself as a closed work that lends itself to rereading and re-interpretation. Thus, the Johannine writings seem to try to meet from the outset what were later to become the criteria of apostolicity, orthodoxy and acceptance by the Church. In other words, from the moment John's gospel and Letters were composed, they were on their way to becoming Scripture.

These three papers on the canonization of groups of early Christian writings are followed by a paper devoted to the early phases of canonization of one single writing, namely the Acts of the Apostles. Jens Schröter (Hamburg) discusses the question why by the end of the second century Acts became one of the Church's authoritative books. He begins by giving an account of the rise of Acts to canonical authority. This rise began relatively late and was connected with the Church's polemics against Marcion and the gnostics. Irenaeus and Tertullian used Acts to demonstrate that the "orthodox" doctrine of the one God was not only taught by Christ and Paul, but also by all the other apostles. Acts served to maintain and warrant the authority of the apostles next to Paul. The authority of these other apostles was confirmed with recourse to the authority of Paul. Thus Acts became a link between the theological testimony of the gospels and that of Paul. The conclusion that this was the theological function Acts intended to fulfil, is confirmed by the various positions Acts takes in manuscripts and canon lists, where Acts figures in different combinations with gospels, Paul and Catholic Epistles.

Acts' rise to special authority occurred independently of that of Luke's gospel. The early Church did not yet look upon these two books as the "two-part Lukan opus". However, the fact that the reception and transmission of Acts took place along different lines from those of Luke's gospel corresponds to (and is historically justified by) the difference in literary nature between Acts and the gospel. The literary character of Acts differs markedly from that of the gospel. The distinct reception of Acts does justice to the way the author conceived of this book. It follows that a canonical interpretation of Acts, if undertaken, should regard the contents of Acts as complementary to, not as conflicting with, the theologies of Luke and Paul. Acts can prevent Luke's Paul and Luke from being seen as incompatible with the Paul of the letters.

The next paper is primarily concerned with the origins of the system of writing *nomina sacra* in Christian Greek manuscripts and the question whether they are evidence of an early canonical form of the New Testament. In it Christopher Tuckett (Oxford) argues that it is less certain than many have assumed that the system is a Christian innovation. It may already have been used by non-Christian Jewish scribes. The system appears to have been applied with less consistency than some have claimed. The phenomenon of *nomina sacra* did not function as a characteristic of a "First edition" of a collection of "canonical" early Christian writings, distinguishing it from other collections of texts (contra D. Trobisch[23]). As to the form of the *nomina sacra*, suspended forms seem to have preceded contracted forms. Early suspensions were gradually replaced by contractions, probably in order to clarify case endings and to facilitate reading. The system of *nomina sacra* can only have been of limited significance, partly because of the limited extent of literacy in antiquity. Further, the use of *nomina sacra* would not have been noticed by a hearer at all. They definitely did not serve any form of devotion, as did the Hebrew tetragrammaton. In fact, the *nomina sacra* may not have been "sacred" signs at all, as appears for instance from the contraction of *anthropos*, "man". Their designation as *sacra* is mistaken. Their original purpose may have been to serve as reading aids. This is suggested, *inter alia*, by the fact that the stroke which is written over *nomina sacra* is also written above proper names that are not abbreviated but written out in full. "Christ" and "Lord", then, may have been treated as proper names. In sum, the *nomina sacra* may partly have been *nomina*, but they are not *sacra*.

Two extensive studies deal with the rise of a Christian canon of the Old Testament and that of the New Testament respectively in the Christian Church of the second century. Marinus de Jonge (Leiden) presents a study on the authority of the Old Testament in the early Church accord-

---

23. D. TROBISCH, *Die Endredaktion des Neuen Testaments* (NTOA, 31), Freiburg, Universitätsverlag; Göttingen, Vandenhoeck & Ruprecht, 1996; translated as *The First Edition of the New Testament*, Oxford, Oxford University Press, 2000.

ing to the testimony of the "Old Testament Pseudepigrapha". This contribution focuses on the question of what was the function of the so-called "pseudepigrapha of the Old Testament" in the early Church? Why did Christians transmit, read, edit, rewrite and even compose these writings? What authority did these writings have among Christians? According to M. de Jonge, the lively interest which early Christians took in the stories about the Protoplasts and Patriarchs can be explained against the foil of Marcion's and some Gnostics' negative assessment of the Creator-God and his revelation, the Old Testament. For instance, the Greek *Life of Adam and Eve*, as a story about the lives and deaths of the Protoplasts, purposes to show that the God who speaks and acts in Gen 3, is the One and Good God, not the lower Creator-God. Consequently, the God of Gen 3 is the same God as the one revered by the Christians. The *Life of Adam and Eve* posits the unity and identity of the God of Genesis with the merciful God of Jesus and the New Testament. The book thus opposes views maintained by Marcion and certain Gnostics according to which the Old Testament God was different from, and inferior to, the God of Jesus and the Christians. Similarly, the *Testaments of the Twelve Patriarchs* can be seen as an attempt to answer the question of how Christians can claim to stand in continuity with the generations from Adam to Moses and yet reject the Jewish interpretation of Israel's Scriptures.

The *Life of Adam and Eve* and the *Testaments of the Twelve Patriarchs*, then, seem to defend the validity of the book of Genesis, and the Old Testament in general, over against Marcion's, the Marcionists' and certain Gnostics' rejection of the Old Testament. The Christian tendency to retain the Old Testament and especially Genesis resulted in the Christian interest in stories about the great biblical figures from Adam to the Patriarchs. Several so-called Pseudepigrapha of the Old Testament can be construed as reflecting the struggle between main stream Christianity and Marcionism with regard to the authority of the Old Testament. These writings mirror a specific stage in the history of the formation of the Christian canon of the Old Testament.

Another contribution to the history of the biblical canon in the second-century Church is the study presented by Joseph Verheyden (Leuven) on the Canon Muratori. In it he examines the arguments put forward by A.C. Sundberg (1973 etc.[24]) and G.M. Hahneman (1992[25]) in

24. A.C. SUNDBERG, *Canon Muratori. A Fourth Century List*, in *HTR* 66 (1973) 1-41. For Sundberg's later publications on the subject see J. VERHEYDEN, *The Canon Muratori. A Matter of Dispute*, below, pp. 487-556, esp. p. 497, n. 43.

25. G.M. HAHNEMAN, *The Muratorian Fragment and the Development of the Canon* (Oxford Theological Monographs), Oxford, Clarendon, 1992.

favour of a fourth-century Eastern origin of the Muratorian Fragment. According to Verheyden, these arguments do not hold water. The Fragment says that "Hermas composed The Shepherd quite recently in our times in the city, while his brother Pius occupied the see of the city of Rome". The most plausible interpretation of this passage is that the Fragmentist was mistaken as to the date of origin of The Shepherd, but wrote his own text not long after Pius' pontificate of Rome, that is, some time during the last quarter of the second century. Against Hahneman, it should be maintained that the Muratorian Fragment, on its traditional dating, is not an anomaly, either in contents, concepts or form. On the contrary, the Fragment shows striking similarities in wording and contents with other late-second-century authors in the West, whereas it clearly disagrees with later Eastern canon lists, for instance, in defending extensively the authority of the four gospels and in omitting Hebrews. In brief, the most plausible explanation of the evidence remains that the Muratorian Fragment originated in the late second century in the West. This early, Western provenance can also account for the fact, generally neglected in earlier research, that the Fragment was used in the West about 400 by Chromatius of Aquileia (Northern Italy) and possibly as early as 354 by the latest redactor of the Liberian Catalogue. If one accepts a late fourth-century origin in the East, this relatively early use of the Muratorian Fragment in the West becomes hard to explain.

In a paper on the theological relevance of the shape of the New Testament canon, Karl-Wilhelm Niebuhr (Jena) examines the consequences of a New Testament exegesis which takes the canonical context seriously. Niebuhr aims to answer the question of what is the theological meaning of the biblical canon, in its final form, taken as a whole. He first discusses the overall structure of the canon and the connections between its constituent parts. In all traditional canons of the Bible (the Jewish Bible, the Christian Old Testament, the New Testament canons according to Athanasius, the Vulgate, the Gelasian Decree and Trent, etc.) the sequence of the biblical books appears to form theologically interesting patterns. For instance, in the Byzantine canon in which Acts precedes Romans, the account of Paul's preaching in Rome at the end of Acts is a significant preparation for Paul's message in Romans. Similarly, predictions of Jesus' second coming in all New Testament books preceding Revelation, cannot but strike the reader as references pointing forward to Revelation. Subsequently, Niebuhr analyzes in more detail the relationships between Acts and the letters included in the New Testament. Pre-Byzantine canons usually insert Hebrews between 2 Thessalonians and 1 Timothy; this position seems to justify a Pauline interpretation of Hebrews. In several early canons, Acts and the Catholic Epistles form a meaningful unit in which the narrative about the apostles on the one hand and their epistolary teaching on the other are brought together (Praxapostolos). In the Byzantine canon, however, Acts' position invites one to see the coherence between the account of Paul's teaching in Acts and his message in the Pauline letters. Niebuhr then examines the patterns that structure the various corpora of New Testament letters and indicates the connections between the letters of each individual corpus of letters. The order of the Catholic Epistles, James, Peter, John (and Jude), for example, mirrors the order in which the "pillars" of the Jerusalem church appear in Gal 2,9. Finally, Niebuhr points out how the various components of the New Testament canon relate to Jesus as the centre of the canon.

Short papers included in the New Testament section of these proceedings concern a variety of aspects of the history and significance of the New Testament as canon. These are the topics that are dealt with: the canonicity of the long ending of Mark and the possibility of recognizing two alternative endings of Mark as canonical (Camille Focant, Louvain-la-Neuve); hermeneutical factors in the harmonization of the gospels and the question of textual authority (Nicholas Perrin, London); the place and claim of Revelation in the biblical canon (Konrad Huber and Martin Hasitschka, Innsbruck); the dispute between Harnack and Overbeck about the formation of the New Testament canon (Martin Rese, Münster); canonical coherence in reading the Masoretic text and the Septuagint with a sequel (Robert Brawley, Chicago); the exegetical consequences of reading Mt 1,1 in the light of Genesis (Thomas Hieke, Regensburg); hermeneutical aspects of the authority of the Bible (Johannes Nissen, Aarhus); and, finally, the interpretation of the Bible as Scripture and canon in contemporary African Christianity (Chris Manus, Nairobi).

Interestingly, the views put forward and defended in the papers presented here turn out to converge on several points.

(1) With regard to a remarkable number of writings later included in the New Testament, it is argued that, by their very claim to apostolic authority, these writings from the outset had the inherent potential to be accepted as canonical. This applies to Paul's letters (Lindemann[26]) and to

---

26. A. LINDEMANN, *Die Sammlung der Paulusbriefe im 1. und 2. Jahrhundert*, see below, pp. 321-351.

the Johannine corpus (Zumstein[27]). But something similar applies to Acts, insofar as the motives that led to its rise to an authoritative status in the second half of the second century, were precisely the same as those that had led Luke to write the book. Luke's intention was to show that the Church's teaching was based on the testimony of a wide range of apostles besides Paul. Precisely this idea made the book such a useful tool in the struggle of the Church against the exclusive use of Paul by the Marcionites (Schröter[28]). The letters of Paul, the Johannine writings and Acts can thus all be said to have had a predisposition to become canonical from the very moment they were written.

(2) Marcion and Marcionism are no longer seen as the main stimuli behind the emergence of the New Testament canon (as they were by Harnack[29]). Yet Marcion continues to be regarded as indirectly responsible for at least two new developments in the history of the Christian Bible. First, Marcion's restrictive canon, which comprised only Luke and Paul, caused other Christians to hold Acts in higher regard (Schröter[30]). Second, Marcion induced other Christians to insist that the God about whom Genesis speaks, is the One and Good God. As a consequence, these Christians took an interest in traditions and books, based on Genesis, concerning the Protoplasts and the Patriarchs figuring in Genesis and regarded as children of the Good God. Second-century Christians not only read and rewrote such books, now designated as "Old Testament Pseudepigrapha", but also composed new ones (M. de Jonge[31]).

(3) Historical research into the history of the New Testament canon, as presented in these proceedings, leads to several convincing results. For instance, a collection of Pauline letters, invested with apostolic authority, was in existence as early as the end of the first century (Lindemann[32]). The Muratorian Fragment was composed in the late second century in the West, not during the fourth century in the East (Verheyden[33]). The four gospels are decidedly nearer to forming a fixed and

---

27. J. ZUMSTEIN, *La naissance de la notion d'Écriture dans la littérature johannique*, see below, pp. 371-394.
28. J. SCHRÖTER, *Die Apostelgeschichte und die Entstehung des neutestamentlichen Kanons*, see below, pp. 395-429.
29. A. VON HARNACK, *Die Entstehung des Neuen Testaments und die wichtigsten Folgen der neuen Schöpfung*, Leipzig, Hinrichs, 1914, and other works.
30. SCHRÖTER, *Die Apostelgeschichte* (n. 28).
31. M. DE JONGE, *The Authority of the "Old Testament" in the Early Church. The Witness of the "Pseudepigrapha of the Old Testament"*, see below, p. 459-486.
32. LINDEMANN, *Die Sammlung* (n. 26).
33. J. VERHEYDEN, *The Canon Muratori. A Matter of Dispute*, see below, pp. 487-556.

closed canon in Irenaeus' works than they are in the works of Justin
Martyr, but Justin's assessment of the gospels is certainly not far removed from that of Irenaeus. In any case, Justin is likely to have known
all the four gospels and to have considered them of the same level of
authority as the Jewish Scriptures (Stanton[34]). The *nomina sacra* have
not served as a characteristic of a "First edition" of the New Testament
to distinguish this "edition" from other collections of Jewish and early
Christian writings (Tuckett[35]).

(4) Several authors whose contributions appear in these proceedings
argue that the interpretation of New Testament writings requires a canonical approach taking into account the whole New Testament or even
the whole Bible (so, with variations, Söding[36], Niebuhr[37] and others).
Others remain concerned about the question how historical-critical research, if taken seriously, can be "domesticated" and reconciled with a
method of theologically inspired exegesis. The great question is of
course to what extent the hermeneutical "translation" of the contents of
biblical writings into a theologically significant message for modern
hearers, belongs to the domain of the exegete. Some insist that it is the
inescapable responsibility of the exegete to speak out theologically, under penalty of being marginalized as irrelevant. Others seem to conceive
of the exegete's task as mainly a literary-historical discipline, without
being absolutely opposed to the idea that, in the final phase of the exegetical operation, theological propositions are put forward developed
with the aid of a canonical approach. Others again remain inclined to
look upon exegesis as a purely historical discipline, hoping that biblical
and systematic theology will reap the benefits of its labour. Opinions remain divided on these questions, but the voice of those who advocate
some form of canonical interpretation sounds clearly and distinctly.

Jean-Marie AUWERS
Université catholique de Louvain
Faculté de théologie
45, Grand-Place
B–1348 Louvain-la-Neuve

Henk Jan DE JONGE
Universiteit Leiden
Faculteit der Godgeleerdheid
P.O. Box 9515
NL–2300 RA Leiden

---

34. G.N. STANTON, *Jesus Traditions and Gospels in Justin Martyr and Irenaeus*, see below, pp. 353-370.

35. C.M. TUCKETT, *"Nomina Sacra" : Yes and No?*, see below, pp. 431-458.

36. SÖDING, *Der Kanon* (n. 21).

37. K.-W. NIEBUHR, *Exegese im kanonischen Zusammenhang: Überlegungen zur theologischen Relevanz der Gestalt des neutestamentlichen Kanons*, see below, pp. 557-584.

COLLOQUIUM BIBLICUM LOVANIENSE
1–50

The *Colloquium Biblicum Lovaniense* held its first meeting in 1949 and, as it was planned from the very beginning, it became an annual meeting, *De Bijbelse Studiedagen te Leuven / Les Journées Bibliques de Louvain*. In 1964 and in 1982 the General Meeting of the Society for New Testament Studies and in 1989 the IOSOT Congress for Old Testament took place in Leuven. This accounts for the fact that there are three vacant years in the list of our yearly meetings. It is, therefore, only now in 2001 (and not in 1998) that we can celebrate our 50th session.

I

This Jubilee Session is not the first celebration in the history of the Colloquium. The tenth anniversary of its foundation coincided with the World's Fair in Brussels (1958) and on that occasion the first *International Catholic Congress for Biblical Studies* was organized by the committee of the former presidents of the Colloquium under the chairmanship of Professor Joseph Coppens. The Proceedings of the meeting relate the presence of about four hundred participants, and some eighty contributions are included in the two volumes of *Sacra Pagina* (BETL 12-13, 1959).

The 25th anniversary in 1974 was another occasion for having a feast, the first *session jubilaire*. The meeting was devoted to one theme of study, the Biblical Notion of God, in two separate sections (Old Testament and New Testament). In many ways this 1974 meeting (BETL 41, 1976) served as the model for the true Jubilee we are celebrating this year.

In 1974 Professor Coppens presented a historical survey: "Vingt-cinq années de Journées Bibliques à Louvain: Un aperçu historique". He could speak, he said, "en qualité de survivant de l'équipe qui en jeta les fondements". He then rephrases the formulation and becomes the only survivor, "*seul* survivant des collègues qui en 1948 (sic) prirent l'initiative de fonder les Journées", and he makes clear, at least for philatelists, that these colleagues were above all Lucien Cerfaux (1883-1968) and Gonzague Ryckmans (1887-1969)[1]. There is no doubt, however,

---

1. *La notion biblique de Dieu* (BETL, 41), Gembloux, Duculot / Leuven University Press, 1976, 23-47, esp. 24-32 (24, cf. 15). See the frontispiece.

that the real founder was Joseph Coppens. For those among us who have known Coppens as an assiduous note-taker, it may appear strange that, "à défaut de notes manuscrites conservées pour la période des origines", he had to rely on memory. My own contacts with the founding fathers, L. Cerfaux and J. Coppens, and my personal recollections, do not reach back beyond the year 1954, when I took up residence in the Pope's College[2].

To the list of presidents of the Colloquium enumerated in Coppens's survey (1949-1974)[3] we can now add the presidents from 1975 to the present: Marinus de Jonge (1975), Mathias Delcor (1976), Jacob Kremer (1977), Maurice Gilbert (1978), Jan Lambrecht (1979), Pierre-Maurice Bogaert (1980), Joël Delobel (1981), Norbert Lohfink (1983), Albert Vanhoye (1984), Johan Lust (1985), Jean-Marie Sevrin (1986), Jacques Vermeylen (1987), Raymond Collins (1988), Adelbert Denaux (1990), Adam van der Woude (1991), Camille Focant (1992), Willem Beuken (1993), Reimund Bieringer (1994), Marc Vervenne (1995), Christopher Tuckett (1996), Antoon Schoors (1997), Joseph Verheyden (1998), André Wénin (1999), Andreas Lindemann (2000), and, now in office, Jean-Marie Auwers and Henk Jan de Jonge.

Professor Mathias Delcor (°1919), president of the session on Qumran in 1976, died in 1992. The obituary in the Bulletin of the Institut Catholique de Toulouse mentions his presidency at our Colloquium as "(le) couronnement de son activité de qumranologue". Last year on the 19th of November we received with deep regret the news of the death of Professor Adam Simon van der Woude (°1927) in Groningen. He also was a famous qumranologue, serving as president for the session on the Book of Daniel in 1991. Other former presidents who have passed away since 1974 are: Willem van Unnik (1910-1978), François Braun (1893-1980), Albert Descamps (1916-1980), Joseph Coppens (1896-1981), Béda Rigaux (1899-1982), Charles Hauret (1907-1991), Jean Giblet

---

2. As one of the *subregentes*. See my reports on the Colloquium in *De Standaard*, 1955, 10-11 September; 1956, 8-10 September. Cf. F. NEIRYNCK, *J. Coppens, fondateur des Journées Bibliques de Louvain*, in *ETL* 57 (1981) 274-284; reprint in *Logia. Mémorial Joseph Coppens* (BETL, 59), 1982, 9-19.

3. L. Cerfaux (1949), J. Coppens (1950), J. Levie (1951), B. Rigaux (1952), P. van Imschoot (1953), G. Ryckmans (1954), J. Heuschen (1955), F. Braun (1956), J. van der Ploeg (1957), J. Coppens (1958), A. Descamps (1959), R. De Langhe (1960), É. Massaux (1961), J. Giblet (1962), C. Hauret (1963), I. de la Potterie (1965), G. Thils - R. Brown (1966), H. Cazelles (1967), F. Neirynck (1968), W.C. van Unnik (1969), M. Sabbe (1970), M. Didier (1971), C. Brekelmans (1972), J. Dupont (1973), J. Coppens (1974).

For the complete list of the presidents and of all published papers, cf. F. NEIRYNCK (ed.), *Colloquium Biblicum Lovaniense 1-50 1949-2001* (SNTA, 19), Leuven, 2001 (henceforth *CBL*).

(1918-1993), Raymond Brown (1928-1998), Jacques Dupont (1915-1998), Gustave Thils (1909-2000), and now recently Marcel Didier (1928-2002) and Joseph Heuschen (1915-2002). *Requiescant in pace.*

II

When the Colloquium started in 1949, it was located in the Pope's College, *Paus Adriaan VI College*, and, without interruption, after half a century, the housing of the Colloquium is still at the Pope's College. Thanks are thus due to its successive 'presidents': professors Joseph Coppens (1949-1967), Maurits Sabbe (1967-1989), and now Lambert Leijssen (since 1989) for their generous hospitality. The announcement of the first Colloquium in August 1949 contains a precise indication of the meeting place: "Les réunions se tiendront dans le Club du Collège du Pape, … in de Clubzaal van het Pauscollege, eerste deur rechts onder het portaal". The door on the right is no longer there and for many years now the plenary sessions of the Colloquium have their traditional location in the more spacious Kleine Aula[4].

The Colloquium started as a two-day programme but changed as early as 1951 to the programme of three days that is maintained up to now. Broadly speaking one can distinguish three periods with regard to the date of the Colloquium: in the beginning of September (1949-1957), the second half of August (1958-1995), and the last week of July (1996-). This last option allows participants to avoid the noisy Leuven kermis in September and the rock festival in the streets of Leuven in August, but there is of course an academic reason: the vacation schedules of some colleagues from abroad and the avoidance of conflicts with other Biblical congresses (in particular the SNTS meeting in the beginning of August).

In this connection I may recall my search for an explanation of the rapid success of the Colloquium in the 1950's (n. 2). One can say that the only real explanation was the prestige and authority then enjoyed by its two founders, Cerfaux and Coppens. The situation of the Scripture professors in Belgian seminaries and theological schools in the postwar period, however, should also be considered. To cite only the New Testament, the Society for New Testament Studies had been meeting annually since 1947, but we had to wait until 1954 before a Catholic exegete from

---

4. *'t Heilig Land*, 1953: "een ander en zeker veel geschikter lokaal, waar we heel wat prettiger zaten" (145). – On the first meeting of CBL, see *Avant-propos*, in *ALBO* II/16 (1950) 7-9.

the Benelux area entered the SNTS[5]. For Catholic exegetes, there were only the meetings in Leuven. That the need for local societies was felt more generally may appear from the foundation of the Dutch Conventus (SNTC) in 1951 and the start in 1955 of the biennial meetings of Catholic Neutestamentler in Germany.

The description of the internal organization of our Colloquium can be brief: there is the growing body of former presidents and there is one member secretary (J. Coppens, F. Neirynck). The former presidents constitute the board of the Colloquium, the CBL Committee, which has to decide on the topics of future meetings and to appoint the president elect (since 1975 strictly alternating Old Testament and New Testament). The acting president proposes the programme of papers and seminars, he chairs all plenary sessions of the Colloquium and is in charge of editing the proceedings for publication in BETL. From the original series of lectures at the Bible Days in French or Dutch, the programme gradually developed and became more varied, with a presidential address, nine main papers by invited speakers (in English, German, or French), four seminars in four different languages (one is in Dutch; and there are two sessions for each), a number of offered papers (the short papers) and the so-called carrefour (an open discussion of the main papers in the evening session of the second day). The number of participants at the Colloquium varies from one hundred to one hundred and fifty.

I may add at this juncture a supplementary observation on the composition of the Committee. From the question concerning the founders of the Colloquium, one might retain the impression that the Colloquium was a matter for University professors. The truth is that, in the first reference to the Committee in 1958, among its nine members, the Committee included Jean Levie, Béda Rigaux, François-Marie Braun, Johannes van der Ploeg, and the Seminary professors Paul van Imschoot and Joseph Heuschen, all six of whom were elected presidents of the Colloquium, and, as former presidents, became *full* members of the Committee.

III

More important to note is the evolution in the themes of study. It was not by accident that the first meetings (1-5, 1949-1953) tended to focus

---

5. J. Dupont (upon proposal by Chr. Butler). He is followed in 1956 by L. Cerfaux, A. Descamps, and B. Rigaux. See my *L'exégèse catholique en deuil: R.E. Brown – J. Dupont*, in *ETL* 74 (1998) 506-516.

on questions common to OT and NT. This is true for the first meeting on Sensus plenior. It was true also for Biblical Theology; Scripture Teaching in the Seminaries; Messianism; and *La piété biblique / Bijbelse vroomheid*. At that time most participants were teaching in their own school both Old Testament and New Testament. It was with some regret that professor Coppens missed this combination of Old and New in the later sessions of the Colloquium. In 1974, upon the invitation by the Committee, he agreed to preside at that jubilee session on one condition – that the topic pertain to both Testaments.

The first session specifically devoted to the Old Testament was presided over by G. Ryckmans in 1954: *L'Ancien Testament et l'Orient*. This meeting was also innovative for another reason. In contrast to the limitation to Benelux and the exclusively Roman Catholic character of previous meetings, the presence of an important delegation from the British Society for Old Testament Study gave the Colloquium for the first time a broader international and ecumenical dimension. The following year (1955, with Joseph Heuschen as president) one of the lecturers was Willem van Unnik, who became a faithful participant at our New Testament meetings, and was appointed president of the Colloquium in 1969. In later years he was followed in that function by Marinus de Jonge (1975), Adam van der Woude (1991), Christopher Tuckett (1996), Andreas Lindemann (2000), and Henk Jan de Jonge (2001).

General Old Testament themes were studied again in 1963, *Aux grands carrefours de la révélation et de l'exégèse de l'Ancien Testament* (C. Hauret); 1967, *De Mari à Qumrân: L'Ancien Testament et son milieu* (H. Cazelles); 1972, *Questions disputées d'Ancien Testament: Méthode et théologie* (C. Brekelmans); to which can be added the OT section in *La notion biblique de Dieu* (1974, ten essays). Of the sessions 1-25, only one session was devoted to a particular OT book (*Le Psautier*, in 1960; R. De Langhe). The opposite situation emerged in the later period. Apart from the Colloquium on Wisdom (1978, *La Sagesse dans l'Ancien Testament*; M. Gilbert) all OT sessions were devoted to individual books, in the following (noncanonical) order: Jeremiah (1980, P.-M. Bogaert), Deuteronomy (1983, N. Lohfink), Ezekiel (1985, J. Lust), Isaiah (1987, J. Vermeylen), Daniel (1991, A.S. van der Woude), Job (1993, W. Beuken), Exodus (1995, M. Vervenne), Qohelet (1997, A. Schoors), and Genesis (1999, A. Wénin).

When we turn to the New Testament, we do not find the same contrast between an earlier and a later period. Already in 1968-1970-1971 redaction criticism came to expression in the separate treatment of the individual Synoptics. Three parts can be distinguished in the New Testament.

The Synoptic Gospels are first studied in 1955 (*La formation des évangiles: Problème synoptique et Formgeschichte*, J. Heuschen); the Gospel of John in 1956 (*L'évangile de Jean: Études et problèmes*, F.-M. Braun) and Paul in 1959 (*Littérature et théologie pauliniennes*, A. Descamps).

The Colloquium returned anew to the Synoptic Gospels in 1965 (*De Jésus aux évangiles. Tradition et rédaction dans les évangiles synoptiques*, I. de la Potterie), followed by the Gospel of Luke in 1968 (F. Neirynck), Matthew in 1970 (M. Didier), and Mark in 1971 (M. Sabbe), and in 1973, concluding the series on the Synoptics, *Jésus aux origines de la christologie* (J. Dupont). The Gospel of John became the focal point again in 1975 (*L'évangile de Jean*, M. de Jonge), followed by the Johannine Apocalypse in 1979 (*L'Apocalypse johannique*, J. Lambrecht). Thirdly and finally attention was turned to *L'apôtre Paul* in 1984 (A. Vanhoye), followed by *The Thessalonian Correspondence* in 1988 (R.F. Collins) and *The Corinthian Correspondence* in 1994 (R. Bieringer).

Besides this repeatedly applied tripartite scheme (Synoptics – John – Paul) we can observe a move from more general to more specific questions: from the Gospel of John in 1975 to *John and the Synoptics* in 1990 (A. Denaux); from the Acts of the Apostles in 1977 (J. Kremer) to *The Unity of Luke-Acts* in 1998 (J. Verheyden); from *Logia: The Sayings of Jesus* in 1981 (J. Delobel) to *The Sayings Source Q and the Historical Jesus* in 2000 (A. Lindemann). In the Gospel studies more specific methodological questions are treated: *The Synoptic Gospels: Source Criticism and the New Literary Criticism* (1992, C. Focant) and *The Scriptures in the Gospels* (1996, C.M. Tuckett).

As yet I did not refer to Apocrypha. For a partial treatment two titles can be cited: *La littérature juive entre Tenach et Mischna* (1969, W.C. van Unnik) and *The New Testament in Early Christianity* (1986, J.-M. Sevrin). More significantly, two entire sessions were devoted to Qumran, in 1957 (J. van der Ploeg) and 1976 (M. Delcor), and Qumran is now again on the programme for next year (now also with a more specific theme: *Wisdom and Apocalypticism in the Dead Sea Scrolls*). One should not forget that it was in the midst of the first Dead Sea fever that the Colloquium was founded. Coppens could write in 1950: "Au cours de ces derniers mois, l'intérêt s'est manifesté déplacé des textes bibliques vers les textes apocryphes. C'était à prévoir … Pour l'instant, c'est A. Dupont-Sommer qui mène la discussion"[6].

6. *ETL* 26 (1950), 580. Besides the specific Qumran meetings in 1957 and 1976 (resp. 11 and 28 contributions), see also J. Giblet 1952; F.-M. Braun 1954; J. Coppens 1956, 1959; E.-J. Kissane, R. Busa, J. van der Ploeg, J. Mejía, J. Caubet Iturbe, G. Bernini, R.E. Murphy: 1958; M. Baillet, M. Delcor: 1960; P. Grelot 1961; A.-M. Denis 1962; H.H. Rowley 1967; M. Black, B. Dehandschutter: 1969; J. Lust 1985; D. Dimant 1991.

IV

With only three exceptions in the early 1950's (nos. 2, 3, 5) each session of the Colloquium was followed by the publication of the proceedings: the first volume in *Analecta Lovaniensia Biblica et Orientalia* (ALBO II/16), two volumes in *Orientalia et Biblica Lovaniensia* (OBL 1 and 4), nine in *Recherches Bibliques* (RechB 1-9), and all other volumes in the *Bibliotheca Ephemeridum Theologicarum Lovaniensium* (BETL). The *Recherches Bibliques* 1-8 deserve our special attention. Presented as published "sous le Patronage du Colloquium Biblicum Lovaniense", the collection of *Recherches Bibliques* exclusively contains proceedings of the Colloquium. It began with the session on messianism (1952), *L'attente du Messie* (1954, ²1958), edited by B. Rigaux and dedicated to J. Coppens "Colloquii Biblici Lovaniensis indefesso promotori". The collection comes to a provisional end in vol. 8 (1967; session 15, 1963) with a retrospective Index of volumes 1-8, referring to J. Coppens as "secrétaire des *Journées Bibliques* et de la rédaction du RB" (= Recherches Bibliques). The publisher of the collection was Desclée de Brouwer. The books were printed in a handy format (14x22), with a total number of pages varying around the 200 (between 190 and 260). All texts were unilingual in French. The use of citations in Greek was restricted to a few Synoptic parallels. This reader-friendly character of the *Recherches Bibliques* has contributed very much to the diffusion of the "Journées Bibliques de Louvain" in the 1950's and the early 1960's.

I may quote here a few words from an address by Rector A. Descamps on the significance of the Colloquium, "de betekenis van de Bijbelse Studiedagen" (1967)[7]:

> Voor de Bijbelwetenschap zowel als voor onze universiteit was de inrichting van de Bijbelse Dagen een van de vruchtbaarste wetenschappelijke initiatieven van de na-oorlogse jaren... De uitstraling van de Bijbeldagen wordt ook verzekerd door de gepubliceerde *Acta*, welke de tastbare uitslagen van studie en bespreking voor een breder publiek beschikbaar stellen... Tenslotte wordt men er normaal toe gebracht, in een reeds lange serie *Acta* (verwijzing naar de *Recherches Bibliques*), het geheel van de grote bijbelse sectoren systematisch te bestrijken, zodat de collectie geleidelijk tot een kleine *summa* uitgroeit, die ook als "Inleiding" tot de twee Testamenten kan fungeren.

Daarbij toch dit corollarium: niet iedereen was onverdeeld gelukkig met de strekking om de *Recherches Bibliques* te bestemmen voor een

---

7. Toespraak A. Descamps, 25 augustus 1967: (BETL, 24), 1969, 75*-77*.

ruim publiek. Niet elk onderwerp leent zich daartoe, en men kan er begrip voor opbrengen dat door toedoen van Prof. R. De Langhe (1911-1963) de reeks *Orientalia et Biblica Lovaniensia* opgericht werd, waarin als eerste volume *L'Ancien Testament et l'Orient* (1957) en als vierde en laatste *Le Psautier* (1962) zijn verschenen. In beide gevallen werd ook afgeweken van de regel om uitsluitend in het Frans te publiceren. In de *Recherches Bibliques* werd die regel strikt gehandhaafd, ondermeer ook voor collega's uit Nederland die, zoals toen gebruikelijk was, op het Colloquium zelf hun referaat in het Nederlands hadden voorgedragen. Dat bracht bijvoorbeeld mee dat in *L'attente du Messie* de bijdragen van de professoren W. Grossouw en J. van der Ploeg ontbreken. Het probleem kreeg een oplossing à la Coppens: voortaan zouden alle Nederlandse en ook Duitse teksten door hem zelf of door zijn zorgen[8] in het Frans vertaald worden.

Si dans les années 1965 à 1969 les Journées Bibliques se déroulent normalement, ce furent des années de transition en ce qui concerne la publication. Transition d'abord de la collection des *Recherches Bibliques* à celle de la *Bibliotheca Ephemeridum Theologicarum Lovaniensium*. Le titre de "Recherches Bibliques" a encore été donné au volume du colloque de 1969 sur la littérature intertestamentaire ("entre Tenach et Mischna"), mais ce n° 9, publié en 1974 par Brill (Leiden), n'a de commun avec les volumes antérieurs que le nom de la série et le fait que l'article de Jan Willem Doeve, qui représente un quart du volume (*Le domaine du temple de Jérusalem*, 118-163) fut traduit par Coppens.

Les colloques 16-19 de 1965-1968, avec une légère inversion dans l'ordre, occupent dans BETL les n°s 25 (1967), 26 (1968), 24 (1969), 32 (1973), et sont publiés par les Éditions Duculot (Gembloux). Le format 16x24 est désormais la règle. Il fut beaucoup moins satisfaisant qu'une très large part du texte de ces quatre volumes se trouve reproduite déjà dans *ETL* antérieurement à la publication dans BETL[9], un procédé qui risquait de compliquer les rapports entre la revue et la collection et qui fut bien vite abandonné. À partir de 1967 la publication de nos colloques est donc intégrée dans celle de la BETL et elle l'est restée jusqu'à présent.

8. J. Heuschen: W.C. van Unnik 1955; I. de la Potterie: W. Grossouw 1956; A. Descamps: 1959*; see the explicit references to J. Coppens: G. Quispel 1956; F. Nötscher 1957; A.S. van der Woude 1957; H. Gross 1963; T. Vriezen 1963; add J.W. Doeve 1955, *et al.* See also J. De Caevel: O. Betz 1957; T. Snoy: W.G. Kümmel, R. Pesch 1968; G. Koerperich: G. Strecker 1970.

9. Cf. *CBL*: n°s 16, nn. 2-6; 17, nn. 1-6; 18, nn. 2-11; 19, nn. 4, 6, 9.

De 1974 à 1980, les volumes du Colloque (BETL n°s 33, 34, 40, 41, 44, 46, 48, 51, 53), tous imprimés sur les presses Duculot et distribués par Duculot, sont régis par un accord spécial de co-publication entre les Éditions Duculot et Leuven University Press. Finalement en 1980, suite à une réorganisation chez Duculot, un accord dans ce sens, mais appliqué à l'ensemble des volumes publiés dans la série, a été conclu entre Leuven University Press et les Éditions Peeters. Depuis lors la *Bibliotheca* a pris un nouvel élan. Une bonne centaine de numéros ont paru depuis, et en ce qui concerne les Journées Bibliques, on peut signaler la réédition ou réimpression de huit numéros (n°s 32, 33, 34, 40, 41, 44, 51, 54) et une augmentation non négligeable du nombre des pages pour les volumes nouveaux (pour atteindre une moyenne qui dépasse les sept cents pages). Précisons encore que les couleurs des couvertures, le bleu pour l'Ancien Testament et le vert pour le Nouveau Testament, ont été choisies en 1989 et n'alludent en rien au contexte actuel de la politique belge.

V

The blue and green colours are relatively well represented in BETL with a variety of Biblical studies. For the last ten years I can refer to several monographs (nos. 145, 151, 154), bibliographic tools (140), collected essays (150), and *Festschriften* (143, 144, 146), along with the three recent Colloquium volumes: Luke-Acts (142), Genesis (155), and the Sayings Source Q (158)[10].

While I wrote down the text of this paper, my reference to volumes 155 and 158 as "recently published" was still a guess: I did see the proofs, at more than one stage, but I had not yet seen the printed books. Whereas two years were needed for the editing of *Studies in the Book of Genesis*, A. Lindemann has faced the challenge of publishing the volume on *The Sayings Source Q* within one year, an achievement that was made possible thanks to the goodwill and cooperation of the Orientalist Printing and Peeters Publishing.

I am particularly happy with the publisher's decision that, starting from 1972, out-of-print volumes are to be made available in reprints or new editions. The OT volume *Questions disputées d'Ancien Testament* (C. Brekelmans 1974) has received a new edition enlarged with supplementary notes (203-222) and even a new title on the dust jacket (*Con-*

___

10. See the list of BETL in *CBL*: ● Colloquium Biblicum Lovaniense, and ○ other Biblical studies (109-116).

tinuing Questions in Old Testament Method and Theology, M. Vervenne 1989). Two other OT volumes can be cited as exemplary instances of a new edition ("Nouvelle édition mise à jour"): *La Sagesse dans l'Ancien Testament* (M. Gilbert 1979, ²1990, 399-406.407-425) and *Le livre de Jérémie* (P.-M. Bogaert 1981, ²1997, 411-417.418-448). Reviews of the new edition bring the impact of the original edition back to mind. I quote here one example[11]:

> Le C.B.L. de 1980 est resté célèbre parmi les connaisseurs du livre de Jérémie pour avoir propagé avec force, en particulier à travers les contributions de P.-M. Bogaert et d'É. Tov, l'idée alors relativement nouvelle d'après laquelle le texte de la Septante reflète une version plus originale, plus courte, (du livre) que le texte massorétique lequel en fournit une rédaction révisée et élargie.

Both volumes, Wisdom and Jeremiah, contain a contribution by Norbert Lohfink, supplemented with substantial additions in the new editions. Lohfink presided the colloquium on Deuteronomy (1983) and more recently he contributed to the volume on Qohelet and the Festschriften for C. Brekelmans and M. Gilbert[12]. It was N. Lohfink who suggested to the Committee to take the Canon as topic for the Jubilee Meeting.

I can hardly resist quoting a fragment from C.E. Clements's comment on *Das Deuteronomium: Entstehung, Gestalt und Botschaft*[13]:

> The annual colloquia in biblical studies at Leuven have come to represent a major contribution to contemporary biblical research by drawing together a wide range of scholarly viewpoints on a specific subject and by allowing

---

11. J. JOOSTEN, in *RHPR* 79 (1999), 257. Cf. P.-M. BOGAERT, 430-432 (additional note). On "diverse text forms" in Jer, see also J. LUST, in *JNSL* 20 (1994) 31-48.

12. Cf. *CBL*: N. Lohfink 1974, 1978 (²1989), 1980 (²1997), 1983*, 1997 (and BETL 133, 143: 1997, 1999).

13. *ETL* 62 (1986) 166-168, 166. Compare the more or less similar appreciation in comments on *L'Évangile de Jean*: "De commissie ... heeft een gelukkige hand in het aantrekken van haar sprekers. Ze brengt mensen bij elkaar die als vertegenwoordigers gelden van een bepaalde richting van exegese, zodat het totaalcongres een momentopname geeft van wat er gaande is. Omdat elk congres ook thematisch beperkt blijft (een bijbelboek, een literair genre, een onderzoeksveld) is de aandacht geconcentreerd en bereikt men een maximum aan effect en impact" (Sj. VAN TILBORG, in *TvT* 18, 1978, 202), and on *The Book of Job*: "a fair selection of the most eminent specialists working in the field of Job studies. Their collected papers reflect the major trends in today's scholarship on the subject" (J. LUST, in *ETL* 71, 1995, 209); "La collection *BETL* publie depuis de longues années les communications faites aux Journées bibliques de Louvain (Colloquium Biblicum Lovaniense). Comme celles-ci portent sur des sujets bien délimités, un livre biblique assez souvent, la publication qui en résulte constitue non seulement un état de la question, mais, mieux encore, une occasion de voir se profiler les travaux en cours et les tendances dominantes" (P.-M. BOGAERT, in *Revue bénédictine* 105, 1995, 3). See also on *Ezekiel and his Book*: "La formule consistant à limiter le thème à un livre a fait ses preuves. Cette fois encore, elle s'est révélée heureuse: elle assure l'homogénéité du colloque et celle de la publication qui suit" (*ibid.*, 97, 1987; 324).

them to express a variety of research methods and techniques. In this respect they offer to the researcher as fully as is reasonably possible an opportunity to discover the state of enquiry on a specific biblical book … To
anyone contemplating starting out on a specific topic of research on the
Deuteronomic writings these lectures provide an excellent starting-point.

As a matter of fact, it is clearly an advantage of this focusing on a
specific biblical book (for the Old Testament, beginning with the session
on Jeremiah, 1980) that specialists in the field are brought together in
confrontation with each other.

No less remarkable are some developments in the viewpoints of contributors. At the start in 1949 the two protagonists were widely known as
representatives of typically Roman Catholic positions, the theory of the
sensus plenior for Coppens and Matthean priority for Cerfaux. In 1966,
at the session on Exegesis and Theology, R.E. Brown was invited by
Coppens to give a paper on the *sensus plenior*. In fact, Brown's presentation was an inventory of "the modern problems that face the theory of
the SP"[14]. I have knowledge only of a brief comment by Coppens: "Que
le 'sens plénier' pose encore des problèmes, R.E. Brown y appelle
l'attention"[15]. There came no real reply, however, and in 1990 Brown
could observe: "there has been virtually no discussion of the SPlen
since 1970"[16].

In a recent exposition on the Synoptic Problem J.S. Kloppenborg
Verbin has a note on L. Vaganay's synoptic solution: "It is not surprising that it has not attracted any significant following. Among its few ad-
herents, Cerfaux 1954"[17]. Cerfaux's reflections on the Synoptics did not
stop in 1954. In 1968, for the colloquium on the Gospel of Luke, he accepted (to my great satisfaction) the responsibility for leading the
French-speaking seminar. His "Introduction du Séminaire" (on Luke's
use of Q) was his last writing on the Gospels. It includes a significant
retraction in a paragraph on the redactional composition of Matthew[18].
Curious coincidence: twelve years later the last manuscript Coppens
was able to make ready for printing was on the Son of Man in Q ("*La
Quelle*")[19]. It can be encouraging for us all that in the end certain pecu-

14. *The Problems of the Sensus Plenior*, in *ETL* 43 (1967) 460-469; BETL 26, 1968,
72-81.
    15. *Le messianisme royal* (LD, 54), Paris, 1968, 157 n. 158. His own emphasis is now
on "relectures" and the "intentionalités des textes".
    16. *NJBC*, 1157 (cf. *JBC*, 1968, 615-618). See also Brown's dissertation (1955) and
CBQ 15 (1953) 141-162; 25 (1963) 262-285.
    17. *Excavating Q*, 2000, 46 (and n. 47). Cf. 319-320.
    18. *L'évangile de Luc*, 1973, 61-69 (= ²1989, 285-293), esp. 64 (= 288).
    19. BETL 55, 159. Cf. F. NEIRYNCK, *Evangelica II* (BETL, 99) Leuven, LUP-Peeters,
410.

liar positions are given up. This is not, however, the only message one can retain from the history of CBL.

VI

Speaking for myself, research items such as the structure of Matthew (1965, cf. 1970), the minor agreements (1965), duality in Mark and the limits of source criticism (1971), John's use of the Synoptics (1975, cf. 1990), the study of Q (1981, cf. 2000), Paul and the sayings of Jesus (1984, cf. 1994) received their first treatment in CBL. Influential essays on the Gospels such as, for instance, W.G. Kümmel's *Lukas in der Anklage der heutigen Theologie* (1968) and G. Strecker's *Die Makarismen der Bergpredigt* (1970) originally appeared in CBL. The meeting on Mark in 1971 (presided by M. Sabbe) was a most typical example, with a seminar session in dialogue with M.-É. Boismard and my lecture on duality which, more than I had expected, inspired the enthusiasm of Norman Perrin and was followed, at the evening carrefour in the conference room of the Pope's College, with an unprecedented clash between Norman Perrin and William Farmer, which up to now remains the vocal climax in the history of CBL. Another memorable session was the meeting on christology in 1973, with the debate on the historical Jesus between Albert Descamps and Ernst Käsemann.

It was in 1979 that I was asked[20] to take over the task of secretary of CBL. In 1992, after a first decade in office (sessions 30-40), I agreed to continue, *Deo volente*, for a second decade (sessions 41-50); possibly because it reminded me of the words of Rector Descamps, "le règlement de l'Université est muet sur l'éméritat d'un organisateur des Journécs Bibliques"[21]. Or, could it be more simply that I was influenced by the charming words addressed by acting presidents? (Cf. BETL 126, VIII: "A special debt of gratitude is due to Emeritus Professor Frans Neirynck ...").

In recent years the international character of the Colloquium has been further developed. A rough count of the articles published since 1975, resulting from main papers, seminars, and offered papers (see the lists in *CBL*), indicates a total number of 750 titles, of which about 600 are written by non-Belgian contributors. At last year's meeting on the Sayings Source Q, presided by Andreas Lindemann, eight of the nine main pa-

---

20. Cf. J. Coppens, in BETL 55, IX: "En mars 1979 je fus subitement, tout à l'improviste, atteint d'une maladie ...".
21. Cf. above, n. 7 (p. 77*).

pers, two of the four seminars, and seventeen of the eighteen offered papers were delivered by non-Belgian colleagues. In sessions 26-50 (1975-2001) one counts nine non-Belgian presidents; in chronological order: M. de Jonge, M. Delcor, J. Kremer, N. Lohfink, A. Vanhoye, A.S. van der Woude, C.M. Tuckett, A. Lindemann, and H.J. de Jonge. I retain excellent memories of my collaboration with all these presidents. More particularly in this year it was a special pleasure for me that I could work together with Henk Jan as one of the acting presidents in preparation of the Jubilee Meeting.

There is one of the former presidents who deserves special mention today as the most faithful participant at our Colloquium. Christopher M. Tuckett started in 1981 with a short paper and, with only one exception, he has been present at every New Testament session and delivered a main paper or led one of the seminars. Christopher, you are in your own way an "indefessus promotor" for our Colloquium, and I thank you for being with us once more.

And I extend my gratitude to all of you for joining us in this celebration of the 50th session of our *Colloquium Biblicum Lovaniense*.

Frans NEIRYNCK
CBL secretary 1979-2001

DER KANON DES ALTEN UND NEUEN TESTAMENTS
ZUR FRAGE NACH SEINEM THEOLOGISCHEN ANSPRUCH

I. DIE FRAGE

Der theologische Anspruch des biblischen Kanons ist enorm. Die Wahrheit des Evangeliums steht auf dem Plan, die Normativität des Ursprungs, die Unüberholbarkeit eines Anfangs, der alles Kommende zu bestimmen beansprucht, und die Notwendigkeit fortwährender Erinnerung an ein vergangenes Geschehen und Zeugnis. Beim Kanon geht es um das Kriterium der Unterscheidung zwischen „wahr" und „falsch" in Sachen des Glaubens, der Hoffnung und der Liebe. Über die Einheit und Vielfalt der Schrift müsste gesprochen werden, über einen Kanon im Kanon und die Mitte der Schrift, über das Verhältnis zwischen den beiden Testamenten und die Beziehungen zwischen Israel und der Kirche, auch über Exegese und Biblische Theologie, Methodik und Hermeneutik, jüdische und christliche Schriftauslegung, geschichtliche Wirkungen und theologische Ansprüche. An der Kanonizität hängt die Verbindlichkeit der Heiligen Schrift, je anders im Judentum und Christentum verstanden und auch noch einmal mit deutlichen Unterschieden in der evangelischen und katholischen Kirche[1].

Der Kanon ist für den theologischen Status und die theologische Verantwortung der Exegese von entscheidender Bedeutung. Ist er aber auch ein *Gegenstand* exegetischer Forschung? Gehört er nicht in das Fachgebiet der Judaistik und der Patristik, dann der Dogmatik und Pastoraltheologie? Ist es nicht anachronistisch, wenn Exegeten, auf die ihnen anvertrauten Texte schauend, vom Kanon sprechen, vom Alten und vom Neuen Testament, von der Bibel, der Heiligen Schrift, gar von Inspiration und Inerranz[2]?

---

1. Ein ambitoniertes ökumenisch-theologisches Projekt aus der Zusammenarbeit exegetischer, historischer und systematischer Theologie ist W. PANNENBERG & TH. SCHNEIDER (eds.), *Verbindliches Zeugnis* I-III (Dialog der Kirchen, 7.9.10), Freiburg/Göttingen, Herder/ Vandenhoeck & Ruprecht, 1992-1998.

2. Jüngst macht sich H. FRANKEMÖLLE diese Bedenken zu eigen: *Das Neue Testament als Kommentar? Möglichkeiten und Grenzen einer hermeneutischen These aus der Sicht eines Neutestamentlers*, in F.-L. HOSSFELD (ed.), *Wieviel Systematik erlaubt die Schrift? Auf der Suche nach einer gesamtbiblischen Theologie* (QD, 185), Freiburg/Basel/Wien, Herder, 2001, pp. 200-278.

A. *Die Alternative des 19. Jh.*

Am Ende des 19. Jh. schien es zur Rechten und zur Linken klar, dass die Exegese als Exegese gerade dann zu sich selbst kommt, wenn sie den Kanon Kanon sein lässt und die Kirche Kirche. WILLIAM WREDE schrieb 1897 in seiner fulminanten Besinnung „Über Aufgabe und Methode der sogenannten neutestamentlichen Theologie": „Keine Schrift des Neuen Testaments ist mit dem Prädikat ‚kanonisch' geboren. Der Satz: ‚eine Schrift ist kanonisch' bedeutet zunächst nur: sie ist *nachträglich* von den maßgebenden Faktoren der Kirche des 2. bis 4. Jahrhunderts – vielleicht erst nach allerlei Schwankungen im Urteil – für kanonisch *erklärt* worden. Wer also den Begriff des Kanons als feststehend betrachtet, unterwirft sich damit der Autorität von Bischöfen und Theologen jener Jahrhunderte. Wer diese Autorität in anderen Dingen nicht anerkennt – und kein evangelischer Theologe erkennt sie an –, handelt folgerichtig, wenn er sie auch hier in Frage stellt"[3]. Bis heute wächst die Zahl derer, die es mit den Geboten der Toleranz und Fairness, der wissenschaftlichen Objektivität und der christlichen Freiheit nicht vereinbaren können, einen Kanon anzuerkennen[4].

Die Kehrseite dieses Argumentes macht das 19. Jh. in einer Spielart römischer Theologie sichtbar, die auf die Kritik bereits des Erstens Vatikanums gestoßen ist[5]. Der Kanon sei das Produkt einer kirchlichen Lehrentscheidung. Allein seine Existenz demonstriere den Primat der Tradition vor der Schrift und des Lehramtes vor der Theologie. Indem die Bischöfe der Alten Kirche den Kanon definiert hätten, erweise sich, dass *sie* die Definitionsgewalt über die Verbindlichkeit des Kanons haben, während die Exegese sich damit begnügen müsse, still und bescheiden die Richtigkeit der *dicta probantia* zu bestätigen, die im Zuge einer durchaus nicht undifferenzierten Dogmenhermeneutik benötigt werden, um die Aussagen des kirchlichen Lehramtes abzustützen.

Gilt diese Alternative auch heute noch? Ist man darauf festgelegt, eine wissenschaftlich saubere Exegese zu treiben und kirchlich folgenlos zu bleiben – oder allenfalls der Geist zu sein, der stets verneint? Muss,

---

3. *Über Aufgabe und Methode der sogenannten Neutestamentlichen Theologie*, Göttingen, Vandenhoeck & Ruprecht, 1897. Wiederabdruck der pp. 7-80 bei G. STRECKER (ed.), *Das Problem der Theologie des Neuen Testaments* (Wege der Forschung, 367), Darmstadt, Wissenschaftliche Buchgesellschaft, 1975, pp. 81-154, bes. p. 85.

4. Vgl. W. RICHTER, *Exegese als Literaturwissenschaft. Entwurf einer alttestamentlichen Literaturtheorie und Methodologie*, Göttingen, Vandenhoeck & Ruprecht 1971, p. 40; H. RÄISÄNEN, *Beyond New Testament Theology*, London, SCM, 1990.

5. Texte bei G. SCHNEEMANN, *Controversiarum de divinae gratiae liberique arbitrii concordia initia et progressus*, Freiburg i.Br., Herder, 1881.

wer theologische Ambitionen hat, die historisch-philologische Konzentration verlieren, darf er nur noch der gehorsame Diener seines kirchlichen Lehrherrn sein? HEINZ SCHÜRMANN hat auf die Frage: „Sind sie Exeget oder Theologe?" mit der Gegenfrage geantwortet: „Sind sie Pianist oder Musiker?" Diese Pointe entspricht nicht nur dem Charisma des Neutestamentlers, sondern spiegelt auch einen Paradigmenwechsel im Verhältnis von Exegese und Dogmatik, der für die Hermeneutik des Kanons von großer Bedeutung ist[6].

B. *Der Paradigmenwechsel im 20. Jh.*

Das 19. Jh. hat unter den Bedingungen der Aufklärung und im Durchbruch des historischen Denkens wesentliche Klärungen geschaffen. Hinter die historisch-kritische Erforschung des Kanons führt kein Weg zurück. Noch die römischen Immunisierungsversuche, die das gescheiterte Antimodernismus-Projekt geprägt haben, zeigen im Rückblick, wie unausweichlich und aussichtsreich sie war und ist.

Freilich gibt es eine Vielzahl von Faktoren, die das Problemfeld Kanon und Exegese zu Anfang des 21. Jh. in einem anderen Licht erscheinen lassen als zu Ende des 19. *Auf der einen Seite* ist die religionsgeschichtliche Methode in die Exegese integriert: Erstens gehören motivgeschichtliche Studien über alle Grenzen religiöser Kulturen hinweg, aber innerhalb der Grenzen möglicher oder nachgewiesener Rezeptionen zum Standardrepertoire der Analysen, sowohl unter genetischen als auch unter phänomenologischen Aspekten; zweitens ist die Lokalisierung der Form und Funktion, der Intention, Aussage und Rezeption eines Textes sowohl im Horizont des Alten Testaments und Judentums als auch im Kontext der altorientalischen und hellenistischen Kulturen ein wesentlicher Aspekt der Textinterpretation[7]. Auch für Exegeten, die dem *canonical approach* zuneigen oder eine Biblische Theologie ins Auge fassen, ist es ziemlich selbstverständlich, den Blick über den Kanon – jedenfalls idealiter – auf alle Texte des antiken Judentums und Christentums auszuweiten und ihnen, so weit es eben möglich ist, historische und theologische Gerechtigkeit widerfahren zu lassen. *Auf der*

---

6. H. SCHÜRMANN, dessen Person und Werk ich dankbar gedenke, hat die wichtigsten Reflexionen katholischer Exegese seiner Generation, der Generation des Zweiten Vatikanum vorgelegt; vgl. *Wort Gottes und Schriftauslegung. Gesammelte Beiträge zur theologischen Mitte der Exegese*, ed. K. BACKHAUS, Paderborn, Schöningh, 1998.

7. Vgl. TH. SÖDING, *Wege der Schriftauslegung. Methodenbuch zum Neuen Testament*. Unter Mitarbeit von CH. MÜNCH, Freiburg/Basel/Wien, Herder, 1998, pp. 173-190. 262-267.

anderen Seite bezweifeln führende Vertreter einer religionsgeschichtlichen Exegese nicht mehr die wissenschaftliche Möglichkeit einer Biblischen, am Kanon orientierten Theologie[8]. Es ist nicht die Zeit der großen Versöhnung angebrochen. Gott sei Dank bleiben die Debatten kontrovers und polemisch. Aber die Diskussion wird unter neuen Vorzeichen geführt. Was sind die Gründe?

1. *Die Krise des Schriftprinzips und die biblische Orientierung der*
Theologie

Die exegetischen Arbeiten der Religionsgeschichtlichen und Form-
geschichtlichen Schule haben es vermocht, ihre Zeit in Gedanken der
Schrift und die Schrift in zeitgemäße Gedanken zu fassen; deshalb haben sie weit in die evangelische und die katholische Kirche ausgestrahlt
und im Verein mit ähnlichen Impulsen aus der Patristik, der Dogmen-
und Reformationsgeschichte tiefgreifende Wirkungen erzielt. Die Kritik
der Verbalinspiration, die historisch-kritische Erforschung der Entstehungsgeschichte des Alten wie des Neuen Testament, die Aufdeckung
der zahlreichen Analogien zwischen kanonischen und nicht-kanonischen, alt- und neutestamentlichen, frühjüdischen und frühchristlichen,
aber auch biblischen und nicht-biblischen Texten, sei es aus der Welt
des Alten Orients, sei es aus der Zeit des griechisch-römischen Hellenismus – all dies hat zu einer tiefen Krise des reformatorischen Schriftprinzips geführt[9], aber in weiten Teilen evangelischer Theologie gerade
nicht zur Auflösung des Kanons, sondern zu einem neuen Kanonverständnis, das sein geschichtliches Werden nicht als Gegensatz, sondern
als Ausdruck seines Wesens erkennen kann, nämlich sowohl als notwendige Voraussetzung wie auch als integraler Bestandteil seiner normativen Kraft[10].

Die formgeschichtliche Schule, von den Konservativen vielfach als li-

8. Vgl. R. ALBERTZ, *Religionsgeschichte Israels in alttestamentlicher Zeit,* 2 Bde.
(ATD.E, 8), Göttingen, Vandenhoeck & Ruprecht, 1992, p. I 37 (der allerdings die
religionsgeschichtliche Orientierung als intellektuell überlegene erachtet); G. THEISSEN,
Die Religion der ersten Christen. Eine Theorie des Urchristentums, Gütersloh: Kaiser,
2000, p. 13f. (der die Unterscheidung nicht im Hinblick auf die Wissenschaftlichkeit,
sondern die Adressaten vornimmt). Freilich ist diese Position auf religionsgeschichtlicher
Seite keineswegs unumstritten; vgl. die Diskussion in *JBT* 10 (1995): *Religionsgeschich-*
te Israels oder Theologie des Alten Testaments; JBT 12 (1997): *Biblische Hermeneutik.*
Vgl. auch zur Möglichkeit einer gegenseitigen Befruchtung O. KEEL, *Religionsgeschichte*
Israels oder Theologie des Alten Testaments?, in F.-L. HOSSFELD (ed.), *Systematik* (Anm.
2), pp. 88-109.

9. Vgl. W. PANNENBERG, *Die Krise des Schriftprinzips* (1962), in ID., *Grundfragen*
systematischer Theologie I, Göttingen, Vandenhoeck & Ruprecht, ³1979, pp. 11-21.

10. Vgl. den Überblick von H.H. SCHMID & J. MEHLHAUSEN (eds.), *Sola Scriptura.*
Das reformatorische Schriftprinzip in der säkularen Welt, Gütersloh, Mohn, 1991.

beral verschrieen, hat – inmitten aller historischen Irrtümer, die sie begangen haben mag – *en gros* und *en detail* deutlich herausgearbeitet, dass die biblischen Schriften in einem eminenten Sinn „Literatur für Leser" (HARALD WEINRICH) sind. Die Entstehung und Tradierung der alttestamentlichen Schriften setzt – in ganz bestimmten und sehr variablen historischen Konstellationen – die Größe Israel voraus, das sich in den Protagonisten seiner Selbstdefinition als Gottesvolk versteht; die neutestamentlichen Schriften sind im Prozess der Konstituierung der Ekklesia entstanden und dienen dem, was Paulus ihren „Aufbau" genannt hat. Es ist kaum ein Zufall, dass die katholische Kirche sich der historisch-kritischen Exegese zu einem Zeitpunkt geöffnet hat, an dem diese Richtung führend und ihre ekklesiale Attraktivität sichtbar geworden war. Das Dokument der Päpstlichen Bibelkommission von 1993 markiert schon mit seinem Titel die Pointe des katholischen Interesses: „Die Interpretation der Bibel in der Kirche"[11]. 50 Jahre zuvor hatte *Divino afflante spiritu* (DH 3825)[12] erstmals die Türen des katholischen Lehrhauses vorsichtig für die fremden Gäste aus den Provinzen der historischen Kritik geöffnet[13], nicht ohne sie ob ihrer Gefährlichkeit misstrauisch zu beäugen[14]. Das Zweite Vatikanische Konzil geht einen großen Schritt weiter und nennt das Studium der Hl. Schrift – mit Worten Leos XIII. (Prov. Deus [Ench. Bibl. 114]) *„universae theologiae anima"* (OT 16) und *„anima Sacrae Theologiae"* (DV 24)[15]. Dabei ist jedoch vorausgesetzt, dass zur Exegese nicht nur die Anwendung historischer und philologischer Methoden, sondern auch die Suche nach der Einheit und Ganzheit

11. Deutsche Ausgabe: *Die Interpretation der Bibel in der Kirche* (Verlautbarungen des Apostolischen Stuhles, 115), Bonn, 1993. Weiterführend: *L'interpretazione della Bibbia nella Chiesa. Atti del Simposio promosso dalla Congregazione per la Dottrina della Fede Roma, settembre 1999* (Atti e Documenti, 11), Città del Vaticano, Libreria editrice, 2001.

12. Zur evangelischen Einschätzung vgl. H. VON SODEN, *Pius XII. über die zeitgemäße Förderung der biblischen Studien*, in ID., *Urchristentum und Geschichte. Gesammelte Aufsätze* II: *Kirchengeschichte und Gegenwart*, ed. H. VON CAMPENHAUSEN, Tübingen, Mohr, 1956, pp. 177-194.

13. In ein freundliches Licht tauchen die römische Entwicklung P. LAGHI, M. GILBERT & A. VANHOYE, *Chiesa e Sacra Scrittura. Un secolo ecclesiastico e studi biblici* (SubBib, 17), Rom, PIB, 1994.

14. Aus dieser Zeit stammt G. EBELINGS Urteil, die katholische Kirche gebe die historische Bibelforschung nur deshalb frei, weil deren Ergebnisse sie in ihrer Lehrentwicklung ohnedies nicht irritieren könnte: *Die Bedeutung der historisch-kritischen Methode für die protestantische Theologie und Kirche* (1950), in ID., *Wort und Glaube* (I), Tübingen, Mohr, ²1962, pp. 1-49.

15. Zur Vorgeschichte der Formel vgl. L. LELOIR, *La Sainte Écriture, âme de toute la théologie*, in *Seminarium* 18 (1966) 880-892. Nach dem Kommentator J. RATZINGER hat DV 24 in Verbindung mit OT 16 „für die Systemgestalt der Theologie eine nahezu revolutionierende Bedeutung": *LTK*.E, 2 (1967) 577.

der Schrift gehört[16].

Der Krise und Reformulierung des Schriftprinzips auf evangelischer Seite entspricht eine biblische Orientierung auch der katholischen Theologie. Beides erweist sich als ökumenisch-theologisch fruchtbar und stellt die exegetische Arbeit in einen neuen kirchenpolitischen und ekklesialen Kontext. Der Bibelwissenschaft wird eine fundamentaltheologische Orientierungsfunktion angesonnen, wenn es gilt, die Wahrheit des Evangeliums im Rückgriff auf das Schriftzeugnis zu bewähren. In diesem Kontext braucht die Exegese ihren Eigensinn nicht prinzipiell gegen die Systematische Theologie zu behaupten, sondern verweist ihrerseits, indem sie als Exegese das Zeugnis der Schrift expliziert, die Systematik an die *norma normans non normata* aller christlichen Theologie[17]. Das freilich setzt voraus, dass sie als Exegese einen Zugang zum Phänomen des Kanons findet und substantiell dazu beitragen kann, im Wort der Schrift das Wort Gottes zu entdecken, wie es der Glaube zu hören vermag. Begründet der Kanon des Neuen Testaments tatsächlich, wie ERNST KÄSEMANN meinte[18], die Vielfalt der Konfessionen oder nicht doch die Einheit der Ekklesia? Die Exegese ist gefragt, mit ihren methodischen Möglichkeiten, d.h. durch die Analyse und Interpretation der einschlägigen Texte, darzutun, was kanonische Normativität im biblischtheologischen Sinn heißen kann. Dass die biblischen Bücherlisten – nicht vor dem 4. Jh. – „Kanon" genannt werden[19], spiegelt die historische Entwicklung wider, dass die Heilige Schrift im Römischen Reich nach der konstantinischen Wende als Grundgesetz des sich entwickelnden Staatskirchentums angesehen wird[20]. Der Ort ihrer siegreichen An-

16. Das Programm einer biblischen Orientierung der gesamten Theologie, dessen Realisierung weitestgehend noch aussteht, postuliert (in *Dei Verbum* 12) eine Exegese, die nicht in einen Selbstwiderspruch gerät, sondern auf den Königsweg gelangt, wenn sie sowohl die Kontexte, Strukturen und Genesen der Texte als auch die Einheit und des Anspruch des Kanons zum Gegenstand ihrer Forschung macht. In weiser Zurückhaltung beschränkt sich DV 12 allerdings auf das Postulat, ohne einen Weg vorzuzeichnen, wie es erfüllt werden kann; vgl. zur Problemanzeige N. LOHFINK, *Der weiße Fleck in Dei Verbum, Artikel 12*, in *TTZ* 101 (1992) 337-342.

17. Vgl. TH. SÖDING, *Neutestamentliche Exegese und Ökumenische Theologie. Probleme, Projekte und Perspektiven*, in K. RAISER & D. SATTLER (eds.), *Ökumene vor neuen Zeiten*. FS Th. Schneider, Freiburg/Basel/Wien, Herder, 2000, pp. 99-131.

18. *Begründet der neutestamentliche Kanon die Einheit der Kirche?* (1951), in Id. (ed.), *Das Neue Testament als Kanon*, Göttingen, Vandenhoeck & Ruprecht, 1970, pp. 124-133, bes. 131.133. Eine Kritik habe ich versucht in TH. SÖDING, *Entwürfe Biblischer Theologie in der Gegenwart. Eine neutestamentliche Standortbestimmung*, in H. HÜBNER & B. JASPERT (eds.), *Biblische Theologie. Entwürfe der Gegenwart* (Biblisch-Theologische Studien, 38), Neukirchen-Vluyn, Neukirchener 1999, pp. 41-103.

19. Vgl. A. VON HARNACK, *Über das Alter der Bezeichnung „die Bücher" (Die Bibel) für die h. Schriften in den Kirchen*, in *Zentralblatt für das Bibliothekswesen* 45 (1928) 337-342.

erkennung als *regula fidei*[21] ist auch der Ort ihrer größten Bedrohung: als Waffe im Kampf gegen Ketzer und Juden eingesetzt zu werden. Umso wichtiger ist es, den Sinn des Kanonbegriffs nicht als gegeben vorauszusetzen (und dann etwa exegetisch bestätigen oder widerlegen zu wollen), sondern allererst aus den biblischen Quellen zu erarbeiten.

2. Die Entdeckung der Jüdischen Bibel und das Projekt Biblischer Theologie

Die historisch-kritische Exegese hat seit ihren Anfängen erheblich dazu beigetragen, die Einheit des Kanons in Frage zu stellen, indem sie die Unterscheidung zwischen dem Alten und dem Neuen Testament auf ihre Fahnen geschrieben hat. Gegen die fraglose Selbstverständlichkeit, mit der im Zuge allegorischer Schriftauslegung die *interpretatio Christiana* des Alten Testaments praktiziert wurde, arbeitete die Exegese, auf eine kurze Formel gebracht, heraus, dass, historisch interpretiert, das Alte Testament so sehr von Jesus, dem Christus schweigt, wie das Neue Testament von ihm spricht. Gleichzeitig wurde im Laufe der Zeit wieder deutlicher, dass zentrale Themen der Theologie – von der Schöpfung über die Geschichte und das Ethos bis zur Eschatologie – grundlegend und unüberholt im Alten Testament zur Sprache kommen. Umgekehrt hat sich in der Exegese des Neuen Testaments gezeigt, dass es nicht etwa, wie RUDOLF BULTMANN noch meinte, das Produkt eines jüdisch-hellenistischen Synkretismus ist[22], sondern entscheidend durch die Vorgabe, Aufnahme und Anverwandlung alttestamentlich-jüdischer, (palästinisch-aramäischer wie hellenistisch-griechischer) Theologie geprägt ist[23], auch wenn (wie schon im Alten Testament und Frühjudentum) die Fähigkeit des Neuen Testaments zur kritisch-integrierenden Rezeption

20. Vgl. TH. SÖDING, *Mehr als ein Buch. Die Bibel begreifen*, Freiburg/Basel/Wien, Herder ³2001 (¹1995), pp. 22-27.

21. Gleichzeitig entwickelt sich die *regula fidei* in Gestalt des Symbolons als (dem Anspruch nach) schriftgemäße Norm der Schriftauslegung; vgl. P. GRECH, *The „regula fidei" as Hermeneutical Principle Yesterday and Today*, in *L'interpretazione* (Anm. 11), pp. 208-231.

22. R. BULTMANN, *Das Urchristentum im Rahmen der antiken Religionen*, Zürich/München, Artemis, ⁵1986 (¹1947).

23. Ins Zentrum Biblischer Theologie gestellt von P. STUHLMACHER, *Biblische Theologie des Neuen Testaments* I-II, Göttingen, Vandenhoeck & Ruprecht, 1992-1999. Die Kritik an einem traditionsgeschichtlichen Kontinuum als Rückgrat Biblischer Theologie, die sich in einem lehrreichen Aufsatz jüngst auch B. JANOWSKI zu eigen gemacht hat (*„Verstehst du auch, was du liest?". Reflexionen auf die Leserichtung des christlichen Bibel*, in F.-L. HOSSFELD [ed.], *Systematik* [Anm. 2], pp. 150-191, bes. p. 155f), muss differenzieren zwischen der These des Neutestamentlers, dass die urchristlichen Schriften nur aus der essentiellen Traditionskontinuität zum Alten Testament heraus verstanden werden können (ohne dass freilich die beeindruckende Fähigkeit zur kritischen Adaption

von Motiven paganer Religionen sehr groß gewesen ist und zur Substanz neutestamentlicher Theologie gehört[24].

Im religionsgeschichtlichen Vergleich zeigt sich ein singuläres Phänomen: Der erste Teil der *Biblia Christiana*, das „Alte Testament", ist die eine und ganze Heilige Schrift der Juden. Hier liegt der Kern des hermeneutischen Problems. Es ist keineswegs nur ein exegetisches. Es fordert die harte Arbeit an einer Neubestimmung des Verhältnisses zwischen dem Christentum und dem Judentum. Die Arbeit gehört zum historischen Auftrag der gegenwärtigen Theologengeneration[25]. Sie fordert nicht nur die historisch-kritische Differenzierungsfähigkeit der Exegese; sie öffnet ihr auch die Augen für geschichtliche Phänomene, die theologisch gedeutet sein wollen.

Zum einen: Historisch betrachtet, gibt es einen zweifachen Ausgang des Alten Testaments: den in das Judentum, dokumentiert durch Talmud und Midrasch, und den in das Christentum, dokumentiert durch das Neue Testament[26]. Wie aber ist dieser Umstand *theologisch* zu bewerten? Ist die *interpretatio Judaica* des „Alten Testaments" in der Perspektive christlicher, also alt- *und* neutestamentlicher Kanonhermeneutik irrelevant? Ist sie eine Konkurrentin, die es auszustechen gilt[27]? Oder ist sie eine Schwester im Geiste, deren Stimme gehört werden muss, wenn die jüngere Tochter, die Ekklesia, sagen will, was ihr vom

paganer Motive relativiert werden dürfte), und der eines Alttestamentlers, die Schrift Israels sei, traditionsgeschichtlich betrachtet, essentiell auf das Neue Testament hin angelegt; vgl. TH. SÖDING, *Alles neu!? Neutestamentliche Anmerkungen zum Verhältnis zwischen den Testamenten,* in G. STEINS (ed.), *Leseordnung. Altes und Neues Testament in der Liturgie* (Sonderheft Gottes Volk), Stuttgart, Katholisches Bibelwerk, 1997, pp. 78-91.

24. Dies hätten Konzepte Biblischer Theologie stärker als in den vorliegenden Entwürfen berücksichtigen; vgl. TH. SÖDING, *Entwürfe* (Anm. 18), pp. 91-101.

25. Wichtige Dokumente zur Gewissenserforschung und Neuorientierung der Kirchen sammeln (mit besonderer Berücksichtigung des deutschen Sprachraumes) R. RENDTORFF & H.H. HENRIX (eds.), *Die Kirchen und das Judentum. Dokumente 1945 bis 1985,* Paderborn/München, Bonifatius/Lembeck, ²1989; H.H. HENRIX & W. KRAUS (eds.), *Die Kirchen und das Judentum. Dokumente 1996 bis 2000,* Paderborn/München, Bonifatius/Lembeck, 2001.

26. Vgl. E. BLUM (ed.), *Die Hebräische Bibel und ihre zweifache Nachgeschichte.* FS R. Rendtorff, Neukirchen-Vluyn, Neukirchener 1990; K. KOCH, *Der Doppelte Ausgang des Alten Testaments in Judentum und Christentum,* in *JBT* 6 (1991) 215-242.

27. Das ist offenkundig über weiteste Strecken der Theologiegeschichte der herrschende Eindruck – bildlich dargestellt im ikonographischen Programm der blinden, geschlagenen Synagoge und der freien, siegreichen Ekklesia. Andere Akzente setzt das Straßburger Münster; vgl. O. V. SIMSON, *Ecclesia und Synagoge am südlichen Querhausportal des Straßburger Münsters,* in L. KÖTZSCHE & P. VON DER OSTEN-SACKEN (eds.), *Wenn der Messias kommt. Das jüdisch-christliche Verhältnis im Spiegel mittelalterlicher Kunst,* Berlin, 1984, pp. 104-125. Seine theologische Konsequenz hat eindrucksvoll H.U. VON BALTHASAR beschrieben: *Die Tragödie und der christliche Glaube* (1965), in ID., *Spiritus Creator. Skizzen zur Theologie* III, Einsiedeln, Johannes, 1967, pp. 347-365, bes. p. 360.

Alten und vom Neuen Testament her zu sagen aufgetragen ist [28]? Welches Gewicht hätte aber dann diese Stimme der Älteren? Ohne weiteres ist klar, dass sie von größter heuristischer Bedeutung ist, um das Alte Testament aus seinen eigenen Voraussetzungen und im Horizont seiner eigenen Zielsetzungen zu verstehen. Aber mit diesem hermeneutischen Hinweis bleibt die Frage nach dem *theologischen* Stellenwert der jüdischen Bibellektüre noch offen. Eine Antwort zu geben, setzt eine Reflexion über das Grundverhältnis zwischen Israel und Kirche voraus und ist selbst ein wesentlicher Aspekt dieser Verhältnisbestimmung.

Zum anderen: Das Neue Testament ist im Alten verwurzelt. Sein großes Thema ist allerdings Jesus Christus. Sein Evangelium ist der neue Wein, der in neue Schläuche gehört (Mk 2,22) so gut der alte auch schmecken mag (Lk 5,38). Nicht eine höhere Moralität oder tiefere Spiritualität begründet die Neuheit des Neuen Testaments[29], sondern Jesus, der Christus. Jesus ist „der Neue", der das Neue Testament zum *Neuen* macht. Doch ohne die Heilige Schrift Israels könnte Jesus gar nicht als Christus wahrgenommen werden. Der Gott Jesu Christi ist kein anderer als der Gott Abrahams, Isaaks und Jakobs (Mk 12,26). Ein starker Zweig der Verwurzelung des Neuen Testaments im Alten Testament ist die Rezeption der Schrift[30]. Die *interpretatio Christiana* des Alten Testaments im Neuen, die der patristischen Exegese die Richtung gewiesen hat[31], steht allerdings in großem Gegensatz nicht nur zu wesentlichen Tendenzen jüdischer Exegese, sondern auch zu vielen Ergebnissen historisch-kritischer und literaturwissenschaftlicher Schriftauslegung. Folgt daraus, dass allein das *Vetus Testamentum in Novo recepto* kanonischen Rang genießt[32]? Ist umgekehrt die christologische Schrifthermeneutik philologisch und theologisch desavouiert[33]?

Die Biblische Theologie[34] stellt sich dem Problem, wie angesichts der

---

28. Dafür plädiert mit Verve E. ZENGER, *Das Erste Testament. Die jüdische Bibel und die Christen*, Düsseldorf, Patmos, 1991 u.ö.; ID., *Einleitung in das Alte Testament*, Stuttgart, Kohlhammer, ³1998 (1995), pp. 12-35.

29. Vgl. E. ZENGER, *Ein Gott der Rache? Feindpsalmen verstehen*, Freiburg/Basel/Wien, Herder, 1994.

30. Unter Berücksichtigung des Intertextualitäts-Modells neu erarbeitet von R.B. HAYS, *Echoes of Scripture in the Letters of Paul*, New Haven/London 1989; C.M. TUCKETT (ed.), *The Scriptures in the Gospels* (BETL, 131), Leuven, Peeters, 1997.

31. Vgl. nur H. DE LUBAC, *Geist aus der Geschichte* (frz. 1950), Einsiedeln, Johannes, 1968; ID., *Der geistige Sinn der Schrift*, Einsiedeln, Johannes 1967; ID., *Exégèse médiévale. Les quatres sens de l'Écriture* (Théologie, 41), 4 Bde., Paris, Aubier, 1959-196; J. DANIÉLOU, *Sacramentum futuri. Etudes sur les origines de la typologie biblique*, Paris, Beauchesne, 1950.

32. In den Mittelpunkt einer Biblischen Theologie gestellt von H. HÜBNER, *Biblische Theologie des Neuen Testaments* I-III, Göttingen, Vandenhoeck & Ruprecht, 1990-1995.

33. Das ist die Tendenz bei G. DAUTZENBERG, *Alter und neuer Bund nach 2Kor 3*, in R. KAMPLING (ed.), „*Nun steht aber diese Sache im Evangelium". Zur Frage nach den Anfängen des christlichen Antijudaismus*, Paderborn, Schöningh, 1999, pp. 229-249;

Zweiheit der Testamente von der Einheit der Schrift gesprochen werden kann[35]. Die Kernfrage lautet: Bedarf es einer Relativierung der Christologie, wenn das Alte Testament als Bibel Israels gewürdigt und die jüdische Schriftauslegung in ihrem theologischen Rang anerkannt werden soll? Oder ist es gerade die Christologie des Neuen Testaments, die den Grund legt für die Unterscheidung beider Testamente, ohne die Einheit der Schrift preiszugeben, und die Achtung des Judentums, ohne die christliche Identität zu relativieren[36]?

3. *Der Kanonische Prozess und die Frage nach dem Ursprung des Kanons*

Seit Ende des 19. Jh. sind große Arbeiten zur Geschichte des Kanons erschienen[37]. Sie unterscheiden sich in vielem, haben aber auf verschiedene Weise die diversen Phasen, Probleme, Konflikte und offenen Fra-

P. FIEDLER, *Antijudaismus als Argumentationsfigur. Gegen die Verabsolutierung von Kampfesäußerungen des Paulus im Galaterbrief*, in *ibidem*, pp. 251-279. Wesentlich differenzierter urteilt N. WALTER, *Zur theologischen Problematik des christologischen Schriftbeweises im Neuen Testament*, in *NTS* 41 (1995) 338-357.

34. Vgl. J. BARR, *The Concept of Biblical Theology*, London, SCM, 1999.

35. Signifikante Positionen werden markiert in CH. DOHMEN & TH. SÖDING (eds.), *Eine Bibel - zwei Testamente. Positionen Biblischer Theologie* (Uni-Taschenbücher, 1893), Paderborn, Schöningh, 1995.

36. Dies ist die These meines früheren Beitrages: *Probleme und Chancen Biblischer Theologie aus neutestamentlicher Sicht*, in *Eine Bibel* (Anm. 35), pp. 159-177. H. FRANKEMÖLLE scheint in seiner Kritik (*Kommentar* [Anm. 2], p. 248 Anm. 135 und 269 Anm. 195) nicht mit der Möglichkeit zu rechnen, dass sich „in Christus" der „Eigenwert" des Alten Testaments für christliche Theologie erschließen könnte. Meine Position habe ich zwischenzeitlich verdeutlicht: *Das Jüdische im Christentum - Verlust oder Gewinn christlicher Identität? Thesen eines Neutestamentlers*, in *TTZ* 109 (2000) 54-76 (span. Übersetzung: *Selecciones de teología* 40 [2001] 197-210).

37. Vgl. (als kleine Auswahl) Th. ZAHN, *Geschichte des neutestamentlichen Kanons I: Das Neue Testament vor Origenes*, Erlangen, Deichert, 1888/1889, *II: Urkunden und Belege zum ersten und dritten Band*, Erlangen/Leipzig, Deichert, 1890/1892; ID., *Grundriß der Geschichte des neutestamentlichen Kanons*, Leipzig, Hinrichs, [4]1904 ([1]1901). Nachdr. Wuppertal, Brockhaus, 1985; A. VON HARNACK, *Das Neue Testament und das Jahr 200: Theodor Zahn's Geschichte des neutestamentlichen Kanons (Erster Band, Erste Hälfte) geprüft*. Freiburg i.Br., Mohr, 1889; ID., *Lehrbuch der Dogmengeschichte* II, Leipzig, Hinrichs, [3]1894; A.C. SUNDBERG, *The Old Testament Canon of the Early Church* (HTS, 20), Cambridge, Mass, Harvard University Press, 1964; H. VON CAMPENHAUSEN, *Die Entstehung der christlichen Bibel*, Tübingen, Mohr, 1968; A. SAND, *Kanon. Von den Anfängen bis zum Canon Muratori* (HDG, I/3a), Freiburg/Basel/Wien, Herder, 1974; S.Z. LEIMAN, *The Canonization of Hebrew Scripture. The Talmudic and Midrashic Evidence*, Hamden, Archon Books, 1976; D. KAESTLI & O. WERMELINGER (eds.), *Le canon de l'Ancien Testament. Sa formation et son histoire* (Le monde de la Bible), Genève, Labor et fides, 1984; R.T. BECKWITH, *The Old Testament Canon of the New Testament Church and its Background in Early Judaism*, Grand Rapids, Eerdmans, 1985; H.Y. GAMBLE, *The New Testament Canon. Its Making and Meaning*, Philadadelphia, Fortress, 1985; E.E. ELLIS, *The Old Testament in Early Christianity. Canon and Interpretation in the Light of Modern Research*, Tübingen, Mohr, 1991; B.M. METZGER, *Der*

gen der Kanonbildung bis zu ihrer vorläufigen Beruhigung im 4. Jh. aus den Quellen aufgearbeitet, die Impulse ebenso wie die Widerstände, die Umwege sowohl als auch die Durchbrüche, unfaire Attacken ebenso wie leidenschaftliches Ringen um die Wahrheit, faule Kompromisse nicht anders als großherzige Friedensangebote. Im christlichen Traditions-raum geht es um die Arbeiten an der Schlussredaktion der Septuaginta[38] und den immer wieder aufflackernden Streit um die *hebraica veritas*[39], um die Sammlung der Paulusbriefe[40] und der Evangelien, die Abwehr Marcions, der nicht nur das Alte Testament ablehnen, sondern auch das sich formierende Neue verstümmeln wollte[41], die Zurückweisung der Gnosis mit ihrer Favorisierung apokrypher Evangelien wie der Apostel-akten[42], die Diskussionen speziell um den Hebräerbrief und die Johan-nesapokalypse, schließlich auch die Aufstellung von Kanon-Listen[43].

Kanon des Neuen Testaments. Entstehung, Entwicklung, Bedeutung (engl. 1987), Düssel-dorf, Patmos, 1993; L.M. MCDONALD, *The Formation of the Christian Bible Canon,* Peabody, Mass, Hendrickson, 1987, ²1995; O.H. STECK, *Der Kanon des hebräischen Al-ten Testamentes. Historische Materialien für eine ökumenische Perspektive,* in W. PANNENBERG & TH. SCHNEIDER (eds.), *Verbindliches Zeugnis,* Bd. I (Anm. 1), pp. 11-33; K.S. FRANK, *Zur altkirchlichen Kanongeschichte,* in *op. cit.,* pp. 128-155; D.M. CARR, *Canonization in the Context of Community. An Outline of the Formation of the Tanakh and the Christian Bible,* in R.D. Weis & D.M. Carr (eds.), *A Gift of God in Due Season. Essays on Scripture and Community in Honour of J.A. Sanders* (JSOT SS, 225), Sheffield, Sheffield Academic Press, 1996, pp. 22-64.

38. Vgl. M. HARL, G. DORIVAL & O. MUNNICH, *La Bible grecque des Septante. Du judaïsme hellénistique au christianisme ancien* (ICA), Paris, Cerf, 1988; M. HENGEL (& R. DEINES), *Die Septuaginta als „christliche" Schriftensammlung, ihre Vorgeschichte und das Problem ihres Kanons,* in ID. & A.M. SCHWEMER (eds.), *Die Septuaginta zwischen Judentum und Christentum* (WUNT 72), Tübingen, Mohr, 1994, 182-284; M. MÜLLER, *The First Bible of the Church. A Plea for the Septuagint* (JSOT SS, 206), Sheffield, Sheffield Academic Press, 1996; K.H. JOBES & M. SILVA, *Invitation to the Septuagint,* Grand Rapids, Baker, 2000.

39. Wichtiges Material und gute Durchdringung des Problems bei CH. MARKSCHIES, *Hieronymus und die „Hebraica veritas",* in M. HENGEL & A.M. SCHWEMER (eds.), *Septuaginta* (Anm. 38), pp. 131-181; weiter: R. HENNINGS, *Der Briefwechsel zwischen Augustinus und Hieronymus und ihr Streit um den Kanon des AT und die Auslegung von Gal 2,11-14* (VigChrSup, 21), Leiden, Brill, 1994; G. MENESTRINI, *Il carteggio Agos-toni – Gerolamo,* in *CrSt* 18 (1997) 387-396.

40. Nicht überzeugend ist die steile These von D. TROBISCH, die meisten Paulusbriefe seien nicht als aktuelle Gemeindebriefe, sondern als literarische Darstellung der pau-linischen Theologie in Briefen zu erklären: *Die Entstehung der Paulusbriefsammlung* (NTOA, 10), Freiburg/Göttingen, Universitätsverlag/Vandenhoeck & Ruprecht, 1989; ID., *Die Paulusbriefe und die Anfänge der christlichen Publizistik* (KT, 135), München, Kaiser, 1994.

41. Große Sympathien brachte seinem Vorstoß noch einmal A. VON HARNACK entge-gen: *Marcion. Das Evangelium vom fremden Gott* (¹1921.²1924), Darmstadt, Wissen-schaftliche Buchgesellschaft, 1985.

42. Vgl. A. BENOIT, *Saint Irénée. Introduction à l'étude de sa théologie* (EHPhR, 52), Paris, Presses Universitaires de France, 1960; H. GRAF REVENTLOW, *Epochen der Bibel-auslegung I: Vom Alten Testament bis Origenes,* München, Beck, 1990, pp. 150-170; J. FANTINO, *La théologie d'Irénée. Lecture des écritures en réponse à l'exégèse gnos-tique; une approche trinitaire* (CoF, 180), Paris, Cerf, 1994.

Das immer neue Abschreiben der Texte spielt eine Rolle[44], ihre Rezeption im Gottesdienst bis hin zum liturgischen Gebrauch[45], die Ausbildung regionaler Profile der Alten Kirche und die schwierigen Bemühungen um einen globalen Gedankenaustausch, die Diskussionen um Apostolizität und Katholizität, um Rechtgläubigkeit und Ketzerei, Wahrheit und Liebe, Gehorsam und Freiheit.

So unterschiedlich die Interessen und Resultate der einschlägigen Arbeiten sind, scheinen sie doch die These nahezulegen, dass der Kanon nicht nur von seinem definierten, jedenfalls faktischen Endergebnis her zu erklären und verstehen ist, sondern im Zuge eines „kanonischen Prozesses", der mit der Entstehung der biblischen Schriften beginnt und mit der Festlegung seines Umfangs nicht endet, sondern sich bis in die Gegenwart bei der Kommentierung und Auslegung ereignet. Dieser kanonische Prozess ist keine stringente Entwicklung, die nach dem Muster einer genetischen Programmierung abläuft, aber auch nicht eine Abfolge von Zufällen oder das Ergebnis von Willkür, sondern ein echter historischer Prozess, der an vielen Stellen anders hätte verlaufen können und doch – wenigstens im Rückblick – als lebendige Tradition erkennbar ist. Vom kanonischen Prozess her zu denken, kann die Exegese vor apologetischem Übereifer bewahren, die Kanontheorie der Alten Kirche historisch-kritisch beweisen zu wollen, stellt aber auch die Frage nach seinem Ausgangspunkt: Inwiefern lässt sich im Rückblick auf die biblischen Schriften exegetisch erklären und verstehen, *dass* es überhaupt einen Kanon gibt? Und inwieweit lässt sich erklären, dass er die Gestalten gewonnen hat, die sich in der jüdischen und christlichen Tradition herausgebildet haben?

4. *Die Gedächtnisgeschichte und die Kriterienfrage*

Die Chancen, das Phänomen des biblischen Kanons historisch zu erklären und theologisch zu verstehen, sind durch die Entwicklung der philosophischen Hermeneutik erheblich verbessert worden. WILHELM

43. Vgl. McDONALD, *Formation* (Anm. 37).

44. Die These von D. TROBISCH, *Die Endredaktion des Neuen Testaments. Eine Untersuchung zur Entstehung der christlichen Bibel* (NTOA, 31), Freiburg/Schw./Göttingen, Universitätsverlag/Vandenhoeck & Ruprecht, 1996, es habe eine „Kanonische Ausgabe" des Neuen Testament im 2. Jh. (wahrscheinlich vom Rom aus) ihren Siegeszug angetreten habe, ist trotz beachtlicher Argumente und vieler wertvoller Einzelbeobachtungen nicht hinreichend begründet.

45. Vgl. zur Schriftlesung im Synagogengottesdienst J. MAIER, *Schriftlesung in jüdischer Tradition*, in A. FRANZ (ed.), *Streit am Tisch des Wortes. Zur Bedeutung des Alten Testaments und seiner Verwendung in der Liturgie*, St. Ottilien, Eos, 1995, pp. 505-559; ferner L. TREPP, *Der jüdische Gottesdienst. Gestalt und Entwicklung*, Stuttgart et al., 1992. Zum urchristlichen Wortgottesdienst vgl. J.CHR. SALZMANN, *Lehren und Ermahnen. Zur Geschichte des christlichen Wortgottesdienstes in den ersten drei Jahrhunderten* (WUNT, 59), Tübingen, Mohr, 1994, pp. 58f.

DILTHEY[46] hat gezeigt, dass jede Interpretation historisch bedingt ist, HANS GEORG GADAMER[47], dass sie die Entwicklung eines wirkungsgeschichtlichen Problembewusstseins voraussetzt. Dies eröffnet neue Möglichkeiten, die Beziehung zwischen Texten und ihrer Tradierung zu erforschen[48]. Literaturwissenschaftlich ist die aktive Rolle des Lesers bei der Konstituierung eines Textsinns vielfach beschrieben worden[49]. Ekklesiologisch ist Rezeption durch YVES CONGAR als Grundzug der Traditionsbildung erklärt worden[50]. Das denkbar intensivste Beispiel der Textrezeption durch eine Interpretationsgemeinschaft ist die Kanonisierung[51]. Es ist gleichzeitig das ekklesiologisch alles entscheidende, besteht doch der *sensus fidelium* nach Lumen Gentium 12 (DH 4130; mit Verweis auf 1 Thess 2,13; vgl. DV 8 [DH 4210]) wesentlich darin, im Wort der Heiligen Schrift das Evangelium zu vernehmen[52].

Wertvolle Anregungen, das Phänomen der Kanonbildung zu beschreiben, lassen sich auf den Exkursionen gewinnen, die JAN ASSMANN von Ägypten aus organisiert, um die „Archäologie der literarischen Kommunikation" zu studieren[53]. Dem unbefangenen Blick des Kulturwissenschaftlers zeigen sich Grundgesetze der Kanonisierung, die *in theolo-*

46. W. DILTHEY, *Die Entstehung der Hermeneutik* (1900), in *Gesammelte Schriften* V, Stuttgart, Teubner, ²1957, pp. 317-338.

47. H.G. GADAMER, *Wahrheit und Methode. Grundzüge einer philosophischen Hermeneutik,* Tübingen, Mohr, ⁶1990 (¹1960).

48. Die Polemik von H. FRANKEMÖLLE gegen den Begriff „Wirkungsgeschichte" für „Rezeptionsgeschichte" (*Evangelium und Wirkungsgeschichte. Das Problem der Vermittlung von Methodik und Hermeneutik in neueren Auslegungen zum Matthäusevangelium,* in L. OBERLINNER & P. FIEDLER [eds.], *Salz der Erde – Licht der Welt. Exegetische Studien zum Matthäusevangelium.* FS A. Vögtle, Stuttgart, Katholisches Bibelwerk, 1991, pp. 31-89, bes. pp. 63-84) reißt auseinander, was zusammengehört: die *intentio auctoris,* den *sensus textus* und die *receptio lectoris*

49. Vgl. W. ISER, *Der Akt des Lesens. Theorie ästhetischer Wirkung,* München, Fink, 1976; differenzierter: U. ECO, *Die Grenzen der Interpretation,* München/Wien, Hanser, 1992. Die gültige Einsicht der Rezeptionsästhetik formuliert bereits MICHEL DE MONTAIGNE: „Un suffisant lecteur descouvre souvant ès escrits d'autruy des perfections autres que celles que l'autheur y a mises et apperceües, et y preste de sens et des visages plus riches" (*Essais* I, Paris, Pléiade, 1962, p. 135 [I 24]).

50. Y. CONGAR, *La „réception" comme réalité ecclésiologique,* in RSPT 56 (1972) 369-403; ID., Die Rezeption als ekklesiologische Realität, in *Conc* (D) 8 (1972) 500-514; vgl. ID., *La tradition et les traditions. Essai historique,* Paris, Fayard, 1960; ID., *La tradition et les traditions. Essai théologique,* Paris, Fayard, 1963. Zur Weiterführung der Diskussion vgl. W. BEINERT (ed.), *Glaube als Zustimmung. Zur Interpretation kirchlicher Rezeptionsvorgänge* (QD, 131), Freiburg/Basel/Wien, Herder, 1991.

51. Vgl. R. VON HEYDEBRANDT (ed.), *Kanon, Macht, Kultur. Theoretische, historische und soziale Aspekte ästhetischer Kanonbildung,* Stuttgart, Metzler, 1998.

52. Vgl. TH. SÖDING, *Wissenschaftliche und kirchliche Schriftauslegung. Hermeneutische Überlegungen zur Verbindlichkeit der Heiligen Schrift,* in W. PANNENBERG & TH. SCHNEIDER (eds.), *Verbindliches Zeugnis* II (Anm. 1), pp. 72-121.

53. A. & J. ASSMANN & C. HARDMEIER (eds.), *Schrift und Gedächtnis. Archäologie der literarischen Kommunikation* I, München, Fink, ²1993; A. & J. ASSMANN (eds.), *Kanon und Zensur. Beiträge zur Archäologie der literarischen Kommunikation* II, Mün-

gicis – nicht ganz ohne Grund – schnell unter moralischen Verdacht gestellt werden: Ohne Traditions- und Sinnpflege, ohne Selektion und Konzentration, ohne Zensur und Affirmation, ohne Häresie-Kritik und Wahrheitspathos gibt es keinen Kanon. Dass es einen Kanon gibt, ist der profilierte Ausdruck dafür, dass sich ein kulturelles Gedächtnis bildet, in dem eine Geschichte nicht vergessen wird, sondern in bestimmter Form lebendig bleibt.

Im kulturgeschichtlichen Vergleich zeigen sich aber auch Spezifika des biblischen Kanons. Israels Schrift speichert nicht nur das kollektive Gedächtnis einer Gemeinschaft, die sich als erwähltes Volk Gottes sieht, sondern proklamiert dieses Gedächtnis als normative Größe. Diese Proklamation, die permanente Bejahung fordert, hängt damit zusammen, dass – nach der theologischen Konstruktion, dem der Kanon ihre Form gibt – im Ursprung nicht Gewohnheit, sondern eine Offenbarung steht, die als solche durch das Medium des Kanons in Erinnerung gehalten und je neu aktualisiert werden soll.

Das Konzept einer Gedächtnisgeschichte zeigt, wo der wissenschaftliche Weg verlaufen kann, auf dem nicht nur besser zu erkennen ist, *dass* ein Zusammenhang zwischen der Entstehung und der Rezeption eines Textes besteht, sondern *worin* er im Falle des biblischen Kanons besteht. Deshalb stellen sich weiterführende Fragen[54]. Wenn nach dem Zeugnis der kanonisierten Schriften im Ursprung des biblischen Kanons das steht, was die neuzeitliche Theologie Offenbarung zu nennen pflegt[55], welche Bedeutung hat dann noch der Text? Wenn die Gedächtnisgeschichte zuverlässig literarische Zeugnisse als Quellentexte analysiert, ist prinzipiell nicht verwehrt, nach dem Ursprungsgeschehen des Gedächtnisses zu fragen. Was wäre das denkbare Ergebnis – im Falle des Alten und im Falle des Neuen Testaments? Gibt es die Möglichkeit, die erinnerte Geschichte noch einmal aus der Erinnerung der Geschichte zu gewinnen und sie kriteriell geltend zu machen? Ist es tatsächlich so, dass jede Wissenschaft den Kanon letztlich auflöst, weil sie dessen entscheidende Voraussetzung, die Offenbarung, nicht teilen kann[56]? Interessiert bei einem Blick auf den Kanon als Kanon nur mehr die Endgestalt[57]?

chen, Fink, 1987; J. ASSMANN & B. GLADIGOW (eds.), *Text und Kommentar. Archäologie der literarischen Kommunikation IV*, München, Fink, 1995; J. ASSMANN, *Fünf Stufen auf dem Wege zum Kanon*, Münster, Lit, 1998.

54. Besonders anregend sind die Reflexionen von M. SECKLER, *Problematik des Biblischen Kanons und die Wiederentdeckung seiner Notwendigkeit*, in *L'interpretazione* (Anm. 11), pp. 150-177.

55. Vgl. P. EICHER, *Offenbarung. Prinzip neuzeitlicher Theologie*, München, Kösel, 1977; A. DULLES, *Models of Revelation*, Garden City, NY, Doubleday, 1983.

56. So A. U. J. ASSMANN, *Kanon und Zensur*, in ID. (eds.), *Kanon und Zensur* (Anm. 53), p. 19.

Oder ist gerade ein Kanon, der vom Primat der Offenbarung ausgeht, um seines theologischen Profiles willen darauf angewiesen, auch in geschichtlicher Perspektive exegesiert zu werden[58]? Ist, mehr noch, die Unterscheidung zwischen „wahr" und „falsch" in der Rede von Gott, die durch den Kanon sanktioniert wird, die Ursache einer aggressiven Religionspolitik und die Keimzelle unfreien Denkens[59]? Oder ist sie im Gegenteil die Voraussetzung dafür, Wahrheit und Freiheit überhaupt als Schwestern im Geiste denken zu können[60]?

C. *Die Aufgabe*

Die Exegese des Alten und Neuen Testaments hat keinen Alleinvertretungsanspruch auf die Analyse und Interpretation des Kanons. Sie braucht die Nachbarschaft anderer Interessenten aber auch nicht zu fürchten. Sie steht von vornherein in einem Dialog mit historischen und dogmatischen Disziplinen, theologischen wie kulturwissenschaftlichen und kann daraus nur lernen, zur Sache zu kommen. Im Rahmen der Theologie ist es ihre Aufgabe, die Ratio der philologischen und historischen Wissenschaft zur Geltung zu bringen; gelingt dies nicht, bleibt die theologische Berufung auf einen Kanon wissenschaftlich obsolet. Umgekehrt ist es die Aufgabe der Exegese, in den Diskurs der Philologen und Historiker die Theologie der interpretierten Schriften einzubringen; ge-

---

57. So J. ASSMANN, *Stufen* (Anm. 53), p. 14: „Mit der Endgestalt ist das geschichtliche Werden des Textes vergessen". Dem folgt der *canonical approach* – allerdings nur im alttestamentlichen Teil, nicht in der traditionsgeschichtlich strukturierten Darstellung des Neuen Testaments; vgl. B.S. CHILDS, *Biblical Theology in Crisis*, Philadelphia, Fortress, 1970; ID., *Introduction to the Old Testament as Scripture,* Philadelphia, Fortress, 1979; ID., *Old Testament Theology in a Canonical Context*, Philadelphia, Fortress, 1985; ID., *The New Testament as Canon*, Philadelphia, Fortress, 1985; ID., *Biblical Theology of the Old and New Testament I-II*, London, SCM, 1992 (deutsch: *Die Theologie der einen Bibel* I-II, Freiburg/Basel/Wien, Herder, 1994.1996.

58. Lk 1,1-4 zeigt, dass das geschichtliche Werden des Textes – in bestimmtem Ausschnitt und starker Färbung – Teil des kanonischen Gedächtnisses ist.

59. So – zugespitzt – die These von J. ASSMANN, *Moses der Ägypter. Entzifferung einer Gedächtnisspur*, München, Hanser, 1998; dazu E. ZENGER, *Was ist der Preis des Monotheismus? Zu heilsamen Provokation von Jan Assmann*, in *Herder Korrespondenz* 55 (2001) 186-191; zum Image des Mose: E. OTTO (ed.), *Mose. Ägypten und das Alte Testament* (SBS, 189), Stuttgart, Katholisches Bibelwerk, 2000. Die These, die Assmann vertritt, ist in ähnlicher Weise zuvor unter philosophischem Blickwinkel von H. BLUMENBERG vertreten worden: *Die Legitimität der Neuzeit,* 3 Bde., Frankfurt/M., Suhrkamp, 1966, bes. Bd. 1: *Säkularisierung und Selbstbehauptung;* ID., *Arbeit am Mythos*, Frankfurt/M., Suhrkamp, 1979, pp. 239-290.

60. Auf der Suche nach einer Antwort darf die Exegese so frei sein, sich der kulturwissenschaftlichen Einsichten zu bedienen, ohne ihren theologischen Impetus, den sie von den biblischen Texten empfängt, gedächtnisgeschichtlich oder konstruktivistisch aufzulösen.

lingt dies nicht, beherrschen die Dogmen der neuzeitlichen Wissenschaftlichkeit die Auslegung der biblischen Texte.

Die besondere Aufgabe der Exegese besteht darin, nicht nur den Ausgangspunkt (oder besser: die Ausgangspunkte) des kanonischen Prozesses historisch und philologisch zu markieren, sondern von den alt- und
neutestamentlichen Schriften aus nach der Kanonizität des Kanons zu
fragen. Der Anspruch des Kanons muss von den kanonisierten Schriften
selbst her bestimmt werden, wenn er sich fundamentaltheologisch rechtfertigen lassen soll. An der Exegese ist es, den Anspruch des Kanons so
zur Geltung zu bringen, wie er sich von den alt- und neutestamentlichen
Schriften her darstellt.

II. DER ANSPRUCH DES KANONS

Ein theologischer Schlüsselbegriff zum Verständnis des Kanons ist
der Begriff der Offenbarung. *Dass* es überhaupt einen Kanon gibt, setzt
eine Offenbarung Gottes voraus. Kein menschlicher Text könnte aus
sich heraus – etwa aufgrund eines bloßen Anspruchs, einer faszinieren-
den Persönlichkeit, einer mitreißenden Idee oder einer sozialen Übereinkunft – jenen Anspruch erheben, der dem jüdischen und christlichen
Kanon seine Gestalt gibt. Offenbarung ist freilich nicht, wie dies in der
Neuzeit weitgehend der Fall war, instruktionstheoretisch zu fassen, sondern – orientiert man sich am Zeugnis der Schrift selbst – heilsgeschichtlich und soteriologisch[61]. Offenbarung ist, neuzeitlich gesprochen, „Selbstmitteilung Gottes", die der Manifestation seines Gottsein
in der Schöpfungs-Geschichte dient und das Ziel verfolgt, den Menschen, die er erwählt, sein Gottsein zu erschließen – wie dies unter den
endlichen Bedingungen von Raum und Zeit möglich ist (vgl. 1 Kor 13).
Jede Fixierung auf extraordinäre Einzelereignisse, so wichtig sie gerade
im Falle der Prophetie und des neutestamentlichen Apostolates sind,
wäre ein Irrweg. Entscheidend ist vielmehr, die Geschichtlichkeit der
Offenbarung zu erkennen: Der Plural der Offenbarungen verweist auf
einen Singular der Offenbarung, der sich seinerseits in jener theozentrischen Perspektive erschließt, die im gesamt-biblischen Bekenntnis
zum *einen* Gott angesprochen wird, der neutestamentlich das Bekenntnis

---

61. Zum Offenbarungsverständnis, wie es im folgenden vorausgesetzt ist, vgl. die Begründung in TH. SÖDING, *Geschichtlicher Text und Heilige Schrift. Fragen zur theologischen Legitimität historisch-kritischer Exegese*, in TH. STERNBERG (ed.), *Neue Formen
der Schriftauslegung?* (QD, 140), Freiburg/Basel/Wien, Herder, 1992, pp. 73-130, bes.
pp. 93-107.

zum *einen* Kyrios entspricht (1 Kor 8,6). Die alt- und neutestamentlichen Schriften sind nach ihrem eigenen Bekunden (soweit sie Auskunft geben) nicht diese Offenbarung selbst, sondern deren Zeugnis, das allerdings zur Wirkungsgeschichte der Offenbarung gehört.

1. *Alttestamentliche Grundlagen*

In seiner Apologie *contra Apion* macht FLAVIUS JOSEPHUS den Kanon biblischer Bücher als Argument für die kulturelle Stärke des Judentums geltend (1,37-41)[62]. Er will keinen neuen Kanon einführen, sondern rekurriert auf die Abgeschlossenheit und das unvergleichlich hohe Alter des vorliegenden Kanons (der sich pharisäischen Traditionen verdanken dürfte). Für Josephus stehen zweiundzwanzig Kanon-Bücher fest: die fünf Bücher Moses, gefolgt von dreizehn Büchern postmosaischer Propheten[63] und flankiert von vier Büchern mit Lobliedern auf Gott und Lebensregeln. Die Dreiteilung des Tanach – *Tora, Nebiim, Ketubim* – ist deutlich zu erkennen[64]. Die kanonischen Bücher gelten dem jüdischen Historiker als zuverlässige Dokumentation der exzeptionellen Geschichte Israels; ihr Umfang und Wortlaut sind sakrosankt. Alle kanonischen Bücher sind inspiriert[65], alle sind in der Zeit von Mose bis Artaxerxes geschrieben, nur bis Esra ist die prophetischen Sukzession ununterbrochen (*Ap.* 1,29.37-41)[66]. Diese theologische Konstruktion, die in rabbinischer Zeit ausgebaut und umfassend abgesichert werden wird[67], steht

---

62. Zur Würdigung vgl. R. MEYER, *Bemerkungen zum literargeschichtlichen Hintergrund der Kanontheorie des Josephus*, in O. BETZ, K. HAACKER & M. Hengel (eds.), *Josephus-Studien.* FS O. Michel, Göttingen, Vandenhoeck & Ruprecht, 1974, pp. 258-299; L.H. FELDMAN, *Use, Authority, and Exegesis of Mikra in the Writings of Josephus*, in M.J. MULDER (ed.), *Mikra* (CRINT, II/1), Assen/Philadelphia, Fortress, pp. 455-518; G. STEMBERGER, *Hermeneutik der Jüdischen Bibel*, in CH. DOHMEN & G. STEMBERGER, *Hermeneutik der Jüdischen Bibel und des Alten Testaments*, Stuttgart et al., Kohlhammer, 1996, pp. 23-132, bes. 33-36; S. MASON, *Josephus on Canon and Scriptures*, in M. SAEBØ (ed.), *Hebrew Bible/Old Testament. The History of Its Interpretation*, Vol. I: *From the Beginnings to the Middle Ages (until 1300)*, Part 1: *Antiquity*, Göttingen, Vandenhoeck & Ruprecht, 1996, pp. 217-235.

63. Akzeptiert Josephus mehr Propheten, als später kanonisiert worden sind? So P. KATZ, *The Old Testament in Palestine and Alexandria*, in ZNW 47 (1956) 191-217; A.C. SUNDBERG, *Old Testament* (Anm. 36); G. WANKE, *Die Entstehungsgeschichte des Alten Testaments als Kanon*, in TRE 6 (1980), pp. 1-8, bes. 5. Anders jedoch D. BARTHÉLEMY, *L'État de la Bible juive depuis le début de notre ère jusqu'à la deuxième révolte contre Rome (131-135)*, in S. AMSLER et al. (eds.), *Le canon de l'Ancien Testament*, Genève, Labor et Fides, 1984, pp. 9-46, bes. 29ff.

64. Die Bezeichnung wird Gamaliel II. zurückgeschrieben.

65. Nach Josephus hat Mose „nach Gottes Diktat und Lehre" geschrieben (*Ant.* 17,159; vgl. 4,183), und zwar in Etappen (*Ant.* 4,196f). Alle prophetisch begabten Verfasser der Bibel haben „unter der Anhauchung Gottes" ihre Werke verfasst (*Ap.* 1,36f).

66. Der Gedanke ist nicht aus der Luft gegriffen, sondern durch Ps 74,9; Sach 13,2-6; Dan 3,38 Th; 1 Makk 4,46; 9,27; 14,41; syrBar 85,3 vorbereitet, wird aber hier – wohl nicht erstmalig – kanonhermeneutisch gewendet.

nicht nur im Interesse des Altersbeweises[68], sondern auch der Rekonstruktion einer normativen Ursprungsgeschichte, an der sich die Gegenwart, die nach der Restitution des Zweiten Tempels in alltäglichen Bahnen zu verlaufen scheint, messen muss.

Josephus steht zu seiner Zeit nicht allein[69], aber die Position, die er sich zu eigen macht, ist nicht unumstritten[70]. Woher erklärt sie sich? Und weshalb hat sie sich (jüdisch wie christlich) im wesentlichen durchgesetzt?

Eine wichtige Zwischenstation markiert der Prolog, mit dem der Enkel des Siraciden seine griechische Übersetzung eingeleitet hat[71]. Er bezieht sich auf „das Gesetz und die Propheten und die anderen ihnen folgenden (Schriften)" (prol. 1f), zu denen er wohl auch das Werk seines Großvaters rechnet[72]. Er ist überzeugt, dass dem Volk Israel („uns") durch diese Schriften „Vieles und Großes" von Gott „gegeben" worden ist. Er meint damit jene „Bildung ($\pi\alpha\iota\delta\varepsilon i\alpha$) und Weisheit ($\sigma o\varphi i\alpha$)", derentwegen Israel das Lob der anderen Völker gebührt. Deshalb wird zugleich daran erinnert, dass allein ein aufmerksames Studium der gesamten Überlieferung in ihrer ganzen Breite die Gewähr dafür bietet, Israels „Bildung und Weisheit" weiter zu fördern (Z. 4-14).

Die Einleitungswissenschaften sind nur annäherungsweise in der Lage, die Vorgeschichte und den Kontext dieser schriftlichen Äußerungen zu erhellen[73]. Es zeigt sich, dass weder mit einer einheitlichen,

67. Einen gewissen Abschluss dokumentiert bBathra 14.15.

68. Vgl. P. PILHOFER, *Presbyteron kreitton* (WUNT, II/39), Tübingen, Mohr, 1990.

69. Eine vergleichbare Auffassung vom Umfang (24 Bücher) und vom Stellenwert, von der Inspiration und Normativität des Kanons hat 4 Esr 14; vgl. J.-D. KAESTLI, *Le récit de IV Esdras 14 et sa valeur pour l'histoire du canon de l'Ancien Testament*, in S. AMSLER et al. (eds.), *Le canon* (Anm. 63), pp. 71-102; CH. MACHOLZ, *Die Entstehung des christlichen Bibelkanons nach 4 Esr 14*, in E. BLUM et al. (eds.), *Die hebräische Bibel und ihre zweifache Nachgeschichte*. FS R. Rendtorff, Neukirchen-Vluyn, Neukirchener, 1990, pp. 379-391. 4Q MMT nennt das „Buch Moses", die „Bücher der Propheten" und „David"; vgl. zu Qumran T.H. LIM, *Holy Scripture in the Qumran Commentaries and Pauline Letters*, Oxford, University Press, 1997; J.C. VANDERKAM, *Revealed Literature in the Second Temple Period*, in: ID., *From Revelation to Canon. Studies in the Hebrew Bible and Second Temple Literature* (JSJ SS, 62), Leiden, Brill, 2000, pp. 1-30. PHILO (*De vita contemplativa* 25) nennt die Gesetze, die prophetischen Orakel, Hymnen und „andere Schriften, durch die Erkenntnis und Frömmigkeit vermehrt und vervollkommnet werden".

70. Die Samaritaner und Sadduzäer akzeptieren bekanntlich nur die Tora. Interessanterweise rekurriert auch der Aristeasbrief, obgleich er die Legende der Septuaginta-Übersetzung tradiert, nur auf die Bücher des Mose. PHILO befasst sich in seinen Allegoresen nur mit der Tora.

71. Vgl. H.-P. RÜGER, *Le Siracide: un livre à la frontière du canon*, in S. AMSLER et al. (eds.), *Le canon* (Anm. 63), pp. 47-69.

72. Im übrigen dürfte er an die Psalmen und die Proverbien, an das Hohe Lied und Hiob, an die Chronikbüchern, an Esra und Nehemia, vielleicht auch an Kohelet gedacht haben; vgl. RÜGER, *Le Siracide* (Anm. 71), pp. 64ff.

durchgängigen, klar gegliederten Entwicklung noch mit zentraler Steuerung oder einem normativen Konzept zu rechnen ist. Kennzeichnend ist vielmehr eine Synchronizität unterschiedlicher Prozesse an verschiedenen Orten und in verschiedenen Strömungen des Judentums. Wo es einerseits bereits deutlich erkennbare Versuche gibt, eine Kanonisierung zu fördern und damit gleichzeitig zu beschließen[74], entstehen andererseits weiterhin Schriften, die sich später in bestimmen Kanonlisten finden. Auf Palästina und die Diaspora lassen sich klare Positionen nicht verteilen, die Verhältnisse sind höchst komplex, die Grenzen durchlässig. Die Debatte erstreckt sich über einen langen Zeitraum. Auch Christen haben sich schließlich aktiv beteiligt, und noch die Rabbinen stehen in argumentativen Kontroversen, die sich im Judentum wie im Christentum erst im 3. und 4. Jh. n. Chr. langsam beruhigen. Das schließt bestimmte Vorentscheidungen nicht aus. Weithin gilt seit der späteren Perserzeit die Tora als (weitgehend) abgeschlossen[75]. Während für wichtige Gruppen im Judentum dies der Kanon war und blieb, setzen sich in anderen, z.B. pharisäischen, essenischen auch die Prophetenbücher durch. Welche dazugehören, steht gegen Ende des 3. Jh. v. Chr. (vorläufig) fest (ohne Daniel)[76]. Sicher ist auch, dass etwa seit dieser Zeit die Psalmen zum festen Bestand zählen, ohne dass sie eigentlich „kanonisiert" zu werden brauchten. Die Diskussion konzentriert sich auf andere „Schriften".

Im Zuge dieser Entwicklung wird die Tora als Orientierungsgröße auch der Propheten und der „Schriften" inszeniert[77]. Die Entstehung und Tradition, Fortschreibung und Relecture, die Sammlung und Re-

---

73. Vgl. S.B. CHAPMAN, *The Law and the Prophets. A Study in Old Testament Canon Formation* (FAT, 27), Tübingen, Mohr, 2000.

74. Vgl. G. STEINS, *Die Chronik als kanonisches Abschlussphänomen. Studien zur Entstehung und Theologie von 1/2 Chronik* (BBB, 93), Bonn, Weinheim, 1995.

75. Vgl. O. KAISER, *Einleitung in das Alte Testament*, Gütersloh, Mohn, [5]1984 ([1]1969), p. 407.

76. Vgl. O.H. STECK, *Der Abschluss der Prophetie im Alten Testament* (BTS, 17), Neukirchen-Vluyn, Neukirchener, 1991.

77. Das Bewußtsein vom einzigartigen Rang der Tora bahnt sich nicht nur in den Schluss-Redaktionen des Pentateuch an, insbesondere mit der Erzählung vom Tod des Propheten Mose Dtn 34; es spiegelt sich auch in den redaktionellen Vorstößen zum „Abschluß der Prophetie" (bes. Mal 3,22ff), in der Komposition des Psalters (Ps 1 portraitiert den idealen, nämlich toratreuen Leser, Ps 2 den idealen, nämlich messianischen Autor), in der Anlage des Danielbuches und in der Konzeption der Chronik-Bücher, die Tora und Nebiim durch eine Neu-Erzählung der Geschichte Israels von Adam bis Kyros miteinander verzahnen. Nicht zuletzt bildet die sich entwickelnde Diskussion über die Vielfalt des Kanons und die ihm zugrundeliegende Einheit geradezu das Motiv des Baruchbuches, das angetreten ist, eine „allen Sondermeinungen vorausliegende, biblisch gegründete, deshalb fundamentale und konsensfähige Grundlage" israelitisch-jüdischer Theologie zu schaffen (vgl. O.H. STECK, *Das apokryphe Baruchbuch* [FRLANT, 160], Göttingen, Vandenhoeck

daktion dieser Schriften, verdankt sich Prophetenschülern, Priestern, Schriftgelehrten und Weisheitsheitslehrern, die an unterschiedlichen Orten, in einem langen Zeitraum, nicht in einer kontinuierlichen Entwicklung, sondern in immer neuen Schüben und flexiblen Antworten auf neue historische Herausforderungen, aber in der ständigen Aneignung und Anreicherung eines wachsenden Erbes das Profil des Jüdischen Kanons herausgebildet und zugleich auch die jüdische Kultur des Gedächtnisses, des Lernens und Lehrens, des Lesens und Auslegens, der Textpflege und des Kommentars geprägt haben[78].

Die Entwicklungsgeschichte des Kanons wird durch besondere Wertschätzungen des Textes flankiert. Die deuteronomischen und weisheitlichen Kanonformeln[79] versuchen, durch das Verbot der Kürzung die Authentizität, durch das Verbot der Erweiterung die Suffizienz und durch das Gebot der genauen Beachtung die Normativität der von ihnen überblickten Schriften für den von ihnen abgesteckten Geltungsbereich zu sichern[80]. Zu den präkanonischen Phänomenen gehört, dass Mose nach Ex 24,3f seine Verkündigung der Tora an das zu Füßen des Sinai versammelte Volk dadurch absichert, dass er „alle Worte des Herrn" aufschreibt; nach Ex 34,27ff schreibt Mose auf ausdrückliche Anweisung Jahwes die „zehn Worte" als „die Worte des Bundes" auf die Tafeln des Gesetzes[81]; in beiden Fällen dient das Schreiben[82] dazu, die dauerhafte Verbindlichkeit des sakrosankten Textes zu sichern[83]. Ohne Zweifel hat das prophetische Pathos inspirierten Sprechens auf die Wert-

& Ruprecht 1993, p. 312); vom Deuteronomium inspiriert, aber auch von der (deuteronomistisch gedeuteten) Prophetie beeinflußt, will das Buch in der Orientierung am ganzen (ihm bekannten) Kanon dessen theologische, spirituelle, ethische und praktische Essenz destillieren. Vgl. den Überblick von E. ZENGER, *Einleitung in das AT* (Anm. 28), pp. 24ff.

78. Vgl. P.R. DAVIES, *Scribes and Schools. The Canonization of the Hebrew Scriptures*, Louisville, Westminster John Knox Press, 1998.

79. Dtn 4,2; 13,1; ferner Koh 3,14; Jer 26,2; Spr 30,6, dann epAr 311 (sowie Mt 5,18f); vgl. CH. DOHMEN & M. OEMING, *Biblischer Kanon – warum und wozu?* (QD, 137), Freiburg/Basel/Wien, Herder, 1992, pp. 68-89.

80. Heben Dtn 4,2 und 13,1 vor allem auf die Normativität des im Dekalog zentrierten Gesetzes ab, so zeichnet sich in Spr 30,5f („Die Gesamtheit des Wortes Gottes ist im Feuer geläutert") der Gedanke einer Kanonizität der ganzen Heiligen Schrift ab (auch wenn deren Grenzen z.T. noch nicht abschließend festgelegt gewesen sind).

81. Zum Zusammenhang beider Texte vgl. CH. DOHMEN, *Der Sinaibund als Neuer Bund nach Ex 19-34*, in E. ZENGER (ed.), *Der Neue Bund im Alten. Zur Bundestheologie der beiden Testamente* (QD, 146), Freiburg/Basel/Wien, Herder, 1993, pp. 51-83.

82. Nach Jub 2,1 hat Mose den Schöpfungsbericht aufgeschrieben, wie es ihm ein Engel Gottes offenbart hat.

83. Nach Jer 36 ist das Aufschreiben der prophetischen Worte nicht nur ein Akt heiligen Ungehorsams gegen den königlichen Maulkorberlass, sondern auch die Keimzelle des prophetischen Buches; vgl. A. GRAUPNER, *Auftrag und Geschick des Propheten Jeremia. Literarische Eigenart, Herkunft und Intention vordeuteronomistischer Prosa im Jeremiabuch* (BTS, 15), Neukirchen-Vluyn, Neukirchener, 1991, pp. 98-111.

schätzung der Bücher abgefärbt; mehr noch: hier dürfte die stärkste Quelle für die spätere Überzeugung von der Inspiration nicht nur der prophetischen Bücher, sondern der gesamten Schrift liegen, zumal auch Mose und David als Propheten erscheinen[84].

Im Lichte dieser Texte kann es nicht verwundern, wenn die Buchform der Tora besondere Erwähnung findet[85] und „Bücher" (Dan 9,2), „heilige Bücher" 1 Makk 2,9), „heiliges Buch" (2 Makk 8,23) zu ihrer technischen Bezeichnung wird. Nach Jes 34,16 wird die Schriftrolle des Propheten einst als „Buch Jahwes" gelesen werden[86]; für Josephus sind die alttestamentlichen Schriften schlicht die „Bücher" oder eben: „die Bibel" (*Ant.* 4,303)[87].

Wiewohl selbst damit noch nicht gemeint ist, was im „dogmatischen" Sinn jüdischer und christlicher Theologie den Begriff des Kanons füllt, darf doch nicht unterschätzt werden, welch hohes Reflexionsbewusstsein von der Bedeutung der Schriftlichkeit, der prinzipiellen Unantastbarkeit des Textes und der Normativität des „Buches", vor allem der Tora, sich in den jüngeren Schichten des Alten Testaments und im Frühjudentum herausgebildet hat. Es kommt nicht von ungefähr, dass die „Schrift" *de facto* einen kanonischen Rang erfährt. Er ist nach dem Zeugnis der Schriften in einem doppelten begründet:

Zum einen sind die kanonisierten Schriften in der Vielzahl ihrer Positionen, als synchronische Ganzheit gelesen, die Zeugen alttestamentlich-jüdischen Glaubens an den Einen Gott (Dtn 6,4f): ein religionsge-

---

84. Darüber hinaus spiegelt es den Vorgang einer aktiven Kanonisierung, wenn große Männer der Geschichte Israels zu Autoren der biblischen Bücher werden oder mit ihren bereits feststehenden Büchern anderen – nicht nur Söhnen (und Töchtern?), sondern auch viel weiter entfernten Verwandten – eine Heimstatt bereitet haben. David wird der Autor sehr vieler Psalmen (vgl. 2 Kön 23,2), Salomo wichtiger Weisheitsbücher. Daniel bietet das Beispiel gezielter Pseudepigraphie; er wird als Prophet gegolten haben (vgl. Mt 24,15 und 4Q 174/4Qflor), hat aber in der Jüdischen Bibel unter den Nebiim keinen Platz mehr gefunden, weil der Teil bereits festgelegt war; vgl. K. KOCH, *Is Daniel also among the Prophets?*, in *Interp* 39 (1985) 117-130. Hiob gelangt mit Hilfe von Ez 14,14 zu Ehren; das Jesajabuch wird zum Dokument einer Fortschreibung, die nahezu die gesamte Wegzeit für die Entstehung des Alten Testaments umfasst.

85. Neh 9,3; 2 Chr 17,9: „Buch der Weisung Jahwes"; Dtn 28,61; 30,10; Jos 1,8: „Buch dieser Weisung"; Jos 8,31; 23,6; 2 Kön 14,6: „Buch der Weisung Moses"; Ex 24,7; 2 Kön 23,2.21: 2 Chr 34,30; 1 Makk 1,57: „Buch des Bundes"; 1 Makk 1,56: „Buch des Gesetzes"; vgl. Josephus, *Ant.* 1,15; 8,159. Ebenso redet das Neue Testament: Mk 12,26: „Buch des Mose" (für die Tora); Gal 3,10: „Buch des Gesetzes"; Hebr 9,19: „das Buch" (für die Tora); Hebr 10,7: „die Buchrolle"; vgl. auch 2 Tim 4,13.

86. Vgl. Lk 3,4: „Buch der Worte des Propheten Jesaja"; Lk 4,17: „Buch des Propheten Jesaja"; Lk 20,42 und Apg 1,20: „Buch der Psalmen"; Apg 7,42: „Buch der Propheten".

87. 2 Makk 2,13 zitiert geläufig die „Bücher der Könige und Propheten". Der Aristeasbrief spricht (mit Blick auf die Tora) von „den jüdischen Büchern" (28; vgl. 36.176.317) – man wird wohl auch übersetzen dürfen: die jüdische Bibel.

schichtliches Unikat, die große Alternative zu den polytheistischen Religionen, meilenweit auch getrennt vom philosophischen Monotheismus. Der Gott, den kein Bild darstellen kann, braucht das dauerhafte und verlässliche Wort der Schrift, um überhaupt als Gott wahrgenommen und verehrt werden zu können.

Zum anderen sind die kanonisierten Schriften die maßgeblichen Zeugen einer Geschichte, die gerade nicht zu den theologischen Adiaphora gehört, wenn anders Gott der Gott Abrahams, Isaaks und Jakobs ist. Ohne die lebendige Erinnerung der Geschichte könnte die Erwählung Israels nicht anschaulich werden, nicht die Bundestreue Gottes und die Sünde des Volkes, nicht Gottes Gericht und die Rettung aus dem Gericht, nicht Gottes Gerechtigkeit und Erbarmen.

Das aber heißt: Die Kanonizität des Kanons hängt nach dem Selbstzeugnis der alttestamentlichen Schriften nicht am Vorgang der Kanonisierung, so gewiss Textpflege und Interpretation in der Gemeinschaft des Gottesvolkes zusammengehören. Sie hängt am Gottsein Gottes selbst und seinem Handeln in der Geschichte. Der Kanon trägt seinen theologischen Anspruch nicht in selbst; er leiht ihn vielmehr vom Anspruch Gottes, dessen geschichtlicher Gestaltungswille und inspirierende Geisteskraft die „Schrift" entstehen lässt, um durch sie dauerhaft die Gemeinschaft des Gottesvolkes zu prägen.

Gibt es aus dem Alten Testament selbst heraus die Möglichkeit eines Zweiten Kanons oder einer besseren Alternative zu ihm? Die Apokryphen, besonders die apokalyptischen Schriften, halten dafür, dass es für die Endzeit Wichtigeres, im Zweifel auch Älteres gibt als den Kanon von Mose bis Esra. Das Jubiläenbuch, die Henoch- und die Esrapokalypse bieten Beispiele. Es dürfte mit der Enttäuschung apokalyptischer Prognosen zu tun haben, dass diese Schriften – obgleich sie formal z.T. die Kanonkriterien eines Josephus hätten erfüllen können – vom Judentum, das sich nach der Zerstörung des zweiten Tempels vor allen durch die Konzentration auf seine „Schrift" konsolidierte, nicht als kanonisch anerkannt worden sind. Nach GERHARD VON RAD ist zwar das Alte Testament „nichts anderes als ein Buch einer ins Ungeheure gewachsenen Erwartung"[88]. Aber – alle Kritik an diesem Urteil beiseitegelassen: Wenn der Messias kommt, so wie er im Alten Testament verheißen wird, braucht es keinen Kanon mehr. Das Alte Testament, historisch verstanden, bedarf aus sich heraus keiner qualitativen Ergänzung, so lange auch über die eine oder andere Erweiterung diskutiert worden ist.

---

88. *Theologie des Alten Testaments* II, München, Kaiser, [4]1965, p. 381.

2. *Die Wertschätzung der „Schrift" im Spiegel des Neuen Testaments*

Für alle urchristlichen Autoren gibt es eine entscheidende Bezugsgröße ihres Denkens und Schreibens, ihres Betens und ihres Ethos: die
„Schrift" (γραφή) oder, wie es häufiger im Plural heißt, die „Schriften"
(γραφαί). Zwar kann sich der Paulus der Areopagrede (Apg 17,28)
im Gespräch mit Epikureern und Stoikern – ohne den Namen zu nennen – auf die *Phainomena* des Aratos von Soloi berufen (5). Die
religionsgeschichtliche Arbeit hat gezeigt, in wie starkem Maße die neutestamentlichen Schriften auch bei den zentralen Themenfeldern der
Theologie ohne größere Berührungsängste sensible Motive paganer Re-
ligiosität rezipieren[89]. Der Blick in diese Richtung zeigt einen für die
Inkulturation des Evangeliums unerlässlichen, im Alten Testament
vorstrukturierten Adaptionsvorgang, der zur Substanz neutestamentlicher Theologie gehört. Die Orientierung an der Schrift zu betonen, bedeutet keineswegs, einen geschlossenen Traditionsraum zu konstruieren,
der gegenüber der paganen Religionsgeschichte abgeschlossen wäre.
Aber derselbe Blick in die Umwelt des frühen Christentums und des frühen Judentums zeigt doch auf der auf der anderen Seite den qualitativen
Unterschied zur *Schrift*rezeption. Es gibt im Neuen Testament keine
Analogie zum Rekurs auf die γραφή. Das spiegelt sich nicht nur in der
Terminologie, es betrifft die Theologie. Die Adaption paganer Theolo-
goumena geschieht in einem theologischen Koordinatensystem, das ent-
scheidend durch die alttestamentliche Theologie vorgegeben ist: die
Einzigkeit Gottes, die Schöpfung, die Unterscheidung zwischen Gott
und Welt, die Geschichte als Herrschaftsraum Gottes, die Gnade und
Barmherzigkeit, das Gericht und das Heil Gottes, die Leiblichkeit und
Sterblichkeit des Menschen, die Hoffnung auf das Reich Gottes, das
Ethos der Zehn Gebote – die Liste der theologischen Positionen ließe
sich erheblich verlängern, die im Neuen Testament durch den Rekurs
auf die Schrift abgedeckt wird und die Rezeption religionsgeschicht-
licher Motive bestimmt. Dass die alttestamentlichen Vorgaben durch die
Christologie noch einmal in ein neues Licht gesetzt werden und neue
Bedeutungsdimensionen gewinnen, setzt deren fundamentale Gültigkeit
gerade voraus.

In Zitaten und Anspielungen, in regelrechten „Schriftbeweisen" und
kühnen Exegesen ist die Schrift nahezu allgegenwärtig[90]. Welchen genauen Umfang sie hatte, mit wievielen Schriftrollen neutestamentliche

---

89. Vgl. G. STRECKER & U. SCHNELLE (eds.), *Neuer Wettstein. Texte zum Neuen Testament aus Griechentum und Hellenismus* II/1-2, Berlin, de Gruyter, 1996.
90. Einen guten Eindruck verschafft H. HÜBNER, *Vetus Testamentum in Novo* II: *Corpus Paulinum*, Göttingen, Vandenhoeck & Ruprecht 1997.

Autoren arbeiten konnten, ob sie vielleicht gar nur in Florilegien ge-
schaut haben[91], von welchem genauen Wortlaut sie ausgegangen sind,
ob sie umstandslos die *Biblia Graeca* zitiert oder einen Seitenblick auf
die hebräischen und aramäischen Versionen riskiert haben[92] – das alles
kann im Einzelfall halbwegs geklärt werden, muss im ganzen aber unter
vielerlei Aspekten offen bleiben. Entscheidend ist: Paulus und Johannes,
Matthäus und Markus, Lukas und Petrus, der Hebräerbrief, nicht zu vergessen: Jesus selbst – sie alle kennen den Begriff γραφή; sie alle setzen
ihn ohne nähere Erläuterung bei ihren Adressaten als bekannt voraus;
ihnen allen steht die „Schrift" als eine feste Größe vor Augen[93], wie
weich auch immer ihre Elemente gewesen sein mögen. Zuweilen fallen
die Namen der „Autoren" biblischer Bücher: Mose und David, Jesaja
und Jeremia, auch dann gelten ihre Bücher dezidiert als Teile der
„Schrift". Man kann, wie in souveräner Lässigkeit der Hebräerbrief,
verschiedene Schriftstellen ohne Quellenangabe zitieren (1,3-14), man
kann, wie in schriftgelehrtem Eifer der Apostel Paulus, Belegverse für
theologische Thesen häufen (Röm 3,9-17)[94]; man kann, wie der Seher
Johannes, ohne jede Zitationsformel sich reichlich aus dem Schatz biblischer Urbilder bedienen – immer ist, ausgesprochen oder unausgespro-
chen, die „Schrift" als eine Ganzheit und als eine Größe *sui generis* die
entscheidende Bezugsgröße.

Keine einzige Schrift, die den Weg in den jüdischen Kanon gefunden
hat, wird vom Neuen Testament ausgeklammert, alle Schriften, die für
das Neue Testament „Schrift" sind, haben zuvor einen quasi-kanoni-
schen Stellenwert jedenfalls in wichtigen Strömungen nicht zuletzt des
hellenistischen Judentums gehabt[95]. In den Grundlinien verbindet das

---

91. Die Diskussion ist nicht ausgestanden, sondern neu interessant; vgl. M.C. ALBL,
*'And Scripture Cannot Be Broken'. The Form and Function of the Early Testimonia
Collections* (SNT, 96), Leiden, Brill, 1999.

92. Wichtige Beobachtungen bei D. BARTHÉLEMY, *Études d'histoire du texte de
l'Ancien Testament* (OBO, 21), Fribourg/Göttingen, Universitätsverlag/Vandenhoeck &
Ruprecht, 1978. Nach den gründlichen Studien von D.-A. KOCH (*Die Schrift als Zeuge
des Evangeliums. Untersuchungen zur Verwendung und zum Verständnis der Schrift bei
Paulus* [BHT, 69], Tübingen, Mohr, 1986) hat Paulus besonders bei Jesaja, aber auch bei
Hiob und im 3. Königsbuch Texte benutzt, die näher am Hebräischen als die Septuaginta
gestanden haben.

93. In Mk 12,10 meint *graphê* die bestimmte Schrift*stelle* (Ps 118,22f[LXX]).

94. Nach Apg 13,33 zitiert Paulus ausdrücklich den „zweiten Psalm".

95. Ausnahmen bestätigen die Regel. Paulus sagt, er zitiere in 1 Kor 2,9 die Schrift,
aber weder im Masoretischen Text noch in der Septuaginta oder der Vulgata oder sonst
einer bekannten Textrezension lässt sich die Quelle finden. Ein Grenzfall ist das Henoch-
Zitat (vgl. äthHen 1,9) in Jud 14ff; vgl. ausführlich A. VÖGTLE, *Der Judasbrief/Der zweite Petrusbrief* (EKK, 22), Neukirchen-Vluyn, Neukirchener, 1994, pp. 71-86. Gehört
„Henoch" für „Judas" zur Schrift? Akzeptiert er den prophetischen Anspruch eines
nicht-kanonischen Autors? Am ehesten zeigt Jud 14ff wohl, dass die Grenzen des Kanons
noch nicht überall geschlossen waren und dass der Kreis inspirierter Schriften in der Antike größer war der kanonisierter.

Schriftverständnis des Urchristentums vieles mit wichtigen Strömungen des Frühjudentums. Wie durch Jesus selbst begründet (vgl. Mk 12,18-27), gibt es keine näheren Beziehungen zur sadduzäische Reduktion auf die Fünf Bücher Mose, wohl aber zum Pharisäismus, zu den Essenern und zu apokalyptischen Kreisen. Eine Parallele freilich zur frühjüdischen Kanondogmatik des Josephus (und des 4. Esra), dass Esra der letzte Prophet sei, findet sich im Neuen Testament nicht. Für Jesus gibt es nur *eine* Grenze: „Gesetz und Propheten" gehen bis Johannes, danach bricht die Zeit der Gottesherrschaft an (Lk 16,16 par. Mt). Auch andere Texte erwecken den Eindruck, dass, auf das Feld der Kanontheologie übertragen, gerade kein garstig breiter Graben zwischen dem Zeitraum alt- und neutestamentlicher Inspiration liegen soll und beide „Epochen" so eng aneinandergerückt werden[96], wie sie durch das Kommen der Basileia klar voneinander geschieden werden.

Die Schrift ist als Ganzheit für das Neue Testament wie für das Frühjudentum keine unstrukturierte Größe. Sie begegnet – auch Jesus hat so gesprochen[97] – als „Gesetz und Propheten" (Joh 1,45; Apg 13,15; 24,14 [27]; 26,22 [retro]; 28,23; Röm 3,21) oder als „Gesetz und Propheten und Psalmen" (Lk 24,44)[98]. An keiner Stelle werden die verschiedenen Kanonteile gegeneinander ausgespielt[99]. Die Differenzierung hat eher plerophorischen Charakter und soll das theologische Gewicht des Rekurses noch erhöhen. Schaut man auf die direkten und indirekten Schriftrezeptionen, zeichnet sich zweierlei ab: das überragende Gewicht derjenigen Schriften, die Bestandteile der *Biblia Hebraica* geworden sind, aber auch die Rezeption solcher Schriften, die zur *Biblia Graeca* gehö-

---

96. In seinem *tractatus de fide,* der zugleich ein *tractatus de populo dei* ist, rechnet der Hebräerbrief zur „Wolke der Zeugen" (12,1) auch die makkabäischen Kämpfer (11,32-38).

97. Vgl. neben Mt 5,17 und 7,12 sowie 22,40 vor allem auch Mt 11,13 par. Lk 16,16; sowie Lk 16,29.31 („Mose und die Propheten") dazu J. BECKER, *Jesus von Nazaret*, Berlin, de Gruyter, 1996, pp. 140ff; ferner (mit einer diskussionswürdigen Interpretation) G. THEISSEN & A. MERZ, *Der historische Jesus*, Göttingen, Vandenhoeck & Ruprecht 1996, pp. 322f. Die Wendung ist frühjüdisch belegt: 2 Makk 15,9; 4 Makk 18,10.

98. Interessant ist die Reihenfolge: Die Psalmen folgen den Propheten. Dies entspricht eher der (späteren) Struktur der hebräischen Bibel als des (späteren) christlichen Alten Testaments.

99. Das ist auch der Fall, wenn nur der Nomos (nicht selten bei Paulus und Johannes) oder die Propheten (Mt 26,56: „die Schriften der Propheten"; Lk 1,70: „durch den Mund seiner heiligen Propheten von Ewigkeit her" [vgl. Apg 3,21]; Lk 18,31: „was geschrieben worden ist von den Propheten"; 24,25: „alles glauben, was die Propheten gesagt haben"; Joh 6,45; Apg 3,18: „angekündigt durch den Mund aller Propheten"; 3,24: „alle Propheten von Samuel an und alle folgenden"; 7,42: „wie im Buch der Propheten geschrieben steht"; 15,15: „darin stimmen die Worte der Propheten überein"; Röm 1,2: „vorangekündigt durch seine Propheten in heiligen Schriften"; Hebr 1,1; Jak 5,10: „die Propheten, die im Namen des Herrn gesprochen haben"; 2 Petr 3,2) oder „das Buch der Psalmen" (Apg 1,20) als Schrift angeführt werden.

ren[100]. An nicht wenigen Stellen ist auch die griechische Sprachgestalt ursprünglich hebräischer Texte die Bezugsgröße neutestamentlicher Schriftzitate[101].

Die Intensität der Schriftrezeption im Neuen Testament drückt nicht nur aus, dass es zur Kultur des Judentums gehört. Es ist weder nur Gewohnheit noch gar traditioneller Ballast, der von judenchristlichen Autoren mitgeschleppt werden müsste. Das Neue Testament kennzeichnet vielmehr eine *theologische* Einschätzung der Schrift, die entschieden, unzweideutig und vorbehaltlos positiv ist. Es gibt keine einzige distanzierende Bemerkung[102]. Nach Paulus sind die Schriften „Wort Gottes" (Röm 3,2) und deshalb „heilig" (1,2)[103]. Der Zweite Timotheusbrief bringt auf den Punkt, was sich seit langem angebahnt hat[104] und feste

100. Jakobus bezieht sich auf die nüchternen Seiten der siracidischen Alltagsweisheit (vgl. H. FRANKEMÖLLE, *Der Brief des Jakobus* I-II [ÖTK, 17/1-2], Gütersloh, Gütersloher, 1994), während Johannes, aber auch die Paulusschule ohne die elaborierte Weisheitsspekulation auch des Sirachbuches und der Sapientia nicht zu denken sind. Paulus bezieht sich auf zahlreiche Seiten der salomonischen Weisheitsschrift (vgl. N. WALTER, *Sapientia Salomonis und Paulus. Bericht über eine Hallenser Dissertation von Paul-Gerhard Keyser aus dem Jahre 1971*, in H. HÜBNER (ed.), *Die Weisheit Salomos im Horizont Biblischer Theologie* [BTS, 22], Neukirchen-Vluyn, Neukirchener, 1993, pp. 83-108), aber in 1 Kor 1,18-31 auch auf Bar 3-4 (vgl. H. HÜBNER, *Der vergessene Baruch. Zur Baruch-Rezeption des Paulus in 1Kor 1,18-31*, in SNTU 9 [1984] 161-173) und Jesus Sirach (vgl. TH. SÖDING, *Das Wort vom Kreuz. Studien zur paulinischen Theologie* [WUNT, 93], Tübingen, Mohr, 1997, pp. 224f). Paulus ist jedenfalls kein Patron für die kanonische Geltung nur des „Masoretischen Kanons"; anders jedoch U. LUZ, *Paulinische Theologie als Biblische Theologie,* in M. KLOPFENSTEIN et al. (eds.), *Mitte der Schrift? Ein jüdisch-christliches Gespräch* (Judaica et Christiana, 11), Bern et al., Lang, 1987, pp. 119-147, p. 123.

101. Das prominenteste Beispiel in einer langen Reihe ist das Zitat von Jes 7,14LXX in Mt 1,23.

102. Auf einem anderen Blatt steht, dass im Hebräerbrief gerade nicht die Schriftform gewürdigt wird, sondern die Lebendigkeit auch eines Wortes, dass Gott „viele Male und auf vielerlei Weise einst zu den Vätern gesprochen hat (1,1); vgl. M. THEOBALD, *Vom Text zum „lebendigen Wort" (Hebr 4,12). Beobachtungen zur Schrifthermeneutik des Hebräerbriefes,* in CHR. LANDMESSER, H.-J. ECKSTEIN & H. LICHTENBERGER (eds.), *Jesus Christus als die Mitte der Schrift. Studien zur Hermeneutik des Evangeliums.* FS O. Hofius (BZNW, 86), Berlin, de Gruyter, 1997, pp. 751-790.

103. Der Zweite Timotheus spricht von „heiligen Buchstaben" (2 Tim 3,15) zum Ausdruck ihrer einzigartigen Würde. Alttestamentliche Gottesrede wird im Neuen Testament durchweg als Gottesrede wiedergegeben; vgl. nur Gen 2,24 und Mk 10,6 par. Mt 19,5 (1 Kor 6,16; Eph 5,31), Gen 25,23 und Röm 9,12, Ex 3,6 und Mk 12,26 parr.; Apg 3,13; 7,32, Ex 33,19 und Röm 9,15, 1 Kön 19,18 mit Röm 11,4; Hos 2,25.1 und Röm 9,25; Mal 1,2f und Röm 9,13. Die Liste ist wesentlich länger.

104. David hat nach Mk 12,26 „im Heiligen Geist" Ps 110 („Setz dich zu meiner Rechten...") gesprochen. Nach Mt 1,23 und 2,15 wird das Schriftwort (Jes 7,14; Hos 11,1) „vom Kyrios durch den Propheten gesprochen". Nach Apg 1,16 hat „der Heilige Geist durch den Mund Davids" im „Buch der Psalmen" (1,20) den Verrat des Messias vorausgesagt (Ps 69,26; 109,8); vgl. noch Apg 3,18.21; 4,25. Nach dem Ersten Petrusbrief geht das prophetische Zeugnis des Alten Testaments auf Offenbarung zurück (1,10ff). Vgl. TH. SÖDING, *Die Schriftinspiration in der Theologie des Westens. Neutesta-*

Überzeugung des Urchristentums geworden ist: „Die ganze Schrift ist von Gott inspiriert (θεόπνευστος)" (3,16)[105]. Sicher zeigen die Art und der Umfang der Schriftrezeption bestimmte Vorlieben: Die Propheten werden als Zeugen eschatologisch-messianischer Verheißungen, die Mosebücher als Dokumente der Schöpfung und des Gesetzes, auch wegen der exemplarischen Glaubens-Biographien, die Psalmen wegen der Intensität ihrer Klagen und der messianischen Implikationen ihrer Königslieder geschätzt. Aber daraus kann nicht abgeleitet werden, dass andere Schriften keine oder prinzipiell geringere Bedeutung hätten. Die positive Einschätzung bezieht sich, soweit erkennbar, auf die Schrift im ganzen und als ganze.

Im neutestamentlichen Zeitraum geht es noch nicht darum, mit Verweis auf das Christusgeschehen die Gültigkeit der Schrift zu begründen, sondern umgekehrt: mit Verweis auf die Schrift die Dimensionen des Christusereignisses. Die Aussage des Jerusalemer Credo 1 Kor 15,3-5, dass Jesu stellvertretender Sühnetod und seine Auferweckung am dritten Tage „gemäß den Schriften" geschehen ist[106], gibt die hermeneutische Leitlinie für das ganze Neue Testament vor[107]. Die Schriftzitate haben im Neuen Testament nicht nur ornamentalen, sondern argumentativen Charakter[108]. Joh 10,35 formuliert: „Die Schrift kann nicht aufgelöst

---

mentliche Anmerkungen, in U. LUZ et al. (eds.), *Auslegung der Bibel in orthodoxer und westlicher Perspektive. Akten des west-östlichen Neutestamentler/innen-Symposiums in Neamt vom 4.-11. September 1998* (WUNT, 130), Tübingen, Mohr, 2000, pp. 169-205, bes. pp 179-191.

105. Selbstverständlich ist der Satz bis in die Übersetzung hinein umstritten. Vgl. zur Diskussion TH. SÖDING, *Schriftinspiration* (Anm. 104), pp. 187f. Der Zweite Petrusbrief springt diesem Verständnis bei (1,20f): „Keine Prophetie der Schrift ist Sache eigenwilliger Auslegung; denn niemals ist eine Prophetie vom Willen eines Menschen ausgegangen, sondern vom Heiligen Geist getrieben haben Menschen von Gott gesprochen".

106. Vgl. (unter Berücksichtigung der Kanonthematik) TH. SÖDING, *Mehr als ein Buch* (Anm. 20), pp. 218-231.

107. Vgl. CH. DOHMEN – F. MUSSNER, *Nur die halbe Wahrheit? Für die Einheit der ganzen Bibel,* Freiburg/Basel/Wien, Herder, 1993, pp. 71f. 87f.

108. Zwar nehmen sich die Autoren zuweilen große Freiheiten im Text und in der Auslegung heraus; aber anderenorts geht es ihnen *strictissime* um den Wortlaut und den Kontext. Zum Beispiel von Röm 1-8 vgl. O. HOFIUS, *Der Psalter als Zeuge des Evangeliums. Die Verwendung der Septuaginta-Psalmen in den ersten beiden Hauptteilen des Römerbriefes,* in H. GRAF REVENTLOW (ed.), *Theologische Probleme der Septuaginta und der hellenistischen Hermeneutik,* Gütersloh, Mohn, 1997, pp. 72-90. Nicht hermeneutische Willkür lässt sich beobachten, sondern die gezielte Anwendung exegetischer Methoden der Zeit und – nicht nur bei Paulus, auch im Hebräerbrief, bei Johannes und Matthäus – eine ziemlich umfassende Schriftkenntnis. *Pars pro toto* sei erwähnt, dass Paulus von den vier Schriftstellen, die als Beleg für seine These der Glaubensgerechtigkeit theoretisch in Frage kommen, drei zitiert (Gen 15,6 in Gal 3,6; Röm 4,3.9; Jes 28,16 in Röm 9,33; 10,11; Hab 2,4 in Gal 3,11; Röm 1,17); es fehlt nur Jes 7,9 – eine Sachparallele zu Jes 28,16. Matthäus kann noch jede Handlung Jesu, die Markus durchaus als Durchbrechung gesetzlicher Vorschriften inszeniert, als Erfüllung der Schrift erklären (vgl. nur Mk 2,13-17 mit Mt 9,9-13 [Hos 6,6]; Mk 3,1-6 par. Mt 12,9-14).

werden"[109]. Der hermeneutische Grundsatz des Paulus lautet: „Nicht über das hinaus, was geschrieben steht" (1 Kor 4,6)[110]. Es ist weder einfach selbstverständlich, mit der Schrift zu leben, noch muss ihr ekklesialer Gebrauch gegen Einwände gerechtfertigt werden. Eher scheint es, als habe der Glaube an Jesus den Christus das Schriftverständnis der urchristlichen Juden stimuliert, weil er es radikal problematisiert hat[111]. Auch wenn das Stichwort nicht fällt: Für das Neue Testament hat das Alte kanonische Bedeutung. Sie ist – wie im Alten Testament selbst angelegt und im Frühjudentum vorprogrammiert – darin begründet, dass sie in aller Klarheit von der Einzigkeit Gottes handelt und von der Notwendigkeit der Nächstenliebe. Das Doppelgebot Jesu (Mk 12,28-34) zeigt, worin die normative Kraft der Schrift aus neutestamentlicher Sicht besteht und dass sie *nur* von der Schrift ausgehen kann. Nirgendwo heißt es im Neuen Testament, die heiligen Schriften seien insuffizient oder ergänzungsbedürftig. Wohl aber ist durchweg in den urchristlichen Texten davon die Rede, dass die „Schrift" im Zeitraum *vor* dem Kommen Jesu Christi entstanden ist. Doch bedeutet dies nicht, dass sie „veraltet" wäre, im Gegenteil: Gerade dies macht sie relevant, dass sie die Länge und Breite und Tiefe der Geschichte Israels erschließt[112]. Wo sich gezielte Kritik an einzelnen Gesetzesworten findet, ist die Gültigkeit des Gesetzes (und damit eines wesentlichen Teiles der Schrift) gerade nicht in Frage gestellt, sondern bestätigt, freilich auf bestimmte Zeiten oder Fälle begrenzt[113]. Die prinzipiell positive Einschät-

---

109. Vgl. H. HÜBNER, *Biblische Theologie* III (Anm. 32), pp. 175ff.

110. Freilich ist der Sinn des Satzes umstritten; zur hier vertretenen Deutung vgl. TH. SÖDING, *Das Wort vom Kreuz* (Anm. 100), pp. 241f.

111. Vgl. D.-A. KOCH, *Art. Schrift*, in *TRE* 30 (1999), pp. 457-471, bes. p. 457: „Weder für Jesus von Nazareth noch für die frühen … Gemeinden stellte sich die Frage nach der ‚Beibehaltung der Schrift'…. Da nirgends ein neuer Gott, sondern ‚nur' ein neues handeln dieses Gottes proklamiert wurde, blieb die Schrift als umfassendes Zeugnis von Gottes Wirken und seinem verpflichtenden Willen notwendigerweise in Geltung – trat jetzt aber in ein Wechselverhältnis gegenseitiger Interpretation mit dem Bekenntnis zum neuen Heilshandeln Gottes in Jesus Christus".

112. Für Johannes bestreitet dies allerdings in einem nachdenkenswerten Beitrag M. THEOBALD, *Schriftzitate im „Lebensbrot"-Dialog Jesu (Joh 6). Ein Paradigma für den Schriftgebrauch des vierten Evangelisten*, in C.M. TUCKETT (ed.), *The Scriptures in the Gospels* (Anm. 30), pp. 327-366.

113. Die deutlichsten Beispiele liefern die sog. Antithesen der Bergpredigt. Nach Mt 5,17-20 stehen sie aber unter dem Vorzeichen, das Gesetz nicht aufzulösen, sondern zu erfüllen. Nach Mk 10,5, ist die Erlaubnis zur Ehescheidung Dtn 24,1 der Hartherzigkeit des Gottesvolkes geschuldet; aber damit wird der Wert der gesetzlichen Regelung gerade bestätigt – auch wenn er für die Zeit Jesu Christi keine Bedeutung mehr haben soll. Für Paulus ist die Geltungsfrist der Beschneidungsvorschrift und der Reinheitsgebote mit dem Kommen Jesu Christi für die Glaubenden abgelaufen – nicht aber für die, die ihre Gerechtigkeit in Gesetzeswerken suchen. Der Hebräerbrief führt lang und breit aus, dass die levitischen Kultvorschriften ihre temporäre Bedeutung durch das Christusgeschehen verloren haben.

zung des Alten Testaments als heilige Schrift auch für die Christen verweist auf Grundlinien neutestamentlicher Israel-Theologie. Für sie ist –
bei gravierenden Unterschieden zwischen verschiedenen Schriften – die
Bejahung der Erwählung Israels entscheidend[114], die Geschichte Israels
und damit auch die Dokumentation der Glaubenserfahrungen Israels in
der Bibel positiv zu schätzen.

3. Die Selbstpräsentation der neutestamentlichen Schriften

Erst an den Rändern des Neuen Testament melden sich erste Vorbo-
ten des – viel – späteren Sprachgebrauchs, dass auch urchristliche Bücher zur „Schrift" gehören[115]. Der Zweite Petrusbrief stellt den „von
den Propheten vorausgesagten Worten" das „Gebot eurer Apostel des
Herrn und Retters" an die Seite (3,2); bei den Aposteln denkt er sowohl
an Petrus, auf dessen (pseudepigraphen) Brief er anspielt (3,1), als auch
an Paulus, dessen Briefe – wohl wegen der überragenden „Weisheit", in
der sie geschrieben sind – nur schwer verstanden werden können und
desto sorgfältiger exegetisiert werden müssen (3,16f).

Typisch ist jedoch nicht sogleich die Parallelisierung mit den heiligen
Schriften Israels, sondern ein eigener Anspruch, der sich auch in eigenen
Formen artikuliert. Paulus[116] schreibt seine Briefe *als* Apostel Jesu Christi an die Ekklesia Gottes[117]. Damit hat er ein Kommunikationsniveau
beschrieben, das sie als Formen schriftlicher Evangeliumsverkündigung
erkennen lässt, den normativen Anspruch auch der sog. Gelegenheits-
schreiben unterstreicht[118], im religionsgeschichtlichen Vergleich ohne

---

114. Besonders stark geschieht dies bei Paulus, wie der große Bogen von Röm 1,16
und 2,9f bis zu Röm 11,26 zeigt. Weitere Texte und die Begründung der These bei
TH. SÖDING, *Kriterien im Neuen Testament für eine Theologie des Alten Testaments,* in
L'interpretazione (Anm. 11), pp. 232-265, bes. pp. 239-247.

115. Der Erste Timotheusbrief (5,18) zitiert nach der Ankündigung „die Schrift sagt"
zuerst Dtn 25,4 („Du sollst dem Ochsen zum Dreschen keinen Maulkorb anlegen") und
dann Mt 10,10 par. Lk 10,7 („Wer arbeitet, ist seines Lohnes wert"), also ein Jesuswort
aus den Evangelien. Der Zweite Timotheusbrief scheint neben den „Büchern" des Alten
Testaments (vgl. 2 Tim 3,16f) als „Pergamente" auch *Neotestamentica*, vermutlich Abschriften der Paulusbriefe, zum apostolischen Bücherschatz des Paulus zu rechnen (2 Tim
4,13); so die Vermutung von E. PLÜMACHER, *Art. Bibel* II, in *TRE* 6 (1980), pp. 8-22, bes.
p. 9; ähnlich A.J. HULTGREN, *I-II Timothy, Titus,* Minneapolis, MN, Augsburg, 1984,
p. 143; auf das AT deutet jedoch L. OBERLINNER, *Pastoralbriefe: Zweiter Timotheusbrief*
(HTKNT, XI 2/2), Freiburg/Basel/Wien, Herder, 1995, pp. 173f. Der sekundäre Schluss
des Römerbriefes, Röm 16,25ff, rechnet den Paulus-Brief selbst zu den prophetischen
Schriften.

116. Vgl. zum folgenden TH. SÖDING, *Das Wort vom Kreuz* (Anm. 100), pp. 196-221.

117. Die stilistischen Variationen der Präskripte untersuchen F. SCHNIDER & W. STEN-
GER, *Studien zum neutestamentlichen Briefformular* (NTTS, 11), Leiden, Brill, 1987.

118. Auch wenn Paulus sich keineswegs immer durchsetzen konnte, wie die turbulen-
te Korrespondenz mit den Korinthern zeigt, ist der Autoritätsanspruch deutlich; er wird in
1 Kor 3 auf denkbar höchste Weise begründet: Der Apostel ist der Architekt der Kirche,
indem er deren Grundstein legt: Jesus Christus.

echte Parallele dasteht[119] und im Urchristentum stilbildend gewirkt
hat[120]. Für den Apostelbrief gibt es in der „Schrift" keine Formvor-
lage[121]; das Medium – aus der Not des Apostels geboren, nicht persönlich mit der Gemeinde sprechen zu können – entspricht dem Evangelium: Es überwindet Entfernungen, die durch die Mission entstanden
sind, und verbindet Räume, die zwischen den *Ekklesiai* liegen; vor allem
bietet es Gelegenheit zu Katechesen und Kontroversen, zu Homilien und
Paraklesen, zu Bekenntnissen und Gebeten, zu persönlicher Zuwendung
und zur Pflege der Gemeinschaft – wie dies alles dem Glaubensprinzip
entspricht, das die Ekklesia Gottes nach Jesu Tod und Auferweckung
überhaupt erst hat entstehen lassen[122]. Paulus will, dass seine Briefe in
der Gemeindeversammlung vorgelesen werden (1 Thess 5,27); damit
hat er selbst die Basis geschaffen, dass sie keine Eintagsfliegen waren,
sondern von den Gemeinden auch in späterer Zeit als Orientierung genutzt werden konnten[123]. Allerdings weiß Paulus zu unterscheiden: Der
Kraft Gottes entspricht die eigene Schwäche, dem Glanz des Evangeliums das eigene Elend: „Wir tragen diesen Schatz in irdenen Gefäßen,
damit das Übermaß der Kraft Gott vorbehalten bleibe und nicht von uns
ausgehe" (2 Kor 4,7), so lautet der Kardinalsatz einer kreuzestheolo-
gischen und pneumachristologischen Kanontheologie, der freilich einzig
in der Bibel dasteht.

Die paulinischen Pseudepigraphen nutzen die Autorität des Apostels[124], um in der bewährten Briefform seine Theologie fortzuschrei-

119. Zu den zahlreichen formalen Parallelen vgl. H.-J. KLAUCK, *Die antike Briefliteratur und das Neue Testament. Ein Lehr- und Arbeitsbuch* (UTB, 2022), Paderborn,
Schöningh, 1998.

120. Sicher in den Briefen der Paulusschule. Ob auch der Hebräerbrief und die Katholischen Briefe sowie die Sendschreiben der Apokalypse die von Paulus gefundene Briefform nutzen, wäre eigens zu erörtern.

121. Entsprechen die Paulusbriefe den Sendschreiben des Hohen Rates an Diaspora-
Gemeinden? So I. TAATZ, *Frühjüdische Briefe. Die paulinischen Briefe im Rahmen der
offiziellen religiösen Briefe des Frühjudentums* (NTOA, 16), Freiburg/Göttingen,
Universitätsverlag/Vandenhoeck & Ruprecht 1991.

122. Zur Form des Briefes und seinem hermeneutischen Potential vgl. (mit etwas anderen Akzenten) H. WEDER, *Neutestamentliche Hermeneutik,* Zürich, Theologischer Verlag, 1986, pp. 314-325.

123. Freilich hat dies den allerersten Korintherbrief (vgl. 1 Kor 5,9) nicht vor dem
Vergessen bewahrt – wenn man ihn nicht literarkritisch aus dem kanonischen Ersten Korintherbrief herausdestillieren will. Grundsätzlich ist keineswegs gesagt, dass im übrigen
alle Briefe des Paulus (oder anderer Apostel) erhalten geblieben sind. Auch das Schicksal
des Briefes an die Laodizener, den Kol 4,16 kennt, ist ungewiss. Der Zufall hat eine Rolle
gespielt.

124. Vgl. zu den kanonhermeneutischen Aspekten der Pseudepigraphie D.G. MEADE,
*Pseudonymity and Canon. An Investigation into the Relationship of Authorship and
Authority in Jewish and Earliest Christian Tradition* (WUNT, 39), Tübingen, Mohr,
1986.

ben[125], in Kontroversen zu behaupten und institutionell abzusichern[126]. Auf diese Weise tragen sie nicht nur zur Heiligsprechung des Apostels, sondern auch zur allmählichen Kanonisierung seiner Theologie bei – freilich um den Preis, nur mehr die Stärke, nicht aber zugleich die Schwäche seiner Verkündigungsworte zu betonen, die dem Kreuz Jesu Christi entspräche. Kol 4,16 regt den Austausch von Briefen an und legt damit den Samen für die Entstehung der Paulusbriefsammlung, die zu einem Keim der neutestamentlichen Kanonbildung geworden ist[127].

Auch die Evangelien sind – bei aller Nähe zu den alttestamentlichen Geschichtsbüchern – eine neue Gattung biblischer Literatur[128]. Ursprünglich ohne Verfasserangaben entstanden[129], weil sie sich ganz in die *Jesus*tradition stellen wollen, eignet ihnen von Anfang an ein erheblicher Anspruch[130]. Markus will in seinem Werk, den alles bestimmenden „Anfang" des Evangeliums darstellen (1,1)[131], Matthäus stellt seinen *Biblos geneseos Iesou Christou* (1,1)[132] der „Schrift" an die Seite[133], beruft sich auf das kirchenkonstitutive Zeugnis des Petrus (Mt 16,16ff) und stellt sich im Lichte des Missionsbefehles 28,16-20[134] als Kompen-

125. Vgl. K. SCHOLTISSEK (ed.), *Christologie in der Paulusschule. Zur Rezeptionsgeschichte des paulinischen Evangeliums* (SBS, 181), Stuttgart, Katholisches Bibelwerk, 2000.

126. Vgl. M. WOLTER, *Die Pastoralbriefe als Paulustradition* (FRLANT, 146), Göttingen, Vandenhoeck & Ruprecht, 1988.

127. Vgl. zu den Katholischen Briefen F. VOUGA, *Apostolische Briefe als „scriptura". Die Rezeption des Paulus in den katholischen Briefen,* in H.J. MEHLHAUSEN (ed.), *Sola scriptura* (Anm. 10), pp. 194-210.

128. Eigener Erörterungen bedarf die Verhältnisbestimmung zu antiken Biographien; sehr weit in der Annahme von Analogien geht D. FRICKENSCHMIDT, *Evangelium als Biographie. Die vier Evangelien im Rahmen antiker Erzählkunst* (TANZ, 22), Tübingen/Basel, Francke, 1997.

129. Selbst wenn man der optimistischen These M. HENGELS zur Frühdatierung der *tituli* folgt (*Die Evangelienüberschriften* [SHAW.PH, 3], Heidelberg 1984), bleibt der Satz prinzipiell richtig.

130. Vgl. zum folgenden TH. SÖDING, *Ein Jesus – Vier Evangelien. Vielseitigkeit und Eindeutigkeit der neutestamentlichen Jesustradition,* in *Theologie und Glaube* 91 (2001), 409-443.

131. Vgl. D. DORMEYER, *Das Markusevangelium als Idealbiographie von Jesus Christus, dem Nazarener* (SBS, 43), Stuttgart, Katholisches. Bibelwerk, 2001, pp. 21-24.

132. Vgl. D. DORMEYER, *Mt 1,1 als Überschrift zur Gattung und Christologie des Matthäusevangeliums,* in F. VAN SEGBROECK et al. (eds.), *The Four Gospels 1992*. FS Frans Neirynck (BETL, 100), Leuven, Peeters, 1992, pp. 1361-1383.

133. Vgl. H. FRANKEMÖLLE, *Das Matthäusevangelium als Heilige Schrift und die Heilige Schrift des Früheren Bundes. Von der Zwei-Quellen- zur Drei-Quellen-Theorie,* in C. FOCANT (ed.), *The Synoptic Gospels. Source Criticism and the New Literary Criticism* (BETL, 110), Leuven, Peeters, 1993, pp. 281-310. (Die Terminologie des Untertitels ist allerdings inadäquat: Die „Schrift" ist für Matthäus keine „Quelle" wie Markus und Q.).

134. Vgl. P. STUHLMACHER, *Zur missionsgeschichtlichen Bedeutung von Mt 28,16-20,* in *Evangelische Theologie* 59 (1999) 108-130.

dium „all" dessen vor, was Jesus seine Jünger „gelehrt" hat, damit sie es weitergeben[135]; Lukas (Lk 1,1-4; Apg 1,2f)[136] schreibt sein Doppelwerk, um den Christen der dritten Generation zu demonstrieren, auf welch sicherer Basis ihre Katechese steht (und vielleicht auch, um die Gebildeten unter den Verächtern des Christentums darüber aufzuklären, wohin der „Weg" Jesu wirklich führt); damit leistet er als Historiker unter den Evangelisten seinerseits eine Fundamentalkatechese mit weitreichendem Anspruch für die Gemeinden (wahrscheinlich des paulinischen Missionsraumes). Den höchsten Anspruch formuliert Johannes (20,30f; vgl. 21,24f): Sein „Buch", das eine gezielte Auswahl und Zuspitzung der Jesustradition bietet[137], dient dazu, den „Glauben der Glaubenden zu wecken"[138]. Die Kraft der Erinnerung, die dem Glauben an Jesus als Messias und Gottessohn dient, ist für Johannes der Geist, der als Paraklet den Jüngern die Wahrheit Jesu (14,6) erschließt[139]; der

135. J. GNILKA, *Das Matthäusevangelium* I-II (HTKNT, I/1-2), Freiburg/Basel/Wien, Herder, 2000 (1988), p. 509: „Ist mit Taufen und Lehren eine Explikation des Zum-Jünger-Machens gegeben, so ist sowohl die sakramentale Eingliederung der für das Evangelium Gewonnenen in die Kirche als auch deren begleitende unterrichtsmäßige Betreuung erforderlich".

136. Zur philologischen, theologischen und hermeneutischen Bedeutung des lukanischen Prooemiums vgl. H. SCHÜRMANN, *Das Lukasevangelium* I (HTKNT, III/1). Freiburg/Basel/Wien, Herder, 2000 ([1]1969), pp. 1-17.

137. Vgl. TH. SÖDING, *Die Schrift als Medium des Glaubens. Zur hermeneutischen Bedeutung von Joh 20,30f,* in K. BACKHAUS & F.G. UNTERGASSMAIR (eds.), *Schrift und Tradition.* FS J. Ernst, Paderborn, Schöningh, 1996, pp. 343-371.

138. J. ZUMSTEIN, *Kreative Erinnerung. Relecture und Auslegung im Johannesevangelium.* Zürich, Pano, 1999, p. 36.

139. Vgl. H. SCHLIER, *Zum Begriff des Parakleten nach dem Johannesevangelium,* in Id., *Besinnung auf das Neue Testament. Gesammelte Aufsätze* II, Freiburg/Basel/Wien, Herder, 1964, pp. 264-271; G. BORNKAMM, *Der Paraklet im Johannesevangelium,* in Id., *Geschichte und Glaube. Gesammelte Aufsätze* 3, München, Kaiser, 1968, pp. 68-89; F. MUSSNER, *Die johanneischen Parakletsprüche und die apostolische Tradition,* in Id., *Praesentia Salutis,* Düsseldorf, Patmos, 1967, pp. 146-158; R.E. BROWN, *The Paraclete in the Fourth Gospel,* in NTS 13 (1967-68) 113-132; U.B. MÜLLER, *Die Parakletenvorstellung im Johannesevangelium,* in ZTK 71 (1974) 31-77; F. PORSCH, *Pneuma und Wort. Ein exegetischer Beitrag zur Pneumatologie des Johannesevangeliums* (FTS, 6), Frankfurt/M., 1974; U. WILCKENS, *Der Paraklet und die Kirche,* in D. LÜHRMANN & G. STRECKER (eds.), *Kirche.* FS G. Bornkamm, Tübingen, Mohr, 1980, pp. 185-203; M. HASITSCHKA, *Die Parakletworte im Johannesevangelium. Versuch einer Auslegung in synchroner Textbetrachtung,* in *Studien zum Neuen Testament und seiner Umwelt* 18 (1993) 97-112; A. DETTWILER, *Die Gegenwart des Erhöhten. Eine exegetische Studie zu den johanneischen Abschiedsreden (Joh 13,31-16,33) unter besonderer Berücksichtigung ihres Relecture-Charakters* (FRLANT, 169), Göttingen, Vandenhoeck & Ruprecht, 1995, pp. 181-189; CH. KAMMLER, *Jesus und der Geistparaklet. Eine Studie zur johanneischen Verhältnisbestimmung von Pneumatologie und Christologie,* in O. HOFIUS & ID., *Johannesstudien* (WUNT, 88), Tübingen, Mohr, 1996, pp. 87-190; CH. DIETZFELBINGER, *Der Abschied des Kommenden. Eine Auslegung der johanneischen Abschiedsreden* (WUNT, 95), Tübingen, Mohr, 1997, pp. 202-226; ID., *Paraklet und theologischer Anspruch im Johannesevangelium,* in ZTK 82 (1985) 398-408.

verlässliche Zeuge ist der Lieblingsjünger[140], der nach Joh 21 zwar einen „Primat" des Petrus[141] (und damit auch ein besonderes Gewicht der synoptischen Tradition anerkennt), aber ohne jeden Verzicht auf das überlegene Glaubenswissen der johanneischen Kommunität. In der Zeit, in der man den Irdischen wie den Auferstanden nicht mehr wie ausnahmsweise noch Thomas sehen kann, ist das „Buch" eine notwendige Stütze für den Glauben, der zu retten vermag.

Bleibt im Johannesevangelium die Inspirationstheologie implizit, wird sie in der Johannesoffenbarung explizit[142]. Der Seher nimmt für sich in Anspruch, das – und nur das – aufzuschreiben, was ihm von Jesus Christus, dem es Gott offenbart hat (1,1f), gezeigt worden ist (1,10f); dem entspricht, dass er zum Abschluss die deuteronomistische Kanonisierungsformel auf sein eigenes Werk anwendet (22,18f): Es präsentiert sich als Prophetie, die gelesen werden soll – unter der Verheißung, dass „selig ist, wer die Worte der Prophetie vorliest" (1,3) und „die Worte der Prophetie dieses Buches bewahrt" (22,7).

Keine dieser Stellen lässt sich so deuten, dass eine neutestamentliche Schrift sich als Ergänzung des „alttestamentlichen" Kanons präsentieren würde. Alle beziehen sich vielmehr auf das Christusgeschehen. Für sie ist die „Schrift" – prinzipiell – abgeschlossen; nicht abgeschlossen ist hingegen der Zeitraum inspirierten, normativen Glaubenszeugnisses, schließlich auch in der schriftlichen Form der neutestamentlichen Texte. Als Zeugnisse des Bekenntnisses zum eschatologischen Heilshandeln Gottes in Christus treten die „neutestamentlichen" Schriften den „alttestamentlichen" an die Seite, unlösbar mit ihnen verbunden und unverkennbar von ihnen unterschieden.

An einigen wenigen Stellen des Neuen Testaments finden sich – kaum schon programmatisch – Sätze, an die in späterer Zeit angeknüpft

140. Heute wird mehr denn je diskutiert, ob der „Lieblingsjünger" eine reine Symbolgestalt ist oder eine stilisierte historische Figur. Für das erste plädieren J. KÜGLER, *Der Jünger, den Jesus liebte. Literarische, theologische und historische Untersuchungen zu einer Schlüsselgestalt johanneischer Theologie und Geschichte. Mit einem Exkurs über die Brotrede in Joh 6* (SBB, 16), Stuttgart, Katholisches Bibelwerk, 1988; U. WILCKENS, *Maria, Mutter der Kirche (Joh 19,26f)*, in R. KAMPLING & TH. SÖDING (eds.), *Ekklesiologie des Neuen Testaments*. FS K. Kertelge, Freiburg/Basel/Wien, Herder, 1996, pp. 247-266; für das zweite M. HENGEL, *Die johanneische Frage* (WUNT, 67), Tübingen, Mohr, 1993.

141. Vgl. R. PESCH, *Die biblischen Grundlagen des Primats* (QD, 187), Freiburg/Basel/Wien, Herder, 2001.

142. Im Formvergleich zeigt sich, dass die Johannesoffenbarung eine besondere Nähe zu Daniel (und frühjüdischen Apokalypsen) aufweist; durch die Sendschreiben, die dem gesamten Buch Briefcharakter geben, entsteht aber ein eigenständiges Gebilde; vgl. M. KARRER, *Die Johannesoffenbarung als Brief. Studien zu ihrem literarischen, historischen und theologischen Ort* (FRLANT, 140), Göttingen, Vandenhoeck & Ruprecht 1986.

werden konnte, wenn es galt, Grenzen zu ziehen. Eine einheitliche Linie bahnt sich im Neuen Testament nicht an. Es gibt vielmehr gegenläufige Tendenzen, die aber gerade in ihren Widersprüchen einen Bezugsrahmen gebildet haben. *Paulus* sieht die Reihe der Urapostel, deren Missionsauftrag eine Erscheinung des Auferweckten zugrundeliegt, definitiv mit seiner Person, die bereits eine Ausnahme von der Regel war, beschlossen (1 Kor 15,1-11). Dieses Kriterium der Apostolizität ist außerordentlich wirkmächtig geworden[143]. *Lukas* rekurriert gleichfalls auf die „Apostel", aber gerade nur auf die Zwölf als die „Augenzeugen und Diener des Wortes" (1,2), denen Paulus als „dreizehnter Zeuge"[144] auf dem Fuße folgt, ohne selbst im eigentlichen Wortsinn „Apostel" sein zu können. Sein Evangelium, so Lukas, gibt (wie vor ihm schon das des Markus, aber nicht in derselben Vollständigkeit) das Zeugnis dieser Zeugen wieder, die aufgrund ihrer Geschichte mit Jesus allein die Garanten der Kontinuität zwischen der Verkündigung Jesu und der Verkündigung der Kirche, aber auch die maßgebenden Verkünder der Auferstehung Jesu sein können. *Johannes* bringt in seinem Evangelium die Perspektive des Lieblingsjüngers ein, der selbst kein „Apostel" und keiner der „Zwölf" ist (wozu man ihn später gemacht hat), sondern der „andere Jünger" (18,15; 20,2ff), der schneller ist, genauer hinschaut und tiefer glaubt – aber dennoch Petrus den Vortritt lässt (20,2-10)[145]. In allen drei Impulsen geht es um die zeitliche und sachliche Nähe zu Jesus und sei-

---

143. Die Protagonisten der Paulusschule machen es stark: bis dahin, dass der Zweite Timotheusbrief, als Testament des Paulus fingiert, einen definitiven Schlusspunkt unter die Produktion von Paulusbriefen zu setzen versucht hat, was im weiteren Prozess der Kanonisierung bestätigt wurde. Der Hebräerbrief sucht mit seinem Postskript Kontakt zur Paulustradition (13,20-25) und ordnet sich mit 2,3 in die apostolische Tradition ein (vgl. 3,14; 13,7); anders jedoch E. GRÄSSER, *An die Hebräer I* (EKK, 17/1), Zürich/Neukirchen-Vluyn, Einsiedeln/Neukirchener, 1990, pp. 106f. Mit Jakobus, Petrus und Johannes finden Briefe den Weg in den Kanon, deren Namen aus Gal 2,9 als die der drei Jerusalemer Säulen (vgl. D. LÜHRMANN, *Gal 2,9 und die katholischen Briefe. Bemerkungen zum Kanon und zur frühchristlichen regula fidei*, in ZNW 72 [1981] 65-87). Judas segelt im Schlepptau des Petrus. Die Evangelien finden schließlich als die zweier Apostel und zweier Apostelschüler Anerkennung. Die Kanonisierung der Apokalypse ist im Zuge der Identifizierung ihres Verfassers mit dem Apostel (und Evangelisten) Johannes erfolgt; denkbar wäre freilich auch ein Rekurs auf Eph 2,20, wonach die Ekklesia auf das Fundament der „Apostel und Propheten" gebaut ist (vgl. 4,17).

144. CH. BURCHARD, *Der dreizehnte Zeuge* (FRLANT, 103), Göttingen, Vandenhoeck & Ruprecht 1970.

145. Der Erste Johannesbrief bezieht sich auf die Anschauung des Evangeliums zurück (1,1-5); vgl. H.-J. KLAUCK, *Der Rückgriff auf Jesus im Prolog des Ersten Johannesbriefes*, in H. FRANKEMÖLLE & K. KERTELGE (eds.), *Vom Urchristentum zu Jesus. FS J. Gnilka*, Freiburg/Basel/Wien, Herder, 1989, pp. 433-451. Signifikant ist auch das „Wir" von 2 Joh 5 im deutlichen Rückbezug auf 1 Joh 2,7-11 vor dem Hintergrund von Joh 13,31-35; vgl. H.-J. KLAUCK, *Der Zweite und Dritte Johannesbrief* (EKK, 23/2), Zürich/Neukirchen-Vluyn, Benzinger/Neukirchener 1992, pp. 49ff.

nem Evangelium; mehr noch geht es um eine persönliche Beziehung, sei es zum Irdischen, sei es zum Auferweckten: Es sind die von Jesus Christus selbst Berufenen, deren Zeugnis normative Bedeutung gewinnt, wenn anders Jesu Wirken, Tod und Auferweckung eschatologische Heilsbedeutung hat[146].

Der theologische Anspruch, der sich auf vielstimmige und vielfach gebrochene Weise in den neutestamentlichen Schriften artikuliert, geht auf den Anspruch Jesu selbst zurück (ohne mit ihm identisch zu sein): Die Unbedingtheit des Rufes Jesu zur Umkehr und zum Glauben (Mk 1,15) folgt aus der Unbedingtheit des von Jesus proklamierten Willens Gottes, seine Herrschaft nahekommen zu lassen; sein Kreuzestod, der diesen Anspruch ein für allemal als frevelhaft erwiesen zu haben schien, wird von seinen Jüngern im Licht des Ostermorgens als definitive Bejahung verstanden, seine Auferstehung nicht nur als Bestätigung seiner Person und Sache, sondern als seine Erhöhung zur Rechten Gottes und als Grund der Evangeliumsverkündigung an alle Völker.

III. THESEN ZUR KANONHERMENEUTIK

Welche Konsequenzen lassen sich aus den exegetischen Beobachtungen ableiten? Neun Thesen seien zur Diskussion gestellt.

1. *Dass* es im Judentum und im Christentum einen Kanon gibt, erklärt sich historisch nicht als frommes Missverständnis oder reiner Zufall, sondern als Ergebnis einer Rezeption, die auf einer prinzipiellen Bejahung des Anspruchs beruht, der den biblischen Texten selbst innewohnt und nach deren Zeugnis aus der Offenbarung folgt, die sie bezeugen. Dass der christliche Kanon als Machtinstrument einer kirchlichen Elite fungiert hat, nötigt nicht zur Auflösung des Kanons, sondern zu einer Theologie des Kanons, die ihn von seinen biblischen Ursprung her erklärt.

2. Der kanonische Anspruch, der von den biblischen Schriften ausgeht, richtet sich – je unterschiedlich im Alten und im Neuen Testament – in umfassender Weise auf die Lehre, das Ethos und den Gottesdienst des Gottesvolkes; umgekehrt sind es gerade die von den im kanonischen

---

146. Alle drei Impulse lassen verstehen, weshalb das Kriterium der Apostolizität in der Alten Kirche zum entscheidenden geworden ist – und dass es in Zweifelsfällen als *theologisches* angewendet worden ist. Im ganzen wird man urteilen müssen, dass nach den im Neuen Testament selbst erkennbaren Parametern die Kanonisierung keiner der neutestamentlichen Schriften überraschen kann – und dass andere Schriften nur geringe Chancen hatten, dauerhaft und umfassend als kanonisch anerkannt zu werden. Der Erste Clemensbrief kam schon deshalb nicht in Betracht, weil er nicht „apostolisch" ist.

Prozess befindlichen Schriften angesprochenen Kommunitäten, denen sich die implizite und explizite Kanonisierung verdankt[147]. Eine Kanontheologie, die „weit oben" bei der Inspiration ansetzt, braucht eine Kanontheologie „von unten", die in historischer Differenziertheit von den Funktionen handelt, die bestimmte Textcorpora zu bestimmten Zeiten und an bestimmten Orten für bestimmte Gruppen ausgeübt haben[148]. Umgekehrt braucht eine Kanongeschichte, die auf die Suche nach den Ursprüngen geht, eine Kanontheologie, wenn überhaupt verstanden werden soll, worum es bei der Kanonbildung geht. Im kanonischen Anspruch, so implizit er bleiben mag, artikuliert sich ein Wahrheitsbewusstsein, das auf Offenbarung beruht, und ein dadurch geprägtes Verständnis des Willens Gottes, der unbedingten Gehorsam verlangt, das ganze Leben bestimmt, dank der „Schriften" in den Grundzügen klar erkennbar ist und in schriftgemäßer Weise fortwährend aktualisiert und appliziert werden muss. Der Kanon macht produktive Interpretation nicht überflüssig, sondern ruft sie hervor. Es gäbe keinen Kanon, wenn er nicht immer neue Interpretationen freisetzte, in denen es, paulinisch ausgedrückt, um die Wahrheit des Evangeliums ginge; es gäbe im jüdischen und christlichen Sinn keine Diskussion um die Wahrheit religiöser Rede, wenn es keinen Kanon gäbe.

3. Der Kanon ist kein papierener Papst. Die kanonisierten Schriften weisen, indem sie theologische Ansprüche stellen, gerade nicht auf sich selbst, sondern auf den, dessen Wirken sie sich nach ihrem eigenen Zeugnis verdanken. Der Anspruch eines Kanons gibt den Anspruch des *einen* Gottes auf gehorsame Anerkennung wieder (Dtn 6,4f; vgl. Ex 20,1-7 par. Dtn 5,6-11) und des einen Kyrios auf Glauben (1 Kor 8,6). Die Schriften sind das Medium der immer neuen Präsentation dieses Anspruchs durch die Zeiten hindurch und über alle räumlichen Grenzen hinaus. Der Kanon setzt die *viva vox evangelii* voraus, indem er sie bezeugt; er begründet die Möglichkeit jeweils neu lebendiger Verkündigung, indem er den bestimmenden Anfang dokumentiert. Deshalb ist die Kanonizität des Kanons weder an einer absoluten Sicherheit des Textes festzumachen noch an der genauen Abfolge der verschiedenen Bücher,

---

147. Die Korrelation zwischen dem kanonisierten Text und der kanonisierenden Gemeinschaft betont zu Recht G. STEINS, *Die „Bindung Isaaks" im Kanon (Gen 22). Grundlagen und Probleme einer kanonisch-intertextuellen Lektüre* (HBS, 20), Freiburg/Basel/Wien, Herder, 1999.

148. Sozial- und religionsgeschichtliche Studien liefern die Konkretionen. Dieses Programm verfolgt S. TALMON, *Heiliges Schrifttum und Kanonische Bücher aus jüdischer Sicht – Überlegungen zur Ausbildung der Größe „Die Schrift" im Judentum*, in M. KLOPFENSTEIN et al. (eds.), *Mitte* (Anm. 100), pp. 45-79 (der allerdings einen Gegensatz zur Kanon*theologie* sieht).

noch nicht einmal an der genauen Fixierung einer Kanonliste. Vielmehr sind die Suche nach dem festen Text wie die zahlreichen Textvarianten, die von der Textkritik dokumentiert werden, die übersichtliche Ordnung wie die Unterschiede der Ordnungen, die Feststellung eines genauen Umfanges wie dessen Diskussion jeweils Teile des kanonischen Prozesses, der das Faktum des Kanons voraussetzt und durch Interpretation dessen Kanonizität zeitigt[149].

4. Über den Umfang des neutestamentlichen Kanons hat es nach dem 2. Jh. kaum noch Auseinandersetzungen gegeben, auch wenn Einzelfälle – jüdisch wie christlich – bis ins 3. und 4. Jh. hinein kontrovers diskutiert worden sind. Im Umfang des alttestamentlichen Kanons stimmen das rabbinische Judentum und das frühe Christentum substantiell überein[150]. Dies erklärt sich aus einem kanonischen Prozess im Frühjudentum, der zu wesentlichen Teile bereits abgeschlossen war und an dem das Urchristentum auf seine Weise partizipiert. Die nicht unerheblichen Differenzen zwischen der *Biblia Judaica* und dem *Vetus Testamentum* erklären sich aus signifikanten Unterschieden im Verständnis der Geschichte und des inspirierenden Waltens des Geistes Gottes. Aus neutestamentlicher Sicht gibt es einen Abschluss des alttestamentlichen Kanons nicht schon mit Esra, sondern erst mit dem Auftreten des Täufers und dem Kommen Jesu. Die Bedeutung der „Septuaginta" ist im Neuen Testament so groß, dass eine christliche Kanon-Theologie nicht nur die *Biblia Hebraica* ins Auge fassen dürfte, sondern auch das *Vetus Testamentum Graece* zu würdigen hat[151] – aber nicht als Gegensatz zum Hebräischen, sondern als Basis des Neuen Testaments, die ihrerseits das Hebräische zur Basis hat, auf der auch das Neue Testament gründet[152].

149. Vgl. dazu – am Beispiel der verschiedenen Kanon-Ordnungen – den Beitrag von E. Zenger in diesem Bd., pp. 111-134.

150. Der exegetische Blick richtet sich berufsbedingt vor allem auf die Differenzen. Es muss aber festgehalten werden, dass vor allen Unterschieden die prinzipielle Übereinstimmung darin besteht, dass nicht nur das „Gesetz", sondern auch die Propheten und die übrigen Schriften, besonders die Psalmen, als kanonisch anerkannt worden sind.

151. Vgl. P. Stuhlmacher, *Die Bedeutung der Apokryphen und Pseudepigraphen für das Verständnis Jesu und der Christologie*, in S. Meurer (ed.), *Die Apokryphenfrage im ökumenischen Horizont*, Stuttgart, Bibelgesellschaft, 1989, pp. 13-25; N. Walter, *„Bücher - so nicht der heiligen Schrifft gleich gehalten…"? Karlstadt, Luther - und die Folgen*, in A. Freund et al. (eds.), *Tragende Tradition*. FS M. Seils, Frankfurt/M. et al., 1992, pp. 173-197; H. Spieckermann, *God's Steadfast Love. Towards a New Conception of Old Testament Theology*, in *Bib* 81 (2000) 305-327, bes. pp. 307f. Skeptisch, ob es möglich ist, eine „Theologie der Septuaginta" zu rekonstruieren, zeigt sich E. Tov, *Die Septuaginta in ihrem theologischen und traditionsgeschichtlichen Verhältnis zur hebräischen Bibel*, in M. Klopfenstein et al. (eds.), *Mitte* (Anm. 100), pp. 237-268. Es käme auf einen Versuch an.

152. H. Gese urteilt zwar in seinen *Erwägungen zur Einheit der biblischen Theologie* (1970): „Ein christlicher Theologe darf den masoretischen Kanon niemals gutheißen" (in

5. Der *christliche* Kanon ist *wesentlich* dadurch geprägt, dass er zwei Teile hat, die beiden Testamente, und dass zuerst das Alte, dann das Neue Testament kommt[153]. Beides spiegelt die Epochenwende, die nach Jesus das Nahekommen der Basileia (Mk 1,15), nach Paulus die Sendung des messianischen Gottessohnes (Gal 4,4), nach Johannes die Inkarnation des Logos (Joh 1,14) herbeigeführt hat; beides spiegelt aber auch die Identität Gottes mit sich selbst wider, die Theozentrik der Christologie und Soteriologie, anders formuliert: die Gerechtigkeit Gottes, der sich selbst treu bleibt und Gerechtigkeit schafft, indem er, nach christlichem Glauben eschatologisch definitiv mit der Sendung des Sohnes, ein „Je Mehr" der Gnade verwirklicht (Röm 5,12-21), das im vollendeten Reich Gottes alles bestimmen wird (1 Kor 15,28). Die starken Theologien des Neuen Testaments lassen erkennen, dass dieser Einschnitt, weil er dem *einen* Gott verdankt ist, die Geschichte Israels nicht vergessen macht oder relativiert, sondern in neuem Licht erstrahlen lässt[154]. Jesus ist gekommen, „die verlorenen Schafe des Hauses Israel" zu sammeln (Mt 15,24; vgl. 10,6), und hat in seinem Volk auch die nicht verworfen, die ihm keinen Glauben geschenkt haben; Paulus hat

ID., *Vom Sinai zum Zion* [BEvT, 64], München, ³1990, pp 11-30, bes. p. 16f). Die Frage lautet, was „gutheißen" meint. Auch als christlicher Theologe hat man m.E. die Entscheidung der Juden für die *Biblia Hebraica* zur Dynamisierung der eigenen Kanontheologie zu nutzen (was die Kirchen der Reformation unter dem Eindruck des Humanismus ja auch getan haben). Deutlich zu unterscheiden hätte man zudem die Sprachen- und die Umfangsfrage. Im Hinblick auf die Übersetzung bleibt der Bescheidenheitstopos des Siraciden-Enkels aufschlussreich (prol. 15-24): „Ihr seid also gebeten, mit Wohlwollen und Aufmerksamkeit die Lektüre zu betreiben und dort Nachsicht zu üben, wo es scheinen könnte, daß wir trotz allen Mühens bei der Übersetzung in gewissen Fällen nicht ganz den rechten Sinn getroffen haben. Denn es hat nicht dieselbe Ausdruckskraft, ob etwas im originalen Hebräisch gelesen oder in eine andere Sprache übertragen wird". Dennoch ist, vom Neuen Testament her geurteilt, das Griechische auch im Alten Testament neben dem Hebräischen eine kanonische Sprache. Richtig ist die Beobachtung, dass für die Kirchen bestimmter Regionen und Zeiten auch Übersetzungen in andere Sprache *ihre* Bibel geworden sind; vgl. A. SCHENKER, *L'Écriture Sainte subsiste en plusieurs formes canoniques simultanées*, in *L'interpretazione* (Anm. 11), pp. 178-186. Doch *aus neutestamentlicher Sicht* ist die Bedeutung der „Septuaginta" so groß, dass noch einmal ein qualitativer Unterschied gemacht werden muss. Im Hinblick auf den Umfang scheint ein transparentes Verfahren günstig: In den Bibelausgaben ist die Grenzfrage des Kanons anzusprechen, wie es die *Guidelines for Interconfessional Cooperating in Translating the Bible* (1987) auch vorsehen.

153. Eine Umstellung aus theologischen Gründen, weil man das Alte Testament nicht ohne das Neue verstehen könne, favorisierte F. SCHLEIERMACHER, *Der christliche Glaube*, ed. M. Redeker, Berlin, de Gruyter, ⁷1960, §132.

154. Unter dieser Rücksicht ist das nicht selten missbräuchlich verzerrte Modell von „Verheißung" und „Erfüllung" hinsichtlich seiner Leistungsfähigkeit, die beiden Testamente zu unterscheiden und in eschatologischer Perspektive zu verklammern, neu zu bedenken; vgl. zu Paulus TH. SÖDING, *Verheißung und Erfüllung im Lichte paulinischer Theologie*, in *NTS* 46 (2001) 146-170.

zu reflektieren gewusst, dass es, solange die Geschichte währt, ein spannungsreiches Nebeneinander von Judentum und Christentum geben wird, das im Zeichen eschatologisch-vollendeter Gemeinschaft im Reich Gottes steht (Röm 11)[155]. Die Orientierung am Kanon zeigt, dass *dies* die normativen Positionen für eine christliche Theologie des Judentums sind. Daraus leitet sich ab, welche theologische Bedeutung es hat, *dass* es die jüdische Auslegung des „Alten Testaments" mit einem innerhalb des Judentums normativen Anspruch gibt. Allein ihr Faktum weist darauf hin, dass Altes und Neues Testament keine bruchlose Einheit bilden. An der Einheit des Kanons festzuhalten, kann nicht die Zweiheit der Testamente relativieren; erst wo die Unterscheidung gelungen ist, kann eine Verbindung versucht werden. Die Unterscheidung setzt den Einsatz der historisch-philologischen Vernunft, also Exegese im neuzeitlichen Wortsinn voraus. Die Verbindung kann nur gelingen, wenn beide Teile bleiben können, was sie gewesen und geworden sind: das Alte Testament das Alte vor dem Neuen und das Neue Testament das Neue im Rückgriff auf das Alte[156]; auch diese Klärung kann nicht dog-

---

155. Dass die Vision einer Rettung ganz Israels kein spontaner Einfall oder ein apokalyptischer Ausfall des Paulus ist, sondern das Ergebnis einer prophetischen Schriftauslegung in den Bahnen paulinischer Evangeliumstheologie, zeigt M. THEOBALD, *Der „strittige Punkt" (Rhet. A. Her. I,26) im Diskurs des Römerbriefes. Die propositio 1,16f und das Mysterium der Rettung ganz Israels,* in R. KAMPLING (ed.), *Evangelium* (Anm. 33), pp. 183-228.

156. Der Ökumenische Arbeitskreis evangelischer und katholischer Theologen (Jaeger-Stählin-Kreis) hat erklärt (*Verbindliches Zeugnis* III [Anm. 1]: „Evangelische und katholische Christen lesen das Alte Testament gemeinsam als verbindliches Wort Gottes (p. 308). … Die tiefen Unterschiede zwischen jüdischer und christlicher Auslegung der gleichen Schriften müssen theologisch gewürdigt und für ein aus den Quellen erneuertes christliches Schriftverständnis genutzt werden" (p. 309f). … Die Antijudaismen christlicher Schrift-Exegesen … gilt es von der Schrift selbst her in ihrer Spannung und Einheit zwischen dem Alten und dem Neuen Testament zu überwinden. Die Beobachtung der z.T. tiefgreifenden Differenz zwischen einer traditionellen interpretatio christiana und dem geschichtlichen Ursprungssinn alttestamentlicher Texte gibt uns Christen auch die Möglichkeit, einen neuen Zugang zum Alten Testament zu gewinnen (p. 310). … [Das Alte Testament bildet] nicht nur als Vorbereitung auf die Christusoffenbarung, sondern auch aus eigenem theologischen und historischen Recht den ersten Teil des christlichen Kanons (ib.). … *Einerseits* setzt das Neue Testament das Alte Testament notwendig voraus. … *Andererseits* zielt das Alte Testament im Horizont des Christusgeschehens auf das Neue: nicht in dem Sinn, dass es, seinem historischen Literalsinn nach betrachtet, bereits offenkundig das Christus-Evangelium bezeugte; wohl aber in dem Sinn, dass die *eschatologische* Selbstoffenbarung des *einen* Gottes, der sich schon in den alttestamentlichen Schriften als er selbst mitteilt, in Leben, Lehre, Tod und Auferweckung Jesu Christi geschieht, wie dies im Neuen Testament zur Sprache kommt. Deshalb lesen Christen die Heilige Schrift Israels von Gottes eschatologischem Heilshandeln durch Jesus Christus her in neuer Weise als Urkunde ihres Glaubens (p. 317). … Von Christus her erweist sich das Alte Testament weder nur als Vorgeschichte des christlichen Glaubens noch allein als dialektisches Gegenüber des Neuen Testaments, wohl aber als Dokument der Erwählung Israels wie seiner Geschichte mit Gott, in der die Christenheit wurzelt (vgl. Röm 11), und als Urkunde einer Hoffnung auf endgültiges Heil für Juden und Heiden, das auf-

matisch, sie muss exegetisch erfolgen, wenn sie den Texten gerecht werden soll[157].

6. Innerhalb des Kanons haben nicht alle Schriften dasselbe Gewicht. Unterschiede werden nicht erst von den Rezipienten gemacht; wesentlich sind die Unterschiede, die darin angelegt sind, *was* die Schriften thematisieren und *wie* sie es thematisieren. Innerhalb des „Alten Testaments" kommt der Tora schon deshalb Erstrangigkeit zu[158], weil sie den Schöpfungsbericht und in den Erzelternerzählungen die grundlegende Erwählungsgeschichte Israels enthält, den Exodus und die Sinaitraditionen mit dem Gesetz des Mose; durch den kanonischen Prozess werden die Propheten wie die Schriften programmatisch auf die Tora bezogen. Innerhalb des Neuen Testaments haben die Evangelien einen ähnlichen Primat inne: weil sie – in vierfacher Form – die Geschichte des Wirkens, des Todes und der Auferweckung Jesu als Christus erzählen, auf die sich alle anderen neutestamentlichen Schriften im Kern beziehen.

7. Eine Auslegung, die dem Kanon als Kanon gerecht werden will, muss zwar über die Einzelexegese hinaus zu theologischen Urteilen kommen, worin seine Verbindlichkeit besteht, darf aber nicht von sich aus oder nur im Lichte bestimmter Rezeptionstraditionen oder Interpretationsplausibilitäten einen „Kanon im Kanon" abgrenzen oder innerhalb der Schriften eine „Mitte" markieren, auf die hin und von der her theologische Exegese (oder exegetische Theologie) zu treiben wäre[159],

grund der Gnadenfülle Gottes die Grenzen von Raum und Zeit sprengt, um Gottes Herrschaft zu vollenden" (pp. 317f). Obwohl dies Kernsätze des Dokumentes sind, sieht W. GROSS Grund zu dem – allerdings ohne jeden Textnachweis aufgestellten – Urteil, es werde von dem Dokument „in massiver Weise" das AT „neutestamentlich und christologisch-systematisch vereinnahmt" (*Ist die biblisch-theologische Auslegung ein integrierender Methodenschritt?*, in F.-L. HOSSFELD [ed.], *Systematik* [Anm. 2], pp. 110-149, bes. p. 137).

157. Vielleicht darf man noch einen Schritt weiter gehen: Das Kanonprinzip geht offensichtlich gut mit Randunschärfen zusammen. Einerseits gibt es nicht nur in den lateinischen Konfessionen, es gab von Anfang an und gibt bis heute in den orientalischen Kirchen unterschiedliche Kanonlisten, ohne dass der Kanon als *locus theologicus* Schaden zu nehmen braucht. Ebenso bleiben nicht geringe Text-Unsicherheiten, keineswegs nur in den alttestamentlichen Spannungen zwischen dem Hebräischen und Griechischen, sondern von Anfang in der Handschriftenüberlieferung. Diese Randunschärfen zeigen, dass der Kanon nicht in erster Linie von seinen Rändern, sondern von seiner Mitte und nicht nur vom Endpunkt, sondern auch vom Ursprung her verstanden werden muss.

158. Üblich ist, die Tora „Kanon im Kanon" zu nennen oder „Mitte der Schrift" (so z.B. S. FRAENKEL, *Die „Mitte des Tanach" aus der Sicht des Rabbinischen Judentums*, in M. KLOPFENSTEIN et al. [eds.], *Mitte der Schrift?* [Anm. 100], pp. 97-118; O. KAISER, *Der Gott des Alten Testaments* I: *Grundlegung* [UTB, 1747], Göttingen, Vandenhoeck & Ruprecht, 1993, pp. 329-353), beide Termini signalisieren Konzepte einer Kanonhermeneutik, deren Leistungsfähigkeit kritisch diskutiert werden muss.

159. Ein konstruktive Kritik alttestamentlicher Vorstellungen übt L. SCHWIENHORST-SCHÖNBERGER, *Einheit und Vielfalt. Gibt es eine sinnvolle Suche nach der Mitte der Schrift?*, in F.-L. HOSSFELD (ed.), *Systematik* (Anm. 2), pp. 48-87. Aus neutestamentlicher Sicht übt eine differenzierte Kritik H. WEDER, *Die Externität der Mitte. Überlegungen*

sondern hat die Texte von dem her auszulegen, was sie bezeugen. Altes und Neues Testament haben im Kreis ihrer Schriften zwar insofern eine „Mitte", als die Tora, die Propheten und Psalmen im Alten Testament, die Evangelien und die Apostelbriefe im Neuen Testament die Gravitationszentren des kanonischen Prozesses bilden. Aber diese Mitte ist kein Kanon. Die biblischen Schriften haben vielmehr vielfältige Perspektiven auf den einen Gott hin, die von unterschiedlichen Standpunkten aus unterschiedliche Aspekte seines Wesens und Handelns erfassen, aber auch typische Formen menschlicher Antwort in der Gemeinschaft des Gottesvolkes[160], im Neuen Testament unter der alles noch einmal neu bestimmenden Sicht des eschatologischen Heilshandelns Gottes durch, mit und ihn Jesus Christus[161], zusammen mit der ursprünglichen Antwort derer, die im Glauben an das Evangelium Jesu Christi verkündet hat, in die Ekklesia Gottes hineingeführt worden sind[162].

8. Das „Neue Testament" kann nie – weder historisch-kritisch noch kanontheologisch – ohne die Voraussetzung des „Alten Testaments" gelesen werden. Was sich motivgeschichtlich als Verwurzelung des Neuen Testaments im Alten Testament nachweisen lässt, bildet die Basis der kanontheologischen Verbindung, die aber entscheidend durch das Christusgeschehen bestimmt wird. Das „Alte Testament" hingegen muss historisch-kritisch, *als Biblia Judaica,* ohne Rücksicht auf das Neue Testament gelesen werden. Hingegen kann es als erster Teil der *Biblia Christiana* nicht ohne seinen zweiten Teil, das Neue Testament, kanonische Geltung beanspruchen. Das bedeutet jedoch nicht, dass der Ursprungssinn christlich-theologisch unbedeutend wäre. Er ist im Gegenteil von fundamentaler Bedeutung, wenn anders die Geschichte zum Wesen der Offenbarung gehört. Kanonhermeneutisch ist also „zuerst" das Alte Testament als Altes Testament auszulegen, d.h. als Dokument der Glaubensgeschichte Israels *ante Christum natum,* danach das Neue Testament als Neues, das *post Christum natum* auf der Basis des Alten den Ursprung des – theozentrischen – Christusglaubens dokumentiert

---

zum hermeneutischen Problem des Kriteriums der Sachkritik am Neuen Testament, in FS O. Hofius (Anm. 102), pp. 291-320.

160. Vgl. B. JANOWSKI, *Der eine Gott der beiden Testamente. Grundfragen einer Biblischen Theologie,* in *ZTK* 95 (1998) 1-36, bes. 29: „Wenn es demnach *die* Mitte des Alten Testaments als *Sinnmitte einer pluriformen Textsammlung* nicht gibt und nicht geben kann, ... so ... doch die *Sach- und Wirkmitte eines Geschehens ...* die Gegenwart/das Wirken JHWHs in Israel *und* das geschichtliche Leben Israels in der Gemeinschaft des Glaubens an seinen Gott ... ist das in den alttestamentlichen Texten bezeugte Identitätszentrum des JHWH-Glaubens und darum seine sachliche ‚Mitte'".

161. Vgl. W. THÜSING, *Die neutestamentlichen Theologien und Jesus Christus. Grundlegung einer Theologie des Neuen Testaments* I-III, Münster, Aschendorff, 1996-1999.

162. Ausführlicher begründet in TH. SÖDING „*Mitte der Schrift" – „Einheit der Schrift". Grundsätzliche Erwägungen zur Schrifthermeneutik,* in W. PANNENBERG & TH. SCHNEIDER (eds.), *Verbindliches Zeugnis* III (Anm. 1), pp. 43-82.

und in diesem Rahmen auch eines neues Verständnis des Alten Testaments[163].

9. Weil das die Kanonizität des Kanons begründende Offenbarungshandeln Gottes in der Geschichte geschieht, muss in der Auslegung des Kanons als Kanon dessen Geschichte zur Sprache kommen. Die Endgestalt hat zwar im Sinne der Kommunität, die sie festlegt, definitive Verbindlichkeit (weshalb im Gottesdienst immer der End-Text verkündet wird), will aber theologisch als *End*gestalt einer längeren Entwicklung erklärt werden[164]. Unter den Bedingungen neuzeitlichen Denkens fordert das Bündnis von Glaube und Vernunft, das – je zu ihrer Zeit – im Alten Testament nicht nur von der Weisheit, im Neuen Testament nicht nur von Paulus und Johannes begründet ist, die Anwendung historischer und philologischer Methoden, die Verbindung von Synchronie und Diachronie *innerhalb* des *canonical approach*. Umgekehrt wird die Exegese aber durch die Beschäftigung mit dem Buchstaben zum Geist der Bibel geführt; nicht erst, wenn sie sich, theologisch entschieden, auf den Weg kanonischer Schriftauslegung begibt, schon wenn sie zu verstehen versucht, wovon die biblischen Texte, ihre Autoren und Adressaten handeln, ist sie gehalten, so oder so auf die Wahrheitsfrage zu antworten[165].

Nienborgweg 24   Thomas SÖDING
D - 48161 Münster

---

163. CH. DOHMEN vertritt das hermeneutische Konzept einer „doppelten Hermeneutik", derzufolge das Alte Testament zuerst ohne das Neue und dann im Lichte des Neuen zu interpretieren ist: *Das Konzept der doppelten Hermeneutik*, in ID. & G. STEMBERGER, *Hermeneutik* (Anm. 62), pp. 211-213. Freilich bleibt zu klären, wie sich die beiden Leseweisen zueinander verhalten.

164. Das arbeitet R. RENDTORFF (*Theologie des Alten Testaments. Ein kanonischer Entwurf* I: *Kanonische Grundlegung*, Neukirchen-Vluyn, Neukirchener, 1999) in seinem Konzept aus: „Eine kanonische Auslegung ... wird vielmehr die verschiedenen Stadien der Textgeschichte mit dem gleichen Respekt behandeln als Bestandteile des kanonischen Prozesses, der schließlich zum kanonischen Text in seiner Endgestalt geführt hat" (p. 154).

165. Vgl. N. LOHFINK, *Alttestamentliche Wissenschaft als Theologie? 44 Thesen*, in F.-L. HOSSFELD (ed.), *Systematik* (Anm. 2), pp. 13-47. - U. WILCKENS (*Schriftauslegung in historisch-kritischer und geistlicher Betrachtung*, in W. PANNENBERG & TH. SCHNEIDER [eds.], *Verbindliches Zeugnis* II [Anm. 1], pp. 13-71) und P. STUHLMACHER (*Der Kanon und seine Auslegung*, in FS O. Hofius [Anm. 102], pp. 262-290) plädieren für die Öffnung historisch-kritischer zu einer geistliche Schriftauslegung in moderner Erneuerung der Lehre vom mehrfachen Schriftsinn. M.E. muss sich die Exegese aber darauf konzentrieren, in strenger Konzentration auf geschichtliches und philologisches Arbeiten die theologische Perspektive der biblischen Schriften zu öffnen – und freilich im Dialog mit der Philosophie und den anderen Wissenschaften ein geschichtliches und philologisches Denken einzuüben, das den Positivismus und Historismus, dem die Exegese von ihren Anfängen an hohen Tribut geleistet hat, aufhebt; vgl. TH. SÖDING, *Inmitten der Theologie des Neuen Testaments. Zu den Voraussetzungen und Zielen der neutestamentlichen Exegese*, in *NTS* 42 (1996) 161-184.

OLD TESTAMENT

MAIN PAPERS

LES VOIES DE L'EXÉGÈSE CANONIQUE DU PSAUTIER

Qu'est-ce qui change lorsque l'exégèse prend au sérieux le canon des Écritures? Depuis que Norbert Lohfink et Erich Zenger ont posé cette question il y a une dizaine d'années[1], un nombre sans cesse grandissant d'études exégétiques sont venues apporter des éléments de réponse. Prenant acte de ces acquis, les pages qui suivent voudraient les ressaisir dans une réflexion globale, illustrée à partir du cas du Psautier – non que ce cas soit isolé ou particulier, mais parce qu'il peut être considéré comme exemplaire.

Parler de «canon», c'est envisager les écrits bibliques à la fois dans leur(s) forme(s) traditionnelle(s) et dans l'espace d'un corpus clos auquel est conféré un statut herméneutique. Ce contexte interprétatif génère des effets de sens différents, selon qu'il est considéré dans sa plus grande extension ou dans une segmentation plus restreinte. Dans cet article consacré à l'interprétation canonique des psaumes, trois espaces herméneutiques successifs seront examinés: le Psautier dans sa forme canonique hébraïque[2], le canon juif des Écritures, et le canon chrétien, volume unique en deux volets[3].

1. LE PSAUTIER COMME EXÉGÈSE DES PSAUMES

Depuis une vingtaine d'années, les exégètes se sont avisés que la forme achevée du Psautier, loin d'être le résultat de pures contingences,

---

1. N. LOHFINK, *Was wird anders bei kanonischer Schriftauslegung? Beobachtungen am Beispiel von Psalm 6*, in *JBT* 3 (1988) 29-53; = ID., *Studien zur biblischen Theologie* (SBAAT, 16), Stuttgart, Katholisches Bibelwerk, 1993, pp. 263-293; E. ZENGER, *Was wird anders bei kanonischer Psalmenauslegung?*, in F.V. REITERER (ed.), *Ein Gott, eine Offenbarung. Beiträge zur biblischen Exegese, Theologie und Spiritualität*. FS N. Füglister, Würzburg, Echter, 1991, pp. 397-413.

2. C.-à-d. le texte massorétique. Je me suis expliqué plus haut («Introduction», p. XIX-XX) sur les raisons pour lesquelles je persistais à parler des «formes canoniques» des livres bibliques.

3. En envisageant ces trois cas de figure, on ne prétend nullement viser à l'exhaustivité. La Septante du Psautier, munie d'une signature davidique (Ps 151), fournit elle aussi une «forme canonique» qui génère des effets de sens particuliers. Cf. P.-M. BOGAERT, *L'ancienne numérotation africaine des Psaumes et la signature davidique du Psautier (Ps 151)*, in *RBén* 97 (1987) 153-162 et les études rassemblées dans E. ZENGER (ed.), *Der Septuaginta-Psalter. Sprachliche und theologische Aspekte* (HBS, 32), Freiburg i. Br., Herder, 2001. — Un Premier Testament incluant les deutérocanoniques constitue bien entendu, à côté du TaNaK, une configuration canonique ayant sa consistance propre, mais les effets de sens produits par la prise en compte des livres absents du canon hébreu ne seront pas envisagés ici.

était porteuse d'une intention théologique[4]. Certes, dans son développement historique, le Psautier est une collection de collections, mais, dans son état final, il se donne à lire comme un livre dont chaque psaume serait un chapitre. Le fait qu'il y a un corpus des psaumes oblige l'interprète à se tenir non seulement devant les pièces individuelles, mais aussi devant l'œuvre achevée dont elles sont devenues les éléments interconnectés. Comme l'écrit Michael D. Goulder: «The oldest commentary on the meaning of the psalms is the manner of their arrangement in the Psalter»[5]. En effet, l'intention théologique qui s'exprime à travers la forme massorétique du livre des psaumes, en même temps qu'elle donne son sens au recueil en tant qu'ensemble, rejaillit sur la signification de chaque pièce prise individuellement. La figure du livre demande à être honorée, et le titre traditionnel de *sefer tehilîm* mérite d'être pris au sérieux[6]: le livre, avec tous ses éléments canoniques, est ainsi un horizon vers lequel regarde l'interprète, avec la conviction que, dans l'assemblage final, chaque psaume est devenu l'élément d'un tout dont il reçoit du sens autant qu'il lui en donne.

En particulier, le travail qui a consisté à «coudre» l'un à l'autre les éléments constitutifs du Psautier, par le procédé de la *concatenatio*, a pour effet de créer une continuité entre les psaumes, qui ne sont plus dès lors à lire comme une succession de pièces hétérogènes, mais comme le déploiement d'une même prière ou le déroulement d'un drame[7]. Les

---

4. Pour un état de la question, je me permets de renvoyer à mon essai de synthèse *La composition littéraire du Psautier. Un état de la question* (CRB 46), Paris, Gabalda, 2000.

5. M.D. GOULDER, *The Psalms of the Sons of Korah* (JSOT SS, 20), Sheffield, Academic Press, 1982, p. 1. On mesure la distance qui sépare ces lignes de ce qu'écrivait H. GUNKEL, *Reden und Aufsätze*, Göttingen, Vandenhoeck & Ruprecht, 1913, p. 93: «In der Sammlung des Psalters steht jedes Lied für sich allein, ohne daß wir das Recht hätten, es mit dem vorhergehenden oder dem folgenden zusammenzunehmen».

6. L'expression ספר תהלים apparaît déjà à Qumrân en 4Q 491, fr. 17, 4, où elle désigne déjà très probablement le livre biblique des Psaumes; nous aurions donc ici, dans un document non autographe de la seconde moitié du Ier s. avant notre ère, la plus ancienne attestation du titre du Psautier, tel qu'il a été conservé par la tradition juive. Cf. M. BAILLET (ed.), *Qumrân Grotte 4. III (4Q 482-4Q 520)* (DJD, 7), Oxford, Clarendon Press, 1982, p. 40; C.-H. HUNZINGER, *Fragmente einer älteren Fassung des Buches Milḥamā aus Höhle 4 von Qumrān*, in ZAW 69 (1957) 131-151; P.W. FLINT, *The Dead Sea Psalms Scrolls and the Book of Psalms* (Studies on the Texts of the Desert of Judah, 17), Leiden, Brill, 1997, pp. 22-23 et 219. Lc 20,42 et Ac 1,20 parlent du βίβλος ψαλμῶν.

7. Voir les inventaires dressés par G. BARBIERO, *Das erste Psalmenbuch als Einheit* (Österreichische Biblische Studien, 16), Frankfurt, P. Lang, 1999, *passim*; C. BARTH, *Concatenatio im ersten Buch des Psalters*, in B. BENZING (ed.), *Wort und Wirklichkeit. Studien zur Afrikanistik*, t. 1, Meisenheim am Glan, Rapp, 1976, pp. 30-40; J.P. BRENNAN, *Psalms 1–8: Some Hidden Harmonies*, in *Biblical Theology Bulletin* 10 (1980) 25-29; ID., *Some Hidden Harmonies of the Fifth Book of Psalms*, in R.F. McNAMARA (ed.), *Essays in Honor of J.P. Brennan*, New York, Rochester, 1977, pp. 126-158; R.L. COLE, *The Shape and Message of Book III (Psalms 73–89)* (JSOT SS, 307), Sheffield, Aca-

mots de tel psaume s'entendent en écho dans le suivant, et l'impression est ainsi créée que c'est la même voix qui s'exprime tout au long des psaumes. Celui qui dit, au Ps 3,1: «YHWH, qu'ils sont nombreux mes adversaires!» est aussi celui qui dit: «Quand je crie, réponds-moi, Dieu de ma justice» (Ps 4,2), «À mes paroles prête l'oreille, YHWH» (Ps 5,2), «Aie pitié de moi, YHWH, car je dépéris» (Ps 6,3), et ainsi de suite. Ce procédé n'a de sens que si les éditeurs ont voulu encourager la lecture du livre *per ordinem ex integro*[8]. Comme il ne peut être question d'entreprendre ici une démonstration exhaustive[9], on se contentera de donner quelques exemples destinés à suggérer la pertinence et l'intérêt d'une telle traversée du livre.

A. *Quelques séquences significatives*

1. Ps 15–19: l'absolu de la Torah

Le thème de la rectitude de la conduite humaine et des normes qui définissent un comportement intègre[10] unifie les Ps 15–19[11]. À la ques-

---

demic Press, 1999, *passim*; P. SCHELLING, *De Asafpsalmen, hun samenhang en achtergrond*, Kampen, Kok, 1985, pp. 235-244; J. SCHREINER, *Zur Stellung von Psalm 22 im Psalter*, in ID. (ed.), *Beiträge zur Psalmenforschung. Psalm 2 und 22* (FzB, 60), Würzburg, Echter, 1988, pp. 241-277, spéc. 259-263.

8. Cf. N. FÜGLISTER, *Die Verwendung und das Verständnis der Psalmen und des Psalters um die Zeitenwende*, in SCHREINER (ed.), *Beiträge zur Psalmenforschung* (n. 7), pp. 319-384, spéc. 350-352; ZENGER, *Was wird anders* (n. 1), p. 397-398; N. LOHFINK, *Psalmengebet und Psalterredaktion*, in *Archiv für Liturgiewissenschaft* 34 (1992) 1-22, pp. 7-13; ID., *Psalmen im Neuen Testament. Die Lieder in der Kindheitsgeschichte bei Lukas*, in K. SEYBOLD & E. ZENGER (eds.), *Neue Wege der Psalmenforschung*. FS W. Beyerlin (HBS, 1), Freiburg i. Br., Herder, 1994, pp. 105-125, spéc. 106-107.

9. Ce qui est le propos de commentaires suivis. Voir en particulier J.A. ALEXANDER, *The Psalms Translated and Explained*, Edimburg, 1873 [rééd. photomécanique: Ann Arbor, MI, Cushin-Malloy, 1977); F.-L. HOSSFELD & E. ZENGER, *Die Psalmen*, t. 1, *Psalm 1–50* (NEB AT, 29), Würzburg, Echter, 1993, p. 50; EID., *Psalmen 51-100* (HTK AT), Freiburg i. Br., Herder, 2000; T. LORENZIN, *I Salmi* (I Libri biblici. Primo Testamento, 14), Milano, Paoline, 2000.

10. Sur 12 emplois de l'adjectif תמים «intègre» dans le Psautier, 6 apparaissent dans les Pss 15-19: 15,2; 18,24.26.31.33; 19,8.

11. Pour ce qui suit, voir en particulier F.-L. HOSSFELD & E. ZENGER, «*Wer darf hinaufziehn zum Berg JHWHs?*». *Zur Redaktionsgeschichte und Theologie der Psalmgruppe 15–24*, in G. BRAULIK, W. GROSS & S. MCEVENUE (eds.), *Biblische Theologie und gesellschaftlicher Wandel*. FS N. Lohfink, Freiburg i. Br., Herder, 1993, pp. 166-182; P.D. MILLER, *Kingship, Torah Obedience, and Prayer. The Theology of Psalms 15–24*, in SEYBOLD & ZENGER (eds.), *Neue Wege* (n. 8), pp. 127-140; BARBIERO, *Das erste Psalmenbuch* (n. 7), pp. 189-324; LORENZIN, *I Salmi* (n. 9), pp. 97-110. — Pour la structure de la section formée par les Pss 15-24, voir aussi P. AUFFRET, *La sagesse a bâti sa maison. Études de structures littéraires dans l'Ancien Testament et spécialement dans les Psaumes* (OBO, 49), Fribourg, Éditions universitaires; Göttingen, Vandenhoeck & Ruprecht, 1982, pp. 407-438.

tion de savoir quelles sont les conditions d'admission dans le Temple, le Ps 15 répond en exigeant une conduite parfaite (חלך תמים «marcher intègre», v. 2), dont il détaille ensuite le contenu en dix préceptes moraux. Dans les deux psaumes suivants, le psalmiste s'emploie à montrer qu'il remplit les exigences de ce contrat. Le «fidèle» du Ps 16 déclare s'être tenu à l'écart du syncrétisme ambiant et de ses abominations pour se vouer tout entier au service du seul vrai Dieu; cette attitude lui vaut de connaître le bonheur de l'intimité divine: il vit avec YHWH constamment devant les yeux (v. 8) et espère être éternellement en présence de sa Face (v. 11); si le Temple n'est pas évoqué au Ps 16 par l'image de la tente, de la montagne sainte (comme en Ps 15,1) ou par une autre périphrase habituelle, il n'en est donc pas moins présent. Le Ps 17 est la protestation d'innocence d'un homme qui affirme être demeuré totalement fidèle aux exigences divines (vv. 1b-4)[12] et se déclare certain que sa justice lui vaudra de contempler la Face de YHWH (v. 15)[13]. Les vv. 21-27 du Ps 18 ne tiennent pas un autre langage: l'intégrité (vv. 24.26) que le psalmiste revendique pour lui est dans la ligne de l'idéal du «petit décalogue» du Ps 15 et des deux proclamations d'impeccabilité qui suivent[14]. De plus, est énoncé ici, en termes généraux, le fondement théologique qui soustend les discours qui précèdent: c'est la rectitude dans la conduite qui attire la bienveillance divine; YHWH est fidèle et intègre avec l'homme fidèle et intègre (vv. 26-27). Le vocabulaire de l'intégrité réapparaît au Ps 19[15], mais pour qualifier d'abord la Torah de YHWH (v. 8), présentée comme un absolu aux effets bienfaisants. Le psalmiste ne peut prétendre à la même perfection que dans la mesure où Dieu l'innocente de ses fautes cachées (v. 13) et le préserve d'une arrogance présomptueuse (v. 14). Ainsi est ouverte une brèche où peut s'introduire la faiblesse humaine et l'aveu du péché. À qui veut jouir de l'intimité divine, le Ps 15 imposait une conduite «parfaite». Au terme du parcours, il est rappelé que, face à

---

12. Pour l'exégèse de ces versets, voir, outre les commentaires: S.-P. IM, *Die «Unschuldserklärungen» in den Psalmen*, Seoul, Logos, 1989, pp. 87-103.

13. Les contacts que le Ps 17 entretient avec le Ps 16 avaient déjà été notés par Franz DELITZSCH, *Biblischer Commentar über die Psalmen* (Biblischer Commentar über das Alte Testament, 4/1), Leipzig, Dörffling und Franke, ⁴1883, p. 174; ⁵1894, p. 161. On relèvera surtout les rencontres verbales suivantes: Pss 16,1 et 17,8: שָׁמְרֵנִי; Pss 16,2.4 et 17,3.5: בַּל; Pss 16,5 et 17,5: תָּמֹךְ ... תּוֹמִיךְ; Pss 16,8 et 17,7: בִּימִינֶךָ ... מִימִינִי et l'emploi l'emploi du nom divin אֵל (16,1; 17,6), rare au premier livre des psaumes. Pour un inventaire exhaustif, voir BARBIERO, *Das erste Psalmenbuch* (n. 7), pp. 215-220. À partir de l'examen de ces correspondances, J. CALÈS, *Le livre des Psaumes*, vol. 1, Paris, Beauchesne, 1936, p. 214 avait conclu que les Pss 16 et 17 étaient l'œuvre d'un seul auteur.

14. Cf. J.-M. AUWERS, *La rédaction du Psaume 18 dans le cadre du premier livre des psaumes*, in *ETL* 72 (1996) 23-40.

15. Les contacts littéraires entre le Ps 18 (en particulier les vv. 21-31) et le Ps 19 sont nombreux. Voir l'inventaire dans BARBIERO, *Das erste Psalmenbuch* (n. 7), pp. 240-249.

l'absolu de la Torah, tout homme est pécheur et ne tient sa justice que de la miséricorde divine.

2. Pss 120–134: un pèlerinage vers le Temple ou vers la Torah?

Dans le Psautier massorétique, comme dans la Septante, les quinze «psaumes des Montées» dessinent un itinéraire qui part du monde païen (Ps 120) pour aboutir dans le Temple de Jérusalem, lieu où officie le clergé aaronide (Ps 133) et d'où YHWH répand sa bénédiction (Ps 134)[16]. La majorité des exégètes admettent que ces psaumes ont effectivement été utilisés lors des fêtes de pèlerinage[17]. Quoi qu'il en soit, intégrés dans un recueil qui peut être utilisé en tout lieu et en tout temps, ils permettent au lecteur du Psautier de refaire pour lui-même un pèlerinage spirituel et, en ce sens, ils sont susceptibles de constituer une sorte de substitut aux liturgies du Temple[18]. La présence de ces psaumes dans le grand rouleau de la grotte 11 de Qumrân[19] témoigne de leur utilisation par les Esséniens, mais dans un autre contexte que celui des fêtes de pèlerinage, auxquelles les sectaires de Qumrân ne participaient plus.

En 11QPs[a], les deux derniers psaumes graduels sont dissociés du reste de la collection: alors que les Pss 121–132 occupent les colonnes 3-6[20],

16. Sur la structure de la collection, voir en particulier: K. SEYBOLD, *Die Wallfahrtpsalmen. Studien zur Entstehungsgeschichte von Psalm 120–134* (Biblisch-Theologische Studien, 3), Neukirchen, Neukirchener Verlag, 1978; É. BEAUCAMP, *L'unité du recueil des montées*, in *Liber Annuus* 29 (1979) 73-90, repris in *Laval Théologique et Philosophique* 36 (1980) 3-15; M. MANNATI, *Les psaumes graduels constituent-ils un genre littéraire distinct à l'intérieur du psautier biblique?*, in *Semitica* 29 (1979) 85-100; H. SEIDEL, *Wallfahrtslieder*, in H. SEIDEL & K.-H. BIERITZ (eds.), *Das Lebendige Wort. Beiträge zur kirchlichen Verkündigung*. FS G. Voigt, Berlin, Evangelische Verlagsanstalt, 1982, pp. 26-40; AUFFRET, *La sagesse a bâti sa maison* (n. 11), pp. 439-531; H. VIVIERS, *The Coherence of the* ma'alôt *Psalms (Pss 120–134)*, in *ZAW* 106 (1994) 262-288; L.D. CROW, *The Songs of Ascents (Psalms 120–134). Their Place in Israelite History and Religion* (SBL DS, 148), Atlanta, GA, Scholars Press, 1996; P. AUFFRET, *Là montent les tribus. Étude structurelle de la collection des Psaumes des Montées, d'Ex 15,1-18 et des rapports entre eux* (BZAW, 289), Berlin – New York, de Gruyter, 1999.

17. Cependant, l'évocation de Méshek et Qédar dès le Ps 120,5 est peut-être une invitation à interpréter (ou à réinterpréter?) ces psaumes comme chants du retour d'exil, évoquant la «montée» vers Jérusalem de la communauté rapatriée. Cf. K. DEURLOO, *Gedächtnis des Exils (Psalm 120–134)*, in *Texte & Kontexte* 55 (1992) 28-34; cf. M.S. SMITH, *The Theology of the Redaction of the Psalter: Some Observations*, in *ZAW* 104 (1992) 408-412, p. 410: «While this title originally referred to pilgrimage, as a collection in their present context in Book V, these psalms represent songs for returning to Jerusalem from exile».

18. Cf. M. MILLARD, *Die Komposition des Psalters. Ein formgeschichtlicher Ansatz* (FAT, 9), Tübingen, Mohr, 1994, pp. 209; E. ZENGER, *Komposition und Theologie des 5. Psalmenbuchs 107–150*, in *BN* 82 (1996) 97-116, pp. 115-116; trad. angl. *JSOT* 80 (1998) 77-102.

19. Édition: J.A. SANDERS, *The Psalms Scroll of Qumrân Cave 11 (11QPs[a])* (DJD, 4), Oxford, Clarendon, 1965.

les Ps 133 et 134 apparaissent beaucoup plus loin dans le manuscrit, respectivement aux col. 23 (entre les Ps 141 et 144) et 28 (après le Ps 140
et avant le Ps 151). Le profil de la collection s'en trouve considérablement modifié: la «trajectoire» décrite par les graduels n'aboutit plus au
Temple de Jérusalem (Ps 134), mais s'achève avec les perspectives messianiques du Ps 132. Il est possible que le compilateur ait eu des raisons
particulières de vouloir rapprocher le Ps 133 du Ps 141 et le Ps 134 du
Ps 140[21]. Cependant, on ne peut manquer d'observer que le Ps 132 fournit à la collection une «chute» beaucoup plus en rapport avec les préoccupations et les attentes des Esséniens[22]. Le fait que, dans ce rouleau, la
série des Pss (120).121–132 soit suivie du Ps 119, est lui aussi significatif. Comme l'a écrit Gerald H. Wilson, «the placement of this Psalm (=
Ps 119) *after* the *ma'alôt* psalms rather than *before* them as in the
canonical psalter has a significant effect. Rather than Torah precipitating
pilgrimage to Jerusalem and temple, pilgrimage, in effect, leads to the
Torah»[23]. L'itinéraire du pèlerinage devient ici un parcours spirituel, qui
nourrit l'espérance messianique.

3. Pss 146–150: la finale du livre

Le Hallel final (Pss 146–150) est greffé sur le dernier verset du Ps
145[24]:

> (21) Que ma bouche dise la louange de YHWH,
>   et que toute chair bénisse son saint Nom,
>   à jamais et pour toujours.

Conformément à ce schéma, qui va de «ma bouche» à «toute chair»,
les Pss 146–150 élargissent progressivement le cercle de ceux qu'ils
invitent à entrer dans la louange[25]: après l'auto-exhortation du Ps 146

---

20. La restitution du Ps 120 au bas de la colonne 2 (mutilée) est hautement vraisemblable. Voir FLINT, *The Dead Sea Psalms Scrolls* (n. 6), pp. 187 et 192.

21. P.W. SKEHAN, *A Liturgical Complex in 11QPs^a*, in *CBQ* 35 (1973) 195-205,
p. 196.

22. MILLARD, *Die Komposition des Psalters* (n. 18), pp. 219-223. Une autre explication est proposée par FLINT, *The Dead Sea Psalms Scrolls* (n. 6), pp. 193-194.

23. G.H. WILSON, *The Qumran Psalms Scroll (11QPs^a) and the Canonical Psalter:
Comparison of Editorial Shaping*, in *CBQ* 59 (1997) 448-464, p. 460 (c'est l'A. qui souligne).

24. G.H. WILSON, *The Editing of the Hebrew Psalter* (SBL DS, 76), Chico, Scholars
Press, 1985, pp. 193-194. — ZENGER, *Komposition und Theologie des 5. Psalmenbuchs*
(n. 18), pp. 106-107 et P.D. MILLER, *The End of the Psalter. A Response to Erich Zenger*,
in *JSOT* 80 (1998) 103-110, pp. 105-107 ont montré que le Ps 145 avait pour fonction à la
fois de conclure les Ps 107-144 et d'introduire le Hallel final.

25. J.S. KSELMAN, *Psalm 146 in its Context*, in *CBQ* 50 (1988) 587-599, pp. 596-599;
N. LOHFINK, *Lobgesänge der Armen. Studien zum Magnifikat, den Hodajot von Qumran
und einigen späten Psalmen* (SBS, 143), Stuttgart, Katholisches Bibelwerk, 1990, pp. 108-

(v. 1: «Loue, ô mon âme, YHWH»), l'appel à louer YHWH est adressé successivement à Jérusalem et à la communauté israélite (Ps 147; cf. vv. 2.12), aux diverses créatures célestes et terrestres (Ps 148,1-6.7-13) et, enfin, à «tout ce qui a un souffle de vie» (Ps 150,6). À l'intérieur de ce mouvement «centrifuge», s'inscrit le mouvement inverse: aux Pss 148-149, la perspective se rétrécit progressivement, de l'univers cosmique (148,1-6) à la terre (148,7-10) et plus précisément aux êtres humains (148,11-14a), puis de l'humanité en général aux «fidèles» d'Israël, qui constituent le peuple «proche de Dieu» (148,14b; cf. 149). Dans cette grande louange œcuménique, où le Psautier voit l'achèvement de l'histoire, tout et tous trouvent à se réjouir en Dieu, mais pour des raisons différentes: le cosmos loue YHWH pour la stabilité de l'ordre de la création (Ps 148,6); la terre le célèbre parce qu'il a relevé son peuple (Ps 148,14a), et celui-ci chante YHWH parce que justice lui a été rendue contre ses ennemis (Ps 149,6-9). Ce double mouvement a pour effet d'indiquer quelle est, dans l'ordre du monde voulu par YHWH, la place spécifique d'Israël et de montrer comment le peuple élu est le médiateur entre les Nations et YHWH: c'est en voyant le Dieu d'Israël agir pour son peuple que «les rois de la terre et tous les peuples» (Ps 148,11) découvrent qui est YHWH et qu'ils peuvent le louer pour la sublimité de son Nom, c'est-à-dire pour ce qu'Il est. Ainsi, le Hallel final peut-il faire de l'élection de quelques-uns l'objet de la louange de tous.

On ne prétend nullement ici que les psaumes qui composent les séquences qui viennent d'être évoquées ont été écrits d'un seul trait de plume; on soutient que les enchaînements ainsi obtenus sont significatifs et que la mise en séquence de ces psaumes leur confère un surcroît de sens. Lu pour lui-même, chacun des psaumes du Hallel final a sa propre perspective théologique; la réunion des cinq poèmes en un ensemble fortement concaténé[26] produit un discours théologique nouveau, qui n'ôte pas leur signification aux pièces individuelles, mais les prolonge et cherche à les unifier. Du reste, la mise en évidence des éléments formels qui assurent la continuité entre les pièces ne manque jamais de renvoyer l'interprète à des questions d'ordre génétique, dès lors que s'il se sent tenu de circonscrire les interventions éditoriales.

125, spéc. 108-109; A. WÉNIN, *Le psaume 1 et l'«encadrement» du livre des louanges*, in P. BOVATI & R. MEYNET (eds.), *«Ouvrir les Écritures»*. FS Paul Beauchamp (LD, 162), Paris, Cerf, 1995, pp. 151-176, spéc. 169-176 (retravaillé dans *Le Livre des Louanges. Entrer dans les Psaumes*, Bruxelles, Lumen Vitae, 2001, pp. 67-96); E. ZENGER, *«Daß alles Fleisch den Namen seiner Heiligung segne» (Ps 145,21). Die Komposition Ps 145-150 als Anstoß zu einer christlich-jüdischen Psalmenhermeneutik*, in *BZ* 41 (1997) 1-27; LORENZIN, *I Salmi* (n. 9), pp. 535-544.

26. Cf. AUWERS, *La composition littéraire* (n. 4), pp. 90-91.

Une exégèse qui envisage les cent cinquante psaumes comme autant d'entités isolées et indifférentes les unes aux autres se condamne à la myopie, car elle ne peut saisir les processus éditoriaux qui ont tissé à travers tout le recueil un réseau de reprises et de renvois et qui ont glosé les textes psalmiques au fil de campagnes de relecture successives coïncidant avec telle ou telle phase de l'édition du Psautier. De ce point de vue, une exégèse soucieuse d'honorer le Psautier comme livre est mieux outillée pour dégager les éléments adventices et reconstituer la préhistoire des pièces[27]. Soit le dernier verset du Ps 148 :

> (14) Il a levé haut la corne de son peuple,
> sujet de louange pour tous ses fidèles,
> pour les fils d'Israël, le peuple qui lui est proche.

Beaucoup d'exégètes estiment que le contenu nationaliste de ce verset tranche trop nettement sur le reste du psaume pour appartenir au poème primitif[28]. À la suite d'Hermann Gunkel, plusieurs commentateurs isolent les deux derniers stiques comme un *Unterschrift*[29]. Mais, si le v. 14 est effectivement un élément adventice, ne faut-il pas plutôt voir ici un élément rédactionnel destiné à assurer la transition avec le Ps 149, dont il annonce directement et le thème et le vocabulaire[30] :

> (1) Chantez à YHWH un cantique nouveau,
> sa louange dans l'assemblée de ses fidèles.
> (2) Qu'Israël se réjouisse en son créateur,
> que les fils de Sion jubilent en leur roi.

B. Les Pss 1–2 : une double clef de lecture

Jesús Enciso Viana s'est jadis employé à montrer que plusieurs collections du Psautier étaient introduites par un «prologue», qui fournissait une clef de lecture[31]. Les Pères de l'Église avaient déjà eu cette in-

---

27. Un des apports majeurs des travaux de F.-L. Hossfeld et E. Zenger (n. 9) est d'avoir fait la preuve que le développement génétique des pièces du Psautier ne se comprend bien qu'à partir de l'histoire de la rédaction du livre lui-même.

28. Voir l'état de la question dressé par W.S. PRINSLOO, *Structure and Cohesion of Psalm 148*, in *OTE* 5 (1992) 46-63, pp. 51-52.

29. H. GUNKEL, *Die Psalmen* (Göttinger Handkommentar zum Alten Testament II/2), Göttingen, Vandenhoeck & Ruprecht, 1926, p. 618; G. CASTELLINO, *Libro dei Salmi* (La Sacra Bibbia), Torino-Roma, Marietti, 1955, pp. 530 et 534; H.-J. KRAUS, *Psalmen* (BKAT, 15), Neukirchen-Vluyn, Neukirchener Verlag, ⁵1978, p. 1141; G. RAVASI, *Il Libro dei Salmi*, vol. 3, Bologna, Dehoniane, 1985, p. 966; K. SEYBOLD, *Die Psalmen* (HAT, I/15), Tübingen, Mohr, 1996, p. 543.

30. On note quatre contacts lexicaux pour deux versets : ישראל, בני, חסידים, תהלה.

31. J. ENCISO, *Los Salmos-prólogos*, in *Estudios Eclesiásticos* 34 (1960) 621-631; = J. SAGÜES, S. BARTINA & M. QUERA (eds.), *Miscelanea Bíblica Andrés Fernández*, Madrid, Fax, 1961, pp. 317-327.

tuition pour le Ps 1, dont ils parlaient comme d'un prologue, d'un porti-
que d'entrée ou de la préface du Saint-Esprit[32].

Les commentateurs admettent généralement que le Ps 1, de facture
récente, a été ajouté avant le Ps 2 pour former avec celui-ci «l'introduction duelle» au livre des Psaumes[33]. Dans cette hypothèse, le Ps 2*[34]
a pu fonctionner à lui seul comme introduction à un Psautier encore
en voie de formation[35]. Il annonce en effet la structure conflictuelle
qui domine les deux premiers tiers du Psautier. Placé en tête d'une
série de poèmes dont il résume en lui tout le drame, le Ps 2 fonctionne
à la manière d'une grille de lecture et propose une identification des
protagonistes. D'une part, il désigne pour «ennemis» le monde païen
hostile à YHWH et à son peuple. D'autre part, il identifie le «je» qui
dit les psaumes avec la communauté israélite et donne une portée collective à des pièces qui, au départ, relevaient peut-être de la piété indivi-

---

32. BASILE, *Homiliae in Ps.* 1, 3, ad v. 1 (PG XXIX, 213D- 216A): «Le rôle que remplit une fondation dans une maison, une quille dans un bateau, ou un cœur dans le corps
d'un être vivant, il me semble qu'à l'égard de tout l'ouvrage des psaumes c'est ce court
prologue qui le remplit»; JÉRÔME, *Tractatus in Ps.* 1 (ed. G. MORIN, CC SL 78, Turnhout,
Brepols, 1958, p. 3): «Grandis itaque porta istius domus primus psalmus est»; ID.,
Commentarioli in Ps. 1, 1 (ed. G. MORIN, CC SL 72, Turnhout, Brepols, 1959, p. 178):
«Quidam dicunt hunc psalmum quasi praefationem esse Spiritus sancti, et ideo titulum
non habere».

33. L'expression est de P.D. MILLER, *The Beginning of the Psalter*, in J. Clinton
McCANN (ed.), *The Shape and Shaping of the Psalter* (JSOT SS 159), Sheffield,
Academic Press, 1993, pp. 83-92 (p. 91). Pour ce qui suit, voir en particulier E. ZENGER,
Der Psalter als Wegweiser und Wegbegleiter. Ps 1–2 als Proömium des Psalmenbuchs,
in A. ANGENENDT & H. VORGRIMLER (eds.), *Sie wandern von Kraft zu Kraft. Aufbrüche,
Wege, Begegnungen. Festgabe für Bischof Reinhard Lettmann*, Kevelaer, Butzon &
Bercker, 1993, pp. 29-47; WÉNIN, *Le psaume 1* (n. 25), pp. 152-169.

34. La finale sapientielle du Ps 2 (vv. 10-12) est littérairement solidaire du Ps 1 et
forme avec celui-ci un cadre rédactionnel permettant la relecture sapientielle du Ps 2,1-9.
Cf. O. LORETZ, *Stichometrische und textologische Probleme der Thronbesteigungs-
Psalmen. Psalmenstudien IV – Anhang I: Ps 2 und Ps 110*, in *UF* 6 (1974) 230-232;
E. ZENGER, *«Wozu tosen die Völker ?», Beobachtungen zur Entstehung und Theologie
des 2. Psalms*, in E. HAAG & F.-L. HOSSFELD (eds.), *Freude an der Weisung des Herrn.
Beiträge zur Theologie der Psalmen*. FS H. Gross (SBB, 13), Stuttgart, Katholisches
Bibelwerk, 1986, pp. 495-511; HOSSFELD & ZENGER, *Psalm 1–50* (n. 9), p. 50; AUWERS,
La composition littéraire (n. 4), pp. 123-127.

35. Cf. C. RÖSEL, *Die messianische Redaktion des Psalters. Studien zu Entstehung
und Theologie der Sammlung Psalm 2-89* (Calwer Theologische Monographien; Reihe A,
Bibelwissenschaft, 19), Stuttgart, Calwer, 1999. La documentation qumrânienne semble
indiquer que les trois premiers livrets du Psautier avaient déjà reçu une forme fixe à une
époque où le dernier tiers du psautier restait encore fluide, ce qui autorise à penser que les
Pss 2–89* ont préexisté au reste du recueil. Cf. J.A. SANDERS, *Cave 11 Surprises and the
Question of Canon*, in D.N. FREEDMAN & J.C. GREENFIELD (eds.), *New Directions in
Biblical Archaeology*, New York, Doubleday, 1971, pp. 113-130; G.H. WILSON, *The Qumran Psalms Manuscripts and the Consecutive Arrangement of Psalms in the Hebrew
Psalter*, in *CBQ* 45 (1983) 377-388; FLINT, *The Dead Sea Psalms Scrolls* (n. 6), pp. 135-
149.

duelle[36]. Le Psautier est ainsi placé sous le signe du combat contre les Nations et reçoit un statut de *Kampf-Liederbuch* national[37].

En même temps qu'il met en place les éléments de l'action dramatique et qu'il distribue les rôles, le Ps 2 ne laisse aucun doute sur l'issue finale. Dès les premiers mots, le lecteur est averti que la révolte des Nations est vouée à l'échec[38]. Le Ps 2 a ainsi une valeur oraculaire et assure Israël, qui crie son désarroi au long des psaumes, que l'ennemi n'aura pas le dernier mot. La confiance du psalmiste est fondée sur le décret divin (חק יהוה) qui est évoqué au v. 7. Quelle que soit l'interprétation précise que l'on donne au stique 7a[39], ce décret nous renvoie en définitive à l'oracle de Nathan. C'est dire que, pour le Ps 2, il n'y a pas de meilleure garantie de salut pour Israël face aux Nations que les promesses faites à David[40].

Le Ps 1 a été comme greffé sur le Ps 2. Entre eux apparaît tout un jeu d'oppositions et de correspondances[41]: opposition entre ceux qui sont

36. Cf. J. BECKER, *Israel deutet seine Psalmen. Urform und Neuinterpretation in den Psalmen* (SBS, 18), Stuttgart, Katholisches Bibelwerk, 1966.

37. L'expression est de B.J. DIEBNER, *Psalm 1 als «Motto» der Sammlung des kanonischen Psalters*, in *DBAT* 23-24 (1987) 7-45, p. 34.

38. La question du v. 1, purement rhétorique, exprime l'étonnement en face d'un acte insensé, qui n'a aucune chance de succès: למה veut dire ici «À quoi bon?».

39. אספרה אל חק יהוה. La plupart des commentateurs négligent la préposition אל pour traduire: «Je publierai le décret de YHWH», ce qui suppose que le contenu du protocole royal est formulé dans les versets qui suivent. Quelques interprètes, cependant, à la suite de J. OLSHAUSEN, *Die Psalmen* (Kurzgefasstes exegetisches Handbuch zum Alten Testament, 14), Leipzig, 1853, p. 41, donnent à la préposition le sens de «au sujet de» (cf. Gn 20,2.13b; Jr 40,16; 2 Ch 32,17). On traduit alors: «je parlerai au sujet du décret de YHWH», c'est-à-dire: «je vais m'expliquer sur le décret», ou: «je vais en montrer le sens». Dans ce cas, le décret divin est celui par lequel le «messie» a été sacré roi sur la sainte montagne de Sion (v. 6), et les vv. 7b-9 seraient «l'exégèse» du protocole royal faite par le roi-messie lui-même.

40. Outre les commentaires, voir en particulier A. ROBERT, *Considérations sur le messianisme du Ps. II*, in *Mélanges Jules Lebreton* [= *RSR* 39 (1951-52)], pp. 88-98, spéc. 94-95; R. PRESS, *Jahwe und sein Gesalbter. Zur Auslegung von Psalm 2*, in *TZ* 13 (1957) 321-334, pp. 329-331.

41. Cf. P. AUFFRET, *Compléments sur la structure littéraire du Ps 2 et son rapport au Ps 1*, in *BN* 35 (1986) 7-13; BARBIERO, *Das erste Psalmenbuch* (n. 7), pp. 34-41. — La LXX renforce les correspondances entre les Pss 1-2, notamment en suremployant le vocabulaire du «chemin»: aux occurrences attendues de ce mot (1,1.6ab; 2,12) s'ajoutent, au Ps 1,3, l'emploi du mot διεξόδους pour rendre פלג (uniquement ici et au Ps 118LXX,136) et celui du verbe κατευοδοῦν pour rendre צלח. Au Ps 2,12 le chemin en dehors duquel les rois païens sont menacés de se perdre est qualifié dans la LXX de chemin de justice (ἐξ ὁδοῦ δικαίας), ce qui renvoie au «chemin des justes» du Ps 1,6. Il est possible que l'addition de ἀπὸ προσώπου τῆς γῆς au Ps 1,4c soit une manière d'anticiper sur τὰ πέρατα τῆς γῆς de Ps 2,8b. Enfin, la traduction de נשקו־בר par δράξασθε παιδείας, au Ps 2,12, est tout à fait dans le ton sapientiel du Ps 1. Cf. P. MAIBERGER, *Das Verständnis von Psalm 2 in der Septuaginta, im Targum, in Qumran, im frühen Judentum und im Neuen Testament*, in SCHREINER (ed.), *Beiträge zur Psalmenforschung* (n. 7), pp. 85-151, spéc. 89-91.

assis au club des moqueurs (1,1) et YHWH qui est assis sur son trône cé-
leste, où il rit des païens (2,4); opposition entre le juste qui murmure la
Torah (1,2) et les peuples qui «murmurent la vanité» (2,1). D'un côté
comme de l'autre, la ruine des pécheurs et celle des païens sont décrites
avec la même image du «chemin qui se perd» (1,6; 2,12). Ces rappro-
chements conduisent à une nouvelle identification des protagonistes.
D'une part, les rois et peuples païens qui se concertent pour attaquer
YHWH et son messie sont assimilés aux pécheurs et au conseil des im-
pies; les גוים du Ps 2,1 deviennent ainsi les «sans-loi», les «païens»
d'où qu'ils soient. D'autre part, l'Oint de YHWH à qui est promise la victoire sur ses ennemis est mis en parallèle avec le juste qui réussit dans
toutes ses entreprises. Le même combat est ainsi transposé dans le cadre
d'un nouveau conflit entre le juste (ou l'assemblée des justes) et les im-
pies. La ligne de démarcation ne passe donc plus entre Israël et les Nations, mais au-dedans d'Israël lui-même pour séparer les hommes religieux des «païens de l'intérieur»: ce qui distingue le juste de l'impie,
c'est leur attitude à l'égard de la Torah. Cette Torah de YHWH que le
juste a sans cesse à la bouche et dans laquelle il trouve le principe de son
action[42] tient ici la place du «décret de YHWH» dans lequel le roi-messie
du Ps 2,7 puise son assurance et ses règles de conduite. La Torah prend
ainsi le relais du décret divin qui fonde la légitimité de l'institution monarchique – ou, si l'on préfère, la relecture du Ps 2 par son cadre
sapientiel surimpose au sens technique de חק (pour désigner le «protocole» d'intronisation royale) le sens de «décret divin» qui est habituel
dans le vocabulaire de l'alliance[43] et qui est aussi le sens du mot à
d'autres endroits du Psautier, notamment au Ps 119[44]; la relecture fait
ainsi du roi-messie du Ps 2 un modèle de soumission à la Torah[45]. Si le

---

42. חפצו (Ps 1,2) est généralement traduit par «son plaisir». Cependant le mot peut
aussi avoir le sens d'«occupation» (Is 46,10; 58,3). Cette signification plus dynamique
est recommandée par le v. 3: «tout ce qu'il entreprend, il le réussit». Cf. A. KAMINKA,
Neueste Literatur zu den Hagiographa (1), in *Monatsschrift für Geschichte und Wissen
schaft des Judentums* 71 (1927) 289-298, p. 295 («nicht Lust, sondern... die Tagesbe-
schäftigung»); R. LACK, *Le Psaume 1. Une analyse structurale*, in *Bib* 57 (1976) 154-
167, p. 157; N. LOHFINK, *Psalmengebet und Psalterredaktion* (n. 8), p. 5.
43. H. RINGGREN, Art. חקק, in *TWAT* 3 (1982), cc. 149-157, spéc. 152-153.
44. A. ROBERT, *Le sens du mot Loi dans le Ps. CXIX (Vulg. CXVIII)*, in *RB* 46 (1937)
182-206, pp. 184 et 188; A. DEISSLER, *Psalm 119 (118) und seine Theologie. Ein Beitrag
zur Erforschung der anthologischen Stilgattung im Alten Testament* (Münchener
Theologische Studien, I/11), Munich, Zink, 1955, pp. 80-81.
45. Cf. T.N.D. METTINGER, *King and Messiah. The Civil and Sacral Legitimation of
Israelite Kings* (CB OT, 8), Lund, Gleerup, 1976, p. 289-290. — Ps 2,3 a pu également
faire l'objet d'une semblable réinterprétation. Dans la logique du poème, l'image des
chaînes et des entraves évoque la servitude politique imposée aux Nations (cf. 1 R 12,4;
Is 9,3; 10,27; 14,25; 47,6; Jr 27,8.11). Celles-ci veulent soulever le joug qui pèse sur elles du fait que YHWH a donné à son Messie autorité sur toute la terre (v. 8). Cependant, on

Ps 2 faisait du recueil qu'il préfaçait un *Kampf-Liederbuch* national, le Ps 1 fait de l'ensemble *das Gebetbuch der Gerechten*[46]. Mais, d'un côté comme de l'autre, l'issue finale du combat ne fait aucun doute: si, par la suite, plusieurs psaumes constateront avec amertume ou avec indignation que le juste n'est pas toujours récompensé et que les sans-loi réussissent trop souvent (Ps 37,1; 49,6-7; 73,4-12), le lecteur aura à se rappeler que la vérité des êtres et des choses sera mise en pleine lumière par le «jugement», devant lequel les רשעים ne tiendront pas (Ps 1,5)[47]. Ainsi donc, le Ps 1, en même temps qu'il a une valeur programmatique, est-il un message d'espérance et de foi adressé au «juste» qui choisit de conformer son existence aux enseignements de la Torah et de faire du Psautier son livre de prière.

On voit une fois de plus que, pour être bien menée, l'exégèse qui est ici mise en œuvre doit faire converger un questionnement d'ordre synchronique et un questionnement d'ordre diachronique. Sa spécificité est même de se tenir à la croisée des deux méthodes et de s'efforcer d'en articuler les résultats. La visée ici recherchée n'est nullement d'harmoniser des psaumes aux théologies fortement individualisées, mais de montrer comment les textes réagissent les uns sur les autres et se complètent mutuellement. La tâche de l'interprète n'est pas achevée lorsqu'il a dégagé les couches rédactionnelles successives, ni même lorsqu'il a précisé la portée des relectures. Le Ps 1, plus récent, n'annule pas le Ps 2 et ne le vide pas de son contenu. L'un et l'autre se tiennent côte à côte dans le Psautier et parlent à la même hauteur. Entrés successivement dans le livre, ils doivent néanmoins pouvoir être lus ensemble. Un tel acte de lecture constitue précisément le défi que cherche à relever l'exégèse canonique, en s'engageant dans un dialogue avec les textes, qui respecte leurs tensions internes tout en cherchant à déployer les virtualités de sens suscitées par leur inscription dans un corpus.

En suggérant que l'hostilité des Nations contre YHWH et son Oint se vérifie et s'actualise dans la lutte que l'homme de Dieu doit soutenir

---

ne peut oublier que, dans les livres sapientiaux, comme plus tard dans les écrits rabbiniques, l'image du joug renvoie à la sagesse ou à la Torah (Sir 6,24.30 [hébreu]; 51,26); cf. G. BERTRAM, Art. ζυγός, in *TWNT* 2 (1935), pp. 898-900, spéc. 900. Il est possible qu'une telle signification apparaisse en surimpression dans le cadre de la relecture sapientiale du psaume, où les rois des Nations sont invités à accueillir un discours de sagesse et à vivre dans la crainte de YHWH.

46. C. LEVIN, *Das Gebetbuch der Gerechten. Literargeschichtliche Beobachtungen am Psalter*, in *ZTK* 90 (1993) 355-381.

47. La nature exacte de ce jugement est discutée; une perspective eschatologique n'est pas exclue. Voir la discussion dans M. CONTI, *Presente e futuro dell'uomo nei Salmi sapienziali* (Spicilegium Pontificii Athenaei Antoniani, 34), Roma, Pontificium Athenaeum Antonianum, 1998, pp. 39-40.

contre les pécheurs, une lecture en diptyque des Pss 1–2 aboutit à mettre en perspective le juste (ou la communauté des justes) et le roi-messie, laissant entendre qu'en un sens tout homme juste – fût-il «opprobre des humains et méprisé du peuple» (Ps 22,7) – est une figure du messie et qu'inversement le messie est une figure corporative de la communauté des justes. Par là est d'emblée indiquée l'inadéquation d'une opposition entre l'individuel et le collectif: l'unique est à la fois singulier et pluriel; le roi-messie (l'élu entre les élus) redouble la figure d'Israël (l'élu entre les nations). «L''individu-peuple' n'est pas une solitude, il appartient à une alliance où les voix s'unissent pour exulter», écrit Paul Beauchamp[48]. Pris comme un tout, les Pss 1–2 instaurent une lecture bi-dimensionnelle du recueil, grâce à laquelle les psaumes royaux ont gardé quelque pertinence après que l'institution monarchique eût disparu.

On voit ici comment la prise en compte du livre permet une «lecture stéréophonique», dont le relief tient à la diversité des contextes qu'une approche de type diachronique permet de dégager[49]. Il s'agit, ni plus ni moins, d'honorer la figure du livre, non seulement dans sa continuité et sa structure, mais aussi dans ses tensions internes.

C. Les titres des psaumes comme horizon interprétatif[50]

«Although the titles are relatively late», écrit Brevard S. Childs, «they represent an important reflection on how the psalms as collection of sacred literature were understood and how this secondary setting became normative for the canonical tradition»[51]. La discussion portant sur les titres des psaumes s'est longtemps limitée à l'examen de leur va-

48. P. BEAUCHAMP, *Le roi, fils de David et fils d'Adam. Messianisme et médiation*, in *Lumière et Vie* 178 (1986) 55-67, p. 65. Cf. aussi N. FRYE, *Le Grand Code. La Bible et la littérature*, traduit de l'anglais, Paris, Seuil, 1984, pp. 144-157, spéc. 144-145.

49. Je reprends l'expression «lecture stéréophonique» à Y.-M. BLANCHARD, *Vers un nouveau paradigme exégétique*, in J. DORÉ & F. BOUSQUET (eds.), *La théologie dans l'histoire* (Sciences théologiques et religieuses, 6), Paris, Beauchesne, 1997, pp. 73-91 (p. 87).

50. Je reprends l'expression «horizon interprétatif» à ZENGER, *Was wird anders* (n. 1), p. 407: «Bei kanonischer Auslegung sind die Psalmenüberschriften als Deutehorizont mitzulesen». Les Pères parlaient de «guide», de «héraut» ou de «clef». Références patristiques dans AUWERS, *La composition littéraire* (n. 4), pp. 148-149.

51. B.S. CHILDS, *Reflections on the Modern Study of the Psalms*, in F.M. CROOS, W.E. LEMKE & P.D. MILLER (eds.), *Magnalia Dei. The Mighty Acts of God. Essays on the Bible and Archaeology in Memory of G. Ernest Wright*, New York, Doubleday, 1976, pp. 377-388 (pp. 383-384). Cf. P.C. CRAIGIE, *Psalms 1–50* (WBC, 19), Waco, TX, Word Books, 1983, p. 31: «They (= the titles) are frequently of more importance for understanding the role of particuliar psalms in the context of the Psalter and in the historical context of Israel's worship than they are for understanding the original meaning and context of the individual psalms».

leur historique, en particulier pour les titres faisant allusion à des événements précis de la vie de David[52]. Le résultat de l'enquête s'étant révélé négatif, les titres ont été jugés sans intérêt. Les travaux de B. S. Childs ont beaucoup contribué à la réhabilitation des titres biographiques du Psautier[53]: ces titres représentent, en effet, l'exégèse la plus anciennement attestée de certains psaumes[54], une exégèse dont on est au moins assuré qu'elle a existé dès l'Ancien Testament. On se contentera de donner ici deux exemples[55].

1. Le Ps 30: «cantique de la dédicace de la Maison»

Le titre du Ps 30 désigne le poème comme un «cantique de la dédicace de la Maison» (שׁיר־הנכת הבית)[56]. On voit généralement ici une allusion à la purification du temple de Jérusalem à l'époque de Juda Maccabée, commémorée annuellement depuis 164[57]. Soph XVIII, 2 (42a)

---

52. Pour l'histoire de la recherche, voir A.M. COOPER, *The Life and Times of King David according to the Book of Psalms*, in R.E. FRIEDMAN (ed.), *The Poet and the Historian. Essays in Literary and Historical Biblical Criticism* (HSS, 26), Chico, CA, Scholars Press, 1983, pp. 117-131; M. KLEER, *«Der liebliche Sänger der Psalmen Israels». Untersuchungen zu David als Dichter und Beter des Psalmen* (BBB, 108), Bodenheim, Philo, 1996.

53. B.S. CHILDS, *Psalm Titles and Midrashic Exegesis*, in *JSS* 16 (1971) 137-150; ID., *Midrash and the Old Testament*, in J. REUMANN (ed.), *Understanding the Sacred Text. Essays in honor of Morton S. Enslin on the Hebrew Bible and Christian Beginnings*, Valley Forge, Judson Press, 1972, pp. 47-59; ID., *Reflections* (n. 51); ID., *Introduction to the Old Testament as Scripture*, London, SCM Press, 1979, pp. 520-522.

54. F.F. BRUCE, *The Earliest Old Testament Interpretation*, in *OTS* 17 (1972) 37-52. Voir aussi E. SLOMOVIC, *Toward an Understanding of the Formation of Historical Titles in the Book of Psalms*, in *ZAW* 91 (1979) 350-380; M. FISHBANE, *Biblical Interpretation in Ancient Israel*, Oxford, Clarendon Press, 1985, pp. 403-407.

55. On lira avec intérêt, comme un prolongement possible aux deux exemples fournis ci-dessous, l'article de S. GILLMAYR-BUCHER, *The Psalm Headings. A Canonical Relecture of the Psalms* publié dans ce volume, pp. 247-254. Voir aussi B.L. TANNER, *The Book of Psalms Through the Lens of Intertextuality* (Studies in Biblical Literature, 26), New York – Bern – Berlin, P. Lang, 2001.

56. Voir, à propos du titre de ce psaume, la discussion entre J.L. MAYS, *The Question of Context in Psalm Interpretation*, dans McCANN (ed.), *The Shape and Shaping of the Psalter* (n. 33), pp. 14-20, spéc. 17-18, R.E. MURPHY, *Reflections on Contextual Interpretation of the Psalms*, *ibid.*, pp. 21-28, spéc. 23-24 et W. BRUEGGEMANN, *Response to James L. Mays, «The Question of Context»*, *ibid.*, pp. 29-41, spéc. 33-34.

57. SLOMOVIC, *Toward an Understanding* (n. 54), p. 369 pensait que le thème du psaume correspondait mieux à la dédicace du site du futur temple salomonien (1 Ch 21–22,1), tandis que C. LATTEY, *The First Book of Psalms (Pss I–XLI)* (Westminster Version of Sacred Scriptures), London – New York – Toronto, 1939, p. 100 estimait que le caractère personnel du psaume invitait plutôt à penser à la dédicace du palais de Salomon. Dans ce cas, ne faudrait-il pas plutôt penser à l'inauguration de la «maison» de David? C'était l'avis de E. KÖNIG, *Die Psalmen*, Gütersloh, Bertelsmann, 1927, p. 55, qui renvoie à 2 S 5,15 (lire 5,11) et 7,1. Une allusion à la dédicace du temple de Zorobabel paraissait plus probable à A.F. KIRKPATRICK, *The Book of Psalms*, Cambridge, 1902, p. 151. B.D. EERDMANS, *The Hebrew Book of Psalms* (OTS, 4), Leiden, 1947, pp. 73-75, de son côté,

assigne en effet le Ps 30 à la célébration annuelle de la Hannukah, et cet usage semble confirmé par Pesikta Rabbati 50 qui prend le Ps 30 comme base des homélies de cette fête[58]. La mention de la dédicace de la Maison, qui étonne en tête d'une action de grâces individuelle pour une guérison, invite à réinterpréter le psaume comme un chant du temple lui-même – et de la communauté qui s'y réunit – célébrant leur restauration[59]. Plusieurs éléments du texte se prêtent à une telle relecture, en particulier les vv. 7-8:

> (7) J'avais dit en ma quiétude:
> «Je ne serai jamais ébranlé!»
> (8) Yahvé, dans ta faveur, tu m'avais établi sur de fortes montagnes,
> tu as caché ta Face, je fus épouvanté.

שַׁלְוִי «quiétude» (v. 7) ne s'emploie dans le Psautier qu'ici et au Ps 122,7 (à propos de Jérusalem). Le v. 7b rappelle Jr 7,4-5.8-10, où le prophète dénonce l'illusion de ceux qui se croient en sécurité dans le temple de YHWH. Le v. 8a, quelle qu'en soit la lecture[60], fait inévitablement penser à Sion (cf. Is 25,6.10; 26,1-2). Le v. 13a: «Que ma gloire te chante et ne se taise pas» prend un autre sens si c'est le temple qui est censé parler.

2. Le Ps 90: «prière de Moïse, homme de Dieu»

Pour fictive qu'elle soit, l'attribution du Ps 90 à «Moïse, homme de Dieu» (v. 1) n'en est pas moins porteuse de sens. Ce psaume fait immédiatement suite à une lamentation sur la ruine de la monarchie davidique (Ps 89) et relance l'interrogation sur la permanence du ḥesed divin (89,2.29.34; 90,14). Or, en donnant la parole à Moïse, le Ps 90 prend un recul qui lui permet de porter l'attention sur un passé plus lointain que l'époque royale:

---

interprétait: cantique pour l'inauguration d'une maison particulière (avec renvoi à Dt 20,5). N.H. TUR-SINAI, *The Literary Character of the Book of Psalms*, in *OTS* 8 (1950) 263-281, p. 277 a vu dans le titre une allusion au rituel de la purification du sanctuaire qui précédait la fête des Tentes. Si le sens premier de la racine est «commencer (à utiliser)», on pourrait risquer la traduction: «for use of the household (or temple)», avec CRAIGIE, *Psalms 1–50* (n. 51), p. 251.

58. L'usage du Ps 30 dans le service synagogal quotidien est tardif, comme l'a montré Y.P. MERHAVIAH, *Psalm 30 and its Place in the Daily Services*, in *Sinai* 40 (1956) 182-196.

59. CHILDS, *Introduction to the Old Testament* (n. 53), p. 519.

60. Une traduction littérale du TM serait: «YHWH, dans ta faveur tu avais fixé pour ma montagne (להררי) une force (ou une forteresse)». Ainsi traduit, le texte s'entend au premier chef de Sion. La LXX porte: «Seigneur, en ta volonté, tu as accordé à ma beauté (τῷ κάλλει μου) une force». Les traducteurs grecs semblent avoir lu להדרי au lieu de להררי. Si la Septante est plus proche de l'original, on peut penser que la leçon du TM vise à infléchir le psaume dans le sens du titre.

(1) Seigneur, tu as été pour nous un refuge de génération en génération.
(2) Avant que fussent nées les montagnes,
    enfantés terre et monde,
    d'éternité en éternité, tu es Dieu.

Moïse est ainsi convoqué pour attester de la fidélité divine: Dieu, qui a été un refuge dans le passé, longtemps avant que la monarchie ait existé, le sera encore maintenant que la monarchie n'existe plus. La voix qui, au Ps 89, interroge sur l'avenir de l'alliance avec David est ainsi renvoyée au passé pré-monarchique d'Israël et aux premières alliances[61].

II. LE PSAUTIER DANS L'ÉCRIN DES ÉCRITURES JUIVES

Dans un second temps, le contexte où prend corps la lecture des psaumes peut être élargi aux dimensions du canon des Écritures juives.

A. Psautier et Torah

On ne s'est peut-être pas assez étonné que le Ps 1, en proclamant le bonheur de l'homme qui médite jour et nuit sur la Torah de YHWH, fasse la promotion d'un autre corpus d'écrits que celui qu'il est censé préfacer. À prendre ce macarisme au pied de la lettre, le lecteur devrait abandonner aussitôt la lecture du Psautier pour s'absorber dans la méditation des cinq livres de Moïse. Les commentateurs n'ont pas manqué de relever que Ps 1,2-3 démarquait d'assez près le prologue de Josué (1,7-8)[62],

---

61. Cf. WILSON, *The Editing* (n. 24), p. 215; LORENZIN, *I Salmi* (n. 9), p. 359. Un rapprochement avec l'historiographie deutéronomiste s'impose; cf. B. GOSSE, *Moïse entre l'alliance des patriarches et celle du Sinaï*, in *SJOT* 11 (1997) 3-15, spéc. 14.

62. Cf. Jos 1,7-8: «Montre-toi fort et aie bon courage pour veiller à agir selon toute la *loi* (ככל־התורה) que t'a prescrite Moïse, mon serviteur! Ne t'en détourne ni à droite ni à gauche afin d'avoir du succès partout où tu iras. Que ce livre de la *loi* (ספר התורה הזה) ne s'éloigne pas de ta bouche; *tu le murmureras jour et nuit* (והגית בו יומם ולילה) afin de veiller à agir selon tout ce qui s'y trouve écrit. Car c'est alors que tu *réussiras* (תצליח) en tes voies et alors tu auras du succès» et Ps 1,2-3: «(Heureux l'homme...) qui *murmure la loi* de YHWH *jour et nuit* (בתורתו יהגה יומם ולילה)... tout ce qu'il fait, *il le réussira* (יצליח)». — La majorité des commentateurs postulent la dépendance de Ps 1,2-3 à l'égard de Jos 1,8: cf. B. JANOWSKI, *Die Kleine Biblia*, in E. ZENGER (ed.), *Der Psalter in Judentum und Christentum* (HBS, 18), Freiburg i Br., Herder, 1998, pp. 381-420, spéc. 407. Cependant, quelques-uns envisagent une relation allant dans le sens inverse: cf. T.C. RÖMER, *Josué, lecteur de la Torah (Jos 1,8)*, in K.-D. SCHUNCK & M. AUGUSTIN (eds.), *«Lasset uns Brücken bauen...». Collected Communications to the XVth Congress of the International Organization for the Study of the Old Testament, Cambridge 1995* (BEATAJ, 42), Frankfurt, P. Lang, 1998, pp. 117-124, spéc. 122-123 – ou encore attribuent les deux textes au même milieu producteur, qui aurait cherché à préciser la bonne utilisation du deuxième et du troisième volet du canon en les corrélant à la Torah: cf. A. ROFÉ, *The Piety of the Torah-Disciples at the Winding-Up of the Hebrew Bible: Josh 1:8; Ps 1:2, Is 59:21*, in H. MERKLEIN, K. MÜLLER & G. STEMBERGER (eds.), *Bibel in jüdischer und christlicher Tradition. FS J. Maier* (BBB, 88), Frankfurt, A. Hain, 1993, pp. 78-85.

dont le but affiché est de rattacher l'œuvre de Josué et le livre qui porte son nom à l'œuvre et au livre de Moïse (au moins au Deutéronome). Dans les termes du prologue, l'histoire de Josué montre comment la fidélité à la Loi est récompensée et l'infidélité, punie. Secondairement, c'est tout le corpus des Prophètes antérieurs (qu'ouvre le livre de Josué) qui se trouve ainsi rapporté à la Torah et invoqué à l'appui de la thèse présentée par le prologue: tout autant que celle de Josué, l'histoire des Juges et celle des rois de Juda et d'Israël montrent que l'attachement à la Torah est condition de vie et de bonheur.

Le Ps 1 remplit une fonction similaire à l'égard du Psautier: il présente le recueil comme une «méditation» de la Torah (v. 2); plus exactement, il invite à voir dans les psaumes une illustration de la thèse mise en exergue: la Torah est un chemin fécond et porteur de vie. Il est significatif que, pour rapporter le livre des psaumes à la Torah, le Ps 1 reprenne les termes mêmes du prologue de Josué, c'est-à-dire qu'il présente le rapport du Psautier vis-à-vis de la Loi mosaïque comme étant similaire à celui des Prophètes antérieurs à l'égard du Pentateuque. Par là, le rédacteur non seulement revendique pour le Psautier une place parmi les livres qui se constituaient en corpus dans le prolongement de la Torah[63], mais initie en outre une lecture des psaumes faite dans la perspective de la Torah.

B. Psautier et geste davidique

Les titres «historiques» sont des éléments éditoriaux qui invitent à lire le Psautier avec, comme arrière-fond, l'expérience à la fois singulière et exemplaire du fils de Jessé. Mais, pour mériter son nom, l'intertextualité doit fonctionner à double sens: une fois établie la relation entre tel psaume et tel épisode de la geste davidique, celui-ci doit pouvoir être relu à la lumière de son complément lyrique. Une lecture de la Bible qui veut honorer la figure du livre et le canon des Écritures doit ainsi faire se croiser les textes plus anciens et ceux dont l'exégèse historico-critique montre qu'ils sont plus récents[64].

---

63. Cf. O.H. STECK, *Der Abschluss der Prophetie im Alten Testament. Ein Versuch zur Frage der Vorgeschichte des Kanons* (Biblisch-Theologische Studien, 17), Neukirchen, Neukirchener Verlag, 1991, pp. 161-166; K. SEYBOLD, *Die Psalmen. Eine Einführung* (Urban-Taschenbücher, 382), Stuttgart, Kohlhammer, 1986, p. 22: «Der Leser des Psalters wird als Leser des Gesetzes (der *Tora*) am Eingang begrüßt und ermahnt. Beides setzt wohl voraus, daß das Buch in der Hand dieses Lesers auch schon zu den heiligen Schriften gezählt wird, welche nach 'Gesetz' und 'Propheten' den dritten Teil des Grundstocks des hebräischen Kanons bilden».

64. On sait que le TM de 1-2 Samuel laisse parfois des espaces libres, dont plusieurs apparaissent dans des récits évoqués par les titres des psaumes. Il est possible que, dans

Un des effets de l'intitulation davidique du Psautier est de compenser les silences de la geste davidique sur la vie intérieure du fils de Jessé. En d'autres termes, là où les livres de Samuel nous mettent en présence d'un chef de bande, le Psautier rappelle que David fut aussi un homme de prière[65]. Quelques exemples: le récit de 2 S 15–18 est discret sur la manière dont David a vécu intérieurement la révolte d'Absalom contre lui; le Ps 3, lu à la lumière de son titre, en dit davantage sur ses sentiments et sur sa prière. Dans l'épisode de Bethsabée, 2 S 12,13 fait simplement dire à David: «J'ai péché contre YHWH»; le Psautier développe la supplication du roi repentant (Ps 51), et on comprend mieux alors la réaction immédiate de Nathan: «YHWH a ôté ton péché, tu ne mourras pas». Avec le Ps 72 «s'achèvent les prières de David, fils de Jessé» (v. 20): il semble que les éditeurs du Psautier ont voulu présenter les Pss 70–72 comme la prière du roi au soir de sa vie et fournir ainsi une plus ample version des «dernières paroles» de David, où le monarque apparaît particulièrement soucieux de l'avenir de son peuple[66].

Des effets de sens similaires pourraient être recherchés pour d'autres corpus, par exemple pour les Sapientiaux: à côté d'une interprétation du livre de Qohèlèt ou du Cantique qui tienne compte de la fiction salomonienne, une exégèse qui prend au sérieux le canon du Premier Testament pourrait accréditer une lecture de la geste de Salomon à la lumière des Sapientiaux[67]. Bien entendu, de telles «lectures croisées dans

ces cas, le פסקה soit un appel au psaume correspondant: on lirait Ps 54 en 1 S 23,4; Ps 132 en 2 S 7,4; Ps 51 en 2 S 12,13; Ps 3 en 2 S 16,13; Ps 34 ou 56 en 2 S 21,10, etc. Cf. Sh. TALMON, *Hebrew Apocryphal Psalms from Qumran*, in *Tarbiz* 35 (1965-66) 214-234 (en hébreu); FISHBANE, *Biblical Interpretation* (n. 54), pp. 405-406; P. ACKROYD, *Doors of Perception. A Guide to Reading the Psalms*, London, SCM, ²1983, pp. 35-36. À l'inverse, M.D. GOULDER, *The Psalms of Asaf and the Pentateuch. Studies in the Psalter, III* (JSOT SS, 233), Sheffield, Academic Press, 1996, p. 178 a suggéré que «the Selahs in the psalm text provided breaks in which our Succession Narrative (2 Sam 11–20; 1 Kgs 1) could be recited». Quoi qu'il en soit de ces hypothèses, l'intitulation davidique du Psautier invite à rapprocher psaumes et récits, qui sont ainsi tenus de s'expliquer mutuellement. Cf. J.-L. VESCO, *Le Psaume 18, lecture davidique*, in *RB* 94 (1987) 5-62, p. 17.

65. Une telle lecture est amorcée par B. COSTACURTA, *Con la cetra e con la fionda. L'ascesa di Davide verso il trono* (Collana Biblica), Roma, Dehoniane, 1994. Cf. aussi VESCO, *Le Psaume 18* (n. 64); B. GOSSE, *L'interprétation des livres de Samuel à partir des Psaumes en 1 Sam 11 1-10*, in *BiOr* 173 (1992) 145-153; ID., *L'insertion de 2 Samuel 22 dans les livres de samuel, et l'influence en retour sur les titres davidiques du Psautier*, in *JANES* 27 (2000) 31-47; et J.-M. AUWERS, *Le David des psaumes et les psaumes de David*, in L. DEROUSSEAUX & J. VERMEYLEN (eds.), *Figures de David à travers la Bible* (LD, 177), Paris, Cerf, 1999, pp. 187-224, spéc. 223-224.

66. Cf. J.-M. AUWERS, *Les Psaumes 70–72. Essai de lecture canonique*, in *RB* 101 (1994) 242-257.

67. Cf. G.T. SHEPPARD, Art. *Canonical Criticism*, in *ABD* 1 (1992), pp. 861-866, spéc. 865.

l'enceinte canonique»[68] ressortissent à une herméneutique centrée sur la lecture des textes davantage que sur leur écriture. On ne prétend nullement que ces potentialités de sens puissent être saisies au niveau de la conscience des auteurs, mais bien qu'une théorie de la réception des textes les rend perceptibles.

C. Le statut du Psautier

La place qui est attribuée à un livre du Premier Testament dans les manuscrits ou dans les listes anciennes est révélatrice du statut qui est reconnu à ce livre dans l'économie du corpus canonique. On ne signalera ici que quelques-unes des nombreuses hésitations qui affectent le Psautier[69]. Dans les manuscrits hébreux qui suivent la tradition Ben Asher, comme le codex d'Alep ou le codex de Saint-Pétersbourg, les Psaumes font immédiatement suite aux Chroniques – ce qui tire le Psautier du côté de la liturgie du Temple, dont les derniers versets des Chroniques annoncent la restauration. Dans la liste du canon hébreu que rapporte Jérôme dans son *Prologus galeatus*, les Psaumes font suite à Job, comme si le *sefer tehilîm* réassumait la souffrance de Job pour la transformer progressivement en louange. Dans la liste du Talmud de Babylone (BB 14b), les Psaumes apparaissent en deuxième position des *Ketûbîm*, juste après le livre de Ruth, qui se termine par la généalogie de David; voilà, sans aucun doute, une manière de mettre en évidence l'attribution davidique du livre. Le même souci justifie la place que l'*Ambrosianus* de la Peshitta donne au Psautier, juste après les livres de Samuel; le récit est ici immédiatement suivi de son complément lyrique. Dans le *Sinaiticus* de la Septante, le Psautier fait la transition entre les écrits prophétiques et les écrits de sagesse, comme s'il relevait des deux genres. Dans l'*Alexandrinus*, il fait suite à 1–4 Mac, ce qui met peut-être en évidence la tension eschatologique qui traverse le recueil. L'hésitation sur la place qui revient au Psautier dans le canon des Écritures révèle une hésitation sur le statut du livre lui-même, et chacune des séquences qui viennent d'être évoquées induit des clefs herméneutiques propres.

---

68. L'expression est de P. RICŒUR, in ID. & A. LACOCQUE, *Penser la Bible*, Paris, Seuil, 1998, p. 447.

69. Ces indications rapides seront prolongées dans ce même volume par E. ZENGER, *Der Psalter im Horizont von Tora und Prophetie. Kanongeschichtliche und kanonhermeneutische Perspektiven*, pp. 111-134. Voir aussi P. BRANDT, *Endgestalten des Kanons. Das Arrangement der Schriften Israels in der jüdischen und christlichen Bibel* (BBB, 131), Berlin, Philo, 2001, *passim*.

III. Le Psautier dans la Bible chrétienne

Dans son extension maximale, le corpus qui sert de contexte à la lecture du Psautier est le canon des deux Testaments. L'exégèse scientifique a abandonné l'interprétation christologique du Premier Testament comme appartenant à un âge révolu de la lecture des livres saints. Brevard S. Childs écrit à ce propos: «While an interpretation of the New Testament in the light of the Old Testament background can be readily defended because of the historical dependence of the New on the Old, the reverse move, namely, an interpretation of the Old in the light of the New, is not at all obvious. Far more than historical continuity of background is being claimed. This latter move obviously has no historical rationale, but rests on the confession of a theological context in which the two parts are seen in a particular relationship»[70]. Une telle exégèse suppose, en effet, que l'unité des Écritures est plus et autre chose que la simple reliure qui, dans une bible chrétienne, tient ensemble les deux Testaments. Cette exégèse est cependant légitime dans la mesure où elle met en évidence des rapports d'intertextualité qui s'établissent dans la synchronie du Livre, ce «grand intertexte» ou ce «grand code», lieu de circulation du sens[71]. Pour en revenir au livre des psaumes, on voit bien que les figures mises en perspective par l'introduction duelle du Psautier – celle du juste, celle de l'impie, celle du roi-messie, celle d'Israël et celle des Nations – sont susceptibles d'effectuations différentes à l'intérieur du recueil[72] comme à l'extérieur de celui-ci[73], puisque la prière des psaumes a pour vocation de se prêter à de perpétuelles réappropriations. Dès lors, en-deçà même d'une adhésion au principe confessant de l'accomplissement des Écritures en Jésus-Christ, on ne voit pas au nom de quoi on refuserait à l'individualité historique du Christ, telle que les écrits du Nouveau Testament nous la donnent à voir, le droit d'informer à son tour les figures du juste et du roi et de leur donner son nom iné-

---

70. B. Childs, *Biblical Theology in Crisis*, Philadelphia, PA, Fortress, 1970, p. 109.

71. Je reprends l'expression «grand intertexte» à P. Ricœur, *Temps biblique*, in Ar*chivo di filosofia* 53 (1985) 23-35, p. 27: «La Bible, ainsi lue, devient un grand intertexte vivant, qui est le lieu, l'espace, d'un travail du texte sur lui-même. Notre acte de lecture veut être la saisie, par l'imagination reconstructrice, de ce travail du texte sur lui-même». — J.A. Sanders, Art. *Canon. Hebrew Bible*, in *ABD* 1 (1992), pp. 837-852 parle de la Bible comme d'un «text compressed into canon» (p. 850; cf. p. 843).

72. Le Ps 83 fournit un excellent parallèle au Ps 2, qui décrit une révolte généralisée des Nations «contre YHWH et contre son messie» (v. 2). Ps 83,7-9 montre comment cette figure des Nations hostiles a pris corps soit dans des ennemis militaires responsables de désastres nationaux, soit dans la descendance d'hommes qui ont représenté pour Israël de profondes blessures.

73. Par exemple: 2 Ch 6,41-42 fait du Ps 132,8-10 la prière de Salomon.

changeable[74], pour autant que cette opération n'aboutisse pas à nier le relief du livre sous prétexte de son unité formelle[75]. Le défi qui attend l'exégète qui accepte de se risquer à une telle interprétation est de faire voir comment «c'est dans le travail du texte sur lui-même que l'anticipation du sens à venir et non encore déployé trouve le gage de sa projection hors de lui-même»[76].

On illustrera brièvement ce propos à partir du Ps 118. À supposer même que ce poème ait été composé à l'occasion d'une libération historique précise[77], il dépasse l'événement qui est à l'origine de sa rédaction pour magnifier le *ḥesed* divin qui fait de l'alliance entre YHWH et son peuple une alliance à jamais (vv. 1b.2b.3b.4b.29b). Pour célébrer l'éternelle fidélité de YHWH, le poème regarde vers le passé d'Israël[78]. Il est vrai qu'à aucun moment il n'évoque de manière explicite un événement précis de l'histoire du peuple élu, mais il ressaisit l'action salvifique de manière globale[79], ce qui le rend propre à accompagner la célébration de toutes les «merveilles» (cf. v. 23b) de Dieu, en particulier celle de

---

74. Cf. Y.-M. BLANCHARD, *Le texte dans son corpus. Enjeux herméneutiques du canon scripturaire*, in J. NIEUVIARTS & P. DEBERGÉ (eds.), *Les nouvelles voies de l'exégèse. En lisant le Cantique des cantiques* (LD, 190), Paris, Cerf, 2002, pp. 295-319: «Pour nous modernes, la question est de savoir s'il suffit de lire le rapport [entre l'A.T. et le N.T.] en un seul sens, rendant compte de l'expression néo-testamentaire à partir de ses précédents vétéro-testamentaires, selon le principe parfaitement juste qui veut que la langue précède son effectuation. Ou bien, considérant le fait même du livre, non seulement disponible en synchronie mais historiquement parlant indissociable du texte particulier, ne faut-il pas relire aussi la figure vétéro-testamentaire à la lumière de son expression néo-testamentaire, étant donné que la langue n'est pas un fonds immuable mais s'enrichit elle-même de ses effectuations concrètes, au sein d'un espace social déterminé, à savoir la communauté linguistique nationale, régionale ou autre? Si nous considérons que la Bible dans son ensemble définit l'espace commun aux diverses confessions chrétiennes, il paraît légitime que le rapport langue-parole, dont nous pensons qu'il traduit bien la notion d'accomplissement et sous-tend la pratique plus technique de la typologie, soit systématiquement exploité comme une règle de lecture canonique, honorant à la fois la spécificité de chaque texte et la réalité du livre dans sa totalité signifiante» (p. 313).

75. J'entends ici l'objection d'E. LÉVINAS, *Personnes ou figures* [1950], in *Difficile liberté. Essais sur le judaïsme* (Présence du judaïsme), Paris, Albin Michel, ²1976, pp. 160-164: «Si tous les personnages purs de l'Ancien Testament annoncent le Messie, tous les indignes, ses bourreaux, toutes les femmes, sa Mère, le Livre des Livres, obsédé par un thème unique, répétant inlassablement les mêmes gestes, ne perd-il pas de sa vie vivante?» (p. 163).

76. P. RICŒUR, *«Comme si la Bible n'existait que lue...»*, in BOVATI & MEYNET (eds.), *«Ouvrir les Écritures»* (n. 25), pp. 21-28, spéc. 22.

77. À la suite de Fr. BAETHGEN, *Die Psalmen* (HKAT, II/2), Göttingen, 1892, p. 358, plusieurs commentateurs pensent à la fête de Sukkôt de 444, après la reconstruction du mur de Jérusalem par Néhémie.

78. Le refrain d'action de grâces des vv. 2-4 et 29 se retrouve en 1 Ch 16,34.41, 2 Ch 5,13; 7,3.6; 20,21; Esd 3,11, pour célébrer des événements marquants de la vie d'Israël.

79. Au v. 17b, les mss hébreux hésitent entre le pluriel («je raconterai les œuvres de Yah») et le singulier («l'œuvre de Yah»).

l'exode[80] – et ce qui explique que ce psaume a pris place en finale du Hallel dit «égyptien»[81]. Cependant, le psaume ne regarde pas seulement vers le passé: il célèbre un salut dont le plein accomplissement est encore à venir. Aussi le psalmiste, après avoir remercié Dieu d'avoir exaucé sa prière (v. 21), supplie-t-il: «De grâce, YHWH, donne donc le salut! De grâce, YHWH, donne donc la réussite» (v. 25). C'est pourquoi «celui qui vient au nom de YHWH» (v. 26), qui a vaincu par ce même Nom qu'il sait invoquer (vv. 5.10-12), représente une «figure» qui, même si elle a trouvé des points d'application dans l'histoire passée d'Israël (cf. 1 S 17,45), tend vers un accomplissement[82]. Affirmer que cet accomplissement réside dans l'avènement du sujet Jésus-Christ plutôt que dans l'apport d'un sens plus élaboré ou plus affiné relève évidemment de l'acte de foi. Il n'en reste pas moins vrai que la lecture messianique que le Nouveau Testament et certains témoins de la tradition juive font de ce psaume est inscrite dans la dynamique même du texte, qui prend appui sur le passé d'Israël pour pointer vers le jour du Seigneur qui vient[83].

Faculté de théologie   Jean-Marie AUWERS
45, Grand-Place
B-1348 Louvain-la-Neuve

---

80. Ps 118,14.28 est à rapprocher Ex 15,2; Ps 118,15-16 rappelle Ex 15,6.

81. Cf. J. SCHRÖTEN, *Entstehung, Komposition und Wirkungsgeschichte des 118. Psalms* (BBB, 95), Weinheim, Beltz Athenäum Verlag, 1995, pp. 91-112.

82. Le v. 22 («La pierre qu'ont rejetée les bâtisseurs est devenue tête d'angle») vient de plus loin que le psaume. Il exprime, probablement sous une forme proverbiale, l'observation d'un fait courant lié aux techniques de construction. La métaphore de la pierre rejetée se trouve évoquée dans le psaume pour souligner tout à la fois la puissance déconcertante de YHWH (telle qu'elle s'est manifestée au cours de l'histoire d'Israël) et la vanité des appréciations humaines. Mais le psalmiste n'entend nullement restreindre la portée de cette vérité d'expérience à un événement précis. La métaphore reste disponible pour une actualisation ultérieure. Cf. M. BERDER, *«La pierre rejetée par les bâtisseurs»: Psaume 118,22-23 et son emploi dans les traditions juives et dans le Nouveau Testament* (EB, N.S. 31), Paris, Gabalda, 1996, pp. 472-365.

83. Sur la notion d'accomplissement des figures, voir en particulier P. BEAUCHAMP, *L'un et l'autre Testament*, 2 vol., Paris, Seuil, 1976-1990; ID., *Le Récit, la Lettre et le Corps* (Cogitatio fidei, 114), Paris, Cerf, 1982; J. CALLOUD, *Le texte à lire*, in L. PANIER (ed.), *Le temps de la lecture. Exégèse biblique et sémiotique* (LD, 155), Paris, Cerf, 1993, pp. 31-63; Fr. MARTIN, *Pour une théologie de la lettre. L'inspiration des Écritures* (Cogitatio fidei, 196), Paris, Cerf, 1996, pp. 324-343.

CANONIZATION OF ANCIENT HEBREW BOOKS
AND HASMONAEAN POLITICS

I

Since the nineties of the 19th century, the so-called three-stage theory of the canonization of the Hebrew Bible, the Old Testament, has been the prevailing hypothesis. The idea is that the three parts of the Hebrew Bible, Law, Prophets, and Writings, were canonized in three successive stages in history: the Law in the fourth century BCE (Ezra), the Prophets a little before 200 BCE, and, finally, the Writings as additional part of the collection about 100 CE at the synod of Jamnia. Thus, the full canon was established, according to this theory, at the beginning of the second century CE.

In recent times, however, it has been argued that this theory can no longer be maintained. One of the major criticisms is that the idea of a synod of Jamnia can no longer be defended. Another point which deserves attention is that it does not do full justice to the early Jewish sources, such as the well-known passage in Josephus' *Contra Apionem* (I, 38-40; see below).

This new situation leaves room for new theories. Roughly speaking, the following new hypotheses have been developed in the last twenty years:

(1) In early Judaism, the full canon of the Old Testament, in the sense of a "closed" one, did not emerge before the second century CE[1].

(2) The collection of the books of the Hebrew Bible, as we know it, was established as a closed canon around 150 BCE[2].

(3) The formation of the OT canon did take place, at least as far as the Law and the Prophets are concerned, at a very early date, namely in the

---

1. See E. ULRICH, *The Canonical Process, Textual Criticism, and Latter Stages in the Composition of the Bible*, in M. FISHBANE & E. TOV (eds.), *"Sha'arei Talmon": Studies in the Bible, Qumran, and the Ancient Near East Presented to S. Talmon*, Winona Lake, IN, 1992, pp. 267-291; = ID., *The Dead Sea Scrolls and the Origins of the Bible*, Grand Rapids, MI, 1999, pp. 51-78; J.A. SANDERS, *The Issue of Closure in the Canonical Process*, in L.M. MCDONALD & J.A. SANDERS (eds.), *The Canon Debate*, Leiden, 2002 (in the press).

2. See S.Z. LEIMAN, *The Canonization of Hebrew Scripture: The Talmudic and Midrashic Evidence* (Transactions of the Connecticut Academy of Arts and Sciences, 47), Hamden, 1976; R.T. BECKWITH, *The Old Testament Canon of the New Testament Church and Its Background in Early Judaism*, London, 1985.

process of a final redaction of groups of books, presumably in the Persian period[3].

II

When one considers these theories several questions arise, the crucial one being that of the definition of "canon" and "canonical".

The last of the just mentioned theories is based on the notion of "canonical" in the sense of a final and intertextual redaction which is meant to establish an interrelationship of a number of books. However, one wonders whether the term canonical is here the appropriate one. It is suggested that passages such as Deut 34, Josh 1,1-9, and Mal 3,22-24 are part of a canonical redaction of the books of the Law and the Prophets. I doubt however, whether, for instance, Josh 1,1-9 is meant to function as an introduction to the (canonical) corpus of the Prophets as a whole. From a redactioncritical point of view this passage is more likely to be seen as part of a redaction of a literary corpus, namely Deuteronomy up to and including Kings, or Genesis up to and including Kings. Furthermore, the reference to "the law of Moses" in Josh 1,7 does not refer to the *torah* in the sense of the Pentateuch, but rather in the sense of the law of Deuteronomy.

The first and second theories mentioned above are based on the use of canon, and canonical, in the sense of a *closed/fixed* canon which at the same time is related to the notion of a *standardized* text. Here we touch upon the concept of a closure of the canon in early Judaism. It is my contention, that, different from Early Christianity, the idea of a closure of the canon in the sense of a decision taken at some moment in history has no basis in any of the (early) Jewish sources. Rather, as I will argue in this paper, a collection of ancient Hebrew books happened to become, in the second century BCE, for some reason or another, "canonical" in the sense of highly authoritative, but this collection should not to be seen as closed or fixed.

As to the idea of a standardized text, one is reminded of the well known statement by Josephus, namely, that the text of the Scriptures,

---

3. See J. BLENKINSOPP, *Prophecy and Canon: A Contribution to the Study of Jewish Origins*, Notre Dame, IN, 1977; O.H. STECK, *Der Abschluss der Prophetie im Alten Testament: Ein Versuch zur Frage der Vorgeschichte des Kanons* (Biblisch-Theologische Studien, 17), Neukirchen-Vluyn, 1991; S. DEMPSTER, *An "Extraordinary Fact": Torah and Temple and the Contours of the Hebrew Canon*, in *Tyndale Bulletin* 48 (1997) 23-56 and 191-218; S.B. CHAPMAN, *The Law and the Prophets. A Study in Old Testament Canon Formation* (FAT, 27), Tübingen, 2000 (p. 106: "canon-conscious-redactions").

consisting of the five books of Moses, the 13 books of the Prophets, and the four remaining books, has been transmitted in a most accurate manner (CAp I,39-42: "no one has ventured either to add, or to remove, or to alter a syllable"). It may well be that this view expressed by Josephus reflects the idea of Jewish circles in the first century CE. However, as has been argued by scholars, "canonical" in the sense of a stabilized or standardized text form does not apply to an earlier period such as the second century BCE[4].

Although the term "canon" is not used in the sense of a list of most important works in pagan antiquity, the idea of listing authoritative works or authors is clearly attested: the Three Tragedians, the Nine Lyric Poets, and the like[5]. There is good reason to believe that this idea goes back to the great Alexandrian scholars of the third and second centuries BCE[6]. The authors of these selected works were known as "the classics" (classici).

As we know, the term "canon" is not used in ancient Judaism either, but the concept of "canonical" in the sense of "authoritative" is present. This is most clearly the case with the passage of Josephus in CAp. According to this passage, elements which underscore the notion of the books as "scriptures" are (a) the claim of an accurate transmission of the text of these books (see above), and (b) "the instinct of every Jew to regard them as the decrees of God, to abide with them, and, if need be, cheerfully to die for them" (I,42). This may reflect the ideas of Jewish circles in the late first century CE. But, as indicated above, there is reason to differentiate regarding the concept of canonical in the course of time, because passages dating to the second century BCE seem to reflect another view.

One of these early passages is found in the Prologue to the Wisdom of Jesus ben Sira. It reads:

> My grandfather Jesus, who had devoted himself for a long time to the study of the Law, the Prophets, and the other books of our ancestors (εἴς τε τὴν τοῦ νόμου καὶ τῶν προφητῶν καὶ τῶν ἄλλων πατρίων βιβλίων ἀνάγνωσιν), and developed a thorough familiarity (ἱκανὴν ἕξιν) with

4. See A. VAN DER KOOIJ, *The Canonization of Ancient Books Kept in the Temple of Jerusalem*, in ID. & K. VAN DER TOORN (eds.), *Canonization and Decanonization. Papers presented to the International Conference of the Leiden Institute for the Study of Religions (LISOR) Held at Leiden 9-10 January 1997* (Studies in the History of Religions, 82), Leiden, 1998, pp. 17-40, esp. 32.

5. J.F.A. SAWYER, *Sacred Languages and Sacred Texts*, London - New York, 1999, p. 60.

6. Cf. B. LANG, *The "Writings". A Hellenistic Literary Canon in the Hebrew Bible*, in VAN DER KOOIJ & VAN DER TOORN (eds.), *Canonization and Decanonization* (n. 4), pp. 41-78, esp. 47.

them, was prompted to write something himself in the nature of instruction and wisdom (ll. 8-12).

Although the Prologue as a whole expresses clearly the importance of the books involved, our passage contains a significant feature which deserves attention: the fact that the third section is called "the other books of the ancestors" means that all the books are considered "ancestral books". They are constituting the literary heritage of the Jewish nation. In antiquity, the notion of being "ancestral" or "ancient" means that the object concerned is considered authoritative[7]. Thus, the collection consisting of the Law, the Prophets, and the other books has a special position in being ancestral, i.e., worthy of respect and sacrosanct. The emphasis here is not on selected authors, but on the idea of "ancient" in the sense of constituting a basic element of a religion and culture.

The notion of "ancestral" marks also the difference of position between these ancient books on the one hand, and the writing of Ben Sira on the other. It indicates that the Wisdom of Ben Sira, at least in the view of the grandson, does not have the same position as the books of the ancestors, although it is also clear from his Prologue that the new book is considered as being significant precisely because it is based on a thorough study of the ancestral ones.

Another element in the Prologue which points to a position of authority of the writings concerned, is the notion of a thorough "study" of these texts. The grandson praises his grandfather as someone who "devoted himself for a long time to the study of the ancient books and as someone who developed a thorough familiarity with them". The terms used here (ἀνάγνωσις, ἕξις) are also found in the Letter of Aristeas (see §§121, 305) where they reflect the standards of Alexandrinian scholarship. This emphasis on the "study" of the ancient books is attested by other documents of the time, such as the so-called Halakhic Letter, 4QMMT, dating to the middle of the second century BCE. In C, 10 it is stated: "We have [written] to you so that you may study the book of Moses and the books of the Prophets and (that/those of[8]?)

---

7. Cf. H.G. KIPPENBERG, *Die jüdischen Überlieferungen als πάτριοι νόμοι*, in R. FABER & R. SCHLESIER (eds.), *Die Restauration der Götter. Antike Religion und Neo-Paganismus*, Würzburg, 1986, pp. 45-60; G.G. STROUMSA, *The Christian Hermeneutical Revolution and its Double Helix*, in L.V. RUTGERS et al. (eds.), *The Use of Sacred Books in the Ancient World* (CBET, 22), Leuven, 1998, pp. 9-28, esp. 11.

8. The interpretation of the reading בדו]יד is uncertain (below, p. 32). See the contribution of E. Ulrich in this volume. Most recently, T.H. Lim has argued that "in David" is probably best understood "as an elliptical reference to David's deeds": *The Alleged Reference to the Tripartite Division of the Hebrew Bible*, in *RQ* 77 (2001) 23-37, esp. 35. It is true that the Hebrew verb בין + the preposition ב can be used in connection with the understanding of the deeds of someone (God, or kings) in Qumran writings, but in the

David"[9]. The Hebrew expression for "to study" is הבין ב[10]. It has to do with the reading and interpretation of ancient books (see, e.g., Dan 9,2). The important thing is that thorough knowledge of the books enabled scribes and scholars to argue on the basis of the ancient texts. The Letter, and other documents from Qumran as well, make fully clear how this was done, namely, by quoting passages from ancient books and by presenting an interpretation of these passages[11]. Thus, also the aspect of study and the use of passages from the ancient books as an *argument* point to a highly authoritative position of the writings concerned in the second century BCE.

III

The passage in the Prologue quoted above, about "the study of the Law, the Prophets, and the other books of the ancestors", seems to testify to a tripartite division of "the books", fully in line with Josephus' statement. However, as has been suggested by scholars, the rather vague name of the third section, "the other books" (cf. line 25: τὰ λοιπὰ τῶν βιβλίων, "the rest of the books"), may indicate that this part was still open-ended and not yet determined[12]. But the difficulty with this idea is that the use of the article, "*the* other books", seems to presuppose that also the third section was a defined one[13], which, by the way, is not the same as a definitive or closed one. It should be noted that Josephus in using a similar designation, "the remaining books" (αἱ λοιπαί), clearly refers to a defined group of books, namely a (small) group of four books (presumably, the Psalms and three books belonging to Wisdom literature).

case of 4QMMT C,10 it stands more to reason to interpret the elliptical expression "in David" in the light of the preceding terminology "in the book, or books of". In the case of "deeds" one would have expected an explicit reference (מעשי) in the text. I owe the reference to the article by Lim to Florentino García Martínez.

9. The text continues thus: "[and the] [events of] ages past". The expression used here (מעשי] דור ודור]) does not refer to writings, pace J.C. VANDERKAM, *Authoritative Literature in the Dead Sea Scrolls*, in *DSD* 5 (1998) 382-402, esp. p. 388, as is clear from 4Q270 (see *DJD* 10, Oxford, 1994, p. 59 [note]).

10. For this verb, see LIM, *Tripartite Division* (n. 8), p. 36.

11. See e.g. J. LUST, *Quotation Formulae and Canon in Qumran*, in VAN DER KOOIJ & VAN DER TOORN (eds.), *Canonization and Decanonization* (n. 4), pp. 79-91; VANDERKAM, *Authoritative Literature* (n. 9), pp. 382-402.

12. See e.g. H.P. RÜGER, *Le Siracide: un livre à la frontière du canon*, in J.D. KAESTLI & O. WERMELINGER (eds.), *Le canon de l'Ancien Testament: Sa formation et son histoire* (Le Monde de la Bible), Genève, 1984, pp. 47-69.

13. Cf. R.T. BECKWITH, *A Modern Theory of the Old Testament Canon*, in *VT* 41 (1991) 385-395, esp. p. 388.

Further, it has been proposed that the phrase "the other books" might refer to books outside the canonical collection[14]. This interpretation is related to the view according to which the designation of "the Law and the Prophets" points to a bipartite division of the collection of canonical books[15]. However, this interpretation of the expression "the other books" is difficult to accept, because the use of the adjective "of the ancestors" clearly suggests that the third section was considered part of the same collection as the first and second sections. As stated above, all books are seen here as ancient books, including the ones designated as "other" or "remaining". Thus, it seems plausible to assume that the Prologue reflects the idea of a threefold division of the canonical collection, the collection of books that were considered "ancestral".

The idea whether a threefold division is also present in 4QMMT, in the passage quoted above, is disputed. However, if the wording "that/those of David" might be taken as referring to book, or books, as seems likely (see note 8, and compare the expression τὰ τοῦ Δαυιδ in 2 Macc 2,13), then this term is best interpreted as a reference to the book of Psalms. A reference to this book reminds one of Luke 24,44, where "the Psalms" seems to be used as a designation to a third grouping ("the Law of Moses, the Prophets, and the Psalms"). The reference to "the Psalms" as a term for the third section would at least make good sense, because, as is stated by Josephus, the book of Psalms, "the hymns" as he terms it, was the first one of the third section, the so-called "the remaining books".

Another passage which is of interest in this connection is to be found in Philo's *De vita comtemplativa* §25. He tells the reader that the houses of the Therapeutae had a special room ("sanctuary"), into which they took with them "laws (νόμους) and oracles delivered through the mouth of prophets (λόγια θεσπισθέντα διὰ προφητῶν) and psalms (ὕμνους) and the other books[16] (τὰ ἄλλα) which foster and perfect knowledge and

14. J. Barton, *Oracles of God: Perceptions of Ancient Prophecy in Israel After the Exile*, London, 1987, p. 44.

15. So J. Barr, *Holy Scripture: Canon, Authority, Criticism*, Oxford, 1983, p. 55; Barton, *Oracles of God* (n. 14), p. 44; E. Ulrich, *The Bible in the Making: The Scriptures at Qumran*, in Id. & J.C. Vanderkam (eds.), *The Community of the Renewed Covenant* (Christianity and Judaism in Antiquity, 10), Notre Dame, IN, 1993, pp. 77-94, esp. 82; D.M. Carr, *Canonization in the Context of Community: An Outline of the Formation of the Tanakh and the Christian Bible*, in R.D. Weis & Id. (eds.), *A Gift of God in Due Season. Essays on Scripture and Community in Honor of James A. Sanders* (JSOT SS, 225), Sheffield, 1996, pp. 22-64, esp. 40-41.

16. F.H. Colson translates as "anything else" (*Loeb Classical Library*, 363, p. 127), but this rendering of τὰ ἄλλα is too imprecise; cf. J.C. Vanderkam, *Revealed Literature in the Second Temple Period*, in Id., *From Revelation to Canon. Studies in the Hebrew Bible and Second Temple Literature*, Leiden, 2000, pp. 1-30, esp. 22 n. 38.

piety". The question is whether the words "the other books" are used for a fourth grouping, as has been proposed by VanderKam[17], or not. In my view, there is reason to believe that the terms "the hymns (psalms)" and "the other books" should be taken together as referring to the third grouping. For Josephus offers a similar, twofold description of the third section: "hymns to God" and "precepts for the conduct of human life". This is the more interesting since the second part, presumably referring to the books of wisdom literature, has a close parallel in the text of Philo: "the other (books) which foster and perfect knowledge (ἐπιστήμη) and piety (εὐσέβεια)".

However, except for these passages, the expression "the Law and the Prophets" seems to have been more common, since it is attested at several places in writings dating to the second and first centuries BCE and the first century CE. It has been suggested by scholars that this points to a twofold division of the collection (see above). However, the fact that a tripartite formula is attested during the same period in which the designation of "the Law and the Prophets" was used, aks for another interpretation. The former expression was apparently the less common one and the latter the more common one, as far as our textual evidence goes. This situation is more easily explained by assuming that the expression "the Law and the Prophets" was used by way of abbreviation, as was also the case in the later rabbinical literature[18]. An interesting passage in this regard is Luke 24: in verse 27, the expression "Moses and the Prophets" is used, whereas in verse 44 the formula "the Law of Moses, the Prophets, and the Psalms" is found. The reason for the abbreviated form is not difficult to guess: the third section of the collection did not carry a specific appellation; it was simply called "the rest of the books", or otherwise ("the Psalms"). Moreover, as I believe, this section was a small one, just as Josephus tells us, the book of Psalms being the first one of the remaining, four, books[19].

IV

Thus, there is evidence that since the second half of the second century BCE a particular collection of ancient Hebrew books was considered "canonical" in the sense of highly authoritative. As has been pointed out

17. VANDERKAM, *Revealed Literature* (n. 16), p. 22.
18. Even the term "Torah" could be used for the Hebrew Bible as a whole; see W. BACHER, *Die exegetische Terminologie der jüdischen Traditionsliteratur*, 1. Teil: *Die bibelexegetische Terminologie der Tannaiten*, Darmstadt, 1965 (= Leipzig, 1899), p. 197.
19. See VAN DER KOOIJ, *Canonization of Ancient Books* (n. 4), p. 30.

by scholars, these books were kept in the temple[20]. Strictly speaking, we do not have specific information about the question which books did belong to this collection. But in the light of the sources of the time, such as the section on the Praise of the Fathers in Ben Sira, one may assume that basically the collection was made up by (the) books which we know as the biblical ones. It seems plausible to assume that the author of the Prologue had a defined collection of ancient books in mind, but, as stated above, this does not mean that this collection was closed or fixed. As a matter of fact, there are indications that in the period from 150 BCE up to the first century CE the number of these books may have varied. In principle, this needs not to surprise us in the light of the pluriformity of ancient Judaism. There is, of course, the fact of the rather limited canon of the Samaritans (the books of Moses only), but I do think here of the Qumran community in which besides "the books of the Law and of the Prophets" also books such as Henoch and Jubilees were held in high esteem[21]. Or to give another example: as has been argued by D. Barthélemy, the books of Esther and Qoheleth seem not to have been part of the collection of books that is reflected by the so-called *kaige*-edition of the Old Greek[22].

The question I would like to deal with now, is whether the picture outlined above also holds true for the pre-Maccabaean period in Judaism, in particular the time of Jesus ben Sira (ca 200 BCE). Did one attach the same weight to the ancient books in those earlier days, as many as were already in existence then[23], as one did afterwards? We will deal with the question by asking whether Jesus the grandfather held the same opinion as his grandson.

In the Prologue the grandson states that his grandfather Jesus had devoted himself for a long time to "the study of the Law, the Prophets and the other books of the ancestors", developing a thorough familiarity with them in order to be able to write his own book. From a rhetorical point of view it strikes one how much emphasis the grandson puts on the idea that his grandfather had written his own book on the basis of a study and thorough knowledge of the ancient books.

20. See e.g. BECKWITH, *Old Testament Canon* (n. 2), pp. 80-86.

21. See VANDERKAM, *Authoritative Literature* (n. 9), pp. 396-401, and ID., *Revealed Literature* (n. 16), pp. 24-29.

22. D. BARTHÉLEMY, *L'état de la Bible juive depuis le début de notre ère jusqu'à la deuxième révolte contre Rome (131-135)*, in KAESTLI & WERMELINGER (eds.), *Le canon de l'Ancien Testament* (n. 12), pp. 9-45, esp. 22.

23. The book of Daniel is of a later date. On the canonization of this book, see now K. KOCH, *Stages in the Canonization of the Book of Daniel*, in J.J. COLLINS & P.W. FLINT (eds.), *The Book of Daniel. Composition and Reception* (SVT, 83/2), Leiden, 2001, pp. 421-446.

But what would Jesus the grandfather have said to this? There is some evidence which suggests that his opinion differed from that of his grandson. The important passage in this respect is ch. 39,1-3:

(1) How different it is with the person
   who devotes himself to reflecting on the Law of the Most High
   he studies the wisdom of all ancients
   and he occupies himself with the prophecies
(2) the stories about/sayings of the famous men he preserves
   and he penetrates the intricacies of proverbs;
(3) he studies the hidden meaning of sayings,
   and he knows his way among riddles of proverbs.

This passage is part of a long discourse about the scribe (ספר/γραμ-ματεύς) in 38,24–39,11. It lists the various subjects which are typical of the study of the scribe. Some scholars believe that v. 1 reflects an ancient three-fold scheme of the canonical collection: the Law, Wisdom, and Prophets[24]. This is far from certain, because the phrase "the wisdom of all ancients" (σοφία πάντων ἀρχαίων) seems to imply a wider literary horizon than the wisdom literature of ancient Israel[25]. An interesting parallel is found in LXX-3 Rg 5,10. According to that text,

(King) Solomon abounded greatly
beyond the wisdom of all the ancients
καὶ ἐπληθύνθη Σαλωμων σφόδρα
ὑπὲρ τὴν φρόνησιν πάντων ἀρχαίων ἀνθρώπων.

King Solomon exceeded all ancient wise men on earth in wisdom (observe the clause that follows: "and beyond that of the wise men of Egypt"). So the Jewish scribe who first of all would have to reflect on the Law, would also have to study the wisdom of the sages of the remote past, regardless their nationality.

It may well be that the apocalyptic books of Enoch were considered to belong to this wider category of wisdom. Note in this connection that, as has been argued by scholars, the original – Hebrew – version of Sir 44,16 refers to Enoch as a sage who had knowledge of astronomy, whereas the Greek version of this passage (and also the Masada version) probably reflects a different view, more in line with the tradition found in (LXX) Gen 5,24[26].

24. See, e.g., J.C.H. LEBRAM, Aspekte der alttestamentlichen Kanonbildung, in VT 18 (1968) 173-189.
25. Opinions differ, see J. MARBÖCK, Sir. 38,24–39,11: Der schriftgelehrte Weise. Ein Beitrag zu Gestalt und Werk Ben Siras, in M. GILBERT (ed.), La Sagesse de l'Ancien Testament (BETL, 51), Leuven, 1979, repr. 1990, pp. 293-316 and 421-423, esp. 312.
26. See J.T. MILIK, The Books of Enoch. Aramaic Fragments of Qumran Cave 4, Oxford, 1976, pp. 10-11, and H.S. KVANVIG, Roots of Apocalyptic. The Mesopotamian Background of the Enoch Figure and of the Son of Man (WMANT, 61), Neukirchen-Vluyn, 1988, pp. 118-126.

As to the last part of v. 1 ("he occupies himself with the prophecies"), together with v. 2a ("the stories about the famous men he preserves"), it could be that both clauses refer to the books written by the prophets which contain stories about famous men[27]. V. 2a may also be related to the Praise of the Fathers in the book of Ben Sira, for the phrase "famous men" is also found in the introduction to that section of the book (see 44,3).

Finally, vv. 2b-3 are about wisdom literature, which should be studied by the scribe. Unlike v. 1, this part of the pericope seems to refer to the wisdom literature of the Jewish tradition. It is to be noted that the phrase "riddles of proverbs" is also used in the passage about Solomon (Sir 47,15.17).

The sources given in 39,1-3 correspond with the contents of the book of Wisdom itself: it contains reflections on the Law, it has a long section called the Praise of the Fathers (cf. the "famous men" of v. 2); and last but not least, its major interest is the wisdom based both on the Jewish literary heritage and on traditions of non-Jewish provenance as well[28]. The great emphasis on wisdom in 39,1-3 is in agreement with the composition of the book as a whole.

As to the sources to be used by a scribe, Sir 39,1-3 presents a picture different from the statement by the grandson in his Prologue. This is important for our discussion. The grandson states emphatically that the book of his grandfather is based on a thorough study of "the books of the ancestors", that is, books which belong to the Jewish tradition. The main points which are typical of this view, and which do not seem to be typical of the view of Jesus himself, are:

– the presentation of these books as a particular collection, with a threefold structure;
– a detailed and thorough study of just these books;
– the exclusive use of "the books of the ancestors".

One notices a shift towards a much stronger emphasis on the significance of "the ancestral books". This does not imply that these books were not previously held as important. Yet, the Prologue clearly reflects a different attitude towards the ancient books.

V

The historical background which may have given rise to this shift is not difficult to guess, for in the period between the grandfather and the

---

27. Note the use of the term "prophecies" beside "the books of the prophets" in the Prologue.

grandson dramatic and incisive events had taken place, between 169 and 161 BCE. According to the literature of the time (Daniel, 1 and 2 Maccabees) the temple state of the Jews and everything that was seen as essentials of that state – city (Jerusalem), temple, cult, laws – was seriously threatened; it can easily be imagined that this crisis resulted in a strong emphasis on everything "ancestral" (πάτριος, πατρῷος), symbolizing the Jewish self-identity, such as the ancient books which happened to be at that time the literary heritage of the Jewish nation.

In terms of canonization it seems that, as a result of the crisis just mentioned, the ancient books which were kept in the temple and which as such had already acquired some significance (cp. Egypt and Mesopotamia), enjoyed a higher status. The new significance attached to these books in the Maccabaean era is related to a shift in the use to which these books were put. The pre-Maccabean book of Ben Sira, particularly its section of the Praise of the Fathers, is based on the contents of these books in a rather loose way[29]; later on, however, writings appear that are characterized by a strong concentration on texts from the ancient books by way of quotations. As is also reflected in the Prologue to the Wisdom of Ben Sira, the books involved became normative, i.e., they became "scripture". A new composition, like that of the grandfather Jesus, was only acceptable if based exclusively on those books.

It is reasonable to assume that this shift was promulgated by leading conservative circles in the Jewish community. It is likely to think here of the leaders of the time, viz. the Hasmonaean/Maccabaean leaders. According to the letter of 2 Macc 1,10–2,18, the restoration of the cult and the rededication of the temple by Judas the Maccabaean went hand in hand with the recollection of ancient books in the temple library or archive. Although it is difficult to say whether this letter provides trustworthy information, it is plausible to assume that Hasmonaean politics of the time had not only to do with the restoration of the cult in Jerusalem and the rededication of the temple, but also with the ancestral books that were kept in the temple[30]. This would explain why, from the second half of the second century BCE onwards, these books are presented as a literary collection that was held highly authoritative. Thus, the identity

28. For the latter aspect, see P.W. SKEHAN & A.A. DI LELLA, *The Wisdom of Ben Sira* (AB), New York, 1987, pp. 46-50.

29. As far as quotations are concerned, only a type of anthology is found, and naturally many allusions. On the issue of citations in Ben Sira, see now M. GILBERT, *Siracide*, in *DBS* 12/71 (1996), cc. 1423-1424.

30. For a similar idea, see P.R. DAVIES, *In Search of Ancient Israel* (JSOT SS, 148), Sheffield, 1992, p. 156; ID., *Scribes and Schools: The Canonization of the Hebrew Scriptures*, Louisville, KY, 1998, p. 178.

crisis in the first half of the second century BCE can be regarded as a crucial moment in the history of the canonical process[31].

Faculteit der Godgeleerdheid   Arie VAN DER KOOIJ
RU Leiden
P.O. Box 9515
NL-2300 RA Leiden

.

---

31. For the significance of the Hellenistic challenge in the second century BCE, see also J.A. SANDERS, *From Sacred Story to Sacred Text: Canon as Paradigm*, Philadelphia, PA, 1987, p. 183.

SEPTUAGINT AND CANON

A. General Remarks

1. *Discrepancies and Canon*

The discrepancies between the Septuagint (LXX) and the Masoretic Text (MT) do have implications for the understanding of the canons of Holy Scriptures accepted by various Jewish and Christian communities[1]. In its critical editions, the Septuagint differs from MT in several respects: two of these are usually given particular attention: first, the Septuagint contains a larger number of books; second, the order of the books is different.

Number of Books. The LXX comprises three types of books: a) a translation of the books of the Hebrew Bible or MT; b) a translation of books written in Hebrew or Aramaic, but not included in MT; c) books written in Greek.

Roughly speaking, b) and c) may be called "deutero-canonical" books; they do not belong to the canon of books of the Hebrew Bible, but to a second canon, used by the early Christians, and formally accepted by the Roman Catholic Church.

Order of Books. The order of books in LXX differs from the order in MT: The Hebrew books are arranged in three groups reflecting different stages of the process of growth and of canonization. The books of the Greek Bible are basically arranged according to their literary character: History, Poetry, Prophetical literature.

---

1. K.H. JOBES & M. SILVA, *Invitation to the Septuagint*, Grand Rapids, MI, 2000, pp. 79-85; H.B. SWETE, *An Introduction to the OT in Greek,* Cambridge, 1900; S. JELLICOE, *The Septuagint and Modern Study*, Oxford, 1968; E. TOV & R. KRAFT, *Septuagint*, in *IDB. Supplementary Volume*, Nashville, TN, 1976, pp. 807-815; N. FERNANDEZ-MARCOS, *Introducción a las versiones griegas de la Biblia*, Madrid, 1979; E. TOV, *Die Griechischen Bibelübersetzungen*, in *Aufstieg und Niedergang der Römischen Welt*, II. 20.1 (1987), pp. 120-189; E. TOV, *The Septuagint*, in J. MULDER (ed.), *Mikra*, Leiden, 1988, pp. 161-188; M. HARL, G. DORIVAL & O. MUNNICH, *La Bible grecque des Septante* (Initiations au christianisme ancien), Paris, 1988, pp. 112-119 (Dorival) and 321-329 (Dorival); B. BOTTE & P.-M. BOGAERT, Art. *Septante et versions grecques*, in *DBS* 12/68 (1993), cc. 536-693; M. CIMOSA, *Guida allo studio della bibbia greca*, Roma, 1995; M. HENGEL & R. DEINES, *Die Septuaginta als "christliche Schriftensammlung", ihre Vorgeschichte und das Problem des Canons*, in M. HENGEL & A.M. SCHWEMER (eds.), *Die Septuaginta zwischen Judentum und Christentum* (WUNT, 72), Tübingen, 1990, pp. 182-284; J.-D. KAESTLI & O. WERMELINGER (eds.), *Le canon de l'Ancien Testament. Sa formation et son histoire* (Le Monde de la Bible), Genève, 1984, pp. 40-45 (D. Barthélemy), 116-120 (É. Junod), 161-165 and 180-195 (O. Wermelinger).

Although this was not the original concern of the human authors and translators of the Bible, behind these diverging sequences one may detect a theological bias. The Hebrew canon is construed around the notion of revelation and the Word of the Lord. God's word was revealed to mankind in the Books of Moses or the Torah. This Law is the core of the revelation and the most venerable and authoritative part of the Bible. After Moses, other prophets in the history of religion proclaimed and reworded this Law in new situations. They are the mediators between the divine Word of the Torah and men. Their instructions and exhortations are the second part of the Hebrew Bible. The third part, including the Psalms, can be seen as the answer of men to God's word.

The order of the books in the Greek canon implies a different theological bias. It expresses a view on the historical aspects of revelation. Its first part is devoted to the past history of Israel. All the books related to that past are grouped together in chronological order. The second part includes Psalms and Wisdom, that is, the books dealing with present life in Israel. The third part is oriented towards the future. It contains the prophetical and apocalyptical books. This implies that the prophets are no longer considered as mediators of the divine word or "forth-tellers", but as "fore-tellers".

This rather straightforward picture of the Septuagint and its differences with MT overlooks a third major type of differences between MT and LXX: the textual differences between the Greek and the Hebrew within the respective books of the Bible. Moreover, it is implicitly based on the assumption of the questionable existence of a pre-Christian Alexandrian form of the Greek Bible in which the number and order of the books was identical with that of our critical editions of the Septuagint. Before turning to matters of textual difference, we have to focus on the notion of the Alexandrian canon.

2. Alexandrian Canon[2]

According to views widely spread in the nineteenth and twentieth centuries, the Jews in the Greek Diaspora, in the early years of Christianity, had a larger and less rigid canon of biblical books than that accepted by the Palestinian Jews. It comprised the books preserved in the

---

2. A.C. SUNDBERG, *The Old Testament of the Christian Church*, in *HTR* 51 (1958) 205-226; ID., *The Old Testament of the Christian Church* (Harvard Theological Studies, 20), Cambridge, MASS, 1964; ID., *"The Old Testament" : a Christian Canon*, in *CBQ* 30 (1968) 143-155, repr. in ID., *The Canon and Masorah of the Hebrew Bible*, ed. S.Z. LEIMAN, New York, 1974, pp. 99-111; DORIVAL, in *La Bible grecque des Septante* (n. 1), pp. 112-125.

ancient codices of the Septuagint. This canon was adopted by the Christians[3]. The second edition of O. Eissfeldt's leading introduction into the Old Testament (1956) strongly defended this theory. In a letter to P. Katz the author writes: "The second edition of my *Einleitung in das Alte Testament* has abandoned the opinion that our Hebrew Bible preserved the original order of the books and that the order in the Alexandrian collection was a transformation of this and merely secondary; and replaces it with the explanation that the extent of a collection of sacred writings as revealed in LXX is based on an older Jewish tradition which was later modified, particularly at the Council of Jamnia, by narrowing the Canon". Eissfeldt's decision to abandon his earlier position was due, firstly, to the essays of P. Katz, and secondly, to the discoveries in the Judaean desert, which, in Eissfeldt's view, clearly show that the indigenous Jewish community in and near Qumran knew a collection of sacred writings similar in extent to the LXX-Canon[4].

Against this thesis, Sundberg lists a series of objections[5] which can be outlined as follows: 1. There is a lack of primary evidence[6]. The main witnesses of the Alexandrian canon are the early Greek codices. The number and the order of the books preserved in them display minor variants. The earliest one, the *codex Vaticanus*, is to be dated to the fourth century of the Christian era. Like all the other early codices, it is a Christian work. 2. The hypothesis of an Alexandrian canon supposes that Alexandria had become a leading centre of Judaism. The historical sources deny this. 3. If the Church adopted the Alexandrian canon, that fact should be demonstrated in the close agreement of Christian usage of the OT and of Christian OT lists with respect to contents. However, the OT quoted in the NT and in the works of the Church Fathers, and the early OT lists, do not correspond to the alleged Alexandrian canon[7]. 4.

3. Sundberg traces the theory of the Alexandrian Canon back to J.S. SEMLER, *Abhandlung von freier Untersuchung des Canons nebst Antwort auf die tübingische Vertheidigung der Apokalypsis*, Halle, 1791 (= Texte zur Kirchen- und Theologiegeschichte, 5, Gütersloh, 1967).

4. P. KATZ, *The Old Testament in Palestine and in Alexandria*, in *ZNW* 47 (1956) 191-217, esp. 203 n. 19a; O. EISSFELDT, *Einleitung in das Alte Testament*, Tübingen, ²1956, p. 706 (§75, 4); the text on the canon remained unchanged in the third edition, translated into English by P. Ackroyd: *The Old Testament. An Introduction*, Oxford, 1966, p. 570.

5. SUNDBERG, *The Old Testament of the Christian Church* (n. 2), pp. 51-79.

6. See already R.H. PFEIFFER, *Introduction to the Old Testament*, New York, 1941, p. 68.

7. Concerning the OT quotations in the NT and in Qumran, and for further bibliography on this item, see J. LUST, *Mic 5,1-3 in Qumran and in the New Testament, and Messianism in the Septuagint*, in C.M. TUCKETT (ed.), *The Scriptures in the Gospels* (BETL, 131), Leuven, 1997, pp. 65-88. Concerning the canon in the early Christian Church, see the works mentioned in note 1, especially the contribution of É. JUNOD, *La formation et la composition de l'Ancien Testament dans l'Église grecque des quatre pre-*

The theory was posited on the assumption that the "deutero-canonical" or "apocryphal" books were composed originally in Greek. More recent research, largely based on the Qumran findings, shows that the great bulk of these books were in fact written in Hebrew or Aramaic, most likely in a Palestine environment.

Sundberg's remarks on the Qumran documents can now be updated. The pre-Christian biblical papyri, including the Qumran fragments, can be listed as follows:

- p942 or pFouad266: fragments of Gn 7; 38; see also p847 and 848[8].
- p805 or p7QLXXEx: Ex 28,4-7; 1-2 century BC[9].
- p801 or 4Q119 or 4QLXXLv[a]: Lv 26,2-16; 1-2 century BC[10].
- p802 or p4Q120 or 4QLXXLv[b]: Lv 2-5; first century BC[11].
- p803 or 4Q121 or 4QLXXNm: Nm 3,30–4,14; 1st century BC[12].
- p819 or 4Q122 or 4QLXXDt: Dt 11,4; second century BC[13].
- p847 or pFouad266: fragments of Dt 11; 31–33; first century BC.
- p848 or pFouad266: fragments of Dt 17–33; first century BC[14].
- p957 or pRyl.Gk.458: Dt 23–28; second century BC[15].
- p804 or p7QLXXEpJer: EpJer 43–44; second/first century BC[16].
- p943 or 8HevXIIgr: Minor Prophets; probably first century BC[17].

---

miers siècles, in KAESTLI & WERMELINGER (eds.), *Le canon de l'Ancien Testament* (n. 1), pp. 105-134; Junod reminds his readers of the fact that the Greek Church has never officially defined the canon of the Books of the Old Testament.

8. W.G. WADDELL, *The Tetragrammaton and LXX*, in *JTS* 45 (1944) 158-161.

9. *DJD* 3, Oxford, 1962, pp. 142-143.

10. Prel. publ.: P.W. SKEHAN, *The Qumran Manuscripts and Textual Criticism*, in *Volume du Congrès. Strasbourg 1956* (SVT, 4), Leiden, 1957, pp. 148-160, esp. 149-160; E. ULRICH, *The Greek Manuscripts of the Pentateuch from Qumran, Including Newly-Identified fragments of Deuteronomy*, in A. PIETERSMA & C. COX (eds.), *The Septuaginta. FS J.W. Wevers*, Mississauga, 1988, pp. 8-79. Official publication: E. ULRICH, in *DJD* 9, pp. 162-165.

11. Very fragmentary; see SKEHAN, *The Qumran Manuscripts and Textual Criticism* (n. 10), pp. 157-158, and ULRICH, *The Greek Manuscripts of the Pentateuch* (n. 10), pp. 79-80. Official publication: E. ULRICH, in *DJD* 9, pp. 167-186.

12. Very fragmentary; see SKEHAN, *The Qumran Manuscripts and Textual Criticism* (n. 10), pp. 155-157, and ID., *4QLXX Num: A Pre-Christian Reworking of the Septuagint*, in *HTR* 70 (1977) 39-50; ULRICH, *The Greek Manuscripts of the Pentateuch* (n. 10), pp. 80-81. Official publication: E. ULRICH, in *DJD* 9, pp. 187-194.

13. Prel. publ. ULRICH, *The Greek Manuscripts of the Pentateuch* (n. 10), pp. 71-82, esp. 74-75. Official publication: E. ULRICH, in *DJD* 9, pp. 195-197.

14. None of these fragments overlap with the Rylands papyri (p957). The preserved portions of p848 are more substantial than the others. A recent photographic edition has been taken care of by Z. ALY & L. KOENEN, *Three Scrolls of the Early Septuagint* (Papyrologische Texte und Abhandlungen, 27), Bonn, 1980.

15. The fragment has been published by C.H. ROBERTS, *Two Biblical Papyri in the John Rylands Library*, Manchester, 1936; = *BJRL* 20 (1936) 219-245.

16. Published in *DJD* 3, p. 143.

17. Prel. publ. by B. LIFSHITZ, *The Greek Documents of the Cave of Horror*, in *IEJ* 12 (1962) 201-207; *Yedi'ot* 26 (1962) 183-190; D. BARTHÉLEMY, *Les devanciers d'Aquila* (SVT, 10), Leiden, 1963. Official publication: E. TOV, in *DJD* 8, Oxford, 1990.

Apart from these fragments, our witnesses to the text of the Septuagint are exclusively Christian. It should be clear that the precious but scanty remainders of pre-Christian Greek biblical fragments do not give any positive support to an Alexandrian Canon supposedly including more books and following another order than the Hebrew Canon. Indeed, only one tiny fragment, p7QLXXEpJer, belongs to the so-called "deutero-canonical" books, but there is no proof whatsoever that it was accepted as canonical[18]. Moreover, within the Minor Prophets' scroll p943, the only preserved document of some length, the sequence of the books follows that of MT, not of LXX. Although this fact does not plead in favour of the existence of a Greek Canon, different from MT, it does not disprove its existence either, because the scroll does not contain the text of the Septuagint strictly speaking, but that of a recension towards the Hebrew text as preserved in MT[19].

Sundberg's critiques of the Alexandrian canon, adopted by most scholars, are sound. They are, however, basically concerned with its place of origin, and with the number and order of the books in that canon. They hardly deal with the text of the individual books. It is our contention that, in several instances, LXX preserved a form of the text that goes back to a pre-Christian Hebrew *Vorlage*. The Septuagint appears to be a witness to a form of the text that was highly respected in pre-Christian times, so much so that it was this form of the text that was deemed worthy of translation. This happened in a period in which the text was not yet strictly uniformed.

3. *Text and Canon*

Although we do not have any proof of an Alexandrian canon with regard to the number and order of the biblical books, we do have traces of a Septuagint canon in as far as the text of the individual books is concerned. In several instances the text of the books in the Greek Bible differs considerably from that in the Masoretic version of the Bible. Many of these divergences are clearly due to the Hebrew *Vorlage* used by the Greek translators, and not to changes brought in by the translators or later redactors, nor to errors in the course of the transmission of the text. This is generally accepted in the case of Jeremiah. 4QJer[b] preserved a fragment of a Hebrew text in which both the order of the text and the

18. About the canonical books in Qumran, see J. LUST, *Quotation Formulae and Canon in Qumran*, in A.VAN DER KOOIJ & K.VAN DER TOORN (eds.), *Canonization and Decanonization. Papers presented to the International Conference of the Leiden Institute for the Study of Religions (LISOR) Held at Leiden 9-10 January 1997* (Studies in the History of Religions, 82), Leiden, 1998, pp. 67-77.
19. BARTHÉLEMY, *Les devanciers d'Aquila* (n. 17), pp. 179-201.

vocabulary correspond to the Septuagint translation of Jeremiah. The Greek scrolls among the Dead Sea finds confirm this. Some of them are very similar to our Septuagint texts, but others are recensions towards MT, which strongly suggests that the original Greek version differed from MT[20].

It is impossible to give here a full survey of each and every difference within the respective books. Some of the major divergences can be categorised and listed as follows[21]:

a. Order. Within a particular book the sequence of chapters, or of verses within a chapter, may differ from that of the Hebrew:

- Genesis: towards the end of chapter 31, the order of verses 46-52 in LXX differs significantly from that in MT.
- Exodus: the sequence of chapters and verses within Ex 36–40, about the execution of the instructions concerning the mansion of the Lord, is considerably different.
- Joshua: the ceremony at Ebal and Gerizim in MT 8,30-35, is located immediately after the report on the hostile gathering of western kings (9,1-2) in LXX.
- 1 Kings: in several chapters, the verses are arranged differently, especially in chapters 4; 5–7, and 10–11, moreover, chapters 20 and 21 are inverted.
- Proverbs: within chapters 15–31, the order of chapters and verses differs.
- Jeremiah 25–51: Hebrew: the oracles against the nations are collected at the end of the book; Greek: in the middle; within chapter 10 the order is different.
- Ezekiel: in chapter 7,1-9 the arrangement of the two editions differs much. Moreover, in p967, the oldest and pre-hexaplaric witness to the Septuagint of Ezekiel, further important deviations occur: ch. 37 with the vision of the dry bones, is placed after the final battles against Gog in chapters 38–39.
- Daniel: in p967 chapters 5–6 are inserted between chapters 8 and 9.

b. Pluses and Minuses. Often the Greek text is shorter ("minuses"), or longer ("pluses").

Minuses:
- Exodus: chapters 36–40 do not only display a different order, they are also substantially shorter in LXX.

---

20. Further confirmation is found in the discussions of the early Fathers of the Church with the Jews. Justin's quotations of the Minor Prophets suggest that he used a text fairly identical with that of the manuscript from Nahal Hever; see BARTHÉLEMY, *Les devanciers d'Aquila* (n. 17), pp. 205-207.

21. Lists of differences between LXX and MT can be found in H.B. SWETE, *An Introduction to the Old Testament*, Cambridge, [2]1914, pp. 231-264: a. differences of sequence; b. differences of subject-matter; O. MUNNICH, *Le texte de la Septante et ses problèmes*, in *La Bible grecque des Septante* (n. 1), pp. 172-182: a. abbreviations and expansions; b. differences of sequence; c. LXX and MT, witnesses to two distinct textual traditions); J. TREBOLLE BARRERA, *La Biblia judia y la Biblia christiana*, Madrid, 1993, pp. 412-427, = *The Jewish Bible and the Christian Bible*, Leiden, 1998, pp. 390-404.

- Joshua: LXX omits 20,4-6.
- The Septuagint version of the story of David and Goliath in 1 Sam 17–18 is about 50 percent shorter than MT.
- 1 Chronicles: 1,10-16.17b-23 are wanting in LXX (Ms B).
- The list in Neh 11, 25-35 (2 Esdr 21) and 12,4-41 are considerably shorter.
- Proverbs: a number of verses in MT do not have a direct equivalent in LXX.
- Job: the text of LXX Job in its pre-hexaplaric version is much shorter than MT. In the critical editions of LXX, the hexaplaric additions are marked with an asterisk.
- Again, the case of Jeremiah is most clear. Its LXX translation is about 15 percent shorter than MT.

Pluses:
- Deuteronomy: in the Song of Moses, the last four distychs of MT (32,43) correspond to eight distychs in LXX.
- Joshua: pluses occur in 24,42a-d, and at the end of the book, in 24,31a and 33a.b.
- 1 Kings: in this book LXX contains a variety of large pluses: most important are: chapter 2,35a-o. 46a-l; 8,53a (poetic summary of 8,12-13); 12,24a-z; 16,28a-h.
- 2 Kings: 1,18a-d.
- 2 Chronicles: 35,19a-d; 36,2a-c.4a.5a-d.
- Esther: the Greek text, both in its LXX and in its Alpha-version contains large additions, usually numbered A-F.
- Proverbs: a number of Greek verses do not have a direct equivalent in MT.
- Jeremiah: the Greek text includes Bar 1,1–3,8.
- Daniel: the Greek text, both in its LXX and in its Theodotion version, has three longer supplements: the stories of Bel and the Dragon and of Suzannah, and the hymn at the end of chapter 3.

c. Other differences of subject matter

In several instances, LXX and MT appear to contain different interpretations of the text. Systematic revisions, responsible for particular divergences spread over several books or over the Bible as a whole, are hardly to be detected. Most of the interpretative deviations are confined to particular books or to particular passages in those books. "Messianism" is an interesting theme in as far as possible encompassing modifications are concerned. Several scholars hold that LXX accentuates the messianic expectations in the Bible. In several contributions I argued that this was not the case, at least in as far as the expectation is concerned of an individual royal messiah[22].

Many interpretative differences are due to adaptations to a new historical situation. Often, these re-interpretations appear to be due to the scribes of the Hebrew texts used by the translators, or to the translators themselves. Not infrequently, however, they seem to have been pro-

22. For references see J. LUST, *Messianism in Ezekiel in Hebrew and in Greek: Ezek 21:15(10) and 18(13)*, in FS E. Tov (forthcoming).

duced by the editors of MT, or to the revised character of their manuscripts.

In several books with a rather free translation, these differences are
due to interpretations of the Hebrew preserved in MT, either by the translators or by the editors of the Hebrew manuscripts laying before them.
The Septuagint translation of Isaiah offers good examples of such adaptations. The work of A. van der Kooij on this topic is particularly significant[23].

In books displaying a more literal translation, the differences are most
often not to be ascribed to interventions of the translator, but to adaptations of the Hebrew text, either in the *Vorlage* of LXX or in MT. An interesting example can be found in Ez 24,15-24 and Ezekiel's wife. The
Hebrew text of the passage contains a remarkable note about the death
of the prophet's wife[24]. The Greek shows some minor, but rather important deviations from the Hebrew text, the most striking being that the
Greek does not mention the death of the prophet's wife. Indeed, it does
not mention her at all.

In as far as all these differences are due to the Hebrew manuscripts,
preferred by the editors of MT, or to those carefully selected for translation, they may be qualified as normative or "canonical" in the Jewish
communities responsible for their selection. When the differences are
due to the translators, however, or to later editorial work on the
Septuagint, other factors come into play. In this context the idea of inspiration may be important.

4. *Canon and Inspiration*

The notions of canon and inspiration are closely related. The introduction to the Holy Scriptures of A. Robert and A. Feuillet presents "the
biblical Canon as the collection of books inspired by God"[25], the criterion of canonicity being the inspiration of the holy books[26]. To my
knowledge the first explicit attestation of the link between canonicity
and inspiration is found in Josephus' works. He notes that religious
books are accepted as belonging to the Bible because their authors, the

23. See recently A. VAN DER KOOIJ, *The Oracle of Tyre. The Septuaginta of Isaiah 23
as Version and Vision* (SVT, 71), Leiden, 1998.
24. See J. LUST, *The Delight of Ezekiel's Eyes. Ez 24:15-24 in Hebrew and in Greek*,
in B. TAYLOR (ed.), *X Congress of the IOSCS, Oslo 1998* (SBL SCS, 51), Atlanta, GA,
2001, pp. 1-26.
25. A. ROBERT & A. FEUILLET, *Interpreting the Scriptures*, New York, 1969, p. 33
(updated version of *Introduction à la Bible*, Vol. 1, Paris - Tournai, 1959).
26. *Ibid.*, p. 51.

prophets, are inspired[27]. Around the same period, the notion of inspiration and its link with the canonicity of a book or text is implicitly present in the use of quotation formulae in the Qumranic literature and in the NT[28]. Later on, in the Roman Church, the relation between canon and inspiration is clearly stated in the decree on revelation of the First Vatican Council: "The Church regards the books of the Old and New Testament as sacred and canonical, not because... they were approved by her authority, nor because they contain revelation without error, but because, written under the inspiration of the Holy Spirit, they have God for their author"[29].

I do not intend to give here a full survey of the relation between the two notions as described in the classical treaties. My point is that this relation was considered to be significant not only for the Hebrew Bible, but also for the Septuagint. Philo does not tell us the exact sequence or number of the books of the Torah that were translated, but he carefully emphasizes the inspired and prophetic character of the translation[30]. This implies that according to him, the Greek text preserved in the individual books was to be accepted as normative, because of its inspired character. The early Fathers of the Christian Church shared that view and applied it to the Bible as a whole. Later on, the fact that the role played in the Church by the Greek version had been forgotten, encouraged theologians to reject the inspiration of the Septuagint. In the middle of the twentieth century, scholars such as P. Benoit and P. Auvray re-animated the theory[31] and looked with favour upon the idea of an overall inspiration of the LXX.

The main conclusion for our topic is that the books of the Septuagint can be considered as inspired, and thus canonical, not only in as far as the text of their *Vorlage* is concerned, but also in respect to the work of the translators. Of course, much then depends on the respective religious communities and their interpretation of inspiration.

The second part of this paper is devoted to the study of some differences between LXX and MT within the book of Ezekiel. It is our conten-

---

27. Josephus, *Contra Apionem* I,38: "the prophets alone had this privilege, obtaining their knowledge through the inspiration which they owed to God".

28. See, e.g., LUST, *Quotation Formulae* (n. 18), pp. 67-77.

29. *De Fontibus revelationis*, canon 4: Denzinger, *Enchiridion symbolorum* (1787).

30. *De Vita Moysis* II,37.

31. P. BENOIT, *La Septante est-elle inspirée?*, in *Vom Wort des Lebens*. FS Meinertz, Münster, 1951, pp. 41-49, = ID., *Exégèse et théologie*, t. 1, Paris, 1961, pp. 3-12; ID., *L'inspiration des Septante d'après les Pères*, in *L'homme devant Dieu*. FS H. de Lubac, t. 1, Paris, 1963, p.169-187, = ID., *Exégèse et théologie*, t. 3, Paris, 1968, p. 69-89; P. AUVRAY, *Comment se pose le problème de l'inspiration de la Septante?*, in *RB* (1952) 321-336; see ROBERT & FEUILLET, *Interpreting the Scriptures* (n. 25), p. 28.

tion that many of these differences are not due to the translators, but to the Hebrew manuscript chosen for translation.

B. THE SHORTER SEPTUAGINT TEXT OF EZEKIEL

The Greek translation of Ezekiel is notably shorter than MT. When one considers the critical editions, the phenomenon is not as obvious as in Jeremiah. In Ezekiel the combined minuses of LXX do not amount to more than 4-5% of the text[32]. This picture changes when one takes into account the minuses in papyrus 967[33]. H.S. Gehman, one of its editors, concluded that of all our Greek Mss, this papyrus preserved a text of Ezekiel closest to the original LXX. In his view, the authority of the *codex Vaticanus* as our best source for the original text must yield to this new evidence. Gehman's high esteem of p967 has been corroborated by Ziegler[34], Payne[35], and has received general adherence. This does not apply to the "minuses" in the papyrus. They have most often been labelled as omissions or corruptions due to *parablepsis*. Elsewhere, I refuted this view and defended the thesis that the three longer minuses (Ez 12,26-28; 32,25-26; 36,23b-38) are not due to errors of scribes or translators. They are witnesses to an earlier Hebrew text in which these sections were not yet added. A fourth set of omissions, in ch. 7, witnessed by all major Mss of LXX, confirms this. Here we do not have to repeat the full argumentation. Our main objective is to point out the

32. E. Tov, *Recensional Differences Between the MT and LXX of Ezekiel*, in *ETL* 62 (1986) 89-101; J. Lust, *The Use of Textual Witnesses for the Establishment of the Text*, in Id. (ed.), *Ezekiel and His Book. Textual and Literary Criticism and Their Interrelations* (BETL, 74), Leuven, 1986, pp. 7-20.

33. The edition of p967 is spread over several books and periods: F.G. Kenyon, *The Chester Beatty Biblical Papyri: Ezekiel* (Fasc. 7), London, 1937; A.C. Johnson, H.S. Gehman & E.H. Kase, *The John H. Scheide Biblical Papyri: Ezekiel*, Princeton, 1938; L.G. Jahn, *Der griechische Text des Buches Ezechiel, nach dem Kölner Teil des Papyrus 967* (Papyrologische Texte und Abhandlungen, 15), Bonn, 1972; M. Fernandez-Galiano, *Nuevas Paginas del codice 967 del A.T. griego*, in *Studia Papyrologica* 10 (1971) 7-76. Fernandez-Galiano (p. 15) mentions three major omissions: 12,26-28; 36,23b-38; 38–39. He overlooked that, although chs. 38–39 are missing in the leaves published by him, they were not missing in the manuscript as a whole. Their transposition is to be studied together with the absence of 36,23b-38. Two of the longer omissions received full attention from F.V. Filson, *The Omission of Ezek 12,26-28 and 36,23b-38 in Codex 967*, in *JBL* 62 (1943) 27-32. The third one, 32,24-26, is most often overlooked. The text of p967 is supported by the *Vetus latina Codex Wirceburgensis*, see P.-M. Bogaert, *Le témoignage de la Vetus Latina dans l'étude de la Septante: Ézéchiel et Daniel dans le p967*, in *Bib* 59 (1978) 384-395.

34. J. Ziegler, *Ezechiel* (Septuaginta: Vetus Testamentum Graecum, 16), Göttingen, 1952, p. 28; Id., *Die Bedeutung der Chester Beatty-Scheide Papyrus 967 für die Textüberlieferung der Ezechiel-Septuaginta*, in *ZAW* 61 (1945-48) 76-94.

35. J. Barton Payne, *The Relationship of the Chester Beatty Papyri of Ezekiel to Codex Vaticanus*, in *JBL* 68 (1949) 251-265.

common tendencies in MT's pluses. The four sections in question appear to deal with eschatological times, proposing a specific view on these matters.

C. IRRELEVANT PROPHECY

1. *The Minus in 12,26-28: An Evaluation*[36]

Before turning to the omission itself, a short survey of its context is in order. In MT, and in the traditional text of LXX, chapter 12 ends with two disputes. The first (12,21-25) begins with the revelation formula opening a major new section. The dispute proper opens with a quote, and deals with prophecy in general, especially with the lack of true prophecy. It prepares for the theme of false prophecy developed in the following chapter. The second dispute (12,26-28), missing in p967, interrupts this connection. Indeed, its theme is that of Ezekiel's visions on the final days, and not that of true and false prophecy in general. The section is probably an insert.

The inserted dispute is most likely concerned with the eschatological or apocalyptic dimensions of Ezekiel's prophecies[37]. The expressions "for distant times" and "for many years ahead", used in the objection quoted in v. 27, point in that direction. The answer in the following verse either suggests that the apocalyptic times are to be identified with the present, or that Ezekiel's words and visions are not eschatological nor apocalyptic, but refer to the present. It "historicizes" Ezekiel's preaching. This should be seen against the background of the fact that the authorities responsible for the Hebrew "canon" appear to have been suspicious in matters of "apocalyptics". The only apocalyptic book that passed their critical judgment was Daniel. It was, however, not admitted among the other books as "prophecy", but as "wisdom". The "plus" in Ez 12,26-28 may have been inserted in order to answer objections against the admission of Ezekiel, with its apocalyptic-coloured visions. A comparison with the other major "pluses" in MT-Ezekiel sheds more light on this.

---

36. FILSON, *The Omission* (n. 33), p. 28. The commentaries do not pay much attention to the problem. L.C. ALLEN, *Ezekiel 1–19* (WBC), Waco, TX, 1994, p. 188 notes that the omission of vv. 26-28 in LXX[967] does not appear to be significant for the Hebrew text. With Filson, he opines that the omission most probably occurred by *parablepsis*. K.-F. POHLMANN, *Der Prophet Hesekiel* (ATD, 21/1), Göttingen, 1996, p. 172, shares that opinion. Earlier, W. ZIMMERLI, *Ezechiel* (BKAT, 13), Neukirchen, 1969, p. 281 expressed a similar verdict. D.I. BLOCK, *The Book of Ezekiel*, vol. 1 (NICOT), Grand Rapids, MI, 1997, and M. GREENBERG, *Ezekiel 1-20* (AB), Garden City, NY, 1983, do not seem to notice the feature.

37. See G. FOHRER, *Ezechiel* (HAT, 13), Tübingen, 1955, pp. 67-68.

2. Elam in the Netherworld: Ez 32,24-26[38]

This second long minus belongs to an oracle against Egypt announcing its descent into Scheol. The middle section of this oracle, vv. 22-30, offers a litany-like panorama of gentile dead that preceded Egypt into Sheol. In this instance the critical editions of LXX, largely based on the text of the major codices, also present a shorter text than MT, but the minus in p967 is more extensive.

In MT verses 22-30 list the following nations that preceded Egypt in the Netherworld: Assyria (22-23), Elam (24-25), Meshech-Tubal (26-28), Edom (29), the northern princes and the Sidonians (30). The basis for the entries in this international roll is not clear. In v. 28 the list is unexpectedly interrupted by a direct address to Pharaoh, between the sections about Meshech-Tubal and Edom.

The shorter Greek text of these verses in p967 is structured differently. It distinguishes between two nations only: Assyria (22-23) and Elam (24-27), and between their leaders: the princes of Assyria (29) and/or the princes of the North (30). The direct address to Pharaoh (v. 28) figures right in the middle, and calls for attention.

The main difference with MT is of course that the Greek is much shorter than the Hebrew. In a first reading, the pluses in MT, vv. 25 and 26, may seem to be simple doublets, shorter variants of v. 24. But a closer reading reveals that there is much more to it. Meshech and Tubal and their shame figure in the pluses of MT. More divergences occur in the immediate context.

A further investigation suggests that the reasons for the insert in LXX[Z] and in MT are similar to those detected in chapter 12. They appear to be related to diverging views on the eschaton and on apocalyptics.

In this context, the mention of Meshech and Tubal may be significant. In the eschatological battle described in Ez 38,2.3 and 39,1 the two also occur as a pair, in the same order, as allies of Gog[39]. Exegetes find it dif-

---

38. H.VAN DYKE PARUNAK, *Structural Studies in Ezekiel*, Ann Arbor, Univ. Microfilms (diss. Harvard), 1978, pp. 406-421; L. BOADT, *Ezekiel's Oracles against Egypt: A Literary and Philological Study of Ezekiel 29-30* (BibOr, 37), Rome, 1980, pp. 150-168; B. GOSSE, *Le recueil d'oracles contre les nations d'Ézéchiel XXV-XXXII dans la rédaction du livre d'Ézéchiel*, in *RB* 93 (1986) 535-562; ID., *Ez 32,17-32 dans le cadre du recueil des oracles contre les nations*, in ID., *Isaïe 13,1–14,23* (OBO, 78), Freiburg - Göttingen, 1988, pp. 170-199; J.B. BURNS, *The Consolation of Pharaoh, Ez 32,17-32*, in *Proceedings Eastern Great Lakes and Midwest Biblical Societies* 16 (1996) 121-125. For text-critical notes see the commentaries: ZIMMERLI, *Ezechiel* (n. 35), pp. 776-778; ALLEN, *Ezekiel 1–19* (n. 36), p. 135; M. GREENBERG, *Ezekiel 21–37* (AB), New York, 1997, pp. 659-660; BLOCK, *The Book of Ezekiel* (n. 36), pp. 219-222; see also D. BARTHÉLEMY, *Critique textuelle de l'Ancien Testament* (OBO, 50/3), Fribourg - Göttingen, 1992, pp. 261-270.

39. In 27,13 they occur in a different order; see also Gen 10,2.

ficult to detect the historical events underlying the reference to the pair Meshech and Tubal. In fact, in chapters 38 and 39 no such historical reference is intended. Meshech and Tubal belong to the more mythical realm and represent forces of the apocalyptic period. In the masoretic text of Ez 32, however, they are put on one line with Assur (v. 22) and Elam (v. 24) which are two nations that dominated the political scene in the recent past. This strongly suggests that the editors of MT attempted to bring them down to the historical level.

In a further support to that attempt, they explicitly assimilated them with the shame of the uncircumcised (vv. 24.25.30), and dissociated them from the *gibbôrîm* (v. 27). In v. 27 MT has a negation without equivalent in the Greek: "And they do *not* lie with the fallen warriors". The *gibbôrîm* or mighty warriors are portrayed as lying in Sheol, but Pharaoh and his hordes, as well as the other nations, will not lie with them. According to MT, the *gibbôrîm* are heroes, entitled to special treatment in the Netherworld. They are not to be mixed with the shame of the uncircumcised[40]. In order to make this clear, MT inserts a negation, absent from the Greek. A similar distinction between the *gibbôrîm* and the uncircumcised was already evoked in MT vv. 19-21. The more original text of v. 21 is preserved in LXX. There the warriors, called giants in the Greek, taunt the Egyptians asking "do you think to be better than we? Come down and lie with the uncircumcised". MT transposes the question to v. 19, taking it out of the mouth of the giants who are again dissociated from the uncircumcised. The Greek has a different appreciation of these beings. It connects them more clearly with the prehistorical *gibbôrîm* mentioned in Gen 6,4. The connection is given not only in the translation (γίγας "giant"), but also in their qualification as ἀπ᾽ αἰῶνος ("of old"), which occurs exclusively in Ez 32,27 and in Gen 6,4. In LXX the giants do not seem to deserve special esteem, and are not to be distinguished from the uncircumcised[41]. At least to some extent, they are seen as responsible for the corruption of mankind on earth. "Their iniquities cling to their bones" (v. 27)[42].

This succinct discussion of the long minus in Ez 32,24-26 leads to the suggestion that p967 preserved the earliest text form. The editors of MT

---

40. נפלים מערלים most likely qualifies the subject of the sentence: "those fallen among the uncircumcised do not lie with the mighty".

41. In MT מערלים replaces מעולם the Hebrew equivalent of ἀπ᾽ αἰῶνος.

42. This phrase fits perfectly the description of the giants in several manuscripts of LXX. In p967 and in the main codices, however, it has been applied to the uncircumcised going down to Sheol. The sentence returns unaltered in MT where it creates tensions with the changed context. For want of a better option, exegetes tend to correct עונתם ("their iniquities") into צנתם ("their shields"). The correction was first proposed by Cornill, and is accepted in the major recent commentaries of Zimmerli, Greenberg, Allen, and Block.

adapted it to their special views on eschatological and apocalyptic themes. They inserted sections on the mythological kingdoms of Meshech and Tubal, aligning them with the historical enemies Assur and Elam, and with Edom which symbolizes Israel's major enemy in the times of the editor of MT. In doing so the editor may have tried to suggest that nations, such as Meshech and Tubal, mentioned in the final battle of chs. 38–39, are no mysterious apocalyptic entities, but historical agents. He probably made an attempt to bring Ezekiel's visions down to earth.

A comparison with the long plus detected in the final verses of ch 12 points in a similar direction. We noted that in 12,21 the prophet begins a dispute about false prophecy, which continues in chapter 13. In MT this dispute is disturbed by an insert (vv. 26-28), absent from p967. In this "plus" the attention is shifted towards Ezekiel's preaching about the final times[43]. As in 32,24-26, MT's addition in 12,26-28 is an almost literal repeat of the immediately foregoing section. Nevertheless, it clearly sets new accents, strongly suggesting that Ezekiel's preaching is not for remote eschatological times, but rather for the present. We will see that similar interests lay behind the intervention of the editor of the final verses of ch. 36 in MT.

D. PRELUDE TO THE VISION OF THE DRY BONES? Ez 36,23Bβ-38

Almost hundred years ago Thackeray argued that the Greek of Ez 36,23bβ-38 differs from that of the rest of Ezekiel[44]. Students of p967, in which the section in question is missing, have inevitably been reminded of Thackeray's observation. Kase and Irwin were the first to suggest that the passage must have been lacking in the Hebrew text used by the translator[45]. Many others tended to treat this minus as *parablepsis*. In 1981 I rejected that solution, defending the case of the originality of the short version[46]. There is no need to repeat the full argumen-

---

43. See J. LUST, *Textual Criticism of the Old and New Testaments: Stepbrothers?*, in A. DENAUX (ed.), *New Testament Textual Criticism and Exegesis*. FS J. Delobel (BETL, 161), Leuven, 2002, pp. 15-31.

44. See H. St. J. THACKERAY, *The Greek Translators of Ezekiel*, in *JTS* 4 (1902-03) 398-411. Ez 36,23 can be subdivided as follows:

23aα	וְקִדַּשְׁתִּי אֶת־שְׁמִי הַגָּדוֹל הַמְחֻלָּל בַּגּוֹיִם
23aβ	אֲשֶׁר חִלַּלְתֶּם בְּתוֹכָם
23bα	וְיָדְעוּ הַגּוֹיִם כִּי־אֲנִי יְהוָה נְאֻם אֲדֹנָי יְהוִה
23bβ	בְּהִקָּדְשִׁי בָכֶם לְעֵינֵיהֶם

45. JOHNSON, GEHMAN & KASE, *The John H. Scheide Biblical Papyri* (n. 33), p. 10; W.A. IRWIN, *Ezekiel*, Chicago, 1943, p. 62-65.

46. J. LUST, *Ezekiel 36–40 in the Oldest Greek Manuscript*, in *CBQ* 43 (1981) 517-531.

tation here. A brief summary may suffice. (1) The section beginning in 36,16 ends in 36,23bα with the recognition formula; verses 23bβ-38, absent from p967, are an appendix. (2) An omission of 1451 letters is too long for an accidental skip of the scribe's eye. (3) An omission of this length is unprecedented in the papyrus. (4) Not even the most absent minded scribe would have overlooked a passage so rich in theological meaning. (5) A closer investigation into the language of the section, both in Greek and in Hebrew, reveals that it is different from that of the more original parts of Ezekiel. It points to an editorial hand other than the ones responsible for the rest of the book. (6) If this were an accidental omission, v. 23bα should have been followed by 37,1, not by 38,1, with ch. 37 in p967 following after ch. 39. (7) Finally, the order of the chapters in p967 has its own logic. Changing that order, MT had to insert 36,23bβ-38 in order to prepare for the transposed chapter 37, with its vision of the infusion of the Lord's spirit into the dry bones of Israel.

A comparison with the two other longer minuses shows striking parallels. In all of them the additions in the Hebrew are largely composed of materials found elsewhere in Ezekiel. Moreover, in the three longer pluses a similar theological interest can be detected. In all of them the editor seems to have tried to downplay the eschatological and apocalyptic tendencies in the book of Ezekiel. In order to discover this implication in 36,23bβ-38, one has to look at the larger context. In p967, chapter 36 is immediately followed by an apocalyptic scene in chapters 38–39. These chapters describe the apocalyptic battle of Gog, chief prince of Meshech and Tubal, against the people of the Lord. The war is terrible and leaves nothing but corpses. The battle report is then followed by a resurrection scene and the announcement of the coming of the messiah: king David (chapter 37). Finally, chapters 40–48 offer a visionary description of the New Ideal Israel and the New Temple in Jerusalem. The editor of MT appears to have diminished the apocalyptic implications of this composition. He put the scene of the dry bones before the battle against Gog. In order to fit this revitalisation scene in its new position, he added a section to chapter 36, in which he announced that the Lord was going to put his spirit within his corrupt people. The suggestion for the audience was that Israel was morally dead, not physically[47].

E. The End and the ṢEFIRAH in Ez 7,1-11

An other important minus, or better, a set of minuses and transpositions, is to be found in Ez 7,1-11. This chapter belongs to the first part of

47. See LUST, *Textual Criticism* (n. 43), pp. 28-31.

Ezekiel which is not preserved in p967. A detailed study has been devoted to it by P.-M. Bogaert[48]. The chapter announces the final day:
"The end has come upon the four corners of the land".

1. The main pluses in MT are the following phrases: v. 5b: "An evil, a
singular evil, see it is coming"; 6b-7a: "the end is coming; it is ripe for
you! See it is coming: the *ṣefirah*"; 10b: "see it has come, the *ṣefirah*
has come forth"; 11c: "and there is no *noah* among them". All these
pluses specify the evil that is coming at the end of the days.

2. The composition in LXX displays a strictly concentric structure. The
end of verse 6 occupies central position: "(I am) the one who strikes (ὁ
τύπτων)". This theme prepares for the vision in ch.9, the only other instance in which this participle occurs (9,5.7.8). The role of the Lord is
emphasized. His punishing action is situated on the "day of the Lord"
(v. 10).

MT presents a reshuffling of the materials. Its structure is also concentric, but more complex. Vv. 3-6 of LXX are transposed and are in MT
vv. 6-9; and vv. 7-9 of LXX are equally transposed and are in MT vv. 3-5.
The central and final notion in MT, the coming of the cryptic *ṣefirah*, is
absent from LXX.

3. The pluses in MT use some words that are new in this context:
צפירה / רעה / אחת. The rare term צפירה receives an emphasis, being
used twice, in a central position, and at the end. Whereas in LXX emphasizes the punishing role of the Lord and the day of the Lord, MT draws
the attention to the צפירה, the instrument of the Lord's fury. The day of
the Lord is not mentioned explicitly in MT.

Given the literal character of the translation, it may be taken for
granted that the differences are not due to the translator. This implies
that they were already present in the Hebrew *Vorlage* of LXX. The comparison between both texts demonstrates that a reorganisation of the materials took place within MT, in order to bring to the fore a new element:
the coming of the צפירה. The identification of this cryptic figure may
give us some information about the historical background of the editors
of MT. In Dan 8,5 the image of the צפיר or "he-goat" refers to Alexander. Inspired by this model, the editor of MT-Ezekiel may have applied
the same image to the Greek people, using the feminine genre. The editor presents a re-reading of the text from his historical point of view, after the events during the reign of Antiochus IV. Additional parallels with
Daniel's report on these events confirm this. In Dan 9,12-14 the coming
of the same Greek empire is described in terms of "a great evil", using

---

48. P.-M. BOGAERT, *Les deux rédactions conservées (LXX et TM) d'Ézéchiel 7*, in
LUST, *Ezekiel and His Book* (n. 32), pp. 21-47.

אחת in a sense very similar to that in Ez 7,6. The use of רעה in Ez 7,6 may then allude to the one horn of the he-goat in Dan 8,9 that refers to Antiochus IV.

F. CONCLUSIONS

1. There is no evidence of an Alexandrian Canon as opposed to a Palestinian Canon. The preserved data do not allow us to draw the conclusion that the Jewish communities in Egypt recognized a larger Canon than MT, comprising more biblical books in a different order.

2. There is sufficient evidence in favour of a less narrow pre-Masoretic Canon in as far as the text of the respective biblical books is concerned. The Septuagint, supported by the Qumranic data, pleads in favour of this assumption. The selection of the manuscripts, used for translation, proves that they were recognized as authoritative, even when they differed from those later accepted as canonical in MT.

3. Theories about the inspiration of the translators support the view that divergences from the Hebrew, due to conscious interventions of the translators, can also be accepted as authoritative.

4. In Ezekiel, the shorter text of LXX, as preserved in p967, offers a good example of a witness to an earlier "canonical" Hebrew text with its own theological accents, differing from those in MT.

van 't Sestichstraat 34   Johan LUST
B-3000 Leuven

QUMRAN AND THE CANON OF THE OLD TESTAMENT

The purpose of this paper is to reassess current views on the canon of the Hebrew Scriptures in light of the new manuscript evidence provided by the discovery of the Qumran scrolls. For clarity in this paper I will present my conclusions first in the form of theses, followed by the evidence and arguments which I believe form the basis of those theses. The conclusions have emerged from my attempt at neutral empirical study of the text of the scriptural scrolls from Qumran for their critical editions.

I. CANON

Thesis 1. It is essential that a clear definition of "canon" be established as the basis of discussion; otherwise, discussion cannot proceed.

One of Plato's legacies to the civilized world is the clarity achieved by defining what we are talking about. In the *Meno* and the *Phaedrus*, Socrates insists on clear definitions in order to gain precision and solid bases for advancing the argument:

> You say this and that about virtue, but what *is* it?
> I believe we rejected the type of answer that employs terms which are still in question and not yet agreed upon....
> ... to define so-and-so, and thus to make plain whatever may be chosen as the topic for exposition. For example, take the definition given just now..., it was that which enabled our discourse to achieve lucidity and consistency[1].

There is confusion in many discussions of canon recently, at times because the term is not sharply defined, at times because authors present definitions that others do not agree with, and at times because some discussions seem to be more directed toward reaching a previously held conclusion than toward accurately describing the evidence.

The definition I present here I intend to be simply the articulation of how the term has been used in theological discussions traditionally. If there are elements missing or not precise, I would eagerly welcome supplements or amendments and suggest that we use that revised definition.

---

1. Plato, *Meno* 75d and 79d, and *Phaedrus* 265d, in E. HAMILTON & J. CAIRNS (eds.), *The Collected Dialogues of Plato*, tr. W. K. C. GUTHRIE & R. HACKFORTH, Princeton, 1961, pp. 362 and 511.

My purpose is to put forward a fully adequate definition that all can agree on, so that our discourse can "achieve lucidity and consistency".

Thesis 2. "Canon", in the sense of the canon of Scripture, is a "technical term in theology designating the collection of inspired books that composes Holy Scripture and forms the rule of faith"[2]. It is the definitive list of inspired, authoritative books which constitute the recognized and accepted body of sacred Scripture, forming the rule of faith of a major religious group, that definitive list being the result of inclusive and exclusive decisions after serious deliberation and wide endorsement by the community.

To arrive at this definition I consulted a number of theological dictionaries, making sure that the selection included Jewish, Catholic, and Protestant dictionaries as well as dictionaries in English, French, German, and Spanish. I have listed these definitions in Appendix 1. My selection was not exhaustive, but I think it was fairly representative. I did not exclude any definitions, for example, because they did not agree with my views. Not every definition is complete in itself, because there are so many aspects to the concept that seldom can they all be included; but none of the definitions conflicts with another. From the collection I believe the following description emerges; again, I would welcome any efforts toward greater precision.

The term is a technical term and thus not open to negotiation or manipulation, just as the notion of "square" is not. It is post-biblical and Christian (though the idea originates in Judaism's growing reverence for the Torah and the Prophets)[3], and it includes a number of factors, all of which must be present to use the term accurately. Although it means both "rule" and "list", the meaning "list" predominates in the discussions, and virtually always when there is discussion of "the canon of the Scripture", it is the contents of the list, not their authoritative quality that is the primary focus. In antiquity the list involves books (not, I would add, the textual form of the books). The list of books is closed or delimited: certain books had been recognized and accepted, through sifting or debate according to current criteria, as belonging on the list, and other books had finally been consciously and intentionally excluded. There was a lengthy process whose end was the canon; and it is inaccurate, anachronistic, and confusing to use the term canon for any of the

2. K. RAHNER & H. VORGRIMLER, *Theological Dictionary*, ed. C. ERNST, tr. R. STRACHAN, New York, 1965, p. 65.

3. For practical purposes, B.M. METZGER, *The Canon of the New Testament: Its Origin, Development, and Significance*, Oxford, 1987, p. v, is correct that "the word 'canon' is Greek; its use in connection with the Bible belongs to Christian times; the idea of a canon of Scripture originates in Judaism".

stages along that trajectory until the end of the process had been reached. Prior to the establishment of the canon one should speak of "the canonical process" or "the road toward canon".

Thesis 3. The notion of canon includes, among others, three important aspects highlighted by Qumran: It involves books, not the specific textual form of the books; it entails reflective judgment; and the canonical list excludes as well as includes books.

I hasten to say that the evidence from Qumran did not add these aspects to the concept of canon; it merely brings the traditional aspects into sharper view. In fact, a principal thesis of this paper is that the definition of canon is an ancient and stable technical term that does not and should not change from time to time.

a. The Book, Not Its Specific Textual Form, Is Canonical

As the definitions of canon amply illustrate, discussions of canon focus on the book considered as a literary opus, not the textual form of the opus. It is the book that is canonical, and there is no attention paid to the particular wording or textual form of the opus. Both in ancient Judaism and in Christianity it is the book of Jeremiah, for example, that is canonical, not the textual form – LXX vs. MT – of the book. For the rabbis it was scrolls, i.e., books, which made the hands unclean[4]. The Mishnah discusses the permissibility of different languages, scripts, materials, and even blank spaces[5], but I have not found any awareness of a concern about variant textual forms of a given book.

Bruce Metzger argues the same point for the Christian canon:

> Eusebius and Jerome, well aware of such variation in the witnesses, discussed which form of text was to be preferred. It is noteworthy, however, that neither Father suggested that one form was canonical and the other was not. Furthermore, the perception that the canon was basically closed did not lead to a slavish fixing of the text of the canonical books.
> Thus, the category of 'canonical' appears to have been broad enough to include all variant readings (as well as variant renderings in early versions)…
> In short, it appears that the question of canonicity pertains to the document *qua* document, and not to one particular form or version of that document[6].

b. Canon Entails Reflective Judgment

In philosophy a reflective judgment is one that is made retrospectly, looking backward and consciously recognizing and explicitly affirming

---

4. *M. Yad.* 3,5; 4,6.
5. *M. Meg.* 1,8; 2,1; *m. Yad.* 3,4; 4,5.
6. METZGER, *The Canon* (n. 3), pp. 269-270.

that which has already come to be. It represents the difference between sense experience and judgment, the difference between pre-conceptual knowledge and scientific knowledge, the difference between living and "the examined life". Thus, the Jewish community for centuries handed down sacred writings which increasingly functioned as authoritative books, but it was not until problematic situations arose, questions were asked, debates joined, and official decisions made that there came to be what we can properly call a canon. "The simple practice of living with the conviction that certain books are binding for our community is a matter of authoritativeness. The reflective judgment, when a group formally decides that it is a constituent requirement that these books which have been exercising authority are henceforth binding, is a judgment concerning canon"[7].

c. The Canonical List Excludes as well as Includes Books

As we saw, the canon is a closed list; certain books are intentionally included, others intentionally excluded. As Bruce Metzger says, the closing of the canon "was a task, not only of collecting, but also of sifting and rejecting"[8]. And as John Barton says, "The crucial element is the question of *closure*... A 'canon' is thus by definition a way of setting *limits* to the books recognized as holy"[9]. Simply having books that are binding for the community is again a matter of authoritativeness; after the reflective judgment and official decision that these books *but not those books* are henceforth authoritative, the community has a canon.

II. PROBLEMS AFFECTING CANON

Thesis 4. One of the problems in the discussion of canon is the mentality or presuppositions of scholars.

In discussions such as ours it is appropriate to operate as a religious historian, as distinct from a dogmatist or an apologist. The task is to find the evidence concerning the canonical process and the resulting canon in the evidence from antiquity[10]. It would seem that there is no place for

---

7. E. ULRICH, *The Dead Sea Scrolls and the Origins of the Bible* (Studies in the Dead Sea Scrolls and Related Literature, 2), Grand Rapids, MI - Leiden, 1999, p. 57.

8. METZGER, *The Canon* (n. 3), p. 7.

9. J. BARTON, *The Significance of a Fixed Canon of the Hebrew Bible*, in M. SÆBØ (ed.), *Hebrew Bible / Old Testament: The History of Its Interpretation*, Vol. 1. Part 1, Göttingen, 1996, pp. 67-83, esp. 70.

10. Three exemplary articles have recently appeared on the state of the developing canon as seen at Qumran. J. TREBOLLE, *A "Canon within a Canon": Two Series of Old Testament Books Differently Transmitted, Interpreted and Authorized*, in *RQ* 19 (2000)

either hostility toward traditional beliefs or overly loyal adherence to traditional beliefs about the canon. Epistemologically, religious beliefs or dogmas are conclusions based on earlier evidence, understood according to the worldviews that were prevalent at the times those conclusions were formulated. If we obtain better evidence that generates new understandings and provides the basis for revised conclusions, so much the better. It is important to work at seeing the evidence and describing it with categories and terminology that are accurate and appropriate for the period, without superimposing modern categories on the ancient evidence – whether consciously or not.

Thesis 5. It is important to locate and assess properly the evidence relating to the canonical process along the complex historical trajectory that moved from national literature to a definitive canon of sacred Scripture.

All would agree that before the third century BCE there was no canon of Scripture and that by the fourth century CE a canon had come to be in the Jewish and Christian communities. Along that trajectory, a number of interwoven developments were taking place that contributed to the canonical process.

First, starting with the Exile, there was a shift from the national literature of Israel to the sacred Scripture of Judaism. For example, the early narrative strands of the Pentateuch, which earlier may well have been perceived more as a national epic than as "Scripture", became part of the Torah of Moses. Prophetic booklets, which earlier might have been viewed as containing some elements of revelation, became revealed books. The Psalms, which were human hymns to God, in the late Second Temple period became the inspired words of God to humanity[11]. These more elevated perceptions of scriptural status were brought about in part by the theologized transformations of late editions of the books – as, e.g., with the addition of Proverbs 1–9 to the more pedestrian earlier edition, and with the postscript of Esther 9,18-32 with its Purim connection.

Second, the destruction of the Temple brought the shift from a religion that was Temple-based to one that was text-based. The gaping absence of Temple ritual and more intense focus on texts understandably entailed heightened reflections and debates concerning the relative status

383-399. J. VANDERKAM, *Authoritative Literature in the Dead Sea Scrolls*, in *DSD* 5 (1998) 382-402, and more recently *Revealed Literature in the Second Temple Period*, in ID., *From Revelation to Canon: Studies in the Hebrew Bible and Second Temple Literature* (JSJ SS, 62), Leiden, 2000, pp. 1-30.
    11. First made explicit in 11QPs[a] 27,11.

of various books, and eventually their textual forms. What may have been a secondary concern of the priests now became one of the few remaining concerns of the religion at large.

Third, the format of the books of the Law and Prophets and other traditional literature shifted from individual scrolls for individual books to the codex which could contain many books. This forced decisions regarding the status of books. Whereas an indefinite number of scrolls can lie on a table or a shelf, certain books and only those must eventually be placed within the fixed covers of the codex. The "table of contents" of the Law and the Prophets (and other writings?) shifted from a *mental notion* to a *physical object*. Again, the question of which books should be included must have stirred critical discussions regarding the scriptural status of various books – discussions which continued up until Aqiba's time.

Thus, we must avoid flawed *middot*, such as excessively wide application of the evidence. The mere mention of the name of a book we now consider Scripture does not necessarily mean that it was considered a book of Scripture in the ancient writer's day. Nor does the mention of one book of Scripture mean that all books we now acknowledge in that category are Scripture (see below). Nor can we extrapolate that, if one author regards a book as Scripture, Judaism at large does.

III. THE QUMRAN SCROLLS OF THE SCRIPTURES

Thesis 6. The scrolls of the Scriptures found in the eleven caves at Qumran display the Scriptures of general Palestinian Judaism in the late Second Temple period. They may not be dismissed as "sectarian" or "vulgar" texts, because they were not composed by the Qumran community but were mainly imported from Jerusalem and elsewhere (or copied faithfully at Qumran), and because they do not show any "sectarian" variants. Rather they are the oldest, the best, and the most authentic evidence we have for the shape of the Scriptures at the time of the beginning of Christianity and rabbinic Judaism. Thus, unless one can for a certain aspect explain why it is not the case, the Qumran scriptural evidence is generally applicable for the text and canon of late Second Temple Palestinian Judaism. The Qumran scriptural scrolls should now become the standard criteria for understanding and judging the Jewish Scriptures in late Second Temple Palestinian Judaism.

Our descriptive language and our categories of classification need refinement. Since we approach this newly found evidence from the recent end of a long history during which many ideas have been debated, many lines of distinction and demarcation have been drawn, and our categories have long since become clear, it is difficult to see ancient reality on its own terms without our current categories anachronistically superimposed. We tend to observe the evidence and ask our questions from the point of view of modern, not ancient, categories. For example, it is presupposed that the MT was the "standard biblical text" during the Qumran period[12]. But the question should not be the presupposition-filled "was the MT the standard biblical text in the Qumran period?", but the more neutral question "what was the text of the Scriptures like in that period?"[13]. That is, there was no "MT" or category of "proto-MT" during the late Second Temple period. Nor was there a "Bible" strictly speaking, nor did Judaism have an acknowledged "standard text", whether MT or otherwise[14].

Even if there were standard texts for each book, presumably they would have to be the texts championed by the Pharisees and then adopted by rabbinic Judaism to be meaningful as the "standard text" that eventually became the Masoretic Text. But is there any evidence to suggest that the Pharisees were aware that they had texts which differed from other textual forms, or that their texts differed from the ones in use by the Temple priests, or that they had the religious authority – acknow-

---

12. That the MT was the "standard biblical text" is the default presupposition (I might rephrase: the faulty presupposition) of many biblical scholars; many commentaries, despite some introductory lip-service to textual matters, turn out to be commentaries merely on the MT. When one compares, for example, the earlier edition of LXX-Jeremiah with the later editon of MT-Jeremiah, how solid can historical studies based on the latter be? Nearly twenty years ago I noted, when contemplating the idea of C. WESTERMANN's *Basic Forms of Prophetic Speech* (Philadelphia, 1967), that "If we take our examples from the MT of Jeremiah, we have approximately a 15% chance of describing, not the basic forms of the speech of the historical prophets, but the basic forms of late editorial practice"; see *Horizons of Old Testament Textual Research at the Thirtieth Anniversary of Qumran Cave 4*, in *CBQ* 46 (1984) 613-636, p. 636. — It is difficult even for the most sophisticated to escape the pervasiveness of this presupposition. See E. TOV, *Textual Criticism of the Hebrew Bible*, Minneapolis, MN - Assen, 1992, pp. 114-117, where the Qumran biblical MSS are categorized according to "(1) Texts Written in the Qumran Practice, (2) Proto-Masoretic Texts, (3) Pre-Samaritan Texts, (4) Texts Close to the Presumed Hebrew Source of ⅏, (5) Non-Aligned Texts". For critique of these categories that are handy and useful but require revision, see E. ULRICH, *The Dead Sea Scrolls and the Biblical Text*, in P.W. FLINT & J.C. VANDERKAM (eds.), *The Dead Sea Scrolls after Fifty Years: A Comprehensive Assessment*, vol. 1, Leiden, 1998, pp. 79-100, esp. 82-84, 92. For illuminating advances see now Tov's recent article, *The Place of the Masoretic Text in Modern Text Editions of the Hebrew Bible: The Relevance of Canon*, in L.M. MCDONALD & J.A. SANDERS (eds.), *The Canon Debate: On the Origins and Formation of the Bible*, Peabody, MA (forthcoming).

13. E. ULRICH, *The Qumran Biblical Scrolls – The Scriptures of Late Second Temple Judaism*, in T.H. LIM et al. (eds.), *The Dead Sea Scrolls in Their Historical Context*, Edinburgh, 2000, pp. 67-87, esp. 67, 69-70.

14. *Ibid.*, pp. 82-87.

ledged by any other groups within Judaism – to claim that their texts were standard and others not so? To my knowledge, there is no such evidence, and Shemaryahu Talmon has reached the same conclusion[15]. Lawrence Schiffman perceptively notes that "the gradual transfer of influence and power from the priestly Sadducees to the learned Pharisees went hand in hand with the transition from Temple to Torah"[16], i.e., during the period after the First Jewish Revolt (66-74). He also candidly points out that "Rabbinic tradition claimed [a dominant or normative] status for Pharisaic Judaism, but it is difficult to consider a minority, no matter how influential, to be a mainstream"[17]. Thus, though scholars had grown accustomed to equating the MT with the text and the contents of Judaism's authoritative Scriptures prior to the two Revolts, that view must be recognized as in serious need of revision.

On the other hand, the biblical texts from Qumran fit perfectly into the broader picture provided by the combined witnesses of the MT, the LXX, the SP, the NT, and Josephus. If one myopically judges all by the MT, then the scrolls are "vulgar texts", the LXX is a "free translation or paraphrase", the SP is "filled with secondary expansions by the Samaritans", and Josephus paraphrases and is guilty of "unscriptural details". But each of those judgments (as generic judgments, not certain particular cases) is wrong. The text of the Jewish Scriptures was pluriform prior to the Revolts, and its variant literary editions for each book as well as the individual textual variants embedded within each simply show up in the manuscripts that happen to get transmitted to posterity. The various witnesses attest authentically to the plurality of text forms that was normal in the Second Temple period.

If one attempts to discover in the Qumran biblical scrolls textual variants that were "sectarian" in origin or motivation, one searches in vain. In an analysis of the individual textual variants highlighted by the Qumran biblical scrolls in contrast with each other and with the MT, the SP, and the Septuagint, I found no variants to indicate that any sect – whether Pharisaic, Sadducean, Samaritan, Essene, Christian, or other – had tampered with Scripture in order to bolster their particular beliefs, except for the two Samaritan beliefs that God "had chosen" Mount Gerizim (cf. Deut 12,5; 14,23; 16,2; 17,8; 18,6; 26,2; etc.) and had commanded the central altar there, and except for the Mount Gerizim / Mount Ebal variant at Deut 27,4. But with respect to this last, the

15. See his essay in E. HERBERT & E. TOV (eds.), *The Bible as Book* (forthcoming).
16. L.H. SCHIFFMAN, *From Text to Tradition: A History of Second Temple and Rabbinic Judaism*, Hoboken, NJ, 1991, p. 112.
17. *Ibid.*, p. 98.

Qumran scroll (4QJosh[a]) apparently preserves the earliest, non-sectarian tradition, while the Samaritan adds the first level of sectarian variant, and it is the MT that changes to yet a later level of sectarian polemical variant[18].

Thus, the textual character exhibited by the biblical scrolls found at Qumran fits perfectly with the character of the biblical text exhibited by the spectrum of other early witnesses: the MT, the SP, the LXX, the quotes in the NT, and the narrative of Josephus's *Jewish Antiquities*.

Why, then, do some people think that the Qumran biblical scrolls are sectarian or vulgar or private copies? I submit that they may be starting off with the presupposition that the received MT is and always was the Hebrew Bible, and anything (whether textual form or canonical collection) that does not match the MT is therefore considered sectarian or vulgar. In contrast, I think that the Qumran biblical scrolls, since they are our only pre-Revolt MSS and display no "sectarian" features, should now become the standard criteria for understanding and judging the Jewish Scriptures in late Second Temple Palestinian Judaism.

Finally, just as the textual character of the variegated biblical MSS from Qumran accurately exemplifies the character of the texts of the Scriptures in late Second Temple Palestinian Judaism, so does the picture painted by the *collection* of MSS exemplify broader Judaism's stage of progress on the road toward what would eventually become the canon.

IV. AUTHORITATIVE SCRIPTURES BUT NO CANON AT QUMRAN

What evidence does Qumran provide concerning the status of the eventual canon of the Hebrew Bible? Does it show clearly that there was a canon, and, if so, what were its contents? Or does it show that there was not yet a canon? Is there evidence of a milestone along the road toward the eventual canon? Or are there at least some clues to provide partial indications?

Thesis 7. There is strong evidence to demonstrate that the writings in the library at Qumran recognized a number of books as containing the word of God, thus as authoritative Scripture, and that they were at times referred to as the Torah and the Prophets. There is no conclusive evidence, however, to determine what the exact contents of the collection were that the community considered the authoritative books of Scrip-

18. E. ULRICH, *47. 4QJosh^a*, in E. ULRICH, F. M. CROSS, *et al.* (eds.), *Qumran Cave 4. IX: Deuteronomy, Joshua, Judges, Kings* (DJD, 14), Oxford, 1995, pp. 143-152.

ture. Thus, there were recognized books of authoritative Scripture, but there is no clear evidence for a canon of Scripture. In particular, I think no sound conclusion about a tripartite canon can be based on 4QMMT.

Criteria that would be conclusive for determining whether the writings found at Qumran provide evidence for a canon of Scripture would be: (a) the clear mention of a title of the canon or its parts, or a list of the books in the canon. Criteria that would in varying degrees be indicative would be: (b) multiple copies of the books; (c) formulae which introduce explicit quotations of Scripture; (d) books explicitly quoted as Scripture; (e) books on which commentaries were written; and (f) books that were translated into the vernacular languages, either Greek or Aramaic.

Let us review the evidence according to these criteria, attempting to judge the evidence appropriately, not granting it too much or too little weight. First, we must be careful to note that there is positive evidence for authoritativeness of certain books, but that our lack of evidence for canon could simply be a *lack* of evidence. That is, it is possible that Qumran had or acknowledged a canon but that the evidence did not survive. Though that is possible, it is unlikely. If we examine the evidence that is preserved, we find that it parallels the evidence of the NT (as we will see below).

a. Titles or Lists

No list of authoritative books has been preserved in the writings found at Qumran. Titles of subcollections of authoritative books do occur; it is common knowledge that the texts speak of the Law and the Prophets, or Moses and the Prophets, as God's revealed and written word. The very beginning of the *Community Rule*, for example, directs that the community's initiates are to learn "to seek God with all their heart and with all their soul, to do that which is good and upright before him, just as he commanded through Moses and all his servants the prophets" (1QS 1,1-3). Later, the important self-identity quotation of Isa 40,3 ("In the desert, prepare the way of [the Lord]") is interpreted thus: "This is the study of the law wh[i]ch he commanded through the hand of Moses, in order to act in compliance with all that has been revealed from age to age, and according to what the prophets have revealed through his holy spirit" (1QS 8,15-16)[19]. The Law and the Prophets is used also in the NT as the title for the Scriptures: e.g., Luke 16,16.29.31; 24,27; Acts

19. The translation is from F. GARCÍA MARTÍNEZ & E.J.C. TIGCHELAAR (eds.), *The Dead Sea Scrolls Study Edition*, vol. 1, Leiden, 1997, pp. 89, 91.

26,22; 28,23. Thus the books of authoritative Scripture were at times grouped under the quasi-title, the Torah and the Prophets[20].

But, with one possible exception, just as the NT never offers a more specific title for the Jewish Scriptures, neither do the Qumran texts – either those composed within broader Judaism or those which bear the stamp of the community's particular theology.

That one exception is the much-discussed and often inflated testimony of 4QMMT (4Q394-399). The editors translate their composite and partly reconstructed text:

> [And] we have [written] to you so that you may study (carefully) the book of Moses and the books of the Prophets and (the writings of) David [and the] [events of] ages past[21].

For accuracy, and to avoid inflated interpretations, it is important to note the following at the palaeographic and textual levels:

(a) For the first word of this line in the "composite text" one of the two overlapping texts, 4Q398, has an anomalous reading that is a variant from 4Q397, and 4Q398 lacks the second word altogether;

(b) The tiny fragment with "[and] in the book[s of]" before "[the p]rophets" is a separate fragment which is plausibly placed here but which also may not have originally been part of this line[22]; it is even questionable whether a *yod* followed the *resh*, thus leaving the word "book" as singular and out of place here;

(c) For "David" only *waw-bet-dalet* ("and in d[ ]") is clear, followed by two vertical strokes and part of a top horizontal stroke connecting them; "and in David" is a fully plausible suggestion, but several other words are also possible, including *bdwr* (note that *dwr* occurs twice in the next line);

(d) Just as the spacing (when the two MSS are lined up to form a "composite text") causes a problem at the beginning of the sentence, so also it causes a problem between "David" and "ages past". That is, the suggested reading does not fit well the spacing requirements of the MSS.

---

20. This paper will be sensitive throughout to another ancient classification that should be generally followed, in contrast to the later Masoretic classification, viz., that Psalms and Daniel were considered among the Prophets, not the Writings (see ULRICH, *Scrolls and Origins* [n.7], pp. 21-22). It should also be recalled that the Twelve Minor Prophets were viewed as comprising one book by the late Second Temple period.

21. E. QIMRON & J. STRUGNELL, *4QMMT "Composite Text"*, C 10-11, in *DJD* 10, Oxford, 1994, pp. 58-59.

22. This is an intelligent placement of this fragment, and if I were editing that text I would probably also place it tentatively here; but it would be good to have a note to the reader, explicitly saying that the placement is conjectural and by no means certain.

At the level of interpretation we note:

(e) Whereas "in the *book* of" precedes "Moses", it is not certain that "in the *book*[*s*] of" precedes "[the p]rophets", and quite importantly "*book*" clearly does not precede "David"; this raises a serious problem for considering the word beginning with *waw-bet-dalet* as a "third section" of a "tripartite canon".

(f) The absolute *bspr ktwb* ("in the book it is written"?) occurs in the next line (C 11). It appears to presume that the identity of that book (singular) is clear, and perhaps thus that only one book had been named in the previous line.

We are now in a position to watch the escalation from a few possible and plausible restorations to "a significant piece of evidence for the history of the tripartite division of the Canon"[23]:

(1) We do not know that "books" of the prophets are mentioned here.

(2) We do not know that "David" is mentioned here.

(3) Even if "David" is mentioned, we do not know whether this is the person or the book. Note that, unlike "the book of Moses", no *book* of David is mentioned; moreover, MMT never otherwise mentions the Psalms but does speak once of the person[24].

(4) Nonetheless, the *DJD* translation presents the text in a way that leads the non-specialist reader to think that "the book of Moses and the books of the Prophets and (the writings of) David" is a fully preserved and clear continuous text, except for "the writings of" – and the parentheses might be interpreted as implying that it is an implicit expression readily supplied, whereas in contrast it is a problematic interpretation.

(5) Now that "the books of the Prophets and (the writings of) David" are in the text, this is then compared to the well-known Lucan phrase "the law of Moses and the prophets and the psalms" (Luke 24,44), which is categorized as a "tripartite 'canon' formula"[25].

(6) The *DJD* edition then stretches further and informs us, in a note on line 10, that "In this context דויד probably refers not only to the Psalms of David, but rather to the Hagiographa. This is a significant

23. QIMRON & STRUGNELL, in *DJD* 10, p. 59 n. 10.

24. "Remember David, he was a pious man, and indeed he was delivered from many troubles and forgiven" (C 25-26). The translation is by M. ABEGG, in M. WISE, M. ABEGG, Jr., & E. COOK, *The Dead Sea Scrolls: A New Translation*, San Francisco, 1996, p. 364. "In the days of Solomon the son of David" (thus person, not book) also occurs in the exhortations regarding blessings and curses (C 18).

25. QIMRON & STRUGNELL, in *DJD* 10, p. 112, n. 6. The qualification is given that "Phrases of this kind occur in other passages that have, perhaps loosely, been called canon lists". But the remainder of the page gives the appearance of endorsing a tripartite canon.

piece of evidence for the history of the tripartite division of the Canon[26]".

(7) Finally, a later section on dating, entitled "דויד as Part of the Description of a Tripartite Canon," adopts, but does not argue, the common view that "a tripartite list is attested in ... the prologue of the grandson of Ben-Sira." It then states that "the title of the third section, whatever it contained, is 'David'", and a note compares it with "the similar tripartite 'canon' formula in Luke 24,44"[27].

My point in all this is not to criticize the editors. They have done a very good job with a highly challenging set of fragments, and it is difficult to draw the line between pedantic precision and user-friendly exposition. Also, it is the editor's task or prerogative to suggest interconnections and paths for future research, and I would assent to the plausibility of many of their conclusions (except the tripartite canon).

My point is rather that biblical scholars using the "composite text" and translation together with the escalated summary formulations will think they are building on stone rather than a mixture of some stone and some sand, i.e., reconstructions. I will give but two illustrations here.

Perhaps I should make myself the first object of my own critique: in my earlier article in the *Encyclopedia of the Dead Sea Scrolls*, I translated the text and commented as follows:

> "[And also] we [have written] to you that you may have understanding in the book of Moses [and] in the book[s of the P]rophets and in Dav[id...]". We can be confident about which books were included in Moses' law and about many that would have been classified among the prophets; but exactly which other texts were subsumed under "prophets" is not obvious, and it is unlikely that "David" here refers to anything beyond *Psalms*. After "David" the damaged sequel in the fragments ("[...] generation after generation") may add yet another book or category – perhaps annals[28]?

So I accuse myself first of over-stepping the link between evidence and conclusion. If given a second chance, I would draw the reader's attention to the limit of plausibility, not certainty, in placing the tiny fragment with "[and] in the book[s of]" before "the [P]rophets" (capitalization overinterpreting?), and the limit of possibility for the restoration "in

---

26. *Ibid.*, p. 59 n. 10. A later summary section (p. 112) does add the qualifier: "It is not clear whether 'David' refers just to the Psalter, or denotes a *Ketubim* collection, either one that was open-ended, or one that was closed". But someone studying the text and its explanation would not necessarily see that later qualifier.

27. *Ibid.*, pp. 111-112.

28. E. ULRICH, *Canon*, in L.H. SCHIFFMAN & J.C. VANDERKAM (eds.), *Encyclopedia of the Dead Sea Scrolls*, New York, 2000, pp. 117-120, esp. 118-119.

Dav[id]". My confidence about Moses' law would include the possibilities that many Jews would consider 4Q364-367 (called "Reworked Pentateuch") as copies of this book, that some would include Jubilees, and that some might include the Temple Scroll[29]. I would still maintain that the contents of the prophets was far from clear[30], and that "David", if correct, does not refer to the Ketubim[31].

I would also suggest, alongside the possibility that line 10 contained a canonical reference (whether tripartite or bipartite), an alternate possibility that it contained simply a reason why "you should study the book of Moses", or an idea or quote from "the book of Moses".

A second illustration is Arie van der Kooij's recent article using 4QMMT for a discussion of an early tripartite canon[32]. He briefly introduces the MMT, then quite understandably quotes the *DJD* translation of the line (which I suggest is an escalated translation as presented), and quotes the *DJD* Hebrew of the line, but without dots or circlets to indicate the uncertainty of letters, and without the type of bracket symbol which indicates that the spatial interrelationship between fragments is unknown (i.e., there is no questioning that "book[s of]" may not precede "prophets").

After his brief introduction and presentation of the text he immediately moves to the editors' exaggerated conclusion: "As is stated by the editors (Qimron and Strugnell), 'this is a significant piece of evidence for the history of the tripartite division of the canon'", and he mentions "'David' as a designation of the third section" which he will discuss

---

29. See J.C. VANDERKAM, *The Dead Sea Scrolls Today*, Grand Rapids, MI, 1994, pp. 156-157. J. LUST, *Quotation Formulae and Canon in Qumran*, in A. VAN DER KOOIJ & K. VAN DER TOORN (eds.), *Canonization and Decanonization* (Studies in the History of Religions, 82), Leiden, 1998, pp. 67-77, esp. 72-75, argues against its "special status and authority" (p. 74 n. 25). But to decide the issue one must ask: is there evidence that Jews were widely asking the explicit question yet whether individual holy books were or were not part of the official Scriptures, or was there even a felt need to ask the question and reach agreement on such issues?

30. Note that Josephus (CAp., 1,40), more than a century later, still counts thirteen books of prophets. I agree with A. VAN DER KOOIJ, *The Canonization of Ancient Books Kept in the Temple of Jerusalem*, in *Canonization and Decanonization* (n. 29), pp. 17-40, esp. 20-23, that Josephus probably attests an earlier grouping of the prophets than that reflected in the MT. I would not agree, however, that Josephus's tripartite canon reflects a tradition two centuries old.

31. 4QMMT does not appear to be interested in hymns or psalms but rather in "the end of days" (see C 14, 16, 21), and thus "David" (if correct) would at most mean the Psalter, viewed as a prophetic book, as the pesharim view the Psalter, and as 11QPs[a] 27:11 explicitly says. The editors would then be correct in making the parallel with the Lucan phrase, since it too is concerned only with the Psalter as a prophetic book, not the Hagiographa. Note the context: "that everything written about me in the law of Moses, the prophets, and the psalms must be fulfilled" (Luke 24,44 NRSV).

32. VAN DER KOOIJ, *Canonization* (n. 30), pp. 17-40.

later[33]. On the same page he states that "the Prologue [to Ben Sira] and 4QMMT very likely refer to the same collection of ancient books" and uses 4QMMT as parallel to other witnesses that he interprets as tripartite canon lists.

Again, my intention is not to criticize Professor A. van der Kooij; he is merely quoting what the editors of the text printed in the *DJD* edition and proceeding logically. My intention is rather to raise our awareness that it is easy, for myself as well as for van der Kooij and others, to draw conclusions that overreach what the evidence will support.

On the one hand, with regard to the Prologue to Ben Sira, I think that the wording provides a reasonably strong foundation for the hypothesis that it may attest a tripartite canon, even though I disagree with that hypothesis. The Prologue also provides a strong foundation for the hypothesis, which I do endorse, of a bipartite grouping of (1) the Scriptures (i.e., the Law and the Prophets) and (2) other important religious literature which is not on the level of Scripture but is helpful toward instruction and wisdom[34]. A parallel might be a bookseller's catalogue with sections listing entries under "Bible" and "Theology", in which "Bible" is replaced with "Law and Prophets", thus "Law and Prophets and Theology". On the other hand, in contrast to the Prologue to Ben Sira which can be reasonably interpreted in either direction, I think that no sound conclusion about a tripartite canon can be based on 4QMMT C, 10[35].

Thus, I maintain that at Qumran we are left with no list of scriptural books and with only "the Law and the Prophets" as the title of the Scriptures; if "David" be the correct reading in 4QMMT C, 10, the claim that it refers to the Psalter is problematic without the preceding word "book of", and there is no basis whatever for extending it to the remainder of the Writings.

b. *Multiple Copies of Books*

That several copies of an individual book were preserved at Qumran is not a conclusive indicator that it was regarded as possessing authoritative status, but it is one indicator, to be used in concert with others, of the importance of a book. Appendix 2 lists as clearly as presently possible the number of copies of the books of the received Masoretic

---

33. *Ibid.*, pp. 26-27.
34. See ULRICH, *Canon* (n. 28), p. 118.
35. Note that a few lines later (C 17) neither a book of "David" nor a "third section" occurs in the similarly questionable "[written in the book] of Moses [and in the books of the Prophets]".

Bible, plus 1 Enoch and Jubilees, due to the large number of MSS preserved[36].

Realizing that the number of copies is only one indicator and that the preservation of the fragmentary scrolls is somewhat random, an attempt at an impartial assessment of the importance and thus perhaps authoritativeness of the books on that list might look like the following:

Quite strong	Strong	Some	Weak	Negligible
the Pentateuch	Jubilees	Jeremiah	Joshua	Proverbs
Psalms	1 Enoch	Ezekiel	Judges	Qohelet
Isaiah	Minor Prophets	Job	Samuel	Esther
1 Enoch?[a]	Daniel[c]		Kings	Ezra
Jubilees?[b]			Ruth	Nehemiah
			Canticles	Chronicles
			Lamentations	

[a] If the nine copies of the Book of Giants were indeed part of 1 Enoch.
[b] With more copies than Numbers and almost as many as Leviticus.
[c] Relative to its small size.

It may be partly due to chance that only one small fragment of the large book of Chronicles was found, whereas many fragments from eight MSS of the relatively small book of Daniel were found in three different caves. But one could also argue that that fact is significant and betrays to some extent the relatively higher status of Daniel for the community. The latter argument is strengthened when one notes that Daniel is quoted as Scripture and that it exercised a strong influence on the apocalyptic thought and terminology of the community.

c. Formulae

Joseph Fitzmyer wrote a classic study of the formulae introducing quotations of the Scriptures in the Qumran texts[37]. He articulated many of the main points that the formulae provide concerning Jewish beliefs about Scripture during the late Second Temple period. Formulae such as "For thus it is written" (1QS 5,15) and "As for what God said" (CD 8,9), which introduce quotations from Scripture, demonstrate that they

---

36. I realize that my presentation there, based on the categories provided by our received MT, is theoretically problematic, but I list it thus because it is a handy expedient and also illustrates the weak case for the "canonicity" of the Ketubim as a third section in this period.

37. J.A. FITZMYER, The Use of Explicit Old Testament Quotations in Qumran Literature and in the New Testament, in NTS 7 (1960-61) 297-333, reprinted in his Essays on the Semitic Background of the New Testament (SBL SBS, 5), Missoula, MT, 1974, pp. 3-58. See also VANDERKAM, Authoritative Literature (n. 10), pp. 391-396.

believed certain written texts to have originated as the word of God. Other formulae such as "As God said through Isaiah the prophet" (CD 4,13) and "As you said through Moses" (1QM10,6) make explicit that writings of Moses and the prophets convey the word of God. This is strong evidence which demonstrates that the writings in the library at Qumran recognized the books so designated as containing the word of God, thus as authoritative Scripture. In this category also the Qumran evidence appears to be representative of Judaism at large, not "sectarian".

d. Books Quoted as Scripture

The next question to ask is which books are quoted with a designation as Scripture at Qumran. This is a vast topic the center of which holds rich data, but the periphery of which is quite difficult to chart precisely. Indeed, for a large percentage of instances it is difficult to prove conclusively that the appeal is to a written authority as Scripture specifically (as opposed to respected national literature). The difficulty in achieving clear criteria for classification is well known from studies of quotations of the OT in the NT, but in general one can say that the quotations in the NT are overwhelmingly from the books of the Pentateuch, Psalms, Isaiah, and the Minor Prophets, with modest representation from Samuel, Kings, Jeremiah, Ezekiel, Daniel, Job, and Proverbs, and virtually no others[38]. If various attempts to catalogue the quotations from Scripture in the Qumran MSS[39] are compared, one is satisfied that the broad lines are clear and sufficient for our purposes, giving a reasonable approximation of the truth. One of the most soberly charted recent lists of quotations introduced by citation formulae is presented by James VanderKam, and his results are listed in Appendix 2[40]. Isaiah and the Minor Prophets are the most frequent, with modest representation from the books of the Pentateuch and Ezekiel; the only others are Psalms, Daniel, Samuel[41], Jeremiah, Proverbs, and Jubilees.

---

38. See, e.g., *Old Testament Quotations in the New Testament*, ed. R.G. BRATCHER, London, ³1987; *Index of Quotations* in K. ALAND et al. (eds.), *The Greek New Testament*, Stuttgart, United Bible Societies, ³1983, pp. 897-898; and TREBOLLE, *Canon within a Canon* (n. 10), pp. 393-395.

39. See, e.g., TREBOLLE, *Canon within a Canon* (n. 10), pp. 389-92; and *Index of References* in WISE, ABEGG & COOK, *The Dead Sea Scrolls* (n. 24), pp. 506-513.

40. VANDERKAM, *Authoritative Literature* (n. 10), pp. 394-395, accepted by TREBOLLE, *Canon within a Canon* (n. 10), p. 389 n. 28.

41. The only quotation from the former prophets is from Nathan's oracle in 2 Samuel 7, thus highlighting the prophetic nature of the book.

That the lack of a formal quotation introduced by a citation formula cannot serve as sufficient evidence to disqualify a book from having been considered authoritative Scripture is clear from the fact that Genesis is not so quoted, and Exodus only once. Nonetheless, it can be stated as a general impression that the citation-formula quotations clearly attest the Scriptural status of the Pentateuch and the Latter Prophets, and give indication of the same for Psalms, Daniel, Samuel, and Proverbs. Note that of the books beyond the Law and Prophets, only Proverbs is so quoted and only once, while Jubilees seems to be quoted once with a formula (in 4Q228 1 i 9; cf. 1 i 2) and referred to once importantly in parallel with the Law of Moses (CD 16,2-4)[42]. From another perspective, I am not aware that any text quoted as authoritative Scripture by one author is rejected as non-scriptural by another.

Thus, there is also a good deal of positive evidence to show that certain books were considered authoritative Scripture – again the Law and the Prophets, but no Writings except Proverbs –, although lack of evidence does not by itself show that a book was not authoritative.

e. Commentaries on Books of Scripture

Continuous commentaries have been identified only on the prophetic books: six on Isaiah[43], seven (possibly nine?) on the Book of the Minor Prophets[44], and three on Psalms[45]. It is widely agreed that these commentaries presuppose that the prophetic books are revealed Scripture. The prophets deal with the end time: "as it is written in the book of Isaiah the prophet about the end of days" (4QFlor 1,15), and "who said concerning the end of days by Isaiah the prophet" (11QMelch 15). The well-known passage in the Habakkuk pesher shows that God, via the ancient prophetic Scriptures, was still offering vital revelation to the chosen through the Teacher of Righteousness (1QpHab 7,1-6). Indeed, "the spirit of prophecy had not ceased at the time of Ezra... [The community] believed that God continued to address his own in order to help them understand the writings of the ancient tradition and to unfold new truths to address the concerns of their times"[46].

---

42. See VANDERKAM, *Authoritative Literature* (n. 10), p. 399.
43. 3Q4 and 4Q161-165.
44. Two on Hosea (4Q166-167), one or two on Micah (1Q14; cf. 4Q168?), one on Nahum (4Q169), one on Habakkuk (1QpHab), two on Zephaniah (1Q15; 4Q170), and possibly one on Malachi (cf. 5Q10?).
45. 1Q16; 4Q171; and 4Q173.
46. VANDERKAM, *Authoritative Literature* (n. 10), p. 401.

Although continuous commentaries appear to be limited to the prophetic books, there are a number of interpretive works on the Torah – more narrative interpretation of Genesis, and more legal interpretation of Exodus to Deuteronomy[47]. These are in addition to the many *ad hoc* references to passages in the Torah concerning halakic matters, often introduced by introductory formulae.

While the halakic and continuous commentaries point strongly to the Torah and certain Prophets (Isaiah, the Minor Prophets, and the Psalter) as books of Scripture, Julio Trebolle interestingly highlights a different class of interpretive works widening the prophetic circle: "parabiblical or apocryphal rewritings on the model of Chronicles… based on narrative sections of the Pentateuch (particularly Gen 1–11) and on books of the second series", i.e., the Former Prophets, Jeremiah, Ezekiel, and Daniel[48]. Note that the witness of the interpretive works from Qumran again points to the Law and the Prophets, but not the Writings, as Scripture.

f. Translations of Books of Scripture

Translations of a work, in antiquity as today, are some indication of the importance with which a work is regarded, though it is good to consider which type of importance is involved. One Aramaic translation of Leviticus (4Q156) and two of Job (4Q157 and 11Q10) were found at Qumran. The importance of Leviticus would presumably be religious or religio-legal, whereas for Job the importance could as easily be literary as religious, or a blend of both. But the fact that a copy of Job is also preserved in the Palaeo-Hebrew script (4Q101), and that it is the only identified work other than the five books of Moses to be preserved in the Palaeo-Hebrew script, lends more weight to the religious importance accorded that book.

Two Greek translations of Leviticus (4QLXXLev[a] and 4QLXXLev[b]) were found in Cave 4, together with one copy each of Numbers (4QLXXNum), and Deuteronomy (4QLXXDeut); a Greek translation of Exodus (7QLXXExod) was found in Cave 7, and a Greek revision of the Septuagint of the Minor Prophets was also found at Nahal Ḥever (8ḤevXII gr). It is difficult to avoid the two conclusions that Genesis had also been available in Greek and that the purpose for the translations was the religious importance accorded the Torah and the (Minor) Prophets.

47. For an informative discussion see M.J. BERNSTEIN, *Pentateuchal Interpretation at Qumran*, in FLINT & VANDERKAM (eds.), *The Dead Sea Scrolls after Fifty Years* (n. 12), pp. 128-159; and TREBOLLE, *Canon within a Canon* (n. 10), pp. 391-393.
48. TREBOLLE, *Canon within a Canon* (n. 10), pp. 383, 397-398.

Conclusion

In conclusion, I will list the main theses presented in this paper:

1. It is essential that a clear definition of "canon" be established as the basis of discussion; otherwise, discussion cannot proceed.

2. "Canon", in the sense of the canon of Scripture, is a "technical term in theology designating the collection of inspired books that composes Holy Scripture and forms the rule of faith"[49]. It is the definitive list of inspired, authoritative books which constitute the recognized and accepted body of sacred Scripture, forming the rule of faith of a major religious group, that definitive list being the result of inclusive and exclusive decisions after serious deliberation and wide endorsement by the community.

3. The notion of canon includes, among others, three important aspects highlighted by Qumran: It involves books, not the specific textual form of the books; it entails reflective judgment; and the canonical list excludes as well as includes books.

4. One of the problems in the discussion of canon is the mentality or presuppositions of scholars.

5. It is important to locate and assess properly the evidence relating to the canonical process along the complex historical trajectory that moved from national literature to a definitive canon of sacred Scripture.

6. The scrolls of the Scriptures found in the eleven caves at Qumran display the Scriptures of general Palestinian Judaism in the late Second Temple period. They may not be dismissed as "sectarian" or "vulgar" texts, because they were not composed by the Qumran community but were mainly imported from Jerusalem and elsewhere (or copied faithfully at Qumran), and because they do not show any "sectarian" variants. Rather they are the oldest, the best, and the most authentic evidence we have for the shape of the Scriptures at the time of the beginning of Christianity and rabbinic Judaism. Thus, unless one can for a certain aspect explain why it is not the case, the Qumran scriptural evidence is generally applicable for the text and canon of late Second Temple Palestinian Judaism. The Qumran scriptural scrolls should now become the standard criteria for understanding and judging the Jewish Scriptures in late Second Temple Palestinian Judaism.

7. There is strong evidence to demonstrate that the writings in the library at Qumran recognized a number of books as containing the word of God, thus as authoritative Scripture, and that they were at times

---

49. RAHNER & VORGRIMLER, *Theological Dictionary* (n. 2), p. 65.

referred to as the Torah and the Prophets. There is no conclusive evidence, however, to determine what the exact contents of the collection were that the community considered the authoritative books of Scripture. Thus, there were recognized books of authoritative Scripture, but there is no clear evidence for a canon of Scripture. In particular, I think no sound conclusion about a tripartite canon can be based on 4QMMT.

I have argued elsewhere that the traditional tripartite canon, properly speaking, was not in place prior to the fall of the Temple in 70 CE and perhaps even somewhat later. Just as there was no "standardized text" neither was there yet a definitive canon of Scripture. Though the Prologue to Ben Sira can be interpreted as reflecting a tripartite grouping of books (not canon), it can also be interpreted as reflecting a bipartite grouping of Scripture (the Law and the Prophets) plus other religious literature, and the latter interpretation is strengthened by the lack of any other mention of a tripartite canon for two hundred years until Josephus[50].

I do not find myself persuaded by van der Kooij's recent argument in favor of a tripartite collection in the Prologue, though his is a possible interpretation. But the second-century BCE testimony of 2 Macc 2,13-14 holds no strength for a canon, and it cannot be propped up "by the fact that 4QMMT already witnesses to the existence of an official collection of ancient books around 150 BCE"[51]. The Prologue is the only second-century BCE witness; it is ambiguous, and it finds no supporting echo for two centuries.

The topic assigned to this paper – the witness from the Qumran scrolls – conforms to the same picture. Although the witness is never as clear as hoped for, no feature appears that sets the Qumran biblical MSS apart from the Scriptures of wider Palestinian Judaism. The combination of factors surveyed here sketches the same picture as for the rest of Judaism: there was no canon as yet, though much of the road toward the eventual canon had been traveled. There seems to be broad consensus that the Law and the Prophets are God's word, with the explicit status of authoritative Scripture. The boundaries of the prophetic collection are unclear (as probably also in wider Judasim) with Psalms and Daniel explicitly and the Former Prophets probably included. There is some indication that Job and Proverbs are accorded scriptural status, but 1 Enoch

50. ULRICH, *Canon* (n. 28), p. 118.
51. VAN DER KOOIJ, *Canonization* (n. 30), p. 37.

and Jubilees appear as stronger candidates. The remainder of the Writings are known, but there is little indication of elevated status[52].

Department of Theology   Eugene ULRICH
University of Notre Dame
Notre Dame, IN 46556
USA

APPENDIX 1: DEFINITIONS OF "CANON" IN THEOLOGICAL DICTIONARIES[53]

Specifically theological dictionaries – Jewish, Catholic, Protestant, and English, French, German, Spanish – provide the following clarity for the definition of "canon":

1. "Canon of Scripture: A technical term in theology designating the collection of inspired books that composes Holy Scripture and forms the rule of faith"[54].

2. "The Greek word *kanōn* means both 'rule' and 'list,' and in the second capacity came to be used by the church at a rather late date... to designate those Scriptural books which were regarded as inspired. The Protestant canon and the Roman Catholic New Testament canon are identical, but Protestants follow the Old Testament canon of the Hebrew Bible..."[55].

3. "The process by which the various books in the Bible were brought together and their value as sacred Scripture recognized is referred to as the history of the canon.... While the OT canon had been formally closed.... The rise of heresy... was a powerful impulse towards the formation of a definite canon. A sifting process began in which valid Scripture distinguished itself from Christian literature in general on the basis of such criteria.... The canon was ultimately certified at the Council of Carthage (397)"[56].

4. "The term [canon] as applied to the Bible designates specifically the closed nature of the corpus of sacred literature accepted as authoritative because it is believed to be divinely inspired.... In the second century, κανών had come to be used in Christian circles in the sense of 'rule of faith'. It was the church Fathers of the fourth century C.E. who first applied 'canon' to the sacred Scriptures. No exact equivalent of this term is to be found in Jewish sources although the phrase Sefarim Ḥiẓonim ('external books': Sanh. 10,1), i.e., uncanonical, is

---

52. If one were to apply to most of the Writings the criteria by which J. LUST, *Quotation Formulae* (n. 29), p. 75, denied special status to the Temple Scroll, Qumran would not be judged as granting special status to the Writings: "there is not one mention of ... in any of the other Qumranic texts. Only two copies were found" and they do "not belong to the collection of canonical scriptures explicitly quoted...".

53. The definitions in this appendix are drawn from my article, *The Notion and Definition of Canon*, in *The Canon Debate* (n. 12).

54. RAHNER & VORGRIMLER, *Theological Dictionary* (n. 2), p. 65.

55. *The Westminster Dictionary of Church History*, ed. J.C. BRAUER, Philadelphia, PA, 1971, p. 156.

56. *Baker's Dictionary of Theology*, ed. E.F. HARRISON, Grand Rapids, MI, 1960, pp. 94-95.

certainly its negative formulation... The concept enshrined in the 'canon' is distinctively and characteristically Jewish... In short, the development of the canon proved to be a revolutionary step in the history of religion, and the concept was consciously adopted by Christianity and Islam"[57].

5. "Canon ... term that came to be applied to the list of books that were considered a part of authoritative Scripture. The fixing of the canon of the Hebrew Bible was a long process about which we know little. ... it is clear that certain books not in the present list were accepted by some communities; also, some in the present canon were evidently not universally accepted"[58].

6. "The term *canon* ... was first used by the fourth-century Church fathers in reference to the definitive, authoritative nature of the body of sacred Scripture. Both Jews and Christians needed to define, out of the available literature, what should be regarded as divinely inspired and hence authoritative and worthy of preservation; the process was one of rejection rather than selection, a weeding out from among books commonly regarded as sacred"[59].

7. "Canon: En grec: règle. (1) Toute décision solennelle.... (2) Nom donné... à la grande prière de la messe... (3) Liste des ouvrages qui font partie du catalogue des livres sacrés, et sont reconnus comme d'inspiration divine et donc canoniques: 'canon des Écritures'"[60].

8. "At.licher Kanon... Vorstufen: Lange bevor die Schriften des AT ... kanonisch wurden..., beanspruchten und erhielten viele ihrer Bestandteile eine Geltung, die der Kanonizität schon verwandt war und den Weg zu ihr hin nachträglich als logisch erscheinen läßt.

Es ist das Besondere der nt.lichen Kanonbildung, daß die Alte Kirche hist. unter deutlicher Beachtung apostolischer Verfasserschaft der Schriften den Kanon abschloß und begrenzte, [und] daß sie ... in der Korrelation von Norm und Schrift herausstellte... Die Kanonbildung selbst ist somit nur aus der Geschichte des Urchristentums, aus ihrem Weg in die Alte Kirche und aus den sie bestimmenden Motiven erklärbar"[61].

9. "Los griegos usan el vocablo *Canon* como sinónimo de *registro* o *catálogo*; y en este sentido lo oímos de los Libros de la Escritura. ... no es canónico, si está fuera del catálogo. El *Canon Bíblico* es el catálogo de libros inspirados y reconocidos como inspirados"[62].

The sources above are unanimous in their general definition of canon, each including many of the essential aspects, although all do not include all of the aspects important for the complete definition. It is not surprising that all were not attentive to all aspects, since usually there has not been such an acute need to clarify the definition so comprehensively. It should be noticed, however, that, though aspects may be missing, there is no hint of disagreement.

---

57. *Encyclopaedia Judaica*, Jerusalem, 1971, vol. 4, pp. 817-818.

58. *Dictionary of Judaism in the Biblical Period: 450 B.C.E. to 600 C.E.*, ed. J. NEUSNER & W.S. GREEN, New York, 1996, vol. 1, p. 112.

59. N. SOLOMON, *Historical Dictionary of Judaism*, Lanham, London, 1998, p. 79.

60. P. CHRISTOPHE, *Vocabulaire historique de culture chrétienne*, Paris, 1991, p. 52.

61. R. SMEND & O. MERK, *Bibelkanon*, in E. FAHLBUSCH *et al.* (eds.), *Evangelisches Kirchenlexikon: Internationale theologische Enzyklopädie*, vol. 1, Göttingen, 1986, pp. 468-474.

62. R. RABANOS, *Propedeutica biblica*, Madrid, 1960, p. 110.

APPENDIX 2: THE NUMBER OF PASSAGES QUOTED AS SCRIPTURE
AND THE NUMBER OF COPIES OF BOOKS OF THE MASORETIC BIBLE

	Quotations	Total copies	Sq.Heb.	Palaeo-Heb.	Greek	Aramaic
Genesis	—	23 (+1?)	20 (+1?)	3		
Exodus	1	18	15	2	1	
Leviticus	4	17 (+2?)	10 (+1?)	4 (+1?)	2	1
Numbers	3	12 (+1?)	10 (+1?)	1	1	
Deuteronomy	5	32 (+1?)	29 (+1?)	2	1	
Joshua	—	3	3			
Judges	—	4	4			
Samuel	1	4	4			
Kings	—	3	3			
Isaiah	9	22	22			
Jeremiah	1	6	6			
Ezekiel	4	7	7			
Minor Prophets	9	10	9		1	
Psalms	2	37 (+2?)	37 (+2?)			
Job	—	6	3	1		2
Proverbs	1	2	2			
Ruth	—	4	4			
Canticles	—	4	4			
Qohelet	—	2	2			
Lamentations	—	4	4			
Esther	—	—	—			
Daniel	2	8	8			
Ezra	—	1	1			
Nehemiah	—	—	—			
Chronicles	—	1	1			
Total		230 (+7?)	208 (+6?)	13 (+1?)	6	3
1 Enoch	—	12 (+9?)	11 (+9?)		1	
Jubilees	1?	14 (+3?)	14 (+3?)			
Tobit	—	5	1			4
Ben Sira	—	2	2			
Letter Jer.	—	1			1	

The numbers for quotations introduced by formulae are from J. VANDERKAM, *Authoritative Literature*, in *DSD* 5/3 (1998) 394-395. The categories for number of copies of each book include Hebrew MSS in the Jewish or square script (plus questionable identifications in the square script) and in the Palaeo-Hebrew script (plus questionable identifications), as well as translations into Greek and Aramaic. Since two books are occasionally copied on the same MS, the number of MSS is slightly less than the number of copies of books listed here.

L'APPORT DES PÈRES DE L'ÉGLISE À LA QUESTION DE LA CLÔTURE DU CANON DE L'ANCIEN TESTAMENT

Est-il possible d'écrire une histoire du Canon de l'Ancien Testament sans faire référence aux Pères de l'Église[1]? C'est apparemment la conviction de l'un des derniers livres parus sur le sujet: Stephen B. Chapman ne cite nulle part les Pères, à l'exception d'une brève note concernant la question du Canon des Sadducéens, à propos duquel il rappelle que nos renseignements viennent d'un texte d'Origène et d'un texte de Jérôme[2]. Il est vrai que Chapman centre sa réflexion sur le couple constitué par la Loi et les Prophètes, qu'il considère comme la plus ancienne réalité canonique que nous puissions atteindre et qu'il fait remonter à l'époque deutéronomiste, vers 550: selon lui, à cette époque, la Loi ne bénéficie d'aucune prééminence par rapport aux Prophètes; elle constitue seulement le début du corpus biblique. À ses yeux, la suprématie de la Loi relève d'une innovation de l'époque rabbinique. Les Écrits, dont il est à peine question dans son livre, forment soit une troisième partie nouvelle, soit plutôt un commentaire de l'ancien corpus unique constitué par la Loi et les Prophètes. On comprend qu'une telle réflexion, qui porte sur le Canon avant l'époque rabbinique, puisse se passer en droit de l'apport des Pères, pour des raisons chronologiques évidentes. Pourtant on est étonné de lire dans le chapitre V une analyse qui repose en partie sur des passages des Paralipomènes, d'Esdras-Néhémie et de Daniel, tous trois considérés comme faisant partie des Prophètes. Mais, dans la Bible massorétique, ces livres appartiennent aux Écrits. L'analyse de Chapman repose donc sur l'idée implicite qu'ils ont d'abord fait partie des Prophètes avant d'être reclassés parmi les Écrits. Or, si l'on excepte un passage du *Florilège* trouvé à Qumrân qui parle du «livre de Daniel le prophète» (4Q174), tous les autres témoignages permettant

---

1. On trouvera en annexe la liste des principales sources patristiques utilisées (p. 109-110). Sauf exceptions justifiées par le sujet traité, je n'ai pas cru nécessaire d'intégrer les sources arabes, arméniennes, coptes, éthiopiennes, géorgiennes, syriaques. – Les abréviations bibliques sont les abréviations de la collection. Toutefois, pour respecter l'usage de la Septante et des Pères grecs et latins, j'utilise Jes, et non Jos, pour Josué, car le titre de ce livre est toujours Jésus (fils de) Navé; 1-4 Rg (où Rg signifie Règnes), et non 1-2 S et 1-2 R; 1-2 Par (pour Paralipomènes), le terme de Chroniques n'étant jamais utilisé; Eccl (et non Qo, pour Qohélet), car les Pères parlent toujours du livre de l'Ecclésiaste. J'utilise encore les abréviations AT et NT, pour désigner l'Ancien et le Nouveau Testament.

2. S.B. CHAPMAN, *The Law and the Prophets. A Study in Old Testament Canon Formation* (FAT, 27), Tübingen, 2000, p. 266 n. 128.

d'établir que les trois livres ont sans doute d'abord appartenu à la collection des Prophètes se trouvent chez les Pères de l'Église, entendus en un sens large: non seulement les auteurs, mais aussi les listes canoniques et les manuscrits bibliques de l'époque patristique. En d'autres termes, Chapman manie l'argument patristique sans le dire et peut-être sans le savoir.

En fait, il n'est pas possible d'écrire une histoire du Canon juif sans faire référence aux Pères: d'autres exemples le montreront dans le cours de l'exposé. Mais, si cela est vrai, à plus forte raison est-il impossible de comprendre la constitution du Canon chrétien de l'Ancien Testament si l'on se coupe des témoignages patristiques. La différence principale qui sépare ces deux Canons est la présence, chez les chrétiens, des deutérocanoniques et de divers compléments à des livres canoniques. Sur ces livres supplémentaires et ces compléments, les sources juives sont peu loquaces, encore qu'elles le soient plus qu'on ne l'a longtemps dit: la présence de certains deutérocanoniques à Qumrân en hébreu ou en araméen (le psaume 151, Tobit) ou celle des suppléments à Esther chez Flavius Josèphe et parmi les Midrashs de ce livre oblige à poser la question du Canon juif en termes plus nuancés qu'on ne le fait parfois. Mais ce sont évidemment les listes canoniques, les manuscrits bibliques des chrétiens et les discussions des Pères sur le statut à accorder à ces livres et leur manière de les citer, ou non, comme Écritures qui constituent l'essentiel de nos informations sur ce point.

Or l'apport des Pères à la connaissance de la Bible juive et de l'Ancien Testament chrétien doit être apprécié dans un contexte scientifique qui rend cette évaluation délicate. La théorie classique d'H.E. Ryle et de ses successeurs est remise en cause[3]. Elle envisageait le Canon rabbinique comme le produit d'un développement historique en trois étapes, situées, pour la Loi, à l'époque d'Esdras vers 450, puis, pour les Prophètes, un peu avant les Maccabées ou sous Judas Maccabée lui-même vers 160, enfin, pour les Écrits, au moment des discussions menées par les rabbins à Jamnia/Yabneh vers 100 de notre ère. Toutes ces datations sont aujourd'hui discutées et d'autres sont proposées, plus anciennes ou plus récentes. L'idée même d'un développement historique en trois étapes est contestée. Certes on n'en revient pas, du moins à ma connaissance, à la théorie d'Élias Lévita (1469-1549), pour qui, sous l'autorité d'Esdras, les hommes de la Grande Assemblée (*knesset ha-gedolah*) avaient établi en une seule fois le Canon biblique en trois parties. Mais, on vient de le voir, l'idée d'un premier Canon, deutéronomiste, en deux

---

3. H.E. RYLE, *The Canon of the Old Testament. An Essay on the Gradual Growth and Formation of the Hebrew Canon of Scripture*, Londres, 1892.

parties, suivi beaucoup plus tard d'un second Canon, rabbinique, en trois parties a ses partisans. Toutefois, la théorie classique n'est pas encore remplacée par une autre théorie. Par conséquent, il paraît utile d'évaluer dans quelle mesure les Pères vont dans son sens, ou si, au contraire, ils vont dans le sens de sa remise en question, voire s'ils entraînent dans d'autres directions.

On voit que la question de la clôture du Canon est au centre des recherches. Le Canon est-il clos dès l'époque d'Esdras, voire auparavant, ou au contraire beaucoup plus tard, sous les Maccabées ou encore à Yabneh? Y a-t-il eu plusieurs clôtures et plusieurs Canons? La clôture ou les clôtures sont-elles définitives, ou bien y a-t-il eu des brèches suivies de nouvelles clôtures? Il ne faut donc pas prendre le terme «clôture» du titre en un sens étroit. Il ne désigne pas uniquement l'état final du Canon de l'Ancien Testament chrétien. L'apport des Pères ne suffirait d'ailleurs pas à traiter ce point, qui a fait l'objet de discussions bien après l'époque patristique, lors des Conciles de Florence (1442) et de Trente (1546) par exemple, ou encore entre les catholiques et les protestants, ou même au sein des différentes églises. Le terme «clôture» attire l'attention sur le fait qu'un Canon est caractérisé par une liste close d'écrits reconnus comme inspirés par l'Esprit et normatifs pour les fidèles. Mais la clôture est normalement sous le signe de la pluralité: l'histoire apprend qu'il y a eu des clôtures successives, et peut-être même parfois des clôtures simultanées. Les Pères de l'Église sont les premiers à illustrer ce phénomène: les listes qu'ils proposent sont rarement identiques entre elles, même si elles contiennent beaucoup d'éléments semblables; les variations concernent les deutérocanoniques, la présence, ou non, d'Esther, des Maccabées et des Psaumes de Salomon. De ce point de vue, à la clôture fermée de la Bible massorétique, on peut opposer la clôture semi-ouverte de l'Église des premiers siècles: à côté d'éléments stables, celle-ci contient des éléments variants.

I. La division du Canon des Hébreux

Les Pères apportent-ils des informations sur la division du Canon des Hébreux? Et que peut-on en tirer pour l'histoire de ce Canon?

1. Le Canon réduit à la Loi

Les Pères savent que, pour certains groupes de Judée-Palestine, le Canon se réduit à la Loi. Origène affirme que les Samaritains et les Sadducéens «reçoivent les livres du seul Moïse» (*Contre Celse* 1,49; voir aussi *Commentaire sur Mt* 17,29). On trouve la même information sur les Samaritains chez Épiphane de Salamine, *Panarion* I 9, 2, et Jérôme, prologue «galeatus»; sur les Sadducéens, chez l'auteur de l'*Élenchos* IX 29, Origène, *Commentaire sur Mt* 17,35-36, et Jérôme, *Commentaire sur Mt* 22,31.

Les renseignements donnés par les Pères sont discutés, surtout dans le cas de la Bible sadducéenne. Mais, comme ce point n'est pas central pour mon propos, je ferai plutôt remarquer que, de cette Bible étroite des Samaritains et des Sadducéens, les Pères ne tirent aucun enseignement pour l'histoire même de la Bible. Cela contraste avec l'époque moderne dont l'argument essentiel pour distinguer une première étape de canonisation de la Loi antérieure à une deuxième étape de canonisation des Prophètes consiste précisément dans l'existence du Pentateuque samaritain. Sur ce sujet donc, l'apport des Pères se révèle décevant. En est-il de même avec la bipartition de la Bible, c'est-à-dire avec la division en Loi et Prophètes?

2. *La bipartition du Canon*

Certains Pères connaissent cette bipartition, ce qui ne peut surprendre de la part de lecteurs de 2 M (où, en 15,9, Judas Maccabée encourage ses troupes «par la Loi et les Prophètes») et du Nouveau Testament, où elle figure en Mt 5,17 et 7,12.

Dans la deuxième moitié du IIe siècle, Méliton de Sardes est conduit à énumérer les livres de la Bible pour la raison suivante: Onésime lui a demandé de composer «des extraits tirés de la Loi et des Prophètes» sur la question du Sauveur et l'a interrogé sur le nombre (ἀριθμός) des livres de l'Ancien Testament et sur leur ordre (τάξις). Méliton est allé en Judée-Palestine et là des informateurs l'ont renseigné, probablement des Juifs chrétiens. Dans l'énumération des livres bibliques, le mot «Loi» n'est pas repris. En revanche, on trouve le mot «Prophètes» au pluriel (προφῆται) devant Is, Jr, les XII, Dn, Ez et Esd. La présence de ce dernier livre parmi les Prophètes doit être notée. En général, il figure après 1-4 Rg et 1-2 Par. Faut-il penser à un déplacement accidentel? Ce serait étonnant de la part de quelqu'un qui dit être particulièrement attentif à la question de l'ordre des Livres. Un autre fait notable doit être noté. On pense d'emblée que tous les livres énumérés avant le mot «Prophètes» relèvent de la Loi. Si la présence parmi eux, et en tête de la liste, des cinq livres de Moïse est attendue, en revanche, il est plus inattendu de constater que sont énumérés, d'une part, Jes, Jg, Rt, 1-4 Rg, 1-2 P, classés en général parmi les Prophètes, d'autre part, Ps, Pr, Eccl, Ct et Jb, dont l'aspect législatif n'est pas l'élément le plus caractéristique. Faut-il penser que les livres énumérés de Jes à Jb appartiennent à une troisième subdivision de la Bible? Mais, outre que cette subdivision comprend des livres qui appartiennent tant aux Prophètes qu'aux Écrits de la Bible massorétique, rien dans le texte de Méliton, qui parle de «la Loi et des Prophètes», n'autorise à aller dans ce sens. En définitive, il semble que l'expression «la Loi et les Prophètes» ait chez Méliton un sens générique et désigne l'ensemble des livres du Canon, sans prétendre décrire une subdivision particulière. Cette conclusion en entraîne une autre: employé seul, le mot «Prophètes» désigne effectivement des livres prophétiques, sans que la liste de ces livres soit nécessairement exhaustive; employé à côté de «la Loi» dans l'expression «la Loi et les Prophètes», il fait référence à l'ensemble des livres bibliques. L'expression «la Loi et les Prophètes» ne renvoie donc pas à une subdivision rigoureuse entre deux catégories de livres. Ce fait ne doit pas étonner: Moïse, l'auteur de la Loi, est aussi le plus grand des Prophètes et il y a des aspects législatifs dans plusieurs des livres extérieurs au Pentateuque, notamment dans 3-4 Rg et dans Esd.

La même expression «la Loi et les Prophètes» se retrouve, à la fin du IVᵉ siècle, chez Rufin d'Aquilée, *Exposition du symbole*, 34-36, qui énumère les cinq livres de Moïse, Jes, Jg avec Rt, 1-4 Rg, P, 1-2 Esd, Est, puis les Prophètes, au pluriel (*Prophetae*), Is, Jr, Ez, Dn et, en outre, les XII, Jb, Ps, les 3 livres de Salomon, Pr, Eccl et Ct. Ces derniers livres, de Jb à Ct, font-ils partie des Prophètes? La Loi comporte-t-elle, outre les cinq livres de Moïse, les livres qui vont de Jes à Est? On fera à propos de Rufin la même observation que pour Méliton: employé seul, le mot «Prophètes» désigne les 4 grands Prophètes et les 12 petits Prophètes, sans qu'on puisse exclure l'appartenance d'autres livres à cette catégorie; employé dans l'expression «la Loi et les Prophètes», il se réfère à l'ensemble des livres bibliques et n'induit pas une subdivision précise.

Apparemment, une autre subdivision figure chez Augustin. Dans son traité *Sur la doctrine chrétienne* II 8, 13, il distingue les livres, de Gn à 1-2 Par, qui appartiennent à l'histoire (*historia*) et les Prophètes (*Prophetae*), qui comprennent Ps, les trois livres de Salomon, Sg et Ecclésiastique, puis les Prophètes au sens propre (*proprie*): les XII, Is, Jr, Dn, Ez. La distinction entre l'histoire et les Prophètes apparaît comme un simple démarquage de la distinction entre «la Loi et les Prophètes». Augustin a remplacé la Loi par l'histoire, parce que ce dernier terme lui apparaît plus approprié que celui de Loi pour décrire le contenu des livres qui vont de Gn à 1-2 Par. On remarque encore qu'il distingue les Prophètes au sens propre des autres Prophètes: il manifeste ainsi l'embarras que ne manque pas de susciter le contenu de certains livres prophétiques. Mais il ne croit pas devoir se soustraire à la contrainte de la classification traditionnelle.

Innocent I est le témoin d'une bipartition qui rappelle celle d'Augustin, tout en s'en écartant. Dans sa *Lettre* adressée à l'évêque de Toulouse, Exsupère, en février 405, il classe le Pentateuque, Jes, Jg, 1-4 Rg, Rt, les 16 livres des Prophètes, les 5 livres de Salomon et le psautier dans une première catégorie, dont il ne donne malheureusement pas le nom, et Jb, Tb, Est, Jdt, 1-2 M, 1-2 Esd et 1-2 Par dans une seconde catégorie, celle des «histoires». Fait-il ainsi écho à la bipartition augustinienne en histoire et prophètes? Une différence majeure sépare les deux auteurs: le Pentateuque, Jes, Jg, 1-4 Rg et Rt appartiennent à l'histoire chez Augustin, mais n'en font pas partie chez Innocent I, puisque les «histoires» ne commencent apparemment qu'avec les livres énumérés en dernier. Certes, on pourrait réconcilier les deux Pères, en supposant qu'Innocent I en réalité énumère d'abord des livres historiques, puis passe aux livres prophétiques et pour finir revient aux livres historiques. Mais rien dans la *Lettre* ne va en ce sens et ne permet de diviser les livres énumérés avant les histoires en livres historiques et livres prophétiques. Cependant il est clair, à la lecture de cette *Lettre*, qu'Innocent I veut simplement donner une liste des livres canoniques à son correspondant. Son propos n'est pas de réfléchir à leur classification. Celle qu'il esquisse ne doit donc pas être trop sollicitée. Et ce qu'il faut en retenir, c'est qu'elle fait probablement écho, sous une forme rédactionnelle maladroite, à la bipartition d'Augustin.

L'ensemble de ces témoignages patristiques va incontestablement dans le sens de la théorie classique du Canon, pour laquelle une bipartition de la Bible a précédé sa tripartition. Elle va aussi dans le sens de l'étude de Chapman, selon qui «la Loi et les Prophètes» désigne le corpus biblique plus qu'une subdivision de ce corpus. Toutefois, il ne signale pas la persistance de cette expression à la fin du IVe siècle, ce qui est un fait remarquable sur lequel il faut réfléchir un instant. Il faut rapprocher des témoignages patristiques les sept témoignages rabbiniques étudiés par S.Z. Leiman où la même expression bipartite se trouve employée[4]. Certes les textes rabbiniques qui parlent de «la Loi, des Prophètes et des Écrits» sont plus nombreux, mais l'existence de sept textes interdit de traiter l'expression «la Loi et les Prophètes» en termes d'exception. Les rabbins peuvent parler de la Bible avec des termes qui évoquent soit sa bipartition soit sa tripartition. Chapman a tendance à opposer une Bible

---

4. S.Z. LEIMAN, *The Canonization of Hebrew Scripture: The Talmudic and Midrashic Evidence*, Hamden, CT, 1976.

judéenne bipartite à une Bible rabbinique tripartite: le témoignage des Pères et des rabbins oblige à nuancer cette opposition: la Bible bipartite et la Bible tripartite ont coexisté. Cette dernière remarque va incontestablement dans le sens de la thèse qui propose une date tardive pour l'établissement et le triomphe de la tripartition biblique.

3. *La tripartition du Canon*

Les Pères connaissent-ils la tripartition rabbinique? Leurs témoignages permettent-ils de trancher entre les argumentations contradictoires qui prennent appui sur les discussions rabbiniques relatives à Ct, Eccl, Est, Ez et Pr pour dater le Canon tripartite soit de l'époque de Judas Maccabée, voire avant, soit de l'époque de Jamnia, ou même plus tard[5]? Dans un cas, on argumente en disant qu'il n'y aurait pas eu de discussions sur ces livres s'ils n'avaient pas déjà fait partie d'un Canon déjà constitué. Dans l'autre cas, on avance que la discussion sur les livres prouve que le Canon est en cours d'élaboration.

En fait les Pères font référence à deux types de tripartition de la Bible bien différentes. En règle générale, la tripartition dont ils parlent n'est pas la tripartition rabbinique. Par exemple, Eusèbe de Césarée, dans ses *Eklogès prophétiques*, un document que les historiens du Canon n'utilisent guère, passe en revue tous les passages de l'AT qui prophétisent Jésus: il parle d'abord du «Pentateuque» (ἡ πεντάτευχος), puis des «Écritures à la suite» (αἱ ἑξῆς γραφαί), qui sont les «Écritures historiques» (αἱ ἱστορικαὶ γραφαί) ou encore les «Prophètes» (Προφῆται); très probablement, à ses yeux, Pentateuque et Prophètes ne font qu'un; ensuite il y a «les livres poétiques» (τὰ στιχήρη), Ps, Pr, Eccl, Ct et Jb; puis viennent «les Écritures prophétiques» (αἱ προφητικαὶ γραφαί). Exemples voisins chez Cyrille de Jérusalem; Grégoire de Nazianze, *Poèmes* I 12 (les 12 livres historiques; les 5 livres poétiques; les 5 livres de l'Esprit prophétique); le Pseudo-Jean Chrysostome (qui énumère successivement τὸ ἱστορικόν, τὸ συμβουλευτικόν, τὸ προφητικόν). Du côté latin, le *Décret* de Gélase, qui peut être plus ancien que l'époque de ce pape et remonter à l'époque de Damase, à la fin du IVe siècle, distingue l'ordre de l'AT (*ordo Veteris Testamenti*), l'ordre des Prophètes (*ordo prophetarum*) et l'ordre des histoires (*ordo historiarum*).

Le second type de tripartition de la Bible connu par les Pères est celui dont parle Jérôme dans le célèbre prologue «galeatus» aux livres de Sa-

---

5. Voir, d'un côté, R.T. BECKWITH, *The Old Testament Canon of the New Testament Church and Its Background in Early Judaism*, Londres, 1985; ID., *Formation of the Hebrew Bible*, in A.J. MULDER (ed.), *Mikra*, Assen - Maastricht - Philadelphia, PA, 1988, p. 39-86; LEIMAN, *The Canonization of Hebrew Scripture* (n. 4); de l'autre côté, L.M. MCDONALD, *The Formation of the Christian Biblical Canon*, Peabody, Mass, 1995.

muel et des Rois. Il faut noter d'emblée que Jérôme prétend décrire ici le Canon hébraïque de son temps, et nullement un Canon grec ou latin. Les livres de la Bible sont divisés en trois ordres (*ordines*): l'ordre des cinq livres de Moïse, que les Hébreux appellent «Thorath, c'est-à-dire Loi (*legem*)»; l'*ordo* des Prophètes; enfin l'*ordo* des hagiographes (Jérôme emploie le terme grec ἁγιόγραφα).

Ce qu'il faut souligner, c'est le caractère complètement isolé de cette description hiéronymienne du Canon biblique. Sauf erreur de ma part, la tripartition des Hébreux n'est signalée par aucune autre source. Certes, on a voulu que certaines listes patristiques fassent écho à la tripartition rabbinique. Mais aucune de ces démonstrations n'emportent l'adhésion, comme je voudrais le montrer en analysant les documents patristiques qui devraient pourtant se prêter le mieux à pareille démonstration: ceux qui décrivent une Bible en usage dans des milieux hébreux. Ces documents sont: la liste de Méliton, la liste d'Origène, la liste de Jérusalem parfois appelée liste de Bryennios, les listes d'Épiphane, la liste de Josippe, la liste de Timothée dans le *Dialogue de Timothée et d'Aquila*. Toutes ces listes offrent l'originalité de mêler les livres des Prophètes avec les livres des Écrits et fournissent donc un argument contre l'ancienneté de la distinction entre Prophètes et Écrits[6]. Certes, il est normal

---

6. Dans le matériau réuni ci-après, seuls les livres des Prophètes et des Écrits sont signalés; chaque livre est suivi de la lettre P, quand il s'agit d'un livre prophétique, et de la lettre E, quand il s'agit d'un Écrit. – La liste de Méliton (fin du IIe siècle) reproduit le canon d'un groupe judéo-chrétien, plutôt que le Canon de Juifs. La voici: Jes, P; Jg, P; Rt, E; Rg, P; Par, E; Ps, E; Pr, E; Ec, E; Ct, E; Jb, E; Is, P; Jr, P; Dn, E; Ez, P; Esd, E. – La liste d'Origène, au début du IIIe siècle, décrit l'AT de certains «Hébreux», qui sont, selon moi, des judéo-chrétiens; voir G. DORIVAL, *Un groupe judéo-chrétien méconnu: les Hébreux*, in *Apocrypha* 11 (2000) 7-36. Elle donne les noms des livres d'abord en grec, puis en hébreu transcrit en lettres grecques. Voici la liste des livres: Jes, P; Jg, P, avec Rt, E; Rg, P; Par, E; Esd, E; Ps, E; Pr, E; Eccl, E; Ct, E; XII, P; Is, P; Jr, P, avec Lm, E, et Lettre, qui est soit la Lettre de Jérémie soit Ba (qui est en effet une lettre), dans les deux cas un texte absent du TM; Dn, E; Ez, P; Jb, E; Est, E. Vient enfin le livre des Maccabaïques, qui est en dehors (ἔξω) des livres précédents. – La liste de Jérusalem donne «les noms des livres chez les Hébreux». Son auteur est anonyme. La date du manuscrit qui la fait connaître est 1056, mais la liste est beaucoup plus ancienne. La présence d'araméismes dans les titres rapproche la liste d'une des listes d'Épiphane: les listes pourraient bien être de la même époque, antérieures à la seconde moitié du IVe siècle. Les noms sont donnés d'abord en hébreu araméisé transcrit en grec, puis en grec: Rt, E; Jb, E; Jg, P; Ps, E; 1-4 Rg, P; Par, E; Pr, E; Eccl, E; Ct, E; Jr, P; XII, P; Is, P; Ez, P; Dn, E; Esd, E; Est, E. – Les listes d'Épiphane sont au nombre de trois. Celle qui figure dans le traité *Sur les poids et mesures* 4, ne peut être prise en compte ici, car elle organise les livres bibliques en quatre Pentateuques qui n'ont rien à voir avec la tripartition rabbinique. En revanche la liste qui figure dans le *Panarion* I 8, 6, 1-4, affirme énumérer les livres des Juifs, qui sont peut-être des judéo-chrétiens: Rt vient à la suite de Jg; Lm, Lettre de Jérémie et Ba regroupés avec Jr; il y a deux livres d'Esdras et, enfin, il y a deux livres «en contestation» (ἐν ἀμφιλέκτῳ), Si et Sg. Voici la liste: Jes, P; Jg, P; Rt, E; Jb, E; Ps, E; Pr; E; Eccl, E; Ct, E; 1-4 Rg, P; 1-2 Par, E; XII, P; Is, P; Jr, P; Ez, P;

que les listes les plus tardives ne fassent pas écho à la tripartition rabbi-nique, dans la mesure où les contacts intellectuels entre chrétiens et Juifs sont alors très peu nombreux. Mais, dans le cas de Méliton, d'Origène, de la liste de Jérusalem, d'Épiphane et de Josippe, qui est peut-être un Juif converti, la chose est plus inattendue. Elle va nettement dans le sens d'une datation tardive de la tripartition biblique. Assurément, il est pos-sible de limiter la portée de cet argument en disant que les auteurs chré-tiens ont été influencés par l'ordre chrétien des livres et qu'ils n'ont pas respecté l'ordre original donné par leurs informateurs. Mais il s'agit là d'une argumentation invérifiable qui n'emporte guère la conviction.

Une autre considération va à l'appui du caractère tardif de la triparti-tion. Il faut reprendre ici le prologue «galeatus» de Jérôme. Au début de ce prologue, Jérôme rappelle que, pour «la plupart» des Hébreux, il y a cinq livres de la Bible doubles (*duplices*), à l'instar des cinq consonnes hébraïques qui s'écrivent de deux façons. Ces livres sont 1-2 S, 1-2 Rg, 1-2 Par, 1-2 Esd et «Jr avec Cinoth», qui est le nom hébreu de Lm. Puis Jérôme décrit les trois *ordines* de la Loi, des Prophètes et des Hagiogra-phes. À propos de l'ordre des prophètes, il explique que le deuxième des huit livres de cet ordre est constitué par Jg auquel les Hébreux «joi-gnent» (*coniungunt*) Rt. Puis il récapitule le total des livres de chaque ordre: 5 pour la Loi, 8 pour les Prophètes et 9 pour les Hagiographes. Il précise alors que, selon «certains» (*nonnulli*), Rt et Cinoth font partie des hagiographes et qu'il faut les compter séparément. Il est facile de calculer qu'en ce cas il y a 11 Hagiographes. Le nombre des livres pro-phétiques reste identique, 8, puisque Rt et Lm étaient regroupés avec Jg et Jr. Ce qu'il faut faire remarquer, c'est que Jérôme signale l'existence, non pas d'une seule tripartition de la Bible hébraïque, mais de deux tri-partitions: celle qui est à ses yeux la plus attestée comprend 5 livres de

Dn, E; 1-2 Esd, E; Est, E. La dernière liste d'Épiphane figure dans le traité *Sur les poids et mesures* 22-23. Elle donne les noms des livres d'abord en hébreu araméisé transcrit en lettres grecques, puis en grec. Les Hébreux dont il est question sont plutôt des Juifs chré-tiens que des Juifs: Rt figure après Jg; il y a deux livres d'Esdras. Voici la liste: Jes, P; Jb, E; Jg, P; Rt, E; Ps, E; Par, E; 1-4 Rg, P; Pr, E; Eccl, E; Ct, E; XII, P; Is, P; Jr, P; Ez, P; Dn, E; 1-2 Esd, E; Est, E. – La liste de Josippe, de la fin du IVᵉ siècle, donne les noms des livres en hébreu transcrit en lettres grecques, puis en grec. Elle est très proche de celle d'Origène, mais elle énumère Rt à part de Jg, ce qui la conduit à mettre Est «en dehors» des livres, sur le même plan que les Maccabaïques. Voici la liste: Jes, P; Jg, P; Rt, E; 1-2 Rg, P; 3-4 Rg, P; Par, E; Esd, E; Ps, E; Pr, E; Eccl, E; Ct, E; XII, P; Is, P; Jr, P; Ez, P; Dn, E; Jb, E. – Le *Dialogue de Timothée et d'Aquila* est une œuvre anonyme qu'on peut dater de la fin du Vᵉ siècle ou du VIᵉ siècle. La scène se déroule à Alexandrie. Le chrétien Timothée dialogue avec le Juif Aquila. Ils dressent ensemble la liste des livres considérés comme inspirés tant par les chrétiens que par les Juifs. Seuls les titres grecs sont donnés: Jes, P; Jg, P, avec Rt, E; 1-2 Rg, P; 3-4 Rg, P; Jb, E; Ps, E; Pr, E; Eccl, E; XII, P; Is, P; Jr, P; Ez, P; Dn, E; Esd, E; Jdt, pourtant absent du TM; Est, E.

la Loi, 8 livres des Prophètes (avec Jg-Rt et Jr-Lm) et 9 livres des Écrits; la tripartition minoritaire parle de 5 livres de la Loi, de 8 livres des Prophètes (sans Rt et Lm) et de 11 livres des Écrits (avec Rt et Lm). Comme c'est cette dernière tripartition qui va l'emporter dans le judaïsme, on peut penser que la première répartition est antérieure à la seconde. Quoi qu'il en soit de ce point de chronologie relative, Jérôme témoigne qu'à son époque la tripartition rabbinique est relativement fluide, ce qui s'explique mieux si elle est récente que constituée depuis longtemps.

Il est temps de récapituler les principaux éléments de l'argumentation en faveur de la datation tardive de la tripartition biblique. D'abord, il est remarquable que les Pères qui décrivent un Canon dont l'origine juive ou judéo-chrétienne ne fait pas de doute, ne parlent pas de tripartition, à l'exception de Jérôme. Ensuite, jamais les Pères n'énumèrent les livres des Prophètes avant ceux des Écrits ou l'inverse, mais les deux catégories de livres sont entremêlées. Enfin Jérôme, qui est le premier à parler de la tripartition, décrit en fait deux tripartitions différentes, ce qui montre la fluidité relative de la Bible tripartite à son époque. Tous ces éléments sont en faveur d'une tripartition apparue peu de temps avant Jérôme et encore sujette à discussion à son époque. Cette conclusion est en contradiction avec la thèse qui situe la tripartition à l'époque des Maccabées. Cette dernière thèse prend appui sur 2 M 2,13-15, le Prologue du Si, 4QMMT (*Miqsat Ma'aseh ha-Torah*, en fait 4Q397, fragments 14-21, lignes 10-11), Philon, *Sur la vie contemplative* 25 et Lc 24,44. Deux observations peuvent être faites sur ce point. D'abord, il est possible que la tripartition ne soit pas un phénomène général en milieu juif, que certains groupes l'aient adoptée très tôt, d'autres beaucoup plus tard. En toute rigueur, le silence des Pères sur la tripartition ne peut pas être interprété comme une preuve de son inexistence, mais comme un simple indice de sa généralisation tardive. En second lieu, la portée des textes utilisés à l'appui de la datation ancienne de la tripartition a peut-être été majorée. Certains d'entre eux décrivent plutôt une quadripartition, comme nous allons le voir maintenant.

4. *La quadripartition du Canon*

La quadripartition de la Bible, dont les Pères attestent l'existence, est-elle une innovation chrétienne ou, au contraire, a-t-elle des antécédents juifs? Examinons d'abord les données patristiques. Le premier auteur qui atteste sûrement une quadripartition est Épiphane de Salamine, qui, dans son traité *Sur les poids et mesures* 4, distingue quatre Pentateuques dans la Bible: les livres législatifs, les livres poétiques (στιχήρεις: Jb, Ps, Pr, Eccl, Ct), les écrits ou hagiographes (γραφεῖα ou ἁγιόγραφα: Jes, Jg avec Rt, 1-2 Par, 1-2 Rg, 3-4 Rg) et le Pentateuque prophétique (προφητικὴ πεντάτευχος: les XII, Is, Jr avec Lm, Lettre de Jérémie et Lettre de Baruch, Ez, Dn). On note que les hagiographes d'Épiphane n'ont rien à voir avec les hagiographes de la tradition rabbinique. Jean Damascène, *Sur la foi orthodoxe* IV 17, reprend les analyses d'Épiphane. En fait, ce premier type de quadripartition résulte d'une construction artificielle, qui s'explique par la volonté de ramener toute la Bible à l'étalon qu'est le Pentateuque. Ce qui démontre le caractère artificiel de cette division, c'est qu'Épiphane et Jean Damascène sont dans l'obligation d'ajouter en fin de liste deux livres isolés: 1-2 Esd et Est. C'est aussi le fait qu'Épiphane propose une énumération des livres de la Bible sans quadripartition en *Panarion* I 8, 6, 1-4 et *Sur les poids et mesures* 23-24.

Les Pères font connaître d'autres Bibles quadripartites tout aussi artificielles. C'est le cas d'Amphiloque d'Iconium, *Iambes à Séleucos* 251-319 et du Pseudo-Léonce de Constantinople (milieu du VIᵉ siècle). Chez les Latins, dans ses *Instituta Regularia Divinae Legis* I, II-VI, Junilius Africanus, qui vivait à Constantinople au milieu du VIᵉ siècle, classe dans l'histoire, *historia* (III), 12 livres de l'AT (de Gn à 1-4 R), ainsi que plusieurs livres qui, selon lui, ne font pas partie des Écritures canoniques (*canonicae scripturae*) et sont absents de la Bible hébraïque: 1-2 Par, Jb, Tb, Esd, Jdt, Est, 1-2 M. Relèvent de la prophétie, *prophetia* (IV): Ps, les XII et les 4 grands Prophètes. Relèvent des proverbes, *proverbia* (V): Pr, Si, ainsi que, selon certains, Sg et Ct. Appartient à la doctrine simple (*simplex doctrina*) sur la foi et les mœurs (VI): Eccl. Cependant, le propos de Junilius n'est pas de réfléchir sur le Canon: il est de classer les livres de l'AT et du NT d'un point de vue rhétorique, selon laquelle il y a quatre espèces de «dictio»: l'histoire, la prophétie, l'espèce proverbiale, l'espèce qui dit très simplement. C'est dire que la quadripartition proposée est totalement artificielle.

Au terme de cette enquête chez les Pères, il semble qu'on atteigne une conclusion décevante sur la quadripartition: elle résulte tantôt d'une volonté de mesurer la Bible à l'aune du Pentateuque, tantôt d'une classification d'origine rhétorique. Et elle n'aboutit pas à un résultat convaincant. On peut cependant se demander si son apparition ne pourrait pas s'expliquer par une volonté de «christianiser» l'Ancien Testament. La bipartition est commune aux Juifs et aux chrétiens. La tripartition est caractéristique de la Bible juive. La quadripartition permet de créer une classification propre aux chrétiens. On aimerait four-

nir des textes à l'appui de cette hypothèse. Apparemment, il n'y en a
pas.

5. *Conclusions sur la division du Canon*

1. Pour ne pas fausser les perspectives, il faut rappeler que nombreux
sont les Pères, d'Origène au Pseudo-Nicéphore[7], qui ne proposent pas
une division du Canon quand ils énumèrent les livres de la Bible.

2. Il faut revenir sur la quadripartition et faire remarquer que les Pères
qui proposent une Bible quadripartite attestent d'une difficulté à classer
les livres bibliques que l'on trouvait déjà dans la littérature juive antérieure, dans des documents que l'on a trop souvent voulu annexer au
profit de la tripartition rabbinique. 2 M 2,13-15 énumère les livres des
Rois et des Prophètes, les livres de David et les lettres des rois sur les
anathèmes; si l'on ajoute les livres de la Loi, on a ici une division en
quatre, voire en cinq, plutôt qu'en trois parties. Dans la reconstitution
actuellement proposée, 4QMMT parle du livre de Moïse, du (ou des)
livre(s) des Prophètes et de David et sans doute des Gestes des générations: la tripartition paraît moins évidente que la quadripartition[8]. Chez
Philon d'Alexandrie, *Sur la vie contemplative* 25, il est question des lois,
des prophètes, des hymnes et des autres (textes): rien ne prouve qu'il
faille mettre les hymnes et les autres (textes) dans la même catégorie; on
est plutôt invité à les distinguer. Ce que révèlent en fait ces textes, c'est
que l'expression «la Loi et les Prophètes» n'est plus considérée comme
satisfaisante pour rendre compte du corpus biblique dans son intégralité,
et cela même si elle continue à être employée dans les mêmes textes, par
exemple en 2 M 15,9 ou en 4QMMT (4Q397, fragments 14-21 ligne
15). Lc 24,44, qui parle de la Loi, des Prophètes et des Psaumes, est souvent utilisé en faveur de l'existence de la tripartition au Ier siècle de notre
ère. Mais une telle conclusion suppose que l'on fasse du mot «psaumes» l'équivalent du mot «Écrits». En définitive, seul le Prologue du Si

---

7. Ce sont: Origène décrivant le Canon des «Hébreux»; Athanase; le Pseudo-Atha-
nase; Josippe; Épiphane (*Panarion* I 8, 6, 1-4); la liste de Jérusalem; le canon 59 du
Concile de Laodicée (avant 381); le canon apostolique 85; le *Dialogue de Timothée et
d'Aquila*; la liste du *Baroccianus* 206; beaucoup plus tard Nicéphore ou le Pseudo-
Nicéphore. Du côté latin, Hilaire de Poitiers; Jérôme (*Lettre 53 à Paulin*, 8); la liste de
Cheltenham d'environ 359 (dite aussi liste de Mommsen); le Canon 36 du Concile de
Carthage de 397; la liste du codex de Bobbio; la liste du codex *Claramontanus*; Isidore
de Séville.

8. Cette reconstitution a fait l'objet d'un débat lors du colloque de Louvain. Acceptée
par Arie van der Kooij, elle est récusée par Eugen Ulrich et Florentino Garcia Martinez, à
l'avis desquels il paraît prudent de se rallier. En ce cas, le passage de 4QMMT ne pourrait
plus être utilisé en faveur de l'existence de la tripartition ou de la quadripartition à
Qumrân.

atteste l'existence de la tripartition à date haute. Mais il s'agit d'un texte lié à un milieu juif particulier. Rien ne prouve que les autres milieux juifs l'aient reçue, ni les qumrâniens, ni Philon, ni les chrétiens. Dès lors, rien d'étonnant si les Pères sont muets à son sujet.

3. Un apport ponctuel des Pères, et singulièrement de Jérôme, doit être signalé. Nous connaissons le nom hébreu de chacune des trois parties de la Bible, *Tôrâh*, *Nebi'im*, *Ketûbim*, mais nous ne savons pas si un terme commun désignait ces trois parties. Jérôme apporte quelque lumière sur ce point. Dans sa description de la Bible hébraïque tripartite (prologue «galeatus»), il emploie le mot latin *ordo* pour désigner les livres de la Loi, puis les Prophètes, enfin les Écrits. Ce mot d'«ordre» désigne d'abord la succession des livres à l'intérieur de chaque catégorie, puis il finit par signifier chaque catégorie de livres. Le même mot *ordo* est employé dans le sens de catégorie de livres par le *Décret* de Gélase et par Rufin. Mon idée est que Jérôme n'est pas l'inventeur de ce mot, mais qu'il traduit un mot hébreu ou araméen utilisé par ses informateurs pour décrire chaque sous-ensemble de la Bible. Or nous savons que la Mishna et les Talmuds sont divisés en six ordres, ou *sedarim*. On peut donc se demander si le mot *séder*, avant d'être employé pour les six grandes divisions de la Mishna et des Talmuds, n'a pas été utilisé pour les trois grandes catégories de textes bibliques. Ce qui va dans ce sens, c'est le traité *Baba' batra'* 14b-15a, où il est question du *sdr* des Prophètes et du *sdr* des Hagiographes: le mot *sdr* semble signifier ici chacune des trois sections de la Bible. L'ensemble des témoignages de *Baba' batra'*, de la Mishna, des Talmuds, de Jérôme va dans le même sens: le mot hébreu et araméen *sdr*, en latin *ordo*, a été employé pour désigner chacune des trois parties de la Bible.

II. LE NOMBRE DES LIVRES CANONIQUES

Une question récurrente posée aux historiens du Canon est celle du nombre des livres de la Bible hébraïque: les sources anciennes hésitent entre 22 et 24 livres. Les Pères fournissent-ils quelque lumière à ce sujet?

1. *Les témoignages patristiques*

Le nombre le plus petit qui est signalé par les Pères est 22. Les Pères affirment souvent qu'il est le chiffre des Hébreux (Athanase, Pseudo-Athanase, Cassiodore parlant de la traduction de Jérôme faite sur l'hébreu). Souvent aussi, ils le mettent en relation avec le nombre des consonnes de l'alphabet hébreu (Grégoire de Nazianze; Épiphane; Pseudo-Athanase, §2 et 41; Timothée dans le *Dialogue de Timothée et d'Aquila*; du côté latin, Hilaire de Poitiers; Jérôme, prologue «galeatus»). Épiphane, *Sur les poids et mesures* 22-23, met aussi 22 en relation avec les 22 œuvres de la création de Dieu, les 22 générations d'Adam à Jacob, les 22 «xestes» qui forment le «modios».

Pour arriver à ce nombre de 22, les Pères se livrent à diverses manipulations: les XII sont comptés pour un; Rt est tantôt compté pour un (Grégoire de Nazianze; Josippe; Pseudo-Athanase; Pseudo-Léonce; du côté latin, troisième Concile de Carthage de 435), tantôt ne fait qu'un avec Jg (Épiphane; Cyrille de Jérusalem; Concile de Laodicée; «certains», τινες, cités par le Pseudo-Athanase, qui pour arriver au total de 22, introduisent Est; Timothée; Jean Damascène; Pseudo-Nicéphore); 1-4 Rg sont comptés pour un (troisième Concile de Carthage de 435), pour deux (Grégoire de Nazianze; Épiphane; Cyrille de Jérusalem; Concile de Laodicée; Hilaire de Poitiers; Timothée; pseudo-Léonce; Jean Damascène; Pseudo-Nicéphore); 1-2 Par sont souvent comptés pour un (Grégoire de Nazianze; Épiphane; Cyrille de Jérusalem; Concile de Laodicée; Hilaire de Poitiers; Timothée; Pseudo-Léonce; Jean Damascène; Pseudo-Nicéphore); 1-2 Esd sont comptés pour un (Grégoire de Nazianze; Épiphane; Cyrille de Jérusalem; Concile de Laodicée; Hilaire de Poitiers; troisième Concile de Carthage de 435; Timothée, qui emploie le mot «Esdras» au singulier; Pseudo-Léonce; Jean Damascène; Pseudo-Nicéphore) ou pour deux; les trois livres de Salomon sont comptés tantôt pour trois, tantôt pour deux (Timothée réunit ensemble Eccl et Ct) tantôt même pour un (troisième Concile de Carthage de 435, qui compte pour un les 5 livres de Salomon, Pr, Eccl, Ct, Sg et Si); Jr et ses suppléments ne font en général qu'un, mais il arrive que Ba soit distingué de Jr (Pseudo-Nicéphore). Enfin, Est est tantôt présent tantôt absent.

Pour procéder à ces manipulations, les Pères affirment qu'ils s'autorisent des pratiques des Hébreux. Par exemple, Cyrille de Jérusalem dit qu'à l'imitation des Hébreux, il compte pour un 1-2 Rg, 3-4 Rg, 1-2 Par et, probablement, 1-2 Esd. Du côté latin, Rufin dit que 1-4 Rg sont comptés pour deux chez les Hébreux tandis que 1-2 Esdras est compté pour un chez eux. Quand il affirme que Rt est compté avec Jg et que les XII ne comptent que pour un, on peut penser que sa source est également hébraïque.

Grâce à ces manipulations, les Pères en arrivent à introduire des livres absents du Canon hébraïque, alors même qu'ils prétendent s'en tenir à lui. Ainsi Timothée, qui introduit Jdt comme vingt-et-unième livre, juste

avant Est. Les suppléments à Jr, Ba et Lettre de Jr, sont également présents chez plusieurs auteurs: Épiphane, *Panarion* I 8, 6, 1-4; *Sur les
poids et mesures* 5; *Dialogue de Timothée et d'Aquila*.

Le nombre de 24 livres est beaucoup moins attesté, et seulement chez
des écrivains latins. Hilaire de Poitiers explique que certains ajoutent
deux livres aux 22 livres, afin d'atteindre le nombre des lettres grecques.
Cette explication n'aurait pas manqué de surprendre les rabbins,
d'autant plus que les deux livres en question sont Tb et Jdt, absents du
Canon du TM. En second lieu, à peu près à la même époque qu'Hilaire,
la liste de Cheltenham rapproche les livres canoniques des 24 vieillards
de l'Ap, ce qui implique que le nombre de ces livres est de 24, et elle
affirme que «nos Anciens sont d'accord pour dire ces livres sont canoniques». Elle suggère ainsi que le nombre de 24 est traditionnel, mais la
documentation à notre disposition ne permet pas de confirmer l'existence de cette tradition. Enfin, Jérôme, dans le prologue «galeatus», signale que «certains» (*nonnulli*) inscrivent Rt et Lm parmi les hagiographes, qui passent ainsi de neuf à onze livres. Le total des livres devient
24 au lieu de 22. Il ne précise pas qui sont ces «certains». Il les rapproche des 24 vieillards de l'Ap qui adorent l'agneau, ce qui pourrait être
un argument pour en faire des chrétiens. Mais, comme, dans le prologue
«galeatus», il parle de la Bible hébraïque de son temps et que, d'autre
part, les vieillards ne peuvent pas ne pas évoquer l'ancien peuple, il est
probable qu'ils sont des Juifs. Le témoignage de Jérôme est en définitive
le seul témoignage chrétien à signaler les 24 livres de la Bible hébraïque.

Le nombre de 26 figure dans le *Dialogue de Timothée et d'Aquila*,
mais est sans doute une erreur de copiste ou d'éditeur pour 27.

Le nombre de 27 livres figure pour la première fois chez Épiphane de
Salamine. Dans son Traité *Sur les poids et mesures* 3-4 (voir aussi 22-23
et *Panarion* I 8, 6, 1-4), il explique que cinq des 22 lettres hébraïques
ont deux formes et que par conséquent 22 et 27 sont équivalents; il faut
compter pour un Jg et Rt, 1-2 Par, 1-2 Rg, 3-4 Rg et 1-2 Esd. La même
explication se retrouve chez Jean Damascène, *Sur la foi orthodoxe* IV
17, qui est pratiquement identique au texte d'Épiphane qui vient d'être
cité. On note qu'aucun des deux Pères ne signale l'importance du nombre 27, qui est le nombre des livres du NT. En montrant que les 22 livres
de l'AT peuvent être comptés pour 27, Épiphane et Jean Damascène
font apparaître que l'AT et le NT forment les deux volets d'un même
diptyque, harmonieusement composé chaque fois de 27 livres.

Le nombre de 34 figure dans les listes de l'*Oxoniensis Baroccianus*
206 et du *Parisinus Coislinianus* 120, le chiffre de 35 dans le *Londinensis Add.* 17469, parce qu'il compte Rt à part. Dans les deux listes, 1-

4 Rg comptent pour quatre livres, mais 1-2 Par pour un livre; il y a un seul Esd; les XII comptent pour douze. Sont décomptés «en dehors» (ἔξω) de ces livres 9 autres livres: Sg, Si, 1-4 M, Est, Jdt et Tb. Le total des livres de l'Écriture est de 60: 34 livres de l'AT et 26 du NT (Ap n'est cité ni parmi les livres canoniques, ni parmi les 9 livres «en dehors», ni parmi les 25 «apocryphes»).

Le nombre de 44 est cité par Augustin, *Sur la doctrine chrétienne* II 8, 13. Il compte pour quatre 1-4 R; pour deux 1-2 Par, 1-2 M, 1-2 Esd; pour douze les XII, tout en affirmant expressément que les XII ne comptent que pour un! On remarque que les livres classés sous la première rubrique «*historia*» sont au nombre de 22, tout comme les livres relevant de la rubrique «*prophetae*». Mais Augustin ne fait aucun rapprochement avec le nombre des livres hébreux, pas plus qu'il ne signale que le nombre de 44 est le double du nombre 22.

Dans sa description de la Bible d'Augustin, Cassiodore signale les 22 livres d'histoire et les 22 livres de prophétie. Il ajoute que ces 44 livres de l'AT et les 27 livres du NT font un total de 71 livres, qui, augmenté du chiffre 1 de la Trinité, donne le nombre 72, qui est caractéristique de la «livre» (*libra*). En effet, la livre comprenait 72 *solidi*. Cassiodore suggère ainsi l'équivalence des *libri* de l'Écriture avec la *libra*, unité de poids et de compte, des livres (saints) avec la livre (profane).

Le même nombre de 44 se retrouve dans le codex de Bobbio, qui contient le *Liber Sacramentorum ecclesiae gallicanae*, et qui propose une liste des livres canoniques qu'on date du VIe ou du VIIe siècle. Cette liste offre plusieurs curiosités: elle regroupe Rt, Est et Jdt, qualifiés de «livres des femmes» (*libri mulierum*); elle omet 1-2 Par, Sg et Si; le nombre total des livres devrait dès lors être de 40; pour atteindre le nombre de 44, la liste compte le psautier («Daviticum») pour 5, ce qui signifie qu'elle compte pour un livre chacun des 5 livres du psautier. Malgré ce·décompte original, le total devrait être de 43, car il y a un seul Esd: il en résulte qu'il faut sûrement corriger «Esdra I» en «Esdra II», qui est le nombre donné par Augustin. Le nombre total des livres des deux Testaments est de 72: 44 de l'AT et 28 du NT (dont le *Liber Sacramentorum* fait partie). La liste de Bobbio ne rapproche pas ce nombre des 72 traducteurs de la LXX.

Enfin le nombre de 45 figure chez Isidore de Séville, où il résulte du décompte à part de Lm chez «certains» (*quidam*). Ce qui signifie que le nombre de référence est 44, celui d'Augustin. La liste donnée par Isidore suit d'ailleurs celle d'Augustin, dans le traité de *Sur la doctrine chrétienne*, à une exception près: Esd, donné après 1-2 M chez Augustin, figure avant ces livres chez Isidore. Pourtant, si l'on additionne les livres énumérés par Isidore, on aboutit au total de 43, car il parle simplement d'«Esdrae», là où, chez Augustin, il est question d'«Esdrae duo». Il faut donc corriger le texte d'Isidore d'après Augustin, ou bien considérer que l'expression «libri duo» qui suit «Macabeorum» est en facteur commun d'Esd et de M.

Chez les autres Pères, le nombre des livres bibliques n'est pas précisé, mais on peut assez souvent le calculer, et l'on aboutit aux nombres qui viennent d'être cités, mais aussi à quelques autres.

2. *L'apport des Pères*

Les Pères fournissent-ils un argument pour décider lequel des deux chiffres des livres de la Bible est le plus ancien, 22 ou 24? Les arguments traditionnels en faveur de 22 sont le témoignage de Flavius Josèphe, qui parle des 22 livres de la Bible (*Contre Apion* I 38-41) et les textes patristiques qui viennent d'être cités. Les arguments en faveur de 24 sont les témoignages de la tradition rabbinique (TB *Baba' batra'* 14b-15a et huit autres passages rabbiniques) et du judaïsme apocalyptique (*4 Esdras* 14,18-47, qui parle des 24 livres du Canon destinés à être publiés et des 70 livres apocalyptiques destinés aux seuls sages d'Israël).

Le texte décisif en la matière est le prologue «galeatus» de Jérôme. Jérôme explique qu'il y a deux tripartitions de la Bible hébraïque de son temps: l'une, où il y a 5 livres de la Loi, 8 livres des Prophètes et 9 livres des Écrits; l'autre, où il y a les mêmes 5 livres de la Loi, toujours 8 livres des Prophètes, mais maintenant 11 livres des Écrits (les mêmes chiffres de 5, 8 et 11, figurent dans le prologue à Daniel). En effet, Rt qui était compté avec Jg et Lm qui était compté avec Jr (*Hieremias cum Cinoth*) ne font plus partie des Prophètes, mais deviennent des livres autonomes de l'ordre des hagiographes. De 22 on passe ainsi à 24.

Or ce que dit Jérôme s'inscrit assez bien dans ce que nous savons de l'évolution de la liturgie juive. À une époque mal connue, mais antérieure au VIIIe siècle de notre ère, qui est la date finale de la composition du traité *Soferim*, on se met à lire Rt lors de la fête de Shavouot et Lm lors du jeûne du Tish'ah be-Av, qui commémore la catastrophe de 586. Cette réalité liturgique a imposé que Rt soit dorénavant séparé de Jg, et Lm de Jr, et que les deux livres soient copiés sur des rouleaux indépendants. Dorénavant, ils ne pouvaient plus être décomptés avec Jg et Jr. Jérôme est donc le témoin de cette innovation liturgique, qui reçoit une traduction dans la Bible hébraïque de son temps. On peut donc dire qu'il est le plus ancien témoin de la constitution en cours des 5 *megillot*. On

note aussi que Jérôme permet de dater l'innovation liturgique et codicologique mieux que ne le permettent les sources rabbiniques.

III. LE DÉCLASSEMENT DE LIVRES PROPHÉTIQUES PARMI LES ÉCRITS

1. *Ruth et Lamentations*

On vient de voir que Jérôme donne un témoignage sûr du fait que Rt
et Lm ont fait partie des Prophètes avant d'être reclassés parmi les
Écrits. À vrai dire, il existe dans la littérature patristique d'autres indices
allant dans ce sens. D'abord, Rt est toujours cité après Jg et, mieux encore, est souvent compté pour un seul livre avec Jg. Ensuite, lorsque,
dans leurs énumérations, les Pères signalent explicitement Lm, ce livre
est toujours associé à Jr (voir Athanase; Épiphane de Salamine; canon
59 du Concile de Laodicée; *Décret de Gélase*; Pseudo-Athanase §39;
Dialogue de Timothée et d'Aquila, 83-84v).

À ces indications tirées des textes patristiques, il faut joindre le dossier des textes rabbiniques, qui confirment les propos des Pères. Selon le
TB *Baba' batra'* 14b-15a, qui affirme rapporter les enseignements des
rabbins, Samuel a écrit son livre, Jg et Rt, tandis que Jérémie a composé
son livre, Rg et Lm. Cette affirmation va dans le sens de l'appartenance
de Rt et Lm aux Prophètes et même du regroupement de Rt avec Jg et de
Lm avec Jr.

2. *Daniel*

Dn fait partie des Écrits de la Bible massorétique. Il n'en va pas ainsi
chez les Pères, où, en règle générale, Dn fait partie du corpus prophétique. Par exemple, pour Méliton, les Prophètes sont Is, Jr, les XII, Dn, Ez
et Esd; dans ses *Eklogès prophétiques*, Eusèbe suit apparemment l'ordre
XII, Jr, Ez, Dn et Is, mais, à la fin du développement qu'il consacre aux
XII, il explique qu'il réserve Is pour le livre IV; il a donc parfaitement
conscience de ne pas respecter l'ordre normal qui est XII, Is, Jr, Ez et
Dn, lequel est donc le dernier des livres prophétiques; chez Athanase,
Dn est le vingt-deuxième et dernier livre du Canon et il suit les XII, Is,
Jr et Ez. Il existe de nombreux autres témoignages patristiques de l'ap-
partenance de Dn aux Prophètes[9]. La seule exception à la règle générale

9. Ce sont: le canon 59 du Concile de Laodicée; Cyrille de Jérusalem; Grégoire de
Nazianze; Amphiloque; le Canon apostolique 85; le pseudo-Athanase; le Pseudo-Jean
Chrysostome; la liste de l'*Oxoniensis Baroccianus* 206; le Pseudo-Léonce de Constantinople; le Pseudo-Nicéphore. Du côté latin, Hilaire de Poitiers cite Dn entre Jr et Ez; dans
la liste de Cheltenham (Mommsen), Dn figure entre Jr et Ez; il en est de même chez

est constituée par Jérôme qui, dans le prologue «galeatus», classe Dn dans l'*ordo agiograforum* et qui, dans le prologue à sa traduction de Dn, explique que ce livre ne figure pas parmi les Prophètes chez les Hébreux. Mais, dans le même prologue, il ne peut s'empêcher de qualifier Daniel de «prophète» et, dans la *Lettre 53* à Paulin, 8, il parle de Daniel, «le dernier parmi les grands prophètes». Même le témoignage de Jérôme va dans le sens de la présence de Dn parmi les livres prophétiques. On note que, dans la description que Cassiodore donne de la Bible de Jérôme, divisée en Loi, Prophètes et Hagiographes, Dn fait partie des Prophètes, et non des Hagiographes. Si grand était le poids qui faisait de Dn un livre prophétique!

Comment rendre compte de la contradiction entre les témoignages patristiques et les sources rabbiniques? Il n'existe pas à ce sujet de témoignage aussi décisif que le prologue «galeatus» dans le cas de Rt et de Lm. Il y a pourtant, à Qumrân, l'indication du *Florilège* de 4Q174, qui parle du «livre de Daniel le prophète». Certes, il n'est pas exclu que le livre d'un prophète puisse être classé parmi les Écrits: c'est ce qui se passe dans le cas des Ps, dont l'auteur, David, est regardé comme un prophète par les traditions chrétienne et juive, et même dans le cas d'Esther, qui est une des femmes qui a prophétisé pour Israël, si l'on en croit TB *Megillah* 14a. Mais Dn n'est pas assimilable à ces deux livres, dont la présence parmi les Écrits paraît due à des raisons cultuelles et liturgiques. En réalité, il est difficile d'admettre que le livre d'un inspiré appelé «prophète» puisse être d'emblée classé parmi les Écrits. Il est beaucoup plus naturel qu'il ait fait d'abord partie du corpus prophétique. On doit d'ailleurs noter qu'à ma connaissance, aucun savant n'a proposé de ranger Dn dans le corpus des quatre livres d'hymnes et de préceptes dont parle Flavius Josèphe: en général, on le classe parmi les treize livres des Prophètes que signale le même auteur. Est-ce à dire que le témoignage de Flavius Josèphe constitue l'élément décisif qui nous manque? En fait Flavius Josèphe n'énumère pas les treize livres et il faut se garder de trop solliciter son propos. Néanmoins, avec le *Florilège* de Qumrân, Flavius Josèphe et les textes patristiques, nous tenons un faisceau d'indices qui vont tous dans le même sens: la présence originelle de Dn parmi les Prophètes. Resterait à comprendre pourquoi Daniel a été déclassé parmi les Écrits. Ce déclassement paraît propre aux rabbins

---

Augustin, *Sur la doctrine chrétienne* II 8, 13; le *Décret* de Gélase classe Dn dans l'*ordo prophetarum*; Rufin énumère Is, Jr, Ez, Dn et «en outre» les XII; chez Innocent I et dans le codex de Bobbio, il est question des «16 livres des prophètes» (*prophetarum libri XVI*), ce qui implique que Dn en fasse partie; Junilius Africanus met Dn dans les livres qui relèvent de la prophétie, entre Ez et Ag.

et doit donc trouver son explication au sein de ce milieu. Faut-il penser à une raison de type cultuel et liturgique, comme on le fait valoir dans le cas de Ps, Rt et Lm? Cette hypothèse a été proposée[10], mais on ne voit pas bien dans quelle occasion cultuelle spéciale Dn a été lu. En revanche, il est facile de remarquer que Dn est le plus apocalypticien des livres bibliques. Il contient des visions et des données numériques qui donnaient des arguments aux partisans juifs des révoltes contre Rome. Or les deux guerres juives et singulièrement la seconde (130-135) ont mis le judaïsme en danger de mort. Il est sûr qu'un courant partisan du repli du judaïsme sur ses traditions, et favorable à une coexistence de fait avec l'empire romain, est apparu parmi les rabbins. On peut faire l'hypothèse que c'est dans ce contexte que Dn a été déclassé: faisant partie des Écrits, il était moins utilisable politiquement. Cependant il s'agit là d'une hypothèse qu'on aimerait étayer sur des textes.

3. *Autres livres bibliques*

Il y a sûrement eu d'autres cas de déclassement: chez Flavius Josèphe, il y a treize Prophètes et seulement quatre «autres» (λοιπά) livres. Les Pères permettent-ils de déterminer quels sont les anciens livres prophétiques? La réponse est négative, mais les Pères permettent au moins de poser des questions sur des déclassements possibles.

Souvent, dans la littérature patristique, 1-2 Par figurent immédiatement à la suite de 1-4 R: c'est un argument en faveur de leur classement parmi les Prophètes. Cet ordre est attesté dans un grand nombre de sources patristiques[11]. Il en va de même pour 1-2 Esd, qui suit immédiatement 1-4 R et 1-2 Par dans beaucoup de sources, mais qui sont un peu moins nombreuses que pour 1-2 Par[12]. De plus, dans le *Vaticanus* de la LXX, 1-4 Rg est suivi de 1-2 Par et de 1-2 Esd. Dans l'*Alexandrinus*, 1-2 Par suit également 1-4 Rg, mais 1-2 Esd figure entre Est, Tb et Jdt, d'une part, et 1-2 M et Ps, d'autre part. Le cas d'1-2 Par est donc mieux argumenté que celui d'1-2 Esd. En outre, chez Méliton de Sardes, la liste

---

10. Notamment par E.E. ELLIS, *The Old Testament in the Early Church*, in MULDER (ed.), *Mikra* (n. 5), p. 653-690.

11. Ce sont: Méliton; Origène; Eusèbe de Césarée; Athanase; Épiphane de Salamine; liste de Jérusalem; Grégoire de Nazianze; Amphiloque; Cyrille de Jérusalem; Josippe; Pseudo-Athanase; Pseudo-Jean Chrysostome; liste du *Baroccianus* 206; Pseudo-Léonce de Constantinople; Jean Damascène; Pseudo-Nicéphore; du côté latin Hilaire de Poitiers; Rufin d'Aquilée; liste de Cheltenham et Augustin; Isidore de Séville. Plusieurs listes canoniques donnent le même témoignage: canon 59 du Concile de Laodicée; canon apostolique 85; du côté latin, *Décret* de Gélase et Concile de Carthage de 397.

12. Mêmes témoignages que précédemment, sauf Épiphane de Salamine; liste de Jérusalem; liste du *Baroccianus* 206; liste de Cheltenham et Augustin; Isidore de Séville; *Décret* de Gélase et Concile de Carthage de 397.

des «Prophètes» comprend Is, Jr, les XII, Dn et Esd. Certes, on peut être tenté d'arrêter les livres prophétiques à Dn et d'en exclure Esd. Mais, ce faisant, on ne respecte pas la lettre du texte. Il semble bien que, pour les informateurs probablement judéo-chrétiens de Méliton, Esd était un livre prophétique.

Le Pseudo-Jean Chrysostome classe «David» dans la partie prophétique. Pour Isidore de Séville, le premier des livres des Prophètes est constitué par le livre des Psaumes. En soi, ces témoignages n'ont rien de choquant: pour la tradition juive et chrétienne, le roi David est aussi un prophète. Mais ce sont des témoignages rares et tardifs, qui ne sont pas recoupés par d'autres textes, en dehors de celui d'un autre auteur tardif, Junilius Africanus, qui affirme que Ps relève de la prophétie. Cependant, la perspective de Junilius est d'ordre rhétorique, et non biblique: il veut simplement dire que les psaumes offrent majoritairement un style prophétique, – une remarque qu'on peut accepter. Faut-il pour autant récuser le Pseudo-Jean Chrysostome et Isidore de Séville? Comme le Pseudo-Jean Chrysostome classe parmi les Prophètes Rt, qui a sûrement appartenu aux Prophètes, on se gardera d'écarter son témoignage, et par conséquent celui d'Isidore de Séville, tout en soulignant que celui de Flavius Josèphe va nettement en faveur de l'appartenance des Ps aux autres livres: ces derniers comprennent des hymnes, dans lesquels il est difficile de voir autre chose que les Ps. Toutefois, il semble bien qu'à Qumrân, les psaumes aient fait partie du corpus prophétique[13].

Le même Pseudo-Jean Chrysostome sait que «certains» attribuent le livre de Jb à Moïse, qui est le premier et le plus grand des prophètes. De fait, cette affirmation figure dans le TB *Baba' batra'* 14b-15a. Est-ce suffisant pour dire que Jb a fait partie des Prophètes, voire même du Pentateuque? En réalité, les sources anciennes sont unanimes sur la Loi et ses cinq livres. L'appartenance aux Prophètes ne peut cependant être exclue. D'ailleurs, dans les tentatives de reconstitution des treize livres des Prophètes selon Flavius Josèphe, Jb est souvent cité parmi eux.

---

13. Voir P.W. FLINT, *The Dead Sea Psalms Scrolls and the Book of Psalms* (Studies on the Texts of the Desert of Judah, 17), Leiden, 1997, p. 218-219, et J. TREBOLLE BARRERA, *The Jewish Bible and the Christian Bible. An Introduction to the History of the Bible*, Leiden, 1998, p. 160. Tous deux font remarquer que les *pesharim* semblent bien être réservés aux livres prophétiques. P. W. Flint ajoute le témoignage de 11QPs[a] (= 11Q5) col. XXVII, ligne 11: David a prononcé 4.050 cantiques; «tous ceux-là il les a dits dans la prophétie (בנבואה) qui lui a été donnée de la face du Très-Haut». Il est juste de signaler que Flint présente aussi des arguments à l'encontre de l'appartenance des psaumes aux livres prophétiques, en particulier le témoignage de 4QMMT en faveur de la tripartition de la Bible. Mais on a vu à quel point la reconstitution proposée ici pour le texte éta᷉ douteuse.

Il est probable que les études qumrâniennes pourront faire avancer la question de la classification des autres livres bibliques. Par exemple, il semble bien que les écrits attribués à Salomon (Pr, Eccl et Ct) aient d'abord fait partie des Prophètes[14], – une hypothèse que les témoignages patristiques ne corroborent cependant pas.

IV. La clôture des Écrits

La question de la datation de la clôture des Écrits divise les spécialistes en deux camps: ceux qui sont favorables à l'époque hasmonéenne et à une date haute; ceux qui pensent à l'époque de Jamnia/Yabneh, voire plus tard. Le témoignage des Pères peut-il nous éclairer?

Les Pères ne font jamais écho aux discussions rabbiniques sur Ct, Eccl, Ez, Pr et Si. Il n'en va pas de même dans le cas d'Est. En effet le statut de ce livre est chez eux contradictoire, ce qui peut s'expliquer, au moins partiellement, par la complexité du statut d'Est chez les rabbins: ces derniers considèrent que ce livre, qui n'a pas été retrouvé à Qumrân, est une addition à la Torah et aux Prophètes (TB *Megillah* 14a) tout en faisant partie du Canon massorétique.

Quelles sont les données patristiques sur Est? Tantôt ce livre figure dans le Canon: c'est le huitième livre dans le canon 59 du Concile de Laodicée; c'est le douzième livre chez Cyrille de Jérusalem; c'est le vingt-et-unième livre selon le Concile de Carthage de 435; c'est le vingt-deuxième et dernier livre du Canon des Hébreux chez Origène, Épiphane de Salamine (*Panarion* I 8, 6, 1-4 et *Sur les poids et mesures* 4), Timothée dans le *Dialogue de Timothée et d'Aquila*; c'est le vingt-septième et dernier livre, qui est aussi le vingt-deuxième, chez Épiphane (*Sur les poids et mesures* 23) et dans la liste de Jérusalem. Est figure également parmi les livres canoniques dans le canon 85 des Apôtres, chez le Pseudo-Chrysostome; du côté latin, dans la liste de Cheltenham, dans le *Décret* de Gélase, dans le canon 36 du Concile de Carthage de 397, chez Rufin, chez Augustin (*Sur la doctrine chrétienne* II 8, 13), chez Jérôme, *Lettre 53* à Paulin 8, chez Cassiodore, chez Isidore de Séville, dans la liste du codex de Bobbio, dans la liste du codex *Claramontanus*.

Tantôt Est ne figure pas dans le Canon. C'est le cas de Méliton (où l'on a supposé une lacune accidentelle, car le total des livres bibliques semble être de 21), de Grégoire de Nazianze et d'Amphiloque d'Ico-

---

14. Voir Trebolle Barrera, *The Jewish Bible and Christian Bible* (n. 13), p. 160.

nium. Dans la Peshitta ancienne, Est est absent, ainsi que 1-2 Par et 1-2 Esd.

Tantôt il y a hésitation sur la place d'Est dans le Canon: à la fin de sa liste des livres bibliques, Amphiloque signale que «certains» (τινες) ajoutent Esther; le Pseudo-Athanase fait de même (§2).

Tantôt, enfin, Est est cité parmi les livres qui ne sont ni canoniques ni apocryphes et qui deviendront beaucoup plus tard les livres deutérocanoniques. Il en va ainsi chez Athanase et le Pseudo-Athanase. Josippe met Est sur le même plan que les Maccabaïques, «en dehors» des livres canoniques (ἐνδιάθετα βιβλία). Il y a la même mise «en dehors» d'Est dans la liste de l'*Oxoniensis Baroccianus* 206. Chez le Pseudo-Nicéphore, Est fait partie des livres contestés (ἀντιλέγεσθαι), mais non apocryphes.

Il arrive même qu'il y ait des contradictions chez un même Père. Dans le *Traité des Principes*, composé à Alexandrie avant son départ pour Césarée de Palestine, Origène cite Est comme Écriture (III 2, 4). Est fait partie du Canon des Hébreux décrit dans le *Commentaire du psaume 1*, lui aussi composé à Alexandrie. Mais, dans l'*Homélie 27 sur les Nb* 1,3, Est est mis sur le même plan que Tb et Sg.

Ainsi les Pères se contredisent entre eux, voire présentent des contradictions internes. Comment expliquer ce double phénomène? Il est tentant de mettre ces contradictions en relation avec les discussions rabbiniques et de les interpréter comme reproduisant les hésitations des rabbins sur la canonicité d'Est. Peut-on préciser davantage? Les contradictions patristiques se comprennent mal dans l'hypothèse où la liste des Écrits aurait été close dès l'époque hasmonéenne: en ce cas, on s'attendrait à ce qu'Est figurât comme livre canonique chez tous les Pères. Les contradictions patristiques se comprennent beaucoup mieux si les Pères ont hérité d'un Canon lui-même contradictoire dans le cas d'Est. Cette considération nous amène au plus tôt à la fin du Ier siècle ou au début du IIe siècle, c'est-à-dire à l'époque de Jamnia/Yabneh. Mais d'autres indices plaident en faveur d'une datation plus tardive, et d'abord le fait qu'au IIe et au IIIe siècles, il y ait des discussions chez les rabbins au sujet d'Est. Par exemple, pour Mar Samuel (mort vers 254), «Est ne souille pas les mains», c'est-à-dire n'est pas canonique (TB *Megillah* 7a). Il y a là un témoignage allant dans le sens d'un Canon clos bien après Jamnia/Yabneh. Évidemment, rien ne prouve que les Pères aient été au courant de ces discussions. Pourtant on ne peut s'empêcher de remarquer qu'Origène change d'opinion sur Est et en fait un deutérocanonique lors de la deuxième période de sa vie, lorsqu'il vit à Césarée de Palestine, où il est en contact avec des rabbins et a des discussions avec eux. À son exemple, les Pères pour qui le refus de la canonicité d'Est relève avant tout d'une tradition ecclésiastique ont pu être encouragés à persévérer dans cette attitude parce qu'ils savaient que leur opinion était partagée par un certain nombre de rabbins. Ces remarques vont dans le sens d'une datation tardive de la clôture des Écrits, pas avant la fin du IIIᵉ siècle, voire plus tard. Peut-on préciser? Jérôme, on l'a vu, est le témoin de deux tripartitions rabbiniques différentes; mais toutes deux mettent Est parmi les livres bibliques. L'époque des discussions rabbiniques a bien l'air d'être close. En ce cas, la clôture des Écrits devrait être datée au plus tard d'un peu avant le séjour de Jérôme en Judée-Palestine. Une date un peu antérieure ne peut être exclue. La prudence invite à proposer une fourchette un peu large: les années 250 à 350.

V. LES LIVRES «DEUTÉROCANONIQUES»

La question du statut des deutérocanoniques dans le judaïsme n'a jamais été vraiment tirée au clair. Les Pères apportent-ils quelque lumière sur ces livres, qui ne furent appelés deutérocanoniques que bien après la période qui nous intéresse?

1. *Les données patristiques*

Face aux deutérocanoniques, le comportement des Pères n'est pas uniforme. Parfois, ils les citent au milieu des autres livres bibliques, sans les classer sous une rubrique particulière. Mais, dans la plupart des cas, ils les énumèrent à part.

Méliton de Sardes cite les Pr de Salomon, «appelés ausi Sg». Peut-être s'agit-il du livre des Pr et, en ce cas, Méliton n'énumère aucun deutérocanonique. Mais peut-être s'agit-il bien de Sg, qui, en ce cas, serait le seul deutérocanonique signalé par Méliton, au milieu des autres livres bibliques. Chez le Pseudo-Jean Chrysostome, 1-2 Par est suivi de 1-2 Esd, Est, Tb, Jdt, puis Jb, puis Sg, puis, après une lacune, Si, Is, Jr, Ez, Dn, les XII. Du côté latin, la liste de Cheltenham et le *Décret* de Gélase citent les deutérocanoniques sur le même plan que les livres canoniques. Il en va de même chez Augustin (*Sur la doctrine chrétienne* II 8, 13: Tb, Est, Jdt et 1-2 M sont cités entre Jb et 1-2 Esd; Sg et Si sont classés parmi les prophètes; *Cité de Dieu* XV 23: Ba est cité comme un prophète).

Dans leur pratique de citateurs, les Pères considèrent souvent les deutérocanoniques comme Écritures. Sg est citée comme Écriture par Clément de Rome, Tatien, *À Diognète*, Irénée, Clément d'Alexandrie,

Cyprien et d'autres. Pour les autres deutérocanoniques, on peut se reporter aux relevés de S.M. Zarb[15]. Voici les deutérocanoniques, auxquels on a joint Est, qu'Origène cite comme Écritures dans le *Traité des Principes*: Est (en III 2, 4); 2 M 7, 28 (en II 1, 5); Sg 11, 20 (en II 9, 1 et IV 4, 8) et 15, 11 (en III 4, 1); Tb 5, 4 (en III 2, 4) et 13, 18 (en II 3, 5); Si 6, 4 (en II 8, 4); 16, 21 (en IV 3, 14); 43, 20 (en II 8, 3); le verset 42 de Suzanne (en III 1, 2 et III 1, 17).

Toutefois, le plus souvent, les Pères traitent les deutérocanoniques à part. Les listes qu'ils en donnent sont plus ou moins fournies. Chez Origène décrivant le Canon des Hébreux, il existe un seul livre «en dehors» (ἔξω) des livres canoniques, celui des «Maccabaïques», dont le titre hébreu est *Sarbêthsabanaiel*, un titre qui a fait couler beaucoup d'encre. Grâce à Jérôme qui, dans le prologue «galeatus», raconte qu'il a trouvé 1 M en hébreu et 2M en grec, nous pouvons identifier les «Maccabaïques» avec 1 M.

Une liste étroite de deux livres figure chez Épiphane, *Panarion* I 8, 6, 1-4 (il s'agit de Sg et Si, deux livres ἐν ἀμφιλέκτῳ, «en contestation», une catégorie qu'Épiphane distingue des apocryphes), *Sur les poids et mesures* 4 (où les mêmes deux livres sont qualifiés d'«utiles» et de «profitables»); chez Josippe (Est et les Maccabaïques sont «en dehors» (ἔξω) des livres canoniques); chez Jean Damascène (les deux Sagesses, Sg et Si, sont qualifiées de «pleines de vertu» (ἐνάρετοι) et de «belles» (καλαί), mais elles ne sont pas comptées avec les livres canoniques). Du côté latin, Hilaire dit que Tb et Jdt sont des livres supplémentaires (*additi*): sans doute sont-ils des deutérocanoniques.

Une liste de taille moyenne de 5 ou 6 livres est attestée chez Athanase (5: Sg, Si, Est, Jdt, Tbt) et chez le Pseudo-Athanase (§2 et 41-46: même liste que chez Athanase). Du côté latin, chez Rufin, qui distingue les livres «ecclésiastiques» et les livres «canoniques»: les 2 Sagesses (c'est-à-dire Sg et Si), Tb, Jdt et les «livres des M», sans doute 1-2 M; chez Jérôme (prologue «galeatus»: les 2 Sagesses, Jdt, Tb, 1-2 M); chez Isidore de Séville, qui signale que «les Hébreux ne reçoivent pas» Tb, Jdt et 1-2 M, mais que «l'Église les compte parmi les Écritures canoniques», et qui donne un renseignement voisin sur Sg et Si.

Une liste large de 9 livres est attestée dans l'*Oxoniensis Baroccianus* 206, où les livres «en dehors» (ἔξω) des livres canoniques sont numérotés de 1 à 9: Sagesse de Salomon, Sagesse de Sirach, 1-4 M, Est, Jdt, Tb. À quoi s'ajoutent les Psaumes de Salomon, le neuvième des vingt-cinq livres «apocryphes» énumérés par le *Baroccianus* 206.

15. S.M. ZARB, *De historia canonis utriusque testamenti*, Rome, 1934, p. 117, 128-142.

Une liste large de 10 livres, sans doute décomptée pour 8, figure chez le Pseudo-Nicéphore (1-3 M, Sg, Siracide, Psaumes et Odes de Salomon, Est, Jdt, Suzanne, Tb).

Une liste large de 13, sans doute décomptée pour 9 figure chez le Pseudo-Athanase (§74: Sg, Si, Est, Jdt, Tb, 1-4 M, Ptolémaïques, Psaumes et Ode (au singulier) de Salomon, Suzanne; cette liste offre deux bizarreries: 1-4 M accompagnés des Ptolémaïques, dont on voit mal ce que c'est sinon 3 M, et Suzanne).

On remarque que le même auteur, le Pseudo-Athanase, peut proposer une liste moyenne (§2 et 41-46) et une liste large (§74).

2. *Les phénomènes de flou*

De la sorte, les deutérocanoniques sont sous le signe de la variabilité. On a signalé une variabilité de même ordre dans le cas d'Est, tantôt rangé dans le Canon, tantôt classé parmi les deutérocanoniques. Mais, ici, cette variabilité devient un vrai flottement qui se traduit par des effets de brouillage. Dans le cas des titres d'abord: Pr reçoit le titre de Sg chez Méliton et de *Sagesse pleine de vertu* (Πανάρετος Σοφία) chez Hégésippe et Irénée cités par Eusèbe de Césarée (*Histoire ecclésiastique* IV 22, 9). Mais il n'est pas exclu qu'il s'agisse en réalité du livre de la Sg. Inversement, Πανάρετος est le nom de Sg chez Épiphane, *Sur les poids et mesures* 4, Jean Damascène et le Pseudo-Athanase. De son côté, Si est cité sous le nom de Sg par Origène (*Traité des Principes* II 8, 3, qui cite Si 43,20), sous le nom de Πανάρετος chez Jérôme et sous le titre de Pr dans un manuscrit hébreu auquel Jérôme a eu accès (prologue aux 3 livres de Salomon). Il faut avouer qu'il y a là de quoi égarer plus d'un lecteur!

Le même brouillage entoure parfois la terminologie. Dans le *Dialogue de Timothée et Aquila*, Timothée appelle apocryphes Tb, Sg et Si, tout en mettant Jdt dans le Canon hébraïque! Jérôme, qui distingue en règle générale les deutérocanoniques des apocryphes, finit par les ranger parmi ces derniers, dans le prologue «galeatus».

Enfin, s'il y a accord chez les Pères pour qualifier les deutérocanoniques d'«utiles et profitables» (selon l'expression d'Épiphane, *Sur les poids et mesures* 4), il n'y a pas de consensus sur la manière de définir cette utilité profitable. Chez Origène, Athanase et le Pseudo-Athanase, la lecture des deutérocanoniques est recommandée à tous ceux qui débutent dans les choses divines, aux catéchumènes. Dans le canon apostolique 85, la lecture est conseillée aux jeunes, qui ne sont pas forcément les catéchumènes. Chez Rufin et chez Jérôme, les deutérocanoniques ser-vent à l'«édification du peuple», mais «non pour confirmer l'autorité des doctrines ecclésiastiques» (prologue aux livres de Salomon). Il est donc possible que le public auquel les deutérocanoniques étaient conseillés ait varié dans le temps et dans l'espace.

3. *Les deutérocanoniques, des livres «extérieurs» et/ou des livres «lus»?*

Sur des bases aussi embrouillées, est-il possible d'aller plus loin? É. Junod a fait observer que les Pères distinguaient trois catégories de livres: les livres «testamentaires»; les «autres livres», nos deutérocanoniques, et les livres «apocryphes». Il a montré que les deux termes techniques «testamentaires» et «apocryphes» remontaient aux Juifs de langue grecque. Il a regretté de ne pouvoir faire la même analyse à propos des «autres livres», dans la mesure où les Pères ne donnent pas le nom de cette catégorie, à supposer que ce nom ait jamais existé[16]. C'est sur ce point précis qu'il est peut-être possible d'avancer un peu.

La première suggestion prend son point de départ dans une expression qu'on trouve chez Origène, Josippe, la liste du *Baroccianus* 206 et le Pseudo-Nicéphore. Ils parlent tous des livres qu'on trouve «en dehors» (ἔξω) des livres canoniques. Certes il n'existe pas de livre «en dehors» dans le judaïsme hellénistique. Mais l'expression grecque ne peut pas ne pas évoquer les livres appelés *ḥiẓonim*, «extérieurs», dans la tradition rabbinique. Le TB *Sanhedrin* 100b explique que, selon un tanna, ces livres extérieurs étaient ceux des hérétiques. Mais le texte continue par un propos de Rabbi Joseph (vers 320): il est interdit de lire le livre de Ben Sira. Si faisait donc partie des *ḥiẓonim* au IVe siècle, et sans doute auparavant. Peut-on généraliser à l'ensemble des deutérocanoniques cette appellation? On peut au moins suggérer cette piste de recherche. Cependant une autre question se pose: les *ḥiẓonim* ont-ils pu désigner les seuls deutérocanoniques? Le texte du TB *Sanhedrin* 100b, qui parle à la fois des livres des hérétiques et du Si, ne va pas en ce sens. Mais là encore une recherche complémentaire reste à mener[17].

---

16. É. JUNOD, *La formation et la composition de l'Ancien Testament dans l'Église grecque des quatre premiers siècles*, in J. -D. KAESTLI & O. WERMELINGER (éds.), *Le Canon de l'Ancien Testament. Sa formation et son histoire* (Le Monde de la Bible), Genève, 1984, pp. 105-151.

17. Il est question des «livres extérieurs» (*soferim ḥiẓonim*) dans la Mishna *Sanhedrin* 10, 1; le TJ *Sanhedrin* 28a; le TB *Sanhedrin* 100b; *Ecclésiaste Rabbah* 12, 12 (voir LEIMAN, *The Canonization of Hebrew Scripture* [n. 4], partie II, §68-71). Les livres visés sont, outre Si, ceux de Ben La'ana et Ben Tigla, dont l'identification est problématique.

Que sont les livres de hérétiques? S'agit-il des Évangiles ou des apocryphes ou d'autres textes? S'il s'agit des Évangiles, ne peut-on faire l'hypothèse que les *ḥiẓonim* auraient d'abord désigné les deutérocanoniques avant que ce terme soit étendu aux livres des hérétiques chrétiens?

Une seconde suggestion peut être avancée. On remarque que plusieurs des sources patristiques insistent sur le fait que les deutérocanoniques font l'objet d'une lecture (Origène, Athanase, Rufin, Jérôme). Le Pseudo-Athanase distingue même «les livres canoniques» (τὰ κανονιζόμενα), les livres «seulement lus aux catéchumènes» (τὰ ἀναγινωσκόμενα μόνον τοῖς κατηχουμένοις) et «les livres apocryphes» (τὰ ἀπόκρυφα). La question est donc la suivante: les livres «lus» ou «seulement lus» ne pourraient-ils pas constituer l'appellation technique que recherchait É. Junod? Il ne semble pas qu'il existe dans la tradition rabbinique une catégorie de livres appelés *qerû'im* ou *miqrâ'im* (terme éventuellement accompagné de *'ak*), qu'il faudrait distinguer des livres «écrits», *ketûbim*. Cependant, dans la même tradition rabbinique, le verbe «écrire» entre en opposition avec plusieurs verbes. L'opposition «lire» *vs* «traduire» de la Mishna *Megillah* 4, 10, ne semble pas éclairante, pas plus que celle qu'on trouve en TJ *Megillah* 74d entre «lire» et «réciter par cœur». En revanche, il existe une opposition entre «lire» *vs* «écrire» qui est différente de la distinction bien connue entre le *qerey* et le *ketib*, dans le TB *Megillah* 7a, où Mar Samuel explique que Est a été dit pour être lu, non pour être écrit. Dans le même traité, en 3b, Rabbi abandonne l'étude de la Torah pour aller écouter la lecture du livre d'Esther, tandis qu'en 14a, selon Rabbi Nahman b. Isaac, la lecture du rouleau d'Esther équivaut à réciter le Hallel. On peut se demander s'il n'y a pas là une opposition entre les livres qui sont soumis à la lecture orale seule et les livres qui font à la fois objets de lecture et d'étude. C'est le moment de rappeler que les deutérocanoniques n'ont pas fait l'objet de commentaires et d'homélies dans les premiers siècles patristiques. On peut suggérer que les Pères étaient sur ce point les héritiers de pratiques juives. Je résume l'hypothèse d'une phrase: les deutérocanoniques chrétiens seraient un groupe de livres juifs qui avaient en commun d'être lus, mais non étudiés; Est aurait fait partie de cette catégorie de livres, puis, pour des raisons au départ cultuelles et liturgiques, serait passé de cette catégorie à celle des *ketûbim*; Si, dont nous savons par le prologue de son traducteur, qu'il était destiné à l'étude, aurait effectué le mouvement inverse.

64, Avenue des Chartreux   Gilles DORIVAL
F-13004 Marseille

SOURCES PATRISTIQUES

On trouvera ci-dessous la liste des principales sources patristiques utilisées, avec référence, le cas échéant, à l'étude de T. ZAHN, *Geschichte des Neutestamentlichen Kanons*, t. 2,1, Erlangen - Leipzig, 1890, qui en a réuni et présenté un grand nombre[18]:

1. Sources grecques

Amphiloque d'Iconium, *Iambes à Séleucos* 251-319 (avant 394), PG 37, 1577-1600 (ZAHN, p. 217-219).

Athanase d'Alexandrie, *Lettre festale 39* (an. 394), PG 26, 1436-1440 et 1176-1180 (ZAHN, p. 210-212). Version copte plus complète: éd. L.-TH. LEFORT, CSCO 151, Louvain, 1951, elle-même à compléter par R. COQUIN, *Les Lettres festales d'Athanase (CPG 2102). Un nouveau complément: le manuscrit IFAO, copte 25*, in *Orientalia Lovaniensia Periodica* 15 (1984) 138-158, pl. X (ce témoin contient la suggestion avancée par Lefort de suppléer le mot Esdras au sein d'une phrase).

Pseudo-Athanase, *Synopse abrégée de la divine Écriture* (Vᵉ siècle?), PG 28, 284-437 (cf. ZAHN, p. 302-318).

Cyrille de Jérusalem, *Homélies catéchétiques* IV 33-36 (fin IVᵉ siècle), PG 33, 453-505 (ZAHN, p. 172-180).

Épiphane de Salamine (fin IVᵉ siècle), *Panarion* I 8, 6, 1-4, éd. K. HOLL, GCS 25, Leipzig, 1915 (cf. ZAHN, p. 219-226); Id., *Sur les poids et mesures* 3-4 et 22-23, PG 43, 237-293 (ZAHN, p. 172-180).

Eusèbe de Césarée, *Eklogès prophétiques* (premier tiers du IVᵉ siècle), PG 22, 1021-1262.

Grégoire de Nazianze, *Poèmes*, I 12 (fin IVᵉ siècle), PG 37, 472-474 (ZAHN, p. 216-217).

Canons des Apôtres 85 (fin IVᵉ siècle?), éd. M. METZGER, *Constitutions Apostoliques* VIII 47, 85, SC 336, Paris, 1987 (ZAHN, p. 180-193).

Pseudo-Jean Chrysostome, *Synopse en abrégé* (Vᵉ siècle?), PG 56, 313-385 (cf. ZAHN, p. 226-233).

Jean Damascène, *Sur la foi orthodoxe*, IV 17 (première moitié du VIIᵉ siècle), PG 94, 789-1228 (ZAHN, p. 295).

Josippe, *Hypomnesticon* I 25 (fin IVᵉ siècle), PG 106, 15-176.

Pseudo-Léonce de Constantinople, *Sur les hérésies* II (milieu du VIᵉ siècle), PG 86, 1193-1268 (ZAHN, p. 293-295).

Méliton de Sardes, *Eklogès* (fin IIᵉ siècle), dans Eusèbe de Césarée, *Histoire ecclésiastique* IV 26, 12-14.

Pseudo-Nicéphore, *Chronographie abrégée* (vers 900), PG 100, 1001-1060 (ZAHN, p. 295-301).

Origène, *Commentaire sur le psaume 1*, dans Eusèbe de Césarée, *Histoire ecclésiastique* VI 25; ID., *Homélies sur les Nombres* 27, 1-3 et 28, 2, 1 (avant 250).

Anonyme, *Dialogue de Timothée et d'Aquila* (Vᵉ-VIᵉ siècles), éd. F.C. CONYBEARE, Oxford, 1898.

---

18. Voir aussi H. B. SWETE, *An Introduction to the Old Testament in Greek*, revised by R. R. OTTLEY, Cambridge, 1902, repr. New York, 1968, p. 201-214.

Canon 59 du Concile de Laodicée (avant 381), éd. P.P. JOANNOU, *Fonti. Fascicolo IX. Discipline générale antique (IVe-IX ^esiècles)*, t. 1,2 *Les canons des Synodes particuliers*, I, 2, pp. 154-155 (ZAHN, p. 202).

Liste de Jérusalem (*Hierosolymitanus* 54, an. 1056) (fin IVe siècle?), éd. J.-P. AUDET, *A Hebrew-Aramaic List of Books of the Old Testament in Greek Transcription*, in *JTS* 1 (1950) 135-154.

Liste du *Londinensis Add.* 17469, de l'*Oxoniensis Baroccianus* 206 et du *Parisinus Coislinianus* 120 (VIe siècle?), éd. ZAHN, p. 290.

2. Sources latines

Augustin, *Sur la doctrine chrétienne* II 8, 12-13, éd. J. MARTIN, CC SL 32, Turnhout, 1962 (ZAHN, p. 253-259); ID., *Cité de Dieu* XV 23, 4 et XVIII 43.

Cassiodore, *Institutio divinarum litterarum* 11-14 (VIe siècle), éd. ZAHN, p. 269-273.

Hilaire de Poitiers, *Tractatus super psalmos*, Instructio psalmorum 15 (milieu du IVe siècle), éd. A. ZINGERLE, CSEL 22, 1891.

Innocent I, *Lettre à Exsupère évêque de Toulouse* (20 février 405), éd. ZAHN, p. 244-246.

Isidore de Séville, *In libros Veteris et Novi Testamenti Proemia* (vers 600), PL 83, 155-160.

Jérôme, *Lettre 53 à Paulin*, 8, éd. J. LABOURT, t. III, CUF, Paris, 1953; ID., prologues sur le Pentateuque, les livres de Samuel et des Rois (prologue «galeatus»), Esther, les 3 livres de Salomon, Daniel, dans *Biblia Sacra iuxta Vulgatam Versionem*, éd. R. WEBER, 2 tomes, Stuttgart, 1969 (4e éd. par R. GRYSON, 1994).

Junilius Africanus, *Instituta Regularia Divinae Legis* I, III-VI, éd. H. KIHN, Fribourg-Br., 1880.

Philastre de Brescia, *Livre des hérésies* 78 (fin IVe siècle), PL 12 (cf. ZAHN, p. 233-239).

Rufin d'Aquilée, *Exposition du symbole*, 34-36, éd. M. SIMONETTI, CC SL 20, Turnhout, 1961 (ZAHN, p. 240-244).

Canon 36 du Concile de Carthage de 397; canon 24 *in causa Apierii*; canon 47 du Concile de Carthage de 435, éd. C. MUNIER, CC SL 149, Turnhout, 1974 (ZAHN, p. 246-253).

Décret de Gélase (document plus ancien que l'époque de Gélase, peut-être l'époque de Damase, fin IVe siècle), éd. E. VON DOBSCHÜTZ, TU 38/4, Leipzig, 1912 (cf. ZAHN, p. 259-267).

Liste du codex de Bobbio (VIe ou VIIe siècle), aujourd'hui *Parisinus lat. 13.246*, éd. ZAHN, p. 285.

Liste de Cheltenham dite aussi liste de Mommsen (milieu du IVe siècle), éd. T. MOMMSEN, *Zur lateinischen Stichometrie*, in *Hermes* 21 (1886) 142-146 (ZAHN, p. 143-145).

Liste du codex *Claramontanus* (avant le VIIe siècle); aujourdhui *Parisinus gr.* 107, éd. ZAHN, p. 158-159.

DER PSALTER IM HORIZONT
VON TORA UND PROPHETIE

Kanongeschichtliche und kanonhermeneutische Perspektiven

Eine der wichtigsten Fragen der derzeitigen Kanondiskussion ist m.E. die Frage nach der *Relevanz des Kanons für das Verständnis der biblischen Texte* im Horizont von Judentum und Christentum. Hat der Kanon nur die Funktion, die als formativ und normativ geltenden Texte festzulegen, ist er also eine letztlich juristische Größe, oder konstituiert der Kanon als strukturiertes Ganzes ein spezifisches Sinngefüge mit eigener Gesamtaussage? Ist der Kanon ein Archiv, der den in ihm aufbewahrten Texten bzw. Büchern zwar eine besondere Dignität, aber keinen ihnen zukommenden besonderen kanonischen Sinn verleiht, oder schafft der Kanon einen Sinnraum, der den Texten einen Bedeutungszuwachs und eine zusätzliche Sinnrichtung gibt? Hat der Kanon Relevanz für die Projekte Biblische Theologie und Theologische Exegese oder sind beide Projekte eigentlich Versuche, denen sich die Exegese als historische Wissenschaft sogar widersetzen muß?

Über diese Frage ist die Exegese derzeit zutiefst gespalten. Es gibt nicht nur diese beiden gegensätzlichen Positionen, sondern zahlreiche Zwischenpositionen[1]. Ich will gleichwohl Vertreter der zwei Gegenpositionen am Anfang meiner Überlegungen kurz zu Wort kommen lassen, da sie gewissermaßen den Rahmen abstecken, in dem mein Vortrag angesiedelt ist.

Die erste Position markiere ich zunächst mit einem Zitat aus Wolfgang Richters einflußreicher Methodologie »Exegese als Literaturwissenschaft«: »Die Existenz des Kanons ist für den Interpreten der Texte bedeutungslos; interessant ist er nur als historisches Faktum, insofern seine Aufstellung dazu geführt hat, daß andere Texte leider verlorengegangen sind und für die Interpretation nicht mehr zur Verfügung stehen«[2]. Daß dies auch für die Kanonstruktur gilt, hält John Barton, einer der aktivsten Teilnehmer an der Kanondiskussion der letzten zwei Jahr-

---

1. Vgl. die Beiträge von E.L. Ehrlich, H. Frankemölle, W. Groß, B. Janowski, O. Keel, K. Lehmann, N. Lohfink, L. Schwienhorst-Schönberger im Sammelband F.-L. Hossfeld (ed.), *Wieviel Systematik erlaubt die Schrift? Auf der Suche nach einer gesamtbiblischen Theologie* (QD, 185), Freiburg i. B., Herder, 2001.

2. W. Richter, *Exegese als Literaturwissenschaft. Entwurf einer alttestamentlichen Literaturtheorie und Methodologie*, Göttingen, Vandenhoeck & Ruprecht, 1970, p. 40.

zehnte, folgendermaßen ausdrücklich fest: »The books of Scripture were not arranged in any particular order from which theological implications can be derived«[3].

Die Gegenposition läßt sich mit zwei Zitaten von Norbert Lohfink charakterisieren: »›Kanon‹ impliziert drei Elemente, die sich zusammengenommen nicht mehr durch historischen Zugriff bewältigen lassen. Erstens umfaßt ein Kanon eine Vielheit von Büchern mit einer Vielheit von Theologien. Zweitens erhebt er inhaltlich einen Einheitsanspruch... Drittens schließt er auf der kanonischen Geltungsebene andere Texte und Zeugnisse aus... Daß diese drei Elemente sich verbinden, hängt damit zusammen, daß der Kanon vor allem von seiner gesellschaftlichen Funktion her definiert werden muß. Er umschreibt den Makrotext, auf den sich eine Rezeptionsgemeinschaft als auf ihre unaufgebbare und allein liturgisch proklamierbare textliche Basis zurückbezieht«[4]. Das aber bedeutet für eine christliche Exegese: »Eigentlich wird die Exegese mit der Auslegung des kanonischen Textes ja überhaupt erst zur Theologie. Erst der Sinn, den die biblischen Texte innerhalb der Einheit der Schrift gewinnen, ist ihr inspirierter und irrtumsloser Sinn. Von ihm allein hat Theologie auszugehen, alles andere ist, wenn auch noch so wichtige und unentbehrliche, Vorstudie«[5].

Im Spannungsfeld dieser beiden Positionen wollen meine Ausführungen die Frage nach der Relevanz des Kanons für schriftgemäßes Verständnis der Psalmen reflektieren. Ich gliedere diese Überlegungen in zwei Teile, die das Problem von zwei unterschiedlichen Seiten her beleuchten sollen. Der erste Teil katalogisiert eine Reihe mir wichtig erscheinender kanongeschichtlicher Beobachtungen. Der zweite Teil bringt kanonhermeneutische Perspektiven, die beim Psalmenbuch selbst ansetzen und dieses kanontheologisch einordnen sowie davon ausgehend einige allgemeinere Schlußfolgerungen über die Funktion des Kanons für die Interpretation der kanonischen Texte andeuten[6].

---

3. J. BARTON, *Oracles of God. Perceptions of Ancient Prophecy in Israel after the Exile*, New York & Oxford, University Press, 1986, p. 44.

4. N. LOHFINK, *Alttestamentliche Wissenschaft als Theologie? 44 Thesen*, in HOSSFELD (ed.), *Wieviel Systematik* (n. 1), pp. 39-40.

5. N. LOHFINK, *Der Begriff »Bund« in der biblischen Theologie*, in N. LOHFINK & E. ZENGER, *Der Gott Israels und die Völker. Untersuchungen zum Jesajabuch und zu den Psalmen* (SBS, 154), Stuttgart, Katholisches Bibelwerk, 1994, p. 27.

6. Aus der Vielzahl meiner bisherigen Beiträge zu diesem Thema nenne ich nur: *Das Erste Testament. Die jüdische Bibel und die Christen*, Düsseldorf, Patmos, ⁵1995; *Die grund-legende Bedeutung des Ersten Testaments. Christlich-jüdische Bibelhermeneutik nach Auschwitz*, in *Bibel und Kirche* 55 (2000) 6-13; *Einleitung in das Alte Testament*, Stuttgart, Kohlhammer, ⁴2001, pp. 11-35.

I. Kanongeschichtliche Vorgaben

1. »Einen (jüdischen) Kanon gibt es streng genommen erst, nachdem eine jüdische Richtung, die pharisäisch-rabbinische, ihre Auffassung durchgesetzt hat, im 3./4. Jahrhundert n.Chr. Aber auch die Rabbinen kämpften noch um die Kontrolle über den normativen Text und benutzten dazu Vorschriften für die Erstellung tauglicher, rituell heiliger Schriftrollen-Exemplare«[7].

2. Strenggenommen sind die Begriffe »Bibel« und »Kanon« für die Heiligen Schriften des Judentums insofern mißverständlich, als sie vom christlichen Bibelverständnis her entwickelt wurden und terminologisch keine hebräischen Entsprechungen haben[8]. »Bibel«, abgeleitet vom kirchenlateinischen *biblia* und als *Singular* verstanden, bezeichnet seit Anfang des 2. Jahrtausends die Gesamtheit der Schriften bzw. »Bücher« des Alten und Neuen Testaments als Einheit, deren Basisstruktur als zweiteilig verstanden wird, wobei nach traditionellem Verständnis der zweite Teil, das Neue Testament, die entscheidenden Perspektiven für das Verständnis des ersten Teils, des Alten Testaments, liefert. Dieses mit »Bibel« verbundene christliche Konzept könnte man zwar einerseits mit dem zweiteiligen jüdischen Konzept von schriftlicher und mündlicher *Tora* parallelisieren, aber dann bleiben die übrigen Schriften des Tanach unberücksichtigt. Andererseits haben diese übrigen Schriften, zumindest die Ketubim, in der synagogalen Liturgie nie jene fundamentale Rolle gespielt, die die (schriftliche) Tora hatte.

3. Entgegen der noch vor zwei Jahrzehnten gängigen Auffassung, *der kanonische Prozeß* zum dreigeteilten Tanach sei geradlinig und sukzessiv in den drei Stadien Tora (4.Jh.), Nebiim (3. bzw. 2.Jh.) und Ketubim (1.Jh. n.Chr.) abgelaufen, wird heute die kanongeschichtliche Situation dieser Epoche – entsprechend der Vielgestaltigkeit des Judentums bzw. der jüdischen Gruppierungen jener Epoche – als viel komplexer beschrieben[9], wie paradigmatisch das folgende Zitat von David Carr belegt:

> In sum, there is no evidence for Jewish consensus on the overall structure of the canon during the Second Temple period, whether tripartite or bipartite. Instead, just as there was a plurality of Jewish groups during this time, there seems to have been a plurality in conceptions of Scripture. Some

---

7. J. Maier, *Zur Frage des biblischen Kanons im Frühjudentum im Licht der Qumranfunde*, in *JBT* 3 (1988) 146.

8. Cf. J. Maier, Art. *Bibel. III. Judentum*, in *LTK* II (³1994), pp. 365-366; G. Veltri, Art. *Kanon. II. Judentum*, in *LTK* V (³1966), p. 1182.

9. Einen guten Forschungsüberblick bietet nun St.B. Chapman, *The Law and the Prophets. A Study in Old Testament Canon Formation* (FAT, 27), Tübingen, Mohr, 2000, pp. 1-70.

groups, such as the Samaritans, Alexandrians, and certain establishment groups in Palestine seem to have focused exclusively or almost exclusively on Torah alone. Others seem to have worked with the Torah and a group of non-Torah, authoritative books termed ›Prophets‹. And finally, we have seen – particularly in certain groups more generally working with a bipartite canon – at least a couple of texts draw an occasional distinction between the ›prophets‹ and a variously described collection of other non-Torah authoritative books, although the contents of such a collection and terminology for it are not standardized. The lines of continuity between these varying conceptions are twofold: Torah is present in all of them, and if there is an additional category, the next one is usually termed ›Prophets‹. Otherwise, variety reigns... The Torah-only canon seems to have been common primarily among groups associated with an ongoing Temple cult (the Sadducees, and certain Priestly circles in Jerusalem, the Samaritans at Mt. Gerizim). In contrast, the broader Tora and Prophets canon seems to have been favored by groups whose base of activity lay primarily outside Temple circles (the Pharisees, Qumran community, and early Christians[10].

4. Im Rahmen dieser kanongeschichtlichen Neuorientierung ist auch die lange Zeit übliche These von einem gegenüber dem pharisäisch-rabbinischen Kanon *umfangreicheren* und konzeptionell anders zu lesenden *alexandrinischen Septuagintakanon* des hellenistischen Judentums, den das Urchristentum übernommen habe, nicht mehr haltbar. Einerseits ist der Septuaginta*kanon* eine Schaffung der christlichen Kirche und andererseits dürfte gerade das alexandrinische Judentum, wie vor allem Philo belegt, nur das Tora-Kanonkonzept vertreten haben[11].

5. Die beiden Kanon-»Mainstreams«, Tora-Kanon und Tora-Prophetie-Kanon, spiegeln sich auch in der Terminologie der Epoche *um die Zeitenwende* wider. Die im Neuen Testament verwendeten *Bezeichnungen* für die heiligen Schriften Israels »Gesetz und Propheten« (Mt 5,17; 7,12; 11,13; 22,40; Lk 16,16; Apg 24,14; Röm 3,21), »Mose und Propheten« (Lk 16,29; 24,27; Joh 1,45), »Propheten und Mose« (Apg 26,22), »Gesetz« (Lk 16,16; Joh 10,34; 12,34; 15,25; Röm 3,19; 1 Kor

---

10. D.M. CARR, *Canonization in the Context of Community: An Outline of the Formation of the Tanakh and the Christian Bible*, in R.D. WEIS & D.M. CARR (eds.), *A Gift of God in Due Season. Essays on Scripture and Community in Honor of James A. Sanders* (JSOT SS, 225), Sheffield, Academic Press, 1996, pp. 45-48. Vgl. auch die Diskussion bei H. FRANKEMÖLLE, *Das Neue Testament als Kommentar? Möglichkeiten und Grenzen einer hermeneutischen These aus der Sicht eines Neutestamentlers,* in HOSSFELD (ed.), *Wieviel Systematik* (n. 1), pp. 227-235.

11. Vgl. hierzu grundlegend: M. HENGEL & A. SCHWEMER (eds.), *Die Septuaginta zwischen Judentum und Christentum* (WUNT, 72), Tübingen, Mohr, 1994; M. MÜLLER, *The First Bible of the Church. A Plea for the Septuagint* (JSOT SS, 206), Sheffield, Academic Press, 1996; N. WALTER, *Die griechische Übersetzung der »Schriften« Israels und die christliche »Septuaginta« als Forschungs- und als Übersetzungsgegenstand,* in H.-J. FABRY & U. OFFERHAUS (eds.), *Im Brennpunkt: Die Septuaginta* (BWANT, 153), Stuttgart, Kohlhammer, 2001, pp. 71-96.

14,21), »Gesetz, Propheten und Psalmen« (Lk 24,44) und »Propheten«
(Röm 1,2; Hebr 1,1) sind keine Neuschöpfungen der neutestamentlichen
Autoren, sondern damals übliche Qualifizierungen dieser Schriften als
inspiriert und normativ, wie die Verwendung dieser Terminologie in den
Makkabäerbüchern (»Gesetz und Propheten«: 2 Makk 15,9; 4 Makk
18,10; TestLev 16,2) und bei Josephus zeigt. Die Bezeichnungen lassen
sich freilich nicht im Blick auf den genauen Kanon*umfang* auswerten,
wie vor allem an den als Einzelbegriffen verwendeten Termini »Gesetz« bzw. »Propheten« abzulesen ist, die auch als Gesamtbezeichnung
der heiligen Schriften Israels auftreten und offensichtlich unterschiedliche Verständnisperspektiven anzeigen. Daß *alle* als heilige Schriften Israels beurteilten Schriften als »Propheten« bezeichnet werden können,
ist z.B. dort zu erkennen, wo in neutestamentlichen Schriften generali-
sierend von »Propheten« die Rede ist, aber zugleich die Mose-Tora im
Blick ist, ohne daß damit eine Aussage über die Kanonstruktur oder den
Kanonumfang verbunden ist. Als Gesamtbezeichnung für alle Schriften
dürfte »Propheten« gemeint sein, »wenn Hebr 1,1 formuliert ›viele
Male und auf vielerlei Weise hat Gott einst zu den Vätern gesprochen
durch die Propheten‹ oder wenn Paulus zu Beginn des Römerbriefes
sein zu verkündendes Evangelium als ›das er *durch seine Propheten* im
voraus verheißen hat in den Heiligen Schriften‹ (Röm 1,2) beschreibt,
oder wenn schließlich Matthäus bei seinem vielfältigen Bezugnehmen
auf die vorliegende Heilige Schrift in bezug auf Nazareth als Wohnort
Jesu generell sagen kann: ›Denn es sollte sich erfüllen, was *durch die
Propheten* gesagt worden ist: Er wird Nazoräer genannt werden‹ (Mt
2,23). Das letzte Beispiel zeigt den generellen Bezug am deutlichsten,
weil sich ein entsprechendes Zitat weder in den Schriftpropheten, noch
im Kanonteil Propheten noch in der Bibel Israels überhaupt findet, so
daß man hier nicht von einem Zitat, sondern von einem Hinweis auf die
›Schriftgemäßheit‹ ausgehen muß, wie er am bekanntesten auch in 1
Kor 15,3-5 vorliegt, wobei... in Mt 2,23 die *Schrift*gemäßheit als
*Propheten*gemäßheit erscheint«[12]. Diese Prophetenperspektive hat freilich ein Fundament im *Text* der Tora selbst. Im sog. Mose-Epitaph Dtn
34,10-12 wird ja einerseits die Tora deutlich als eigener Komplex von
den Nebiim abgegrenzt, aber andererseits wird darin Mose ausdrücklich
prophetisiert und damit zugleich die Tora zur Prophetie erklärt.

   6. Kanongeschichtlich auswertbare Hinweise der Epoche um die Zeitenwende auf eine kanonhermeneutische Relevanz der *Anordnung der*

12. CH. DOHMEN, *Hermeneutik des Alten Testaments*, in CH. DOHMEN & G. STEM-
BERGER, *Hermeneutik der Jüdischen Bibel und des Alten Testaments*, Stuttgart, Kohlhammer, 1996, p. 152.

heiligen Schriften, sei es der Abfolge von Kanonteilen sei es der Abfolge der einzelnen Schriften innerhalb der Kanonteile, sind nicht nur zah-
lenmäßig gering, sondern in der Forschung neuerdings sehr kontrovers
diskutiert. Dies gilt bekanntlich für 2 Makk 2,13, für Sir 44–50, und für
den Prolog zum griechischen Sirachbuch, für Josephus Contra Apionem
I,38-40 und für die viel bemühte Baraita aus dem babylonischen Talmud
Baba Bathra 14b, aber auch für den Lehrbrief 4QMMT. Die komplexe
Diskussion kann und muß hier nicht dargestellt werden[13]. Doch soll festgehalten werden, daß alle diese Textstellen den von ihnen implizit oder
explizit genannten Schriften einen *Sonderstatus* innerhalb der Literatur
Israels zusprechen und daß diese Schriften *in Gruppen eingeteilt bzw.
klassifiziert* werden. Freilich ist unsicher, ob gerade die Klassifizierung
in Gruppen und das Arrangement aus kanonischem Interesse geschieht
bzw. kanonisches Bewußtsein widerspiegelt. Das Problem läßt sich exemplarisch an Josephus Contra Apionem erkennen, wo Josephus nicht
als Kanontheologe, sondern als Historiker die von ihm als kanonisch
qualifizierten (aber nicht namentlich bestimmten) 22 Bücher in drei
Gruppen von 5, 13 und 4 Büchern nach historischen Gesichtspunkten
einteilt:

> Bei uns gibt es nicht Myriaden von Büchern die nicht zusammenstimmen
> und (einander) widerstreiten, sondern nur zweiundzwanzig Bücher, welche
> *die Niederschrift der (gesamten) vergangenen Zeit* enthalten und mit Recht
> vertrauenswürdig sind. Fünf davon sind die des Mose, welche die Gesetze
> enthalten und die Tradition von der Menschenschöpfung bis zum Ende
> des Mose; diese Zeitspanne erstreckt sich ungefähr auf 3000 Jahre. –
> Vom Ende des Mose bis zu Artaxerxes... haben die Propheten nach Mose
> die Geschehnisse gemäß (dem von) ihnen (Erlebten) in dreizehn Büchern
> niedergeschrieben. – Die restlichen vier (Bücher) enthalten Hymnen auf
> Gott und Lebensregeln für die Menschen. – Von Artaxerxes bis hin zu
> unserer Zeit ist zwar alles aufgeschrieben worden, aber (das) wird nicht
> des gleichen Vertrauens gewürdigt wie die (Bücher) vor ihnen, weil
> nicht die genaue Aufeinanderfolge der Propheten gegeben war (Ap. I,38-
> 41)[14].

Leider können wir nur vermuten, welche Bücher Josephus mit den
»restlichen vier Büchern« meint; möglicherweise sind es die Psalmen,
das Buch der Sprichwörter, Kohelet und Hoheslied (dann läge ebenfalls
das historische Kriterium der Abfolge David – Salomo zugrunde). Be-

---

13. Vgl. den Forschungsüberblick bei P. BRANDT, *Endgestalten des Kanons. Das Arrangement der Schriften Israels in der jüdischen und christlichen Bibel* (BBB, 131), Berlin, Philo, 2001, pp. 62-73.95-124.
14. Übersetzung nach B.J. DIEBNER, *Erwägungen zum Prozeß der Sammlung des
dritten Teils der antik-jüdischen (hebräischen) Bibel, der Ketubim*, in DBAT 21 (1985),
p. 178.

merkenswert ist allerdings, daß die Schriftengruppe »von Artaxerxes bis hin zu unserer Zeit« wegen ihres fehlenden prophetischen Bezugs als nicht kanonisch beurteilt wird.

7. Für die *Frühzeit der jüdischen Kanongeschichte* und für die damit verbundene Frage nach einer *Sachstruktur* des Kanons in der Abfolge der Bücher dürften neben der bereits genannten Baba Bathra-Stelle vier Quellen besonders relevant sein, auf die neuerdings wieder Peter Brandt in seiner Bonner Dissertation nachdrücklich aufmerksam gemacht hat[15]. Es sind zunächst die bei Eusebius überlieferten Kanonlisten des Melito von Sardes (um 170 n.Chr.) und des Origenes (frühes 3.Jh.), sodann der Prologus galeatus des Hieronymus, d.h. das Vulgata-Vorwort zu Sam und Kön, sowie schließlich das sog. Bryennios-Manuskript. Alle diese Texte spielen in der neueren Diskussion über Umfang und Sachstruktur des jüdischen Kanons eine wichtige Rolle. Während Baba Bathra 14 und der Prologus galeatus als Zeugnisse für den *jüdischen* Kanon spätestens des 4.Jh. gelten, ist umstritten, inwieweit Melito, Origenes und das Bryennios-Manuskript für die Rekonstruktion der *jüdischen* Kanongeschichte relevant sind. Ohne dies hier näher begründen zu können, bin ich der Auffassung, daß auch diese drei Quellen aussagerelevant für jüdische Kanonformationen sind, vor allem dahingehend, daß ihre Differenzen keine Fehler sind, sondern unterschiedliche kanontheologische Interessen widerspiegeln.

Ich will dies kurz erläutern und beginne mit einem vergleichenden Blick auf Baba Bathra 14 und den Prologus, die folgende Büchersequenzen mit ausdrücklichen Gruppenbildungen bieten[16]:

Baba Bathra	Prologus
	»quinque libri Mosi, quos proprie Thorath, id est, legem appelant«
	Gen Ex Lev Num Dtn
»die Reihenfolge der Propheten« (סדרן של נביאים)	»secundum Prophetarum ordinem«
Jos Ri Sam Kön Jer Ez Jes Dod	Jos Ri+Rut Sam Kön Jes Jer Ez Dod
»die Reihenfolge der Schriften« (סדרן של כתובים)	»tertius ordo agiografa«
Rut Ps Ijob Spr Koh Hld Klgl Dan Est Esr Chr	Ijob Ps (»David quem quinque incisionibus, et uno Psalmorum volumine comprehendunt«) Salamon (= Spr Koh Hld) Dan Chr Esr/Neh Est

15. BRANDT, *Endgestalten* (n. 13).
16. Im Anschluß an BRANDT, *Endgestalten*, pp. 62-68.125-130.

Beide Listen stimmen in ihrer Dreiteilung TNK und weitgehend auch in der Abfolge der einzelnen Bücher überein. Allerdings sind einige Differenzen bemerkenswert:

– Im Prophetencorpus nimmt der Prologus Ri und Rut zusammen (»iudicum librum; et in eundem compingunt Ruth, quia in diebus iudicum facta narratur historia«)

– Jes ist in beiden Listen unterschiedlich plaziert: während Jes im Prologus die Reihe der Schriftpropheten eröffnet, steht Jes in Baba Bathra erst hinter Jer und Ez.

– Klgl dürften unterschiedlich positioniert sein: Im Talmud gehören sie zur Gruppe der Schriften; der Prologus, wo sie explizit nicht genannt sind, dürfte sie mit Jer zusammendenken (das legt sich von anderen Hinweisen des Hieronymus her nahe).

– Die Reihenfolge der ersten Bücher in der Gruppe »Schriften« ist verschieden: während der Talmud die Abfolge Rut – Ps – Ijob hat, dreht der Prologus die Bücher Ps – Ijob zur Abfolge Ijob – Ps um.

– Die Reihenfolge der letzten Bücher in der Gruppe »Schriften« ist verschieden, insbesondere fällt der unterschiedliche Schluß mit Chr im Talmud bzw. mit Ester im Prologus auf.

Die weitgehende Übereinstimmung dürfte die Thesen, die Liste von Baba Bathra habe technische Funktion als Anweisung für die bibliothekarische Aufbewahrung der Schriftrollen[17] oder als Vorgabe für die Schreiber von Schriftrollen[18] gehabt, als höchstens sekundäre Erklärungen erscheinen lassen; primär geht es um eine unter sachlichen Gesichtspunkten erfolgende Reihung – und das heißt eben doch: Hier liegt eine *kanonhermeneutische Perspektive* vor.

Dies bestätigt auch ein kurzer Blick auf die Kanonlisten von Melito und Origenes sowie des Bryennios-Manuskripts, die zwar aus christlicher Hand stammen, aber höchstwahrscheinlich (auch) *jüdische Perspektiven* wiedergeben[19]:

17. Cf. N.M. SARNA, Art. *Bible: Canon*, in *Encyclopaedia Judaica* IV (1971), cc. 827-828.
18. Cf. M. HARAN, *Archives, Libraries, and the Order of the Biblical Books*, in *JANES* 22 (1993) 51-61.
19. Vgl. zum folgenden BRANDT, *Endgestalten* (n. 13), pp. 73-80.

Melito	Origenes	Bryennios
Gen	Gen	Gen
Ex	Ex	Ex
Num	Lev	Lev
Lev	Num	*Jos*
Dtn	Dtn	Dtn
Jos	Jos	Num
Ri	Ri	Rut
Rut	Rut	Ijob
1–4 Kön	1–4 Kön	Ri
1–2 Chr	1–2 Chr	*Ps*
	1–2 Esr	1+2 Sam
Ps	*Ps*	1+2 Kön
Spr	Spr	1+2 Chr
Koh	Koh	Spr
Hld	Hld	Koh
Ijob		Hld
Jes	(Dod)	Jer
Jer	Jes	Dod
Dod	Jer	Jes
Dan	Klgl	Ez
Ez	EpJer	Dan
	Dan	
	Ez	
Esr	Ijob	1+2 Esr
	Est	Est

Die drei Listen haben zunächst jeweils auffallende *kanonsystematische Eigenheiten*:

a. Am überraschendsten sind die Divergenzen im Bereich *der Tora/ des Pentateuch* bei Melito und im Bryennios-Manuskript.

– Melito bietet die Abfolge Num – Lev. Da sich die Abfolge Num – Lev auch in anderen von Melito nicht abhängigen Listen befindet, muß hier eine kanonsystematische Idee vorliegen, die S.Z. Leiman so auf den Punkt bringt: »The sequence probably reflects an attempt to connect the narrative portions of the Pentateuch. Leviticus was perhaps considered a continuation and elaboration of the sacrificial legislation in Numbers 28 and 29«[20].

20. S.Z. LEIMAN, *The Canonization of Hebrew Scripture. The Talmudic and Midrashic Evidence* (Transactions of the Connecticut Academy of the Arts and Sciences, 47), Hamden, CT, Archon Books, 1976, p. 165.

– Das Bryennios-Manuskript bietet die ersten sechs Bücher im Vergleich mit der üblichen Reihenfolge so, daß die ersten drei Bücher Gen – Ex – Lev wie üblich angeordnet sind, während die nächsten drei Bücher in der umgekehrten Anordnung Jos – Dtn – Num folgen. Will man hier nicht einen unbeabsichtigten Fehler[21] oder nur die Kunstvariante der Konzentrik bzw. Palindromie[22] annehmen, läge eine pointierte theologische Programmatik vor, die einerseits die Landnahme in die Gründungsgeschichte Israels hineinnimmt und andererseits den so geschaffenen Hexateuch doch wieder vor der Landnahme enden läßt, und sei es nur in einem als Rückblick zu lesenden Bücherzusammenhang Dtn – Num, wie Num 36,13 dann als Kolophon betonen würde.

b. Bei Melito und Origenes ist die Abfolge *Jos – Chr* identisch. Sie orientiert sich an der Chronologie und ordnet deshalb Rut hinter Ri ein. Danach folgen die *poetischen Bücher*, ebenfalls chronologisch angeordnet: Ps (David) – Spr/Koh/Hld (Salomo). Hier bietet das Bryennios-Manuskript abermals eine Abfolge, die kanontheologisch originell ist, insbesondere was die Psalmen betrifft. Zunächst stehen hier Rut und Ijob *vor* Ri. Diese Zusammenstellung von Rut und Ijob könnte mit der in Baba Bathra 15b auf Rabbi Eleazar/Eliezer zurückgeführten Auffassung zusammenhängen, Ijob habe zur Zeit der Richter gelebt[23]. Dann könnte man die Sequenz Rut – Ijob – Ri so deuten, daß diese drei Bücher der Zeit der Richter zugeordnet wären, und zwar so, daß zunächst zwei wichtige Einzelgestalten (Rut+Ijob) auftreten, ehe dann im Richter-Buch die Epoche selbst zur Sprache kommt. Analog könnte man dann die Positionierung von Ps vor Sam – Kön – Chr verstehen: Der Psalmendichter und Psalmenbeter David wird vor die Erzählungen über die Königszeit (Sam – Kön – Chr) gestellt.

c. Das Corpus der *Schriftpropheten* wird in drei unterschiedlichen Fassungen geboten. Am auffallendsten ist hier die Abfolge Dan – Ez bei Melito und Origenes, während das Bryennios-Manuskript die sonst in griechischen Codices üblichere Abfolge Ez – Dan bietet. Über die Gründe dieser Abweichung kann man nur spekulieren; wahrscheinlich hängt diese Position von Ez zumindest bei Melito mit dem in Schlußposition stehenden Buch Esr/Neh zusammen, das dann als Ausführung von Ez 40–48 verstanden wäre.

21. J.-P. AUDET, *A Hebrew-Aramaic List of Books of the Old Testament in Greek Transcriptions*, in *JTS* 1 (1950), p. 150.
22. P. KATZ, *The Old Testament Canon in Palestine and Alexandria*, in *ZNW* 47 (1956), p. 206.
23. bBB 156: »R. Eleazar sagte, Ijob lebte zur Zeit der Richter, denn es heißt: *Ihr alle habt es ja gesehen, warum ergebt ihr euch eitlem Wahn* [Ijob 27,12], und das Zeitalter, das ganz eitel war, ist das Zeitalter der Richter«.

d. Sowohl bei Melito als auch bei Origenes überrascht die Positionierung von Ijob in unmittelbarer Nähe zum Block der Schriftpropheten, bei Melito vor diesem Block und bei Origenes hinter diesem Block. Dies könnte mit einer Deutung des Ijob als eines leidenden bzw. geduldigen Propheten zusammenhängen, wie sie auch im Jakobusbrief (vgl. Jak 5,10f) bezeugt ist.

e. Auffallend ist die Schlußposition von Est bei Origenes und im Bryennios-Manuskript; warum Est bei Origenes fehlt, ist unklar.

f. Eine eigene Diskussion wäre notwendig, um das Problem der mit »Esr« bezeichneten Schriften (Esr + Neh, 1–4 Esr?) bestimmen zu können.

Jenseits dieser kurz kommentierten (und auch jenseits der hier nicht kommentierten) Einzeldifferenzen erscheint mir *noch bedeutsamer*, daß *allen drei Listen* eine *Basis-Struktur* mit Tora und Schriftprophetie in Außenposition *gemeinsam* ist, also jene Struktur, die typisch ist für den sog. Septuagintakanon, über den gleich noch zu reden sein wird. Sollte die Annahme richtig sein, daß die drei Listen einen primär *jüdischen* Hintergrund haben, wird zumindest die These fragwürdig, die Schlußpositionierung der Prophetie sei typisch christlich.

8. Die von Peter Brandt nunmehr durchgeführte *Untersuchung der hebräischen Handschriften* ab ca. 800 n.Chr. und der *Frühdrucke der jüdischen Vollbibeln* erbrachte für den uns hier interessierenden *Block der Ketubim* folgendes Ergebnis[24]: Die beherrschende Hauptform ist die *dreiteilige Abfolge* von Tora, Nebiim und Ketubim, wobei sowohl bei den Nebiim wie bei den Ketubim unterschiedliche Reihenfolgen auftreten. Bei den Ketubim dominieren folgende drei Ordnungen:

Östliche Ordnung:	Rut Ps Ijob Spr Koh Hld Klgl Dan Est Esr/Neh Chr
Westliche Ordnung:	Chr Ps Ijob Spr Meg (Rut Hld Koh Klgl Est) Dan Esr/Neh
Rabbinerbibel:	Ps Spr Ijob Meg (Hld Rut Klgl Koh Est) Dan Esr/Neh Chr

a. Das Bücherarrangement der *östlichen Ordnung* (Talmud) läßt sich folgendermaßen erklären:

»Die Ordnung des Talmud ist zunächst durch ein chronologisches Gerüst strukturiert: Mit der historischen Abfolge von David, Salomo, Jeremia, Exil und nachexilischer Zeit sind die Bücher Ps – Spr/Koh/Hld – Klgl – Dan – EN bereits fixiert. Die übrigen Positionen ergeben sich wie folgt: Rut dient wegen der Genealogie Davids als Einleitung zum Psalter. Die enge Bindung wird in bBB 14b anhand eines ›und‹ deutlich, das nur an ausgesuchten Stellen zwischen Buchtiteln steht. BECKWITH[25] geht so

24. Vgl. BRANDT, *Endgestalten* (n. 13), pp. 132-171.
25. R.T. BECKWITH, *The Old Testament Canon of the New Testament Church and its Background in Early Judaism*, London, SPCK; Grand Rapids, Eerdmans, 1985, p. 112.

weit zu behaupten, Rut sei als ein Teil des größeren Werkes aufgefaßt
worden, weshalb man Ps auch in dieser Ordnung als das erste Buch
der Ketubim bezeichnen könne. Ijob hielten einige Rabbinen für einen
Zeitgenossen der Königin von Saba (bBB 15b), so daß sich von daher
die Plazierung zwischen Ps (David) und Spr (Salomo) nahelegte. Eine
andere Erklärung liefert RIEDEL[26] Rut und Ps seien aus der Chronologie
herausgehoben, die erst mit Ijob einsetze, welcher vorn stehe wegen seiner ›vorisraelitischen‹ Herkunft... Für die Abfolge Spr – Koh – Hld
kann eine Ordnung nach Größe erwogen werden, die ermöglicht, daß Spr
an der Seite der beiden anderen ›großen Ketubim‹ bleiben konnte. Die Position von Est vor EN hat ihre Wurzeln in der rabbinischen Meinung, Ester
habe vor Esra gelebt (bBB 15a)... Die Verbindung von Est zu Dan wird
durch die Verklammerung mit ›und‹ als enger ausgewiesen als die zu
EN«[27].

Die Schlußposition von Chr könnte zunächst damit zusammenhängen, daß nach bBB 15a die Chr als Werk von Esra und Nehemia galten;
dementsprechend schließt die Baraita 15a die Chr auch mit »*und*« an
Esr/Neh an. Wenn gleichwohl Chr nicht, wie die chronologische Ordnung erwarten ließe, vor Esr/Neh gesetzt wird, dürfte dies mit der Absicht zusammenhängen, Chr gezielt als rekapitulierenden Schluß des
Tanach (Rückblick bis an den Anfang »von Adam an...«) zu präsentieren.

b. Das Arrangement der *westlichen Ordnung* (Adath Deborim 1207
n.Chr.) unterscheidet sich vor allem in zwei Punkten von der östlichen
Ordnung: Zum einen stehen hier die Megillot als Gruppe zusammen,
wobei Rut und Ester in Außenposition stehen und so dem chronologischen Prinzip der Ketubim angepaßt sind (Rut als »Rückblende« und
Ester als »Vorblende«). Zum anderen steht Chr hier am Anfang, was
sich mit P. Brandt so erklären läßt: »Chr eröffnet den Reigen mit einem
Bogen von Adam bis David und Salomo, deren Schriften (Ps und Spr)
folgen, bevor die nachexilischen Bücher Dan und EN den Abschluß bilden«[28].

c. Das Arrangement der *Rabbinerbibel* (Jakob ben Chajjim 1524
n.Chr.) ist eine Mischform aus der östlichen und der westlichen Ordnung. Auffallend sind vor allem zwei Eigenheiten: Die Megillot werden
nach liturgischen Gesichtspunkten, d.h. nach der Abfolge der Feste, deren Festrolle sie sind, angeordnet. Die Chronik steht wieder programmatisch am Schluß.

---

26. W. RIEDEL, *Namen und Einteilung des alttestamentlichen Kanons*, in ID., *Alttesta-*
mentliche Untersuchungen I, Leipzig, Deichert, 1902, p. 102.
27. BRANDT, *Endgestalten* (n. 13), pp. 151-153.
28. *Ibid.*, p. 154.

d. Allen drei Ordnungen ist gemeinsam, daß *der Psalter* hervorgehoben ist, entweder in absoluter Spitzenposition oder durch entsprechende »Vorworte« (Rut bzw. Chr).

e. Diese Arrangements der Ketubim sind auch bei *heutigen Ausgaben des Tanach* bestimmend. Es gibt Ausgaben nach der westlichen (masoretischen) Ordnung (z.B. Breuer[29]) oder nach der Rabbinerbibel-Ordnung (z.B. Koren[30]). Die BHS, die wie BHK mit der Handschrift L auch deren (westliche) Ordnung wiedergibt, ändert diese Ordnung, indem sie mit der östlichen Ordnung und der Rabbinerbibel-Ordnung Chr an den Schluß stellt und bietet so eine »Mischform«. Ebenfalls eine (freilich andere) Mischform bietet JPS von 1985 (Ps – Spr – Ijob – Meg [Hld – Rut – Klgl – Koh – Est] – Dan – Esr – Neh – Chr) mit folgender Erklärung: »The Leningrad Codex reflects a sequence found in Middle Eastern and Spanish manuscripts. But the Writings are arranged differently in modern Bibles, following the German manuscript tradition. We chose the modern sequence – more likely to be familiar to our readers – for quicker navigation«[31].

9. Die *Kanongeschichte des christlichen Alten Testaments* ist aus vielen Gründen viel komplexer als die jüdische Kanongeschichte. Allerdings ist auch hier das externe und interne Gruppenarrangement nach Gattungsmerkmalen und nach chronologischen Gesichtspunkten bestimmend. Auffallend ist, daß neben nur christlich belegten Anordnungen vereinzelt sogar typisch jüdische Ordnungen auftreten. Auch hierzu findet sich eine reiche Dokumentation in der Dissertation von Brandt[32]. Ich wähle für unseren Zusammenhang nur die drei Haupttypen des Bücherarrangements der griechischen (Codex Alexandrinus 5.Jh.), lateinischen (Amiatinus um 700) und der syrischen (Ambrosianus 6.-7.Jh.) Tradition aus, um auch so die *kanongeschichtliche Positionierung des Psalter* zu beleuchten[33]:

---

29. M. BREUER, Bd. 1-3, Jerusalem, 1977-1982.
30. M. KOREN, Jerusalem, 1966.
31. *JPS Hebrew-English Tanakh. The Traditional Hebrew Text and the New JPS Translation*, Philadelphia, PA, The Jewish Publication Society, 1999, p. XVI.
32. BRANDT, *Endgestalten* (n. 13), pp. 172-341.
33. Die folgende Tabelle findet sich bei BRANDT, *Endgestalten*, p. 354.

Alexandrinus	Amiatinus	Ambrosianus
Gen bis Dtn	**Gen bis Dtn**	**Gen bis Dtn**
		Ijob
Jos – Ri – Rut	Jos – Ri – Rut	Jos – Ri
Sam	Sam	Sam
		Ps
Kön	Kön	Kön
Chr	Chr	
	Ps	
	Spr	**Spr**
	Weish Sir	
	Koh – Hld	**Koh – Hld**
Dod		
Jes	*Jes*	*Jes*
Jer – Bar – Klgl – EpJer	*Jer – Klgl – Bar*	*Jer – Klgl – Bar*
Ez	*Ez*	*Ez*
Dan – Sus – Bel	*Dan – Sus – Bel*	*Dod*
	Dod	*Dan – Bel*
	Ijob	Rut – Sus
Est – Tob – Jdt	Tob – Est – Jdt	Est – Jdt
		Sir – Chr – EpBar – 4 Esr
1-2 Esdras	1-2 Esdras	EIN
1-4 Makk	1-4 Makk	1-4 Makk
Ps – Ijob		
Spr – Koh – Hld – Weish – Sir		

Folgende kanonhermeneutisch relevante Merkmale möchte ich her-
vorheben:

a. Alle drei Kanongestalten zeigen ein *Gruppenarrangement*: Bücher
des Pentateuch (am Anfang), Geschichtsbücher, Prophetenbücher und
poetische Bücher, freilich in unterschiedlicher Gruppen-Reihenfolge.
»Auf die Geschichtsbücher folgen entweder die prophetischen oder die
poetischen Bücher. Daß in den Beispielen in zwei Fällen die poetischen
vor den prophetischen Büchern stehen, aber nur in einem Falle die prophetischen vor den poetischen, dürfte in der Tendenz ungefähr dem Verhältnis entsprechen, das eine Quantifizierung der handschriftlichen Text-
zeugen insgesamt ergibt«[34]. In jedem Fall ist sowohl im Blick auf den
Septuaginta*kanon* als auch im Blick auf die christliche Kanongestalt
festzuhalten: »Die Rede von der *generellen* Schlußstellung der Prophe-

34. *Ibid.*, p. 355.

ten im [christlichen] AT ist unbedingt als Klischee zu entlarven. Weder in der lateinischen noch in der syrischen, am ehesten in der griechischen Tradition kann sie beobachtet werden – doch auch hier eher in den Kanonlisten als in den Bibeln, und selbst in den Listen oft nur dank einer Klassifizierung bestimmter Bücher der Propheten, die nach westlichem Verständnis so nicht genannt werden: Ijob, Est, Esdras«[35].

b. Die *Gruppe der poetischen Bücher* ist in den drei Überlieferungen unterschiedlich umfangreich. Gemeinsam ist allen der Kern der drei »salomonischen Bücher« Spr – Koh – Hld. Die griechische und die lateinische Tradition positioniert dazu auch die Bücher Weish und Sir.

c. Das *Buch Ijob* nimmt in allen drei Formationen eine unterschiedliche Positionierung ein. Im Alexandrinus steht Ijob (nach Ps) vor den salomonischen Büchern. Im Amiatinus steht Ijob nicht bei den poetischen Büchern, sondern eröffnet einen Block von Erzählungen, die von den »klassischen« Geschichtsbüchern deutlich abgesetzt sind. Dies entspricht einer breiter belegten altlateinischen Tradition, die unter der Bezeichnung »Historiarum« eine Büchergruppe bildete, zu der Ijob, Tob, Est, Jdt und Esdras, gelegentlich auch Makk und Chr gehören.

d. Nur am Rande möchte ich auf *zwei Besonderheiten*, die an der Positionierung von *Rut* erkennbar sind, hinweisen. Zum einen: Sowohl Alexandrinus als auch Amiatinus dokumentieren die später breit bezeugte christliche Tradition eines Oktateuch Gen – Rut, der insgesamt höchstwahrscheinlich als »kanonische« Genealogie Davids mit messianisch-christologischer Perspektive verstanden wurde. Zum anderen: Im Ambrosianus eröffnet Rut die Gruppe der (in der westsyrischen Tradition beliebten) Frauenbücher Rut – Sus – Est – Jdt[36].

e. Was den *Psalter* angeht, belegen Alexandrinus und Amiatinus seine kanonhermeneutisch relevante Position an der Spitze der poetischen Bücher, was einerseits der Chronologie David – Salomo entspricht, aber andererseits auch mit der theologischen Bedeutung von Ps (s.u.) zusammenhängen dürfte. Auffallend ist die Positionierung von Ps im Ambrosianus, wo der Psalter zwischen Sam und Kön plaziert ist. Das hinter dieser Positionierung stehende Kanonkonzept ist erkennbar, wenn man zugleich die Positionierungen von Ijob und der im Ambrosianus reduzierten Gruppe der (salomonischen) poetischen Bücher Spr – Koh – Hld in den Blick nimmt. Diese Bücher werden hier nach chronologischen Gesichtspunkten jeweils passend eingereiht: Ijob steht nach dem Pentateuch (der als feststehende Gruppe nicht aufgebrochen wird bzw. werden

---

35. *Ibid.*, pp. 357-358.
36. Vgl. dazu nun: I. FISCHER, *Rut* (HTKAT), Freiburg i. B., Herder, 2001, pp. 110-111.

kann) entweder weil Mose als Autor von Ijob angenommen wird (vgl.
bBB 15a) oder weil Ijob mit Jobab von Gen 36,33f (vgl. Ijob 42,17G)
identifiziert wird. Analog wird der Psalter zwischen Sam und Kön eingereiht, vielleicht als Fortführung des »psalmistischen« Schlusses von 2
Sam 22–23 bzw. des »kultischen« Abschlusses 2 Sam 24. Analog folgt
dann der Kern der salomonischen Bücher Spr – Koh – Hld nach Kön.

f. In der Tradition lateinischer Handschriften bzw. Kanonlisten werden die *Psalmen* gelegentlich ausdrücklich zur *Gruppe der Propheten*
gerechnet (z.b. bei der Zweiteilung des AT in »Historiae« und »Prophetae« bei Augustinus und Cassiodor)[37].

g. Der *Einfluß der »jüdischen« Kanonsystematik* des Prologus galeatus des Hieronymus ist sowohl bei griechischen Vätern (z.b. Rufin, Leon-
tius, Junilius[38]) als auch in der lateinischen Tradition mehrfach festzu-
stellen (z.b. Isidor, Hrabanus Maurus, Petrus Venerabilis[39]).

II. KANONHERMENEUTISCHE IMPLIKATIONEN

1. Was *ergibt unsere kanongeschichtliche Skizze* im Hinblick auf un-
sere eingangs gestellte Frage nach der hermeneutischen Relevanz des
Kanons bzw. im Blick auf die kanontheologische Interpretation des
Psalters? Ich halte folgende Punkte für bedeutsam:

a. Der *kanonische Prozess*, d.h. die Kanonwerdung, ist nicht mit der
Festlegung des *Umfangs* des Kanons (»Kanonschließung«) beendet,
sondern setzt sich in dem Bemühen um eine *Sachstruktur* des Kanons
fort, die in der Zusammenfassung von Einzelschriften zu Gruppen und
in der Anordnung dieser Gruppen in einer aussagerelevanten Makro-
struktur des Kanons sichtbar wird. Der Vorgang der Kanonisierung umfaßt demnach *drei Aspekte*: Kanonwerdung, Kanonschließung und Kanonstrukturierung. Die als Zusammenfassung der neueren Kanonfor-
schung von H.-J. Fabry präsentierte These: »Der Kanon der Heiligen
Schriften ist primär nicht ein wohlgeordnetes Sinnganzes, sondern trägt
alle Züge eines Produktes, das durch negative Ausgrenzung entstanden
ist«[40], ist weder kanongeschichtlich gedeckt noch ist sie geeignet, von
ihr aus *kanontheologische* Perspektiven zu entwickeln, wie dies jüngst

---

37. Vgl. dazu BRANDT, *Endgestalten* (n. 13), pp. 243-260.
38. *Ibid.*, pp. 195-196.211-212.
39. *Ibid.*, pp. 256.297. »Judaisierender« Einfluß findet sich sogar in der Vulgata-Liste
von Papst Innozenz I (pp. 255-256).
40. H.-J. FABRY, *Die Qumrantexte und das biblische Kanonproblem*, in S. BEYERLE *et
al.* (eds.), *Recht und Ethos im Alten Testament*. FS H. Seebaß, Neukirchen-Vluyn, Neukirchener Verlag, 1999, p. 254.

W. Groß tut, wenn er dem Kanon ein *inhaltliches* Profil abspricht[41]. Die kanongeschichtlich erkennbare Suche nach einer *Sachstruktur* in der Anordnung der Heiligen Schriften ist bei aller Divergenz eine *Sachauslegung*, hinter der das Bemühen steht, einen theologisch relevanten Makrotext zu komponieren. Dieser Makrotext hat, wie im folgenden weiter ausgeführt wird, Konstanten und Varianten, wobei die Konstanten strukturell besonders bedeutsam sind.

b. Als feststehende Gruppierung halten sich im *kanongeschichtlichen* Prozeß die *beiden Größen »Tora« und »Prophetie«* durch, wobei die Reihenfolge der Einzelschriften im Prophentenblock variiert[42]. Diese Basisform der heiligen Schriften Israels hat sich auch in der Bezeichnung »Gesetz und Propheten« niedergeschlagen. In der christlichen Tradition gibt es daneben auch eine starke Oktateuch-Tradition, die vermutlich eine messianisch-christologische Perspektive darstellt.

c. Die neben »Tora« und »Prophetie« *übrigen Schriften* werden unterschiedlich und offensichtlich nach unterschiedlichen Kriterien ausgewählt und eingeordnet[43]. Hier gibt es vor allem Differenzen zwischen der hebräischen und der griechischen Tradition bzw. zwischen der jüdischen und der christlichen Bibel, wenngleich diese in der Überlieferung erkennbare christlich-jüdische Differenz wahrscheinlich bereits auf eine *innerjüdische* Kanondivergenz zurückgeht, die mit der kanonischen Basisstruktur Tora - Prophetie zusammenhängt. Ich halte den von Ch. Dohmen gemachten Vorschlag für sehr plausibel, wonach sich hier zwei unterschiedliche Erweiterungen der um 200 v.Chr. vorliegenden Tora-

---

41. W. GROSS, *Ist biblisch-theologische Auslegung ein integrierender Methodenschritt?*, in HOSSFELD (ed.), *Wieviel Systematik* (n. 1), pp. 129-131.

42. Die *Entstehung* der beiden Größen Tora (Gen–Dtn) und Prophetie (Jos–2 Kön + Schriftpropheten) kann und braucht hier nicht weiter diskutiert zu werden. Was meine eigene Position betrifft, verweise ich auf ZENGER, *Einleitung* (n. 6), pp. 119-124.467-472. Einerseits ist es keine Frage, daß sich beide Größen bei ihrer Entstehung wechselseitig beeinflußt haben, andererseits gilt solche Wechselseitigkeit nicht für die Frage der *Kanonstrukturierung*. Beide Aspekte müssen stärker auseinander gehalten werden als dies bei CHAPMAN, *The Law* (n. 9) der Fall ist.

43. Daß und wie »die Schriften« unterschiedliche Gemeinde- bzw. Lebenskonzepte im Spannungsfeld von Tora und Prophetie realisieren, hat gut herausgearbeitet: D.F. MORGAN, *Between Text and Community. The »Writings« in Canonical Interpretation*, Minneapolis, MN, Fortress Press, 1990, pp. 30-75. Demgegenüber erscheint mir die originelle These von B. Lang, die Auswahl der 12 »Schriften« sei als hellenistisch inspirierter »literarischer Kanon« neben dem »liturgischen Kanon« von Tora und Prophetie entstanden, weder literaturgeschichtlich (!) hinreichend begründet noch kanongeschichtlich abgesichert: vgl. B. LANG, *The ›Writings‹: A Hellenistic Literary Canon in the Hebrew Bible*, in A. VAN DER KOOIJ & K. VAN DER TOORN (eds.), *Canonization and Decanonization. Papers presented to the International Conference of the Leiden Institute for the Study of Religions (LISOR) held at Leiden 9-10 January 1997* (Studies in the History of Religions, 82), Leiden, Brill, 1998, pp. 41-65.

Nebiim-Schrift niedergeschlagen haben, was angesichts der kanongeschichtlichen Pluralität um die Zeitenwende nicht verwundert.

Etwas vereinfacht lassen sich die beiden verschiedenen Kanonstrukturen…
auf unterschiedliche inhaltliche Rezeptionen der Tora-Nebiim-Schrift zurückführen. Während der Tanach mit seinem dritten Kanonteil ganz deutlich an der Tora als Ausgangspunkt der ganzen Schrift orientiert bleibt –
d.h. sowohl die Propheten (Nebiim) als auch die Schriften (Ketubim)
werden von der Tora her gelesen und verstanden…, bildet die Prophetie
den Ausgangspunkt der Rezeptionslinie, die [in nochmals erweiterter
Form] im späteren Alten Testament greifbar wird. Die Wirkungsgeschichte
zeigt somit, daß die zu Beginn des 2. Jahrhunderts v.Chr. vorliegende *Bibel
Israels aus Tora und Nebiim* sozusagen von ihrem einen und von ihrem
anderen Ende her rezipiert werden kann und rezipiert wird. Es ergibt
sich daraus folglich eine Art Tora-Perspektive und eine Propheten-
Perspektive für die weitere Aufnahme von Schriften in einen Kanon der
Bibel Israels[44].

d. Im Block der Ketubim und in der Gruppierung der poetischen
Schriften der (jüdischen und christlichen) griechischen Bibel nimmt *der
Psalter* mit auffallender Konstanz die Spitzenposition ein; Abweichungen lassen sich, wie wir oben angedeutet haben, mit jeweils besonderen
Systematisierungen erklären. Die Spitzenposition in der hebräischen
Kanonsystematik hängt mit der genannten Tora-Perspektive zusammen,
die auch beim Prozeß der Schlußredaktion des protomasoretischen Psalmenbuchs leitend war; andererseits zeigt auch die Schlußgestalt des im
pharisäisch-rabbinischen Kanon überlieferten Psalmenbuchs[45] eine Prophetie-Perspektive. Darüber hinaus ist erkennbar, daß der sog. Septuaginta-Psalter – ganz im Sinne der eben skizzierten Wachstumshypothese
der Bibelsammlung des hellenistischen Judentums (im Mutterland) – die
Prophetie-Perspektive verstärkt hat. Beides soll abschließend kurz kon-
kretisiert werden.

2. Die *Tora-Perspektive des protomasoretischen hebräischen Psalters*
läßt sich an folgenden mit der Endkomposition des Psalters in Verbindung stehenden Psalmen bzw. Strukturmerkmalen erkennen:

a. Der den Psalter eröffnende *Psalm 1* zeichnet das Porträt des Gerechten, der sich von der Tora JHWHs leiten läßt. Der gleich zweimal in
Ps 1,2 gesetzte Begriff Tora hat einerseits programmatische Signal-
funktion für alle weiteren Tora-Vorkommen (Ps 19; 37; 40; 78; 89; 94;

44. DOHMEN, *Hermeneutik* (n. 12), p. 153.
45. Das Problem der unterschiedlichen Gestalt(en) des Psalmenbuchs in Qumran lasse
ich hier unberücksichtigt; doch vgl. dazu zuletzt U. DAHMEN, *Psalmentext und Psalmen-
sammlung. Eine Auseinandersetzung* mit P.W. Flint, in ID., A. LANGE & H. LICHTEN-
BERGER (eds.), *Die Textfunde vom Toten Meer und der Text der Hebräischen Bibel*, Neukirchen-Vluyn, Neukirchener Verlag, 2000, pp. 109-126.

105; 119) bzw. Tora-Konzepte (z.B. Ps 15; 24; 25; 29; 34; 73; 86; 93;112; 148) des Psalters. Andererseits bindet Ps 1 den Psalter an die Tora JHWHs, wie sie im Pentateuch vorliegt, zurück. »Nach Ps 1 macht der Psalter explizit, was Pentateuch (und Propheten) als Tora Jhwhs für das Leben eines Gerechten implizieren«[46].

b. Die redaktionelle Erweiterung *Ps 2,10-12* macht aus dem »Gottessohn« des vorexilischen Königspsalms Ps 2,1-9 einen Toralehrer für die Völker[47].

c. Der *Torapsalm 119* ist die Mitte der Komposition des von der Schlußredaktion geschaffenen 5. Psalmenbuches Ps 107–145[48].

d. Auch das *Finale des Psalters, Ps 146–150*, ist toratheologisch imprägniert (vgl. besonders Ps 147,15.18-20; Ps 148,6.14)[49].

e. Die Schlußredaktion hat den Psalter durch *eigens geschaffene* und an herausragender Stelle positionierte *Psalmen* ausdrücklich in den Horizont der Sinai-Tora-Theologie gestellt. Dies gilt vor allem von dem das 5. Psalmenbuch abschließenden und das Schlußfinale Ps 146–150 vorbereitenden Ps 145, aber auch von dem die königstheologisch bzw. messianisch konzipierte Komposition Ps 3–89 mit der theokratisch bestimmten Komposition Ps 90–145 verkettenden redaktionellen Ps 86. Sowohl Ps 86 als auch Ps 145 sind stark von den Gottesprädikationen Ex 34,6f her entworfen[50].

f. Da der Psalter insgesamt von vorne nach hinten gewachsen ist, ist die mit diesem Wachstum verbundene »*Mosaisierung*« bzw. »*Pentateuchisierung*« als Charakteristikum jener Redaktionsstufen zu beurteilen, die die Endkomposition des Psalters geschaffen haben. Die Mose- bzw. Pentateuchperspektive beginnt pointiert mit dem auch redaktionell ausdrücklich als Mosepsalm gekennzeichneten Ps 90, in dem Mose in seiner von Ex 32,7-14 her bekannten Rolle des Fürbitters Israel vor dem Vernichtungszorn Gottes bewahrt. Mose wird durch die als «Mose-Komposition« zu lesende Psalmenfolge Ps 90–92 zum Verkünder der

---

46. R.G. KRATZ, *Die Tora Davids. Psalm 1 und die doxologische Fünfteilung des Psalters*, in *ZTK* 93 (1996), p. 11.

47. Vgl. zu dieser These: E. ZENGER, *Der Psalter als Wegweiser und Wegbegleiter. Ps 1-2 als Proömium des Psalmenbuchs*, in A. ANGENENDT & H. VORGRIMLER (eds.), *Sie wandern von Kraft zu Kraft. Festgabe für Bischof Reinhard Lettmann*, Kevelaer, Butzon & Bercker, 1993, pp. 29-47.

48. Vgl. E. ZENGER, *The Composition and Theology of the Fifth Book of Psalms, Psalm 107-145*, in *JSOT* 80 (1998) 77-102.

49. Vgl. E. ZENGER, *»Daß alles Fleisch den Namen seiner Heiligung segne« (Ps 145,21). Die Komposition Ps 145-150 als Anstoß zu einer christlich-jüdischen Psalmenhermeneutik*, in *BZ* 41 (1997) 1-27.

50. Vgl. J. VORNDRAN, *»Alle Völker werden kommen«. Studien zu Psalm 86* (BBB, 133), Berlin, Philo, 2002.

dann in Ps 93–100 proklamierten universalen Königsherrschaft JHWHs. Diese »Mose-Botschaft« ist die Antwort der Psalmenkomposition auf die am Ende des 3. Psalmenbuchs in Ps 89 erhobene Klage über den Niedergang des davidischen Königtums. Deshalb verwundert es nicht, wenn im letzten Drittel des Psalters die großen pentateuchischen Themen in den Vordergrund treten. Das wird vor allem in den Geschichtspsalmen Ps 105 106 135 136 und in dem stark von der Exodustheologie her geprägten Pesach-Hallel Ps 113–118 sichtbar[51]. Zu dieser «Pentateuchisierung» des Psalters gehört auch die Verstärkung der Schöpfungstheologie im letzten Drittel des Psalters, vor allem im Psalterfinale, das mehrfach explizit auf Gen 1–9 zurückgreift. So ist unübersehbar: Der Psalter hat seine Endgestalt im Horizont der Tora des Mose erhalten. Während er in seinen ersten Entstehungsphasen eine Sammlung von Klage- und Bittgebeten mit punktuellen hymnischen Perspektiven war, ist er nun eine große geschichts- und schöpfungstheologische Komposition – und als solche eine poetische Aneignung bzw. Aktualisierung von Tora und Prophetie[52].

g. Die Pentateuchisierung des Psalters wird schließlich auch strukturell in seiner *Einteilung in die fünf Bücher* Ps 3–41.42–72.73–89.90–106.107–145 (mit Ps 1–2 und Ps 146–150 als Rahmen) sichtbar. Diese Fünfteilung kam m.E. dadurch zustande, daß die Schlußredaktion ihr bereits vorgegebene Strukturierungen im Bereich Ps 3–89 aufnahm und weiterführte[53].

h. Die Pentateuchisierung des Psalters hat ein *Vorbild* in der Einfügung der Psalmen Ex 15 und Dtn 32 in den Pentateuch. Gerade diese beiden Pentateuchtexte werden ihrerseits im Psalter vielfach aufgegriffen[54].

3. Eine *Prophetie-Perspektive* ist *im hebräischen Psalter* bereits in vielen Einzelpsalmen durch Aufnahme von Prophetenbüchern, insbesondere durch wörtliche oder motivliche Einspielungen der Bücher Jesaja[55] und Jeremia[56] gegeben. Dazu hat bekanntlich die sog. anthologische

51. Vgl. E. ZENGER, *Das schöne Confitemini. Perspektiven christlicher Psalmenhermeneutik am Beispiel des 118. Psalms* (Festschriftbeitrag im Druck, 2002).

52. Vgl. zu diesen Perspektiven besonders die Bonner Dissertation: E. BALLHORN, *Zum Telos des Psalters. Der Textzusammenhang des vierten und fünften Psalmenbuchs (Ps 90-150)*, Diss. Bonn 2000.

53. Vgl. E. ZENGER, *Der Psalter als Buch. Beobachtungen zu seiner Entstehung, Komposition und Funktion*, in ID. (ed.), *Der Psalter in Judentum und Christentum* (HBS, 18), Freiburg im Breisgau, Herder 1998, pp. 27-31.

54. Zur Rezeption von Ex 15 vgl. z.B. Ps 74; 77; 86; 118 und von Dtn 32 vgl. z.B. Ps 82 und 92.

55. Zur Rezeption des Jesajabuchs vgl. z.B. Ps 72; 84; 85; 86; 87; 96; 97; 102; 147.

56. Zur Rezeption des Jeremiabuchs vgl. z.B. Ps 51; 55; 79; 137.

Psalmenexegese viele Beobachtungen zusammengetragen. Auch die sog. Davidisierung bzw. Messianisierung vor allem im Bereich der ersten drei Psalmenbücher stellte den Psalter in den Horizont der Samuel-bücher (vordere Propheten), wodurch Psalter und Samuelbücher gerade-zu zu Komplementärtexten wurden[57]. In unserem Zusammenhang er-scheint mir freilich wichtiger, daß abermals die späten Wachstumspha-sen des Psalters, nämlich die Formation des vierten und fünften Psal-menbuchs, und insbesondere das Finale Ps 146–150 den Psalter »pro-phetisierten«, indem sie ihm eine dominierende eschatologische Per-spektive gaben. Diese kündigt sich bereits in der Komposition der JHWH-König-Psalmen an, wo das in Ps 93 entworfene Konzept von JHWHs Weltkönigtum sukzessiv universalisiert und eschatologisiert wird (vgl. besonders Ps 94 97 99). Die Prophetisierung wird paradig-matisch sichtbar im Schlußpsalm Ps 118 des Pesach-Hallel, der als poe-tisch inszenierte Kurzfassung der sog. Jesaja-Apokalypse Jes 24–27 und als eschatologische Aktualisierung der Zionstheologie des Jesajabuchs überhaupt verstanden werden will, wobei bei Ps 118 gerade eine Ver-schmelzung von Mosetora und Zionsprophetie vorliegt. Die Eschatolo-gisierung des Psalters zeigt sich insbesondere bei der Ausgestaltung des Themas Israel und die Völker, das in den Spätphasen der Psalter-entstehung ins Zentrum des Interesses rückt. Vor allem aber stellt das Psalterfinale den Psalter in einen prophetisch-eschatologischen Hori-zont. Ich gebe dazu nur einige Hinweise:

a. Die explizite Eschatologisierung beginnt bereits mit der Schlußbitte von Ps 146,10 »Es herrsche als König JHWH auf ewig«, die das Offenbarwerden der universalen Königsherrschaft JHWHs, die im un-mittelbar vorangehenden Ps 145 entworfen wird, herbeisehnt.

b. Die Eschatologisierung wird verstärkt in Ps 147, der mit der Meta-pher vom Bau Jerusalems die eschatologische Sammlung und Heilung der Kinder Zions beschwört.

c. Der in Ps 148 kunstvoll gestaltete Aufruf zum kosmischen Lobpreis zeichnet die eschatologische Vollendung, deren Realisierung der Lob-preis Israels, wie er im Psalter in seiner Endkomposition vorliegt, schon jetzt vorwegnimmt und zugleich durch seine Inszenierung näherkommen läßt.

d. Am deutlichsten ist Ps 149 von einer Perspektive bestimmt, die sich an der eschatologischen Prophetie inspiriert und zugleich als Trans-

---

57. Vgl. dazu M. KLEER, *Der liebliche Sänger der Psalmen Israels. Untersuchungen zu David als Dichter und Beter der Psalmen* (BBB, 108), Bodenheim, Philo, 1996, pp. 11-128; D. ERBELE-KÜSTER, *Lesen als Akt des Betens. Eine Rezeptionsästhetik der Psal-men* (WMANT, 87), Neukirchen-Vluyn, Neukirchener Verlag, 2001, pp. 54-85.

formation der JHWH-König-Psalmen Ps 93–100 gelesen werden will.
Der prophetische Horizont wird vor allem im zweiten Teil des Psalms in
V 5-9 erkennbar, wo das von JHWH aus dem Tod erweckte Israel der
Armen als Instrument des eschatologischen Gerichts an den Königen
und Machthabern der Völker gezeichnet wird. Ps 149 entwirft mit seinen
Metaphern die Vollendung der universalen Königsherrschaft JHWHs –
und zwar als im Lobpreis sich vollziehende Prolepse.»Ps 149 schildert
ein Geschehen, das erst in eschatologischem Rahmen stattfinden wird.
Aber das geschieht gerade nicht in Form einer Reportage, sondern als
Hymnus. Die Besonderheit liegt darin, daß Israel jetzt schon – proleptisch – mit dem Gebet des Psalters in den eschatologischen Jubel ausbricht. Die Vorausschau auf die kommende Welt im Modus des Lobes
läßt erkennen, daß dem Psalter eine doppelte Sprachform eignet: er stellt
sich an seinem Ende als Lobgebet dar, gleichzeitig aber auch als prophetisches Buch, das die Zukunft Gottes in bezug auf Israel schildert«[58].

e. Auch Ps 150 steht im Horizont der eschatologischen Prophetie.
Hier geht es nicht um die Aufforderung zu einem Festgottesdienst im
Jerusalemer Tempel, sondern um die poetisch-proleptische Inszenierung
des endzeitlichen Gotteslobs im vollendeten (»neuen«) Kosmos.

4. Der sog. *Septuaginta-Psalter* verstärkt – gemäß seiner kanonsystematischen Einordnung – die *prophetisch-eschatologische Perspektive*
des Psalmenbuchs. Gerade dies bedürfte einer detaillierteren Darstellung. Ich verweise diesbezüglich auf die Münsteraner Dissertation von
Holger Gzella[59], sowie auf den von mir selbst herausgegebenen Band
über den Septuaginta-Psalter[60]. Aus der Vielzahl der Beobachtungsfelder
will ich nur einige kurz benennen:

a. Noch vorgängig zu allen inhaltlichen Einzelphänomenen, die das
eschatologische Profil des Septuagintapsalters konturieren (wie z.B. die
individuelle bzw. persönliche Eschatologie oder die Messianologie), ist
eine den ganzen griechischen Psalter prägende sprachlich erkennbare
Futurisierung der Darstellungsperspektive zu nennen. Die im hebräischen Psalter oftmals schwierige und kontroverse Frage, wie die Zeitstufen zu bestimmen sind, ist hier durch die klaren Futurbildungen eindeutig entschieden. Die Futurisierung geht soweit, daß teilweise sogar
Vergangenheitsaussagen des hebräischen Psalters so futurisiert werden,
daß daraus nun Endzeitaussagen werden. Als eindrucksvolles Beispiel

---

58. BALLHORN, *Zum Telos* (n. 52), p. 371.
59. H. GZELLA, *Lebenszeit und Ewigkeit. Studien zur Eschatologie und Anthropologie
des Septuagintapsalters* (BBB, 134), Berlin, Philo, 2002.
60. E. ZENGER (ed.), *Der Septuaginta-Psalter. Sprachliche und theologische Aspekte*
(HBS, 32), Freiburg i. B., Herder, 2001.

nenne ich Ps 29 = Ps 28 G, der die in Ps 29 in der mythischen Vorzeit geschilderte Theophanie in die Endzeit transponiert und dabei zusätzlich das messianische Motiv von der Vernichtung der Götzen in den Psalm einträgt[61].

b. Der griechische Psalter zeigt in mehreren Differenzen zum hebräischen Psalter eine auffallende Nähe zur apokalyptischen Theologie, die hinter der Endredaktion des Danielbuches steht, so daß sogar vermutet werden kann, daß hinter beiden ähnliche anti-makkabäische apokalyptische Kreise stehen.

c. Der griechische Psalter wird nun durch mehrere zusätzliche Überschriften (Ps 145–148 G: Ἀλληλουια· Ἀγγαιου καὶ Ζαχαριου; Ps 64,1: Εἰς τὸ τέλος· ψαλμὸς τῷ Δαυιδ ᾠδή Ιερεμιου καὶ Ιεζεκιηλ ἐκ τοῦ λόγου τῆς παροικίας ὅτε ἔμελλον ἐκπορεύεσθαι) ausdrücklich mit Gestalten der Schriftprophetie korreliert (wie immer diese Überschriften zu deuten sind, was hier nicht detaillierter erörtert werden kann[62]). Ps 137 = Ps 136 G wird in einigen Handschriften neben David auch Jeremia (mit Genitiv Ιερεμιου) zugeschrieben.

d. Eine dezidierte Eschatologisierung liegt gewiß in der Übersetzung der sog. Psalmendedikation למנצח mit εἰς τὸ τέλος vor[63].

e. Auch die Übersetzung des Überschriftenelements משכיל »Weisheitslied« mit σύνεσις ist höchstwahrscheinlich als eschatologisierender Lesehinweis gemeint, wie M. Rösel durch die Diskussion der einschlägigen Stellen zeigt, die er folgendermaßen bündelt: »So wage ich zusammenfassend die Behauptung, daß auch die mit σύνεσις gebildeten Überschriften die in Jesaja und Daniel deutlich gemachte Konnotation eines auf die Endzeit gerichteten Verstehens haben können«[64].

f. Vor allem aber vollzieht der als Nachwort bzw. als Metatext zum griechischen Psalter fungierende Ps 151 eine ausdrückliche Prophetisierung des griechischen Psalters[65]. Diesen »Psalm« hat die Redaktion ausdrücklich als »kanonisierendes« Nachwort qualifiziert, das dem Psalter eine doppelte Prophetisierung geben soll. Zum einen verändert der Psalm das im Psalter selbst dominierende Bild vom verfolgten und

---

61. Vgl. H. GZELLA, *Das Kalb und das Einhorn. Endzeittheophanie und Messianismus in der Septuaginta-Fassung von Ps 29(28)*, in ZENGER (ed.), *Der Septuaginta-Psalter* (n. 60), pp. 257-290.

62. Die Korrelation von Ps 145 G–148 G mit Hag und Sach betont, daß diese Psalmen nun im Licht der Jerusalem- und Tempelprophetien von Hag und Sach gelesen werden sollen.

63. Vgl. dazu M. RÖSEL, *Die Psalmenüberschriften des Septuaginta-Psalters*, in ZENGER (ed.), *Der Septuaginta-Psalter* (n. 60), pp. 137-139.

64. RÖSEL, *Die Psalmenüberschriften* (n. 63), p. 137.

65. Zu Ps 151 G vgl. besonders BALLHORN, *Zum Telos* (n. 52), pp. 395-466; ERBELE-KÜSTER, *Lesen* (n. 57), pp. 86-107.

leidenden David und macht ihn zum geistbegabten Retter seines Volkes und Verteidiger des wahren Gottes. Davids Erwählung wird dabei nach dem Muster der Retter- und Prophetenberufung ausgestaltet. Zum anderen rückt die Überschrift mit dem Element οὗτος ὁ ψαλμὸς ἰδιό-γραφος David ausdrücklich in die Reihe der »Schriftpropheten« ein[66] und gibt dem Psalter so die Dimension der von JHWH selbst eingegebenen Worte und Texte. Deren rettende Kraft im Kampf gegen die Bösen und das Böse wird ohnedies in Ps 151 G gleich zweimal benannt. Sowohl die Überschrift[67] als auch der zweite Teil von Ps 151 (V 6-7) hebt die prophetische Gotteskraft heraus, die dem Psalmendichter und *Psalmenverfasser* David zueigen ist und die er seinen Psalmen gewissermaßen eingestiftet hat. Das ist eine kanonhermeneutische Perspektive, die im übrigen bereits im synchron gelesenen Erzählzusammenhang 1 Sam 16–18 gegeben ist[68]. Doch dies ist ein eigenes Thema[69].

Westfälische Wilhelms-Universität Münster   Erich ZENGER
Seminar für Zeit- und
Religionsgeschichte des AT
Johannisstraße 8-10
D-48143 Münster

66. Vgl. das Niederschreiben prophetischer Worte bzw. Gottesbotschaften vor allem bei Jesaja, Jeremia, Ezechiel und Habakuk und besonders das Niederschreiben des Mosepsalms Dtn 32 durch den Propheten par excellence Mose.

67. Die in der Überschrift hergestellte Beziehung zur David-Goliat-Erzählung 1 Sam 17 schlägt einen Bogen zurück zum »messianischen« David-Psalm 143 G, der mit seiner Überschrift ebenfalls auf 1 Sam 17 hinweist.

68. Vgl. dazu E. ZENGER, *David as Musician and Poet: Plotted and Painted*, in J.C. EXUM & S.D. MOORE (eds.), *Biblical Studies/Cultural Studies* (JSOT SS, 266), Sheffield, Sheffield Academic Press, 1998, pp. 263-298.

69. Dieser Beitrag entstand im Kontext meines Projekts »Religiöse Dichtung als Konstituierung von Gegenwelten« im Sonderforschungsbereich »Funktionen von Religion in antiken Gesellschaften des Vorderen Orients« an der Universität Münster.

TEXTUAL DIVERSITY AND CANONICAL UNIFORMITY

1. *Introduction*

Dogmatic statements about the extent and effect of Jewish and Christian canons seem to be relatively uncomplicated[1]. Somewhere during the early Christian era synods made decisions as to the extent of the canon. In the Jewish tradition the hypothetical *Knesset Gedolah* fulfilled a similar function[2]. However, when the subject matter, the texts, are considered then it becomes evident that the issue is infinitely more complicated. The textual reality of a *plurality of texts* is the result of a multitude of factors (social, political, ideological, etc.).

This paper endeavours to address the fact that textual material as deviant as some of the freely translated units in the Septuagint, as well as some of the fragments/scrolls that were unearthed at the Dead Sea and vicinity, could be seen as part of a canon, seemingly without creating dogmatic problems. This article focusses on the Septuagint, and more specifically on the Greek version of Proverbs which is used as a case study in order to demonstrate the plurality of textual material during the early Judaic period. Even though it differs dramatically from the Massoretic text (and other textual witnesses) in some respects, the Septuagint was used in the early Christian community and also for a period of time in Jewish communities. These differences seemingly did not cause "dogmatic" problems to the "believing" communities. In order to demonstrate the relevance of the LXX for canonical issues some Qumran texts/fragments related to the Septuagint are also analysed.

2. *Textual Variety*

Even though scholars are aware, or at least are progressively becoming more aware, of the importance of the Septuagint for a number of

---

* This paper is the result of the English seminar that I conducted during the congress. Prof. Magne Saebø acted as referent. It was prepared during my stay as senior fellow at the KULeuven during the year 2000-2001. I want to express my appreciation to the vice-rector, Prof. M. Vervenne, and to Prof. J. Lust who jointly invited me to their institution.

1. Cf. S.Z. LEIMAN, *The Canonization of Hebrew Scripture. The Talmudic and Midrashic Evidence* (Transactions of the Connecticut Academy of the Arts and Sciences, 47), Hamden, CT, Archon Books, 1976 and J. BARTON, *The Significance of a Fixed Canon of the Hebrew Bible*, in M. SÆBØ, *Hebrew Bible/Old Testament. The History of its Interpretation*, Vol. 1. *From the Beginnings to the Middle Ages (until 1300)*, Part 1. *Antiquity*, Göttingen, Vandenhoeck & Ruprecht, 1996, pp. 67-106.

2. F.E. DEIST, *Witnesses to the Old Testament*, Pretoria, DRCPublishers, 1988, p. 15.

hermeneutical issues[3], not many actually deal with this corpus of ancient texts systematically. This applies also to the issue of canon. Philip Davies[4], for example, in a recent book on the canonization of the Hebrew scriptures, addresses a whole array of questions relating to canon; inter alia, he devotes a whole chapter to "Canons and the Dead Sea Scrolls"; however, he hardly ever refers to the Septuagint. To be sure, he does actually in one instance make mention of LXX Proverbs, but then only as an indication of a possible new heading in Prov 22,17 with a superficial comment ("if we follow the Greek and identify a new heading 'The Words of the Wise'")[5]. One could ask whether this a relic of a past approach in which the Septuagint was solely utilized as a source for understanding the Hebrew. As I will indicate shortly the order of the chapters followed in the MT and LXX respectively differs substantially and cannot be "mixed".

Magne Saebø, on the contrary, makes use of the insights of the Septuagint in his search for the "Way to Canon"[6]. In an enlightening chapter, "From Collections to Book: A New Approach to the History of Tradition and Redaction of the Book of Proverbs", he endeavours to come to terms with the redactional implications of this differing order of chapters. He also refers to the pluses (in comparison to MT) in chapter 9,12.18[7]. He succeeds in implementing text-critical perspectives for a better understanding of the textual and social processes at work in the formation of canons (cf. his first chapter).

That these textual phenomena have implications for all sorts of "theological" questions, including the canon, should become clear in the course of this article. However, before these texts are dealt with some methodological issues need to be addressed.

3. *Methodological Issues*

a. One should remember that the subject matter of this reflection is texts on vella or papyrus and not books/codices or bibles that are much later developments. To take one example: the Masoretic text published

---

3. Cf. my *The Septuagint of Genesis - Text and/or Interpretation?* in A. WÉNIN (ed.), *Studies in the Book of Genesis - Literature, Redaction and History* (BETL, 155), Leuven, University Press - Peeters, 2001, pp. 315-329.

4. P.R. DAVIES, *Scribes and Schools. The Canonization of the Hebrew Scriptures.* Louisville, KY, Westminster John Knox Press, 1998.

5. *Ibid.*, p. 135.

6. M. SÆBØ, *On the Way to Canon. Creative Tradition History in the Old Testament,* Sheffield, University Press, 1998.

7. *Ibid.*, p. 257.

in the Biblia Hebraica Stuttgartensia is based on the medieval codex Leningradensis that dates from circa 1008 A.D. It is effectively a late text, even though it certainly contains ancient traditions!

b. It is indicative to reflect on a suitable "text theory". The well-known "Ur-text theory" (de Lagarde), the Targum- or Vulgar-text theory (Kahle), the Recensional theory (Rosenmüller), the Local-text theory (Cross *et al.*) and the multiple-text theory (Talmon & Tov) are relevant in this regard[8].

c. The Septuagint, generally speaking, dates from a period prior to the Hebrew (the *Vorlage* of MT). It, therefore, in general represents a Hebrew parent text older than the MT's *Vorlage*.

d. This Greek translation nevertheless has its own intricate history of origin and transmission that has to be kept in mind constantly. It underwent various Jewish and Christian recensions. It is therefore necessary to make a distinction between the original, Old Greek text and the later recensions. Strictly spoken the term Septuagint refers only to the pentateuch.

e. Most books in the Septuagint exhibit a unique transmission history. Whereas in the book of Job one must distinguish between the Old Greek and the Theodotionic text, in Proverbs hexaplaric influence is to be found.

f. The person(s) responsible for Proverbs followed a free translation technique. This is observed on a *micro-* and a *macro-level*. As far as the first goes, some individual lexical items are rendered consistently, many are varied[9]. This approach can be described as one of *diversity* and *unity*. Also on the *macro-level* this translation unit exhibits unique features. The order of some chapters towards the end of the book (24–31) that differ from MT should be ascribed to its translator(s), as is the removal of the names of Agur and Lemuel who are mentioned as authors of some Proverbs in the Hebrew[10]. In the final analysis this interpretative approach is ascribed to the translator's ideology[11], which is characterised by a fundamentally conservative religious attitude. This inference is, inter alia, based upon the prominent role of the law of Moses in LXX Proverbs[12].

8. *Ibid.*, pp. 36-46.
9. J. Cook, *Ideology and Translation Technique – Two Sides of the Same Coin?* in R. Sollamo & S. Sipilä (eds.), *Helsinki Perspectives on the Translation Technique of the Septuagint*, Göttingen, Vandenhoeck & Ruprecht, 2001, pp. 195-210.
10. J. Cook, *The Septuagint of Proverbs - Jewish and/or Hellenistic Proverbs? Concerning the Hellenistic Colouring of LXX Proverbs* (SVT, 69), Leiden, Brill, 1997.
11. Cf. J. Cook, *Theological/Ideological Tendenz in the Septuagint - LXX Proverbs a case study*, in S. Sipilä (ed.), *Proceedings of IOSCS Basel 2001* (forthcoming).
12. J. Cook, *The Law of Moses in the Septuagint Proverbs*, in *VT* 49 (1999) 448-461.

g. The LXX should be read holistically, contextually, in order to determine the content of whole passages. One should not, at least as far as LXX Proverbs goes, concentrate on the *micro-level*, the lexeme, but move to the *macro-level*, that of the story!

h. The Old Greek of the Septuagint version of Proverbs has not yet been determined. It is one of the books that has not been prepared yet in the Göttingen edition. Before a specific reading and/or strophe/verse is analysed one should therefore make certain that it indeed represents the Old Greek text and not a later hand. The edition of Holmes/Parsons[13] is of utmost importance in this regard.

4. *LXX Proverbs*[14]

a. Chapter 1

This chapter is shaped differently in the LXX. To mention one example: on a syntactic level vv. 22-33 are structured differently to MT.

Verse 22

עַד־מָתַי פְּתָיִם תְּאֵהֲבוּ פֶתִי וְלֵצִים לָצוֹן חָמְדוּ
לָהֶם וּכְסִילִים יִשְׂנְאוּ־דָעַת

Ὅσον ἄν χρόνον ἄκακοι ἔχωνται
τῆς δικαιοσύνης, οὐκ αἰσχυνθή-
σονται·
οἱ δὲ ἄφρονες, τῆς ὕβρεως ὄντες ἐπι-
θυμηταί,
ἀσεβεῖς γενόμενοι ἐμίσησαν αἴσθη-
σιν

How long, O simple ones, will you love being simple?
How long will scoffers delight in their scoffing and fools hate knowledge?

As long as the innocent *hold on* to *righteousness they will not be ashamed*,
but the *foolish* since they are lovers of pride,
after they became impious they hated insight.

Verse 30

לֹא־אָבוּ לַעֲצָתִי נָאֲצוּ כָּל־תּוֹכַחְתִּי

οὐδὲ ἤθελον ἐμαῖς προσέχειν βου-
λαῖς,
ἐμυκτήριζον δὲ ἐμοὺς ἐλέγχους.

They would have none of my counsel, and despised all my reproof.

Neither would they have my counsels, *and* despised my reproofs.

---

13. R. HOLMES & J. PARSONS, *Vetus Testamentum Graecum cum variis lectionibus*, Oxford, Clarendon Press, 1732.

14. These passages were discussed extensively during the seminar. The printed version here is based upon my monograph *The Septuagint of Proverbs* (n. 10).

Verse 31

וְיֹאכְלוּ מִפְּרִי דַרְכָּם וּמִמֹּעֲצֹתֵיהֶם יִשְׂבָּעוּ

τοιγαροῦν ἔδονται τῆς ἑαυτῶν ὁδοῦ τοὺς καρποὺς καὶ τῆς ἑαυτῶν ἀσεβείας πλησθήσονται·

Therefore they shall eat the fruit of their way
and be sated with their own devices.

Therefore they shall eat the fruits of their own ways,
and be filled with their own *ungodliness.*

The Hebrew has a temporal clause in the first stich of v. 22 which the translator has changed into a conditional clause with the particle ἄν. The *apodosis* (οὐκ αἰσχυνθήσονται) also has no equivalent in the Hebrew text. V. 23 is connected to v. 22 by changing the subject of the sentence from 2nd to 3rd person plural. V. 26 is the *apodosis* of the conditional clause that commences in v. 24. The Hebrew particle גם is used in MT whereas the Septuagint applies τοιγαροῦν, the result is that the conditional sentence now ends in a final clause. The beginning of the conditional clause is also expressed differently in the LXX. For the particle יען the translator used ἐπειδή. The Hebrew particle expresses causality whereas the Greek equivalent carries temporal implications. The following conditional clause in v. 27 is also rendered differently in the LXX. In MT an infinitive plus a preposition בבא as introduction to the *protasis* occurs twice. In the Greek the particles ὡς ἄν plus a subjunctive are used as the equivalent. The *apodosis* in v. 28 is expressed in the MT by means of the particle אז plus an imperfect. In the LXX the translator used the phrase ὅταν ἐπικαλέσησθε for his translation.

Verse 32

כִּי מְשׁוּבַת פְּתָיִם תַּהַרְגֵם וְשַׁלְוַת כְּסִילִים תְּאַבְּדֵם

ἀνθ' ὧν γὰρ ἠδίκουν νηπίους, φονευθήσονται,
καὶ ἐξετασμὸς ἀσεβεῖς ὀλεῖ.

For the simple are killed by their turning away,
and the complacence of fools destroys them;

For *because* they wronged the innocent they will be slain,
and *an inquiry* will ruin the ungodly.

Verse 33

וְשֹׁמֵעַ לִי יִשְׁכָּן־בֶּטַח וְשַׁאֲנַן מִפַּחַד רָעָה

ὁ δὲ ἐμοῦ ἀκούων κατασκηνώσει ἐπ' ἐλπίδι
καὶ ἡσυχάσει ἀφόβως ἀπὸ παντὸς κακοῦ.

but he who listens to me will dwell secure
and will be at ease, without dread of evil.

However, those who listen to me will dwell in hope,
and will rest without fear from *all* evil.

The translator had a different view on v. 32 that has implications for the macro-structure of practically the whole passage. He made a subtle connection between vv. 32 and the previous verses. The κακοί of v. 28 onwards, which in the final analysis go back to and also include the "fools" (οἱ δὲ ἄφρονες) of v. 22, are made the subjects of those who wronged the innocent. They are then killed and not the innocent as seen by MT.

The Greek translator thus followed the syntax of the Hebrew to some extent, but expressed the individual clauses in a typically Greek linguistic manner. In some instances he does bring about nuanced changes in order to deliberately express specific meanings. This is the case in vv. 22, 23 and 32, where he clearly has structured his translation in order to emphasise a religious theme, the contrast between the good and the bad. Religious considerations thus have an impact on a syntactic level as well. This applies to the next passage too.

b. Chapter 2

This chapter also has a different structure than MT. It can be divided into two major parts. Thus the exclamation particle ὦ in v. 13 has a pertinent syntactic function introducing the second large sense division in this chapter. The first 13 verses describe the "good realm" and the rest of the verses (13-22) the "bad realm". The κακὴ βουλή (bad counsel) in v. 17 is central to this realm. It has no equivalent in the Hebrew and seems to be part of the translator's literary strategy to depict his translation in terms of the dualisms that are already present in the Hebrew text. The antecedent of this combination occurs in v. 11, βουλὴ καλή (good counsel), and on a semantic level it is the second part of the dualism of the good and bad advice by which man can organise his life. This "dualism" represents a follow-up of the theme in chapter 1. As a matter of fact this religious category is used more extensively in the LXX of Proverbs than is the case in MT[15].

c. Chapter 6

Again the Greek text is structured uniquely, inter alia, by the addition of three strophes in v. 8 and one in v. 11a.

---

15. Cf. J. COOK, *Contrasting as a Translation Technique*, in C.A. EVANS & S. TAL-MON (eds.), *From Tradition to Interpretation: Studies in Intertextuality in Honor of James A. Sanders*, Leiden, Brill, 1997, pp. 403-414.

Verse 8

תָּכִין בַּקַּיִץ לַחְמָהּ אָגְרָה בַקָּצִיר מַאֲכָלָהּ

ἐτοιμάζεται θέρους τὴν τροφὴν
πολλήν τε ἐν τῷ ἀμήτῳ ποιεῖται τὴν
παράθεσιν.

She prepares her food in summer,
and gathers her sustenance in harvest.

it prepares (its) food in the summer
and it provides *ample* food in the harvest.

8a Or go to the bee
and learn how industrious she is,
and how seriously she performs (her)
work,
8b and whose products kings and com-
moners use for (their) health
and she is respected by all and re-
nowned.
8c Although she is physically weak,
by honouring wisdom she has been
honoured (obtained distinction).

8a ἢ πορεύθητι πρὸς τὴν μέλισσαν
καὶ μάθε ὡς ἐργάτις ἐστὶν
τήν τε ἐργασίαν ὡς σεμνὴν ποιεῖται,
8b ἧς τοὺς πόνους βασιλεῖς καὶ ἰδιῶ-
ται πρὸς ὑγίειαν προσφέρονται,
ποθεινὴ δέ ἐστιν πᾶσιν καὶ ἐπί-
δοξος·
8c καίπερ οὖσα τῇ ῥώμῃ ἀσθενής,
τὴν σοφίαν τιμήσασα προήχθη.

The translator has utilised specific Greek lexemes that occur in prominent Greek classical writings. It would seem as if the *hapax legomenon*
ἐργάτις in v. 8a was taken directly from Aristotle's *Historia Animalium*.
In addition to the fact that this is the sole example of this noun in the
Septuagint, the position of the simile of the bee, following directly after
that of the ant, as in Aristotle, is of crucial importance for the question
as to the origin of this addition. The overriding theme is that diligence is
a sure safeguard against poverty. In vv. 6-8 in the LXX the sluggard is
referred to the ant and in v. 11a he is contrasted directly with the "dili-
gent".

This addition thus represents a plus compared to MT (and the other
extant textual witnesses) that has no direct bearing upon the Hebrew and
that reflects the "ideology" of the translator.

d. Chapter 8

Chapter 8 contains one of the classic creation passages in the OT. It
has been composed beautifully in the Hebrew and has a structure of four
sections: vv. 1-11; 12-21 (MT formally has only one section indicated –
vv. 1-21); 22-31 which in the MT are of roughly the same length; the
unit is ended off with a peroration in vv. 32-36. In the Masoretic Text
the first and third sections are made up of 22 lines, whereas the middle
section has only 21 lines. The number of the consonants in the Hebrew
alphabet (22) was apparently utilised by the author(s) as a structural pattern (acrosticon). This literary device is employed extensively in Ben

Sira too. The closing section (vv. 32-36), on the contrary, contains only 11 lines.

There are many differences between the Septuagint and the MT. A prominent one is that this significant structure of 22 lines is followed in the Septuagint in the second section as well, except for v. 13, which contains three hemistichs and which corresponds with MT. There is, however, an added stich in the Septuagint in v. 21, which balances the pattern of 22, excepting of course v. 13. The fact that in the LXX the second sub-section has twenty-three half verses could naturally be the work of the translator or could be retroverted to a deviating Hebrew *Vorlage*. The same possibilities are also available as theoretical options for the other differences between LXX and MT.

One of the less obvious differences between MT and LXX occurs in vv. 30-31, and more specifically concerns the interpretation of אמון.

Verse 30

וָאֶהְיֶה אֶצְלוֹ אָמוֹן וָאֶהְיֶה שַׁעֲשֻׁעִים יוֹם יוֹם מְשַׂחֶקֶת לְפָנָיו בְּכָל־עֵת	ἤμην παρ' αὐτῷ ἁρμόζουσα, ἐγὼ ἤμην ᾗ προσέχαιρεν. καθ' ἡμέραν δὲ εὐφραινόμην ἐν προσώπῳ αὐτοῦ ἐν παντὶ καιρῷ,
then I was beside him, like a master workman; and I was daily his delight, rejoicing before him always,	I was next to him fitting together, I was the one in whom he took delight, and each day I rejoiced in his presence continually.

This verse is the *locus classicus* concerning the so-called Stoic colouring of the LXX. The verbal form ἁρμόζουσα has been taken as "to join, to accommodate, bring into harmony", which is then seen as an idea expressing "the Stoic view of nature"[16]. This is based on flimsy evidence. The Greek lexeme ἁρμόζω appears only in 10 passages in the LXX: 2 Kings 6,5 (*) and 14 (עז?); Ps 151,2 (-); Prov 8,30 (אמון), 17,7 (נאוה), 19,14 (שכל), 25,11 (אפן) (only in S2); Nahum 3,8 (אמון); 2 Macc 14,22 and 3 Macc 1,19. As can be seen it is used to render different lexemes in Proverbs. In Prov 17,7 the Hebrew contains a contrast between the speech of a fool and of a king: לֹא־נָאוָה לְנָבָל שְׂפַת־יֶתֶר אַף כִּי־ לְנָדִיב שְׂפַת־שָׁקֶר. The LXX has the following translation: οὐχ ἁρμόσει ἄφρονι χείλη πιστὰ οὐδὲ δικαίῳ χείλη ψευδῆ. In this context the nuance of "fitting" clearly prevails.

16. G. GERLEMAN, *The Septuagint Proverbs as a Hellenistic Document*, in *OTS* 8 (1950), p. 26.

Nahum 3,8 is the closest parallel to the passage under discussion.

הֲתֵיטְבִי מִנֹּא אָמוֹן הַיֹּשְׁבָה בַּיְאֹרִים מַיִם סָבִיב
לָהּ אֲשֶׁר־חֵיל יָם מִיָּם חוֹמָתָהּ

ἑτοίμασαι μερίδα, ἅρμοσαι χορδήν,
ἑτοίμασαι μερίδα, Αμων ἡ κατοι-
κοῦσα ἐν ποταμοῖς, ὕδωρ κύκλῳ
αὐτῆς, ἧς ἡ ἀρχὴ θάλασσα καὶ
ὕδωρ τὰ τείχη αὐτῆς.

Are you better than Thebes that sat by the Nile, with water around her, her rampart a sea and water her wall?

Prepare a portion, tune the cord, prepare a portion for Ammon; she that dwells among the rivers, water is around her, whose dominion is the sea, and whose walls are water.

The Greek seems to be an interpretation of the Hebrew and the verb ἅρμοσαι could therefore be related to אמון as suggested by HR. The problem is that the Hebrew lexeme is also rendered literally as Αμων.

The nuance of "harmonizing" suggested by G. Gerleman[17] is, therefore, not imperative in anyone of these passages. I would consequently argue that it is also not necessarily to be accepted in the one under discussion. In extra-biblical writings this lexeme is used with other connotations. In Wisd 36,17 it has the sense of "adapt, accommodate", and in Hegesipp Com the nuance of "to prepare" applies. Also the nuance of "joining, fit together" occurs in classical Greek sources. It is used, inter alia, to describe the work of a joiner in Od 5.247. Pi N 8.11 applies it in the meaning of "to regulate, set in order and to govern". It also appears in the meaning of "fitting", namely clothes or armour that fit well (Pi P 4.80).

It is therefore not easy to determine what the translator actually had in mind in this case. The Hebrew lexeme אמון is already a problematic one, for it appears only twice in the Hebrew Bible. The main Greek mss also have no text available for Jer 52,15. אמון as a proper noun is also used for the Egyptian god Amun and it can also be related to the root אמן (support, assist, bind together). Some scholars have indeed connected it with אָמָן "master-workman, craftsman"[18], which is also how the author of the Wisdom of Solomon understood it. In Wisd 7,21 and 8,6 wisdom is described as τεχνῖτις. Read against the Hellenistic milieu in which he lived, it is possible that he could have interpreted it in a Platonic manner according to the idea of the Demiurge, or that he simply understood the Hebrew אמון in that manner[19].

17. Cf. also A. BARUCQ, *Le livre des Proverbes* (Sources Bibliques), Paris, Gabalda, 1964, p. 94.

18. R.B.Y. SCOTT, *Proverbs*, (AB), New York, Ktav, 1965, p. 72.

19. Cf. O. KEEL, *Die Weisheit spielt vor Gott. Ein ikonographischer Beitrag zur Deutung des mᵉsaḥäqät in Sprüche 8,30f*, Freiburg i. Br., Universitätsverlag, 1974, p. 17; G. BERTRAM, *Die religiöse Umdeutung altorientalischer Lebensweisheit*, in *ZAW* 13

Because of the limited application of the Greek verb, it remains difficult to decide what nuance the translator actually had in mind. Consequently the context must provide the decisive evidence. To me it is unacceptable to formulate a theory of possible external influence on account of limited evidence, as was done by Gerleman regarding Stoic perspectives adopted by the translator. Hengel[20] followed Gerleman in this regard and on the basis of the passage under discussion talks about "popularphilosophischen Züge". Indications of such signs, according to him, are the preexistence of wisdom (v. 22); the fact that she was created for the sake of God's works (v. 22) and the question of wisdom experiencing joy (vv. 30b and 31). Hengel poses the question whether the description of wisdom is not to be seen "als eine Art von Weltseele"[21], which is the way it functions in Plato's Timaeus. He opts for this explanation because the typical Stoic notion of the identification of God and matter would certainly have been a problem for a Jewish translator. According to Hengel the Platonic version with its reference to Demiurges as personal creation gods would have been more acceptable to Jews.

I do not regard the small number of references to typical Stoic or popular philosophical traits mentioned by the above-mentioned scholars as convincing evidence. The connotations of "to join, prepare, harmonize" for ἁρμόζουσα, which are certainly found in extra-biblical writings, need not to be reconstructed in this context. The verb ἁρμόζουσα actually describes wisdom's relationship with the creator. It is not used to depict her relation towards creation. This relationship is being described in the rest of the verse as well. The Greek ἐγὼ ἤμην ᾗ προσέχαιρεν, "I was the one in whom he took delight", is less ambiguous than MT. The addition of the personal pronoun ἐγώ is important in this regard. It could be a case of stressing the subject, underlining the privileged role wisdom actually had beside God.

The emphasis of the whole pericope in its Greek version is thus on God's activity in the creation process. Wisdom has no other role to play than that of being happy and joyful, which also need not to be seen as an exclusive characteristic of Stoicism. Therefore I translate ἁρμόζουσα with "fitting together", a nuance that appears in specific contexts. In my view the translator underscores the creative role of God in the creation and deliberately underplays the active role of wisdom.

(1936), p. 162; GERLEMAN, *Hellenistic Document* (n. 16), p. 26 and M. HENGEL, *Judentum und Hellenismus*, Tübingen, Mohr, 1973, p. 285.

20. *Ibid.*, p. 292.
21. *Ibid.*, p. 293.

Again this chapter contains unique additions and interpretations compared to MT.

e. Chapter 9

In the Hebrew this chapter falls into three parts: a. wisdom's invitation (vv. 1-6); b. the mocker and the wise (vv. 7-12); and c. the invitation of Madame Folly (vv. 13-18), even though the Masoretes indicated
only two delimitations (1-9 and 10-18). This chapter also contains by far
the largest number of pluses of any of the first nine chapters in the LXX
Proverbs. All in all there are 17 extra stichs and several individual pluses
in comparison to MT. It is naturally of crucial importance to determine
what the origin of these pluses is.

12   *Son*, if you are wise for yourself, *you should be wise for your neighbours as well*,
      however, if you turn out wicked, you will bear the *evil* solely.
12a   *He that sets himself upon falsehood, he attempts to rule the wind,*
      and it is he that pursues birds in their flight.
12b   *For he has forsaken the ways of his own vineyard,*
      and has caused the axles of his own farm to go astray.
12c   *Yes, he travels through an arid desert*
      and a land destined to drought,
      indeed he gathers barrenness with the hand.

The pluses in connection with v. 12 depict the foolish, the translator
making use of farming terminology. It is instructive to observe that the
first set of pluses occurs exactly before the foolish woman is contrasted
with the wise woman. The translator therefore evidently intended to describe the man foolish enough to follow the invitation of the foolish
woman. He is likened unto one who has lost all sense of direction, for he
no longer knows his trade, namely how to farm properly. He is busy
with futile things, attempting to rule the wind and gathering barrenness
with his hands.

The same intention is followed with regard to the constellation of
pluses in v. 18.

18a   *However, run away, do not delay in this place,*
      neither fix your eyes upon her,
18b   *for thus will you go through foreign water*
      and pass through a foreign river.
18c   *However, abstain from foreign water,*
      and do not drink from a foreign fountain,
18d   *that you may live for a long time*
      and years of life may be added to you.

Again the translator uses ancient traditions in order to warn the reader
against the inherent dangers of Dame Folly. In the process he depicts

Hades in reference to the tale of Sodom, using a similar description to the one that appears in Gen 19,26: "Therefore, run away, do not delay in this place, neither fix your eyes upon her". The point the translator evidently wants to make is that her fate will be the same as that of Lot's wife. Utter destruction is what awaits those foolish enough to accept her invitation.

The reference to "foreign water" is also significant. Water is one of the central issues in Proverbs and in 5,15-17 the springs and channels of water are equated with the male sperm, which is a reference to the dangers of sexuality. In the present context, however, this reference is a metaphorical one, as is the case with the reference to the foreign river. The metaphor of water for wisdom is an ancient one. According to J. Marböck[22] it was already used in prominent Babylonian traditions. It is used in a similar way in Sir 15,1-3. Sir 21,13 reads: "The knowledge of the wise wells up in abundance, and his counsel is a life-giving spring". Interesting is also the reference to bread which occurs in the current chapter in v. 17 too.

In the present context the reference to water is therefore an indirect, metaphorical one. The translator in my opinion applies this metaphor in an extremely ingenious manner on more than one level. He is not only relating wisdom directly to water, but the water is firstly related to other, foreign literary traditions in v. 18b. I think that the translator is using a well-known Greek tradition, namely the myth concerning the river Styx, which is traversed on the way to Hades. He does not, however, use the link in a positive manner, but, on the contrary, negatively connects the tradition with the foolish woman. In this way he warns the novice of the lurking dangers hiding at Dame Folly's (whore)house. It is instructive that these pluses are located in the context of Hades.

The uninitated are also warned not to drink of foreign waters and a foreign fountain in v. 18c. This is yet another metaphorical reference to foreign wisdom. I have argued in another context that the translator of Proverbs has approached the figure of the אשּׁה זרה[23] systematically to a large extent. He draws a detailed parallel between the strange woman, on the one hand, and foreign wisdom, on the other hand. It is therefore instructive to analyse the way he had depicted the different shady ladies in Prov 1–9. He applies an interesting metaphor in the description of the strange woman and foreign, anti-Israelite/Jewish wisdom. As a matter of

---

22. J. MARBÖCK, *Weisheit im Wandel. Untersuchungen zur Weisheitstheologie bei Ben Sira* (BBB, 37), Bonn, P. Hanstein, 1971, p. 78.

23. J. COOK, אשּׁה זרה *(Prov 1-9 in the Septuagint), a Metaphor for Foreign Wisdom?*, in *ZAW* 106 (1994) 458-476.

fact, the ladies mentioned in Prov 2,16-19; 5,1-11 and 15-23; 6,20-35; 7 and 9 are all metaphors for the foreign wisdom. In my opinion the foreign wisdom against which the reader is warned is indeed the "dangerous" foreign wisdom of the time, namely Greek philosophy of the kind encountered in the Hellenistic period. To me it is clear that the Greek translator of Proverbs has an apprehensive disposition towards the Hellenism of his day. He himself, as is the case with Ben Sira too, clearly had an excellent international, classical, Greek education and consequently has a remarkable competency in the Greek language. Yet I would argue that he utilised this competence to demonstrate the inherent dangers lurking in Hellenism, for in the final analysis he was a conservative Jewish scribe.

f. Chapter 31 *vis-à-vis* Chapters 30, 25 and 29

The latter part of this book has a different sequence of chapters from that found in the MT. Whereas the first 23 chapters are the same as MT, the last 8 chapters differ in order. The LXX has the following schema *vis-à-vis* MT[24]:

I-III	1,1–24,1-22	
VI, part 1	30,1-14	The words of Agur, 1st part
IV	24,23-34	Words of the wise
VI, part 2	30,15-33	The words of Agur, 2nd part
VII	31,1-9	The words of Lemuel, 1st part
V	25–29	
VIII	31,10-31	The words of Lemuel, 2nd part

The first 9 verses of Proverbs 31 in the LXX has as overriding theme the King. This theme occurs also in vv. 1-8 in Chapter 25. I have therefore argued[25] that this different order of chapters is the result, not of a recensionally different Hebrew edition[26], but of an adaptation of passages by the translator(s) on account of thematical considerations. I recently discovered that the King also is central in the verses that precede LXX Prov 31, namely 30,31-33!

Finally, Prov 29,27 and the beginning of the acrosticon (31,10) were linked by the translator on account of the contrast between the ἀνήρ

24. E. Tov, *Textual Criticism of the Hebrew Bible*, Minneapolis, MN, Fortress Press; Assen/Maastricht, Van Gorcum, 1992, p. 337.

25. Cook, *The Septuagint of Proverbs* (n. 10), pp. 304-308.

26. E. Tov, *Recensional Differences between the Masoretic Text and the Septuagint of Proverbs*, in H.W. Attridge et al. (eds.), *Of Scribes and Scrolls. Studies on the Hebrew Bible, Intertestamental Judaism, and Christian Origins Presented to John Strugnell*, Lanham, MD, 1990, p. 52.

ἄδικος and γυναῖκα ἀνδρείαν. Whereas the end of Prov 29 refers to the unrighteous man, the tenth verse of Prov 31 commences with the virtuous wife. Here is an evident contrast between these two persons. If one takes into account how a translator proceeds it can be argued that the translator of Proverbs, after completing these chapters, realised that these two verses actually related better to each other than the beginning of Prov 30 does with the end of Prov 29. He then decided to adapt the order of these chapters.

It could, however, also be argued that the Hebrew of these verses already witnesses to this relationship. Whereas Prov 29,27 mentions the איש עול, Prov 31 contrasts this with the reference to the אשת חיל. However, unfortunately there is no primary textual evidence of such a text. In the MT these verses are separated by Prov 30 and the first 9 verses of Prov 31! Therefore, even though it is theoretically possible that these differences already existed in the *Vorlage*, there is no primary evidence, excepting of course the Septuagint, which in this case is secondary, versional evidence. It must therefore also be possible that these are indeed translational differences.

5. *LXX Gen 1,9 and 4 QGen*[hl, k]

The Hebrew (MT) and LXX formats of first chapter of Genesis differ rather extensively. This applies especially to the so-called *Hexaemeron* (vv. 1-31), which is built up in 6 days and 8 works. The following general structure obtains in these 31 verses[27]: A. "Wortbericht"; B. "Tatbericht"; C. Namegiving; D. Ending formula; E. Ending formula.

A closer scrutiny of these versions brings to light a number of differences. There is an apparent anomaly in v. 9 in that the MT does not include a *Tatbericht*, which does appear in LXX. It is also clear that the LXX has a more consistent and seemingly harmonised structure than MT. The equivalent of the formula "and it was so", for example, appears with regular consistency in the LXX.

Formerly scholars argued that the LXX actually represents an harmonization of the whole of the chapter[28]. The arguments run as follows: This translator actually became aware of the conspicuous differences between MT and LXX and interpreted them as anomalies. He then "corrected" these differences by simply filling them in in the Greek. This clearly rests upon the assumption that Greek translators would have

27. Cf. Cook, *The Septuagint of Genesis* (n. 3).
28. *Ibid.*, pp. 318f.

been apt to adapt their parent texts. Taking the translation technique into account that was followed by this translator – he was not a free renderer of his *Vorlage*, at least not as free as LXX Proverbs – I would suggest not to consider this theoretical possibility too seriously.

It is also possible to infer that the LXX actually represents a deviating Hebrew *Vorlage*. This is indeed suggested by two fragments from Qumran cave 4.

a. 4 QGen[h1]

This fragment consists of a few words of Gen 1,8-10. In the publication by J.R. Davila[29] (who was responsible for Genesis) the scanty fragments can be observed (the plates at the back of the publication represent the original films). Line 1 (v. 8) contains the remains of a shin (שׁ) and could be the first letter of שׁמים or שׁני in v. 8. Line 2 (v. 9) has the noun מקוה that corresponds with the Septuagint reading εἰς συναγωγήν in the first part of the verse.

Here we therefore have primary textual evidence that there existed a Hebrew text at Qumran that had the reading מקוה in its *Vorlage*. This important variant is mentioned by Davila on page 62 stating that it occurs in 4QGen[h1], LXX and La against מקום in 4QGen[b], MT, Sam pent, the Targumim, Peshitta, and the Vulgate.

Even though this is only a small fragment it should not be underestimated. The important point in this regard is that the Septuagint witnesses to a Hebrew reading that could shed light on the "pluses" in the LXX of Gen 1. However, this is not direct evidence of the existence of the whole plus in v. 9 in LXX, even though Davila does think that there actually existed such a longer reading. According to him this reading was omitted because of *homoioarchton* – the eye of the scribe accidentally jumped from ויקוו in v. 9 to ויקרא in v. 10 (cf. below). The next fragment is decisive for our evaluation.

b. 4 QGen[k]

This fragment contains only two words ותרא היבשה. The small circle on top of the בּ indicates that it is partly faded. This phrase is the Hebrew for the Greek phrase καὶ ὤφθη ἡ ξηρά (and the dry land became visible) which occurs in v. 9 as part of the major addition compared to MT. According to Davila (cf. his discussion of the variants on page 76), this

---

29. J.R. DAVILA, in E. ULRICH, F.M. CROSS *et alii* (eds.), *Qumran cave 4.VII: Genesis to Numbers* (DJD, 12), Oxford, Clarendon Press, 1994, p. 62.

"phrase could be an explicating plus, based on the descriptions of the other acts of creation in 1,12.16.25. But the rigid structure of the creation account makes it more likely that the phrase is original and was lost by *homoioarchton* in MT".

I agree with Davila that this is primary and at the same time weighty evidence that there existed a Hebrew text that actually contained this "plus". I disagree that it got lost on account of a mechanical error. The differences between the two Hebrew verbs, ויקו and ויקרא are too large for the eye to simply have jumped.

Looking at the words/phrases in the LXX of Gen 1 that are pluses compared to MT it is amazing that the major differences between MT and LXX actually occur in connection with those passages where water is referred to in Genesis 1. Firstly, in v. 6 where the waters are mentioned; the equivalent of the phrase "and it was so" appears only in LXX. Secondly, in v. 9 where the whole *Tatbericht* ("and the waters assembled...") is missing in MT. Thirdly, v. 20 where the equivalent of the phrase "and it was so" is not found in MT, but in LXX. Thus these apparent anomalies in comparison with LXX appear where water comes in play.

To me it is clear what has happened here. This is evidence of redactional activity by some "conservative" redactor on the Hebrew side. In parts of the ancient Near East water played a primary role in the creation of the earth. Therefore the person who was responsible for the Hebrew text of the *Vorlage* of MT actually found the possibility that the water could be seen as the generating force behind the creation as "theologically" unacceptable. This "conservative" redactor therefore emended his Hebrew text by simply removing the Hebrew phrases that refer to the role of water. The more harmonising structure that appears in LXX was in my view part of the Hebrew *Vorlage* used by the translator of Gen 1. To this translator as also to the person(s) responsible for its *Vorlage* water created no theological problem. However, the redactor(s) of the MT parent text thought it would undermine the omnipotence of God, the almighty creator of heaven and earth!

Thus, here we have significant versional evidence that there existed a Hebrew text that differed from MT somewhere in the pre-Christian era. This text was, however, adapted on account of "theological/ideological" reasons somewhat later, perhaps during the Maccabean era[30].

---

30. Cf. A. VAN DER KOOIJ, *Perspectives on the Study of the Septuagint: Who are the Translators?*, in F. GARCÍA MARTÍNEZ & E. NOORT (eds.), *Perspectives in the Study of the Old Testament and Early Judaism* (SVT, 73), Leiden, Brill, 1998, pp. 214-229.

6. *LXX Jeremiah 43(50) - The Difference in the Order of Books*

The book of Jeremiah has a complex transmission history which is evidenced in the large number of extant texts. The major differences between LXX and MT were formerly explained as the result primarily of the assumed free approach of the Septuagint translator. However, after the discoveries of the Dead Sea scrolls new possible explanations were formulated. There are remarkable correspondences between these extant texts/fragments, especially between 4QJer[d] and the LXX. Because of its fragmentary state the Qumran material should be approached with extreme caution. Nevertheless there appears to be evidence of Hebrew texts corresponding to the Septuagint. Jeremiah 43 in the MT, which is 50 in the LXX, seems to represent a Hebrew text that is older than the *Vorlage* of the MT[31].

7. *Concluding Theses*

a. The Greek translator of Proverbs was a creative interpreter of his parent Semitic text that did not differ extensively from MT.

b. On a *text-historical level* the diversity of (Hebrew) textual material in the pre-Masoretic era, even though it undoubtedly existed (Qumran texts), should not be overstated. The *Vorlage* of LXX Proverbs corresponds to a large extend with MT. It should therefore be treated with the utmost caution when utilized for text-critical purposes.

c. The relationship between the Semitic *Vorlagen* and the translated Greek texts as *Urbild* and *Abbild* as suggested by R. Hanhart[32] should also be addressed in an endeavour to understand the canonical value of the Septuagint[33].

d. The rabbis did not create a scriptural canon. They inherited a more-or-less agreed set of writings[34] – holy books.

---

31. Cf. J. COOK, *The Difference in the Order of the Books of the Hebrew and Greek versions of Jeremiah - Jer 43 (50): A Case Study*, in OTE 7/2 (1994) 175-192 and TOV, *Textual Criticism* (n. 24), pp. 319-329.

32. R. HANHART, *Textgeschichtliche Probleme der LXX von ihrer Entstehung bis Origenes*, in M. HENGEL & A. M. SCHWEMER (eds.), *Die Septuaginta zwischen Judentum und Christentum* (WUNT, 72), Tübingen, Mohr, 1994, pp. 1-19.

33. J. COOK, *Septuagint Proverbs and Canonization*, in A. VAN DER KOOIJ & K. VAN DER TOORN (eds.), *Canonization and Decanonization. Papers Presented to the International Conference of the Leiden Institute for the Study of Religions (LISOR) Held at Leiden 9-10 January 1997* (Studies in the History of Religions, 82), Leiden, Brill, 1998, pp. 79-91.

34. DAVIES, *Scribes and Schools* (n. 4), p. 167.

e. There is a creative element in the formation of the canon, for in the process 'From Pluriformity to Uniformity' "the creative element did continue in the various forms of the transmission of the text, in its Hebrew form as well as in the non-Hebrew versions"[35].

f. Sociological factors played determinative roles in the fixation of texts/canons[36].

g. Ideological factors had an impact on newly shaped texts (Proverbs LXX and Gen 1,9).

h. The obvious differences between texts of which the rabbis must have been aware clearly did not create dogmatic problems to them (cf. the paper by E. Ulrich in this volume).

i. Harmonisation of apparent discrepancies is found in both Christian and Jewish sources (cf. the Samaritan Pentateuch).

Department of Ancient Studies   Johann COOK
University of Stellenbosch
South Africa

---

35. SÆBØ, *On the Way to Canon* (n. 6), p. 44.
36. *Ibid.*, p. 45.

AUX ORIGINES DE LA FIXATION DU CANON
SCRIPTORIA, LISTES ET TITRES

LE *VATICANUS* ET LA STICHOMÉTRIE DE MOMMSEN

Les implications matérielles des démarches successives et progressives aboutissant à la délimitation du canon dans les Églises chrétiennes sont connues, mais rarement étudiées comme telles. Elles font partie de cette loi d'incarnation qui caractérise le christianisme. Je les rappelle brièvement, avant de les analyser.

1. C'est au cours du IVe siècle seulement que tous les livres ont pu être regroupés en un seul codex. Les plus anciens exemples sont le *Sinaiticus* et le *Vaticanus*. Et même s'il faut réserver l'existence possible de témoins perdus, plus anciens, aucun spécialiste n'a jamais envisagé l'existence de *codices* de cette ampleur avant 300. L'observation, d'ailleurs, ne vaut que pour le grec; dans le domaine latin il faut attendre le milieu du VIe siècle (Cassiodore), dans les autres espaces linguistiques vraisemblablement plus tard encore.

L'évolution antérieure est maintenant connue. Les œuvres littéraires sont transmises sur rouleau (la bibliothèque d'Herculanum, antérieure à 79 de l'ère chrétienne, est le plus bel exemple). Et le rouleau ne peut guère contenir plus qu'un livre biblique. Il semble même que pour les livres les plus longs, la Genèse, Jérémie, il en ait fallu deux[1]. À partir du IIe et au cours du IIIe siècle, l'emploi du codex se généralise. L'outil se perfectionne petit à petit, de telle sorte que le codex peut porter la copie de plus d'un livre biblique[2]. Ainsi le manuscrit 967 de la Septante, codex de papyrus fait d'un seul cahier de 59 bifeuillets (118 folios), donne Ézéchiel, Daniel, Esther. La technique consistant à superposer des cahiers, ternions, quaternions, quinions, permet de fabriquer des *codices* plus importants, mais il n'y a pas d'exemple de *codices* pouvant comporter toute la Bible avant les grands onciaux S et B. Sans doute n'était-ce possible que sur parchemin.

Au début, la canonicité d'un livre ne peut se manifester par sa seule présence dans un codex caractérisé comme biblique. Il n'est pas rare

---

1. Cette conclusion ressort des différences de langue ou de grammaire distinguant les deux moitiés d'un même livre: H. St J. THACKERAY, *The Bisection of Books in Primitive Septuagint*, in *JTS* 9 (1907-08) 88-98; et déjà ID., *The Greek Translators of Jeremiah*, in *JTS* 4 (1902-03) 245-266. Pour la Genèse, voir O.J. BAAB, *A Theory of Two Translators for the Greek Genesis*, in *JBL* 52 (1933) 239-241.

2. E.G. TURNER, *The Typology of the Early Codex*, University of Pennsylvania, 1977; J. VAN HAELST, *Les origines du codex*, in A. BLANCHARD (éd.), *Les débuts du codex* (Bibliologia, 9), Turnhout, 1989, pp. 12-35.

qu'en Égypte, pour laquelle nous sommes très bien documentés, un même codex contienne tel livre canonique et tel autre qui, à notre connaissance, n'a aucune prétention à ce statut. En revanche, lorsqu'il devient possible de regrouper tous les livres bibliques, la présence de tel livre dans cet ensemble est une indication en faveur de sa canonicité. Mais jusque-là et bien plus tard, l'existence de listes sera le mode le plus normal pour définir la canonicité d'un livre.

2. Les listes de livres ont dû jouer très tôt un rôle. Elles n'ont pas eu toutes le même statut. Eusèbe cite les listes de Méliton et d'Origène[3]. Nous reviendrons sur la *Lettre Festale* d'Athanase. Autour de 400, les conciles africains (et Augustin dans le *De doctrina christiana*), un appendice aux canons du concile de Laodicée et la lettre d'Innocent Ier à Exsuperius prennent la peine d'énumérer les livres canoniques. À côté de ces listes qui tiennent leur autorité de grands noms de l'exégèse ou des Églises, il y a aussi des listes établies à l'initiative, semble-t-il, de «libraires» ou de «scriptoria». Le cas le plus manifeste est le Canon de Mommsen qui atteste un usage africain latin au milieu du IVe siècle et qui énumère les livres bibliques (A.T. et N.T.) ainsi que les œuvres de Cyprien, chaque titre étant accompagné de sa stichométrie.

Ces listes (et d'autres) n'ont donc pas toutes la même portée dans l'histoire de la fixation du canon, même s'il est vraisemblable que les libraires tenaient compte des usages ecclésiaux. Ajoutons que, au cours de leur transmission, les listes ont fait parfois l'objet d'ajustements, les apparats critiques en témoignent. Il est facile de comprendre que les copistes ultérieurs ont été tentés de tenir pour faute ou omission ce qui ne correspondait pas à leur usage.

3. Les listes sont faites essentiellement d'une succession de titres, souvent très brefs[4]. Se pose dès lors la question de l'univocité des appellations. Lorsque chaque liste avait pour correspondant tel codex ou telle série de *codices* chez tel «libraire», le risque d'équivoque restait limité. Mais lorsque la liste n'est pas accompagnée, et en particulier lorsqu'il

---

3. *Eusebius Werke*. II. *Die Kirchengeschichte*, edd. E. Schwartz & Th. Mommsen (GCS), Leipzig, 1903, 1908, pp. 386-389, 571-575. – On se rappellera que ces listes sont à pondérer par l'usage effectif que les auteurs font des livres bibliques. Voir J. Ruwet, *Duo textus Origenis de canone Antiqui Testamenti*, in *Bib* 2 (1921) 57-60; Id., *Les «Antilegomena» dans les œuvres d'Origène*, in *Bib* 23 (1942) 18-42 (N.T.) et 24 (1943) 18-58 (A.T.); Id., *Clément d'Alexandrie: canon des Écritures et apocryphes*, in *Bib* 29 (1948) 77-99, 240-268, 391-408.

4. En 1994, un colloque s'est tenu à Chantilly sur ce sujet: J.-Cl. Fredouille *et al.* (eds.), *Titres et articulations du texte dans les œuvres antiques* (Collection des Études Augustiniennes. Série Antiquité, 152), Paris, 1997.

n'y a pas encore de *codices* bibliques reconnaissables et vraiment distincts des autres, l'ambiguïté est possible, et certains ont pu essayer d'en profiter à des fins personnelles. La stichométrie, en fixant la dimension de l'œuvre, limite les risques sans les supprimer.

Ces considérations assez générales demandent à être appuyées par des exemples concrets, qui mettent en évidence l'interaction des multiples facteurs évoqués ci-dessus: d'une part, le support (rouleau et codex), les listes et les titres; d'autre part, les libraires (au sens large: scriptoria, copistes) et les autorités ecclésiastiques. Deux exemples seront l'objet de cet article; ils sont presque contemporains, la Stichométrie de Mommsen, de 359, pour le monde latin (bibles en une dizaine de *codices*), et le *Vaticanus* (la bible grecque en un codex), du milieu du IVe siècle, en relation avec le canon d'Athanase pour le monde grec.

I. LE *VATICANUS* (B) ET LE CANON D'ATHANASE

L'origine du *Vaticanus* (sigle: B; Biblioteca Apostolica Vaticana, Vat. gr. 1209) pose des questions difficiles, peut-être insolubles, mais que les érudits ne se lasseront pas de soulever, tant ce manuscrit est précieux aux yeux de tous. Avec le *Sinaiticus* (S dans l'A.T., א dans le N.T.), il est la plus ancienne bible conservée en un volume, et il a contenu d'emblée l'Ancien et le Nouveau Testament. Un récent colloque tenu à la Faculté autonome de théologie protestante de Genève le 11 juin 2001, suite à la publication d'un très beau fac-similé du manuscrit[5], a débattu de ces questions que Theodore C. Skeat avait soulevées à nouveau fin 1999 dans un article du *Journal of Theological Studies*[6].

Dans le cadre d'un article sur le canon, elles n'ont pas toute la même importance. Et je ne traiterai ici que de la question du rapport entre le canon d'Athanase tel que nous le connaissons grâce à sa *Lettre Festale* 39 et l'ordre des livres contenus dans le *Vaticanus*. J'évoque brièvement les questions en suspens, ainsi que mon opinion à leur sujet.

1. Il est raisonnable de tenir que le *Vaticanus* et le *Sinaiticus* (S) sont issus du même scriptorium. L'ornementation discrète de certains colophons est identique, et les écritures sont très voisines. Cependant,

5. *Bibliothecae Apostolicae Vaticanae Codex Vaticanus Graecus 1209. Bibliorum Sacrorum Graecorum Codex Vaticanus B*, Roma, 1999. Un volume de *Prolegomena* accompagne le somptueux fac-similé et comporte trois contributions: P. CANART, *Notice paléographique et codicologique*, pp. 1-6; P.-M. BOGAERT, *Le texte de l'Ancien Testament*, pp. 7-26; St. PISANO, *The Text of the New Testament*, pp. 27-41.

6. H.J. MILNE & T.C. SKEAT, *Scribes and Correctors of the Codex Sinaiticus.* Including a Contribution by D. COCKERELL, London, 1938; T.C. SKEAT, *The Codex Sinaiticus, the Codex Vaticanus, and Constantine*, in *JTS*, N.S. 50 (1999) 583-625.

d'après Skeat, S serait dicté, tandis que B est copié[7]. La mise en page est aussi très différente, 4 colonnes habituellement dans S, trois dans B. L'ordre des livres bibliques de l'Ancien Testament (avec des implications sur le canon) est très différent, alors que c'est un point sur lequel le responsable d'un scriptorium peut imprimer sa marque. Si donc on admet que B et S sont issus du même scriptorium, il faut en même temps placer entre eux deux un intervalle de temps suffisant.

2. Skeat a montré que l'emploi du parchemin est beaucoup plus économe dans B que dans S. Une seule peau donne quatre bi-feuillets au lieu de deux[8]. J'observe dans le même sens qu'il y aussi moins de feuillets blancs (souvent détachés aujourd'hui) dans B que dans S. Avec Skeat, j'en conclus que S est antérieur à B. Cette conclusion est inéluctable si les deux manuscrits ont été exécutés dans le même scriptorium[9]. B marque un progrès évident sur S en matière de fabrication du codex.

3. Skeat, reprenant sa thèse de 1938, estime pouvoir montrer que S a été écrit à Césarée. L'argument principal est la présence de deux fautes trahissant l'origine césaréenne du scribe: en Mt 12,54, la leçon αντιπατριδα au lieu de πατριδα n'a pas de sens, mais peut venir à l'esprit d'un scribe de Césarée; en Ac 8,5, on peut expliquer de la même façon, le remplacement de σαμαρειας par καισαρειας. De plus, le manuscrit porte des notations hexaplaires du VIe s., qui font supposer que le manuscrit est resté à Césarée[10]. – Aucun des deux arguments n'est contraignant, car les fautes «césaréennes» peuvent avoir été commises en amont de S, et les annotations hexaplaires étaient largement connues hors de Césarée vers 500. D'autre part, B n'a, pour l'Ancien Testament, aucune des caractéristiques du texte origénien (O) ou césaréen, sinon le texte d'Isaïe (l'exception confirmant la règle). Il n'a pas non plus les canons d'Eusèbe. Quant à S, on n'y trouve aucun texte origénien ou césaréen de première main. B et S représentent le plus souvent le texte égyptien en accord avec le copte et l'éthiopien. Voir le Tableau 1.

4. A. Rahlfs mettait B en relation avec une commande de l'empereur Constant Ier à Athanase[11]. Skeat de son côté le rattache à une commande de Constantin à Eusèbe[12]. S'il faut choisir, la première solution, Cons-

7. T.C. SKEAT, *The Use of Dictation in Ancien Book-Production*, in *Proceedings of the British Academy* 42 (1956) 179-208.

8. SKEAT, *The Codex* (n. 6), pp. 612-614.

9. Si B et S n'ont pas été écrits dans le même atelier, on peut envisager une évolution plus lente dans celui de S.

10. SKEAT, *The Codex*, pp. 617-619: les correcteurs Ca et CPamph sont à mettre en relation avec le texte «césaréen».

11. A. RAHLFS, *Alter und Heimat der vatikanischen Bibelhandschrift*, in *Nachrichten ... Göttingen*, Philol.-Hist. Kl. 1899, pp. 72-79.

12. SKEAT, *The Codex* (n. 6), pp. 605-609 et déjà pour S, en 1956, SKEAT, *The Use of Dictation* (n. 7).

tant Ier, est préférable, car la liste des livres dans B est apparentée au canon d'Athanase de plusieurs façons. Mais il se peut aussi que B soit postérieur. Voyons ce qu'il en est.

A. *Le canon alexandrin*

Pour l'étude du canon alexandrin, il existe un point de repère assuré[13]. Dans sa *Lettre Festale* 39, datée de 367, Athanase énumère les livres de la Bible selon un ordre et avec un contenu particuliers. Alfred Rahlfs a mis en lumière la parenté (non l'identité) de ce canon athanasien, donc alexandrin, avec B[14]. Le contenu et l'ordre des livres de S n'ont rien de commun avec ce canon, sauf la présence du *Pasteur d'Hermas*. Theodore Skeat a rappelé les différences entre le canon athanasien et B, et il a fait intervenir la version sahidique, publiée entre-temps, qui présente un ordre légèrement différent des épîtres pauliniennes[15]. Je voudrais montrer que les différences ne parviennent pas à cacher une vraie parenté.

D'abord, l'absence totale des Maccabées dans B est caractéristique du canon athanasien qui comporte par ailleurs des livres absents de l'hébreu, soit dans la catégorie des livres pour débutants, οἱ ἄρτι προσερχόμενοι (Esther, Judith, Tobie, Sagesse, Siracide), soit dans son Ancien Testament (suppléments de Daniel, Baruch et la Lettre de Jérémie). Mais surtout B garde groupés les livres non chrétiens pour débutants (donc à l'exclusion de la *Didachè* et du *Pasteur* qui sont chrétiens): Sagesse, Siracide, Esther, Judith, Tobie, dans le même ordre que le canon d'Athanase.

Cependant il ne faudrait pas trop vite conclure du canon d'Athanase à celui d'Alexandrie, ni du canon d'Athanase en 367 à celui d'Alexandrie tout au long du IVe siècle. Le pontificat d'Athanase (328-373) a été interrompu par des exils ou des empêchements, à Trèves de 335 à 337, à Rome de 339 à 346, chez les moines de 356 à 362, de 362 à 363, de 365

---

13. Sur le canon alexandrin, d'une façon générale, voir les articles cités à la n. 3, et sur Athanase, voir J. RUWET, *Le canon alexandrin des Écritures. Saint Athanase*, in *Bib* 33 (1952) 1-29; D. BRAKKE, *Canon Formation and Social Conflict in Fourth Century Egypt: Athanasius of Alexandria's Thirty-Ninth Festal Letter*, in *HTR* 87 (1994) 395-420. Sur 1–4 M, voir H. DÖRRIE, *Die Stellung der vier Makkabäerbücher im Kanon der griechischen Bibel*, in *Nachrichten von der Gesellschaft der Wissenschaften zu Göttingen*, Philol.-Hist. Kl. Fachgr. Religionswissenschaft, N.F., Bd. I, Nr. 2, Göttingen, 1937, pp. 45-54. Voir encore J. LEEMANS, *Athanasius and the Book of Wisdom*, in *ETL* 73 (1997) 349-368, ainsi que sa contribution au présent volume (pp. 265-277).

14. RAHLFS, *Alter und Heimat* (n. 11).

15. SKEAT, *The Codex* (n. 6), pp. 600-603. – Dans *Le texte de l'Ancien Testament* (n. 5), j'ai signalé, p. 8, n. 6, qu'il fallait considérer dorénavant aussi R. G. COQUIN, *Les Lettres Festales d'Athanase (CPG 2102). Un nouveau complément: le manuscrit IFAO, copte 25*, in *Orientalia Lovaniensia Periodica* 15 (1984) 138-158, pl. X (avec mention des deux livres d'Esdras, omis dans le manuscrit utilisé par L.-Th. Lefort).

à 366, ce qui signifie que d'autres que lui, ses adversaires peut-être, ont pu imprimer leur marque aux productions manuscrites bibliques de la grande cité.

Autrement dit, la parenté spéciale du canon d'Athanase avec B n'empêche nullement une origine alexandrine de S, très différent pour ce qui touche le canon et l'ordre des livres, si elle est vraisemblable par ailleurs.

B. *La suite des livres dans B et le canon alexandrin*

Dans les *Prolegomena* à l'édition en fac-similé, j'ai proposé de voir dans l'organisation de B un compromis entre un usage établi et le canon athanasien[16]. D'une part, les «livres pour commençants» relatifs à l'Ancien Testament se retrouvent groupés, mais, d'autre part, ils sont placés à l'intérieur de l'Ancien Testament, entre les Sapientiaux et les Prophètes. Voir le Tableau 1. La marque du canon athanasien est donc manifeste, mais la logique du canon athanasien n'est pas respectée. Cette observation amène à placer la copie de B *après* le canon athanasien, mais pas nécessairement après 367, car la publication du canon dans la *Lettre Festale* 39 n'est vraisemblablement pas une innovation. Du moins, les termes introduisant la liste donnent à penser qu'il s'agit surtout d'une confirmation.

L'ordre des épîtres pauliniennes a été examiné par Skeat, et il faut y revenir. Trois ordres sont à prendre en compte.

1. L'ordre sahidique attesté par les manuscrits sahidiques des lettres pauliniennes et par la version sahidique de la *Lettre Festale*: Hébreux vient après Romains et 1–2 Corinthiens[17].

2. Une capitulation marginale dans B suppose l'ordre Romains, 1–2 Corinthiens, Galates, Hébreux, etc. Au dire de Skeat, cette capitulation n'est pas de la main d'un des deux scribes de B[18]. Il s'agit d'une addition postérieure, qui ne peut parler pour l'origine. Cependant la place particulière de Hébreux intrigue. Elle est unique certes, mais aussi très proche de l'ordre sahidique, et elle s'explique mieux dans un contexte égyptien.

---

16. Bogaert, *Le texte de l'Ancien Testament* (n. 5), pp. 8-9.

17. Pour l'ordre des épîtres pauliniennes en sahidique, voir H. Thompson, *The Coptic Version of the Acts of the Apostles and the Pauline Epistles in Sahidic Dialect*, Cambridge, 1932, p. xxviii: «The Sahidic has an order peculiar to itself, ranking Hebrews next after 2 Cor. and before Gal. This was due doubtless to its importance in point of length. It is the order found in all Sahidic manuscripts containing the Epistles or so much of them as to reveal their order including Be (Beatty) and both Morgan manuscripts».

18. Skeat, *The Codex* (n. 6), p. 601.

3. L'ordre attesté par le texte grec du canon d'Athanase, par la liste attachée aux canons du concile de Laodicée (date incertaine, vers 400), et suivi dans B ainsi que dans de nombreux onciaux et minuscules grecs: Hébreux avant les épîtres pastorales (1–2 Timothée, Tite, Philémon)[19].

Quoi qu'il en soit, l'ordre des épîtres pauliniennes dans B ne peut pas être un argument contre son origine égyptienne, puisqu'il rejoint à cet égard la forme grecque de la *Lettre Festale*.

Il convient d'ajouter un mot sur la succession des trois livrets Esther, Judith, Tobie (dorénavant EJT), qui varie d'un témoin à l'autre. Il est intéressant d'observer que B a, sur ce point, l'ordre d'Athanase. B n'est pas seul, mais il est le seul des grands onciaux. Voici les données, avec utilisation des sigles du «Septuaginta-Unternehmen» de Göttingen[20]:

    EJT: B 46 58 76 107 130 311
    ETJ: A S 64 243 248 249 534
    JET: 19 55 108
    TEJ: 583
    E...TJ: N(V)
    T...EJ: 542.

C. *Observations codicologiques sur B*

C'est avec prudence que je propose ici des observations codicologiques sur B. Avec plus de prudence encore que je propose leur interprétation. Mais des hommes de métier y trouveront peut-être matière à plus ample conclusion.

1. La mesure du quinion, et en particulier du demi quinion (5 feuillets, 10 pages) me paraît avoir présidé à l'organisation de la copie. Les Livres historiques occupent 33 quinions et un demi, les Sapientiaux commençant en haut du recto du folio 6 de ce même quinion (p. 625). De même, les Prophètes commencent avec un nouveau quinion (50) et s'achèvent avec le milieu d'un quinion (64), le Nouveau Testament commençant en haut du recto du folio 6 de ce quinion (p. 1235). Autrement dit, les Sapientiaux, les Prophètes, le Nouveau Testament commencent soit avec

---

19. C'est l'ordre de plusieurs onciaux du Nouveau Testament, outre S = ℵ et B, A C H I P 0150 0151. Voir surtout H.J. FREDE, *Epistulae ad Philippenses et ad Colossenses* (Vetus Latina, 24/2), Freiburg i. Br., 1966-1971, pp. 290-303 («Die Ordnung der Paulusbriefe und der Platz des Kolosserbriefs im Corpus Paulinum»), spéc. p. 293; on notera cependant que l'ordre des Épîtres pauliniennes dans la version sahidique de la *Lettre Festale* 39 d'Athanase n'est pas A4, mais A3: Rm Co He Ga Ep Ph Col Th Tm Tt Phm.

20. D'après A. RAHLFS, *Verzeichnis der griechischen Handschriften des Alten Testaments* (Mitteilungen des Septuaginta-Unternehmens, 2 = *Nachrichten... Göttingen*, Beiheft 1914), Berlin, 1915, passim.

un nouveau quinion (les Prophètes), soit sur la seconde moitié d'un quinion (Sapientiaux, Nouveau Testament). Cette disposition suppose un scriptorium organisé.

2. Dans B, Esther–Judith–Tobie occupent sur trois colonnes les p. 893 (une colonne) à 944 (une colonne et demie), soit près de 51 p., soit encore la matière de 2 quinions (40 p.), d'un demi quinion (10 p.) et d'une page.

Si ces trois livres étaient copiés, comme il n'est pas rare (dans S et 55 par exemple), à la suite de B Esdras, ils commenceraient à la p. 624, presque blanche actuellement dans B, et s'achèveraient à la fin d'un quinion, p. 674*, occupant les onze dernières pages du quinion 33* (p. 624*-634*) et les quinions 34* et 35*, soit 51 pages. (Les astérisques indiquent le quinion ou la page dans l'hypothèse envisagée.)

Dans cette hypothèse (EJT à la suite de B Esdras), non seulement les Livres historiques s'achèveraient exactement avec un quinion (35*), mais encore les Sapientiaux qui suivent (sept livres, avec Psaumes et Job), écrits sur deux colonnes, occuperaient alors exactement 14 quinions moins 3 pages (une page et un folio) laissées blanches (ce seraient les q. 36* à 49*)[21]. Dans la disposition actuelle, ils commencent avec un milieu de quinion (p. 625) et s'achèvent (p. 893, première colonne) à l'intérieur d'un quinion. Après quoi, les Prophètes commencent avec le quinion 50 dans la réalité et dans l'hypothèse proposée.

Considérant le caractère singulier de l'organisation des livres dans B, il est satisfaisant de constater qu'une organisation moins étrange donnerait une répartition régulière des quinions selon les grandes subdivisions, Livres historiques avec EJT, Sapientiaux, Prophètes, Nouveau Testament. Je fais donc l'hypothèse que le scriptorium de B a connu avant la copie de B une ordonnance des livres de l'A.T. plus commune:

> Les Livres historiques avec EJT: 35 quinions;
> Les Sapientiaux: 14 quinions, sur deux colonnes;
> Les Livres prophétiques: 14 quinions et demi;
> Le Nouveau Testament: commençant exactement avec la seconde moitié du q. 64.

3. L'observation précédente est fondamentale. Il faut cependant en ajouter une autre. Le groupe athanasien des «livres pour débutants» se trouvait, d'après la *Lettre Festale*, à la suite du Nouveau Testament. Je compte aussi avec une autre possibilité, celle que les livres proprement vetero-testamentaires de ce groupe aient été placés entre l'Ancien Testa-

---

21. Soit l'équivalent de un demi quinion + 13 quinions + 7 pages. Pour les calculs, il faut prendre garde que le quinion 37 original, dans les Psaumes, est perdu et remplacé par un trinion, ce qui perturbe la numérotation des pages, normalement vingt par cahier.

ment et le Nouveau. Les cinq «livres pour débutants» occupent dans B les p. 809 (2ᵉ col.) à 944, près de 136 pages, soit en théorie 7 quinions, moins 2 folios. En réalité, ils commencent vers le début d'un quinion et s'achèvent trop tôt vers la fin d'un quinion dont le dernier folio blanc a été retranché.

Dans le premier cas, ces cinq livres se trouvaient après le Nouveau Testament et sont donc à retrancher du compte de l'Ancien Testament, ce qui amène à sortir de la mesure du demi quinion. Il n'y a donc pas lieu de la poursuivre. D'ailleurs, B est fruste de la fin.

Dans la seconde hypothèse, en revanche, nous aurions:

Genèse à B Esdras: 32 q. et demi;
Prophètes: 14 q. et demi;
Sapientiaux (avec Sg et Si) + EJT: 16 q. et demi, à la suite comme dans B[22];
Nouveau Testament: commençant exactement avec la seconde moitié du q. 64.

4. Partant de ces observations, je défends la vraisemblance (rien de plus) de la séquence historique suivante.

a. Dans un scriptorium aguerri à la copie de très longs textes et donc aussi à leur mensuration, l'on pouvait copier la Bible grecque dans un ordre fréquemment attesté et ancien – celui de S – de la façon suivante:

Livres historiques + EJT: 32 q. et demi + 2 q. et demi = 35 q.;
Sapientiaux: 14 q. (sur deux colonnes) = q. 36* à 49*;
Prophètes: 14 q. et demi = q. 50* à 64* première moitié;
N.T.: commençant exactement avec la seconde moitié du q. 64.

Dans ce système, l'interversion Prophètes – Sapientiaux serait sans conséquence.

b. Sous l'influence du canon athanasien – et sans qu'il faille tenir la date de 367 pour contraignante –, on disposa la matière de telle sorte que les «livres pour débutants» soient rangés entre l'Ancien et le Nouveau Testament. Il suffisait pour cela de déplacer EJT (deux quinions et demi) après les Sapientiaux, ce qui entraînait le regroupement des «livres pour débutants» (Sg, Si, EJT). Le résultat respectait la mesure du demi quinion et permettait de regrouper les livres copiés sur deux colonnes en 14 quinions complets exactement, les quinions 48* à 61*, ce qui facilitait la réglure:

Livres historiques jusqu'à B Esdras: 32 quinions et demi (q. 1 à 33 1/2);
Prophètes: 14 quinions et demi (q. 33 2/2* à 47*);

___

22. Dans B, cet ensemble occupe un demi quinion (q. 33, deuxième moitié) et 16 quinions (q. 34 à 49). Dans l'hypothèse «athanasienne», il occupe de façon équivalente 16 quinions (q. 48* à 63*) et un demi (q. 64*, première moitié).

> Sapientiaux (s'achevant sur Sg et Si): 14 quinions moins 3 pages, sur 2 colonnes (q. 48* à 61*, 1 feuillet blanc);
> EJT: 2 quinions et demi (q. 62* à 64*, première moitié);
> N.T.: commençant exactement avec la seconde moitié du q. 64.

c. En réaction contre cette disposition particulière, qui n'avait d'ailleurs pas d'avenir, en réaction peut-être aussi contre Athanase, le même scriptorium déplaça les Prophètes, de telle sorte que les «livres pour débutants» rentrent dans le rang. La seule trace, mais caractéristique, de l'ordonnance athanasienne est la place singulière de EJT après Sagesse – Siracide. C'est l'ordre du *Vaticanus* (B):

> Livres historiques jusqu'à B Esdras: 32 quinions et demi;
> Sapientiaux s'achevant sur Sg, Si, suivis de EJT: 16 quinions et demi;
> Prophètes: 14 quinions et demi;
> N.T.: commençant exactement au milieu d'un quinion.

Les trois dispositions (a, b, c) sont fondées sur le demi quinion. La troisième (c), singulière, a le mérité d'exister. C'est celle de B. La deuxième (b), correspondant mieux au canon athanasien, rend compte de la singularité de la troisième. La première (a) correspond à une ordonnance ancienne et destinée à survivre; elle groupe les Livres historiques, y compris EJT; elle se distribue sur les quinions de façon très régulière, en fonction des grandes parties de la Bible grecque et de la disposition des sept livres sapientiaux sur deux colonnes en un nombre exact de quinions, commençant avec un quinion.

Comment l'atelier des scribes pouvait-il calculer à l'avance l'étendue de sa copie? Une fois mise en évidence une mesure, le demi quinion, il faut se demander si elle peut avoir un rapport avec la stichométrie. Ayant fait des calculs pour la plupart des livres de l'Ancien Testament, je ne suis arrivé à des résultats vraiment significatifs que pour l'Octateuque. Comme il ressort d'une étude qui sera publiée par ailleurs, le nombre de lignes dans B est pour ces livres exactement (on ne peut guère s'attendre à plus de précision) le double du chiffre donné par les listes stichométriques[23]. En dehors de l'Octateuque, on ne retrouve cette précision que pour certains livres (des Prophètes). Les erreurs dans la transmission des chiffres n'expliquent pas tout. Ainsi pour les quatre Livres des Règnes, le rapport n'est pas de 1 à 2, mais de 1 à 2,2 ou à 2,3. Il faudrait des calculs précis (nombre moyen de caractères par ligne dans les diverses parties de B) pour avancer.

Jusqu'à plus ample informé, je préfère croire que c'est l'occupation du parchemin, et donc la mesure du demi quinion, qui a conduit le scribe

---

23. Notre communication au colloque de Genève donne les justifications nécessaires.

à écrire plus large ou plus serré. Cependant il ne pouvait apprécier l'espace nécessaire que sur la base de calculs et, pourquoi pas?, d'une stichométrie.

Conclusion

À partir d'observations codicologiques simples, mettant en évidence l'importance du demi-quinion dans la mesure des quantités pour l'organisation du travail de copie, j'ai visé à montrer que la série des «livres pour débutants», caractéristique du canon d'Athanase apporte une clé pour comprendre l'ordre des livres de l'Ancien Testament dans B. Poussant plus loin la thèse de Rahlfs et la présentation que j'en ai donnée dans les *Prolegomena*, je crois qu'un même scriptorium a pu organiser et mesurer sa copie selon trois modèles successifs:

le premier, ancien et destiné à prévaloir finalement, laisse groupés les livres historiques, y compris Esther, Judith et Tobie;

le deuxième rejoint au plus près le canon athanasien, groupant les livres non chrétiens pour débutants entre l'Ancien et le Nouveau Testament;

le troisième, attesté dans B, revient à la tradition; elle garde des traces très nettes du canon athanasien, puisque les livres pour débutants restent groupés et que les Maccabées font défaut, mais elle renonce à mettre en évidence les livres pour débutants et à disloquer pour cela la série des Sapientiaux.

Le passage d'un modèle à l'autre ne trouble pas l'emploi de la mesure du demi quinion ou du quinion entier.

En amont de ce travail de copie, se trouvaient ou bien des rouleaux ne contenant qu'un seul livre biblique, ou bien vraisemblablement déjà de petits *codices* en réunissant quelques-uns. On peut penser que seul l'emploi du parchemin a permis la fabrication d'une bible en un seul codex. Ce passé rend compte du peu d'homogénéité du contenu de B, très sensible pour l'Ancien Testament. Quoi qu'il en soit de la succession des trois stades telle que je l'ai proposée, le rôle pivot du canon athanasien est certain dans B, et il fait peser lourdement la balance en faveur de son origine égyptienne et alexandrine. Aucun indice en faveur d'une origine césaréenne ne le contrebalance.

Tout ceci, que l'on pourrait développer plus en détail, montre au moins que, s'il est un domaine où les responsables d'un scriptorium pouvaient exercer leur influence d'une manière décisive, c'est bien, en l'absence de décisions ecclésiastiques indiscutables, la liste des livres et surtout leur ordre.

II. LA STICHOMÉTRIE DE MOMMSEN

En préparant pour les *Monumenta Germaniae Historica* l'édition d'une ancienne Chronique (révision du «Chronographe de 354»), dont la date est 359, Theodor Mommsen découvrit un *indiculum* des livres bibliques et des œuvres de Cyprien, accompagné de leurs stichométries[24]. La liste est clairement d'origine latine et presque certainement africaine[25]. Elle précède donc celle des Conciles d'Afrique (à partir de 393) et celle d'Innocent Ier (405); elle ne peut avoir subi l'influence de Jérôme. Elle a ceci de particulier, j'essaierai de le montrer, qu'elle se trouve au confluent des besoins d'une Église et des pratiques commerciales d'un libraire. Cette stichométrie est une liste, faite de titres, dont le contenu est précisé tant bien que mal par la dimension des œuvres en stiques. C'est même la seule définition que nous ayons du stique, mesure servant au calcul du prix des copies. En 1878, Charles Graux avait montré que la mesure du stique était l'hexamètre épique[26]. La liste de Mommsen l'a confirmé pour le latin: la mesure est bien le vers virgilien de seize syllabes.

Quoniam indiculum uersuum in urbe Roma non aliquidum (ad liquidum *Mommsen*) sed et alibi auaritiae causa non habent integrum, per singulos libros computatis syllabis posui numero xvi uersum Virgilianum omnibus libris numerum adscribsi.

Puisque dans la ville de Rome l'on ne détient pas d'*indiculum* des stiques qui soit clair et puisque ailleurs, par goût du lucre, on n'en détient pas qui soit fidèle, après avoir fait pour chaque livre le compte des syllabes, j'ai estimé le vers virgilien à seize (syllabes et) j'ai joint le résultat à tous les livres.

---

24. Th. MOMMSEN, *Zur lateinischen Stichometrie*, in *Hermes* 21 (1886) 142-156; ID., *Zur lateinischen Stichometrie (Nachtrag zu Bd. XXI S. 142f)*, in *Hermes* 25 (1890) 636-638; *Chronographus anni CCCLIIII*, ed. Th. MOMMSEN (Monumenta Germaniae Historica, Auct. antiquissimorum t. 9; Chronica minora, 1), Berlin, 1892, pp. 80-81, 89-90. – À toute fin pratique, on utilisera l'édition, très commode, de Erwin PREUSCHEN, *Analecta*, Freiburg i. Br. - Leipzig, 1893, pp. 138-141.

25. S. BERGER, *Histoire de la Vulgate pendant les premiers siècles du moyen âge*, Nancy, 1893, pp. 320-321, s'est trompé. Il faut suivre W. SANDAY, *The Cheltenham List of the Canonical Books of the Old and New Testament and the Writings of Cyprian* et C.H. TURNER, *The Cyprianic Stichometry*, in *Studia Biblica et Ecclesiastica*, 3, Oxford, 1891, pp. 217-303 et 304-325; Th. ZAHN, *Geschichte des neutestamentlichen Kanons*, t. 2,1, Erlangen Leipzig, 1890, pp. 1007-1012; P. MONCEAUX, *Histoire littéraire de l'Afrique chrétienne*, t. 3, Paris, 1905, pp. 229-230; P.-M. BOGAERT, *Tobie, Esther et Judith dans la stichométrie de Mommsen*, in P. COCKSHAW, M.-C. GARAND & P. JODOGNE (eds.), *Miscellanea codicologica F. Masai dicata* (Les Publications de Scriptorium, 8), Gand, 1979, pp. 545-550 – Voir *Addendum*, p. 172.

26. Ch. GRAUX, *Nouvelles recherches sur la stichométrie*, in *Revue de philologie, de littérature et d'histoire anciennes*, N.S. 2 (1878) 97-143.

A. *Les titres*

Fiunt libri VII, écrit la liste de Mommsen pour l'ensemble qui va de Genèse aux Juges, sans Ruth. Le titre *Eptaticus* n'est pas employé ici explicitement. J'ai montré ailleurs que cette dénomination, empruntée au grec, a désigné anciennement chez les Latins les sept premiers livres de la Bible, à l'exclusion de Ruth rattaché aux Livres des Règnes comme ici ou au groupe des *Libri mulierum*[27]. La chose existe aussi sans le mot. Divers commentaires latins portent sur ces sept livres. Plus tard, lorsque la version hiéronymienne prévalut, le mot *Eptaticus*, reçu par l'usage, engloba occasionnellement Ruth, le mot «octateuque» restant exceptionnel et savant en latin.

Hiesu Naue, Libri Regnorum (pour 1–2 Samuel et 1–2 Rois) sont des décalques de l'usage des Septante. En revanche le mot *Eptaticus*, qui vient certainement du grec, n'est plus attesté par les écrivains grecs chrétiens, chez qui l'appellation Octateuque (avec Ruth) a prévalu.

Il est à noter que la dénomination d'*Eptaticus*, répandue dans le monde latin, a eu pour effet de concurrencer celles de Pentateuque, de Livres de la Loi, ou de Livres de Moïse et, comme la notion d'Octateuque, de faire prévaloir l'histoire sainte sur la loi.

B. *La liste et ses particularités*

1. *Les subdivisions et les sous-totaux dans la stichométrie.* – Au moment et au lieu où est rédigée la liste, dans le monde latin, vers 350, il est improbable qu'une bible complète ait pu être copiée en un seul codex. Du moins, il n'y a aucune mention ou exemple de la copie d'un ensemble aussi vaste (biblique ou non) sur un seul codex avant Cassiodore. Les sous-totaux proposés par la liste correspondent peut-être à l'usage des libraires de regrouper l'*Eptaticus*, les quatre *Libri Regnorum* avec Ruth, les *Libri Salomonis*, les Prophètes (la liste mentionne les *Prophetae maiores... numero IIII*, mais la stichométrie paraît bien englober les Petits Prophètes) et les quatre évangiles dans des *codices* distincts.

2. *L'ordre des livres.* – On notera ici surtout que les particularités dans l'ordre des livres ne sont pas accidentelles, puisqu'elles sont attestées aussi ailleurs. Il en est ainsi pour l'ordre Nombres–Lévitique[28], Daniel–Ézéchiel[29], ainsi que pour les évangiles énumérés par les deux té-

27. P.-M. Bogaert, Eptaticus: *le nom des premiers livres de la Bible dans l'ancienne tradition chrétienne grecque et latine*, in Fredouille *et al.* (eds.), *Titres et articulations* (n. 4), pp. 313-337.
28. P.-M. Bogaert, art. *Septante*, in *DBS* 12/68 (1993), cc. 536-692, spéc. c. 577.
29. *Ibid.*, c. 646.

moins selon un ordre différent: Mt–Jn–Mc–Lc dans le ms. Saint-Gall, Stiftsbibliothek, 133, Mt–Mc–Jn–Lc dans le ms. Cheltenham, Phillipps 12266 (non localisé aujourd'hui à ma connaissance)[30].

3. *Livres attendus et inattendus.* – Sont absents de la liste les livres d'Esdras, normalement en grec *A Esdras* et *B Esdras*, dans notre usage *III Esdras* et Esdras–Néhémie. Il s'agit peut-être d'un oubli, mais j'ai noté leur absence dans plusieurs autres listes[31]. Dans le Nouveau Testament, manquent l'Épître aux Hébreux[32] – ce qui ne surprendra pas dans le milieu latin vers 350[33] – ainsi que les Épîtres de Jacques et de Jude. C'est leur absence qui permet d'arriver au chiffre de vingt-quatre livres. Il est rare en revanche de voir mentionner explicitement le chiffre de 151 psaumes comme fait la liste, mais la présence du Ps 151 est très répandue dans les psautiers latins[34].

4. *Trois ou cinq sapientiaux?* – Combien la liste compte-t-elle de livres sapientiaux, trois (selon l'hébreu) ou cinq? Inclut-elle la Sagesse et l'Ecclésiastique? L'appellation *Salomonis* n'est accompagnée d'aucune précision, sinon de la stichométrie du total, 5 500 ou 6 500. Le second chiffre est suffisamment haut pour autoriser leur présence; les deux chiffres sont trop hauts pour Proverbes, Ecclésiaste, Cantique seulement. On sait que les Églises d'Afrique ont normalement les cinq livres, et le Siracide y est attribué anciennement à Salomon[35]. Il faut donc en venir à l'examen austère de la stichométrie.

30. P.-M. BOGAERT, *Ordres anciens des évangiles et tétraévangile en un seul codex*, in *RTL* 30 (1999) 297-314; voir les ordres E4 et E2 – Voir *Addendum*, p. 172.

31. P.-M. BOGAERT, *Les livres d'Esdras et leur numérotation dans l'histoire du canon de la Bible latine*, in *Revue bénédictine* 110 (2000) 5-26, spéc. p. 13-14. – J'ai observé depuis lors que les deux livres d'Esdras manquent aussi dans deux témoins du *De doctrina christiana* d'Augustin (voir l'apparat critique dans CC SL, t. 32, p. 39) et dans les meilleurs témoins de la tradition latine (attribuée à Isidore) de la liste des livres bibliques attachée aux canons de Laodicée (ed. C.H. TURNER, Oxford, 1939, p. 390, ligne 19).

32. La liste mentionne 13 épîtres de Paul d'après Chelt.; il faut comprendre ainsi le texte: *n(umero) xiij*, qui ne peut se rapporter à des stiques (en latin: *uersus*). Le chiffre 13 000 est impossible.

33. H.J. FREDE, *Lateinische Texte und Texttypen im Hebräerbrief*, in R. GRYSON & P.-M. BOGAERT (eds.), *Recherches sur l'histoire de la Bible latine* (Cahiers de la Revue Théologique de Louvain, 19), Louvain-la-Neuve, 1987, pp. 138-153, spéc. pp. 148-153.

34. P.-M. BOGAERT, *Le psautier latin des origines au XIIᵉ siècle. Essai d'histoire*, in A. AEJMALAEUS & U. QUAST (eds.), *Der Septuaginta-Psalter und seine Tochterübersetzungen. Symposium in Göttingen 1997* (Mitteilungen des Septuaginta-Unternehmens, 24, = Abhandlungen der Ak. der Wiss. in Göttingen, Phil.-Hist. Kl., III, 230), Göttingen, 2000, pp. 51-81, spéc. 57-58.

35. Voir W. THIELE, *Zum Titel des Sirachbuches in der lateinischen Übersetzung*, in GRYSON & BOGAERT (eds.), *Recherches sur l'histoire de la Bible latine* (n. 33), pp. 43-49. Pour D. DE BRUYNE, *Le titre, le prologue et la finale de l'Ecclésiastique*, in ZAW 47 (1929) 261, le titre *Ecclesiasticus Salomonis* est primitif.

C. *La stichométrie*

La transmission des chiffres romains est toujours quelque peu aléatoire dans les manuscrits. Dans le cas présent, il y a des variantes entre les deux témoins de la liste. Il y a cependant un troisième terme. Les témoins de la version hiéronymienne (Vulgate) ont parfois gardé, à la fin de chaque livre, une indication stichométrique qui ne lui était pas destinée. Ces chiffres, collationnés par Samuel Berger[36], peuvent être complétés par certaines éditions critiques parues depuis lors. Ils appartiennent au même système que ceux de la stichométrie de Mommsen.

Le calcul des rapports entre les chiffres de la stichométrie de Mommsen et la dimension réelle des œuvres permet d'y reconnaître un système dominant et deux autres marginaux.

Le système dominant vaut pour les livres de l'Ancien Testament, à mesurer selon les Septante, la Vulgate ou même selon la *Vetus Latina* quand celle-ci a été faite sur un modèle grec particulier ou perdu. Il vaut aussi pour les œuvres de Cyprien. D'une part, ce système est calculé sur l'hexamètre épique latin; de l'autre, il n'est pas emprunté aux systèmes grecs, dont il se distingue par des valeurs plus petites. Dans les évaluations réduites à la «ligne de Migne» pour permettre une comparaison entre livres bibliques et œuvres de Cyprien, le nombre de lignes de Migne est légèrement plus élevé que le chiffre donné par la stichométrie. Cette évaluation a été contrôlée sur les nombres de mots donnés pour chaque livre de la Vulgate[37] par le Centre Informatique et Biblique (CIB, Maredsous) et pour les œuvres de Cyprien par le CETEDOC (Louvain-la-Neuve): le rapport entre le nombre de mots latins et le chiffre de la stichométrie est très voisin de 7 à 1. Pour Cyprien, je me suis aidé du tableau de Hans von Soden[38]. Voir les Tableaux 2 et 3.

Le deuxième système ne fonctionne que pour les évangiles. Le rapport entre le nombre de mots latins (CIB) et la stichométrie de Mommsen est de 6 pour 1 dans Mt, Mc et le total des quatre évangiles. Il faut donc corriger la stichométrie de Luc de 3 300 en 3 000 et celle de Jean de 1 800 en 2 300 (MDCCC à corriger en MMCCC). Ces considérations ne sont pas totalement satisfaisantes, mais les stichométries grecques don-

---

36. BERGER, *Histoire de la Vulgate* (n. 25), pp. 313-327 et 363-368.

37. Pour les livres où il n'y pas de différence quantitative entre l'hébreu et le grec, on peut compter que le nombre de mots est sensiblement le même dans la Vulgate et dans la *Vetus Latina*. C'est sur ces livres que j'ai établi mes calculs.

38. H. VON SODEN, *Die Cyprianische Briefsammlung. Geschichte ihrer Entstehung und Überlieferung* (TU, 25/3), Leipzig, 1904, pp. 43-50. Voir aussi C.H. TURNER, *Studies in Early Church History. Collected Papers*, Oxford, 1912, pp. 263-265. – J'ai pris comme test des œuvres pour lesquelles H. von Soden pouvait accepter tels quels les chiffres de la stichométrie.

nent des chiffres identiques ou presque, si bien que l'on peut tenir ces chiffres pour empruntés au grec. Voir le Tableau 4.

Pour les Actes et pour l'Apocalypse, le rapport du nombre de mots latins à la stichométrie est de 4,6 à 1. Le calcul est précis. Les Actes ont presque exactement le double de mots que l'Apocalypse, et la stichométrie des Actes est exactement le double de celle de l'Apocalypse. Voir le Tableau 4. Toutefois, ce système ne peut être fondé sur l'hexamètre épique ni en latin, ni en grec. Je renonce à exploiter les chiffres globaux de 1–3 Jn et de 1–2 Pi.

D. *Les vingt-quatre Anciens et le nombre des livres bibliques chez les Latins*

La tradition juive ancienne paraît avoir connu un compte des livres bibliques au nombre de 22 (Flavius Josèphe, *Contra Apionem* I,VIII,38-41) ou de 24 (*IV Esdras* 14,44-47; *BTaanith* 8a, explicite sur le chiffre 24). Ces deux chiffres ont été mis assez tôt en relation avec les lettres de l'alphabet hébreu (au moins depuis Origène, suivi par Hilaire de Poitiers) et de l'alphabet grec (Hilaire de Poitiers, apparemment seul)[39].

Au moins depuis Victorin de Poetovio, qui se réfère à des *Epitomae Theodori* (on corrige parfois en *Theodoti*), les 24 Anciens de l'Apocalypse (4,5) sont dits représenter les 24 livres de l'Ancien Testament[40]. Cette explication vient cependant en concurrence avec une autre qui y voit les deux Testaments, les douze patriarches et les douze apôtres. Jérôme reprend sans les modifier ces deux interprétations de Victorin dans la refonte qu'il fait du commentaire de son prédécesseur[41]. De plus, dans son Prologue à Esdras, il tient le chiffre 24 pour décisif: «ce qui est en dehors des 24 Anciens doit être rejeté», tandis que, dans son Prologue aux *Libri Regum IV*, il rappelle d'abord le nombre de 22 et ajoute celui de 24, à condition de distinguer Ruth et Lamentations, selon les Anciens de l'Apocalypse[42].

Alors qu'Hilaire, partant du chiffre 22 du canon hébreu (qu'il reçoit d'Origène), ajoute Tobie et Judith pour atteindre 24, et qu'il se réfère aux deux alphabets, Jérôme passe de 22 à 24 sans changer de contenu, celui du canon hébreu qu'il subdivise autrement, et en référence aux

---

39. ORIGÈNE, *In Ps.*, dans EUSÈBE, *Hist. Eccl.* 6,25 (ci-dessus, n. 3), pp. 572-579; HILAIRE, *Tract. in Ps.*, Instr. 15 (CC SL 61, pp. 12-13).
40. VICTORIN DE POETOVIO, *Sur l'Apocalypse. Introduction, texte critique, traduction, commentaire et index par* M. DULAEY (SC, 423), Paris, 1997, pp. 66-67, 70-71.
41. CSEL 49, pp. 51, 55 et 57 (ed. I. HAUSSLEITER).
42. *Biblia Sacra iuxta vulgatam versionem*, Stuttgart, ⁴1994, p. 638, lignes 20-21; p. 365, lignes 44-48.

Anciens de l'Apocalypse. Par ailleurs, les autres commentateurs latins anciens de Ap 4,5, quand ils se réfèrent aux deux Testaments, le *Carmen adversus Marcionem* IV, 215-219 du Pseudo-Tertullien[43] et Primasius (qui dépend souvent de Tyconius)[44], n'évoquent pas les livres bibliques.

Au regard de ces traditions latines, la Stichométrie de Mommsen a une position originale. Voici le texte:

Sed ut in apocalypsi Iohannis dictum est: *uidi xxiiii seniores mittentes coronas suas ante thronum*, maiores nostri probant hos libros esse canonicos et hoc dixisse seniores.	Mais selon qu'il est dit dans l'Apocalypse de Jean: «J'ai vu les 24 Anciens déposant leurs couronnes devant le trône», nos prédécesseurs font la preuve que ces livres sont canoniques et que telle est l'affirmation des Anciens.

a. L'*indiculum* se réfère explicitement aux vingt-quatre Anciens pour l'Ancien Testament, même si nous ne savons pas de façon certaine comment il arrivait concrètement à ce chiffre.

b. Est-ce par hasard que le chiffre 24 s'applique aussi au Nouveau Testament? Le compte est facile à faire: 4 évangiles, 13 épîtres pauliniennes, les Actes et l'Apocalypse, 3 épîtres de Jean et 2 de Pierre.

c. Tout se passe donc comme si la liste s'appuyait sur les deux interprétations de Ap 4,5 attestées par Victorin, en les mêlant. Il y a bien 24 livres de l'Ancien Testament. Cependant les deux Testaments sont visés. Dès lors, le compte des livres n'est pas deux fois douze, mais deux fois vingt-quatre[45]. Nous ne pouvons savoir quelle fut l'autorité de cette interprétation. Elle pourrait être donatiste (voir *Addemdum*, p. 172). En 359, les Églises – et en particulier l'Église d'Afrique – n'ont pas encore légiféré définitivement sur le canon. On a vu que l'Épître aux Hébreux a été lente à se faire admettre chez les Latins. Il faut compter aussi avec des omissions dues à des circonstances accidentelles, ainsi celle de A et B Esdras.

Conclusions

1. Ap 4,4-5 pourrait bien avoir été le lieu biblique auquel les chrétiens latins ont accroché leur première réflexion sur une fixation du canon. Déjà les Quatre Vivants ont été identifiés aux quatre évangiles pour ré-

---

43. CC SL 2, p. 1448 (ed. R. WILLEMS).
44. CC SL 92, p. 48 (ed. A.W. ADAMS).
45. Gilles Dorival a montré une symétrie semblable pour le chiffre 27 chez Épiphane de Salamine et chez Jean Damascène: voir dans ce volume, *L'apport des Pères de l'Église à la question de la clôture du Canon de l'Ancien Testament*, p. 95.

soudre l'aporie de l'Évangile un et quatre, et les plus anciens témoins de
ce raisonnement, Irénée et Victorin, vraisemblablement aussi Hippolyte,
s'appuient sur l'Apocalypse (indépendamment ou non d'Ez 1,10)[46]. Les
vingt-quatre Anciens paraissent aussi avoir servi assez tôt de mesure
pour la fixation du nombre des livres bibliques, de quelque façon
d'ailleurs qu'on s'en soit accommodé, puisque le canon de Mommsen et
Jérôme l'appliquent différemment. Quant à Hilaire, il ne se réfère pas
aux Anciens de l'Apocalypse. Mais son intérêt pour le chiffre vingt-quatre pourrait s'expliquer par la volonté de réunir un chiffre traditionnel
chez les Latins et l'explication d'Origène par le nombre des lettres de
l'alphabet. Je ne sais si la division de l'Iliade et de l'Odyssée chacun en
vingt-quatre chants désignés par les lettres de l'alphabet grec ont pu
jouer un rôle dans le choix de ce chiffre.

2. La liste de Mommsen donne le «canon» des œuvres de Cyprien,
traités et lettres, à la suite du canon des Écritures. Cette association révèle la très grande autorité dont la personne et les écrits du martyr joui-
rent très vite. Une deuxième liste (ms. Würzburg M.p.theol.fol. 145)[47],
et deux autres, plus allusives, le sermon 313C (Morin Guelf. 26)
d'Augustin[48] et la *Vita Cypriani*[49], inventorient l'activité littéraire du
saint évêque. La liste de Mommsen confirme donc pour le milieu du IVe
siècle ce que l'on sait par ailleurs. Cyprien a été très tôt reconnu comme
le premier Père de l'Église latine.

3. Mais la liste de Mommsen n'a pas été rédigée par une autorité ecclésiastique; elle est un outil de libraire. La note sur le calcul incorrect
des stiques à Rome répond à la volonté d'établir le prix exact des copies.
Il est intéressant d'observer que la plus ancienne liste latine complète
des livres bibliques (le Canon de Muratori est plus ancien, mais frag-
mentaire) est due à cette nécessité pratique, sans souci visible d'exclure
des apocryphes.

CONCLUSIONS GÉNÉRALES

1. La Stichométrie de Mommsen et le *Vaticanus* se trouvent, tous les
deux, au carrefour de plusieurs facteurs: le scriptorium (avec ses copistes) et la librairie (avec ses clients) d'abord, une liste agréée de livres

46. Th. ZAHN, *Forschungen zur Geschichte des neutestamentlichen Kanons und der
altkirchlichen Literatur*. II. *Der Evangeliencommentar des Theophilus von Antiochien*,
Erlangen, 1883, pp. 257-275; P.-M. BOGAERT, *Les Quatre Vivants, l'Évangile et les évangiles*, in *RTL* 32 (2001) 457-478.
47. PL, Suppl. 1, 70-71.
48. PL, Suppl. 2, 609-511.
49. A.A.R. BASTIAENSEN (ed.), *Vita di Cipriano...* (Vita dei Santi, 3), Verona, 1975,
pp. 18-20.

ensuite, qui suppose que l'on s'entende sur les titres et leur contenu, enfin des *codices* ou même des rouleaux qui ont servi comme modèles immédiats ou lointains et dont l'homogénéité est a priori incertaine ou improbable.

2. Chez les Latins, un consensus officiel sur le canon est acquis autour de 400[50], longtemps donc avant que l'œuvre de Jérôme, qui deviendra la partie la plus importante de la Vulgate, connaisse une large diffusion. C'est pour cette raison que l'on n'a plus été en mesure de comprendre des dénominations telles que *Eptaticus*, *Esdrae libri II* (*III Esdras* + Esdras–Néhémie), *Hieremias* (y compris Baruch), pour cette raison que Esdras (notre Esdras–Néhémie) a été divisé en deux livres et que Baruch a disparu de la plupart des bibles latines pendant cinq siècles, de 700 (*Amiatinus*) à 1200 environ[51].

3. Ces considérations restent d'actualité. S'il n'y a plus aujourd'hui d'équivoque fondamentale, les divergences dans les titres des livres entraînent encore des erreurs. Combien d'érudits ne confondent-ils pas 1 Rg (le premier livre des Règnes ou 1 Samuel) et 1 Rois, l'Ecclésiaste et l'Ecclésiastique? Le contenu des livres n'est pas nécessairement identique: Tobie, Siracide. Les exigences des éditeurs, des libraires ou des *stationarii* de jadis, restent déterminantes dans certains choix. Sans parler des différences confessionnelles touchant le canon, l'ordre des livres a une signification, ainsi le regroupement des livres historiques.

4. L'exemple de Rufin d'Aquilée achèvera utilement cet exposé qui met en évidence les aspects physiques de la transmission des Écritures. En 405, ayant pris le parti de rendre en latin, tout en l'abrégeant de moitié, le commentaire d'Origène sur l'Épître aux Romains, qui comportait quinze rouleaux (*uolumina*), évalué à un total de 40 000 stiques, Rufin se plaignait qu'aucune bibliothèque ne les possédait tous les quinze. Henry Chadwick et Caroline P. Hammond Bammel se sont rendu compte que certaines parties de l'Épître, traitées très rapidement, l'étaient à l'aide d'extraits d'autres œuvres d'Origène. Ils en ont conclu que Rufin n'avait pu se procurer les tomes 11 et 14 et avait rempli les lacunes comme il pouvait[52]. Nous avons un peu oublié aujourd'hui la difficulté qu'il y avait à se procurer des exemplaires d'œuvres même répandues.

---

50. Les conciles africains depuis 393, la lettre d'Innocent Ier en 405.

51. La liste des bibles où Baruch est ajouté de seconde main est significative à cet égard. Voir P.-M. BOGAERT, *Le nom de Baruch dans la littérature pseudépigraphique: l'Apocalypse syriaque et le livre deutérocanonique*, in W. C. VAN UNNIK (éd.), *La littérature juive entre Tenach et Mischna* (Recherches bibliques, 9), Leiden, 1974, pp. 56-72, spéc. 66-69.

52. C.P. HAMMOND BAMMEL, *Der Römerbrieftext des Rufin und seine Origenes-Übersetzung* (Aus der Geschichte des lateinischen Bibel, 10), Freiburg i. Br., 1985, pp. 93-103.

5. Comment expliquer entre les listes des livres canoniques des divergences notables et qui ont pu être plus grandes qu'il n'y paraît aujourd'hui? Les Églises chrétiennes ont reçu pour leur Ancien Testament les livres que les communautés juives voisines tenaient pour Écriture. L'usage de ces communautés juives pouvait différer de l'une à l'autre sur la liste des K^{e}tûbîm, non seulement pour des raisons de principe, mais aussi pour des raisons pratiques: la dispersion en de nombreux rouleaux rendait difficile la possession effective de tous les livres reconnus.

6. Le théologien observera que, dès que ce fut codicologiquement possible, les libraires chrétiens présentèrent en un seul codex les deux Testaments.

Une «physique» du canon, tel était l'objet de cet article. Il va de soi que tout n'est pas dit par ce biais. Mais on comprendra mieux, je l'espère, après l'analyse de ces deux exemples, à quelles difficultés se heurtait toute décision en la matière, alors même que la foi catholique et tout simplement la bonne foi des acteurs n'étaient pas en cause.

Abbaye de Maredsous   Pierre-Maurice BOGAERT
B-5537 Denée

Addendum. – En décembre 2001 a paru l'étude de Richard ROUSE & Charles MCNELIS, *North African Literary Activity: A Cyprian Fragment, the Stichometric Lists and a Donatist Compendium*, in *Revue d'histoire des textes* 30 (2000) 189-233. – D'après les auteurs, la stichométrie de Mommsen serait d'origine donatiste comme certains au moins des textes qui l'entourent. Le ms. de Cheltenham est aujourd'hui à Rome, *Biblioteca Nazionale Centrale*, Vitt. Em. 1325; il a été copié à Nonantola au Xe ou au début du XIe s. Un antique bifolio de Cyprien (Marburg, *Hessisches Staatsarchiv* I,1; CLA 1728), d'origine africaine, est copié en lignes de 16 syllabes.

TABLEAU 1: DESCRIPTION DU *VATICANUS* (A.T.)

q., p., scribes	col.	B (dans l'ordre)			S[53]	55
p. 1-334		Gn		affinité avec 56	o (+)	+
		Ex			o	+
q. 1 à 18		Lv		affinité avec A	o (+)	+
(44 lignes)		Nb			o (+)	+
		Dt			o	+
		Jos			o	+
		Jg		recension *Kaige-Théodotion*	o (+)	+
	3 col.	Ru		affinité avec A	o	+
scribe A		1 Rg → 19,11a		affinité de 1–4 Rg avec	o	+
p. 335-624		1 Rg 19,11b -		la version éthiopienne	o	+
		2 Rg			o	+
q. 19-33 1/2		3 Rg			o	+
(42 lignes,		4 Rg			o	+
sauf q. 29,		1 Par		affinité avec S	(+)	+
à 40 lignes)		2 Par			o	+
		A Esd		affinité avec 55, éthiopien	o	+
scribe B		B Esd		affinité avec 55, S, éthiopien	+	+
p. 625-944		Ps			+	
		Prov			+	
q. 33 2/2-49		Eccl (Qo)			+	
(42 lignes)	2 col.	Ct			+	
		Jb		même place de Job en 46	+	
		Sg (p. 809, c. 2)	pour		+	
		Sir (→ p. 893)	les		+	
		Est (p. 893, c. 2)	débu-	affinité avec S, 55	+	+
		Jdt	tants	affinité avec 55	+	+
scribe A		Tb (→ p. 944)		affinité avec 55, 46 (S diffère)	+	+
p. 945-1518		XII Proph		affinité avec S	+	
		Is		recension *O* (S diffère)	+	
q. 50-64 1/2		Jr Ba Lm Ep		affinité avec S	+	
(42 lignes)		Ez			o	
scribe B	3 col.	Dn (Th)			o	
p. 1235-1518		Nouveau			+	
		Testament				
q. 64 2/2-78						
(42 lignes)						

53. La présence d'un livre (ou du moins d'une partie de ce livre) est indiquée par le + ou (+). Le o indique qu'un livre n'est pas conservé, mais devait se trouver dans le manuscrit. Les feuillets découverts au Sinaï il y a une vingtaine d'années ne sont pas encore publiés, mais on sait à quels livres ils appartiennent.

TABLEAU 2: STICHOMÉTRIE DE L'ANCIEN TESTAMENT (HEPTATEUQUE)

	Nombre de mots latins (Vulg.)[54]	b/a	Nombre de mots grecs (Rahlfs)[55]	Stichométrie de Mommsen		Bibles latines (mss)	Chiffres retenus	a/c	b/c
	a	b/a	b	Chelt.	St-Gall		c	a/c	b/c
Gn	25749	1,26	32566		3700	3070, 1084, 3070, 4308, 4900	3700	6,96	8,80
Ex	20468	1,21	24816		3000	3000, 1209	3000	6,82	8,27
Lv[56]	13961	1,37	19082		2300	2300, 1300, 2400, 2600	2300 (corr. 2000?)	6,07! (corr. 6,98)	8,30 corr.: 9,54!
Nb	19629	1,28	25059		3000	3000	3000	6,54	8,35
Dt	18720	1,22	22990		2700	2600, 2700, 1750	2600	7,20	8,84
Jos	12441	1,20	14896		1750	1750, 1701	1750	7,11	8,51
Jg	12976	1,23 1,20	A15947 B15580		1750	1750, 1850, 2600	1850	7,01	A8,62 B8,42
total				18100	18100 (en fait: 18200)		18200		

54. Selon les chiffres du CENTRE INFORMATIQUE ET BIBLE (CIB), *Databank. List of Data and Services*, Turnhout, 1981, pp. 30-31 (Bible grecque), pp. 33-34 (Vulgate).

55. Selon les chiffres du CIB, *Databank* (n. 54).

56. Dans le Lévitique, le rapport mots latins/mots grecs est inattendu.

TABLEAU 3: STICHOMÉTRIE DE CYPRIEN, COMPARÉE À CELLE
DE L'ANCIEN TESTAMENT

Le tableau de H. von Soden donne souvent des valeurs 32 : 41 (ou 32 :
40, ou 32 : 42) pour le rapport entre le nombre de lignes de l'édition du
CSEL et la stichométrie de Mommsen[57]. Cette valeur est certainement
correcte, et elle permet de corriger quelques-uns des chiffres aberrants.
Si alors on choisit deux traités où cette valeur est respectée, le *De
mortalitate* (426 lignes du CSEL, 550 stiques) et le *De zelo et liuore*
(322 lignes du CSEL, 420 stiques) qui représentent respectivement 574
et 440 lignes de Migne, on constate qu'une ligne de Migne est légèrement plus courte qu'un stique. On peut faire le même calcul pour certains livres dont la stichométrie est sûre. Ainsi Ruth a 245 lignes dans
Migne (PL 28) et 250 stiques; le Deutéronome 2 768 lignes dans Migne
et 2 700 stiques. Le même calcul peut se faire à partir du nombre de
mots (CIB pour la Vulgate[58]) ou de formes (CETEDOC pour Cyprien[59]):

	Nombre de stiques[60]	Nombre de formes	Lignes de Migne	c/a	b/a
	a	b	c		
Deutéronome	2600	18720	2768	1,06	7,20
Ruth	250	1819	245	0,98	7,28
De mortalitate	550	3912	574	1,04	7,11
De zelo et liuore	420	2934	440	1,05	6,99

57. VON SODEN, *Die Cyprianische Briefsammlung* (n. 38), pp. 44-45.
58. Selon les chiffres du CIB, *Databank* (n. 54).
59. *Thesaurus Sancti Cypriani*. Series A – Formae, curante CETEDOC (Corpus
Christianorum Thesaurus Patrum Latinorum), Turnhout, 1997, p. XIX.
60. D'après la stichométrie de Mommsen.

TABLEAU 4: LES TROIS TYPES DE STICHOMÉTRIE
(ÉVANGILES, ACTES–APOCALYPSE, ANCIEN TESTAMENT)

	Nombre de mots latins (Vulgate)[61]	b/a	Nombre de mots grecs (Rahlfs)[62]	Stichométrie de Mommsen	b/c	a/c
	a		b	c		
Syst. 2						
Mt	16458	1,11	18344	2700	6,79	6,10
Mc	10297	1,11	11304	1700	6,65	6,06
Lc	18034	1,08	19479	3300!	5,90!	5,46!
				corr. 3000	corr. 6,49	corr. 6,01
Jn	14049	1,11	15636	1800!	8,69!	7,80!
				corr. 2300[63]	corr. 6,80	corr. 6,11
total	58838		64763	10000	6,48	5,88
				corr 9700	corr. 6,68	corr. 6,07
Syst. 3						
Act	16631	1,11	18450	3600	5,12	4,62
Apoc	8358	1,18	9851	1800	5,47	4,64
Syst. 1[64]						
Anc. Test.					8,5	7
Syst. 2						
Evg					6,7	6
Syst. 3						
Act, Apoc					5,2	4,6

61. Selon les chiffres du CIB, *Databank* (n. 54).
62. Selon les chiffres du CIB, *Databank* (n. 54).
63. IDCCC à corriger en IICCC (ou MDCCC en MMCCC).
64. Voir Tableau 2: a/c et b/c

DER BIBELKANON ALS DENKMAL UND TEXT

ZU EINIGEN METHODOLOGISCHEN ASPEKTEN KANONISCHER SCHRIFTAUSLEGUNG

EINLEITUNG

In Deutschland wird jeweils am Ende eines Jahres von verschiedenen Gesellschaften zur Pflege der deutschen Sprache ein »Wort des Jahres« und ein »Unwort« ausgerufen. Mit dieser Aufgabe im Blick auf ihr Fach betraut, müsste die Bibelexegese wahrscheinlich den Begriff »Kanon« – je nach Standort – als Wort oder Unwort der letzten beiden Jahrzehnte auswählen: War das Thema »Kanon« lange Zeit vorrangig ein Thema der »Allgemeinen Einleitungswissenschaft«, so steht es gegenwärtig im Fokus der Diskussion um biblische Hermeneutik, Methodik und Theologie[1]. Hinsichtlich der Notwendigkeit, der konkreten Ausgestaltung, ja der wissenschaftlichen Seriosität und der Leistungsfähigkeit von Ansätzen einer »kanonischen Schriftauslegung«, des »canonical approach«, einer »kanonisch-intertextuellen Lektüre« – oder wie die unterschiedlichen Spielarten eines kanonischen Zugangs in der Bibelauslegung immer bezeichnet werden mögen – gehen die Meinungen weit auseinander.

Die zahlreichen, in den unterschiedlichen Diskussionszusammenhängen aufgeworfenen Probleme lassen sich in der Frage zusammenfassen, ob eine »kanonische Schriftauslegung« als eine *wissenschaftliche* Gestalt von Exegese im Kontext der kritischen Moderne/Post-Moderne überhaupt möglich ist. Die Antwort auf diese Frage hängt entscheidend davon ab, wie die Eigenart des Bibelkanons näher bestimmt wird: Handelt es sich um einen Text oder eine Textsammlung? Ist »Kanon« möglicherweise gar nicht als literarisches Phänomen zu fassen, sondern eine juristische Qualifizierung, also eine Aussage über die Bedeutung von Texten für eine Rezeptionsgemeinschaft? Jede Antwort auf die *Frage nach der Textqualität von Kanon* hat Implikationen für den interpretierenden Umgang mit den biblischen Texten.

1. Cf. *JBT* 3 (1988); C. DOHMEN & M. OEMING, *Biblischer Kanon warum und wozu? Eine Kanontheologie* (QD, 137), Freiburg im Breisgau, Herder, 1992. Die aktuelle Kanondiskussion hängt auf das engste zusammen mit den beiden anderen Grundlagendebatten gegenwärtiger Bibelwissenschaft, der Diskussion unter dem Titel »Religionsgeschichte Israels oder Theologie des Alten Testaments?« (cf. *JBT* 10 [1995]) und der Frage nach Notwendigkeit und Möglichkeit einer »Biblischen Theologie« (cf. B. JANOWSKI, Art. *Biblische Theologie* I., in *RGG*, ⁴1999, vol. 1, pp. 1544-1549).

Die Auseinandersetzung um die Rolle des Kanons ist Teil einer größeren, die Exegese und die Theologie überschreitenden Debatte um die Grundlagen des Textverstehens. Der seit dem Beginn des 19. Jh. etablierte Konsens über die Grundlagen des Textverstehens unter dem Paradigma »Quellenkritik und Geschichte« ist zerfallen; eine neue Position, die eine ähnlich dominierende Stellung einnehmen könnte, ist nicht in Sicht[2]. Stattdessen sind wir Zeuginnen und Zeugen einer sehr lebendigen Debatte, in der sich Vieles neu strukturiert. Kommunikationsprobleme zwischen klassischen Positionen biblischer »Hermeneutik« und »post-modernen« Ansätzen lassen sich nicht leugnen; sie sind alles andere als eine Frage persönlicher Präferenzen, sondern haben ihre Entsprechungen in den philosophischen und literaturtheoretischen Kontroversen der letzten Jahrzehnte. Diese Einsicht kann die zum Teil sehr scharf geführte Debatte innerhalb der Exegese[3] entspannen und zugleich Impulse freisetzen für eine angemessene Behandlung der methodologischen und methodischen Fragen innerhalb der Exegese. Ohne Bezug auf diese größeren Theoriehorizonte ist ein innerexegetischer Fortschritt nicht zu erwarten. Aber werden diese Debatten in der innerexegetischen Diskussion hinreichend berücksichtigt? Diese Frage stellt sich mir, weil die Bezugnahmen auf die »großen« literaturtheoretischen Diskussion in der gegenwärtigen Exegese im deutschen Sprachraum selten sind. Stattdessen wird eher mit fragwürdigen Konzepten von »Autorintention« und »ursprünglicher Textbedeutung« (s.u. II.) als vermeintlich sicheren Bezugspunkten der Exegese zum Schutz vor willkürlichen Bedeutungszuweisungen in der Lektüre operiert[4].

I. DIE UMSTRITTENE ROLLE DES BIBELKANONS
IN DER GEGENWÄRTIGEN BIBELAUSLEGUNG

Das Thema »Kanon« steht spätestens seit B.S. Childs' 1979 erschienenem epochalen Werk *Introduction to the Old Testament as Scripture*[5]

2. Zur ersten Orientierung über die aktuellen Theoriediskurse cf. A. NÜNNING (ed.), *Metzler Lexikon Literatur und Kulturtheorie. Ansätze – Personen – Grundbegriffe*, Stuttgart, J.B. Metzler, ²2001.

3. Vgl. die bis in die jüngste Zeit hinein äußerst polemisch geführte Diskussion zwischen J. BARR und B.S. CHILDS; zuletzt in J. BARR, *The Concept of Biblical Theology. An Old Testament Perspective*, London, SCM, 1999, pp. 47-51.378-451.

4. Einen aktuellen Einblick in die Spannweite und die Spannungen der gegenwärtigen Diskussion vermittelt F.-L. HOSSFELD (ed.), *Wieviel Systematik erlaubt die Schrift? Auf der Suche nach einer gesamtbiblischen Theologie* (QD 185), Freiburg im Breisgau, Herder, 2001; cf. darin etwa die »klassische« Position von W. Groß mit den Ansätzen von N. Lohfink und L. Schwienhorst-Schönberger, die den neueren Literaturtheorien aufgeschlossen gegenüberstehen und sie für ihre Überlegungen fruchtbar machen.

5. B.S. CHILDS, *Introduction to the Old Testament as Scripture*, London, SCM, 1979.

auf der exegetischen Agenda, eigentlich jedoch schon seit K. Stendahls Artikel *Biblical Theology* im ersten Band von *The Interpreter's Dictionary of the Bible* von 1962[6]. Die grundlegenden damit verbundenen Fragen werden jedoch erst nach und nach in größeren Teilen der Exegese erkannt und aufgenommen.

Stendahl arbeitet die Frage nach dem Kanon als Schlüsselfrage der Exegese als einer *theologischen* Disziplin heraus:

> The Question as to the meaning of the bible in the present – as distinguished from the meaning in the past as stated by descriptive biblical theology – receives its theological answer from the canonical status of scripture. In its most radical form, the question was: Do these old writings have any meaning beyond their significance as sources for the past? On what basis could it be valid to translate them into new modes of thought? On what basis could such an original – and such a translation – have a normative function for the life of the church? Such questions can be answered only within the consciousness of the church. The answer rests on the act of faith by which Israel and its sister by adoption, the church, recognizes its history as sacred history, and finds in these writings the epitome of the acts of God. As such these writings are meaningful to the church of any age. It is as canon, and only as canon, that there is a Bible, an OT and a NT as well as the whole Bible of the Church as a unity. The old question of whether the Bible rests on the Church or the church on the bible is a misleading question from the point of view of the historical alternative. To be sure the church 'chose' its canon. But it did so under the impact of the acts of God by which it itself came into existence. The process of canonization is one of recognition, not one of creation *ex nihilo* or *ex theologia*[7].

Diese Position blieb lange Zeit eine Randposition in dem Sinne, dass die von Stendahl beschriebenen Zusammenhänge von Bibelkanon, Exegese und Glaubensgemeinschaft eher in der systematisch-theologischen Reflexion als der bibelwissenschaftlichen Methodologie Beachtung fanden. Nach der einflussreichen 1971 erschienenen Methodenlehre *Exegese als Literaturwissenschaft. Entwurf einer alttestamentlichen Literaturtheorie und Methodologie* von W. Richter hat der Bibelkanon keine positive Bedeutung für die Exegese der biblischen Texte:

> Die Existenz des Kanons ist für den Interpreten der Texte bedeutungslos; interessant ist er nur als historisches Faktum, insofern seine Aufstellung dazu geführt hat, daß andere Texte leider verlorengegangen sind und für die Interpretation nicht mehr zur Verfügung stehen. Die Entstehung des Kanons muß er den Kirchengeschichtler verfolgen lassen, seine Gestaltung sowie Fragen der Inspiration und Irrtumslosigkeit muß er dem Dogmen-

---

6. K. STENDAHL, Art. *Biblical Theology, Contemporary*, in *IDB*, 1962, Vol. 1, pp. 418-432.

7. STENDAHL, *Biblical Theology* (n. 6), p. 429.

geschichtler und Dogmatiker, geistesgeschichtlich bedingte Wertungen wie 'historisch' dem Theologiegeschichtler überlassen[8].

Richter entwickelt ein ausschließlich negatives Kanonkonzept: Der Bibelkanon entsteht durch Ausgrenzung und führt zum Verlust antiker Quellen, die für historische Forschungen hilfreich wären. Man kann die Kanondebatte der letzten Jahrzehnte als Überwindung dieses rein äußerlichen Kanonkonzeptes lesen, denn ein wichtiges Ergebnis dieser Debatte ist die Einsicht, dass der Redaktionsprozess koextensiv zum Kanonprozess ist[9].

Aber auch, wenn dem Kanon eine positive Bedeutung als Zusammenstellung »heiliger« Schriften einer Gemeinschaft zukommt, bleibt der *texttheoretische* Status des Kanons nach W. GROSS offen, denn es sei

> nicht geklärt, mit welchem Recht die unterschiedlichen Schriften des AT und des NT, nur weil sie im christlichen Kanon zusammengestellt sind, als *ein* Text betrachtet werden, der als solcher mit *literarischen* Methoden analysiert werden könnte. Vielleicht ist der Kanon eher nach Analogie einer juristischen Größe zu verstehen[10].

Hier wird die Bedeutung des Kanons ebenfalls in den »äußeren« Bereich der Exegese verlagert; es geht um Fragen der Verbindlichkeit. Für das literaturtheoretische Design der Bibelauslegung wird dem Kanon keine Bedeutung zugesprochen, weil seine Textqualität nicht geklärt sei.

Die »Kanondefinition« von C. Seitz kann geradezu als Gegenposition zu W. Gross gelesen werden, da Seitz die Besonderheit des biblischen Textes pointiert von seiner Kanonqualität her bestimmt und diese mit dem literarischen Entstehungsprozess untrennbar verbunden sieht:

> »Kanon« ist keine von außen herangetragene Wertung, die den Umfang und die Zahl der Texte begrenzt und sie in irgendeiner Weise für verbindlich erklärt. Der Begriff »kanonisch« wird vielmehr gebraucht, um die größtmögliche Kontinuität zw.(ischen) der abschließenden Anerkennung der Autorität eines Textes und dem Umgang mit der Tradition, der dem gesch.(ichtlich) vorausging, anzuzeigen. Das endgültige lit.(erarische) Werk ist kanonisch aufgrund seiner Gesch.(ichte) innerhalb des Gottesvolkes Israel, welches das Wort empfangen und im Geheimnis von Gottes Vorsehung der Nachwelt in einer bestimmten Form überantwortet hat. Der

---

8. W. RICHTER, *Exegese als Literaturwissenschaft. Entwurf einer alttestamentlichen Literaturtheorie und Methodologie*, Göttingen, Vandenhoeck & Ruprecht, 1971, pp. 40-41.

9. Vgl. J. JEREMIAS, *Das Proprium der alttestamentlichen Prophetie*, in *TLZ* 119 (1994) 483-494; O.H. STECK, *Der Abschluß der Prophetie im Alten Testament. Ein Versuch zur Vorgeschichte des Kanons* (Biblisch-theologische Studien, 17), Neukirchen-Vluyn, 1991; DOHMEN & OEMING, *Biblischer Kanon* (n. 1).

10. W. GROSS, *Ist biblisch-theologische Auslegung ein integrierender Methodenschritt?*, in HOSSFELD (ed.), *Wieviel Systematik* (n. 4), pp. 110-149, p. 145.

schriftliche Charakter ergibt sich aus der Eigenart des Gegenstandes, nämlich das Wort des lebendigen Gottes zeitübergreifend zu vermitteln[11].

Dezidiert als Text, genauer als Makrokontext der Teiltexte, wird der Kanon in der neueren Diskussion von L. Schwienhorst-Schönberger beschrieben:

> Ihre letztlich normative Bedeutung gewinnen die Texte der Bibel nicht als Einzeltexte, sondern als Teiltexte eines Makrokontextes, den wir als Kanon bezeichnen (vgl. B. CHILDS). Der kanonische Text ist (letztlich) als *ein* Text zu verstehen... Der Kanon schreibt eine begrenzte Vielstimmigkeit (Polyphonie) fest... Kanonische Texte sind gegenüber einer radikal dekonstruktivistischen Interpretation insofern gefeit, als sie in einem doppelt abgegrenzten Kontext überliefert sind, dem literarischen (sprachlichen) Kontext des Kanons und dem lebensweltlichen (kulturellen) Kontext der Rezeptions- und Interpretationsgemeinschaft...[12].

Ähnlich hatte schon drei Jahrzehnte früher N. Füglister formuliert:

> Die ganze Schrift ist der Kontext, der die einzelne Aussage determiniert, modifiziert, retardiert, in und aus dem sie Stellenwert und Sinn, Bedeutung und Funktion erhält[13].

Diese Aussage setzt voraus, dass der Kontext mehr ist als eine »äußere« Verbindlichkeitsaussage, sondern dass die Textualität eines Bibeltextes nicht ohne den biblischen Kontext gefasst werden kann.

Mit N. Lohfink lässt sich die texttheoretische Beschreibung des Bibelkanons weiter präzisieren:

> Es gibt in beiden Büchergruppen (= AT u. NT: G.St) eine bei allen Variationen doch so stabile Anordnung und darüber hinaus so viele literarische Verstrebungen, daß man mit mehr rechnen muß als nur einer Reihe von in sich selbständigen Büchern. Beide Kanones bilden in sich geschlossene Sinngefüge. Das wird erst in unseren Jahren durch die Forschung nachgewiesen, scheint aber schon genügend gesichert zu sein. Damit entsteht innerhalb der beiden Büchergruppen eine neue, intensivere Art von Intertextualität. Das hat beträchtliche Folgen für den Sinn der einzelnen Bücher, ja der einzelnen Aussagen in ihnen. Die Konsequenzen sind kaum schon gezogen... Wie eine entsprechende theoretische Hermeneutik aussehen würde, wäre erst Schritt für Schritt zu erarbeiten. Ich kenne keine vorhandenen Theorien, die diesem Ansatz entsprechen und zugleich auf exegetischer Erfahrung aufruhen würden. Im Endeffekt hatte wohl auch die

---

11. C. SEITZ, Art. *Canonical Approach* in *RGG*, [4]1999, vol. 2, pp. 53-54, spez. 54 (Ergänzungen: G.St.).

12. L. SCHWIENHORST-SCHÖNBERGER, *Einheit und Vielfalt. Gibt es eine sinnvolle Suche nach der Mitte des Alten Testaments?*, in HOSSFELD (ed.), *Wieviel Systematik* (n. 4), pp. 48-87, p. 67.

13. N. FÜGLISTER, *Vom Mut zur ganzen Schrift. Zur Eliminierung der sog. Fluchpsalmen*, in *Stimmen der Zeit* 184 (1969) 186-200, p. 197.

Theorie vom mehrfachen Schriftsinn nicht genügend Atem. Die Entwicklung einer differenzierteren Theorie wäre sowohl für den »systematischen«
(an Sachfragen orientierten) als auch für den »exegetischen« (Texte
entlanggehenden) Teil der Theologie dringend erfordert. Zu Theologie, das
heißt reflexer Vermittlung des im Kanon enthaltenen Wortes Gottes, wird
der Umgang mit der Bibel auf jeden Fall erst, wenn der kanonische Text
synchron unter Berücksichtigung der innerkanonisch gegebenen Strukturen
erschlossen wird. Alle andere Auslegungsarbeit, und sei sie noch so unentbehrlich, bleibt Vorstufe und ist noch keine Theologie im christlichen
Sinn[14].

Die weit reichenden Konsequenzen für die exegetische Methodologie
und Methodik deutet Lohfink an, wenn er bemerkt:

> Die in der Bibelwissenschaft entwickelte historische Erforschung der Ent-
> stehungsgeschichte der biblischen Texte und die dabei benutzten Techni-
> ken literarischer Kritik zur Erschließung von Texten sind außerordentlich
> wichtig und hilfreich. Sie verbinden sich jedoch faktisch (keineswegs we-
> sensnotwendig) weithin mit Interessenausrichtungen, die eher der Bibel als
> allgemeinem Kulturgut und historischem Phänomen zuzuordnen sind, we-
> niger der Bibel als Kanon. So sucht eine letztlich romantische Grundein-
> stellung stets nach den ältesten Textzuständen. Eine am Genie interessierte
> Grundeinstellung fragt nach den großen Schriftstellerpersönlichkeiten. Das
> sind oft keineswegs die Endredaktoren unserer Bücher. Eine sozialge-
> schichtlich interessierte Grundeinstellung fragt nach sukzessiven Textbear-
> beitungen und der Geschichte der Anpassung eines Textes in seiner Vorge-
> schichte an immer neue historische Konstellationen. Das sind alles legitime
> Fragen, ihre Beantwortung führt stets sowohl zu diachronen als auch zu
> synchronen Betrachtungen. Sie bleiben auch unentbehrlich als Vorarbeiten
> zu jener Fragestellung, die allein der Bibel als Kanon entspricht…: zur Er-
> schließung des synchronen Textsinns der in gesellschaftlichen Gruppen
> wie den christlichen Kirchen als Bibel akzeptierten kanonischen Schriften
> in ihrem nun festliegenden Text[15].

14. N. Lohfink, *Eine Bibel – zwei Testamente*, in C. Dohmen & T. Söding (eds.),
Eine Bibel – zwei Testamente. Positionen Biblischer Theologie, Paderborn, F. Schöningh,
1995, pp. 71-81, spez. 79. Die Kritik von Gross, *Biblisch-theologische Auslegung* (n.
10), pp. 127-129 an diesen und ähnlichen Äußerungen Lohfinks basiert letztlich auf der
Tatsache, dass für Gross Textsinn und Autorintention untrennbar verbunden sind; mit der
Differenzierung des Begriff der Intention (Autorintention - Textintention - Leserintention,
vgl. H. Utzschneider, *Text – Leser – Autor. Bestandsaufnahme und Prolegomena zu einer Theorie der Exegese*, in *BZ* 43 [1999] 224-238) einerseits und der unumgänglichen
Relativierung der Bedeutung der Autorintention für die Interpretation in der neueren
Literaturtheorie andererseits (vgl. H. Steinmetz, *Sinnfestlegung und Auslegungsvielfalt*,
in H. Brackert & J. Stückrath [eds.], *Literaturwissenschaft. Ein Grundkurs [re
55523]*, Reinbek bei Hamburg, Rowohlt, ⁵1997, pp. 475-490) wird die theoretische
Grundlage dieser Kritik brüchig. Lohfinks Konzept erscheint im Lichte dieser Entwicklungen nicht mehr als eine theologische Überforderung oder Überfremdung exegetischer
Arbeit an den biblischen Texten, sondern als literaturtheoretisch gut begründete Position,
die einer Selbstisolierung der Bibelwissenschaft innerhalb der kulturwissenschaftlichen
Diskurse aufgrund fehlender theoretischer Innovationsbereitschaft wehrt.
15. Lohfink, *Eine Bibel* (n. 14), p. 78.

Damit ist die Frage nach dem Fokus der exegetischen Arbeit gestellt: Geht es um historische Rekonstruktion oder um gegenwärtige »Textaneignung«, die selbstverständlich der historischen Arbeit schon allein deshalb bedarf, weil wir es bei den biblischen Texten mit literarischen Produkten einer fremden und fernen Kultur zu tun haben.

Avant la lettre hatte M. Buber bereits in den 30er Jahren des vergangenen Jahrhunderts Überlegungen zur Bedeutung des Bibelkanons für die Auslegung einzelner biblischer Texte vorgetragen, die nicht nur eine hohe Sensibilität für die Architektonik des Kanons und die dadurch eröffneten Sinnmöglichkeiten seiner Teiltexte erkennen lassen, sondern im Horizont einer post-modernen, nicht mehr oder nicht mehr primär und ausschließlich autorbezogenen Exegese, äußerst interessant erscheinen. BUBER nimmt sowohl die konstitutive Bedeutung von Intertextualität für die Textualität der Bibeltexte, als auch die Idee des kanonischen Prozesses als die entscheidende Form der Kanonisierung vorweg. Bubers These lautet: »Biblische Texte sind als Texte der Bibel zu behandeln…«, und er erläutert:

> … das heißt: einer Einheit, die, wenn auch geworden, aus vielen und vielfältigen, ganzen und fragmentarischen Elementen zusammengewachsen, doch eine echte organische Einheit und nur als solche wahrhaft zu begreifen ist. Das bibelstiftende Bewußtsein, das aus der Fülle eines vermutlich weit größeren Schrifttums das aufnahm, was sich in die Einheit fügte, und in den Fassungen, die dieser Genüge taten, ist nicht erst mit der eigentlichen Zusammenstellung des Kanons, sondern schon lange vorher, in allmählichem Zusammenschluß des Zusammengehörigen, wirksam gewesen. Die Kompositionsarbeit war bereits »biblisch«, ehe die erste Vorstellung einer bibelartigen Struktur erwachte; sie ging auf eine jeweilige Zusammenschau der verschiedenen Teile aus, sie stiftete Bezüge zwischen Abschnitt und Abschnitt, zwischen Buch und Buch, sie ließ den tragenden Begriff durch Stelle um Stelle klären, ließ die heimliche Bedeutung eines Vorgangs, die sich in der einen Erzählung nur eben leicht auftat, in einer andern sich voll erschließen, ließ Bild durch Bild und Symbol durch Symbol erleuchten. Manches von dem, was man »Midrasch« nennt, ist schon in der Bibel selbst, in diesen Zeugnissen einer zur biblischen Einheit strebenden Auslese- und Koordinationsarbeit zu finden, deren stärkstes Werkzeug eine diskret folgerichtige Verwendung von Wiederholungen, Motivworten, Assonanzen war.

Er scheint den kühnen wissenschaftsgeschichtlichen Vorgriff zu ahnen, wenn er hinzufügt: »Wir stehen hier erst am Anfang einer methodischen Erkenntnis. Es gilt den Blick für diese Entsprechungen und Verknüpfungen und überhaupt für die Einheitsfunktion in der Bibel zu schärfen«[16].

16. M. BUBER, *Ein Hinweis für Bibelkurse*, in M. BUBER & F. ROSENZWEIG, *Die Schrift und ihre Verdeutschung*, Berlin, Schocken, 1936, pp. 310-315, spez. 314-315.

Die von W. Gross in der neueren Diskussion scharf akzentuierte Alternative zwischen einer interpretierbaren autorintendierten Intertextualität und dem »Wildwuchs«[17] der von Leserinnen und Lesern erzeugten Intertextualität stellt sich in der Sicht M. Bubers weniger bedrohlich dar: Der Leseakt, der zwangsläufig Leseerfahrungen aktiviert und über das Verfahren der Intertextualität in den Lese- und Deutungsprozess einspielt, setzt den Prozess fort, in dem die Bibel entstanden ist:

> Die hebräische Bibel will als Ein Buch gelesen werden, so daß keiner ihrer Teile in sich geschlossen bleibt, vielmehr jeder auf jeden offengehalten wird; sie will ihrem Leser als Ein Buch in solcher Intensität gegenwärtig werden, daß er beim Lesen oder Rezitieren einer gewichtigen Stelle, die auf sie beziehbaren, insbesondere die ihr sprachidentischen, sprachnahen oder sprachverwandten erinnert und sie alle einander erleuchten und erläutern, sich miteinander zu einer Sinneinheit, zu einem nicht ausdrücklich gelehrten, sondern dem Wort immanenten, aus seinen Bezügen und Entsprechungen hervortauchenden Theologumenon zusammenschließen. Das ist nicht eine von der Auslegung nachträglich geübte Verknüpfung, sondern unter dem Wirken dieses Prinzips ist eben der Kanon entstanden, und man darf mit Fug vermuten, daß es für die Auswahl des Aufgenommenen, für die Wahl zwischen verschiedenen Fassungen mitbestimmend gewesen ist. Aber unverkennbar waltet es schon in der Komposition der einzelnen Teile: die Wiederholung lautgleicher oder lautähnlicher, wurzelgleicher oder wurzelähnlicher Wörter und Wortgefüge tritt innerhalb eines Abschnitts, innerhalb eines Buches, innerhalb eines Bücherverbands mit einer stillen, aber den hörbereiten Leser überwältigenden Kraft auf. Man betrachte von dieser Einsicht aus die sprachlichen Bezüge etwa zwischen Propheten und Pentateuch, zwischen Psalmen und Pentateuch, zwischen Psalmen und Propheten, und man wird immer neu die gewaltige Synoptik der Bibel erkennen[18].

II. Thesen zur Methodologie kanonischer Schriftauslegung

Vor dem Hintergrund der aktuellen Kontroverse um die Rolle des Bibelkanons für die Bibelauslegung werden im Folgenden Überlegungen zur Unumgänglichkeit der Beachtung des Bibelkanons für die Auslegung formuliert. Die Thesen verstehen sich als ein pointierter Diskussionbeitrag, mit dem Ziel, die fehlende literaturtheoretische Fun-

17. O.H. Stecks in diesem Zusammenhang gern zitierte Warnung vor einem »Wildwuchs synchroner Entdeckungen« (cf. W. GROSS, *Biblisch-theologische Auslegung* [n. 10], p. 124-125) ist sicher berechtigt; es sollte aber nicht vergessen werden, dass der Wildwuchs *diachroner* Entdeckungen aus den letzten 200 Jahren bereits ganze Bibliotheken füllt.

18. M. BUBER, *Zu einer neuen Verdeutschung der Schrift*, Beilage zu: *Die fünf Bücher der Weisung*, verdeutscht von M. BUBER in Gemeinschaft mit F. ROSENZWEIG, Köln, Jakob Hegner, 1968, p. 13-14.

dierung vorhandener Ansätze einer »kanonischen Bibelauslegung« zu überwinden und Ansatz- und Eckpunkte für eine Operationalisierung einer solchen Auslegung zu formulieren. Der gegenwärtige Diskussionsstand lässt nur ein tentatives Vorgehen zu, dem die Thesenform am besten entspricht[19].

These 1: Die Eigenschaft der biblischen Literatur, die mit dem Terminus »Kanon« erfasst wird, ist kein sekundäres Phänomen: Die Bindung an die jüdische bzw. christliche Glaubensgemeinschaft tritt nicht nachträglich zur Bibel als Heiliger Schrift hinzu (etwa erst mit einem synodalen Kanonentscheid), die biblischen Schriften *werden* nicht erst zum Kanon, sondern sie entstehen *als* Kanon[20]. Die kanonische Qualität der biblischen Texte ist daher kein Gesichtspunkt neben anderen, sondern hat die Auslegung von Anfang an zu bestimmen.

Solange »Kanon« als ein sekundäres Phänomen konzipiert wurde, das eine nachträgliche Bestimmung über die Verbindlichkeit zum Ausdruck bringt, bleiben die Konsequenzen für die Bibelauslegung marginal. Mit der Ausweitung des Kanonkonzeptes nach vorne, d.h. auf den Entstehungsprozess der Bibeltexte (der einzelnen Bücher, nicht nur Sammlungen) gewinnen die eine einzelne Perikope und ein einzelnes Buch überschreitenden literarischen Phänomene notwendigerweise größeres Gewicht in der Auslegung. Parallel dazu muss sich das Interesse von der »ursprünglichen Autorintention« und der Bestimmung des Textsinnes auf dieser Basis (was in sich bei weitgehend anonymer oder in theologischer Pseudonymität überlieferter Literatur schon äußerst problematisch ist) verlagern auf die vorliegende Textgestalt und ihre Funktion in der Glaubensgemeinschaft[21]. Im Blick auf die Problematik der Rekonstruktion von Autorenintentionen ist das eine Entlastung exegetischer Arbeit.

These 2: In den gegenwärtigen theologischen Debatten um die Bibel und ihre Auslegung, vor allem um die Rolle des Kanons, tut mehr Theo-

---

19. Fast jede dieser Thesen wäre in einer eigenen längeren Studie zu entwickeln und theoretisch zu fundieren; cf. G. STEINS, *Die »Bindung Isaaks« im Kanon (Gen 22). Grundlagen und Programm einer kanonisch-intertextuellen Lektüre* (HBS, 20), Freiburg i. Br., Herder, 1999.

20. Cf. C. DOHMEN & G. STEINS, Art. *Schriftauslegung*, in *LTK*, ³1993, Vol. 9, pp. 253-256.

21. Cf. STENDAHL, *Biblical Theology* (n. 7), der den Kanon zutreffend als Ergebnis eines »Anerkennungs-/Rezeptionprozesses«, nicht eines »Schöpfungsvorgangs« beschreibt. Es kann nur nachdrücklich betont werden: Der Bibelkanon ist ein Rezeptionsphänomen; er wurde nicht als Kanon geschaffen, sondern in einem längeren Prozess »angenommen«. Dass sich kein Datum für seine Entstehung angeben lässt, spricht nicht gegen die Existenz eines Kanons, sondern ist eine Folge dieser »Rezeptionslogik«.

rie Not[22]. Über das Konzept »Kanon« ist ein Anschluss der bibel-
hermeneutischen Diskussion an gegenwärtige literaturwissenschaftliche
Theoriedebatten möglich[23].

Angesichts des Kanons ist die gegenwärtige Wissenschaft keineswegs
methodologisch und methodisch hilflos, wenn sie die theologischen
Funktionen des Kanons literaturtheoretisch reformuliert und dabei die
post-moderne literaturtheoretische Diskussion aufnimmt[24]. In einem erweiterten literaturwissenschaftlichen Theoriekontext erweist sich der hi-
storisch-rekonstruktive Blick als einseitig und als der Komplexität der
Texte oft wenig angemessen, ohne dass genaues Lesen und die Wahrnehmung der Geschichtlichkeit der Texte dabei auf der Strecke bleiben
müssten[25].

22. A. REICHERT, *Offene Fragen zur Auslegung neutestamentlicher Texte im Spiegel
neuerer Methodenbücher*, in *TLZ* 126 (2001) 993-1006, p. 1005 konstatiert einen Nach-
holbedarf an methodologischer Reflexion in der gegenwärtigen Exegese; ebenso diagno-
stiziert UTZSCHNEIDER, *Text – Leser – Autor* (n. 14), p. 224 eine »'Theorievergessenheit',
ja 'Theorievermeidung' der gegenwärtigen exegetischen Wissenschaft«. Das Problem
liegt jedoch tiefer und betrifft nicht nur die Exegese der letzten 10 bis 15 Jahre; es fällt
auf, dass ein so einflussreiches Werk wie RICHTER, *Exegese* (n. 8), das aus 1971 erschien,
bereits an der in den 60er Jahren entwickelten Rezeptionstheorie vorbei geht, obwohl diese für die Auslegung der Bibel eine nicht zu unterschätzende Bedeutung hat. Offensichtlich ist das szientistische Paradigma hier so dominant geworden, dass für hermeneutische
Reflexionen keine Anschlussmöglichkeiten mehr bestehen; cf. N. LOHFINK, *Rezension zu
W. Richter, Exegese als Literaturwissenschaft. Entwurf einer alttestamentlichen Literaturtheorie und Methodologie*, in *BZ* 17 (1973) 286-294; die Folgen dieser Vernachläs-
sigung der Hermeneutik in der Bibelwissenschaft belasten bis heute den exegetischen
Diskurs.
23. Cf. die anregende Skizze einer post-modernen neutestamentlichen Literaturtheorie
von E. REINMUTH, *Diskurse und Texte. Überlegungen zur Theologie des Neuen Testaments nach der Moderne*, in *Berliner Theologische Zeitschrift* 16 (1999) 81-96; J. TENG
KOK LIM, *Historical Critical Paradigm. The Beginning of an End*, in *Asia Journal of
Theology* 14 (2000) 252-271; U.H.J. KÖRTNER, *Der inspirierte Leser. Zentrale Aspekte
biblischer Hermeneutik*, Göttingen, Vandenhoeck & Ruprecht, 1994; P. ENGELMANN
(ed.), *Postmoderne und Dekonstruktion. Texte französischer Philosophen der Gegenwart*,
Stuttgart, Reclam, 1999.
24. Cf. J.P.H. WESSELS, *Implications of a Postmodernist Reading of the Old Testament for Textual Meaning*, in *OTE* 11 (1998) 600-614. — In der Theologie anzutreffende
Vorbehalte gegenüber post-modernen Literaturtheorien finden interessanterweise in dem
Dokument *Die Interpretation der Bibel in der Kirche* der Päpstlichen Bibelkommission
von 1993 keinen Widerhall; im Gegenteil wird eine einseitig historische Ausrichtung der
Exegese als literaturtheoretisch überholt und den Bibeltexten unangemessen bezeichnet,
ja auf weite Strecken wird die nordamerikanische Kanondebatte ebenso positiv rezipiert
wie die Erkenntnisse der post-modernen Literaturwissenschaften und philosophischen
Hermeneutiken, cf. Dt. Bischofskonferenz (ed.), *Verlautbarungen des Apostolischen
Stuhls* 115, Bonn, 1993, pp. 68; 80-81; der Originaltext des Dokumentes ist publiziert in
Bib 74 (1993) 451-528.
25. Cf. das n. 24. genannte Dokument der Päpstlichen Bibelkommission: »Das ganze
Bemühen der historisch-kritischen Exegese geht dahin, den genauen Wortsinn diese oder
jenes biblischen Texte in der Situation seiner Entstehung zu bestimmen. Doch läßt sich
diese Theorie heute angesichts der Erkenntnisse der Sprachwissenschaften und der philo-

These 3: Mit Hilfe text- und literaturtheoretischer Erkenntnisse der kritischen Moderne/Post-Moderne lassen sich die starren Alternativen in der Beschreibung des Bibelkanons (zum Beispiel: Text *oder* Sammlung; literarische Einheit *oder* Rahmen eines Textensembles; Interpretationsvorgabe *oder* Zufallsprodukt, geschlossenes Sinngefüge *oder* Interpretationshorizont) überwinden. Ein »kritisches« Textkonzept ermöglicht die methodologische Integration einiger Charakteristika des Bibelkanons, die in der historisch-kritischen Methodik nicht hinreichend berücksichtigt werden.

In der gegenwärtigen Diskussion wird besonders das textkonstitutive Moment der innerbiblischen Intertextualität intensiv bearbeitet[26]. Ein ebenso bedeutsames Arbeitsfeld wäre ein positiver Zugang zur innerbiblischen Vielstimmigkeit[27]; der klassische Zugang einer sukzessiven Monologisierung der innerbiblischen Vielstimmigkeit durch eine Projektion der biblischen Texte auf die Zeitleiste einer hypothetischen Literaturgeschichte kann zwar die Herkunft der Texte erklären, gewinnt aber damit noch keinen interpretatorischen Zugang zur synchronen Polyphonie: Die synchrone Vielstimmigkeit ist – pointiert gesagt – nicht verstanden, wenn sie diachron aufgelöst wird.

These 4: Der Bibelkanon ist als Sammlung, Thesaurus, Rahmen eines Textensembles, juristische Größe o.ä. texttheoretisch unterbestimmt.

---

sophischen Hermeneutiken, die die Polysemie geschriebener Text anerkennen, so nicht mehr halten« (p. 68). »In der Tat kann die historisch-kritische Methode ja kein Monopol beanspruchen. Sie muß sich ihrer Grenzen bewußt werden und auch der Gefahren, denen sie ausgesetzt ist. Die jüngsten Entwicklungen der philosophischen Hermeneutiken und was wir in Bezug auf die Interpretation der Heiligen Schriften innerhalb der biblischen Tradition und der Tradition der Kirche feststellten, haben das Interpretationsproblem in einem neuen Licht erscheinen lassen, das die historisch-kritische Methode nicht immer wahrnehmen wollte. Die alles beherrschende Ansicht dieser Methode, den Sinn der Texte zu bestimmen, indem sie diese in ihren ursprünglichen historischen Kontext einordnet, macht sie in der Tat manchmal weniger offen für den dynamischen Aspekt der Bedeutung und die Möglichkeiten einer weiteren Entwicklung des Sinnes« (p. 115). Zur Bedeutung dieses Dokumentes cf. P.S. WILLIAMSON, *Catholic Principles for Interpreting Scripture. A Study of the Pontifical Biblical Commission's The Interpretation of the Bible in the Church* (Subsidia Biblica, 22), Rom 2001.

26. Cf. den Überblicksartikel von P. TULL, *Intertextuality and the Hebrew Scriptures*, in *Currents in Research. Biblical Studies* 8 (2000) 59-90; Tull stellt fest: »... by removing artificially imposed boundaries between texts and texts, between texts and readers, by attending to the dialogical nature of all speech, intertextual theory invites new ventures in cultural and literary perception that will certainly introduce shifts in the ways biblical scholarship is carried out for many years to come« (p. 83). Ferner cf. G. STEINS, *Amos und Mose rücken zusammen. Oder: was heißt intertextuelles Lesen der Bibel?*, in *Religionsunterricht an höheren Schulen* 44 (2001) 20-28.

27. Cf. C.A. NEWSOM, *Bakhtin, the Bible, and Dialogical Truth*, in *Journal of Religion* 76 (1996) 290-306; B. GREEN, *Mikhail Bakhtin and Biblical Scholarship. An Introduction* (SBL SS, 38), Atlanta, GA, 2000.

Unter Rückgriff auf neuere literaturtheoretische Ansätze lässt sich der Kanon als ein Text im Sinne von *Intertext, Metatext, Kontext, Hypertext* und *Diskurs* theoretisch präziser beschreiben.

Das Konzept der Intertextualität[28] problematisiert die Geschlossenheit des Textes: Texte lassen sich beschreiben als Schnittpunkte verschiedener Texte, die im Lesevorgang eingespielt werden (können). Intertextualität ist nicht allein und zuerst ein Phänomen der Textproduktion (das wäre ein Arbeitsfeld der Einflussforschung), sondern ein Prozess der Textkonstitution in der Rezeption. Intertextualität ist daher kein Begleitphänomen von Texten, sondern konstitutiv: Textualität ist als Inter-Textualität zu begreifen.

Nicht nur der Autor kodiert in der Textproduktion – bewusst oder unbewusst – ein Intertextualitätspotential. Auch die Rezipierenden erbringen darstellbare und diskutierbare Intertextualisierungen. Nur wer den Autor über den Leser stellt, den Autor gewissermaßen als Herrn aller zukünftigen Rezeptionsakte begreift und die schöpferische Rolle der Rezeption im Ansatz unterbewertet, wird allein die auf Autorintentionen zurückführbare Intertextualität als relevant betrachten. Der Text wird damit jedoch nicht der Willkür seiner Rezipienten ausgeliefert. Dass es im Text selbst eine Steuerung seiner Rezeption gibt (unabhängig von einer hypothetischen Autorintention) zeigt sich stets in Kontroversen über die Textauslegung, in denen nicht aus der Biographie des Autors zitiert wird, um eine befremdliche Position zu bestreiten, sondern auf den Text verweisen wird.

Intertextualität liegt nicht nur dort vor, wo sie markiert ist und/oder auf Autorintention zurückgeführt werden kann. Im Kanon entsteht selbst durch lockere Juxtaposition ein intertextuelles Gefüge, weil der Einzeltext nicht mehr allein wahrgenommen wird. Das Hohelied zum Beispiel wird mit der Einfügung in den kanonischen Kontext ein anderer Text, wie seine Wirkungsgeschichte in Juden- und Christentum hinreichend demonstriert[29].

---

28. Cf. P. STOCKER, *Theorie der intertextuellen Lektüre. Modelle und Fallstudien*, Paderborn, F. Schöningh, 1998; M. GROHMANN, *Intertextualität als Vermittlungsmodell zwischen jüdischer und christlicher Hermeneutik*, in *Wiener Jahrbuch für Theologie* 2 (1998) 265-284; S. GILLMAYR-BUCHER, *Intertextualität. Zwischen Literaturtheorie und Methodik*, in *Protokolle zur Bibel* 8 (1999) 5-20; STEINS, *Die »Bindung Isaaks«* (n. 19), pp. 45-83; R. ULMER, *Postmoderne Talmudische Hermeneutik*, in *Zeitschrift für Religions- und Geistesgeschichte* 46 (1994) 352-365; P.D. MISCALL, *Text, More Texts; a Textual Reader and a Textual Writer*, in *Semeia* 69/70 (1995) 247-260.

29. Cf. L. SCHWIENHORST-SCHÖNBERGER, *Das Hohelied und die Kontextualität des Verstehens* (unveröffentl. Vortragsmanuskript 2001): »Nun wissen wir aber inzwischen alle, dass die Bedeutung eines Textes kein zeitlich abgeschlossenes Phänomen ist. Sie ist weder einfachhin identisch mit der Intention des Autors noch mit der Bedeutung, die in

In einem semantischen Kanonmodell sind zwei Bedeutungen von Kanon zu unterscheiden: Kanon (1) = der (kanonisierte) Text der Bibel, und Kanon (2) = der Kanon als Metatext. Die Zusammenfassung aller in einer Glaubensgemeinschaft akzeptierten und für normativ erklärten Texte schafft einen Metatext, der zwei Funktionen hat: Erstens ermöglicht er das Verständnis des Einzeltextes durch die Etablierung eines Verständnisrahmens (»Rahmen« meint sowohl Spielraum als auch Begrenzung); zweitens begrenzt der Kanon als Metatext die Vieldeutigkeit, die jedem Text eigen ist[30]. Die metatextuellen Funktionen des Kanons sind texttheoretisch beschreibbar und nicht allein »äußere« Aspekte von Text im Sinne von Aussagen über den normativen Status.

Die Rezeptionstheorie[31] hat in der Überwindung eines Modell der stabilen, singulären und inhärenten Textbedeutung gezeigt, dass jede Interpretation durch aktive Re-kontextualisierung geschieht. Pointiert formuliert transportieren Texte keine Bedeutungen, sondern Bedeutungs*potentiale*, die in je neuen Rekontextualisierungen realisiert und auf Vereindeutigungen hin selektiert werden. Die Anerkennung der Polyvalenz von Texten bedeutet also nicht den Verzicht auf Bedeutung; aber Eindeutigkeit entsteht offensichtlich nicht aus dem Text, sondern ist das Ergebnis komplexer Konstellationen textueller und der außertextueller Bezugspunkte.

Das Konzept der Hypertextualität[32] scheint eine faszinierende Analogie zum Funktionieren des Bibelkanons zu eröffnen: Als Hypertext befähigt die Bibel die Rezipierenden zu einem interaktiven Aufbau von Textensembles in nicht-linearer multi-sequentieller Form[33], nicht anders, als es bereits im Entstehungsprozess der Bibel geschehen ist. Die ältere

---

einer ersten Rezeptionsphase konstituiert wird. Ändert sich der Rezeptionskontext, ändert sich auch die Bedeutung. Mit 'Rezeptionskontext' meine ich jetzt sowohl den literarischen als auch den lebensweltlichen 'Zusammenhang'«. Daher stellt sich letztlich nicht die Frage, *ob* die Exegese beim Kanon anzusetzen hat, sondern allein *wie* dies in methodologisch reflektierter und methodisch nachvollziehbarer Weise geschehen kann.

30. Cf. M. WELKER, *Das vierfache Gewicht der Schrift*, in D. HILLER & C. KRESS (eds.), *»Daß Gott eine große Barmherzigkeit habe«. Konkrete Theologie in der Verschränkung von Glaube und Leben*. FS G. Schneider-Flume, Leipzig, Evangelische Verlagsanstalt, 2001, pp. 9-27, hier 14-16.

31. Cf. H.L. ARNOLD & H. DETERING (eds.), *Grundzüge der Literaturwissenschaft*, München, Deutscher Taschenbuch Verlag, ⁴2001; J. FREY, *Der implizite Leser und die biblischen Texte*, in *Theologische Beiträge* 23 (1992) 266-290; STEINS, *Die »Bindung Isaaks«* (n. 19), pp. 84-102.

32. Vgl. A. NÜNNING, *Lexikon Literatur- und Kulturtheorie* (n. 2), p. 261; T. BEAUDOIN, *Virtual Faith. The Irreverent Spiritual Quest of Generation X*, San Francisco, Jossey-Bass, 2000, pp. 125-127.

33. Cf. N. LOHFINK, *Moses Tod, die Tora und die alttestamentliche Sonntagslesung*, in G. STEINS (ed.), *Leseordnung. Altes und Neues Testament in der Liturgie*, Stuttgart, Katholische Bibelwerk, 1997, pp. 122-137, hier pp. 130-132.

Exegese hatte dies lange vor dem Computerzeitalter mit Begriffen wie
»anthologischer Stil« oder »Midraschmethode« zu erfassen gesucht
und damit sowohl ein produktions- wie ein rezeptionsorientiertes Verfahren formuliert[34].

Exegese ist Teil eines Diskurses, d.h. einer Konstellation, die dem
Gegenstand nicht äußerlich bleibt, sondern ihn erst konstituiert. Das
diskurstheoretische Verständnis von Text[35] macht es möglich, die »festen« Positionen von Autor, Text und Leser jeweils in ihren Verfloch-
tenheiten und Bedingtheiten zu sehen. Diskurse sind geschichtlich bedingte Sprach-Räume, die den Teilnehmern jeweils vorgegeben sind;
Textsinn (nicht nur die Textproduktion) ist abhängig von gesellschaft-
lich konstituierten Kommunikationshorizonten. Die Theorie der Diskur-
sivität von Texten hat weitreichenden Folgen für die klassische Autor-
Text-Leser-Triade: Sie ist nicht einfach gegeben, sondern selbst Funktion von Bedingungen einer höheren Stufe.

These 5: »Moderne« Exegese beruht seit B. de Spinoza auf zwei Prämissen: erstens der Unterstellung des einen/einzig richtigen dem Text
inhärenten Sinnes, dem Exegese sich immer mehr annähern kann, und
zweitens dem methodischen Individualismus, d.h. dass dieser Sinn von
dem allein mit Vernunft arbeitenden und von jedem kontextuellen
Einfluss befreiten einzelnen Forschersubjekt gefunden werden kann.
Beide Prämissen sind von der modernitätskritischen / post-modernen Literaturwissenschaft problematisiert und durch eine Theorie der Sinn-
offenheit/-vielfalt und der Kontextualität allen Verstehens ersetzt worden[36].

These 6: Das Problem der Beliebigkeit im Umgang mit Texten kann
nicht durch eine Ausrichtung auf die Autorintention beseitigt werden.
Die Autorintention ist nur spekulativ zu ermitteln, sie ist eine Projektion

---

34. Zu aktuellen Reformulierungen dieser Ansätze cf. D. BANON, *Kritik und Tradition. Jüdische und christliche Lektüre der Bibel,* in *Judaica* 52 (1996) 23-39; N. DOUGLAS-
KLOTZ, *Midrash and Postmodern Inquiry. Suggestions Toward a Hermeneutics of In-
determinacy,* in *Currents in Research. Biblical Studies* 7 (1999) 181-193; M. OEMING,
*Lob der Vieldeutigkeit. Erwägungen zur Erneuerung des Verhältnisses jüdischer und
christlicher Hemeneutiken,* in *Trumah* 9 (2000) 125-145; L. TEUGELS, *Two Centuries of
Midrash Study. A Survey of Some Standard Works on Rabbinic Midrash and Methods,* in
NTT 54 (2000) 125-144.

35. Cf. J. FOHRMANN & H. MÜLLER, *Diskurstheorien und Literaturwissenschaft,*
Frankfurt, Suhrkamp Verlag, 1988; M. TITZMANN, *Kulturelles Wissen – Diskurs – Denk-
system. Zu einigen Grundbegriffen der Literaturgeschichtsschreibung,* in *Zeitschrift für
französische Sprache und Literatur* 99 (1989) 47-61; J. LINK & U. LINK-HEER, *Diskurs/
Interdiskurs und Literaturanalyse,* in *Zeitschrift für Literaturwissenschaft und Linguistik*
77 (1980) 88-99.

36. Cf. SCHWIENHORST-SCHÖNBERGER, *Einheit und Vielfalt* (n. 12), pp. 62-66.

einer Sinnmöglichkeit des Textes. Der Terminus »Autorintention« suggeriert einen mit dem Text-»Ursprung« verbundenen normativen Anspruch (»genau so und nicht anders, als der Autor es wollte, muss der Text von *allen* späteren verstanden werden«), der die Sinnmöglichkeiten eines Textes unzulässig begrenzt in Richtung des einen richtigen Sinnes[37].

Statt von Autorintention sollte besser von der *Enzyklopädie* des Textes (dem kulturellen Kontext seiner Entstehung im weitesten Sinne) und seiner Bedeutung für hypothetisch erschlossene Erstadressaten gesprochen werden[38]. Die Enzyklopädie des Bibeltextes ist vor allem auf dem Wege historischer Forschung (Philologie, Archäologie, Religionsgeschichte etc.) zu rekonstruieren. Historische Forschung hat also in der Exegese nicht nur ein begrenztes »Aufenthaltsrecht«, sondern ist für das Verstehen literarischer Artefakte einer fremden Kultur unverzichtbar. Die Frage der kulturellen Enzyklopädie ist jedoch zu unterscheiden von der Suggestion einer allen späteren Rezeptionen überlegenen »ursprünglichen« Bedeutung.

Der Text bleibt auch gegenüber der ursprünglichen Textverwendung polyvalent; sein Sinnreichtum ist größer als die hypothetisch erschlossene Ursprungsbedeutung, d.h. die Bedeutung zum Zeitpunkt seiner Entstehung. Rezeption ist ein kreativer, sinnanreichernder Prozess und kein »Nachstellen der Ursprungssituation«, ohne dass dabei die Mächtigkeit des Anfangs geleugnet werden müsste. »Der Text kann seinen Anspruch nur entfalten, wenn er vorher nicht im historisch-antiquarischen Interesse auf die Vergangenheit seiner Entstehung fixiert worden ist«[39]. Das

37. Zur Problematisierung des Rekurses auf Autorintentionen in der Textinterpretation cf. M. PROUST, *Gegen Sainte-Beuve*, in *Marcel Proust Werke*, III Bd. 3, Frankfurt, Suhrkamp, 1997, pp. 9-43.

38. Nach U. ECO, *Zwischen Autor und Text. Interpretation und Überinterpretation*, München, Carl Hanser, 1994, p. 154 bewegt sich jede Textinterpretation zwischen drei Polen: (1) dem Text, (2) der Leserin/dem Leser mit einem spezifischen Erwartungshorizont, (3) der »kulturellen Enzyklopädie«. Das Weltwissen einer Kultur ist der letzte Bezugspunkt der Interpretation. Die Metapher der Enzyklopädie verdeutlicht, daß das Wissen nicht in einem Lexikon erfaßt werden kann, sondern einer umfangreichen Bibliothek gleicht, in der Werke unterschiedlichster Art aus den verschiedenen Wissensbereichen nebeneinander stehen. Die unverzichtbare Bedeutung historisch-kritischer Arbeit für die Bibelexegese ist in diesem theoretischen Rahmen präzise beschreibbar. Ihr Ziel sind nicht Mutmaßungen über Intentionen des Verfassers des auszulegenden Textes und über mögliche frühere Rezeptionen, sie dient vielmehr der Rekonstruktion der von jeder Äußerung des fremden (»alten«) Textes vorausgesetzten Weltsicht. Die Arbeit an der Wiedergewinnung einer teilweise versunkenen Enzyklopädie des fremden Textes wahrt das Eigenrecht des Textes in der Rezeption und verhindert so eine Überwältigung durch die Gegenwartsinteressen von Leserin und Leser.

39. H. SPIECKERMANN, *Die Verbindlichkeit des Alten Testaments. Unzeitgemäße Betrachtungen zu einem ungeliebten Thema*, in *JBT* 12 (1997) 25-51, p. 26.

Problem der Beliebigkeit wird nicht durch eine Festlegung möglicher Bedeutungen auf eine Ursprungsbedeutung überwunden, sondern allein im komplexen Zusammenspiel von Vorgaben des Textes und ausweisbaren Sinnfindungen in je aktuellen Rezeptionen.

These 7: Der Kanon bewahrt historische Konstellationen nicht als solche auf. Schon aus dem Redaktionsprozess ist ersichtlich, dass der Fokus nicht die Vergangenheit, sondern die Gegenwart und die Öffnung für zukünftige Rezeptionen ist. Ältere Textstufen werden nicht unversehrt und in gleichsam archivalischem Interesse addiert, sondern in anamnetischer Absicht de-kontextualisiert und re-kontextualisiert. Als Traditionsliteratur konserviert der Kanon nicht die Spuren der Geschichte als Quellen und Überreste, sondern *stilisiert* sie zu Gunsten der »Erinnerung«. Der Bibelkanon hat »Denkmalcharakter«, er transportiert nicht Vergangenheit, sondern »erinnerte Zukunft«, einen narrativen Entwurf der Identität der zugehörigen Glaubensgemeinschaft[40].

Daher mahnt P. Stuhlmacher zu Recht: »Die Anamnese gehört zu den Grundelementen einer nicht nur sekundär an den biblischen Kanon herangetragenen, sondern von ihm selbst vorgegebenen Hermeneutik, und an diesem Sachverhalt sollte man nicht länger einfach vorbeigehen«[41].

Die in der alttestamentlichen Wissenschaft häufig anzutreffende Beschreibung großer Teile des AT als »Historiographie« ist problematisch, denn nicht nur das nachbiblische Judentum, sondern bereits die Bibel

---

40. Cf. zu dieser Zentralfrage biblischer Hermeneutik den ausgreifenden Essay von J. SCHRÖTER, *Die Frage nach dem historischen Jesus und der Charakter der historischen Erkenntnis*, in A. LINDEMANN (ed.), *The Sayings Source Q and the Historical Jesus* (BETL, 158), Leuven, University Press - Peeters, 2001, pp. 207-254. Wenn Schröter als ein Ergebnis festhält, die »Frage nach dem historischen Jesus« sei umzuformulieren in »diejenige nach einem an die Quellen gebundenen Entwurf des *erinnerten* Jesus als Inhalt des sozialen Gedächtnisses des Urchristentums« (p. 233), bedeutet das nicht weniger als eine epochale Reformulierung der exegetischen Aufgabe, die analog auch für das Alte Testament gilt. Mit dieser durch historische Rekonstruktion nicht überholbaren, sondern betonten Bindung an den narrativen Entwurf der Quellen ist ein wesentlicher Einwand gegen eine kanonische Schriftlektüre hinfällig; zu diesem »historistischen«, die Schrift als eminentes Erinnerungsphänomen überspielenden Einwand cf. J. TREBOLLE BARRERA, *The Jewish Bible and the Christian Bible. An Introduction to the History of the Bible*, Leiden, Brill, 1998, p. 418: »The tendency of canonical criticism to give emphasis to the final stages of the formation of the Bible *does not correspond to the very dynamic* of scripture. The Bible places stress on the oldest traditions and on the founders, Moses and Jesus. The biblical books are always attributed to ancient authors, not to the redactors of recent periods«. Zu diesem Problemkomplex s.a. J.B. GREEN, *Modernity, History and the Theological Interpretation of the Bibel*, in *Scottish Journal of Theology* 54 (2001) 308-329.
41. P. STUHLMACHER, *Anamnese. Eine unterschätze hermeneutische Kategorie*, in W. HÄRLE (ed.), *Befreiende Wahrheit*. FS E. Herms (Marburger theologische Studien, 60), Marburg, 2000, pp. 23-38, hier p. 33.

ist – so paradox es klingen mag – »mehr am Sinn der Geschichte als an Geschichtsschreibung interessiert«[42]; ein Indiz dafür ist die zunehmende Ritualisierung in den Kernteilen der Geschichtsüberlieferung, die gerne als spätere Redaktorenarbeit und damit – gegen den Sinn der vorliegenden Texte – als *quantité negligeable* gehandelt wird (vgl. Ex 3,15b und die durchgängige Akzentuierung des »Heute« in Ex 12–14; ferner Ex 19,1). Im Dtn wird Geschichte vollends zum memorierbaren Paradigma; *mutatis mutandis* gilt Entsprechendes auch in den zu paränetischen Exempla umgestalteten »Königs*bildern*«[43] der Chronikbücher. Es scheint, dass in der exegetischen Wissenschaft erst langsam die Sensibilität für die im Zuge der historistischen Verwissenschaftlichung verlorengegangenen Charakteristica der biblischen Literatur wiedergewonnen wird – nicht ohne den Anstoß durch eine besondere Art von kulturwissenschaftlicher »Fremdprophetie«[44].

Die Grenze der klassischen historisch-kritischen Methodik liegt darin, dass sie, »indem sie hinter den Text zu dringen versucht, in die umgekehrte Richtung im Vergleich zu dem eigenen Verlauf der Texte schreitet, die vorwärts auf die Empfänger blicken«[45]. Das heißt: »Analyse, die den Sinn eines Textes primär hinter dem Text sucht, tut dies gegen den Verlauf der Textentstehung und somit auf die Gefahr höchst verzerrender Sinnwahrnehmung hin«[46]. Traditionsliteratur wie die Bibel wird nicht angemessen konzeptualisiert, wenn sie in sukzessive Autorenliteratur verwandelt wird.

These 8: Der Endtext (»final form«) wird daher nicht angemessen verstanden und in seinen Sinnmöglichkeiten erkannt, wenn er als Summe der Vorstufen erfasst und linear in einer Redaktionsgeschichte (die als allein angemessene Lesemöglichkeit behauptet wird) rekonstruiert wird. »Endgestalt« meint zudem anderes als »Endgestaltung« im Sinne einer autorintendierten »Ausgabe letzter Hand«, das Produkt »Text« ist

---

42. V. LENZEN, *Wesen der Erinnerung und jüdische Gedächtniskultur*, in *Lebendiges Zeugnis* 56 (2001) 254-264, p. 261 mit Bezug auf Y.H. YERUSHALMI, *Zachor: Erinnere Dich! Jüdische Geschichte und jüdisches Gedächtnis*, Berlin, Klaus Wagenbach, 1996.

43. Der Ausdruck scheint mir treffender zu sein als die übliche Rede von den Königs*geschichten* der Chronik, denn der Chronist zeigt an allen Königen immer dasselbe: Wer das Hauptgebot beachtet, erfährt Segen, wer es missachtet, wird bestraft.

44. Hier ist vor allem J. ASSMANN zu nennen, vgl. jüngst, *Religion und kulturelles Gedächtnis*, München, C.H. Beck, 2000.

45. T. VEIJOLA, *Text, Wissenschaft und Glaube. Überlegungen eines Alttestamentlers zur Lösung des Grundproblems der biblischen Hermeneutik*, in *JBT* 15 (2000) 313-339, p. 328.

46. H. SPIECKERMANN, *Psalmen und Psalter. Suchbewegungen des Forschens und Betens*, in F. GARCÍA MARTÍNEZ & E. NOORT (eds.), *Perspectives in the Study of the Old Testament and Early Judaism* (SVT, 73), Leiden, Brill 1998, pp. 137-153, hier p. 145.

autonom gegenüber dem Produktionsvorgang, es »funktioniert« unabhängig von diesem[47]. Das unterschiedlichen historischen Konstellationen entstammende Material ist im Endtext zu einem vielstimmigen, gegebenenfalls auch kontrastiven und konträren Ensemble zusammengefügt, das allein dem uneinholbaren Thema (Gott - sein Handeln an seinem und durch sein Volk - für die Völker) gerecht wird und zugleich eine Fülle von Anschlussstellen für zukünftige Diskurse bereithält.

These 9: Bibelauslegung ist vom Lektüreparadigma her zu konzipieren. Auch eine so genannte diachron orientierte Exegese »entgeht« nicht der Lektüre, die im Umgang mit Texten nicht eine Vorstufe der Auslegung, sondern deren Rahmen ist. Auch Aussagen über Ursprungsbedeutungen sind auf einen hypothetischen Entstehungskontext projizierte aktuelle Lektüreerfahrungen.

Die neuere texttheoretische Diskussion sprengt den Textbegriff auf[48]. Der Text ist nicht etwas Statisches, Fertiges, in sich Ruhendes. Auch ein Text hat Zeichencharakter: Das Signifikat eines literarischen Textes ist nicht festzulegen wie die lexikalische Eintragung einer Wortbedeutung; es muss jeweils auf der Grundlage des Signifikanten vom Zeichenbenutzer neu generiert werden (vgl. den drei-poligen Zeichenbegriff von C.S. Peirce). Als Konsequenz der veränderten Zeichenbedeutung kann das Zeichen nicht länger als »Faktum« aufgefasst werden. Gegen eine Tendenz zum Objektivismus in der biblischen Exegese ist festzuhalten, dass Text und Rezipient nicht einfach als Objekt und Subjekt einander gegenüber stehen. Die verbreitete Vorstellung eines Dialogs zwischen Text und Rezipierenden holt die Komplexität des Kommunikationsprozesses nicht hinreichend ein. Wenn die Zuweisung von Signifikant und Signifikat das Ergebnis einer Interpretationsleistung ist, gehören die

47. Cf. STEINS, *Die »Bindung Isaaks«* (n. 19), p. 29.
48. Cf. G. MARTENS, *Was ist ein Text? Ansätze zur Bestimmung eines Leitbegriffs der Textphilologie*, in *Poetica* 21 (1989) 1-25; unter dieser Rücksicht ist eine Position wie die von J. BARTON, *Canon and Old Testament Interpretation*, in E. BALL (ed.), *In Search of True Wisdom. Essays in Old Testament Interpretation in Honour of Ronald E. Clements* (JSOT SS, 300), Sheffield, Academic Press, 1999, pp. 37-52 als vortheoretisch zu bestimmen, cf. p. 52: »Biblical critics' obligations are to the text, not to the Church or to theology, and they have the duty of reporting what the text says, not what the theologian wants to hear. The idea that there is a special 'canonical' level of meaning above the natural sense of the text has been widespread in Christian history and has, of course, an extremely distinguished pedigree; but it is not compatible with biblical criticism as this has developed since the Reformation, and nothing is gained by pretending that it can be made compatible. The best service biblical critics can render to religious believers (among whom they as often numbered themselves) is to tell the truth about what the text seems to them to mean, not to be talked into believing that it means something more helpful, more edifying or more theologically correct than it does«.

Offenheit der Bedeutung und die Veränderbarkeit der Sinnzuweisung notwendigerweise in den Textbegriff hinein. Das ist die eigentliche Sinnspitze eines post-traditionalen Textbegriffs.

Der Text ist eine Kommunikationsbasis. Die Funktion der Lektüre ist folglich neu zu bestimmen, denn sie ist dem Text nicht äußerlich, sondern »schafft« ihn erst. Damit einher geht eine Problematisierung von »Selbstverständlichkeiten«: die Bindung der Textbedeutung an die Autorintention und die Vorstellung des einen (richtigen) Sinnes. Offenheit und Vieldeutigkeit sind aber nicht gleichzusetzen mit Beliebigkeit: der Text bleibt eine Vor-Gabe. Pluralität begegnet in der Bibel nicht nur im Nebeneinander der unterschiedlichen Texte, oder im rekonstruierten Hintereinander der »Schichten« eines Textes, sondern bereits in den Sinnmöglichkeiten des einzelnen Textes.

These 10: Im Blick auf ihren Gegenstand, den Bibeltext als Kanon, hat die Exegese als wissenschaftliche Disziplin eine doppelte Aufgabe zu erfüllen: Sie rekonstruiert die verloren gegangenen Enzyklopädien des divergenten kanonischen Materials als unabdingbare Voraussetzungen eines angemessenen Verstehens, und sie schützt und erinnert die Sinnmöglichkeiten des kanonischen Textes. Sinnfindung/-festlegung mit normativem Anspruch ist keine Aufgabe der Exegese als Wissenschaft, sondern der *community/ies of faith and practice* bzw. der darin für solche Orientierungsleistungen zuständigen Instanzen. Die Auslagerung normativer Ansprüche entlastet den wissenschaftlichen Diskurs und erweitert seine Spielräume.

These 11: Der Kanon mag von seiner Entstehung her (historisch) das Produkt vieler Zufälle und Beliebigkeiten sein[49]. In der *Lektüre* bibli-

---

49. In der Debatte über die Entstehung des alttestamentlichen Kanons spielt zwar das Konstrukt einer »Synode von Jamnia« keine Rolle mehr; erstaunlicherweise halten aber viele an dem in der älteren Debatte damit verbundenen Abschlussdatum (ca. 100 n.Chr.) fest. Wie das Beispiel von J. BARTON, *The Significance of a Fixed Canon of the Hebrew Bible*, in M. SÆBØ (ed.), *Hebrew Bible/Old Testament. The History of its Interpretation*, Vol I, Part 1, Göttingen, Vandenhoeck & Ruprecht, 1996, pp. 67-83 zeigt, werden zwar kanongeschichtlich bedeutsame Befunde registriert und interpretiert, es fehlt aber eine Metareflexion auf die für die Rekonstruktion der Kanongeschichte verwendeten Modelle. So hält J. Barton Beweglichkeiten im zweiten und dritten Kanonteil bis weit in die christliche Zeit hinein fest und wertet sie als Beleg für die Offenheit des Kanonisierungsprozesses. Das fraglos vorausgesetzte Modell ist dabei offensichtlich das einer *einlinig* verlaufenden Kanongeschichte, die gewissermaßen zunehmend stärker den kanonischen Prozess gerinnen lässt, bis am Ende der Kanon dasteht. Dafür spricht wenig; die Befunde lassen sich besser in ein Modell der Mehrgleisigkeit integrieren, ganz analog zu den Erkenntnissen der Textgeschichte. Es ist nicht wahrscheinlich, dass die Textgeschichte und die Kanongeschichte erst spät zusammenkommen. Textüberlieferung *und* Kanonformie-

scher Texte ist er keine Zufallserscheinung, sondern der *primäre* Kontext, in dem uns ein Bibeltext begegnet. Alle anderen Kontexte (z.b. Entstehungssituation des Textes; ältere literarische Kontexte/Vorstufen; religionsgeschichtliche Hintergründe) sind hypothetisch erschlossen. Daher verdient der Kanon besondere Beachtung in der Exegese. Der Kanon ist somit auch beschreibbar als privilegierter Intertext und privilegiertes Feld der Rekontextualisierung in der Lektüre.

These 12: Gegenüber Integrations- oder Exklusivmodellen in der Zuordnung exegetischer Methodenschritte ist festzuhalten: Eine kanonische Lektüre ist kein Methodenschritt, der ergänzend zum Ensemble etablierter historisch-kritischer Methoden (und deren Erweiterungen, z.B. in der Formkritik) hinzutritt, sie ersetzt auch nicht diese klassischen Methoden. Eine kanonische Lektüre ist eine *eigene* Art des »Umgangs« mit einem Bibeltext, die nicht auf Rekonstruktion (etwa der Intentionen von Autoren und Redaktoren) abzielt, sondern in einer vorsichtigen Annäherung an den gegebenen Bibeltext diesen im Raum der privilegierten Intertextualität des Kanons liest[50]. Ihr Ziel ist es, die Vielfalt von Sinnmöglichkeiten des Textes im Raum des Kanons aufzuzeigen oder offen zu halten [51].

rung sind gruppenspezifische Vorgänge, daher ist eine Reflexion auf Beweglichkeiten im Kanonisierungsprozess immer unvollständig und nicht aussagefähig, wenn sie nicht begleitet wird von Reflexionen auf die Trägergruppen. In einem solchen Referenzrahmen erscheint auch eine frühe (hasmonäische) Ansetzung des erst in rabbinischer Zeit »universalisierten« Kanons nicht länger problematisch; cf. jetzt auch P.R. DAVIES, *Scribes and Schools. The Canonization of the Hebrew Scriptures*, Louisville, Westminster, John Knox Press, 1998, p 182: »The likely creators of the canon that the rabbis inherited were… the Hasnomeans… 'Judaism' as defining a religious system was in a sense a product of Hellenism, and so was its canon. Both are of course related to each other and came about through a combination of imitation of, and reaction to, the foreign culture«. Ein weiteres Problem gegenwärtiger Kanondebatten ist die Verwendung des maximalistischen Kanonbegriff der nachreformatorischen Kontroverstheologie, so als ob erst dort zulässig von einem Kanon gesprochen werden könnte, wo eine feste Textform flächendeckend aufgrund eines belegbaren autoritativen Kanonentscheids anerkannt wird. In der Kanongeschichte ist gegenwärtig vieles in Bewegung; es erscheint sehr fraglich, ob das traditionelle Modell der sukzessiven Kanonisierung der drei Kanonteile noch länger aufrecht erhalten werden kann; schon die Beobachtung einer engen Verbindung von »Tora« und »Propheten« auf einer späten Redaktionsstufe (das Kürzel R^P ist an vielen Stellen als »*prophetische* Redaktion« des Pentateuch zu dechiffrieren) wirft Fragen auf, die mit dem dreistufigen Modell nicht zu lösen sind; cf. S.B. CHAPMAN, *The Law and the Prophets. A Study in Old Testament Canon Formation* (FAT, 27), Tübingen, Mohr Siebeck, 2000.

50. Cf. die Position M. Bubers unter I.

51. Vgl. SEITZ, *Canonical Appraoch* (n. 11), p. 54: »Der C.A. kombiniert also nicht wie die hist.-krit. Exegese Methoden (Literar-, Form- und Traditionsgesch.), sondern focussiert sie in einer bes. Art der Anwendung, in der die theol. Intention des Textes nicht als dem endgültigen Gestaltungsprozess und seiner Rezeption vorgelagert verstanden wird«.

These 13: Die Erarbeitung der kanoninternen Intertextualität schafft mit ihrem text- und kontextnahen Vorgehen die Grundlage und die Orientierung (»bei der Sache bleiben«) für weitere kanonüberschreitende intertextuelle Konstellationen. Rezeption wird nicht als Wiederholung vergangener Sinnbildungen verstanden, sondern als offener Prozess der Sinnanreicherung[52].

These 14: Ein solches Vorgehen ist mit dem Begriffspaar »Diachronie und Synchronie« nicht einzuholen, eine kanonische Lektüre ist als »synchron« oder »holistisch« nicht treffend beschrieben. Sie bezieht jedoch diachrone und synchrone Erkenntnisse zum Text ein[53]. Das Arrangement der exegetischen Methoden könnte als Feldstruktur gedacht werden[54], in dem die drei Pole Produktion/»Autor« – Text – Rezeption je

52. Cf. die kritische Überlegung von H.G. GADAMER, *Wahrheit und Methode. Grundzüge einer philosophischen Hermeneutik* (Gesammelte Werke, 1), Tübingen, Mohr Siebeck, 1990, p. 172: »Nun ist die Wiederherstellung der Bedingungen, unter denen ein überliefertes Werk seine ursprüngliche Bedingungen erfüllte, für das Verständnis gewiß eine wesentliche Hilfsoperation. Allein, es fragt sich, ob das, was hier gewonnen wird, wirklich das ist, was wir als die *Bedeutung* des Kunstwerkes suchen, und ob das Verstehen richtig bestimmt wird, wenn wir in ihm eine zweite Schöpfung, die Reproduktion der ursprünglichen Produktion, sehen. Am Ende ist eine solche Bestimmung der Hermeneutik nicht minder widersinnig als alle Restitution und Restauration vergangenen Lebens«.

53. Zur Rolle diachroner Betrachtungen in der Exegese vgl. REICHERT, *Offene Fragen* (n. 22), p. 1001: »Die diachrone Betrachtung verändert nichts an den für die Textauslegung relevanten Textdaten, und sie verändert nichts an der Auswertung von Beobachtungen, sofern diese zur Bestimmung der Mitteilungs- und Wirkabsicht des Textes führen soll... Die Analyse der textuellen Vorgeschichte eines Textes/Teiltextes hat für dessen Auslegung keine konstitutive Funktion... Die Bestimmung der textuellen Vorgeschichte kann für die Auslegung des Textes in seiner vorliegenden Gestalt unmittelbar nichts austragen, weil sie dem vorliegenden Text nichts hinzufügt und nichts wegnimmt. Sie kann aber gegebenenfalls die synchrone Auslegung auf deren eigene Grenzen aufmerksam machen. Gegen diese eingeschränkte Funktionsbestimmung diachroner Betrachtungsweise ist folgender Einwand denkbar: Kann denn nicht gerade die diachrone Betrachtung – jedenfalls in bestimmten Fällen – zu einem deutlicheren Bild von der Intention des Textautors verhelfen?«. Diesem Einwand begegnet Reichert mit folgender Überlegung: »Unabhängig von den Möglichkeiten eines Rückschlusses auf empirischen Autor(sic!)/ empirische Adressaten stellt sich... die Frage nach der Notwendigkeit ihrer Berücksichtigung im Auslegungsverfahren. Die Antwort auf diese Frage scheint mir tendenziell negativ ausfallen zu müssen... Gegen Beobachtungen zum Text und deren Auswertung lässt sich nicht einmal eine gewisse Erkenntnis des Autors und seiner Intention ausspielen. Analoges gilt natürlich erst recht für die Adressatenseite... Damit ist deutlich: Weder der empirische Autor mit seiner Intention noch die empirischen Adressaten mit ihrer Rezeption können im Verfahren der Textauslegung eine notwendige, eine konstitutive Rolle spielen« (p. 1004). Insofern erscheint die von GROSS, *Biblisch-theologische Auslegung* (n. 10), p. 123 vorgeschlagene Ausrichtung der Textauslegung auf die Ermittlung der Intentionen des empirischen Autors und der von ihm intendierten Adressaten zur Absicherung gegen Interpretenwillkür wenig aussichtsreich. Sind nicht gerade die Hypothesen über Autorintentionen die Gelegenheit zur Camouflage willkürlicher Interpretationen?

54. Cf. L.C. JONKER, *On Plotting the Exegetical-Hermeneutical Landscape*, in *Scriptura* 59 (1996) 397-411.

unterschiedlich zur Geltung kommen. Innerhalb diese Ensemble gibt es jedoch ein »Gravitationszentrum«, dem »Dialog« von Text/Kanon und Rezipierenden in der je aktuellen Lektüre.

SCHLUSS

Die gegenwärtigen Diskussion über die Rolle des Bibelkanons in der Bibelauslegung ist keine Debatte neben vielen anderen im internationalen exegetischen Diskurs, sondern betrifft die Identität von Bibelauslegung als wissenschaftlich-theologisches Unternehmen: »Die Kanonfrage erweist sich immer mehr als Schlüsselfrage sowohl für die Interpretation der Bibel in der Kirche im weiteren Sinne als auch für die theologische Identität einer dazu dienlichen Bibelwissenschaft«[55]. Die Exegese steht vor der Frage, ob sie weiterhin »jenseits« des Kanons ansetzen will, oder ob sie den Kanon als dem geschichtlich gewordenen Ort der Gottesoffenbarung in der Haltung modernitätskritischer Selbstbescheidung zu ihrem Ausgangs- und Bezugspunkt macht. Mit der Berücksichtigung des Bibelkanons werden in der exegetischen Methodologie und Methodik die Karten neu gemischt. »Wir stehen hier erst am Anfang...«[56].

Institut für Kath. Theologie   Georg STEINS
Universität Osnabrück
Schloßstrasse 4
D-49069 Osnabrück

---

55. M. SECKLER, *Über die Problematik des biblischen Kanons und die Bedeutung seiner Wiederentdeckung*, in *Theologische Quartalschrift* (2000) 30-53, p. 49; es ist bedauerlich, dass Seckler das Verständnis des Kanons als Rezeptionsphänomen und vergleichzeitigte Vielstimmigkeit nicht durchhält, sondern pp. 52-53 wieder zu Gunsten der üblichen diachron orientierten Exegese verlässt. Die Sinnspitze des Kanons besteht doch gerade darin, dass die Kopräsenz des Widerstreitenden und unterschiedlichen Kontexten Entstammenden den Endtext bleibend bestimmt und als solche verstanden werden muss, nicht aber über eine Abbildung auf eine hypothetische Literaturgeschichte, die *de facto* das Problem und die Herausforderung des Widerstreits durch Historisierung entschärft; die Notwendigkeit historischer Forschung in der Exegese ist davon nicht berührt (s.o.).
56. S.o. Abschnitt I. das Zitat von M. Buber.

CANONICAL APPROACHES ANCIENT AND MODERN

I. INTRODUCTION

The "canonical approach" to reading the Bible, especially the Old Testament, is a new feature of biblical scholarship in the last twenty-five years or so. It was formulated as a conscious programme by Brevard S. Childs with the publication of his *Biblical Theology in Crisis*[1], and developed in his crucially important study *Introduction to the Old Testament as Scripture*[2]. It arose from the perceived demise of the North American "Biblical Theology" movement of the post-Second World War period, which had attempted to produce a grand theological synthesis in biblical studies by moving beyond "historical" criticism to an analysis of the underlying theological concepts of the Bible. By the late 1970s this kind of biblical theology was no longer very fashionable: its linguistic basis had been demolished by James Barr[3], and many of its leading concepts called in question by others.

Rather than simply rejecting the constructive agenda of the "biblical theologians" – who had wanted above all to make the Bible fruitful for the work of theologians and ordinary believers – Childs proposed a new way of approaching the matter. He fully shared biblical theology's concern for the essential unity and religious importance of the Bible, but argued that this unity was not to be perceived, as they had thought, at the level of the Bible's leading concepts, or in a kind of "Hebraic thinking" which distinguished the Bible from modern modes of thought and had to be painfully reconstructed so that we could learn to adjust our own ideas to match the biblical witness. On the contrary, the unity of the Bible lay not beneath its surface but in its final form, which the Church had accepted as its canon. What was needed was close attention to the Bible as it stands, rather than an excavation of the text as if it were merely another ancient document of purely historical interest to us. He argued that if we began, as historical critics do, by ignoring the Bible's religious claim on us, and studying it as though it were a document that had just happened to turn up from the ancient world, we should be bound to have

---

1. B.S. CHILDS, *Biblical Theology in Crisis*, Philadelphia, PA, Fortress Press, 1970.
2. B.S. CHILDS, *Introduction to the Old Testament as Scripture*, Philadelphia, PA, Fortress Press, 1979.
3. J. BARR, *The Semantics of Biblical Language*, Oxford, University Press, 1961 is the major work concerned here.

difficulty in subsequently making connections with our own belief. But the problem would be of our own making. If you take Christianity's sacred text and insist on ignoring its sacredness, then you are bound to find it hard to move from the mode of study you have chosen back into a theological appropriation. What the Christian who studies the Bible should do, on the contrary, is to *begin* by treating the Bible as the Church's book. That will not preclude asking historical questions about it; but such questions will be clearly seen as secondary to the task of expounding the text as it is, in the form in which Christians (and Jews) have canonized it.

There can be no doubt that this represents a new position in modern biblical studies. As I have tried to argue elsewhere[4], it was clearly anticipated in some measure by earlier biblical scholars. Gerhard von Rad already sought an appreciation of the whole text, beyond the fragmentation brought about by source criticism; and there is a general movement of thought going back to Karl Barth (a clear influence on von Rad) that insists on reading the Bible as the Word of God, and not merely as an ancient document. The "Biblical Theology" movement, as Childs himself stresses, had the same vision of biblical study as part of the Church's theological task, rather than as an "antiquarian" pursuit. But in the form it now takes Childs's programme is certainly a new departure. Childs has not had many direct disciples, though one may think of G.T. Sheppard and Christopher Seitz among American scholars, and among British ones of Walter Moberly. The recent Festschrift for Childs, *Theological Exegesis*[5], bears witness to his influence on many other scholars too. But his whole approach has stimulated many who do not subscribe to it in full to ask questions about the Bible "as Scripture" in a new way, and it is now normal to read papers and books concentrating on the "final form" of the biblical text and treating the Bible as a whole in a way that would have been distinctly unusual thirty years ago. The whole ethos of current biblical studies, especially in North America, owes much to the new questions Childs has placed on the agenda.

II. MISUNDERSTANDINGS OF THE CANONICAL APPROACH

There are four points on which I believe Childs is sometimes misunderstood, and which could benefit from some clarification.

4. See J. BARTON, *Canon and Old Testament Interpretation*, in E. BALL (ed.), *In Search of True Wisdom: Essays in Old Testament Interpretation in Honour of Ronald E. Clements* (JSOT SS, 300), Sheffield, Academic Press, 1999, pp. 37-52.

5. C. SEITZ & K. GREENE-MCCREIGHT, *Theological Exegesis: Essays in Honor of Brevard S. Childs*, Grand Rapids, MI, Eerdmans, 1999.

1. The first matter is the interest of "canonical" interpreters in the "final form" of the biblical text. "Final form" exegesis is at present very much in the air because of the growing interest in literary study of the Bible. Literary critics tend in general to be uninterested in genetic questions, showing little concern for the sources underlying our present texts and not caring much about their cultural roots: they direct attention to the text as a finished artefact. Indeed, for literary critics of a more postmodern variety the whole question of the origins of texts is a matter of complete indifference, since what is interesting to them is the interplay between text and reader.

This creates a superficial resemblance to the canonical approach, which many have commented on[6]. In both cases we are urged to look at what lies before us on the page, not at what may (or may not) have preceded it in the text's long history of composition and transmission. But appearances deceive. When Childs talks of the "final form" of the text he does not mean the text as a unified aesthetic object, but (Barth-like) as the communication of the word of God. This communication may in some cases be aided by recognizing features of the history of the text: for example, the Deutero-Isaiah hypothesis is illuminating for faith, because it enables us to see that words once directed to a specific set of circumstances have been incorporated into a larger work (the book of Isaiah) and so set free to speak to all generations. The question is not: what does the final form mean as a literary unity?, but: what word of God is communicated through this passage? Since church and synagogue have canonized a particular form of the text, it must be through that form that theological insight is meant to be generated. It may well be illuminated in some ways by our knowing about the background of the text – historical, archaeological, text-critical, even source-critical – in some cases. But the essential point to hold on to is what our exegesis should be directed to: knowledge of God through Scripture. That aim can never be attained if we ignore the form in which the Bible has come down to us, as though the church had canonized 'J' or 'Proto-Isaiah'. Knowledge of the process that led up to canonization can certainly be illuminating, but only so long as it is recognized as *ancillary* to the theological task.

2. Secondly, some confusion has been generated by Childs's use of the word "canon". Though he speaks of "the canonical approach", his seminal book used the phrase "as Scripture" (*Introduction to the Old*

6. See my own comments in J. BARTON, *Reading the Old Testament: Method in Biblical Study*, London, Darton, Longman & Todd, 1984, [2]1996, pp. 100-103.

Testament as Scripture) rather than "as canon". In practice he often
seems to use the two terms interchangeably. This has led some to think
that he is interested in canon formation as a historical process, and produces objections based on that understanding – for example, that the
church and the synagogue canonized two different collections as Hebrew Scriptures and Old Testament respectively, or that the "canon" is
really a post-scriptural phenomenon[7]. If Childs is speaking of the canon
as the principle whereby the *exact* contents of the Bible are delineated
and defined, then it is not hard to show that his position lands him in
some odd conclusions. For example, it seems to commit him to exegesis
of the Bible as it existed in the second or third centuries AD, or even in
the eighth or ninth if the Masoretic Text is regarded as the authoritative
version of the canon: and why, people ask, should that be more determinative for modern Christians than the Bible as it existed in, say, the New
Testament period? Or again, why should we not be interested in the
process of canonization, as James Sanders is, arguing that there is something authoritative in each stage of the development that led to the final
form of Scripture[8].

But this is to misunderstand. In saying "canon" Childs does not primarily mean the Bible considered as an official list, but the Bible considered as the authoritative word for the church. That is, it is the *binding*
character of the canon he is concerned with, not its character as an authoritative *selection* of particular books. I have argued at some length
that much clarity could be gained if we agreed to distinguish sharply between these two concepts, using "scripture" for the first and "canon"
for the second, and I am quite sure that this is so[9]. But it is equally clear
that Childs does not use the two terms in that way, but in speaking of a
"canonical approach" intends what others might express by saying that
the Bible is meant to be read as "holy" or as "authoritative" or indeed
"as Scripture". To call the Bible "canon" for Childs is, I believe, another way of saying that it is Christians' sacred book. Of course it may
be slightly fuzzy at the edges, and I do not think that is a problem for
him, though as a rule of thumb he recommends that we should work

7. On this see especially J. BARR, *Holy Scripture: Canon, Authority, Criticism*, Oxford, University Press, 1983.
8. See J.A. SANDERS, *Torah and Canon*, Philadelphia, Fortress Press, 1972; ID., *From
Sacred Story to Sacred Text*, Philadelphia, PA, Fortress Press, 1987.
9. See J. BARTON, *Oracles of God: Perceptions of Ancient Prophecy in Israel after
the Exile*, London, Darton, Longman & Todd, 1984, pp. 55-82; ID., *The Spirit and the
Letter: Studies in the Biblical Canon*, London, SPCK, 1997, pp. 1-24 (the American edition is called *Holy Writings, Sacred Text: The Canon in Early Christianity*, Louisville,
KY, Westminster/John Knox).

with the Hebrew canon of the Masoretes. Far more important than any marginal disagreements about the exact content of the canon, however, is the fact that it is the church's scripture, and therefore not to be read "like any other book". Christians go to the Bible expecting to find in it the word of life: that is what Childs means by calling it "canonical". To me it seems a pity to have two terms, "scripture" and "canon", yet to use them as though they were complete synonyms. But my strong impression is that that is what Childs does, and that we understand his meaning best by glossing "canon", wherever it occurs, by "Holy Scripture".

3. Thirdly, from the beginning other scholars have referred to Childs's programme as "canonical criticism". He himself has always rejected this term, arguing that it tends to suggest that there is simply a progression from one kind of 'criticism' to another: source criticism, form criticism, redaction criticism, traditio-historical criticism, canonical criticism. On the contrary, the canonical approach is compatible with all these other "criticisms", provided they leave room for the overarching question about the text's authority as Scripture, but with none of them if they are presented as asking the only appropriate questions and seeing these as historical in character. The problem is that all the standard "criticisms", in Childs's view, have been absolutized. His own canonical approach is meant to raise a wholly fresh issue, and to ask the only question that really ought to be absolute for the Christian scholar: what does this text tell us of the God to whom Scripture bears witness? This question takes us completely outside the purview of historical criticism of any kind, and into a directly theological engagement with the text. Canonical criticism is thus a misleading, because relativizing term, which seeks to reduce his approach to merely the latest in a long line of methods when in reality it is an attempt to engage with the text at a wholly new level.

4. Fourthly, it is important not to confuse what Childs is advocating with the history of interpretation. Study of earlier interpreters has always been one of Childs's great strengths as a biblical scholar, and his commentary on Exodus[10] shows just how broad is his acquaintance with patristic and Reformation commentators. It established a new model for the commentary form. Not many scholars followed it at the time, but recently we have seen the history of interpretation (*Wirkungsgeschichte*)

10. B.S. CHILDS, *Exodus* (OTL), London, SCM, 1974.

moving to the top of the agenda for a number of biblical scholars. While it is true that the history of interpretation has come to dominate many of the humanities, within biblical studies Childs has surely been instrumental in raising its profile, and leading scholars to think that the quest for the "original meaning" is not the only worthy goal that a commentary might set itself. But the canonical approach is certainly not conceived as a history of biblical interpretation, even though it may use this history and give it a far more honoured place than it has traditionally occupied since the rise of biblical criticism. The canonical approach is focused on establishing what the text communicates of theological truth, and the reading of past interpreters is ancillary to that.

III. ANCIENT ROOTS OF THE CANONICAL APPROACH

But the history of interpretation *is* crucial for Childs in another aspect. His conviction is that so-called "pre-critical" interpreters read the Bible in a way much closer to his own canonical approach than has been usual since the rise of "critical" methods at the Enlightenment. The fact that the canonical approach is a novelty within modern biblical scholarship must not disguise its historic importance for most Bible-readers. What Childs is proposing, in his view, is not the invention of a new style of criticism but essentially a return to something that was taken more or less for granted until "historical critics" began to assume control of professional biblical studies in the seventeenth and eighteenth centuries. Most interpreters in all generations (including, in fact, our own, if by interpreter we mean "reader of the Bible") have gone to Scripture because they have expected to find there the word of life. They may or may not have been interested in how the Bible came to be, but they have certainly been interested in what it has to say – now. One could put it this way: seen from a foreshortened, modern perspective, "critical" biblical scholarship seems to dominate the landscape, and the canonical approach is a minor feature. But if we take a bird's eye view over the whole study of the Bible from ancient to modern times, biblical criticism represents a brief and unsatisfactory interlude in a long history of the reverent study of Scripture by believers seeking theological insight. The Fathers and the Reformers are thus not drawn on simply because they were important in the past, but because they are likely to show us the way back to a proper theological appropriation of the biblical text.

Childs's aim is thus not so much to invent a new mode of Bible study as to reconnect us all with an old one. In his eyes the canonical approach is ancient, rather than modern. To accept it is at once to rehabilitate the thousands of past interpreters conventionally dismissed as "pre-critical", as well as ordinary believers today who read the Bible not for the historical or literary information they can extract from it, nor out of an interest in the history of the text, but because they have a faith which is seeking understanding. Indeed, in a certain sense Childs is not only trying to bring back past modes of biblical study, but to re-validate what ordinary Christians do anyway when they study the Scriptures privately or in Bible-study groups. One reason why his approach has been influential well beyond the bounds of those who consciously adopt it as an academic programme is that it resonates with what so many non-academic Christians do when they open a Bible: they ask what it is saying to them in the here and now. It is not surprising that the canonical approach often appeals to people training for Christian ministry. They hear it as an academically respectable support for the kind of Bible study they want to do anyway, as part of the pastoral task of getting from the Bible insights applicable to the people to whom they are going to minister. The canonical approach makes the Bible profitable for the Christian reader, or better, it endorses the questions Christian readers tend to put to the Bible, such as: What must I do? What must I believe? What is God saying to me?

It is only in this sense that the canonical approach is committed to a "final form" reading of the biblical text. This is just as well, because with most biblical books older interpreters seldom practised the kind of "holistic" reading we have come to experience from modern literary critics. Many such critics have great respect for patristic or rabbinic commentators (the use of rabbinic interpretation is specially noticeable in the work of Robert Alter[11] and Gabriel Josipovici[12]), but they seem generally not to notice that rabbinic commentary is seldom holistic in their sense. The rabbis treat biblical books as wholes in the sense that they do not divide them up into sources, but they hardly ever pay attention to them as finished "works": rather, they treat them as collections of individual verses, any one of which can be interpreted in isolation. That is already how St Paul treats the Old Testament text. The Fathers are more varied in this respect, and many patristic commentaries do attend to the overall shape of biblical books; but even so, it is not uncommon for them to treat individual sayings as *dicta probantia* in a way that rides roughshod over the integrity of the book containing them. And one

11. See R. ALTER, *The Art of Biblical Narrative*, London, George Allen & Unwin, 1981.
12. See G. JOSIPOVICI, *The Book of God*, New Haven - London, Yale University Press, 1988.

might say the same of the Reformers. "Final form" exegesis as now practised is not all that much like the commentaries of the past. But, as we have seen, Childs is not committed to a final form reading in that sense of the term, with a premium set on seeing the book as an aesthetic whole or "work". What he sees as a whole is the Bible in its complete form, and there he is certainly at one with many earlier interpreters.

The canonical approach treats the Bible as unlike any other book, as a text to be read with quite different questions from those we put to other ancient (or modern) texts. And in that it is certainly at one with much "pre-critical" exegesis, and with modern "non-critical" reading by ordinary Christians. Like them, it works with the principle that the meaning that can correctly be found in this book is always a meaning compatible with its status as Holy Scripture: an edifying meaning, a "confessional" meaning, a worthy meaning, a consistent meaning. Scripture is special. Different criteria of meaning, truth, and consistency apply in reading Scripture from those we regularly employ in reading other books. To put it in more technical vocabulary, there is a "special hermeneutic" applicable in reading the Bible which is distinct from the "general hermeneutic" that applies to all other texts.

What this approach produces is an account of the meaning of biblical books which is holistic, not in the sense of treating each of them as a coherent "work", but in the sense that the whole Bible is felt to have a single overall "message" or thrust. Childs is at one with the Fathers and the Reformers in this way of thinking about the Bible. How is this overall message to be established? In the case of the Fathers it may be provided by the "rule of faith", a basic quasi-credal outline of Christian belief; for Reformation commentaries, it is sometimes derived from a Confession. In either case, of course, the writers in question would themselves have claimed that it derived from the very Scriptures for which it then provided the proper interpretative framework! Childs does not overtly begin from a confessional account of Christian truth, but seeks to derive the coherence of the biblical message from within the Bible itself: but he can only do so, of course, because he has a commitment to the Bible's internal integrity and truth-filled character, and that commitment itself necessarily derives from a confessional point of view – which is in fact broadly a Reformed one. When he begins to outline the message of the Bible taken as a whole, in *Biblical Theology of the Old and New Testaments*[13], the generally Reformed character of the enterprise becomes even more apparent. This is the strength of the project,

---

13. B.S. CHILDS, *Biblical Theology of the Old and New Testaments: Theological Reflection on the Christian Bible*, London, SCM, 1992.

but also its weakness, for how could the canonical approach be applied by Christians with a different conception of the relationship between Scripture and belief – Catholics or Lutherans, for example?

But leaving that question aside, we may certainly say that something like the canonical approach can be encountered in many past ways of conceptualizing the essential meaning of the Bible. All of Scripture was thought to contribute to a single coherent message. For the Fathers, applying to Scripture the "rule of faith", the biblical material was interpreted as being about four things: creation, fall, the coming of Christ, and the final consummation[14]. Everything had to be fitted into this framework, and all the individual books were to be read as illustrations or exemplifications of some part of this pattern of belief. The sufferings of Job made sense as part of the Bible because they prefigured those of Christ; the sinful backslidings of Israel in Kings illustrated the fallenness of humankind; the prophets foretold the final consummation. In this way all the disparate parts of the Bible could be made to cohere with each other in a harmonious whole. The fact that the ideas of creation and fall, for example, were not present in some parts of the scriptural record did not matter, because they were there in the Bible taken in its "final form" and could quite properly be read from one book into another. The Bible as a finished whole bore an even and steady witness to these major themes, and to read bits of it as though one were unaware of the themes would have been to read it against the grain.

As Childs says when speaking of the covenant idea in the Old Testament (and I take this example as typical of many), "there is a basic hermeneutical issue at stake ... On the one hand, it is evident from critical research that Israel's religion underwent a history of development. Its pre-exilic form differs from its post-exilic, and Deuteronomic theology is also distinct from that of Isaiah's [*sic*] ... On the other hand, it is equally evident that the compilers of the Old Testament did not collect and order their material from the perspective of modern critical scholarship. Rather, the Hebrew scriptures were formed and structured for predominantly theological concerns"[15]. Historical reading may thus validly point to elements of change and development, and may find a theme present in one book but lacking in another; but a canonical reading will look to the finished product, and seek to find an overarching meaning to which all the parts contribute. That would also have been a common

---

14. This way of putting the matter depends on the illuminating work of R. KENDALL SOULEN, *The God of Israel and Christian Theology*, Minneapolis, MN, Fortress Press, 1996.

15. CHILDS, *Biblical Theology of the Old and New Testaments* (n. 13), p. 415.

patristic or Reformation understanding, I believe; it is also the normal rabbinic position. Childs thus shows what ancient credentials his canonical approach can claim.

My intention so far has been to try to clarify what is meant by the canonical approach, and to present it so far as possible in terms that I hope Childs and its other proponents would accept. It seems to me that the canonical approach is a proposal about how Christians should read the Bible within the context of faith. As such it is in a way insulated from critical enquiry. So far as "canonical" readers are concerned, the truth about the historical development and original context of biblical texts is interesting (or may be so), but it has nothing to contribute to a Christian reading (or "construal", to use a favourite term of Childs) of the Bible. The canonical approach, though it is about the Bible, does not belong to biblical studies in the sense commonly accepted nowadays, but to systematic or constructive theology: it is a theory about how we should *use* the Bible in seeking to deepen and ground faith. As such it is a theory that biblical critics need have no quarrel with, so long as it is not used as an instrument for opposing their work or for suggesting that it is illegitimate: Childs himself generally avoids this, though not all of his followers do so. But of course there is built into the canonical approach, as into any new programme, the implication that it is a better use of the theologian's time than other pursuits – among them above all "historical criticism", which is felt not to have contributed much to a religiously fruitful understanding of Scripture. Historical criticism is legitimate but largely useless: that is the message that most people get from exponents of canonical criticism. Or, if it does have some use, its usefulness is small enough to be out of all proportion to the amount of time traditionally spent on it in theological education and scholarship!

My purpose in this paper has been not to criticise the canonical approach, but to describe it, and to identify its roots. In the process I have argued that Childs is quite correct in claiming that it represents a return to pre-critical exegesis: not in the sense that we should use the methods of pre-critical interpreters (he is not hospitable to allegorization, for example), but in the sense that like them we should approach the text of the Bible as a finished whole and look for religious edification in it as it stands. "Critical" analysis is not illegitimate, but it is not productive spiritually (it is *unergiebig*, as one would say in German). The "canonical" interpreter is like the Fathers or the Reformers in seeking what is religiously edifying in the biblical text and in looking for coherence, depth, consistency, and spiritual truth there: that, indeed, is what is meant by calling it "scripture" or, in Childs's use of the term, "canon".

The question that remains on the table, of course, is whether it is really a good idea to go back to the interpretative concerns of the classic commentators of the patristic or Reformation periods. Granted that that is indeed what Childs is seeking to do, is he correct in thinking that it will make the Bible "come alive" again for modern readers? I have raised critical doubts about the canonical approach in other places, and will not repeat them here[16]. In the present paper I will say only this. To practise "canonical" exegesis of the Bible before the questions characteristic of "critical" scholarship had been raised was not the same thing as it is to practise it now that they have. Biblical criticism is not in the end concerned merely with questions of "Introduction" – date, place of writing, authorship – as Childs sometimes appears to suggest. It is concerned with a systematic attempt to discover whether the Bible does indeed say what the tradition (as encapsulated, for example, in the patristic "rule of faith", the creeds, the Reformation confessions) claims that it says, by applying the normal criteria we apply to all texts in trying to discover their meaning. It dethrones the "special" hermeneutic that traditional reading reserved for biblical texts, and applies instead a general hermeneutic such as one would use in reading anything else. It is exceedingly doubtful whether this genie can be pushed back into the bottle once it has emerged. Much more than the mere assertion that we need to "get back behind" biblical criticism is called for if the canonical approach is to be established on a firm foundation: nothing less than a complete change in mental perspective. Childs is well aware that this is what he is calling for; it is important that it should be generally recognized that this is how far-reaching a change the canonical approach requires.

Oriel College   John BARTON
Oxford OX1 4EW
United Kingdom

16. See BARTON, *Reading the Old Testament* (n. 6), pp. 89-103.

OFFERED PAPERS

UNE ÉTAPE MAJEURE DANS LA FORMATION
DU CANON DES ÉCRITURES
L'ŒUVRE DEUTÉRONOMISTE

L'histoire de la formation de la Bible hébraïque est assurément longue et complexe. La décision de la communauté croyante d'attribuer à un corps littéraire bien délimité une autorité normative[1], d'en faire son «Écriture sainte», n'a été possible qu'au terme d'un long processus de maturation, dont nous ne pouvons connaître tous les détours[2]. Assez souvent, les spécialistes font commencer cette histoire à l'époque d'Esdras-Néhémie[3]. Au cours de cette brève communication, je voudrais montrer comment l'œuvre littéraire de l'école deutéronomiste du VIᵉ siècle avant notre ère marque à cet égard un premier seuil d'importance décisive.

Je développerai ma réflexion en quatre parties. Je commencerai par rappeler ce qu'on peut dire de la littérature israélite à la fin de l'époque royale. Ensuite, j'expliquerai pourquoi on peut parler de l'œuvre deutéronomiste comme d'un «canon avant la lettre». Dans une troisième partie, je tenterai de discerner pourquoi cette entreprise était utile et nécessaire à ce moment-là de l'histoire d'Israël. J'esquisserai enfin une hypothèse sur la destinée ultérieure de ce premier canon.

---

1. C'est au moins une définition possible du canon. Pour d'autres définitions, voir B.J. DIEBNER, *Entre Israël et Israël, le canon*, in O. ABEL & F. SMYTH-FLORENTIN (eds.), *Le livre de traverse. De l'exégèse biblique à l'anthropologie* (Patrimoines), Paris, Cerf, 1992, pp. 101-112.

2. La bibliographie est immense. Parmi les propositions multiples sur l'histoire du canon, voir notamment D.N. FREEDMAN, *The Formation of the Canon of the Old Testament. The Selection and Identification of the Torah as the Supreme Authority of the Postexilic Community*, in E.B. FIRMANCE *et al.* (eds.), *Religion and Law: Biblical-Judaic and Islamic Perspective*, Winona Lake, IN, Eisenbrauns, 1990, pp. 315-331; J. TRUBLET, *Constitution et clôture du canon hébraïque*, in Ch. THÉOBALD (ed.), *Le Canon des Écritures. Études historiques, exégétiques et systématiques* (Lectio Divina, 140), Paris, Cerf, 1991, pp. 77-187; J.W. MILLER, *The Origins of the Bible. Rethinking Canon History*, New York, 1994; D.M. CARR, *Canonization in the Context of Community: An Outline of the Formation of the Tanakh and the Christian Bible*, in R.D. WEIS & D.M. CARR (eds.), *A Gift of God in Due Season*. FS J.A. Sanders (JSOT SS, 225), Sheffield, Academic Press, 1996, pp. 22-64; J. TREBOLLE BARRERA, *The Jewish Bible and the Christian Bible. An Introduction to the History of the Bible*, Grand Rapids, MI, Eerdmans; Leiden, Brill, 1997, pp. 156-167.

3. Ainsi, TRUBLET, *Constitution et clôture du canon hébraïque* (n. 2), pp. 79-85.

1. *La littérature israélite à la fin de l'époque royale*

Le temps n'est plus où l'on croyait pouvoir reconstituer avec assurance une histoire de la littérature israélite à l'époque royale. Qu'il s'agisse de la formation du Pentateuque, de l'«histoire deutéronomiste» ou des recueils prophétiques, les évidences anciennes sont soumises au feu de la critique, et les discussions portent sur des questions essentielles. Il me paraît cependant possible de s'accorder sur un état global de la littérature israélite à la fin de la période royale.

Dressons d'abord un rapide inventaire: quels sont les écrits dont on peut raisonnablement penser qu'ils remontent, sous une forme ou sous une autre, à l'époque de la monarchie? À la veille de la catastrophe qui frappera Jérusalem en 587, il devait exister:

- des recueils législatifs promulgués par l'autorité politique: les noyaux du *Bundesbuch* (Ex 21–23*) et du Deutéronome (Dt 12–26*), édicté par Josias;
- des recueils d'oracles prophétiques (noyaux du Proto-Isaïe, d'Osée, d'Amos, de Michée);
- des recueils de proverbes (collections «salomoniennes» de Pr 10–29*);
- des récits sur les origines de la monarchie (Saül, David, Salomon), qui formaient peut-être déjà une large fresque (de 1 S 1 à 1 R 11*)[4];
- des récits qui formeront plus tard le squelette des livres de la Genèse et de l'Exode, même si l'on peut discuter de leur teneur[5];
- sans doute aussi d'autres récits sur l'histoire d'Israël, qui racontent en particulier la prise de possession de la terre promise (éléments du livre de Josué), l'époque pré-monarchique (éléments du livre des Juges) et l'histoire du prophète Élisée.

À cette liste, il faut vraisemblablement ajouter des psaumes (mais étaient-ils déjà consignés par écrit?) et des pièces d'archives qui seront exploitées plus tard par l'historien deutéronomiste; de même, on peut imaginer que certains matériaux aujourd'hui inclus dans le Lévitique formaient déjà un embryon de loi cultuelle, et il faut compter avec l'existence d'écrits aujourd'hui perdus[6]. Quoi qu'il en soit, les diffé-

---

4. Je me permets de renvoyer à mon livre *La loi du plus fort. Histoire de la rédaction des récits davidiques, de 1 Samuel 8 à 1 Rois 2* (BETL, 154), Leuven, University Press - Peeters, 2000.

5. Faut-il encore parler d'un «document J», éventuellement complété par des éléments de type E? Les récits des Origines, des Patriarches, de la sortie d'Égypte et du Sinaï étaient-ils indépendants? Quels liens ces récits avaient-ils avec l'histoire de Josué? Je ne puis entrer ici dans la discussion.

6. Nb 21,14 fait référence à un «Livre des Guerres de YHWH»; il est aussi question d'un «Livre du Juste» (Jos 10,13; 2 S 1,18), d'un «Livre de l'Histoire de Salomon»

rents recueils dont nous avons connaissance étaient indépendants les uns des autres, et ils ne disposaient pas tous du même type d'autorité.

a. Les recueils de lois formaient la législation imposée par le pouvoir royal, lui-même longtemps soumis à la tutelle assyrienne, puis à celle de Babylone. Les lois formaient la règle qui s'imposait à tous pour la vie sociale et bénéficiaient évidemment de l'autorité royale. Bien plus, comme dans tout le Proche-Orient, elles étaient censées exprimer la pensée divine. La dimension religieuse est d'ailleurs explicite dans l'*Ur-Deuteronomium*, qui accorde une place importante à la centralisation du culte[7].

b. D'autres livrets devaient avoir un statut officiel ou quasi-officiel. Je songe en particulier aux récits concernant les origines de la monarchie, qui exposent les fondements idéologiques du pouvoir. Peut-être faut-il en dire autant des autres écrits historiques, et notamment de ceux qui concernent les origines de l'humanité, les patriarches et les événements du temps de Moïse et Josué. Ces derniers écrits étaient importants comme expressions de la conscience nationale.

c. Les recueils d'oracles prophétiques, en revanche, formaient une littérature «privée». Les grands prophètes ayant critiqué – parfois d'une manière acerbe – la politique royale, il n'est pas imaginable que leurs oracles aient été diffusés par l'autorité politique, et encore moins qu'ils aient reçu un statut officiel. Leur autorité n'est pas imposée par le pouvoir en place, mais elle est liée au prestige de telle ou telle figure prophétique.

d. Le statut des recueils de proverbes est moins clair. Les analogies avec les écrits égyptiens donnent cependant à penser que ces recueils ont servi à l'éducation des fonctionnaires de la cour. Ce seraient ainsi des livrets destinés à l'usage d'un groupe particulier.

À la veille de 587, il existait donc sans doute à Jérusalem un ensemble de textes indépendants les uns des autres. Certains étaient revêtus de l'autorité officielle et s'imposaient à l'ensemble de la population; ils se distinguaient cependant les uns des autres par leurs genres littéraires.

(1 R 11,41), d'un «Livre des Annales des rois d'Israël» (1 R 14,19; 15,31; 16,5, etc.) et d'un «Livre des Annales des Rois de Juda» (1 R 14,29; 15,7.23; etc.). «Peut-être n'avons-nous en réalité que 10 % de ce qu'on pouvait lire à l'ombre du Temple durant la grande époque de la théologie royale pré-exilique», écrit J.A. SANDERS, *Identité de la Bible. Torah et Canon* (Lectio Divina, 87), Paris, Cerf, 1975, p. 19. Mais comment le savoir?

7. Cet élément, qui a pu être inséré par Josias lui-même, a par ailleurs une portée politique évidente.

D'autres écrits provenaient de groupes particuliers, et leur autorité était plutôt de type moral. Rien n'indique que ces différents éléments étaient reliés les uns aux autres. En d'autres termes, cette littérature ne constitue pas encore ce que nous pourrions appeler un «canon».

2. *L'œuvre deutéronomiste: un canon des Écritures avant la lettre*[8]

De la littérature hétéroclite dont il est question plus haut, l'école deutéronomiste du temps de l'Exil va faire un ensemble cohérent. Je sais que la littérature dite «deutéronomiste» fait aujourd'hui l'objet de débats particulièrement animés[9] et que plusieurs auteurs[10] réagissent contre ce qu'ils appellent le «pan-deutéronomisme». Il me semble pourtant raisonnable d'admettre que les différents livrets écrits à l'époque royale ont été interprétés et réédités dans le contexte du grand malheur de Jérusalem avec une perspective largement commune. Chaque fois, il s'agissait de réfléchir aux raisons pour lesquelles le malheur s'était abattu sur Juda et, en particulier, pourquoi ses élites avaient été déportées.

Commençons, encore une fois, par établir un inventaire des textes concernés, en notant comment ils sont utilisés. Cette fois, on peut parler de trois blocs.

---

8. Voir déjà D.N. FREEDMAN, *The Earliest Bible*, in M.P. O'CONNOR & D.N. FREEDMAN (eds.), *Backgrounds of the Bible*, Winona Lake, IN, Eisenbrauns, 1987, pp. 29-37; J. BLENKINSOPP, *The Pentateuch. An Introduction to the First Five Books of the Bible*, London, SCM, 1992, pp. 233-237; Th. RÖMER, *L'école deutéronomiste et la formation de la Bible hébraïque*, in ID. (ed.), *The Future of Deuteronomistic History* (BETL, 147), Leuven, University Press - Peeters, 2000, pp. 179-193. Freedman considère que la «Bible» éditée à l'époque exilique contient un texte très proche de l'ensemble Genèse-Rois (y compris les textes P) et des recueils prophétiques (y compris Ézéchiel) dans la Bible hébraïque actuelle. Ma position se rapproche davantage de celle de Römer; elle s'en distingue cependant sur deux points au moins: je ne suis pas convaincu par la localisation de l'école deutéronomiste à Babylone, et je pense qu'il faut distinguer deux, sinon trois rédactions Dtr successives à l'époque exilique, ce qui permet d'ailleurs d'expliquer certaines incohérences entre les textes. S.B. CHAPMAN, *The Law and the Prophets. A Study in Old Testament Canon Formation* (FAT, 27), Tübingen, Mohr Siebeck, 2000, parle d'un «canon deutéronomiste», mais les hypothèses qu'il propose n'ont pas grand chose en commun avec les miennes.

9. Voir par exemple les diverses contributions rassemblées dans RÖMER (ed.), *The Future of Deuteronomistic History* (n. 8).

10. Voir notamment R.R. WILSON, *Who Was the Deuteronomist? (Who Was Not the Deuteronomist?): Reflexions on Pan-Deuteronomism*, in L.S. SCHEARING & S.L. MCKENZIE (eds.), *Those Elusive Deuteronomists. The Phenomenon of Pan-Deuteronomism* (JSOT SS, 268), Sheffield, Academic Press, 1999, pp. 67-82, et l'ensemble de cet ouvrage.

a. Le Tétrateuque (en fait la Genèse, l'Exode et les Nombres). Qu'il ait existé ou non un document J plus ancien, nous avons à présent une vaste fresque qui va des origines de l'humanité à l'histoire de Moïse et qui inclut le *Bundesbuch*[11]. Chaque fois que la chose est possible, le récit montre la justice divine et oriente le lecteur vers la cause du grand malheur: l'infidélité à l'Alliance[12].

b. L'«Histoire deutéronomiste», du Deutéronome au second livre des Rois[13]. L'auteur s'est servi de divers documents plus anciens, dont le Deutéronome primitif, les récits sur la prise de possession de la terre promise et les débuts de la royauté, l'histoire d'Élisée et des documents d'archives. À nouveau, le récit expose l'engagement solennel de tout Israël dans l'Alliance, puis la succession des infidélités du peuple et du roi. Les notices des règnes donnent pour chacun d'entre eux un jugement à l'aune de l'attitude par rapport à la Loi d'Alliance et, en particulier, de l'interdit de l'idolâtrie. On trouve ce qui sonne

11. La perspective d'une composition deutéronomiste de ce qui deviendra plus tard le Pentateuque est aujourd'hui proposée, sous diverses formes, par de nombreux auteurs. C'est par exemple le «J tardif» de H.H. SCHMID, *Der sogenannte Jahwist. Beobachtungen und Fragen zur Pentateuchforschung*, Zürich, Theologische Verlag, 1976; c'est aussi la «composition D» de E. BLUM, *Studien zur Komposition des Pentateuch* (BZAW, 189), Berlin - New York, de Gruyter, 1990. Voir aussi J. BLENKINSOPP, *Deuteronomic Contribution to the Narrative in Genesis-Numbers: A Test Case*, in SCHEARING - MCKENZIE (eds.), *Those Elusive Deuteronomists* (n. 10), pp. 84-115.

12. Prenons trois exemples. Comme ses homologues mésopotamiens, le récit ancien du Déluge ne motivait guère la décision divine de détruire la terre. Dtr explique que tous les hommes commettaient sans cesse le mal (Gn 6,5-6); la catastrophe ne frappe donc que des coupables, et YHWH agit selon la stricte justice. De même, Dtr motive la destruction de Sodome et Gomorrhe (image du malheur de Jérusalem) par le péché de toute la population sans exception, «depuis les jeunes jusqu'aux vieux» (Gn 19,4); non seulement YHWH est juste (les innocents échapperont au feu du ciel), mais il était prêt à pardonner si la ville renfermait dix justes (18,22-32). Enfin, l'histoire du veau d'or (Gn 32) apparaît comme un paradigme: aussitôt après s'être engagé à observer la Loi d'Alliance (Ex 24,3-8), Israël la transgresse d'une manière caractérisée; YHWH pardonne, et il le fera encore bien souvent, jusqu'au jour où il devra se résoudre à punir le peuple coupable (cf. 34,6-7). Sur l'histoire du veau d'or et ses rédactions successives, voir J. VERMEYLEN, *L'affaire du veau d'or (Ex 32–34). Une clé pour la «question deutéronomiste»?*, in ZAW 97 (1985) 1-23.

13. Déjà M. NOTH, *Überlieferungsgeschichtliche Studien I*, Halle, 1943, considérait Dt 1–3 comme l'introduction primitive de l'Histoire deutéronomiste; pour la discussion de la question, voir H.D. PREUSS, *Deuteronomium* (EdF, 164), Darmstadt, Wissenschaftliche Buchgesellschaft, 1982, pp. 75-84. H.-Ch. SCHMITT, *Das spätdeuteronomistische Geschichtswerk Genesis I–II Regum XXV und seine theologische Intention*, in J.A. EMERTON (ed.), *Congress Volume Cambridge 1995* (SVT, 66), Leiden, Brill, 1997, pp. 261-279, croit pouvoir reconnaître une même strate littéraire deutéronomiste tardive dans le Tétrateuque et dans l'ensemble Deutéronome-Rois; il parle d'une seule grande œuvre littéraire. En fait, ce «Dtr tardif» serait postérieur à P, et certains passages seraient caractérisés par le mélange de conceptions P et Dtr.

comme une conclusion générale en 2 R 24,20a («Oui, par la colère de YHWH cela arriva à Jérusalem et à Juda, jusqu'à ce qu'il les chasse de devant sa face») et 25,21b («Et Juda fut déporté de sur sa terre»).

c. Les recueils d'oracles prophétiques. Le cas le plus évident est celui du livre de Jérémie[14]. Il faut y joindre au moins ceux d'Osée[15], d'Amos[16] et de Michée[17]. Malgré les objections formulées en particulier

14. C'est aujourd'hui l'opinion commune. Voir, parmi d'autres publications, W. THIEL, *Die deuteronomistische Redaktion von Jeremia 1–25* (WMANT, 41), Neukirchen-Vluyn, Neukirchener Verlag, 1973; ID., *Die deuteronomistische Redaktion von Jeremia 26–45* (WMANT, 52), Neukirchen-Vluyn, Neukirchener Verlag, 1981. Quelques auteurs ont cru pouvoir opposer l'histoire deutéronomiste et la rédaction de Jérémie généralement attribuée à la même école deutéronomiste; voir encore tout récemment R. ALBERTZ, *In Search of the Deuteronomists*, in RÖMER (ed.), *The Future of the Deuteronomistic History* (n. 8), pp. 1-17. L'enquête menée par Th. RÖMER, *Y a-t-il une rédaction deutéronomiste dans le livre de Jérémie?*, in A. DE PURY *et al.* (eds.), *Israël construit son histoire. L'his-toriographie deutéronomiste à la lumière des recherches récentes* (Le Monde de la Bi-ble), Genève, Labor et Fides, 1996, pp. 419-441, conduit à conclure: «Il n'y a pas de différence idéologique entre HD et Jr dtr» (p. 436). Voir aussi Th. RÖMER, «La conver-sion du prophète Jérémie à la théologie deutéronomiste», in A.H.W. CURTIS & Th. RÖ-MER (eds.), *The Book of Jeremiah and Its Reception – Le livre de Jérémie et sa réception* (BETL, 128), Leuven, University Press - Peeters, 1997, pp. 27-50. Tant pour l'ensemble Deutéronome-Rois que pour le livre de Jérémie, il faut compter avec plus d'une rédaction Dtr.

15. Les affinités entre le livre d'Osée et le Deutéronome sont bien connues. On a sou-vent parlé d'une influence d'Osée sur l'école deutéronomiste. Mais le livre d'Osée lui-même n'a-t-il pas connu une édition deutéronomiste, qui expliquerait une part au moins de ces affinités? À ma connaissance, cette question n'a pas encore fait l'objet d'une recherche systématique. L'intervention d'un rédacteur deutéronomiste a cependant été reconnue ici et là. Voir par exemple B. RENAUD, *Le livret d'Osée 1–3. Un travail com-plexe d'édition*, in *Revue des Sciences Religieuses* 56 (1982) 159-178, spéc. pp. 169-171; M. NISSINEN, *Prophetie, Redaktion und Fortschreibung im Hoseabuch. Studien zum Werdegang eines Prophetenbuches im Lichte von Hos 4 und 11* (AOAT, 231), Kevelaer, Butzon und Bercker; Neukirchen-Vluyn, Neukirchener Verlag, 1991; J. VERMEYLEN, *Osée 1 et les prophètes du VIIIe siècle*, in R.G. KRATZ et al. (eds.), *Schriftauslegung in der Schrift. FS O.H. Steck* (BZAW, 300), Berlin - New York, de Gruyter, 2000, pp. 193-206. D'autres auteurs parlent d'une «édition exilique», sans mentionner explicitement l'école deutéronomiste.

16. Cf. W.H. SCHMIDT, *Die deuteronomistische Redaktion des Amosbuches*, in *ZAW* 77 (1965) 168-193; M. ALVAREZ BARREDO, *Relecturas deuteronomisticas de Amos*, diss. Urbaniana, Roma, 1993; J. JEREMIAS, *Der Prophet Amos* (ATD, 24/2), Göttingen, Vandenhoeck und Ruprecht, 1995, p. xxi.

17. Cf. B. RENAUD, *La formation du livre de Michée* (Études bibliques), Paris, Ga-balda, 1977, pp. 387-399; S.L. COOK, «Micah's Deuteronomistic Redaction and the Deuteronomists' Identity», in SCHEARING & MCKENZIE (eds.), *Those Elusive Deutero-nomists* (n. 10), pp. 216-231. J. NOGALSKI, *Literary Precursors to the Book of the Twelve* (BZAW, 217), Berlin - New York, de Gruyter, 1993, et ID., *Redactional Processes in the Book of the Twelve* (BZAW, 218), Berlin - New York, de Gruyter, 1993, pp. 274-275, parlent d'un corpus littéraire deutéronomiste comprenant les livres d'Osée, d'Amos, de Michée et de Sophonie.

par Ch. Brekelmans[18], je crois pouvoir maintenir que le livre d'Isaïe est marqué, lui aussi, par une rédaction deutéronomiste[19].

Si cet inventaire est exact, l'école deutéronomiste a réédité l'ensemble de la littérature publique connue à son époque, à la seule exception possible des collections de proverbes, dont nous avons vu que l'usage était sans doute destiné à un groupe particulier. De là à penser que ce groupe avait l'intention de faire paraître un ensemble «complet»[20], une interprétation globale et cohérente de toutes les traditions israélites, il n'y a qu'un pas[21].

Il faut aller plus loin: les trois grands blocs de la littérature deutéronomiste ne sont pas isolés les uns des autres, mais ils forment un seul corps littéraire, où tout est interconnecté[22]. Non seulement on trouve partout la même théologie de l'Alliance et le même souci apologétique, mais il faut aussi noter des «références croisées» ou, plus exactement, des textes qui font système, alors qu'ils appartiennent à des ensembles littéraires distincts.

a. Il y a correspondance entre l'Exode (Décalogue + *Bundesbuch*, lois d'application pour le temps de la marche au désert avec Moïse) et le Deutéronome (Décalogue + législation des chap. 12–26, lois d'application pour le temps de Josué). Il existe une loi pour les pères, qui mourront au désert, et une autre loi pour les fils, qui entreront dans la terre promise. Une génération manquera de confiance, l'autre pas.

b. Jr 36, qui forme le sommet d'une série de récits sur la persécution du prophète (19,1–20,6; 26; 36; 37–43), correspond par antithèse au ré-

---

18. C. BREKELMANS, *Deuteronomistic Influence in Isaiah 1–12*, in J. VERMEYLEN (ed.), *The Book of Isaiah – Le livre d'Isaïe* (BETL, 81), Leuven, University Press - Peeters, 1989, pp. 167-176; voir aussi L. PERLITT, *Jesaja und die Deuteronomisten*, in V. FRITZ *et al.* (eds.), *Prophet und Prophetenbuch*. FS O. Kaiser (BZAW, 185), Berlin - New York, de Gruyter, 1989, pp. 133-149; = ID., *Deuteronomium-Studien* (FAT, 8), Tübingen, Mohr, 1994, pp. 157-171.

19. J. VERMEYLEN, *Du prophète Isaïe à l'apocalyptique*, 2 vol. (EB), Paris, Gabalda, 1977-1978; O. KAISER, *Der Prophet Jesaja. Kapitel 1–12* (ATD, 17), 5ᵉ éd., Göttingen, Vandenhoeck und Ruprecht, 1981; ID., *Der Prophet Jesaja Kapitel 13–39* (ATD, 18), Göttingen, Vandenhoeck und Ruprecht, ³1983. Voir aussi T. COLLINS, *The Mantle of Elijah. The Redaction Criticism of the Prophetical Books* (The Biblical Seminar), Sheffield, Academic Press, 1993, pp. 39-40.

20. Cette intention serait cohérente avec l'insistance de Dtr sur la présence de «tous» les Israélites, qui se sont engagés sur «toute» la Loi d'Alliance; cf. Ex 24,3-8; Jos 24,1-28.

21. Cette volonté de synthèse correspond à la rédaction de «résumés historiques» comme Dt 6,20-25; 26,5-9; Jos 24,2-13.

22. Pour plus détails et l'argumentation, voir J. VERMEYLEN, *L'école deutéronomiste aurait-elle imaginé un premier canon des Écritures?*, in RÖMER (ed.), *The Future of Deuteronomistic History* (n. 8), pp. 223-240. Je ne puis ici que donner un très bref résumé.

cit de 2 R 22[23]. Lorsqu'il prend connaissance du rouleau de la Loi, Josias a déchiré ses vêtements, il a fait appel à une prophétesse et il a mis la Tôrah en pratique; son fils Jojaqim, en revanche, déchire et brûle le rouleau des paroles de Jérémie, et il veut s'emparer du prophète. La fidélité du père s'oppose à l'infidélité du fils.

c. De même, il y a opposition entre l'attitude d'Achaz (Is 7) et celle de son fils Ézéchias (Is 36–37 ou 2 R 18–19)[24], dans des circonstances semblables et dans le même lieu. Là où le père refuse la parole du prophète, le fils la sollicite. Les liens entre ces textes et l'ensemble 2 R 22 / Jr 36 sont multiples[25].

Ces interconnexions renforcent d'une manière considérable la cohérence de la littérature éditée par l'école deutéronomiste: ce ne sont pas seulement des livres juxtaposés, mais un seul ensemble complexe, chaque partie majeure renvoyant aux autres.

De quelle autorité cette œuvre immense pouvait-elle se prévaloir? On peut écarter d'emblée deux hypothèses. Même si l'école deutéronomiste a pu commencer à travailler sous Sédécias (cf. la «conclusion» fournie par 2 R 24,20a et 25,21b), elle n'avait pas la caution du roi, car Dtr porte sur les souverains d'Israël et de Juda un regard critique et même souvent un regard de condamnation. Ce travail n'était pas non plus commandité par le sacerdoce car, dans l'ensemble, les prêtres et les préoccupations sacerdotales n'y sont guère à l'honneur[26]. En revanche, Dtr est l'héritier de la prédication des grands prophètes, dont en particulier Jérémie[27], et il accorde une grande place au prophétisme: non seulement il réédite des recueils d'oracles, mais il fait de Moïse le prophète par excellence (cf. Dt 18,18-22) et met en valeur les récits concernant les prophètes[28]. Isaïe, Michée et Jérémie avaient annoncé le malheur de Jérusalem, s'attirant

---

23. Des analogies profondes entre Jr 36 et Jon 3 peuvent également être relevées, mais elles ne peuvent intervenir ici, car le livre de Jonas est plus récent (époque perse ou, plus probablement, époque hellénistique).

24. Contrairement à l'opinion classique, je pense qu'Is 36–37 forme le texte primitif par rapport à 2 R 18–19. En outre, je considère que le récit «B1» (Is 36,2–37,9a.38*) est d'origine deutéronomiste. Sur tout cela, voir J. VERMEYLEN, Hypothèses sur l'origine d'Isaïe 36–39, in J. VAN RUITEN & M. VERVENNE (eds.), Studies in the Book of Isaiah. FS W.A.M. Beuken (BETL, 132), Leuven, University Press - Peeters, 1997, pp. 95-118.

25. J. VERMEYLEN, L'école deutéronomiste (n. 22), pp. 230-235.

26. Le contraste avec les textes P (qu'il faille parler ici d'un document ou d'un travail de relecture de documents antérieurs) est éloquent!

27. Voir H.W. WOLFF, Das Kerygma des Deuteronomistischen Geschichtswerkes, in ID., Gesammelte Studien (TB, 22), München, Kaiser, pp. 308-324, spéc. p. 323.

28. Ainsi, il accorde une place essentielle à Élie. La tendance est générale; cf. W. DIETRICH, Prophetie im deuteronomistischen Geschichtswerk, in RÖMER (ed.), The Future of the Deuteronomistic History (n. 8), pp. 47-65; J. VERMEYLEN, La loi du plus fort (n. 4), spéc. pp. 646-648.

les moqueries de leurs adversaires. Mais ce qu'ils avaient dit s'était révélé tragiquement exact: ils avaient eu raison! L'œuvre Dtr, qui interprète les écrits et les traditions antérieures à la lumière de leur prédication, bénéficiait sans doute de l'autorité prophétique. C'est une autorité «morale», qui s'impose à la conscience, et non une autorité qui tient à l'exercice du pouvoir et repose en définitive sur la contrainte. De plus, le souci premier de l'auteur (ou des auteurs) est d'ordre théologique: il ne s'agit pas seulement de rapporter l'histoire, mais aussi et surtout de l'interpréter à la lumière de catégories comme «Alliance», «péché», «justice», «rétribution divine». En d'autres termes, cette œuvre s'adresse à la conscience du croyant, avec l'autorité venue des grands prophètes.

Il faut cependant se demander si ce qui précède peut expliquer la parution d'un tel monument, qui devait requérir des sommes importantes et touchait des questions politiquement sensibles. Une telle entreprise est-elle imaginable sans l'accord ou même le soutien actif du pouvoir babylonien? C'est assez peu probable. L'école deutéronomiste a eu accès aux archives royales, ce qui suppose une autorisation en bonne et due forme. On se souvient aussi que Jérémie appartenait au parti pro-babylonien; ce sont les officiers de Nabuchodonosor qui le délivrèrent de la cour de garde où il était enfermé (Jr 39,14), à la suite de quoi il accompagna Godolias, le gouverneur nommé par le nouveau pouvoir (40,5-6). Les rédacteurs deutéronomistes appartenaient sans doute au même parti favorable à Babylone; ils montraient d'ailleurs que le malheur de Jérusalem n'a pas été causé par l'impérialisme mésopotamien, mais par le péché de Juda. On peut donc imaginer que l'œuvre Dtr a été écrite à tout le moins en accord avec les autorités babyloniennes. Avait-elle un statut plus ou moins officiel, comme plus tard la Torah d'Esdras? Quoiqu'une réponse assurée à cette question me paraisse impossible dans l'état actuel de nos connaissances, un élément au moins va dans le sens d'un grand prestige auprès des Judéens: après le retour des déportés, la littérature deutéronomiste n'a pas été abandonnée ou supplantée par l'écriture sacerdotale (P, puis l'œuvre chroniste), mais elle a conservé un rôle central dans la communauté croyante de Jérusalem.

Ainsi, la littérature Dtr présente les caractéristiques d'un «canon des Écritures» avant la lettre. C'est un ensemble littéraire à la fois ample et délimité, qui reprend dans une lumière nouvelle les divers recueils importants, à un titre ou à un autre, pour les Judéens de l'époque royale. Bien plus, s'il rassemble des écrits de genres littéraires et de provenances diverses, cet ensemble ne se présente pas comme une bibliothèque dont les divers ouvrages seraient simplement juxtaposés, mais plutôt comme un corps d'écriture à la fois structuré et unifié, avec des renvois d'un bloc à l'autre. Il propose une lecture théologique aussi cohérente que possible de l'histoire du peuple, depuis son origine; il exprime ainsi l'identité à la fois nationale et religieuse d'Israël et propose une éthique correspondante. Sans doute reconnue, voire soutenue par les autorités babyloniennes, cette littérature n'était pas attachée à un groupe particulier parmi les Judéens; elle semble avoir été reconnue d'une manière assez officielle ou, en tout cas, bénéficier d'un prestige suffisant pour subsister après l'effondrement de Babylone, l'avènement du régime perse et le retour des déportés à Jérusalem. Pour expliquer cela, il fallait que cet ensemble littéraire fasse autorité, qu'il soit largement reconnu comme normatif.

3. *Essai d'interprétation historique*

Le travail immense de l'école deutéronomiste a pris du temps. Sans doute peut-on distinguer deux phases essentielles, qui correspondent pour certains textes au moins à deux éditions successives. Dès ce moment, on peut parler d'une «dynamique du canon».

La première étape se situe dans le climat du grand malheur qui vient de frapper Jérusalem: le siège et la déportation de 598, puis, quelques années plus tard, le nouveau siège, la nouvelle déportation, la fin de la royauté judéenne, le démantèlement des remparts et la destruction du Temple. Coup sur coup s'effondrent la croyance en l'inviolabilité de Sion comme centre du monde et la protection inconditionnelle de YHWH, puis l'institution royale avec son idéologie. La foi en YHWH comme Dieu de salut et l'identité nationale sont remises en question jusque dans leurs fondements. C'est dans ce contexte qu'un groupe d'hommes sensibles à la prédication des prophètes a entrepris de sauver ce qui pouvait l'être et de fonder une nouvelle conscience commune. Le plus urgent était de comprendre la catastrophe et ses raisons profondes, sans remettre en cause la justice de YHWH. En réponse à cette nécessité, l'école deutéronomiste a repris systématiquement les écrits plus anciens en les interprétant dans la ligne de la théologie de l'Alliance, offerte généreusement par YHWH mais sans cesse trahie par son peuple. Le grand rassemblement littéraire dont il est question plus haut a donc dû être commencé sous Sédécias ou au lendemain de 587, dans les premières années du grand malheur. Ce travail peut être désigné à l'aide du sigle DtrH, tel que l'école de Göttingen le propose au sujet de l'Histoire deutéronomiste.

Une deuxième édition importante de l'œuvre deutéronomiste date du milieu de l'époque exilique, aux alentours de 560; elle correspond plus ou moins au DtrP de l'école de Göttingen, et c'est pourquoi j'utilise le même sigle. En une génération, les questions se sont déplacées. La réflexion sur la catastrophe et ses causes demeure vive, mais les années ont passé, et l'on se demande combien de temps le malheur va encore durer. Ceux qui étaient trop jeunes pour avoir leur part de responsabilité dans le malheur de Jérusalem vont-ils payer pour le péché de leurs pères[29]? La réponse est négative: chaque génération sera rétribuée en fonction de sa propre conduite (cf. Jr 31,29-30). Les contrastes relevés plus haut entre la génération de Moïse et celle de Josué, entre la conduite d'Achaz et celle de son fils Ézéchias, entre l'attitude de Josias et celle de son fils Jojaqim ont été introduits à ce niveau littéraire. Les connexions étroites entre les trois blocs littéraires (Tétrateuque, Histoire deutéronomiste, recueils d'oracles prophétiques) remontent à cette deuxième édition deutéronomiste. C'est à propos de cette édition qu'on peut véritablement parler d'un premier «canon des Écritures» avant la lettre.

Quoi qu'il en soit de la distinction entre les deux éditions, la formation du «corps» littéraire deutéronomiste correspond à la dispersion d'Israël comme corps social et donc à la nécessité de réfléchir à sa propre identité[30]. Au contraire d'autres peuples, Israël avait déjà, au temps de l'Exil, une vive conscience de sa particularité, de son lien vital avec YHWH; il lui était donc interdit de se dissoudre parmi les autres nations. Mais comment faire corps, alors qu'il n'y a plus d'autorité politique israélite? Puisque l'autorité du pouvoir faisait défaut, il fallait recourir à un autre type d'autorité: celle de la persuasion de la conscience. Typique est, à cet égard, l'introduction massive de la parénèse dans le livre du Deutéronome: puisque la loi israélite n'est plus imposée par le pouvoir politique (Juda est devenu province babylonienne), il faut convaincre de la nécessité morale de l'observer[31]. À l'autorité du roi, qui ne règne plus, s'est substituée l'autorité du prophète Moïse, porte-parole du Dieu de l'Alliance. Tel est le principe d'unité du corps littéraire

---

29. On a remarqué depuis longtemps l'importance de la distinction entre les générations dans le livre du Deutéronome, qui parle souvent des «pères». Comme le montre par exemple Dt 30,4-5, ces «pères» ne sont pas toujours les patriarches, mais représentent dans plus d'un cas la génération précédente. Voir à ce sujet l'étude fouillée de Th. RÖMER, *Israels Väter. Untersuchungen zur Vaterthematik im Deuteronomium und in der deuteronomistischen Tradition* (OBO, 99), Freiburg, Universitätsverlag; Göttingen, Vandenhoeck und Ruprecht, 1990.

30. Sur le lien entre identité et formation du Canon, voir surtout J.A. SANDERS, *Torah and Canon*, Philadelphia, PA, Fortress, 1972, traduit en français sous le titre *Identité de la Bible* (n. 6).

31. Voir J. VERMEYLEN, *Un programme pour la restauration d'Israël. Quelques aspects de la loi dans le Deutéronome*, in C. FOCANT (ed.), *La loi dans l'un et l'autre Testament* (LD, 168), Paris, Cerf, 1997, pp. 45-80.

deutéronomiste. Le Tétrateuque culmine avec la révélation de la Loi et la conclusion de l'Alliance. Dans l'ensemble Deutéronome-Rois, c'est sur la base de la Loi instaurée par YHWH et transmise par son prophète que la conduite d'Israël et de ses dirigeants est sans cesse évaluée. Quant aux recueils d'oracles, ils disent la parole de nouveaux prophètes qui ont pris le relais de Moïse pour rappeler à leur tour les exigences de l'Alliance.

La constitution d'un premier canon des Écritures a donc pour fonction de rassembler Israël sur des bases nouvelles, alors que son unité est mise à mal sur le plan politique et qu'il faut prévenir le danger d'une assimilation parmi les nations païennes. Ce n'est évidemment qu'une étape, car l'autorité de l'Écriture ainsi rassemblée n'était pas encore telle, qu'on n'ose plus la retravailler.

4. *Le destin ultérieur de ce canon avant la lettre*

Ce «canon», qu'est-il devenu au cours des siècles suivants? Je ne puis ici que proposer quelques hypothèses schématiques.

À la fin de la période exilique et au cours de la première moitié de l'époque perse, on assiste à une croissance du corps littéraire par l'adjonction de nouveaux matériaux à l'intérieur de chacun des livres qui le composent. Pour le Tétrateuque, ce seront surtout les matériaux d'origine sacerdotale, mais il faut noter que les autres blocs de la littérature deutéronomiste recevront, eux aussi, divers compléments[32]. Le phénomène de l'addition est révélateur du poids que l'on accordait à ces écrits, et le fait que le Tétrateuque ait été davantage retravaillé que les autres ouvrages pourrait indiquer que son prestige était spécialement grand.

L'étape suivante est marquée par l'œuvre d'Esdras, auquel on peut attribuer la formation définitive de la Torah (Pentateuque), reconnue par le pouvoir perse comme loi s'imposant à l'ensemble du monde juif de Transeuphratène (cf. Esd 7,25). Le Pentateuque est une construction littéraire qui a pour centre le Lévitique et englobe désormais le Deutéronome, lui-même détaché de l'Histoire deutéronomiste. Ce Pentateuque, toujours placé sous l'autorité de Moïse, reçoit un statut nouveau, officiel cette fois; il forme le noyau de ce qui sera plus tard le canon la Bible hébraïque. Mais il faut remarquer que cette mise à part n'altère pas nécessairement l'autorité reconnue depuis longtemps aux autres parties du

---

32. Ainsi, les livrets prophétiques sont transformés par le procédé de la relecture-réécriture, mais ils sont aussi complétés par l'adjonction du livre d'Ézéchiel, dont il n'est pas évident qu'il ait connu une rédaction Dtr.

corps littéraire rassemblé par Dtr. D'une certaine manière, le nouveau statut octroyé au Pentateuque n'en fait pas le canon, mais plutôt un canon à l'intérieur du canon. On remarquera par ailleurs que le bloc formé par les «prophètes antérieurs» ou l'«histoire deutéronomiste» ne subira plus de modification significative après l'époque d'Esdras, comme s'il n'était plus permis de le retravailler; ce phénomène pourrait être révélateur d'un statut supérieur accordé à cette littérature[33].

Dans le Nouveau Testament, on désigne fréquemment les Écritures «canoniques» par l'expression «la Loi et les Prophètes»[34]. On considère souvent que l'inclusion des *Nebi'îm* (prophètes «antérieurs» et prophètes «postérieurs») parmi les ouvrages «qui souillent les mains» est intervenue au cours de la première moitié du IIe siècle[35]. Quoi qu'il en soit des nuances qu'il faudrait apporter à cette affirmation classique, l'ensemble de la littérature deutéronomiste voit son autorité confirmée à l'époque hellénistique[36]. Notons que ce nouveau périmètre du «canon des Écritures en devenir» intervient, encore une fois, dans un contexte d'éclatement du judaïsme, dont une large partie s'hellénise. À nouveau, la recomposition du corps social s'effectue par la définition d'un corps littéraire.

Diverses contributions à ce volume montrent que la clôture définitive de la Bible hébraïque relève d'une problématique complexe et qu'il faut compter avec une diversité de situations. Une étape décisive semble cependant avoir été franchie en Palestine à la fin du premier siècle de notre

---

33. Si les additions à un ensemble littéraire montent le prestige qu'on lui accorde, l'arrêt de ces additions peut indiquer soit un désintérêt, soit au contraire la perception du caractère «intouchable» des textes en question. Ici, c'est évidemment la deuxième hypothèse qui s'impose.

34. Mt 5,17; 7,12; 11,13, etc. L'usage de l'expression ne signifie pas automatiquement l'existence d'un canon en deux parties clairement distinctes; voir à ce sujet les contributions de G. Dorival et E. Zenger dans ce volume (pp. 81-110 et 111-134).

35. Plusieurs livres prophétiques recevront des compléments apparentés à la littérature apocalyptique; voir par exemple Is 24,16b-18a. Plusieurs auteurs pensent que le Siracide atteste déjà l'appartenance des Prophètes à ce qui sera défini plus tard comme «canon des Écritures»: O.H. STECK, *Der Abschluß der Prophetie im Alten Testament. Ein Versuch zur Frage der Vorgeschichte des Kanons* (Biblisch-Theologische Studien, 17), Neukirchen-Vluyn, Neukirchener Verlag, 1991, pp. 136-144; ID., *Die Prophetenbücher und ihr theologisches Zeugnis. Wege der Nachfrage und Fährten zur Antwort*, Tübingen, Mohr, 1996, p. 130; J.-L. SKA, *L'éloge des Pères dans le Siracide (Si 44–50) et le canon de l'Ancien Testament*, in N. CALDUCH-BENAGES & J. VERMEYLEN (eds.), *Treasures of Wisdom. Studies in Ben Sira and the Wisdom of Solomon*. FS M. Gilbert (BETL, 143), Leuven, University Press - Peeters, 1999, pp. 181-193. D'autres auteurs, au contraire, estiment que le témoignage du Siracide ne permet pas de trancher; voir surtout D.M. CARR, *Canonization in the Context of Community* (n. 3), pp. 39-40.

36. La série des prophètes postérieurs est complétée par l'addition du livre d'Ézéchiel, s'il n'y a pas été introduit à une étape antérieure; les livres d'Osée, d'Amos et de Michée se voient adjoindre divers recueils, pour former le livre des XII prophètes.

ère, lorsque les *Ketubîm* sont inclus dans le canon juif des Écritures[37]. Ce troisième bloc est formé de livres qui n'appartenaient pas à la littérature deutéronomiste. Encore une fois, cependant, la formation du canon est liée à la nécessité de rassembler Israël après la rupture causée par la Guerre juive et la fin du Second Temple.

Ainsi, tant l'inclusion des *Nebi'îm* que celle des *Ketubîm* confirment l'hypothèse que j'ai proposée au sujet de la constitution du canon deutéronomiste: la nécessité de redéfinir un corps littéraire qui fait autorité doit répondre à l'éclatement ou à un ébranlement grave du corps social d'Israël.

5. *Conclusion*

Jusqu'à la fin de l'époque royale, il ne pouvait exister aucune littérature que nous pouvons qualifier de «canonique», mais des écrits aux statuts variés. Le rassemblement d'une vaste littérature destinée à faire autorité sur le plan de la foi et de la morale est l'œuvre de l'école deutéronomiste du temps de l'Exil; les ouvrages édités ou réédités à ce moment forment un véritable canon des Écritures avant la lettre, rendu nécessaire par la disparition du pouvoir politique israélite. Les définitions ultérieures du canon confirmeront l'autorité normative accordée à cette littérature.

Avenue H. Conscience 156   Jacques VERMEYLEN
B-1140 Bruxelles

---

37. Voir G. STEMBERGER, *Jabne und der Kanon*, in *JBT* 3 (1988) 163-174.

SIMSON UND DAS ENDE DES RICHTERBUCHES

EIN BEISPIEL EINER KANONEXEGESE ZWISCHEN KOMPOSITIONS-
UND WIRKUNGSGESCHICHTLICHER AUSLEGUNG

1. *Grundlagen*

Der Kanon ist in der gegenwärtigen Bibelhermeneutik von entscheidender Bedeutung[1]. Der »Canonical Approach« hat aber ein weites Spektrum: So benutzt B.S. Childs die »Community of Faith« als Brückenglied von der Gemeinschaft der ersten Textproduzenten und Textrezipienten zu den gegenwärtigen Lesern. Häufig wird der »Canonical Approach« jedoch mit dezidiert literarisch orientierten Ansätzen verbunden (z.B. »Literary Approach«, »New Literary Criticism« oder »Intertextualität«)[2].

Jede Interpretation vereindeutigt, indem sie aus den möglichen Bedeutungen des Textes auswählt oder bestimmten Textteilen mehr Aufmerksamkeit widmet als anderen. Kanonische Exegese steht bei ihren Kritikern entsprechend in dem Verdacht, unzulässig zu vereindeutigen, weil sie die sogenannte Endgestalt des Textes und nicht die zahlreichen postulierten Vorformen als interpretationsleitenden Gegenstand einfordert. Doch die Exegese der sogenannten Endgestalt erweist sich mehrfach als Erhebung einer Vielfalt:

Schon die Definition des Kanons ist unterschiedlich, je nachdem, ob der Kanon des Tenach, der Septuaginta oder der christlichen Bibel einschließlich dem Neuen Testament Ausgangspunkt ist.

Es ist textkritischer Befund, dass die sogenannte Endgestalt in verschiedenen Manuskripten überliefert ist. Ein Teil dieser Überlieferung lässt sich in Gruppen zusammenordnen, die durch eine gemeinsame Sprache, einen gemeinsamen gesellschaftlichen oder lokalen Kontext[3]

---

1. Vgl. als Einzelexegese G. STEINS, *Die »Bindung Isaaks« im Kanon (Gen 22). Grundlagen und Programm einer kanonisch-intertextuellen Lektüre* (HBS, 20), Freiburg i. B., 1999, dort weitere Literatur, und als Gesamtdarstellung R. RENDTORFF, *Theologie des Alten Testaments. Ein kanonischer Entwurf.* Bd. 1. *Kanonische Grundlegung*, Neukirchen-Vluyn, 1999, p. 4-6.

2. Neuer Überblick: M. OEMING & A.-R. PREGLA, *New Literary Criticism*, in *TR* 66 (2001) 1-23.

3. Die Theorie von lokalen Textfamilien (bes. W.F. Albright und F.M. Cross) wird u.a. durch die gemeinsamen Funde unterschiedlicher Texttypen in Qumran in Frage gestellt: H.-J. FABRY, *Der Text und seine Geschichte*, in E. ZENGER *et al.*, *Einleitung in das*

gebildet werden. Die textliche Vielfalt ist bereits Teil der Vielfalt der Auslegungen, aber selbst ein gemeinsamer Ausgangstext kann durch unterschiedliche Auslegungen in seiner Bedeutung weiter differenziert werden. Manche unterschiedliche Auslegungen realisieren innertextliche Polyvalenzen, wie sie z.B. durch Leerstellen – »gaps« – innerhalb des Textes entstehen[4]. Solche Polyvalenzen entstehen auch durch das umfängliche und innerhalb der verschiedenen Überlieferungsstränge unterschiedliche literarisch-kontextuelle Umfeld, in dem ein einzelner Text unterschiedliche Bedeutungen annehmen kann. Die Endgestalt des Textes gibt es damit weder textkritisch noch interpretativ.

Die Variation, das Wachsen und Spezifizieren der Bedeutung eines Textes, ist mit der Etablierung eines Kanons nicht abgeschlossen. In jeder Trägergruppe treten maßgebliche Texte zu den eigentlich kanonischen Texten hinzu, die deren Interpretation prägen.

Die hier vorliegende Variante einer kanonischen Exegese ist wesentlich dadurch geprägt, dass sie der im Kanon vorgegebenen Einteilung des Textes in Bücher hohes Gewicht beimisst. Die Einteilung in Bücher ist eine der Größen, die allen Kanonformen gemeinsam ist[5]. Ein biblischer Text ist Teil des Kanons, weil er Bestandteil eines biblischen Buches ist. Die Buchbetrachtung ist damit ein wichtiger Bestandteil einer kanonischen Interpretation. Die Betrachtung der Bucheinteilung eröffnet auch eine Verbindung zwischen der synchronen Betrachtung einer vorliegenden Textform und der historisch-kritischen Frage nach der Textgenese.

2. Unterschiedliche Interpretationen der biblischen Gestalt Simson

Wählen wir die Simsongeschichte als Beispiel. Es scheint ungünstig gewählt: Grundlegende Fragen des Verstehens der Simsongeschichte sind nicht eindeutig beantwortet, eine Interpretation der Simsongeschichte im Zusammenhang mit dem Richterbuch geht selten über lite-

---

Alte Testament (Kohlhammer Studienbücher Theologie, 1,1), Stuttgart, ³1998, pp. 59-62, bes. p. 62, ähnlich E. Tov, *Der Text der Hebräischen Bibel. Handbuch der Textkritik*, Stuttgart, 1997, pp. 154-161. Diskutabel bleibt für Fabry eine Theorie von Gruppentexten in Anschluss an Sh. Talmon (dazu Fabry, *Text*, p. 62). Demgegenüber gehen E. Tov und J. Trebolle Barrera von einer Vielzahl von Texttraditionen aus. Die ältere Theorie eines Übergabepunktes, nach dem Redaktionen abgeschlossen sind und die Textüberlieferung begann, ist nicht haltbar.

4. Grundlegend M. Sternberg, *The Poetics of Biblical Narrative. Ideological Literature and the Drama of Reading*, Bloomington, IN, 1985.

5. Der Schluss des Richterbuches ist u.a. in Qumran bezeugt (Lücke nach Ri 21,25 in 4QJudg^b Frag.3 Zeile 13), so: E. Ulrich, F. M. Cross, *et al.* (eds.), *Qumran Cave 4.IX: Deuteronomy, Joshua, Judges, Kings* (DJD, 14), Oxford, 1995, p. 167).

rarhistorische Vermutungen hinaus[6]. Eine kanonische Interpretation des Richterbuches ist nicht etabliert[7].

Die Auslegungsgeschichte zeigt sehr unterschiedliche Interpretationen der biblischen Gestalt Simson. In der neueren theologischen Interpretation überwiegt eine kritische Sicht Simsons[8]. Demgegenüber wird Simson bereits im Hebräerbrief, Hebr 11,32, in eine Reihe von Glaubenshelden nach Gideon und Barak, aber vor Jefta, David, Samuel und die Propheten gestellt[9].

Exemplarisch möchte ich zwei antike Interpretationen darstellen. Sie gehören zur Gattung der »rewritten bible« und werden mit *antiquitates* betitelt: Für Josephus ist Simson eine überaus positive Gestalt. Josephus hebt an Simson in seiner abschließenden Beurteilung seine Tapferkeit und Stärke hervor.

> Bewundernswert ist er wegen seiner Tugend und Stärke und wegen seines großen Mutes an seinem Ende und seines Zorns gegen die Feinde bis zu seinem Ende.
> Und dass er von einer Frau überlistet wurde, muss der Natur der Menschen zugerechnet werden, die dem Wesen nach sündig ist.
> Ihm muss aber bezeugt werden, dass er in jeder anderen Hinsicht tugendhaft gewesen ist[10].

Josephus kennt zwar negativ beurteilte Handlungen von Simson, meint aber den Helden durch den Verweis auf Frauen, die ihn verführen, entschuldigen zu können. Entsprechend findet sich eine Verurteilung von Simson bei Josephus nur als Nebenbemerkung:

> Später verließ er (Simson) die väterlichen Gesetze und übertrat die häusliche Lebensweise, er ahmte die fremden Gewohnheiten nach, und dies ist der Anfang vom Übel[11].

6. Literarhistorisch gilt die Simsongeschichte als ein später Anhang der älteren Sammlung von Richtererzählungen (Ri 3–9*), seit W. RICHTER, *Traditionsgeschichtliche Untersuchungen zum Richterbuch* (BBB, 18), Bonn, 1963, pp. 323-328. Das Interpretationsdefizit gilt auch für die Sternberg-Schülerin Y. AMIT, *The Book of Judges. The Art of Editing* (Biblical Interpretation Series, 38), Leiden, 1998: Sie arbeitet die Schlussstellung der Simsongeschichte innerhalb der Richterzyklen heraus (p. 45), doch die Interpretation dieser Stellung bleibt fraglich (p. 263).

7. Das Richterbuch kann zwar als Beispiel für die gelungene Präsentation eines breiten exegetischen Spektrums gelten (G.A. YEE [ed.], *Judges and Method. New Approaches in Biblical Studies*, Minneapolis, 1995), eine Kanoninterpretation fehlt aber.

8. So z.B. G. VON RAD, *Theologie des Alten Testaments*. Bd. 1. *Die Theologie der geschichtlichen Überlieferungen Israels*, München, [10]1992, pp. 345-346 (ein Exkurs). Das Gesamturteil über Simson lautet: »So zeigen also auch die Simsongeschichten das Scheitern eines Charismatikers und das Bild einer vertanen Gotteskraft« (p. 346).

9. Die positive Deutung dieser Figuren ist durch Hebr 11,33f. gesichert. Die Reihenfolge der Aufzählung bleibt unklar.

10. FLAVIUS JOSEPHUS, *Ant. Jud.* 5,317 (*Opera*. Vol. I. *Antiquitatum Iudaicarum Libri I-V*, ed. B. NIESE, Berlin, Weidmann, 1887).

11. *Ibid.* 5,306.

Ein anderes Bild von Simson zeichnen die *Antiquitates Biblicae*, deren Autor hilfsweise *Pseudo-Philo* genannt wird. Auch bei Pseudo-Philo wird Simson wegen Delila getadelt (*Ant. Bib.* 43,5)[12]. Doch ähnlich wie die biblischen Texte selbst enthält sich diese Nacherzählung einer ausdrücklichen Wertung. Da Pseudo-Philo verschiedene Teilerzählungen stark ineinander verschränkt, bekommt diese eine negative Wertung jedoch hohes Gewicht, zumal eine positive Wertung fehlt.

Die negative Sicht Simsons bei Pseudo-Philo wird auch in weiteren Details deutlich. So wird Simson von Pseudo-Philo beschuldigt, dass er sich durch Delila hat betrunken machen lassen (*Ant. Bib.* 43,6), obwohl seine Mutter nach *Ant. Bib.* 42,3 auf seine Alkoholabstinenz verpflichtet sei. Beide Notizen schließen sich frei an das vorgeburtliche Alkoholverbot für die Mutter Simsons in Ri 13,4.7.14 an.

3. *Ambivalenzen in der biblischen Simsongeschichte*

Die verschiedenen Interpretationen der biblischen Gestalt Simson repräsentieren unterschiedliche Aspekte der biblischen Erzählungen. Eine Interpretation Simsons hebt beispielsweise seine Frömmigkeit hervor[13]. In der Simsongeschichte finden sich mehrere Gebete Simsons: Nach seiner ersten Befreiung aus der philistäischen Gefangenschaft betet er um Wasser (Ri 15,18), seine positive Gebetserfahrung nutzt er dann zu seinem Selbstmordattentat (Ri 16,28). Dass er hier auf die Erfahrung eines erhörten Gebetes zurückgreifen kann, zeigt die Formulierung:

> Adonaj, JHWH, denke an mich und gibt mir Kraft, noch dies eine Mal, Gott... (Ri 16,28bα).

Simson gelingt am Schluss seiner zweifelhaften Tätigkeit als Befreier Israels erstmalig eine durch ein Gebet bewusste Einbindung Gottes in seine Aktivität.

Es bleibt fraglich, wie und mit welchem Gewicht dieser Einzelzug der Simsongeschichte interpretierbar ist. Andere Geschichten zeigen ihn als den exemplarischen Sünder, der sich wenig um den Willen Gottes kümmert, man denke nur an seine notorische Neigung zu jeweils unpassenden Frauen. Beides, Simson als frommer Beter und seine menschlichen Züge, erinnern den Leser an David, der innerbiblisch mit einem ähnlichen Spektrum präsentiert wird.

---

12. *Pseudo-Philo's Liber Antiquitatum Biblicarum*, ed. G. KISCH (Publications in Mediaeval Studies, 10), Notre Dame, IN, 1949.
13. So Ch. EXUM, *The Theological Dimension of the Samson Saga*, in *VT* 33 (1983) 30-45, bes. pp. 39-43 und 45.

Die Simsongeschichte hat eine Reihe von subtilen Bezügen hin auf die Texte von der Entstehung des Königtums. Simson wird als Kriegsheld gezeichnet, der es von den zahlenmäßigen Leistungen her mit den größten Recken Davids aufnehmen könnte, der aber als isolierter Einzelkämpfer keine Führungsqualitäten erkennen lässt und insofern die Führungsfigur David vorbereitet. Reflektieren wir deshalb kurz den biblischen Erzählzusammenhang, innerhalb dessen die Verbindung zwischen Simson und David zu denken ist. Wir wählen wieder die frühen Interpretationen als Beispiel.

4. Eine Nachzeichnung des Erzählzusammenhanges der Simsongeschichte gemäß der Auslegungsgeschichte

Beide interpretierenden Nacherzählungen der Simsongeschichte sind nicht auf die Einzelerzählung beschränkt, sondern stehen im Zusammenhang einer Interpretation des Kontextes. Das eher negative Bild Simsons bei Pseudo-Philo fügt sich in den aus der hebräischen Bibel bekannten Zusammenhang: Nach der Simsongeschichte folgen bei Pseudo-Philo die Erzählungen Ri 17–21 in freier Ausschmückung[14]. Vor die Konstituierung des Königtums, die mit der Geburtsgeschichte Samuels ihren Ausgangspunkt nimmt, fügt Pseudo-Philo noch eine kleine Erzählung ohne biblische Vorlage ein, die zu diesem Neuanfang einen Kontrast bildet: Elkana wird vergeblich per Los als König über Israel bestimmt (*Ant. Bib.* 49).

Die Interpretation Simsons als Helden Israels bei Josephus setzt sich demgegenüber in einer anderen Sicht des Zusammenhanges fort. Nach der Simsongeschichte folgt in der Darstellung von Josephus die Nacherzählung des Buches Rut (*Ant. Jud.* 5,9), das dann mit der Geburtsgeschichte Samuels zum von Samuel begründeten Königtum Sauls und Davids überleitet. Während der Zusammenhang Richterbuch, Rut und Samuelbuch von biblischen Handschriften und insbesondere von der Überlieferung des griechischen Kanons her[15] begründbar ist, ist die Behandlung von Ri 17–21 Teil der Interpretation von Josephus, die sich zunächst einmal nicht vom biblischen Text her nahelegt. Josephus rückt den Zusammenhang Ri 19–21, in dem die Ermordung der Nebenfrau eines Leviten zur Auslöschung fast des gesamten Stammes Benjamin

---

14. Vgl. z.B. das Gebet des Pinchas (PSEUDO-PHILO, *Ant. Bib.*, 46,4ff.).

15. R. BECKWITH, *The Old Testament Canon of the New Testament Church and Its Background in Early Judaism*, London, 1985, p. 194 (Codex Vaticanus und Alexandrinus).

führt, vor die Wiedergabe der Othnielnotiz (Ri 3,7-11)[16]. Die Erzählung von der Wanderschaft des Stammes Dan Ri 17f. wird bei Josephus sogar nur in aller Kürze dazwischen gestellt (*Ant. Jud.* 5,175-178). Der Schluss des biblischen Richterbuches dient Josephus zur Illustration eines Chaos, in dem Israel zum Götzendienst kommt, das aber bereits die Richter beseitigen können, weil Josephus dieses Chaos vom Ende zum Anfang des Richterbuches transferiert[17].

Das Nachzeichnen des Erzählzusammenhanges in beiden Interpretationen zeigt, dass die Interpretationsdifferenz der Simsongeschichte einer anderen Auffassung des größeren biblischen Erzählzusammenhanges entspricht.

5. *Die Simsongeschichte im biblischen Richterbuch*

Die Reihenfolge der Erzählungen des Richterbuches ist innerhalb der biblischen Überlieferung textkritisch unbestritten. Dennoch wird die Reihenfolge der Erzählungen von modernen Interpreten gelegentlich umgestellt. Dafür gibt es einen biblischen Anlass:

> Und in diesen Tagen suchte der Stamm Dan für sich ein Erbteil zum Wohnen,
> denn es war ihm bis zu diesem Tag noch nicht zugefallen mitten in den Stämmen Israels (Ri 18,1b).

Der Text verweist auf die Schwierigkeiten des Stammes Dan, das in Jos 19,40-46 zugewiesene Siedlungsgebiet zu halten. Diese Probleme sind in Jos 19,47 und Ri 1,34 bereits erwähnt. Die auslegungsgeschichtliche Einordnung der Gewinnung neuen Landbesitzes durch den Stamm Dan Ri 18 an den Anfang des Richterbuches realisiert damit eine Möglichkeit, die der biblische Text selbst als eine Leseperspektive anbietet. Doch ist Ri 18 im biblischen Erzählzusammenhang nicht isoliert. Ri 18 ist eng mit Ri 17 verbunden, da das vom Stamm Dan geraubte und mit in den Norden genommene Heiligtum in Ri 17 begründet wird. Doch ist die Texteinheit Ri 17–18 auch mit der biblisch vorhergehenden Simsongeschichte Ri 13–16 als Erzählung des Stammes Dan verbunden. Die Simsongeschichte setzt den Westen Judas als Gebiet des Stammes Dan voraus. Insofern ist der biblische Zusammenhang, der den Stamm

---

16. FLAVIUS JOSEPHUS, *Ant. Jud.* 5,182-184.
17. Josephus lässt u.a. die Geschichte von der Herstellung eines Ephod durch Gideon aus, der in der biblischen Darstellung Ursache für einen Götzendienst ist (*Ant. Jud.* 5,213-232). Dazu L.H. FELDMAN, *Studies in Josephus' Rewritten Bible* (JSJ SS, 58), Leiden, 1998, p. 551. Josephus entlastet die biblische Figur.

Dan erst nach dem Abschluss der Simsongeschichte nach Norden wandern lässt, erzählerisch gut begründet[18]. Außerdem gibt es subtile Verbindungen zwischen beiden Textzusammenhängen, so geht einer namenlosen Frau mit 1100 Silberstücken in Ri 17 genau die Summe verloren, die die letzte Geliebte Simsons namens Delilah in Ri 16 für die Preisgabe Simsons gewinnt[19].

Innerbiblisch hat Ri 17–18 damit eine ambivalente Stellung: Einerseits legt sich eine Anordnung von Ri 17–18 nach der Simsongeschichte nahe, andererseits weist die Wanderung der Daniten Richtung Norden auf eine deutlich früher erzählte Zeit. Machen wir deshalb ein gedankliches Experiment. Die Probleme der erzählerisch verspäteten Nordwanderung wären gelöst, wenn der Schluss des Richterbuches einschließlich der Simsongeschichte geschlossen an den Anfang des Buches transferiert würde. Die Radikalität des durch die Verknüpfung von Ri 17f. mit Jos 19,47 und Ri 1,34 möglichen und bei Josephus teilweise realisierten Eingriffes verdeutlicht, dass das Richterbuch und insbesondere sein Schluss eine gestaltete Größe ist. Die Simsonerzählung ist sowohl Abschluss der Richtererzählungen als auch Teil des sogenannten Anhangs Ri 17–21.

6. Thesen zu einer kanonorientierten Interpretation

a. Die kanonische Interpretation hat von literarischen Zäsuren auszugehen. Die hebräische Bibel hat eine scharfe Zäsur zwischen Richter- und Samuelbuch. Simson erscheint damit im Zusammenhang mit den das Königtum befürwortenden Texten, die die Notwendigkeit des Königtums mit dem wachsenden Chaos begründen.

b. Simson ist der letzte in einer Reihe von Richtern im Richterbuch. Der nachfolgende Richter Samuel organisiert den Übergang von der

18. Zum historischen Problem der Nordwanderung des Stammes Dan vgl. die ältere Stellungnahme von M. NIEMANN, *Die Daniten. Studien zur Geschichte eines altisraelitischen Stammes* (FRLANT, 135), Göttingen, 1985. Hier datiert Niemann die Nordwanderung des Stammes Dan vor die Zeit, in der er die erzählte Zeit der Simsongeschichte ansiedelt. Insofern muss Niemann hier von einer im Süden verbliebenen danitischen Sippe um Simson ausgehen. Die neuere, auf einem Oberflächensurvey der nördlichen Umgebung von Bet Schemesch beruhende Hypothese von G. Lehmann, M. Niemann und W. Zwickel bestreitet demgegenüber die Historizität der Nordwanderung der Daniten. Aus fehlenden Belegen in der Eisen-I- und Eisen-IIa/b-Zeit schließen die Autoren, dass die Erzählung von einer Nordwanderung der Daniten ihre als Flüchtlinge nach 720 eingenommenen Gebiete im Westen Judas legitimieren soll: G. LEHMANN, M. NIEMANN & W. ZWICKEL, *Zora und Eschtaol. Ein archäologischer Oberflächensurvey im Gebiet nördlich von Bet Schemesch*, in *UF* 28 (1996) 343-442, bes. p. 405.

19. Deswegen heißt die Mutter Michas bei Pseudo-Philo Dedila (*Ant. Bib.* 44,2).

Richter- in die Königszeit. Insofern liegt es nahe, die Simsongeschichte und das Richterbuch als Vorbereitung der Königszeit zu verstehen. Simson ist dabei in seiner Ambivalenz als Einzelfigur sowohl Proto- als auch Antityp zu Samuel und David.

c. Das Buch Rut füllt in der üblichen Anordnung der griechischen Bibel die in der hebräischen Bibel starke Zäsur zwischen Richter- und Samuelbuch auf. In dieser Anordnung antwortet das Samuelbuch nicht mehr auf die negativen Herausforderungen am Ende des Richterbuches, sondern auch eine Heldin wie Rut wird zur Wegbereiterin des Königtums[20]. Die Stellung des Buches Rut zwischen Richter- und Samuelbuch ermöglicht eine stärkere Hervorhebung der positiven Aspekte der Simsonfigur. Die Ambivalenz des Verstehens der Simsongestalt spiegelt damit eine Differenz im Verstehen verschiedener Kanonformen: Das Verstehen der Einzelgeschichte und das des Makrokontextes bis hin zum jeweiligen Kanon entsprechen sich.

Bülowstr. 27   Matthias MILLARD
D–32756 Detmold

---

20. Es gibt weitere Bezüge zwischen Richterbuch und Rut: Rut handelt so selbständig wie die Frauen am Anfang des Richterbuches, die erstaunliche Leistungen in typisch männlichen Rollen vollbringen: Achsa (Ri 1,12-15), Debora und Jael (Ri 4–5) sowie die unbekannte Frau, die Abimelech tötet (Ri 9,53). Das Buch Rut funktioniert auch als Gegengewicht z.B. zur problematischen Haltung gegenüber Fremden im Richterbuch, die im Kontext der Septuaginta Schwierigkeiten bereitet und die deshalb im literarischen Nahkontext relativiert wird.

ΟΙ ΟΥΚ ΟΝΤΕΣ ΘΕΟΙ
IN DER SEPTUAGINTA DES JEREMIABUCHES
UND IN DER EPISTEL JEREMIAS

EIN BEITRAG ZUR FRAGE NACH DEM WERDEGANG
DES SOGENANNTEN ALEXANDRINISCHEN KANONS

Unser Wissen über die Kanonbildung stützt sich grundsätzlich auf die externe Evidenz, bzw. auf die Rezeptionsgeschichte der hebräischen Schriften im Judentum und im Christentum. Daraus entnehmen wir, daß die Voraussetzung für die Aufnahme eines Buches in den alttestamentlichen Kanon die Befürwortung durch eine von allen anerkannte Autorität war, die ihre Entscheidung abhängig von bestimmten Kriterien machte. Nämlich, daß das Buch a) als göttlich inspiriert und b) als altehrwürdig bekannt war[1]. Doch die Begriffe der göttlichen Inspiration (θεοπνευστία) und des Alters eines alttestamentlichen Buches sind nicht eindeutig und abschließend auf ihren Inhalt geprüft. Ebensowenig geklärt ist die endgültige Zusammenstellung des Kanons. Wir kennen zwar zwei Fassungen des Kanons a) die engere palästinische, die die sogenannten protokanonischen Bücher umfaßt, und b) die weitere alexandrinische Fassung, welche auch die sogenannten deuterokanonischen Schriften enthält. Man ist sich aber noch nicht einig darüber, welcher Kanon der ältere ist und worin sich die Vertreter des jeweiligen Kanons unterscheiden oder der gleichen Meinung sind. Ch.H. Dodd begann seine epochemachende Studie *The Bible and the Greeks* von 1935 mit der erwähnenswerten Bemerkung, daß der Charakter des Judentums sich mehr oder weniger unter dem Einfluß des Griechentums geändert hat, so daß das palästinische und das alexandrinische Judentum nicht mehr als identische Phänomene in der Geistesgeschichte angesehen werden können, sondern als unterschiedliche, die einer Sonderbehandlung bedürfen. Doch diese Hypothese sollte nicht zum Ausgangspunkt unserer Betrachtung des Werdegangs des alexandrinischen Kanons werden, sondern sie muß aufgrund von alttestamentlichen Aussagen widerlegt oder nachgewiesen werden. Somit wird die Frage aufgeworfen,

* Dieser Vortrag stellt zusammenfassend Forschungsergebnisse eines auf Einladung von Herrn Professor Christoph Elsas zweimonatigen Aufenthaltes (März-April 2000) im Religionsgeschichtlichen Institut der Philipps-Universität Marburg mit Unterstützung des DAAD dar. Hiermit sei mein herzlichster Dank ausgesprochen.

1. JOSEPHUS, *Contra Apionem*, I 7 20ff. Dazu P.J. BRATSIOTIS, Εἰσαγωγὴ εἰς τὴν Παλαιὰν Διαθήκην, Athen, 1936, repr. 1975, pp. 486-522, insbesondere p. 488f.

welche internen Kriterien[2] sind für die kanonische Wertung der sogenannten deuterokanonischen Schriften maßgebend geworden? Dieser
Frage möchte ich anhand der Bezeichnung der Götter als οἱ οὐκ ὄντες
θεοί in der LXX des Jeremiabuches und in der Epistel Jeremias nachge-
hen.

I

Die Bezeichnung οἱ οὐκ ὄντες θεοί begegnet uns nur in Jer 5,7 in
einem Gotteswort, welches sich auf den Eidspruch des untreuen Volkes
an die falschen Götter bezieht. Es handelt sich eigentlich um eine substantivierte Wortverbindung, die aus dem negierten aktiven Partizip des
Verbes εἰμί und dem Plural des Appelativums θεός besteht und als
Präpositionalobjekt des Verbes ὀμνύω dient.

οἱ υἱοί σου ἐγκατέλιπόν με   בניך עזבוני
καὶ ὤμνυον ἐν τοῖς οὐκ οὖσι θεοῖς   וישבעו בלא אלהים

Sollten kontextunabhängige Bedeutungskomponenten, die mit einer
möglichen Ersetzung des griechischen Ausdrucks durch ein dynami-
sches Übersetzungsäquivalent wie z.B. »Götzen« einhergehen, vermieden werden, so würde er im Deutschen mit »die nichtseienden Götter«
wortwörtlich übersetzt werden, unter der Voraussetzung, daß sein Inhalt
näher erklärt werden soll.

Als erstes fällt nun auf, daß neben der nominalisierten Formulierung
οἱ οὐκ ὄντες θεοί an zwei Stellen des Jeremiabuches (Jer 2,11; 16,20)
auch die verbale Form (οὗτοι) οὐκ εἰσι θεοί belegt ist. Diese steht im
Zusammenhang mit der Klage Gottes über sein Volk, das, obwohl es
seine Herrlichkeit kennt und erlebt hat, ihn verworfen hat, um sich den
selbstgemachten, unnützen Göttern hinzugeben. Beide LXX-Varianten
geben denselben hebräischen Ausdruck im Griechischen wieder, nämlich לא אלהים[3] (= Nichtgötter, Ungötter). Im Unterschied zum hebräischen Jeremiabuch, wo das Dasein, Bestehen und Existieren von beleb-

---

2. In der heutigen exegetischen Diskussion wird diese Frage in Bezug auf die hebräischen Schriften des engeren Kanons thematisiert. Die Schriften des weiteren Kanons werden daher kaum oder gar nicht berücksichtigt. Erkennt man dies als exegetisches Problem, dann sollte man die Fragestellung entsprechend abändern.

3. Der Ausdruck לא אלהים begegnet uns sonst noch in 2 Kön 19,18 = Jes 37,19
(LXX: οὐ θεοί εἰσιν); 2 Chr 13,9 (LXX: ὁ μὴ ὢν θεός) und Hos 8,6 (LXX: οὐ θεός
ἐστιν). Der Ausdrucksweise und dem Sinngehalt von Ex 7,1 (נתתיך אלהים לפרעה –
δέδωκα σε θεὸν Φαραώ) vgl. Ps 81(82),6; Ez 28,9 (לא אל – οὐ θεός versus אלהים אני –
θεός εἰμι ἐγώ) werde ich einen anderen Aufsatz widmen.

ten und unbelebten Dingen sowie ihre Verneinung durch לֹא[4] oder אֵין[5]
vor allem mit Nominalsätzen bezeichnet wird, ist im Griechischen in
den entsprechenden Fällen der Gebrauch des Verbes εἰμί unentbehrlich.
Εἰμί entspricht dem hebräischen היה, welches mit dem gleichklingenden
Verb חיה graphisch leicht verwechselt werden kann. Im Jeremiabuch
wird zwischen den beiden Verben aber bewußt unterschieden und sie
werden richtig gebraucht und übersetzt[6]. Dies zeigt sich besonders in
den Gebrauchsweisen des Verbes חיה – ζῆν in theologischem Kontext
bzw. in der Schwurformel חי יהוה – ζῇ Κύριος[7], die mit der Gottesbezeichnung אלהים חיים – θεὸς ζῶν[8] engstens zusammenhängt.

An den soeben erwähnten theologischen Aussagen sind zweierlei
Betrachtungs- und Darstellungsweisen erkennbar, die auf zwei unterschiedliche Denkarten hinweisen: Erstere wird durch die Gleichung
היה — εἰμί gekennzeichnet und hat am ehesten abstrahierenden Charakter, denn sie setzt Einsichten voraus, die auf logischer Deduktion beru-
hen; letztere drückt sich aber durch חיה – ζῶ aus, ist deskriptiv und ver-
anschaulichend durch ausgeprägt bildhafte Sprache. Sollte die erste Ausdrucksweise repräsentativ für logisches Denken sein, dann scheint die
letztere an das empirische Denken angeglichen zu sein. Empirisches und
logisches Denken scheinen im Jeremiabuch miteinander zu harmonisie-
ren. Aber ihr Verhältnis zueinander im jeremianischen Schrifttum hinsichtlich der Götterwelt ist bisher weder einheitlich noch überhaupt ausreichend erklärt und beurteilt worden. Wie ist es nun möglich, diesen
Vorgang begreifbar zu machen?

II

Die Negation οὐκ führt ein verneinendes Urteil über den Seins-
charakter der Götter ein. Dieses Urteil setzt voraus, a) daß es etwas gibt,
was θεός genannt wird und b) daß auch von θεοί geredet wird, die mit
θεός nicht zusammenfallen. Um den Gegensatz zwischen θεός und
θεοί sichtbar zu machen, fügt der hebräische Text dem Appelativum
אלהים die näheren Bestimmungen אחרים oder נכר(ים) bei, die im Griechischen abwechselnd durch ἕτεροι oder ἀλλότριοι wiedergegeben
werden. Zwischen οἱ οὐκ ὄντες θεοί und θεοὶ ἕτεροι bzw. θεοὶ
ἀλλότριοι, die als abstrakte, einander bedingende Götterbezeichnungen

---

4. Vgl. Jer 10,16; 11,23; 14,5.15 u.a.
5. Vgl. Jer 10,20; 12,11f; 14,6 u.a.
6. Vgl. Jer 21,9 = 45(38),2.
7. Vgl. Jer 4,2; 5,2; 12,16 u.a.
8. Vgl. z.B. Dtn 4,33(LXX); 5,26.

in LXX-Jeremia gebraucht werden, besteht ein scheinbarer Widerspruch, denn die erste Bezeichnung schließt auf den ersten Blick die letzten beiden aus. Wie auch aus dem Vorkommen der Partikel ὄντως[9] (= wirklich) in der LXX hervorgeht, ist die Bezeichnung οἱ οὐκ ὄντες θεοί in der Bedeutung »die Götter, die gar nicht vorhanden sind bzw. eigentlich nicht existieren« zu verstehen. Wenn sie aber gar keine Götter sind, wieso heißen sie »andere bzw. fremde Götter«? Das Problem kann m.E. folgendermaßen gelöst werden. Hinsichtlich ihrer Verwendungsweise besteht zwischen den soeben genannten Bezeichnungen ein sachlicher Unterschied. Erstere gilt als eine Wesensbestimmung der Götter an sich, während die beiden letzten Relationsbegriffe bezogen auf menschliche Vorstellungen des Göttlichen sind. Die Bezeichnung θεοὶ ἕτεροι weist zunächst auf die Heterogenität der Göttervorstellungen im Vergleich mit dem geoffenbarten Jahwebild hin; die Bezeichnung θεοὶ ἀλλότριοι aber führt zu einem biblischen Verständnis des Begriffs der Entfremdung, die vom allgemeinen Verhältnis zwischen Gott und Volk ausgeht und sich in alle Äußerungen des menschlichen Lebens ausweitet (Jer 7,9).

Die Gattungsbezeichnung אלהים – θεός / θεοί bezieht sich eigentlich auf die menschlichen Vorstellungen von einem höchsten Wesen als Gegenstand religiöser Verehrung. Jahwe ist nicht identisch mit den menschlichen religiösen Vorstellungen von der Gottheit. Er erfüllt aber ein menschliches Verlagen und wird zu Gott, indem er sich seinem auserwählten Einzelnen und seinem Volk entsprechend ihrer Aufnahmefähigkeit offenbart. In LXX-Jer 7,23 lesen wir: Ἀκούσατε τῆς φωνῆς μου, καὶ ἔσομαι ὑμῖν εἰς θεόν, καὶ ὑμεῖς ἔσεσθέ μοι εἰς λαόν. Das erste Gebot »Du sollst keine anderen Götter neben/außer mir haben«, das die Einzigkeit und den Ausschließlichkeitsanspruch des Gottes Israels zum Ausdruck bringt, bedeutet eigentlich, daß von dem Moment an, wo Jahwe sich als Gott geoffenbart hat, alle bisherigen Göttervorstellungen hinfällig sind. Der Grund dafür, daß das Volk trotz der Selbstoffenbarung Jahwes weiterhin bei den nichtseienden Göttern schwört, wird auf eine ganz besondere Weise in LXX-Jer 9 gezeigt. Gott sagt, sie haben mich nicht erkannt (9,2), weil sie mich nicht erkennen wollten (9,5). Deshalb wird in LXX-9,9 festgestellt: ἐξέλιπον παρὰ τὸ μὴ εἶναι ἀνθρώπους· οὐκ ἤκουσαν τὴν φωνὴν τῆς ὑπάρξεως (= sie sind zugrunde gegangen, weil sie keine Menschen sind; sie haben »die Stimme der Existenz« nicht gehört). Der singuläre Ausdruck φωνὴ τῆς ὑπάρξεως, der das hebräische קול מקנה ersetzt, ist von ausgesprochener

---

9. Num 22,37; 1 Kön 12,24f; Weis 17,13; Jer 3,23; 10,19.

theologischer Bedeutung, denn er hat in LXX-Jer 9,9 den Aussagewert der oft im Deuteronomium vorkommenden Wendung φωνὴ Κυρίου τοῦ Θεοῦ bzw. φωνὴ Θεοῦ ζῶντος[10]. Andererseits bedeutet die ihm entgegengestellte Aussage τὸ μὴ εἶναι ἀνϑρώπους nicht, daß sie als Menschen nie existiert haben (οὐκ), sondern daß sie wegen ihrer gewollten Unkenntnis Gottes von der Existenz in die Inexistenz geraten sind (μή). Daraus ergibt sich, daß die Existenz der Götter vom Glauben der Menschen an sie ganz abhängig ist, während die Existenz der Menschen von Jahwe als die Existenz κατ᾽ ἐξοχήν bedingt ist.

III

Die verbale Formulierung οὐκ εἰσι ϑεοί kommt gehäuft in der Epistel Jeremias vor (V. 14.22.28.49.51.64.71) u.zw. als Epexegese der Aussage ψευδῆ εἰσί (V. 7), in der die nominale Formulierung οἱ ψευδεῖς ϑεοί (V. 58, 3mal) ihre Begründung findet. Betrachtet man beide nominalen Formulierungen οἱ οὐκ ὄντες ϑεοί und οἱ ψευδεῖς ϑεοί, so kommt man auf den Gedanken, daß der οὐκ ὤν des Jeremiabuches dem ψευδής der Epistel Jeremias entspricht. Somit aber stellt sich klar und deutlich die Frage nach dem Verhältnis der Inexistenz und der Unwahrheit in Bezug auf die Götter, die in LXX-Jeremia durch den Gebrauch der Negation οὐκ (und nicht μή) zum Ausdruck kommen. Diese bewusste Wortwahl weist darauf hin, daß Götter an sich nie existiert haben; nur handgemachte Götterbilder (ἔργα τῶν χειρῶν αὐτῶν – מעשׂי ידיהם)[11] sind den Menschen bekannt. Also: Weder taucht Jahwe aus dem Nichts auf, noch hebt sich die Religion Israels aus der Asche der fremden Religionen empor. Wenn nun in LXX-2Chr 13,9 die Bezeichnung ὁ μὴ ὤν ϑεός (im Sing.) für לא אלהים auftritt, so besagt sie nicht, daß es einst Jahwe nicht gegeben hat, sondern daß das Volk ihn als Gott durch die Vertreibung seiner rechtmäßigen Priester außer Wirksamkeit setzen will. Sie bezieht sich also auf ein falsch verstandenes Jahwe-Bild und dem daraus resultierenden falschen Dienst an ihm[12].

Die Bezeichnung οἱ ψευδεῖς ϑεοί hat keine hebräische Entsprechung. In MT-Jer 10,14 = 28(51),17; 13,25 begegnet uns aber die Bezeichnung שֶׁקֶר ohne weitere Bestimmung und dient zur Charakterisierung nicht der Pseudoprophetie sondern der Götterbilder. In LXX-Jer 16,17 tritt anstelle des einfachen hebräischen שֶׁקֶר die erweiterte griechi-

---

10. Siehe z.B. Dtn 5,25f.
11. Jer 1,16; 25,6. EpJer 50 vgl. V. 7.45f.
12. Vgl. LXX-Jer 5,12; 7,4

sche Form ψευδῆ εἴδωλα in der Bedeutung etwa »Trugbilder«. Wenn man unter εἴδωλον das Abbild einer objektiven Wirklichkeit versteht[13], dann sind die Götterbilder deshalb trügerisch, weil sie keine Wirklichkeit getreu darzustellen vermögen. Daher wird der Glaube an sie in LXX-Jeremia als Glaube εἰς οὐθέν (ohne hebräische Entsprechung)[14], εἰς κενόν – לשוא[15] bezeichnet. In Jer 10,14; 28(51),17 sowie in EpJer 24 wird die Wesenlosigkeit der Götterbilder folgendermaßen definiert: ψευδῆ ... οὐκ ἔστι πνεῦμα ἐν αὐτοῖς – ולא־רוח בם ... שקר: Es ist zu bemerken, daß πνεῦμα – רוח nicht näher bestimmt wird. Daher bleiben mehrere Deutungsmöglichkeiten offen. In EpJer 24.50 wird aber πνεῦμα – רוח eindeutig mit dem göttlichen Geist identifiziert, der weder auf die Bilder noch auf ihre Hersteller eingewirkt hat. Was sie eigentlich sind kommt im Jeremiabuch durch den Ausdruck לבם הרע שררות (= Starrsinn ihres bösartigen Herzens) zur Sprache, welcher die Bilder als bloße Projektionen der Subjektivität des Menschen erklärt und in der LXX auffallend variierend wiedergegeben wird: Nämlich durch a) ἐνθυμήματα (= Einfälle) τῆς καρδίας αὐτῶν τῆς πονηρᾶς (Jer 3,17) bzw. τῆς κακῆς (7,24) und b) τὰ ἀρεστὰ (= Gegenstand des Wohlgefallens) τῆς καρδίας ὑμῶν τῆς πονηρᾶς (16,12; vgl. 18,12) bzw. τῆς κακῆς (9,13MT).

Somit ergibt sich in der LXX etwa die Gleichung οὐκ εἰσὶ θεοί = ψευδεῖς εἰσί = οὐκ ἔστι πνεῦμα ἐν αὐτοῖς = לא־רוח = שקר = לא אלהים = בם), bei der der Begriff ψευδής – שקר zum Übergang vom abstrakten zum bildhaften Reden über die Götterverehrung und zur Verbindung der Abgötterei mit der Pseudoprophetie in Israel dient. Ψευδεῖς sind die Götter, weil sie nicht unabhängig vom subjektiven Bewußtsein existieren, und ψευδῆ sprechen ihre Diener, die Pseudopropheten (LXX-5,13). Darüber hinaus finden wir in 16,19f. die Gleichung ψευδῆ ... εἴδωλα = οὐκ ἔστιν ἐν αὐτοῖς ὠφέλημα (אין־בם מועיל = שקר ... הבל). Daran schließt sich die Gleichung μάταια = ἔργα ἐμπεπαιγμένα (10,15) bzw. μεμωκημένα (28[51],18; מעשׂה תעתעים = הבל). Besonders Aufmerksamkeit verdient die Bezeichnung μάταια ἀλλότρια für הבלי נכר (8,19), die die Fremdartigkeit sowie die Unangemessenheit des Glaubens an die Götter zum Ausdruck bringt. Das Jeremiabuch und sein(e) Übersetzer gehen anscheinend von folgendem Gedanken aus: Das Volk weiß, daß der Begriff »Gott« das Allerhöchste umfassen muß, was man sich vorstellen kann. Trotzdem erhebt es das Allerniedrigste für sich zum Gott.

---

13. Plato, Σοφιστής, 266b-c: Εἴδωλον (=Abbild) im Unterschied zu φάντασμα (= Phantasiegebilde).
14. Jer 3,9.
15. Jer 6,29; 18,15.

Der Begriff der Entfremdung, dessen Quintessenz auch in Hab 2,18-19 zusammengefaßt wird, erfährt im Jeremiabuch in mehreren Textvariationen mit wechselnder Intension und Intensität seine feste Bestimmung. Am eindrucksvollsten sind m.E.: a) Jer 2,13, wo als Gottesklage die Aussage vorgebracht wird: ἐμὲ ἐγκατέλιπον, πηγὴν ὕδατος ζωῆς καὶ ὤρυξαν ἑαυτοῖς λάκκους συντετριμμένους οἳ οὐ δυνήσονται ὕδωρ συνέχειν (vgl. 17,13), b) 2,27: ἔστρεψαν ἐπ᾽ ἐμὲ νῶτα καὶ οὐ πρόσωπα αὐτῶν (39[32],33 vgl. LXX-7,24). In diesem Sinne sind die nichtseienden Götter als θεοὶ ἀλλότριοι zu betrachten, u.zw. in radikalem Gegensatz zum Gott Israels, der laut Jer 23,23 ein θεὸς ἐγγίζων und οὐχὶ θεὸς πόρρωθεν ist.

IV

Neben dem Ausdruck οἱ οὐκ ὄντες θεοί tritt im Jeremiabuch[16] die Formulierung ὁ ὤν (= der Seiende) für Gott auf, die anstelle eines hebräischen אהה gebraucht zu werden scheint. Somit aber taucht in der LXX eine Lesart auf, die keine hebräische Entsprechung hat und klar und deutlich an LXX Ex 3,14 erinnert und als Oppositionsbegriff zu οὐκ ὄντες θεοί dient. Man fragt sich: a) Hat die LXX des Jeremiabuches diese Lesart vorgefunden?; b) Hat sie sie erfunden; oder c) hat man einfach den hebräischen Text schlecht lesen bzw. verstehen können und daher nach dem Sinne des Pentateuchs ergänzt?; d) Was hat dazu bewogen, gerade diese Wortwahl zu treffen, die das Gott-Götter-Verhältnis erneut in den Vordergrund rückt?; e) Welche weiteren Konsequenzen sind daraus zu ziehen?

Es kann kein Zufall sein, daß ὁ ὤν im Jeremiabuch nicht als irgendeine beliebige Gottesbezeichnung, sondern m.E. als der geoffenbarte Name Gottes am brennenden Dornbusch LXX-Ex 3,14[17] verwendet wird. Darauf weist die syntaktisch-stilistische Beschaffenheit des Textes hin.

In der hebräischen Formulierung אהיה אשר אהיה (Ex 3,14) hat man eine volksetymologische Erklärung des Namens יהוה gesehen, die man mit »ich bin der ich bin« oder »ich werde sein, der ich sein werde« wiedergibt. An dieser Stelle, die ausgesprochen theologischen Charakter hat, bevorzugt die LXX statt einer wörtlichen Wiedergabe die Interpretation ἐγώ εἰμι ὁ ὤν. Das substantivierte Partizip ὁ ὤν erinnert an das ὄν

---

16. So z.St. J. ZIEGLER (Hg.), *Ieremias, Baruch, Threni, Epistula Ieremiae*, (Septuaginta Gottensis, 15), Göttingen, ²1976. Anders aber z.St. A. RAHLFS (Hg.), *Septuaginta. Id est Testamentum graece iuxta interpretes. Duo volumina in uno*, Stuttgart, (1935) 1979.

17. Anders Ch.H. DODD, *The Bible and the Greeks*, London, 1935, p. 4.

bzw. μὴ ὄν von Parmenides[18], unterscheidet sich aber deutlich darin, daß es nicht ein Neutrum (τὸ ὄν), sondern ein Maskulinum (ὁ ὤν) ist, u.zw. ohne weitere Bestimmung. Er ist also der absolut Seiende, ὁ ὄντως ὤν[19], der alles aus dem Nichts geschaffen hat (2Makk 7,28).

Der Name Gottes ὁ Ὤν ist im Jeremiabuch von anderen Gottesbezeichnungen umgeben, nämlich: Δεσπότης (אדני) und Κύριος (יהוה). Aus dem näheren Kontext ergeben sich noch weitere Eigenschaften Gottes.

In Jer 1,6 haben wir eine bekenntnisartige Formulierung, die in V. 5 und 7 näher bestimmt wird: a) V. 5: Der Seiende ist der Schöpfer eines jeden Menschen und kennt seine Geschöpfe bis ins Herz hinein; b) V. 7: Er greift in den Lebensweg des erwählten Einzelnen bzw. seines wahren Propheten ein und gibt ihm Kraft, Gottes Willen zu verkünden und zu erfüllen.

In Jer 4,10 hätte man erwartet, daß der wahre Prophet, bzw. Jeremia, klar und deutlich den Pseudopropheten den Vorwurf macht, sie hätten das Volk getäuscht. Aber Jeremia übergeht die Pseudopropheten und wendet sich direkt an Gott mit einer Frage, auf die man keine positive Antwort erwarten kann: »Hast du, Der Seiende, der Gebieter, der Herr, dieses Volk getäuscht?«. Damit soll gezeigt werden, daß Lüge und Wahrheit einander ausschließen, und der Seiende, der die Quelle der Wahrheit ist, nicht zugleich der Urheber der Lüge sein kann. In Jer 14,13, wo ebenfalls als Name Gottes »der Seiende« gebraucht wird, wird dieser Sachverhalt verdeutlicht.

Laut Jer 39(32),17ff. ist »der Seiende« der allmächtige und allwissende Schöpfer sowie der gnädige und gerechte Richter der ganzen Welt. An diese universalen Aussagen schließen sich andere, die die Erwählung des Volkes und das rettende Eingreifen Gottes in seine Geschichte schildern. Dies geschieht in Analogie zu Jer 1,16, wo von der Erschaffung und Erwählung des Einzelnen die Rede ist (vgl. Ex 3). Damit will man betonen, daß der Seiende der Herr alles Seins ist. Die Götter als die Nichtseienden können daher nicht über die Seienden verfügen. Diese Feststellung wird in der Epistel Jeremias näher beschrieben[20].

V

Obwohl die Aussage οὗτοι οὐκ εἰσὶ θεοί ganz selten, aber doch mit erkennbarer Absicht, im Jeremiabuch vorkommt, tritt sie in der Epistel

---

18. Parmenides (F 2.8ff. vgl. F 3.22; ausführlich F 7-8) in H. Diels & W. Kranz (Hg.), *Die Fragmente der Vorsokratiker*. Bd. I, Dublin – Zürich, [14]1969, pp. 231. 234-240.
19. Vgl. etwa Plato, Ἐπινομίς, 976c:8.
20. EpJer 33-37.52-53.58.63.65-67.

Jeremias auffallend oft auf, sie hat textgliedernde Funktion und wird zu ihrem Zentralthema. Die sprachliche und gedankliche Beschaffenheit der sich wiederholenden Gedanken über die nichtseienden Götter deutet m.E. eher auf griechischen Ursprung hin und scheint dem Text als ordnendes Element beigefügt worden zu sein.

Die Epistel Jeremias ist eigentlich in der Form einer Disputation angelegt, in der ein Fragekomplex erörtert wird. Die Hauptfrage, ob es neben Jahwe, dem Gott Israels andere Götter gibt, zerfällt dort in zwei Teilfragen. Erstere wird durch die gesammte Argumentation impliziert und lautet: Was sind eigentlich die Götter? Letztere wird explizit in V. 29 gestellt: Wieso werden sie denn Götter genannt? Erklärt wird dies mit einer Namensätiologie bzw. Pseudoetymologie, ein Stilmittel, welches nur auf den ersten Blick an Ex 3,14 erinnert: Θεοί, ὅτι γυναῖκες παρατιθέασιν θεοῖς... Es ist m.E. anzunehmen, daß man dadurch auf Begriffe wie φύσει und θέσει θεός anspielen wollte, was jedoch explizit in Gal 4,8 (οἱ φύσει μὴ ὄντες θεοί) enthalten ist.

Konkrete abwertende Götterschilderungen und abstrakte Begrifflichkeit wechseln sich in der Epistel Jeremias ab, wobei die abstrakte Begrifflichkeit dem Nachweis dient, daß die Göttervorstellungen nicht nur falsch sind, sondern längst überholt. An deren Stelle trat in der hellenistischen Zeit im Griechentum zunehmend eine Art von theoretischem Atheismus auf, während im Judentum ein praktischer Atheismus wuchs, d.h. sie verließen ihren wahren Gott und sein Gesetz zugunsten von selbstgemachten Göttern.

Im Unterschied zum Jeremiabuch, wo die Aussagen in polemischem Kontext in Bezug auf die Pseudoprophetie und die Abgötterei zu finden sind, nimmt die Epistel Jeremias eine nüchterne apologetische Stellung gegenüber der Degradierung und Depotenzierung der Götterwelt ein. Dies geschieht aufgrund philosophisch-theologischer Reflexion, die sich vor allem in den Verbaladjektiven νομιστέον[21], κλητέον[22], ἐκδεκτέον[23], γνωστέον[24] zeigt. Umgeben wird sie von einer satirischen Veränderung des allgemein bekannten alttestamentlichen Stoffes bezogen auf das Gott-Götter-Verhältnis[25], so daß der so offensichtliche Sarkasmus des Jeremiabuches nun ins Komische gezogen wird[26].

---

21. Nur in EpJer 39.44.56.63.
22. Nur in EpJer 39.44.63.
23. Nur in EpJer 56.(63A) (wahrscheinlich ein Neologismus).
24. Nur in EpJer 51.
25. R.G. KRATZ, *Der Brief des Jeremia* (ATD.Apokryphen, 5), Göttingen, 1998, pp. 77-79.
26. Dazu siehe H.D. PREUSS, *Verspottung fremder Religionen im Alten Testament* (BWANT, 92), Stuttgart, 1971, p. 262ff.

Ohne auf die Einzelheiten der Exegese einzugehen, wollen wir einige bedeutungserklärende Punkte ihres eigentümlichen philosophisch-theologischen Gedankenganges zusammenfassen.

1) Schon in V. 3 ist ein grundsätzlicher Unterschied zwischen Schein und Sein der Götter zu erkennen. Es handelt sich nicht um die Wirklichkeit der Gottheit, sondern um die Darstellung einer Fiktion. Die Aufgabe des Gewissens (διάνοια), also der weisen Gesinnung, ist, zwischen Wirklichem und Fiktivem zu unterscheiden.

2) Hinter dem Schein steckt nach V. 7 die Lüge. Die Götter haben keine Sprache[27]. Daran erkennt man, daß sie keine Götter sind. Demnach müssen die Menschen ihr Bewußtsein und ihre Einstellung den Göttern gegenüber ändern, um zum wahren Gott zurückkehren zu können.

3) Hinsichtlich ihrer Entstehung sowie ihrer Existenz widersprechen sie den empirischen Gegebenheiten des israelitischen Glaubens (V. 15). Es ist auch bezeichnend für die Epistel Jeremias, daß sie, indem sie versucht, die Götterbilder graduell abzubauen/-werten, zeigt, was das geltende Gottesbild in Israel ist.

4) Erst am Ende sagt der Verfasser der Epistel Jeremias (V. 72) was die Götter wirklich sind, nämlich εἴδωλα d.h. materielle Verobjektivierungen von fiktiven Gedanken, eigentlich absurde und widersinnige psychologische Hypostasierungen der Ängste der Menschen vor dem Nichts. Somit wird aber die Akzeptanz von völlig unnatürlichen und unlogischen, subjektiven Äußerungen über die Götter widerlegt.

VI

Der Gebrauch der abstrakten Begriffe ὁ ὤν und ἡ ὕπαρξις für Gott und οἱ οὐκ ὄντες θεοί für die Götter charakterisiert vor allem die Übersetzungssprache des Jeremiabuches, die bewußt an LXX-Ex 3,14 anknüpft. In der Urfassung sind aber schon abstrakte Formulierungen vorhanden, wie z.B. הבל, שקר, לא אליהם. Das bedeutet, daß der/die Übersetzer des jeremianischen Schrifttums anerkannt habe/n, daß die Abstraktionen auch zu Jeremias Zeit üblich waren. Die Tatsache, daß die Vorsokratiker ähnliche oder vergleichbare Formulierungen in Bezug auf die Gottheit getroffen haben, läßt die Vermutung aufkommen, daß entweder a) schon zu der Zeit der Abfassung des Jeremiabuches – und nicht erst in der hellenistischen Zeit – ein Einfluß des Griechentums auf die Sprach- und Denkstrukturen des Alten Testaments zu spüren war,

---

27. 1 Kor 12,2.

oder b) ein gegenseitiger Austausch stattgefunden hat, oder aber auch c) daß es sich um zwei parallele Phänomene in der Entwicklungsgeschichte des menschlichen Geistes handelt, die als solche erst in der hellenistischen Ära, wo Griechentum und Judentum sich aufs engste berühren, anerkannt werden. Dies schlägt sich auch in der Sprache der LXX und der deuterokanonischen Schriften nieder.

Die theologischen Ideen, die in der Epistel Jeremias abgehandelt werden, sind schon im Jeremiabuch vorhanden. Dort wird einerseits die Zwecklosigkeit, die Wirkungslosigkeit sowie die Nichtigkeit der Götter geschildert, andererseits aber auch die Eitelkeit der Menschen, die sich zu Gott machen wollen, indem sie aus dem Nichts die Nichtseienden entstehen lassen, aber statt über sie zu herrschen, von ihnen beherrscht werden[28]. Somit wird die Quintessenz der Götzenverehrung aufgezeigt, die von der Epistel Jeremias aufgenommen und authentisch ausgelegt wird. Dies dürfte m.E der entscheidende Grund dafür sein, daß die Epistel Jeremias unter den Diaspora-Juden kanonische Anerkennung fand.

Septuaginta Unternehmen
Theaterstr. 7
D-37073 Göttingen

Evangelia G. DAFNI

---

28. Gal 4,8.

THE PSALM HEADINGS
A CANONICAL RELECTURE OF THE PSALMS

The psalm headings offer the readers a variety of informations. Advices for a musical performance, specifications about the genre, the kinds of prayer or references to a historical person are presented to the readers before they begin to read a psalm.

Within exegesis it has long been recognized that the psalm titles do not belong to the psalm texts themselves but are an editorial addition. While this realization often caused a neglect of the titles within an interpretation focusing on the single psalms, for a canonical exegesis the psalm headings offer important informations. The repeated elements of the psalm titles are considered valuable elements for the reconstruction of the growing of the Psalter. Furthermore those headings that add a reference to a well-known historical person or situation encourage a canonical relecture as they provide links between the psalms and texts of other biblical books.

How this relecture unfolds and how it offers the readers a new perspective on their own political situation will be shown by using those psalms that are linked to David.

1. *The Communicational and Intertextual Function of the Psalm Headings*

With the addition of a psalm title the communicational situation as well as the context of a psalm changes. Looking at the communicational situation of the text it becomes obvious that the psalm headings add a new level of communication. Beside the voice of the lyrical speaker of a psalm there is now the voice of someone who attaches informations to this psalm. Subsequently there is also a new addressee, someone who not only perceives the psalm text but also includes the information of the psalm heading to his or her understanding and/or usage of the text. If a title refers to a historic person or situation this information allows the readers to assign the psalm to a specific situation or even an author. The readers then perceive the text through the eyes of a historical subject or with this person in mind.

Furthermore such headings establish links to other biblical texts and thus lead the readers to an intertextual reading. When the title points out another text the readers will add this information to their understanding of the psalm. Subsequently the texts will start to interfere with one another, adding information as well as changing the point of view. Thereby this interaction will affect all involved texts that are the psalms as well as the historical texts. Thus the intertextual dimension of the psalm titles ties up different texts from the scriptures and subsequently encourages a new reading that understands one text in the light of the other[1]. In this way the psalm titles clearly initiate a canonical reading of the psalms.

2. *David in the Psalm Headings*

From all the psalm headings referring to a historic person those pointing to David are by far the most numerous[2] ones. Out of the 73 psalm titles containing the notice לדוד[3], 13[4] provide more than a general reference to a historic person[5] including references to the life of David according to the description of the books of Samuel. In most of these headings the reference to the historical situation is given quite accurately and it points the readers to one specific situation in the life of David[6].

1. Cf. J.L. MAYS, *The David of the Psalms*, in *Interpratation* 40 (1986) 143-155, p. 54.

2. Other persons mentioned are Asaph (12 occurrences), sons of Korah (11 occurrences), Solomon (2 occurrences), Heman, Moses (1 occurrence).

3. As recent studies have shown the frequently used לדוד did at first not point to a Davidic authorship, but marked the psalm as a prayer spoken by David. Only later לדוד was understood as information about authorship. Cf. M. KLEER, *"Der liebliche Sänger der Psalmen Israels"*. *Untersuchungen zu David als Richter und Beter der Psalmen* (BBB, 108). Frankfurt am Main, Athenäum, 1996, pp. 78-86; C. RÖSEL, *Die messianische Redaktion des Psalters. Studien zu Entstehung und Theologie der Sammlung Psalm 2–89** (Calwer theologische Monographien. Reihe A: Bibelwissenschaft, 19), Stuttgart, Calwer Verlag, 1999, pp. 161-166.

4. Ps 3; 7; 18; 34; 51; 52, 54; 56; 57; 59; 60; 63; 142.

5. From all the psalm headings referring to David those of the second book of the Psalter are considered the oldest ones, whereas the other Davidic psalm titles may have been inserted according to this example. Cf. F.L. HOSSFELD & E. ZENGER, *Psalmen 51–100* (HTK/AT), Freiburg i. B., Herder, 2000, p. 33; RÖSEL, *Die messianische Redaktion* (n. 3), p. 169.

6. There are no definite criteria according to which the references to the historical texts are made. Mostly it are "general parallels between the situation described in the Psalm and some incident in the life of David": B.S. CHILDS, *Psalm Titles and Midrashic Exegesis*, in *JSS* 16 (1971) 137-150, p. 147. Nevertheless, most of the references are quite unambiguous. This is mainly achieved by the use of proper names combined with a short summary of the alluded situation. For a comprehensive discussion, cf. E. SLOMOVIC, *Toward an Understanding of the Formation of Historical Titles in the Book of Psalms*, in *ZAW* 91 (1979) 350-380; J.-M. AUWERS, *Le David des psaumes et les psaumes de David*, in L. DESROUSSEAUX & J. VERMEYLEN (eds.), *Figures de David à travers la Bible. XVIIe congrès de l'ACFEB (Lille, 1er – 5 septembre 1997)* (LD, 177), Paris, Cerf, 1999, pp. 187-225, esp. 213-217.

Asking for the function of these references it is generally assumed that David serves as a figure of identification. David is seen as the ideal praying king as well as the suffering righteous one or the one who is saved by God in all situations, even from sin. The readers may identify with David and his distress and speak the same prayer in their own difficult situation. Doing so they might gain confidence, because they know that the prayers of David were answered. Hence David is a general example with whom the readers can identify[7].

Looking at the psalm texts, however, it becomes obvious that this explanation does only cover one aspect. While the images of the conflicts and enemies in the psalms are open for identification in all kind of distress the figure of David restricts these possibilities. Although a prayer David himself said or even wrote might be ascribed more efficiency it also limits its possible usage. Only somebody who sees himself/herself in a similar situation like the one the psalm heading mentions for David can pray the psalm like David did. Therefore it appears that there is still another way of identification with David.

3. *The Transformation of the Context*

Focusing on the process of identification it becomes obvious that this causes a change of the psalm's context. The transformation of the context that is initiated by the psalm headings can be viewed as a twofold process. Adapting the text for a situation in the life of David is only the first step. Thereby the ritual or spiritual context of the psalm as a text for everybody declines and it becomes a text of David, providing some insight into his inner life and his intimate thoughts[8]. So both texts, the psalm itself and the story of David, fuse together. When, as a second step, a reader identifies with David, the psalm is again removed from its settings and put into a new context, the one of the reader. And it is this context that encourages the identification with David. The answer to the question why it seemed desirable to pray like David did can therefore be found in the reconstruction of this specific context.

The starting point for a reconstruction of the reader's context is the information given in the psalm titles. Both their content and the time when they probably were added to the psalms have to be considered.

---

7. Cf. MAYS, *The David of the Psalms* (n. 1), p. 152; N. FÜGLISTER, *Die Verwendung und das Verständnis der Psalmen und des Psalters um die Zeitenwende*, in J. SCHREINER (ed.), *Beiträge zur Psalmenforschung. Psalm 2 und 22* (FzB, 60). Würzburg, Echter Verlag, 1988, pp. 319-384, esp. 370-371.

8. Cf. CHILDS, *Psalm Titles* (n. 6), p. 149.

Although the time of origin of these psalm titles cannot be given exactly it nevertheless appears to be a common agreement that the historical information was added in postexilic times, as a way of interpreting and actualising already existing biblical texts[9]. Looking at the content the most striking element of those headings pointing to the life of David is the accumulation of references to the same situation, the conflict between David and Saul[10].

The query for the function of these psalm headings hence starts with the question for the relevance of the conflict between David and Saul in the postexilic period. Thereby two interweaving traces may be followed: one identifying David and Saul with the representatives of southern and northern Israel and the other recognizing David as the hoped for (messianic) king.

3.1. *Saul and David as a Personification of Israel and Judah*

Focusing on the two historical persons, Saul and David, they may be seen as representatives of the two kingdoms of Israel, Israel in the north and Judah in the south. If they are viewed as personifications of the competing kingdoms, the conflict between David and Saul is a controversy of current interest from the sixth century onwards. According to the books of Ezra and Nehemiah the people returning from Babylonian exile are competing with the inhabitants of the land, especially those of northern Samaria. Although in the beginning Judah was part of the province of Samaria and therefore politically dependent from the north, the people returning from exile wanted to draw a clear dividing line between themselves and those who remained in Israel. They tried to exclude them from any activity going on in Jerusalem. While Samaria had a positive interest, political as well as religious, in the events in Jerusalem, the exiles from Jerusalem did not accept the inhabitants of Samaria – neither the descendents of the former Israelites, who worshiped YHWH, nor the descendents of the deportees from Assyria – as a genuine religious partner[11]. Furthermore the demand for exclusiveness of Jerusalem

---

9. Cf. CHILDS, *Psalm Titles* (n. 6), pp. 148-149; SLOMOVIC, *Toward an Understanding* (n. 6), p. 350; KLEER, *Der liebliche Sänger* (n. 3), pp. 82-83; HOSSFELD & ZENGER, *Psalmen 51–100* (n. 5), p. 30.

10. From the thirteen biographical psalm titles eleven refer to a situation of a conflict. Six psalms refer to the conflict between David and Saul (Ps 18, 52, 54, 57, 59, 142); Ps 3 and 63 refer to the conflict between David and Absalom, Ps 34 and 56 to a conflict with Philistines; Ps 18 and 60 are related to a general situation of fight; the reference of Ps 7 remains uncertain. Cf. SLOMOVIC, *Toward an Understanding* (n. 6), pp. 365-377.

11. Cf. F. DEXINGER, *Der Ursprung der Samaritaner im Spiegel der frühen Quellen*, in ID. & R. PUMMER (eds.), *Die Samaritaner* (Wege der Forschung, 604), Darmstadt, Wissenschaftliche Buchgesellschaft, 1991, pp. 67-140, esp. 91-92.

lead to similar demands in Samaria and thus prolonged and increased the confrontation. This conflict went on until the separation of Samaria, most probably in the second century BC[12].

In this situation the returning exiles might have felt like David pursued by Saul. In the image of Saul as representative of northern Israel the assumptions of the syncretic north, were there is no true worship of YHWH, are resumed. The exiles of Jerusalem were convinced that they were the true Israel, the chosen remains of the pre-exilic Israel. They alone had to rebuild Jerusalem, the temple as well as the city, and to re-establish the cult. In this situation prayers of David can function as a point of identification, giving hope and confidence during these difficult times.

3.2. David as the Hoped for King

Connected with the mention of David there are also some traces of a nationalistic hope, an expectation that the Davidic kingdom might rise again and regain independence. However, this hope has certainly not been dominant in the early post-exilic times. Especially the books of Ezra and Nehemiah provide a very un-Davidic picture of their time. Although a descendant of David, Zerubbabel, appears among the leaders of the people, his royal descent of Jehoiachin, king of Judah, is never mentioned. Rather the Persian kings are shown as undisputed kings, through whom God acted on Israel. The worldview of Ezra and Nehemiah shows an almost total acceptance of the given political situation and no interest in any perspective of change[13]. Consequently there is no place for the house of David as a symbol for national unity in this kind of political thought[14].

But this picture is not the only one of that time. Beside this view traces of a Davidic hope can be found in the prophets Haggai and Zechariah. Although their positions differ, their prophecies show that the returning exiles were stirred by some eschatological hopes. These expectations were linked to Zerubbabel, son of Shealtiel (cf. Hag 2,23). He is of Davidic origin, and he further is strongly related to the restoration

---

12. Cf. A.H. GUNNEWEG, *Geschichte Israels: von den Anfängen bis Bar Kochba und von Theodor Herzl bis zur Gegenwart* (Theologische Wissenschaft, 2), Stuttgart, Kohlhammer, [6]1989, p. 170.

13. S. JAPHET, *Sheshbazzar and Zerubbabel. Against the Background of the Historical and Religious Tendencies of Ezra-Nehemiah*, in *ZAW* 94 (1982) 66-98, esp. 72.

14. But nevertheless in Neh 9,36f also another tendency might be observed. According to JAPHET, *Sheshbazzar and Zerubbabel* (n. 13), p. 79, there is "a feeling of despair in the face of the present and its sufferings, and in that feeling there is a latent hope of change".

of the temple (Ezra 3, Hag 1), two aspects that mark him as the ideal candidate. The period of restoration thus also was a time of ferment, containing messianic hopes as well as hopes for liberation, independence and redemption[15].

During this period the psalm headings referring explicitly to the struggles of David on his way to become Israel's king can provide a link to the actual situation of the returning exiles. Far from calling for a revolution the psalm titles keep alive the hope for a Davidic king, who despite all challenges will succeed. This gives hope to people in their own difficult situations. They can look forward to the restoration of the house of David. For the understanding of the psalms this means that, while the identification of the enemies stays the same, the lyrical subject of the psalms is not understood as anybody or Israel as a whole, but as a king like David[16]. As David was threatened and his becoming or being king seemed almost impossible, so it is now. The hope for a re-establishing of a Davidic king is small, but with the point of view of the psalms the hopes are supported by God.

3.3. *The Time of the Maccabean Uprising*

The political dimension of the Davidic psalm headings is of interest once again during the Maccabean uprising[17]. The possibility for an identification with David and Saul is thereby further extended. The parallels to the conflict between David and Saul are not restricted to Judah against Israel, but can be compared to the situation of the Maccabees fighting against an almost overwhelming enemy. As David had to flee before Saul, Mattatias flees before Antiochus IV, seeking shelter in the mountains. In this context the references to the conflict between Absalom and his father David also can be read politically. Like David the Maccabees have to stand their ground against resistance from their own

---

15. The books Ezra and Nehemiah describe these times from a historical distance "and after a period of time during which those hopes and ferments flickered and were suppressed" (JAPHET, *Ibid.*, p. 79).

16. Rösel sees this function not in the psalm headings but in the redaction of the messianic Psalter, Ps 2–89. There David appears as a king appointed by God and the promises he received nurture the hope that there also exists a future for the Davidic kingdom. The political dimension of this collection of psalms encourages the hopes for a restoration of the kingdom and the Davidic dynasty. Cf. RÖSEL, *Die messianische Redaktion* (n. 3), pp. 201-213.

17. A literary connection between David and the Maccabees has been observed for the literary construction of the first book of Maccabees, as it is structured similar to the history of the Israelite kingdom in the times of David and Salomon.

people[18]. Nevertheless, the conflict between Judah and Samaria still existed. When the Hasmonean king Hyrkanos made use of a power-political vacuum between the Greek and Roman empires and increased the Hasmonean empire to the south and to the north, claiming regions from Samaria (135/4-104 BCE), the old political and religious rivalry was again revived[19].

The political situation in the time of the Maccabean uprising could easily be understood in the light of history. The parallel story of David provided hope and encouragement as well as justification to the readers of the psalm, who understood the text from the view of David and in this way gained a new perspective on their own situation.

4. Re-reading the Psalms

The psalm headings point to an active and creative re-reading process that is not restricted to one actualisation or interpretation. Nor does the editing of the psalms, as it becomes obvious in the titles, occur as a systematic exegesis of the psalms. The exegetical activity that took place in the addition of the psalm titles rather appears to be a lively process that was continued over many years[20], and took into consideration the changing situation of the readers of the psalms.

The connection to historical texts, to stories about the life of David, his ascent, conflict with Saul, his son Absalom, as well as his enemies in general, add a political dimension to the re-reading of the psalm texts. The titles point to a political situation that is very much similar to the one the readers live through. Thereby David is the point of identification as he experiences similar incidents of trouble and danger from enemies as the readers of the psalms. Although David is never portrayed as a king in the psalm headings, the readers know that he succeeded and became king despite all hardship. This makes him a desirable point of identification. As history seems to repeat itself, confidence and encouragement may be drawn from the historical events and this may help to overcome one's own doubts and sense of insecurity. The reading of the

18. Cf. S. VON DOBBELER, *Die Bücher 1–2 Makkabäer* (Neuer Stuttgarter Kommentar. Altes Testament, 11), Stuttgart, Katholisches Bibelwerk, 1997, p. 44.

19. Cf. DEXINGER, *Der Ursprung der Samaritaner* (n. 11), p. 135.

20. As new titles were added the image of David changed again and he became the royal author of the psalms. Cf. for example the headings of the LXX Psalter were more and also different references to the life of David were added. Cf. SLOMOVIC, *Toward an Understanding* (n. 6), pp. 356-364; A. PIETERSMA, *David in the Greek Psalms*, in *VT* 30 (1980), 213-226. A similar activity is also evident from the Targum and the Peshitta. Cf. CHILDS, *Psalm Titles* (n. 6), p. 143.

psalms in light of generally acknowledged texts and the recollection of David and his life assures the readers of their own way and raises their hopes. Thus a canonical relecture of the psalms initiated by the psalm headings is not restricted to an inner-biblical re-reading process, but it links the situation of the readers with the texts and thus enables them to find answers to their most urgent questions as well as a new perspective on their own life.

Theologische Fakultät Erfurt   Susanne GILLMAYR-BUCHER
Domstraße 10
D-99084 Erfurt

SIRACH AND WISDOM: A PLEA FOR CANONICITY

Today the majority of Christian denominations agree on the canonicity of the 27 books that comprise the New Testament, but there is still disagreement on the content of the Old Testament canon. However, several facts seem to leave open the possibility for agreement on an extended Old Testament canon. For one, historically, a parallel situation seems to have occurred in relation to the New Testament. Not only did Luther judge the books he designated Old Testament "Apocrypha" as of lesser status, but he made a similar judgment in regard to Hebrews, James, Jude and Revelation. In both the Old and New Testament, the books Luther judged to be of "inferior quality" were placed at the end of the Old and New Testament, respectively, in his 1534 German edition. This practice was followed in the Tyndale editions until 1539, when the grouping of the New Testament books returned to the traditional order, which has since been followed in English editions of the New Testament[1]. Thus an earlier disagreement was eventually resolved. Additionally, it can be pointed out that in insisting on the shorter Old Testament canon, Luther and other Reformers were themselves departing from more than a millennium of tradition in Western christendom which had accepted the more inclusive canon.

This presentation will first survey the history of the development of the Old Testament canon and then the recent argumentation for a wider canon, finally focusing more specifically on additional reasons that seem to support the acceptance of a canonical status for the Books of Sirach and Wisdom.

1. *History of Development of the Old Testament Canon*

The history of Israel reflects differences in regard to accepted authoritative sacred writings; the Samaritans, for example, accepted only the Pentateuch. Nonetheless, the group of authoritative writings continued to expand until the Christian period, and Raymond Brown has noted that a book like Jubilees was composed and read by various groups of Jews,

---

1. R.F. COLLINS, in ID. & R.E. BROWN, Art. *Canonicity*, in R.E. BROWN, J.A. FITZMEYER & R.E. MURPHY (eds.), *The New Jerome Biblical Commentary*, London, Chapman, 1990, pp. 1042-1043, §45-46, p. 1051, §86.

including the Qumran community, even though in some points and laws it was not in harmony with the Pentateuch, which was accepted as sacred scripture by 400 BCE[2].

Already during the patristic period, there was disagreement regarding the number of books in the Old Testament canon. Eusebius (*H.E.* IV.xxvi.13) notes that Melito (2nd century) returned from the East with what seems to have been intended as a list of 22 books, evidence of the influence of the Jewish canon, and that Origen (3rd century) likewise knew of a list of 22 books (*H.E.* VI.xxv). Nonetheless, in regard to the reading of passages, even entire books, Origen distinguished between "their scriptures" (those of the Jews) and "our scriptures" (those of the church = LXX)[3].

In opting for the shorter canon, Luther was following the view of Jerome, who regarded the "Palestinian canon" as equivalent to the Scriptures used by Jesus. Augustine, Jerome's contemporary, disagreed and accepted all the books in the Septuagint canon, and his influence was decisive in the West. Albert Sundberg maintains, however, that even in the East the impact of the Jewish canon on the church was that of a list of books, not a canonical text, and refers to both Athanasius and Epiphanius in the East as attempting to preserve Christian usage within the strictures of the Jewish list, much as Origen had done[4]. Conversely, in the West, Hilary of Poitiers appears to be following Origen's list of the Jewish canon, but nonetheless utilizes Judith, Tobit, Wisdom, Baruch, and Susanna similarly to the way in which he cites Jewish canonical scriptures[5]. Thus while the influence of Augustine won the day for the longer canon in the West until the time of Luther, even in the East there seem to be indications that the Jewish canon was not completely determinative.

A canonical theory commonly accepted until the 1960s[6] held that the longer "Alexandrian" or "Septuagint" canon constituted the Sacred Scripture of the Alexandrian Jews, while the shorter "Palestinian" or

2. *Ibid.*, p. 1039, §26.
3. A.C. SUNDBERG, *The "Old Testament": A Christian Canon*, in *CBQ* 30 (1968) 143-155, p. 148.
4. *Ibid.*, p. 149.
5. H.H. HOWORTH, *The Influence of St. Jerome on the Canon of the Western Church. II*, in *JTS* 11 (1909-10) 323-325.
6. J.T. LIENHARD, *The Bible, the Church, and Authority: The Canon of the Christian Bible in History and Theology*, Collegeville MN, Liturgical Press, 1995, pp. 68-69, notes two earlier theories that were successively discarded. The first maintained that the NT quotes only the books in the shorter canon and that the Christian OT was thus defined by Jesus and the apostles. However in 1713 the earliest collection of NT use of the "Apocrypha" was published in Amsterdam by G. Surenhusius. In the 16th century, the Jewish scholar Elias Levita contended that the Jewish canon had been closed in the time of Ezra and thus was the only authentic canon. Abraham Kuenen refuted this theory in 1876.

"Hebrew" canon, consisting of only the books eventually declared canonical by the Pharisaic rabbis near the end of the first century CE, was the Bible of the Palestinian Jews, including those in the Age of the Apostles. According to this theory, it was the Alexandrian canon which the Christian church accepted as its official list of canonical books. The theory has long since been discredited, most notably by Sundberg, beginning with an article in 1958[7], taking into account the data from Qumran.

2. Recent Argumentation on the Christian OT Canon

From the Protestant perspective the 20th-century argumentation for canonicity of the "Apocrypha" began in 1958 with Sundberg's article *The Old Testament of the Early Church*, followed by a monograph with the same title in 1964[8]. In 1966 the *Catholic Biblical Quarterly* published the texts of three papers by Samuel Sandmel, a Jewish scholar, Roland Murphy, a Roman Catholic exegete, and Sundberg; these had been presented at a symposium on the canon held at the previous annual meeting of the Society of Biblical Literature.

a. Samuel Sandmel

Sandmel first briefly asserts that Jewish inquiry into the history of the canon reflects the general trend in biblical scholarship. Secondly, he uses the word "quasicanonical" to refer to the Jewish rabbinic literature, noting that it has functioned within Judaism as if innately merged with Scripture, "co-authoritative" with Scripture. Finally, from Sandmel's particular scholarly perspective, canon must be viewed as both a logical development and one determined by fortuitous circumstances; it only reflects the sanctity which a given era happens to assign to a given number of books[9].

b. Roland Murphy

Murphy begins by insisting on the relation between inspiration and canonicity. While inspiration has to do with God's influence on the

---

7. A.C. SUNDBERG, *The Old Testament of the Early Church*, in *HTR* 51 (1958) 205-226 and ID., *The Old Testament of the Early Church* (Harvard Theological Studies, 20), Cambridge, MA, Harvard University Press; London – Oxford, 1964; see also J.P. LEWIS, *What Do We Mean by Jabneh?*, in *Journal of Biblical Research* 32 (1964) 125-132 and S.Z. LEIMAN, *The Canonization of Hebrew Scripture: The Talmudic and Midrashic Evidence*, Hamden, CT, Archon, 1976, pp. 120-124.

8. *Ibid.*

9. S. SANDMEL, *On Canon*, in *CBQ* 28 (1966) 203-207, quotation from p. 204.

composition of the Old Testament, canonicity is the external attestation of such inspiration in regard to a particular book. Correspondingly, while history can provide data relative to the formation of the canon, ultimately it cannot establish the motivation for adherence to an inspired and normative canon, since such adherence is an act of faith. Historically, the interaction between Christianity and Judaism seems to have been a powerful factor in canonization.

Murphy next raises the question: Is it the book that is canonical, or the text? Some scholars have argued that specifically the text of the LXX is inspired. Others, following Luther's principle, have contended that the early Christian sacred scripture was somewhat fluid, and was heard and acknowledged insofar as it directed towards Christ. Murphy insists that such a position is too vague and needs to be complemented by other criteria, such as agreement with orthodox doctrine and use in the churches. He notes that while some of the Conciliar Fathers at Trent wanted to provide a scholarly basis for decisions on canonicity, in fact the decision was ultimately based on the practice of the church[10].

c. Albert Sundberg

Sundberg begins by briefly reviewing the history of the exclusion of the "Apocrypha" in the Reformed tradition and the reconsideration of the issue in the 18th century, a reconsideration that resulted from the inescapable fact of the use of this literature in the New Testament and that led to the formation of the Alexandrian canon hypothesis. Sundberg notes that Bruce Metzger, in his 1957 work *An Introduction to the Apocrypha*, essentially affirms Luther's position that canon should be decided by the internal worth of a book. Both F.V. Filson (1956) and Metzger, who hold similar positions, appear to view the Hebrew canon as having been determined before the time of Jesus and thus regard the inclusion of the "Apocrypha" in Christian Old Testament Scriptures as ensuing from a mistaken understanding of the Jewish circumstances of canon[11].

Relying on reference to his 1964 monograph for fuller argumentation, Sundberg questions whether the traditional Protestant position on the Old Testament canon is still tenable, given that the bases of this position are both misleading and historically inaccurate, since there was no closed Hebrew canon in Jesus' day, nor did a Hebrew canon paralleling

10. R. MURPHY, *The Old Testament Canon in the Catholic Church*, in *CBQ* 28 (1966) 189-193.
11. A.C. SUNDBERG, *The Protestant Old Testament Canon: Should It Be Re-Examined?*, in *CBQ* 28 (1966) 194-203, pp. 194-199.

the subsequent Jamnia canon exist at that time. Rather, what existed was a closed collection of Law and Prophets, and a large undifferentiated number of Jewish religious writings. It was this combined group that passed from Judaism into Christianity as the Scriptures of the early church[12].

Further, Sundberg contends, Filson's argument that Jesus and the New Testament authors do not quote the "Apocrypha" is anachronistic, first, because there was no collection designated as such at that time, and secondly, because if direct quotation is meant, a number of books accepted by Protestants would have to be excluded, as even Metzger concedes. However Metzger's criterion of internal worth, following Luther, is likewise invalid, since, though it seems to situate the criteria of canonicity within the internal self-witness of a writing to its own worth, in reality the decision is made by the person arguing the case. Thus canonicity depends on subjective judgment[13].

Regardless of the history of the canonical situation within Judaism, Sundberg insists that in fact the usage within Judaism is not the real issue. The Jewish canon is valid within Judaism, but in appealing to a (now known to be) historically inaccurate notion of an early Jewish canon, Christians were more fundamentally basing their claims on what was perceived to be the usage of Jesus and the early Church. Though this perception has also been demonstrated to be inaccurate, nonetheless canonization is a community process, and for Christians, the only legitimate criteria is Christian usage. Such usage was the ultimate basis of Jerome's claims as well as of those of Tertullian and Augustine.

Similarly, it is incorrect to apply the Jamnia doctrine of inspiration to the Christian doctrine of the canon, as was done by the Calvinists in the Westminster Confession of 1647. Not even Jerome sought to argue that the books of the "Apocrypha" were not inspired. Even in the case of the Pseudepigrapha, exclusion from the Christian Old Testament was done on the basis of doubtful authenticity, not on the question of inspiration. The Calvinistic doctrine was an innovation arising from applying a Jewish doctrine of canon to Christian practice and divorcing subsequent Protestant doctrine of Scripture from previous doctrine of the Church.

Thus Sundberg concludes, in its perspective on the Old Testament canon Protestantism has broken away from its historical heritage, based on a mistaken understanding that earliest Christian Old Testament usage corresponded to that in the Jewish canon. Now that the mistake is evi-

---

12. *Ibid.*, p. 199, with reference to *The Old Testament of the Early Church* (n. 7), pp. 81-103.
13. *Ibid.*, pp. 200-201.

dent Protestant Christians should either return to their historical heritage or evolve a new apologetic for their Old Testament canon[14].

d. Reaction to Sundberg

James Sanders has expressed appreciation for Sundberg's convincing demonstration that Christianity continued to view as canonical literature what had earlier been regarded as sacred within the Jewish tradition but later excluded from the Jewish canon[15]. Beginning in 1972, Sanders has written several works contending that the possibility must be taken seriously that the hermeneutics utilized within the Bible, even if not recorded in it as text, may be just as canonical for today's believing communities as anything explicit in the biblical literature[16].

John Goldingay, an Anglican priest, briefly takes issue with Sundberg's argumentation, to my mind unconvincingly, but is more concerned with developing his own notion of an open canon[17]. In 1995 Joseph Lienhard, a Roman Catholic scholar, published a book on canon based on lectures given in 1989. While his main concern is with the New Testament, in his discussion of canon history since the Reformation he basically follows Sundberg and remarks that Sundberg's book has not received the attention it deserves[18]. More recently another Catholic scholar, Daniel J. Harrington, has maintained that the real issue is not some kind of official acknowledgment of canonical status, but the recognition that the Old Testament "Apocrypha" should be read and studied on their own merits as important resources for recognizing the Jewishness of Jesus and the Early Christian movement[19].

3. Ben Sirach and Wisdom

More specific arguments have been adduced in regard to the case for canonical status for Sirach and Wisdom based on both Jewish and Christian usage. David Winston notes that the text of Wisdom is preserved

14. *Ibid.*, pp. 201-203.

15. J.A. SANDERS, *From Sacred Story to Sacred Text*, Philadelphia, PA, Fortress, 1987, pp. 81, 145.

16. J.A. SANDERS, *Torah and Canon*, Philadelphia, PA, Fortress, 1972; ID., *Canon and Community: A Guide to Canonical Criticism* (Guides to Biblical Scholarship), Philadelphia, PA, Fortress, 1984; ID., *From Sacred Story* (n. 15).

17. J. GOLDINGAY, *Models for Scripture*, Grand Rapids, MI, Eerdmans, 1994, pp. 168-182.

18. LIENHARD, *The Bible, the Church, and Authority* (n. 6), pp. 67-72.

19. D.J. HARRINGTON, "The Old Testament Apocrypha in the Canon Debate", a paper presented at the annual meeting of the Catholic Biblical Association, Loyola Marymount University, Los Angeles, CA, August 5-8, 2000.

entirely or in part in Codices A, B, C, S and V; in S and A Wisdom is preceded by the Song of Songs (in B by Job) and followed by Sirach, with the prophetic books immediately following. Additionally, Wisdom 7,26 is used by Origen, Dionysius of Alexandria, and Theognostus in Christological argumentation[20]. The placement would seem to indicate that both Wisdom and Sirach are considered canonical in these manuscripts.

While conceding that the extant evidence is insufficient to decide exactly which books were considered uniquely authoritative in 100 BCE, James C. VanderKam considers the possibility that the grandson of Ben Sira considered his grandfather's writings to be on a par with the Law and the Prophets[21]. He takes particular note of the last sentence in the second paragraph of the prologue[22]: "Not only this book [Sirach], but even the Law itself, the Prophecies, and the rest of the books differ not a little when read in the original"[23]. Since the first sentence of the prologue refers to "the Law and the Prophets and the others that followed them"[24], this could indicate a threefold division of Scripture, with the third being less precise. VanderKam also refers to Philo's categories of laws, oracles of prophets, and "psalms and anything else"[25].

Alexander Di Lella points out that before the rabbis excluded Sirach from the Jewish canon, it was clearly considered one of the sacred writings by Greek-speaking Jews in Palestine as well as the Diaspora, since it was incorporated into the LXX. Secondly, the Jewish community at Masada in the first century BCE possessed a Hebrew copy of the book written stichometrically, and the same writing practice was utilized in two first century BCE Hebrew fragments of Sirach found in Cave 2 at Qumran. This writing procedure, normally reserved for books later received as canonical, shows the reverence that the Essenes and other Palestinian Jews bestowed upon Sirach. Finally, from early in the first century BCE the work underwent successive Hebrew and Greek recensions

20. D. WINSTON, *The Wisdom of Solomon* (AB, 43), Garden City NY, Doubleday, 1979, pp. 65-69.

21. C. HAGERTY, *The Authenticity of the Sacred Scriptures*, Houston TX, Lumen Christi Press, 1969, p. 114, had earlier asserted this with much more certainty. For Hagerty, it is the younger Sirach's assumption that his grandfather's book was the equal of other inspired Scriptures that is cited as evidence that the Writings had not yet been definitely fixed.

22. In Skehan's translation, this would be sentence no. 7 (numbering by Di Lella); cf. P.W. SKEHAN & A. DI LELLA, *The Wisdom of Ben Sirach* (AB, 39), New York, Doubleday, 1986, p. 131.

23. J. VANDERKAM, *The Dead Sea Scrolls Today*, Grand Rapids, MI, Eerdmans; London, SPCK, 1994, pp. 143-144.

24. *Ibid.*, p. 143.

25. *Ibid.*, p. 145.

in Palestine, indicating that at least some Jews there accepted it as sacred and inspired. Even in the later rabbinic tradition, Sirach is cited with approval in the Talmud and other writings, sometimes with the introductory formula "it is written", a formula normally reserved for quotations from the canonical Scriptures[26].

Earlier Sundberg had noted that, in distinction to the more properly termed apocryphal writings, Sirach and Wisdom remained in circulation in Judaism after the closing of the Jewish canon. The Talmud twice cites Sirach by name and a third time refers to it as being from the Writings[27]. In the 13th century, Nachmanides was familiar with and utilized an Aramaic text of Wisdom[28]. Within the Christian tradition, Di Lella points out that the early church regarded Sirach as canonical, as evidenced in the *Didache*, Clement of Rome, Irenaeus, and Tertullian. In fact, "The fathers of the Church attest more frequently to the canonicity of Sirach than to several protocanonical books"[29]. Sundberg notes that Epiphanius (*Panarion*, lxxvi) valued both Wisdom and Sirach so highly that, though he acknowledged their exclusion from the Old Testament, he incorporated them into the New Testament[30].

In the East, Athanasius followed the listing favored by Jerome, but Johan Leemans has pointed out that, nonetheless, in citing passages from the book of Wisdom, Athanasius links them with protocanonical writings in such a way as to make it appear that the citations from Wisdom are viewed as Scripture: "we have had ample opportunity to see Athanasius treating his quotations from Wisdom on an equal footing with those from the 'canonical books' … it is clear that citations from Wisdom are used to support theological reflection and are important elements in his argumentation in defence of the divinity of the Spirit"[31].

While both Sundberg and Metzger have rightly questioned the mere presence in the New Testament of quoted material from the "Apocrypha" as a criteria for canonicity, I believe that for both Sirach and Wis-

---

26. SKEHAN & DI LELLA, *The Wisdom of Ben Sira* (n. 22), p. 20.

27. SUNDBERG, *The "Old Testament" : A Christian Canon* (n. 3), pp. 151-152.

28. A. MARX, *An Aramaic Fragment of the Wisdom of Solomon*, in *JBL* 40 (1921) 57-69.

29. A. DI LELLA, *Sirach*, in R. E. BROWN et al. (eds.), *The New Jerome Biblical Commentary* (n. 1), pp. 496-509, p. 497, §6.

30. SUNDBERG, *The "Old Testament" : A Christian Canon* (n. 3), p. 149.

31. J. LEEMANS, *Athanasius and the Book of Wisdom*, in *ETL* 73 (1997) 349-368, pp. 366-367; quotation from p. 367. HAGERTY, *Authenticity* (n. 21), p. 124 had earlier remarked that the practice of Athanasius, as well as that of Origen and Jerome, belied the theory because in the course of their argumentation they quoted deuterocanonical books as if accepting them as inspired and authoritative.

dom a case can be made on the basis of usage in, at least, the undisputed letters of Paul. It is not simply that material from these writings can be identified explicitly or implicitly in Paul's writings, but the importance of the subject for which they are utilized. Like Job and Qoheleth, both Sirach and Wisdom are less optimistic about simple retributive justice for those who follow the path pointed out by Wisdom. While Sir 24 takes the hitherto unprecedented step of identifying Wisdom with Torah[32], Paul identifies Christ with Wisdom, but even as superior to Torah[33].

When the New Testament writers, most particularly Paul, sought a way to understand the utter shame and disgrace of the crucifixion, they looked to their Scriptures and found an answer in the divine reversal of perspective, what Di Lella has termed the "existential wisdom", of books like Job, Sirach, and Wisdom[34]. This is particularly evident in Philippians and the Corinthian correspondence. It is precisely the crucified Christ that Paul identifies as the power and wisdom of God (1 Cor 1,24) and as the one whom God has made our wisdom (1 Cor 1,30)[35]. Some degree of Wisdom background is acknowledged by most scholars in Phil 2,5-11[36]. The description of Christ as the one for whom Paul regarded all things as loss and garbage in Phil 3,7-11 is modeled on the depiction of the incomparability of Wisdom in Wis 7[37], which also appears to have influenced the author of Col 1,15-20 and Heb 1,1-3. The gospels strongly emphasize the reversal of the perspective of human wisdom in insisting that Christian discipleship is a way of the cross (Mark 8,34-35) and Christian leadership should involve service, not lording it over others (Mark 9,35; 10,31.42-45); Christians are to wash one another's feet because that is what their Lord and Teacher does (John 13,13-15).

---

32. A. WEISER, *Introduction to the Old Testament*, London, DLT, 1961, p. 409 (= ID., *The Old Testament: Its Formation and Development*, New York NY, Association, 1961), proposes that it was the identification of Wisdom and Torah that led to the exclusion of Sirach from the Jewish canon.

33. For an overview of recent scholarly literature on Paul and the Law, see V. KOPERSKI, *What Are They Saying About Paul and the Law?*, Mahwah NJ, Paulist, 2001.

34. SKEHAN & DI LELLA, *The Wisdom of Ben Sirach* (n. 22), pp. 33-36.

35. For full discussion see V. KOPERSKI, *Knowledge of God and Knowledge of Christ in the Corinthian Correspondence*, in R. BIERINGER (ed.), *The Corinthian Correspondence* (BETL, 125), Leuven, University Press - Peeters, 1996, pp. 183-202.

36. V. KOPERSKI, *The Knowledge of Christ Jesus my Lord: The High Christology of Philippians 3:7-11* (CBET, 16), Kampen, Kok Pharos, 1996, pp. 298-299.

37. *Ibid.*, pp. 299-301; see also pp. 301-319 for an overview of the wisdom ambience in all the undisputed letters of Paul. The connection between Phil 3,7-1 and Wis 7 was first noted by Dionysius the Carthusian, *In omnes beati Pauli epistolas commentaria*, Paris, Poncetus le Preux, 1552, pp. 88-89.

It has been almost 40 years since Sundberg challenged Protestantism to either accept the "Apocrypha" as part of the Old Testament or come up with new justification for not so doing. If usage, in particular liturgical usage, is a primary criterion for canonicity, as Augustine argued, some change can be detected. What initially spurred my interest in this subject was the homiletical writing I do for an ecumenical publication. I noticed that "Apocrypha" were turning up among the Sunday Scripture readings within the Protestant tradition. Winston pointed out in 1979 that the British Anglican Church Lectionary contained 44 Lessons from the Apocrypha and the American Protestant Episcopal Church Lectionary included 110 such Lessons[38].

Sundberg tells of his preaching on a text from Sir 38 at an ecumenical Labor Day service with Baptist, Methodist, and Congregationalist participants in a Baptist church which had a very old pulpit Bible – old enough to contain the "Apocrypha". When challenged by some Baptist participants as to where he had found the text he preached on, he replied "Well, from your Bible". He was not questioned further.

Dept. of Theology & Philosophy   Veronica KOPERSKI
Barry University
11300 N.E. Second Ave.
Miami Shores, FL 33161-6695
USA

---

38. WINSTON, *Wisdom of Solomon* (n. 20), p. 67.

CANON AND QUOTATION
ATHANASIUS' USE OF JESUS SIRACH

1. *Introduction*

The *Festal Letter* Athanasius of Alexandria wrote for the year 367 stands out as a key-text in the history of the canon[1]. The text is fragmentarily preserved: parts of it survive in Greek, Coptic and Syriac, often in collections of canon law[2]. In this letter the Alexandrian bishop writes that he wants "to set forth in order the canonized and transmitted writings (τὰ κανονιζόμενα καὶ παραδοθέντα), those believed to be divine books (πιστευθέντα τε θεῖα εἶναι βιβλία), so that those who have been deceived might condemn the persons who led them astray, and those who have remained pure might rejoice to be reminded (of those things)"[3]. Then he enumerates the 22 books of the Old Testament

---

1. See e.g. the following: É. JUNOD, *La formation et la composition de l'Ancien Testament dans l'Église grecque des quatres premiers siècles*, in J.-D. KAESTLI & O. WERMELINGER (eds.), *Le canon de l'Ancien Testament. Sa formation et son histoire* (Le Monde de la Bible), Genève, Labor et Fides, 1984, pp. 105-151, esp. 141-144; B.M. METZGER, *The Canon of the New Testament: Its Origin, Development, and Significance*, Oxford, Clarendon, 1987, pp. 210–12; L.M. McDONALD, *The Formation of the Christian Biblical Canon*, Peabody MA, Hendrickson, 1995, pp. 220–222; J. TREBOLLE BARRERA, *The Jewish Bible and the Christian Bible: An Introduction to the History of the Bible*, Grand Rapids MI, Eerdmans, 1998, pp. 236–57. For additional bibliography, see D. BRAKKE, *Canon Formation and Social Conflict in Fourth Century Egypt: Athanasius of Alexandria's Thirty-Ninth Festal Letter*, in *HTR* 87 (1994) 395-420, p. 397 n. 5.

2. The most recent edition of the Greek text is by P.P. JOANNOU, *Discipline générale antique (IVᵉ-IXᵉ s.). II. Les canons des Pères Grecs* (Fonti, 9), Grottaferrata, 1963, pp. 71-80. Of large portions of the text, a Coptic translation is extant: cf. L.-Th. LEFORT (ed.), *St. Athanase. Lettres festales et pastorales en Copte* (CSCO, 150-151), Leuven, CSCO, 1955, pp. 58-62 (Coptic text) and pp. 31-41 (French translation). Additional Coptic fragments were published by R.-G. COQUIN, *Les lettres festales d'Athanase (CPG 2102). Un nouveau complément: Le manuscrit IFAO, Copte 25*, in *OLP* 15 (1984) 133-158 and E. LUCCHESI, *Un nouveau complément aux Lettres festales d'Athanase*, in *Analecta Bollandiana* 119 (2001) 255-261. The Syriac translation is edited by W. CURETON, *The Festal Letters of Athanasius Discovered in an Ancient Syriac Version*, London, Society for the Publication of Oriental Texts, 1848 (Appendix). An English translation of a composite text can be found in D. BRAKKE, *Athanasius and the Politics of Asceticism*, Baltimore, John Hopkins University Press, 1998; = *Athanasius and the Politics of Asceticism* (Oxford Early Christian Studies), Oxford, University Press, 1995, pp. 326-332. See also his *Canon Formation and Social Conflict* (n. 1).

3. *Ep. Fest* XXXIX: ἐκθέσθαι τὰ κανονιζόμενα καὶ παραδοθέντα, πιστευθέντα τε θεῖα εἶναι βιβλία, ἵνα ἕκαστος, εἰ μὲν ἠπατήθη, καταγνῷ τῶν πλανησάντων, ὁ δὲ καθαρὸς διαμείνας χαίρῃ πάλιν ὑπομιμνησκόμενος. The text is quoted according to Joannou (n. 2); the translation is taken from BRAKKE, *Athanasius and Asceticism* (n. 2), p. 329.

followed by those of the New Testament. These books are "the springs of salvation" (πηγαὶ τοῦ σωτηρίου). "In these books *alone* the teaching of piety is proclaimed. Let no one add or subtract from them" (ἐν τούτοις μόνοις τὸ τῆς εὐσεβείας διδασκαλεῖον εὐαγγελίζεται· μηδεὶς τούτοις ἐπιβαλλέτω, μηδὲ τούτων ἀφαιρείσθω τι). After τὰ κανονιζόμενα the Alexandrian bishop introduces a second and third category of books:

> But for the sake of greater accuracy, I add this, writing from necessity. There are other books, in addition to these, which have not been canonized, but have been appointed by the ancestors to be read to those who newly join us and want to be instructed in the word of piety: the Wisdom of Solomon, the Wisdom of Sirach, Ester, Judith, Tobit, the book called Teaching of the Apostles, and the Shepherd. Nevertheless the former books are canonized, the latter are (only) read; and there is no mention of the apocryphal books. Rather (the category of apocrypha) is an invention of heretics, ...[4].

Athanasius then continues with a severe rejection of the apocryphal books that are misleading the simple folk. While this is not surprising, the distinction between the first and second category deserves a closer look. The passages I quoted above make it abundantly clear that to Athanasius there is a clear difference between the "canonized writings" (τὰ κανονιζόμενα)[5] and the other books (ἕτερα βιβλία) that are traditionally read to the catechumens. While the second are certainly not without value, only the former are styled "the springs of salvation" and it is explicitly stated that in the canonized books *alone* the teaching of piety is proclaimed.

The different value *vis-à-vis* the canonized writings Athanasius attaches to the Wisdom of Solomon, the Wisdom of Jesus Sirach, Ester, Judith, Tobit, the Didache and the Shepherd of Hermas at first does not really surprise us. After all, the canonical status of all these writings has always been in doubt. The latter two have not made it into the canon, the other do not belong to the Jewish canon and are also excluded by some Christian denominations while being accepted by others.

Within the framework of Athanasius' writings, however, the assertion is rather startling because, as this paper will demonstrate, nowhere in his

4. Ἀλλ' ἑνεκά γε πλείονος ἀκριβείας προστίθημι καὶ τοῦτο γράφων ἀναγκαίως, ὡς ὅτι ἔστι καὶ ἕτερα βιβλία τούτων ἔξωθεν, οὐ κανονιζόμενα μέν, τετυπωμένα δὲ παρὰ τῶν πατέρων ἀναγινώσκεσθαι τοῖς ἄρτι προσερχομένοις καὶ βουλομένοις κατηχεῖσθαι τὸν τῆς εὐσεβείας λόγον· Σοφία Σολομῶντος καὶ Σοφία Σιρὰχ καὶ Ἐσθὴρ καὶ Ἰουδὶθ καὶ Τωβίας καὶ Διδαχὴ καλουμένη τῶν ἀποστόλων καὶ ὁ Ποιμήν. Καὶ ὅμως, ἀγαπητοί, κἀκείνων κανονιζομένων, καὶ τούτων ἀναγινωσκομένων, οὐδαμοῦ τῶν ἀποκρύφων μνήμη, ἀλλὰ αἱρετικῶν ἐστιν ἐπίνοια, ... (Translation BRAKKE, p. 330).

5. In what follows "the canonized books" is shorthand for "the books Athanasius describes in his *Festal Letter* of 367 as τὰ κανονιζόμενα".

writings he treats these writings in a different way than the "canonized" ones. To prove this point I will review all the passages in which the Alexandrian bishop is quoting or alluding to Jesus Sirach. In each case I will assess which purpose the quotation or allusion serves. Special attention will thereby be given to the question whether the borrowing from Sirach is treated at an equal level with one of the canonized books. I will also study how each quotation is introduced and whether this constitutes any difference with the way quotations of canonized books are introduced. A few years ago I studied Athanasius' use of the Wisdom of Solomon along these lines and concluded that there is no difference whatsoever in the way Athanasius used citations from Wisdom in comparison to those from the writings he styled as "canonized"[6]. I hope to show that the same conclusion can be reached with regard to Sirach.

2. A Survey of Athanasius' Use of Jesus Sirach

a. Establishing a Secure Basis

I started my inquiry by collecting all passages in which Athanasius seemingly quoted from the book of Sirach[7]. To that end I used the Scriptural index of the *Lexicon Athanasianum*, the Scriptural indexes of the existing text-editions and translations, as well as the Scriptural index compiled by James Ernest as part of his recent doctoral dissertation[8]. This resulted in a list of some twenty passages in which Athanasius – according to the judgment of at least one scholar – used the book of Sirach. This result is more or less in agreement with Maurice Gilbert's observation: "In seinem Schriften zitiert er 17 Sir.-Verse"[9].

Unfortunately, matters are not as straightforward as this. In order that our conclusions should be valid, we must first establish a secure basis to build on. First of all this means the exclusion of the passages in the corpus Athanasianum which are not written by the Alexandrian bishop. Among the passages to be excluded on this ground are two passages from a treatise *On Virginity* (CPG 2248) which by now is generally con-

---

6. J. Leemans, *Athanasius and the Book of Wisdom*, in *ETL* 73 (1997) 349-369.

7. Quotations from Sirach are according to the edition of J. Ziegler (ed.), *Sapientia Iesu Filii Sirach* (Septuaginta: Vetus Testamentum Graecum, 12/2), Göttingen, Vandenhoeck & Ruprecht, 1965.

8. J.D. Ernest, *Uses of Scripture in the Writings of Athanasius of Alexandria*, Ph.D. dissertation, Boston College, 2000. I would like to thank Dr. Ernest for providing me with this valuable resource.

9. M. Gilbert, Art. *Jesus Sirach*, in *Reallexikon für Antike und Christentum* 17 (1996), cc. 878-906, esp. 893.

sidered as inauthentic[10]. On the same ground four passages[11] from the *Expositions on the Psalms* must be excluded from further consideration[12]. A letter written by Alexander of Thessaloniki and quoted by Athanasius in his *Second Apology against the Arians* is also left aside. In this document Sir 30,4 is quoted and unequivocally introduced by a ὥς που ἡ ἱερά φησι γραφή[13]. Since the letter was not written by Athanasius we cannot use it in our inquiry. A fourth passage, to be excluded on similar grounds, is a fragment from the speech of Anthony, preserved as part of the *Life of Anthony*. This contains a quasi-literal quotation of Sir 1,25 (βδέλυγμα δε ἁμαρτωλῷ θεοσέβεια) which is woven into the text with the help of the particle γάρ[14]. Since it cannot be entirely ruled out that Athanasius did use tradition material going back to the hermit himself, it is perhaps wisest to disregard this passage.

The second kind of texts to be excluded from further consideration are passages of which it cannot be said with certainty that Athanasius actually borrowed from Sirach. There are many of this kind. Very often editors have taken great pains in recognizing even the faintest trace of Scriptural borrowings. While this line of inquiry is important, e.g. for somebody wishing to study the influence of the Scriptures on Athanasius' language and thought, for our purpose we need exactly the opposite: only quotations of or unequivocal reminiscences to the book of Sirach can be included. The following examples may clarify what I mean. In the *Apology for his Flight* Athanasius argues that taking flight in a situation of persecution is permitted until the moment of one's *kairos* has come. Hence the writer's attention for the concept of time in the Scriptures. In this context, Athanasius writes: "Since God promised to those who truly worship him 'I will fulfill the number of your days', Abraham died full of days..." (Τοῦ δὲ Θεοῦ ἐπαγγελλομένου τοῖς

---

10. The passages in question can be found in *De Virginitate*, ed. E. VON DER GOLTZ (TU, 29/2), Leipzig, 1905, p. 48, l. 8-10 (Sir 13,1) and p. 53, l. 16-17 (Sir 15,16). It is to be noted that the first case is a quotation introduced by λέγει γὰρ ἡ θεία γραφή. See for the inauthenticity of the work D. BRAKKE, *The Authenticity of the Ascetic Athanasiana*, in *Orientalia* 63 (1994) 17-56, pp. 47-49.

11. Sir 15,9 in *Expositiones in Psalmos*, XLIX (*PG* 27, c. 236 B13-14). Sir 2,1 in *Expositiones in Psalmos*, CXVII (*PG* 27, c. 476 D2-3) and in *Expositiones in Psalmos*, CXVIII (*PG* 27, c. 489 C10-12). Sir 18,6 in *Expositiones in Psalmos*, CXVIII (*PG* 27, c. 498 C14-16).

12. The authenticity of the work is a matter of debate. A recent survey of scholarship on the question and a defense of Athanasius' authorship, proposing an early date in the first half of the 330's, can be found in P.F. BOUTER, *Athanasius van Alexandrië en zijn uitleg van de Psalmen. Een onderzoek naar de hermeneutiek en theologie van een Psalmvertaling uit de vroege kerk*, Zoetermeer, Boekencentrum, 2001, pp. 20-39.

13. *Apologia Secunda contra Arianos*, 66.1, ed. H.G. OPITZ, *Athanasius' Werke. II/1. Die Apologien*, Berlin – Leipzig, Walter de Gruyter, 1935, p. 145, l. 3-6).

14. *Vita Antonii*, 28.7, ed. G. BARTELINK (SC, 400), Paris, Cerf, 1994, p. 214, l. 30-32.

γνησίως αὐτῷ λατρεύουσιν, ὅτι "τὸν ἀριθμὸν τῶν ἡμερῶν σου ἀναπληρώσω", ὁ μὲν Ἀβραὰμ πλήρης ἡμερῶν ἀποθνήσκει)[15]. Szymusiak recognizes here a quotation of Sir 17,2a. This verse, however, reads, ἡμέρας ἀριθμοῦ καὶ καιρὸν ἔδωκεν αὐτοῖς. Only the first two words are identical and while the thought expressed is certainly not entirely different, I would be very hesitant to consider this an explicit and conscious quotation of Sirach. While one could here still side with the editor and plea for some leniency, the second example is much clearer. In his third chapter of *On the Incarnation*, Athanasius writes ἀλλὰ κατὰ τὴν ἑαυτοῦ εἰκόνα ἐποίησεν αὐτούς[16] Sir 17,3b reads καὶ κατ' εἰκόνα αὐτοῦ ἐποίησεν αὐτούς. The metaphor of man created in the image of God is so universal in patristic thought (probably informed by Gen 1,26) that it seems, despite the obvious similarity in wording, rather superfluous to make the connection with Sir 17,3b. A third example of a doubtful reminiscence of Sirach occurs in the treatise *On Charity and Continence*[17]. Athanasius writes that wine in itself is a good thing on condition that one does not drink too much of it[18]. Although Sir 34,36 contains the same admonishment (οἶνος πινόμενος ἐν καιρῷ αὐτάρκης), I do not see any reason to seek behind such a very general parenetic statement a direct reference to any Scriptural passage.

Several other passages have been excluded from closer consideration on the same grounds[19]. What we are left with, is a rather small but se-

15. *Apologia de fuga sua*, 14, l. 17, ed. J. SZYMUSIAK (SC, 56bis), Paris, Cerf, 1987, p. 208.
16. *De Incarnatione Verbi* 3.3, ed. C. KANNENGIESSER (SC, 199), Paris, Cerf, 1973, p. 270, l. 23-24. The connection with Sirach was suggested by Ernest, albeit between brackets, indicating that it concerns only the vaguest of reminiscences.
17. For a long time this work was considered as inauthentic and thus neglected. D. Brakke, however, made a strong case for its authenticity. Cf. BRAKKE, *Authenticity* (n. 10), pp. 34-36.
18. *De caritate et temperantia*, ed. LEFORT, p. 118 (transl. p. 96).
19. Sir 1, 21: *De caritate et temperantia* (ed. LEFORT, p. 115-116; transl. p. 93). Sir 5,7: *Fragmenta de vita moralia* (ed. LEFORT, p. 124; transl. p. 104). Sir 6,16 (φάρμακον ζωῆς): *De caritate et temperantia* (ed. LEFORT, p. 117; transl. p. 95). Sir 7,17: *Vita Antonii*, 5.6 (ed. BARTELINK, pp. 144-145). Sir 16,11: *Fragmenta de vita moralia* (ed. LEFORT, p. 124; transl. p. 104). Sir 18,17: *Ep. Fest XIX*; translation from A. ROBERTSON, *Select Writings and Letters of Athanasius, Bishop of Alexandria*, p. 546). Sir 21,13 (πηγὴ ζωῆς): *CA* III,1.7 (ed. K. METZLER & K. SAVVIDIS, in *Athanasius' Werke. I/1. Die Dogmatische Schriften*, Berlin-New York, Walter de Gruyter, 2000, p. 307). Sir 29,20: *Vita Antonii*, 3.1 (ed. BARTELINK, pp. 134-137). Sir 44,16 (Ἐνωχ μετετέθη): *CA* III,52.1 (ed. METZLER & SAVVIDIS, p. 363). — In the passages mentioned above in this footnote, the reference to Sirach is all too vague or insecure to style it a conscious borrowing of any sort (quotation, allusion, reminiscence). In the following two cases, however, we found that the reference to Sirach mentioned by the editor to be mistaken: Sir 20,20 in *De caritate et temperantia* (ed. LEFORT, p. 115; transl. p. 93) reflects rather James 3,6 and in the Latin translation of *Ep. Fest XI*, 5 as given in PG 26, c. 1407 A2-3, it concerns a quotation from Eccl 8,10 and not of Sir 27,29 as is indicated in the note.

cure basis of six texts which might allow firm conclusions regarding the practical canonical status of Sirach and therefore deserve closer scrutiny. In the remainder of this paper I propose to take a closer look at these texts.

b. A Survey of Athanasius' Use of Sirach and the Book's "Practical Canonical Status"

Sir 1,9-10 in *Contra Arianos* II, 79

The second book of the *Contra Arianos*, written in Rome in ca. 340, is largely devoted to a discussion about the theological meaning of Prov 8,22 (chapters 18-72). After a short treatment of Prov 8,23-25 (73-78), the book ends with a meditation on divine Wisdom (79-81). This Wisdom of God, synonymous to the Logos, is called the Creator of all things. God is said to be pleased to send His Wisdom to earth, to impart a semblance of its image on all creatures, so that what was made would be worthy of Him. This means that it is possible to recognize, in and through creation, the Word of God and, via the Logos, God Himself. On the other hand it also follows that this image, this imprint of divine Wisdom is present in the created world. To prove this point, Athanasius adduces a series of Scriptural texts: 1 Cor 1,21; Wisd 6,24; Prov 14,16; Prov 24; Eccl 8,1 and 7,10. The final text is from Sirach:

> But if, as the Son of Sirach says, 'He poured her out upon all His works; she is with all flesh according to his gift, and He had given her to them that love Him' (Sir 1,9-10), and this outpouring is a note, not of the Essence of the Very Wisdom and Only-begotten, but of that wisdom which is imaged in the world, how is it incredible that the All-framing and true Wisdom Itself, whose impress is the wisdom and knowledge poured out in the world, should say, as I have already explained, as of Itself, 'The Lord created me for his works' (Prov 8,22)?[20]

The Scriptural passage quoted in the beginning of this fragment is a literal rendering of Sir 1,9c-10b. In Athanasius' interpretation, this quotation proves that in our present world an imprint, an image of divine Wisdom is still present. He precises that it is not an image of the pure,

20. *CA*, II, 79.2: Εἰ δέ ἐστιν, ὥσπερ οὖν καὶ ὁ τοῦ Σιράχ φησιν· Ἐξέχεεν αὐτὴν ἐπὶ πάντα τὰ ἔργα αὐτοῦ μετὰ πάσης σαρκὸς κατὰ τὴν δόσιν αὐτοῦ καὶ ἐχορήγησεν αὐτὴν τοῖς ἀγαπῶσιν αὐτόν, εἰ δὲ ἡ τοιαύτη ἔκχυσις οὐ τῆς οὐσίας τῆς αὐτοσοφίας καὶ μονογενοῦς ἐστι γνώρισμα, ἀλλὰ τῆς ἐν κόσμῳ ἐξεικονισθείσης· τί ἄπιστον εἰ αὐτὴ ἡ δημιουργὸς καὶ ἀληθινὴ Σοφία, ἧς τύπος ἐστὶν ἡ ἐν κόσμῳ ἐκχυθεῖσα σοφία καὶ ἐπιστήμη, ὡς περὶ ἑαυτῆς ἐστι, καθὰ προεῖπον, λέγουσα· Κύριος ἔκτισέ με εἰς ἔργα αὐτοῦ (ed. TETZ, in *Athanasius' Werke.* I/1, 1998, p. 307) p. 256; ET ROBERTSON, *Select Writings* (n. 19), p. 391.

divine essence of God but of the incarnated wisdom of the Father. The quotation from Sirach is introduced with a precise ὁ τοῦ Σιράχ φησιν which indicates its provenance and in this regard is very much akin to similar introductions to quotations from writings styled as "canonized"[21]. Moreover the quotation from Sirach is adduced in support of a theological point and stands on equal footing with several other quotations, most of which from "canonized writings". Thus it would seem that not only the writings he styled "the springs of salvation" are a source for theology in its literal sense of speaking about God. Though on itself not conclusive, this case points to quotations from Sirach being handled on exactly the same way as those of 'canonical writings'.

Sir 15,9 in *Epistula Encyclica*, 3 and *Festal Letter* VII

Sirach 15,9a reads as follows: Οὐχ ὡραῖος αἶνος ἐν τῷ στόματι τοῦ ἁμαρτωλοῦ ("Praise is not seemly in the mouth of a sinner"). The quotation occurs twice in the corpus of Athanasius' authentic writings[22]. A first time it is used in his *Circular Letter to the Bishops of Egypt and Libya*, one of the polemical writings the Alexandrian bishop composed in the 350's. The *Circular Letter* starts with a description of the activities of the Devil to deceive mankind. Athanasius points out how he deceived Eve and through her Adam, but also how his continuous deceiving activities now are detected so that we can be on our guard against this Archdeceiver.

> And although, again, he (sc. the Devil) conceal his natural falsehood, and pretend to speak truth with his lips; yet are we "not ignorant of his devices" (2 Cor 2,11), but are able to answer him in the words spoken by the Spirit against him; "But unto the ungodly, said God, why do you preach

21. To the examples given in LEEMANS, *Athanasius and the Book of Wisdom* (n. 6), p. 357 n. 27, the following, chosen at random, can be added: John 1,1.3 (φησι καὶ ὁ θεολόγος ἀνήρ) in *Contra Gentes*, 42; Lk 19,10 (ἢ φησι καὶ αὐτὸς ἐν τοῖς Εὐαγγελίοις) in *DI*, 14.2 (ed. KANNENGIESSER, p. 314, l. 10-12); 1Cor 1,21 (ὁ Παῦλός φησι) in *DI*, 15.1 (ed. KANNENGIESSER, p. 318, l.5); Eph 2,2 (καὶ περὶ τούτου φησὶν ὁ Ἀπόστολος) in *DI*, 25.5 (ed. KANNENGIESSER, p. 356, l. 25); Jer. 1,5; Is 66,2; Is 44,24; Ps 118,73; Is 49,5 (καὶ τοῦτο ὁ θεὸς αὐτὸς τῷ μέν Ἰερεμίᾳ, ὡς προεῖπον, φησίν· .... Περὶ δὲ τῶν πάντων ἔλεγεν· .... Καὶ πάλιν διὰ Ἡσαΐου φησίν· ..... Ὁ δὲ Δαυὶδ τοῦτο γινώσκων ἔψαλλεν· .... Καὶ ὁ ἐν τῷ Ἡσαΐᾳ λέγων ...) in *De Decretis*, 9.2 (ed. OPITZ, p. 8); Acts 1,1; John 3,17 (ὡς ἔγραψεν ὁ Λουκᾶς ... ὡς ὁ Ἰωάννης φησίν) in *Epistula ad episcopos Aegypti et Libyae*, 1.1 (ed. TETZ, *Athanasius' Werke* I/1, 1996, p. 39-40); Eccl 7,24.25 (Ὁρῶν τοίνυν ὡς ἐν τῷ Ἐκκλησιαστῇ γέγραπται) in *Epistula ad Monachos*, 2.1 (ed. OPITZ, p. 181); Prov 29,12 (ὁ μὲν οὖν Σολομών φησι) in *Historia Arianorum*, 69.2 (ed. OPITZ, p. 221); Prov 23,32 (καθὼς ἐν ταῖς Παροιμίαις γέγραπται), in *Historia Arianorum*, 77.2 (ed. OPITZ, p. 226); Jos 7,18-26 (ὡς ἐν τῷ Ἰησοῦ τῷ τοῦ Ναυῆ γέγραπται), in *Epistula ad episcopos Aegypti et Libyae*, 11.3 (ed. TETZ, p. 51); Is 38,19-20 (ὡς ἐν τῷ Ἡσαΐᾳ γέγραπται) in *CA II*, 4.5 (ed. TETZ, p. 181).

22. As well as a third time in the *Expositiones in Psalmos*. Cf. supra, n. 11.

my laws?" (Ps 49,16ab LXX) and "Praise is not seemly in the mouth of a sinner" (Sir 15,9a)[23].

In this passage the literal quotation of Sirach 15,9 flows naturally out of Athanasius' pen and is fitted neatly into his train of thought. It is not adduced to sustain a theological argument but is one possible answer Christians could give to Satan when he approaches them. Athanasius gives two possible answers; the first is a quotation from Ps 49,16ab (τῷ δὲ ἁμαρτωλῷ εἶπεν ὁ Θεός· διὰ τί σὺ διηγῇ τὰ δικαιώματά μου;). The quotation from Sirach is connected with that from Ps 49,16 LXX by a simple καί and thus clearly stands at an equal level with the former one. Moreover, both answers to the Devil are described as "words spoken by the Spirit against him" (τὰ ὑπὸ τοῦ Πνεύματος εἰς αὐτὸν εἰρημένα). The quotation from Sirach is thus considered as a word spoken by the Spirit. These two elements in his use of Sirach in this passage prove that in practice Athanasius used Sirach in exactly the same way as the "canonized writings", whatever he might have to say about this topic in his much later *Festal Letter* of 367.

The same conclusion can be reached with regard to the quotation of Sir 15,9 in Athanasius' *Seventh Festal Letter*[24]. Interestingly enough, there this quotation is also accompanied by the one from Ps 49,16. In his *Festal Letters* the Alexandrian bishop exhorts his flock to make the most of the season of Lent for their spiritual life. He encourages them to focus on the heavenly feast and to transcend their attachment to the material world. More concrete this meant an increased attention towards fasting, acts of charity, study of the Scripture, sexual renunciation and a more intense prayer life. This withdrawal from the world found a symbolic expression in the Oldtestamentic Exodus-motif: Christians were to travel from Egypt (the world) to Israel, the Promised Land (heaven). This proces of withdrawal was supposed to go on during the Christians' entire lifetime, but especially during Lent, culminating in the feast of Easter. The sacrament of baptism was a kind of passport, a *rite de pas-*

---

23. *Epistula encyclica ad episcopos Aegypti et Libyae*, 3.1: Ἐὰν δὲ καὶ πάλιν τὸ ἴδιον κρύψῃ ψεῦδος καὶ λαλεῖν ὑποκρίνηται διὰ χειλέων τὴν ἀλήθειαν· ἀλλ᾿ οὐκ ἀγνοοῦντες αὐτοῦ τὰ νοήματα δυνάμεθα λέγειν τὰ ὑπὸ τοῦ Πνεύματος εἰς αὐτὸν εἰρημένα· τῷ δὲ ἁμαρτωλῷ εἶπεν ὁ Θεός· διὰ τί σὺ διηγῇ τὰ δικαιώματά μου; καὶ Οὐχ ὡραῖος ὁ αἶνος ἐν τῷ στόματι τοῦ ἁμαρτωλοῦ. Οὐδὲ γὰρ οὐδὲ τὴν ἀλήθειαν λέγων ἀξιόπιστός ἐστιν ὁ πανοῦργος (ed. Tetz, pp. 41-42); ET Robertson, *Select Writings* (n. 19), p. 224.

24. The date of this letter cannot be established with certainty. Possible dates are 335, 340, and 346. For a survey of the problems related to the chronology of Athanasius' *Festal Letters*, see T.D. Barnes, *Athanasius and Constantius. Theology and Politics in the Constantinian Empire*, Cambridge, MA, Harvard Univ. Press, 1993, pp. 183-191.

sage to enter this process of maturation[25]. Thus, Athanasius does not only encourage his flock to start and endure this ascetic practices in their daily lives, but he also reacts against the presence of non-Christians in Church. The feast of Easter is a Christian feast and Jews or gentiles have no right to attend.

> Therefore, although wicked men press forward to keep the feast, and as at a feast praise God, and intrude into the Church of the saints, yet God expostulates, saying to the sinner:'Why do you talk of my ordinances?' (Ps 49,16 LXX). And the gentle Spirit rebukes them, saying, 'Praise is not comely in the mouth of a sinner' (Sir 15,9)[26].

Both quotations are at the same level and are used within the context of the same argument. Moreover, the Sirach-quotation is introduced with the explicit statement that the words were uttered by the Spirit. Thus it is fair to conclude that this is another case in which a quotation from Sirach is treated in exactly the same way as one from the "canonized writings".

Sir 4,28 in *Apologia de Fuga Sua*, 22 and *Apologia Secunda*, 90,3

In the *Apology for his Flight* Athanasius defends himself against the charge of cowardice, levelled against him by the Arians on the occasion of his third exile (356 AD). Athanasius argues that it is lawful to flee for persecution until one's *kairos*, *i. e.* the right moment to die, had come. Therefore, it is not wrong to take flight for persecution, on condition that, when one is apprehended and one's *kairos* has come, then one must be prepared "to fight for the truth until death" (ἀγωνίζεσθαι ὑπὲρ τῆς ἀληθείας μέχρι θανάτου)[27]. This is a clear reminiscence of Sir 4,28 (ἕως θανάτου ἀγώνισαι περὶ τῆς ἀληθείας) which is weaved into the text without any introductory formula. There is no clear purpose here: it is simply an example of the fact that Athanasius' language is thoroughly coloured by his intimate knowledge of the Scriptures.

The same text from Sir 4,28 is quoted in Athanasius' so-called *Second Apology against the Arians*. This writing, the result of a composition in several stages probably finished ca. 357[28], contains a lot of documents

---

25. Cf. the analysis of the *Festal Letters* from this viewpoint in BRAKKE, *Athanasius and Asceticism* (n. 2), pp. 181-201.

26. *Ep. Fest. VII*, 4. ET ROBERTSON, *Select Writings* (n. 19), p. 524.

27. *Apologia de fuga sua*, 22: εἶναι μέντοι τούτους ἑτοίμους, ὥστε καιροῦ καλέσαντος καὶ κρατηθέντας "ἀγωνίζεσθαι ὑπὲρ τῆς ἀληθείας μέχρι θανάτου" (ed. SZYMUSIAK, p. 230, l. 9-11).

28. Cf. BARNES, *Athanasius and Constantius* (n. 24), pp. 192-195.

and testimonies in support of his position in ecclesiastical politics. They are craftily collected and connected by a narrative, which, thanks to omissions and misrepresentations, makes the work a convincing defence of what were in some cases at best doubtful actions of the Alexandrian bishop. These collected testimonies and documents, says Athanasius in the final chapter of the work,

> are memorials and records against the Arian heresy, and the wickedness of false accusers, and afford a pattern and model for those who come after, *to contend for the truth unto death*, and to abominate the Arian heresy which fights against Christ, and is a forerunner of the Antichrist and not to believe those who speak against me[29].

Here too we have a clear borrowing from Sir 4,28a. The text flows naturally out of Athanasius' pen and it seems only a halfconscious quotation. On the other hand Athanasius' text in our opinion resembles that of Sirach closely enough to speak of a clear reminiscence or allusion. The text is used for polemical purposes, in lign with borrowings from 'canonized writings' adopted for similar purposes[30].

Sirach in *Contra Arianos* I,4.3

Another example of a borrowing from Sirach for polemical purposes occurs in the opening chapters of the *Orations against the Arians*, which are overall casted in a vigorous polemical tone with the purpose of discrediting his Arian opponents. Just like other heretics, who are not standing in the tradition of the Church but are as it were composing their own invented heretic faith, Arians have taken their name from the inventor of their heresy. They are not Christians but, like the Marcionites, the Novatians, the Valentinians, Basilidians and Manichaeans, these heretics are named after the founder of their heresy. Moreover, Arius did not only invent his own heresy, he also gave it a literary form in his *Thalia* and in other writings, all of them newish things he invented himself by putting thoughts from other heresies together leading to a result not con-

---

29. *Apologia Secunda contra Arianos* 90,3: ἔστι δὲ ὑπομνήματα μὲν καὶ στηλογραφία κατὰ τῆς ἀρειανῆς αἱρέσεως καὶ τῆς πονηρίας τῶν συκοφαντῶν, ὑπογραμμὸς δὲ καὶ τύπος τοῖς μετὰ ταῦτα γιγνομένοις ἀγωνίζεσθαι μὲν ὑπὲρ τῆς ἀληθείας μέχρι θανάτου, ἀποστρέφεσθαι δὲ τὴν ἀρειανὴν αἵρεσιν χιστομάχον οὖσαν καὶ τοῦ ἀντιχρίστου πρόδρομον, μὴ πιστεύειν δὲ τοῖς καθ' ἡμῶν ἐπιχειροῦσι λέγειν (ed. OPITZ, p. 168); ET ROBERTSON, *Select Writings* (n. 19), p. 147.

30. The following examples of Scripture in the service of polemics, all taken from the *Apologia de fuga sua*, may suffice to illustrate this point: John 8,44 (*AF*, 1, 1. 11-12; ed. SZYMUSIAK, p. 176); 1 Cor 6,10 (1, 1. 12-13 (ed. SZYMUSIAK, p. 176); 1 Tim 1,7 (2, 1. 26; ed. SZYMUSIAK, p. 180); Is 47,6 (9, 1. 16; ed. SZYMUSIAK, p. 196); Ps 69,27 (9, 1. 17-18; ed. SZYMUSIAK, p. 196); John 8,44 (10, 1. 9-10; ed. SZYMUSIAK, p. 196); Is 5,20 (23, 1. 15-16; ed. SZYMUSIAK, p. 232).

sonant with the faith that was handed down from generation to generation by the Church since the time of the Apostles. In none of the writings reflecting this received faith, a *Thalia* is found. Moreover, this "new" belief is put forth in ludicrous songs which have more to do with pleasuremaking then with the rendering into writing of the revered Catholic faith. Having brought forward these objections against Arius and his *Thalia*, Athanasius adduces Scriptural quotations to denounce this practice:

> "While a man", as Wisdom says, "is known from the utterance of his word", so from these (songs) should be seen the writer's effeminate soul and corruption of thought[31].

Athanasius found in the Scriptural passage ἀπὸ ἐξόδου λόγου γινώσκεται ἀνήρ surely a fitting text to sustain his polemical attack against the Arians. It is less clear, however, which passage exactly is meant. Several passages are quite similar to the text as Athanasius has it, but none of them is a quasi-literal quotation. The beginning of Dan 9,25a reads καὶ γνώσῃ καὶ συνήσεις· ἀπὸ ἐξόδου λόγου τοῦ ἀποκριθῆναι καὶ τοῦ οἰκοδομῆσαι. Sir 4,24 reads ἐν γὰρ λόγῳ γνωσθήσεται σοφία καὶ παιδεία ἐν ῥήματι γλώσσης, a text which is in meaning closer to Athanasius' use of it than the passage from Daniel, but has not soo many literal similarities. The formulation of Sir 11,28b is more in line with the one employed by Athanasius: καὶ ἐν τέκνοις αὐτοῦ γνωσθήσεται ἀνήρ. Sir 9,29, finally, conveys a similar meaning as the passage adduced by Athanasius, but differs in wording: ἀπὸ ὁράσεως ἐπιγνωσθήσεται ἀνήρ, καὶ ἀπὸ ἀπαντήσεως προσώπου ἐπιγνωσθήσεται νοήμων. None of these Scriptural passages is entirely parallel to the one Athanasius quotes. In most cases, however, the idea is very much akin. Moreover, the explicit introduction ὥσπερ ἡ σοφία φησίν, which puts the quotation in the mouth of Lady Wisdom, shows that the Alexandrian bishop was most probably quoting from a book pertaining to the wisdom Literature rather than from the prophetical literature to which Daniel belongs. In the case of this quotation we can with some caution conclude that Athanasius is using Sirach for similar purposes as he does with canonized writings. Both can be used for polemical purposes, as is the case here.

---

31. *Contra Arianos*, I, 4.3: Τί γὰρ ἔπρεπε ποιεῖν αὐτὸν ἢ θέλοντα κατὰ τοῦ Σωτῆρος ὀρχήσασθαι τὰ δύστηνα ἑαυτοῦ ῥημάτια τῆς ἀσεβείας ἐν ἐκλύτοις καὶ παρειμένοις μέλεσι σημαίνειν; ἵν', ὥσπερ ἡ Σοφία φησίν, Ἀπὸ ἐξόδου λόγου γινώσκεται ἀνήρ, οὕτως ἀπ' ἐκείνων τὸ τῆς ψυχῆς μὴ ἀνδρῶδες καὶ τῆς διανοίας ἡ φθορὰ τοῦ γράψαντος γινώσκηται (ed. TETZ, p. 113); ET ROBERTSON, *Select Writings* (n. 19), p. 308.

3. *Conclusion*

This article started with the distinction Athanasius makes in his *Festal Letter XXXIX* between the "canonized writings" and the writings to be read by the catechumens. The question was whether this theoretical distinction is reflected in his other writings. Though the textual basis an answer can be safely built upon is rather small, there are enough indications to conclude that there is no difference whatsoever between his use of Sirach and of the "canonized writings". Athanasius introduces the quotations of Sirach in the same way as the canonical writings. He takes both categories of writings as a point of departure for his theological reflection, considers them both as inspired by the Spirit and ocasionally uses them both for the same (polemical) purpose. All this is in agreement with my conclusions with regard to the Alexandrian bishop's use of the book of Wisdom.

From this dichotomy between Athanasius' theoretical qualification of Sirach and his practical use of it, however, it does not necessarily follow that he changed his mind on the canonicity of Sirach and therefore relegated it to the category "to be read by the catechumens". After all, the canonical status of this second category is at the time not yet entirely clear. Athanasius styles these writings as "appointed by the ancestors to be read to those who newly join us and want to be instructed in the word of piety" (τετυπωμένα δὲ παρὰ τῶν πατέρων ἀναγινώσκεσθαι τοῖς ἄρτι προσερχομένοις καὶ βουλομένοις κατηχεῖσθαι τὸν τῆς εὐσεβείας λόγον). Since εὐσεβεία in Athanasius usually means "orthodox faith", the difference between the two categories is not that wide and seems to be situated rather on the practical than on the "canonical level". This practical distinction does not tell much about the canonicity in the sense of the inspired character of the writings in question. A quote from Sirach is considered to be inspired by the Spirit, as are other so-called "canonical" quotes. Moreover, Athanasius was not the only one whose theoretical position and practical use differed. Cyril of Jerusalem and Epiphanius of Salamis were also very hesitant to call Sirach Holy Scripture while in practice not making any difference in using passages from Sirach[32]. Athanasius' distinction shows an awareness that some books read to catechumens were no part of the Jewish canon and that there is not (yet) a consensus on including those writings as a part of a "Christian" canon. Rather than inconclusiveness or incoherence it shows that in the second half of the fourth

32. GILBERT, art. *Jesus Sirach* (n. 9), esp. cc. 892-893.

century the process of canonization was still full of uncertainties and far from closed[33].

Faculty of Theology   Johan LEEMANS
St. Michielsstraat 6
B-3000 Leuven

33. See JUNOD, *La formation* (n. 1); GILBERT, art. *Jesus Sirach* (n. 9), cc. 888-904; C.S. SHAW, *Ecclesiasticus, Book of (or Wisdom of Jesus Sirach)*, in H.J. HAYES (ed.), *Dictionary of Biblical Interpretation*, Vol. I, Nashville, TN, Abingdon Press, 1999, pp. 314-316, esp. 314.

LE CANON ET LA QUESTION DU SALUT

Le nom de Jésus, ישוע, est mis en relation avec le verbe hébreu ישע en Mt 1,21. Le nom de ישוע est rappelé dans le sommaire de Lc 4,14-15. À la suite de ce sommaire[1], ישוע apparaît, comme le lecteur du livre du prophète ישעיהו, en Lc 4,17: «On lui remit le livre du prophète Isaïe (ישעיהו) et déroulant le livre, il trouva le passage où il était écrit». Suit une citation du livre d'Isaïe, dont le nom a pour signification potentielle «Yahvé mon salut», citation qui reprend en grande partie Is 61,1-2a en Lc 4,18-19: «L'esprit du Seigneur est sur moi (רוח אדני יהוה עלי), parce qu'il m'a consacré par l'onction (יען משח יהוה אתי), pour porter la bonne nouvelle aux pauvres (לבשר ענוים שלחני). Il m'a envoyé annoncer aux captifs la délivrance et aux aveugles le retour à la vue, renvoyer en liberté les opprimés, proclamer une année de grâce du Seigneur (לקרא שנת־רצון ליהוה)». Or le terme ישועה joue un rôle important dans le livre d'Isaïe, en rapport au retour de l'exil, et encore plus dans la rédaction de synthèse du livre selon le double parallélisme synonymique משפט צדקה / ישועה צדקה[2]. Certes dans le passage d'Is 61,1-2, le terme ישועה n'apparaît pas. Mais il ne faut pas oublier que le nom du lecteur rappelé en Lc 4,14-15, est justement celui de ישוע, et que c'est en sa personne même que s'accomplit le salut, selon ce qui est suggéré en Lc 4,21. En fait la citation d'Is 61,1-2 insiste sur les destinataires privilégiés du «salut» que sont les ענוים. Du reste la question du «salut» dans le livre d'Isaïe a été largement reprise et méditée dans le Psautier. Dans cette perspective le «salut» et les «pauvres», ont été clairement rapprochés en Ps 149,4b: יפאר ענוים בישועה[3]. On peut relever que le verbe פאר de Ps 149,4 est utilisé en Is 61,3. Les destinataires privilégiés du salut sont encore précisés en Lc 7,22. Ce verset reprend lui aussi divers passages du livre d'Isaïe,

---

1. Sur Lc 4,16-30, voir C.J. SCHRECK, *The Nazareth Pericope. Luke 4,16-30 in Recent Study*, in F. NEIRYNCK (ed.), *L'évangile de Luc. The Gospel of Luke* (BETL, 32), Leuven, University Press – Peeters, ²1989, pp. 399-471.

2. B. GOSSE, *Isaïe 56-59. Le livre d'Isaïe et la mémoire du prophète Isaïe*, in *Henoch* 19 (1997) 267-281. Voir tableaux pp. 277-278.

3. B. GOSSE, *L'influence du livre du prophète Isaïe (yš'yhw) sur la présentation du «salut (yšw'h)» par les cantiques et récits bibliques, et la chute de Jérusalem comme archétype des catastrophes des origines*, in *Henoch* 22 (2000) 3-34; ID., *Le Psaume CXLIX et la réinterprétation postexilique de la tradition prophétique*, in *VT* (1994) 259-263.

4. B. GOSSE, *Le quatrième livre du Psautier, Psaumes 90-106, comme réponse à l'échec de la royauté davidique*, in *BZ* (à paraître en 2002).

Is 35,5-6; 42,7; 26,19 et finalement Is 61,1. Le lien entre l'annonce de la bonne nouvelle et la venue du salut est d'ailleurs souligné par un passage comme Ps 96,2b: בשרו מיום־ליום ישועתו[4]; voir encore Is 52,7[5]. Mais la citation d'Is 61,1-2 en Lc 4,18-19, s'explique avant tout parce que «Jésus», en tant que «sauveur», se reconnaît lui-même dans le personnage qui s'exprime en Is 61,1-2. Ce personnage est «oint», comme le souligne l'usage du verbe משׁח, mais dans le cadre du livre d'Isaïe, en tant que recevant l'esprit de Yahvé, il se situe dans la continuité du personnage d'Is 42,1. Cette double qualité de «Messie» et de «Serviteur», est marquée par les deux variantes textuelles de Lc 3,22: 1) «Tu es mon fils bien-aimé, tu as toute ma faveur» (voir Is 42,1); 2) «Tu es mon fils; moi, aujourd'hui, je t'ai engendré» (voir Ps 2,7)[6]. Que le baptême de Jésus corresponde à une onction dans la perspective de l'ensemble Luc-Actes, est confirmé par Ac 10,38. Dans l'Évangile de Luc, Jésus est présenté comme le Messie-Serviteur, ce qui est du reste conforme à Ac 4,27. Mais dans le cadre des Actes, le Messie-Serviteur devient Messie-Seigneur après la résurrection, en fonction d'une interprétation de la citation du texte de la Septante du Ps 110,1 en Ac 2,34: «Le Seigneur (יהוה) a dit à mon Seigneur (לאדני)», ce qui permet d'affirmer en Ac 2,36: «Que toute la maison d'Israël le sache donc avec certitude: Dieu l'a fait Seigneur (יהוה = אדני) et Christ (משׁיח), ce Jésus (ישוע) que vous, vous avez crucifié». Après la résurrection nous avons donc un Messie-Seigneur, alors qu'avant celle-ci les deux titres correspondent d'une part à Jésus (Messie), et d'autre part à Yahvé (Seigneur), comme en témoigne Ac 4,26 (voir Ps 2,2). Si le Ps 2 a pu être cité en Lc 3,22, cela est conforme au fait qu'en Lc 4,18-19 la citation d'Is 61,1-2 doit se comprendre dans le cadre de la relecture du livre d'Isaïe par le Psautier et plus spécialement dans ce cas Ps 149,4. Or il faut encore relever que finalement Ps 149,8 répond à Ps 2,2-3. Toujours est-il qu'en dehors même de la citation d'Is 61,1 en Lc 4,18-19, le livre d'Isaïe a eu une large influence sur Luc-Actes. Voir Is 6,9-10 et Ac 28,26-27; Is 40,3-5 et

---

5. Yahvé est roi parce qu'il sauve son peuple. Voir encore Ex 15.

6. O. MAINVILLE, *Le messianisme de Jésus. Le rapport annonce / accomplissement entre Lc 1,35 et Ac 2,33*, in J. VERHEYDEN (ed.), *The Unity of Luke-Acts* (BETL, 142), Leuven, University Press – Peeters, 1999, pp. 313-327, considère que l'intronisation messianique n'intervient qu'à la résurrection. À propos de Lc 4,18-19, p. 324 note 35, elle estime qu'il s'agit de la consécration d'un prophète. Or il n'y a jamais eu d'onction prophétique. Le seul texte équivoque se trouve en 1 R 19,15-16, et il s'agit en fait d'un effet de parallélisme. Voir B. GOSSE, *Sur l'identité du personnage d'Isaïe 61,1*, in *Trans* 5 (1992) 45-58. J.J. KILGALLEN, *Your Servant Jesus Whom You Anointed*, in *RB* 105 (1998) 185-201 considère, lui, que l'onction est une expérience post-baptismale. En fait dans l'évangile de Luc, Jésus est présenté comme le Messie–Serviteur, et dans les Actes, après la résurrection, comme le Messie–Seigneur.

Lc 3,4-6; Is 42,7 et Ac 26,18; Is 53,7-8 et Ac 8,32-33. Ainsi le Messie-Serviteur, en lequel se reconnaît Jésus dans la citation d'Is 61,1-2, devient Messie-Seigneur par sa résurrection, et apporte le «salut» (ישועה), comme le signale son nom.

Ces éléments soulignent le lien privilégié établi entre la personne de «Jésus» et le livre d'Isaïe. Or dans le livre d'Isaïe le terme ישועה joue un rôle important en rapport au retour de l'exil comme en témoigne par exemple Is 52,7, mais encore plus dans le cadre de la synthèse d'ensemble en ישועה צדקה / משפט צדקה. Cette perspective de la venue du «salut» a été étendue à ce que l'on considère habituellement comme la première partie du livre d'Isaïe, avec le triple usage du terme ישועה en Is 12,2-3. En Is 12 nous avons une mise en parallèle des événements de l'exode avec ceux du retour de l'exil, voir Is 11,16 et les similitudes entre Ex 15,2 et Is 12,2. Cela correspond également aux relations entre Is 35,9-10 et Is 51,10-11, avec 35,10 = 51,11, et le fait que les גאולים de 35,9 correspondent à ceux qui reviennent d'exil, alors qu'en 51,10 il s'agit de ceux qui ont connu l'exode. Le thème du salut a également été repris dans le Psautier, et en s'appuyant sur ce dernier, le «Messie-Serviteur», a pu ensuite être présenté comme le «Messie-Seigneur». En ce qui concerne le Psautier, il faut rapprocher la mention de ישועתי צדקתי en Is 56,1, de celle de ישועתו צדקתו en Ps 98,2. Mais dans le Psautier le terme ישועה, tout en continuant à faire allusion aux «saluts» collectifs de l'histoire d'Israël, peut aussi par ailleurs se rapporter au «salut» espéré par le psalmiste du second Temple en rapport à sa vie propre. Dans les psaumes 42–43 et 44[7], le terme ישועה apparaît en Ps 42,6.12; 43,5; 44,5. En Ps 42,6.12; 43,5, nous trouvons le refrain: «Qu'as-tu, mon âme, à défaillir et à gémir sur moi? Espère en Dieu: à nouveau je lui rendrai grâce le salut de ma face (ישועות פני) et mon Dieu». Il s'agit de l'expression du désir de l'expérience de salut que va constituer la participation à la reprise du culte au retour de l'exil. Par contre nous trouvons en Ps 44,5: «C'est toi, mon roi, mon Dieu qui décidais les saluts de Jacob (ישועות יעקב)». Dans ce cas les «saluts» passés et collectifs de l'histoire d'Israël sont le gage de l'espérance à venir. Le lien entre la perspective «individuelle» de Ps 42–43, et celle «collective» de Ps 44, est souligné par l'usage de termes communs comme לחץ (Ps 42,10; 43,2; 44,25, sans autre emploi dans le Psautier), mais encore par le fait qu'alors que Ps 44,27 s'appuie sur Is 35,10; Ps 42,2 en fait de même avec Is 35,6. Dans le Psautier la perspective individuelle de salut est encore présente dès le Ps 3, en Ps 3,3.9. Le Ps 3, a par ailleurs été intégré dans la série

---

7. B. GOSSE, *L'insertion des psaumes des chantres-lévites dans l'ensemble rédactionnel livre d'Isaïe – Psautier et les revendications des lévites*, in *Trans* 19 (2000) 145-158.

des Psaumes attribués à David par Ps 3,1. Cette collection de Psaumes renvoie à des événements de la vie de David pour la plupart rapportés en 1 S 16 – 2 S 22. Aussi si on suit l'ordre des références aux livres de Samuel, la série de Psaumes se conclut en 2 S 22 = Ps 18, avec en 2 S 22,51: «Il magnifie les saluts (ישועות) de son roi et il agit avec fidélité envers son oint, envers David et sa descendance à jamais».

Les liens entre les trois ensembles que constituent, le livre d'Isaïe, le Psautier, et les cantiques de Gn – 2 R, sont encore soulignés par les correspondances entre: Ex 15,2a = Ps 118,14 (עזי וזמרת יה ויהי־לי לישועה) et Is 12,2b (כי־עזי וזמרת יה יהוה ויהי־לי לישועה). Le Ps 118 correspond également à la célébration du salut «collectif» de l'exode. Mais les Psaumes des Montées en appliquent la perspective au psalmiste du second temple[8]. Lui aussi bénéficiera finalement de l'expérience de salut, mais dans le cadre du culte, comme en témoigne Ps 132,16: «ses prêtres je les vêtirai de salut (ישע) et ses fidèles crieront de joie». Dans les cantiques de Gn – 2 R, on trouve ישועה en 49,18, voir Gn 49,17 et Ex 15. En ce qui concerne le ישועה d'Ex 14,13, ce verset est lui-même à rapprocher de la tradition hymnique. L'expression d'Ex 14,13 וראו את־ישועת יהוה a des correspondances en Is 52,10 et Ps 98,3 ראו...את ישועת אלהינו. On relèvera encore ישועה en Dt 32,15, dans le cantique de Moïse, et en 1 S 2,1 dans le Cantique d'Anne. Le ישועה de 1 S 14,45, concerne Jonathan précurseur de David[9]. En 2 S 10,11 il s'agit d'une victoire des généraux de David. L'usage de ישועה en Gn – 2 R correspond à des «saluts» antérieurs à l'espérance de salut de retour de l'exil. Or ce dernier «salut» se situe au-delà de la perspective des livres des Rois qui se terminent par l'annonce de la venue du malheur (רעה) contre «ce lieu» (המקום הזה) en 2 R 22,20[10]. De l'usage du terme ישועה en Gn – 2 R, il faut encore rapprocher les cas de 1 Ch 16,23 et 2 Ch 20,17. Le cas de 1 Ch 16,23 correspond à la citation de Ps 96,2, en fait dans le cadre du culte du second Temple. Si les cantiques de Gn – 2 R doivent permettre de participer aux «saluts» passés de l'histoire d'Israël, le cantique est conçu dans les Chroniques comme permettant au psalmiste du second Temple d'espérer son propre salut. Ce point apparaît particulièrement si on compare Ex 14,13: «Moïse dit au peuple: Ne craignez pas! Tenez ferme et vous verrez ce que Yahvé va faire pour vous sauver aujourd'hui (אל־תיראו התיצבו וראו את־ישועת יהוה אשר־יעשה לכם היום), car les Égyptiens que

---

8. B. GOSSE, *Ex 15, Ps 120-134 et le livre d'Isaïe, le salut d'Israël et celui du psalmiste*, in *Bibbia e Oriente* (à paraître).

9. A. CAQUOT & P. DE ROBERT, *Les livres de Samuel* (CAT, 6), Genève, Labor & Fides, 1994, p. 168.

10. B. GOSSE, *L'«histoire deutéronomique»: La rédaction des livres des Rois et ses relations avec les parallèles du livre d'Isaïe*, in *Trans* 18 (1999) 29-57.

vous voyez aujourd'hui, vous ne les verrez plus jamais» et 2 Ch 20,17 «Vous n'aurez pas à y combattre, Tenez-vous là, prenez position, vous verrez le salut que Yahvé vous réserve. Juda et Jérusalem ne craignez pas (התיצבו עמדו וראו את־ישועת יהוה עמכם יהודה וירושלם אל־תיראו), ne vous effrayez pas, partez demain à leur rencontre et Yahvé sera avec vous». En Ex 14–15, le cantique d'Ex 15 suit le récit du succès militaire de Yahvé évoqué en Ex 14, et il en constitue la célébration. En prenant à son compte le cantique d'Ex 15, le psalmiste du second temple pouvait participer à l'expérience de salut d'Israël, salut déjà réalisé. Mais en 2 Ch 20, le cantique est alors promesse de salut à venir. Le salut doit rejoindre le psalmiste dans sa propre vie. Selon ce schéma, et en fonction du récit se rapportant à un épisode guerrier de l'histoire d'Israël, en 2 Ch 20 le cantique précède cette fois le succès militaire comme en témoigne 2 Ch 20,21-22. Cette présentation souligne qu'à l'époque du second Temple, le culte est le cadre de l'expérience de salut, voir par exemple Ps 132,16 ou Is 52,7. Le salut passé d'Israël est un gage du propre salut à venir du psalmiste. Cette prise en compte des Chroniques dans la continuité de l'ensemble Gn – 2 R, pour former une inclusion, est conforme à Lc 11,51.

Dans les autres livres bibliques, le terme ישועה apparaît encore au sujet d'un salut personnel en Jb 13,16; 30,15; Jon 2,10, et au sujet d'un salut guerrier en Ha 3,8. Il ne faut pas négliger non plus les autres usages de la racine ישע. Nous avons déjà vu par exemple que le ישע de Ps 132,16 devait se comprendre dans la continuité du ישועה de Ps 118,14. Le terme תשועה apparaît treize fois dans le Psautier, trois fois dans le livre d'Isaïe, neuf fois en Gn – 2 R (dont cinq fois en 1–2 S) et trois fois en 1–2 Ch. Il faut encore ajouter Jr 3,23; Lm 3,26, et surtout Pr 11,14; 21,31; 24,6. Le livre des Proverbes présente des liens étroits avec le livre d'Isaïe, tout en allant dans le sens d'une démocratisation, comme le fait le Psautier (voir par exemple Is 59,21 et Pr 1,23)[11]. Le substantif ישע se trouve dans les ensembles déjà mentionnés, vingt fois dans le Psautier; cinq fois dans le livre d'Isaïe; quatre fois en 2 Sm 22–23 (voir Psautier); 1 Ch 16,35 (voir Psautier); Jb 5,4.11; Mi 7,7; Ha 3,13.13.18. Quant au verbe ישע il est d'un usage plus courant. Dans le livre de Jérémie les emplois du verbe ישע sont nombreux. Malgré les rédactions successives, la présentation du salut en lien avec le retour de l'exil, à la suite de la chute de Jérusalem apparaît encore clairement dans des passages comme Jr 30,11 ou Jr 31,7. C'est autour de Jr 30–31 que la rédaction

---

11. B. GOSSE, *L'universalisme de la Sagesse face au sacerdoce de Jérusalem au retour de l'exil (Le don de «mon Esprit» et de «mes paroles» en Is 59,21 et Pr 1,23)*, in *Trans* 19 (1997) 39-43.

massorétique du livre de Jérémie a été réorganisée, avec l'annonce de la venue du malheur contre Babylone en Jr 50–51: les nations n'afflueront plus à Babylone (נהר Jr 51,44), et les exilés afflueront (נהרו Jr 31,12) à Jérusalem. En Jr 1–51 TM le «salut» de Jérusalem est lié à la venue du malheur contre Babylone[12]. Dans le livre d'Ezéchiel, le verbe ישע n'y apparaît que trois fois (Ez 34,22; 36,29; 37,23). Mais une très large première partie du livre d'Ezéchiel est orientée vers l'annonce de la chute de Jérusalem. Dans le livre d'Ezéchiel le «salut» correspond bien au retour de l'exil, même s'il est mis l'accent sur une «purification» par rapport aux comportements préexiliques[13]. Dans le rouleau des douze petits prophètes, on peut relever l'usage du verbe ישע en Za 8,7.13; 9,9.16; 10,6; 12,7. À propos du salut en rapport à la chute de Jérusalem on peut noter Za 8,7-8: «Ainsi parle Yahvé Sabaot. Voici que je sauve (מושיע) mon peuple des pays d'orient et des pays du soleil couchant. Je les ramènerai pour qu'ils habitent au milieu de Jérusalem. Ils seront mon peuple et moi je serai leur Dieu, dans la fidélité et la justice».

Ainsi Gn – 2 R conduit le récit jusqu'à la chute de Jérusalem, par rapport à laquelle s'affirmera le salut dans les livres prophétiques. Mais à travers les cantiques insérés en Gn – 2 R se célèbre également des «saluts» antérieurs, présage du salut du retour de l'exil. Dans la continuité du livre d'Isaïe, le Psautier et les Chroniques situent le salut dans le cadre du culte du Temple. Au-delà de la célébration des «saluts» antérieurs, y compris de ceux de l'histoire d'Israël par les cantiques, il s'agit de mettre en valeur la perspective de salut dans la vie même du psalmiste à travers ses propres épreuves. Qu'en est-il des autres livres de la Bible hébraïque non encore abordés? Dans le livre des Proverbes nous avons déjà relevé la mention du «salut». Par ailleurs Pr 1,23 se situe dans une perspective de démocratisation par rapport à Is 59,21. L'accueil de la Sagesse doit permettre à tous de surmonter les épreuves[14]. Il est clair que les livres de Sagesse deutérocanoniques ont pu s'appuyer sur ces perspectives, en lien avec un contexte contestataire en faveur des valeurs universelles. Dans la bible hébraïque, il faut encore relever le

---

12. B. GOSSE, *Trois étapes de la rédaction du livre de Jérémie. La venue du malheur contre ce lieu (Jérusalem), puis contre toute chair (Juda et les nations), et enfin de nouveau contre ce lieu, mais identifié cette fois à Babylone*, in ZAW 111 (1999) 508-529.

13. Ez 36,29: «Je vous sauverai (והושעתי) de toutes vos souillures. J'appellerai le blé et le multiplierai, et je ne vous imposerai plus de famine»; et Ez 37,23.

14. B. GOSSE, *La création en Proverbes 8,22-31 et Isaïe 40,12-24*, in NRT 115 (1993) 186-193; ID., *L'établissement du droit (mšpt) et de la justice (ṣdqh), et les relations entre les rédactions d'ensemble des livres d'Isaïe et des Proverbes*, in SJOT 14 (2000) 275-292; ID., *La Sagesse comme alternative aux alliances nouvelles des livres prophétiques dans la perspective d'une restauration de la religion d'Israël*, in Studi Epigrafi e Linguistici 16 (1999) 73-78.

groupe de cinq livres, Rt–Ct–Qo–Lm–Est. Ce groupe de livres, au-delà même de l'«alternative» des Proverbes, présente un caractère contestataire. Le livre d'Esther à la suite de l'histoire de Joseph relève d'une contestation de la fidélité à la terre. Le livre de Ruth conteste lui l'interdiction des mariages avec les étrangers[15]. Le livre du Cantique et celui de l'Ecclésiaste en référence à Salomon, témoignent d'une contestation plus radicale avec une ouverture sur l'universel.

Le livre de Daniel concerne des épreuves ultérieures de l'histoire d'Israël. Mais le livre de Daniel présente celles-ci dans le cadre d'une fiction se situant pendant l'exil à Babylone. Ainsi les espérances de «salut» ultérieures sont situées en continuité de celles du retour de l'exil. Les livres d'Esdras et de Néhémie se rapportent au retour de l'exil. En ce qui concerne les deutérocanoniques, nous avons déjà noté que les livres de Sagesse, pouvaient s'appuyer sur le rôle joué par le livre des Proverbes. On peut relever particulièrement le livre de la Sagesse, et celui de l'Ecclésiastique ou Siracide, que l'on peut situer à la frontière du Canon[16].

Les livres des Maccabées se rapportent à une mise en cause de la religion d'Israël comme dans le cas de Daniel. Le livre de Baruch attribué au secrétaire de Jérémie a une connotation de Sagesse. Le livre de Tobie se rapporte fictivement à l'époque de la déportation assyrienne, et va dans le sens d'une démocratisation des préoccupations des textes. Le livre de Judith s'enracine dans le cadre de la déportation de Nabuchodonosor. Nous trouvons donc des variations sur le thème de la chute de Jérusalem ou de la déportation.

Ainsi il apparaît qu'en accord avec le texte du Nouveau Testament, et avec le nom même de Jésus, le canon de l'Ancien Testament est structuré autour de la question du «salut» en rapport à l'événement de la chute de Jérusalem. Dans ce cadre le livre d'Isaïe joue bien entendu un rôle central. Les autres livres ont apporté leurs corrections voir leurs contestations. Le «salut» à venir a pu être conçu dans la continuité de ce «salut» du retour de l'exil. Toutefois on peut penser que c'est à cause de nouvelles épreuves que le «Canon» de la Bible hébraïque a été fermé[17].

---

15. R. ALTER, *Canon and Creativity*, New Haven, CT, Yale University Press, 2000, spéc. pp. 27-30; B. GOSSE, *Structuration des grands ensembles bibliques et intertextualité à l'époque perse* (BZAW, 246), Berlin & New York, de Gruyter, 1997, pp. 153-154.

16. P. RÜGER, *Le Siracide: Un livre à la frontière du Canon*, in J.D. KAESTLI & O. WERMELINGER (eds.), *Le Canon de l'Ancien Testament. Sa fonction et son histoire* (Le Monde de la Bible), Genève, Labor & Fides, 1984, pp. 47-69. Il relève les citations de Si 4,1 en Mc 10,19; Si 5,1 en Jc 1,19 et Si 17,26 en 2 Tm 2,19.

17. D. BARTHÉLEMY, *L'état de la Bible Juive depuis le début de notre ère jusqu'à la dernière révolte contre Rome (131-133)*, in KAESTLI & WERMELINGER (eds.), *Le Canon de l'Ancien Testament* (n. 16), pp. 9-45.

En effet il ne s'agissait plus seulement d'une contestation radicale, à laquelle on pouvait répondre en s'appuyant sur les traditions liées à la
chute de Jérusalem, il existait également des différences d'interprétations à l'égard des textes.

4, Résidence Opéra   Bernard GOSSE
F-92160 Antony

THE CHRISTIAN CANON A PALIMPSEST?

1. *Introduction*

While reading and preparing for the Colloquium I stumbled across two statements which acted as catalysts in the writing of this paper. The first one was by George Nickelsburg in a publication celebrating the fiftieth anniversary of the discovery of the Dead Sea Scrolls. He wrote: "Fiftieth anniversaries are usually occasions for celebration. They also provide opportunity for retrospection and reflection"[1]. The second was a statement by Albert Baumgarten in the preface to his book *The Flourishing of Jewish Sects in the Maccabean Era: An Interpretation.* He said: "Believing as I do that there is an intimate connection, best explicitly acknowledged, between the work produced by a scholar and the world in which he or she lives, I conclude by noting the Israeli context of the discussion to follow"[2].

The *Colloquium Biblicum Lovaniense* celebrates its fiftieth anniversary. The first meeting was held in 1949, four years after the end of World War II – a war which will always remind people of the Holocaust. The organizers of this fiftieth meeting thought it fit to make the biblical canons the focus, since in this way both Old and New Testament scholars can take part in the celebration. By doing this they (perhaps unintentionally) also gave scholars the opportunity to reflect on the relationship between Judaism and Christianity. We do share the same religious documents, after all.

Being an Old Testament scholar living in South Africa with a past history of colonialisation and apartheid I am inclined to focus on societies and communities when reading and reflecting on biblical texts. Biblical texts did not originate in a vacuum. They originated in a specific era and area and they were written by people influenced by religious

* The author hereby acknowledges grants received from the National Research Foundation and the Research Committee of the University of South Africa to attend the *Colloquium Biblicum Lovaniense.*

1. G.W.E. Nickelsburg, *Currents in Qumran Scholarship: The Interplay of Data, Agendas, and Methodology*, in R.A. Kugler & E.M. Schuller (eds.), *The Dead Sea Scrolls at Fifty: Proceedings of the 1997 Society of Biblical Literature Qumran Section Meetings* (Early Judaism and Its Literature, 15), Atlanta, Scholars, 1999, pp. 79-99, esp. 79.

2. A.I. Baumgarten, *The Flourishing of Jewish Sects in the Maccabean Era: An Interpretation* (JSJ SS, 55), Leiden, Brill, 1997, p. xiii.

convictions and ideologies. To talk about two Testaments which make up one Bible and to reflect on how this came about without paying attention to the religious communities involved is, to my mind, a thing of the past. Recent developments in linguistics, semiotics, hermeneutics and theory of literature have made us aware of the role readers play in creating meaning. To use the words of Gunnar Hansson: "[M]eanings are not 'found' or 'discovered' in the text, but they are taken out of the mind of the individual reader and from there attributed to the text"[3]. But it is not merely individual readers who attribute meaning to texts; in every society there exists *interpretive communities* which influence individual readers' understanding of biblical texts. To use another quote from the article by Hansson: "Thus, instead of 'the text itself' there is now every reason to pay attention to the *interpretive community*... which each human being is part of, has been formed by, and consciously or unconsciously shares experiences, evaluations, and linguistic or other convictions with"[4].

In South Africa we had the experience that Christians from different Church traditions read and understood the Bible in such a way that it either supported or opposed the policy of apartheid[5]. The existence of different *interpretive communities* in a society has nowhere else been so prominent than in our country.

With these remarks as my background I would like to look at two *interpretive communities* which existed alongside each other in the eastern Mediterranean countries during the first century of the common era (viz. the Jewish and Christian communities) and reflect on how Psalm 8 was read and understood by the author of the letter to the Hebrews. By doing this I hope to produce warrants for my view that the Christian canon (or the Christian Bible) can be compared to a palimpsest (or as it is called in Latin: *codex rescriptus*).

2. *Interpretive Communities*

Although ordinary Christians still cherish the idea that Christianity superseded the religion of the Jews, critical study of the Bible[6] and the

---

3. G. HANSSON, *Reading and Understanding the Bible*, in ID. (ed.), *Bible Reading in Sweden: Studies Related to the Translation of the New Testament 1981*, Stockholm, Almqvist & Wiksell, 1990, pp. 105-116, esp. 109.

4. *Ibid.*, p. 112.

5. Cf. J.W. DE GRUCHY, *Church Struggle in South Africa*, Cape Town, David Philip, 1979; J.A. LOUBSER, *The Apartheid Bible: A Critical Review of Racial Theology in South Africa*, Cape Town, Maskew Miller Longman, 1987.

6. Cf. L. GROLLENBERG, *Unexpected Messiah, or How the Bible Can Be Misleading*, London, SCM, 1987; R.P. CARROLL, *Wolf in the Sheepfold: The Bible as a Problem for Christianity*, London, SPCK, 1991.

early history of Christianity[7] have made this notion untenable. Christianity originated as yet another group (or sect, if you like) in Judaism of the first century CE. Christians developed their own identity while reflecting on the life and teachings of Jesus. They more than often used the Septuagint to interpret the events which took place during and after the lifetime of their teacher. One could say that another *interpretive community* originated in Judaism. At that stage quite a number of different interpretive communities existed in Palestine. Lester Grabbe[8] identified at least four different currents in Judaism: (1) a priestly and scribal current, (2) a political and "messianic" current, (3) an apocalyptic current, and (4) a gnostic current. Although the different currents do not exactly overlap with the different *interpretive communities*, they do give one an idea of the complexity of Judaism during the first century.

The existence of different interpretive communities and the destruction of the Temple in 70 CE posed an enormous threat to the survival of Judaism. This led to a number of meetings of religious leaders to weather the storm. At Jamnia religious leaders defined what Judaism would entail in future and which books would form part of their canon[9]. During these deliberations the Pharisaic form of Judaism (reflecting the priestly and scribal current) gained the upper hand[10]. The decisions which were taken also brought about a break between Judaism and Christianity and the result was that Christians who were still members of synagogues were obliged to leave them[11].

Towards the end of the first century two opposing interpretive communities thus existed alongside each other. The one cherished the Hebrew scriptures and adhered to the laws of Moses. The other one focused on the life and teachings of Jesus and used the Septuagint (the Greek translation of the Hebrew scriptures) in its interpretations and reflections.

The Jewish leaders were not pleased with the Christian appropriation of their scriptures and in later years a negative attitude developed towards the Septuagint[12]. When one reads the books of the New Testament it becomes evident why Christians had a preferential option for this

7. E. TROCMÉ, *The Childhood of Christianity*, London, SCM, 1997.

8. L.L. GRABBE, *An Introduction to First Century Judaism: Jewish Religion and History in the Second Temple Period*, Edinburgh, T. & T. Clark, 1996.

9. R.B. COOTE & M.P. COOTE, *Power, Politics, and the Making of the Bible: An Introduction*, Minneapolis, Fortress, 1990, p.114.

10. TROCMÉ, *The Childhood* (n. 7), pp. 83 and 121.

11. *Ibid.*, pp. 83-84.

12. M. SAPERSTEIN, *Moments of Crisis in Jewish-Christian Relations*, London, SCM, 1989, pp. 3 and 65.

translation. It often supported their production of meaning. To give but one example I would like to read Ps 8,4-7 and Heb 2,5-9 as they are translated in the *Revised English Bible*.

3. *Psalm 8 and Hebrews 2*

Psalm 8,4-7

⁴ כי־אראה שמיך מעשי אצבעתיך ירח וכוכבים אשר כוננתה:

When I look up at your heavens, the work of your fingers,
at the moon and the stars you have set in place,

⁵ מה־אנוש כי־תזכרנו ובן־אדם כי תפקדנו:

what is a frail mortal, that you should be mindful of him,
a human being, that you should take notice of him?

⁶ ותחסרהו מעט מאלהים וכבוד והדר תעטרהו:

Yet, you have made him **little less** than a **god**
crowning his head with glory and honour.

⁷ תמשילהו במעשי ידיך כל שתה תחת־רגליו:

You make him master over all that you have made,
putting everything in subjection under his feet.

⁴ ὅτι ὄψομαι τοὺς οὐρανούς, ἔργα τῶν δακτύλων σου,
σελήνην καὶ ἀστέρας, ἃ σὺ ἐθεμελίωσας.

⁵ τί ἐστιν ἄνθρωπος, ὅτι μιμνήσκῃ αὐτοῦ,
ἢ υἱὸς ἀνθρώπου, ὅτι ἐπισκέπτῃ αὐτόν;

⁶ ἠλάττωσας αὐτὸν βραχύ τι παρ' ἀγγέλους,
δόξῃ καὶ τιμῇ ἐστεφάνωσας αὐτόν·

⁷ καὶ κατέστησας αὐτὸν ἐπὶ τὰ ἔργα τῶν χειρῶν σου,
πάντα ὑπέταξας ὑποκάτω τῶν ποδῶν αὐτοῦ,

Hebrews 2,5-9

⁵ For it is not to angels that he has subjected the world to come, which is our theme.

⁶ There is somewhere this solemn assurance:
What is man, that you should remember him
a man, that you should care for him?

⁷ *You made him for a **short while** subordinate to **the angels**;*
with glory and honour you crowned him;

⁸ *you put everything in subjection beneath his feet.*
For in subjecting everything to him, God left nothing that is not made subject. But in fact we do not yet see everything in subjection to man.

⁹ What we do see is Jesus, who for a short while was made subordinate to the angels, crowned now with glory and honour because he suffered death, so that, by God's gracious will, he should experience death for all mankind.

⁵ Οὐ γὰρ ἀγγέλοις ὑπέταξεν τὴν οἰκουμένην τὴν μέλλουσαν, περὶ ἧς λαλοῦμεν.

⁶ διεμαρτύρατο δέ πού τις λέγων,
Τί ἐστιν ἄνθρωπος ὅτι μιμνήσκῃ αὐτοῦ,
ἢ υἱὸς ἀνθρώπου ὅτι ἐπισκέπτῃ αὐτόν;

⁷ ἠλάττωσας αὐτὸν βραχύ τι παρ' ἀγγέλους,
δόξῃ καὶ τιμῇ ἐστεφάνωσας αὐτόν,

⁸ πάντα ὑπέταξας ὑποκάτω τῶν ποδῶν αὐτοῦ.
ἐν τῷ γὰρ ὑποτάξαι [αὐτῷ] τὰ πάντα οὐδὲν ἀφῆκεν αὐτῷ ἀνυπότακτον. νῦν δὲ οὔπω ὁρῶμεν αὐτῷ τὰ πάντα ὑποτεταγμένα·

⁹ τὸν δὲ βραχύ τι παρ' ἀγγέλους ἠλαττωμένον βλέπομεν Ἰησοῦν διὰ τὸ πάθημα τοῦ θανάτου δόξῃ καὶ τιμῇ ἐστεφανωμένον, ὅπως χάριτι θεοῦ ὑπὲρ παντὸς γεύσηται θανάτου.

The author of the letter to the Hebrews did not use the Hebrew text of Psalm 8 but the Greek text (Septuagint). When we compare the two texts interesting changes catch the eye. The changes are printed in bold.

According to Ps 8,6 God created humans so that they are almost god-like. The Septuagint translated the Hebrew word אלהים ("God/ gods") as ἀγγέλους ("angels") and thus changed the meaning slightly. God created humans so that they are almost like angels. Moreover, the Hebrew word מעט which means "a little less" is translated with the Greek words βραχύ τι ("a short while"). This phrase does not carry the same meaning as the Hebrew word. The Hebrew word מעט reflects *ranking* but the Greek phrase reflects *duration*. These changes in the translation contributed to the new meaning which Christians were "reading from" the old scriptures. By means of a different translation and a *pesher*-like interpretation an allusion to the passion and exaltation of Jesus has been deduced from Ps 8,4-7.

The creation and eventually canonization of new meaning took some years but there were factors which sped up the process. One of these was the conviction that words and texts had more than one meaning. Christians did not increasingly allegorize the old scriptures. On the contrary, they continued a practice which was applied to religious documents by all well trained interpreters during the early centuries. The only difference between the Jewish and Christian interpreters was the meaning which they "discovered" in the text[13]. It is, however, thanks to modern biblical research that the "original" meanings of the psalms (and other biblical texts) have been discovered.

Living long before the rise of the kind of historical self-consciousness which has characterized modern times, New Testament writers were largely untroubled by questions as to what the Old Testament authors might have meant by their words in their own day. Modern critical studies on the other hand have revealed that Psalm 8 is a hymn in which the relationship between Creator and creature is the focal point. The psalm reflects a Hebrew poet's understanding of what it entails to be a human being. Humans are totally insignificant but in spite of this God has appointed them to have dominion over the earth and all other living beings[14]. This meaning of the text was blurred when the Psalms were translated in Greek and the author of the letter to the Hebrews took advantage of this. The Septuagint assisted him in producing new meaning. The religious texts which Jews and Christians (the two interpretive com-

---

13. J. BARTON, *The Spirit and the Letter: Studies in the Biblical Canon*, London, SPCK, 1997, p. 61.

14. J.A. LOADER, *Gedagtes oor gekontroleerde eksegese*, in *Hervormde Teologiese Studies* 34 (1978) 1-40, esp. pp. 35-40.

munities) used were more or less the same, but the readers were different and belonged to different interpretive communities. This necessarily led to the production of different meanings.

4. *The Creation of New Meaning*

In his book on primitive Christian religion Gerd Theissen defined religion as a system of interpretation. "Human beings", he wrote, "cannot exist in their environment as they find it. They have to change it. They do that on the one hand by work and technology, and on the other by interpretations"[15]. When we discuss the issue of the biblical canons we need to take this into account. The religious writings of the early Christians reflect their efforts to make sense of their world. They created new meaning and this meaning was eventually canonized[16].

Christianity originated in Palestine amongst believers of Jewish origin and the destruction of the Temple in Jerusalem in 70 CE affected them as well[17]. The writers of the New Testament read the Septuagint in order to make sense of the life and teachings of Jesus and of the events that happened in 70 CE. They not only had to interpret the death of the one who gave new meaning to their lives, but they also had to deal with the destruction of the most holy place they ever knew. The Greek translation of the Hebrew scriptures played an important role in their interpretations. These interpretations were written down and circulated amongst the different Jesus groups in Palestine, Syria and Asia Minor. In a short period of time their writings became more important than the old scriptures which they used in their interpretations. One could say that the "old texts" were erased and "new ones" were written on top. At a later stage in history some Christians (like Marcion) suggested that Christians should not pay attention to the old texts anymore, but that they should focus more on the new texts[18]. Had Christians done this the two interpretive communities would have moved further away from each other and the enmity between them might have ceased.

5. *Conclusion*

Paul Joyce once said in a sermon "Judaism and Christianity should not be thought of as 'mother' and 'daughter', but perhaps as two sisters,

---

15. G. THEISSEN, *A Theory of Primitive Christian Religion*, London, SCM, 1999, p. 2.

16. R.J. HOFFMANN, *Afterword*, in M. SMITH & R.J. HOFFMANN (eds.), *What the Bible Really Says*, San Francisco, HarperCollins, 1993, pp. 239-243, esp. 243.

17. COOTE & COOTE, *Power, Politics* (n. 9), pp. 112-113.

18. SAPERSTEIN, *Moments of Crisis* (n. 12), p. 3.

whose stories have been distinctive and particular"[19]. Our duty as scholars is to inform ordinary believers about the changes in the study of the Bible, the changes in our understanding of religion and the role which religion play in the production of meaning. Christianity did not supersede the religion of the Jews. In our study of the canons this should be emphasised. The Hebrew scriptures, from which the Christian Old Testament derived, are of course the property of Judaism and are legitimately interpreted within that community. These scriptures (especially in the Greek translation) assisted the early Christians in their interpretations, but during this process they almost "erased" the old text. Thanks to wise leaders this was not done. However, the texts which Christians wrote had a detrimental effect on the other interpretive community. That community was looked upon as a falsifier of the scriptures and was almost eradicated when Christian readers ignored the history of their own religion and forgot that their scriptures could be seen as a palimpsest.

Department of Old Testament   I.J.J. SPANGENBERG
University of South Africa
PO Box 392
Pretoria 0003
Republic of South Africa

19. P. JOYCE, *A Tale of Two Sisters: Judaism and Christianity*, in *Theology* 96 (1993) 384–390, esp. p. 388.

LA STRUCTURE SYMÉTRIQUE DE LA BIBLE CHRÉTIENNE

L'étude du canon, compris comme une liste normative de livres, a suivi la tendance générale des études bibliques qui furent surtout diachroniques. Beaucoup de recherches ont été consacrées à expliquer la formation et la clôture du canon de l'Ancien et du Nouveau Testament, en d'autres mots à comprendre comment on est arrivé à la présente liste des livres. Des études synchroniques plus récentes offrent d'autres richesses de compréhension. Elles montrent que certains textes bibliques, malgré leur longue préhistoire, présentent dans leur forme finale une unité littéraire, fréquemment selon une structure parallèle, chiastique ou concentrique[1]. Elles essaient aussi d'expliquer l'unité de certains groupes de livres, comme les douze petits prophètes, ou les cinq livres du Psautier. La présente étude veut aborder d'une façon synchronique le canon chrétien tel qu'il existe maintenant – peu importe comment on y est arrivé – pour dégager la structure qui donne unité à ce canon dans ses sections majeures. On suit ici l'ordre des livres qui s'est imposé dans les bibles catholiques depuis l'invention de l'imprimerie et qui était déjà largement répandu à l'époque.

1. *Les sections majeures du canon*

Chaque bibliothèque suit un système pour classifier les livres. Certaines personnes placent leurs livres n'importe comment, leur principe de classification est qu'il n'y a pas de principe. Ce n'est pas le cas pour la plupart des personnes et certainement pas pour des bibliothèques d'institutions publiques. Les livres peuvent être classés selon l'ordre chronologique de leur publication ou acquisition, selon leur format ou grandeur, mais généralement selon des systèmes plus complexes. Les livres sont placés dans des sections majeures définies par le sujet et à l'intérieur de

---

1. Voir J.P. FOKKELMAN, *Narrative Art in Genesis: Specimens of Stylistic and Structural Analysis* (SSN, 17), Assen, Van Gorcum, 1975; ID., *Narrative Art and Poetry in the Books of Samuel*, 4 vol. (SSN, 20.23.27.31), Assen, Van Gorcum, 1981, 1986, 1990, 1993; ID., *Major Poems of the Hebrew Bible: At the Interface of Hermeneutics and Structural Analysis*, 2 vol. (SSN, 37.41), Assen, Van Gorcum, 1998, 2000; J. BRECK, *Chiasmus as a Key to Biblical Interpretation* et R.F. ELLIS, *Inclusion, Chiasm, and the Division of the Fourth Gospel*, in *St.Vladimir's Theological Quarterly* 42 (1999) 249-268 et 269-338.

chaque section les livres individuels sont groupés selon d'autres principes. Comme la Bible n'est pas un livre mais une collection de livres et
donc une bibliothèque, il serait surprenant que le canon serait une collection arbitraire d'écrits sans aucun principe d'unité[2]. Il paraît beaucoup
plus probable qu'un système a été suivi dans la composition du canon.
Si la structure de cet ensemble était une des trois structures mentionnées, il faudra en conclure qu'elle est le résultat d'une planification
consciente, faite avec l'intention de guider le lecteur dans cette bibliothèque.

L'Ancien Testament des chrétiens est divisé en quelques sections majeures, et cette division est différente de celle de la Bible hébraïque des
Juifs. Même les chrétiens comme les Protestants qui n'acceptent comme
canoniques que les livres de cette Bible hébraïque ne suivent pourtant
pas sa division. La Bible hébraïque a trois grandes parties: Torah – Prophètes (antérieurs et postérieurs) – Écrits. L'Ancien Testament en a quatre: Pentateuque – Livres Historiques – Livres Sapientiaux (ou didacti-
ques) – Prophètes. Il y a beaucoup de ressemblance entre les deux divisions, mais aussi des différences importantes. Les Prophètes antérieurs
sont devenus les Livres Historiques et certains livres des Écrits (Chroniques, Esdras–Néhémie) ont été placés parmi les Livres Historiques pour
compléter ainsi toute l'histoire d'Israël. Le changement le plus significatif est le déplacement des Prophètes (postérieurs) de leur deuxième position vers la fin de l'Ancien Testament. De tels changements sont sans
aucun doute intentionnels pour donner un autre message à la collection[3]. Qui est responsable de ce changement? Tel est le sujet des études
diachroniques sur la formation et la clôture du canon. Certains cher-
cheurs suggèrent que les chrétiens auraient introduit ce changement, et
non pas les Juifs[4]. Mais peu importe cette discussion, le judaïsme et le

2. E.T. OAKES, *The Usurped Town: The Canon of Scripture in Postmodern Aesthetics*, in *Communio* 17 (1990) 261-280: «The study of the Bible in academic circles now
mirrors in some respects what is happening to the literary texts: there is a conspicuous
hostility to the notion that the canon represents anything more than an arbitrary selection
which contains within it no obviously visible principle of unity» (p. 270).

3. J.L. SKA, *Il canone ebraico e il canone cristiano dell'Antico Testamento*, in *Civiltà
cattolica* 148 (1997) n° 3531-3532, 213-225; J.A. SANDERS, *"Spinning" the Bible: How
Judaism and Christianity Shape the Canon Differently*, in *BibRev* 14/3 (1998) 22-29 et
44-45; ID., *Intertextuality and Canon*, in S.L. COOK & S.C. WINTER (eds.), *On the Way to
Nineveh. Studies in Honor of Georges M. Landes* (American School of Oriental Research
Books, 4), Atlanta, Scholars, GA, 1999, pp. 316-333, spéc. 319-321.

4. Voir les travaux de A.C. SUNDBERG, *The Old Testament of the Early Church (A
Study in Canon)*, in *HTR* 51 (1958) 205-226; ID., *The Old Testament of the Early Church*,
(Harvard Theological Studies, 20), Cambridge, Mass, 1964; ID., *The Protestant Old Tes-
tament Canon: Should It Be Re-examined?*, in *CBQ* 28 (1966) 194-203; ID., *The "Old
Testament": A Christian Canon*, in *CBQ* 30 (1968) 143-155.

christianisme optent maintenant chacun pour sa propre classification de la bibliothèque.

Le Pentateuque raconte les grandes actions de Dieu qui de créateur devient sauveur, les Livres Historiques continuent l'histoire du peuple de Dieu. Freedman appelle l'ensemble du Pentateuque et des Livres Historiques «the Primary History»[5]. Dans tous ces livres, même si Dieu parle, son action domine: *Dieu agit*[6]. Les Livres Sapientiaux sont très différents: dans ces livres *Israël parle*. G. von Rad considérait ces livres comme «la réponse d'Israël»[7]. Et finalement dans les Livres Prophétiques Dieu reprend le rôle majeur, *Dieu parle*.

Les chrétiens n'ont pas seulement pris une décision sur le canon de l'Ancien Testament mais aussi sur le canon du Nouveau Testament. Ils devaient choisir, parmi leurs propres livres qui commençaient à circuler, ceux qu'ils voulaient inclure dans ce canon, et ensuite selon quels principes ils allaient les classifier. Il est certain qu'ils n'ont pas suivi une classification par auteur. Luc est identifié comme l'auteur de deux ouvrages (Lc 1,1-4; Ac 1,1), pourtant ils sont séparés l'un de l'autre par l'Évangile de Jean. Jean est considéré comme l'auteur d'un évangile, de trois lettres et de l'Apocalypse, pourtant des écrits d'autres auteurs sont insérés entre les trois blocs de la littérature johannique. Ils n'ont pas non plus suivi l'ordre chronologique. Les épîtres de Paul sont plus anciennes que les Évangiles, pourtant ces derniers ont reçu priorité.

On décrit fréquemment la structure du Nouveau Testament comme Évangile et Épître, surtout en Occident, ou bien comme Évangile et Apôtre, en Orient. Les Évangiles occupent la première place et ils sont suivis par la tradition des Apôtres[8]. Mais il y a plus: la tradition des Apôtres est divisée en trois: Actes des Apôtres, Épîtres, et Révélation. Par conséquent, le Nouveau Testament comme l'Ancien a quatre sections: Évangiles – Actes – Épîtres – Révélation.

---

5. D.N. FREEDMAN, *The Unity of the Hebrew Bible*, Ann Arbor, The University of Michigan Press, 1993, p. 6.

6. J'adopte avec un léger changement les catégories de J. MILES, *God: A Biography*, New York, A.A. Knopf, 1995, pp. 15-19 («The Order of the Canon and the Course of God's Life»).

7. G. VON RAD, *Théologie de l'Ancien Testament*, Vol. 1 *Théologie des traditions historiques d'Israël*, Genève, Labor et Fides, 1963, dans lequel il étudie le Pentateuque et les Livres Historiques et conclut: «Si l'on réduit... Yahvé est intervenu de façon particulière dans l'histoire d'Israël» (p. 306). À la fin de ce volume, pp. 306-397, dans la section D, «Israël devant Yahvé (La réponse d'Israël)», il étudie les Écrits: «Israël n'est pas resté muet sur ces actes salutaires» (p. 307).

8. F. BOVON, *The Canonical Structure of the New Testament: The Gospel and the Apostle*, in W.R. FARMER (ed.), *The International Bible Commentary: A Catholic and Ecumenical Commentary for the Twenty-First Century*, Collegeville, MN, Liturgical Press, 1998, pp. 212-214.

Les Évangiles et les Actes constituent ce qu'on pourrait appeler «Primary History», comme on l'a fait pour le Pentateuque et les Livres Historiques de l'Ancien Testament. Cet ensemble raconte les débuts et les premiers développements du christianisme, ce qu'on peut de nouveau résumer comme *Dieu agit*, même s'il y a aussi bien des paroles. Dans les Épîtres l'*Église parle*, et le canon du Nouveau Testament se conclut par la Révélation dans laquelle *Dieu parle*.

Les chrétiens auraient pu insérer leurs propres écrits à l'intérieur des quatres sections de l'Ancien Testament. Les Évangiles et les Actes auraient facilement pu être placés à la fin des Livres Historiques pour montrer la continuation de l'histoire du peuple de Dieu. C'est ainsi d'ailleurs que les chrétiens comprirent l'événement du Christ. Le début de l'Évangile de Matthieu le suggère par la généalogie de Jésus dans laquelle Jésus vient à la fin d'une longue liste de personnes de l'histoire d'Israël qu'on trouve dans l'Ancien Testament (Mt 1,1-17). Les Épîtres, les «écrits» chrétiens, auraient pu être ajoutées aux livres sapientiaux qui sont les Écrits juifs. Et l'Apocalypse aurait pu être mise avec les Prophètes parmi lesquels le livre de Daniel, un livre apocalyptique appartenant aux Écrits, avait trouvé place. Tel n'a pourtant pas été le choix des chrétiens: ils ont gardé l'Ancien et le Nouveau Testament séparés. En plus, ils n'ont pas mis ces écrits récents, qui étaient pourtant les leurs et qu'ils devaient chérir d'une façon particulière, avant les livres plus anciens de l'Ancien Testament, mais après, donnant ainsi une réorientation profonde à l'histoire de Dieu avec son peuple. Ceci est sans aucun doute également le résultat d'une planification voulue et intentionnelle. Il existe beaucoup de travaux sur le lien théologique entre l'Ancien et le Nouveau Testament[9], mais presque rien sur la structure de cette nouvelle grande bibliothèque[10] qui est construite selon une structure symétrique de deux fois quatre parties qui se correspondent.

9. W. VOGELS, *God's Universal Covenant: A Biblical Study*, Ottawa, University of Ottawa Press, 1986, pp. 10-14 («The One God's Revelation»); E.H. SCHEFFER, *Die verhouding tussen die Ou en Nuwe Testament*, in *Theologica Evangelica* 16 (1983) 38-52; H. CAZELLES, *L'unité canonique des saintes Écritures*, in *Istina* 36 (1991) 160-181; J.Y. THÉRIAULT, *Approches sémiotiques du canon biblique*, in *Église et théologie* 29 (1998) 163-178.

10. Voir pour la Bible hébraïque, FREEDMAN, *The Unity of the Hebrew Bible* (n. 5); pour la Bible protestante qui n'accepte que les livres de la Bible hébraïque, D.L. CHRISTENSEN, *The Center of the First Testament within the Canonical Process*, in *Biblical Theology Bulletin* 23 (1993) 48-53; ID., *The Pentateuchal Principle within the Canonical Process*, in *Journal of the Evangelical Theological Society* 39 (1996) 537-548. Ma proposition qui se limite aux sections majeures du canon s'applique ainsi à toute Bible chrétienne.

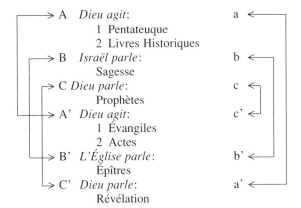

Chose remarquable, dans cette symétrie entre les grandes sections de la Bible on note en même temps une structure parallèle et une structure chiastique. Pour le montrer je porterai une attention particulière au début et à la fin de chacune des différentes sections. D'autres liens pourraient être développés dans des études ultérieures.

2. *La structure parallèle du canon chrétien*

Un parallèle significatif existe entre (A 1) «Dieu agit: Pentateuque» et (A' 1) «Dieu agit: Évangiles». Ces deux sections sont chacune fondamentale: ce que la Torah est pour l'Ancien Testament, les Évangiles le sont pour le Nouveau. Le parallèle apparaît dans leurs débuts. Matthieu, le premier Évangile, s'ouvre par la généalogie de Jésus, ce qui relie intimement la nouvelle histoire à l'histoire ancienne. Il fait remonter les ancêtres de Jésus jusqu'aux patriarches du début du Pentateuque: «Livre de la genèse de Jésus Christ, fils de David, fils d'Abraham: Abraham engendra Isaac…» (Mt 1,1-2). Matthieu continue avec une longue liste de noms; il relie ainsi son Évangile non seulement au Pentateuque mais aussi aux Livres Historiques, donc à toute la «Primary History». Jean ouvre son Évangile avec un prologue: «Au commencement était le Verbe… Il était au commencement auprès de Dieu… Tout fut par lui, et sans lui rien ne fut… et la lumière luit dans les ténèbres» (Jn 1,1-5). Ces versets renvoient aux premiers versets du livre de la Genèse qui ouvre le Pentateuque: «Au commencement, Dieu créa le ciel et la terre… Dieu dit: 'Que la lumière soit' … et Dieu sépara la lumière et les ténèbres» (Gn 1,1-5). Le lien entre Évangile et Pentateuque est clair. Tout montre ainsi la continuité entre (A 1) et (A' 1) mais aussi la nouveauté. Le parallèle entre (A 1) et (A' 1) est renforcé par leurs finales. Le Pentateuque finit avec la mort de Moïse, juste avant l'entrée d'Israël dans la terre promise. Cet événement joue un rôle important non pas seulement pour clôturer cette section importante du canon (Dt 34), mais aussi dans la formation du canon dans son ensemble puisque la mort de Moïse laisse l'histoire de l'exode incomplète et exige une continuation[11]. Le texte fait référence au tombeau de Moïse: «Jusqu'à ce jour nul n'a connu son tombeau» (v. 6). Ce détail est à l'origine de plusieurs spéculations sur l'assomption de Moïse. La mort de Jésus met également fin à une section importante du canon, mais laisse de nouveau l'histoire incomplète et exige une suite. Les Évangiles font aussi référence au tombeau de Jésus, dont le lieu est connu, mais qui est vide. Jésus est ressuscité et il apparaît à ses disciples avant son ascension. On note les ressemblances mais également la nouveauté entre les deux sections.

Il y a un parallèle entre (A 2) «Dieu agit: Livres Historiques» et (A' 2) «Dieu agit: Actes». Moïse a fait sortir Israël du pays d'Égypte, et il a souvent parlé au peuple de la terre promise que Dieu leur donnerait. Lui-même ne peut pas y entrer, il meurt de l'autre côté du Jourdain, mais l'histoire doit continuer. Israël reçoit un nouveau chef pour entrer dans la terre promise. Ceci constitue le début de la section des Livres Historiques: «Yahvé parla à Josué…: 'Moïse, mon serviteur, est mort; maintenant, debout! Passe le Jourdain que voici, toi et tout le peuple, vers le pays que je donne aux Israélites'» (Jos 1,2-3). La présence terrestre de Jésus finit également avec sa mort, mais cette histoire continue aussi dans une nouvelle direction vers des terres nouvelles. La section des Actes s'ouvre par: «Mais vous allez recevoir une force, celle de l'Esprit Saint qui descendra sur vous. Vous serez alors mes témoins à Jérusalem, dans toute la Judée et la Samarie, et jusqu'aux extrémités de la terre» (Ac 1,8).

Entre (B) «Israël parle: Sagesse» et (B') «L'Église parle: Épîtres» il y a un parallèle remarquable. Les écrits des sages sont basés sur leur propre expérience humaine, les sages n'invoquent pas ou ne se basent pas sur une inspiration divine. Comme un refrain le sage dit: «Moi - Je»: «Moi, Qohélet, j'ai été roi d'Israël… j'ai mis tout mon cœur… j'ai regardé toutes les œuvres… je me suis dit à moi-même… j'ai amassé… j'ai pénétré toute sorte de sagesse… j'ai mis tout mon cœur à comprendre… et j'ai compris…» (Qo 1,12-17). L'expérience que le sage a acquise le guide dans sa vie personnelle et le pousse à la partager avec ses enfants: «Écoute, mon fils, l'instruction de ton père» (Pr 1,8). La sa-

---

11. N. LOHFINK, *Moses Tod, die Tora und die alttestamentliche Sonntagslesung*, in *TP* 71 (1996) 481-491; ID., *La morte di Mosè e la struttura del canone biblico*, in *Civiltà cattolica* 150 (1999) n° 3579-3580, 213-222.

gesse essaie de découvrir comment trouver la voie vers une vie pleine, heureuse et harmonieuse et de partager cette découverte[12]. Les Épîtres emploient ce même langage. Paul dit continuellement: «Moi - Je»: «Je remercie mon Dieu... à qui je rends un culte... je fais mémoire de vous... j'ai un vif désir de vous voir... je ne veux pas vous laisser ignorer... j'ai souvent projeté... j'en fus empêché jusqu'ici... je me dois... je ne rougis pas...» (Rm 1,8-16; cf. 1 Co 15,1-5). Ces Épîtres ne se réfèrent pas à une communication inspirée et leur premier but est d'organiser et de maintenir l'harmonie dans les communautés. Comme les Écrits des sages, ces Épîtres essaient de conduire les individus et les communautés à une vie chrétienne heureuse[13]. La section (B) «Israël parle: Sagesse», aussi appelée «Livres poétiques», contient les Psaumes. Dans ces prières formulées en différents genres littéraires, des hommes parlent, parfois directement à Dieu en chantant ses louanges, en suppliant, ou en rendant grâce, mais ils font aussi une proclamation à d'autres personnes. Ceci correspond avec ce qu'on trouve dans (B') «L'Église parle: Épîtres». Paul remercie souvent Dieu, et il proclame ses merveilles: «Je remercie mon Dieu...» (Rm 1,8), «Je rends sans cesse grâces à mon Dieu en faisant mémoire de toi dans mes prières...» (Phm v. 4), et il conclut parfois sa lettre par une doxologie (Rm 16,25-27).

Finalement (C) «Dieu parle: Prophètes» et (C') «Dieu parle: Révélation» sont aussi en parallèle. Beaucoup de livres prophétiques commencent par un titre qui affirme que le livre contient les paroles et les visions que le prophète a reçues de Dieu: «Paroles d'Amos... Ce qu'il vit...» (Am 1,1; cf. Is 1,1; Jr 1,1-2). Le livre de l'Apocalypse commence par un titre semblable: «Révélation de Jésus Christ: Dieu la lui donna... Il envoya son Ange pour la faire connaître à Jean son serviteur, lequel a attesté la Parole de Dieu et le témoignage de Jésus Christ: toutes ses visions. Heureux le lecteur et les auditeurs de ces paroles prophétiques...» (Ap 1,1-3). Les premiers versets présentent le livre de l'Apocalypse comme une «révélation», une «vision» (cf. aussi Ap 5,11), une «parole», une «prophétie» de Dieu (cf. aussi Ap 22,18-19). Ainsi quand le prophète parle, son «Moi - Je» ne se réfère pas au prophète lui même, mais à Dieu, et, par conséquent, il introduit son oracle par: «Ainsi parle Yahvé» (Am 1,3.6.9.11.13; 2,1.4.6). L'auteur du livre de la Révélation

---

12. W. VOGELS, *Words of Wisdom: Proverbs for Everyday Living*, Ottawa, Novalis, 1999, pp. 15-29 («What is Wisdom?»).

13. H. KOESTER, *Writings and the Spirit: Authority and Politics in Ancient Christianity*, in *HTR* 84 (1991) 353-372: «Paul's letters were seen as instruments of the organization of the Churches... There is little appeal to inspiration, and theological themes are secondary» (p. 363).

parle de la même façon dans chacune de ses lettres aux Églises: «Celui qui a des oreilles, qu'il entende ce que l'Esprit dit aux Églises» (Ap 2,7.11.17.29; 3,6.13.22). L'Ancien Testament s'achève sur Dieu parlant par les Prophètes, il est donc orienté vers l'avenir; le Nouveau Testament s'achève sur Dieu parlant une fois de plus et orientant une dernière fois vers l'avenir «car le Temps est proche» (Ap 1,3). La longue liste des Prophètes finit par Malachie qui annonce dans ses derniers versets la venue d'un messager (Ml 3,1.23-24) ouvrant ainsi l'Ancien Testament vers l'avenir, et cette annonce trouve son accomplissement dans les Évangiles comme on le verra. De la même façon, le livre de l'Apocalypse, le dernier livre du Nouveau Testament et donc de toute la Bible, finit à l'avant-dernier verset avec la promesse de la venue de quelqu'un: «Le garant de ces révélations l'affirme: 'Oui, mon retour est proche!' Amen, viens, Seigneur Jésus!» (Ap 22,20).

3. *La structure chiastique du canon*

Chose curieuse, le canon de la Bible, composé selon cette structure parallèle, présente aussi une structure chiastique[14]. Une connexion remarquable existe entre (c) «Dieu parle: Prophètes» et (c' 1) «Dieu agit: Évangiles». Tout lecteur note combien les Évangiles se réfèrent aux textes prophétiques[15]. Matthieu le souligne dans ses deux premiers chapitres. Après avoir raconté un événement de l'enfance de Jésus, il ajoute chaque fois: «Or tout ceci advint pour que s'accomplît cet oracle prophétique du Seigneur» (Mt 1,22-23 = Is 7,14; Mt 2,5-6 = Mi 5,1; Mt 2,15 = Os 11,1; Mt 2,17-18 = Jr 31,15; Mt 2,23 =?). Cette insistance de Matthieu peut bien être la raison pour laquelle son Évangile fut placé en première position, car il fait ainsi une belle transition entre les deux Testaments. Marc montre cette même préoccupation dès son verset d'ouverture: «Commencement de l'Évangile de Jésus Christ, fils de Dieu. Selon qu'il est écrit dans Isaïe le prophète: 'Voici que j'envoie mon messager...'» (Mc 1,1-3). Seule la seconde partie de la citation (v. 3) est prise d'Isaïe (Is 40,3), la première partie concernant le messager (v. 2b) vient du prophète Malachie (Ml 3,1). Ceci est d'autant plus intéressant que Malachie est le dernier prophète et donc le dernier livre du canon de l'Ancien Testament, juste avant le Nouveau Testament. Un des derniers versets de l'Ancien Testament correspond ainsi à un des premiers de

---

14. On peut découvrir des structures différentes dans une même unité littéraire. La question ne se pose donc pas de savoir quelle est la structure «exacte» et laquelle est «fausse».

15. G.K. BEALE (ed.), *The Right Doctrine from the Wrong Texts? Essays on the Use of the Old Testament in the New*, Grand Rapids, MI, Baker, 1991.

Marc. Luc suit la même procédure. Lui aussi commence son Évangile (Lc 1,17) par une référence aux derniers versets de Malachie, le dernier prophète: «Voici que je vais envoyer Élie le prophète, avant que n'arrive le Jour de Yahvé...» (Ml 3,23-24). Ces mêmes derniers versets du dernier prophète jouent aussi un rôle important dans les autres Évangiles synoptiques (Mt 11,14; 17,10-13; Mc 9,11-12).

La relation entre (b) «Israël parle: Sagesse» et (b') «L'Église parle: Épîtres» reste la même dans la structure chiastique comme dans la structure parallèle.

La dernière section (a') «Dieu parle: Révélation» a certains liens intéressants avec (a) «Dieu agit: Pentateuque». Le récit de la création qui ouvre le livre de la Genèse, le premier livre du Pentateuque et de tout le canon, dit au premier verset: «Au commencement, Dieu créa le ciel et la terre» (Gn 1,1). Le livre de l'Apocalypse, le dernier livre de tout le canon, dit: «Puis je vis un ciel nouveau, une terre nouvelle» (Ap 21,1). Ceci donne une première inclusion entre le début et la fin de toute la Bible. Un rapprochement entre le deuxième récit du livre de la Genèse et certains textes de l'Apocalypse donne une deuxième inclusion. L'histoire du paradis mentionne «l'arbre de vie» offert à l'humanité (Gn 2,9.16), mais qui, à cause du péché, ne lui est plus accessible (Gn 3,22). Même l'entrée au paradis lui est interdite: «Il (Yahvé Dieu) bannit l'homme et il posta devant le jardin d'Éden les chérubins et la flamme du glaive fulgurant pour garder le chemin de l'arbre de vie» (Gn 3,24). Cet arbre de vie disparaît complètement du reste de la tradition biblique (excepté Pr 3,18), mais il réapparaît soudainement dans l'Apocalypse, le dernier livre de la Bible, et même plusieurs fois. Les dernières mentions se trouvent vers la fin du livre: «Heureux ceux qui lavent leurs robes; ils pourront disposer de l'arbre de Vie, et pénétrer dans la Cité, par les portes»(Ap 22,14); par ailleurs, «Et qui oserait retrancher aux paroles de ce livre prophétique, Dieu retranchera son lot de l'arbre de Vie et de la Cité sainte» (Ap 22,19; cf. 2,7; 22,1-2). Même *adam*, l'«homme» du jardin (Gn 2,7), réapparaît dans le «Fils d'homme» (Ap 1,13), et également la «femme» dans sa lutte avec le «serpent» (Gn 3,15 et Ap 12,13-17). Le jardin qui fut fermé est de nouveau grandement ouvert. La structure du canon suggère ainsi que pour avoir accès à la vie et au bonheur, il faut passer à travers tout le canon, du début à la fin.

4. *Conclusion*

À première vue la Bible peut paraître une étrange collection de livres disparates. Ils furent écrits durant une période couvrant plusieurs siècles; leur origine, leurs formes et genres littéraires sont très variés. On peut ainsi se poser des questions sur l'unité d'une telle bibliothèque. La structure parallèle - chiastique des sections majeures de la Bible suggère que cette collection est le résultat d'une planification soigneuse d'éditeur(s) et de compilateur(s). La structure parallèle montre que Dieu agit dans l'histoire humaine (A) et qu'il y parle (C); avec la venue du Christ, ceci est répété comme un nouveau commencement: Dieu agit une fois de plus en entrant dans l'histoire humaine (A') et il y parle (C'). La structure chiastique explique davantage la relation entre l'action et les paroles de Dieu. Ce que Dieu a dit par les prophètes (c) est accompli dans la nouvelle action de Dieu en Jésus Christ (c'); et ce que Dieu a fait au début (a), il promet de le restaurer à la fin (a'). Si Dieu a été fidèle à sa parole la première fois, on peut être certain que ses dernières paroles s'accompliront aussi et que notre espérance n'est pas vaine. Dieu est l'acteur principal de la Bible, qui s'ouvre par l'affirmation concernant Dieu: «Au commencement était Dieu» (Gn 1,1) et finit par: «Il est, Il était et Il vient» (Ap 1,4), «Je suis l'Apha et l'Oméga, le Premier et le Dernier, le Principe et la Fin» (Ap 22,13; cf. 1,8). Mais la Bible ne concerne pas seulement Dieu, les hommes aussi y jouent un rôle actif. Entre l'action de Dieu (A et A') et sa parole (C et C') il y a, dans la structure parallèle comme dans la structure chiastique, la parole de l'homme ou sa réponse (B et B'); il réfléchit, il prie et il proclame. Le canon se présente ainsi comme un dialogue entre Dieu et son peuple.

Université Saint-Paul   Walter VOGELS
223 Main Street
Ottawa, Ontario
K1S 1C4
Canada

NEW TESTAMENT

MAIN PAPERS

THE NEW TESTAMENT CANON

I. THE NEW TESTAMENT CANON FROM SEMLER TO CHILDS

The modern study of the canon of the New Testament has taken a strange course. One of the first theologians to apply critical methods to the study of the biblical canon was Johann Salomo Semler (1725-1791), professor of theology at Halle (1753-1791). Among the one hundred and twenty volumes which he produced in his lifetime, most of them utterly unreadable, four constitute his epoch-making *Abhandlung von freier Untersuchung des Canons*[1]. In this work he argued that, in the light of the new historical insights into the genesis of the books included in the Bible, Holy Scripture cannot be identical with God's Word. At most the Word of God can be said to be contained in Holy Scripture. Several books of the Bible, among them the Apocalypse, had had importance only for their own time, not for the Church of later centuries. Here we see how Semler moves over from a theological to a historical approach to the Bible. He also argued that all canon lists of biblical books drawn up and accepted in the early Church had no more than local or regional validity. As a result, the traditional canon of the New Testament could not claim to be binding for the Church as a whole or for all its members. Consequently, individual Christians are not obliged to accept the entire New Testament as canonical; they are free to look in the New Testament for what they themselves regard as authoritative and, in a way, to select their own canon.

More recently, in 1984, Brevard Springs Childs (°1923), professor at Yale, published his *The New Testament as Canon: An Introduction*[2]. In this work and in similar works on the Old Testament, Childs tries to combine the classical theological concerns of the Church with the results of critical scholarship. He argues that the proper context for the theological interpretation of biblical books is the canon itself[3]. The canon is not to be regarded as a loose collection from which each document may be set apart and individually interpreted in the light of the historical circum-

---

1. Halle, Hemmerde, 4 vols., 1771-1775.
2. B.S. CHILDS, *The New Testament as Canon: An Introduction*, London, SCM Press, 1984.
3. See J.A.M. SNOEK, *Canonization and Decanonization: An Annotated Bibliography*, in A. VAN DER KOOIJ & K. VAN DER TOORN (eds.), *Canonization & Decanonization*, Leiden, Brill, 1998, pp. 435-506, esp. 450-451.

stances in which it originated. The normative theological meaning of a given writing is to be determined by appealing to the canonical shape of each text, and to the conceptual relationships configured by the canon between that text and other texts. The canonical meaning, which is not necessarily identical with the historical meaning, is theologically and religiously authoritative.

Between Semler's and Childs' positions there are conspicuous discrepancies. Whereas Semler sought to open up a more historical approach to the books of the Bible, Childs tries to regain a more theological understanding of the Bible by taking seriously the fact that each and every book of the Bible has only come down to us as part of the canon. It must be admitted that, in spite of the considerable differences between Semler's and Childs' hermeneutical views, the two scholars agree to some extent, namely in so far as for both of them the Bible remains the source of theological and Christian truth. Furthermore it should be borne in mind that it is Childs' intention, not to neglect the results of historical exegesis, but to integrate them in his theological exegesis. Yet we may say that the direction canonical studies take in the work of Childs is contrary to that in the work of Semler. Times change, and biblical criticism with them. It might also be argued that the historical study of the Bible to which Semler gave such a strong impetus was bound to elicit, sooner or later, a reaction inspired by theological concerns such as that given by Childs.

When we cast a quick glance at the period that elapsed between Semler and Childs, we cannot but be impressed by the contributions of two giants in the field of research into the New Testament canon: Theodor Zahn (1838-1933) and Adolf Harnack (1851-1930). Zahn, professor at Erlangen and Leipzig, published his fundamental and impressive *Geschichte des neutestamentlichen Kanons* in 1888-1892[4], and his pioneering *Forschungen zur Geschichte des neutestamentlichen Kanons* from 1881 to 1929[5]. Zahn held that the New Testament canon came into existence as early as about the end of the first century. He developed this view in opposition to Harnack's claim that the New Testament canon did not take shape until the end of the second century. Harnack, professor at Giessen, Marburg, and Berlin, published his views on the New Testament canon first in his *Lehrbuch der Dogmengeschichte* ([1]1886-1889), later in his *Das Neue Testament um das Jahr 200* of 1889, and in his *Die Entstehung des Neuen Testaments und die wichtigsten Folgen*

---

4. Th. ZAHN, *Geschichte des neutestamentlichen Kanons*, 2 vols., Erlangen, Deichert; Leipzig, Böhme, 1888-1892.
5. Th. ZAHN, *Forschungen zur Geschichte des neutestamentlichen Kanons und der altkirchlichen Literatur*, 10 vols., Erlangen, Deichert; Leipzig, Böhme, 1881-1929.

der neuen Schöpfung of 1914[6]. Harnack held that not Gnosticism, but Montanism had given the decisive impetus to the formation of the New Testament canon.

The debate between Zahn and Harnack has been analysed and evaluated by some more recent scholars, among them Bruce Metzger in his *The Canon of the New Testament* (1987)[7] and especially John Barton in his *The Spirit and the Letter* (1997)[8]. Barton has pointed out that the controversy between Zahn and Harnack originated from the two scholars' fundamentally different ideas of what the nature of the New Testament canon was. For Zahn the canon was a product of continued collection, augmentation and growth. Harnack, on the other hand, looked upon the New Testament canon as the result of a process of delimitation and exclusion. Consequently, Zahn's concept of the canon was less strict than Harnack's and, as a result, Zahn's date for the canon earlier than Harnack's.

It will be wise to keep Barton's lessons in mind: both sides of the formation process of the New Testament canon have to be reckoned with: its growth and its delimitation[9]. These two developments took place independently. The growth came first, delimitation and exclusion occurred later. The notion "Scripture" has to be distinguished from the notion "canon". The former is an open collection of authoritative books, a collection with only vague contours; books can still be added to it, or removed from it. A canon however is a closed and exclusive list of books regarded as authoritative. The more strictly one defines "canon", the later the date of its origin. Taking into account Barton's insights, the canon of the New Testament cannot be said to have come into existence until the second half of the fourth century. It is no coincidence that the earliest evidence for the use of the Greek word *kanon* in the sense of "exclusive list of the authoritative books of Holy Scripture" dates from the middle of the fourth century. The earliest attestation occurs in Athanasius' treatise on the resolutions of the Council of Nicea[10], which dates from 350 or 351 AD.

6. A. HARNACK, *Lehrbuch der Dogmengeschichte*, Freiburg i. B., Mohr (Siebeck), [1]1886-1889; [2]1888, see vol. 1, pp. 304-328; [3]1894; English translation, *History of Dogma*, London, Williams & Norgate, 1896-1899, pp. 38-60; ID., *Das Neue Testament um das Jahr 200*, Freiburg i. B., Mohr (Siebeck), 1889; ID., *Die Entstehung des Neuen Testaments und die wichtigsten Folgen der neuen Schöpfung*, Leipzig, Hinrichs, 1914.
7. B.M. METZGER, *The Canon of the New Testament. Its Origin, Development, and Significance*, Oxford, Clarendon, 1987, pp. 23-24.
8. J. BARTON, *The Spirit and the Letter. Studies in the Biblical Canon*, London, SPCK, 1997, pp. 1-6.
9. BARTON, *Spirit and Letter* (n. 8), pp. 24-31.
10. Athanasius, *Epistola de decretis Nicaenae synodi* (PG 25, cols. 415-476; 18), where the Shepherd of Hermas is described as "not belonging to *the canon*"; see METZGER, *Canon* (n. 7), p. 292.

Moreover, it should be remembered that the fixation of the New Testament canon in Athanasius' 39th Festal Letter of 367 and in the acts of the Synods of Hippo Regius of 393, confirmed by the Synods of Carthage of 397 and 419, was only temporary and provisional[11]. In later sources, canon lists show hardly less variation than before 367[12]. The first really effective measures were the decisions of the Council of Trent of 1545[13], and the inclusion of canon lists in a series of early confessions of faith drawn up by Protestants. These Protestant confessions include the *Confession de foy* or *Confessio Gallicana* of the French (Reformed) Churches established in Paris in 1559[14], and the *Confession de foy* or *Confessio Belgica* drawn up in 1561 by Guy de Brès and adopted by the Reformed Churches in the Netherlands in the sixties and seventies of the sixteenth century[15].

II. THE CRITERION OF ORTHODOXY

One of the topics usually considered in discussions of the history of the New Testament canon is the criteria that were applied in determining whether or not early Christian writings were authoritative. It should be noticed in passing that these so-called criteria of canonicity were often used, not to determine *a priori* whether or not a writing was authorita-

---

11. The texts of the four documents mentioned are conveniently accessible in F.W. GROSHEIDE (ed.), *Some Early Lists of the Books of the New Testament* (Textus minores, 1), Leiden, Brill, 1948, nos. 8 & 11. For English translations, see METZGER, *Canon* (n. 7), pp. 312-313 (Athanasius' 39th Festal Epistle) and pp. 314-315 (Councils of Hippo Regius and Carthage).

12. Take for instance the canon inserted in the sixth-century Codex Claromontanus of the epistles of Paul (D, 06). This canon includes Barnabas, Pastor of Hermas, Acts of Paul and the Apocalypse of Peter, but Philippians, 1 and 2 Thessalonians and Hebrews are missing; see GROSHEIDE (n. 11), pp. 16-17. For the variation in biblical canons from the 5th to the 16th century, see B.F. WESTCOTT, *The Bible in the Church*, London – Cambridge, MacMillan, 1870, pp. 191-244; J. LEIPOLDT, *Geschichte des neutestamentlichen Kanons*, 2 vols., Leipzig, Hinrich, 1907-1908, II, pp. 1-13.

13. The Council of Trent decided on the contents of the biblical canon on 8 April 1546. For the text of the decision and the list of books accepted as canonical, see H. DENZINGER & C. RAHNER, *Enchiridium symbolorum*, Barcelona, Freiburg i.B., Rome, Herder, [31]1957, pp. 279-280, Nr. 784.

14. For the text of this *Confessio Gallicana* or "Confession of Paris", later called "Confession of La Rochelle", see J.N. BAKHUIZEN VAN DEN BRINK, *De Nederlandse belijdenisgeschriften*, Amsterdam, Bolland, 1976, pp. 70-142. The canonical books of the New Testament are listed in art. III, p. 74. For a recent edition, see P.C. MARCEL & C. VAN LEEUWEN (eds.), *Confession de La Rochelle*, Krimpen aan den IJssel, Fondation d'Entraide Chrétienne Réformée, 1988; see p. 20.

15. For the French, Dutch and Latin texts of the *Confessio Belgica*, see BAKHUIZEN VAN DEN BRINK, *Belijdenisgeschriften* (n. 14), pp. 70-146. The canonical books of the New Testament are listed in article IV, pp. 74-75.

tive, but to justify *a posteriori* the high respect in which a writing had already been held for some time past, or the disapproval it had already incurred. At any rate, in assessing and qualifying certain writings as authoritative or objectionable, early Christian authors used a great variety of criteria.

Modern authors on the subject usually try to cluster these numerous criteria into a limited number of dominant criteria of a broader scope, but they differ in the way they do this. Harry Gamble in his *The New Testament Canon. Its Making and Meaning* (1985) distinguished four criteria: apostolicity, catholicity, orthodoxy, and traditional usage[16]. Bruce Metzger in his *The Canon of the New Testament* (1987)[17] mentions only three criteria: orthodoxy, apostolicity, and consensus among the churches. In Metzger's third criterion, continuous acceptance and usage by the Church at large, Gamble's second and fourth criteria (catholicity and traditional usage) are telescoped. The most thorough, or at least the most extensive and detailed investigation of the criteria for determining canonicity is Karl-Heinz Ohlig's *Die theologische Begründung des neutestamentlichen Kanons in der alten Kirche* of 1972[18]. Ohlig shows that early Christian authors used at least eleven different criteria in determining whether a book had to be recognized as authoritative or to be rejected. His list includes the following criteria: 1. apostolicity, sometimes taken in the narrow meaning of authenticity, but more often in the broader sense of deriving either from an apostle or from a follower of an apostle; apostolic could even mean "in keeping with the pure and right teaching of the apostles"; 2. the age of the document in question; 3. the historical likelihood of its contents (obviously fictitious and fantastic stories are often a ground for rejecting the book in which they occur); 4. orthodoxy; 5. the agreement with the Scriptures of the Old Testament; 6. the edifying nature of the document at issue; 7. its being directed to the Church as a whole (catholicity); 8. clarity and meaningfulness (the contents must not be absurd); 9. spirituality of the contents; 10. acceptance by the Church at large; 11. use for public lessons in the Church.

It has often been observed that these criteria were applied with striking inconsistency. For instance, not all writings attributed to an apostle succeeded in being accepted as canonical, as the fate of the Gospel of

---

16. H.Y GAMBLE, *The New Testament Canon. Its Making and Meaning*, Philadelphia, Fortress, 1985, pp. 67-70.

17. METZGER, *Canon* (n. 7), pp. 251-254.

18. K.-H. OHLIG, *Die theologische Begründung des neutestamentlichen Kanons in der alten Kirche*, Düsseldorf, Patmos, 1972, pp. 57-309.

Thomas or that of the Gospel of Peter may illustrate. 1 Clement is probably considerably older than such writings as 2 Peter and Jude; yet the latter two were eventually received into the canon, whereas the former was not. It will not do to argue that the author of 1 Clement was not known to be an apostle or an apostle's follower, for the author of the letter to the Hebrews was not known at all which did not prevent this wrriting from being highly esteemed in the eastern Church and, eventually, from being canonized both in the East and the West. Finally, several writings that were included in the list of authoritative books did not meet the criteria applied to justify the recognition of other writings. For instance, it is hard to maintain that such Pauline letters as those to Philemon or to the Galatians are addressed to the Church as a whole. In brief, the so-called criteria of canonicity were used with notable flexibility and irritating inconsistency.

Actually this inconsistency should not surprise us. One has to take into consideration that the growth and delimitation of the New Testament canon was a process of centuries, moreover that this process took place in a space as wide as the Mediterranean world, and that the people involved in this process, both individuals (such as clergymen and scholars) and groups (such as church councils and synods), operated at various social levels and with different intentions and interests. Given these circumstances, the last thing one can expect to observe is that criteria for determining canonicity were applied consistently.

Yet the question must be asked whether the inconsistency with which criteria were used to confirm or deny the authority of early Christian writings, is not partly due to the tendency in our sources (that is, in the authors behind our sources) to prefer the use of seemingly objective criteria (such as age, apostolicity, early and wide acceptance) to one more essential, but also more vulnerable criterion, namely orthodoxy. I think it can be argued that in confirming or rejecting the authority of early Christian writings, ecclesiastical authors tended to adduce other grounds than the one they actually had in mind, namely orthodoxy. In other words, the criterion of orthodoxy played a more important role than is revealed by our sources. In my view, orthodoxy was a fundamental, but often tacit criterion.

To be sure, the criterion of orthodoxy is often used explicitly. Two examples may suffice to illustrate this. Serapion, bishop of Antioch about 200, admonishes the Christian community at Rhossus, a town in his diocese, to stop reading the Gospel of Peter[19]. He probably means

---

19. Eusebius, *H.E.*VI 12.

that his addressees should stop using that gospel for the public lessons in their gatherings. The reason Serapion gives to justify his admonition is that the work in question shows traces of a Docetic view of Christ. To quote another example, in his History of the Church (ca. 324) Eusebius includes an account of the writings which the churches accepted as sacred and those they did not accept as such[20]. In this passage, Eusebius distinguishes three categories of books: recognized books, disputed books, and rejected books. According to Eusebius, the third category consists of writings published by heretics. They include the Gospels of Peter, Thomas, Matthias, and others, as well as the Acts of Andrew, John, and other apostles. In an effort to characterize this third category of writings, he observes: "Their ideas and implications are so irreconcilable with true orthodoxy that they stand revealed as the forgeries of heretics"[21]. Here we see the criterion of orthodoxy used explicitly.

In other instances, however, the criterion of orthodoxy seems to be used only tacitly. A case in point is a passage on the Gospels in the Muratorian Fragment. This document was usually dated to the last quarter of the second century, until A.C. Sundberg (1973) argued for a fourth-century date[22]. Sundberg's view was endorsed or accepted by R.F. Collins (1983), G.M. Hahneman (1992), G.A. Robbins (1992), and J. Barton (1997)[23]. In my opinion, however, the arguments for an early date continue to outweigh those for a later date[24]. In particular, the apologetic and polemical tendencies reflected in the document seem to point to a late second-century context rather than a fourth-century situation.

The author of the Muratorian Fragment defends the four Gospels of Matthew, Mark, Luke and John against several possible objections[25]. One problem, among others, is the fact that the Gospels' accounts of Jesus' ministry do not agree. The author tries to play down the seriousness

---

20. Eusebius, *H.E.* III 25. GROSHEIDE, *Lists* (n. 11), pp. 14-15. METZGER, *Canon* (n. 7), pp. 309-310.

21. Translation by G.A. WILLIAMSON, *Eusebius, The History of the Church*, Harmondsworth, Penguin, 1965, p. 135.

22. A.C. SUNDBERG, *Canon Muratori: A Fourth-Century List*, in *HTR* 66 (1973) 1-41.

23. R.F. COLLINS, *Introduction to the New Testament*, Garden City, NY, Doubleday, 1983, p. 35; G.M. HAHNEMAN, *The Muratorian Fragment and the Development of the Canon* (Oxford Theological Monographs), Oxford, Clarendon, 1988; G.A. ROBBINS, *Eusebius' Lexicon of "Canonicity"*, in *SP* 25 (1993) 134-141; BARTON, *Spirit and Letter* (n. 8), p. 10.

24. On the issue of the date of the Muratorian Fragment, see especially J. VERHEYDEN, *The Canon Muratori. A Matter of Dispute*, in the present volume, pp. 487-556.

25. For the Latin text of the Canon Muratori, see GROSHEIDE, *Lists* (n. 11), pp. 6-11. For English translations, see GAMBLE, *Canon* (n. 16), pp. 93-95, and METZGER, *Canon* (n. 7), pp. 305-307.

of this problem by stating that "all things in all [the Gospels] are declared by one supreme Spirit: concerning the [Lord's] birth, his passion, his resurrection, his converse with his disciples, and his twofold advent: the first in lowliness, when he was despised, which has taken place, the second glorious with royal power, which is still in the future"[26]. The author fails to explain why he singles out for mention the details enumerated. A clue may be found, however, in other passages of the Fragment, in which the author strongly opposes Gnosticism and denounces explicitly the teachings of Valentinus and Basilides[27]. It is reasonable to assume, therefore, that the author's summary of the four Gospels' contents as an account of Jesus' birth, passion, resurrection, and conversations with the disciples is meant to evoke the idea that the earthly Jesus' humanity, sufferings, and resurrection in the body were real rather than apparent. Christ was not a divine being who descended from heaven and temporarily assumed someone else's body or a phantasmal human appearance. He was really embodied in human flesh. Similarly, the reference to Christ's second coming seems to allude to the traditional idea that salvation can only be reached on the future Day of Judgement, in contradistinction to the Gnostic idea that salvation is the return of the divine, spiritual spark in man unto God.

If this reading of the Muratorian Fragment is correct, the authority of the four Gospels is vindicated here on the ground that they present a traditional Christology distinct from that of Gnosticism. The standard by which the Fragment assesses the four Gospels, is the criterion of orthodoxy. But this criterion is not mentioned explicitly; it is used tacitly.

In about 210, Gaius, a presbyter at Rome, rejected the Gospel of John, ostensibly because the differences between it and the synoptic Gospels proved that John's Gospel was unreliable[28]. In reality, however, Gaius

26. Lines 19-26: " (cum) ... declarata sint in omnibus omnia: de nativitate, de passione, de resurrectione, de conversatione cum discipulis suis ac de gemino eius adventu, primo in humilitate despectus, quod fuit, secundo in potestate regali praeclaro, quod futurum est".

27. Lines 81-84: "Arsinoi [Bardesanis?] autem seu Valentini vel Miltiadis nihil in totum recipimus, qui etiam novum Psalmorum librum Marcioni conscripserunt una cum Basilide Asiano".

28. ZAHN, *Geschichte des ntl. Kanons* (n. 4), II, p. 991; H. VON CAMPENHAUSEN, *Die Entstehung der christlichen Bibel* (BHT, 39), Tübingen, Mohr, 1968, p. 279; METZGER, *Canon* (n. 7), p. 105: "the differences between the Synoptic Gospels and John's Gospel were taken [by Gaius] to prove that the latter is wrong and so ought not to be included among the books recognized by the Church". See also Hippolytus *apud* Dionysius Bar Salibi (12th century), *In Apocalypsim, Actus et Epistolas Catholicas* (ed. I. SEDLACEK; Corpus Scriptorum Christianorum Orientalium, Scriptores Syri, series II, t. 101), Rome, de Luigi; Paris, Poussielge; Leipzig, Harassowitz, 1910, pp. 1-2: "Hippolytus Romanus dixit: Apparuit vir, nomine Caius, qui asserebat Evangelium non esse Iohannis (...)".

rejected John because he (Gaius) was strongly opposed to Montanism. Since the Gospel of John was one of the books on which the Montanists based their claims, Gaius questioned the authority of the book, not by calling it downright heretical, but by claiming that it was historically unreliable. The criterion of historical trustworthiness thus takes the place of that of orthodoxy.

Another instance of the tacit application of the criterion of orthodoxy occurs in a Catechetical Lecture delivered by Cyril, bishop of Jerusalem, in about 350[29]. Cyril states that one should accept "four Gospels only, for the other ones have inscriptions with false indication of the author and are harmful". The criteria applied here are those of authenticity and the edifying nature of the writing at issue, but what Cyril really means to say appears from the sentence with which he follows the one just quoted. There he disqualifies a Gospel of Thomas because it is a work produced by Manichaeans that destroys the souls of the simple-minded. The reason which Cyril alleges for dismissing other Gospels than the four generally accepted, is that they are inauthentic and harmful. The underlying and hidden reason, however, is that their contents are heretical.

A fourth-century Commentary on the Catholic Epistles, attributed (probably correctly) to Didymus the Blind, designates 2 Peter as not belonging to the New Testament, in spite of its being used in public lessons in the churches[30]. The reason Didymus gives for excluding 2 Peter from the canon is that it is a forgery (*falsata*). Thus the criterion by which 2 Peter is assessed seems to be that of authenticity. The reason adduced, however, is not Didymus' real reason. His real reason for rejecting 2 Peter is that the eschatological scenario of 2 Pet 3,12-13 contradicts the one taught by Jesus in Lk 17,26. Whereas according to Jesus the transition from the present world to the world to come will be a more or less smooth and gradual change, 2 Pet 3,13 describes this transition as an abrupt, brief and total crisis, an extremely violent and incisive event, involving the conflagration of all things and the coming into being of an entirely new heaven and an entirely new earth. Didymus' criticism of 2 Peter thus concerned its eschatology, which he considered unorthodox, and not primarily the authorship of the letter. Yet in the way Didymus presents the matter, the criterion of authenticity takes the place of that of orthodoxy.

---

29. Cyril of Jerusalem, *Catechesis* IV, 36, PG 33, c. 500B; Greek text also in GROSHEIDE, *Lists* (n. 11), p. 15; English transl. in METZGER, *Canon* (n. 7), p. 311.

30. Didymus the Blind, *In Epistolam S. Petri Secundam Enarratio*, PG 39, cc. 1771-1774, see 1774A: "Non igitur ignorandum, praesentem Epistolam esse falsatam, quae licet publicetur, non tamen in canone est".

The examples mentioned show that the criterion of orthodoxy, that is, the test whether the contents of a writing agreed with the traditional teaching of the Church, played a more important part than our sources suggest at first sight. Whatever argument ecclesiastical authors adduce for dismissing a book, their hidden motive may always have been their tendency to fend off heresy. For, as Ohlig says, the criterion of orthodoxy "ist nicht nur wichtiger als andere Kriterien, sondern deren letzter Sinn; er entscheidet nicht nur über die Kanonizität einer Schrift, sondern auch z.B. über ihre Apostolizität"[31]. Indeed apostolicity often means orthodoxy, especially when it does not denote apostolic authenticity but agreement with apostolic teaching. In the final analysis it was mostly the criterion of orthodoxy that decided a writing's fate.

III. The Relevance of the Criterion of Orthodoxy for the Quest of the Historical Jesus

The preceding observations and considerations lead me to a bold conclusion. It is true that the rise of the New Testament canon was a process guided by ideological, theological, especially christological motives. It should also be admitted that, unfortunately, several very early writings seem to have been lost; for instance, Q, the "previous letter" of Paul (1 Cor 5,9) and his "painful letter" (2 Cor 2,4). Moreover, we do not know what will yet turn up from the deserts of Egypt or Judea. But, as we have seen, there was a strong tendency in early Christianity to accept and preserve writings whose contents were in agreement with the teaching of earlier generations, and to dismiss writings that did *not* meet this criterion of orthodoxy. What this orthodoxy implied is indicated, among other sources, by the Muratorian Fragment: the recognition of the real humanity of Jesus Christ, and the expectation of his second coming. In other words: *no redemption without incarnation and eschatological judgement.*

The list of books corresponding to this "orthodoxy" in the Muratorian Fragment is identical with the New Testament canon of twenty-seven writings advocated by Athanasius, except that the Muratorian list lacks Hebrews and four Catholic epistles, and includes the Apocalypse of Peter (though marked as disputed) and Wisdom of Solomon. Roughly speaking, the theological outlook of the Muratorian Fragment corresponds to that of Paul and the four evangelists, that is, to the core of the New Testament canon now generally accepted.

31. OHLIG, *Begründung* (n. 18), p. 170.

Now the crucial question is of course whether those who happened to be in a position to control the acceptance and preservation of Christian writings and traditions during the period from 30 to 70 AD (that is, from Jesus to Paul and the synoptics), were led by the same interest in "orthodoxy" as we saw leading churchmen were in the second and later centuries[32]. If this question can be answered in the affirmative, it follows that the New Testament books vindicated by the Muratorian Fragment, recognized (as ἐνδιάθηκοι) by Eusebius, and propagated as canonical by Athanasius and Augustine, form the best foundation for reconstructing the outlines of Jesus' ministry and teaching. In that case Jesus was an apocalyptic who preached that the Kingdom of God was imminent, and his followers believed that they could be saved through participation in his death and resurrection.

I realize that I mentioned a condition ("If …") and a "question". Further research is needed to answer the question and to fulfil the condition, and this is not the moment to undertake this research. Yet I suspect that Johannes Leipoldt will turn out to have been right when he wrote, now almost a century ago: "Die Erkenntnis, dass unser Neues Testament wirklich die besten Quellen zur Geschichte Jesu enthält, ist die wertvollste Erkenntnis, die wir aus der älteren Kanonsgeschichte entnehmen"[33].

Zeemanlaan 47   Henk Jan DE JONGE
2313 SW Leiden
The Netherlands

---

32. "Orthodoxy" is taken here in the sense of *congruity* of a given document with the basic theological, especially christological ideas accepted as normative by earlier generations of the Church.

33. LEIPOLDT, *Geschichte* (n. 12), I, p. 269.

DIE SAMMLUNG DER PAULUSBRIEFE
IM 1. UND 2. JAHRHUNDERT

Die im Neuen Testament enthaltenen Paulusbriefe sind zu unterschiedlichen Zeiten und in unterschiedlichen Situationen verfaßt worden, und sie richteten sich an unterschiedliche Adressaten. Wie kam es dazu, daß diese Briefe zu einem *Corpus Paulinum* zusammengefaßt und dann in dieser Form tradiert wurden? Welche durch Texte gesicherten Indizien gibt es für den Prozeß der *Sammlung* der paulinischen Briefe? Diese Frage ist nicht identisch mit der Frage nach der „Kanonisierung"[1] der Paulusbriefe innerhalb des „Neuen Testaments"[2]. Aber die Frage, wie und wann die Briefe des Apostels Paulus im formalen Sinn als in der Kirche nicht nur allgemein anerkannte, sondern zugleich auch theologisch verbindliche Schriften verstanden und verwendet wurden, braucht gar nicht gesondert erörtert zu werden. Denn wir kennen in der Geschichte der Entstehung des neutestamentlichen Kanons keine Phase, in der die Zugehörigkeit der Paulusbriefe zum Kanon irgendwie umstritten gewesen wäre; vielmehr gilt ihre Zugehörigkeit offensichtlich von allem Anfang an als selbstverständlich. Die einzige Ausnahme scheint die Frage der Zugehörigkeit des Hebräerbriefes zum Kanon gewesen zu sein. Doch die Unsicherheit, die sich mit dieser Schrift verband, ging in erster Linie darauf zurück, daß ihre Abfassung durch Paulus umstritten war; mit der (irrtümlichen) Annahme der paulinischen Herkunft zumindest ihrer theologischen Gedanken war zugleich auch ihre Kanonizität gesichert[3]. Das vermutlich älteste erhaltene Kanons-

---

1. „Kanon" bedeutet: Der Textbestand ist verbindlich festgestellt, jede Abweichung gilt als „häretisch". Zur Entwicklung der Bedeutung des Wortes κανών (*canon*) vgl. die knappe, aber sehr instruktive Darstellung bei A.F.J. KLIJN, *Die Entstehungsgeschichte des Neuen Testaments*, in *ANRW* II/26.1, Berlin, de Gruyter, 1992, S. 64-97, hier 65f. S. auch u. Anm. 107.

2. Zur Anwendung des Begriffs „Neues Testament" auf eine Sammlung urchristlicher Literatur s. W. KINZIG, Καινὴ διαθήκη: *The Title of the New Testament in the Second and Third Centuries*, in *JTS* 45 (1994) 519-544. Er vermutet (S. 535-541) unter Verweis auf Tertullian Adv Marc IV 6,1, daß Marcion seiner Textsammlung aus Lk und den Paulusbriefen die Bezeichnung „Neues Testament" gegeben habe; von dort habe die große Kirche diese Bezeichnung nach anfänglichem Widerstand (Justin und Irenäus verwenden den Begriff noch nicht) übernommen, wie der Sprachgebrauch Tertullians erkennen lasse (S. 542-544).

3. Vgl. dazu K.-H. OHLIG, *Die theologische Begründung des neutestamentlichen Kanons in der alten Kirche* (KBANT), Düsseldorf, Patmos, 1972, S. 67-75; ferner H.-F. WEISS, *Der Brief an die Hebräer* (KEK, 13), Göttingen, Vandenhoeck & Ruprecht, 1991, S. 115-125.

verzeichnis, das Muratorische Fragment[4], nennt die Paulusbriefe, wenn auch in einer für uns ungewöhnlichen Reihenfolge[5]; ausdrücklich heißt es im Canon Muratori, daß die „Paulusbriefe" an die Laodicener und an die Alexandriner als marcionitische Fälschungen gelten und deshalb von der *catholica ecclesia* nicht rezipiert werden[6]. Etwa hundert Jahre später rechnet Euseb zu den Schriften der καινὴ διαθήκη offenbar ganz selbstverständlich „die Briefe des Paulus", wenn auch ohne alle weiteren Angaben[7]. Aber schon das um das Jahr 150 bei Marcion vorliegende Corpus der nach seinem Urteil verbindlichen Schriften enthielt neben dem Lukasevangelium die paulinischen Briefe, mit Ausnahme der Pastoralbriefe.

Welche Geschichte haben die Briefe des Apostels durchlaufen, von ihrer Entstehung in den 50er und 60er Jahren des 1. Jahrhunderts bis zu ihrer mehr oder weniger definitiven Zusammenstellung um die Mitte des 2. Jahrhunderts? Diese Frage ist schwerer zu beantworten, als es zunächst scheinen möchte. Denn die handschriftliche Überlieferung der Paulusbriefe wie ja überhaupt des Neuen Testaments reicht nicht bis in den hier zu untersuchenden Zeitraum zurück. Die ältesten erhaltenen Paulusbriefhandschriften, beginnend mit 𝔓[46], setzen bereits die Existenz einer Paulusbrief*sammlung* voraus[8]; aber daraus kann nicht ohne weite-

---

4. Die Datierung des Canon Muratori ist ebenso wie seine geographische Herkunft umstritten. A.C. SUNDBERG, *Canon Muratori: A Fourth-Century List*, in *HTR* 66 (1973) 1-41 datiert ihn ins 4. Jahrh. und nimmt als Entstehungsort nicht Rom, sondern den Osten an. Dem widerspricht mit guten Argumenten E. FERGUSON, *Canon Muratori. Date and Provenance* in Elizabeth E. LIVINGSTONE (ed.), *Studia Patristica XVII/2* Oxford, Pergamon Press, 1982, S. 677-683. Vgl. jetzt vor allem J. VERHEYDEN, *The Canon Muratori: A Matter of Dispute,* in diesem Band S. 487-556.

5. Dazu s.u. S. 349.

6. Vgl. dazu E. VERHOEF, *Pseudepigraphy and Canon*, in *BN* 106 (2001) 90-98. Ob der kleine lateinisch überlieferte „apokryphe" Laodicenerbrief mit dem im Canon Muratori erwähnten identisch ist, läßt sich nicht sicher sagen; vermutlich ist es nicht der Fall, zumal er marcionitische Züge nicht aufweist. Vgl. W. SCHNEEMELCHER, *Der Laodicenerbrief*, in DERS. (ed.), *Neutestamentliche Apokryphen in deutscher Übersetzung. II. Band: Apostolisches, Apokalypsen und Verwandtes*, Tübingen, Mohr Siebeck, [5]1989, S. 41-43 (Text in deutscher Übersetzung 43f.), sowie VERHEYDEN, *The Canon Muratori* (s. Anm. 4), S. 539-541. Über den „Alexandrinerbrief" läßt sich gar nichts sagen.

7. Euseb h.e. III 25,2. Euseb erklärt kurz zuvor, Paulus sei zwar der wortgewaltigste und kundigste aller (sc. Apostel) gewesen (πάντων ἐν παρασκευῇ λόγων δυνατώτατος νοήμασίν τε ἱκανώτατος γεγονώς), doch habe er schriftlich nur ganz kurze Briefe hinterlassen, obgleich er „zahlreiche Geheimnisse" hätten mitteilen können (III 24,4 unter Anspielung auf 2 Kor 12,2-4). Zum Kanon bei Euseb vgl. A.D. BAUM, *Der neutestamentliche Kanon bei Eusebios (Hist.Eccl III,25,1-17) im Kontext seiner literaturgeschichtlichen Arbeit* in *ETL* 73 (1997) 307-348.

8. Der erhaltene Textbestand des im allgemeinen „um 200" datierten 𝔓[46] beginnt mit Röm 5,17; es folgen Hebr, 1 und 2 Kor, Eph, Gal, Phil, Kol sowie (teilweise) 1 Thess; dann bricht der Papyrus ab. Ob 𝔓[46] sämtliche Paulusbriefe enthielt und also womöglich als eine vollständige „Paulusbriefsammlung" anzusehen ist, oder ob er womöglich noch weitere urchristliche („neutestamentliche") Schriften umfaßte, läßt sich nicht sagen. (Diese Auskunft verdanke ich Professor Keith Elliott.)

res geschlossen werden, die Weitergabe paulinischer Briefe an andere als die ursprünglich intendierten Adressaten sei immer schon in Form von Sammlungen geschehen[9]. Gibt es Anzeichen dafür, daß die Gemeinden von sich aus begannen, die an sie gerichteten Briefe des Apostels weiterzugeben und so allmählich deren Sammlung vorzubereiten? Geht dieser Prozeß zumindest in seinen Anfängen womöglich schon auf Paulus selber zurück?

Gefragt wird im folgenden danach, welche einigermaßen sicheren Textzeugnisse es im 1. und 2. Jahrhundert für die Anfänge des Prozesses der Weitergabe bzw. der Rezeption der Paulusbriefe gibt, wobei zugleich die Frage gestellt werden soll, welche theologischen Entscheidungen damit verbunden gewesen sein könnten. Abschließend soll dann noch in aller Kürze bedacht werden, welche hermeneutischen Probleme sich daraus ergeben, daß wir die Paulusbriefe nicht als isolierte Einzeltexte besitzen, sondern daß sie uns im Rahmen einer Sammlung vorliegen und dabei überdies als Teil eines größeren neutestamentlichen Kanons[10].

I

Die Briefe des Apostels Paulus stellen in der antiken Briefliteratur in gewisser Weise eine Besonderheit dar: Ein einzelner Mensch schreibt an eine Gruppe von Menschen, die in einer mehr oder weniger weit entfernten Stadt bzw. im Fall der ἐκκλησίαι τῆς Γαλατίας sogar in einem offenbar relativ ausgedehnten Territorium[11] leben; der Schreiber vertraut dabei darauf, daß sein Brief den jeweiligen Adressaten auch tatsächlich zur Kenntnis gebracht werden wird. Zwar kann man darauf verweisen, daß beispielsweise der Kaiser Claudius im Herbst 41 einen Brief „An die πόλις der Alexandriner" richtete[12]; aber angesichts der sehr anderen äußeren Gegebenheiten ist das keine wirkliche Parallele zu den Briefen des Paulus.

9. Vgl. dazu K. ALAND, *Die Entstehung des Corpus Paulinum*, in DERS., *Neutestamentliche Entwürfe* (TB, 63), München, Chr. Kaiser, 1979, S. 302-350.

10. Man kann ja die (vermutlich sehr hypothetische) Frage stellen, ob ein neu aufgefundener, unbezweifelbar echter Paulusbrief „kanonisch" wäre oder nicht; die Antwort kann am Ende nur negativ sein, wobei hinzukäme, daß es keine Instanz gibt, die eine „Kanonisierung" beschließen könnte.

11. Dies gilt unabhängig davon, ob Γαλατία die römische Provinz *Galatia* bezeichnet oder aber die gleichnamige Landschaft im Norden dieser Provinz; vgl. dazu F. VOUGA, *An die Galater* (HNT, 10), Tübingen, Mohr Siebeck, 1998, S. 10-12.

12. Text und engl. Übersetzung bei J.L. WHITE, *Light from Ancient Letters* (Foundations and Facets), Philadelphia, Fortress Press, 1986, S. 133-137. Deutsche Übersetzung bei J. LEIPOLDT - W. GRUNDMANN (ed.), *Umwelt des Urchristentums II. Texte zum neutestamentlichen Zeitalter*, Berlin, Evangelische Verlagsanstalt, 1967, S. 250-253.

Der vermutlich älteste erhaltene Paulusbrief, der *Brief an die Thessa-lonicher*[13], ist ausdrücklich an eine offenbar fest überschaubare Gruppe gerichtet, an die ἐκκλησία Θεσσαλονικέων (1,1)[14]; angesprochen wird damit in concreto eine Mehrzahl von Menschen, was sich auch dar-an zeigt, daß der Plural der Anrede den gesamten Brief beherrscht[15]. Am Ende des Briefes (5,27) steht die im wahrsten Sinne des Wortes „be-schwörende" Aufforderung an die Adressaten (ὑμᾶς), der Brief solle al-len ἀδελφοί vorgelesen werden[16]. Die Dringlichkeit dieser von Paulus sehr betont vorgetragenen Bitte (ἐνορκίζω, 1. Pers. Sing., verbunden mit τὸν κύριον) ergibt sich offenbar nicht aus dem Inhalt des Schrei-bens – man sieht jedenfalls nicht, welche Aussagen im 1 Thess hätten Anlaß geben können, die Verlesung des Briefes womöglich einem Teil der ἐκκλησία vorzuenthalten oder den Brief nur in Auszügen verlesen zu lassen. Aber möglicherweise nahm Paulus an, der an die ἐκκλησία gerichtete Brief werde nicht sofort nach seinem Eintreffen in Thessalonich „von allen" gelesen bzw. gehört werden. Der Brief wurde ja von einem Boten vermutlich bei einer bestimmten einzelnen Person bzw. in deren „Haus" abgegeben[17]; angeredet wird dann zwar die

---

13. Die Echtheit und Frühdatierung des 1 Thess wird in der neueren Forschung kaum bestritten. Vgl. K.P. DONFRIED and J. BEUTLER (eds.), *The Thessalonians Debate. Methodological Discord or Methodological Synthesis?*, Grand Rapids MI, Eerdmans, 2000. Kritisch zu diesem weitgehenden Konsens jetzt aber Marlene CRÜSEMANN, *Die Briefe nach Thessaloniki und das gerechte Gericht. Studien zu ihrer Abfassung und zur jüdisch-christlichen Sozialgeschichte*, Diss. Kassel, 1999. Sie nimmt mit durchaus beacht-lichen Gründen an, 1 Thess sei als, angeblich von den drei im Präskript genannten Auto-ren verfaßter, pseudepigrapher Brief zu verstehen. Ob sich ihre Argumentation, die Posi-tionen des 19. Jahrh., vor allem K. Schrader und F.C. Baur, aufnimmt (Forschungsüber-blick, S. 157-186) in der Debatte wird durchsetzen können, bleibt abzuwarten.

14. Vgl. dazu E. VON DOBSCHÜTZ, *Die Thessalonicher-Briefe* (KEK, 10), Göttingen, Vandenhoeck & Ruprecht, [7]1909 (= 1974), S. 58: ἐκκλησία Θεσσαλονικέων bezeich-net die christliche Ortsgemeinde, „aber für griechische Ohren ist damit das Christen-häuflein in kühner Zuversicht aufmunternd der ganzen Stadtgemeinde gleichgesetzt". Umgekehrt verweist E. VERHOEF, *De brieven aan de Tessalonicenzen*, Kampen, Kok, 1998, 66 darauf, daß die innerhalb der Paulusbriefe ganz ungewöhnlich formulierte Adresse, nähme man sie strikt im buchstäblichen Sinne, mögliche „Nicht-Thessalo-nicher" in der Gemeinde von Thessalonich, also beispielsweise Römer und Galater, aus-schlösse. „Paulus heeft een dergelijke beperking natuurlijk niet bedoeld. Het lidwoord wordt bij namen van volkeren vaak niet gebruikt".

15. Inwieweit der Plural der Absender im buchstäblichen Sinne aufzufassen ist („wir", schon in 1,2 und dann immer wieder, wären dann entsprechend 1,1 Paulus sowie Silvanus und Timotheus), läßt sich nicht sicher sagen. Nach 3,2.6 waren „wir" zeitweilig von Timotheus getrennt; aber in 3,5 steht das sing. ἔπεμψα kommentarlos neben dem plur. ἐπέμψαμεν von V. 2. Vgl. auch die 1. Pers. Sing in 5,27 (s.u.).

16. S. dazu R.F. COLLINS, *„I Command That This Letter Be Read": Writing as a Manner of Speaking*, in DONFRIED-BEUTLER, *The Thessalonians Debate* (s. Anm. 13), S. 319-339.

17. Die „Postanschrift" stand wahrscheinlich außen auf der Briefrolle, sofern man nicht annehmen will, der mit der Überbringung des Briefes beauftragte Bote habe die

ἐκκλησία als ganze, aber die ersten Leser erfahren erst nachdem sie den Text vollständig gelesen haben, daß der Brief unbedingt *allen* ἀδελφοί in der Stadt vorgelesen werden soll. Paulus scheint allerdings keinen Unterschied zu machen zwischen den „Erstlesern" und „allen Brüdern"[18]; die von ihm angeredeten Adressaten („ihr") sind offensichtlich in dem ganzen Brief durchgängig alle Glieder der ἐκκλησία Θεσσαλονικέων, wie die von ihm vergleichsweise sehr häufig (14mal) gebrauchte und dabei „Brüder" wie „Schwestern" gleichermaßen betreffende Anrede ἀδελφοί erkennen läßt. Traugott Holtz folgert aus der Aufforderung in 5,27, durch sie werde „dem apostolischen Brief von Anfang an ein gewichtiger Ort angewiesen, ein allererster Schritt in Richtung auf seine Kanonisierung ist damit getan", auch wenn die Autorität des Briefes noch ganz an die gegebene Situation gebunden sei[19]. Zu beachten ist aber, daß Paulus nicht lediglich „von außen" autoritativ in die internen Angelegenheiten der Gemeinde eingreift; vielmehr fällt gerade auf, daß der Apostel die Adressaten immer wieder zum wechselseitigen Handeln untereinander auffordert[20].

Folgt man den Angaben der lukanischen Apostelgeschichte, so spricht alles für die Annahme, daß 1 Thess in Korinth verfaßt wurde, wohin Paulus nach seinem in Apg 17,15-18,1 beschriebenen und in 1 Thess 3,1 erwähnten Besuch in Athen weitergewandert war. Der Brief selber läßt freilich nichts vom Aufenthalt des Apostels in Korinth erkennen; es gibt

---

Anschrift ohnehin gekannt. Vgl. O. ROLLER, *Das Formular der paulinischen Briefe. Ein Beitrag zur Lehre vom antiken Briefe* (BWANT, IV/6), Stuttgart, W. Kohlhammer, 1933, S. 45f.; Anne KOLB, Art. *Nachrichtenwesen II B,2* in *DNP* 8, Stuttgart, J.P. Metzler, 2000, S. 668f.

18. Der Hinweis auf das ἀναγνωσθῆναι πᾶσιν τοῖς ἀδελφοῖς wäre andernfalls eher am Anfang des Briefes zu erwarten. Oder setzt Paulus mit 1,1 von vornherein voraus, der Brief werde selbstverständlich in der ἐκκλησία als der konkret *versammelten* Gemeinde verlesen werden? Dann käme durch die Bemerkung in 5,27 die Sorge zum Ausdruck, dies könne wider Erwarten doch nicht geschehen sein. Vgl. aber T. HOLTZ, *Der erste Brief an die Thessalonicher* (EKK, 13), Zürich, Benziger - Neukirchen-Vluyn, Neukirchener Verlag, 1986, S. 274: Die Bemerkung hänge „doch wohl nur mit der Besonderheit unseres Briefes zusammen, der ein erster an eine eben gebildete, noch traditionslose Gemeinde ist, vermutlich sogar der erste apostolische Brief an eine eigene Gemeinde des Absenders überhaupt". Vielleicht sei der Brief zunächst von Leuten „aus dem Kreis der Funktionsträger, die 5,12 nannte", gelesen worden, und Paulus dränge nun darauf, daß er nicht nur „durch allgemeine Information" oder „teilweise Verlesung" in der ganzen Gemeinde bekannt gemacht werden solle, sondern durch vollständige Verlesung in der Gemeindeversammlung. Ähnlich VERHOEF, *Tessalonicenzen* (s. Anm. 14), S. 231, der noch eine weitere Deutung für möglich hält: „Misschien drukt Paulus zich zo kras uit omdat deze brief zijn eigen prediking moet vervangen".

19. Problematisch ist es freilich, wenn Holtz hinzufügt, vor dem Apostel sei „die funktional gegliederte Gemeinde eine Einheit, die seinem Wort unterstellt ist" (S. 275).

20. Fünfmal begegnet ἀλλήλων (erstmals in 3,12, dann in 4,9.18; 5,11.15); besonders auffällig ist es am Ende der Gedankengänge von 4,13-18 und 5,1-11.

insbesondere keinerlei Anzeichen dafür, daß Paulus bei der Abfassung des 1 Thess auch noch an andere Leser als die Christen in Thessalonich gedacht und der Brief sich sozusagen indirekt womöglich auch an die Korinther gerichtet haben könnte. Andererseits darf allerdings auch nicht übersehen werden, daß Paulus nicht nur von den Auswirkungen des Glaubens der Thessalonicher auf das übrige Mazedonien spricht (1 Thess 1,7f.; 4,10), sondern ebenso von dessen Ausstrahlung auf Achaja (1,7f.), womit ganz konkret in erster Linie Korinth gemeint gewesen sein dürfte.

Eine nicht geringe Wahrscheinlichkeit spricht für die Annahme, daß die *Gefangenschaftsbriefe* an die Philipper und an Philemon in Ephesus geschrieben wurden, beide Briefe also vergleichsweise „früh" zu datieren sind[21]. In der Adresse des *Philipperbriefes* unterscheidet Paulus erstaunlicherweise zwischen „allen Heiligen" und den zusätzlich genannten ἐπίσκοποι und διάκονοι in Philippi (1,1). Man kann erwägen, ob es – unabhängig von der Frage, welche Funktion die so bezeichneten Personen im einzelnen hatten[22] – diese direkt genannte und dadurch jedenfalls hervorgehobene, vermutlich recht kleine Gruppe war, der der Brief unmittelbar zugestellt werden sollte; eine Antwort ist freilich kaum möglich. Jedenfalls läßt auch dieser Brief nicht erkennen, daß ein über Philippi hinaus gehender weiterer Adressatenkreis angesprochen werden sollte, obwohl Paulus auf die Tatsache, daß die Adressaten in einen größeren Kontext hineingehören, durchaus hinweist (4,15f.)[23]. Im *Philemonbrief* wendet sich Paulus nach V. 1.2a zwar an mehrere Personen (Philemon sowie Apphia und Archippos); daß tatsächlich aber allein

21. Die Angaben im Phil sprechen dafür, daß der Aufenthaltsort des Paulus nicht allzu weit von Philippi entfernt zu denken ist; daß das Leben des Paulus in Ephesus besonders bedroht gewesen war, geht aus 1 Kor 15,32 und 2 Kor 1,8 hervor (vgl. auch Apg 19,23-40). Für Caesarea oder Rom als Abfassungsort (und damit für eine Spätdatierung) des Phil könnten nur die Angaben der Apg über den Prozeß des Paulus sprechen, nicht aber Indizien innerhalb des Briefes selber. Anders u.a. U. SCHNELLE, *Einleitung in das Neue Testament* (UTB, 1830), Göttingen, Vandenhoeck & Ruprecht, ⁴2002, S. 153-156, der eine Abfassung in Rom und damit eine „Spätdatierung" für wahrscheinlich hält.

22. Nach Schnelle (s. die vorige Anm.) ist dies ein Indiz für eine späte Abfassung des Phil, denn der „Terminus ἐπίσκοπος (Aufseher) setzt ein Fortschreiten der Gemeindesituation in Richtung auf die Pastoralbriefe [!] voraus" (S. 154). Sehr viel näher als dieser schon im Blick auf die Chronologie problematische Erklärungsversuch der ungewöhnlichen Adresse in Phil 1,1 liegt der Vorschlag von P. PILHOFER, *Philippi. Band I. Die erste christliche Gemeinde Europas* (WUNT, 87), Tübingen, Mohr Siebeck, 1995, S. 146, die ἐπίσκοποι „zunächst als spezifisch philippisches Phänomen" anzusehen (vgl. im ganzen S. 140-147).

23. Dies gilt unabhängig von der Frage, ob der Brief – wie m.E. wahrscheinlich – als literarische Einheit anzusehen ist oder ob er – wie oft vermutet wird – aus zwei oder mehr ursprünglich selbständigen Briefen sekundär zusammengestellt wurde.

Philemon gemeint ist, zeigen sowohl gleich zu Beginn der Hinweis auf die κατ' οἶκόν σου ἐκκλησία (V. 2) als auch die innerhalb des Briefes oft begegnende Anrede in der 2. Pers. Sing.[24]. Der „Bittbrief"[25] des Paulus verfolgt allein den Zweck, Philemon als den unmittelbaren Adressaten zu einem bestimmten Handeln zu bewegen; an eine Rezeption des Briefes durch weitere Leser hat Paulus ganz offensichtlich nicht gedacht[26].

Die bisherigen Beobachtungen zu den direkten Adressaten der paulinischen Briefe werden durch die Korrespondenz mit Korinth im wesentlichen bestätigt. Wenn der Apostel in der Adresse des *Ersten Korintherbriefes* neben der ἐκκλησία in Korinth ausdrücklich auch „alle, die den Namen unseres Herrn Jesus Christus anrufen", erwähnt (1,2), dann ist dies wohl nicht so zu verstehen, als wende sich Paulus mit seinem Brief nicht allein an die Kirche von Korinth, sondern gleichsam „weltweit" an alle Christen; gegen eine solche Annahme spricht schon, daß der Brief zu sehr spezifischen Problemen gerade in der korinthischen Gemeinde Stellung nimmt. Mit der „ökumenischen" Adresse will Paulus den Korinthern vermutlich von Anfang an bewußt machen, daß sie in einen „weltweiten" Kontext hineingehören und daß sie dies bei ihrer in dem Brief dann oft kritisch kommentierten gemeindlichen Praxis berücksichtigen sollen[27]. Besonders bemerkenswert im Zusammenhang unserer Fragestellung ist die Tatsache, daß es am Ende des Briefes heißt, αἱ ἐκκλησίαι τῆς Ἀσίας und daneben auch die ἐκκλησία im Hause des Aquila und der Prisca ließen Grüße bestellen (1 Kor 16,19). Sofern

24. Die 2. Pers. Plur. nur in Phlm 22 und im Gnadenwunsch V. 25.

25. Zur Gattung s. M. WOLTER, *Der Brief an die Kolosser. Der Brief an Philemon* (ÖTK, 12), Gütersloh, Gütersloher Verlagshaus - Würzburg, Echter, 1993, S. 236f.

26. Es bleibt eine nicht wirklich beantwortbare Frage, warum und auf welche Weise Phlm erhalten blieb. Die einfachste Erklärung wäre noch die Annahme, daß „die ἐκκλησία im Hause des Philemon" in Wahrheit zugleich eine Ortsgemeinde war. In der Alten Kirche wurde dem Brief bisweilen Bedeutungslosigkeit attestiert; ausdrücklich wird er von Hieronymus gegen Kritik an seiner Zugehörigkeit zum NT verteidigt; vgl. P. STUHLMACHER, *Der Brief an Philemon* (EKK, 15), Zürich, Benziger - Neukirchen-Vluyn, Neukirchener Verlag, 1975, S. 18f.

27. Alle „katholischen" Bemerkungen innerhalb des 1 Kor (1,2; 4,17; 7,17; 11,16) sind m.E. von diesem Ziel her zu deuten; vgl. A. LINDEMANN, *Der Erste Korintherbrief* (HNT, 9/I), Tübingen, Mohr Siebeck, 2000, S. 27.116.170.246. Etwas anders L. HARTMAN, *On Reading Others' Letters*, in DERS., *Text-Centered New Testament Studies. Text-Theoretical Essays on Early Jewish and Early Christian Literature*, ed. by D. HELLHOLM (WUNT, 102), Tübingen, Mohr Siebeck, 1997, S. 167-177, hier 173: „Although the matters he dealt with in 1 Corinthians were ‚occasional' and particular, Paul discussed them in such a way that the letter could serve as an apostolic message to other churches as well". Keinesfalls handelt es sich bei den erwähnten Bemerkungen um sekundäre Glossen; die Ausnahme ist 14,33b, wo die entsprechende Formulierung m.E. Teil der tatsächlich als Interpolation anzusehenden *mulier-taceat*-Passage ist (vgl. LINDEMANN [s.o.], S. 315f. sowie die beiden Exkurse S. 316-321).

diese Notiz im buchstäblichen Sinne aufzufassen sein sollte, würde sie
voraussetzen und zugleich den Korinthern explizit signalisieren, daß die
genannten Kirchen zumindest über das Faktum der Korrespondenz des
Paulus mit der Kirche in Korinth informiert sind, darüber hinaus vielleicht sogar über den Inhalt des Briefes[28], auch wenn dies wohl nicht
bedeuten würde, daß sie als Mitabsender zu gelten haben oder umgekehrt indirekt als Adressaten „mitgemeint" sind.

Die innerhalb des „Zweiten Korintherbriefes" redaktionell zusam-
mengestellten Briefe[29] richteten sich, in unterschiedlichen Situationen,
durchweg an die korinthische Gemeinde; eine Ausnahme ist vielleicht
der „Kollektenbrief" 2 Kor 9[30], mit dem sich Paulus offenbar an Christen im übrigen Achaja wendet (vgl. 9,2; möglicherweise wird deshalb
nicht nur die ἐκκλησία τοῦ θεοῦ in Korinth als Adressatin genannt,
1,1, sondern daneben auch „alle Heiligen ἐν ὅλῃ τῇ ᾿Αχαΐα", 1,2).
Sollte die These einer redaktionellen Entstehung des jetzigen 2 Kor zu-
treffen[31], so liegt die Vermutung nahe, daß diese Redaktion durch die
Absicht der Korinther veranlaßt wurde, die an sie gerichteten Briefe des
Apostels auch anderen Gemeinden zugänglich zu machen. Der Vorgang
der „Redaktion" wäre vor allem dann plausibel, wenn der umfangreiche
Erste Korintherbrief immer schon eine literarische Einheit war; man
würde sich dann in Korinth dazu entschlossen haben, aus den vorhandenen weiteren, kürzeren Briefen des Apostels einen dem ersten Brief entsprechenden, also ähnlich umfangreichen zweiten Paulusbrief nach Korinth zu schaffen[32]. Dieser „zweite" Korintherbrief wäre dann ein indi-

28. Paulus hält sich zum Zeitpunkt der Abfassung des 1 Kor in Ephesus, also der
größten Stadt der ᾿Ασία, auf (16,8). Daß er sich mit seinem Gruß „zum Sprecher von
Gemeinden ganzer Provinzen macht" (so W. SCHRAGE, Der erste Brief an die Korinther.
4. Teilband. 1 Kor 15,1-16,24 [EKK, 7/4], Düsseldorf, Benziger - Neukirchen-Vluyn,
Neukirchener Verlag, 2001, S. 466), vermag ich der Formulierung so nicht zu entnehmen.
     29. Meine Analyse der im 2 Kor erkennbaren ursprünglich selbständigen Briefe und
die Rekonstruktion der späteren Redaktion habe ich knapp dargestellt in H. CONZELMANN
- A. LINDEMANN, Arbeitsbuch zum Neuen Testament (UTB, 52), Tübingen, Mohr Siebeck,
¹³2000, S. 271-273.
     30. Zur Analyse s. H.D. BETZ, 2. Korinther 8 und 9. Ein Kommentar zu zwei Verwal-
tungsbriefen des Apostels Paulus (Hermeneia), Gütersloh, Chr. Kaiser - Gütersloher Verlagshaus, 1993, S. 162-165.
     31. Für die Annahme, daß es zum Zeitpunkt der Abfassung von 2 Kor 10-13 in Ko-
rinth bereits mehrere Paulusbriefe gab, spricht jedenfalls die von Paulus referierend dar-
gestellte Kritik in 10,10: Wenn in Korinth festgestellt wird, αἱ ἐπιστολαί des Paulus sei-
en gewichtig, die körperliche παρουσία hingegen sei schwächlich, dann setzt dies mit
großer Wahrscheinlichkeit die Kenntnis mehrerer Briefe (und darüber hinaus wohl auch
mehrere Aufenthalte des Paulus in Korinth) voraus.
     32. Vgl. dazu A. LINDEMANN, Paulus im ältesten Christentum. Das Bild des Apostels
und die Rezeption der paulinischen Theologie in der frühchristlichen Literatur bis
Marcion (BHT, 58), Tübingen, Mohr Siebeck, 1979, S. 22f. D. TROBISCH, Die Entstehung

rekter Beleg für die Weitergabe paulinischer Briefe an andere Gemeinden und damit wohl auch für den Beginn von deren bewußter Sammlung. Leider läßt sich die Redaktion des 2 Kor nicht datieren. Ohnehin sind sichere Belege für eine explizite Benutzung des 2 Kor (in welcher Gestalt auch immer) nur schwer auszumachen; denkbar ist immerhin, daß der Bericht von der Flucht des Paulus aus Damaskus in Apg 9,23-25 literarisch von 2 Kor 11,32f. abhängig ist[33], obwohl es sich hier natürlich auch um (im Wortlaut dann freilich sehr feste) mündlich überlieferte Personaltradition handeln könnte.

Der *Galaterbrief* ist nach 1,2 an die ἐκκλησίαι τῆς Γαλατίας gerichtet. Wir können allerdings nicht erkennen, auf welche Weise dieser Brief mehreren Kirchen in einem geographisch doch wohl größeren Gebiet zugänglich gemacht werden sollte[34]. Aus Gal 6,11 könnte gefolgert werden, daß es nicht mehrere Exemplare, also Abschriften desselben Textes gab, sondern daß Paulus annahm, das Original werde kursieren, denn andernfalls hätte der besondere eigenhändig geschriebene Schluß ja gar nicht als solcher identifiziert werden können[35]. Andererseits wurde aber die Notiz von 6,11 in den Abschriften unverändert weitergegeben, und dies könnte natürlich auch schon für die Ursprungssituation gegolten haben.

Auch der *Römerbrief* schließlich läßt nicht erkennen, daß Paulus die Absicht hatte, mit seinen Ausführungen andere Adressaten als die „Ge-

---

der Paulusbriefsammlung. Studien zu den Anfängen christlicher Publizistik (NTOA, 10), Freiburg/Schweiz, Universitätsverlag - Göttingen, Vandenhoeck & Ruprecht, 1989, S. 123-128 führt 2 Kor in der vorliegenden Form auf eine von Paulus selber in Korinth vorgenommene „Autorenrezension" zurück; dabei habe der Apostel die einzelnen Briefe (nach Trobischs Analyse: 1,3-2,13; 2,14-7,3; 7,4-9,15; 10,1-13,10) ihrer ursprünglichen chronologischen Abfolge entsprechend geordnet. Trobisch geht allerdings nicht auf die Inhalte der jeweiligen Briefe ein.

33. Vgl. LINDEMANN, *Paulus im ältesten Christentum* (s. die vorige Anm.), S. 167.

34. Vgl. dazu VOUGA, *Galater* (s. Anm. 11), S. 9f.: „Entweder ist der Brief von einer Gemeinde zur anderen weitergegeben worden (cf. Kol 4,16). In diesem Falle muß der Absender mit Wechselwirkungen zwischen der Argumentation des Briefes und dem Austausch der Gemeinden über ihre Rezeption rechnen. Es fehlen aber sowohl Anweisungen für den Umlauf (s. 1 Thess 5,27) als auch Hinweise auf Mitarbeiter, die die Aufgabe des Briefträgers hätten übernehmen sollen (cf. 2 Kor 8,23; Phil 2,25-30). Oder der Brief ist in mehreren Exemplaren an die verschiedenen Gemeinden geschickt worden. Die Kopien müssen nicht völlig identisch gewesen sein". Als Muster für die in der Paulusbrief-*sammlung* publizierte Textfassung könne entweder eine in Ephesus vorhandene Abschrift oder aber „eine Kopie aus dem Archiv des Verfassers benutzt worden sein"; für die erste der beiden Möglichkeiten verweist Vouga auf D. TROBISCH, *Die Paulusbriefe und die Anfänge der christlichen Publizistik* (KT, 135), Gütersloh, Gütersloher Verlagshaus, 1994, S. 125f.

35. Zu beachten ist, daß es in Gal 6,11 anders als in 1 Kor 16,21 nicht allein um die persönliche „Unterschrift" geht, sondern daß Paulus gerade die besondere äußerlich erkennbare Art des Schreibens hervorhebt.

liebten Gottes" ἐν Ῥώμῃ zu erreichen[36]. Ähnlich wie in 1 Kor 16,19 findet sich auch im Röm der Hinweis darauf, daß Kirchen Grüße bestellen lassen; dabei ist nun aber nicht nur von Kirchen einer bestimmten Region die Rede, sondern Paulus spricht von αἱ ἐκκλησίαι πᾶσαι τοῦ Χριστοῦ (Röm 16,16[37]), und dies legt nun allerdings die Vermutung nahe, daß Paulus sich zumindest hier eher einer Floskel bedient als daß er konkret ihm aufgetragene Grüße weitergibt[38].

Wenn die bisherigen Beobachtungen zu der von Paulus intendierten Rezeption seiner Briefe durch die Adressaten im wesentlichen zutreffend sein sollten, dann bedeutet dies, daß die Annahme, der Apostel habe bei der Abfassung dieser Briefe andere als die direkt angesprochenen Adressaten im Blick gehabt, als sehr unwahrscheinlich anzusehen ist. Es ließen sich auch keine Indizien dafür finden, daß Paulus selber eine Edition seiner Briefe vorgenommen und damit deren weitere Verbreitung vorbereitet haben könne.

> Damit wird vor allem der These David Trobischs widersprochen, die Geschichte der Paulusbriefsammlung sei durch eine Autorenredaktion, also durch Paulus selber, in Gang gesetzt worden. Trobisch untersucht antike Briefsammlungen und erklärt dann, er wolle auf dieser Basis „mit derben Strichen ein Bild der Entstehungsgeschichte der Paulusbriefsammlung"

---

36. Die Debatte über den Abfassungszweck des Röm, etwa über Jerusalem als „heimliche Adresse", braucht in unserem Zusammenhang nicht berücksichtigt zu werden; als *Brief* ist Röm ohne jeden Zweifel an die Christen in Rom gerichtet. Das Fehlen der Ortsangabe in Röm 1,7.15 im Codex G (in 1,7 außerdem in 1739[mg] und 1908[mg] sowie bei Origenes) läßt freilich das Interesse erkennen, diesem Brief eine „katholische" Adresse zu verschaffen. Zur Frage nach dem Abfassungszweck des Röm vgl. jetzt vor allem Angela REICHERT, *Der Römerbrief als Gratwanderung. Eine Untersuchung zur Abfassungsproblematik* (FRLANT, 194), Göttingen, Vandenhoeck & Ruprecht, 2001.

37. In der „westlichen" Überlieferung steht dieser Hinweis nicht in 16,16, sondern in 16,21.

38. E. KÄSEMANN, *An die Römer* (HNT, 8a), Tübingen, Mohr Siebeck, [4]1980, S. 400 verweist darauf, daß in ähnlicher Weise in 16,4 „von allen heidenchristlichen Gemeinden gesprochen wurde und das fraglos eine Übertreibung darstellt"; wenn Paulus jetzt beanspruche, „im Namen der ganzen Christenheit zu sprechen", so sei zu beachten, daß er nach 16,21ff. „Delegaten der Gemeinden um sich hat (Dodd)". Nach U. WILCKENS, *Der Brief an die Römer. 3. Teilband. Röm 12-16* (EKK, 6/3), Zürich, Benziger - Neukirchen-Vluyn, Neukirchener Verlag, 1982, S. 137f. kommt es Paulus bei seinem so umfassend formulierten Gruß darauf an, „daß wirklich *alle* Gemeinden Christi in dem Evangelium übereinstimmen, wie er es im Briefkorpus dargelegt hat, so daß, wie in der Kollekte alle Heidenchristen ihre Einheit mit den Judenchristen in Jerusalem bezeugen, auch im Ja zum Römerbrief alle Christen übereinstimmen. Das ökumenische Ziel des Briefes zeigt sich so in Röm 16,16b besonders deutlich". – Die oft diskutierte Frage, ob Kap. 16 ursprünglicher Bestandteil des Röm ist, braucht hier nicht im einzelnen diskutiert zu werden. Nach KÄSEMANN, *Römer*, S.393f. handelt es sich um einen selbständigen Empfehlungsbrief, doch hat die neuere Diskussion mit guten Gründen die ursprüngliche Zugehörigkeit zum Röm erwiesen; vgl. W.-H. OLLROG, *Die Abfassungsverhältnisse von Röm 16*, in D. LÜHRMANN - G. STRECKER (eds.), *Kirche*. FS G. Bornkamm, Tübingen, Mohr Siebeck, 1980, S. 221-244; K. P. DONFRIED, *A Short Note on Romans 16*, in ID. (ed.), *The Romans Debate*. Revised and Expanded Edition, Peabody, MA, Hendrickson, 1991, S. 44-52.

skizzieren, in der „Zuversicht, daß der Umgang mit den zahlreich ein-
gesehenen antiken Briefsammlungen meine Phantasie vielleicht in richtige
Bahnen gelenkt hat"[39]. Die von ihm entwickelte Hypothese zur Vorge-
schichte des Corpus Paulinum sieht dann so aus[40]: „Vielleicht war es der
Galaterbrief, der ihn [sc. Paulus] das Medium des Briefes entdecken ließ.
Der an ganz bestimmte Personen zu ganz bestimmten Problemen formulierte Brief wird weitergegeben und gerät in die Hände Dritter", die diesen
Brief sei es kritisch, sei es dankbar aufnehmen. „Der Gal war nicht der erste Brief, den er schrieb, aber doch der erste Brief, der über den konkreten
Zweck und konkreten Adressat hinaus Wirkung auslöste." Dadurch habe
sich Paulus veranlaßt gesehen, „seine Lehre der Nachwelt zu hinterlassen", dies nicht zuletzt auch angesichts des Ausbleibens der Parusie. „Zum
ersten Mal greift Paulus zur Feder und erstellt aus seiner Korrespondenz
mit Korinth den sogenannten *1. Korintherbrief*", der auf ein überwältigen-
des „Leserinteresse" stößt. „Über Nacht wird Paulus zum Schriftsteller.
Man möchte mehr lesen", zumal der in 2 Kor 10,10 beschriebene Vorwurf
gegen Paulus durchaus „treffend" ist. Paulus verläßt Ephesus, und während einer Reise durch die von ihm gegründeten europäischen Gemeinden
faßt er dort vorhandene Korrespondenzen zu größeren Texteinheiten zusammen und gibt ihnen, „vor allem durch die Zusammenfassung in nur
eine Schrift und das erweiterte Präskript, einen testamentarischen An-
strich". So entstehen 1 Thess und Phil in Thessalonich bzw. in Philippi, in
Korinth wird die jüngste Korrespondenz zum 2 Kor zusammengefaßt. Anschließend entsteht der Römerbrief, „in seinen Augen die Krönung seines
Werkes"; Abgesandten aus Ephesus, die er während seiner Reise nach Jerusalem trifft, übergibt er „eine Abschrift des Röm, an die er noch persönliche Grüße und letzte Wünsche anfügt, zusammen mit einer Abschrift des
2Kor"[41]. „Ohne es zu wissen", so Trobisch weiter, hat Paulus „damit den
Grundstock zu einer Sammlung gelegt, aus der dann über Zwischenstufen
das Corpus Paulinum erwächst, die meistgelesene Briefsammlung der
Weltliteratur." Die Gesandtschaft der Epheser habe Röm und 2 Kor mit
dem in Ephesus bereits vorhandenen 1 Kor verbunden und eine Abschrift
des Gal „aus dem Archiv geholt", womit die „*Ursammlung* Röm 1Kor
2Kor Gal" entstanden sei. „Daneben" sei dann „die *katholische Briefsammlung* zusammengestellt" worden: „Sie besteht aus dem 1Kor, der ersten und für Paulus bahnbrechenden Schrift, dem als paulinisches Rund-
schreiben überlieferten Eph und dem Hb"[42].

39. TROBISCH, *Entstehung* (s. Anm. 32), S. 128f. Zu den antiken Briefsammlungen
s.u.
40. Alle folgenden Zitate ohne Einzelnachweis bei D. TROBISCH, *Entstehung* (s. Anm.
32), S. 129f. Hervorhebungen jeweils im Original.
41. Für den Römerbrief wird eine zweifache Rezension (ohne und mit Kap. 16) des
öfteren erwogen, einschließlich der Möglichkeit, daß Paulus selber mehrere Fassungen
versandt habe. Vgl. dazu N.A. DAHL, *The Particularity of the Pauline Epistles as a Problem in the Ancient Church* (1962), in DERS., *Studies in Ephesians. Introductory
Questions, Text-&Edition-Critical Issues, Interpretation of Texts and Themes*, ed by
D. HELLHOLM, V. BLOMKVIST and T. FORNBERG (WUNT, 131), Tübingen, Mohr Siebeck,
2000, S. 165-178, hier 171f.
42. Vom Hebr nimmt Trobisch an, daß er von Paulus selber in Kap. 13 „mit einem
empfehlenden Nachwort" versehen worden sei. „Dadurch wird der Hb zur letzten schriftlichen Mitteilung, die von Paulus erhalten ist".

Einer solchen Rekonstruktion der Entstehung der Paulusbriefsammlung zuzustimmen, fällt schwer; denn textinterne Indizien für ihre Richtigkeit werden von Trobisch nicht einmal ansatzweise sichtbar gemacht[43]. Die von ihm sehr instruktiv vorgestellten und zum Vergleich herangezogenen antiken Briefsammlungen, die auf bewußter Editionstätigkeit basieren, enthalten durchweg ausdrückliche Vermerke darüber, daß und wie die Edition angelegt ist. Michaela Zelzer zufolge war Plinius d.J., „soweit bekannt, der erste, der eine Sammlung kunstvoll gestalteter eigener B[riefe] herausbrachte, die nach den Regeln der B[rief]-Theorie den persönlichen Verhältnissen und Interessen der Empfänger angepaßt sind. Nach dem Stilprinzip der *variatio* verteilte er sie auf 9 B[ücher]"[44]. Plinius leitet in Ep I,1 die Sammlung ausdrücklich mit der an den Adressaten Septicius gerichteten editorischen Vorbemerkung ein, er habe auf dessen Anregung hin seine Briefe, jedenfalls die einigermaßen sorgfältig stilisierten, gesammelt und veröffentlicht[45]. M. Tullius Cicero hatte, wie er an Atticus schreibt, eine Edition seiner Briefe selber ins Auge gefaßt[46]; die Briefe wurden dann aber erst geraume Zeit nach Ciceros Tod tatsächlich ediert.

Selbst wenn man es – ungeachtet fehlender expliziter Belege – für möglich hält, daß der Apostel Kopien seiner Briefe anfertigen und archivieren ließ, so spricht doch nichts dafür, daß er selber damit die Absicht verbunden gehabt hätte, diese Kopien in womöglich redigierter Form als Briefsammlung(en) in Umlauf zu bringen. Die Paulusbriefe, jedenfalls die uns erhaltenen, weisen irgendwelche editorischen Vermerke ihres Verfassers an keiner Stelle auf. Mithin spricht nichts für die Vermutung,

43. Kritisch zu Trobisch SCHNELLE, *Einleitung* (s. Anm. 21), S. 397; vgl. auch meine Rez. in *TLZ* 115 (1990) 682f. Zur Sammlung der Paulusbriefe und zum Werden des Kanons vgl. den Exkurs bei SCHNELLE, *Einleitung*, S. 395-410.

44. M. ZELZER, Art. *Epistel. H. Briefsammlungen*, in *DNP* 3, Stuttgart - Weimar, Metzler, 1997, S. 1165; das zehnte Buch wurde später angefügt.

45. Plinius Ep I,1 erklärt, da er ja kein Geschichtswerk bieten wolle, habe er die Briefe „ohne Rücksicht auf die zeitliche Folge" zusammengestellt, sondern so „wie mir das einzelne Stück gerade in die Hände fiel:" *collegi non servato temporis ordine (neque enim historiam componebam), sed ut quaeque in manus venerat* (C. Plinius Caecilius Secundus, *Epistularum Libri Decem. Lateinisch-deutsch*, ed. H. Kasten, München, Heimeran, ³1976). Selbst wenn man diese Bemerkung nicht allzu wörtlich zu nehmen braucht, so spricht doch wenig für die Interpretation von TROBISCH, *Entstehung* (s.o. Anm. 32), 91, Plinius habe sich „dafür *rechtfertigen* [müssen], daß die Briefe der Sammlung nicht chronologisch geordnet sind" (Hervorhebung von mir).

46. Cicero schreibt (Cic Att XVI 2 [5], 5): „Eine Sammlung meiner Briefe existiert nicht, aber Tiro hat etwa 70 beieinander. Auch Du könntest welche beisteuern. Ich muß sie aber erst durchsehen und korrigieren, ehe sie herausgegeben werden". *Mearum epistularum nulla est* συναγωγή; *sed habet Tiro instar septuaginta; et quidem sunt a te quaedam sumendae, eas ego oportet perspiciam, corrigam; tum denique edentur* (Marcus Tullius Cicero, *Atticus-Briefe. Lateinisch-deutsch*, ed. H. Kasten, München, Heimeran Verlag, ²1976).

daß die Sammlung der Paulusbriefe vom Apostel vorbereitet oder gar definitiv eingeleitet wurde. Nach allem, was wir in den Briefen selber erkennen können, läßt sich der Beginn des Prozesses der Sammlung dieser Briefe nicht unmittelbar auf ihren Autor zurückführen.

II

Nur kurze Zeit nach dem Tode des Paulus kam es zur Abfassung von pseudopaulinischen Briefen[47]. Allein diese Tatsache macht es bereits wahrscheinlich, daß die Existenz von Paulusbriefen schon verhältnismäßig früh auch in solchen Gemeinden nicht unbekannt war, die – soweit wir wissen – nicht selber Adressatinnen eines Paulusbriefes gewesen waren. Der vermutlich älteste dieser pseudepigraphischen Briefe, der *Kolosserbrief*, setzt die Kenntnis zumindest eines der echten Paulusbriefe voraus und läßt dessen direkte literarische Benutzung erkennen[48]. Für die hier erörterte Frage ist Kol aber vor allem deshalb von besonderer Bedeutung, weil es in diesem Brief – vermutlich fiktional – ausdrücklich heißt, die Adressaten in Kolossä sollten den an sie gerichteten Brief mit einem nach Laodicea gerichteten austauschen (4,16)[49]. Leider

47. Die im Neuen Testament enthaltenen „frühen" pseudepigraphischen Paulusbriefe, vor allem Kol und Eph, unterscheiden sich deutlich von den späteren („apokryphen") „Paulusbriefen", dem Laodicenerbrief und dem „3. Korintherbrief" (s. dazu u. Anm. 62) oder gar dem Briefwechsel zwischen Seneca und Paulus. Während die frühen „Deuteropaulinen" darum bemüht sind, den Apostel in theologisch reflektierter Weise in die Gegenwart hineinsprechen zu lassen, sind die späteren Pseudepigraphen ebenso wie die apokryphen Apostelakten eher daran interessiert, eine Art „historischer Neugier" zu befriedigen; das gilt insbesondere für den Laodicenerbrief (der die durch Kol 4,16 aufgerissene „Lücke" füllen soll) und den Briefwechsel mit dem Philosophen Seneca, es deutet sich freilich auch schon in dem als „Testament des Paulus" gestalteten neutestamentlichen 2 Tim an.

48. Die Grußliste Kol 4,10-14 setzt Phlm 23f. unmittelbar voraus; vgl. A. LINDE-MANN, *Der Kolosserbrief* (ZBK.NT, 10), Zürich, Theologischer Verlag, 1983, S. 73-75. Kol will in derselben Situation geschrieben sein, in der Phlm entstand.

49. M.E. dient die Aufforderung in 4,16 dazu, die tatsächliche Adresse des Kol, nämlich die Gemeinde von Laodicea, in den Brieftext einzutragen; vgl. A. LINDEMANN, *Die Gemeinde von „Kolossä". Erwägungen zum „Sitz im Leben" eines pseudopaulinischen Briefes*, in DERS., *Paulus, Apostel und Lehrer der Kirche. Studien zu Paulus und zum frühen Paulusverständnis*, Tübingen, Mohr Siebeck, 1999, S. 187-210. Es fällt auf, daß in bezug auf Laodicea ausdrücklich von einer ἐκκλησία gesprochen wird, während im Blick auf Kolossä weder im Präskript (1,2) noch dann in 4,16 dieser Begriff verwendet ist. L. HARTMAN, *On Reading* (s.o. Anm. 17), S. 169f. nimmt an, Kol sei von einem Mitarbeiter des Paulus (eventuell Timotheus, vgl. 1,1) verfaßt worden, während sich Paulus in Rom in Gefangenschaft befand; die Tatsache, daß Kol Anspielungen auf alle früheren Paulusbriefe enthalte, spreche für die Vermutung, daß Paulus Kopien seiner Briefe besaß und diese seiner „Schule" zur Verfügung standen. Aber auch im Falle der definitiven Pseudonymität des Kol spreche alles dafür, daß dem Autor Kopien der Paulusbriefe zur Verfügung standen. Kol läßt aber durchaus nicht die Bekanntschaft mit *sämtlichen*

läßt die Art der Formulierung der hier zum erstenmal begegnenden Aufforderung nicht erkennen, ob der „Paulus" des Kol einen derartigen
Austausch als bereits übliche Praxis darstellen will bzw. ein solcher
Austausch von den Gemeinden tatsächlich bereits praktiziert wird, oder
ob er den Gedanken an einen derartigen Austausch apostolischer Briefe
jetzt erstmals in die kirchliche Praxis einbringen möchte[50].

Der *Epheserbrief* ist literarisch zumindest vom Kolosserbrief direkt
abhängig, wie allein schon die Übereinstimmungen der Rahmenstücke
deutlich belegen[51]. Sollte die Adresse ἐν Ἐφέσῳ in 1,1 textgeschichtlich sekundär sein, dann wäre diese Schrift offenbar von vornherein bewußt als ein „katholischer Brief" konzipiert worden; der Autor würde
den Lesern vermittelt haben wollen, daß sich Paulus zumindest mit diesem Brief, der das Thema ‚Kirche' ganz ins Zentrum rückt, an die Kirche als ganze wendet und nicht lediglich an eine einzelne Gemeinde[52].
Freilich liegt von der Textüberlieferung her die Annahme näher, daß der
Brief immer schon als ein „Brief des Paulus an die Heiligen in Ephesus"
gelesen werden sollte und sich seine (natürlich fiktive) Zuweisung an die

Paulusbriefen erkennen (vgl. LINDEMANN, *Paulus im ältesten Christentum* [s. Anm. 32],
S. 114-122), auch wenn man nicht so weit gehen wird wie W.-H. OLLROG, *Paulus und
seine Mitarbeiter. Untersuchungen zu Theorie und Praxis der paulinischen Mission*
(WMANT, 50), Neukirchen-Vluyn, Neukirchener, 1979, S. 228, der erklärt: „Eine literarische Abhängigkeit des Kolosserbriefs von den Paulusbriefen läßt sich nicht nachweisen,
auch nicht zum Philemonbrief (wohl aber kennt der Verfasser die paulinischen Brief-
gepflogenheiten)".

    50. Nach E. SCHWEIZER, *Der Brief an die Kolosser* (EKK), Zürich, Benziger - Neu-
kirchen-Vluyn, Neukirchener Verlag, 1976, S. 179 ist der Vorschlag zum Briefaustausch
„wahrscheinlich so etwas wie die erste Anregung zu einer Paulusbriefsammlung, falls
sich nämlich die Gemeinden von anderen Briefen Abschriften zu machen begannen"; der
erwähnte Laodicenerbrief sei nicht erhalten, „falls es sich nicht um den Philemonbrief
handelt". Schweizers Erwägungen sind von seiner Annahme her zu lesen, daß Kol etwa
zeitgleich mit Phlm verfaßt wurde, möglicherweise von Timotheus, und daß der Brief
also jedenfalls nicht „nachpaulinisch" (wenn auch durchaus pyseudonym) ist (S. 23-27).
Nach WOLTER, *Kolosser* (s. Anm. 25), S. 221 setzt der „Weitergabevermerk" in Kol 4,16
den bereits bestehenden Prozeß der Weitergabe und Sammlung der Paulusbriefe schon
voraus, und er „benützt ihn, um den Kol als einen der Paulusbriefe zu identifizieren, die
in den von Paulus und seinen Mitarbeitern gegründeten Gemeinden zirkulieren und dadurch sein nachträgliches Auftauchen in der Gemeinde der faktischen Adressaten zu begründen"; diese Intention korrespondiere „mit der universalisierenden Dimensionierung
der paulinischen Missionstätigkeit in 2,1".

    51. Eph 1,1f. entspricht Kol 1,1f., Eph 6,21f. entspricht Kol 4,7f. Vgl. im übrigen
A. LINDEMANN, *Der Epheserbrief* (ZBK.NT, 8), Zürich, Theologischer Verlag, 1985,
S. 10f.

    52. Denkbar wäre in diesem Fall, daß der Verfasser beabsichtigte, diesen Charakter
der Paulusbriefe grundsätzlich neu einzuführen. Die oft vorgeschlagene Hypothese, Eph
könne als ein „Rundbrief" entworfen worden sein, wobei dann in 1,1 der jeweilige Ortsname eingesetzt werden sollte, ist ohne Textbasis; die Masse der Handschrift liest ἐν
Ἐφέσῳ, nur sehr wenige Handschriften (s.u. Anm. 53) enthalten keine Ortsangabe, ein
weiterer Ortsname neben Ephesus ist nicht überliefert.

Christen in dieser Stadt also nicht erst dem Einfall eines späteren Ab-
schreibers verdankt[53]. Dann aber setzt die Tatsache der Abfassung gerade eines pseudepigraphischen Briefes ausgerechnet nach *Ephesus* voraus, daß zumindest der Verfasser mit dem Faktum der Existenz mehrerer
Paulusbriefe bereits vertraut war und er das Fehlen eines Briefes ausgerechnet nach Ephesus als besonders auffällig empfand[54]. Zugleich aber
ist es durchaus verständlich, daß einige Abschreiber meinten, die Adresse ἐν Ἐφέσῳ sei zu tilgen; denn der Brief läßt ja keinerlei persönliche
Beziehungen zwischen dem Absender und den Adressaten erkennen,
und das konnte im Blick auf die aus anderen Texten, insbesondere auch
aus der Apostelgeschichte bekannte enge Beziehung des Paulus zu
Ephesus Befremden auslösen[55]. Der unter dem Pseudonym „Paulus"
schreibende Autor wählte die Adresse „Ephesus" vermutlich gerade
deshalb, weil er mit seinem Schreiben eben nicht eine bestimmte einzelne Gemeinde mit ihren möglicherweise ganz spezifischen Problemen im
Auge hatte; vielmehr war sein Thema die Kirche als ganze, und dieses
Thema glaubte er in der Gestalt eines Briefes des Paulus an die Christen
in der für den Apostel so bedeutsamen Stadt besonders angemessen darstellen zu können[56].

Leider ist es kaum möglich, den Kolosser- und den Epheserbrief einigermaßen sicher zu datieren; unter Berücksichtigung der erkennbaren
kirchen- und theologiegeschichtlichen Situation dürfte eine Abfassung

53. Vgl. A. LINDEMANN, *Bemerkungen zu den Adressaten und zum Anlaß des Ephe-
serbriefes* (1976), in DERS., *Paulus, Apostel und Lehrer* (s. Anm. 49), S. 211-227. Zur
Diskussion vgl. H. HÜBNER, *An die Kolosser. An die Epheser. An Philemon* (HNT, 12)
Tübingen, Mohr Siebeck, 1997, S. 129f.; ferner A.T. LINCOLN, *Ephesians* (WBC, 42),
Dallas,TX, Word Books, 1990, S. 1-4. P. POKORNÝ, *Der Brief des Paulus an die Epheser*
(THK, 10/II), Leipzig, Evangelische Verlagsanstalt, 1992, S. 34-37 hält die Lesart ἐν
Ἐφέσῳ für sekundär, meint aber zugleich, „daß die wichtigste Gruppe, die der Ephe-
serbrief erreichen sollte, die Gemeinde in Ephesus war" (37), wofür aber nichts in dem
Brief spricht, wenn der Hinweis auf Ephesus in 1,1 sekundär wäre.

54. Sollte Paulus wirklich keinen Brief an die Epheser geschrieben haben, so wäre das
durchaus nicht erstaunlich, da diese Stadt jedenfalls in dem für uns überschaubaren Zeitraum der paulinischen Missionstätigkeit eine Art „Hauptquartier" des Apostels war. Natürlich ist überhaupt nicht auszuschließen, daß es einen Paulusbrief nach Ephesus gab, der
verlorengegangen ist.

55. Es darf nicht übersehen werden, daß ἐν Ἐφέσῳ nur in 𝔓[46] und in ℵ* sowie B*,
ferner in den Minuskeln 424ᶜ und 1739 fehlt. Die sekundäre Streichung ist wesentlich
leichter zu erklären als eine sekundäre Hinzufügung der Adresse; es kommt hinzu, daß
die Lesart ohne ἐν Ἐφέσῳ sprachlich unmöglich ist.

56. Man kann fragen, ob der pseudonyme Epheserbrief in der Nähe der fiktiven Rede
des Paulus an die πρεσβύτεροι von Ephesus in Apg 20,18-35 steht; zumindest bemerkenswert ist, wie sich – bei allen Unterschieden im einzelnen – vor allem die Aussagen in
Eph 4,11-16 mit denen in Apg 20,28-30 berühren. Es ist aber auch denkbar, daß zwischen
Eph und Ephesus (abgesehen von 1,1) überhaupt keine Beziehung besteht; der Brief muß
keineswegs in „Asien" entstanden sein.

im Zeitraum der siebziger oder achtziger Jahre des 1. Jahrhunderts wahrscheinlich sein. In jedem Fall zeigt die Existenz des „Epheserbriefes", daß die Paulusbriefe nur wenige Jahrzehnte nach dem Tode des Apostels bereits als auch überörtlich relevante Texte verstanden werden konnten. Daß man im letzten Viertel des 1. Jahrhunderts von der Existenz gefälschter paulinischer Briefe wußte oder sie jedenfalls für möglich hielt, zeigt der ja selber pseudepigraphische „*(Zweite) Thessalonicherbrief*" (2,2; 3,17)[57]. Dessen Autor bemüht sich darum, die Naherwartung der Endzeitereignisse und damit eine – wie er es offenbar sieht – Fehlinterpretation eschatologisch-apokalyptischer Aussagen, wie sie sich in 1 Thess 4,13-5,11 finden, zurückzuweisen. Er tut dies, indem er „Paulus" erklären läßt, eine sich auf ihn berufende Überlieferung (λόγος) bzw. ein entsprechender Brief (ἐπιστολή) – bei dem es sich nur um unseren 1 Thess handeln kann – seien in Wahrheit unecht (2,2; vgl. 3,17). In dem nun vorliegenden angeblich echten Thessalonicherbrief läßt der Verfasser den Apostel schreiben, die Parusie, „der Tag des Herrn" (2,2), stehe keineswegs unmittelbar bevor oder sei gar schon eingetroffen (ἐνέστηκεν), denn es müsse noch auf etliche Endzeitereignisse gewartet werden (2,3-12). Der „zweite" Thessalonicherbrief läßt nicht erkennen, ob dem Autor über 1 Thess hinaus weitere Paulusbriefe oder gar eine Paulusbriefsammlung – welchen Umfangs auch immer – bekannt waren oder ob er entsprechendes Wissen bei seinen Adressaten voraussetzt. Der Brief ist im Gegenteil (bewußt?) unter der Voraussetzung formuliert, daß „die Thessalonicher"[58], die von ihm angesprochen werden, nur 1 Thess kennen; dabei kann offen bleiben, ob dies für die gemeinten Adressaten tatsächlich zutrifft, oder ob es der Fiktion des Briefes entspricht, da ja auch im 1 Thess nicht von anderen Paulusbriefen die Rede ist. Die Leser erfahren jetzt jedenfalls, daß der ihnen bekannte Brief (= 1 Thess) nicht von Paulus geschrieben wurde und daß ihnen mit dem nun vorliegenden Brief, also unserem 2 Thess, „*der* Thessalonicherbrief des Paulus" zugänglich wird. Die Absicht des Verfassers, seinen Brief als „den" echten paulinischen Brief an die Thessalonicher erscheinen zu lassen, wird schon dadurch deutlich, daß im 2 Thess jeder Hinweis dar-

---

57. Vgl. A. LINDEMANN, *Zum Abfassungszweck des Zweiten Thessalonicherbriefes* (1977), in DERS., *Paulus, Apostel und Lehrer* (s. Anm. 49), S. 228-240.

58. Die tatsächlichen Adressaten müssen durchaus nicht in Thessalonich beheimatet gewesen sein; es genügt, wenn sie den 1 Thess kennen; die ungewöhnliche Adresse τῇ ἐκκλησίᾳ Θεσσαλονικέων (s.o.) steht auch in 2 Thess 1,1. Sollten die Adressaten tatsächlich in Thessalonich zu Hause gewesen sein, so sollten sie durch 2 Thess die Information erhalten, bislang einen unechten Paulusbrief aufbewahrt zu haben; ob sie dies akzeptierten, bleibe dahingestellt – immerhin sind uns beide Thessalonicherbriefe erhalten geblieben.

auf fehlt, dieser Brief sei der zweite an dieselben Adressaten (vgl. dagegen 2 Petr 3,1). Den Adressaten wird mitgeteilt, daß sich „Fälschungen" wie eben jener ihnen bisher bekannte Brief leicht daran erkennen lassen, daß in ihnen das „in jedem Brief" enthaltene Echtheitszeichen fehlt (3,17) – und tatsächlich weist 1 Thess dieses „Zeichen" nicht auf[59].

Die Existenz der drei uns bekannten vergleichsweise früh entstandenen und dabei im einzelnen recht unterschiedlichen pseudopaulinischen Briefe Kol, Eph und 2 Thess belegt, daß im letzten Viertel des 1. Jahrhunderts das Vorhandensein von Paulusbriefen in der Kirche weithin bekannt war, und zwar, wie zumindest Kol zeigt, auch in nicht von Paulus gegründeten Gemeinden. Die Existenz einer regelrechten *Sammlung* läßt sich damit aber noch nicht wahrscheinlich machen. Gegen die Annahme einer so frühen Sammlung spricht ja gerade die Abfassung der pseudopaulinischen Briefe selber; deren Rezeption zumindest in den Gemeinden wäre vermutlich recht schwierig gewesen, wenn diese Gemeinden bereits über so etwas wie ein *Corpus Paulinum* verfügt hätten.

III

Eine veränderte Situation zeigt sich in den *Pastoralbriefen*, die eine kirchliche Situation voraussetzen, die ihre Abfassung etwa um das Jahr 100 wahrscheinlich macht[60]. Wenn die These von Michael Wolter zutrifft, daß diese Briefe von vornherein als ein Corpus von drei Briefen konzipiert wurden[61], dann könnte dies für die Vermutung sprechen, daß es zum Zeitpunkt ihrer Abfassung bereits eine erste größere Sammlung von Paulusbriefen gab, die nun nicht mehr ohne weiteres durch andere „paulinische Gemeindebriefe", hätte ergänzt werden können. Dementsprechend stellen sich die Pastoralbriefe, anders als Kol, Eph und 2 Thess, als quasi „private", persönliche Briefe des Apostels an seine Mitarbeiter bzw. „Schüler" Timotheus und Titus dar; ihr relativ spätes Auftauchen mochte sich von daher leichter erklären lassen – anders als es bei der späten „Entdeckung" eines oder gar mehrerer bisher unbe-

---

59. Fragen kann man, ob die Notiz in 2 Thess 3,17 als Indiz dafür zu gelten hat, daß der Autor (und seine Adressaten) 1 Kor 16,21 und/oder Gal 6,11 kennt, wo freilich der eigenhändige Gruß des Paulus keineswegs als „Echtheitszeichen" Verwendung findet. Denkbar ist natürlich auch, daß der Autor meinte, eine derartige „eigenhändige" *subscriptio* sei gleichsam unwiderleglich.

60. Das deutlichste Indiz für diese Datierung ist m.E. die starke Nähe der Pastoralbriefe zu der im 1. Clemensbrief erkennbaren Ekklesiologie; 1 Clem dürfte in den neunziger Jahren geschrieben worden sein.

61. M. WOLTER, *Die Pastoralbriefe als Paulustradition* (FRLANT, 146), Göttingen, Vandenhoeck & Ruprecht, 1988.

kannter paulinischer Gemeindebriefe der Fall gewesen wäre[62]. Zwar enthalten die Pastoralbriefe keinerlei Hinweis darauf, daß Briefe des Paulus in der Kirche bereits gesammelt werden, ja, sie erwähnen die Existenz („weiterer") paulinischer Briefe nicht einmal; aber ihre Entstehung als solche dürfte als ein indirekter Beleg für das Vorhandensein und für die faktische Rezeption einer ersten Paulusbriefsammlung in den Gemeinden zu werten sein.

Etwa zeitgleich mit den Pastoralbriefen, vielleicht auch schon etwas früher, wurde in Rom der an die Gemeinde in Korinth gerichtete *Erste Clemensbrief* geschrieben. Dieser sehr umfangreiche, seiner Gattung nach im Urchristentum analogielose Brief[63] ist für unsere Fragestellung insofern von großer Bedeutung, als sich hier der erste *sichere* Beleg für das Vorhandensein eines Paulusbriefes an einem anderen als dem ursprünglichen Bestimmungsort findet. In 1 Clem 47,1-4 erwähnt der Verfasser explizit den paulinischen (ersten) Brief an die Korinther, wobei er nachdrücklich an dessen kritische Aussagen zum Thema „Parteien" erinnert. Die knappe Aufforderung ἀναλάβετε τὴν ἐπιστολήν setzt es als selbstverständlich voraus, daß man in Korinth den betreffenden Paulusbrief[64] auch mehr als vierzig Jahre nach dessen Abfassung sofort

62. Später verfaßte pseudopaulinische Gemeindebriefe wie der „Laodicenerbrief" und der „Dritte Korintherbrief" treten mit einem deutlich geringeren theologischen Anspruch auf als die im Neuen Testament enthaltenen unechten Paulusbriefe (s.o. Anm. 47); vgl. SCHNEEMELCHER, *Der Laodicenerbrief* (s. Anm. 6), S. 42: „Der Verf. scheint möglichst allgemein gehaltene Verse aus Paulusbriefen zusammengesucht zu haben, um mit seinem Machwerk eine Lücke im Corpus Paulinum zu schließen, die allerdings jedem Bibelleser auffallen konnte", nämlich das Fehlen des in Kol 4,16 erwähnten Briefes. Zum 3 Kor s. jetzt die sorgfältige Studie von V. HOVHANESSIAN, *Third Corinthians. Reclaiming Paul for Christian Orthodoxy* (Studies in Biblical Literature, 18), New York, Peter Lang, 2000; dazu meine Rez. in *TR* 67 (2002) 494-496. Hovhanessian rückt 3 Kor sachlich in die Nähe der Pastoralbriefe und ordnet ihn zeitlich in die zweite Hälfte des 2. Jahrh. ein; 3 Kor war „an assertion of an emerging Christian orthodoxy in the late second century against the misappropriation of Paul's authority by those outside the pale" (S. 137); leider argumentiert er auch mit der These, Paulus habe im zweiten Jahrhundert (mehr oder weniger) als „der Apostel der Häretiker" gegolten (zu dieser Formulierung bei Tertullian Adv Marc III 5,4 s. aber LINDEMANN, *Paulus im ältesten Christentum* [s. Anm. 32], S. 393f.).

63. Vgl. dazu A. LINDEMANN, *Die Clemensbriefe* (HNT, 17. Die Apostolischen Väter 1), Tübingen, Mohr Siebeck, 1992, S. 13; H.E. LONA, *Der erste Clemensbrief* (KAV, 2), Göttingen, Vandenhoeck & Ruprecht, 1998, S. 23. Eine gewisse Parallele bietet 2 Makk 1,1.

64. LONA, *Clemensbrief*, S. 506 hält es für „möglich, daß die zwei Briefe an die Korinther unter dem Titel ἐπιστολὴ Παύλου τοῦ ἀποστόλου kopiert wurden", und dies könne sogar für die Paulusbriefsammlung als ganze gegolten haben. Lona beruft sich dafür auf R. KNOPF, *Die Lehre der zwölf Apostel. Die zwei Clemensbriefe* (HNT Erg.; Die Apostolischen Väter 1), Tübingen, Mohr, 1920, S. 123. Dieser stützt sich seinerseits auf W. HARTKE, *Die Sammlung und die ältesten Ausgaben der Paulusbriefe*, Bonn, 1917, der seine Annahme daraus ableitet, daß bei Iren Haer III 16,5ff. die Johannesbriefe als *epistola Ioannis* bezeichnet seien; tatsächlich aber zitiert Irenäus Haer III 16,5 nahezu wörtlich 1 Joh 2,18f.21f., d.h. ebenso wie in 1 Clem 47,1 ist sofort klar, daß sich die Aus-

zur Hand hat; es braucht den Adressaten in Korinth nicht erklärt zu werden, daß und warum eine Abschrift des paulinischen Briefes nach Korinth in Rom vorhanden bzw. dessen Text hier zumindest bekannt ist. Eine definitive *Sammlung* von Paulusbriefen läßt sich aus 1 Clem 47 allerdings weder für Rom noch für Korinth erschließen, wenngleich der Autor außer dem paulinischen (Ersten) Korintherbrief zumindest auch den paulinischen Römerbrief gekannt haben dürfte[65]. Daß dem Brief des Paulus eine besondere Autorität zugewiesen wird, steht außer Frage; die Formulierung, Paulus habe den Korinthern ἐπ' ἀληθείας πνευματικῶς geschrieben (47,3), bedeutet aber wohl nicht, daß der Paulusbrief bereits als in gleicher Weise vom Geist „inspiriert" gilt wie die im 1 Clem oft zitierte und ausdrücklich so bezeichnete „Heilige Schrift" (γραφή bzw. ἱεραὶ γραφαί, vgl. vor allem 45,2)[66].

Sehr deutliche Indizien für das Vorhandensein einer wirklichen *Paulusbriefsammlung* zeigen nun aber die Briefe des *Ignatius von Antiochia*. Hier ist allerdings die Forschung insofern in Bewegung geraten, als sowohl die Echtheit der Briefe wie auch insbesondere ihre traditionelle Frühdatierung (um 110) neuerdings wieder nachdrücklich bestritten werden[67]. Während die These einer womöglich bewußt antignos-

sage *Iohannes domini discipulus ... in epistola sua sic testificatus est nobis* mit folgendem Zitat unmittelbar auf 1 Joh bezieht. Richtig ist, daß Irenäus in III 16,8 ein Zitat aus 2 Joh 7f. folgen läßt, eingeleitet mit der Wendung *Iohannes in praedicta epistola ... praecipit dicens*; doch darauf folgt unmittelbar (*Et rursus in epistola ait*) das Zitat von 1 Joh 4,1-3; es liegt also die Vermutung nahe, daß Irenäus die Aussage aus 2 Joh 7f. irrtümlich dem von ihm auch sonst des öfteren zitierten 1 Joh zuweist. Keinesfalls ist die Stelle ein Beleg dafür, im 1 Clem könne eine Paulusbrief*sammlung* als ἐπιστολὴ Παύλου τοῦ ἀποστόλου bezeichnet worden sein.

65. 1 Clem 47,1 läßt leider auch keine Antwort auf die Frage zu, ob es bereits einen „Zweiten Korintherbrief" gab bzw. ob dieser in Rom bekannt war; auch ist die Formulierung der rhetorischen Frage in 47,2 (τί ... ἐν ἀρχῇ τοῦ εὐαγγελίου ἔγραψεν;) kein Beleg dafür, daß man den paulinischen Philipperbrief (vgl. Phil 4,15) in Rom kannte. Freilich ist πρῶτον ... ἐν ἀρχῇ wohl auch nicht so zu verstehen, als habe 1 Clem den 1 Kor für den ältesten Brief gehalten und dieser habe deshalb an der Spitze der Paulusbriefsammlung gestanden (das wird gelegentlich aus der Abfolge der Briefe im Canon Muratori geschlossen; s. dazu u. Anm. 101).
Die Frage, ob 1 Clem die Kenntnis des Hebräerbriefes erkennen läßt (vgl. 1 Clem 36,2-5 mit Hebr 1,3...13, spielt für unseren Zusammenhang keine Rolle (vgl. dazu LINDEMANN, *Clemensbriefe* [s. Anm. 63], S. 19f. und die dort genannte Literatur; m.E. ist die Frage zu bejahen, aber es fehlt jedes Indiz dafür, daß der Autor des 1 Clem den Hebr für einen Paulusbrief gehalten haben könnte).
66. A.C. SUNDBERG, Art. *Canon of the NT* in IDB Suppl, Nashville, TN, Abingdon, [8]1988, S. 138 sieht dagegen eine direkte Parallele zu den Aussagen über alttestamentliche Texte in 1 Clem 13,1 und 16,2; aber dort ist explizit davon die Rede, daß τὸ πνεῦμα τὸ ἅγιον etwas sage (nämlich Jer 9,23f. bzw. Jes 53,1-12); das Adverb πνευματικῶς hat diese volle Bedeutung nicht. Jedenfalls gehören die Paulusbriefe für 1 Clem offensichtlich nicht zu den „heiligen Schriften" (45,2), aus denen bestimmte Beispiele angeführt werden können (45,3-8).
67. Vgl. R.M. HÜBNER, *Thesen zur Echtheit und Datierung der sieben Briefe des Ignatius von Antiochien*, in ZAC 1 (1997) 44-72.

tischen literarischen Fälschung[68] angesichts des Charakters der Briefe
freilich als recht unwahrscheinlich gelten kann[69], wird von der Annahme
einer Datierung der Briefe auf die Zeit Trajans wohl Abschied genommen werden müssen; denn es gibt tatsächlich keine textimmanenten Indizien, die auf diese relativ frühe Entstehungszeit verweisen[70]. Die
Ignatiusbriefe dürften um 130 verfaßt worden sein, also in zeitlicher
Nähe zum neutestamentlichen „Zweiten Petrusbrief", jedenfalls noch
vor dem Auftreten Marcions. Ebenso wie der Autor des 2 Petr spricht
auch Ignatius ausdrücklich von mehreren Paulusbriefen; er setzt also
eine – wenn auch ihrem Umfang nach nicht näher erkennbare – *Sammlung* dieser Briefe voraus. An die Epheser (12,2) schreibt Ignatius, er
wolle „gefunden werden in den Spuren des Paulus", der „euch", also
die Epheser, in jedem Brief (ἐν πάσῃ ἐπιστολῇ) erwähne. Unabhängig
von der Frage, wie wörtlich wir diese Aussage des Ignatius zu nehmen
haben[71], ist jedenfalls klar, daß Ignatius von mehreren Briefen des Paulus weiß; er nimmt an, daß für die Epheser dasselbe gilt. Denn der Sinn
der Aussage in Eph 12,2 kann es ja nicht sein, die Leser über die ihnen
bisher womöglich unbekannte Tatsache zu informieren, daß sie ἐν πάσῃ
ἐπιστολῇ des Paulus Erwähnung finden; vielmehr will Ignatius seinen
Adressaten in Ephesus offensichtlich demonstrieren, daß diese für sie so
ehrenvolle Tatsache auch ihm bekannt ist.

Derselbe Sachverhalt zeigt sich im Brief des *Polykarp von Smyrna* an
die Philipper[72]. Polykarp erwähnt, Paulus habe ihnen (ὑμῖν) aus der Fer-

---

68. Vgl. TH. LECHNER, *Ignatius adversus Valentinianos? Chronologische und theolo-
giegeschichtliche Studien zu den Briefen des Ignatius von Antiochien* (VigChrSup, 47),
Leiden, Brill, 1999, der die Ignatiusbriefe als ein um 165/175 verfaßtes antivalentinia-
nisches Textcorpus deutet; s. meine Rez. in *ZAC* 6 (2002) 157-161.

69. Vgl. A. LINDEMANN, *Antwort auf die „Thesen zur Echtheit und Datierung der sieben Briefe des Ignatius von Antiochien"*, in *ZAC* 1 (1997) 185-194. Vgl. jetzt vor allem
auch A.O. MELLINK, *Death as Eschaton. A Study of Ignatius of Antioch's Desire for
Death*, Diss. Amsterdam, 2000, S. 5-50.

70. Insoweit dürfte LECHNER, *Ignatius* (s. Anm. 68) zuzustimmen sein, vgl. vor allem
S. 68-115. Aber die Datierung nahezu in die Zeit von Irenäus Adv Haer (also um 180),
wo die Ignatianen erstmals bezeugt seien (zu Polykarp s.u. Anm. 72), wird dem literarischen Charakter der Briefe nicht gerecht und verfehlt deren theologie- und kirchenge-
schichtlichen Ort.

71. Muß man annehmen, daß sich Ignatius hier allein auf solche paulinischen Briefe
bezieht, in denen Ephesus tatsächlich erwähnt wird (1 Kor 15,32; 16,8; Eph 1,1; 1 Tim
1,3; 2 Tim 1,18; 4,12; eventuell auch Röm 16,5 und 2 Kor 1,8: Ἀσία)? Oder handelt es
sich einfach um ein überschwengliches Kompliment für die Adressaten? Zur Interpretation vgl. LINDEMANN, *Paulus im ältesten Christentum* (s. Anm. 32), S. 84f., ferner DERS.,
Der Apostel Paulus im 2. Jahrhundert, in J.-M. SEVRIN (ed.), *The New Testament in Early
Christianity* (BETL, 86), Leuven, Peeters, 1989, 39-67, 44f. (= LINDEMANN, *Paulus, Apostel und Lehrer* [s. Anm. 49], S. 294-322, 299f.).

72. Mit der Bestreitung der Echtheit der Ignatiusbriefe verbindet sich bei LECHNER,
Ignatius (s. Anm. 68) auch eine entsprechende Kritik am überlieferten Polykarpbrief; er

ne (ἄπων) Briefe (Plur.!) geschrieben (ἔγραψεν ἐπιστολάς), die auch gegenwärtig die Auferbauung des Glaubens zu fördern vermögen (3,2). In Phil 11,2 zitiert Polykarp ausdrücklich 1 Kor 6,2[73], und er erwähnt dann, daß Paulus in Philippi gewirkt und sich der Philipper *in omnibus ecclesiis* gerühmt habe (11,3)[74]. Da nun aber Philippi, außer natürlich im paulinischen Philipperbrief selber, von Paulus nur in 1 Thess 2,2 erwähnt wird, wird man aus dieser Formulierung keine klare Folgerung für die Anzahl der dem Polykarp bekannten Paulusbriefe ableiten dürfen[75]. Bemerkenswert ist, daß Polykarp unmittelbar anschließend (12,1) den Christen in Philippi bescheinigt, sie seien „in den heiligen Schriften wohl bewandert" (*confido enim vos bene exercitatos esse in sacris literis*). Ist dies möglicherweise als ein Indiz dafür anzusehen, daß Polykarp die paulinischen Briefe zumindest implizit zu den *sacrae literae* rechnet? Ausgeschlossen ist es jedenfalls nicht; und es würde dazu passen, daß Polykarp in demselben Zusammenhang Eph 4,26 zitiert, und zwar ausdrücklich verbunden mit der einleitenden Wendung *ut his scripturis dictum est*. Bei Eph 4,26a handelt es sich zwar um ein Zitat von Ps 4,5 (ὀργίζεσθε καὶ μὴ ἁμαρτάνετε), Polykarp könnte mit seiner Charakterisierung des Textes als *scriptura* mithin das Psalmwort gemeint haben; aber auf die Mahnung *irascimini et nolite peccare* folgt als Fortsetzung die Aussage *et sol non occidat super iracundiam vestram*, und dieser Satz stammt nun zweifellos nicht aus Ps 4, sondern aus Eph 4,26b. Der Befund im ganzen legt also wohl doch die Annahme nahe, daß Polykarp den Paulusbriefen bereits einen Rang als „Schrift" zuweist[76].

Den klarsten frühen Beleg für das Vorhandensein einer *Sammlung* von Paulusbriefen bietet der *Zweite Petrusbrief*: „Petrus", der sich an

---

nimmt an, daß PolPhil 1,1b und Kap. 13 insgesamt in einen um 150 verfaßten echten Polykarpbrief interpoliert wurden, und zwar durch den Autor der Ignatianen selber. Die Verwendung des Namens „Ignatius" gehe auf den in Kap. 9 erwähnten gleichnamigen Märtyrer aus Philippi zurück (aaO., 6-65).

73. *Aut nescimus, quia sancti mundum iudicabunt? sicut Paulus docet.*

74. Dabei ist bemerkenswert, daß Polykarp das Alter der Gemeinde von Philippi hervorhebt: Sie gehöre zu den Kirchen *quae deum solae tunc cognoverant*, während eine Gemeinde in Smyrna noch gar nicht existierte (*nos autem nondum cognoveramus*).

75. Vielleicht läßt sich PolPhil 11,3 als eine etwas eigenwillige Interpretation des von Paulus in Phil 4,15b ausgesprochenen Danks (οὐδεμία μοι ἐκκλησία ἐκοινώνησεν ... εἰ μὴ ὑμεῖς μόνοι) verstehen.

76. J. LEIPOLDT, *Geschichte des neutestamentlichen Kanons. Erster Teil. Die Entstehung*, Leipzig, Hinrich, 1907 (= 1974), S. 191 meint allerdings, „nach allem, was wir wissen", sei es „ausgeschlossen, daß Polykarp den Epheserbrief als Heilige Schrift bezeichnete"; entweder sei die Übersetzung ungenau, „oder Polykarp hat irrtümlicher Weise gemeint, das Zitat aus dem Epheserbriefe stünde im Alten Testamente", wobei Letzteres aber wohl doch wenig wahrscheinlich ist.

einen ganz offenen Adressatenkreis wendet[77], spricht in 3,15 davon, daß
Paulus „euch" geschrieben habe „entsprechend der ihm verliehenen
Weisheit"[78]; in „allen Briefen", die freilich zum Teil „schwer verständlich" seien, habe Paulus die auch von „Petrus" im vorliegenden Brief
vertretene These der durchaus noch nicht als nahe anzusehenden Parusie
(ἡμέρα κυρίου, 3,10) gelehrt. Allerdings gebe es unkundige und
ungefestigte Gemüter, die den Sinn des von Paulus Gesagten verdrehten,
und dies täten sie zu ihrem eigenen Verderben ja auch mit „den übrigen
Schriften". Ähnlich wie in PolPhil 12,1 muß der Hinweis auf die
(λοιπαὶ) γραφαί nicht unbedingt bedeuten, daß der Autor des 2 Petr die
Paulusbriefe unmittelbar zu „den (heiligen) Schriften" rechnet, zumal
das etwas pauschale Adjektiv λοιπός doch recht erstaunlich ist[79]. Andererseits aber wird in der urchristlichen Literatur der Begriff γραφή/
γραφαί durchgängig auf die Bibel, d.h. auf das Alte Testament bezogen.
Das legt nun doch die Vermutung nahe, daß der Autor des 2 Petr die
Paulusbriefe, wenn auch ohne jede Betonung, den γραφαί zurechnet;
das bedeutet nicht, daß über den Umfang einer solchen im Entstehen be-
griffenen erweiterten Gruppe von „Schriften" und gar über die Entwicklung hin zu einem, entsprechend den (alttestamentlichen) γραφαί womöglich bereits als „kanonisch" anzusehenden, „Neuen Testament" Ge-
naueres gesagt werden könnte[80].

---

77. Die Adresse in 2 Petr 1,1 weicht erheblich von derjenigen in 1 Petr 1,1 ab, obwohl
in 2 Petr 3,1 ausdrücklich gesagt wird, dies sei schon der zweite Brief an die Adressaten
(ταύτην ... δευτέραν ὑμῖν γράφω ἐπιστολήν).
    78. Die Wendungen ὁ ἀγαπητὸς ἡμῶν ἀδελφός und κατὰ τὴν δοθεῖσαν αὐτῷ
σοφίαν sind durchaus nicht herablassend gemeint und alles andere als Versuche des
Verfassers („Petrus"), die Bedeutung des Paulus in irgendeiner Weise zu schmälern.
Vgl. dazu H. PAULSEN, Kanon und Geschichte. Bemerkungen zum Zweiten Petrusbrief
in DERS., Zur Literatur und Geschichte des frühen Christentums. Gesammelte Aufsätze,
hg. von Ute E. EISEN (WUNT, 99), Tübingen, Mohr Siebeck, 1997, S. 154-161, bes.
158f.
    79. LEIPOLDT, Geschichte (s. Anm. 76), S. 186: Vorausgesetzt sei, daß „alle" Paulus-
briefe „leicht zugänglich, also gesammelt sind"; doch bedeute dies durchaus nicht
„Kanonisation", d.h. die Paulusbriefe galten noch nicht als „Heilige Schrift". „Es liegt
wohl eine ungenaue Ausdrucksweise vor: in ihrer Ungenauigkeit ist sie allerdings eine
Andeutung der kommenden Entwickelung". Vgl. auch H. PAULSEN, Der Zweite Petrusbrief und der Judasbrief (KEK, XII/2), Göttingen, Vandenhoeck & Ruprecht, 1992,
S. 175: „Solche ‚übrigen Schriften' könnten analog zum sonstigen Sprachgebrauch des
frühen Christentums Texte der ‚Schrift' bezeichnen, dagegen spricht aber, daß der Vf. in
1,19-21 jene bereits durch die Kennzeichnung als προφητικὸς λόγος hervorgehoben
hatte".
    80. SUNDBERG, Canon (s. Anm. 66), S. 137 betont, die Begriffe „scripture" und
„canon" dürften nicht synonym gebraucht werden. Vgl. DERS., Towards a Revised
History of the New Testament Canon in StEv IV. Part 1: The New Testament Scriptures
(TU, 102), Berlin, Akademie-Verlag, 1968, S. 452-461.

IV

Um die Mitte des 2. Jahrhunderts verfügt *Marcion* über eine Sammlung von Paulusbriefen („Apostolos"), die er zusammen mit dem (Lukas-)„Evangelium" als verbindlich ansieht[81]; über die Details werden wir vor allem durch Tertullian informiert. Zwischen Marcion und Tertullians gegen ihn gerichteten großen Werk *Adversus Marcionem* liegen allerdings etwa fünfzig Jahre, so daß sich kaum sicher sagen läßt, ob der von Tertullian vorausgesetzte marcionitische Text des Corpus Paulinum nach Umfang und Wortlaut völlig identisch ist mit der Paulusbriefsammlung Marcions[82]. Daß Marcion der erste Schöpfer eines im eigentlichen Sinne als „kanonisch" aufzufassenden zweiteiligen Corpus urchristlicher Schriften („Neues Testament") war, ist eher unwahrscheinlich[83]; gegen eine solche Vermutung spricht schon die Tatsache, daß Marcion – die Richtigkeit der Ausführungen Tertullians im wesentlichen vorausgesetzt – vor allem die paulinischen Briefe offenbar nicht uner-

81. Vgl. dazu Barbara ALAND, Art. *Marcion/Marcioniten*, in *TRE* 22, Berlin, de Gruyter, 1992, S. 89-101, vor allem 91-93.

82. Zu Marcions Textfassung der Paulusbriefe s. U. SCHMID, *Marcion und sein Apostolos. Rekonstruktion und historische Einordnung der marcionitischen Paulusbriefausgabe* (ANTF, 25), Berlin, de Gruyter, 1995. Vgl. auch J.J. CLABEAUX, *A Lost Edition of the Letters of Paul. A Reassessment of the Text of the Pauline Corpus Attested by Marcion* (CBQ.MS, 21), Washington, DC, The Catholic Biblical Association of America, 1989 (s. dazu meine Rezension in *TLZ* 115 [1990] 594f.).

83. Die These, Marcion sei als der Begründer eines neutestamentlichen Kanons anzusehen, wird insbesondere vertreten von H. VON CAMPENHAUSEN, *Die Entstehung der christlichen Bibel* (BHT, 39), Tübingen, Mohr Siebeck, 1968 (vgl. vor allem S. 207-209). Zunächst seien in der großen Kirche die vier Evangelien zu einer Sammlung zusammengefügt worden, d.h. es war „der erste katholische Kanon zuerst ‚eingliedrig' oder ‚einteilig' konzipiert". „Aber durch Markions Bibel war nun auch die weitere Frage nach dem Rang und und dem Platz der Paulusbriefe unabweisbar geworden" (207). Doch die Erwägung, der „Rang" der Paulusbriefe habe in der großen („katholischen") Kirche in Frage gestanden, hat an den uns bekannten Texten des 2. Jahrh. keinerlei Anhalt; vgl. LINDEMANN, *Paulus im ältesten Christentum* (s. Anm. 32), S. 379-383. Richtig m.E. immer noch W.G. KÜMMEL, *Notwendigkeit und Grenze des neutestamentlichen Kanon,* in E. KÄSEMANN (ed.), *Das Neue Testament als Kanon. Dokumentation und kritische Analyse zur gegenwärtigen Diskussion,* Göttingen, Vandenhoeck & Ruprecht, 1970, S. 62-97, bes. 72: Marcion habe „schwerlich die Kanonbildung der Kirche angeregt, wohl aber beschleunigt und in Nebenpunkten beeinflußt". Etwas anders B. ALAND, *Marcion* (s. Anm. 81), S. 91: „Marcion beansprucht für seine Bibel streng ausschließliche Geltung, die der gesamten Alten Kirche bis hin noch zu Irenäus (vgl. haer. 2,35) fremd gewesen ist. Als erster in der Geschichte der Christenheit entwickelt er daher den Begriff eines geschlossenen, allein gültigen biblischen Kanons". Wenn Irenäus (Haer II 35,4) zu seiner antignostischen Argumentation erklärt, mit ihr stimme überein (*consonat*) „die Predigt der Apostel, die Lehre des Herrn, die Ankündigung der Propheten, die Vorschrift der Apostel, der Dienst der Gesetzgebung" (*praedicatio apostolorum et domini magisterium et prophetarum adnuntiatio et apostolorum dictatio et legislationis ministratio*), dann zählt er damit inhaltlich alles auf, was die Bibel an Autoritäten aufzuweisen hat.

heblich „redigierte", weil er sie in ihrer authentischen Form anscheinend nicht hätte rezipieren können[84]. Die marcionitische „Redaktion" der Paulusbriefe legt den Schluß nahe, daß bereits eine „kirchliche" Sammlung der Paulusbriefe in einer vermutlich relativ festen Textfassung vorlag, deren Existenz sich durch die Beobachtungen zu Ignatius, Polykarp und 2 Petr ja bereits nahegelegt hatte.

Ob und in welchem Sinne eine solche, anscheinend um 120/140 entstandene Sammlung bereits als „kanonisch" bezeichnet werden könnte[85], muß offenbleiben. Auch über die genaue inhaltliche Zusammensetzung der zu vermutenden „kirchlichen" Paulusbriefsammlung und über die Reihenfolge der darin enthaltenen Briefe läßt sich Sicheres nicht sagen, zumal die uns erhaltenen literarischen Quellen aus der Zeit zwischen 2 Petr bzw. Ignatius einerseits und Irenäus andererseits, insbesondere die Schriften der Apologeten, die Paulusbriefe kaum erwähnen[86]. Freilich

---

84. Ähnliches berichtet Euseb h.e. IV 29,6 auch von Tatian; dieser habe nicht nur das Diatessaron geschaffen, sondern man sagt, er habe es auch gewagt, einige Sätze des Paulus umzuschreiben, um seine Ausdrucksweise zu verbessern (τὸ δ᾿ ἀποστόλου φασὶ τολμῆσαί τινας αὐτὸν μεταφράσαι φωνάς, ὡς ἐπιδιορϑούμενον αὐτῶν τὴν τῆς φράσεως σύνταξιν). Daß Tatian damit „eine eigene, den Wortlaut glättende und überarbeitende Ausgabe der Paulusbriefe veranstaltet" habe mit dem ausdrücklichen Ziel „der ‚Rettung' des Apostels" (so VON CAMPENHAUSEN, Entstehung [s. die vorige Anm.], S. 210), kann man dem Euseb-Text nicht entnehmen. Zum Verhältnis der vormarcionitischen Paulusbriefsammlung und dem „Kanon" Marcions s. SCHMID, Marcion und sein Apostolos (s. Anm. 82), S. 284-298, vor allem 296-298. Schmid nimmt an, daß die Reihenfolge der Briefe in der „Bibel" Marcions (einschließlich des Fehlens von Röm 15-16) auf diese Ausgabe zurückgeht; zahlreiche üblicherweise als „marcionitisch" geltende Lesarten gingen durchaus nicht erst auf Marcion zurück: „Sein Beitrag beschränkt sich auf die Streichung präzise eingrenzbarer Textabschnitte in Gal (3,6-9.14-18.29: mentiones Abrahae), in Röm (2,3-11: Gericht nach den Werken; 4,1ff (?): Abraham als Vater aller Glaubenden; 9,1ff (?); 10,5ff (?) 11,1-32 (?): Israel als Träger der Verheißungen und positiver Anknüpfungspunkt) und in Kol (1,15b-16: Schöpfungsmittlerschaft Christi); möglicherweise weitere ‚kleine' Änderungen betreffen die Auslassungen zur σάρξ Christi (Eph 2,14; Kol 1,22). Diese Eingriffe in den Text sind schwerwiegend genug, aber alle weitergehenden Textänderungen … sind nicht zu halten". Der marcionitische Text unterscheide sich „nicht wesentlich von einem großen Teil der übrigen frühen ntl. Textüberlieferung, wie sie in den Papyri vorliegt".

85. Vgl. dazu A.M. RITTER, Zur Kanonbildung in der Alten Kirche, in DERS., Charisma und Caritas. Aufsätze zur Geschichte der Alten Kirche, Göttingen, Vandenhoeck & Ruprecht, 1993, S. 265-280, bes. 267: Es „scheint alle Wahrscheinlichkeit dafür zu sprechen, daß es zur Ausbildung eines zweiteiligen neutestamentlichen Kanons (welchen Umfangs auch immer) auch ohne Markion, rein aus innerkirchlichen Ansätzen und Antrieben gekommen wäre. Das Auftreten Markions wird dann aber diese Entwicklung wesentlich beschleunigt und einen tiefen, lange nachwirkenden Schock ausgelöst haben", nicht zuletzt durch die hinzukommende „Herausforderung durch die ‚Gnosis'". Ähnlich beschreibt H. PAULSEN, Die Bedeutung des Montanismus für die Herausbildung des Kanons, in DERS., Zur Literatur und Geschichte (s. Anm. 79), S. 310-343 das Verhältnis des Montanismus zur Entwicklung des neutestamentlichen Kanons.

86. Eine besondere Ausnahme bildet der Diognetbrief, dessen Datierung freilich umstritten ist. C.M. NIELSEN, The Epistle to Diognetus: Its Date and Relationship to Marc-

enthalten auch die Schriften der späteren kirchlichen Autoren in dieser Hinsicht keine präzisen Informationen: Irenäus zitiert zwar häufig aus den paulinischen Briefen, aber er bietet keine Liste dieser Briefe. Tertullian erklärt zwar, Marcion überliefere die Paulusbriefe nur in verstümmelter Form, und dies *etiam de numero* (Adv Marc V 5 1,9); doch in seiner Auseinandersetzung mit Marcion orientiert er sich dann offenbar ohne weiteres an der von diesem vorgegebenen Reihenfolge. Origenes zitiert in c Cels III 19 zum Stichwort σοφία 1 Kor 2,6-8 unter Hinweis auf „Paulus" als Quelle; er erwähnt dann (III 20) die einzelnen Paulusbriefe und empfiehlt deren Lektüre, aber ohne die beiden Korintherbriefe und den Galaterbrief. In den Acta Scilitanorum antworten die angeklagten Märtyrer auf die Frage des Prokonsuls Saturninus, was für Gegenstände sie in ihrem Behälter mit sich trügen (*Quae sunt res in capsa vestra?*), es handele sich um „Bücher und Briefe des Paulus, eines gerechten Mannes" (*Libri et epistulae Pauli viri iusti*)[87]; aber welche „Bücher" und vor allem welche *epistulae Pauli* es im einzelnen sind, erfährt man nicht – es dürfte in der gegebenen Situation freilich auch kaum von Bedeutung gewesen sein[88]. Selbst Euseb verweist in seinem schon eingangs erwähnten Hinweis auf das Neue Testament (h.e. III 25) zunächst auf die „heilige Vierzahl der Evangelien" und die Apostelgeschichte; dann spricht er von den Briefen des Paulus (μετὰ δὲ ταύτην [sc. Apg] τὰς Παύλου καταλεκτέον ἐπιστολάς), doch er sagt dabei nicht, um welche Briefe es sich im einzelnen handelt[89].

V

Die Frage, wie wir uns die Zusammensetzung und den Aufbau der um die Mitte des 2. Jahrhunderts offenbar vorhandenen paulinischen Brief-

ion in *ATR* 52 (1970) 77-91, S. 88 meint, der Autor des Dg verwende die paulinischen Briefe bereits als Heilige Schrift. Das läßt sich freilich nur indirekt aus der intensiven Verwendung der Paulusbriefe erschließen, eine entsprechende explizite Aussage fehlt. Vgl. dazu A. LINDEMANN, *Paulinische Theologie im Brief an Diognet*, in DERS., *Paulus, Apostel und Lehrer* (s. Anm. 49), S. 280-293.

87. Text nach G. KRÜGER (ed.), *Ausgewählte Märtyrerakten*, mit einem Nachtrag von G. RUHBACH (SQS NF, 3), Tübingen, Mohr Siebeck, [4]1965, S. 29.

88. Aus der Bezeichnung des Paulus als eines *vir iustus* ist nur abzuleiten, daß die Angeklagten in der Prozeßsituation die für sie offenbar wichtigsten (allein wichtigen?) Schriften als im juristischen Sinne unbedenklich erweisen wollen. Der Prokonsul erfährt nicht, wer Paulus ist und um welche Art von Briefen es sich handelt; er scheint sich mit der Auskunft, die er erhält, zufrieden zu geben.

89. Es fällt auf, daß er anschließend im Blick auf 1 Joh und 1 Petr erklärt, diese seien als echt anzusehen, und sie gehörten zusammen mit der Apk zu den Homologumena. Das Thema „Echtheit" wird von Euseb im Blick auf die Paulusbriefe ebensowenig erwähnt wie im Blick auf die vier Evangelien und die Apg.

sammlung im einzelnen vorzustellen haben, läßt sich nicht beantworten.
Die Tatsache, daß die erhaltenen frühen Handschriften der Paulusbriefe
noch im 3. Jahrhundert und teilweise darüber hinaus eine unterschiedliche Abfolge dieser Briefe bieten[90], ist jedenfalls ein Beleg dafür, daß es
offenbar keine mit umfassender Autorität ausgestattete Instanz gewesen
war, die den Prozeß der Sammlung einleitete – dies wohl schon deshalb
nicht, weil es eine solche Instanz vermutlich gar nicht gab. Fragen kann
man, ob mit der Sammlung zugleich auch eine Auswahl verbunden war:
Ist es denkbar, daß nur bestimmte Briefe gesammelt, andere dagegen
womöglich gezielt ausgeschieden wurden? Theodor Zahn hat dies ausdrücklich angenommen, wobei er außer auf 1 Kor 5,9 auch auf 2 Petr
3,15, wo ein sonst unbekannter Paulusbrief an jüdische Christen erwähnt
sei, sowie auf Phil 3,1 verweist[91]. Aber der Verfasser des 2 Petr spielt in
3,15 nicht auf einen unbekannten Paulusbrief an, ebensowenig läßt Phil
3,1 einen solchen erkennen[92]. Der in 1 Kor 5,9 erwähnte früher tatsächlich existierende Brief des Paulus nach Korinth dürfte mit hoher Wahrscheinlichkeit wirklich verlorengegangen sein[93], aber doch wohl kaum
aufgrund einer von einer kirchlichen Autorität bewußt getroffenen Entscheidung gegen diesen Brief, sondern eher aus sehr äußerlichen Gründen.

An welchem Ort man mit der Sammlung der Paulusbriefe begann,
läßt sich kaum sagen. Durchaus denkbar ist es, daß diese Anfänge in

90. Umfassend dazu K. ALAND, *Entstehung* (s.o. Anm. 9), vor allem S. 313-350; vgl.
ferner TROBISCH, *Entstehung* (s. Anm. 32), S. 12-62; dazu SCHMID, *Marcion und sein
Apostolos* (s.o. Anm. 82), S. 284-296.

91. TH. ZAHN, *Grundriß der Geschichte des neutestamentlichen Kanons*, Leipzig,
Hinrichs, ²1904, S. 36f. Vgl. DERS., *Geschichte des Neutestamentlichen Kanons. Erster
Band: Das Neue Testament vor Origenes. Zweite Hälfte*, Erlangen - Leipzig, Deichert,
1889, S. 834f. Zahn nimmt an, daß der Autor des 2 Petr (nach seinem Urteil: vermutlich
Petrus selber) die im 1 Clem und bei Polykarp vorausgesetzte kirchliche Sammlung der
Paulusbriefe noch nicht kennt, da er sich ja ausdrücklich auf einen Paulusbrief berufe, der
nicht in jene Sammlung aufgenommen wurde.

92. Aus dem „Bruch" zwischen Phil 3,1 und 3,2 wird oft die Notwendigkeit einer
Teilung des Phil abgeleitet, wobei dann aber nicht selten die Trennung zwischen 3,1a und
3,1b vorgenommen wird. Nach J. GNILKA, *Der Philipperbrief* (HTK, X/3), Freiburg, Herder, ²1976, S. 185 läßt die Aussage von V. 1b „keinen Zweifel daran, daß er sinnvoller-
weise nur als Einleitung der folgenden Warnungen aufgefaßt werden kann", d.h. mit 3,1b
beginne der „Kampfbrief" Phil 3,1b-4,1.8-9. Nach G. BARTH, *Der Brief an die Philippe*
(ZBK.NT, 9), Zürich, Theologischer Verlag, 1979, S. 54f. gehört 3,1 dagegen im ganzen
zur Schlußmahnung des eher freundlich gehaltenen Briefes 1,1-3,1; 4,4-9. M.E. kann Phil
ohne Schwierigkeiten als literarisch einheitlich angesehen werden.

93. Vgl. LINDEMANN, *Erster Korintherbrief* (s.o. Anm 27), S. 129f. Die Anfänge einer
ersten Sammlung der Paulusbriefe brauchen nicht unbedingt in Korinth, sondern können
durchaus in Ephesus zu suchen sein; möglicherweise geht der Verlust des ursprünglich
„ersten" Korintherbriefes des Paulus einfach darauf zurück, daß kein Exemplar dorthin
gelangte. Selbstverständlich kann dies aber auch in Korinth geschehen sein.

Ephesus zu suchen sind[94]; für diese Annahme würde sprechen, daß die oben erwähnten ersten Indizien für das Vorhandensein einer solchen Sammlung (Ignatius und Polykarp) jedenfalls nach Kleinasien weisen, und auch 2 Petr muß ja durchaus nicht in Rom, sondern kann ebenfalls in Kleinasien verfaßt worden sein. Als ein Kriterium für die Aufnahme eines Briefes in die Sammlung sah es Zahn an, daß die betreffenden Briefe des Paulus „nach Form und Inhalt geeignet" waren, „der versammelten Gemeinde wiederholt zu ihrer Erbauung vorgelesen zu werden"[95]. Aber diese Erwägung setzt im Grunde das Vorhandensein einer Institution voraus, die über die entsprechende Eignung der Briefe autoritativ hätte entscheiden können; eine solche Institution aber gab es vermutlich gar nicht, weder in den einzelnen Gemeinden noch gar überörtlich bezogen auf die Kirche als ganze; und als es dann entsprechende Institutionen gab, waren die Paulusbriefsammlungen längst vorhanden. Insofern ist Kurt Aland zuzustimmen: „Die kirchlichen Instanzen des 2. und der folgenden Jahrhunderte vollzogen mit ihrer Festsetzung des Kanons die Entscheidungen *nach*, welche bei den Gemeinden, genauer gesagt bei den einzelnen Gläubigen, vorher vollzogen worden waren. Die verfaßte Kirche als solche hat den Kanon nicht geschaffen, sie hat den geschaffenen Kanon anerkannt"[96].

Lars Hartman vertritt die eingangs bereits erwähnte These, schon Paulus selber habe die Möglichkeit explizit ins Auge gefaßt, auch andere als die im Briefpräskript genannten Adressaten könnten seine Briefe lesen, und für diese These beruft er sich vor allem auf das Präskript des Ersten

---

94. Nach Zahn spricht gegen Ephesus die nach seinem Urteil irrtümliche Lesart ἐν Ἐφέσῳ in dem von ihm als echt angesehenen Epheserbrief. Aber die m.E. textgeschichtlich ursprüngliche Adresse in Eph 1,1 (s.o. S. 334f.) spricht durchaus nicht gegen eine Entstehung der Sammlung in Ephesus; die dortige Gemeinde könnte diesen theologisch sehr ausgearbeiteten Text bewußt als an sich selber gerichtet aufgefaßt und im Zusammenhang der Sammlung der Briefe die persönlichen Bemerkungen gar nicht vermißt haben.

95. ZAHN, *Geschichte I/2* (s. Anm. 92), S. 838.

96. K. ALAND, *Das Problem des neutestamentlichen Kanons*, in E. KÄSEMANN (ed.), *Das Neue Testament als Kanon* (s. Anm. 83), S. 134-158, hier 147 (Hervorhebung im Original gesperrt, der ganze zitierte Text im Original kursiv). Es heißt bei ihm dann weiter: „Weder die Herrenworte noch die Paulusbriefe noch die vier Evangelien erhalten ihre Stellung durch den Spruch irgendeiner kirchlichen Instanz. Die Herrenworte sind Autorität kraft ihrer Herkunft, kraft ihres vollmächtigen Inhalts. Die Paulusbriefe werden von den Gemeinden angenommen und anerkannt, an die sie gerichtet sind … Man hält die Briefe auch nach dem Tod des Paulus in Ehren und ist bemüht, möglichst alle zu besitzen, um die Stimme des Paulus weiter hören zu können. So entsteht das Corpus der Paulusbriefe". Ohne wirkliche Belege vermutet Aland allerdings, die Korintherbriefe seien „erst nach Schwierigkeiten" in Korinth anerkannt worden, die Galaterbrief sei „mindestens bei einem Teil der Empfänger" abgelehnt worden; damit aber schließe man sich „aus dem Kreis der paulinischen Gemeinden aus und wird zu einer Sondergemeinschaft, die anderen Autoritäten folgt" (ebenda).

Korintherbriefs (1,2)[97]. Aber daß die Adresse in 1 Kor 1,2 für eine so weit reichende Annahme ausreicht, scheint mir zweifelhaft zu sein; grundsätzlich wichtig ist aber Hartmans Beobachtung, daß der Beginn jenes Prozesses, der dann zur Sammlung der Paulusbriefe führte, tatsächlich das Urteil voraussetzt, die ursprünglich an bestimmte Adressaten gerichteten und auf deren zum Teil sehr spezifischen Probleme eingehenden Briefe seien auch für andere Leser und damit auch für Christen in späterer Zeit von Bedeutung[98]. Die Sammlung setzte die Vorstellung voraus und verstärkte sie zugleich, daß die Briefe als zeitlose, oder vielleicht richtiger: als „überzeitliche" Dokumente zu verstehen seien. Damit zugleich dürfte dann auch der Prozeß einer „aktualisierenden" Auslegung begonnen haben, insofern nun gefragt werden mußte, was die einstigen beispielsweise auf Philippi oder Korinth bezogenen Aussagen des Paulus nun „heute", mit Blick auf eine ganz andere Gemeinde und ganz andere Verhältnisse, bedeuten könnten.

Eine derartige hermeneutische Reflexion zeigt sich ansatzweise schon im Ersten Clemensbrief, insofern dieser ausdrücklich die zur Zeit des Paulus bestehenden, also längst vergangenen Verhältnisse in Korinth zu der gegenwärtig bestehenden Situation in Beziehung setzt (1 Clem 47,1-4). Es blieb also, wie auch später noch bei Polykarp erkennbar ist, das Bewußtsein durchaus erhalten, daß die Paulusbriefe von Hause aus keineswegs an „die Kirche" als ganze gerichtet gewesen waren. Die römische Kirche am Ende des 1. Jahrhunderts weiß, daß Paulus „euch", also der Kirche von Korinth, einen kritischen Kommentar zu ihrer „Parteienbildung" geschrieben hatte; der Verfasser des 1 Clem unterscheidet dabei bewußt zwischen den damals gegebenen Verhältnissen einerseits und der zwar ähnlichen, aber doch auch anders gearteten gegenwärtigen Entwicklung andererseits, die den jetzigen Brief ja überhaupt erst ausgelöst hatte[99]. Ebenso weiß Polykarp, daß sich Paulus „einst" (τότε) in Philippi aufgehalten und daß er sich brieflich an die Philipper gewandt hatte; wenn er jetzt die Adressaten anredet („ihr"), so unterscheidet er,

---

97. HARTMAN, *Reading* (s. Anm. 27), S. 173 mit Anm. 32; er verweist außerdem auf 2 Kor 1,1 und auf Formulierungen im 2 Thess sowie im Kol.

98. Vgl. *ibid.*, S. 174: „When asking what the text meant we should ask for two intentions of Paul: the one regarding the specific occasion and, secondly, the one related to more general interest. To turn from the author's side of the communication to the recipient's, we should ask for two understandings of a text: the one in the original letter situation and, secondly, the ones where the letter was reread (e.g., Ephesus)".

99. Vgl. 1 Clem 47,4f.: Mit der damaligen Parteineigung (ἡ πρόσκλισις ἐκείνη) habt „ihr" euch geringere Sünde zugezogen (ἥτονα ἁμαρτίαν ὑμῖν προσήνεγκεν) als mit dem, was „ihr" jetzt zu bedenken habt (νυνὶ δὲ κατανοήσατε). Die Angeredeten („ihr") sind die Korinther als Gemeinde; der Autor nimmt gewiß nicht an, es handele sich heute wie damals um dieselben Personen.

wie PolPhil 3,2 zeigt, allerdings sprachlich nicht zwischen der damaligen Gemeinde als einstiger Adressatin der Paulusbriefe und der jetzigen Gemeinde als Leserin dieser Briefe.

Selbst die knappen Beschreibungen der Paulusbriefe im Canon Muratori setzen voraus, daß man sich der ursprünglichen Abfassungsverhältnisse durchaus bewußt war, auch wenn es dort ausdrücklich heißt, Paulus habe seine Briefe an die ganze Kirche in der οἰκουμένη geschrieben[100]. Nils Alstrup Dahl hat gute Gründe für die These genannt, daß das Muratorische Fragment die paulinischen Briefe nicht in einer von ihm vorausgesetzten „kanonischen" Reihenfolge aufzählt, sondern deren chronologische Abfolge zu bieten glaubt[101]. Dem hat Kurt Aland widersprochen unter Hinweis darauf, daß „der Canon Muratori in seiner Aufzählung der Paulusbriefe einer ihm vorliegenden Handschrift folgt"[102]. Aber unabhängig von der Frage, welche dieser beiden Deutungen des Befundes als die richtige anzusehen ist, bestätigt der Befund im Canon Muratori jedenfalls, daß selbst bei einer im wesentlichen unkommentierten, puren Aufzählung der Briefe noch um das Jahr 200 der „historische" Charakter der Paulusbriefe durchaus im Bewußtsein war und noch nicht der Gedanke überwog, die Briefe seien Zeugnisse einer „zeitlosen" Wahrheit.

VI

Diese Anmerkungen leiten bereits über von der rein historischen Fragestellung hin zu dem hermeneutischen Problem, auf das freilich abschließend nur noch skizzenhaft hingewiesen werden soll[103]: Wie sind

100. S. dazu VERHEYDEN, *Canon Muratori* (s. Anm. 4), S. 520-528.

101. N.A. DAHL, *Welche Ordnung der Paulusbriefe wird vom Muratorischen Kanon vorausgesetzt?* (1961), in DERS., *Studies in Ephesians* (s. Anm. 41), S. 147-163, bes. 157: „Zunächst werden, mit kurzer, antihäretischer Inhaltsangabe diejenigen Briefe genannt, die sowohl im NT der Kirche wie in Marcions *Apostolikon* an erster Stelle stehen, wobei die chronologische Folge dieser Briefe betont wird; in der folgenden chronologisch gemeinten Liste sind es nur diese Briefe, die an einem von der kanonischen Reihenfolge abweichenden Platz erscheinen". Dahl nimmt an, der Verfasser des Muratorianum habe „die paulinischen Briefe in der kanonischen Ordnung vorgefunden", weshalb die These, es habe eine Sammlung gegeben, die mit 1 Kor eröffnet und mit Röm abgeschlossen wurde, „aus der Diskussion über die Frühgeschichte der Paulusbriefe überhaupt auszuscheiden" habe. Dahl hält es allerdings für „nicht ausgeschlossen", daß Marcions Apostolikon ein Indiz für eine mit den Korintherbriefen beginnende Sammlung sein könnte, wobei lediglich Gal aus dogmatischen Gründen vorangestellt worden wäre (S. 158 Anm. 35). Vgl. auch DERS., *The Origin of the Earliest Prologues to the Pauline Letters* (1978), in DERS., *Studies in Ephesians* (s.o.), S. 179-209, vor allem 193-199 („Early Editions of Paul").

102. K. ALAND, *Entstehung* (s.o. Anm. 9), S. 302-350, 329. Der Begriff *ordo* in Zeile 50ff. beziehe sich auf die Textanordnung, nicht auf die Chronologie.

103. Vgl. dazu K.-W. NIEBUHR in diesem Band, S. 557-584.

die paulinischen Briefe heute zu lesen? Sind sie von vornherein als Teil einer Sammlung, letztlich also: als Teil des Neuen Testaments im ganzen, aufzufassen, so wie sie uns ja faktisch überkommen sind? Oder ist es hermeneutisch angemessener, von der in den Texten selber ja durchaus bewahrten Ursprungssituation auszugehen und die Briefe tatsächlich primär als Einzeldokumente zu lesen? Im erstgenannten Fall besteht die Gefahr, daß die inhaltlichen Aussagen der einzelnen Briefe unscharf werden und daß man sich dazu ermutigt fühlt, theologisch als womöglich anstößig Geltendes in dem einen Brief sofort von anderen Aussagen des Paulus (oder sogar vom übrigen Neuen Testament im ganzen) her abschwächen oder korrigieren zu sollen[104]. Im zweiten Fall kann es umgekehrt geschehen, daß die Briefe überwiegend oder sogar ausschließlich als historische Dokumente gelesen werden, als Texte einer vergangenen Zeit, die jedenfalls nicht mehr die unsere ist. Mir scheint gerade der Tatbestand von entscheidender Bedeutung zu sein, daß die Paulusbriefe zwar im Rahmen einer Sammlung, dabei aber doch in ihrer ursprünglichen Form als einzelne Briefe Eingang in den kirchlichen Kanon gefunden haben und daß sie offensichtlich nicht – anders als etwa die alttestamentlichen Prophetenbücher[105] – einer womöglich theologisch oder auch nur literarisch einheitlichen Redaktion bzw. „Zensur" unterzogen wurden[106]. Es gibt jedenfalls keine Indizien dafür, daß die Briefe des Paulus in dem Prozeß, der schließlich zu ihrer „Kanonisierung" führte[107], einzeln „überprüft" worden wären. Die Gemeinden scheinen im Gegenteil davon überzeugt gewesen zu sein, daß diese Briefe als solche einen dauernden Wert besitzen – die Entscheidung über ein Ja

104. So ist es ein durchaus nicht unübliches Verfahren, etwa die Aussagen in 1 Thess 2,14-16 oder in Gal 3,19-22 durch Hinweise auf Röm 7,12 oder auch Röm 9-11 (bzw. meist einzelne Aussagen innerhalb dieses langen Textabschnitts) zu „entschärfen".

105. Die alttestamentliche Forschung rechnet hier oft mit „deuteronomistischer" Redaktion; vgl. etwa W.H. SCHMIDT, *Alttestamentlicher Glaube*, Neukirchen-Vluyn, Neukirchener Verlag, 1996, S. 318.

106. Die Entstehung des in seiner vorliegenden Form m.E. tatsächlich sekundär geschaffenen 2 Kor geht nicht auf eine im Zusammenhang der Entstehung der Paulusbriefsammlung tätig werdende „kirchliche Redaktion" zurück; 2 Kor dürfte primär aus praktischen Gründen entstanden sein, um dem m.E. literarisch einheitlichen 1 Kor einen etwa gleich langen weiteren Brief an die Seite zu stellen. Daß man dabei gleichwohl durchaus „kritisch" vorging, zeigen allerdings 2 Kor 8,18.22; vieles spricht dafür, daß hier ursprünglich der Name eines ἀδελφός genannt war, der dann vermutlich im Zusammenhang der Redaktion des 2 Kor gestrichen wurde (vgl. auch 2 Kor 9,3).

107. Der Begriff „Kanonisierung" ist in sich im Grunde schon problematisch, weil der neutestamentliche Kanon jedenfalls in der Alten Kirche niemals von irgendeiner Instanz „beschlossen" wurde; auch der berühmte 39. Osterfestbrief des Athanasius bestätigt nur etwas, was bereits gültig ist. Vgl. dazu und zur Problematik im ganzen D. LÜHRMANN, *Gal 2,9 und die katholischen Briefe. Bemerkungen zum Kanon und zur regula fidei*, in ZNW 72 (1981) 65-87.

oder ein Nein hinsichtlich der kirchlichen Rezeption eines oder mehrerer Briefe hat vermutlich niemals zur Debatte gestanden[108]. Die Zugehörigkeit der Paulusbriefe zum Neuen Testament ist mithin nicht das Ergebnis einer die urchristliche Überlieferung kritisch bewertenden kirchlichen Zensur; vielmehr wurden diese Briefe ihrerseits zum kritischen Maßstab (κανών) für die verbindliche Rezeption anderer Texte bzw. späterer theologischer Positionen. Darin liegt ihr bleibender Wert, und zwar gerade in ihrer ursprünglichen Form als einzelne, durchaus situationsbezogene („kontextuelle") Texte innerhalb einer alle (erhaltenen) Briefe umfassenden Sammlung und dann auch innerhalb des Neuen Testaments bzw. schließlich innerhalb der ganzen christlichen Bibel Alten und Neuen Testaments. Die Kirche im 2. Jahrhundert scheint dies nicht anders gesehen zu haben als es die Kirchen, gleich welcher Konfession, auch heute tun.

An der Rehwiese 38   Andreas LINDEMANN
D-33617 Bielefeld

---

108. Ein indirekter Beleg dafür ist die Art der antipaulinischen Polemik des gesetzestreuen Judenchristentums des 2. und 3. Jahrh., wie sie sich vor allem in den Quellenschriften der Pseudo-Clementinen niedergeschlagen hat, aber auch schon die (direkte oder indirekte) Pauluskritik des neutestamentlichen Jak. Diese Kritik konnte offensichtlich nicht in offener Form vorgetragen werden, weil Paulus bereits als gleichsam „sakrosankt" angesehen wurde; vgl. LINDEMANN, *Paulus im ältesten Christentum* (s. Anm. 32), S. 104-109 und 240-252, ferner G. LÜDEMANN, *Paulus, der Heidenapostel. Band II. Antipaulinismus im frühen Christentum* (FRLANT, 130), Göttingen, Vandenhoeck & Ruprecht, 1983, S. 228-257.

JESUS TRADITIONS AND GOSPELS IN JUSTIN MARTYR
AND IRENAEUS

The status of Jesus traditions and of the "canonical" Gospels gradually grew in the course of the second century. At the beginning of the century there was widespread respect for "words of the Lord" and for "*the* Gospel" (whether oral or written) in which Jesus traditions were embedded. By the end of the century the early church seemed to be within a whisker of accepting a "canon" of four written gospels, no more no less.

I do not intend to discuss all the developments and factors which led to the sea change which took place during the second century. In order to do so I would need to offer many hostages to fortune, for at crucial points the evidence is disputed, particularly with reference to the first half of the second century. For example, although the Didache has usually been dated to the first decades of the second century, it is now generally accepted that it contains several layers of traditions, the dating of which is problematic. A major challenge has been mounted to the consensus that Ignatius wrote seven letters in the early years of the second century. I do not think the challenge is likely to be successful, but discussion of it would be a distraction from my primary task. And do we know the date of 2 Clement?

I shall focus my attention on two second century giants whose substantial surviving writings can be dated with some confidence, Justin Martyr and Irenaeus. There is general agreement that their writings are important for my topic – and for many others. It will be my contention that some of their evidence for the status and use of Jesus traditions and of Gospels has been misconstrued or overlooked in recent discussion. All too often their writings have been subject to what I call "cherry picking": tasty morsels have been plucked in order to garnish a grand theory, often at the expense of a close reading of the texts. As we shall see, there has been no shortage of grand theories.

I shall not attempt to discuss in any detail the text form or the source of the Jesus traditions. It is important to try to establish whether quoted Jesus traditions are from this Gospel or that, from oral or from written sources, from a pre- or a post-synoptic harmony. These questions have received plenty of scholarly attention. I shall not avoid these fascinating issues, but in line with the theme of this Colloquium, I shall concentrate on a different, somewhat neglected set of questions. What *status* do Justin and Irenaeus give to Jesus traditions and to the Gospels? Are they merely respected traditions? Are they cited as authoritative texts? Are they considered to be Scripture? Do they have the same standing in the church as the Old Testament writings? How close are we to the later emergence of the concept of a canon, an agreed list of authoritative writings which cannot be altered?

I. JUSTIN MARTYR

Justin's comments on the Septuagint and the alleged Jewish deletions and modifications to the text of what Justin regards as Scripture have often been noted[1]. The hermeneutical principles which underly Justin's thorough Christianization of the Old Testament have been discussed less frequently, but they are of considerable importance for Christian theology. However the theme of this Colloquium encourages us to turn our attention elsewhere.

Where are we to place Justin in the story of the eventual emergence of the New Testament canon? Is he, as C.H. Cosgrove has claimed, a reactionary figure who stands four square against second century trends towards regarding apostolic writings as canon[2]? Can we accept Cosgrove's claim that Justin even devalues the authority of the emerging New Testament canon, limiting himself to the sayings of Jesus, with misgivings about the emerging canonical status of the Gospels[3]? Or does Justin have a very high regard for the sayings of Jesus and the Gospels and consider them to be as authoritative as the Old Testament writings?

1. We now have available Miroslav MARCOVICH's much-needed critical editions of the Greek text, *Iustini Martyris Apologiae pro Christianis* (Patristische Texte und Studien, 38), Berlin, De Gruyter, 1994, and *Iustini Martyris Dialogus cum Tryphone* (Patristische Texte und Studien, 47), Berlin, De Gruyter, 1997. Marcovich regularly proposes additions and corrections to the Codex Parisinus, the one surviving manuscript of any importance; this huge codex is dated 11 September 1363. Although Marcovich's own editorial proposals may be a touch too radical for some, they are indicated very clearly in his printed text and can be readily ignored if necessary; details of the editorial emendments made by his predecessors are also indicated. Marcovich's editions provide a solid platform for fresh study of these fascinating writings; nonetheless they remind us that the text of Justin's writings is in a parlous state.

2. C.H. COSGROVE, *Justin Martyr and the Emerging Christian Canon. Observations on the Purpose and Destination of the Dialogue with Trypho*, in *VigChr* 36 (1982) 209-232. There are several weaknesses in Cosgrove's case, the most important of which is his failure to consider the evidence of Justin's Apologies.

3. *Ibid.*, pp. 226-227.

At first sight Justin's writings seem to offer limited evidence for our quest, for only once does he refer to an individual New Testament writing by name[4]. However, as in the interpretation of any writing, whether ancient or modern, genre and context must not be ignored. Justin's Apologies and his Dialogue with Trypho are apologetic writings, with two very different audiences in view. Perhaps Justin does hope that his Apologies will win over the Emperor Marcus Aurelius and the leading Gentile opinion formers of his day to the Christian "philosophy". Perhaps he does hope that Trypho and other Jewish teachers will acknowledge that Jesus is the Messiah promised in Scripture. In my view, however, it is more likely that Justin's extant writings were all intended to provide Christian members of his philosophical school in Rome with apologetic material which they could use in their encounters with both Jews and Gentiles.

In either case, reference to the names of the authors of the New Testament writings would not have been appopriate. As J.B. Lightfoot noted, "In works like these, addressed to Heathens and Jews, who attributed no authority to the writings of Apostles and Evangelists, and for whom the names of the writers would have no meaning, we are not surprised that he refers to those writings for the most part anonymously and with reserve"[5].

Justin's writings provide us with plenty of evidence to assess, though that task is not easy[6]. The First Apology was written very shortly after 150 AD, the Dialogue with Trypho only a few years later in the same decade. However it is unwise to try to trace development in Justin's thinking. Some sections of the Dialogue may well have been written before the Apology and inserted into that long rather rambling account of Justin's conversations with Trypho[7].

---

4. The Revelation of John (Dialogue 81,4).

5. *Essays on the Work Entitled Supernatural Religion*, London, 1893, p. 33. I owe this reference to C.E. HILL, *Justin and the New Testament Writings*, in E.A. LIVINGSTONE, (ed.), *Studia Patristica*, 30, Leuven, Peeters, 1997, p. 43.

6. E.F. OSBORN, *Justin Martyr*, Tübingen, Mohr, 1973, p. 120 notes that in 1877 B.L. Gildersleeve claimed that "the battle over the question whether Justin's Memoirs of the Apostles are identical with our canonical gospels has lasted nearly a century. Begun by Stroth in 1777, it is safe to say that the fight is going on at this very moment in the powder magazine of some theological review".

7. For discussion of Justin's possible use of earlier sources or his own earlier compositions, see O. SKARSAUNE, *The Proof from Prophecy. A Study in Justin Martyr's Proof-Text Tradition: Text-Type, Provenance, Theological Profile* (SNT, 56), Leiden, Brill, 1987, and Luise ABRAMOWSKI, *Die "Erinnerungen der Apostel" bei Justin*, in P. STUHLMACHER (ed.), *Das Evangelium und die Evangelien*, Tübingen, Mohr, 1983, pp. 341-354.

1. *Jesus Traditions: "The Words of the Saviour" (Dialogue 8,2)*

The opening chapters of the First Apology underline the importance Justin attaches to the teachings of Christ and to their careful transmission (4,7; 6,2; 8,3). In all three passages Justin emphasizes that Christians teach (or hand over, παραδίδωμι) what they have been taught by Christ whom they "worship and adore" along with "the most true God" (6,1). The teachings of Christ are clearly authoritative, but nothing further is said about their status in these chapters.

At the climax of the Apology, however, three related passages leave little doubt that the carefully transmitted traditions Justin refers to include the *written* memoirs of the apostles. The prayer following the baptism of "the one who has been illuminated" asks that Christians show by their deeds that they are "good citizens and guardians of what has been commanded" (65,5 ἐντέλλομαι). Only those who "live as Christ handed down" (66,1 παραδίδωμι) are permitted to participate in the baptismal eucharist. The food "eucharistized" through "the word of prayer" that is from Jesus Christ is life-giving (66,2). Then follows a much discussed passage to which we shall return: "For in the memoirs composed by them, called Gospels, *the apostles handed down what they had been commanded*: that Jesus took bread and having given thanks said: ... This is my body ...". (66,3 παρέδωκαν ἐντετάλθαι αὐτοῖς). Justin is adamant that traditions of the sayings and actions of Jesus have been transmitted carefully in the written memoirs by the apostles, and are handed on and carried out by his fellow Christians. Their ultimate source is Jesus Christ himself. Their authoritative status could hardly be underlined more firmly, even though they are not referred to as "Scripture".

In chapter 14 of the Apology Justin provides an important full introduction to no fewer than twenty-six sayings of Jesus organised topically into ten groups[8]. Christians "pray for their enemies" and try to persuade those who hate them unjustly "to live according to the good suggestions of Christ" (14,4). Justin then states that he is about to cite some of the teachings given by Christ. He makes two comments on their character.

(a) They are "short and concise sayings" (βραχεῖς δὲ καὶ σύντομοι παρ' αὐτοῦ λόγοι, 14,5), for Christ was no sophist. Justin assumes that his addressees will be familiar with long-winded sophists and thus be impressed by the pithy sayings of Jesus. In an effort to impress Trypho,

---

8. A.J. BELLINZONI, *The Sayings of Jesus in the Writings of Justin Martyr* (SNT, 17), Leiden, Brill, 1967, pp. 49-100, examines in detail the text form and source of these sayings. However, he fails to comment on Justin's important introductory remarks in chapter 14.

the sayings of Jesus are also said to be "short" (βραχέα λόγια) at Dialogue 18,1.

(b) Justin claims that the "commandments" (14,4 δογμάτα) which are about to be quoted are the word of Christ, and "his word was the power of God" (14,5 δύναμις θεοῦ ὁ λόγος αὐτοῦ ἦν). This introductory comment is clearly intended to establish the importance and authoritative status of the twenty-six sayings of Jesus which follow in chapters 15-17.

Justin himself opens each set of sayings by announcing its theme; the sayings are then introduced with simple phrases in the aorist tense: "he said", "he taught", "he commanded". For example, "Concerning chastity, he said this ..."; this introduction is followed by four sayings linked only by καί (15,1-4). The fourth set of sayings is introduced by Justin as follows: "And that we should share with the needy ... he said these things ..."; eight sayings linked only twice with καί are juxtaposed (15,10-17).

This pattern is repeated almost identically ten times over. The penultimate paragraph is the single exception (17,1-2). Here Justin insists that Christians pay taxes "as we have been taught by him" and then sets out a much abbreviated version of the pronouncement story concerning payment of tribute to Caesar, Mark 12,13-17 and parallels.

The ten sets of Jesus traditions are linked to their present context very loosely. With the partial exception of Dialogue 35,3, where Justin cites one set of four sayings concerning false teachers and false prophets, there are no comparable passages in his writings. These ten sets of sayings of Jesus were almost certainly collected and arranged by Justin himself for catechetical purposes in his school in Rome. Their status is underlined by Justin's introduction of them as "the power of God" and by Justin's repeated claim that his fellow-Christians transmit and live by the sayings of Jesus which have been carefully handed on to them. For our present purposes, we may leave open whether the twenty six sayings of Jesus quoted in chapters 15-17 have been taken from oral or from written sources.

From the First Apology we turn to the Dialogue. Here Justin includes explicit statements concerning the sayings of Jesus in his account of his conversion to Christianity which he dubs "philosophy safe and simple" (8,1). He tells his Jewish opponent Trypho that at the time of his conversion he experienced a passionate desire for the prophets, and for those men who are the friends of Christ, presumably the apostles. He then expresses the hope that all people should be as keen as he is not to distance themselves from the Saviour's words (μὴ ἀφίστασθαι τῶν τοῦ σωτη-ρος λόγων), for they evoke *profound awe* (δέος). Their innate power puts to shame those who turn aside from the right way, while pleasant rest (ἀνάπαυσις) comes to those who carry them out (8,2). Here a version of the "two ways" ethical tradition is linked to the effect the dynamic sayings of Jesus have.

In his vigorous reply Trypho claims that in his conversion to Christianity Justin has been led astray by false statements and has followed men who are not at all worthy. From the context the latter can only be "the friends of Christ", i.e. the apostles. Trypho soon concedes that he has taken some trouble to *read* the admirable and great commands of Christ "in the so-called Gospel" (10,2), a point Justin repeats at 18,1. At Dialogue 88,3, shortly before the 13 references to "the memoirs of the apostles" in chapters 100-107, Justin states that "the apostles of this our Christ" have *written* that the Spirit fluttered down on Jesus at his baptism like a dove. This is clearly a reference to at least two apostles' writings.

So long before the 13 references in the Dialogue to "the memoirs of the apostles" are reached in chapters 100-107, the reader can hardly avoid the conclusion that the powerful words of the Saviour may be *read* in the writings of the apostles, the friends of Christ.

This key point emerges again in a particularly dramatic passage in Dialogue 113 and 114. Justin states that the words of Jesus are the sharp knives by which Gentile Christians in his own day have experienced the "second circumcision" (of their hearts). The first physical circumcision is for Jews. The second circumcision "which circumcises us from idolatry, and in fact all vice" is carried out by "by the words spoken *by the apostles* of the Corner Stone" (Dialogue 113,6-7; 114,4). Given the preceding references to reading and writing, we can be all but certain that written traditions are in mind here. The authoritative status of those traditions could hardly be underlined more strongly.

How does Justin understand the relationship of the sayings of Jesus transmitted through the writings of the apostles to Scripture? In First Apology 61,3 sayings of Jesus are set alongside cited words of Isaiah with the clear implication that they have the same status. The words of Christ, "Unless you are born again …" are followed almost immediately by a version of Isa 1,16-20, "Thus spoke Isaiah the prophet" (61,4-8). The introductory formulae are almost identical: "Christ said", and "Isaiah the prophet thus spoke".

In the next chapter the burning bush theophany is Christianized: "our Christ" converses with Moses in the form of fire out of the bush and said, "Unloose your sandals and come near and hear" (62,3). This is followed by a citation of Isa 1,3, introduced as words of the prophetic Spirit through Isaiah the prophet (63,1). Justin then cites two sayings of Jesus, introduced as "Jesus Christ said" and "Our Lord himself said" (63,3-5).

The first readers of the Apology are encouraged to conclude that sayings of Jesus have the same status as the words of Isaiah, though they are left to draw this conclusion for themselves. Justin makes this key point more explicitly in the Dialogue. With a rather quaint rhetorical touch Justin says to his Jewish opponent Trypho, "Since you have read what our Saviour taught, as you have yourself acknowledged, I think I have not acted in an unseemly fashion by adding some short sayings of his (Christ's) to those found in the prophets" (18,1). The immediate context is significant. In the preceding chapter three passages from Isaiah are linked (52,5; 3,9-11; 5,18-20) as a preface to three sayings of Jesus. The first of the latter sayings is a version of Matt 21,13, words of Jesus addressed to the money-changers in the temple. Jesus refers to Jer 7,11 with the words, "it is written: 'My house is a house of prayer, but you have made it a den of robbers'". Justin's version is much closer to Matt 21,13 than to the LXX (Dialogue 17,3), so in all probability Justin has used Matthew's Gospel at this point.

There is a further example of the use of γέγραπται in a quotation from Matthew at Dialogue 78,1. Here the quotation of Micah 5,2 at Matt 2,5 is referred to. One might have expected Justin to have imitated this New Testament usage in his own introductions to some of the sayings of Jesus he cites, thus placing them on all fours with the Old Testament passages he quotes so frequently. However, although Justin is familiar with the term ἡ γραφή for Scripture (e.g. Dialogue 56,12.17), he never uses γέγραπται to introduce either an OT quotation or a saying of Jesus as Scripture[9].

Nonetheless it would be a grave mistake to claim that the sayings of Jesus are in any way inferior to Scripture. This emerges very clearly from Dialogue 119,6. "For as he [Abraham] believed the voice of God, and it was imputed to him for righteousness, in like manner we, having believed God's voice spoken through the apostles of Christ, and preached to us through the prophets, have renounced even to death all the things of the world". Charles Hill comments appropriately: "Here it

9. H. VON CAMPENHAUSEN, *The Formation of the Christian Bible*, Philadelphia, Fortress, 1972, p. 170, notes that in the "later anti-Jewish Dialogue" Justin introduces a dominical saying with the words "it is written", and suggests cautiously that this is Justin's way of referring to texts which are to be acknowledged as authentic and normative. I do not think that the three uses of γέγραπται in question (49,5; 100,1; 105,6) bear this weight.

is God's own 'voice' which has spoken 'through' the apostles of Christ, and here Justin explicitly and boldly places this 'inspiration' on a par with that of the Old Testament prophets"[10].

Justin attaches considerable significance to the teachings of Christ. Their authority and power is clear. Justin's readers are left in no doubt that the sayings of Jesus have the same standing as the words of the prophets. Justin returns to this point in the closing pages of the Dialogue. With an ironical touch he rounds on Trypho: "If the teaching (διδάγματα) of the prophets *and of Christ* disquiet you, it is better for you to follow God rather than your unintelligent and blind teachers" (134,1). As we have noted above, in several passages Justin notes that "the words of the Saviour" have been conveyed in the writings of the apostles. So it is appropriate that we should now consider the status Justin attaches to "the memoirs of the apostles".

2. *The Gospels: "The Memoirs of the Apostles" (First Apology 66,3)*

At the climax of the First Apology Justin refers twice to "the memoirs of the apostles" (τὰ ἀπομνημονεύματα τῶν ἀποστόλων, 66,3; 67,3) in contexts which underline their importance; the phrase is used a further 13 times in one section of the Dialogue (chs. 100-117).

In his account of the origin and significance of the Christian eucharist, Justin quotes Jesus' words of institution as they are recorded in the memoirs written by the apostles "which are called Gospels" (First Apology 66,3 ἃ καλεῖται Εὐαγγέλια). The status of the memoirs could hardly be clearer. But is the explanatory reference to the Gospels a later addition to the text? This is the only time Justin refers to the noun εὐαγγέλιον in the Apologies, so it is not surprising that some scholars have claimed that the clause is a later gloss. We cannot ignore the fact that this is the first time the plural "Gospels" is used in early Christian writings. Even a generation after Justin, Irenaeus only rarely used the phrase "Gospels" in the plural; he much preferred "the Gospel", or "the Gospel according to ..."[11].

On the other hand, Justin is in the habit of adding explanatory phrases or clauses, especially (as here) when his putative readers may have been baffled by his terminology[12]. So, with this one exception, Justin may have felt that it was quite unnecessary to explain that "the memoirs of

---

10. HILL, *Justin and the New Testament Writings* (n. 5), p. 48.

11. See A. BENOIT, *Saint Irénée. Introduction à l'étude de sa théologie*, Paris, Presses Universitaires de France, 1960, pp. 103-150.

12. See further ABRAMOWSKI, *Die "Erinnerungen"* (n. 7), p. 323. First Apology 65,1; 65,5 and Dialogue 10,2 are noted as parallels to this explanatory clause.

the apostles" were "Gospels". A decision is difficult, but I have already noted plenty of evidence (and more will follow) to establish that the "memoirs" were the writings which became known as "the Gospels".

The second and final reference in the First Apology to the memoirs of the apostles occurs in Justin's account of what takes place in his own day in the Sunday gathering of Christians. "The memoirs of the apostles or the writings of the prophets are read, as long as time permits" (67,3 μέχρις ἐγχωρεῖ). This is the earliest extant reference to the reading of "the Gospels" in the context of Christian worship. The reading is followed by an exposition given by "the Ruler" (ὁ προεστώς). There is no lectionary; the only constraint on the length of the passage read is the time available. The "memoirs of the apostles" are considered to be of equal importance to "the writings of the prophets". Indeed they may even be given a measure of precedence by being referred to before the prophets[13]. The liturgical setting provides further evidence that the status of the memoirs was very high indeed.

How many Gospels does Justin know? Justin uses the noun εὐαγγέλιον twice in the singular in the Dialogue. At 10,2 Trypho is allowed to express admiration for the precepts of Christ recorded "in the so-called Gospel" (ἐν τῷ λεγομένῳ Εὐαγγελίῳ); he has even taken the trouble to read them! Justin introduces his version of Matt 11,27 = Luke 10,22 with "it is written in the Gospel, saying …" (100,2). In both cases, as in several other early Christian writings, the singular is used to refer to the "one Gospel" in which sayings of Jesus are written.

The phrase "the memoirs of the apostles" could be taken to refer to the "one Gospel", but this is most unlikely. We have already noted the explanatory clause in the First Apology 66,3, "the memoirs which are called Gospels" and the important comment at Dialogue 88,3: "*the apostles* of this our Christ" have *written* that the Spirit fluttered down on Jesus at his baptism like a dove.

Confirmation that in his references to "the memoirs of the apostles" Justin has in mind more than one written Gospel is provided by two of the thirteen references to the memoirs in the Dialogue. At 103,8 an explanatory clause follows a reference to the memoirs: "which, I say, were composed by his apostles and those who followed them". This comment on the composition of the memoirs implies that they were written by

---

13. Although it has sometimes been suggested that the prophets are Christian prophets, this is unlikely given Justin's repeated references to and respect for the Old Testament prophets. The possibility of choice between a reading from the Gospels *or* (ἤ) a reading from the prophets is puzzling. Since this is out of line with later liturgical practice, the text is unlikely to be faulty.

more than one apostle, and more than one follower of an apostle, i.e. Justin accepts at least four Gospels, though unlike Irenaeus, he does not name them or discuss their differences[14]. It is a natural, but not a necessary inference that Justin has in mind Gospels written by the apostles Matthew and John, and by followers of the apostles, Mark and Luke. However, caution is necessary. As we shall see in a moment, it is possible that Justin considered Mark's Gospel to be one of the memoirs of the apostles, i.e. to stem from Peter; and we cannot be confident that Justin had John's Gospel in mind when he penned the phrase "memoirs composed by his apostles and those who followed them".

Dialogue 106,3 is more problematic: "We are told that he (Christ) changed the name of one of the apostles to Peter, and it is written in his memoirs (ἐν τοῖς ἀπομνημονεύμασιν αὐτοῦ) that this took place ...". Whose memoirs are referred to here? If we take without emendation the text of the sole witness, the fourteenth century Parisinus codex, there are two possibilities. The memoirs could be Christ's or Peter's. Justin does not refer elsewhere to the memoirs of one individual; only once does he ever name the author of any earlier Christian writing (the Revelation of John, Dialogue 81,4). Nonetheless both Zahn and Harnack interpreted this sentence as a reference to Peter's memoirs, i.e. to Mark's Gospel, as does Luise Abramowski[15]. Miroslav Marcovich, however, is unimpressed, and proposes that "of the apostles" (τῶν ἀποστόλων) should be added to the text at this point; this would bring it into line with the phrase used in the next sentence (106,4): "in the memoirs *of his apostles*", i.e. Christ's apostles. An influential earlier editor of Justin's writings, J.C.Th. von Otto (1847), proposed a similar emendment.

A decision is difficult, especially when we recall the parlous state of the Parisinus codex. Justin's repeated use of the phrase "memoirs of the apostles" does suggest that emendation may be appropriate. However, the more difficult reading of the Parisinus codex is undoubtedly preferable. It is the context which confirms that Justin is here referring to Peter's memoirs, i.e. Mark's Gospel. In the same very complex sentence in which he refers to the change of Peter's name, Justin refers to the change of names of the sons of Zebedee to "Boanerges, which is sons of thunder" (106,3), a phrase found in Mark 3,17, but not in the parallel passages in Matthew and Luke.

---

14. OSBORN, *Justin Martyr* (n. 6), seems to have missed this important passage. He notes that τὰ ἀπομνημονεύματα may have a singular meaning. "If plurality of authorship were important, some further description of the apostles and their writings could be expected" (p. 124).

15. ABRAMOWSKI, *Die "Erinnerungen"* (n. 7), pp. 334-335.

There is a strong cumulative argument for Justin's acceptance of at least four Gospels. Although the Gospels are not named individually, there is no doubt that Justin used Matthew's and Luke's Gospels extensively, and Mark to a more limited extent. But what about John's Gospel? This is a controversial question which can only be referred to briefly here[16]. There is only one quotation to be considered, First Apology 61,4-5: "Christ also said: 'Unless you are born again, you will not enter the kingdom of heaven'; for it is clear to all that 'it is impossible for those who have once been born to enter into their mothers' wombs'"[17]. This is a free rendering of John 3,4-5, not out of line with the way Jesus traditions are quoted elsewhere in Justin's writings[18]. The phrase "kingdom of heaven" (as in the similar tradition at Matt 18,3) is found in several manuscripts of John 3,3 (including the first hand of Sinaiticus) as well as in numerous Patristic witnesses[19]. Justin may have known the text of John 3,3 in this form, or he may have harmonised John's and Matthew's phraseology, as others certainly did.

In addition to this free quotation, there are numerous allusions to passages in the Fourth Gospel, to say nothing of the probability that Justin knew and developed the evangelist's Logos doctrine[20]. In 1943 J.N. Sanders noted 23 possible allusions to John's Gospel; others have compiled their own similar lists[21] There is a strong cumulative case, though this raises two obvious problems. The more clearly one discerns the influence of John's Gospel, the more difficult it is to explain why Justin quotes it only once. And as we noted above, Justin refers to the sayings

---

16. For bibliography see J.W. PRYOR, *Justin Martyr and the Fourth Gospel*, in *The Second Century* 9 (1992) 153-169, esp. p. 153 n. 1.

17. Καὶ γὰρ ὁ Χριστὸς εἶπεν· "Ἂν μὴ ἀναγεννηθῆτε, οὐ μὴ εἰσέλθητε εἰς τὴν Βασιλείαν τῶν οὐρανῶν. Ὅτι δὲ καὶ ἀδύνατον εἰς τὰς μήτρας τῶν τεκουσῶν τοὺς ἅπαξ γεννωμένους ἐμβῆναι, φανερὸν πᾶσίν ἐστι.

18. See PRYOR's full discussion, with good bibliography, *Justin Martyr* (n. 16), p. 163-166. Pryor accepts that First Apology 61,4-5 stems from John 3,3-5, but "it is not a case of direct borrowing by Justin himself, for the saying of Jesus does bear the marks of having been changed under the influence of Matthew 18,3" (166). OSBORN, *Justin Martyr* (n. 6), p. 138, notes that Justin's theology is not openly derived from the Fourth Gospel. "The influence is shown on particular points and not on the shape of the whole".

19. For details see esp. A. HUCK & H. GREEVEN (eds.), *Synopse der drei ersten Evangelien*, Tübingen, Mohr, 1981, *ad. loc.*

20. See M.J. EDWARDS, *Justin's Logos and the Word of God*, in *Journal of Early Christian Studies* 3 (1995) 261-280. Edwards claims that the roots of Justin's Logos are in the Biblical tradition. Justin's acquaintance with the Fourth Gospel is left open.

21. J.N. SANDERS, *The Fourth Gospel in the Early Church*, Cambridge, CUP, 1943, pp 27-32. OSBORN, *Justin Martyr* (n. 6), p. 137, lists some twenty "coincidences of thought and expression". PRYOR, *Justin Martyr* (n. 16), pp. 158-159, adds some further examples of allusions to Sanders's list, but notes that some are more convincing than others.

of Jesus as "short and concise", hardly a natural way to refer to Jesus traditions in John's Gospel.

J.W. Pryor has recently argued that while Justin knows the Fourth Gospel, there is no evidence that he includes it among "the memoirs of the apostles". I do not think we can rule out so firmly the possibility that Justin's reference to memoirs written by "apostles and those who followed them" includes the Fourth Gospel. I prefer to leave this as an open question.

While Justin does know a handful of traditions which did not find their way into the canonical Gospels[22], there is no evidence that he knew or used an apocryphal Gospel[23]. Did he know or compose a harmony of several Gospels? Helmut Koester has recently claimed that the sayings Justin included in his catechism were already harmonized in his *Vorlage*. In composing this source, Justin or his "school" did not intend to construct a catechism, but was composing the *one* inclusive new Gospel which would make its predecessors, Matthew and Luke (and possibly Mark), obsolete[24]. Although Koester's theory has won some support[25], the limited evidence he cites can be explained more plausibly along other lines. It is much more likely that sayings of Jesus from the synoptic Gospels were harmonized for inclusion in the topically organized sets of sayings mentioned above. While some of Justin's harmonized traditions do seem to have been used in his pupil Tatian's more thoroughgoing harmony[26], there is no evidence to support the view that Justin intended to *replace* the synoptic Gospels. As we have seen, Justin's own comments confirm that he had a very high regard for Gospels "written by the apostles and their followers" (Dialogue 103,8). So his *preference* for one single harmonized Gospel is inherently unlikely. There is no reason at all why Justin should not have composed harmo-

22. The most notable are the references to the birth of Jesus in a cave (Dialogue 78,5); to the fire kindled at the baptism of Jesus (Dialogue 88,3); and to an agraphon at Dialogue 47,5: Our Lord Jesus Christ said: "In whatsoever I overtake you, in that I will also judge you." On the latter, see A.J. BELLINZONI, *The Source of the Agraphon in Justin's Dialogue with Trypho 47,5*, in *VigChr* 17 (1963) 65-70.

23. See especially OSBORN, *Justin Martyr* (n. 6), pp. 129-130; similarly, T.K. HECKEL, *Vom Evangelium des Markus zum viergestaltigen Evangelium*, Tübingen, Mohr, 1999, p. 326.

24. H. KOESTER, *The Text of the Synoptic Gospels*, in W.L. PETERSEN (ed.), *Gospel Traditions in The Second Century*, Notre Dame, IN, University of Notre Dame Press, 1989, pp. 28-33.

25. A.J. BELLINZONI, *The Gospel of Matthew in the Second Century*, in *The Second Century* 9 (1992) 197-258, esp. pp. 239-242. MARCOVICH (ed.), *Iustini Martyris Apologiae* (n. 1), p. 29, refers approvingly to Koester's theory, but does not discuss it.

26. See W.L. PETERSEN, *Textual Evidence of Tatian's Dependence upon Justin's AΠOMNHMONEYMATA*, in *NTS* 36 (1990) 512-534.

nized collections of sayings of Jesus for catechetical purposes and have used them alongside his use of written Gospels. Indeed, in my view, he almost certainly did just that.

Justin's high regard for *written* Gospels should by now be clear. Two considerations provide further support. (a) In several passages Justin refers to "reading". I have already noted that Justin's opponent Trypho is twice said to have *read* appreciatively the sayings of Jesus "in the Gospel" (Dialogue 10,2; 18,1). In the Second Apology Justin's opponent Crescens is accused of "running us down without having *read* the teachings of Christ … or if he has *read* them, he has not understood them …". In his own summary of Luke 24,25-6 and 44-6 and Acts 1,8-9 Justin notes that the risen Jesus "taught the disciples to *read* the prophecies in which all these things were predicted as coming to pass …" (I Apology 54,12 καὶ ταῖς προφητείαις ἐντυχεῖν)[27]. Luke's narrative implies oral teaching – indeed it would have been difficult to *read* scrolls on the road to Emmaus. At this point, as in numerous other passages, Justin's narrative is very "bookish".

(b) But what of the term "memoirs" (ἀπομνημονεύματα)? Does this square with the above observations concerning the "bookish" character of Justin's writings? Although the term can refer to mere "notes", it has now been established by Niels Hyldahl that in Justin's writings the term has clear literary connotations. Hyldahl quotes Martin Dibelius approvingly: "An apologetic tendency is operative which is lifting up Christendom into the region of culture. By means of the title 'Memoirs' the Gospel books would be classified as literature proper". Hyldahl notes that Socrates has such a distinctive place in Justin's writings that it was natural for him to allude to Xenophon's *Memorabilia* concerning Socrates in his choice of the term ἀπομνημονεύματα[28].

While it is easy to see why Justin would want to underline the literary credentials of the Gospels for apologetic purposes, we need not conclude that he was exaggerating his case. I have recently argued that the Oxyrhynchus papyri published in 1997 and 1998 suggest that by the second half of the second century, much earlier than has been usually assumed, the literary qualities of the Gospels and their authoritative status for the life and faith of the Church were widely recognized. The often-repeated claim that the Gospels were considered at first to be utilitarian

27. Justin uses ἐντυγχάνω as "read" in a number of passages; see, for example, First Apology 14,1; 26,8; 42,1; 44,12.13; 45,6; Second Apology 3,6.8; 15,3.

28. N. HYLDAHL, *Hegesipps Hypomnemata*, in *ST* 14 (1960) 70-113. The quotation from M. Dibelius is from his *From Tradition to Gospels*, London, 1934, p. 40. See especially ABRAMOWSKI's full discussion in *Die "Erinnerungen"* (n. 7).

handbooks written, by and large, in a "reformed documentary" style now needs to be modified, and we need to remember that we do have a handful of second-century codices with literary texts[29].

For Justin "the words of the Saviour" were transmitted by the apostles in written "upmarket" memoirs which were known as Gospels, though of course he may well have known sayings of Jesus in other written or oral forms. A close reading of all the evidence confirms the high regard in which Justin held both the sayings of Jesus and the "memoirs of the apostles". While it is true that Justin does not refer explicitly either to the sayings or to the memoirs as "Scripture", he comes within a whisker of doing so. Like the "Scriptural" prophets, the "memoirs" are read at length and expounded in the liturgical Sunday gatherings of Christians.

II. IRENAEUS

Irenaeus wrote his *Adversus Haereses* about 180 AD, barely a generation after Justin composed his Apologies and Dialogue. Irenaeus knows Justin's writings[30], and may even have met him in Rome. Although both writers hold the Gospels and especially the words of Jesus in high regard, there are important differences. Whereas Justin made limited use of John's Gospel, Irenaeus has no hesitation in accepting its authority. Indeed it is arguable that this Gospel influenced Irenaeus's theological thought more deeply than any other writing.

Justin seems to have known four Gospels, though he never names any of the evangelists and in only one passage does he show even the slightest interest in the plurality of the Gospels[31]. Irenaeus is more specific: two Gospels (Matthew and John) were written by named apostles or disciples, and two (Mark and Luke) by their followers (*Adv. Haer.* III.10.1; 10.6; 11.1). His lengthy and sophisticated defence of the fourfold Gospel takes us far beyond Justin. His line of argument strongly suggests that he is not making a case for a recent innovation, but underpinning what he and others had long accepted, i.e. that the church had been given one Gospel in fourfold form – four authoritative writings, no more, no less.

29. See G. N. STANTON, *The Early Reception of Matthew's Gospel*, in D.E. AUNE (ed.), *The Gospel of Matthew in Current Study*, Grand Rapids, MI, Eerdmans, 2001, pp. 42-61.

30. The extent of this knowledge merits further investigation. For discussion of the similar use of Matt 7,15 by Justin and Irenaeus, see D.J. BINGHAM, *Irenaeus's Use of Matthew's Gospel in Adversus Haereses* (Traditio Exegetica Graeca, 9), Leuven, Peeters, 1998, pp. 27-32.

31. Dialogue 103,8. See above, pp. 360-363.

Both writers give the same status to the Gospels as they do to the Old Testament writings. Although Justin is familiar with the term ἡ γραφή for Scripture (e.g. Dialogue 56,12.17), he never uses this term to refer to a Gospel, nor does he himself use γέγραπται to introduce either an Old Testament quotation or a saying of Jesus as Scripture. Irenaeus, however, does refer to the Gospels explicitly as "Scripture": *Cum itaque universae Scripturae, et prophetiae et evangelii ... praedicent ... (Adv Haer.* II.27.2). At the end of Book II, he announces that in his next Book he will support his argument from "divine Scripture"; in Book III there are very many more references to the Gospels than to the Old Testament, so there is a clear implication that they are "Scripture".

Nonetheless Irenaeus remains somewhat coy about referring to the Gospels as Scripture. Only once does he introduce a saying of Jesus with "Scripture says", and even in this case Matt 13,18 is alluded to rather than quoted (IV.41.2). In a handful of places he introduces a verse from the Gospels with "it is written"; see, for example, II.22.3; IV.20.6. For Irenaeus "Scripture" is first and foremost the Old Testament, though it is quite clear that the Gospels and sayings of Jesus enjoy the same level of authority as the Old Testament[32].

We noted above that Justin is adamant that traditions of the sayings and actions of Jesus have been transmitted carefully in the written Gospels by the apostles, and are handed on and carried out by his fellow Christians. In the introductory sections of the First Apology Justin emphasizes the careful transmission of tradition by using repeatedly the verb παραδίδωμι. The same points are made even more strongly by Irenaeus. In his introduction to Book III where he is concerned above all with the status of the Gospel in fourfold form, he stresses that the oral proclamation of the Gospel by the apostles was "later handed down to us in the Scriptures" (III.1.1: *in Scripturis nobis tradiderunt*; ἐν γραφαῖς παρέδωκαν ἡμῖν)[33]. Irenaeus then refers briefly to the origin and authorship of the individual Gospels. His comment on Mark, the disciple and interpreter of Peter, echoes the phraseology just quoted: *ipse quae a Petro adnuntiata per scripta nobis tradidit* (III.1.1). At this point we have Eusebius's version of the original Greek: καὶ αὐτὸς τὰ ὑπὸ Πέτρου κηρυσσόμενα ἐγγράφως ἡμῖν παραδέδωκεν (*H.E.* V.8.3).

At the close of his extended comments on the origin and authority of the Gospels, Irenaeus summarizes his key points. The Gospel has been

---

32. For these comments on Irenaeus's use of "Scripture" I am indebted to BENOIT, *Saint Irénée* (n. 11), pp. 120-122.

33. I have cited the Latin text and Greek retroversion from Irenaeus, *Contre les hérésies*, ed. A. ROUSSEAU and L. DOUTRELEAU (SC, 211), Paris, Cerf, 1974.

transmitted in written form by the apostles; since God made all things in due proportion and adaptation, it was fit also that the outward aspect of the Gospel should be well arranged and harmonized (III.11.12: *oportebat et speciem Euangelii bene compositam et bene compaginatam esse*). In this closing section Irenaeus states three times over that the Gospels can be neither more nor fewer in number than they are (III.11.8: *neque autem plura numero quam haec sunt neque rursus pauciora capit esse Euangelia*; cf. 11.9. 1 and 9.12, where almost identical terminology is used).

"No more, no less" almost becomes a slogan for Irenaeus. His terminology is so closely related to a "canon formula" widely known in antiquity that it is most surprising that Irenaeus does not draw on it[34]. As W.C. van Unnik noted, the canon formula "neither add nor take away" has deep roots in both Biblical and Greek thought[35]. Irenaeus knows the concepts in the same order, "no more, no less".

From Aristotle onwards, a "canonical" work was defined as one to which nothing could be added and from which nothing could be subtracted *without harming its aesthetic unity*. Aristotle states that "neither add nor take away" is a proverbial expression[36]. The "canon formula" was a well-known slogan in the Hellenistic world in the realm of *aesthetics*. Irenaeus places a great deal of weight on the aesthetic unity of the fourfold Gospel, so that his failure to quote the slogan is baffling, especially as Eusebius refers to it[37].

Justin emphasizes the importance and power of the words of Jesus. As we noted above, several passages confirm that he is concerned primarily with their written form rather than with continuing oral tradition. Justin does not state that "the words of the Saviour" are available anywhere but in "the memoirs of the apostles". I am convinced that this is also the case with Irenaeus, though here I am somewhat out of line with the current consensus. Hans von Campenhausen claims that Irenaeus does not think of the Gospels as sources for the words of Jesus. Their purpose is simply to provide documentary evidence of the teaching of "that apostle" who wrote down the gospel; the words of the Lord are treated on their own without reference to the Gospels[38]. Y.-M. Blanchard has re-

34. See, however, IV.33.8: *neque additamentum, neque ablationem recipiens.*

35. W.C. VAN UNNIK, *De la règle Μήτε προσθεῖναι μήτε ἀφελεῖν*, in *VigChr* 3 (1949) 1-36. See also C. DOHMEN & M. OEMING, *Biblischer Kanon, warum und wozu? Eine Kanontheologie*, Freiburg, Herder, 1992, esp. pp. 78-89; J. BARTON, *The Spirit and the Letter. Studies in the Biblical Canon*, London, SPCK, 1997, pp. 133-134.

36. Aristotle, *Ethica Nicomachea* II.1106b.

37. At *H.E.* V.16.3 Eusebius cites an anonymous letter which refers to the formula with reference to the "canon" of the New Testament.

38. VON CAMPENHAUSEN, *The Formation of the Christian Bible* (n. 9), pp. 191 and 202. Barton summarizes approvingly von Campenhausen's position in his *The Spirit and the Letter* (n. 35), pp. 82-84.

cently gone much further down this path: «ainsi, au temps d'Irénée, la mémoire vivante des logia du Seigneur paraît constituer le canal privilégié de la Tradition chrétienne"[39]. According to Blanchard, the Gospels are of secondary importance; pride of place among the four is given to Luke[40].

Irenaeus does attach special importance to the sayings of Jesus, but it is a Christological, not a hermeneutical priority[41]. Irenaeus does not single out the words of Jesus as a "canon within the canon". He sees the Gospels as the records of the teaching of Jesus. This is nowhere clearer than in the Preface to Book III: "The Lord of all gave to his apostles the power to proclaim the Gospel, and from them we have known the truth, that is to say the teaching of the Son of God. And it is to them that the Lord said: 'Anyone who hears you hears me ...'". Irenaeus devotes Book IV to the "words of the Lord", but at IV.6.1 there is a further clear indication that they are not to be thought of in isolation from their written form in the Gospels[42]. Irenaeus cites Matt 11,27 = Luke 10,22, and then comments: "Thus has Matthew set it down, and Luke similarly, and also Mark; for John omits this passage". He is, of course, mistaken about Mark, but that is beside the point. In several passages in Book IV the narrative context of the cited "words of the Lord" in one of the Gospels (usually Matthew) is retained; in other passages the deeds of Jesus are referred to or summarised[43].

It would be rash to claim that Irenaeus does not know oral traditions of the sayings of Jesus. But his vigorous exposition of the fourfold form of the Gospel leaves little room for continuing oral tradition. If one were to ask either Justin or Irenaeus where one could find the sayings of Jesus, the answer would surely be, "in the writings of the apostles and their followers".

CONCLUSIONS

Justin and Irenaeus both hold the sayings of Jesus and the Gospels in high regard, and on a level with the Old Testament Scriptures. In this respect the similarities between the two second-century giants are as important as the differences. Although Irenaeus takes several more steps

---

39. Y.-M. BLANCHARD, *Aux sources du canon. Le témoinage d'Irénée* (Cogitatio Fidei, 174), Paris, Cerf, 1993, p. 221.

40. *Ibid.*, pp. 206 and 229.

41. See especially the Preface to Book IV, and IV.1.1. See also BINGHAM, *Irenaeus' Use of Matthew's Gospel* (n. 30), pp. 97-98.

42. Not surprisingly, Blanchard fails to discuss this passage.

43. For the former, see, for example, IV.12.4-5; 10.1; 29.1. For the latter: IV.8.2.

towards acceptance of a "canon" of four written Gospels than does Justin, the great teacher of the new "philosophy of Christ" paves the way. I have emphasized more strongly than most the importance of *written* Jesus traditions for both Justin and Irenaeus. There is an obvious corollary: we may have allowed Papias's preference for "the living voice" over "the written word" to influence too strongly our reading of both Justin and Irenaeus.

The physical appearance of early Christian writings at the time in question is regularly overlooked in discussions of their status. I have argued elsewhere that the emergence of the four-Gospel canon is related to the dissemination of the four Gospels in codex form. Justin may well have had a four-Gospel codex in his catechetical school in Rome by about 150 AD. As long ago as 1933 F.G. Kenyon suggested that Irenaeus may have been accustomed to the sight of codices which contained all four gospels. The evidence for this conclusion is now much stronger than it was 70 years ago[44]. Today when we hear vociferous claims on behalf of the Gospels of Peter and Thomas, we need to recall that there is no manuscript evidence for the acceptance of any "fifth" gospel alongside one or more of the writings of the fourfold Gospel. Codex and canon go hand in hand, but that is another story.

In discussions of the emergence of the canon, whether of the Old Testament or the New Testament writings, definitions are all important, and the devil is in the detail. Even though Irenaeus does not use the term "canon" in its now customary sense, his insistence that the one Gospel proclaimed by the apostles is found in four written Gospels, no more no less, implies a "closed" Gospel canon. If our definition of "Gospel canon" includes reference to an agreed list of widely accepted authoritative writings, then it did not exist at the end of the second century. Irenaeus was a towering figure, but we must not assume that his views on the fourfold Gospel were accepted universally. Justin Martyr influenced Irenaeus strongly, but his pupil Tatian, whose *Diatessaron* almost won the day, took a very different path.

The Faculty of Divinity   Graham STANTON
West Road
Cambridge CB3 9BS
England

---

44. G.N. STANTON, *The Fourfold Gospel*, in *NTS* 43 (1997) 317-346.

LA NAISSANCE DE LA NOTION D'ÉCRITURE
DANS LA LITTÉRATURE JOHANNIQUE

INTRODUCTION

Paul Ricœur a récemment rappelé que le canon n'est pas un phénomène périphérique de la foi chrétienne, mais au contraire un élément
constitutif dans la définition de son identité. Il écrit: «La clôture du canon devient le phénomène majeur qui sépare des autres textes ceux qui
font *autorité* pour les communautés, lesquelles, en retour, se comprennent elles-mêmes à la lumière de ces textes fondateurs, distingués de
tous les autres textes, y compris des commentaires les plus fidèles»[1]. Et
il ajoute, soulignant ainsi la portée éminente de ce processus de sélection: «Ce qui me paraît constitutif du religieux, c'est donc le fait de faire
crédit à une certaine parole, selon un certain code, dans les limites d'un
certain canon»[2]. La constitution du canon chrétien renvoie donc à un
geste spécifiquement religieux: adhérer «à une parole réputée venir de
plus loin et de plus haut que moi»[3].

La littérature johannique participe à ce processus. Très tôt, elle a été
comptée au nombre des écrits fondateurs du christianisme naissant.
Comme l'attestent le fragment de Muratori, à la fin du IIe s., Origène
dans la première moitié du IIIe s., puis Eusèbe de Césarée au début du
IVe s., le quatrième évangile et la première épître de Jn firent d'emblée
partie de la liste des livres réputés canoniques alors que le statut de la
deuxième et de la troisième épître de Jn demeurait controversé. Cependant, dans sa 39ème lettre festale, datée de 367, Athanase d'Alexandrie
confirma l'appartenance de l'ensemble du corpus johannique au canon
néotestamentaire. Ce point d'histoire est bien établi et peut être considéré comme acquis.

Pour indiscutable qu'il soit, ce jugement historique mérite d'être ap-
profondi. Il convient notamment de se poser la question suivante. Quelles étaient les conditions que devait remplir un écrit chrétien primitif
pour accéder au rang de parole fondatrice? Quelles étaient, du point de
vue de l'Église ancienne, les critères qui présidaient à un tel choix? À

---

1. P. RICŒUR, *La critique et la conviction. Entretiens avec François Azouvi et Marc
de Launay*, Paris, Calmann-Lévy, 1995, p. 217.
2. *Ibid.*, p. 219.
3. *Ibid.*

parcourir l'histoire du canon, il s'avère que l'Église ancienne a mis en œuvre trois critères principaux[4] lors de la constitution du Nouveau Testament. Il s'agit de l'apostolicité, de l'orthodoxie et de la reconnaissance par les grandes Églises. Même s'ils furent appliqués de façon souple et avec une pondération variable, il n'y a pas lieu de mettre en doute leur rôle déterminant.

Le premier critère, celui de *l'apostolicité*, pose la question de l'identité de l'instance auctoriale et de l'autorité qui lui est liée. La notion d'apostolicité doit être comprise au sens large: elle tient pour décisive l'attribution d'un écrit à un membre du cercle des Douze (Matthieu, Jean) ou à une personne liée à un membre du collège apostolique (Marc, Luc). Par ailleurs, déjà dans le fragment de Muratori, l'autorité liée à l'apostolicité ne réside pas seulement dans la qualité de témoin oculaire. Ce document précise, en effet, à propos de Jean: «32 Par là en effet, il se proclame non seulement témoin oculaire et auditeur, 33 mais aussi écrivain (qui a consigné) toutes les merveilles du Seigneur dans l'ordre»[5].

Le second critère est celui de *l'orthodoxie* (ὁ κανὼν τῆς πίστεως, *regula fidei*). Pour être retenu dans le canon, un écrit doit être en consonance théologique avec les traditions fondamentales auxquelles l'Église ancienne attribue une valeur normative. Le fragment de Muratori est conscient de cette exigence lorsqu'il rappelle «67 (qu') il ne convient en effet pas de mélanger le miel avec le fiel»[6]. Certes Bauer[7] et, plus récemment, Dunn[8] ont appelé à la prudence et souligné, à juste titre, la diversité des premiers christianismes. Il n'en reste pas moins que le corpus johannique déjà, pour ne prendre que cet exemple, lutte pour la défense de la foi réputée véritable par opposition à des expressions déviantes de cette même foi. Les épîtres de Jn ont, en cette matière, valeur d'exemple.

Le troisième critère est lié au phénomène de la *réception*. Pour prendre rang dans le canon, un écrit doit être accepté dans la majorité des églises et être en usage dans leur pratique liturgique.

4. Cf. H.Y. GAMBLE, *The New Testament Canon. Its Making and Meaning*, Philadelphia, Fortress, 1985, pp. 67-72; B.M. METZGER, *Der Kanon des Neuen Testaments. Entstehung, Entwicklung, Bedeutung*, Düsseldorf, Patmos, 1993, pp. 238-243.

5. Cf. la traduction du fragment de Muratori proposée par J.-D. Kaestli, in D. MARGUERAT (éd.), *Introduction au Nouveau Testament. Son histoire, son écriture, sa théologie* (MoBi, 41), Genève, Labor et Fides, 2000, pp. 471-473, spéc. 472.

6. *Ibid.* Sur le critère de l'orthodoxie, cf. H.J. DE JONGE, *The New Testament Canon*, dans ce volume, pp. 312-319.

7. Cf. W. BAUER, *Rechtgläubigkeit und Ketzerei im ältesten Christentum* (BHT, 10), Tübingen, Mohr (Siebeck), ²1964.

8. Cf. J.D.G. DUNN, *Unity and Diversity in the New Testament*, London, SCM, & Philadelphia, TPI, 1991.

L'existence et l'application de ces trois critères soulèvent cependant une question fondamentale qui a fait l'objet de nombreux débats[9], et qui a la teneur suivante. Ces critères ont-ils été appliqués indépendamment de *l'intentio operis* des écrits retenus, si bien que la canonisation des écrits néotestamentaires n'aurait pas d'appui dans les textes eux-mêmes, mais serait une décision imputable, au premier chef, au magistère de l'Église ancienne? Ou, au contraire, les problématiques liées à ces critères de canonicité ont-ils déjà été l'objet d'une réflexion explicite dans les écrits qui appartiendront plus tard au canon? En d'autres termes, à l'heure de leur rédaction, les écrits néotestamentaires – ou du moins certains d'entre eux - prétendaient-ils déjà au statut d'Écriture[10]? Revendiquaient-ils déjà pour eux-mêmes une autorité sacrée et appelée à être reconnue par l'auditoire auquel ils s'adressaient?

Nous souhaiterions réfléchir à cette question en prenant l'exemple de la littérature johannique. Nous référant aux critères traditionnels de la canonicité dans l'Église ancienne, nous nous poserons successivement trois questions. Premièrement, comment la notion d'autorité auctoriale est-elle élaborée dans le quatrième évangile? Deuxièmement, le problème de l'orthodoxie a-t-il été l'objet d'un débat explicite dans la littérature johannique? Troisièmement, enfin, comment le problème de la reconnaissance et de l'usage de l'évangile s'est-il posé dans le milieu johannique?

I. LA NOTION D'AUTORITÉ AUCTORIALE DANS LE QUATRIÈME ÉVANGILE

Le premier problème proposé à notre réflexion porte sur la façon dont l'autorité auctoriale est présentée dans le quatrième évangile. À cet égard, la fameuse «question johannique»[11] qui a tant marqué l'histoire de l'exégèse, et qui consiste à savoir si Jean le Zébédaïde est l'auteur de l'évangile, ne nous est pas d'un grand secours. Elle appartient, en effet, à l'histoire de la réception du quatrième évangile[12]. Or, ce qui nous inté-

---

9. Cf. METZGER, *Kanon* (n. 4), p. 266.

10. Cette question a été récemment traitée par D.M. SMITH, *When Did the Gospels Become Scripture?*, in *JBL* 119 (2000) 3-20.

11. Sur la fameuse question johannique, cf. F.-M. BRAUN, *Jean le théologien et son évangile dans l'Église Ancienne* (EB), Paris, Gabalda, 1959, pp. 301-392; K.H. RENGSTORF (éd.), *Johannes und sein Evangelium* (Wege der Forschung, 82), Darmstadt, Wissenschaftliche Buchgesellschaft, 1973. Plus récemment: M. HENGEL, *Die johanneische Frage. Ein Lösungsversuch. Mit einem Beitrag zur Apokalypse von J. Frey* (WUNT, 67), Tübingen, Mohr (Siebeck), 1993.

12. Sur l'histoire de la réception de la figure de l'apôtre Jean, cf. R.A. CULPEPPER, *John, the Son of Zebedee. The Life of a Legend*, Minneapolis, Fortress, 2000 (première édition Columbia SC, University of South Carolina Press, 1994).

resse, c'est la manière dont le texte lui-même de l'évangile statue sur cette question. Il le fait d'une double manière. D'une part, il met en scène deux instances qui confèrent une autorité éminente au témoignage rendu par le quatrième évangile au Christ. Il s'agit du Paraclet et du disciple bien-aimé. D'autre part, il s'inscrit explicitement dans une tradition déjà constituée de la notion d'Écriture, celle qu'il hérite de la tradition vétérotestamentaire-juive. Reprenons brièvement ces deux points.

A. *Le Paraclet et le disciple bien-aimé*

Le quatrième évangile évoque avec force deux figures revêtues d'autorité et qui se portent garantes du témoignage rendu au Christ durant l'époque post-pascale. Il s'agit du Paraclet et du disciple bien-aimé.

1. *Le rôle du Paraclet*

Dans les discours d'adieu (14,31-16,33), le Paraclet est présenté à la fois comme celui qui fait mémoire du Christ johannique après Pâques et comme son herméneute (14,26)[13]. Il assure ainsi la présence du Christ johannique parmi les siens de façon illimitée dans le temps et dans l'espace (14,16-17). Cette présence se concrétise dans une anamnèse actualisante de la personne de Jésus et de son enseignement (14,26). Elle prend la forme d'un témoignage formulé qui, à son tour, institue les disciples dans la condition de témoins (15,26-27). Le Paraclet ne s'épuise pourtant pas dans une fonction rétrospective. Le témoignage rendu au Christ est ouvert sur l'avenir et déchiffre cet avenir à la lumière de la révélation (16,13).

Le lecteur attentif ne manque pas de noter que le Paraclet est ainsi mis en rapport avec des notions qui vont précisément être choisies par l'école johannique pour désigner les différents aspects de sa production littéraire. La terminologie du témoignage (μαρτυρεῖν) est utilisée pour nommer l'œuvre du disciple bien-aimé[14], celle de la proclamation (ἀναγγέλλειν) décrit le message transmis par 1 Jn[15], celle de l'ensei-

---

13. Sur la notion de Paraclet dans les discours d'adieu, cf. A. Dettwiler, *Die Gegenwart des Erhöhten. Eine exegetische Studie zu den johanneischen Abschiedsreden (Joh 13,31-16,33) unter besonderer Berücksichtigung ihres Relecture-Charakters* (FRLANT, 169), Göttingen, Vandenhoeck & Ruprecht, 1995, pp. 181-189.203-207; Chr. Dietzfelbinger, *Der Abschied des Kommenden* (WUNT, 95), Tübingen, Mohr (Siebeck), 1997, pp. 202-226.

14. La notion de μαρτυρία est utilisée en 19,35 et en 21,24 pour qualifier l'œuvre du disciple bien-aimé. En 21,24, elle est explicitement mise en rapport avec la composition de l'évangile.

15. Cf. 1 Jn 1,5; 3,11. La notion ἀγγελία est peut-être le terme technique dont l'école johannique s'est servie pour désigner l'évangile comme œuvre littéraire. Dans cette hypo-

gnement (διδάσκειν) la doctrine invoquée par l'Ancien dans 2 Jn[16]. Il n'est donc pas sans fondement de prétendre que l'évangile johannique est le fruit de l'Esprit. La figure du Paraclet explique à la fois sa naissance et le permanent effort de relecture qui le traverse. En fait, l'évangile réalise le programme annoncé dans les discours d'adieu et prêté à l'activité du Paraclet.

2. Le disciple bien-aimé

À côté du Paraclet et en concurrence avec lui, se profile une autre figure revêtue d'autorité, celle du disciple bien-aimé, fondateur du mouvement johannique et figure de proue de son école[17].

Le lecteur ne manque, en effet, pas de remarquer que le disciple bien-aimé remplit la même fonction que le Paraclet. D'une part, il est le témoin privilégié des hauts lieux du kérygme chrétien. Présent devant la croix (19,26), devançant Pierre dans l'inspection du tombeau vide le matin de Pâques (20,3-10), le disciple bien-aimé devient l'irremplaçable dépositaire de la mémoire de la foi pour la communauté à venir. Mais, d'autre part, il n'est pas que le porteur du souvenir du destin du Christ johannique, il en est aussi l'interprète privilégié et insurpassable. Sa position lors du dernier repas – couché sur le sein de Jésus (13,23)[18] – dit sa proximité avec le Christ, et, par là-même, sa capacité à le comprendre en vérité. Son intelligence du mystère pascal est soulignée (20,8; cf. aussi 21,7). Mais surtout, la parole que lui adresse le Christ en croix

---

thèse, les deux passages cités feraient allusion au quatrième évangile (cf. R.E. BROWN, *The Epistles of John* [AB, 30], Garden City, NY, Doubleday, 1982, p. 193). Sans être aussi affirmatif, H.-J. KLAUCK (*Der erste Johannesbrief* [EKK, 23/1], Zürich & Braunschweig, Benziger, Neukirchen-Vluyn, Neukirchener Verlag, 1991, p. 80) qui voit également dans ἀγγελία l'équivalent fonctionnel de la notion chrétienne primitive d'évangile.

16. La notion de διδαχή apparaît trois fois en 2 Jn 9-10. Elle désigne l'enseignement dispensé par le Christ, mais tel qu'il est déjà fixé dans des formules traditionnelles. Cf. la discussion de l'expression ἐν τῇ διδαχῇ τοῦ Χριστοῦ chez BROWN, *Epistles* (n. 15), pp. 687-689; H.-J. KLAUCK, *Der zweite und der dritte Johannesbrief* (EKK, 32/2), Zürich & Braunschweig, Benziger, Neukirchen-Vluyn, Neukirchener Verlag, 1992, pp. 61-62.

17. Sur le disciple bien-aimé, cf. CULPEPPER, *John* (n. 12), pp. 56-88; J. KÜGLER, *Der Jünger, den Jesus liebte. Literarische, theologische und historische Untersuchungen zu einer Schlüsselgestalt johanneischer Theologie und Geschichte. Mit einem Exkurs über die Brotrede in Joh 6* (SBB, 16), Stuttgart, Katholisches Bibelwerk, 1988; G. STRECKER, *Theologie des Neuen Testaments* (de Gruyter Lehrbuch), Berlin - New York, de Gruyter, 1996, pp. 485-490. Cf. notre propre position dans: *Le disciple bien-aimé*, in J. ZUMSTEIN, *Miettes exégétiques* (MoBi, 25), Genève, Labor et Fides, 1991, pp. 225-235.

18. L'utilisation de la notion de κόλπος en 13,23 est à mettre en relation avec 1,18. Le disciple bien-aimé occupe par rapport au Christ, la position même que ce dernier a par rapport à Dieu. Ainsi de même que le Fils est le représentant de Dieu pour le monde, le disciple bien-aimé est-il le lieu-tenant du Fils pour la communauté.

(19,26-27)[19] est sans ambiguïté: c'est lui, le disciple bien-aimé, qui est appelé à représenter le Fils après sa mort auprès des croyants. C'est lui qui est appelé à occuper la place laissée vacante par le crucifié. C'est par son témoignage et sa compréhension achevée de la révélation du Fils que le disciple bien-aimé va assurer, au sein de la communauté post-pascale, sa fonction de «lieu-tenant» du Christ désormais retourné auprès du Père. Et le chap. 21 va achever la mise en place du monument dédié au disciple bien-aimé en précisant que ce témoignage décisif et unique va prendre la forme d'une écriture, appelé à devenir Écriture (21,24-25).

3. Une dualité significative

Comment faut-il alors articuler l'activité de ces deux figures éminentes du récit johannique, qui semblent impliquées à égalité de rang dans la naissance du quatrième évangile? Toutes deux ne sont-elles pas présentées comme les témoins et les herméneutes du Christ pour l'époque post-pascale? Même si les discours d'adieu n'en disent rien, les traits qu'ils prêtent au Paraclet incitent le lecteur à établir un rapport entre l'activité de l'Esprit et le témoignage du disciple bien-aimé[20].

Pourtant, un fait incontournable demeure. Même si l'évangile johannique est le fruit du Paraclet, il est explicitement présenté comme étant l'œuvre du seul disciple bien-aimé. Comment faut-il comprendre cela? Notre hypothèse est la suivante: Alors que le Paraclet est, selon les discours d'adieu, l'acteur d'une anamnèse et d'une relecture infinie de la Révélation, le disciple bien-aimé introduit l'élément de clôture, nécessaire à la naissance d'une écriture. Avec l'œuvre du disciple bien-aimé, le témoignage ouvert et sans cesse renouvelé du Paraclet se fixe et prend une forme stable. Il s'objective dans le témoignage du disciple bien-aimé[21].

---

19. Sur Jn 19,25-27, cf. J. ZUMSTEIN, *Johannes 19,25-27*, in *ZTK* 94 (1997) 131-154; = ID., *Kreative Erinnerung. Relecture und Auslegung im Johannesevangelium*, Zürich, Pano, 1999, pp. 156-177.

20. Au niveau narratif, on remarquera que la scène johannique de la crucifixion est simultanément le lieu où le disciple bien-aimé est installé dans sa responsabilité de représentant du Christ pour la communauté post-pascale (19,26-27), et celui de l'effusion de l'Esprit (19,30b). Certes l'expression καὶ τὴν κεφαλὴν παρέδωκεν τὸ πνεῦμα est ambiguë et peut signifier aussi bien la mort de Jésus que l'effusion de l'Esprit, mais les discours d'adieu ont indiqué clairement que départ de Jésus et venue de l'Esprit vont de pair (cf. par exemple 16,7).

21. Sur le rapport entre la dimension de l'écriture liée au disciple bien-aimé et celle de la parole orale, spécificité du Paraclet, cf. aussi G. THEISSEN, *Die Religion der ersten Christen. Eine Theorie des Urchristentums*, Gütersloh, Kaiser & Gütersloher Verlagshaus, 2000, p. 279.

On remarquera alors que, par cette décision, l'école johannique anticipe la démarche qui dominera plus tard la constitution du canon néotestamentaire. Ce n'est pas l'inspiration de l'Esprit (la théopneustie) qui est élevée au rang de critère déterminant[22] lors de la canonisation d'un écrit, mais bien son attribution à une personne faisant partie du groupe des premiers disciples de Jésus.

Au terme de cette première enquête, un bref bilan s'impose. L'école johannique a formulé en toute clarté dans l'évangile lui-même l'autorité auctoriale qu'elle entend lui attribuer et lui voir reconnaître. L'évangile ne saurait être détaché de l'activité du Paraclet, mais il est – au niveau des médiations historiques – l'œuvre du témoin privilégié et de l'herméneute insurpassable du Christ johannique, le disciple bien-aimé. Placé sous ce double patronage, l'évangile selon Jn revendique une autorité absolue à l'égard de ses destinataires. Ce faisant, il prétend à un statut comparable à celui qui est ordinairement attribué à l'Écriture. Se pose alors la question de savoir si le quatrième évangile connaît une notion élaborée de l'Écriture et, dans l'affirmative, comment il se situe par rapport à elle. Si notre brève enquête sur le Paraclet et le disciple bien-aimé nous a permis de préciser comment l'école johannique a défini l'autorité auctoriale de l'évangile en se référant à sa propre tradition de foi, l'examen du lien liant l'évangile johannique à la Bible hébraïque autorise un élargissement de la perspective. L'autorité de l'évangile est alors située par rapport à une autorité déjà admise aussi bien par la Synagogue que par l'Église.

B. *La notion d'Écriture*

1. *Le quatrième évangile et l'Ancien Testament*

À l'évidence, le quatrième évangile présuppose une conception élaborée de la notion d'Écriture. Comme le montrent les nombreuses citations et allusions à l'Ancien Testament qui parsèment son œuvre, l'auteur implicite s'inscrit dans la tradition vétérotestamentaire-juive[23]. C'est ce que

---

22. Cf. METZGER, *Kanon* (n. 4), p. 242; GAMBLE, *Canon* (n. 4), pp. 71-72.
23. Sur le rapport du quatrième évangile à l'Ancien Testament, cf. C.K. BARRETT, *The Gospel according to St. John*, Philadelphia, Westminster Press, ²1978, pp. 27-30; F.-M. BRAUN, *Jean le théologien II: Les grandes traditions d'Israël et l'accord des Écritures selon le quatrième Évangile*, Paris, Gabalda, 1964; M. HENGEL, *Die Schriftauslegung des 4. Evangeliums auf dem Hintergrund der urchristlichen Exegese*, in *JBT* 4 (1989) 249-288; R. SCHNACKENBURG, *Das Johannesevangelium* (HTK, 4/1), Freiburg - Basel - Wien, Herder, ³1972, pp. 103-106. Pour une étude plus spécifique sur les citations vétérotestamentaires dans le quatrième évangile, cf. M.J.J. MENKEN, *Old Testament Quotations in the Fourth Gospel. Studies in Textual Form* (CBET, 15), Kampen, Pharos, 1996.

confirme sa fréquente utilisation de la terminologie désignant le phénomène de l'Écriture[24].

L'usage johannique de cette conceptualité attire notre attention sur
trois aspects. Ce champ sémantique décrit tout d'abord l'Écriture vétérotestamentaire-juive. En plein accord avec le christianisme naissant,
l'auteur implicite du quatrième évangile en reconnaît l'autorité sans la
moindre restriction. Même dans les passages polémiques de son œuvre,
l'Écriture est partie intégrante de son argumentation[25]. Le conflit porte,
en effet, non pas sur la validité de l'Écriture, mais sur son interprétation
et son appropriation. Ainsi, avec les traditions juive et chrétienne primitive de son temps, Jn postule que Dieu se révèle à travers l'Écriture et
que cette Écriture, référence incontournable pour la formulation de la
foi, appelle un devoir d'interprétation. Cette observation, en soi banale,
est d'importance, car elle montre que l'école johannique reprend un concept déjà élaboré de l'Écriture.

On notera, en second lieu, que l'Écriture ne décrit pas simplement la
tradition ancestrale de la foi vétérotestamentaire-juive, mais que l'auteur
implicite établit une passerelle entre l'Écriture juive et le Christ. Dans de
nombreux passages, le destin du Christ – et notamment sa Passion – sont
présentés comme l'accomplissement de l'Écriture (πληροῦν)[26], voire
comme son achèvement (τελειοῦν)[27]. L'Écriture est ainsi le registre
herméneutique qui permet d'interpréter le destin du Christ, mais, à l'inverse, ce destin auquel l'évangile rend témoignage, est déjà mystérieuse-
ment inclus dans cette Écriture.

Un troisième phénomène, enfin, mérite attention. Dans quelques passages, le témoignage johannique rendu au Christ est hissé au niveau de
l'Écriture juive. Ainsi en 2,22, le texte affirme que «lorsque Jésus se re-
leva d'entre les morts, ses disciples se souvinrent qu'il avait parlé ainsi,
et ils crurent à l'Écriture (γραφῇ) ainsi qu'à la parole (λόγος) qu'il avait
dite». Écriture et parole de Jésus ont désormais la même autorité en matière de foi. Par ailleurs, il est symptomatique que, dans la narration
johannique, le phénomène de l'accomplissement de l'Écriture ne s'applique plus seulement à l'Ancien Testament, mais s'étende également
aux paroles du Christ johannique (18,9.32)[28]. Enfin, il faut faire état des

24. L'évangile utilise ainsi 12 fois le terme γραφή pour désigner l'Ancien Testament
et 10 fois le verbe γράφειν pour le même usage. Cf. aussi la présence des termes νόμος
(9 fois), Μωϋσῆς (1 fois) et προφῆται (1 fois) pour désigner l'Écriture.

25. Cf. par exemple Jn 6 et 8.

26. Cf. 12,38; 13,18; 15,25; 17,12; 19,24.36.

27. Cf. 19,28.

28. Dans les deux cas, l'auteur implicite utilise la formule classique dénotant l'accomplissement de l'Écriture: 18,9 ἵνα πληρωθῇ ὁ λόγος ὃν εἶπεν; 18,32 ἵνα ὁ λόγος τοῦ
Ἰησοῦ πληρωθῇ ὃν εἶπεν.

affirmations où la terminologie servant à nommer l'Écriture est utilisée pour caractériser la narration johannique elle-même. Si tout au long de l'évangile, le parfait passif γέγραπται et le participe parfait passif γεγραμμένος désignent de façon stéréotypée l'Écriture vétérotestamentaire, en 20,30 le γεγραμμένα et en 20,31 le γέγραπται s'appliquent désormais à l'évangile lui-même[29].

Le bilan de ce survol n'est pas sans intérêt. Il permet de mieux cerner la conception johannique de l'autorité attribuée à l'évangile. Il montre que l'école johannique a établi une relation différenciée entre l'Écriture vétérotestamentaire-juive et sa propre production littéraire. D'une part, partageant en cela la position du christianisme primitif, elle a discerné dans la Bible hébraïque l'Écriture de l'Église. Ensuite, sa lecture de cette Écriture l'a amené à affirmer que la personne et le destin du Christ étaient préfigurés en elle. De ce fait, la révélation johannique était mise en relation directe et à égalité de rang avec la révélation vétérotestamentaire. Ce qui était dit dans l'Écriture vétérotestamentaire et ce qui était annoncé dans l'Évangile prétendaient à la même origine divine et à la même validité. Enfin, alors même qu'elle revendiquait pour le quatrième évangile la plus haute autorité et l'avait de facto hissée au rang d'Écriture, l'école johannique n'a jamais franchi le pas qui aurait abouti à faire de son évangile un livre appartenant à la collection de la Bible hébraïque et la complétant. La distinction entre l'Écriture juive dans sa forme traditionnelle et l'Écriture chrétienne en voie de constitution est ici anticipée.

2. Le prologue et l'épilogue, lieux de réflexion sur l'Écriture

Le prologue et l'épilogue sont, enfin, d'un grand intérêt pour notre problématique, car il s'agit de passages en surplomb de la narration, dans lesquels l'auteur implicite réfléchit sur le statut dont jouit son œuvre. Tandis que le prologue établit l'origine de l'Écriture johannique et sa filiation vétérotestamentaire, l'épilogue s'interroge sur l'autorité auctoriale de l'évangile.

Le *prologue* (Jn 1,1-18) fixe le cadre herméneutique dans lequel l'œuvre doit être lue[30]. Il attire notamment l'attention du lecteur sur la

---

29. On remarquera avec intérêt que ces formulations désignant l'Écriture n'apparaissent jamais dans les épîtres johanniques pour caractériser le travail de l'auteur.

30. Sur le prologue et sa fonction, cf. M. THEOBALD, *Die Fleischwerdung des Logos. Studien zum Verhältnis des Johannesprologs zum Corpus des Evangeliums und zu 1 Joh* (NTA NF, 20), Münster, Aschendorff, 1988. Voir notre position dans: J. ZUMSTEIN, *Le prologue, seuil du quatrième évangile*, in *RSR* 83 (1995) 59-69; = ID., *Erinnerung* (n. 19), pp. 78-98, version allemande.

problématique qui sera au centre du récit. Pour ce qui est de notre sujet, deux réflexions sont d'importance.

D'une part – et ce point a été peu souligné dans la recherche -, le prologue articule le rapport existant entre la Parole et l'Écriture. Comme Ricœur l'a rappelé à juste titre[31], dans la tradition biblique, l'Écriture est toujours la mise en écriture d'une Parole reçue et venant d'ailleurs. Le prologue rend compte de ce processus: il annonce la venue de la Parole (ὁ λόγος) dans le monde, son incarnation – qui va être la révélation de Dieu pour les hommes. La narration qui suit est la mise en récit de la venue de la Parole (1,18 ἐκεῖνος ἐξηγήσατο). Ce faisant, le prologue confère un statut éminent à la narration évangélique. De même que la Bible hébraïque trouve son origine dans la parole divine, ainsi en est-il du quatrième évangile qui se veut témoignage suscité par le Logos divin et rendu à ce même au Logos.

D'autre part, le prologue fait écho aux grands thèmes de la Bible hébraïque[32]; il s'adosse à l'Écriture et s'inscrit ainsi dans sa trajectoire. Il s'ouvre par une réminiscence de la Genèse («Au commencement était le Logos …», cf. 1,1). Cette allusion délibérée signifie que l'auteur implicite entend situer d'emblée son récit dans la perspective de la Bible juive et, par cette référence, lui conférer autorité. La suite du prologue reste dans la même ligne: elle aussi se réfère aux grands thèmes de la Bible hébraïque: la création (1,3.10), Moïse, la Loi (1,17)[33]. Par ailleurs, la venue du Logos dans le monde est formulée dans des termes qui rappellent ceux utilisés pour caractériser la Sagesse vétérotestamentaire.

L'épilogue (Jn 21)[34] aborde un autre problème, celui de l'auteur de l'évangile. Pour ce faire, ce chapitre articule l'autorité du disciple bien-

---

31. Cf. P. Ricœur, *Phénoménologie de la religion,* in Id., *Lectures 3. Aux frontières de la philosophie*, Paris, Seuil, 1994, pp. 263-271, spéc. 268-269. Il écrit notamment: «La religion juive et la religion chrétienne se disent fondées sur une parole reçue comme parole de Dieu; mais cette parole n'est nulle part accessible hors d'écritures tenues pour saintes (…). La Parole est tenue pour l'instance fondatrice de l'Écriture et l'Écriture pour le lieu de manifestation de la Parole» (p. 268).

32. Sur cette question, cf. B.C. Childs, *The New Testament as Canon. An Introduction*, London, SCM, 1984, pp. 136-137.

33. Si comme une partie de la critique le prétend, les vv. 17-18 sont rédactionnels, alors le lien avec la tradition vétérotestamentaire-juive n'est pas seulement un élément de l'hymne pré-johannique, mais correspond à la volonté expresse de l'auteur implicite. Cf. par exemple, l'analyse de J. Becker, *Das Evangelium nach Johannes*, Bd. 1: Kapitel 1-10 (ÖTK, 4/1), Gütersloh, Gütersloher Verlag, & Würzburg, Echter Verlag, ³1991, pp. 81-87.

34. Sur le chap. 21, cf. en particulier, E. Ruckstuhl, *Zur Aussage und Botschaft von Johannes 21*, in Id., *Jesus im Horizont der Evangelien* (SBAB, 3), Stuttgart, Katholisches Bibelwerk, 1988, pp. 327-353. Cf. notre position dans: J. Zumstein, *La rédaction finale de l'évangile de Jean (à l'exemple du chap. 21)*, in Id., *Miettes* (n. 17), pp. 207-230; = Id., *Erinnerung* (n. 19), pp. 192-216, version allemande.

aimé à celle de Pierre, personnage emblématique du cercle des Douze et de la communauté primitive. Il statue ainsi avec précision sur l'autorité dont jouit chacune de ces deux figures dans l'Église. Alors que le signification éminente reconnue à Pierre est liée à sa charge pastorale et à son martyre glorieux, celle du disciple bien-aimé l'est à l'évangile qu'il a écrit. C'est par l'entremise de son œuvre qu'il demeure présent dans l'Église jusqu'au retour de son Seigneur[35]. Le quatrième évangile n'est ainsi pas un écrit de circonstance, né d'une initiative tout humaine, il résulte de la vocation que le Christ ressuscité a adressée au disciple bien-aimé.

II. LA NOTION D'ORTHODOXIE

L'orthodoxie est le deuxième critère déterminant en matière de canonicité. Si l'usage du couple «orthodoxie – hérésie» s'avère pertinent dans l'interprétation de l'histoire de l'Église ancienne, il faut, en revanche, faire preuve de la plus grande retenue dans l'application de cette terminologie aux écrits néotestamentaires[36]. Faute de quoi, le risque de succomber au danger d'anachronisme est grand. À titre heuristique, il est néanmoins légitime de se demander si le souci de rectitude doctrinale a existé dans le milieu johannique et s'il a donné lieu à des affrontements intra-ecclésiaux.

Avant d'aborder cette question et pour la bonne conduite de l'enquête, il convient de clarifier un point d'importance. A notre avis – et en cela, nous partageons l'opinion majoritaire de la recherche –, l'évangile, dans ses différentes rédactions, a été composé avant les épîtres johanniques[37]. Dans notre reconstruction de l'histoire du mouvement johannique[38], cela signifie donc que 1 Jn est postérieur à l'évangile et en présuppose l'existence.

---

35. À notre avis, la prophétie du Christ johannique sur le destin du disciple bien-aimé (21,22) ne saurait être séparée de 21,24. Bien que son décès semble contredire la prédiction du Ressuscité, le disciple bien-aimé demeure, en fait, par l'écriture de l'évangile postulée au v. 24, lequel durera jusqu'à la parousie.

36. Sur la question de l'hérésie dans le Nouveau Testament, cf. U. MELL, *Häresie*, in *RGG*[4] 3, Tübingen, Mohr (Siebeck), 2000, cc. 1441-1442.

37. Nous avons exposé notre position, dans: J. ZUMSTEIN, *La tradition johannique*, in D. MARGUERAT (éd.), *Introduction* (n. 5), pp. 345-386, spéc. 375-377. Autre position défendue à la suite de G. STRECKER par U. SCHNELLE, *Einleitung in das Neue Testament* (UTB.W, 1830), Göttingen, Vandenhoeck & Ruprecht, [3]1999, pp. 447-452.

38. Cf. J. ZUMSTEIN, *Zur Geschichte des johanneischen Christentums*, in *TLZ* 122 (1997) 417-428; = ID., *Erinnerung* (n. 19), pp. 1-14.

A. *La question de l'orthodoxie dans le quatrième évangile*

La question de l'orthodoxie est-elle débattue dans le quatrième évangile? À notre avis, et bien que ce point soit controversé[39], le quatrième évangile ne fait pas explicitement état d'une fausse conception de la foi chrétienne présente dans son environnement ecclésial, et qu'il s'attacherait à dénoncer. L'opposition dominante qui est mise en récit est celle existant entre la foi et l'incrédulité – que ce soit l'incrédulité des «Juifs», du monde ou même des disciples[40]. Par ailleurs, dans les discours d'adieu et dans la prière sacerdotale, textes qui abordent les problèmes inhérents à l'époque post-pascale, le clivage déterminant est celui qui existe entre la communauté des disciples et le monde, et non pas un clivage à l'intérieur même de la communauté[41]. La polémique menée par l'auteur implicite de l'évangile est, en premier lieu, une polémique ad extra[42].

Si donc il est hasardeux de voir dans l'évangile l'écho d'affrontements intra-ecclésiaux, il est, en revanche, incontestable que l'auteur implicite de l'évangile entend formuler avec beaucoup de précision sa conception novatrice de la foi chrétienne. Mais sa position consiste moins à polémiquer contre des positions existantes plutôt qu'à les approfondir et à les recadrer. Trois exemples suffisent à le montrer.

L'évangéliste se garde bien de critiquer explicitement l'eschatologie traditionnelle ou de l'exclure de son discours; il préfère prendre appui sur la foi communément admise pour ensuite formuler sa position[43]. La

---

39. Cf. par exemple la position de U. SCHNELLE qui voit dans le quatrième évangile l'expression profilée d'une christologie antidocète (*Antidoketische Christologie im Johannesevangelium. Eine Untersuchung zur Stellung des vierten Evangeliums in der johanneischen Schule* [FRLANT, 144], Göttingen, Vandenhoeck & Ruprecht, 1987, pp. 34.249-258).

40. Sur les «Juifs» dans le quatrième évangile, cf. H. KUHLI, Ἰουδαῖοι, in *EWNT II*, Stuttgart u.a., Kohlhammer, 1981, cc. 479-480; R.A. CULPEPPER, *Anatomy of the Fourth Gospel. A Study in Literary Design* (Foundations & Facets: New Testament), Philadelphia, Fortress, 1983, pp. 125-132; G. STRECKER, *Theologie* (n. 17), pp. 514-520. Sur l'incrédulité du monde, cf. *Ibid.*, 513-514. Les disciples, quant à eux, ne sont – à l'exception de Judas – pas fondamentalement présentés comme frappés d'incrédulité; cependant, comme le montrent les exemples de Pierre (13,8-10.36-38; 18,17.25-27), de Philippe (14,8) et de Thomas (20,25), mais aussi la crise évoquée au chap. 6 (vv. 60-66), leur foi est sujette au malentendu.

41. Le dualisme entre la communauté et le monde est développé de façon programmatique dans les discours d'adieu (chap. 14-16), puis dans la prière sacerdotale (cf. DIETZFELBINGER, *Abschied* [n. 13], pp. 241-246).

42. Il faut penser ici, d'une part, à la polémique menée contre le judaïsme pharisien, d'autre part, au mouvement baptiste. Cf. ZUMSTEIN, *Tradition* (n. 37), pp. 357-358.361.

43. Cf. l'état de la question établi par BECKER, *Johannes I* (n. 33), pp. 293-296. Histoire détaillée de la recherche chez J. FREY, *Die johanneische Eschatologie, Bd. I: Ihre Probleme im Spiegel der Forschung seit Reimarus* (WUNT, 96), Tübingen, Mohr (Siebeck), 1997.

pneumatologie fournit un second exemple de cette attitude. Tout en reprenant à son compte la conception de l'Esprit communément admise
dans le christianisme primitif, il n'hésite cependant pas à développer sa
propre vision du rôle de l'Esprit dans les discours d'adieu en recourant
au concept jusqu'alors inconnu de Paraclet[44]. Dernier exemple: l'évangéliste cite, sans émettre de réserves, les conceptions messianiques en
honneur dans le christianisme naissant pour aussitôt conduire son lecteur
à la découverte de sa christologie de l'envoyé[45]. Le dispositif argu-
mentatif de l'évangile est ainsi placé sous le signe de l'herméneutique
étagée[46]: il s'agit de faire passer le lecteur d'une conception élémentaire
de la foi à une conception achevée, c'est-à-dire johannique.

Mais l'histoire du mouvement johannique ne s'arrête pas là. Si, en effet, l'évangile ne fait pas état de disputes confessionnelles déchirant les
communautés johanniques, et centrées sur l'interprétation «orthodoxe»
de la foi, tout autre est la situation dans les épîtres johanniques. Dans les
trois lettres, il est question de violentes controverses portant sur la formulation authentique de la foi. Avec Conzelmann[47], on peut donc dire,
que, dans le mouvement johannique, le débat sur l'orthodoxie commence avec la *prima johannis*.

B. *La question de l'orthodoxie dans 1 Jn*

A la différence de l'évangile, la première épître de Jn fait explicitement état de divisions à l'intérieur des communautés johanniques
(2,18s). Ces divisions sont en lien avec l'interprétation de la foi (2,22s;
4,2-3.15) et portent sur la confession de foi christologique. Le lecteur

---

44. Abstraction faite des discours d'adieu, l'évangile développe une pneumatologie
qui est en consonance avec celle attestée dans les grands courants du christianisme primitif (par exemple, Paul et Luc). Pour désigner l'Esprit, il utilise alors le concept πνεῦμα.
En revanche, dans les discours d'adieu où apparaît en toute clarté sa propre conception, il
se sert du concept παράκλητος. Cf. sur ce point J. BECKER, *Das Evangelium nach
Johannes*, Bd. 2: Kapitel 11-21 (ÖTK, 4/2), Gütersloh, Gütersloher Verlag, und Würzburg, Echter Verlag, ³1991, p. 566; DETTWILER, *Gegenwart* (n. 13), p. 205.

45. Sur les titres christologiques dans le quatrième évangile, cf. STRECKER, *Theologie*
(n. 17), pp. 508-510; A. WEISER, *Theologie des Neuen Testaments II: Die Theologie der
Evangelien* (Studienbücher Theologie, 8), Stuttgart - Berlin - Köln, Kohlhammer, 1993,
pp. 191-196. Sur la christologie de l'envoyé, cf. BECKER, *Johannes II* (n. 44), pp. 484-
494.

46. Le concept d'herméneutique étagée a été esquissé en premier lieu par C.H. DODD,
The Interpretation of the Fourth Gospel, Cambridge, University Press, 1953, puis repris
par G. THEISSEN, *Religion* (n. 21), pp. 255-272, et développé par J. ZUMSTEIN, *L'évangile
johannique, une stratégie du croire*, in ID., *Miettes* (n. 17), pp. 237-252; = ID.,
Erinnerung (n. 19), pp. 31-45.

47. Cf. H. CONZELMANN & A. LINDEMANN, *Arbeitsbuch zum Neuen Testament*
(UTB.W, 52), Tübingen, Mohr (Siebeck), ¹¹1995, p. 381.

découvre une situation où la vérité de la foi chrétienne est devenue objet de controverse dans un milieu ecclésial donné. La question de l'orthodoxie s'avère ainsi être un enjeu débattu explicitement par l'épître. L'émergence de cette nouvelle problématique est attestée par deux indices significatifs.

Le premier indice tient dans la transformation de la notion de λόγος. Alors que dans le prologue de l'évangile, cette notion désignait la personne du Christ préexistant, puis incarné, et était donc un titre christologique, dans le prologue de la première épître de Jn (1,1), le λόγος désigne le message de la foi[48]. Il est assimilé à une parole formulée, appelée à être transmise et enseignée, mais aussi interprétée.

Le rapport entre Jn et 1 Jn nous fournit un second indice. Si Brown[49] a raison de prétendre que 1 Jn a pour mission d'ouvrir la voie à une lecture fondée de l'évangile, d'en fournir en quelque sorte le commentaire «orthodoxe», alors la problématique subsumée dans l'histoire subséquente de l'Église ancienne par le couple orthodoxie-hérésie, est au centre même de la *prima johannis*. Cette lettre prétend en effet distinguer une interprétation fidèle de la tradition reçue, d'une interprétation fautive. Elle se donne pour objectif d'extirper du sein des communautés johanniques une compréhension déviante de la foi christologique et d'en restaurer l'expression authentique. Ce surgissement de la problématique de l'orthodoxie[50] dans la première épître de Jn est reconnaissable à une série de traits littéraires bien identifiables. Rappelons-en quelques-uns.

En premier lieu, l'expression «depuis le commencement» est l'une des catégories à l'aide desquelles l'auteur implicite aime à argumenter[51]. Ce qui fait foi pour l'école johannique et pour les lecteurs auxquels elle s'adresse, c'est la référence au «commencement», par quoi il faut entendre la révélation christologique telle qu'elle a été transmise dans la prédication adressée aux communautés[52]. L'accès à la vérité se fait par le retour à la parole fondatrice. Le conflit actuel des interprétations peut

---

48. Cf. BROWN, *Epistles* (n. 15), pp. 164-165, et KLAUCK, *Der erste Johannesbrief* (n. 15), pp. 64-65.

49. Cf. BROWN, *Epistles* (n. 15), pp. 90-91, suivi par SMITH, *Scripture* (n. 10), p. 12. Cf. aussi F. VOUGA, *Die Johannesbriefe* (HNT, 15/3), Tübingen, Mohr (Siebeck), 1990, p. 12.

50. Cf. CONZELMANN & LINDEMANN, *Arbeitsbuch* (n. 47), p. 381, qui écrivent de façon profilée: «1Joh ist im Neuen Testament *das* Dokument über das Bewusstwerden von 'Rechtgläubigkeit und Ketzerei' innerhalb der christlichen Kirche».

51. L'expression ἀπ' ἀρχῆς apparaît en 1,1; 2,7.13.14; 3,11.

52. Présentation de la discussion par BROWN, *Epistles* (n. 15), pp. 155-158, qui conclut, p. 158: «'What was from the beginning' means the person, words, and deeds of Jesus as this complex reflects his self-revelation (…) to his disciples after his baptism». Dans le même sens KLAUCK, *Der erste Johannesbrief* (n. 15), p. 60, ou VOUGA, *Johannesbriefe* (n. 49), p. 25.

être tranché par cet acte d'anamnèse. Mais – et ce point est d'importance pour notre problématique – l'argument selon lequel l'origine est fondatrice, est typique d'une démarche habitée par le souci de l'orthodoxie.

En second lieu, un procédé littéraire, chère à la *prima johannis*, consiste à mettre en opposition deux interprétations de la foi. En se servant de formulations antithétiques[53], l'auteur implicite est en mesure d'indiquer quelle est la formulation correcte de la foi. Ou alors en recourant à des affirmations commençant par la formule «à ceci nous savons que» (ἐν τούτῳ γινώσκομεν)[54], il exprime sa ferme intention de définir avec exactitude la portée de cette même foi. Ou encore, les assertions débutant par la formule «celui qui dit que» (ὁ λέγων)[55] permettent de citer une thèse théologique pour aussitôt en souligner la vérité ou l'erreur.

Enfin, on ne manquera pas de remarquer que les deux autorités qui cautionnaient l'évangile, le Paraclet et le disciple bien-aimé, ne sont pas mentionnées dans 1 Jn. À nos yeux, ce silence est explicable. D'une part, dans la crise qui ravage les communautés johanniques, la figure du disciple bien-aimé ne saurait être invoquée pour trancher le débat. Ce n'est, en effet, pas le témoignage rendu au commencement et donc l'évangile du disciple bien-aimé qui est mis en question, mais bien son interprétation. Il en va autrement de l'Esprit. Si le nom du Paraclet est tu, c'est parce que les adversaires de l'école johannique en revendiquent la pleine possession[56]. La préoccupation de l'école johannique est dès lors de réguler la voix de l'Esprit, en la conformant à la tradition de la foi.

C. *La notion d'orthodoxie dans 2 et 3 Jn*

La deuxième épître de Jn est dominée par un affrontement entre juste et fausse interprétation de la foi, entre orthodoxie et hérésie. La constellation des concepts, qui domine le corps de la lettre, est typique. Alors que les notions de commencement (ἀρχή) et d'enseignement (διδαχή) caractérisent la position de l'école johannique, celles de Séducteur (πλάνος) et d'Antichrist (ἀντίχριστος) stigmatisent celle des opposants. Quiconque ne partage pas la confession de foi christologique dé-

---

53. Cf. par exemple 1 Jn 2,10s.23; 5,12.
54. Cf. par exemple 1 Jn 2,3.5; 3,16.19; 4,2.13; 5,2.
55. Cf. par exemple 1 Jn 2,4.6.9; cf. aussi 4,2s.
56. Sur ce point, cf. KLAUCK, *Der erste Johannesbrief* (n. 15), pp. 41-42; P. VIEL-HAUER, *Geschichte der urchristlichen Literatur. Einleitung in das Neue Testament, die Apokryphen und die Apostolischen Väter*, Berlin - New York, de Gruyter, 1975, pp. 470-472.

fendue par l'Ancien, n'a pas accès à Dieu et doit être empêché d'entrer en contact avec la communauté.

La troisième épître de Jn permet d'entrevoir la réalité d'une église où l'adhésion à une interprétation de la foi plutôt qu'à une autre, établit ou rompt la communion ecclésiale. Le conflit des interprétations de la tradition interfère avec la pratique ministérielle. L'orthodoxie s'arme du bras de la discipline pour préserver la pureté doctrinale de la communauté[57].

Faisons un bref bilan. La question de l'orthodoxie qui deviendra centrale dans l'histoire de la constitution du canon, est déjà présente dans l'histoire du mouvement johannique. Elle a été déclenchée par la réception conflictuelle de l'évangile au sein des communautés destinataires. Ce conflit des interprétations s'est focalisé sur la formulation de la foi christologique et il a donné naissance à une tradition d'interprétation «orthodoxe» dont 1 Jn est l'exemple privilégié. Mais il a également abouti à des décisions de nature disciplinaire dont 2 et 3 Jn conservent la trace douloureuse.

III. La notion de reconnaissance

Nous en venons brièvement au troisième critère de canonicité que l'Église ancienne s'est donné. Il s'agit de la notion de reconnaissance ecclésiale. Pour avoir accès au canon, un écrit chrétien primitif devait avoir été accepté et être en usage dans les Églises importantes.

Or, avant même que la question de la reconnaissance ne soit liée à celle du canon, elle s'est posée d'une double manière dans le milieu johannique. Tout d'abord, au niveau de l'auteur implicite de l'évangile qui a lui-même indiqué à quelle reconnaissance il aspirait de la part de son auditoire intentionnel. Ensuite, au niveau du milieu johannique qui a réservé un accueil encore identifiable à l'œuvre centrale de son école: le quatrième évangile.

A. *La reconnaissance attendue du lecteur implicite*

Le quatrième évangile ne laisse planer aucun doute sur la nature de la reconnaissance à laquelle il aspire de la part de son lecteur implicite. Il se veut un témoignage sur le Christ, revêtu de la plus haute autorité, et appelé à fonder la foi des communautés johanniques, puis de la Grande Église.

---

57. Etat de la discussion chez BROWN, *Epistles* (n. 15), pp. 685-693.743-748; KLAUCK, *Der zweite und dritte Johannesbrief* (n. 16), pp. 22-23.106-110.

1. La prétention du récit à la reconnaissance

Trois éléments dans la construction du récit montrent à quelle reconnaissance l'évangile aspire.

Tout d'abord, le *prologue* (1,1-18) reprend un hymne christologique en usage dans les communautés johanniques[58]. En procédant de cette façon, l'auteur implicite s'appuie sur la foi commune qu'il partage avec son environnement ecclésial. Le «nous» du v. 16, qui est un «nous» communautaire[59], signe le pacte de conviction qui unit l'auteur à ses destinataires. Auteur et lecteur implicite sont unis par la même foi christologique.

La *conclusion* de l'évangile (20,30-31) – et c'est le second point – se situe sur la même ligne. Le but du récit, de «ce qui a été écrit» (20,31 γέγραπται), consiste à appeler les croyants à la foi dans la personne du Christ et ainsi à leur donner accès au salut[60]. La prétention ainsi affichée est très élevée. La lecture de l'œuvre est supposée permettre la découverte de l'identité décisive du Fils et donc de Dieu, et ce faisant d'ouvrir l'accès à la vie éternelle. En d'autres termes, les biens religieux les plus hauts sont conférés par l'Écriture que l'auteur implicite a produite à l'intention de son environnement ecclésial.

Le *corps de l'évangile* – et c'est notre troisième point – confirme ce que laissaient entrevoir le prologue et la conclusion. L'ensemble de la narration est en effet structurée par une stratégie perceptible[61]. Comme le montre la mise en intrigue centrée sur l'opposition entre foi et incrédulité, comme le confirment ces procédés littéraires typiquement johanniques que sont le malentendu, l'ironie et le langage symbolique,

---

58. Sur la relation entre l'hymne pré-johannique et sa réception par le quatrième évangile, cf. BECKER, *Johannes I* (n. 33), pp. 81-104; R. SCHNACKENBURG, *Logos-Hymnus und johanneischer Prolog*, in *BZ NF* 11 (1957) 69-109. Sur l'histoire de la recherche, cf. H. THYEN, *Aus der Literatur zum Johannesevangelium*, in *TR* 39 (1974) 1-69, spéc. 53-69; J. BECKER, *Aus der Literatur zum Johannesevangelium*, in *TR* 47 (1982) 305-347, spéc. 317-321; E. HAENCHEN, *Johannesevangelium. Ein Kommentar*, éd. par U. BUSSE, Tübingen, Mohr (Siebeck), 1980, pp. 132-154.

59. Les grands commentaires sont unanimes sur ce point: R. BULTMANN, *Das Evangelium des Johannes* (KEK, 2), Göttingen, Vandenhoeck & Ruprecht, [10]1941, p. 53; R.E. BROWN, *The Gospel according to John*, volume 1: chapters i-xii (AB, 29), Garden City, NY, Doubleday, 1966, p. 15; SCHNACKENBURG, *Johannesevangelium I* (n. 23), p. 251. Plus récemment dans le même sens, U. SCHNELLE, *Das Evangelium nach Johannes* (THK, 4), Leipzig, Evangelische Verlagsanstalt, 1998, p. 42; U. WILCKENS, *Das Evangelium nach Johannes* (NTD, 4), Göttingen, Vandenhoeck & Ruprecht, 1998, p. 35.

60. Il convient de souligner le statut métalinguistique de la conclusion. L'auteur implicite quitte le monde du récit pour se prononcer en toute clarté sur l'intention de la narration et dévoiler ainsi sa prétention à la reconnaissance.

61. Sur la stratégie mise en œuvre par le récit johannique, cf. ZUMSTEIN, *Stratégie* (n. 46).

l'évangile est traversé par une herméneutique étagée dont l'enjeu consiste à faire passer le lecteur d'une foi ébranlée et élémentaire à une foi achevée au sens johannique. La conséquence qui s'impose est que le quatrième évangile est conçu comme un livre de foi dont l'ambition est de s'adresser à un auditoire de croyants pour affermir et structurer leur conviction.

Bref, par son organisation narrative, le quatrième évangile se présente comme un livre de foi. La reconnaissance qu'il entend susciter est une adhésion sans réserve. De la qualité de cette adhésion dépend l'accès à Dieu et à la vie.

2. La reconnaissance du témoignage du disciple bien-aimé

La reconnaissance élevée à laquelle aspirait l'évangile a trouvé un fort écho dans les cercles johanniques. Elle apparaît notamment dans la reconnaissance inconditionnelle que ces derniers ont accordée au témoignage du disciple bien-aimé. Deux lieux textuels attestent cette reconnaissance.

L'autorité du disciple bien-aimé est, tout d'abord, reconnue à l'intérieur de l'évangile lui-même. Dans la scène de la Passion qui voit le soldat percer le flanc du Christ, l'auteur implicite introduit un commentaire (19,35) qui célèbre la valeur inestimable du témoignage d'un témoin oculaire. La logique narrative – et notamment la scène qui se joue entre le Christ en croix, sa mère et le disciple bien-aimé (19,25-27) – permet l'identification de ce témoin: il s'agit du disciple bien-aimé[62]. Ce personnage est non seulement reconnu comme témoin oculaire de la crucifixion de Jésus, mais encore comme l'auteur d'un témoignage dont la véracité ne saurait être mise en cause (καὶ ἀληθινὴ αὐτοῦ ἐστιν ἡ μαρτυρία), et dont le but est d'amener le lecteur à la foi (ἵνα καὶ ὑμεῖς πιστεύ[σ]ητε). L'auteur implicite de l'évangile reconnaît ainsi explicitement, sous la forme d'un commentaire inséré dans le récit, l'autorité qui donne crédit à son œuvre et qui en détermine le but.

Le second texte qui est d'importance est l'épilogue de l'évangile (Jn 21). Ce chapitre – nous l'avons déjà vu[63] – traite dans une perspective proprement johannique de l'autorité qu'il convient d'accorder à deux personnages-clefs du christianisme primitif.

---

62. Dans ce sens, T. LORENZEN, Der Lieblingsjünger im Johannesevangelium (SBS, 55), Stuttgart, Katholisches Bibelwerk, 1972, pp. 53-59; A. DAUER, Die Passionsgeschichte im Johannesevangelium (StANT, 30), München, Kösel, 1972, pp. 332-333; KÜGLER, Jünger (n. 17), pp. 265-267; CULPEPPER, John (n. 12), pp. 65-66. Cf. aussi parmi les commentateurs récents, BECKER, Johannes II (n. 44), p. 708; G.R. BEASLEY-MURRAY, John (WBC, 36), Waco, Word Books, 1987, p. 354; SCHNELLE, Johannes (n. 59), p. 293.

63. Cf. I.B.2.

Le premier personnage est *Pierre*. Réhabilité par le Ressuscité, il se voit conférer la tâche de pasteur de l'Église universelle et prédire le destin d'un martyr glorieux (21,15-19). Cette position illustre lui est pleinement reconnue par l'école johannique qui admet ainsi la légitimité du christianisme de la Grande Église[64]. Mais parallèlement à cette vocation de Pierre, un autre personnage apparaît sur le devant de la scène: c'est *le disciple bien-aimé*. La tâche qui lui est impartie et qui assure sa pérennité jusqu'à la parousie dans la mémoire de l'Église est lié à un travail d'écriture, la rédaction de l'évangile (21,20-24)[65]. L'évangile acquiert ainsi un statut normatif pour l'ensemble de l'Église dans la mesure où il identifie dans la personne du disciple bien-aimé son auteur et dans la mesure où le disciple bien-aimé a été distingué pour cette tâche par le Christ ressuscité en personne. Mais cette vocation particulière du disciple bien-aimé fait – et c'est le point décisif – l'objet d'une reconnaissance explicite par l'école johannique dans le commentaire du v. 24: καὶ οἴδαμεν ὅτι ἀληθὴς αὐτοῦ ἡ μαρτυρία ἐστιν.

La conclusion qui s'impose est claire: l'école johannique reconnaît dans le disciple bien-aimé la figure qui donne autorité à l'évangile qu'elle édite. Elle statue déjà dans cet écrit sur la question de l'apostolicité, qui sera au centre des préoccupations de l'Église ancienne.

B. *La notion de clôture*

La reconnaissance de l'autorité d'un écrit par son environnement ecclésial est ensuite attestée par le phénomène de la clôture. Par clôture, il faut entendre qu'un écrit a acquis son caractère définitif; son texte n'est désormais plus susceptible d'être remanié ou modifié[66]. Il a revêtu un caractère normatif pour son auditoire. Il est devenu Écriture. Le phénomène de la clôture est attesté dans le quatrième évangile par les deux phénomènes littéraires suivants.

En premier lieu, le quatrième évangile se caractérise par l'existence d'une *double conclusion* (20,30-31; 21,25). Alors même que l'évangile avait été l'objet de plusieurs rédactions, lorsque l'école johannique a ajouté l'épilogue à la version de l'évangile dont elle disposait, elle a considéré qu'il ne lui était plus possible de déplacer la conclusion initiale de l'évangile et de la mettre à la fin de l'épilogue. Elle a respecté la

---

64. Par «Grande Église», nous entendons les communautés nourries par les traditions de Paul et de son école, et par les évangiles synoptiques.

65. Cf. I.B.2.

66. Sur la définition de la notion de clôture, cf. A.J. GREIMAS & J. COURTÉS, *Sémiotique, Dictionnaire raisonné de la théorie du langage*, Paris, Hachette, 1993, pp. 38-39.

clôture du texte, puis ajouté l'épilogue en le munissant d'une seconde conclusion. Cette manière de faire prouve que l'évangile avait déjà acquis une forme reconnue par la communauté de ses lecteurs, qu'il n'était plus possible de modifier[67].

En second lieu, le phénomène de *relecture*[68] tel qu'il est conduit dans les discours d'adieu nous confronte à un état de fait similaire. Le fameux «Levez-vous, partons d'ici» (14,31)[69] qui clôt le premier discours d'adieu (13,31-14,31) signale un fait important et souvent mal compris par la «Literarkritik». Lorsque l'école johannique a procédé à la relecture et à l'actualisation du premier discours d'adieu en lui en adjoignant un second (15-16), elle ne s'est pas sentie autorisée à déplacer cet ordre du Christ qui clôturait le premier discours pour le mettre après le chap. 16, voire après le chap. 17. Le processus de relecture, tel qu'il est cultivé par l'école johannique, va de pair avec le respect du texte existant.

Concluons sur ce point. Le phénomène de clôture est d'importance pour notre problématique, car il démontre, d'une part, que l'évangile a été reçu et lu dans les communautés johanniques, d'autre part, qu'à partir d'un certain moment, il n'a plus été possible de procéder à des révisions internes.

C. *La notion de reconnaissance dans 1 Jn*

Le phénomène de la clôture génère un processus qui, une fois encore, a été bien observé par Paul Ricœur. Tout texte qui accède au rang d'Écriture génère une tradition d'interprétation[70]. La littérature johannique témoigne, elle aussi, d'un tel processus, comme le montre la relation entre le quatrième évangile et la première épître de Jean. Trois observations viennent à l'appui de cette thèse.

Tout d'abord, la première épître de Jn s'ouvre par un prologue (1,1-4) et s'achève par un épilogue (5,14-21), lui-même précédé d'une conclusion (5,13). Cette disposition qui imite celle de l'évangile veut suggérer que l'épître se situe dans la continuité de l'évangile et qu'elle lui fait écho[71]. Quel rôle 1 Jn joue-t-il alors par rapport à l'évangile?

---

67. Sur la définition et le genre littéraire de l'épilogue, cf. ZUMSTEIN, *Rédaction finale* (n. 34), pp. 260-261.

68. Sur la notion de relecture, cf. DETTWILER, *Gegenwart* (n. 13), pp. 46-52; J. ZUMSTEIN, *Der Prozess der Relecture in der johanneischen Literatur*, in NTS 42/3 (1996) 394-411; = ID., *Erinnerung* (n. 19), pp. 15-30.

69. Sur ce point, cf. l'analyse de DETTWILER, *Gegenwart* (n. 13), pp. 37-41.

70. Cf. RICŒUR, *Critique et conviction* (n. 1), pp. 217-219.

71. Cf. BROWN, *Epistles* (n. 15), pp. 91-92; KLAUCK, *Der erste Johannesbrief* (n. 15), p. 31.

Comme nous l'avons déjà signalé[72] – et c'est notre deuxième observation –, 1 Jn a pour objectif de montrer comment l'évangile doit être lu. Il se donne comme une consigne de lecture, comme un cadrage herméneutique qui permet de comprendre Jn dans le sens voulu par l'école johannique[73].

S'il en est ainsi – et c'est notre troisième observation –, c'est parce qu'un conflit a éclaté dans les communautés johanniques à propos de l'interprétation de la tradition de foi, et, en particulier, de l'évangile. Ce conflit des interprétations – dont nous avons déjà fait état[74] – suggère tout à la fois la reconnaissance d'une tradition reconnue comme normative pour la foi – le quatrième évangile – et simultanément l'existence d'une lutte pour la juste interprétation de cette tradition. Ainsi, la composition même du corpus johannique nous montre que l'évangile, reconnu comme Écriture, appelle le surgissement d'une tradition d'interprétation. De ce fait, elle nous fait entrevoir que le phénomène de la reconnaissance d'une Écriture fondatrice est partie intégrante de l'histoire des communautés johanniques. Encore faut-il ajouter que la reconnaissance de l'Écriture n'entraîne pas nécessairement celle de la tradition d'interprétation comme le suggère le problème évoqué par 3 Jn[75].

D. *La notion de reconnaissance dans l'histoire subséquente*

Le phénomène de la reconnaissance par les églises johanniques de Jn comme Écriture n'est pas un fait isolé. Il se poursuit au moment-même où l'évangile déborde le milieu johannique pour être offert à la lecture d'un public ecclésial plus large. Deux indices au moins le démontrent.

Tout d'abord, comme l'atteste le papyrus 66, le quatrième évangile a été très rapidement muni du titre εὐαγγέλιον κατὰ Ἰωάννην[76]. Ce titre appartient à l'histoire de la réception de l'évangile et révèle la reconnaissance dont a fait l'objet cet écrit. Par l'attribution de la qualité d'«évangile», il lui a été reconnu le même rang que celui accordé aux synopti-

---

72. Cf. point II.B.

73. Il est intéressant de constater que les listes canoniques ont maintenu le lien étroit qui existe entre Jn et 1 Jn. Le fragment de Muratori (lignes 26-33), par exemple, assied l'autorité de l'évangile et précise sa fonction en citant le prologue de la première épître de Jn.

74. Cf. notre point II.B.

75. La troisième épître de Jn montre comment une interprétation de la tradition de foi autre que celle de l'école johannique a pu s'imposer dans certaines communautés johanniques.

76. Sur la question du titre de l'évangile, cf. M. HENGEL, *Die Evangelienüberschriften* (SHAW.PH, 1984/3), Heidelberg, Winter Universitätsverlag, 1984; ID., *Frage* (n. 11), pp. 204-209.

ques. Il entre dans cette collection, ce qui lui assure un statut privilégié dans la littérature chrétienne primitive[77]. En le plaçant ensuite sous l'autorité de Jean – et il faut probablement penser au Zébédaïde –, l'histoire de la réception identifie le disciple bien-aimé à un membre du cercle apostolique et lui reconnaît ainsi l'autorité indiscutable qui assurera sa canonisation.

Un second indice atteste la reconnaissance du quatrième évangile par un milieu ecclésial plus large et extérieur au milieu johannique. Il s'agit de sa mention dans le document de Muratori. Cette citation de Jn au nombre des écrits reconnus indique qu'à la fin du IIe siècle, Jn, mais aussi les épîtres placées sous son nom – à tout le moins la première – s'étaient acquis la reconnaissance ecclésiale et avaient accédé au statut d'Écriture. La conclusion qui s'impose est claire. Le processus de reconnaissance revendiqué par le texte de l'évangile lui-même et reconnaissable dans l'histoire mouvementée du christianisme johannique, s'universalise. La trajectoire canonique s'affirme.

IV. Conclusion

Nous avons introduit notre réflexion en posant la question suivante: l'évangile selon Jn est-il devenu Écriture parce qu'il a été retenu pour faire partie du canon ou est-il devenu partie intégrante du canon parce qu'il prétendait déjà au statut d'Écriture? S'il faut se méfier des réponses simples, notre analyse nous permet à tout le moins d'affirmer que le corpus johannique occupe une place particulière dans la littérature néotestamentaire, car il reflète une réflexion explicite et structurée sur le phénomène de l'Écriture. En effet, les trois critères qui seront ensuite prépondérants pour opérer la sélection canonique sont déjà présents dans le champ de préoccupation de l'école johannique. Rappelons brièvement les résultats de notre enquête.

Le premier critère, celui de l'apostolicité, est anticipé dans la réflexion sur la notion d'autorité auctoriale. Cette réflexion est construite, d'une part, en lien avec la notion d'Écriture héritée de la tradition vétérotestamentaire juive. Elle intègre, d'autre part, des instances proprement chrétiennes et typiques de la théologie johannique, à savoir le Paraclet[78] et le disciple bien-aimé.

77. Il est possible que l'expression τὰ γραφόμενα βιβλία utilisée en 21,25, désigne l'existence d'autres évangiles, peut-être celle d'un ou de plusieurs évangiles synoptiques (cf. SMITH, *Scripture* [n. 10], pp. 19-20).

78. Cf. P. STUHLMACHER, *Biblische Theologie des Neuen Testaments. Bd. 2: Von der Paulusschule bis zur Johannesoffenbarung. Der Kanon und seine Auslegung*, Göttingen,

Le second critère, celui de l'orthodoxie, surgit avec 1 Jn, c'est-à-dire dès l'instant où se pose le problème de la transmission de la tradition fondatrice et de son interprétation. Le critère choisi pour distinguer la vérité de l'erreur est celui du retour à l'origine, à ce qui a été dit «au commencement». Cette parole fondatrice tient dans la confession de foi christologique centrée sur l'affirmation de l'incarnation du Christ et de sa mort salvatrice.

Le troisième critère essentiel dans la naissance d'une Écriture est celui de la reconnaissance ecclésiale. Dans la littérature johannique, cette problématique est travaillée aussi bien au niveau de la reconnaissance attendue que de la reconnaissance obtenue. La reconnaissance attendue apparaît, d'une part, dans l'adhésion sans réserve que réclame l'évangile, livre de foi, prétendant décider de l'accès à la vie. Elle se manifeste, d'autre part, dans sa prétention à être pour l'ensemble des chrétiens l'œuvre du témoin et de l'herméneute privilégié du Christ. La reconnaissance obtenue, elle, transparaît, tout d'abord, dans le phénomène de la clôture. Elle est attestée ensuite dans une série de commentaires métalinguistiques qui expriment explicitement la reconnaissance de l'autorité du disciple bien-aimé par les cercles johanniques. Cette reconnaissance obtenue affleure enfin dans la tradition de réception et d'interprétation qu'attestent les épîtres. Ce processus de reconnaissance se poursuit dans l'ajout d'un titre à l'évangile, dans les citations patristiques[79] et dans les premières listes canoniques.

Si l'on peut donc dire, sans grand risque de se tromper, que la littérature johannique a réfléchi sur le statut qu'elle entendait se donner, il n'en reste pas moins que cette réflexion s'est effectuée en plusieurs étapes encore identifiables.

La première étape coïncide avec la rédaction de l'évangile. Le lien étroit tissé avec l'Ancien Testament qui est fait à la fois de continuité et de différentiation, le rôle majeur reconnu au Paraclet dans la naissance du témoignage postpascal forment le socle de la notion johannique d'Écriture. La conclusion de Jn 20,30-31 constitue un premier repère. Le

---

Vandenhoeck & Ruprecht, 1999, qui écrit à ce propos (p. 215): «Der Wahrheitsanspruch, der alle johanneischen Schriften prägt, ist nicht mehr zu überbieten. Als vom Geist eröffnete und eingegebene Rede ist ihr jeweiliges (Christus-)Zeugnis unanfechtbar».

79. Sur la question des citations du quatrième évangile dans la littérature patristique, cf. J.-M. POFFET, *Indices de réception de l'évangile de Jean au IIe siècle, avant Irénée*, in J.-D. KAESTLI, J.-M. POFFET, J. ZUMSTEIN (éds.), *La communauté johannique et son histoire. La trajectoire de l'évangile de Jean aux deux premiers siècles* (MoBi, 20), Genève, Labor et Fides, 1990, pp. 305-321; T. NAGEL, *Die Rezeption des Johannesevangeliums im 2. Jahrhundert. Studien zur vorirenäischen Aneignung und Auslegung des vierten Evangeliums in christlicher und christlich-gnostischer Literatur* (Arbeiten zur Bibel und ihrer Geschichte, 2), Leipzig, Evangelische Verlagsanstalt, 2000.

quatrième évangile se veut un livre de foi appelant à la foi, il prétend à une autorité comparable à celle reconnue à l'Écriture vétérotestamentaire-juive[80].

L'inscription du disciple bien-aimé dans la narration et l'adjonction de l'épilogue constituent une seconde étape. Une identité prestigieuse est attribuée à l'auteur de l'évangile: il s'agit du disciple que Jésus aimait. La question de l'apostolicité garantissant la vérité de l'écrit est ainsi débattue dans le récit lui-même. L'épilogue du chap. 21 poursuit, quant à lui, l'ambition de dire la validité de l'évangile désormais clôturé pour l'ensemble de l'Église.

La troisième étape est franchie avec 1 Jn qui soulève le problème de l'orthodoxie. L'évangile est certes le livre de foi des communautés johanniques, mais son interprétation est controversée et appelle une régulation. La confession de foi christologique axée sur l'incarnation et la mort du Christ est érigée en critère doctrinal permettant de distinguer la vérité de l'erreur. 2 et 3 Jn signalent pourtant que cette tradition d'interprétation n'est pas acceptée par l'ensemble des communautés johanniques. Le geste disciplinaire vient alors se greffer sur le débat théologique.

La quatrième étape achève la mise en Église de l'évangile, désormais mis en rapport avec d'autres œuvres du christianisme naissant. La suscription dont est nanti l'évangile, les citations dont il fait l'objet dans des écrits de l'Église ancienne, sa mention dans les premières listes canoniques signalent que l'Écriture johannique est en voie de devenir Écriture du Nouveau Testament. L'ambition prêtée au disciple bien-aimé par le récit est devenue réalité.

Faculté de théologie   Jean ZUMSTEIN
de l'Université de Zurich
Kirchgasse 9
CH-8001 Zürich

---

80. A. OBERMANN, *Die christologische Erfüllung der Schrift im Johannesevangelium. Eine Untersuchung zur johanneischen Hermeneutik anhand der Schriftzitate* (WUNT, 2/83), Tübingen, Mohr (Siebeck), 1996, p. 430.

DIE APOSTELGESCHICHTE UND DIE ENTSTEHUNG DES NEUTESTAMENTLICHEN KANONS
BEOBACHTUNGEN ZUR KANONISIERUNG DER APOSTELGESCHICHTE UND IHRER BEDEUTUNG ALS KANONISCHER SCHRIFT

Die Apostelgeschichte ist in gewisser Weise der Schlüssel zum Verständnis der Idee des kirchlichen Neuen Testaments und hat es zu dem Organismus, wie er vor uns steht, gemacht. Indem sie an die Spitze des „Apostolus" trat, ermöglichte sie erst die Zweiteilung und rechtfertigte die Verbindung der Paulusbriefe mit den Evangelien. Man könnte auch von einer Dreiteilung sprechen, in welcher die Apostelgeschichte (samt den katholischen Briefen und der Joh.-Apokalypse) das Mittelstück bildet[1].

Mit diesen Sätzen faßt Adolf von Harnack seine These über die Entstehung des Neuen Testaments und die Rolle der Apg in diesem Prozeß zusammen. Entwickelt hatte er diese Auffassung nicht zuletzt in der bekannten Kontroverse mit Theodor Zahn, in der es vor allem um die Frage ging, ob das Neue Testament auf einen Prozeß der Selbstdurchsetzung autoritativer Schriften zurückzuführen oder aber als eine bewußte Schöpfung der Kirche am Ende des 2. Jahrhunderts zu beurteilen sei[2]. Bekanntlich setzte sich Harnack – dessen Position Hans von Campenhausen später aufgegriffen und noch einmal zugespitzt hat[3] – vehement für die letztere Option ein und begründete sie u.a. damit, daß die Kirche durch Markion und die gnostischen Schulen des 2. Jahrhunderts zur Festlegung eines Schriftenkanons gezwungen worden sei. Dieser sei deshalb „nicht durch Sammlung … sondern primär durch Ausscheidung" zustande gekommen[4]. Die Aufnahme der Apg sah Harnack als einen entscheidenden Schritt innerhalb dieser Festlegung an, da sie mehreren Zwecken zugleich dienstbar gemacht wurde:

1. A. VON HARNACK, *Beiträge zur Einleitung in das Neue Testament VI: Die Entstehung des Neuen Testaments und die wichtigsten Folgen der neuen Schöpfung*, Leipzig, Hinrichs, 1914, p. 46. Cf. ID., *Lehrbuch der Dogmengeschichte, I: Die Entstehung des kirchlichen Dogmas*, Tübingen, Mohr, [4]1909, pp. 382-384, n. 2.

2. Cf. ID., *Das Neue Testament um das Jahr 200. Theodor Zahn's Geschichte des neutestamentlichen Kanons (Erster Band, Erste Hälfte)*, Freiburg, Mohr, 1889, sowie die Antwort von T. ZAHN, *Einige Bemerkungen zu Adolf Harnack's Prüfung der Geschichte des neutestamentlichen Kanons (Erster Band, Erste Hälfte)*, Erlangen & Leipzig, Deichert, 1889.

3. H. VON CAMPENHAUSEN, *Die Entstehung der christlichen Bibel*, Tübingen, Mohr, 1968, p. 237 u.ö.

4. A. VON HARNACK, *Dogmengeschichte* (n. 1), pp. 372-399, esp. 375.

- Legitimiert durch die Verfasserschaft eines bereits als kanonischer Schriftsteller anerkannten Autors, erzählte sie die Taten und Verkündigung *aller* Apostel, wenn auch nur durch den Mund des Petrus.
- Sie lieferte eine Darstellung der Urgeschichte der Kirche, einschließlich des auf einem Beschluß der Urgemeinde beruhenden Übergangs von der Juden- zur Heidenmission.
- Gemeinsam mit den Briefen (vor allem) des Petrus und Johannes füllte sie die Lücke apostolischer Schreiben neben den Paulusbriefen aus.
- Durch die Verbindung des Paulus mit dem Zwölferkreis ermöglichte sie es, dessen Briefe „nach der kirchlichen communis opinio zu deuten" und „benahm ihnen das Bedenkliche und Unzureichende"[5].

Die Apg ist deshalb für Harnack diejenige Schrift, die die verschiedenen Teile des neutestamentlichen Kanons – Evangelien, Paulusbriefe, katholische Briefe – miteinander verbindet und die hinter dieser Zusammenstellung erkennbar werdende Intention zum Ausdruck bringt. Diese bestimmte Harnack als eine „Logik der Selbsterhaltung", die dazu geführt habe, gegen deren Bestreitung durch Markion und die Gnostiker die Übereinstimmung des Apostolischen mit der Verkündigung Christi zu erweisen, es zudem mit dem AT zu verschmelzen und auf diese Weise die alleinige Autorität der Auslegung zu sichern[6].

Für Harnack stand freilich zugleich außer Frage, daß Anspruch und Wirklichkeit nirgendwo so weit auseinanderklaffen wie bei einer derartigen Inanspruchnahme der Apg. Sie sei nur „faute de mieux in den Kanon gekommen"[7] – nämlich in Ermangelung eines Buches, das die Wirksamkeit des Zwölferkreises *tatsächlich* schildern würde. Ihre kirchliche Aufnahme sei deshalb von „colossalen Übertreibungen" begleitet, die sie zu einem Bericht über die „Taten aller Apostel" hochstilisierten[8] und Lukas zu einem „Begleiter und Mitarbeiter *der Apostel*, vor allem aber des Paulus", machten[9]. Der Apostelteil des Neuen Testament sei somit durch Eigenschaften legitimiert worden, die die Apg gar nicht besitze, die vielmehr künstlich in sie eingetragen worden seien. Die

5. Cf. ID., *Entstehung* (n. 1), pp. 44-45 (Zitat p. 45); *Dogmengeschichte* (n. 1), pp. 381-382 (Zitat p. 382).
6. ID., *Dogmengeschichte* (n. 1), pp. 380-381.
7. *Ibid.*, p. 383, n. 2.
8. So im CanMur, l. 34: acta omnium apostolorum.
9. So Iren.haer. 3,14,1: non solum prosecutor sed et cooperarius fuerit apostolorum, maxime autem Pauli.

Apg, eigentlich alt und zuverlässig, sei somit „im Hinblick auf den Kanon" eine junge Schrift[10].

Die pointierte Position Harnacks soll als Ausgangspunkt der folgenden Überlegungen zur Rolle der Apg im Entstehungsprozeß des neutestamentlichen Kanons dienen[11]. In der Tat verlangt die Frage, warum die Apg seit dem Ende des 2. Jahrhunderts zu den verbindlichen Schriften der Kirche gerechnet wurde, nach einer anderen Antwort als im Fall der Evangelien und der Paulusbriefe. Harnacks Position indiziert diesbezüglich ein Problem, das auch gegenwärtig noch virulent ist, nämlich das Verhältnis von historisch-kritischer Betrachtung und Bestimmung der kanonischen Bedeutung einer Schrift. Bei Harnack fallen diese Aspekte in bezug auf die Apg weit auseinander. Die Kanonisierung der Apg wäre demnach weniger auf ihren *Inhalt*, als vielmehr auf kirchenpolitische Konstellationen des ausgehenden 2. Jahrhunderts zurückzuführen.

Die historisch-kritische Forschung hat diese Linie nach Harnack weitergeführt, auch wenn die Akzente dabei oft anders gesetzt wurden. Sie hat uns gelehrt, die Apg kritisch auf das Verhältnis von Geschichtsdarstellung und zugrundeliegenden Ereignissen der urchristlichen Geschichte hin zu durchleuchten und nicht naiv mit der Wirklichkeit der Frühzeit zu identifizieren; sie hat uns gelehrt, das lukanische Paulusbild als eine eigene Verarbeitung seines Wirkens zu betrachten, die nicht an der in seinen Briefen entwickelten Theologie orientiert ist; sie hat uns gelehrt, die Apg als zweiten Teil des lukanischen Doppelwerkes zu interpretieren und ihre inhaltlichen Charakteristika innerhalb dieses Zusammenhangs zu erörtern.

Die historisch-kritische Lektüre der Apg hat auf diese Weise unverzichtbare Erkenntnisse für deren Interpretation zutage gefördert, hinter die nicht mehr zurückgegangen werden kann. Die Frage nach ihrer kanonischen Bedeutung spielte dabei eine vergleichsweise geringe Rolle. Ob Harnacks These eines kirchlichen Interesses, das mit dem Inhalt der Apg nicht zur Deckung zu bringen sei, ja z.T. sogar in Widerspruch zu diesem stehe, jedoch eine befriedigende Antwort auf die Frage nach dem Verhältnis von historischer und kanonischer Bedeutung dieser Schrift darstellt, wird anhand der betreffenden Quellen zu prüfen sein. Im Blick auf das Thema „Biblischer Kanon" weist die Aufnahme der Apg unter die verbindlichen Schriften jedenfalls – das hat Harnack völlig zu Recht

---

10. ID., *Dogmengeschichte* (n. 1), p. 384, n. 2.
11. Diese Frage ist, soweit ich sehe, monographisch nur einmal behandelt worden, nämlich in der (unveröffentlichten) STM Thesis von D.W. KUCK, *The Use and Canonization of Acts in the Early Church*, Yale Divinity School, 1975. Herrn Kuck sowie der Yale Divinity School Library sei an dieser Stelle für die Bereitstellung der Arbeit gedankt.

betont – über die *Sammlung* solcher Schriften hinaus auf die Ausbildung der Merkmale eines neutestamentlichen *Kanons*[12]. Insofern stellt dieser Prozeß einen wichtigen Bestandteil der neutestamentlichen Kanongeschichte dar.

Ich wende mich in einem ersten – ausführlicheren – Teil der Rezeption der Apg in der Alten Kirche zu, konfrontiere diese im zweiten – kürzeren – Teil mit der Tatsache, daß sich die Apg als Fortsetzung des LkEv zu erkennen gibt und frage schließlich im dritten – noch kürzeren – Teil nach Implikationen einer kanonischen Lektüre der Apg.

I. DIE APOSTELGESCHICHTE IM PROZESS DER ENTSTEHUNG DES NEUEN TESTAMENTS

A. Anfänge der Rezeption: Die externen Zeugnisse des 2. Jahrhunderts

Erste Bezugnahmen auf die Apg lassen sich frühestens in der Mitte des 2. Jahrhunderts feststellen. Versuche, ihre Kenntnis in Spätschriften des NT oder bei den Apostolischen Vätern nachzuweisen, sind von Ernst Haenchen, David Kuck, Gerhard Schneider und neuerdings noch einmal von Charles Kingsley Barrett besprochen und mit Recht als nicht erweisbar beurteilt worden[13]. Die in diesen Schriften begegnenden Anklänge an Formulierungen, die sich auch in der Apg finden, lassen sich durchgehend auf unabhängige Aufnahme urchristlicher Traditionen zurückführen, wogegen für eine Benutzung der Apg die Indizien fehlen[14].

12. Ich unterscheide „Sammlung" und „Kanon" in der Weise, daß eine *Sammlung* von Schriften, wie sie bei den Evangelien und den Paulusbriefen vorgenommen wurde, noch nicht an der Vorstellung von deren *alleiniger Verbindlichkeit* – und damit der Ausgrenzung anderer Schriften – orientiert ist. Dies ist dann allerdings die Intention der Festlegung eines *Kanons*, der somit gleichermaßen eine positiv-bewahrende wie eine negativ-ausgrenzende Funktion besitzt.

13. E. HAENCHEN, *Die Apostelgeschichte* (KEK, 3), Göttingen, Vandenhoeck & Ruprecht, ⁷1977, pp. 17-22; KUCK, *Use* (n. 11), pp. 11-22; G. SCHNEIDER, *Die Apostelgeschichte. I. Teil* (HTK[NT], 5/1), Freiburg et al., Herder, 1980, pp. 170-171; C.K. BARRETT, *The Acts of the Apostles* (ICC), Edinburgh, T & T Clark, 1994, I, pp. 34-38.

14. Zwei Beispiele seien genannt: 1. In 2 Tim 3,11 ist von den διωγμοὶ καὶ παθήματα die Rede, welche Paulus ἐν Ἀντιοχείᾳ, ἐν Ἰκονίῳ, ἐν Λύστροις erlitten hat. Dies entspricht der Darstellung der Ereignisse auf der 1. Missionsreise, wo Paulus und Barnabas in ebendiesen Städten Nachstellungen ausgesetzt sind. Das Fehlen jeglicher konkreter Anspielungen macht es jedoch unmöglich, eine Kenntnis der Apg nachzuweisen. Der Verfasser von 2 Tim greift offenbar unabhängig von der Apg auf Paulustraditionen zurück. 2. Bei IgnSm 3,3 heißt es μετὰ δὲ τὴν ἀνάστασιν συνέφαγεν αὐτοῖς καὶ συνέπιεν ὡς σαρκικός, καίπερ πνευματικῶς ἡνωμένος τῷ πατρί. Dies stellt eine Analogie zu Apg 10,41 dar: οἵτινες συνεφάγομεν καὶ συνεπίομεν αὐτῷ μετὰ τὸ ἀναστῆναι αὐτὸν ἐκ νεκρῶν (cf. auch 1,4; Lk 24,30.42f.; Joh 21,12f.). Die

Als früheste Quellen einer externen Bezeugung kommen damit Justin sowie die EpAp in Betracht. Bei ersterem kann allerdings eine Benutzung der Apg ebenfalls nicht zweifelsfrei festgestellt werden[15]. Die als entscheidender Beleg angeführte Stelle 1 apol. 50[16], in der Menschwerdung, Passion, Himmelfahrt sowie anschließende Geistverleihung erzählt werden, geht in der Beschreibung der Aufnahme Jesu als eines den Jüngern sichtbaren Vorgangs[17] über den Bericht des LkEv hinaus[18]. Darüber hinaus könnte die Formulierung δύναμιν ἐκεῖθεν αὐτοῖς πεμφθεῖσαν παρ' αὐτοῦ λαβόντες Apg 1,8 (λήμψεσθε δύναμιν) anklingen lassen. Allerdings könnte auch – analog zum sekundären Mk-Schluß (Mk 16,19) – eine eigene Rezeption der Überlieferung von Himmelfahrt und Geistverleihung im Anschluß an Lk 24,49.51[19] vorliegen. Die durchaus vielfältigen urchristlichen Zeugnisse über die Erhöhung bzw. Himmelfahrt Christi gemahnen jedenfalls zur Zurückhaltung, eine literarische Vermittlung über die Apg zu postulieren, wenn die Indizien hierfür nicht eindeutig sind.

Wertet man die Stelle dagegen als Beleg für eine Kenntnis der Apg seitens Justin, so wäre sie eher geeignet, die *geringe Bedeutung* zu bestätigen, die sie für Justin besaß[20]. Am auffälligsten ist diesbezüglich zweifellos sein völliges Schweigen über Paulus und die Konzentration auf die Jesusüberlieferung. Beides weist darauf hin, daß Justin – anders als die Apg – das Christentum auf die Schriften Israels und die Autorität Jesu, jedoch nicht zusätzlich auf diejenige des Paulus oder eines anderen Apostels gründet[21]. Unabhängig von der Frage, ob die genannte Stelle Justins Kenntnis der Apg verrät und ob seine (unstrittige) Bekanntschaft mit dem LkEv eine solche Kenntnis zusätzlich nahelegen

Stelle deutet allerdings eher auf eine allgemeine Tradition über das Essen des Auferstandenen mit seinen Jüngern hin als auf eine Benutzung der Apg. Dies wird durch die Bemerkung des Hieronymus (vir.ill. 2) verstärkt, Ignatius habe in 3,2 ein evangelium quod appellatur secundum Hebraeos benutzt. Cf. BARRETT, *Acts* (n. 13), p. 36.

15. Bezweifelt wird eine solche von W.A. STRANGE, *The Problem of the Text of Acts* (SNTS.MS, 71), Cambridge, University Press, 1992, pp. 180-181. Cf. auch das zurückhaltende Urteil bei BARRETT, *Acts* (n. 13), p. 44. Anders jedoch HAENCHEN, *Apg* (n. 13), pp. 22-23; SCHNEIDER, *Apg* (n. 13), p. 172.

16. Cf. HAENCHEN, *Apg* (n. 13), p. 23. Die anderen Stellen sind für die Frage einer literarischen Kenntnis der Apg von geringerem Gewicht.

17. εἰς οὐρανὸν ἀνερχόμενον ἰδόντες καὶ πιστεύσαντες.

18. Cf. T. ZAHN, *Geschichte des neutestamentlichen Kanons (Erster Band, Zweite Hälfte)*, Erlangen & Leipzig, Deichert, 1889, pp. 508-509.

19. καθίσατε ἐν τῇ πόλει ἕως οὗ ἐνδύσησθε ἐξ ὕψους δύναμιν ... καὶ ἐγένετο ἐν τῷ εὐλογεῖν αὐτὸν αὐτοὺς διέστη ἀπ' αὐτῶν καὶ ἀνεφέρετο εἰς τὸν οὐρανόν.

20. Cf. BARRETT, *Acts* (n. 13), p. 44.

21. Cf. A. LINDEMANN, *Paulus im ältesten Christentum. Das Bild des Apostels und die Rezeption der paulinischen Theologie in der frühchristlichen Literatur bis Marcion* (BHT, 58), Tübingen, Mohr, 1979, pp. 353-367.

könnte[22], bleibt somit festzuhalten, daß die Apg für ihn ebensowenig wie die Paulusbriefe eine den Evangelien vergleichbare Bedeutung für die Fixierung der christlichen Tradition besaß.

Ein etwas anderer Befund stellt sich beim Blick auf EpAp ein. Diese im 2. Jahrhundert, vermutlich vor Irenäus, verfaßte Schrift[23] enthält in c. 31 (p. 42) einen Bericht über die Erblindung des Paulus, seine Audition sowie seine nachfolgende Wirksamkeit als Verkündiger unter den Heiden. Berührungen mit den entsprechenden Berichten der Apg sind dabei unverkennbar. Besonders augenfällig sind die doppelte Namensnennung Saul – Paulus, die Erwähnung seiner zeitweiligen Blindheit sowie seine Bezeichnung als „Heil der Heiden". Andere Elemente, wie sein Judesein, die ehemalige Verfolgertätigkeit sowie sein Bekennen vor Königen, könnten dagegen auch aus einer frei umlaufenden „Pauluslegende" stammen, deren Existenz z.B. durch Gal 1,23; 2 Tim 3,11 und 1 Klem 5 belegt wird. Die Zeichnung des Weges des Paulus von Kilikien nach Damaskus in c. 33 (p. 44) steht dagegen in Widerspruch zur Darstellung in Apg 9,1f.

Inhaltlich ist von Bedeutung, daß in EpAp eine Verbindung des Apostelkreises mit der Person des Paulus hergestellt wird, ohne daß dazu auf die Theologie des Paulus oder seine Briefe rekurriert würde. Dies stellt zunächst eine interessante Analogie zur Apg dar. Freilich ist nicht zu übersehen, daß sich EpAp – anders als dann Irenäus – abgesehen von der Bekehrung nicht an der Paulusdarstellung der Apg orientiert. In EpAp ergänzt Paulus den Kreis der elf Apostel, er wird von ihnen belehrt und auf diese Weise dem Eintreten der Apostel für die rechte Lehre gegen Kerinth und Simon zugeordnet. Anders als bei Justin finden wir in EpAp also eine explizite Verbindung der Apostel mit Paulus, für die neben den Evangelien offensichtlich auch auf die Apg zurückgegriffen wird. Dabei erhält die Rolle des Paulus jedoch kein eigenständiges Gewicht. Die entscheidende Autorität ist vielmehr der Kreis der elf Jünger, die die Offenbarungsempfänger sind und innerhalb dieser Offenbarung auch über die Bekehrung des Paulus informiert werden.

Die fehlende Bezugnahme auf die Apg bei den Apostolischen Vätern sowie das Zeugnis von Justin und EpAp zeigen somit, daß sich bis zur Mitte des 2. Jahrhunderts zur Sicherung der Grundlagen des christlichen

---

22. So F. OVERBECK, *Ueber das Verhältniss Justins des Märtyrers zur Apostelgeschichte*, in ZWT 15 (1872) 305-349, pp. 314-316; ZAHN, *Geschichte I/2* (n. 18), pp. 579-580.

23. Cf. C. SCHMIDT, *Gespräche Jesu mit seinen Jüngern nach der Auferstehung. Ein katholisch-apostolisches Sendschreiben des 2. Jahrhunderts* (TU, 43), Leipzig, Akademie-Verlag, 1919, pp. 361-402. Die Entscheidung fällt nach sorgfältiger Abwägung der Indizien „... auf die zweite Hälfte des zweiten Jahrhunderts, genauer auf 160-170".

Glaubens nicht auf die Apg berufen wurde. Dies bedeutet einen gegenüber den Evangelien sowie den Paulusbriefen markanten Unterschied, denn deren Rezeptionsgeschichte beginnt deutlich früher[24]. Zwei signifikante Tendenzen lassen sich gleichwohl erkennen: Justin bindet das Jesuszeugnis an die Schriften der Apostel bzw. Apostelschüler, was schon in seiner Bezeichnung der Evangelien als ἀπομνημονεύματα τῶν ἀποστόλων zum Ausdruck kommt[25]. Diese, möglicherweise antignostisch ausgerichtete Bezeichnung[26] deutet bereits auf das Bestreben der Sicherung der Jesusüberlieferung durch die Autorisierung der schriftlichen Evangelien hin, wie sie dann in der Kanonbildung immer stärker zur Geltung kommt[27]. Die zweite Tendenz ist die Einordnung des Paulus in das gesamtapostolische Zeugnis. Auch diese, in EpAp zum ersten Mal auftretende Thematik wird für die Kanongeschichte bedeutsam werden.

Ganz anders als bei den bislang genannten Schriften stellt sich die Lage bezüglich der Apg bei Irenäus und Tertullian dar[28]. Die entscheidenden Passagen über die Apg bei Irenäus finden sich im dritten Buch von Adversus Haereses. Nachdem er in den ersten beiden Büchern die gnostischen Lehren dargestellt und widerlegt hatte, führt Irenäus nunmehr den Beweis für die Richtigkeit der Lehre, daß es nur einen Gott, Schöpfer von Himmel und Erde, gibt und einen Christus, Gottes Sohn (3,1,2). Die Wahrheit dieser Lehre wird durch ihren apostolischen Ursprung sowie ihre reine Bewahrung in der Kirche verbürgt. Mit diesem Argument wendet sich Irenäus gegen die Herabsetzung der apostolischen Autoritäten sowie die Behauptung der Unvollkommenheit ihrer Lehre (3,1,1). Den inhaltlichen Nachweis führt er sodann anhand des Schriftzeugnisses (6,1-4), desjenigen des Paulus (6,5-7,2) sowie des Herrn selbst (8,1-2). Hierauf folgt das apostolische Zeugnis der Evangelien über Gott und Jesus Christus, das in der symbolischen Ausdeutung des εὐαγγέλιον τετράμορφον gipfelt (3,9,1-3,11,8). Im Anschluß wendet sich Irenäus sodann dem Zeugnis der übrigen Apostel und deren Auffassung von Gott zu[29]. Diese Stelle bildet den Übergang von den vier

24. Cf. unten Abschnitt C. *Die Apg und die Entstehung des neutestamentlichen Kanons.*

25. Iust. 1apol. 66,3; 67,3 sowie dreizehnmal in dial.

26. Cf. L. ABRAMOWSKI, *Die „Erinnerungen der Apostel" bei Justin*, in P. STUHLMACHER (ed.), *Das Evangelium und die Evangelien*, Tübingen, Mohr, 1983, pp. 341-353.

27. Cf. W. SCHNEEMELCHER, *Bibel III. Die Entstehung des Kanons des Neuen Testaments und der christlichen Bibel*, in *TRE* 6, 1980, pp. 22-48, esp. 32.

28. Zeugnisse für eine Kenntnis der Apg liegen des weiteren in dem Brief der Märtyrer von Lugdunum und Vienna (Eus.h.e. 5,1) sowie evtl. in der Erzählung über die Steinigung des Jakobus bei Hegesipp (Eus.h.e. 2,23) vor, in der die Szene der Hinrichtung des Stephanus anklingt.

29. *Ibid.*, 3,11,9: Examinata igitur sententia eorum qui nobis tradiderunt evangelium ex ipsis principiis ipsorum, veniamus et ad reliquos apostolos et perquiramus sententiam eorum de Deo.

Evangelien zur Apg und damit den frühesten Beleg für diejenige Abfolge der neutestamentlichen Schriften, die sich auch bei Tertullian, in CanMur sowie in späteren Kanonverzeichnissen findet[30].

Der erste explizite und ausführliche Rekurs auf die Apg erfolgt somit im Zusammenhang der Abwehr der Lehren Markions und Valentins[31]. Die Darstellung des Inhaltes, vornehmlich der Reden der Apg in haer. 3,12 hat zum Ziel, die Lehre von dem einen Gott und seinem Sohn Jesus Christus, wie sie von Petrus, der Jerusalemer Gemeinde, Philippus, Paulus, Stephanus sowie auf dem Apostelkonzil vertreten wurde, als einheitlich, in Übereinstimmung mit dem Zeugnis der Schrift befindlich und damit die Lehren Valentins und Markions widerlegend, darzustellen.

Ein zweites Ziel der Darstellung des Irenäus richtet sich auf eine Integration des Paulus in die apostolische Tradition. Waren Bekehrung sowie die Predigt des Paulus vor Heiden[32] bereits bei der Wiedergabe der Apg dargestellt worden (3,12,9), so wendet er sich in 3,13 Paulus noch einmal gesondert zu. Dies erfolgt zum einen im Widerspruch gegen die Behauptung, ausschließlich Paulus sei in einer Offenbarung die Wahrheit zuteil geworden[33], zum anderen gegen dessen Ablehnung. Die Übereinstimmung des Paulus mit Petrus und den anderen Aposteln (3,13,1-2), die seiner Isolierung von diesen widerspreche, erfolgt durch den Hinweis, Paulus selbst bestätige in seinem Brief an die Galater, daß Petrus und er von ein und demselben Gott den Auftrag zur Mission erhielten[34]. Daß Paulus andere Apostel neben sich anerkenne, werde zudem durch

---

30. In den Listen des 4. Jahrhunderts traten dann des öfteren die katholischen Briefe zur Apg hinzu (cf. n. 74). Die Reihenfolge Evangelien – Apg – Paulusbriefe – katholische Briefe findet sich dagegen bei Greg.Naz.carm. 1,12,5 sowie bei Amphilochius von Ikonium, deren Verzeichnisse auf der trullanischen Synode von 692 angenommen wurden. Cf. T. ZAHN, *Geschichte des neutestamentlichen Kanons (Zweiter Band, Erste Hälfte)*, Erlangen & Leipzig, Deichert, 1890, pp. 212-219 (dort auch die Texte). Cf. auch den auf der dritten Synode von Karthago verlesenen Kanon der Synode von Hippo regius (ZAHN, *ibid.*, pp. 246-253).

31. Cf. den expliziten Rekurs *ibid.*, 3,12,5.

32. Irenäus kommt bezeichnenderweise nur auf die Areopagrede sowie die Rede des Paulus in Lystra zu sprechen, auf Passagen also, in denen sich Paulus ausdrücklich an Heiden wendet. Bezüglich der Rede in Athen erwähnt er sogar explizit, daß kein Jude anwesend war (non adsistentibus Iudaeis).

33. Im Hintergrund steht die von Irenäus' Gegnern offenbar zur Begründung herangezogene Stelle Eph 3,3. Interessant ist das Vorgehen des Irenäus, um diese Deutung der Stelle zu entkräften: In 12,9 zieht er sie in Verbindung mit Apg 9,19-20 und Phil 2,8 heran und bezieht das geoffenbarte Mysterium auf die Gottessohnschaft sowie den Kreuzestod Jesu. In 13,1, wo er sie als Argument seiner Gegner noch einmal zitiert, widerlegt er sie durch Stellen aus Gal, Röm und 1 Kor, die zeigen, daß Paulus selbst von mehreren spricht, die die Wahrheit verkünden. Beide Male ist es also das Zeugnis des Paulus selbst, anhand dessen die „richtige" Deutung dargelegt wird.

34. *Ibid.* 3,13,1: Eos autem qui dicunt solum Paulum veritatem cognovisse … ipse Paulus convincat eos dicens unum et ipsum Deum operatum Petro in apostolatum circumcisionis, et sibi in gentes. Ipsius ergo Dei Petrus erat apostolus cuius et Paulus.

weitere Äußerungen in seinen Briefen[35] sowie durch den von ihm ange-
strebten Konsens auf dem Apostelkonzil belegt (3,13,3). In diesem Zusammenhang weist Irenäus auch darauf hin, daß der Zeitpunkt, den man
aus der Apg für das Apostelkonzil ermitteln könne, mit der Angabe des
Paulus übereinstimme[36].

Die Ablehnung des Paulus wird dagegen mit dem Argument zurückgewiesen, der Bericht des Lukas sei bereits durch das Evangelium als
wahrhaftig ausgewiesen. Daraus folge, daß der Bericht über die Erwählung des Paulus zum Apostel für die Heiden nicht in Zweifel gezogen
werden dürfe. Wer dies dennoch tue, trenne sich von der Gemeinschaft
der Apostel[37].

Zwischen diesen beiden, auf Paulus bezogenen Teilen steht derjenige
Passus, in dem Irenäus die Zuverlässigkeit des Berichtes der Apg thematisiert (3,14). Diese wird zum einen dadurch erwiesen, daß die Apg
durch einen Paulusbegleiter verfaßt wurde. Irenäus belegt dies durch einen Rekurs auf die Wir-Passagen der Apg, die ihrerseits durch Paulus
selbst bestätigt würden, der Lukas an zwei Stellen seiner Briefe erwähnt[38]. Zum anderen argumentiert Irenäus, Lukas sei bereits durch das
Evangelium legitimiert, da sich in diesem etliche Stücke fänden, die nur
durch ihn überliefert seien. Bezweifle man also die Zuverlässigkeit der
Apg, so verwerfe man zugleich das Evangelium – womit Irenäus nicht
das *LkEv*, sondern das Evangelium als autoritativen Bericht über das
Wirken Jesu überhaupt meint[39].

Der Rekurs des Irenäus auf die Apg weist somit folgende Merkmale
auf:

– Gegen Markion und die Gnostiker wird erwiesen, daß das Zeugnis der
Personen, von denen die Apg berichtet, in Übereinstimmung mit demjenigen der Evangelien steht.

– Gegen Markion wird festgehalten, daß Paulus nicht aus dem Gesamtzeugnis der Apostel isoliert werden darf, sondern innerhalb dessen interpretiert werden muß.

---

35. Irenäus zitiert Röm 10,15 (Jes 52,7) sowie 1 Kor 15,11, wo Paulus selbst zu erkennen gebe, daß das Evangelium von vielen übereinstimmend gepredigt werde.

36. *Ibid.*, 3,13,3: Si quis igitur diligenter ex actibus apostolorum scrutetur tempus de
quo scriptum est ascendisse Hierosolymam propter praedictam quaestionem, inveniet eos
qui praedicti sunt a Paulo annos concurrentes.

37. *Ibid.*, 3,15,1: Qui igitur non recipiunt eum qui sit electus a domino ut fiducialiter
portet nomen eius in quas praediximus gentes, electionem domini contemnunt et seipsos
segregant ab apostolorum conventu.

38. *Ibid.*, 3,14,1-2. Irenäus zitiert 2 Tim 4,10-11 sowie Kol 4,14 (die er natürlich als
authentische Paulusbriefe betrachtet), soweit die lateinische Übersetzung erkennen läßt,
fast wörtlich. Auf den Λουκᾶς aus der Grußliste des Phlm bezieht er sich dagegen nicht.

39. Dies geht aus der Formulierung „Plurima enim et magis necessaria evangelii per
hunc [sc.: Lucam] cognovimus …" (3,14,3) eindeutig hervor.

– Die Glaubwürdigkeit des Berichtes der Apg wird durch die Paulus-
begleiterschaft sowie durch die Identität des Verfassers mit demjenigen des Lukas-Evangeliums erwiesen.

Lenken wir an dieser Stelle den Blick zurück auf die eingangs zitierten Äußerungen Harnacks, so sind sie in bezug auf Irenäus an einer
wichtigen Stelle zu korrigieren: Irenäus benutzt nicht die Apg, um den
Paulusbriefen „das Bedenkliche und Unzureichende" zu nehmen. Dagegen spricht zum einen, daß er bereits vor der Passage, in der er vom
Evangelienzeugnis auf dasjenige der übrigen Apostel übergeht, auf Paulus rekurriert und dessen Zeugnis in Auseinandersetzung mit seinen
Gegnern auslegt (3,6,5-3,7,2). Dies folgt aber auch daraus, daß die Über-
einstimmung des Paulus mit den anderen Aposteln aus *dessen eigenen
Briefen* hergeleitet wird, die damit die Gegner widerlegen[40]. Dies folgt
schließlich drittens daraus, daß sowohl der Bericht des Lukas über das
Apostelkonzil als auch die Wir-Passagen durch Paulus bestätigt werden,
nicht umgekehrt[41]! Es geht Irenäus also nicht darum, mit Hilfe der Apg
Paulus kirchlich zu „domestizieren". Dafür hätte er den Erweis ihrer
Zuverlässigkeit kaum mit einem Rekurs auf den Gal beginnen können.
Vielmehr steht für ihn die Autorität des Paulus unbezweifelbar fest und
führt – gerade umgekehrt – dazu, aus dieser auch diejenige der Apg als
des Werks eines Paulusbegleiters abzuleiten[42].

Abschließend zu diesem Punkt ist auf die Erwähnung der Apg durch
Tertullian hinzuweisen. Tertullian kommt häufig und in unterschiedlichen Zusammenhängen auf die Apg zu sprechen[43]. Dabei zeigen die Rekurse auf die Apostel als moralische Vorbilder und Autoritäten[44], daß er
die Berufung auf diese Schrift als keiner besonderen Legitimation be-
dürftig ansah. Sie zeigen zugleich, daß er diese Schrift in wesentlich
stärkerem Maß als Irenäus als historisches Zeugnis über die Frühzeit der
Kirche heranzog.

Für die hier verfolgte Frage sind zwei Passagen von besonderer Bedeutung. In praesc. 22 setzt sich Tertullian mit der Behauptung auseinander, den Aposteln seien bestimmte Teile der Lehre Jesu verborgen geblieben bzw. sie hätten nicht alles weitergegeben[45]. In seiner Erwiderung

---

40. Cf. 3,13,1: … ipse Paulus convincat eos ….
41. Cf. die Argumentation in 3,13,3, die vom Gal ausgeht und dann das Zeugnis der
Apg als damit übereinstimmend bezeichnet.
42. Cf. R. NOORMANN, *Irenäus als Paulusinterpret. Zur Rezeption und Wirkung der
paulinischen und deuteropaulinischen Briefe im Werk des Irenäus von Lyon* (WUNT, 2/
66), Tübingen, Mohr, 1994, p. 51 mit n. 72.
43. Cf. KUCK, *Use* (n. 11), pp. 46-59.
44. Cf. etwa orat. 24; scorp. 15; ieiun. 8; bapt. 12-13; Prax. 17; pud. 21; res. 39.
45. Tert.praesc. 22: Solent dicere non omnia apostolos scisse, eadem agitati dementia
… omnia quidem apostolos scisse, sed non omnia omnibus tradidisse.

verweist Tertullian neben Stellen aus den Evangelien auch auf die Apg. Diese belege die Herabkunft des Heiligen Geistes auf die Apostel, welcher nach Jesu eigenen Worten (Tertullian bezieht sich hier auf Joh 16,12f.) die Jünger in alle Wahrheit einführen wird. Hieraus folge die Notwendigkeit, diese Schrift zu akzeptieren, um den Heiligen Geist zu erkennen[46].

Die zweite Stelle findet sich innerhalb der Behandlung der paulinischen Briefe in Marc 5. Tertullian befaßt sich in 5,2-4 mit dem Gal und führt den Nachweis, daß Paulus keinen anderen Gott verkünde als denjenigen, der schon immer aus dem Gesetz bekannt war. Auch betone er selbst, daß es nur ein Evangelium gebe. Zugleich bestätige er die Apg, in der dieser Brief zusammengefaßt sei, sowohl durch den Bericht von seiner Bekehrung als auch durch denjenigen über das Apostelkonzil[47]. Es sei somit offensichtlich, warum Markion die Apg ablehne: Sie lehre in Übereinstimmung mit Paulus, daß es keinen Gott außer dem Schöpfer gebe, keinen Christus außer demjenigen des Schöpfers, denn die Verheißung des Heiligen Geistes werde nirgendwo anders dargelegt als in dem Zeugnis der Apg[48].

Für Tertullian spielt also die Bezeugung des Heiligen Geistes durch die Apg eine zentrale Rolle. Auf diese bezieht er sich zum Beleg der Glaubwürdigkeit der Apostel, diese erwähnt er im Zusammenhang des Apostelkonzils (über den Text der Apg hinaus) noch einmal ausdrücklich[49], diese Bezeugung stellt er schließlich als das Einzigartige der Apg heraus[50]. Ihre Bedeutung wird also zum einen durch das in ihr zu findende Zeugnis über den einen Gott und seinen Christus gesichert, das in

---

46. *Ibid.*: Et utique implevit repromissum, probantibus actis apostolorum descensum spiritus sancti. Quam scripturam qui non recipiunt, nec spiritum sanctum possunt agnoscere discentibus missum.

47. Tert.Marc. 5,2,7: Exinde decurrens ordinem conversionis suae de persecutore in apostolum scripturam Apostolicorum confirmat, apud quam ipsa etiam epistulae istius materia recognoscitur, intercessisse quosdam qui dicerent circumcidi oportere et observandam esse Moysi legem … (es folgt eine Erwähnung der Übereinkunft auf dem Apostelkonzil).

48. *Ibid.*: Quodsi et ex hoc congruunt Paulo Apostolorum Acta, cur ea respuatis iam apparet, ut deum scilicet non alium praedicantia quam creatorem, nec Christum alterius quam creatoris, quando nec promissio spiritus sancti aliunde probetur exhibita quam de instrumento Actorum.

49. *Ibid.*: … tunc apostolos de ista quaestione consultos ex auctoritate spiritus renuntiasse … Der anschließend erwähnte Beschluß referiert den Rat des Petrus aus Apg 15,10 (τί πειράζετε τὸν θεὸν ἐπιθεῖναι ζυγὸν ἐπὶ τὸν τράχηλον τῶν μαθητῶν ὃν οὔτε οἱ πατέρες ἡμῶν οὔτε ἡμεῖς ἰσχύσαμεν βαστάσαι; Tert.: non esse imponenda onera hominibus quae patres ipsi non potuissent sustinere), wobei die Darstellung Tertullians eine Verallgemeinerung darstellt, insofern sie diesen Rat als gemeinsamen, auf der Autorität des Geistes gründenden Beschluß darstellt.

50. Cf. n. 48.

Übereinstimmung sowohl mit den Evangelien als auch mit Paulus steht, sie wird darüber hinaus durch dasjenige über den Heiligen Geist ergänzt. Ebenso wie bei Irenäus spielt die Apg zudem eine Rolle im Streit um Paulus. In diesem Zusammenhang setzt sich Tertullian gegen ihre Verwerfung zur Wehr, die er Markion und seinen Anhängern vorwirft[51]. Dabei findet sich insofern eine vergleichbare Tendenz, als es auch bei Tertullian Paulus ist, der die Apg bestätigt, wogegen der Streit um die richtige Paulusdeutung anhand von dessen Briefen geführt wird. Das Zeugnis der Apg hat dabei eine stützende Funktion, muß jedoch seinerseits erst gesichert werden.

Bemerkenswerterweise bezieht sich Tertullian – anders als Irenäus – an den genannten Stellen hierzu allerdings weder auf dieselbe Verfasserschaft von Apg und LkEv noch auf die Verbindung Lukas/Paulus, die ihm jedenfalls bekannt war. Ersteres könnte darauf zurückzuführen sein, daß er in seiner Auseinandersetzung mit Markion das LkEv auf die Vermittlung der Lehre der Urapostel an Paulus zurückführt. Es stammt also gewissermaßen „aus dritter Hand"[52]. Insofern wäre dieses Argument wenig geeignet gewesen, die Autorität der Apg zu stützen. Daß Tertullian die Beziehung Lukas/Paulus nicht stärker ins Feld führt (etwa indem er daraus die historische Glaubwürdigkeit der Apg ableitet), fällt demgegenüber weniger ins Gewicht, da er diese auf jeden Fall für gegeben ansieht und die Apg von daher als einen unbezweifelbaren Bericht über Paulus betrachtet[53]. Es könnte allerdings damit zusammenhängen, daß er die Apg nicht so stark wie Irenäus auf die Übereinstimmung des apostolischen Zeugnisses mit den Evangelien und Paulus hin auslegt, sondern als einen historischen Bericht über Leben und Wirken der Apostel überhaupt ansieht.

Fassen wir diesen Befund zunächst zusammen, so zeigt sich: Um die Mitte des 2. Jahrhunderts läßt sich ein Einfluß der Apg am deutlichsten in der EpAp, weniger deutlich dagegen bei Justin erkennen. Es findet sich jedoch – anders als im Fall der Evangelien und der Paulusbriefe – keine explizite Erwähnung einer zweiten Schrift des Lukas, ebensowenig wie sich ein Einfluß der geschichtstheologischen Konzeption der Apg feststellen läßt. Die Apg tritt vielmehr in einer Situation in den Blickpunkt des Interesses, in der es um die Sicherung des apostolischen

---

51. Cf. auch praesc. 22,11; 23,3.

52. Cf. Tert.Marc 4,2,4: Porro Lucas non apostolus, sed apostolicus … quanto posterioris apostoli sectator, Pauli sine dubio. Wir finden hier somit eine analoge Autorisierung des LkEv (nicht der Apg!) durch Paulus wie bei Iren.haer. 3,1,1: Καὶ Λουκᾶς δέ, ὁ ἀκόλουθος Παύλου, τὸ ὑπ' ἐκείνου κηρυσσόμενον εὐαγγέλιον ἐν βίβλῳ κατέθετο sowie in CanMur (cf. n. 61) und bei Origenes (cf. n. 64).

53. Cf. etwa Tert.praesc. 23.

Zeugnisses geht. Insofern wird man dem Urteil Barretts zustimmen können: „The fact is that the church of the next two or three generations after its composition did not know what to do with Acts"[54]. Barrett bringt diese Tatsache mit dem einmaligen Befund des Apg-Textes innerhalb der neutestamentlichen Textüberlieferung zusammen, dessen Variabilität mit der vergleichsweise geringen Autorität der Apg als verbindlicher Schrift zusammenhängen könnte. Wurde jedoch das Evangelienzeugnis mit der Berufung auf weitere, mündliche Überlieferung konfrontiert und zugleich Paulus für eine dem biblischen Befund sowie dem Zeugnis der Urapostel widersprechende Position in Anspruch genommen, so ergab sich für die sich formierende Kirche die Notwendigkeit, auf diese Herausforderungen zu reagieren. Dies ist die Konstellation, in der man sich in dem oben beschriebenen Sinn auf die Apg berief, indem man sie als Bindeglied zwischen den Evangelien und Paulus interpretierte und als historischen Bericht über das Wirken der Apostel heranzog.

B. *Die Apg im Umkreis kanonischer Schriften: Manuskripte und Kanonverzeichnisse seit dem ausgehenden 2. Jahrhundert*

Ich wende mich nunmehr einigen Zeugen der handschriftlichen Überlieferung sowie den frühen Kanonverzeichnissen zu. Zeitlich wird damit der Raum seit dem ausgehenden 2. Jahrhundert in den Blick genommen. Die frühesten diesbezüglichen Zeugnisse liegen also zeitlich etwa parallel zu Irenäus und Tertullian. Sachlich wird nach der Funktion der Apg innerhalb des sich herausbildenden Kanons gefragt.

Die frühesten Manuskripte, in denen die Apg gemeinsam mit anderen Schriften überliefert ist und die somit Aufschluß über ihre Zuordnung zu einer Schriftengruppe geben könnten, sind P^{45}, P^{53} sowie die großen Codices 01, A, B und D. Auf dem Chester-Beatty Papyrus P^{45} (3. Jahrhundert) finden sich Teile der Apg im Anschluß an Fragmente aus allen vier Evangelien. Eine Zusammenordnung von Evangelien und Apg wird dadurch allerdings nicht zweifelsfrei belegt, denn es ist nicht sicher, ob der Papyrus zusätzlich die Katholischen Briefe enthalten hat und die Apg diesem Corpus zuzurechnen ist[55]. P^{53} besteht aus zwei Teilen mit dem Text von Mt 26,29-40 und Apg 9,33-10,1[56], kann jedoch aufgrund

---

54. Cf. C.K. BARRETT, *The Acts of the Apostles* (ICC), Edinburgh, T & T Clark, 1998, II, pp. lxix-lxx.

55. Cf. D. TROBISCH, *Die Endredaktion des Neuen Testaments. Eine Untersuchung zur Entstehung der christlichen Bibel* (NTOA, 31), Freiburg (Schweiz), Universitätsverlag; Göttingen, Vandenhoeck & Ruprecht, 1996, pp. 52-53.

56. Cf. die Publikation von H.A. SANDERS, in R.P. CASEY et al. (eds.), *Quantulacumque. Studies presented to Kirsopp Lake*, London, Christophers, 1937, pp. 151-161.

des fragmentarischen Charakters keine sicheren Aufschlüsse über eine Zuordnung der Apg zu anderen Schriften geben[57]. Für das 2. und 3. Jahrhundert lassen sich somit aus der handschriftlichen Überlieferung keine eindeutigen Schlüsse für die Stellung der Apg innerhalb der kanonischen Schriften ziehen.

Blicken wir auf die Kanonverzeichnisse, in denen die Apg seit dem ältesten bekannten Verzeichnis ohne Ausnahme enthalten ist, so ist zunächst auf CanMur einzugehen[58]. In diesem wird die Apg im Anschluß an die Evangelien und vor den Paulusbriefen eingeordnet. Dies bestätigt ihre bei Irenäus und Tertullian anzutreffende Behandlung als Fortsetzung des Evangelienzeugnisses durch dasjenige der Apostel[59]. Wie die entsprechenden Ausführungen bei Irenäus und Tertullian belegen, diente diese Reihenfolge dazu, das einheitliche apostolische Zeugnis als Bindeglied zwischen demjenigen der Evangelien einerseits, Paulus andererseits, herauszustellen. Dies kann dann auch für die Bezeichnung acta *omnium* apostolorum im CanMur angenommen werden. Weniger deutlich ist dagegen, ob sich diese Formulierung – wie bei Irenäus – gegen eine isolierte Berufung auf Paulus richtet. Die Bemerkungen des CanMur sind deutlich an der Augenzeugenschaft der Verfas-

---

57. Es ist zudem nicht ganz sicher, ob die Fragmente von demselben Manuskript stammen. Cf. K. ALAND, *Repertorium der griechischen christlichen Papyri* 1, Berlin & New York, de Gruyter, 1976, p. 283.

58. Faksimile-Ausgabe von S.P. TREGELLES, *Canon Muratorianus. The Earliest Catalogue of the Books of the New Testament*, Oxford, Clarendon, 1867. Abgedruckt bei H. LIETZMANN, *Das Muratorische Fragment und die monarchianischen Prologe zu den Evangelien* (Kleine Texte für theologische und philologische Vorlesungen und Übungen I), Bonn, A. Marcus & E Weber's Verlag, 1921, der auch einen Rekonstruktionsversuch bietet. Cf. den Anhang, p. 428. Zur Interpretation cf. VON CAMPENHAUSEN, *Entstehung* (n. 3), pp. 282-303; C.-J. THORNTON, *Der Zeuge Lukas. Studien zum Werk eines Paulusbegleiters*, Diss.masch., Tübingen, 1990, pp. 53-72. (Ich danke Herrn Dr. Thornton, daß er mir diese, in der publizierten Fassung seiner Dissertation nicht abgedruckten Seiten zur Verfügung gestellt hat.) Auf die seit A.C. SUNDBERG, *Towards a Revised History of the New Testament Canon*, in *StEv* 4 (1968) 452-461; ID., *Canon Muratori: A Fourth Century List*, in *HTR* 66 (1973) 1-41 sowie G.M. HAHNEMAN, *The Muratorian Fragment and the Development of the Canon*, Oxford, Clarendon, 1992) in die Diskussion geratene Frage der Datierung des Muratorischen Fragments gehe ich hier nicht ein. Der Versuch der Spätdatierung hat sich nicht durchgesetzt, weshalb ich weiterhin von der traditionellen Ansetzung um 180-200 ausgehe. Zur grundsätzlichen Kritik der Spätdatierung cf. den Beitrag von J. VERHEYDEN in diesem Band (pp. 487-556). Cf. weiter E. FERGUSON, *Canon Muratori: Date and Provenance*, in *SP* 18 (1982) 677-683; G.N. STANTON, *The Fourfold Gospel*, in *NTS* 43 (1997) 317-346, pp. 322-323 sowie die Rezension der Untersuchung Hahnemans von E. FERGUSON, in *JTS* 44 (1993) 691-697.

59. Neben dem oben besprochenen Irenäus-Text cf. Tert.pud. 7-11 (Beispiele aus den Evangelien); 12 (die gemeinsame Vereinbarung der Apostel auf dem Apostelkonzil); 13-18 (das Zeugnis der Paulusbriefe); es folgt der Verweis auf die johanneischen Schriften sowie auf Hebr (den Tertullian hier dem Barnabas zuschreibt); ähnlich res. 39-54. Cf. auch T. ZAHN, *Geschichte des neutestamentlichen Kanons (Erster Band, Erste Hälfte)*, Erlangen, Deichert, 1888, pp. 195-196.

ser orientiert[60]. Hatte der Fragmentist bereits in bezug auf Markus ange-
merkt, daß er nur teilweise bei den berichteten Ereignissen zugegen war,
so wird in bezug auf Lukas ausdrücklich notiert, daß er, ebensowenig
wie Paulus, auf dessen Veranlassung er sein Evangelium schrieb[61], den
Herrn im Fleisch gesehen habe, also kein Augenzeuge des Berichteten
gewesen sei[62]. Dem korrespondiert, daß Lukas hinsichtlich der „Taten
aller Apostel" aufgrund seiner Beziehung zu Paulus sehr wohl als Augenzeuge eingeführt werden kann.

In diesem Sinne wird die Zuordnung des Lukas zu Paulus in l. 35-39
aufgenommen, wo es um die Apg geht. Die Formulierung conprindit
[recte: comprendit] quia sub praesentia eius singula gerebantur (l. 36-
37) stellt die Augenzeugenschaft des Lukas bei den in der Apg berichteten Ereignissen heraus. Sie läßt sich – wie schon die Erwähnung seiner
Heranziehung durch Paulus in l. 4-5 – vermutlich mit den Wir-Berichten

60. Dies geht besonders aus den Bemerkungen zum JohEv (l. 29-34) hervor. Cf. auch
VON CAMPENHAUSEN, *Entstehung* (n. 3), p. 295: „[D]er Kanon Muratori [ist] in erster Li-
nie nicht am apostolischen >Prinzip< interessiert, sondern er fragt lediglich nach solchen
Schriften, die alt und verläßlich sind." sowie H. BURCKHARDT, *Motive und Massstäbe der
Kanonbildung nach dem Canon Muratori*, in *TZ* 30 (1974) 207-211.

61. Lucas ... cum eo [recte: eum] Paulus quasi ut iuris studiosum secundum
adsumsisset numeni [recte: nomine] suo ex opinione concribset [recte: conscripsit] ...
(l. 3-6). Entscheidend hierbei ist, wie die Wendung nomine suo ex opinione gedeutet
wird. ZAHN, *Geschichte II/1* (n. 30), p. 29, emendiert ex opinione zu ex ordine, hinter dem
das καθεξῆς aus Lk 1,3 läge (cf. auch die griechische Rückübersetzung, *ibid.*, p. 140).
Liest man dagegen ex opinione, so bedeutet die Wendung entweder „nach [allgemeiner]
Meinung" (so B.M. METZGER, *Der Kanon des Neuen Testaments. Entstehung, Entwicklung, Bedeutung*, Düsseldorf, Patmos, 1993, p. 287) oder sie bezieht sich auf Paulus zurück (so z.B. die Übersetzung bei W. SCHNEEMELCHER, *Neutestamentliche Apokryphen I:
Evangelien*, Tübingen, Mohr, ⁶1990, p. 28: „nach <dessen> [sc: des Paulus, J.S.] Meinung") oder sie ist an dem ἔδοξε κἀμοί aus Lk 1,3 orientiert und mit „gemäß seinem
Urteil" zu übersetzen. Diese Lösung vertritt z.B. THORNTON, *Lukas* (n. 58), pp. 67-68. Die
erste Deutung ist sachlich vorstellbar, sprachlich allerdings schwierig (cf. ZAHN, *ibid.*).
Bei einem Bezug auf Paulus ergibt sich das Problem, daß die Fortsetzung (besonders das
prout assequi potuit in l. 6, das an dem παρηκολουθηκότι aus Lk 1,3 orientiert sein
könnte) hierzu nicht recht zu passen scheint. Dadurch wird nämlich betont, daß Lukas
sein Evangelium aufgrund *eigener* Nachforschungen schrieb. Die zuletzt genannte Deutung ist deshalb die nächstliegende. Bei dem nomine suo bestehen wiederum die Möglichkeiten eines Bezugs auf Paulus oder Lukas selbst. Auch hier liegt letzteres näher (so
auch ZAHN, *ibid.*, pp. 28-29). Bei einem Bezug auf Paulus wäre zum einen nomine eius zu
erwarten, zum anderen legt es sich nahe, daß die eigene Autorschaft des Lukas gerade
aufgrund seines zuvor herausgestellten Verhältnisses zu Paulus betont wird. Die obige
Formulierung bezieht sich deshalb auf die Notiz, daß Lukas von Paulus als Schrift-
kundiger herangezogen, durch ihn also erst mit der christlichen Überlieferung bekanntge-
macht wurde.

62. Die Diskussion, ob sich das post ascensum Christi (l. 3) auf conscripsit, also auf
die Abfassung des Evangeliums, oder aber auf cum ... adsumsisset, also auf die Heranziehung durch Paulus, bezieht, ist für die Interpretation nicht von großer Bedeutung. Die
Wendung erklärt sich vermutlich am besten als Bezugnahme auf die nur bei Lukas berichtete Himmelfahrt.

in Zusammenhang bringen[63]. Der Hinweis auf das Fehlen eines Berichtes über das Martyrium des Petrus und die Spanienreise des Paulus verstärken diese Deutung. Sie setzen offenbar voraus, daß Lukas diese Ereignisse deshalb nicht berichtete, weil er sie nicht persönlich miterlebt hatte. Wir haben hier also eine analoge Tendenz wie in der Formulierung des Irenäus, Lukas sei non solum prosecutor sed et cooperarius apostolorum, maxime autem Pauli, gewesen (haer. 3,14,1) vor uns: Die Beziehung des Lukas zu *Paulus* wird auf *alle Apostel* ausgedehnt und als Zeugnis der Glaubwürdigkeit seines Berichts über diese gewertet.

Das Muratorianum ist somit für unsere Fragestellung zum einen deshalb von Interesse, weil es die auch bei Irenäus, Tertullian und Origenes begegnende[64] Verbindung Lukas/Paulus bestätigt. Diese wird – ebenfalls in Übereinstimmung mit den Genannten – jedoch nicht aus der Apg abgeleitet. Deutlich ist vielmehr, daß der Name Lukas bereits am Evangelium haftete und von dort auch auf die Apg übertragen wurde[65]. Dieser Befund wird dadurch unterstützt, daß es angesichts der Beobachtungen zur Vier-Evangelien-Sammlung (cf. unten unter C.) als ganz unwahrscheinlich gelten kann, daß das LkEv lange Zeit anonym umlief und erst im Zuge der Aufnahme der Apg dem Paulusbegleiter Lukas zugeschrieben wurde. Die Zuschreibung des dritten Evangeliums an Lukas ist vielmehr eine alte, spätestens im Zusammenhang der Evangelienüberschriften entstandene Tradition[66]. Worauf diese zurückzuführen ist, bleibt ei-

63. Cf. ZAHN, *Geschichte II/1* (n. 30), pp. 54-56.

64. Cf. Tert.Marc. 4,2,4; Iren.haer. 3,1,1 (n. 52) sowie Origenes bei Eus.h.e. 6,25: καὶ τρίτον τὸ κατὰ Λουκᾶν, τὸ ὑπὸ Παύλου ἐπαινούμενον εὐαγγέλιον τοῖς ἀπὸ τῶν ἐθνῶν πεποιηκότα.

65. Cf. C.-J. THORNTON, *Der Zeuge des Zeugen. Lukas als Historiker der Paulusreisen* (WUNT, 56), Tübingen, Mohr, 1991, p. 78: „Es fällt überhaupt auf, daß der Name des Lukas sehr viel enger am Evangelium haftet als an Acta. Nirgends wird eine umgekehrte Übertragung erkennbar". Ähnlich J. JERVELL, *Die Apostelgeschichte* (KEK, 3), Göttingen, Vandenhoeck & Ruprecht, 1998, p. 80: „Es ist völlig undenkbar, dass die Verfasser der ältesten Zeugnisse von sich aus durch Rückschlüsse [sc.: aus der Apg, J.S.] gerade auf Lukas als Verfasser kamen. Es gab ja mehrere Reisebegleiter und Mitarbeiter des Paulus, und mehrere, die viel geeigneter als der nicht sehr prominente Lukas ... erschienen". Die häufig vertretene These – in neuerer Zeit cf. etwa R. PESCH, *Die Apostelgeschichte (Apg 1-12)* (EKK, 5/1), Zürich et al., Benziger; Neukirchen-Vluyn, Neukirchener, 1986, pp. 25-27; J. WEHNERT, *Die Wir-Passagen der Apostelgeschichte. Ein lukanisches Stilmittel aus jüdischer Tradition* (GTA, 40), Göttingen, Vandenhoeck & Ruprecht, 1989, pp. 54-66 –, die Zuschreibung der Apg an Lukas sei über die Wir-Berichte erfolgt und dann auch auf das Evangelium übertragen worden, läßt sich mit diesem Befund nur schwer in Einklang bringen. Wahrscheinlicher ist, daß die Apg als Werk desselben Verfassers erkannt wurde, der auch das εὐαγγέλιον κατὰ Λουκᾶν verfaßt hatte, und dieser dann mit Hilfe der Wir-Berichte mit dem Paulusbegleiter aus 2 Tim 4,10-11 und Kol 4,14 identifiziert wurde.

66. Zum Alter der Evangelienüberschriften cf. HARNACK, *Entstehung* (n. 1), p. 47; ZAHN, *Geschichte I/1* (n. 59), pp. 150-192; M. HENGEL, *Die Evangelienüberschriften* (SHAW.PH, 3/1984), Heidelberg, Winter, 1984, pp. 11-12.

nigermaßen rätselhaft. Auffällig ist jedenfalls, daß die nachträgliche Erfindung einer Tradition über den Evangelienschreiber Lukas erst das Problem produziert hätte, dieses Evangelium zu legitimieren, da man sich hierfür – anders als bei Mt und Joh, anders auch als bei Mk, das wenigstens durch die Autorität des Petrus gestützt wurde – nicht auf einen Augenzeugen berufen konnte[67].

Die im 2. Jahrhundert auftauchende und von da ab bis heute immer wieder vorgenommene Identifizierung dieses Lukas als eines *Paulusbegleiters* ist dann offensichtlich nicht erst über die Apg erfolgt. Hierfür spricht, daß sowohl die vermutlich vorirenäische Tradition in haer 3,1,1 als auch CanMur, Tertullian und Origenes diese Verbindung herstellen *ohne* dazu auf die Apg zu rekurrieren. Dieser Befund könnte dadurch unterstützt werden, daß evtl. auch für Markion „der überlieferungsgeschichtliche Zusammenhang mit Paulus" den Ausschlag für die Wahl des LkEv gegeben haben kann[68]. Wenn Markion gerade dieses Evangelium bevorzugt, auch ohne den Namen des Lukas zu erwähnen und ohne auf die Apg zu rekurrieren, so könnte dies ein Indiz dafür sein, daß die Tradition über die Nähe dieser Schrift zum paulinischen Überlieferungskreis bereits älteren Datums ist und nicht erst über die Apg hergestellt wurde. Für die Kanonisierung der lukanischen Schriften ist dies insofern von Bedeutung, als sich hier eine Möglichkeit eröffnete, die Übereinstimmung des Paulus mit den Jerusalemer Uraposteln bereits über das LkEv zu sichern: Wenn dessen Inhalt durch Paulus autorisiert war, dann war es bereits von dorther unmöglich, Paulus aus dem apostolischen Gesamtzeugnis herauszubrechen[69].

Das Muratorianum macht zum anderen deutlich, daß die Apg als Darstellung der Taten *aller* Apostel eine über die Paulusdarstellung hinausgehende Bedeutung besitzt. Damit zeigt sich hier dieselbe Tendenz wie bei den Aussagen über die Paulusbriefe. Bezüglich seiner Gemeindebriefe (und ähnlich der Privatschreiben) wird vermerkt, sie seien zwar an einzelne Gemeinden gerichtet, besäßen aber aufgrund ihrer Siebenzahl, ebenso wie die Sendschreiben der Offb, eine Bedeutung für die Gesamtkirche (l. 54-63). Diese generalisierende Interpretation findet sich auch in bezug auf die Apg. Sie zeigt eine – neben der an der Paulusdeutung orientierten – zweite Rezeptionslinie auf. Diese läßt sich anhand der

---

67. Hierauf weist THORNTON, *Zeuge* (n. 65), pp. 69-81, zu Recht hin.

68. So A. VON HARNACK, *Marcion. Das Evangelium vom fremden Gott. Eine Monographie zur Geschichte der Grundlegung der katholischen Kirche. Neue Studien zu Marcion*, Leipzig, Hinrichs, ²1924 (unveränderter Nachdruck Darmstadt, Wissenschaftliche Buchgesellschaft, 1996), p. 42.

69. In exakt diesem Sinn argumentiert Tertullian gegen Markion. Cf. Marc. 4,2,5.

Codices und Kanonverzeichnisse ab dem 4. Jahrhundert weiterverfol-
gen.

In den Codices 01, A und B wird die Apg mit den katholischen Briefen zusammengeordnet. Sie steht hier also nicht zwischen Evangelien
und Paulusbriefen[70]. Dabei kann die Reihenfolge der Corpora wechseln.
Folgt in 01 auf die Evangelien zunächst das Corpus Paulinum[71] und
dann erst der Teil mit Apg und katholischen Briefen, so stehen in A und
B die Paulusbriefe hinter Apg+katholische Briefe. Diese Anordnung
(Evangelien – Apg+katholische Briefe – Paulusbriefe) ist die am weitesten verbreitete. Sie zeigt ein gegenüber Irenäus, Tertullian und CanMur
erweitertes (bzw. verändertes[72]) Stadium der Kanonbildung auf: Apg+
katholische Briefe stellen nunmehr *gemeinsam* das apostolische Zeugnis
vor Paulus dar, an das sich dann dasjenige des Paulus anschließt.

Die Apg hat keinen den Evangelien oder den Paulusbriefen vergleich-
bar festen Platz innerhalb einer Schriftengruppe. Dies erklärt ihre wech-
selnde Stellung in den verschiedenen Canones. Daß sie jedoch dort, wo
sie in ein Corpus eingebunden wird, gemeinsam mit den katholischen
Briefen einen der Schriftenkomplexe des neutestamentlichen Kanons
darstellt, dagegen offenbar weder mit der Vier-Evangelien-Sammlung
noch mit den Paulusbriefen – und schon gar nicht mit dem LkEv – zusammengestellt wurde, wird durch folgende Beobachtungen unterstützt:
– In etlichen Manuskripten werden nur Apg und katholische Briefe
  überliefert[73], wogegen sich die Zusammenstellungen Evangelien+Apg
  bzw. Apg+Paulusbriefe nicht finden (mit den erwähnten Ausnahmen
  P[45] und P[53] sowie D, die diesen Befund jedoch nicht grundsätzlich in

---

70. Bei D ist dies nicht mit gleicher Sicherheit zu behaupten. Der Text des Codex
bricht nach Apg 22,29 ab, enthält also nur Evangelien und Apg. Man kann jedoch vermuten, daß auch hier Evangelien und Apg+katholische Briefe ein Corpus gebildet haben,
zumal ein Stück von 3 Joh erhalten ist und mehrere Seiten aus dem Codex herausgerissen
wurden. Cf. D.C. PARKER, *Codex Bezae: An Early Christian Manuscript and its Text*,
Cambridge, University Press, 1992. Cf. auch den Anhang, unten, p. 428.

71. Es versteht sich von selbst, daß hierzu immer auch die deuteropaulinischen Briefe
gehören. Eine Sonderrolle spielte jedoch der Hebr, dessen paulinische Verfasserschaft
schon in der Alten Kirche bestritten wurde. An seiner unterschiedlichen Einordnung innerhalb des Corpus Paulinum läßt sich diese Problematik noch erkennen. Allerdings wurde er, wenn er in Kanonlisten auftauchte, immer im Zusammenhang des Corpus Paulinum
angeführt und niemals als katholischer Brief betrachtet. Cf. W.H.P. HATCH, *The Position
of Hebrews in the Canon of the New Testament*, in *HTR* 29 (1936) 133-151.

72. In CanMur werden die Schriften in der Reihenfolge Evangelien – Apg – Paulusbriefe – katholische Briefe (Jud+2 Johbriefe) – Weish – Offb+ApkPetr angeführt.

73. Cf. K. & B. ALAND, *Der Text des Neuen Testaments. Einführung in die wissenschaftlichen Ausgaben sowie in Theorie und Praxis der modernen Textkritik*, Stuttgart,
Deutsche Bibelgesellschaft, [2]1989, p. 92. Dort wird die Gesamtzahl der Manuskripte für
Apg+katholische Briefe mit 662 angegeben. Hierin enthalten sind 407 vollständige Handschriften und 46 Fragmente, die *nur* diese Schriftengruppe überliefern.

Frage stellen). Deshalb konnten Apg und katholische Briefe von den Herausgebern des Novum Testamentum Graece auch zu einer Schriftengruppe zusammengefaßt werden. Dies entspricht dem Befund in einigen Kanonlisten des 4. Jahrhunderts[74].

– Auch wo die Evangelien so angeordnet sind, daß das LkEv am Ende steht[75], erfolgt dies offensichtlich nicht aus dem Grund, Lk und Apg aufeinander folgen zu lassen. Im Canon Mommsenianus (Cheltenham-Kanon) folgen auf die Evangelien die Paulusbriefe, dann Apg, Offb und katholische Briefe. In der dem Codex Claromontanus angefügten Kanonliste folgen auf die Evangelien ebenfalls die Paulusbriefe, vor den katholischen Briefen, Barn, Offb und Apg[76]. Im Cureton-Syrer sowie bei Theophilus finden sich nur die Evangelien, so daß sich auch hieraus keine Zusammenstellung von Lk und Apg ableiten läßt.

– Die Zusammenstellung Apg+katholische Briefe erklärt sich schließlich auch daraus, daß es sich in beiden Fällen um Schriften handelt, die erst später als Evangelien und Paulusbriefe in die Geschichte der Sammlung verbindlicher Corpora eintreten, längere Zeit dagegen als Einzelschriften umliefen. Die auch später noch anzutreffende Einordnung der Apg hinter die katholischen Briefe, sogar hinter die Offb, zeigt dies ebenso an wie die sich schließlich durchsetzende (freilich schon früher gelegentlich anzutreffende) Abfolge Evangelien – Apg – Paulusbriefe – katholische Briefe – Offb[77].

Ich fasse den dargestellten Befund wiederum zusammen. Das Muratorische Verzeichnis bestätigt, daß die Autorität des Paulus, die bereits für das LkEv in Anspruch genommen wird, bei der Legitimierung der Apg als kanonischer Schrift eine wichtige Rolle spielt. Es macht des weiteren die Tendenz deutlich, die Apg als die kirchlich anerkannte Darstellung über das Wirken der Apostel zu betrachten. Ihre Rezeptions-

---

74. Cf. Cyr.catech. 4,36; Canon 60 der Synode von Laodicea; Ath.ep.fest. 39. Texte und Besprechung bei ZAHN, *Geschichte* II/1 (n. 30).

75. Diese Anordnungen (nämlich Joh – Mt – Mk – Lk; Mt – Mk – Joh – Lk bzw. Mt – Joh – Mk – Lk) sind sehr selten. Die zuerst genannte ist nach ZAHN, *Geschichte* II/1 (n. 30), pp. 371-374, nur für Ägypten belegt und durch die Bevorzugung des Joh veranlaßt. Die zweite findet sich im Cureton-Syrer, im Canon Mommsenianus sowie im Evangelienkommentar des Theophilus. Die zuletzt genannte Reihenfolge begegnet im Codex Claromontanus.

76. Cf. unten, p. 429. METZGER, *Kanon* (n. 61), hat dies offenbar übersehen. Er führt die genannten Listen zwar an (*ibid.*, pp. 292-293), schreibt jedoch wenige Seiten zuvor: „ Ob die Reihenfolge nach c) und d) [sc.: mit Lk am Ende, J.S.] möglicherweise dadurch bedingt war, daß Lukas/Apostelgeschichte zusammenstehen sollten, wissen wir nicht" (*ibid.*, p. 279). Problematisch bei Metzger ist auch, daß er die Zusammenstellung der Apg mit den katholischen Briefen nicht stärker berücksichtigt (cf. *ibid.*, pp. 277-282).

77. So nach Irenäus, Tertullian und CanMur etwa Eus.h.e. 3,25,1-7.

geschichte setzt sich in den Kanonlisten sowie in den Anordnungen der neutestamentlichen Schriften in den Codices sodann dergestalt fort, daß die Apg, nachdem sie einmal als autoritative Schrift anerkannt war, zumeist die Funktion einer Einleitung zu den katholischen Briefen übernimmt. Mit diesen zusammen stellte sie den Apostelteil des Kanons dar, wogegen die Paulusbriefsammlung seit jeher für sich stand und keiner Legitimierung durch die Apg bedurfte. Die katholischen Briefe, von denen lange Zeit nur 1 Petr und 1 Joh unumstrittene Anerkennung genossen, konnten dagegen durch ein Buch, in dem von Jakobus, Petrus und Johannes die Rede war, als zum Kanon gehörig aufgewiesen werden. Dies korrespondiert der seit Irenäus erkennbaren Absicht, das Zeugnis des Paulus durch dasjenige der Urapostel zu erweitern, eine Funktion, die nunmehr auch durch die katholischen Briefe übernommen wurde[78]. Dabei dürfte für die schließlich erfolgte Zusammenstellung der katholischen Briefe zu einem eigenen Schriftencorpus des Kanons nicht zuletzt die Siebenzahl eine Rolle gespielt haben[79].

Im nächsten Abschnitt soll ein kurzer Blick auf die Sammlungen verbindlicher urchristlicher Schriften geworfen werden, um das gewonnene Ergebnis dadurch abzurunden.

C. *Die Apg und die Entstehung des neutestamentlichen Kanons*

Es besteht kein Zweifel daran, daß die Vier-Evangelien-Sammlung sowie die Paulusbriefsammlung früher und unabhängig von der Aufnahme der Apg in den Umkreis verbindlicher Schriften entstanden sind. Bezüglich der ersteren sprechen verschiedene, in der neueren Forschung wieder stärker betonte Indizien dafür, daß ihre Anfänge in die erste Hälfte des 2. Jahrhunderts zurückreichen[80]. Diese Indizien sind:

1. Die Evangelienüberschriften der Gestalt εὐαγγέλιον κατά + Name wurden bereits von Zahn und Harnack als „Das Evangelium in der Fassung von …" gedeutet[81]. Neben dem sprachlichen Befund[82]

---

78. Cf. D. LÜHRMANN, *Gal 2,9 und die katholischen Briefe. Bemerkungen zum Kanon und zur regula fidei*, in ZNW 72 (1981) 65-87, p. 72.

79. Nur am Rande sei vermerkt, daß sich hieran deutlich zeigt, wie sich das Verständnis des Kanons bei Luther gegenüber diesen Intentionen verändert hat: Er löst den Hebr aus dem Corpus Paulinum, Jak und Jud aus demjenigen der katholischen Briefe und ordnet sie aus inhaltlichen Gründen gemeinsam mit der Offb ans Ende.

80. Cf. STANTON, *Fourfold Gospel* (n. 58); T.K. HECKEL, *Vom Markusevangelium zum viergestaltigen Evangelium* (WUNT, 120), Tübingen, Mohr, 1999, pp. 266-355.

81. ZAHN, *Geschichte I/1* (n. 59), pp. 164-167; HARNACK, *Entstehung* (n. 1), pp. 47-48.

82. Es gibt keine Analogien, die es erlauben würden, die Form κατά + Autorname als gängigen Buchtitel zu verstehen. Cf. HENGEL, *Evangelienüberschriften* (n. 66), pp. 9-10 mit n. 8.

spricht hierfür die vor Irenäus nahezu durchgehende[83] Bezeichnung dieser Schriften mit dem Singular τὸ εὐαγγέλιον. Dies weist zunächst auf die Vorstellung der *Einheit* des Evangelienzeugnisses in *mehrfacher Gestalt* hin.

2. Daß sich dieses einheitliche Zeugnis auf die *Vier-Evangelien-Sammlung* bezieht, wird zunächst durch die Codices P[45] und P[75] nahegelegt, in denen sich einmal Fragmente aller vier Evangelien (+ Apg), einmal solche aus Lk und Joh finden[84]. Dazu kommt jetzt, den Beobachtungen T.C. Skeats zufolge, ein aus P[64], P[67] und P[4] bestehender Codex, der die Zusammenstellung der vier Evangelien in einem Codex bereits für das späte 2. Jahrhundert belegen könnte[85]. Dagegen ist kein einziges Manuskript bekannt, in dem jemals ein apokryphes Evangelium gemeinsam mit einem der Vierersammlung überliefert worden wäre. Ebensowenig taucht ein anderes als die vier Evangelien, unterschieden durch die Zusätze κατὰ Ματθαῖον, Μᾶρκον, Λουκᾶν und Ἰωάννην, jemals in einer Kanonliste auf. Bei einer späten Entstehung des Vier-Evangelien-Kanons gegen Ende des 2. Jahrhunderts wäre eine derart einheitliche Überlieferungslage kaum zu erwarten, wie die wesentlich weniger eindeutigen Abgrenzungen bei den Briefen und Apokalypsen deutlich zeigen.

3. Wenn Irenäus die Viergestalt des einen Evangeliums durch den Verweis auf die vier Weltgegenden, die vier Hauptwinde und die vier Cherubim symbolisch ausdeutet[86], dann greift er hierbei vermutlich eine bereits ältere Tradition auf, die es erlaubt, die Zusammenstellung der vier Evangelien als vorirenäisch zu beurteilen[87]. Das Bewußtsein für die Einheit des Zeugnisses der vier Evangelien findet sich des weiteren bei Clemens und Origenes, wenn sie diese vier als die verbindlichen ansehen und andere Evangelien diesen entweder unterordnen oder gänzlich ablehnen[88].

---

83. Iust.dial 66,3, setzt zu der Erwähnung der ἀπομνημονεύματα τῶν ἀποστόλων erläuternd hinzu: ἅτινα καλεῖται εὐαγγέλια. Hengel, *Evangelienüberschriften* (n. 66), p. 14, n. 24, weist des weiteren auf ein Fragment des Apollinaris von Hierapolis (Chronicon Paschale, 13f.), hin.

84. T.C. Skeat erwägt die Möglichkeit, daß auch P[75] ursprünglich ein Vier-Evangelien-Codex, bestehend aus zwei zusammengenähten Bänden, gewesen sei. Cf. Id., *The Origin of the Christian Codex*, in ZPE 102 (1994) 263-268. Der Papyrus wäre dann ein weiteres Zeugnis für die frühe gemeinsame Überlieferung der Vier-Evangelien-Sammlung.

85. Cf. T.C. Skeat, *The Oldest Manuscript of the Four Gospels?*, in *NTS* 43 (1997) 1-34.

86. Iren.haer. 3,11,8.

87. Cf. T.C. Skeat, *Irenaeus and the Four-Gospel Canon*, in *NT* 34 (1992) 194-199. Anders Von Campenhausen, *Entstehung* (n. 3), p. 232.

88. Cf. Cl.Al.strom 3,93,1: Πρῶτον μὲν οὖν ἐν τοῖς παραδεδομένοις ἡμῖν τέτταρσιν εὐαγγελίοις οὐκ ἔχομεν τὸ ῥητόν, ἀλλ᾿ ἐν τῷ κατ᾿ Αἰγυπτίους.

4. Martin Hengel hat wichtige Argumente dafür vorgebracht, daß die Fassung εὐαγγέλιον κατά + Name die gegenüber der Kurzform ohne εὐαγγέλιον ältere Form darstellt. Hierfür spricht vor allem der handschriftliche Befund von P[66] (ΕΥΑΓΓΕΛΙΟΝ ΚΑΤΑ ΙΩΑΝΝΗΝ), P[75] (ΕΥΑΓΓΕΛΙΟΝ ΚΑΤΑ ΛΟΥΚΑΝ) sowie P[4+64+67] ΕΥΑΓΓΕΛΙΟΝ ΚΑΤΑ ΜΑΘΘΑΙΟΝ)[89]. Diese Papyri aus dem späten 2. bzw. frühen 3. Jahrhundert legen die Vermutung nahe, daß die später begegnende Kurzform ohne ΕΥΑΓΓΕΛΙΟΝ sekundär ist. Diese einheitliche Bezeichnung ist ein weiteres Indiz für das hohe Alter der Vier-Evangelien-Sammlung.

Am Rande sei notiert, daß sich die gegenwärtig mancherorts beliebte These einer jedenfalls bis Justin frei umlaufenden Jesusüberlieferung, die noch keine Spuren einer literarischen Verfestigung aufweise, im Lichte dieser Ergebnisse vermutlich etwas anders darstellt. Es ist sicher zutreffend, daß sich die außerhalb der Vier-Evangelien-Sammlung tradierte Jesusüberlieferung nicht in toto auf eine literarische Abhängigkeit von jener zurückführen läßt. Die Quellenlage zeigt jedoch zum einen, daß die außerkanonischen Schriften in ihrer vorliegenden Gestalt die Verschriftlichung der Jesustradition in den vier Evangelien in der Regel bereits voraussetzen[90], zum anderen, daß die Bezeichnungen εὐαγγέλιον κατὰ Θωμᾶν, κατ᾽ Αἰγυπτίους κτλ. offensichtlich Analogiebildungen zu den in der Vierersammlung enthaltenen Schriften darstellen. Die Vorstellung, die Vier-Evangelien-Sammlung sei am Ende des 2. Jahrhunderts aus kirchenpolitischen Gründen geschaffen worden und habe andere Überlieferungsstränge als „häretisch" ausgegrenzt[91], wird dagegen weder den Beobachtungen zum Alter dieser Sammlung noch denjenigen zum Verhältnis der apokryphen Jesusüberlieferung zu der in dieser Sammlung aufbewahrten gerecht.

Die Apg hat, obwohl sie die Jesusgeschichte fortsetzt und an eines der Evangelien unmittelbar anknüpft, nie einen Bestandteil dieser Sammlung gebildet. Daß das LkEv unabhängig von der Apg in die Evangeliensammlung integriert werden konnte und auch nach der Kanonisierung der Apg – trotz der Anerkennung der Identität seines Verfassers mit demjenigen des LkEv – in der Alten Kirche nirgendwo die Idee eines

Or.hom.Luc. 1,2: Ecclesia quatuor habet evangelia, haeresis plurima … Sed in his omnibus nihil aliud probamus nisi quod ecclesia, id est quatuor tantum evangelia recipienda.

89. Cf. HENGEL, Evangelienüberschriften (n. 66), pp. 9-12.

90. Cf. etwa die Bemerkungen zu PapEg, EvPetr und EpAp bei HECKEL, Evangelium (n. 80), pp. 273-329. Dieser Befund wird durch die Tatsache, daß in den außerkanonischen Schriften weitere, nicht über die Vierersammlung überlieferte Traditionen begegnen, nicht außer Kraft gesetzt.

91. Cf. H. KOESTER, Writings and the Spirit: Authority and Politics in Ancient Christianity, in HTR 84 (1991) 353-372, esp. p. 369.

„lukanischen Doppelwerkes" anzutreffen ist, deutet vielmehr auf den selbständigen Status beider Schriften hin, auf den in Teil II noch zurückzukommen sein wird.

Bezüglich der Paulusbriefsammlung sei an dieser Stelle lediglich auf die Zeugnisse aus 2 Petr 3,15 und den Ignatianen sowie die Ausführungen von Andreas Lindemann verwiesen[92]. Es ist festzuhalten, daß die Paulusbriefe unzweifelhaft seit dem frühen 2. Jahrhundert gesammelt wurden. Sie stellen damit neben den Evangelien ein zweites Corpus verbindlicher Schriften dar, dessen Anfänge in die Zeit vor Marcion zurückreichen. Trotz ihrer Orientierung an Paulus und trotz der seit Tertullian, Irenäus und CanMur bezeugten, möglicherweise aber schon älteren Lukas/Paulus-Tradition wurde die Apg nie mit der Paulusbriefsammlung verbunden. Dies kann auf unterschiedliche Überlieferungswege zurückzuführen sein, die sich auch in der jeweiligen Paulusrezeption widerspiegeln: Die Deuteropaulinen und Ignatius sind an der in den Paulusbriefen entwickelten Theologie bzw. seiner apostolischen Autorität orientiert, Marcion repräsentiert einen extremen Paulinismus und lehnt die Apg dabei ab, wogegen die Apg an dem missionarischen Redner Paulus, nicht an dem Briefschreiber, ausgerichtet ist[93].

Im Blick auf die Apg ergibt sich hieraus, daß sie zu einem Zeitpunkt in den Kreis kanonischer Schriften eintritt, zu dem die Sammlung verbindlicher Schriften bereits zur Ausbildung zweier Corpora geführt hat. Eines von diesen (nämlich die Evangeliensammlung) war dabei auch bezüglich des Umfangs bereits fest abgegrenzt. Dies erklärt zunächst, warum sie niemals einer dieser beiden Sammlungen zugerechnet wurde, obwohl sie aufgrund ihrer Verfasserschaft bzw. des Inhalts zu beiden zweifellos stärkere Beziehungen besitzt als zu den katholischen Briefen. Daß in der Alten Kirche die Vorstellung eines „lukanischen Doppelwerkes" nirgendwo nachweisbar ist, obwohl die Abfassung der Apg durch Lukas ausdrücklich anerkannt wurde[94], zeigt zudem, daß die Apg vom Beginn ihrer Aufnahme an als eine neben dem zur Evangeliensammlung gehörigen LkEv selbständige Schrift betrachtet und im Blick auf ihre kanonische Funktion auch entsprechend gedeutet wurde. Hatte bereits Markion

---

92. A. LINDEMANN, *Zeugnisse für die Sammlung der Paulusbriefe im 1. und 2. Jahrhundert* (in diesem Band, pp. 321-351, spez. 342-346).

93. Diese unterschiedlichen rhetorischen Situationen sind in neuerer Zeit stärker ins Blickfeld getreten und fordern dazu heraus, die Opposition „Paulus der Briefe vs. lk Paulus" neu zu überdenken. Cf. S.E. PORTER, *The Paul of Acts. Essays in Literary Criticism, Rhetoric, and Theology* (WUNT, 115), Tübingen, Mohr, 1999, pp. 98-125. 187-206. Cf. auch S. WALTON, *Leadership and Lifestyle. The Portrait of Paul in the Miletus Speech and 1 Thessalonians* (SNTS.MS, 108), Cambridge, University Press, 2000.

94. Deren Bestreitung wurde ebenso zurückgewiesen wie die Ablehnung der Apg als verbindliche Schrift. Cf. PsTert.haer. 6,1; Eus.h.e. 4,29,5; Chrys.hom.Act. (PG 60, p. 13).

durch die Verbindung einer Evangelienschrift mit Paulusbriefen einen Kanon verbindlicher Schriften abgegrenzt, so bot die Apg der Kirche die Möglichkeit, die bereits bestehenden Sammlungen aufeinander zu beziehen und ihren Kanon damit auf das Zeugnis Jesu und der Apostel zu gründen, mit dem dann auch dasjenige des Paulus übereinstimmt.

Im nächsten Teil wende ich mich mit diesem Resultat der Apg als dem zweiten Teil des lukanischen Doppelwerkes zu, um auf diese Weise die eingangs erwähnte Frage nach dem Verhältnis von kanonischer Bedeutung und historisch-kritischer Lektüre voranzutreiben.

II. Die Apg und das lukanische Doppelwerk

Eine der wichtigsten Entwicklungen innerhalb der Lk-Forschung des 20. Jahrhunderts kann in der Betonung der Tatsache gesehen werden, daß es sich bei Lk und Apg um ein einheitliches Werk in zwei Teilen handelt. Dieser Umstand wird nicht zuletzt dadurch dokumentiert, daß das Colloquium Biblicum Lovaniense 1998 unter dem Titel „The Unity of Luke-Acts" stand, nachdem zuvor beide Schriften (1968 bzw. 1977) separat behandelt worden waren[95]. In neueren Arbeiten zu beiden Werken kommt diese Wende in der Lk-Forschung deutlich zum Tragen[96], und Barrett hat die Sicht der Einheitlichkeit zu der These ausgebaut, das lukanische Werk lasse sich als „das erste Neue Testament" bezeichnen, weil hier bereits alles bereitgestellt werde, was für die Kirche notwendig sei: Lehre und Wirken Jesu sowie dessen Fortsetzung durch die Apostel[97].

Es geht mir nicht im geringsten darum, die Bedeutung dieser Erkenntnis in Frage zu stellen. Es kann kein Zweifel daran bestehen, daß sie zu wichtigen Einsichten für die Interpretation beider Schriften geführt hat. Ist die Jesusgeschichte des LkEv bereits im Blick auf die Apg erzählt, so

---

95. Cf. die Hinweise bei J. VERHEYDEN, *The Unity of Luke-Acts. What are we up to?*, in ID. (ed.), *The Unity of Luke-Acts* (BETL, 142), Leuven, Peeters, 1999, pp. 3-56, esp. 3.

96. Ich verweise exemplarisch auf J.T. SQUIRES, *The Plan of God in Luke–Acts* (SNTS.MS, 76), Cambridge, University Press, 1993; M.L. STRAUSS, *The Davidic Messiah in Luke–Acts. The Promise and its Fulfillment in Lukan Christology* (JSNT SS, 110), Sheffield, Academic Press, 1995; P. POKORNY, *Theologie der lukanischen Schriften* (FRLANT, 174), Göttingen, Vandenhoeck & Ruprecht, 1998; G. WASSERBERG, *Aus Israels Mitte – Heil für die Welt. Eine narrativ-exegetische Studie zur Theologie des Lukas* (BZNW, 92) Berlin & New York, de Gruyter, 1998.

97. C.K. BARRETT, *The First New Testament*, in *NT* 38 (1996) 94-104, pp. 102-103. Cf. ID., *The Third Gospel as a Preface to Acts? Some Reflections*, in F. VAN SEGBROECK et al. (eds.), *The Four Gospels 1992*. FS F. Neirynck (BETL, 100), Leuven, Peeters, 1992, II, pp. 1451-1466.

hätte Lukas seine Konzeption von Beginn an im Blick und der Prolog ließe sich mit guten Gründen auf das Gesamtwerk beziehen[98]. Sachliche und terminologische Bezüge, wie etwa die Anklänge des Martyriums des Stephanus an die Passion Jesu, aber auch die analoge Gestaltung des Wunderwirkens Jesu und der Apostel, lassen sich darüber hinaus als bewußte literarische Mittel des Verfassers interpretieren, dessen beide Schriften aufeinander abgestimmt sind[99].

Im Folgenden möchte ich dennoch nach den Grenzen dieser Betonung der Einheitlichkeit des lukanischen Werkes fragen. Ausgangspunkt ist dabei die bereits genannte Beobachtung, daß die Apg in der Alten Kirche stets als selbständige Schrift rezipiert worden ist, obwohl die Identität des Verfassers mit demjenigen des LkEv nicht nur nicht bezweifelt wurde, sondern sogar zu ihrer Legitimation diente[100]. Handelt es sich hierbei lediglich um ein – für die historisch-kritische Forschung letztlich belangloses – Rezeptionsphänomen[101], so hätte dies auch Konsequenzen für ein heutiges Verständnis der Apg als kanonischer Schrift. Man könnte dann nämlich in der Tat fragen, warum das lukanische Doppelwerk nicht auch bei der Anordnung der kanonischen Schriften als ein solches behandelt wird. Wäre die Apg dagegen trotz ihrer Verbindung zum LkEv als ein *selbständiges* Werk zu betrachten, so würde dies auch die altkirchliche Rezeption in einem anderen Licht erscheinen lassen.

Ich setze ein bei der schon oft konstatierten Tatsache, daß LkEv und Apg unterschiedlichen Gattungen angehören. Ist das Evangelium als eine biographische Erzählung zu beurteilen, so gehört die Apg in den Bereich der hellenistischen Historiographie. Diese Tatsache schränkt die in neuerer Zeit vor allem von Robert Tannehill vertretene These einer *narrativen* Einheit beider Schriften[102] insofern ein, als eine solche Einheit auf der *inhaltlichen*, jedoch nicht auf der *pragmatischen* Ebene rea-

---

98. Cf. M. KORN, *Die Geschichte Jesu in veränderter Zeit. Studien zur bleibenden Bedeutung Jesu im lukanischen Doppelwerk* (WUNT, 2/51), Tübingen, Mohr, 1993, pp. 19-32.

99. Cf. hierzu auch die bei BARRETT, *Third Gospel* (n. 97), pp. 1453-1461 notierten Verbindungen zwischen beiden Schriften.

100. Hierauf macht auch STANTON, *Fourfold Gospel* (n. 58), p. 335, aufmerksam: „We are so accustomed to treating Luke and Acts as one single writing in two parts that it is easy to overlook the fact that in the second century Luke's Gospel and Acts circulated separately. Even in later centuries they were not brought together".

101. In diesem Sinne cf. etwa VERHEYDEN, *Unity* (n. 95), p. 6, n. 13: „There is no undisputable manuscript or other external evidence that Lk and Acts were ever transmitted as one body of literature .... However, it is far more common to regard the question of the canonization of Luke's work as a different one from that of its compositional or theological unity .... Canonical disunity may be no more than a regrettable accident".

102. R.C. TANNEHILL, *The Narrative Unity of Luke-Acts. A Literary Interpretation*, Philadelphia, Fortress, I, 1986; II, 1990.

lisiert wird. Lukas bedient sich in beiden Werken unterschiedlicher literarischer Mittel, um eine Kommunikation mit seinen Lesern aufzubauen[103]. Dies läßt sich an folgenden Merkmalen verdeutlichen:

– In der Apg spielt das Stilmittel der Wiederholung eine herausgehobene Rolle. So wird die Bekehrung des Paulus nach dem Bericht des Ereignisses durch den Erzähler noch zweimal von Paulus selbst erzählt und dadurch den Lesenden in ihrer Bedeutung vor Augen gestellt. Ebenso wird die Begegnung zwischen Petrus und Cornelius mit nur geringfügigen Abweichungen im unmittelbaren Anschluß an ihre Darstellung durch den Erzähler von Petrus selbst noch einmal berichtet. Schließlich wird die Jesusgeschichte in den Reden des Petrus und Paulus (mit Variationen) immer wieder erzählt. Eine derartige Verwendung von Wiederholungen findet sich im LkEv nicht.

– Für die Geschichtsdarstellung in der Apg spielen die Reden der Protagonisten eine herausragende Rolle. In diesen wird das Geschehen auf seinen tieferen Sinn hin gedeutet und zugleich vorangetrieben. Die Reden des Stephanus, des Petrus in 10,34-43 sowie des Paulus in 20,18-35 haben dabei noch einmal eine herausgehobene Stellung, insofern sie an wichtigen Wendepunkten der Geschichtsdarstellung der Apg gehalten werden. Auch dieses, der hellenistischen Historiographie zuzurechnende Darstellungsmittel findet im LkEv keine unmittelbare Entsprechung. Die dortigen Reden Jesu sind von denjenigen der Apg vielmehr formal und funktional verschieden. Des öfteren begegnen innerhalb dieser Gleichnisse, eine Gattung, die in der Apg nicht verwandt wird.

– In den Wir-Passagen stellt sich der Verfasser der Apg als unmittelbarer Teilnehmer der berichteten Ereignisse dar. Wie immer das Rätsel dieser Texte zu lösen sein mag, deutlich ist, daß hier ein darstellerisches Mittel – nämlich dasjenige der Autorpartizipation – gewählt wird, das keine Analogie im LkEv besitzt. Auch wenn dieser Umstand darauf zurückzuführen ist, daß sich das Evangelium schon durch den Prolog als eine spätere, nicht auf Augenzeugenschaft beruhende Erzählung zu erkennen gibt, so ändert dies nichts daran, daß die Einführung der 1. Person Plural im Zusammenhang des Paulusberichtes als ein pragmatisches Mittel des Autors der Apg zu erklären ist, dessen Verwendung eine bestimmte Intention verrät.

Zu diesen Unterschieden in der Wahl der jeweiligen narrativen Gestaltungsmittel treten weitere Merkmale, die beide Teile des lukanischen Werkes voneinander unterscheiden. So fällt auf, daß sich in der

---

103. Cf. M.C. PARSONS & R.I. PERVO, *Rethinking the Unity of Luke and Acts*, Minneapolis, Fortress, 1993, pp. 45-83.

Apg, abgesehen von dem Prolog, nirgendwo ein *expliziter* Rückbezug auf den πρῶτος λόγος oder eine Anspielung auf ein dort begegnendes Wort oder Ereignis findet. Im Gegenteil, die Rekurse auf die Jesus-geschichte sind von den allgemeinen Topoi Johannestaufe, voll-mächtiges, geisterfülltes Wirken Jesu, Kreuzestod, Auferweckung ge-kennzeichnet, zu denen dann dasjenige der Zeugenschaft tritt. Sie setzen jedoch keine Kenntnis der *im LkEv erzählten* Jesusgeschichte voraus.

Diese Beobachtung wird durch drei Stellen verstärkt[104]. In Apg 11,6 zitiert Petrus das Jesuswort Ἰωάννης μὲν ἐβάπτισεν ὕδατι, ὑμεῖς δὲ βαπτισθήσεσθε ἐν πνεύματι ἁγίῳ. Dieses Wort findet sich nicht im LkEv, sondern in Apg 1,5. In 20,35 zitiert Paulus das Wort μακάριόν ἐστιν μᾶλλον διδόναι ἢ λαμβάνειν. Es findet sich jedoch weder im LkEv noch sonst irgendwo in den erhaltenen Texten eine Zuschreibung dieses Wortes an Jesus. In 13,25 wird Johannes von Paulus mit den Worten zitiert τί ἐμὲ ὑπονοεῖτε εἶναι; οὐκ εἰμὶ ἐγώ· ἀλλ᾽ ἰδοὺ ἔρχεται μετ᾽ ἐμὲ οὗ οὐκ εἰμὶ ἄξιος τὸ ὑπόδημα τῶν ποδῶν λῦσαι. Die Formulierung dieses Wortes weist in der Auslassung des ἰσχυρό-τερος aus den synoptischen Fassungen sowie der Verwendung von ἄξιος anstelle von ἱκανός stärkere Berührungen mit der johanneischen Fassung als mit derjenigen aus Lk 3,16 auf. Auch an diesen Beispielen wird somit deutlich, daß die Apg nicht in dem Sinne als Fortsetzung des LkEv konzipiert ist, daß sie die impliziten Leser auf dort bereits Erzähl-tes verweisen und so an dieses anknüpfen würde, daß dessen Kenntnis vorausgesetzt wäre. Dies läßt sich gerade anhand des deutlichsten Bei-spiels einer inhaltlichen Verknüpfung, nämlich der doppelten Erzählung von Jüngerbeauftragung und Himmelfahrt am Ende des LkEv und am Beginn der Apg, demonstrieren.

Das viel diskutierte Phänomen dieser modifizierten Reproduktion des Schlusses der lukanischen Jesuserzählung in Apg 1,4-11 bestätigt näm-lich exakt den dargestellten Befund. Deutlich ist zunächst, daß sich die Abweichungen aus der jeweiligen narrativen Funktion erklären[105]. Sind die Belehrungen des Auferstandenen sowie die Himmelfahrt bei Lk das Ende der Erzählung, so stellen sie in der Apg den Beginn eines neuen Werkes dar. Wird diese je eigene Funktion schon an der Wahl der unter-schiedlichen Orte (Betanien bzw. Ölberg) und Zeiten (cf. die Zeitspanne von 40 Tagen in Apg 1,3 mit Lk 24,13) deutlich, so geht sie aus Apg 1,5-8 noch einmal besonders hervor:

---

104. Cf. BARRETT, *Third Gospel* (n. 97), pp. 1461-1462; PARSONS & PERVO, *Rethinking* (n. 103), p. 60.

105. Cf. M.C. PARSONS, *The Departure of Jesus in Luke-Acts. The Ascension Narra-tives in Context* (JSNT SS, 21), Sheffield, Academic Press, 1987, pp. 189-199.

- An die Stelle der Johannestaufe tritt die Geisttaufe als Voraussetzung der Zeugenschaft.
- Die Erwartung der Restitution der βασιλεία τοῦ Ἰσραήλ (V. 6) wird durch den Auftrag der Zeugenschaft für Jesus (ἔσεσθέ μου μάρτυρες, V. 8) inhaltlich neu gefüllt.
- Der durch die Apostel wirkende Geist tritt damit an die Stelle Jesu.

Diese inhaltliche Neufüllung der Ereignisse nach der Auferstehung wird schließlich dadurch unterstützt, daß sich am Ende des LkEv keinerlei Vorausverweis auf ein zweites Werk findet. Dies unterscheidet die lukanischen Schriften von anderen, in mehreren Büchern konzipierten Werken, die zum Vergleich der Prologe oft herangezogen werden[106]. Der zweimalige Bericht dient also dazu, beide Werke als je eigenständige zu profilieren: Er schließt das erstere ab, ohne auf eine Fortsetzung zu verweisen, er versieht das zweite mit einer eigenen Einleitung.

Zusammenfassend läßt sich somit feststellen: Die Einheit des lukanischen Werkes ist in erster Linie eine *inhaltliche*. Beide Bücher sind von einer einheitlichen Perspektive auf die Jesusgeschichte, deren Verwurzelung in der Geschichte Israels sowie ihre Fortsetzung durch die von ihm berufenen Zeugen aus konzipiert. Diese Einheit kann jedoch nicht ohne weiteres auf den *literarischen Charakter* beider Werke übertragen werden. Es gibt vielmehr deutliche Indizien dafür, daß sie als eigenständige Bücher konzipiert wurden, die die Kenntnis des jeweils anderen bei den Lesern nicht voraussetzen. Der einzige explizite Verweis, die Erwähnung des πρῶτος λόγος in Apg 1,1, setzt diese Beobachtung nicht ins Unrecht. Dieser Verweis informiert lediglich darüber, daß ein solches Buch über das ποιεῖν τε καὶ διδάσκειν Jesu existiert, ohne daß jedoch ein Verständnis der Apg auf dessen *konkreten Inhalt* angewiesen wäre.

Daß die Apg, wie oben dargelegt, erst vergleichsweise spät in den Umkreis der verbindlichen Schriften eingetreten ist, hat seine Ursache in den in dieser Zeit aufbrechenden Kontroversen um die Legitimität und Alleinverbindlichkeit des apostolischen Zeugnisses über Jesus sowie die Interpretation der paulinischen Theologie. Daß das LkEv zudem bereits früh fester Bestandteil der Vier-Evangelien-Sammlung wurde, hat die separate Behandlung der Apg zudem zweifellos zusätzlich gefördert. Diese Beobachtungen ändern jedoch nichts an dem Befund, daß auch die literarischen Merkmale des lukanischen Doppelwerkes selbst Anhaltspunkte für eine Eigenständigkeit beider Teile bieten. Dies eröffnet die

---

106. Cf. Ios.ap. I.II; Philo Mos. I.II. PARSONS & PERVO, *Rethinking* (n. 103), pp. 61-64, machen zu Recht darauf aufmerksam, daß in diesen Fällen das erste Buch jeweils mit einer Ankündigung der Fortsetzung abgeschlossen wird.

Möglichkeit, die Apg nicht nur als Fortsetzung des LkEv zu lesen – was sie zweifelsohne *auch* ist –, sondern darüber hinaus als eine historische Darstellung[107] der Frühzeit der Kirche.

Die altkirchliche Rezeption der Apg steht in dieser Hinsicht somit nicht im Widerspruch zu einer am literarischen Befund orientierten Lektüre des lukanischen Doppelwerkes. Vielmehr treffen wir auf zwei distinkte, jedoch nicht konträre Lektüreweisen, die beide an der Apg Anhalt haben: Als Teil des lukanischen Doppelwerkes weist die Apg etliche Merkmale auf, die sie mit dem LkEv verbinden und es auf diese Weise erlauben, von einer „lukanischen Theologie" zu sprechen, die sich auf beide Teile des Werkes bezieht. Als Darstellung der Frühzeit der Kirche sowie der paulinischen Mission gelesen, entwirft sie dagegen ein Bild von der Entwicklung der Kirche in den ersten Jahrzenten, der Verbindung von Paulus und dem Zwölferkreis sowie der Phase der paulinischen Mission. Daß dieses Bild im Blick auf eine Geschichte des Urchristentums aus heutiger Perspektive kritisch zu analysieren und mit weiteren, in der Apg nicht berücksichtigten Quellen zu vermitteln ist, versteht sich von selbst. Im Blick auf eine *kanonische* Lektüre läßt sich dagegen festhalten, daß sich die Apg nicht nur als zweiter Teil des LkEv, sondern *auch* als konzeptionell und literarisch eigenständige Darstellung der Geschichte des Urchristentums präsentiert. Dies führt zu dem dritten, hier zu besprechenden Aspekt, der Bedeutung der Apg als kanonischer Schrift.

III. IMPLIKATIONEN EINER KANONISCHEN LEKTÜRE DER APG

Läßt sich die Apg aufgrund ihrer literarischen Merkmale als eigenständige Schrift beurteilen, so stellt sich abschließend die Frage nach dem Verhältnis einer *historischen* zu einer *kanonischen* Lektüre. Wie eingangs deutlich wurde, grenzte Harnack beide strikt voneinander ab und sah die altkirchliche Rezeption im schroffen Widerspruch zu den Eigenschaften der Apg selbst stehen. Diese Auffassung war Teil seiner dogmengeschichtlichen Perspektive, der zufolge der Kanon als eines der Merkmale der sich herausbildenden frühkatholischen Kirche im späteren

---

107. In die Debatte um die historische Zuverlässigkeit der Apg trete ich an dieser Stelle nicht ein, sondern merke lediglich an, daß die Apg zahlreiche Merkmale aufweist, die sie gattungsmäßig als ein historiographisches Werk kennzeichnen. Daß dieses dann im Blick auf ihre historische Referenz sowie ihre Stellung innerhalb der antiken Historiographie genauer zu bestimmen wäre, steht außer Zweifel, hier jedoch nicht zur Diskussion.

2. Jahrhundert durch Abstoßung bestimmter Schriften von der ältesten Tradition seitens der Kirche zustande gekommen sei. Dabei habe es erst die Apg ermöglicht, die Paulusbriefe sowie die katholischen Briefe dem Kanon zuzugesellen, dessen alleinigen Grundstock die Evangelien gebildet hätten. Die historisch-kritische Forschung nach Harnack hat die entscheidende Differenz dagegen zumeist nicht zwischen dem historischen Wert der Apg und ihrer späteren Kanonisierung, sondern zwischen den Ereignissen der urchristlichen Geschichte und deren Darstellung in der Apg gesehen. In den voranstehenden Ausführungen wurden einige Indizien gesammelt, die beide Sichtweisen modifizieren und damit die genannten Diskrepanzen weniger gravierend erscheinen lassen könnten:

– Evangelien und Paulusbriefe stellen zwei etwa gleichzeitig, offensichtlich jedoch unabhängig voneinander entstandene Vorstufen des neutestamentlichen Kanons dar. In dem Augenblick, wo beide *gleichermaßen* als autoritativ anerkannt wurden, stellte sich die Frage nach ihrem gegenseitigen Verhältnis. Die Apg verhalf dazu, auf diese Frage in Auseinandersetzung mit Markion und den Gnostikern eine Antwort zu finden. Harnacks These über die Kanonbildung ist somit, insbesondere bezüglich des Verhältnisses der Vorstufen des Kanons zu dessen späterer Fixierung, etwas einseitig. Dies ist heute weitgehend anerkannt, es hat dann auch Konsequenzen für die Beurteilung der Rolle der Apg in diesem Prozeß.

– Weder Irenäus noch Tertullian oder CanMur rekurrieren auf die Apg, um die Paulusbriefe als „unbedenkliche" kirchliche Schriften zu erweisen. Die Autorität des Paulus steht vielmehr außer Frage und wird ihrerseits genutzt, um das Zeugnis der Apg zu stärken.

– Der Rekurs auf den prosecutor et cooperarius apostolorum, maxime autem Pauli kann sich – was Harnack auch nicht bestreiten würde – auf die Lukas/Paulus-Tradition stützen, die ihrerseits älter ist als die Zuschreibung der Apg an Lukas. Die Ausweitung dieser Tradition auf *alle* Apostel bei Irenäus – die sowohl in CanMur als auch in der Zusammenstellung Apg+katholische Briefe Analogien besitzt – läßt sich somit als eine Kombination der Lukas/Paulus-Tradition mit dem Inhalt der Apg auffassen und steht nicht im Widerspruch zu diesem.

– Die Apg liefert literarische Indizien dafür, sie als historische Darstellung der Frühzeit der Kirche zu lesen. Besonders Tertullian hat sie in dieser Weise rezipiert. Dies kann durchaus als eine von der Apg implizierte Lektüre angesehen werden.

– Die neuere Forschung zum Paulusbild der Apg hat die hier erfolgte Paulusrezeption als eine spezifische Perspektive aufgewiesen, die an

Paulus als Repräsentant einer bestimmten Epoche der Ausbreitung des Christentums orientiert ist. Daraus ergeben sich bestimmte Akzentverschiebungen gegenüber den paulinischen Briefen, die jedoch nicht notwendig als unvereinbare Widersprüche aufgefaßt werden müssen. Die Alternative „Lukas oder Paulus" erscheint damit in einem anderen Licht.

Im Blick auf eine kanonische Lektüre der Apg ergeben sich hieraus folgende Aspekte: Harnack hat die Verbindungen der Apg zu den drei maßgeblichen Corpora des neutestamentlichen Kanons – Evangelien, Paulusbriefe, katholische Briefe – zu Recht herausgestellt. Die kanonische Bedeutung der Apg läßt sich von hier aus gut erfassen. Sie besteht in erster Linie darin, die Apostel als die legitimen Bewahrer der Jesusüberlieferung darzustellen (eine Funktion, die dann durch die Zusammenstellung mit den katholischen Briefen verstärkt wurde) und das Paulusbild der Apg als in Übereinstimmung mit demjenigen der Briefe zu erweisen. Diese Orientierung an der Legitimität der apostolischen Verkündigung ist für ein Verständnis des neutestamentlichen Kanons in der Tat konstitutiv, da dieser nicht zuletzt auf einer Abgrenzung legitimen Zeugnisses von häretischem basiert.

Die von Harnack vorgenommene Entgegensetzung einer historischen und einer kanonischen Lektüre erscheint angesichts der neueren Apg-Forschung dabei jedoch ebenso überzogen wie die in einer bestimmten forschungsgeschichtlichen Situation entwickelte Antithese des historischen und des lukanischen Paulusbildes. Unbeschadet der Einsichten der historischen Kritik führt eine kanonische Lektüre nicht notwendigerweise zu derartigen Oppositionen. Ich nenne hierfür drei Indizien:

– Die Legitimität des apostolischen Zeugnisses über Jesus ist kein der Apg sekundär imputiertes Interesse, das an der Schrift selbst keinen Anhalt besitzen würde. Vielmehr kann die exklusive Bindung des Jesuszeugnisses an den Zwölferkreis gerade als ein Merkmal der Geschichtskonzeption der Apg betrachtet werden.

– Der Titel acta omnium apostolorum ist, gemessen an dem Inhalt der Apg, zweifellos eine Übertreibung. Er ebnet auch den Befund ein, daß die Apg eine klare Unterscheidung zwischen dem Zwölferkreis als den Aposteln und Paulus als dem „dreizehnten Zeugen" vornimmt. Dennoch erfaßt er darin etwas Richtiges, daß die Apg in der Tat beansprucht, das Wirken des Zwölferkreises, der Hellenisten sowie des Barnabas und Paulus in seinen wesentlichen Facetten zu schildern. Daß dies de facto nur *exemplarisch* geschieht, ändert nichts daran, daß das Konzept der Apg durchaus darin gesehen werden kann, einen *vollständigen* Verlauf dieser Ereignisse zu bieten.

– Die Übereinstimmung des Paulus mit den Jerusalemer Aposteln hat in der Paulusrezeption der Apg zweifellos guten Anhalt. Wenn Irenäus und Tertullian deren Spezifikum darin sehen, Paulus in Übereinstimmung mit dem gesamtapostolischen Zeugnis zu schildern, dann ist die Intention der Apg damit recht gut getroffen.

Es gibt somit gute Gründe dafür, die altkirchliche Rezeption der Apg mit deren eigener Intention näher zusammenzurücken, als Harnack dies getan hatte. Die Intentionen, die Harnack der Kirche des ausgehenden 2. Jahrhunderts zuschrieb, ließen sich damit mutatis mutandis bereits für den Abfassungszweck der Apg selbst in Anschlag bringen. Die Apg als „Konsensdokument" des 1. Jahrhunderts wäre demzufolge, ca. 100 Jahre nach ihrer Entstehung, unter veränderten, aber analogen Bedingungen rezipiert worden, um auseinanderstrebende Deutungen auf das einheitliche Zeugnis der Apostel sowie des Paulus zu verpflichten[108].

Es bleibt abschließend die Frage, wie sich dieser Befund mit einer historisch-kritischen Lektüre der Apg vermitteln läßt. Hier kann es nicht darum gehen, Distinktionen einebnen und Differenzen leugnen zu wollen, die eine solche Lektüre bezüglich des Verhältnisses von Geschichtsdarstellung und zugrundeliegenden Ereignissen zutage fördert. Es ist aber auch deutlich, daß erst die Einbettung dieser Lektüreform in eine umfassendere, hermeneutisch fundierte Texttheorie vom historischen *Erklären* zum *Verstehen* führt. Die Apg mit den Augen des historisch-kritisch geschulten Exegeten als eine *kanonische* Schrift zu lesen, ist kein Widerspruch. Eine solche Lektüre orientiert sich an der Bedeutung, die die Apg den berichteten Ereignissen beimißt. Diese Bedeutung erschöpft sich nicht in der Frage ihrer historischen Faktizität, die dadurch gleichwohl nicht unwichtig wird. Auch für eine historisch-kritisch informierte Lektüre stellt die Apg jedoch die Herausforderung dar, das urchristliche Zeugnis im Blick auf seine Kohärenz zu betrachten. Wirkungsgeschichtlich wäre eine solche Kohärenz angesichts der im Kanon versammelten Schriften zu reflektieren.

Eine kritische Betrachtung der urchristlichen Geschichte wird somit zweifellos nicht zu dem Bild von deren Einheit gelangen[109]. Andererseits kann kein Zweifel daran bestehen, daß die *Bedeutung* der Vergangenheit nicht in den Quellen selbst enthalten ist, sondern durch deren *Interpretation* hervorgebracht wird[110]. Die geschichtstheologische Kon-

---

108. Cf. C.K. BARRETT, *Acts and Christian Consensus*, in P.W. BØCKMAN & R.E. KRISTIANSEN (eds.), *Context*. FS P.J. Borgen, Trondheim, Tapir, 1987, pp. 19-33.

109. Cf. J. SCHRÖTER, *Partikularität und Inklusivität im Urchristentum*, in GuL 16 (2001).

110. Cf. J.G. DROYSEN, *Historik* (Historisch-kritische Ausgabe von Peter Leyh), Stuttgart & Bad Canstatt, 1977, pp. 425-435.

zeption der Apg sowie ihre spätere Kanonisierung lassen sich deshalb als hermeneutische Herausforderungen begreifen, der Geschichte des Urchristentums eine Bedeutung abzugewinnen, die trotz der nicht zu bestreitenden *Mannigfaltigkeit* in ihrer *Kohärenz* liegt. Angesichts des Befundes, daß die Differenzen zwischen den neutestamentlichen Schriften auf der einen und den gnostischen Dokumenten sowie Markion auf der anderen Seite ungleich gravierender sind als diejenigen *innerhalb* der in den Kanon aufgenommenen Schriften, erscheint eine solche Sicht auch aus neuzeitlich-kritischer Perspektive als eine vor den Quellen verantwortete Rekonstruktion. Es ist dies sicher nicht die *einzig mögliche* Lektüreform der Apg. Sie ist jedoch vom literarischen Befund her gut zu begründen, sie wird hermeneutisch durch die Wirkungsgeschichte unterstützt, sie kann schließlich dazu verhelfen, historischen Textsinn und Gegenwartsbedeutung der Apg miteinander zu vermitteln.

Sedanstrasse 19   Jens SCHRÖTER
D-20146 Hamburg
Deutschland

ANHANG

Canon Muratori

1 quibus tamen interfuit et ita posuit
2 tertio euangelii librum secundo lucan
3 lucas ist medicus post asecensum xpi
4 cum eo paulus quasi ut iuris studiosum
5 secundum adsumsisset numeni suo
6 ex opinione concribset dnm tamen nec ipse
7 uidit in carne et ide prout asequi potuit

…

34 … acta aute omniu apostolorum
35 sub uno libro scribta sunt Lucas obtime theofi
36 le conprindit quia sub praesentia eius singula
37 gerebantur sicuti et semote passione petri
38 euidenter declarat sed et profectione pauli ab ur
39 be ad spania proficiscentis …

wobei er doch zugegen war und es so hingestellt hat.
Das dritte Buch des Evangeliums nach Lukas.
Dieser Arzt Lukas hat es nach Christi Himmelfahrt,
da ihm Paulus als der Schrift Kundigen
herangezogen hatte, unter seinem Namen
gemäß seinem Urteil verfaßt. Doch hat auch er den Herrn nicht
im Fleisch gesehen, und daher beginnt er so, wie es ihm erreichbar war.

…

… Die Taten aller Apostel aber
sind in einem Buch aufgeschrieben. Lukas faßt für den besten Theophilus zusammen, was in seiner Gegenwart im einzelnen
geschehen ist, wie er das auch durch Weglassen des Leidens des Petrus
deutlich macht, ebenso durch dasjenige der Reise des Paulus, der von Rom
nach Spanien reiste …

Anordnungen der neutestamentlichen Schriften

Sinaiticus	Alexandrinus	Vaticanus	Bezae Cantabrigiensis
Evangelien	Evangelien	Evangelien	Evangelien
Paulusbriefe	Apg + kath. Briefe	Apg + kath. Briefe	Apg (bis 20,28)
Apg + kath. Briefe	Paulusbriefe	Paulusbriefe	Fragment von 3 Joh
Offb	Offb		
Barn	1/2 Klemens		
PastHerm			

Verzeichnisse mit Lukas am Ende der Vier-Evangelien-Sammlung

Cheltenham-Canon	Liste im Codex Claromontanus	Cureton-Syrer/Theophilus
Matthäus	Matthäus	Matthäus
Markus	Johannes	Markus
Johannes	Markus	Johannes
Lukas	**Lukas**	**Lukas**
Paulusbriefe	Paulusbriefe	
Apg	1/2 Petr	(keine weiteren Schriften)
Offb	Jak	
Johannesbriefe	1-3 Joh	
Petrusbriefe	Jud	
	Barn	
	OffbJoh	
	Apg	
	PastHerm	
	Paulusakten	
	OffbPetr	

"NOMINA SACRA": YES AND NO?

The phenomenon of *nomina sacra*, the abbreviation of a number of key words and indicated as such by a supralinear line, is a well known feature of Christian manuscripts. A fundamental work on the subject remains the monograph of L. Traube[1], who is widely credited with having first coined the description "nomina sacra" itself. Since then, there have been important studies published by A.H.R.E. Paap[2], C.H. Roberts[3], and most recently L. Hurtado[4], as well as other books, essays and various briefer and more general summaries of the phenomenon[5].

A widely accepted view of the situation would be as follows. The number of key words appears generally to have been limited to 15 specific words. Of these 15, a group of 4 are widely believed to have formed the "primary" group, as being the earliest attested and almost uniformly abbreviated in this way: these are θεός, Ἰησοῦς, κύριος and χριστός. The remaining words – πνεῦμα, ἄνθρωπος, σταυρός, υἱός, πατήρ, σωτήρ, μήτηρ, Ἰσραήλ, Δαυείδ, Ἰερουσαλήμ, οὐρανός – are abbreviated less consistently and may have come into the scheme later at various stages. The abbreviations generally have the form of a contraction, including the first and last letters and omitting (most if not all) the letters in between, rather than a suspension which includes the initial letters and omits the subsequent ones. Thus the abbreviation for

---

1. L. TRAUBE, *Nomina Sacra. Versuch einer Geschichte der christlichen Kürzung*, Munich, Beck, 1907.

2. A.H.R.E. PAAP, *Nomina Sacra in the Greek Papyri in the First Five Centuries*, Leiden, Brill, 1959.

3. C.H. ROBERTS, *Nomina Sacra: Origins and Significance*, ch. 2 of his *Manuscript, Society and Belief in Early Christian Egypt*, London, Oxford University Press, 1979, pp. 26-48.

4. L. HURTADO, *The Origin of the Nomina Sacra: A Proposal*, in *JBL* 117 (1998) 655-673.

5. E.g. B.M. METZGER, *Manuscripts of the Greek Bible,* Oxford, Oxford University Press, 1961, pp. 36-37; C.H. ROBERTS, *Books in the Graeco-Roman World and in the New Testament*, in P.R. ACKROYD & C.F. EVANS (eds.), *Cambridge History of the Bible* 1, Cambridge, Cambridge University Press, 1970, pp. 60-61; S. BROWN, *Concerning the Origin of the Nomina Sacra*, in *SP* 9 (1970) 7-19; H. GAMBLE, *Books and Readers in the Early Church*, New Haven, Yale University Press, 1995, pp. 74-78; D. TROBISCH, *Die Endredaktion des Neuen Testaments* (NTOA, 31), Freiburg, Universitätsverlag; Göttingen, Vandenhoeck & Ruprecht, 1996, pp. 16-31; translated as *The First Edition of the New Testament*, Oxford, Oxford University Press, 2000. The evidence from the early papyri is also usefully presented in J. O'CALLAGHAN, *"Nomina Sacra" in papyris graecis saeculi III neotestamentariis* (AnBib, 46), Rome, Pontifical Biblical Institute, 1970.

θεός is $\overline{\theta\varsigma}$ not $\overline{\theta\varepsilon}$. (The abbreviation for Ἰησοῦς is however not quite so consistent: some manuscripts have the suspended form $\overline{\iota\eta}$, although more common is the contraction $\overline{\iota\varsigma}$, whilst some have a mixed form $\overline{\iota\eta\varsigma}$.) The contracted forms thus serve to distinguish these from abbreviations found in other Greek documents which are regularly in the form of suspensions[6].

There has been great debate about the origin of the practice, and also whether the contractions are earlier than, or quite independent of, any suspended forms. There has been debate too about which logically was/ were the original abbreviation/s from which the rest may have derived. Nevertheless, there is widespread agreement that (a) the practice is well-established and consistently applied in the earliest Christian MSS we possess (and hence must go back earlier still), (b) that it is *not* a simple space-saving device[7], (c) it is probably a *Christian* innovation[8], (d) it represents an attempt to reflect the *sacred*, religiously "special" nature of the referents of the nouns being abbreviated in this way: hence the description "nomina *sacra*"[9], (e) such sacredness is probably to be related to the reverence shown in Judaism to the divine name[10].

This general set of claims about the phenomenon does however in my view raise a number of questions. Moreover, some of the general claims may be a little more doubtful than is sometimes thought to be the case. In what follows I am primarily concerned with the *origins* of the system of writing *nomina sacra*. I will therefore consider mostly the *earliest* evidence in the earliest manuscripts (although inevitably the quantity of evidence here is not always as extensive as one might like). I shall also confine attention for the most part to the Greek evidence. Some variation

6. Cf. PAAP, *Nomina Sacra*, p. 2; ROBERTS, *Manuscript*, p. 27; HURTADO, *Origin*, p. 658; for abbreviations in other Greek manuscripts, cf. A. BLANCHARD, *Sigles et abréviations dans les papyrus documentaires grecs: recherches de paléographie*, London, Institute of Classical Studies, 1974.

7. Cf. ROBERTS, *Manuscript*, p. 26, who notes that there are often spaces around the *nomen sacrum* and in any case, with the drawing of the extra line above, not much time (or space) would have been saved overall. See too PAAP, *Nomina Sacra*, p. 2; HURTADO, *Origin*, p. 659; TROBISCH, *First Edition*, pp. 16-17.

8. This has been argued for very influentially by Roberts, who is followed by Hurtado. So too Trobisch, who sees the device as characteristic of the "redactor" of the first "edition" of the New Testament (on which see below). For dissenting voices in the modern era, cf. K. TREU, *Die Bedeutung des Griechischen für die Juden im römischen Reich*, in *Kairos* n.f. 15 (1973) 123-144, esp. pp. 141-142; also R.A. KRAFT, *The "Textual Mechanics" of Early Jewish LXX/OG Papyri and Fragments*, published on the internet at http://ccat.sas.upenn.edu/rs/rak/earlypap.html.

9. PAAP, *Nomina Sacra*, p. 2; O'CALLAGHAN, *Nomina Sacra*, p. 15; ROBERTS, *Manuscript*, p. 26; HURTADO, *Origin*, p. 655 n. 1.

10. PAAP, *Nomina Sacra*, p. 124; ROBERTS, *Manuscript*, pp. 28-9; GAMBLE, *Books*, p. 75.

is visible in later manuscripts, but by then the standardisation process may have been fairly well established.

I. Christian or Jewish?

The question of whether the practice of using *nomina sacra* is Christian or Jewish in origin is not easy to determine. Not the least part of the problem arises from the difficulty in determining whether a particular manuscript has been written by a Christian scribe or by a Jewish one (if indeed one can draw a hard and fast distinction between the two)[11]. Sometimes too the decision itself is settled by referring to the presence (or absence) of *nomina sacra* as the criterion by which to determine the issue: the existence of *nomina sacra* is taken as a clear indication that a manuscript is Christian, and the absence of such as implying that it is non-Christian. Such a use of the phenomenon as a criterion clearly begs the issue. It *may* be that other factors can assist in determining whether a manuscript is Jewish or Christian[12]; nevertheless we must be careful not to allow the argument to become circular, predetermining the answer in advance.

Part of our difficulty arises from the fact that we have relatively few manuscripts that are clearly identifiable as Jewish which can provide us with relevant information here. Greek manuscripts of Jewish texts which can be dated as pre-Christian (and hence are indubitably Jewish, rather than Christian, because of their date) show no evidence of the use of *nomina sacra*. The same is true even if one focuses on instances in such manuscripts where the divine name appears (and where, if anywhere, one might expect a *nomen sacrum* to be used if the system had been known). Such manuscripts include the Leviticus fragment from Qumran (4Q120 = pap4QLXXLev^b), the minor prophets scroll from Nahal Hever (8HevXIIgr) and PFouad 266b (Rahlfs 848). However, the divine name here is treated in various ways: thus in 4Q120 the divine name is represented by the letters ιαω[13], in 8HevXIIgr the divine name appears in old

11. See especially TREU, *Bedeutung*, pp. 140ff. who takes issue with the arguments of Roberts and others which appeal to (a) the use of the LXX, (b) the use of a codex, and (c) the use of *nomina sacra* as decisive evidence for a Christian provenance of a manuscript.

12. Cf. the use of the LXX or the use of a codex, but see previous note. For appeals to such criteria, cf. ROBERTS, *Manuscript*, pp. 74-78.

13. P.W. SKEHAN, E. ULRICH, J.E. SANDERSON, P.J. PARSONS (eds.), *Qumran Cave 4: IV, Palaeo-Hebrew and Greek Biblical Manuscripts* (DJD, 9), Oxford, Oxford University Press, 1992, esp. pp. 168-169.

Hebrew characters[14], and in PFouad 266b it appears in square Hebrew characters[15]. There thus appears to be no precedent here for the use of *nomina sacra* as contractions for the divine name with supralinear lines. Nor too is there any evidence from the Hebrew manuscripts from Qumran for such a device, even though the manuscripts adopt a variety of strategies for dealing with the divine name (e.g. using dots or using old Phoenician characters)[16]. *Nomina sacra* thus start to appear when Christian manuscripts start to appear.

The easiest inference is of course that the use of *nomina sacra* is a Christian invention and characterises Christian manuscripts. One must however be a little circumspect, if only because of the uncertainties surrounding any attempt to identify a manuscript as clearly Christian or non-Christian without begging the question. For example, POxy 7.1007, a fragment of Genesis probably from the 3rd century CE, has θεός contracted as a *nomen sacrum*; but the divine name itself is written as two *yod*'s with a line through them. The latter feature looks more distinctively Jewish, since Christian scribes would probably have written κύριος (in contracted form) here[17]. If then this indicates that the manuscript was written by a Jewish scribe[18], it would provide evidence of Jewish use of a *nomen sacrum* (for θεός at least)[19].

To account for POxy 7.1007, Roberts appealed to the persistence of a Jewish form of Christianity in Oxyrhynchus and hence "a possible explanation of th[is] ... eccentric text would be that [it is] the work of a Jewish-Christian scribe"[20]. This however may prove too much. Since so many of our manuscripts apparently come from Oxyrhynchus (though it is not certain how many were actually written there), and if there were a strong Jewish form of Christianity established there, it is very surprising

14. E. Tov (ed.), *The Greek Prophets Scroll from Nahal Hever (8HevXIIgr): (The Seiyal Collection)* (DJD, 8), Oxford, Oxford University Press, 1990, esp. p. 12.

15. Z. Aly, *Three Rolls of the Early Septuagint: Genesis and Deuteronomy* (PTA, 27) Bonn, R. Aabett, 1980.

16. Cf. Roberts, *Manuscript*, pp. 30-31.

17. The question of whether Jews ever wrote κύριος for the divine name is hotly disputed. See the very full discussion of J.A. Fitzmyer, *The Semitic Background of the Kyrios-Title*, in *A Wandering Aramean: Collected Aramaic Essays*, Chico, Scholars Press, 1979, pp. 115-142.

18. So Treu, *Bedeutung* (n. 8), p. 142; also listed by Kraft, *Textual Mechanics* (n. 8), as a potentially Jewish (and *not* Christian) production; it is taken as Christian by Roberts, *Manuscript*, pp. 33-34; Hurtado, *Origin*, p. 662.

19. Other manuscripts which use *nomina sacra* and which are taken as Jewish by Treu and Kraft include POxy 9.1166 (3rd century, Genesis) and POxy 8.1075 (3rd century, Exodus).

20. Roberts, *Manuscript*, p. 34; cf. too Hurtado, *Origin*, p. 662. Roberts also included POxy 4.656 in this judgement: on this see below.

if this affected only one or two of the mass of Christian manuscripts which we now have from Oxyrhynchus.

Although from a rather later period, we have clear evidence of a Jewish scribe using a *nomen sacrum* for the divine name: in the (6th-century) manuscript of Aquila from the Cairo Genizah, the scribe usually uses old Hebrew letters to represent the divine name; but at one point (2 Kings 23,24), the scribe (perhaps under pressure at the end of the line) has written $\overline{\kappa\upsilon}$ with a supralinear line[21]. One can of course write this off as "the exception which proves the rule"[22], but it remains a piece of clearly Jewish evidence which does not fit the "standard" paradigm.

The provenance of one of the few other manuscripts we possess of Aquila's version, the text of Gen 1 found in PAmh 1.3 (4th century), is also uncertain. This has four instances of $\vartheta\varepsilon\acute{o}\varsigma$ abbreviated as $\overline{\vartheta\varsigma}$. The fact that this is a version of Aquila's text might suggest that it is clearly Jewish[23]; however, Roberts claims that this is an exception to the general rule as the text appears on the verso of a Christian letter[24].

The fact remains that all we can probably say is that the beginnings of the practice of using *nomina sacra coincided* (roughly) with the start of the appearance of Christian manuscripts. But whether it was a specifically Christian innovation as such, or whether it was also used by non-Christian Jewish scribes as well, is not quite so certain.

II. CONSISTENCY

I consider next the issue of how consistently the system of abbreviation was applied. As with all historical work, it is perhaps all too easy to create rather more consistency and order in the alleged system by one's own description of the evidence, dismissing other parts of the evidence which do not fit as aberrations or mistakes (or consigning them to unread or semi-read footnotes!)[25]. Certainly there are some questions

---

21. See FITZMYER, *Semitic Background*, p. 122.
22. So explicitly ROBERTS, *Manuscript*, p. 33.
23. So PAAP, *Nomina Sacra*, p. 4.
24. ROBERTS, *Manuscript*, p. 75 n.2.
25. ROBERTS, *Manuscript*, appears at times to fall into this trap, dismissing pieces of evidence that do not fit his overall theory by references to scribes as e.g. "amateur or careless" (p. 27), "obviously unskilled or ignorant" (p. 28), "conveniently careless" (p. 39) or "palpably amateurish" (p. 45), manuscripts which do not fit the pattern as "eccentric" (p. 34), any exceptions to the "rule" are "such rare exceptions as to be insignificant" (p. 28), or to abbreviations as "correctly" and "incorrectly" written (p. 38f. as if there were a standard norm), or to features which do not fit as due to "scribal error" (p. 38).

which can be legitimately raised about the consistency of the whole phe-nomenon. These can be raised in relation to two aspects: (a) whether the four "primary" words were regularly and consistently abbreviated, and (b) whether the system of *nomina sacra* was confined to the "standard" list of 15.

In fact the picture is generally not quite as uniform as some general descriptions would suggest. It is widely agreed that the 11 *nomina sacra* of the 15 "standard" ones beyond the "primary" four do occur slightly unevenly and certainly not uniformly or consistently. Some rudimentary "history" in their development may be discernible[26]. For example, the contracted forms of οὐρανός, Δαυείδ and Ἰερουσαλήμ seem to have developed relatively late[27], and σωτήρ in abbreviated form does not ap-pear to be extant in any manuscript before the 4th century[28]. ἄνθρωπος seems to occur rather irregularly: it is already present in e.g. the Chester Beatty papyrus of Numbers + Deuteronomy (2nd century)[29] and in the Bodmer papyrus P[66], but not in others[30]. Nevertheless, despite this varia-tion at the "fringes" of the system, the claim is often made that the four "primary" nouns are (all but) always abbreviated. Thus Roberts claims that "the abbreviations [of these four] ... in their sacral meaning may be said to be invariable", and "the abbreviations [of these four] occur, with such rare exceptions as to be insignificant, in written material of all kinds from the earliest period of which we have evidence, the first half of the second century"[31]. Brown claims that these four *nomina sacra* occur in contracted form in all early papyri[32].

There are however some exceptions which may be noted.
(i) POxy 3.407 is an early Christian prayer text, dated to the 3rd century by the original editors. It has no contractions and writes θεός, Ἰησοῦς and χριστός in full (as well as, for what it is worth, σωτήρ and

26. *pace* TROBISCH, *First Edition*, p. 12, who claims that no clear growth in the system can be identified. He refers to the variety in the forms of the abbreviations in the Chester-Beatty manuscripts, and also contrasts e.g. Codex D (which has only 4 abbreviations) with e.g. P[66] (which abbreviates e.g. υἱός and ἄνθρωπος). But this is not relevant to the question of whether other words started to be abbreviated only relatively late.
27. Cf. PAAP, *Nomina Sacra*, p. 119.
28. Cf. O'CALLAGHAN, *Nomina Sacra*, p. 79. PAAP, *Nomina Sacra*, p. 119, can find no instance of this in abbreviated form until the end of the 4th century.
29. This is the date accepted by many, and was the date assigned to the manuscript by Kenyon in the initial publication. See however the discussion in ROBERTS, *Manuscript*, pp. 78-81, arguing that it might be safer to assign it to the "second/third" century.
30. Evidence in PAAP, *Nomina Sacra*, esp. p. 105; O'CALLAGHAN, *Nomina Sacra*, pp. 41-44.
31. *Manuscript*, pp. 27, 28.
32. BROWN, *Concerning* (n. 5), p. 18; cf. too GAMBLE, *Books*, p. 75: these four "were consistently contracted".

οὐρανός)[33]. It is true that this is not a biblical manuscript, but whether this is significant is not certain[34].

(ii) The evidence of P[52] (2nd century and arguably the earliest New Testament manuscript we possess)[35] is unclear. The preserved part of the fragment itself contains no *nomina sacra*, nor are there any words which one might expect to be abbreviated (i.e. none on the "standard" list of 15). Nevertheless, a consideration of the line-lengths might suggest that two references to "Jesus" in parts of lines missing from the fragment were in fact written in full[36]. If so, then P[52] might provide evidence of a 2nd-century manuscript where "Jesus" was *not* abbreviated with a *nomen sacrum*[37].

(iii) One of the extant fragments of the Gospel of Mary, POxy 50.3525 (3rd century) appears to have a κυριε uncontracted. There is some doubt about the reading as only the tops of the letters are visible. (The letters are all marked with dots by the original editors, and in part the reconstruction depends on the fuller Coptic version of the text in BG 8502, with of course the assumption that the Greek fragment corresponds closely enough to the Coptic to enable such reconstruction to take place.) If the reading is correct, it provides an instance where one of the four "primary" words was *not* abbreviated with a *nomen sacrum* (although an occurrence of ἄνθρωπος earlier is abbrevi-

---

33. However, the latter two are generally accepted as relative late-comers into the list, so their appearance here in uncontracted form is not perhaps surprising.

34. ROBERTS, *Manuscript*, p. 27, dismisses such exceptions to his "rule" as tending to occur "in private letters *or prayers* or in e.g. magical texts, often the work of an amateur or careless scribe" (my stress; for the reference to the scribe as "amateur and careless", cf. n. 25 above also). But whether there was any clear distinction drawn between biblical and non-biblical manuscripts in the convention of using *nomina sacra* is not at all certain. It is clear that a large number of non-"biblical" texts do use the system. See below on the discussion of Trobisch's theory about the existence of a "First Edition" of the New Testament.

35. Originally dated to the first half of the 2nd century, some would now date it a little later, i.e. into the second half of that century. Cf. A. SCHMIDT, *Zwei Anmerkungen zu P. Ryl. III 457*, in *APF* 35 (1989) 11-12. Nevertheless it is clearly still very early and indeed still one of the earliest New Testament manuscripts we possess.

36. So Roberts in his initial publication of the fragment: C.H. ROBERTS, *An Unpublished Fragment of the Fourth Gospel in the John Rylands Library*, Manchester, Manchester University Press, 1935, pp. 17-19. See also my *P[52] and Nomina Sacra* in *NTS* 47 (2001) 544-548, seeking to strengthen Roberts' early view. (By the time of his later discussion in *Manuscript*, he may have changed his mind: certainly there is no mention in his later work of this aspect of P[52].)

37. ROBERTS, *Fragment*, p. 19, regarded the lack of *nomina sacra* as confirmation of the very *early* date which he had assigned to the manuscript on palaeographic grounds. If in fact the manuscript is slightly later (cf. above), then the (possible) lack of *nomina sacra* may become even more significant in showing that any alleged "uniform" practice was not as uniformly established as some have suggested.

ated)[38]. The scribe thus does appear to know the system of using abbreviations in this way, but has evidently not chosen to use it in relation to κύριος.

(iv) In the Michigan papyrus fragment of the *Shepherd of Hermas* (PMich 130, probably 2nd century), there is an example of θεῷ written in full[39].

(v) POxy 4.656 (? early 3rd century) is a papyrus codex with parts of Genesis. It has θεός uncontracted. The original scribe appears to have left a blank space for the divine name (whether to be filled in later by himself or someone else is unknown), and a later hand has added κύριος, again in full. It is much debated as to whether this should be regarded as a Christian or a Jewish product[40]. The use of the codex *might* suggest a Christian origin, in which case the manuscript would provide evidence of another very early Christian scribe, *and* perhaps a later "corrector", who did *not* use the system of *nomina sacra*. However, the difficulty of determining whether a scribe was Christian or Jewish, and the danger of circular argumentation (cf. above), means that one cannot be certain[41].

(vi) P[72] has a number of peculiar features in relation to its apparent use of *nomina sacra*[42]. Here we may note that on three occasions κύριος is written in full and unabbreviated (1 Pet 3,12[43]; 2 Pet 1,2; 2,9). Also at 2

38. Of others on the "standard" list, the use of σωτήρ here is not abbreviated (as also in the Rylands fragment of Gospel of Mary PRyl 458); but both manuscripts are 3rd-century and it appears that σωτήρ was not abbreviated at all until the 4th century (cf. n. 28 above). The two fragments are thus not anomalous in writing σωτήρ in full.

39. Campbell BONNER, *A Papyrus Codex of the Shepherd of Hermas (Similitudes 1-9). With a Fragment of the Mandates*, Ann Arbor, University of Michigan Press, 1934, dates the fragment (of the *Mandates*) to "the third quarter of the second century" (p. 129). In col. 1 line 7 (= *Mand.* 2.6), θεῷ appears in full. This is dismissed by ROBERTS, *Manuscript*, p. 38, n. 4, as "probably a scribal error since considerations of space make it certain that κύριος was contracted". But this simply assumes what is to be shown, viz. that all the four "primary" words were uniformly and consistently abbreviated. Certainly the abbreviation of κύριος does not necessarily imply that the non-abbreviation of θεῷ is a mistake!

40. Cf. ROBERTS, *Manuscript*, pp. 33f., 76f., eventually deciding that it is Jewish. Roberts notes that P. KAHLE originally argued that *any* use of κύριος in a manuscript for the divine name was a clear sign of Christian origin, but later claimed that this manuscript was Jewish (*The Cairo Genizah*, New York, Praeger, 1969, p. 219). It is taken by TREU, *Bedeutung* (n. 8), p. 142, and by KRAFT, *Textual Mechanics* (n. 8), as Jewish.

41. Whether one can explain the situation here by reference to a "Jewish Christian" scribe (cf. n. 20 above) is also uncertain.

42. It is admittedly slightly later than some, being usually dated to the end of the 3rd, or beginning of the 4th century. However, according to the original editors of *Papyrus Bodmer VII-IX*, Cologny – Genève, Bibliotheca Bodmeriana, 1959, p. 7, the New Testament parts of the codices edited here (i.e. including P[72]) are 3rd-century.

43. In this verse there are two occurrences of κυρίου. On the first occasion, the word *is* abbreviated as a *nomen sacrum*, as κ̄ῡ; but at the second occurrence κυρίου is written out in full.

Pet 2,20 the scribe wrote κυρίου in full but also wrote a supralinear line above it.

(vii) Finally one should note that there are a number of other instances of uses of κύριος left unabbreviated, but these appear to be mostly uses where the referent(s) is/are clearly secular and not God or Jesus: cf. P[45] in Acts 16,16.19; P[46] in 1 Cor 8,5; Eph 6,5.9; Col 3,22[44]. These may not be so relevant here. Alternatively it may show that at least some scribes did regard the use of the contracted forms as significant. Thus, for example, the scribe of P[46] has κύριοι unabbreviated in 1 Cor 8,5 when referring to the other gods and lords whom others recognise, but has an abbreviated $\overline{κς}$ in the very next verse when referring to Jesus as the one Lord whom Christians acknowledge[45].

If now we consider the other side of the coin and ask how far words *out*side the "standard" list of 15 appear in abbreviated form and/or as *nomina sacra* (with a supralinear line), then the following evidence emerges[46].

(i) The most famous manuscript in this context is probably Papyrus Egerton 2 (2nd century)[47] which in addition to abbreviations for nouns on the "standard" list ($\overline{κς}$, $\overline{θς}$, $\overline{ιη}$, $\overline{πρα}$) has a number of other words abbreviated in the same way: $\overline{μω}$ (= Μωϋσῆς), $\overline{προφας}$ (= προφήτας), $\overline{βαλευσιν}$ (= βασιλεῦσιν), $\overline{η[σας}$ (= Ἡσαίας) and $\overline{επροφσεν}$ (= ἐπροφήτευσεν)[48]. Clearly the scribe of this MS is not working with a

44. See O'CALLAGHAN, *Nomina Sacra*, p. 54.

45. A very similar situation recurs in Eph 6,9 and Col 3,22. However, as we shall see later, this does not apply to all the *nomina sacra* used by any manner of means.

46. Such lists are provided by PAAP, *Nomina Sacra*, pp. 113-114; O'CALLAGHAN, *Nomina Sacra*, 39; K. ALAND, *Repertorium der griechischen christlichen Papyri. I. Biblische papyri. Altes Testament, Neues Testament, Varia, Apokryphen* (PTS, 18), Berlin – New York, De Gruyter, 1976, pp. 420-428. I have though here arranged the evidence by manuscript.

47. Originally dated to the first half of the second century, it is now usually dated a little later, to the second half of that century, partly as a result of one feature (the hooked apostrophe) found in PKöln 255, a fragment now identified as a part of PEg 2: see M. GRONEWALD, *Unbekanntes Evangelium oder Evangelienharmonie (Fragment aus dem Evangelium Egerton)*, in *Kölner Papyri (P. Köln)* 6, Cologne, Westdeutscher Verlag, 1987, 136-145; also Jon B. DANIELS, *The Egerton Papyrus: Its Place in Early Christianity* (PhD dissertation), Claremont Graduate School, 1990, p. 3. For the significance of the apostrophe in relation to dating, cf. E.G. TURNER, *Greek Manuscripts of the Ancient World*, Oxford, Clarendon, 1971, p. 13. See also the references in HURTADO, *Origin*, p. 657, n.7, including the reference to a personal communication from T.C. SKEAT, one of the original editors of the text who has evidently changed his view on the date of the manuscript in light of the new evidence from the Cologne fragment.

48. ALAND, *Repertorium*, also lists $\overline{ιοανου}$ as an abbreviation for Ἰορδάνου (on fr. 2 v., line 7). This is however not justifiable: there is no supralinear line; and there is a gap in the middle of the word due to a piece of the fragment being missing with space for two letters quite easily. This is not therefore a contraction by the scribe but simply a lacuna in the extant fragment.

list of possible abbreviations which is remotely like the "standard" list of 15 nouns.

(ii) The early Chester Beatty papyrus P[45] of the gospels and Acts (3rd century) has the unusual χρανους (= χριστιανούς) at Acts 11,26 (perhaps though simply formed by derivation from an abbreviation for χριστός).

(iii) The Chester Beatty papyrus of the epistles P[46] (c. 200 CE) has a number of unusual abbreviations: αναστρες (= ἀνασταυροῦντες[49]) in Heb 6,6, πνκον (= πνευματικόν, twice in 1 Cor 15,46 and πνκος (= πνευματικός) in 1 Cor 15,47, as well as πνς for πνευματικός in 1 Cor 2,15, for πνευματικοῖς in 1 Cor 3,1, and for πνευματικῶς in 1 Cor 2,14. It also has συνεστραι for συνεσταύρωμαι in Gal 2,19, though all these may well be formed by derivation from the abbreviations for σταυρός and πνεῦμα respectively.

(iv) POxy 1 (c. 200 CE), one of the Greek fragments of the Gospel of Thomas from Oxyrhynchus, has πριδι for πατρίδι (line 19), perhaps formed somewhat mechanically on the basis of the abbreviation for πατήρ.

(v) P[15] (3rd century) has κμου for κόσμου at 1 Cor 7,31 and 7,33, an abbreviation not attested elsewhere.

(vi) P[72] again has some unusual features. Thus δυμι for δυνάμει appears at 1 Pet 1,5, and χρς for χρηστός in 1 Pet 2,3 (perhaps simply a mistake, taking this erroneously as χριστός and abbreviating accordingly); πνατικος and πνατικας appear for πνευματικός/-άς in 1 Pet 2,5. There are also a number of other proper names which are written in full but with a supralinear line drawn, indicating apparently a *nomen sacrum*. Thus we get here νωε (1 Pet 3,20; 2 Pet 2,3), σαρρα (1 Pet 3,6), αβρααμ (1 Pet 3,6), μιχαηλ (Jude 9) and ενωχ (Jude 14).

(vii) The text of Melito preserved in one of the Bodmer papyri (PBodmer XIII) has δνιν, δυιν, δυνι (for δύναμιν/δύναμει); it also has αδαμ, νωε, ιακωβ and μωυσής uncontracted but with supralinear lines, and also αβρμ for ἀβραάμ, as well as αβρααμ in full with a supralinear line – both on the same line of the text!

It is difficult to assess all these and categorise them under a single heading. Some may be simple, almost mindless mistakes (e.g. χρς for χρηστός: cf. above)[50]. Others such as abbreviations for πνευματικός

---

49. Presumably implying this reading: all other manuscripts read ἀνασταυροῦντας (or at least no variant reading is recorded in NA[27]).

50. Cf. too the reading of P[75] at John 3,8, where the scribe evidently mistook the verb πνεῖ as a contracted form of πνεῦμα and then drew a supralinear line over it, suggesting that it was a *nomen sacrum*. On the other hand, it may be worth noting that these mistakes

and ἀνασταυροῦν are clearly derived from the more "standard" abbreviations for πνεῦμα and σταυρός respectively. It would be easy perhaps to ascribe them to the activity of one or more stupid scribes[51]. But in any case, rather than the almost total uniformity claimed by some, the phenomenon appears to have been more variable than some have implied.

Certainly too, even if we confine attention to the list of the "standard" 15 nouns, it is clear that the list grew over the course of time and did not remain static. We have already noted that e.g. σωτήρ does not appear in abbreviated form in early (i.e. 2nd or 3rd-century) manuscripts. So too there is widespread variation in whether (and how) words like ἄνθρωπος, πνεῦμα, πατήρ are abbreviated[52]. It would appear that the list had a tendency to expand rather than to contract, at least after the earlier period. But equally the earliest period to which we have access also shows some considerable variety.

III. NOMINA SACRA AS EVIDENCE OF A "FIRST EDITION" OF THE NEW TESTAMENT?

A number of aspects of the evidence assembled so far may also cast doubts on the theory, recently advocated by David Trobisch, of a "first edition" of the New Testament published very early[53]. There is not enough time or space here to discuss all of Trobisch's arguments for his theory. However, part of the evidence he adduces is the phenomenon of *nomina sacra* which, he claims, provides a distinctive feature of New Testament manuscripts and which may then reflect "a conscious editorial decision made by a specific publisher"[54]. The system is thus a new feature of this peculiarly Christian *collection* of texts, "a characteristic editorial feature of this Christian edition, which clearly distinguishes this

---

are qualitatively rather different: confusing χρηστός for χριστός might be an error in hearing as a text was dictated; the case of John 3,8 must presumably be a *visual* error by someone seeing the text and mistaking the letters seen as an abbreviation for a longer word. Could this perhaps suggest that at least some of the signs for abbreviations were inserted after the time of the actual writing of the manuscript? Perhaps this may indicate that we should not make the phenomenon too uniform.

51. Cf. ROBERTS, *Manuscript*, p. 39, n. 5, who refers to the scribe of P[72] as "both amateurish ... and ignorant, and not much importance should be attached to his practice". Cf. n. 25 above for other similar examples in Roberts' discussion.

52. Evidence in PAAP, *Nomina Sacra*; O'CALLAGHAN, *Nomina Sacra*.

53. TROBISCH, *First Edition*, pp. 11-19.

54. *Ibid.*, p. 19, referring also to the work of U. WILCKEN, *Grundzüge und Chrestomathie der Papyruskunde*, Erster Band: *Historisches Teil*, Leipzig, 1912, p. xlv, who argued that the system goes back to the work of a single individual.

edition from competing publications". Further, such a feature may have contributed to a process of "group definition", or group identity, enabling the Christian movement to distinguish its sacred literature, and hence itself, from its neighbours. "With one glance Christian readers were now able to recognize the Canonical Edition and distinguish it from Jewish-Hellenistic publications and other competing editions of apostolic writings"[55].

Such a theory is highly intriguing in many respects, and would, if established, throw much light on an otherwise very obscure period of Christian history. It must however remain rather conjectural (if only because the period is question is so obscure, precisely because direct evidence is lacking). Further, it is doubtful if the phenomenon of *nomina sacra* can really sustain the theory as advanced here.

First, I have already noted that the phenomenon is not so clearly confined to Christian texts in this period as some have suggested. In an earlier section, I argued that some manuscripts of the Christian era may in fact have been written by Jewish, non-Christian scribes. The phenomenon of using *nomina sacra* seems to coincide with the start of the Christian era in that (so far) no clearly pre-Christian examples of the phenomenon have been identified. But the doubts that still remain about a number of manuscripts mean that we cannot necessarily regard the phenomenon as exclusively Christian too quickly.

Second, we have to note the fact that the phenomenon of *nomina sacra* is attested across the widest range of Christian literature, both "canonical" and non-"canonical", as early as our extant sources allow us to see. In earlier sections, I have referred to some exceptions in relation to the (perhaps slightly exaggerated) claims about the universality of the phenomenon in Christian manuscripts. Yet such exceptions are for the most part just that: and the fact remains that *nomina sacra* are used in a very wide range of early Christian manuscripts. And for the present purposes one may note that they are distributed among "biblical" and non-"biblical" manuscripts alike. Clearly some care is needed in using such a description of texts at a period when the boundaries of the canon may not yet have been fixed[56]. Thus a text such as the *Shepherd of Hermas* may have been regarded as "canonical" by some but not by others. Whether texts like the Gospel of Thomas, or the Gospel of Mary, or Pa-

---

55. *Ibid.*, p. 68.

56. Though one of the main features of Trobisch's study is to challenge the prevailing view that the boundaries around the canon were only drawn much later. Yet he is never quite clear where he thinks the boundaries of the "First Edition" were drawn! But presumably he thinks in terms of boundaries which are very similar to those of our modern New Testaments.

pyrus Egerton 2 were ever regarded as "biblical" or "canonical" is not at all certain. Certainly it seems very doubtful whether the works of people like Irenaeus or Melito were ever regarded as "canonical".

However, the phenomenon of *nomina sacra* seems to cross any possible boundaries between "canonical" and non-"canonical" without any compunction. Thus *nomina sacra* seem to appear in virtually all Christian manuscripts (at least in general terms), whether the texts concerned are "canonical" or not. Thus one may refer to the (probable) abbreviation of κύριος in the 2nd-century fragment of Hermas' *Mandates* (PMich: cf. n. 39 above); the Oxyrhynchus fragments of the Gospel of Thomas (POxy 1, 654: 655 is too fragmentary) use the system of abbreviations freely as do the Greek fragments of the Gospel of Mary (cf. above). We have also seen that PEg 2 is replete with such abbreviations. Equally the very early Oxyrhynchus fragment of Irenaeus (POxy 3.405: cf. POxy 4, pp. 264-5), dated to a time not long after the autograph, uses *nomina sacra*.

All this must place a question mark over Trobisch's claim that *nomina sacra* characterise a particular edition, or collection, of Christian writings with clear boundary lines drawn around the collection serving (among other things) to "distinguish it from ... other competing editions of apostolic writings"[57]. *If* Trobisch's theory is correct, then it must also be the case that the system of using (at least some of) these abbreviations must have spread almost immediately to be used by virtually every Christian scribe writing every Christian text. It does *not* appear to be a feature which distinguishes Christian *scripture* (whatever limits one places on "scripture" at this period).

If one could establish that the phenomenon is a uniquely Christian practice (or perhaps was invented and inaugurated by Christians and was not used by non-Christians for some time at least), then Trobisch's point about the practice in relation to group identity, as serving to demarcate Christians from others socially, might have some validity. However, it would seem that the evidence is not strong enough to establish that the practice served to demarcate a specific collection of Christian texts from other texts, both Christian and non-Christian. The use of the phenomenon of *nomina sacra* to try to establish the existence of a "First Edition" of the New Testament, with roughly the same boundaries as our present New Testament, probably puts rather more weight on the evidence that it can easily bear.

---

57. *First Edition*, p. 68, quoted above. However, Trobisch never specifies what these other "competing editions of apostolic writings" might be.

IV. CONTRACTION OR SUSPENSION?

There has been some debate about whether the origin of the system of *nomina sacra* lies in a contracted or a suspended form. Most have assumed that the contracted form is the more original. Certainly too, as many have pointed out, it is the contracted form which is highly distinctive in relation to other Greek documents[58]. In other texts, a suspension is regularly used, and the system of *nomina sacra* is often regarded as distinctive precisely because of the (predominantly) contracted forms which occur. On the other hand, one must try to explain the suspended form of the name Ἰησοῦς (as ι̅η̅) in a number of very early MSS, notably PEg 2 and P[45] [59].

Hurtado has recently argued that the suspended form of the name Ἰησοῦς is in fact the *fons et origo* of the whole system. He refers to the well known passage in Barn 9,8 where "Barnabas" finds Christian significance prefigured in the number "318", the number of Abraham's men mentioned in Gen 14,14. Using the standard system of representing numbers by letters in Greek, "Barnabas" notes that 318 is in letter form τιη: the τ is then interpreted as a prefiguring of the cross, and the ι̅η̅ of Jesus. It is however hard to see here anything relating directly to the origin of the *nomina sacra*, if only because τ is never used elsewhere as an equivalent *nomen sacrum* for σταυρός. However, Hurtado argues that this shows an earlier, well established belief that Ἰησοῦς could be abbreviated as ι̅η̅ and that this was taken as the equivalent of the number 18. He then speculates that this might have originated in the numerical value of the *Hebrew* word for "life", חי (ח = 8, י = 10)[60]. In this way too he seeks to explain the supralinear lines marking the *nomina sacra* in MSS: just as supralinear lines are regularly used above single letters which serve as numerals (β̅ = 2, γ̅ = 3), so the line above the *nomina sacra* may be a vestige of an original line signalling that the letters are to be taken as the equivalent of a number.

The last suggestion about the supralinear lines is not fully convincing. Hurtado must be given credit for taking full account of the otherwise very unusual line. Nevertheless, the line must be functioning rather differently in the *nomina sacra* compared with the way in which it functions in numerals. In the latter case, the line indicates that the letter(s) is/are not to be read as they stand but *as* numbers. Hence presumably β̅ is read (out) as "δύο", ι̅ as "δέκα". In one way the lines marking *nomina*

58. See n. 6 above.
59. PAAP, *Nomina Sacra*, p. 107, notes that this occurs in 7 sources. Most of them are very fragmentary, providing at most one example of the suspension. However, PEg 2 and P[45] seem to provide evidence of a consistent form of this abbreviation.
60. HURTADO, *Origin*, p. 667.

sacra function similarly in that they indicate that the letters written are not to be read as they stand. But the letters are *not* then read as the equivalent number. Thus τῃ̄ is indeed not to be read as a single syllable sound – but it *is* to be read as Ἰησοῦς and not as δέκα ὀκτώ! Further, Hurtado's suggestion only works in the case of τῃ̄: it does not explain the other abbreviations, nor does it explain why all the other abbreviations have the form of contractions[61]. Further, it is not easy to envisage readers or writers of Greek texts using cryptic references to numbers which depend for their significance on a Hebrew word.

Nevertheless, Hurtado's suggestion that an original suspension preceded contracted forms may be more persuasive. We can certainly see that contractions came to swamp any suspended forms very early. Hence it seems easier to assume that earlier suspensions were taken over and eventually replaced by more popular contractions, rather than original contractions being supplemented by an occasional suspension which surfaced and then disappeared.

Certainly we do see a number of suspensions in some early MSS. I have already referred to the use of τῃ̄ present in some relatively early manuscripts. P[45] also has the suspended form χ̄ρ̄ rather than χ̄ς̄ (Acts 16,18)[62]. Perhaps too we should note the presence of the suspended form of Μωϋσῆς as μ̄ω̄ in PEg 2. Also it *may* be that a suspended form of Ἡσαίας as η̄ς̄ occurred there as well[63]. (However, even if this were the case, we must note that it is still uncertain whether this is a suspension or a contraction: the *sigma* in the abbreviation could be either the second or the final letter of the unabbreviated name.)

Why then did contracted forms replace suspensions? Given the highly unusual nature of the contracted form when compared with other Greek MSS, some attempt at an explanation seems desirable. Hurtado rather bypasses the issue, suggesting only that, with the growing list of words, a standardised system was felt desirable[64]. But this scarcely explains why a system using contractions was developed (with no real contemporary analogy) in preference to a system of suspensions.

---

61. See A. MILLARD, *Reading and Writing in the Time of Jesus*, Sheffield, Sheffield Academic Press, 2000, p. 71.

62. Cf. T.J. KRAUS, *Ad fontes: Gewinn durch die Konsultation von Originalhandschriften am Beispiel von P. Vindob. G 31974*, in *Biblica* 82 (2001) 1-16, on pp. 9-10, who notes the difficulty this makes for relating the form τῃ̄ too closely to Barn 9,8.

63. One difficulty arises from the fact that the abbreviation comes just at the point where the fragment breaks off so that all that is visible is the η and the supralinear stroke. Nevertheless, a consideration of line lengths makes it likely that the abbreviations consisted of only two letters rather than the four letters η̄σᾱς̄ suggested by the original editors. See too G. RUDBECK, *De nominibus sacris adnotatiunculae*, in *Eranos* 33 (1935) 146-151.

64. *Origin*, p. 669.

If one could venture a guess, one might suggest that it may have been simply because of possible ambiguity in the forms of abbreviation. Above all, perhaps, a suspended form gives no information about a case ending. Thus the abbreviation κυ, if it is a suspension, could be κύριος, κύριε, κυρίου or κυρίω. If though it is a contraction there is no ambiguity at all: it must be κυρίου. Contractions would thus make the ending absolutely clear in a way that suspensions would not. Could it be that contractions were developed to replace suspensions, simply in order to clarify case endings and hence to ease the reading process? That this may have been one of the main reasons for developing the system in the first place will be suggested below.

Such a suggestion might also cohere with what meagre evidence we have about Christian use of written materials in the earliest period of Christian history. For the most part we are largely in the dark. If one asks about standards of "literacy", most include both reading and writing together in this category. The two are of course different and it may be that one should not equate standards of writing with standards of reading. However, since we have nothing else to go on, it may be not unreasonable to correlate the two. If so, it may be worth noting that the standard of writing by early Christian scribes is generally deemed to be reasonably competent but not outstanding. The handwriting used is generally described as "documentary" (or "reformed documentary") rather than "literary"[65]. Christian scribes were thus not incompetent fools or idiots; but they may not have been of the highest calibre either.

If then it is legitimate to deduce something about the *readers* of the MSS, i.e. those who actually read the text aloud to others[66], then it may be not unreasonable to assume that Christian readers too were not total idiots but not of the highest calibre either. Might it be than that a system of contractions replaced an original system of suspended forms for the (relatively mundane) purpose of avoiding ambiguity (e.g. in case endings) for any potential reader?

V. HOW INFLUENTIAL?

What was the significance of the system of *nomina sacra*? Perhaps though one should ask first for whom the practice might have been significant.

---

65. See ROBERTS, *Manuscript*, pp. 14-15; GAMBLE, *Books*, p. 71.
66. The days of silent, private reading are some way in the future. And in talking about a "reader" here, I am talking about the person actually responsible for reading the manuscript to others. The "others" are then strictly speaking hearers, not readers themselves.

There are perhaps two issues here. The first is the chronological one: the significance of the *nomina sacra* may have changed over the course of time. Hence the significance at the earliest period may not have been the same as the significance at a later period[67]. Here I shall be concerned with the earlier period to which we can have access. There is however another issue which is rarely if ever considered. At any one time, *who* would have seen any significance in the use of *nomina sacra*?

I would suggest that, in relation to this second issue, the use of *nomina sacra* would have had an extremely limited influence. It clearly affected the scribe writing the manuscript in question. It would clearly have also affected those who actually read the manuscript (aloud and presumably to others). That alone should indicate its somewhat limited influence if only due to the fact that it can only have affected those who were literate. A reasonable estimate for the extent of literacy in the ancient world would appear to be a figure of between 10% and 20% of the population as a whole as being capable of reading and/or writing[68]. And it has generally been thought that Christian groups would not have been very different from the population at large in this respect: hence it seems reasonable to work with a figure of no more than c. 15% of any Christian group as being literate.

However, in the case of *nomina sacra* as used in Christian manuscripts, we have to consider not only how many people *could* read a manuscript, but also how many *did* read any one manuscript. It is generally accepted that the period of the first two centuries of the Christian era predate by some time any activity of private and/or silent reading. Reading would thus be a public activity in which a (single?) lector read to an assembled group who would then be *hearers* of the text, not readers. Thus even if an average Christian group contained 15% or so people who *could* read if required to do so, this does not mean that even these people actually *did* read the manuscript in question. At any one time at which a manuscript was read (in public), the only person who would have noted the system of *nomina sacra* would have been the lector.

Further, there is no evidence (as far as I am aware) that the *nomina sacra* led to any change in the pronunciation of the key words: as far as hearers were concerned, the presence or absence of a *nomen sacrum*

---

67. Such seems to be implied by Hurtado's overall theory: the initial symbolism of the numerical value of the name of "Jesus" (in *Hebrew* letters) led to the initial suspended form of the name, but this was lost or forgotten as the system developed with the use of contracted forms of others words (all in *Greek*).

68. Cf. W.V. HARRIS, *Ancient Literacy*, Cambridge MA, Harvard University Press, 1989; GAMBLE, *Books*, pp. 2-10.

would have led to exactly the same end-result. The use of a *nomen sacrum* is a signal to the *reader* that some letters in the manuscript being read out are to be pronounced otherwise than written. But then whether the manuscript has κύριος or κ̅ς̅, the end result would be the same: what is said – and heard – will have been κύριος in full[69].

This then is quite *un*like the situation with regard to the divine name YHWH. As is well known, some Jewish manuscripts adopt a variety of devices for writing (or avoiding writing) the divine name. In each case too it is clear that, if the divine name is written, the expectation is that the name will *not* be pronounced. The devices used in the manuscripts varied: e.g. writing the name in old Hebrew letters in a Greek text, using two *yod*'s, leaving a blank space, using the letters ιαω[70]. But in each case this is a clear signal to the reader that something *other* than the name is to be uttered. And because this "something other" is then said, it is also heard by the listeners. Thus the difference in sound is something shared by both speaker/reader and hearers. The difference would have had significance for *all* those engaged in the process of participating in the reading of the text.

Yet this is precisely what does not seem to have happened with the use of Christian *nomina sacra*, and hence any supposed analogy between the use of *nomina sacra* and Jewish reverence for the divine name may be misleading[71]. Thus when Roberts says, referring to the use of the four "primary" *nomina sacra*, that "their full meaning was only apparent to the faithful to whose attention it was brought whenever the sacred books … were read"[72], his words may be accepted at face value[73], but the likelihood is that "the faithful to whose attention it was brought" would probably only have been the one person actually engaged in the process of converting the signs on the page to audible sound, i.e. the lector. For all other "readers", i.e. hearers, the significance of the *nomina sacra* in the manuscript being read out must have been minimal if not completely non-existent. Roberts' suggestion that "the abbreviation would constitute a warning signal to the reader and may have served as the occasion *for some mark of reverence* on his part" is, as far as I am

---

69. I am not aware that anyone has suggested that the word would have been pronounced as written (i.e. as a vowel-less "kiss", or "kss", sound). The line above the word is usually taken as indicating that the word is to be read and uttered in a *different* way from what is written on the papyrus/parchment. See too PAAP, *Nomina Sacra*, p. 123.

70. See above.

71. Cf. too TROBISCH, *First Edition*, p. 14.

72. ROBERTS, *Manuscript*, p. 48.

73. Though it does seem clear from the context that Roberts does not think in terms of such limited influence at all!

aware, without foundation[74]. Claims then that the system represents any *broadly based* "theology" or whatever must be regarded with not a little suspicion. It *may* have represented a "theology" (on which see below); but the circle affected by such a theology must have been extremely limited.

VI. SIGNIFICANCE

Some very far-reaching claims about the possible significance of the system of *nomina sacra* have been made by a number of scholars, notably by Roberts and Hurtado. As noted earlier, almost all have concurred with the theory implied in Traube's original description – that these are "nomina *sacra*", intended to emphasise the "sacred" character of the words so abbreviated[75]. Brown even claims that the four "original", or "primary", abbreviations are "not simply *nomina sacra* but rather *nomina divina*"[76]. Hurtado too at one point slips into the same language: "if the *nomina sacra* began with the special abbreviation of Jesus' name, it appears that very quickly the other early-attested *nomina divina* (θεός, κύριος, χριστός) were also accorded special reverence and written as sacred abbreviations"[77]. Roberts and Hurtado then want to trace the whole system back to an important *theological* idea of reverence for the name of Jesus in earliest Christianity[78].

All this may however overplay the evidence which we have very considerably. A statement such as that of Brown presupposes that the four "primary" words abbreviated (i.e. θεός, Ἰησοῦς, κύριος, χριστός) do in fact form the *original* basis of the system (as well as making some

74. ROBERTS, *Manuscript*, p. 29 (my stress). One might imagine this in relation to a reference to God, or Jesus (in the manner in which in some churches today people make a small sign bowing their head whenever the name of Jesus is mentioned); but as we shall see shortly, a significant number of these abbreviations are decidedly *un*-sacred. Is one seriously to imagine wholesale bowing of the head whenever ἄνθρωπος is mentioned (at just the points where the word is abbreviated, but not where it is written in full?), or whenever Joshua's name cropped up in the reading of the Chester Beatty Numbers papyrus?!

75. See above.

76. BROWN, *Concerning* (n. 5), p. 19. Cf. too F. BOVON, *Names and Numbers in Early Christianity*, in *NTS* 47 (2001) 267-288, on p. 277: "The system of the *nomina sacra* corresponds to a double theological movement. First, it offers a special way of writing the divine name detaching it from the human network. Second, it relates the Son more closely to the Father by including both of them in a sphere secluded from the realm of creation".

77. HURTADO, *Origin*, p. 669. Yet how appropriate is it to call χριστός a "divine" name? And is κύριος always a reference to a "divine" figure?

78. ROBERTS, *Manuscript*, pp. 41ff.; HURTADO, *Origin*, p. 671f.

considerable further assumptions in calling them "divina"). Yet while it is true that, by the time any evidence reaches the light of day for us, the abbreviation of these four words seems well established and (at least moderately!) consistent, we still lack any evidence that shows clearly that at an earlier stage these were the *only* four abbreviations used. Certainly if this were the case, there are still some awkward parts of the evidence which would not be accounted for very easily.

(a) Above all there is the presence of ἄνθρωπος in the list of *nomina sacra*. We may note that ἄνθρωπος is abbreviated in some very early manuscripts, e.g. the Chester Beatty Numbers + Deuteronomy (2nd century)[79], as well as in POxy 1 (c. 200 CE) and also P[46] (also c. 200 CE). It is true that the abbreviation is not always consistent[80]. But does this lack of consistency show that it did not belong to an "original" system presumed to be highly consistent and regular (containing just the four "primary" words)? Or does it simply show that, at the earliest point we can reach, the system was *not* so regulated at all but displayed considerable variation? The existence of widely different (in this respect) texts such as PEg 2 (with almost a riot of abbreviations) and P[52] (with perhaps none) should perhaps incline us to the second possibility.

But ἄνθρωπος may also be significant in that it is one of the most *un*-"sacred" words in many respects. Several have tried to classify the abbreviations by whether the words are used in a "sacred" or "profane" sense[81]. And it is notable how many of the occurrences of ἄνθρωπος as a *nomen "sacrum"* are in fact what could only be called a "profane" sense. To take one example among many, POxy 1 line 19 has an abbreviated $\overline{\alpha\nu\omega\nu}$ in its version of saying 28 of the Gospel of Thomas: "My soul became afflicted for the sons of men; because they are blind in their hearts and do not see ...". The context scarcely suggests that the ἄνθρωποι here are regarded as very "sacred"! Similarly, in P[46] ἄνθρωπος is frequently abbreviated in 1 Cor 2,6-16 in relation to the ψυχικὸς ἄνθρωπος and the πνευματικὸς ἄνθρωπος indiscriminately (cf. vv. 11, 14, though conversely ἄνθρωπος is always written in full in 1 Cor 15, referring to both the first and the second man, e.g. in v. 47)[82].

79. Though cf. n. 29 above.
80. It is abbreviated 4 times in the Chester Beatty Numbers + Deuteronomy and written in full 19 times (cf. PAAP, *Nomina Sacra*, p. 7); in P[46] it is abbreviated 10 times and written in full 68 times (*ibid.*, p. 8). The occurrence in POxy 1 is the only occurrence of the noun in the extant text.
81. PAAP seeks to divide the usages up into these two categories (*Nomina Sacra*, p. 5 and then in all his lists); O'CALLAGHAN tries to sub-divide the possibilities more precisely into four categories (cf. *Nomina Sacra*, pp. 25-31, and then in turn also in his lists).
82. So too all the (four) abbreviations of ἄνθρωπος in the Chester Beatty Numbers + Deuteronomy papyrus are classified by PAAP as profane (*Nomina Sacra*, p. 6). For P[66]

One of the few to have implicitly noted the difficulty and sought to respond to it was Roberts, who claimed:

> It [an abbreviated form for ἄνθρωπος] is found in the Chester Beatty Numbers and Deuteronomy, once again in a secular sense which implies that its use as a sacral term is earlier. Gnostic usage apart, it must owe its position to the title of Jesus as Son of Man[83].

This was then for Roberts a further indication of the very early date of the system as a whole, since "Son of Man" disappears as a significant christological title quite quickly.

However, such an argument is in danger of putting the cart before the horse. To say that an established "secular" usage implies that a "sacral" usage must pre-date this simply assumes that such a "sacral" usage exists at all and indeed that the whole system is indeed based on a set of "sacred" names. But it is precisely the occurrence of a word like ἄνθρωπος which calls this assumption into question. Further, there is, as far as I am aware, no clear evidence that the use of ἄνθρωπος in the phrase ὁ υἱὸς τοῦ ἀνθρώπου can be regarded as significant in determining the origin of the practice of abbreviating ἄνθρωπος. Certainly little consistency can be shown in our extant early manuscripts for a tendency to abbreviate the word in this phrase specifically.

> Excursus on "Son of Man" in early papyri:
> The fragmentary nature of so many early papyri means that the phrase "Son of Man" is not always preserved in the parts of the text which have survived. Perhaps the most support for Roberts' theory that the abbreviation for ἄνθρωπος owes its origin to the use of the phrase ὁ υἱὸς τοῦ ἀνθρώπου applied to Jesus comes from P[75]. Here the phrase is written as ο υιος του $\overline{\alpha\nu\text{ου}}$ on 15 occasions (but *not* abbreviating υἱός!); four times both nouns are abbreviated (Luke 9,44; John 3,13; 6,27; 12,23); but on two occasions ἄνθρωπος (and υἱός) are written in full (Luke 18,8; John 12,34). In the use of the phrase "Son of Man" in P[66], ἄνθρωπος is abbreviated 7 times (John 6,53.62; 9,35; 12,23.34 (twice); 13,31, but written in full on 4 occasions (John 3,13.14; 5,27; 8,28).

Paap counts 23 as "profane" and 12 as "sacred" (*ibid.*, p. 10). O'CALLAGHAN, *Nomina Sacra*, pp. 41-42, gives 29 instances in P[66] marked with an asterisk (indicating "improperly sacred or used in a profane sense" [p. 27]); for P[75], he gives 30 instances of an abbreviated form of the word with an asterisk. The same would also apply in the case of e.g. πνεῦμα: abbreviated forms of the word are used equally for human, or indeed "demonic", "spirits" quite as much as for God's Holy Spirit. To take some examples at random, $\overline{\pi\nu\alpha}$ is used in Acts 16,16 to refer to the spirit of divination, and in Luke 13,11 to refer to the "spirit of sickness" suffered by the woman. Similarly $\overline{\pi\varsigma}$ (for πατρός) is used in Acts 16,2 of Timothy's (presumably not very sacred!) father.

83. ROBERTS, *Manuscript*, p. 40.

In P⁴⁵ where the phrase is extant, ἄνθρωπος is always written in full (Mark 9,31; Luke 9,58; 12,8.10)[84].

In P⁵⁹ ἀνθρώπου is (probably) abbreviated at John 1,51 (no other uses are extant).

In P⁹⁵ ἀνθρώπου was probably written in full at John 5,28 (to judge from the line lengths).

P³⁷ has ἀνθρώπου in full at Matt 26,24.25.

P⁴⁷ has ἀνθρώπου in full at Rev 14,14 (despite the unusual form α̅θ̅ν̅ in Rev 9,15.18.20).

Overall there seems little indication that scribes in these early papyri display any consistency in abbreviating ἀνθρώπου specifically in the phrase ὁ υἱὸς τοῦ ἀνθρώπου. And, as we noted earlier, there are plenty of instances in these early papyri of ἄνθρωπος being abbreviated in contexts where the word has no "sacred" connotation at all.

(b) We may also note the way in which Ἰησοῦς can sometimes be abbreviated in a non-"sacral" way. Thus in the Chester Beatty Numbers + Deuteronomy papyrus, ι̅ς̅ is sometimes used for Joshua. Roberts writes again:

> The use for Jesus was so well established in the second half of the second century that to write it wherever the name occurred was second nature to the scribe. This would again seem to carry the system back to at least the turn of the century[85].

Again this may assume too much. Do we *know* that a "sacred" form of the abbreviation – for Jesus alone – *must* predate such an abbreviation for Joshua here? Again Roberts appears to assume offhand that all these abbreviations are indeed "sacred". But perhaps the early evidence is just what calls that into question.

(c) Similarly we may note the use of the unusual π̅ρ̅ι̅δ̅ι̅ in POxy 1 line 32. This is presumably formed on the basis of a fairly mechanical abbreviation for πατήρ, the first four letters of πατρίδι being mistakenly thought to come from πατήρ. But the almost mechanical nature of the "error" can itself highlight the way in which the word itself appears to be virtually ignored by the scribe. Certainly the word πατρίς here has no "sacred" meaning at all. Any abbreviation is made apparently on an almost rote basis, not on any awareness of the sacred nature of the word itself in its context.

---

84. However, it should be noted that P⁴⁵ never abbreviates ἄνθρωπος: cf. PAAP, *Nomina Sacra*, p. 12.

85. ROBERTS, *Manuscript*, p. 38.

(d) We must also consider the evidence provided by PEg 2, as well as possibly the slightly later P[72] and PBodmer XIII. Certainly the evidence of PEg 2 would suggest that, as one moves back earlier in time, the "system" may become more haphazard rather than less, with considerably more words being abbreviated in this way. Some of these could be said to have a small element of "sacredness" (e.g. Moses, Isaiah, prophets, prophesy)[86]. But e.g. "kings" has at most a very derivative element of "sacredness" associated with the word (e.g. God or Jesus as a "king"), and in PEg 2 itself the word is used in a highly *un*-"sacral" way[87]. Also any "sacredness" attaching to the figures of Moses, Isaiah or the prophets did not generally lead to other Old Testament figures being singled out for similar treatment in other manuscripts[88].

Could all this perhaps suggest that Traube's initial description of the phenomenon as "nomina *sacra*" has led people astray? Traube of course wrote well before the publication of PEg 2 and other papyri (e.g. the Chester Beatty and Bodmer papyri). But the cumulative evidence of this newer material might suggest that the nouns abbreviated in this way in the earliest manuscripts are *not* quite so "sacra" after all. Further, the initial period may have been characterised by more freedom and variety than uniformity.

Were there though any limits to the nouns which were singled out for such treatment in writing manuscripts? It has always been a puzzle why the "standard" list is at it is, and why it does not include such special ("sacred"?) words such as λόγος, σοφία, ἄρτος, αἷμα, σῶμα, οἶνος to name but a few[89]. One answer may be that the list was never intended to be primarily nouns with high Christian theological significance.

---

86. DANIELS, *Egerton Gospel* (n. 47), pp. 3-4, argues that the fact that these words are abbreviated shows that "prophetic" elements of Jewish history and tradition held some special place for the scribe (and perhaps the author) the fragment (or for the tradition in which s/he was trained); he thus finds in this added support for his claim that the text comes from a Jewish Christian milieu. (Strictly, however, such an argument could only show at most something about the scribe of the fragment, not the author of the text itself [if the two were different].)

87. It refers here to the secular "kings" with the question raised as to whether one should pay them what belongs to them (presumably by way of taxes, cf. Mark 12,13-17 and pars.). DANIELS, *Egerton Gospel* (n. 47), p. 163, argues that the abbreviated form of βασιλεῦσιν here may indicate a belief (by the scribe or the author) that God is one of the "kings" referred to in the question. This however seems very forced. But even if this were the case, the fact that the noun is in the plural implies that there are several other "kings" apart from God in mind as well, and they are still referred to by the abbreviated form of the noun.

88. Except possibly P[72] and PBodmer XIII: see below.

89. Cf. ROBERTS, *Manuscript*, p. 40. There is though one occurrence of αἷμα with a supralinear line (though no abbreviation) in P[46] at Heb 9,13; also ἰχθύς occurs with a

But equally it may be significant that a number of the "unusual" abbreviations which one sees in some extant manuscripts are in fact proper names, names of people. Roberts himself, raising the question of why the "standard" list is as it is, claims that "the inevitable four apart ... the list is limited to proper names and nouns"[90]. As a statement about the 11 nouns of the "standard" 15 beyond the "primary" 4, this is surely simply not true. Words like ἄνθρωπος, σταυρός or οὐρανός are not proper names; and other nouns such as πατήρ, μήτηρ or υἱός can barely be described as such (even if in a very few contexts they might verge on becoming proper names). However, it remains the case that some *other* "nomina sacra" are proper names. Thus "Moses" and "Isaiah" are abbreviated in PEg 2; προφήτης (and derivatively ἐπροφήτευσεν) might just come in this category (though βασιλεῦσιν will not so easily, at least in the sense that it is used here in PEg2, i.e. in a decidedly secular sense). It may be worth noting too the presence of what appear to be similar phenomena in the supralinear lines written above the names Νῶε, Ἀβραάμ, Σάρρα, Μιχαήλ, Ἐνώχ in P[72], though the names themselves are all written out in full. So too in PBodmer XIII, Ἀδάμ, Νῶε, Ἰακώβ are treated similarly, whereas Ἀβραάμ once is both abbreviated and given a supralinear stroke, i.e. it has both the characteristics of the other "*nomina sacra*". The presence of the supralinear lines may indicate that the scribes here thought that these were being treated in a similar way to the other "standard" "*nomina sacra*". But could it perhaps be that these were indicated in this way *because they were proper names*, not necessarily because they were thought of as especially "sacred" terms? Clearly this would apply only derivatively in some cases, and admittedly not at all in others. Thus θεός, κύριος and χριστός are only semi-"proper" names rather than descriptions. However, as God's own name is never pronounced, θεός becomes virtually the equivalent of a proper name; so too *if* κύριος was the spoken equivalent for the divine name among Greek-speaking Jews (and certainly also for Christians)[91], then κύριος functions in many respects as a proper name. Similarly χριστός, although not strictly a name, seems to have become one at a very early stage of christological development (cf. 1 Cor 15,3!). However, such an explanation clearly will not work for words such as ἄνθρωπος or σταυρός, and only in some instances for πατήρ, μήτηρ or υἱός.

supralinear line but not abbreviated in the Gospel of the Egyptians (cf. PAAP, *Nomina Sacra*, p. 114).

90. ROBERTS, *Manuscript*, p. 40. To speak of "the *inevitable* four" does slightly beg the question!

91. Cf. above.

What then was the primary or original purpose of the *nomina sacra*? I would suggest that they may have functioned primarily as *reading aids* to assist some who were perhaps not as proficient as others to read the text more easily[92].

A certain amount has been written on the nature of the scribal hands we now see in early Christian manuscripts, with a fair measure of agreement that these hands are not of a high "literary" quality but are rather "documentary", perhaps though with some aspirations to a higher quality and hence sometimes called "reformed documentary"[93]. The high "literary" hands all write in a continuous script with no breaks at all or concessions to the reader, except perhaps at the end of long sections. It is a well known feature of "documentary" hands to break this principle via a variety of means, e.g. by having small breaks between words or smaller sections, enlarging the first letter of a section or a page, using letters (with supralinear lines) to denote numbers, and sometimes too using an apostrophe to separate syllables or words, to mark a doubled consonant, and (sometimes) to indicate a proper name[94].

---

92. The possibility is raised also by TROBISCH, *First Edition*, pp. 17-18, though he claims that the system is too uniform to suggest that this was the original reason for it.

93. See above, though see the reservations about this general claim raised by G.N. STANTON, *The Early Reception of Matthew's Gospel: New Evidence from Papyri?*, in D.E. AUNE (ed.), *The Gospel of Matthew in Current Study. Studies in Memory of William G. Thompson S.J.*, Grand Rapids, Eerdmans, 2001, pp. 42-61. The evidence of the newly published Oxyrhynchus New Testament papyri (to which Stanton refers) may indicate that the quality of early Christian manuscripts was a little more varied than some have suggested in the past; but the evidence of the rest of the early Christian written evidence remains.

94. See generally ROBERTS, *Manuscript*, 14-19 for these points; for the apostrophe, see TURNER, *Greek Manuscripts* (n. 47 above), p. 13. Cf. too B. LAYTON, in ID. (ed.), *Nag Hammadi Codex II,2-7 Volume One* (NHS, 20), Leiden, Brill, 1989, p. 15: "The value of the apostrophe for the ancient reader would have been as *an aid to reading, like the superlinear stroke*". He is writing about Coptic, but the same applies equally well to Greek. In Coptic the supralinear stroke is of course very common; thus attempts to read into its use a crypto-*nomen sacrum* are probably wide of the mark. Hence contra e.g. R. VALANTASIS, *The Gospel of Thomas*, London, Routledge, 1997, pp. 144-145, who takes the line over the Coptic word *hmhal* ("servant") in Thomas 65 as implying that the servants in the parable here are being regarded as "divine figures", with wide-ranging implications drawn. He fails to note that the word *hmhal* is regularly written with a supralinear line and this is a feature of Coptic language and writing, not a *nomen sacrum* of profound theological significance!

Roberts himself drew a sharp distinction between the Christian texts, which displayed these features fairly consistently, and Jewish texts, which he claimed showed rather more sophistication and "literary" quality. Such a distinction is however questioned by Kraft especially (see his *Textual Mechanics* [n. 8 above]): precisely these features may characterise Jewish texts just as much (cf. especially the use of spacings in the Rylands Deuteronomy fragments, or the use of spacings and enlarged letters in the 8HevXIIgr scroll.

One must also remember the very high level of expertise required by anyone who read from a manuscript written in continuous script. Most of us today have become so used to reading modern script that we forget the enormous sub-conscious assistance which is provided by the spacings between (every!) word, as well as other helps and indications from capitalisation, punctuation, paragraphing, use of separate lines (e.g. in verse) etc. It has indeed become standard in literary studies to point out how a text can change its nature radically depending on whether it is set out in straight prose or in verse lines[95]. So too at a more mundane level, we have become accustomed to be able to make the necessary mental adjustment to enable us to recognise proper names by the fact that they are (usually) capitalised.

All such aids were of course unavailable to a reader of ancient manuscripts written in continuous script. Presumably some of the features which distinguish documentary hands from literary hands were designed to assist the *reading* process, to enable the reader to pick up and interpret the sense more easily in a way we do today, unthinkingly for the most part, by our systems of spaces between words, capitalisation and other punctuation. No doubt the rudimentary spacing which one sees in some documentary hands is working in this way. So too perhaps was the (apparent) system of using an apostrophe to signal proper names.

I would suggest that perhaps the use of *nomina "sacra"* was developed and operated for just these reasons. Some of the words so abbreviated were obviously "key" words in some ways in that they occurred with reference often to key figures in Christian discourse (God, Jesus, Lord, Christ). But the purpose of the abbreviation system may not have been to highlight particular reverence for God or Jesus. That was done in other ways! Rather, the intent may been simply to enable the reader to get his/her bearings a little more easily when reading the text, to identify one or two key words in a passage and make the necessary mental adjustments (e.g. by fixing on at least one point where there was a word break) more easily[96].

---

95. See S. FISH, *Is There a Text in This Class?*, Cambridge, MA, Harvard University Press, 1980, esp. ch. 14 "How to Recognize a Poem when You See One", pp. 322-337.

96. A possible difficulty for this theory, raised in discussion at the seminar, is that, whilst the supralinear line might function as an aid to readers to get their mental bearings, the abbreviation itself might make the actual reading process harder rather than easier. This is true, though we know of no instance of an abbreviation without the supralinear line which provides the mental help. And while an abbreviated form on its own would undoubtedly make for a much harder text to decipher, the abbreviation *with* the line is much clearer. (Cf. the illustration of TROBISCH, *First Edition*, p. 18 [together with n. 51 on p. 117] who prints the text of Jude 25 with the abbreviations but without spaces or supralinear lines, and then prints the text with the lines.)

This too might explain why the system developed the use of contractions, since it would then clarify unambiguously the case ending (perhaps not usually a difficulty, but it could be so in one or two instances), and perhaps enable the reader to recognise these instantly. It might also explain why one or two rather *un*-"sacred" words are abbreviated in this way, e.g. especially ἄνϑρωπος or πνεῦμα (in many instances: cf. above). If the aim was not necessarily to provide a list of sacred terms, but simply to provide a reference point to the reader for one or two key terms in reading, it may not be surprising if a word like ἄνϑρωπος was used in this way. It has sometimes been argued that the "sacred" nature of the list, and the fact that it is not just a space-saving device, is shown by the fact that commonly occurring words are not abbreviated[97]. This however may miss the point. The aim may not have been necessarily to save space, nor indeed to overuse the device since a flood of supralinear lines would simply have created confusion. If these lines were to function as markers enabling readers to get their mental bearings, then the list would have to be relatively small and related to words that do *not* occur every other line (e.g. καί). A word like ἄνϑρωπος would seem to be ideally suited, as would "key" words in Christian discourse (e.g. God, Jesus, but perhaps too "cross" etc.). Such a theory would, as noted earlier, also fit with what (little) we know of the general standard of Christian writers (and hence *perhaps* readers) at this early period: Christian writers were competent but perhaps not of the highest quality; and hence maybe Christian readers were also competent, but perhaps not of the highest quality.

This might also explain why some proper names are marked in this way (some abbreviated, some not but still with the supralinear line). We know of the use of an apostrophe for this purpose in some documentary texts[98]. If then the system of abbreviations with lines is operating in the same way, it may not be surprising that in the Christian manuscripts we have the common abbreviations for Jesus and God, as well as then the abbreviations of proper names in this way in PEg 2, P[72] and PBodmer XIII, as we have seen (as well as possibly the Chester Beatty papyrus of Numbers and Deuteronomy using ιη̅ for Ἰησοῦς = Joshua[99]).

---

97. Cf. PAAP, *Nomina Sacra*, p. 122.

98. Cf. TURNER, *Greek Manuscripts*, p. 11. The usage is quite frequent in some of the Chester Beatty texts.

99. However, it must be admitted that this manuscript does not abbreviate any of the (many!) other proper names which occur.

Conclusion

It may be that Traube was half right, but perhaps only half right, in his famous description of the phenomenon as "nomina sacra". They may be "nomina" – yes (or at least in part and perhaps in origin); but "sacra" – no!

Theology Faculty Centre   Christopher M. TUCKETT
41 St Giles
Oxford OX1 3LW
England

THE AUTHORITY OF THE "OLD TESTAMENT" IN THE EARLY CHURCH: THE WITNESS OF THE "PSEUDEPIGRAPHA OF THE OLD TESTAMENT"

I. INTRODUCTION

1. *The Term "Pseudepigrapha of the Old Testament"*

This essay will deal with the question why the writings commonly classified among the "Pseudepigrapha of the Old Testament" were transmitted by Christians and how they functioned in the Early Church. The fact that a number of writings dealing with important biblical figures was handed down at all shows that Christians regarded as important what people as Adam, Enoch, the patriarchs, Moses, Elijah or other prophets had done and said. The documents under discussion bear witness to the authority of the Jewish Bible as the "Old Testament" of the church.

This typically Christian term "Old Testament" is getting into use at the end of the second century as designation of the Jewish holy books, accepted as part of the Christian Bible by (at least a substantial part of) Christendom. The use of this term in the present context will prove to be warranted.

The use of the expression "Pseudepigrapha of the Old Testament", however, is questionable. It is regularly used as a designation of a group of writings that are assumed to be of Jewish origin and to date from the period between around 200 BCE and 100 CE ("the time of the second temple", "the intertestamentary period"). Though commonly used for lack of a better term, this is not a very suitable expression, for several reasons. First, there is by no means consensus on the question which writings should be reckoned to the Old Testament pseudepigrapha and which should not. Second, there is much difference of opinion about the provenance and the transmission history of many documents. Next, the designation "pseudepigraphon" (in the sense of: a writing from antiquity ascribed to somebody else than the real author) is, strictly speaking, applicable only in the case of a relatively small number of the books commonly brought together in collections "Pseudepigrapha of the Old Testament". Let me explain this briefly[1].

---

1. For details see the Appendix.

2. *The Term "Pseudepigrapha" in Most Cases Inapplicable*

Since the publication in the beginning of the twentieth century of the collections "Apocrypha and Pseudepigrapha" edited by E. Kautzsch and R.H. Charles, the term "Pseudepigrapha of the Old Testament" is used for those Jewish writings from the period between 200 BCE and 100 CE which never belonged to the "Apocrypha". E. Kautzsch's two volumes were succeeded by the series "Jüdische Schriften aus hellenistisch-römischer Zeit". Here the words "pseudepigrapha" and "apocrypha" were avoided, but the period in which the documents were supposed to have originated was maintained. Charles's collection was followed by *The Apocryphal Old Testament* edited by H.F.D. Sparks. He, too, avoided the term "pseudepigrapha" but, in his introduction, he also distanced himself from Charles's view that the writings under discussion were written during the "intertestamentary period", and therefore of eminent importance for our knowledge of early Judaism and (particularly) of early Christianity. According to Sparks, one could not do them justice by regarding them only as "background literature". Most of the writings will indeed be of Jewish origin, but often we find Christian elements, result of Christian interpolation or redaction. Sometimes we have Christian texts incorporating Jewish material, or documents composed by Christians with the help of elements taken from the Old Testament. Sparks states categorically that in preparing *The Apocryphal Old Testament* "our single criterion for inclusion has been whether or not any particular item is attributed to (or is primarily concerned with the history or activities of) an Old Testament character (or characters)".

The criterion employed by Sparks is, in my opinion, the right one. Moreover it should be stressed that the literature that interests us in this essay was transmitted to us by Christians. In 1984 M.E. Stone edited a volume with the title *Jewish Writings of the Second Temple Period*, with the subtitle "Apocrypha, Pseudepigrapha, Qumran Sectarian Writings, Philo, Josephus". In his introduction he states: "The present volume includes material that was not transmitted by Jewish tradition. Part was preserved by the various Christian churches and part was uncovered by archeological chance".

3. *The Old Testament Pseudepigrapha as Part of Christian Literature*

A central question is thus why the "pseudepigrapha" (and other writings) were transmitted by Christians and how authoritative they were. The next question is, obviously, what authority they may have had for (certain groups among) Jews–either as we know them or in an earlier form (see, for instance, the fragments of Enoch and Jubilees found near the Dead Sea).

R.A. Kraft has repeatedly reminded us that in the reconstruction of the history of transmission one should not apply the terms "Jewish" or "Christian" too easily. Not everything that is not evidently "Christian" is "Jewish"[2]. It is also not easy to remove Christian elements as later interpolations. Often one should speak of redaction rather than interpolation, and the reconstruction of a supposedly original, Jewish document is very seldom a simple undertaking – as a long period of research on the *Testaments of the Twelve Patriarchs* has taught me. I may also point to the following remark by Kraft on the *Oracula Sibyllina*, applicable to similar writings as well: "The overtly Christian portions are themselves quite diverse in content and origin, and the total work provides an excellent example of how some types of literature were not 'authored' in any normal sense of the word, but *evolved* in stages over the years"[3].

4. In sections III and IV below, the proposed approach will be illustrated by means of an analysis of a number of passages taken from the Greek *Life of Adam and Ev*e and the *Testaments of the Twelve Patriarchs*. First, however, it is helpful to look somewhat further into the question of the attitude towards the Jewish authoritative writings among Christians in the second century.

II. THE PLACE OF THE JEWISH AUTHORITATIVE WRITINGS AMONG CHRISTIANS IN THE SECOND CENTURY

In the writings that were later brought together in the "New Testament" the books that had authority for Jews are presented as authoritative for the followers of Jesus as well. Their status is not argued, it is simply taken for granted. In his contribution about the interpretation of Scripture in the New Testament, D.-A. Koch describes the situation as

---

2. See, in particular, his *The Multiform Jewish Heritage of Early Christianity*, in J. NEUSNER (ed.), *Christianity, Judaism and other Greco-Roman Cults*. FS Morton Smith, Leiden, Brill, 1975, vol. 3, pp. 174-199; *Reassessing the Recensional Problem in the Testament of Abraham*, in G.W.E. NICKELSBURG (ed.), *Studies in the Testament of Abraham* (SBL SCS, 6), Missoula, MT, Scholars, 1976, pp. 202-226; *The Pseudepigrapha in Christianity*, in J.C. REEVES (ed.), *Tracing the Threads. Studies in the Vitality of Jewish Pseudepigrapha* (SBL EJL, 6), Atlanta, Scholars, 1994, pp. 55-86. KRAFT also kindly sent me a copy of his contribution "Setting the Stage and Framing Some Central Questions", to the seminar "Early Jewish Writings and the New Testament" during the SNTS meeting in Tel Aviv in August 2000 (published in *JSJ* 32 [2001] 371-395).
3. KRAFT, *The Multiform Jewish Heritage* (n. 2), pp. 184-185.

follows: "Weder für Jesus von Nazareth noch für die frühen (palästinisch- oder hellenistisch-) judenchristlichen Gemeinden stellte sich die Frage nach der 'Beibehaltung der Schrift' .... Da nirgends ein neuer Gott, sondern 'nur' ein neues Handeln dieses Gottes proklamiert wurde, blieb die Schrift als umfassendes Zeugnis von Gottes Wirken und seinem verpflichtenden Willen notwendigerweise in Geltung – trat jetzt aber in Wechselverhältnis gegenseitiger Interpretation mit dem Bekenntnis zu dem neuen Heilshandeln Gottes in Jesus Christus"[4]. Koch mentions here some matters that remained important also in the second century (and later). How can one demonstrate continuity in God's actions? How should Christians read and interpret the Scriptures? How do Christians, in discussions with Jews who refer to the same Scriptures, justify their point of view? How does one deal with the elements of discontinuity – eventually leading to the question: Can one really speak of a continuous acting and speaking of one and the same God?

Later Christians, in increasing numbers of non-Jewish descent, are more and more confronted with the necessity of self-defence in a Hellenistic milieu. How does the appeal to the Scriptures function in such a context? The debate between Christian and non-Christian philosophers becomes interrelated with that between Christians and Jews, and with inner-Christian discussions and controversies. In what follows some major issues will be indicated. Following Hans von Campenhausen[5] and John Barton[6] (and others) I shall pay special attention to the views of Marcion and those of Justin Martyr.

1. *The Canon*

Many scholars have emphasized that questions concerning the fixation of a list of "biblical" books did not play an important role in the first three centuries CE. For Jews and Christians the important point was the appeal to "a collection of authoritative books". One does not yet feel the need for a precise description and exact delimitation of "an authoritative collection of books"[7]. To formulate this differently: one possessed "Scriptures", but did not worry about the delimitation of a "canon"[8].

4. D.-A. KOCH, in *TRE* 30 (1999) 457-471, esp. p. 457.
5. H. VON CAMPENHAUSEN, *Die Entstehung der Christlichen Bibel* (BHT, 39), Tübingen, Mohr (Siebeck), 1968.
6. J. BARTON, *The Spirit and the Letter. Studies in the Biblical Canon*, London, SPCK, 1997.
7. This distinction is made by B.M. METZGER in his *The Canon of the New Testament. Its Origin, Development and Significance*, Oxford, Clarendon, 1987, p. 282.
8. See BARTON, *Spirit and Letter* (n. 6), p. 9 (and *passim*, following A.C. Sundberg). For canon questions in Judaism and Christianity see, for instance, Roger T. BECKWITH &

We also do not note any friction between Jews and Christians in this period about the question which books are authoritative or not. In chapters 71-73 of his *Dialogue with Trypho* Justin accuses the Jewish teachers of omitting crucial passages in the Septuagint; the authority of the books as such is not a subject of discussion[9].

> In this context it is interesting to look for a moment to the appeal to the testimony of Enoch in Jude 14, where the words προεφήτευσεν δὲ καὶ τούτοις ἕβδομος ἀπὸ 'Αδὰμ 'Ενὼχ λέγων are followed by a quotation from *1 En* 1,9 (known to us in an Ethiopic and a Greek, plus a very fragmentary Aramaic, version)[10]. Enoch, the patriarch from the period before the Flood, was clearly a man of authority, also for the author of the Epistle of Jude. But, in the words of Richard Bauckham, "while this word (he means προεφήτευσεν) indicates that Jude regarded the prophecies in *1 Enoch* as inspired by God, it need not imply that he regarded the book as canonical Scripture"[11]. A. Vögtle rightly adds that, in the case of the Epistle of Jude, one should not use the term "canonical": "Er schrieb ja lange vor der Zeit, da "inspiriert" und "kanonisch", "Schrift" und "Kanon" identische Begriffe wurden"[12].

A key text in support of this view on the relation between "Scripture" and "canon" is Eusebius's report on Melito, bishop of Sardis around 170 CE. In H.E. 4.26, 13-14 he tells us that a list of τῶν ὁμολογουμένων τῆς παλαιᾶς διαθήκης γραφῶν, can be found in the preface of Melito's 'Εκλογαί. In this preface Melito addresses his "brother Onesimus" who had asked him several times for ἐκλογαί from the Law and the Prophets respecting the Saviour and the Christian faith in general. Onesimus had also asked for exact information concerning the number and the order of the "old books" (τῶν παλαιῶν βιβλίων). In order to

---

E. Earle ELLIS, in M.J. MULDER & H. SYSLING (eds.), *Mikra. Text, Translation, Reading and Interpretation of the Hebrew Bible in Ancient Judaism and Early Christianity* (CRINT, 2,1), Assen–Maastricht, Van Gorcum; Philadelphia, Fortress, 1988, resp. "Formation of the Hebrew Bible", pp. 39-86 and "The Old Testament Canon in the Early Church", pp. 653-690.

9. See ELLIS, "The Old Testament Canon" (n. 8), p. 655.

10. For details see R. BAUCKHAM, *Jude. 2 Peter* (WBC, 50), Waco, TX, Word, 1983, pp. 93-101, and A. VÖGTLE, *Der Judasbrief. Der zweite Petrusbrief* (EKK, 22), Solothurn–Düsseldorf, Benziger; Neukirchen-Vluyn, Neukirchener, 1994, pp. 71-84. See also B. DEHANDSCHUTTER, in J.J.A. KAHMANN & B. DEHANDSCHUTTER, *De Tweede Brief van Petrus en de Brief van Judas*, Boxtel, Katholieke Bijbelstichting, 1983), pp. 138-139 and in his contribution *Pseudo-Cyprian, Jude and Enoch. Some notes on 1 Enoch 1:9*, in J.W. VAN HENTEN, H.J. DE JONGE et al. (eds.), *Tradition and Re-interpretation in Jewish and Early Christian Literature*. FS J.C.H. Lebram (SPB, 36), Leiden, Brill, 1986, pp. 114-120. Beside the quotation in v. 14 the epistle shows acquaintance with *1 En.* 6-16 in vv. 6-7 and, very probably, with *Ass. Mosis* in v. 9. Unfortunately, this passage is lacking in the fragmentary Latin version of this document, the only one known.

11. *Jude. 2 Peter* (n. 10), p. 95.

12. *Der Judasbrief* (n. 10), p. 85.

give an answer to these questions, Melito travelled to the East, "the place where these things were proclaimed and done". There he accurately ascertained the books of the Old Testament (ἀκριβῶς μαθὼν τὰ τῆς παλαιᾶς διαθήκης βιβλία)–which he duly lists.

This is the first time the question of the number and the order of the Jewish writings that are authoritative for Christians is raised explicitly. Interestingly, not only Eusebius in his introduction, but also Melito himself uses, beside the expression "the old books", also the term "the books of the Old Covenant/Testament". From this time onwards this is a current expression among Christians for the authoritative writings taken over from Israel[13].

2. *Text*

The problem of the text(s) of the "Old Testament" available to Christians during the first two or three centuries, and the question of how they cited them, need not be solved here. In general they used the Septuagint, or Hebraizing recensions of the Greek translation. Deviations from the text and the textual variants now found in critical editions of the various books of the Septuagint can be explained by the use of local traditions, quotation from memory, or the desire to bring the witness of the Scriptures in agreement with that concerning God's revelation in Jesus Christ. A striking example is Justin's reproach to the Jews in *Dial.* 71-73 (already referred to). According to him the Jews have omitted sayings by Ezra and Jeremiah, as well as the words "from the wood" after "The Lord reigns" in Ps 95(96),10 (cf. also *1 Apol.* 41,1-4). Justin follows here a christianized *Vorlage*, probably in a collection of proof-texts[14].

It is difficult to be certain about the number of Christian communities or authors that will have had a complete collection of "old books" at their disposal. In the second century there certainly existed collections of quotations ("florilegia", "testimonia-books"). A number of scholars have assumed Christian use of similar anthologies also for the first century (already in the epistles of Paul)[15].

---

13. Zie G.W.H. LAMPE, *A Patristic Greek Lexicon*, Oxford, Clarendon, 1961, p. 348, s.v. διαθήκη sub 3 (cf. p. 268, s.v. ἐνδιάθηκος) and VON CAMPENHAUSEN, *Entstehung* (n. 5), pp. 305-311 (with references to Clement of Alexandria and Origen). On the expression ἐπὶ τῇ ἀναγνώσει τῆς παλαιᾶς διαθήκης in 2 Cor 3,14 see (still) H. WINDISCH, *Der zweite Korintherbrief* (KEK), Göttingen, Vandenhoeck & Ruprecht, 1924 (reprint 1970), p. 121.

14. See, among others, O. SKARSAUNE, *The Proof from Prophecy. A Study in Justin Martyr's Proof-Text Tradition: Text-Type, Provenance, Theological Profile* (SNT, 56), Leiden, Brill, 1987, pp. 35-42.

15. See recently Martin C. ALBL, *'And Scripture Cannot Be Broken'. The Form and Function of the Early Testimonia Collections* (SNT, 96), Leiden, 1999.

3. *The Gnostics and Marcion*

Harnack's well-known thesis that the Gnostics, in a process of acute Hellenization of Christianity, would have rejected the "Old Testament", has proved no longer tenable. Von Campenhausen is of the opinion that the Gnostics were indeed very much interested in ancient writings, including the Scriptures of Judaism and the traditions connected with them[16]. In a considerable number of Gnostic documents we find expositions of "Old Testament" texts, particularly also of the first chapters of Genesis. Of course these writings and traditions are used critically, and judged by the standards of the Gospel as understood by the specific Gnostic authors. Also "spiritual" standards (derived from Hellenistic philosophy) are applied, but in general the reliability and authority of the Jewish Scriptures are not questioned.

Birger Pearson has described the situation as follows: "The Bible ('Old Testament') was part of the Christian heritage, as it was of the Gnostic heritage. But there was considerable variety in the way Gnostic Christians looked upon it. Three basic attitudes emerged: (1) open rejection of the Old Testament; (2) whole-hearted acceptance of it; and (3) an intermediate position according to which the biblical text was inspired by the lower Creator or lesser powers, but nevertheless contained 'spiritual truth' to be ferreted out by means of a spiritual (allegorical) exegesis. Authorization for this procedure was found in revelation attributed to the Saviour and various of his apostles"[17].

Marcion was far more radical. For him the only authoritative writings were the "Euangelion" (a thoroughly redacted version of the Gospel of Luke) and the "Apostolikon" (the epistles of Paul, that is the Corpus Paulinum without the Pastorals, also cleansed of supposed interpolations). These contained the revelation of the One, true God who had made himself known through Jesus Christ. According to Harnack Marcion played a central role in the formation of the canon of the "New Testament", but Metzger adds a significant qualification: "It was in opposition to Marcion's criticism that the Church first became fully conscious of its inheritance of apostolic writings". He quotes with approval a statement by R.M. Grant: Marcion "forced more orthodox Christians to examine their own presuppositions and to state more clearly what

---

16. Von Campenhausen, *Entstehung* (n. 5), pp. 88-108.

17. B. Pearson, *Use, Authority and Exegesis of Mikra in Gnostic Literature*, in Mulder & Sysling (eds.), *Mikra* (n. 8), pp. 635-652; quotation on p. 652. See also his *Jewish Sources in Gnostic Literature*, in M.E. Stone (ed.), *Jewish Writings of the Second Temple Period* (CRINT, 2,2), Assen, Van Gorcum; Philadelphia, Fortress, 1984, pp. 443-481.

they already believed"[18]. Marcion also forced his "orthodox" opponents to examine their presuppositions in their use of the Jewish authoritative writings. In an interesting chapter "Marcion Revisited" John
Barton has argued that Marcion took the Jewish Scriptures very seriously indeed[19]. "The old Scriptures were, in fact, a Jewish book through
and through, but they were a wholly reliable and trustworthy Jewish
book". These Scriptures did not speak, however, of the good God, the
Father of Jesus Christ, but contained the revelation of a lower Creator-
god. Opposed to all allegorical interpretation, Marcion could in no way
connect the message of the Jewish Scriptures with that in his "Euangelion" and "Apostolikon". "For Marcion's gospel is the good news
that mankind has been freed from the thrall of the Old Testament god;
and unless one knows this (proscribed!) text, and also knows why it is
wrong, one cannot properly welcome the gospel message". In order to
make this clear, and also to demonstrate the many contradictions and in-
congruities in the Scriptures of the Jews, Marcion wrote his *Antitheses*,
for his followers a book of great importance and authority. This book,
according to Barton, "provided the essential content of Marcionite faith
by way of an interpretation of Scripture".

Over against Marcion and the Marcionites (some of them, like
Apelles, even more radical than their master) "orthodox" Christians
held on to the conviction that the One, true God can be found in both the
ancient books of the Jews and in the Gospel(s) together with Epistles.
This made further reflection on the hermeneutics of the "Old Testament" indispensable. To quote Barton again: "In insisting on the identity of God the creator and God the redeemer, orthodox Christians found
themselves necessarily committed to the Old Testament, which they restored to a more central role".

An important contribution to this reflection was given by Justin Martyr, as will be made clear in the next subsection. Later, in section III, in
an analysis of the Greek *Life of Adam and Eve*, I hope to demonstrate
that this document, essentially a story about the life, death and departure
of Adam and Eve, wants to show that the God who speaks and acts in
Genesis 3 is the One, true God and not an inferior Creator-god.

4. *Justin Martyr*

According to Von Campenhausen Justin is the first Christian theologian with something like a "doctrine of Holy Scripture". As a man of

18. METZGER, *Canon* (n. 7), pp. 91-99; quotation, on p. 99, from R.M. GRANT, *The
Formation of the New Testament*, London, Hutchinson University Library, 1965, p. 126.
19. BARTON, *Spirit and Letter* (n. 6), pp. 35-62; the following quotations are found on
pp. 43, 51 and 65 respectively.

authority in the church of Rome, around the middle of the second century, he is active on various fronts. He writes his first and his second *Apology* to make Christianity acceptable for Hellenistic philosophers and to secure a place for it within the structures of the Roman empire. He has to defend Christian ideas, as Von Campenhausen puts it, "vor dem Richterstuhl der platonischen Überzeugung"[20]. At the same time he does not shun the debate with the Gnostics and Marcion, and in this debate he employs arguments used of old in the discussions between Christians and Jews. Justin's most extensive work is his *Dialogue with Trypho*. As C.H. Cosgrove has argued, this book is not an apology directed against the Jews, even less a missionary treatise, but rather an inner-Christian attempt to clarify the position of the church in God's history of salvation–over against groups of judaizers as well as over against Marcion and the Marcionites. "Indeed the main themes of the *Dialogue* are among the most serious faced by the church of the second century; the problem of the Mosaic law, that of the Old Testament as canon, and especially the question of Christian self-definition over against Judaism and yet in terms of the Old Testament"[21]. Reflecting on this problem Justin develops a view on the Bible at the centre of which is the question of the authority of the Scriptures taken over from the Jews[22].

It is worthwhile highlighting a number of points from Von Campenhausen's clear exposition of Justin's ideas concerning Scripture. Justin is firmly convinced that it is God himself who speaks in these writings, through his Logos or through the Spirit of prophecy. Their inspired status gives us the certainty that it is God whom we meet in every word contained in them. There are, therefore, no contradictions in the Scriptures, although Justin often has to go all out in order to solve problems

---

20. Von Campenhausen, *Entstehung* (n. 5), pp. 106-122; quotation on p. 115.

21. C.H. Cosgrove, *Justin Martyr and the Emerging Christian Canon. Observations on the Purpose and Destination of the Dialogue with Trypho*, VigChr 36 (1982) 209-232; quotation on p. 218. Cosgrove's view is shared by Barton, *Spirit and Letter* (n. 6), pp. 56-57. Strikingly Cosgrove considers the possibility that the first Apology also served an inner-Christian purpose; in the end, however, he remarks: "... the problem of persecution faced by the second-century church demands that a real external dialogue be regarded as the primary focus of this work" (n. 41). Yet earlier, in n. 7, he says: "There were no doubt internal needs for self-definition and self-justification vis-à-vis the Hellenistic world as well". For a discussion of various views on the *Dialogue* see R.S. MacLennan, *Early Christian Texts on Jews and Judaism* (Brown Judaic Studies), Atlanta, Scholars, 1990, pp. 49-88 and S.G.J. Sanchez, *Justin apologiste chrétien. Travaux sur le Dialogue avec Tryphon de Justin Martyr* (CRB, 50), Paris, Gabalda, 2000. MacLennan opts for "an apologetic essay written to Christians" (p. 84); Sanchez emphasizes: "Justin a décidé d'écrire un *dialogue* entre un Juif et un chrétien et non un *adversus Judaeos*" (p. 253).

22. Justin does not yet formulate a theory concerning the "New Testament"; see Cosgrove, *Justin Martyr* (n. 21), pp. 221-224 and, in a broader perspective, Barton, *Spirit and Letter* (n. 6), pp. 79-91.

with the help of allegorical and typological interpretation. In order to demonstrate the continuity in God's words ands actions he repeatedly uses the well-known scheme of prediction and fulfilment. Of this Von Campenhausen says: "Er stammt aus der älteren christlichen Tradition, dient jetzt aber in charakteristisch veränderter Zielsetzung weniger dazu, den Christusglauben vor der Schrift auszuweisen, als vielmehr umgekehrt, die bedrohte Autorität der Schrift aufs Neue zu begründen"[23].

At the same time Justin is convinced that all truth found in the works of prominent Greek philosophers comes from God as well. He uses the argument found in the works of Hellenistic-Jewish apologists that those philosophers are dependent on the Bible. Plato derived his wisdom from Moses who, after all, lived many centuries earlier[24]. Christians have a strong case in their debates with Jews as well as gentiles. It may seem that they are mere newcomers in the history of humanity, but they are the ones to whom God has granted the right understanding of all he has revealed all through the ages. Justin takes great pains to prove this with a variety of arguments. At a certain moment in his discussion with Trypho he points to the testimonies of David, Isaiah, Zechariah and Moses, and asks: "Do you acknowledge those, Trypho? They are laid down in your Scriptures, or rather in our Scriptures, not yours. For we believe in them, but you read them without understanding their meaning" (Dial. 29,2)[25].

In his controversy with the Gnostics and Marcion Justin wants to demonstrate that the entire Law comes from God, and that it contains nothing that is unworthy of him. There is also no reason to accuse him of inconsistency, arbitrariness or ignorance (Dial. 23,1-2; 30,1; 92,5)[26]. Insofar as commandments show people how to lead a pious and righteous life, they are universally valid. Also commandments that can be

---

23. Von Campenhausen, Entstehung (n. 5), p. 109.

24. Von Campenhausen, Entstehung (n. 5), p. 109, n. 162. Von Campenhausen mentions also Justin's doctrine of the λόγος σπερματικός. See also John G. Gager, Moses in Greco-Roman Paganism (SBL MS 16), Nashville–New York, Abingdon, 1972, pp. 76-79. As defenders of the thesis of Moses' priority vis-à-vis the Greeks, Gager mentions Aristobulus, Eupolemus, Artapanus, Philo and Josephus, and among Christians Justin, Tatian, Clement of Alexandria, Origen and Eusebius.

25. Robert L. Wilken, The Christians as the Romans (and Greeks) Saw Them, in E.P. Sanders (ed.), Jewish and Christian Self-Definition, vol. 1, London, SCM, 1980, pp. 100-125, has pointed out that the Christians in their discussions with gentiles had to prove that the Jewish interpretation of the "Old Testament" was wrong. "Attempts to legitimate Christian religious claims had to deal not only with the philosophical objections of pagans, but with scriptural and historical arguments, offered by pagans (and Jews), but supported by the existence of a rival tradition of interpretation" (p. 123).

26. Von Campenhausen, Entstehung (n. 5), pp. 112-116, and, in more detail, also Th. Stylianopoulos, Justin Martyr and the Mosaic Law (SBL DS 20), Missoula, MT, Scholars, 1975.

explained as references to the mystery of Christ present no problem. But how are the many rules of the "ceremonial law" (to use a later term) to be reconciled with God's eternal will? Justin declares that these rules were intended for the Jews only, because of their σκληροκαρδία. They were additionally given to keep this people on the right track and to bring it to repentance. It is important to note how Justin stresses that a great number of God's commandments were meant for a particular period in history only[27]. He divides the history of salvation into three periods. The time of the righteous before Moses, the interim period of the extra regulations in the Mosaic law intended for Israel in particular, and the new dispensation inaugurated by Jesus Christ[28].

In an earlier discussion of Justin's often complex treatment of the relation between God and the Law[29] I have pointed out that Justin's insistence on the fact that the faithful in the period before Moses (sometimes called "patriarchs") obeyed God without detailed regulations, together with his conviction that Jesus Christ has been given as an "eternal and definitive law" (*Dial.* 11,2) helps us to understand how the *Testaments of the Twelve Patriarchs* were understood by Christians in the latter part of the second century, and later. The *Testaments* bring to the fore the essential and abiding elements in God's commandments, and they announce that all who obey those, in Israel and among the gentiles, will have a share in God's kingdom after the coming of Christ. Below, in section IV, we shall return to this in a discussion of *Test. Benjamin* 10.

III. THE GREEK *LIFE OF ADAM AND EVE* AND THEOPHILUS, *AD AUTOLYCUM* 24-28

1. *The* Life of Adam and Eve

The *Life of Adam and Eve* has come down to us in Greek, Armenian, Georgian, Latin and Slavonic. There are considerable differences between

---

27. See especially STYLIANOPOULOS, *Justin's Historical Interpretation of the Law*, in ID., *Justin Martyr and the Mosaic Law* (n. 26), pp. 153-163; cf. pp. 51-67.

28. "Der Gegensatz zum alten Gesetz ist für Justin nicht durch das Evangelium und den Glauben, sondern durch das vollkommene Gesetz bestimmt, das die Patriarchen gekannt und die Propheten verkündigt haben und das durch Jesus, den neuen Gesetzgeber, endlich vollkommen und mit erlösender Kraft verkörpert ist", so VON CAMPENHAUSEN, *Entstehung* (n. 5), p. 117.

29. *The Pre-Mosaic Servants of God in the Testaments of the Twelve Patriarchs and in the Writings of Justin and Irenaeus*, VigChr 39 (1985) 157-170, later published in a collection of my essays, *Jewish Eschatology, Early Christian Christology and the Testaments of the Twelve Patriarchs. Collected Essays*, ed. H.J. DE JONGE (SNT, 63), Leiden, Brill, 1991, pp. 263-276.

the versions[30]. I restrict myself to the Greek version (often wrongly
called the *Apocalypse of Moses*) that can be shown to be the earliest of
all[31]. All Greek manuscripts were copied by Christian scribes, just as
those of the other versions. As so often the question has to be asked
whether we are dealing here with a Jewish document (with Christian interpolations or adaptations) or with a Christian writing. To answer this
question we have to look for elements that determine the structure and
meaning of this writing[32]. Individual parallels in clearly Jewish and
Christian sources do not help us very much in determining its origin.
The decisive question is: what are the features that make the Greek *Life
of Adam and Eve* to what it wants to be?

Notwithstanding the deficiencies of the final redaction the Greek text
presents a clear structure. Its core is a "Testament of Eve" (chs. 15-30)
that gives the story of Genesis 3, and ends (in true testamentary fashion)
with the words: "Now then, children, I have shown you the way in
which we were deceived. But take heed that you yourselves do not for-
sake the good" (30,1). It is preceded by an overall introduction (chs. 1-
4), a brief account by the dying Adam about what happened in Paradise
(chs. 5-8) and the story of the failed attempt by Eve and Seth to get "the
oil of mercy" from the Garden, to alleviate Adam's pains (chs. 9-14).

The sin of Adam and Eve is described as a transgression of God's
commandments. Eve in particular is to blame; this is the central point in
her description of what happened in the Garden. But also Adam is held
responsible and he explicitly acknowledges his fault (27,2-3). Their
common enemy is Satan, acting through the serpent in order to deceive
Eve, and using Eve to deceive Adam. In accordance with Genesis 3 God
curses the serpent (not Satan) in ch. 26.

The Greek *Life of Adam and Eve* does not end with chapter 30. An
account of Adam's death and departure follows. God shows mercy; Eve
and Seth see how angels bring Adam to the Paradise in the third heaven
and how his body is buried with that of Abel, near the earthly Paradise
(chs. 32-41). The picture given in these chapters is very complex and not
always internally consistent, but one thing is clear: Adam is pardoned,

---

30. See M. DE JONGE & J. TROMP, *The Life of Adam and Eve and Related Literature*
(Guides to Apocrypha and Pseudepigrapha), Sheffield, Sheffield Academic Press, 1997.

31. See my *The Literary Development of the Life of Adam and Eve*, in G.W. ANDER-
SON, M.E. STONE, J. TROMP (eds.), *Literature on Adam and Eve. Collected Essays* (SVTP,
15), Leiden, Brill, 2000, pp. 239-249.

32. On the following see, in more detail, my essay *The Christian Origin of the Greek
Life of Adam and Eve*, in ANDERSON, STONE, TROMP (eds.), *Literature* (n. 31), pp. 347-
363. For a different view see M. ELDRIDGE, *Dying Adam with his Multiethnic Family.
Understanding the Greek Life of Adam and Eve* (SVTP, 16), Leiden, Brill, 2001.

he shares in heavenly bliss, and he is promised a share in the resurrection to come "with all persons belonging to your seed" (41,3). Six days after Adam Eve dies; she is buried with Adam and shares Adam's lot (chs. 42-43).

Chapters 27-29, at the end of Eve's testament, prepare the reader for these developments. Adam confesses his sin and asks for forgiveness. He is punished, for God's judgment and punishment are righteous–as is expressly underscored. But when God refuses Adam access to the tree of life, he tells him: "... if you, after your departure from Paradise, guard yourself from all evil, prepared (rather) to die (then to transgress), I shall raise you at the time of the resurrection. From the tree of life will be given to you and you will be immortal for ever" (28,3-4). In 37,5 this promise is confirmed when God grants Adam a glorious *post mortem* existence until the day of God's reckoning, when God will raise him with the entire human race descended from him (see also 41,3).

The essential elements of the Greek *Life of Adam and Eve,* I think, are to be sought in its final section, chs. 31-43, the part of the writing that relates what is not told in Genesis 3. It wants to make clear that God, the creator of heaven and earth, who brought the protoplasts into being and put them into the Garden of Eden, is righteous and merciful for all who try to live in accordance with his commandments and are prepared to repent wholeheartedly when they sin.

The observation in the last paragraph invites us to try out the following approach: Over against all who, like the Marcionites and a number of Gnostics, picture the god of Genesis 3 as incompetent, jealous or malicious, "orthodox" Christians, in the second century and later, had to maintain that also in this crucial chapter it is the One, true God who acts and speaks. Are we able to show that the Greek *Life of Adam and Eve* defends the "orthodox" point of view in the form of a story followed by apocalyptic visions?

Before following this line of investigation, however, it is necessary to remark that we find very few typically, let alone exclusively, Jewish or Christian elements. It has often been remarked that in a Christian writing one would expect at least a reference to Rom 5,12-20, the passage in which Paul describes how Adam's transgression led to condemnation and death for humanity, and how these effects were annulled by the obedience of Jesus Christ, leading to eternal life in unity with him. Neither do we find any hint of the interesting "recapitulation theory" developed by Irenaeus, with Jesus Christ, the Son of God as the new, true Adam and Mary as the new Eve (*Adv. Haer.* 3.21,10-23,7)[33]. We do find, how-

---

33. Compare already Justin, *Dial.* 100,3-6 (cf. 84,2; 88,4; 103,6). Moreover, Gen 3,15 is not explained as a "proto-Gospel" (as in *Adv. Haer.* 3.23,7).

ever, an evidently Christian element in 37,3 where we hear how Adam is immersed three times in the water of the Acherusian Lake–an essential detail in the story told in chapters 33-37[34]. There is no doubt that the Greek *Life* is Christian in its present form, but are we perhaps dealing with a Christian edition of an originally Jewish document? Against this one should remark that we find very few typically Jewish elements too. Not only does Jesus not come into the picture, but also commandments specifically connected with Moses are not mentioned. Exhortations such as φυλάξεις ἑαυτὸν ἀπὸ παντὸς κακοῦ in 28,4 or ὑμεῖς δὲ φυλάξατε ἑαυτοὺς μὴ ἐγκαταλιπεῖν τὸ ἀγαθόν in 30,1 (the closing verse of the testament of Eve) remain very general. True, it cannot be excluded that the *Life of Adam and Eve* once existed in some Jewish form. We do not need to assume the existence of such a document, however, to explain the present Greek *Life*, once we are able to show that the main concern of the latter can directly be linked to the discussion about Genesis 3 among Christians in the latter part of the second and the beginning of the third century. In the next subsection (III,2) I shall try to prove this connection in a short analysis of *Ad Autolycum* 2,24-28 of Theophilus of Antioch, dating from shortly after 180[35].

2. *Theophilus,* Ad Autolycum *2,24-28*

Theophilus calls the books of the Old Testament "sacred writings" or "prophetic writings" (1,14)[36]. What the prophets taught should be read together with the contents of the Gospels διὰ τὸ πάντας πνευματοφόρους ἑνι πνεύματι θεοῦ λελαληκέναι (3,12). In 2,33 Theophilus even declares: "... all the rest were in error and ... only the Christians have held the truth–we who are instructed by the Holy Spirit who spoke in the holy prophets and foretold everything". Interestingly, in 2,9 the Sibyl is put on a par with the prophets. "There were not just one or two of them but more at various times and seasons among the Hebrews, as well as the Sibyl among the Greeks. All of them were consistent with

---

34. See M. DE JONGE & L.M. WHITE, *The Washing of Adam in the Acherusian Lake (Greek Life of Adam and Eve 37:3) in the Context of Early Christian Notions about the Afterlife* (forthcoming). In 36,3 God is called "Father of lights", an expression only found in Jas 1,17 and Christian texts referring to it.

35. See R.M. GRANT, *Theophilus of Antioch. Text and Translation*, Oxford, Clarendon, 1970 (whose translation I have used), and M. MARCOVICH, *Tatiani Oratio ad Graecos. Theophili Antiocheni Ad Autolycum* (PTS, 43/44), Berlin – New York, De Gruyter, 1995. For parallels in the works of Irenaeus en Tertullian see my essay *The Christian Origin* (n. 32 above).

36. Here we also find the notion that later poets and philosophers borrowed ideas from the sacred writings in order to make their own teaching look trustworthy.

one another" (*i.e.*, in their description of events in the past and present, and in their prediction of those in the future). For Theophilus the words of the Sibyl are of equal value as those of the prophets. In 2,36 two long passages from the Sibyl are introduced with the phrase: Σίβυλλα δέ, ἐν Ἕλλησιν καὶ ἐν τοῖς λοιποῖς ἔθνεσιν γενομένη προφῆτις ....

Turning now to chapters 24-28 of *Ad Autolycum* we find that in 24,5-8 man in Paradise is pictured in an intermediary state, "neither entirely mortal nor entirely immortal, but capable of either state". Paradise itself occupied an intermediate position between heaven and earth. When God placed man in Paradise, he gave him an opportunity for progress; he wanted him to grow, to become mature/perfect (τέλειος). In this way, even having been declared god (θεὸς ἀναδειχθείς) he would ascend to heaven, possessing immortality. God's command to man to "work" in the Garden of Eden implied "no other task than keeping the commandment of God, lest by disobedience he destroy himself–as he did through sin (καθὼς καὶ ἀπώλεσεν διὰ ἁμαρτίας)".

In chapter 27 Theophilus returns to the question of mortality and immortality. Man was meant to win immortality by keeping the commandments of God; that holds true before *and* after man's disobedience described in Genesis 3. Man forfeited his immortality δι' ἀμελείας καὶ παρακοῆς. Now, however, God grants it to him διὰ ἰδίας φιλανθρωπίας καὶ ἐλεημοσύνης, *when man obeys him.* "For as by his disobedience man gained death for himself, so by obedience to the will of God whoever will can obtain eternal life for himself". Commentators have pointed here to the parallel with Rom 5,18-19, noting, of course, one important difference: disobedience and obedience are not connected with Adam and Christ respectively, but with Adam alone, as the man to whom God, in his mercy, gives a second chance–just as in the Greek *Life of Adam and Eve* 28.

In chapter 25 Theophilus twice refers to opinions of "some people" (ὡς οἴονταί τινες) with whom he is in disagreement. The fruit of the tree of knowledge was not lethal, as they suppose; no, death was the result of man's disobedience. It is also not true that Genesis 3 would teach that God was jealous of Adam and begrudged him anything when he ordered him not to eat of the tree of knowledge. He simply wanted to test him; he wished to see whether Adam would be obedient to him, as a child to his father[37]. "It was not that the tree of knowledge contained

---

37. Cf. Apelles's question in Ambrose, *De Paradiso* 7,35, "... unde mors acciderit Adae, utrum a natura ligni eiusmodi an vero a Deo". For these and other parallells see the apparatus in the edition of MARCOVICH *ad locum.* Cf. also M. DE JONGE, *The Christian Origin* (n. 32), pp. 360-362 for parallels in some Gnostic writings.

anything evil, but that through disobedience man acquired pain, suffering and sorrow, and finally fell victim to death".

By expelling man from Paradise God conferred a great benefit on him, chapter 26 tells us. When God called Adam and asked: "Where are you, Adam?" he was not ignorant (again a contention of those who saw a lower Creator-god at work here), but patient. He gave Adam "an occasion for repentance and confession". Man was banished from Paradise so that through punishment he might expiate his sin in a fixed period of time and might be recalled. Therefore Genesis μυστηριωδῶς mentions twice (in 2,8 and in 2,15) that man was placed in Paradise.

Finally, in chapter 28, Theophilus speaks about Eve and the serpent. At the end of this chapter he calls Eve, who was deceived by the serpent, "the pioneer of sin" (ἀρχηγὸς ἁμαρτίας)". The serpent was no more than an instrument of Satan, also called "demon" and "dragon" (Rev 12,9); he was originally an angel. One may compare here a number of points in the story of the Fall in chapters 15-30 of the Greek *Life of Adam and Eve*[38].

3. *Summary*

Summing up we may say:

a. In the Greek *Life of Adam and Eve* we find very few typically Jewish or Christian elements; in its present form the document is Christian, however.

b. Its central message is that God the Creator, who placed the first human beings in Paradise, but expelled them after they had transgressed his command, was and is righteous and merciful. He granted forgiveness to these two people, and forgives all their descendants if and when they repent and live in accordance with God's commandments. He gives them a share in eternal life and in the resurrection at the end of days.

c. This message agrees with that of Christian theologians around 200 (and later) who take pains to demonstrate, over against the Marcionites and some Gnostics, that the God of Genesis 3 and the Father of Jesus Christ are one and the same.

d. The Greek *Life of Adam and Eve*, therefore, represents one of the attempts to show that Genesis, just as other Jewish authoritative writings, should retain its place among the Scriptures of the Early Church.

---

38. And also in 39,3, hinting at an expulsion of Satan from heaven. This expulsion is described in chapters 12-16 of the Armenian, Georgian and Latin versions of the *Life of Adam and Eve*.

IV. JUSTIN MARTYR ON THE "PATRIARCHS" AND *TEST. BENJAMIN* 10

1. *Justin Martyr on the "Patriarchs"*

Taking up what has been said in II,4 about Justin's views on the authority of the Jewish sacred writings for Christians we shall now discuss a number of passages from his *Dialogue with Trypho* in which he speaks about different categories of believers who will have a share in God's future kingdom. I mention here *Dial.* 25,6-26,1; 45,2-4; 80,1; 130,1-2 in particular. Justin is concerned about the relation between Jews and Christians, but mentions repeatedly believers from the time before Moses (sometimes called "patriarchs", as we have seen) and the prophets in this connection. Those passages shed light on *Test. Benjamin* 10 and related texts in the Testaments[39].

In 25,6-26,1 Justin gives an answer to Trypho's question: "Do you intend to say that none of us shall inherit anything on the holy mountain of God?" Justin replies that those who persecuted Christ and those who still persecute him, and do not show repentance, will indeed be excluded. The gentiles, however, who have come to believe in him, and repented about their sins, will inherit "with the patriarchs and the prophets and all the righteous born from Jacob". Those gentiles are not required to observe the sabbath, or to be circumcised, or to keep the festivals.

In 45,2-4 observant Jews are expressly included among those who will be saved. Here Trypho asks: "Will those who live according to the Law ordained by Moses live at the resurrection of the dead, just as Jacob and Enoch and Noah, or not?" Justin answers that one's descent does not count (cf. 44,1) but that each person will be saved because of his or her own righteous deeds, also those who have lived in accordance with the Law of Moses. For, beside all sorts of precepts that were included only because of the σκληροκαρδία of the Jewish people, this Law contains τὰ φύσει καλὰ καὶ εὐσεβῆ καὶ δίκαια. All who did the things that are universally, naturally and eternally good are pleasing to God, and therefore also these pious Jews will be saved "by means of this Christ" in the resurrection, "together with the righteous before them, Noah and Enoch and Jacob, and any others there may be, together with those who recognize this Christ as the son of God". Similarly, in 130,1-2 Justin quotes Deut 32,43 and continues: "By saying this he means that

---

39. See also my essay *The Pre-Mosaic Servants* (n. 29 above). For the *Dialogue* I used the edition of M. MARCOVICH, *Iustini Martyris Dialogus cum Tryphone* (PTS, 47), Berlin – New York, De Gruyter, 1997.

we gentiles rejoice with his people, I mean Abraham and Isaac and Jacob and the prophets, and in fact all from that people that are pleasing to God". Others belonging to this people will, however, be punished for their wrong-doings (cf. 120,5).

In chapters 80-81 Justin shares Trypho's expectation of a rebuilding of Jerusalem. He answers affirmatively, when Trypho asks him whether Christians believe in a new Jerusalem in which "your people will be gathered and rejoice with Christ, together with the patriarchs and prophets and the saints of our race or even of them who became proselytes before your Christ came". Justin adds that this is his own position and that of many others; and in support of it he quotes Isa 65,17-25 and Rev 20,4-6. He emphasizes, however, that other respectable Christians think differently in this matter.

In short: In Justin's view the patriarchs and the prophets will have a share in God's kingdom, together with the Israelites who have kept the essential precepts of the Law and the gentiles who believe in Christ and keep these same commandments.

2. *The* Testament of Benjamin *10*

We now turn to the final section in the *Testament of Benjamin*, the last of the *Testaments of the Twelve Patriarchs*, with many Christian phrases essential to the argument[40]. Chapter 10 in particular gives a neat summary ot the views and intentions of the author(s) of the *Testaments*.

In 10,3 the dying patriarch summarizes his paraenesis in very general terms:

> "You must do truth and righteousness each one to his neighbour and jus-
> tice unto preservation
> and keep the Law of the Lord and his commandments".

Benjamin teaches these things as a spiritual testament that has to be handed down from generation to generation. In this he follows Abraham, Isaac and Jacob (v. 4).

> "They gave us all these things for an inheritance, saying:
> Keep the commandments of God
> until the Lord will reveal his salvation to all the nations" (v. 5).

---

40. For details see H.W. HOLLANDER and M. DE JONGE, *The Testaments of the Twelve Patriarchs. A Commentary* (SVTP, 8), Leiden, Brill, 1985, based on M. DE JONGE *cum aliis* (eds.), *The Testaments of the Twelve Patriarchs. A Critical Edition of the Greek Text* (PVTG, 1,2), Leiden, Brill, 1978. Salient features are, for instance, the passage on the rending of the temple-veil at Jesus's death in *T. Benj.* 9,4 (cf. *T. Levi* 10,3) and the prediction of the coming of the Benjaminite Paul as apostle to the gentiles in *T. Benj.* 11.

At that moment Enoch, Noah and Shem will rise on God's right hand with gladness, together with the patriarchs mentioned earlier (v. 6). Also the sons of Jacob will rise each over his tribe,

> "worshipping the king of heaven
> who appeared on earth in the form of a man of humility;
> and as many as believed in him on earth, will rejoice with him" (v. 7)[41].

The Lord will judge all, in Israel and among the nations, who did not believe in him when he appeared on earth (vv. 8-10). But the chapter ends on a positive note:

> "But you, if you walk in holiness before the face of the Lord,
> you will again dwell safely with me;
> and all Israel will be gathered together unto the Lord" (v. 11).

The *Testaments* are in essence a paraenetical writing, speaking about the contents of God's Law in very general terms (often referring to one or both of the great commandments[42]). They are cast in the form of final exhortations of the twelve sons of Jacob directed towards the twelve tribes of Israel. Israel has to obey what is permanently valid in God's commandments and is asked to believe in Jesus Christ. In that way the children of the patriarchs will receive eternal salvation on the same conditions as the believers among the gentiles.

3. *Parallels between the* Testaments *and Justin's* Dialogue

The parallels between the message of the *Testaments* and the views of Justin as expressed in his *Dialogue with Trypho* are obvious. It is possible, perhaps even probable, that the *Testaments*, like the *Dialogue*, do not primarily want to address the Jews, but are meant for inner-Christian use. However that may be, the Christian readers of this book will have understood that the sons of Jacob, in their exhortations as well as in their predictions concerning God's future, wanted to fix the attention of gentiles and Jews on the essential points of God's message to humanity. As righteous believers from ancient times, the period before Moses, the patriarchs were authorities in this matter and were entitled to a hearing.

---

41. Compare *T. Sim.* 6,7; *T. Levi* 18,14; *T. Jud.* 25 and, in particular, *T. Zeb.* 10,2 "For I shall rise again in the midst of you as a ruler in the midst of his sons, and I shall rejoice in the midst of my tribe as many as have kept the Law of the Lord and the commandments of Zebulun their father". *T. Benj.* 9:2 reminds us of Justin, *Dial.* 80-81: "But the temple of God will be in your portion, and the last will be more glorious than the first; and there the twelve tribes and all the gentiles will be gathered together, until the Most High will send forth his salvation in the visitation of an only-begotten prophet".

42. See my *The Two Great Commandments in the Testaments of the Twelve Patriarchs*, in *NT* 44 (2002) 371-392.

Also the *Testaments of the Twelve Patriarchs* show how important it was for Christians in the second century to emphasize the connection between the church, living from the witness of God in Jesus Christ, and the believers of the Old Dispensation, particularly those living in the time before the Law of Moses.

V. READING THE "PSEUDEPIGRAPHA/APOCRYPHA OF THE OLD TESTAMENT" IN A CHRISTIAN CONTEXT

Our investigations in sections III and IV have shown, I hope, that it makes sense to study the "Pseudepigrapha/Apocrypha of the Old Testament" as part of the literature of early Christianity. They are witnesses to the authority of the books of the "Old Testament" for (a considerable part of the) Christians in the second century and later. The Christians who accepted these books as authoritative were interested in what was otherwise known about Adam, Enoch, Moses, Elijah and other important figures. Their words carried weight, their faith and righteous conduct were exemplary.

A precise demarcation of a collection "Pseudepigrapha" or "Apocrypha" has proved a difficult undertaking. (We should do well to use another term anyhow, but no one seems to have found any so far.) It is impossible to limit the collection to *Jewish* writings, and then to those from the period between 200 BCE and 100 CE. Some of the documents under discussion are, at least in fragmentary form, known from undoubtedly Jewish sources, but the great majority has come down to us transmitted by Christians. And because Christians were convinced of the continuity in God's revelation through the great figures of the "Old Testament" *and* through Jesus Christ and his apostles, the distinction between "Jewish" and "Christian" was for them only of relative importance. What is not evidently "Christian" need not therefore be "Jewish". That is why it is often difficult to decide whether a particular document goes back to a pre-Christian original and was perhaps later interpolated, or more or less thoroughly redacted, or whether it is a Christian composition incorporating Jewish sources or traditions.

In any case the study of these writings should not limit itself to—or even be primarily concerned with—the possible Jewish origin of a document and its place within Judaism around the beginning of the common era. We shall have to begin with an analysis of the Christian transmission—a process that continued into late in the Middle Ages (and even after that)—and to make an attempt to trace its earliest history. We shall have to determine its function and meaning in and for (specific groups of) early Christians. In certain cases we shall be able to ask even further back, and investigate the history of a writing, in its present or in an earlier form, in pre-Christian Judaism.

APPENDIX

WHAT DO WE MEAN BY "PSEUDEPIGRAPHA / APOCRYPHA
OF THE OLD TESTAMENT"?

The term "Pseudepigrapha of the Old Testament" has become fashionable since the beginning of the twentieth century when two collective works appeared in which this word played an important role[43]. First *Die Apokryphen und Pseudepigraphen des Alten Testaments*, two volumes edited by E. Kautzsch[44], and somewhat later *The Apocrypha and Pseudepigrapha of the Old Testament* edited by R.H. Charles (also in two volumes)[45]. The titles of these two volumes betray the Christian viewpoint of these two scholars, and the distinction "apocrypha–pseudepigrapha" their typical Protestant stance. The Protestant "Apocrypha of the Old Testament" are regarded as "deuterocanonical" by Roman-Catholics, who use the term "apocrypha" for the books that Protestants call "pseudepigrapha"[46]. But whichever of the two terms is chosen, the question remains which books should be classified as such. Kautzsch and Charles limited the "Pseudepigrapha of the Old Testament" to books written by Jews in the period between 200 BCE and 100 CE, but not belonging to the Apocrypha of the church. Comparison between their two collections shows that already these two scholars did not entirely agree as to which writings should be counted among the Old Testament Pseudepigrapha.

43. Much earlier, in the first decades of the eighteenth century, J.A. FABRICIUS published his *Codex Pseudepigraphus Veteris Testamenti*, 2 vols., Hamburg, Felginer, 1713 (^{2}1722-1723).

44. Tübingen, Mohr, 1900 (^{2}1921; repr. Darmstadt, Wissenschaftliche Buchgesellschaft, 1961).

45. Oxford, Clarendon, 1913 (several reprints).

46. Compare in the nineteenth century J.-P. MIGNE, *Dictionnaire des apocryphes*, 2 vols., Paris, 1856 and 1858 (repr. Turnhout, Brepols, 1989). In this collection MIGNE also deals with the New Testament Apocrypha. In the "Corpus Christianorum" J.-C. HAELEWYCK recently published a *Clavis Apocryphorum Veteris Testamenti*, Turnhout, Brepols, 1998. A.-M. DENIS, who published, successively, an *Introduction aux pseudépigraphes grecs d'Ancien Testament* (SVTP, 1), Leiden, Brill, 1970, a *Concordance grecque des pseudépigraphes d'Ancien Testament,* Louvain-la-Neuve, Institut Orientaliste, 1987, and a *Concordance latine des pseudépigraphes d'Ancien Testament,* Turnhout, Brepols, 1993, finally chose for the second edition of his completely revised Introduction (published posthumously, with the assistance of J.-C. HAELEWYCK) the title *Introduction à la littérature religieuse judéo-hellénistique*, 2 vols., Turnhout, Brepols, 2000.

Others avoided the term "Pseudepigrapha" or used it for a much smaller number of writings. So, for instance, E. Schürer in the third volume of his *Die Geschichte des jüdischen Volkes*, that is mainly devoted to Jewish literature[47]. He spoke about "palästinisch-jüdische Literatur" in general (beside the "hellenistisch-jüdische") and reckoned only some writings to the category "Prophetische Pseudepigraphen". Later, in 1928, P. Riessler brought together a very large number of "ausserkanonische Schriften des Judentums" under the title *Altjüdisches Schrifttum ausserhalb der Bibel*[48]. As successor of Kautzsch's two volumes we may regard the series of monographs appearing since the 1970s under the title *Jüdische Schriften aus hellenistisch-römischer Zeit* (JSHRZ)[49]. It consists of an extensive collection of books, divided into five groups: "Historische und legendarische Erzählungen", "Unterweisung in erzählender Form", "Unterweisung in lehrhafter Form", "Poetische Schriften", "Apokalypsen".

Among other collections mention may be made of the French *La Bible. Écrits intertestamentaires*[50] of 1987. It gives translations of nineteen "Pseudépigraphes de l'Ancien Testament" preceded by some "Écrits qoumrâniens" (taking up about a quarter of the book). There also appeared in the 1980s the Italian *Apocrifi dell' Antico Testamento*[51] and the five volumes of the Spanish *Apócrifos del Antiguo Testamento*[52]. Comparison of these last two collections shows that, as might be expected, the problem of selection and limitation is also there for those who prefer the term "apocrypha" to that of "pseudepigrapha".

In 1984 M.E. Stone edited the book *Jewish Writings of the Second Temple Period* in the series "Compendia Rerum Iudaicarum ad Novum Testamentum"[53]. As its subtitle tells us, it deals with "Apocrypha, Pseudepigrapha, Qumran Sectarian Writings, Philo, Josephus". It classifies the sources according to literary genre (though differently from JSHRZ) or provenance. There is no special chapter devoted to the "Pseudepigrapha"; the writings found near the Dead Sea are dealt with separately. Important for our purpose is what Stone says about the dif-

---

47. Leipzig, Hinrichs, [4]1909; see especially pp. 258-370.

48. Heidelberg, Kerle & Rühling, 1928 (reprint Darmstadt, Wissenschaftliche Buchgesellschaft, 1966).

49. Published by Gütersloher Verlagshaus Gerd Mohn.

50. A. DUPONT SOMMER & M. PHILONENKO (eds.), *La Bible. Écrits intertestamentaires* (Bibliothèque de la Pléiade, 337), Paris, Gallimard, 1987.

51. Originally two volumes, edited by P. SACCHI, Torino, Unione Tipografico-Editrice Torinese, 1981 and 1989; later three additional volumes appeared, see n. 68.

52. Edited by A. DÍEZ MACHO and others, Madrid, Ediciones Cristiandad, 1983-1987.

53. Assen, Van Gorcum; Philadelphia, Fortress, 1984. The book appeared in the second section of "Compendia", devoted to Jewish literature.

ference between the volume edited by him and the next, entitled *The Literature of the Sages*[54]. I quote: "The volume on rabbinic literature comprises material relevant to the history of Jewish literature and thought transmitted within the Jewish tradition and in Semitic languages. The present volume includes material that was not transmitted by Jewish tradition. Part was preserved by the various Christian churches and part was uncovered by archeological chance" (p. xix). The discovery of a great number of writings, some of them already known earlier, near the Dead Sea has indeed considerably broadened and deepened our knowledge of the literature, history and the religious ideas of Judaism in the period around the beginning of the Common Era. It is very important that in this case we are likely to deal with documents hidden in the time of the Jewish war against the Romans, which consequently must have been written before that date. The discovery of the Qumran Scrolls meant a great boost for the research into the writings already known, including the Pseudepigrapha; they could now be studied in a wider context and from new viewpoints[55]. Stone rightly stresses, however, that many of those, like the works of Philo and Josephus, were only transmitted by Christians. This basic fact should not be overlooked in the study of these writings, and in the use of the material transmitted by Chris-

54. S. Safrai (ed.), *The Literature of the Sages. First Part* (CRINT II, 3a), Assen, Van Gorcum; Philadelphia, Fortress, 1987.

55. It should be noted, however, that the caves at Qumran yielded only a few Apocrypha or Pseudepigrapha already known before the discoveries near the Dead Sea. Peter W. Flint, in his contribution *'Apocrypha', Other Previously-Known Writings, and 'Pseudepigrapha' in the Dead Sea Scrolls*, to P.W. Flint & J.C. Vanderkam (eds.), *The Dead Sea Scrolls after Fifty Years. A Comprehensive Assessment*, Leiden, Brill, 1999, vol. 2, pp. 24-66, mentions only: Tobit, Sirach, the Epistle of Jeremiah (with a question mark), Psalm 151A and B, Psalm 154 and 155, Enoch and Jubilees. He rightly classifies a number of fragments of the Aramaic Levi Document, 4Q TNaph and some fragments that, according to some people, can be connected with Judah and Joseph, plus fragments connected with Qahat and Amram, among "material related to the Testaments of the Twelve Patriarchs" (note the "related to"!). An entirely different question is whether other Qumran documents should be reckoned to the "Pseudepigrapha of the Old Testament". Flint refers here to M.J. Bernstein's essay *Pseudepigraphy in the Qumran Scrolls: Categories and Functions*, in E.G. Chazon, M.E. Stone, A. Pinnick (eds.), *Pseudepigraphic Perspectives. The Apocrypha and Pseudepigrapha in Light of the Dead Sea Scrolls* (STDJ, 31), Leiden, Brill, 1999, pp. 1-26. Defining "pseudepigrapha" as "texts falsely attributed to an author (usually of great authority) in order to enhance their authority and validity", this author distinguishes between different uses of the term. Beside "authoritative pseudepigraphy" proper, there is "convenient pseudepigraphy" ("where the work is anonymous but individual voices are heard within it") and "decorative pseudepigraphy" ("where the work is associated with a name without a particular regard for content or to achieve a certain effect"; for these definitions, see pp. 1-7 and p. 25). In this light Bernstein and Flint discuss a number of documents; a definitive, generally accepted classification is still outstanding.

tians, for the reconstruction of Jewish history and Jewish religious ideas in the period before 70 CE.

We shall have to pay special attention to two collections in English that may be regarded as successors to R.H. Charles's Pseudepigrapha volume. Its direct successor at the Clarendon Press, edited by H.F.D. Sparks, received the title *The Apocryphal Old Testament*[56]. This book serves as a companion volume to *The Apocryphal New Testament* by M.R. James[57], published by the same publisher. Sparks expressly avoids the term "pseudepigrapha" and distances himself from Charles's view that the writings under discussion are Jewish, date from the "intertestamental" period, and are, as such, of great importance for our knowledge of the Judaism of the period and the background of early Christianity. Sparks does not want just to present background literature for students of the New Testament, nor can the writings involved be treated as that. Most of the books may indeed be of Jewish origin, he says, but often we find Christian elements as result of interpolation or redaction. There are also Christian apocryphal texts using Jewish material; moreover we must allow for the likelihood that Christians, influenced by what they read in the Old Testament, composed writings of their own. Sparks writes: "Our single criterion for inclusion has been whether or not any particular item is attributed to (or is primarily concerned with the history or activities of) an Old Testament character (or characters)"[58]. Not everything that satisfied this criterion could be included, but Sparks tried to present at least the most important and interesting documents; he did not include wrtings (only) found at Qumran.

The second collection to be mentioned here are the two volumes *The Old Testament Pseudepigrapha*, edited by J.H. Charlesworth[59]. Volume 1 is devoted to "Apocalyptic Literature and Testaments", volume 2 to "Expansions of the 'Old Testament' and Legends, Wisdom and Philosophical Literature, Prayers, Psalms and Odes; Fragments of Lost Judeo-Hellenistic Works". Apart from the fragments just mentioned Charlesworth has included no less than fifty-two writings. Qumran

---

56. H.F.D. SPARKS (ed.), *The Apocryphal Old Testament*, Oxford, Clarendon, 1984.

57. M.R. JAMES (ed.), *The Apocryphal New Testament*, Oxford, Clarendon, 1924, many times reprinted. Recently revised and expanded in J.K. ELLIOTT (ed.), *The Apocryphal New Testament*, Oxford, Clarendon, 1993.

58. See H.F.D. SPARKS, *Apocryphal Old Testament* (n. 56), "Preface", pp. ix-xviii; quotation from p. xv.

59. J.H. CHARLESWORTH, *The Old Testament Pseudepigrapha*, 2 vols., Garden City, NY, Doubleday, 1983-1985. Among the many reviews I mention that by S.P. BROCK in *JJS* 35 (1984) 200-209 en 38 (1987) 107-114. See also the reviews of the works of Sparks and Charlesworth together, by M.E. STONE & R.A. KRAFT in *RSR* 14 (1988) 111-117.

documents are lacking, just as in the collection of Sparks. Charlesworth declares that he deliberately chose to present a large collection. He noticed, he says, a "consensus that the Pseudepigrapha must be defined broadly so as to include all documents that conceivably belong to the Old Testament Pseudepigrapha". After this he continues:

> "The present description of the Pseudepigrapha is as follows: Those writings 1) that, with the exception of Ahiqar, are Jewish or Christian; 2) that are often attributed to ideal figures in Israel's past; 3) that customarily claim to contain God's word or message; 4) that frequently build upon ideas and narratives present in the Old Testament; 5) and that almost always were composed either during the period 200 B.C. to A.D. 200 or, though late, apparently preserve, albeit in an edited form, Jewish traditions that date from that period".

He adds:

> "Obviously, the numerous qualifications ... warn that the above comments do not define the term "pseudepigrapha"; they merely describe the features of this collection"[60].

The fact that the word "pseudepigrapha" figures so prominently and is used as an inclusive–and at the same time elusive–term, is remarkable. Charlesworth retains it notwithstanding "the numerous qualifications". Also other publications from his hand show abundantly that he is aware of the complexity of the situation[61]. His survey article "Pseudepigrapha of the Old Testament" in the *Anchor Bible Dictionary*[62] begins with the observation that many of these documents were composed by Jews, that others were expanded or rewritten by Christians, and that some are Christian compositions depending in various degrees on pre-70 Jewish documents or oral traditions. Nevertheless: however difficult it may be to determine in detail what is Jewish and what not, the importance of the entire collection lies for Charlesworth in its being "essential reading for an understanding of early Judaism (ca. 250 BCE to 200 CE) and of Christian origins"[63].

---

60. J.H. CHARLESWORTH, *Old Testament Pseudepigrapha* (n. 59), "Introduction for the General Reader", p. xxv.

61. See, for instance, his *The Pseudepigrapha and Modern Research* (SBL SCS, 7), Missoula, MT, Scholars, 1976 (second expanded edition 1981) and *The Old Testament Pseudepigrapha and the New Testament* (SNTS.MS, 54), Cambridge, University Press, 1985 (new edition with new preface [pp. vii-xxiv], Harrisburg, Trinity International, 1998).

62. J.H. CHARLESWORH, art. *Pseudepigrapha of the Old Testament*, in D.N. FREEDMAN (ed.), *ABD*, New York, Doubleday, 1992, vol. 5, pp. 537-540.

63. See not only the article just mentioned (n. 62), but also *Old Testament Pseudepigrapha* (n. 59), vol. 1, pp. xxvii-xxix and *In the Crucible. The Pseudepigrapha as Biblical Interpretation*, in J.H. CHARLESWORTH & C.A. EVANS (eds.), *The Pseudepigrapha and Early Biblical Interpretation* (JSPSup, 14), Sheffield, Sheffield Academic Press, 1993, pp. 20-43.

In stating this repeatedly and emphatically Charlesworth stands in the tradition starting with Kautzsch and Charles. Including so many extra writings in his selection does not make it easier, however, to substantiate this claim in each individual case. But quite apart from that, the case can be made that it makes at least as much sense to study these documents "as part of the continuous flow of Jewish and Christian creativity which in good part derives from preoccupation with the 'canonical books'", as Stone remarked in his review of Charlesworth's two volumes[64]. Stone refers there to an earlier article from his hand in which he observes that documents for which there is no independent corroboration or other compelling evidence cannot, without more ado, be used as sources for our knowledge of Judaism in the period of the Second Temple. "Before the Pseudepigrapha and similar writings are used as evidence for that more ancient period, they must be examined in the Christian context in which they were transmitted and utilized"[65].

A very special and individual approach to the Pseudepigrapha problem is found in J.-C. Picard's essay *L'apocryphe à l'étroit. Notes historiographiques sur le corpus d'apocryphes bibliques*[66]. He prefers to speak about a "continent apocryphe", one could say "an apocryphal world", in which people lived for a long time. His aim is to take account of the entire complex of apocryphal biblical traditions in Antiquity and in the Middle Ages (and even later), among Jews, Christians and Muslims[67]. These apocryphal traditions functioned as myths, as basic, foundational stories in the communities that transmitted them, orally and in writing, and naturally in many variants. They require a literary and historical as well as an ethnological approach. A purely text-critical or source-critical analysis of these writings, with a view to reconstructing their earliest form, and using this earliest form as evidence in the study of early Judaism or early Christianity, does not do justice to the apocryphal tradition as a complex process. Such a completely one-sided approach has also led to the formation of very limited collections of "Pseudepigrapha of the Old Testament" (as in the case of Kautzsch and Charles), and similarly limited collections of "Apocrypha of the New

64. See note 59; quotation from p. 112.
65. M.E. STONE, *Categorization and Classification of the Apocrypha and Pseudepigrapha*, in *Abr-Nahrain* 24 (1986) 167-177; quotation from pp. 172-173.
66. J.-C. PICARD, *L'apocryphe à l'étroit. Notes historiographiques sur le corpus d'apocryphes bibliques*, in *Apocrypha. Le champ des apocryphes* 1 (1990) 69-117. This essay was reprinted in ID., *Le continent apocryphe: Essai sur les littératures apocryphes juive et chrétienne* (Instrumenta Patristica, 36), Steenbrugis, In Abbatia S. Petri; Turnhout, Brepols, 1999, pp. 3-51. In this book, a posthumous collection of Picard's most important publications, one finds an introduction to Picard's ideas about the "apocryphal world" by Francis SCHMIDT; see pp. xix-xxviii.

Testament" (Hennecke & Schneemelcher). One can, of course, always consider including more or different documents in such collections, but what is really needed is a completely different approach to apocryphal literature.

Many comments could be made in the margin of Picard's characterization of Pseudepigrapha research since the end of the nineteenth century as one-sided and reductionist. To me, at any rate, it would seem perfectly legitimate to attempt to reconstruct the first stages in a transmission process. In the case of the writings under discussion it makes sense to consider in which cases it is possible to trace the origins of this process back to Christian circles in the first two or three centuries, or even to Jewish groups around the beginning of the Common Era. In trying to achieve this goal one will have to apply all available philological, literary and historical methods bearing in mind, of course, the great complexity of the entire process of transmission. Remarkable is Picard's positive assessment of the works of H.F.D. Sparks and J.H. Charlesworth, to which he refers briefly at the end of his essay. In their approach he notices "une rupture définitive avec les présupposés trop réducteurs et le réductionnisme méthodologique illustrés, au debut de ce siècle, par les recueils de Kautzsch et de Charles".

Finally I would like to draw attention to a recent article by P. Sacchi, which serves at the same time as the introduction to volumes 3 and 4 of the *Apocrifi dell' Antico Testamento*[68]. He continues to prefer the term "apocrypha" to "pseudepigrapha". He accepts the literary criterion that the writings concerned must be ascribed to and/or have to deal with figures from the Old Testament. At the same time, however, he would like to hold on to the Catholic interpretation of the term "apocrypha", which in his view provides a clear historical criterion. This term "has a precise historical meaning which can be retained even nowadays …: thus it is possible to define a corpus of texts which cannot extend beyond the beginning of the second century CE"[69]. In the end Sacchi distinguishes between "intertestamental" apocrypha (Jewish, before 100), Jewish Old Testament apocrypha (after 100), Christian Old Testament apocrypha (after 100), and Jewish medieval (post-talmudic) apocrypha. Sacchi re-

---

67. He praises the collections by J.A. FABRICIUS, who edited not only the *Codex pseudepigraphus Veteris Testamenti* mentioned in note 43, but earlier also a *Codex apocryphus Novi Testamenti*, Hamburg, Schiller, 1703, ²1719.

68. See note 51. Published in 1999 and 2000 by Paideia in Brescia (which had already in 1997 published volume 5, an appendix with the works of Jewish-Hellenistic writers from the diaspora). SACCHI's article *Il problema degli apocrifi dell'Antico Testamento* appeared in *Henoch* 21 (1999) 97-129.

69. From the English summary on p. 129.

gards the survival of the "genre" as interesting, and he does realize that the apocrypha/pseudepigrapha were transmitted by Christians–yet he is of the opinion that the distinctions he proposes are practicable and meaningful.

Summing up:

a. In the end the term "Pseudepigrapha of the Old Testament" is not very useful, for several reasons:

1. There is no consensus as to which writings should be regarded as belonging to this category.

2. This lack of consensus is due to the different ways the term has been used in the past and in the present. On the one hand it is used for all documents in which one or more biblical figures play an important role, but on the other hand a historical criterion is often applied and the term is restricted to writings dating from the period between about 200 BCE and 100 CE that are supposed to be of Jewish origin.

3. It is also not unimportant that only in a relatively restricted number of instances can one properly speak of "pseudepigraphy", and that a number of books that were later incorporated in the Jewish Bible/the Christian Old Testament and in the New Testament may be called "pseudepigrapha".

b. Yet it remains meaningful to pay attention to those writings which have in common that they are concerned with the lives, activities and words of a great figure (or great figures) in the Jewish Bible/the Old Testament. It is also worthwhile to concentrate on the earliest stages in the transmission of such writings, particularly in those cases where we are able to go back to early Christianity, or perhaps even to Jewish groups in the same period or just before. It is important to keep in mind the great complexity of the transmission process.

Libellenveld 19
NL-2318 VE Leiden
The Netherlands

Marinus DE JONGE

THE CANON MURATORI
A Matter of Dispute

"Pro captu lectoris habent sua fata libelli". The famous words of the Roman grammarian Terentianus Maurus (fl. ca. 200 AD)[1] are, in many respects, applicable to the loose fragment of text now commonly referred to as the Muratorian Fragment or, perhaps less neutrally, as the Canon Muratori. The author who originally composed the document would probably never have guessed that later generations would come to cherish his little text as a fundamental witness to the process through which the Church formed its New Testament. Moreover, the scribe, who in the eighth (or perhaps the late-seventh) century did such a miserable job of copying the text, would surely be equally surprised to learn that the fruits of his labour would one day be cited, and thus saved from oblivion, as an example of the deplorable state of letters in early-medieval Italy. Indeed, Lodovico Antonio Muratori, who in 1740 published the fragment from a manuscript he had found in the Ambrosiana Library and which had once belonged to the Bobbio monastery, was rather more interested in the terrible quality of its language than in its content[2]. Since

---

1. J.-W. BECK (ed.), *Terentianus Maurus. De Syllabis* (Hypomnemata. Untersuchungen zur Antike und zu ihrem Nachleben, 102), Göttingen, Vandenhoeck & Ruprecht, 1991, p. 122 (l. 1286). The sole known manuscript of this work is now lost. It came from the monastery at Bobbio. If one accepts the traditional dating of the Fragment, Terentianus would have been a contemporary of its author.

2. L.A. MURATORI, *Antiquitates Italicae Medii Aevi*, III, Milan, Typographia Societatis Palatinae, 1740, pp. 851-856 (text on pp. 854-855). The section is a part of *Dissertatio xliii*, "De literarum statu, neglectu et cultura in Italia post barbaros in eam invectos usque ad Annum Christi Millesimum Centesimum" (pp. 809-880). Muratori calls the text a "fragmentum de Apostolis" and a "fragmentum antiquissimum ad Canonem divinarum Scripturarum spectans" (p. 851). In his comment he quotes Jerome: "Nam quod est ad indoctos, vel suo tempore Sanctus Hieronymus ad Lucinium scribens, incusabat 'imperitiam Notariorum, Librariorumque incuriam, qui scribunt non quod inveniunt, sed quod intelligunt: & dum alienos errores emendare nituntur, ostendunt suos'" (p. 855). The quotation is from the letter to Lucinus (*Ep.* 71,5) and differs slightly at the beginning ("non mihi debes inputare, sed tuis et inperitiae … incuriae").

Several other transcriptions and/or editions of the Fragment have been published, often with considerable emendations. See, e.g., H. LIETZMANN, *Das Muratorische Fragment und die Monarchianischen Prologe zu den Evangelien* (Kleine Texte, 1), Bonn, Marcus-Weber, 1902, pp. 1-10. S. RITTER, *Il Frammento Muratoriano*, in *Rivista di archeologia cristiana* 3 (1926) 215-267, pp. 246-254 (with retroversion into Greek). See also below, n. 3. Hereafter, the text is quoted (with the usual orthographical adjustments) as it is found in the transcription of G.M. HAHNEMAN, *The Muratorian Fragment and the Development of the Canon* (Oxford Theological Monographs), Oxford, Clarendon, 1992, pp. 6-7 (henceforth abbreviated as HMF). – On the date of the manuscript, see E.S. BUCHANAN,

its publication, scholars have invested much energy in studying it. In the process, they have also demonstrated such an amazing amount of ingenuity in suggesting interpretations and reconstructions, that one wonders whether it is still possible to say anything new about it. And yet that is precisely what has happened in the last few years. It is these most recent attempts that provide us with an incentive for yet another close-up look at both the text and its related problems.

I. Chaos and Consensus

It is not an exaggeration to say that every word of the Fragment has been scrutinized, often with the result that several explanations are defended for one and the same expression[3]. Discussion has not been lim-

The Codex Muratorianus, in *JTS* 9 (1907) 537-545, p. 538: "possibly the seventh". A date in the eighth century is more commonly accepted.

3. From earlier literature one should mention the monograph by S.P. Tregelles, who took up many of the observations previously made by B.F. Westcott, F.D. Hesse, J. Schuurmans Stekhoven, and G. Kuhn. T. Zahn wrote a chapter of 143 pages on the Fragment for his *Geschichte des Neutestamentlichen Kanons*, and A. Harnack often returned to it in his publications, sometimes in direct response to Zahn. The Fragment received its due in the general surveys on the formation of the canon by, a.o., Westcott, K.G. Credner, J. Leipoldt, and M.-J. Lagrange. Cf. S.P. TREGELLES, *Canon Muratorianus. The Earliest Catalogue of the Books of the New Testament*, Oxford, Clarendon, 1867 (with a transcription of the text and a reprint of Muratori's comment on pp. 11-13). F.H. HESSE, *Das Muratori'sche Fragment neu untersucht und erklärt*, Giessen, Ricker, 1873. J. SCHUURMANS STEKHOVEN, *Het Fragment van Muratori*, Utrecht, van Huffel, 1877. G. KUHN, *Das Muratorische Fragment über die Bücher des Neuen Testamentes*, Zürich, Höhr, 1892. T. ZAHN, *Geschichte des Neutestamentlichen Kanons*, II.1, Erlangen-Leipzig, Deichert, 1890, pp. 1-143. A. HARNACK, *Tatians Diatessaron im muratorischen Fragment nachgewiesen*, and *Der polemische Abschnitt im muratorischen Fragment als Schlüssel für ein geschichtliches Verständniss desselben*, in *Zeitschrift für die lutherische Theologie und Kirche* 35 (1874) 276-288 and 445-464 (with "Nachtrag" in 1875, 207-208); *Das muratorische Fragment und die Entstehung einer Sammlung apostolisch-katholischer Schriften*, in *ZKG* 3 (1879) 358-408; *Das Neue Testament um das Jahr 200*, Freiburg, Mohr, 1889, passim; *Über den Verfasser und dem literarischen Charakter des Muratorischen Fragments*, in *ZNW* 24 (1925) 1-16. B.F. WESTCOTT, *A General Survey of the History of the Canon of the New Testament*, Cambridge–London, MacMillan, 1855, [5]1881, pp. 212-220 and 521-538 (Latin text). In addition, see K.A. CREDNER, *Zur Geschichte des Kanons*, Halle, Buchhandlung des Waisenhauses, 1847, pp. 69-94; ID., *Geschichte des Neutestamentlichen Kanon*, ed. G. Volkmar, Berlin, Reimer, 1860, pp. 141-170 and 341-363 (Volkmar). F. OVERBECK, *Zur Geschichte des Kanons*, Chemnitz, 1880, repr. Darmstadt, Wissenschaftliche Buchgesellschaft, 1965, pp. 71-142 (in discussion with Harnack). J. LEIPOLDT, *Geschichte des neutestamentlichen Kanons*, 2 vols., Leipzig, Hinrich, 1907-08, passim. H. LIETZMANN, *Wie würden die Bücher des Neuen Testaments heilige Schrift? Fünf Vorträge*, Tübingen, Mohr, 1907, pp. 52-63. C.R. GREGORY, *Canon and Text of the New Testament*, New York, Scribner, 1907, pp. 129-133. M.-J. LAGRANGE, *Introduction à l'étude du Nouveau Testament. I. Histoire ancienne du Canon du Nouveau Testament*, Paris, Gabalda, 1933, pp. 59-84. See also the detailed articles by H. LECLERCQ, *Muratorianum*, in *DACL* 12 (1935) 543-560, and G. BARDY, *Muratori (Canon de)*, in *DBS* 5 (1957) 1399-1408.

ited to the details of the text. In fact, every single aspect has been a matter of dispute: its content and structure, its author and date, its provenance and sources, its original language, its genre and purpose, its reception and role in the formation of the canon, even its authenticity and textual quality. Thus, the remarkable thing is perhaps not that in recent years still other interpretations have been proposed, but that, amidst the chaos, some sort of consensus (in part a negative one) has been reached with regard to most of the aforementioned issues.

No one has dared to repeat F. Thiersch's suspicion that the Fragment might be a hoax from the pen of Muratori[4] or G. Volkmar's conclusion that nothing is wrong with this text and that the manuscript is "most correct"[5]. As a matter of fact, the text is in a terrible state, which is one of the reasons why it is so difficult to interpret. Detailed study of the orthography has revealed that Muratori's conclusion about the quality of the text was correct, but that the copyist is not solely responsible. Right after the Fragment, the scribe copied the same excerpt from Ambrosius' *De Abraham* twice on opposite pages. It is a stunning example of the carelessness of the copyist, but it should also be observed that these copies are quite identical, a probable indication that at least some of the orthographical and grammatical errors in the Fragment (esp. case endings) were already present in his model[6].

Among the more recent surveys which discuss the Fragment, see esp. H. VON CAMPENHAUSEN, *Die Entstehung der christlichen Bibel* (BHT, 39), Tübingen, Mohr, 1968, pp. 282-303 (ET 1972). I. FRANK, *Der Sinn der Kanonbildung. Eine historisch-theologische Untersuchung der Zeit vom 1. Clemensbrief bis Irenäus von Lyon* (Freiburger theologische Studien, 90), Freiburg, Herder, 1971, pp. 178-189. A. SAND, *Kanon. Von den Anfängen bis zum Fragmentum Muratorianum* (Handbuch der Dogmengeschichte, 1.3a.1), Freiburg, Herder, 1974, pp. 60-63. B.M. METZGER, *The Canon of the New Testament. Its Origin, Development, and Significance*, Oxford, Clarendon, 1987, ²1997, pp. 191-201 and 305-307 for an English translation. It is this translation which is quoted in this study. There is another in H.Y. GAMBLE, *The New Testament Canon. Its Making and Meaning*, Philadelphia, PA, Fortress, 1985, pp. 93-95 and in L.M. MCDONALD, *The Formation of the Christian Biblical Canon*, Peabody, MA, Hendrickson, 1995, pp. 209-220.

4. Thiersch considered some of the errors so bizarre, "dass sie uns fast wie ein Scherz vorkommen und schon mehrmals den Verdacht in uns erweckten, ob nicht das ganze Fragment eine spasshafte Mystification des Herausgebers Muratori sein könnte" (*Versuch zur Herstellung des historischen Standpuncts für die Kritik der neutestamentlichen Schriften*, Erlangen, 1845, p. 385).

5. "Das MS. ist so wenig ein corruptes, dass es vielmehr zu den correctesten gehört". This is the first line of the Appendix Volkmar added to the edition of Credner's *Geschichte des Neutestamentlichen Kanon* (n. 3), pp. 337-416, here p. 341. Contrast Credner's "Der Text unseres Fragmentes ist ein über alle Maassen verdorbener" (*Zur Geschichte* [n. 3], p. 72).

6. Cf. ZAHN, *Geschichte*, II.1 (n. 3), pp. 9-14. HMF (n. 2), pp. 10-17. A different solution is suggested by P. HENNE, *Le Canon de Muratori. Orthographe et datation*, in *Archivum Bobiense* 12-13 (1990-91) 289-304, p. 302: "Une autre possibilité serait que deux scribes d'origines diverses auraient chacun écrit une partie du codex" (the Fragment and the excerpt from Ambrose). However, this is rather improbable. The text of *De Abraham* is reproduced with commentary by TREGELLES, *Canon Muratorianus* (n. 3), pp. 21-28.

The Fragment (85 lines, 31 lines on a page) begins in the middle of a clause on top of f. 10r and ends abruptly in the middle of l. 23 of f. 11r. It mentions, in this order, two of the canonical gospels (Luke and John, followed by a quotation from 1 John), thirteen letters of Paul (Hebrews is missing), some apocryphal letters assigned to Paul, three of the Catholic epistles (Jude and two letters of John), the Revelations of John and of Peter, the Shepherd of Hermas, and a number of works by heretics that are to be rejected. There is no reason to suspect that this order had ever been rearranged[7]. It is possible that the copyist possessed the Fragment's beginning since the codex gives indications that some pages (a quire?) just before f. 10 might be missing. While there has been some discussion about the interpretation of the first line[8], it is commonly agreed that the text must have mentioned the gospels of Matthew and Mark, since it continues on lines 2 and 9 with "tertio evangelii librum secundo Lucan" and "quarti evangeliorum Iohannis". Generally, scholars are more hesitant to speculate about whether the text also mentioned the books that had been accepted as comprising the Old Testament or included some sort of an introduction. Since the Fragment breaks off after "constitutorem" and is immediately followed in the codex by the excerpt from *De Abraham*, it is reasonable to assume that the scribe copied the text as he found it. Because the text of lines 81-85 is very confused it is difficult to decide whether or not the clause is complete[9].

The question of the authorship is a stalemate: scholars have simply never been able to arrive at a consensus. Among the names that have been proposed, often with little or no argumentation, are Caius, Papias, and Hegesippus[10]. The first of these is known to have criticized the Gospel of John, which makes him an unlikely candidate given the detailed treatment this gospel receives in lines 9-16. With Papias the Fragment would have to be dated very early in the second century. If Hegesippus was the author it is almost incomprehensible that Eusebius of Caesarea would have been unaware of this[11]. A more substantial case has been

7. Ctr. G. KOFFMANE-KUNITZ, *Das wahre Alter und die Herkunft des sogenannten Muratori'schen Kanons*, in *Neue Jahrbücher für deutsche Theologie* 2 (1893) 163-223, p. 221, who argued that in the "Vorlage" of the Fragment Revelation preceded the Catholic Epistles.

8. Most scholars take "quibus" to be a relative pronoun, but some have thought it was originally part of an "aliquibus" (so ZAHN, *Geschichte* [n. 3], II.1, p. 18).

9. The latter is the more exceptional position defended by Zahn (*Geschichte* [n. 3], II.1, pp. 126 and 143).

10. Respectively, these names were first suggested by MURATORI, *Antiquitates* (n. 2), p. 851; S. DE MAISTRE, *Daniel secundum LXX ex Tetraplis Origenis*, Rome, Propaganda Fides, 1772, p. 467; and C. BUNSEN, *Analecta Ante-Nicaena*, London, Longman, 1854, I, pp. 125-127.

11. As noted earlier by CREDNER, *Geschichte des Neutestamentlichen Kanon* (n. 3), pp. 142-143; cf. also TREGELLES, *Canon Muratorianus* (n. 3), p. 5.

made for Hippolytus of Rome[12]. Others can live with the idea of an anonymous document[13].

Hermas wrote the Shepherd "nuperrime temporibus nostris … sedente cathedra urbis Romae ecclesiae Pio" (ll. 74-76). Pius was bishop of Rome sometime between 138 and 155. It has commonly been accepted that this indication, together with the references to Marcion in ll. 65 and 83 and to the "Cataphrygians" (i.e., the Montanists) in l. 84, point to the last two decades of the second or the first two decades of the third century as the date of the Fragment's original composition. Westcott thought it could not be "placed much later than 170 A.D."[14]. With Hippolytus we are in the early third century[15]. The few scholars who have argued for a later date have long been silenced[16].

12. This was first proposed by J.B. Lightfoot, who not only argued that the Fragment represents an excerpt of one of Hippolytus' ᾠδαὶ εἰς πάσας τὰς γραφάς, but also offered a retroversion of the original Greek poem. His suggestion for the authorship was taken up by T.H. Robinson, by Zahn (though he remained skeptical in his *Geschichte*; cf. II.1, pp. 137-138), and by Lagrange, who defended it against the criticism of Harnack, who had himself once suggested Rhodon but later thought that the Fragment had been composed in the circles of Pope Victor I or Pope Zephyrinus (*Verfasser* [n. 3], p. 15). Cf. J.B. LIGHTFOOT, *The Muratorian Fragment*, in *The Academy* 36/907 (1889) 186-188; ID., *Clement of Rome*, London, ²1889, II, pp. 405-413. T.H. ROBINSON, *The Authorship of the Muratorian Canon*, in *The Expositor* 7th ser., 1 (1906) 481-495. T. ZAHN, *Hippolytus, der Verfasser des Muratorischen Kanons*, in *NKZ* 33 (1922) 417-436, repr. in his *Forschungen zur Geschichte des neutestamentlichen Kanons*, 10, Leipzig, Deichert, 1929, pp. 58-75. M.-J. LAGRANGE, *L'auteur du Canon de Muratori*, in *RB* 35 (1926) 83-88; *Le Canon d'Hippolyte et le Fragment de Muratori*, in *RB* 42 (1933) 161-186; *Histoire ancienne* (n. 3), pp. 78-84. Note too that if Hippolytus were the author, the Fragment would then be the work of a dissident.

13. See TREGELLES, *Canon Muratorianus* (n. 3), p. 5, who compares it to the Epistle *ad Diognetum*, "of which we know nothing. And this in the absence of all evidence is the only course to be adopted if we would avoid speculation". Nevertheless, a new name was added to the list by J. Chapman, who argued that the Fragment preserved an excerpt from the *Hypotyposes* of Clement of Alexandria: *L'auteur du Canon Muratori*, and *Clément d'Alexandrie sur les évangiles, et encore le Fragment de Muratori*, in *RBén* 21 (1904) 240-264 and 369-374. Yet another suggestion was made by V. BARTLET, *Melito the Author of the Muratorian Canon*, in *The Expositor* 7th ser., 2 (1906) 214-224.

14. WESTCOTT, *Canon* (n. 3), p. 212.

15. Zahn (*Hippolytus* [n. 12], p. 71) argued for a slightly earlier date (ca. 210) than Lagrange, who suggested the period 217-222 (*Histoire ancienne* (n. 3), pp. 78-84). A similarly late date was defended by C. ERBES, *Die Zeit des Muratorischen Fragments*, in *ZKG* 35 (1914) 331-362.

16. See CREDNER, *Zur Geschichte* (n. 3), p. 93 (F.T. Zimmermann, 1805; Hug, 1847). Cf. WESTCOTT, *Canon* (n. 3), p. 213: "The opinions of those who assign it to the fourth century, or doubt its authenticity altogether, scarcely deserve mention", with a reference to Credner. J. DONALDSON, *A Critical History of Christian Literature and Doctrine from the Death of the Apostles to the Nicene Council*, London, 1866, III, pp. 210-211, dated the Fragment ca. 250 and regarded the passage on Hermas (ll. 73-75) as an interpolation by the fourth-century translator (see below, n. 71). The isolated view of KOFFMANE-KUNITZ, *Das wahre Alter* (n. 7), who as late as 1893 continued to argue for a fifth-century date, was, after being refuted by H. Achelis, largely forgotten. See H. ACHELIS, *Zum Muratorischen Fragment*, in *ZWT* 37 (1894) 223-232. Cf. now SUNDBERG, *Canon Muratori* (cf. also below, n. 43), p. 3 n. 13 and BOLGIANI, *Frammento Muratoriano* (below, n. 46), p. 461.

Expressions such as "in catholicam ecclesiam recipi non potest"
(ll. 66-67), "recipimus" (l. 72), "nihil in totum recipimus" (l. 82), "legi
in ecclesia" (l. 73), "in catholica [ecclesia?] habentur" (l. 69), or "in
honorem ecclesiae catholicae … scificatae [sanctificatae?] sunt" (ll. 61-
63) can sometimes be found in official Church documents or in other
writings. However, the Fragment nowhere mentions the use of written
sources[17]. With regard to the traditional date, the oft quoted material
from Irenaeus or Tertullian is better explained as coincidental parallels
(in content and in wording) from contemporary authors, than as a possible source for the Fragmentist.

As far as I have been able to discover, the conclusion that the Fragment was composed in the West was never seriously disputed in the earlier literature. Two important arguments in this respect are its positive
appreciation of the Book of Revelation, which was long disputed in the
East, and the absence of Hebrews[18]. That the text originated in Rome is
primarily derived from the mention of the city in ll. 74-75 ("in urbe
Roma Herma conscripsit")[19]. The evidence may be less compelling than
has been suggested[20]. Yet, it is obvious that the Fragmentist pretends to
know certain traditions about Pope Pius and likes to use this kind of information to situate (or maybe, lend authority to?) his work.

While Harnack's conclusion that the text was originally composed in
Latin was not novel when he made it, and, while it has been repeated by
others[21], it has always remained a minority opinion and even seems to
have been largely abandoned nowadays. In this regard, much has been
made of the remark about mixing gall with honey on l. 67 ("fel enim
cum melle misceri non congruit"). It is argued that it is impossible to
imagine a Greek original in which this paronomasia sounds as good as it
does in Latin. However, the Greek may have been inspired by similar

17. Westcott found it difficult to determine "the exact character" of the Fragment and
speculated that it might have been derived from an anti-heretical tract. Ultimately, however, he decided that it was probably composed from various sources in the way patristic
authors such as Eusebius often compiled their quotations (*Canon* [n. 3], pp. 213 and 219).
    18. Cf. VON CAMPENHAUSEN, *Entstehung* (n. 3), p. 283 n. 192.
    19. Cf. HARNACK, *Verfasser* (n. 3).
    20. H. Koch argued, against Harnack, that if the author lived in Rome he would prob-
ably not have referred to the city in this way but have written "in (hac) urbe". H. KOCH,
*Zu A. v. Harnack's Beweis für den amtlichen römischer Ursprung des Muratorischen
Fragments*, in *ZNW* 25 (1926) 154-160 (with a reply by Harnack on pp. 160-162). See
already ZAHN, *Geschichte*, II.1 (n. 3), pp. 132-134, esp. 132 n. 2.
    21. HARNACK, *Verfasser* (n. 3). Cf. DONALDSON, *Critical History* (n. 16), III, pp. 210-
211; HESSE, *Das Muratori'sche Fragment* (n. 3), pp. 25-39; STEKHOVEN, *Fragment* (n. 3),
pp. 27-40. A.A.T. EHRHARDT, *The Gospels in the Muratorian Fragment*, in *Ostkirchliche
Studien* 2 (1953) 121-138; repr. in *The Framework of the New Testament Stories*, Cambridge, MA, UP, 1964, pp. 11-36. Additional references in ZAHN, *Geschichte* (n. 3), II.1,
p. 12 n. 3.

images in other texts and may have played on the words χολή-μέλι[22]. In fact, this is how Zahn retroverted the text into Greek, while simultaneously offering other illustrations of how translators struggled to render a Greek paronomasia into Latin or of how they created a new one for their translations[23]. On the hypothesis that the Fragment is a clumsy translation from the Greek, a plausible explanation can be found for at least some of its rather cumbersome modes of expression. Zahn tentatively suggested a date and provenance for the translation in fifth- or sixth-century Gaul. However, he was never forceful about this conclusion. It is also worth noting that the parallels he gives are from a *Peregrinatio* that dates from the late-fourth century[24]. J. Campos has now convincingly demonstrated that the translation is best placed in the late-fourth (or possibly the early-fifth) century[25].

The Fragment is clearly not a random collection of writings. Neither does the Fragmentist seem interested in communicating his personal opinion or in propagating anything particularly novel. His aim is to inform the reader that such is "the practice of 'the Catholic Church'"[26]. The text does emit a certain air of authority, although it must also be admitted that there are no overt clues that would allow us to take it as an official document of the Roman church[27]. The Fragmentist does not offer a mere list of the books that are "accepted" and "held in esteem" in the Church. He also adds a comment about the authorship and authenticity of some of the writings, a fact which has led several scholars to suggest a comparison between it and the so-called "New Testament Introduction" genre[28].

22. Cf. Hermas, *Mand.* 5,1 (μέλι-πικρόν). For an earlier discussion, see TREGELLES, *Canon Muratorianus* (n. 3), p. 49.

23. ZAHN, *Geschichte*, II.1 (n. 3), pp. 86-87 ("festina lente": "Eile mit Weile") and 142: χολὴν γὰρ μέλιτι, with alternatives μετὰ μέλιτος and σὺν μέλιτι (p. 86 n. 2). Zahn especially drew attention to the passage in Irenaeus, *Adv. Haer.* 3,17,4, in which it is said that it is wrong to mix the plaster of the doctrines of the Gnostics with the milk of the word of God: "In Dei lacte gypsum male miscetur" (ed. Rousseau-Doutreleau, SC 211, pp. 342-343: θεοῦ γάλακτι γύψος πονηρῶς μίγνυται). Cf. also ZAHN, *Hippolytus* (n. 12), pp. 61-62.

24. *Geschichte*, II.1 (n. 3), p. 131.

25. J. CAMPOS, *Epoca del Fragmento Muratoriano*, in *Helmantica* 11 (1960) 485-496. Cf. HMF (n. 2), pp. 12-13. See already KUHN, *Das Muratorische Fragment* (n. 3), pp. 3-16. HENNE, *Orthographe* (n. 6), pp. 301-302, on the other hand, situates the model from which the Fragment was copied (which is not necessarily the oldest version) in seventh-century, northern Gaul.

26. WESTCOTT, *Canon* (n. 3), p. 220.

27. See the discussion between Harnack and Koch (cf. above, n. 20).

28. So LIETZMANN, *Bücher* (n. 3), p. 53. More recently, see VON CAMPENHAUSEN, *Entstehung* (n. 3), p. 285 (for the quote see below, n. 42) and D. TROBISCH, *Die Entstehung der Paulusbriefsammlung. Studien zu den Anfängen christlicher Publizistik* (NTOA, 10), Freiburg, Universitätsverlag – Göttingen, Vandenhoeck & Ruprecht, 1989, p. 42.

One of the most famous disputes over the Fragment is that which was waged between Zahn and Harnack concerning the text's purpose[29]. Zahn was always reluctant to admit that the text was in any sense polemical. In his view, the formation of the canon was a gradual, intra-ecclesial process that began very early and took a long time to reach its culmination. The Church's canon was not the result of any crisis. For Harnack, the church formed its New Testament canon as a firm rebuttal to the acute danger it perceived in Marcion's attempts to formulate his own "edited version" of the accepted books, even if the details required some time to be finally worked out. Harnack's interpretation has never lacked critics. Early on, Lagrange duly noted that Harnack had greatly overestimated Marcion's impact[30]. Nevertheless, one cannot deny that Harnack's conclusions have been highly influential. In spite of his critique, Lagrange did recognize that the Fragment contains a polemical undertone. He saw that undertone as reflecting Hippolytus' struggle with Caius and his refutation of the Montanists, a group that was then active in Rome. Von Campenhausen even went so far as to characterize the Fragment as "ein fester Bollwerk gegen alle irgend bekannten Ketzerschriften und Ketzereien"[31]. And even Zahn finds a reminiscence of the Marcionite crisis in the way some apocryphal letters of Paul are rejected, even if he could not admit that it was this event which initially compelled the Fragmentist to make his composition[32].

It is hardly surprising that scholars who accept the traditional dating have used it to establish the Fragment as a core document for the recon-

29. For a good survey of this controversy as well as a solid attempt at appreciating the presuppositions and the implications of both positions, see now J. BARTON, *The Spirit and the Letter. Studies in the Biblical Canon*, London, SPCK, 1997, pp. 1-34 and 35-62 (Marcion). For Zahn, cf. also U. SWARAT, *Alte Kirche und Neues Testament. Theodor Zahn als Patristike*r, Wuppertal – Zürich, Brockhaus, 1991, pp. 253-352, esp. 264-267 (Canon Muratori).

30. LAGRANGE, *Histoire ancienne* (n. 3), p. 67: "C'est grossir démesurément l'influence que Marcion a pu avoir sur l'Église".

31. *Entstehung* (n. 3), p. 289. Cf. H. PAULSEN, *Die Bedeutung des Montanismus für die Herausbildung des Kanons*, in *VigChr* 32 (1978) 19-52: the final section of the Fragment with the list of authors and writings that are to be rejected "hat eine deutliche Aufgabe: sie soll den endgültigen Abschluss und die Begrenzung des Kanons unterstreichen" (p. 44).

32. That is how he interpreted the reference to "the heresy of Marcion" in l. 65. According to Zahn, it gives the reason why the Epistle to the Laodiceans and that to the Alexandrians ought to be rejected. The Fragmentist does not want to say that these were actually written or used by the Marcionites. He only wants to counter the opinion that they might be included in the readings of the church. To accomplish this, he reaches back to an argument that had already proven successful and claims that these letters contained Marcionite teaching (*Geschichte*, II.1 [n. 3], pp. 83-85). The second mention of Marcion in l. 83 is dismissed as a mistake of the translator reading μαρκιων for μακράν (p. 125; cf. 143 -όν).

struction of the early history of the canon. Harnack saw its primary significance in the answer it offered to the challenge posed by Marcion. Lagrange preferred to emphasize the fact that the content of the Fragment was largely identical with the canon that the Church would later accept[33]. Many scholars have expressed surprise at how little attention this important document has received in the ancient church. For example, in his *Geschichte*, Zahn observed with regard to the reception of the Fragment: "Ein Citat aus unserem Kanon sucht man in der vorhandenen altkirchlichen Literatur vergeblich. Dass Victorin von Pettau ihn gekannt hat, ist vielleicht wahrscheinlich zu nennen; aber citirt hat auch dieser ihn nicht"[34]. Later on, however, Zahn became less sceptical and, with characteristic zeal, argued that Victorinus († ca. 304) had known the Fragment and had borrowed from it while commenting upon the letters of Paul[35]. He also compared Victorinus' comment with one found in the writings of the twelfth-century Syriac author Dionysius bar Salibi and assigned by him to Hippolytus. Victorinus would thus offer indirect proof that Hippolytus was the author of the Fragment. Lagrange likewise concluded that Hippolytus certainly was a major source for Victorinus and that the latter no doubt did depend upon the Fragment[36]. Regarding Paul's letters the Fragmentist wrote: "cum ipse beatus apostolus Paulus sequens prodecessoris sui Iohannis ordinem nonnisi nomenatim septem ecclesiis scribat" (ll. 47-50) and "una tamen per omnem orbem terrae ecclesia diffusa esse dinoscitur. Et Iohannis enim in apocalypsin licet septem ecclesiis scribat tamen omnibus dicit" (ll. 55-59). This passage must have been the source of Victorinus' comment on Rev 1,20: "Septem autem ecclesiae, quas nominatim vocabulis suis vocat, ad quas epistolas facit, non quia illae solae <sint> ecclesiae aut principes, sed quod uni dicit omnibus dicit"[37]. In his comment on Rev 1,4 (not 1,20), Dionysius writes: "Hippolytus dicit: 'Scribens septem ecclesiis scripsit, sicut Paulus epistulas suas tredecim septem ecclesiis scripsit'". Interestingly, he also appends to this a reminder that Heb has not been mentioned. Perhaps he did this because Hippolytus thought it had been composed by Clement[38]. Victorinus' comment is much closer to the text of

---

33. "C'était exactement l'image du Canon d'aujourd'hui, sauf cette faveur accordée à l'Apocalypse de Pierre" (*Histoire ancienne* [n. 3], p. 84). Of course, this is an exaggeration. For Lagrange, however, it was less so: he conjectured that the Fragment originally did mention Heb and the Catholic Epistles.
34. *Geschichte*, II.1 (n. 3), p. 137.
35. *Hippolytus* (n. 12), p. 66.
36. *Histoire ancienne* (n. 3), pp. 81-82.
37. Ed. Dulaey, SC 423, p. 52.
38. For a Latin translation of the Syriac, see ed. Sedlacek, CSCO 101, pp. 2-3.

the Fragment than that of Dionysius. If the identification of Dionysius is correct, it might indicate that Hippolytus had access to the Fragment, but it certainly cannot be used to prove that he must have been its author. As a matter of fact, given the way Dionysius renders Hippolytus' view, the latter would have seriously misunderstood his own comment in the Fragment; he no longer maintains the distinction between the seven letters to the churches and the letters that were addressed to individuals, a decidedly conspicuous feature of both the Fragment and Victorinus[39]. Clearer evidence of the use of the Fragment can be found in a Prologue to Paul's letters that is preserved in four manuscripts of the eleventh and the twelfth century. The Prologue opens with the text of ll. 42-50 ("primo ... ordine tali"); towards the end there follows, in this order and as one bloc, the text of ll. 63-68 ("fertur ... congruit"), 81-85 ("Arsinofa ... constitutorem"), and 54-57 ("verum ... dinoscitur"). The passages are not identified as quotations. Because this version of the text is better than that of the eighth-century manuscript, it is probably best to maintain that it was not immediately derived from it[40].

Some might say that it is too optimistic to speak of a (relative) consensus. Still, that is exactly how many authors of New Testament Introductions and histories of canon formation have written about it. For example, W.G. Kümmel describes the document as follows: "(Dieses) Fragment in nicht immer verständlicher lat. Sprache gibt einen höchstwahrscheinlich aus dem Griechischen in schlechtes Latein übersetzten Text wieder, der am Anfang und vielleicht auch am Ende verstümmelt ist. Der unbekannte Verf. schreibt gegen Ende des 2. Jhr. in Rom; dass er der römische Gegenbischof Hippolyt war, ist unwahrscheinlich; es handelt sich auch schwerlich um ein offizielles römisches Dokument, wohl aber um ein autoritatives Verzeichnis der in der kath. Kirche 'angenommenen' und öffentlich zu lesenden Schriften unter ausdrücklicher Ablehnung von Schriften, denen andere kirchliche Christen oder Ketzer gleiche Würde beimessen wollen"[41].

39. *CommRev* 1,20: "Denique, sive in Asia sive in toto orbe, septem ecclesias omnes; et septenatim nominatas unam esse catholicam Paulus docuit. ... postea singularibus personis scripsit", with the "logical" explanation, "ne excederet numerum septem ecclesiarum" (ed. Dulaey, SC 423, pp. 52-54). On the exegetical work of Victorinus, see M. DULAEY, *Victorin de Poetovio, premier exégète latin* (Études augustiniennes, 139), Paris, Institut d'Études augustiniennes, 1993, 2 vols., esp. vol. I, pp. 160-161 and 305.

40. The text of the Prologue is edited in *Miscellanea Cassinese*, I.1, Montecassino, Pubblicazioni Cassinesi, 1897, pp. 1-5, and by A. HARNACK, *Excerpte aus dem Muratorischen Fragment (saec. xi et xii)*, in *TLZ* 23 (1898) 131-134, and again in *Miscellen* (TU, 20/3), Leipzig, Hinrich, 1900, p. 112. Text reproduced in HMF (n. 2), pp. 9-10. For further evidence of the use of the Fragment, see below, pp. 552-555.

41. *Einleitung in das Neue Testament*, Heidelberg, Quelle & Meyer, [21]1983, pp. 434-435 (ET, p. 492).

H. von Campenhausen, while recognizing that many hypotheses ("Wald der Hypothesen") have been advanced, gives a similar description: "Fest steht, dass das Muratorium ins Abendland gehört und nicht lange vor oder nach der Wende vom zweiten zum dritten Jahrhundert verfasst sein muss. Die namentlich von Harnack verfochten Annahme, es handle sich um ein amtliches Dokument des römischen Bischofs, lässt sich nicht halten und ist heute wohl allgemein aufgegeben. Solche offiziellen Festsetzungen beginnen erst anderthalb Jahrhunderte später und sind in unserer Zeit nirgends nachweisbar. Es handelt sich um die private Arbeit eines betont katholisch-kirchlich denkenden Theologen, der natürlich auch Bischof gewesen sein kann. Man hat besonders an Hippolyt als Verfasser gedacht; doch lassen sich auch gegen diese Zuschreibung erhebliche Bedenken anmelden. In jedem Fall dürfte der vorliegende Text nur die Übersetzung einer griechischen Vorlage darstellen. Seiner Art nach erinnert das Fragment an die 'Vorsatzstücke', wie sie in vielen alten Bibelhandschriften auftauchen, um den Leser nach Art unserer 'Einleitungen' kurz über die Entstehungsverhältnisse, den Verfasser und den Inhalt der einzelnen Bücher zu orientieren. ... Solche Texte sind stets rein sachlich gehalten, auch dort, wo sie dazu dienen sollen, eine bestimmte Sicht polemisch-apologetisch zu rechtfertigen"[42].

II. THE CHALLENGE

In recent years Albert C. Sundberg and Geoffrey M. Hahneman have challenged some of these conclusions. Their critique concentrates on two issues that had previously raised little discussion and that seemed all but settled: the Fragment's date and its Western provenance. Obviously, if such challenges were to succeed, they would have serious consequences for the interpretation of other aspects of the Fragment and of the formation history of the canon. In their opinion, the text was originally composed in the East in the fourth century (Hahneman: late fourth-century) at a time when several other such lists were in circulation. Sundberg has presented his views in a number of publications, most notably in a long article published in 1973[43]. His conclusions were criti-

---

42. *Entstehung* (n. 3), pp. 283-286.
43. *Canon Muratori. A Fourth Century List*, in HTR 66 (1973) 1-41 (henceforth: SCM); *Dependent Canonicity in Irenaeus and Tertullian*, in *Studia Evangelica* 3 (1964) 403-409; *Towards a Revised History of the New Testament Canon*, in *Studia Evangelica* 4 (1968) 452-461; *The Making of the New Testament Canon*, in C.M. LAYMAN (ed.), *The Interpreter's One-Volume Commentary on the Bible*, Nashville, TN, 1971, pp. 1216-1224; *The Biblical Canon and the Christian Doctrine of Inspiration*, in Interp 29 (1975) 352-371; *Canon of the New Testament*, in *The Interpreter's Dictionary of the Bible. Supplement Volume*, Nashville, TN, 1976, pp. 136-140.

cized, "demolished" according to one critic, by, among others, E. Ferguson, B.M. Metzger, and P. Henne[44]. Despite this "demolition", his arguments were taken up and further elaborated by Hahneman in his 1992 monograph *The Muratorian Fragment and the Development of the Canon*[45]. This work has elicited similar critical reactions from J.-D. Kaestli, C.E. Hill, and F. Bolgiani to name but three[46]. However, it must also be noted that, while support for Sundberg and Hahneman has remained quite marginal, their conclusions have generated some positive responses from various scholars. One of the first was N.A. Dahl who, in spite of having initially defended the anti-Marcionite character of the Fragment, later switched camps under Sundberg's influence[47]. In his Introduction R.F. Collins concludes, on the basis of Sundberg's "significant studies" and his "careful analysis", that "Canon Muratori represents a fourth-century Eastern list rather than the second-century Roman product which it is commonly thought to be"[48]. P. Vallin was also per-

44. E.F. FERGUSON, *Canon Muratori. Date and Provenance*, in *Studia Patristica* 17/2 (1982) 677-683. METZGER, *Canon* (n. 3), p. 193. P. HENNE, *La datation du Canon de Muratori*, in *RB* 100 (1993) 54-75.

45. See above, n. 2. The book is a revised version of the author's 1987 Oxford dissertation. See also ID., *More on Redating the Muratorian Fragment*, in *Studia Patristica* 19 (1989) 359-365.

46. J.-D. KAESTLI, *La place du* Fragment de Muratori *dans l'histoire du canon. À propos de la thèse de Sundberg et Hahneman*, in *Cristianesimo nella storia* 15 (1994) 609-634. C.E. HILL, *The Debate over the Muratorian Fragment and the Development of the Canon*, in *Westminster Theological Journal* 57 (1995) 437-452. F. BOLGIANI, *Sulla data del Frammento Muratoriano. A proposito di' uno studio recente*, in *Rivista di Storia e Letteratura Religiosa* 31 (1995) 461-471. See also the reviews in *JTS* 44 (1993) 691-697 (E. Ferguson); *CBQ* 56 (1994) 594-595 (M.W. Holmes); *CritRR* 7 (1994) 192-194 (B.M. Metzger); *NT* 36 (1994) 297-299 (J.K. Elliott); *ScotJT* 47 (1994) 418-419 (L.R. Wickham); *WTJ* 56 (1994) 437-438 (C.E. Hill); *Bijdragen* 56 (1995) 82-83 (M. Parmentier); *JEC* 3 (1995) 89-91 (R.F. Hull); *JEH* 46 (1995) 128-130 (J.N. Birdsall). Hill uses several examples to demonstrate that Hahneman has plagiarized passages from Gamble's monograph (cf. above, n. 3). Though a serious accusation, it, of course, does nothing to invalidate Hahneman's arguments.

47. Cf. *Welche Ordnung der Paulusbriefe wird vom Muratorischen Kanon vorausgesetzt?*, in *ZNW* 52 (1961) 39-53; and cf. his *The Origin of the Earliest Prologues to the Pauline Letters*, in *Semeia* 12 (1978) 233-277, p. 237.

48. *Introduction to the New Testament*, Garden City, NY, Doubleday, 1983, p. 35; cf. also p. 421. Collins draws special attention to Sundberg's analysis of the evidence Eusebius gives for Origen (HE 6,25,3-11), evidence which would prove that Origen did not possess a list of New Testament books and, most probably, had not even addressed the question. I have not been able to identify the reference in Collins to F.F. Bruce's being supportive of Sundberg. It is probably a mistake, as Bruce has continued to defend the traditional dating against Sundberg: see his *New Light on the Origins of the New Testament Canon*, in R.N. LONGENECKER – M.C. TENNEY (eds.), *New Dimensions in New Testament Study*, Grand Rapids, MI, Eerdmans, 1974, pp. 3-18, here 17 n. 59; *Some Thoughts on the Beginning of the New Testament Canon*, in *BJRL* 65 (1983) 57; compare *New Testament History*, London, Nelson, 1969, p. 36, and *Tradition Old and New*, Grand Rapids, MI, Zondervan, 1970, pp. 140-141.

suaded by Sundberg's arguments: "je tiens les hypothèses de Sundberg pour solides, et j'estime qu'une datation vers 300 est vraisemblable"[49]. G.A. Robbins is open for the possibility of a fourth-century dating[50], and R.M. Grant argues that what the Fragment says about John's gospel in ll. 9-16 may have been taken from Eusebius' *Church History*, a work mentioned as the source for a similar story by Jerome. Grant goes on to add that "other aspects of this account of the canon clearly suggest a date late in the fourth century or early in the fifth"[51]. In his survey of the formation of the canon L.M. McDonald repeatedly refers to Hahneman's views on the Fragment[52]. He is impressed by the "important objections" of Sundberg and Hahneman and he rightly observes that, depending on the period in which one situates the text, it becomes "either the 'final proof' or the 'Achilles' heel' of New Testament canonical research for evidence of a late second-century New Testament canon"[53]. A few passing references to the Fragment can be found in J. Barton's *The Spirit and the Letter*. In the first of these, Barton admits that the arguments of Hahneman are "generally convincing", while diplomatically adding that an early date for the Fragment is still not necessarily fatal to Sundberg's major thesis that the New Testament canon was not closed until the fourth century[54].

Before moving to a discussion of Sundberg's and Hahneman's principle arguments, it should be pointed out that both do accept some of the majority views regarding the Fragment. For Sundberg, it is an anonymous document that speaks with authority and was originally composed in Greek and translated into Latin in the late-fourth century[55]. Hahneman, whose presentation is somewhat more argumentative, agrees that the question of authorship is irresolvable and that Greek was the original

---

49. *La formation de la Bible chrétienne*, in C. THEOBALD (ed.), *Le Canon des Écritures. Études historiques, exégétiques et systématiques* (LD, 140), Paris, Cerf, 1990, pp. 189-236, here 221 (cf. 235-236).

50. *Eusebius' Lexicon of "Canonicity"*, in *SP* 25 (1993) 134-141, p. 140 ("an entirely different climate") and n. 16.

51. *Heresy and Criticism. The Search for Authenticity in Early Christian Literature*, Louisville, KY, Westminster – J. Knox, 1993, p. 110 (where he refers to Sundberg and Hahneman's dissertation). See also his review of HMF (n. 2) in *CH* 64 (1995) 638-640.

52. *Formation* (n. 29), pp. 212 and 213-215.

53. *Ibid.*, p. 209.

54. *Spirit and Letter* (n. 29), p. 10. A good example of how Sundberg's theories have divided scholarly opinion can be found in W.R. Farmer's and D.M. Farkasfalvy's *The Formation of the New Testament. An Ecumenical Approach*, New York, Paulist, 1983. The latter points to a twofold weakness in the hypothesis (p. 161 n. 1: "a theological preconception" on the closing of the canon and the incorrect interpretation of the time indication in l. 74). Elsewhere, Farmer writes that, thanks to Sundberg's criticism, "I have rested nothing on the *Muratorian Canon*" (p. 94 n. 83).

55. SCM (n. 43), pp. 2-3.

language. By way of example he discusses the evidence from ll. 68-70, a passage which contains comments on the Johannine epistles and on the Wisdom of Solomon. The confusion in the extant text is the result of an erroneous translation from the Greek[56]. From the faulty translation Hahnemann concludes that, "if the traditional dating of the Fragment is questioned", the document must have originated in the East, due to the fact that, in the West, Greek had been rapidly declining as the church's dominant language since the third century[57]. Sundberg rightly points out that there are no indications that the present translation is a revision of an earlier one made as an attempt to adapt it to the Vulgate[58]. Of course, if one accepts the traditional dating, one must recognize that it took a long time before the text was translated into Latin. About this one can only speculate, even though the Fragment was not unique in receiving this kind of treatment[59]. In fact, it could help to explain why the Fragment went practically unnoticed for so long. Moreover, it is probably not a coincidence that it was Victorinus of Pettau (an author who knew Greek and whose style, according to Jerome, had been very much influenced by that tongue) who probably quoted some of its lines in a (his own?) translation[60]. Finally, since Victorinus did not identify his source for the quotation, he was probably of no help in furthering the text's circulation.

Hahneman offers a detailed description of the contents of the manuscript that contains the Fragment[61]. Not all of the texts in the codex can be identified[62], but those that can be all belong to the fourth or the fifth century. While admitting that an early work, by way of exeception, may have been included in the codex[63], Hahneman finds in this fact corroboration for a late date. The codex contains (excerpts from) works by Eucherius of Lyons, Ambrosius, John Chrysostom, and probably Ambrosiaster. No specific guiding criterion has been found to explain these selections except for the fact that all these authors wrote in the second half

56. HMF (n. 2), pp. 13-16.
57. HMF, pp. 16-17.
58. SCM, p. 2 n. 8.
59. See the discussion regarding the date of the Latin translation of Irenaeus's Ἔλεγχος (Adv. Haereses), which some have assigned to the end of the fourth or the beginning of the fifth century.
60. De vir. ill. 74: "non aeque Latine ut Graece noverat. Unde opera eius grandia sensibus viliora videntur compositione verborum".
61. HMF, pp. 17-22.
62. Besides the Fragment, there is a short passage entitled De Abraham on f. 71-73 and the detached leaf (now f. 74 and interrupting the text of f. 73v-75) which contains an "Expositio fidei catholice".
63. HMF, p. 22: "It is of course quite possible, if the Fragment dates from the late-second century, that an earlier work was included with the several later ones".

of the fourth century. But if the Fragment had been translated at that time the compiler of the codex could easily have assumed that it was simply another contemporary document. Hahneman also adds a corroborative argument for his theory of an eastern provenance when he observes that "almost two-thirds" of its contents consists of material from eastern sources[64]. It is worth noting both that this estimation is, strictly speaking, less-than-inaccurate[65] and that three out of the four authors that are mentioned in the codex are Westerners. Like the Fragment itself (f. 10r-11r, in between fragments from Eucherius and Ambrosius), their works are to be found in the initial section of the codex.

III. THE SHEPHERD OF HERMAS AND THE DATE OF THE FRAGMENT

The information in the Fragment about the date of the Shepherd has always been regarded as a major argument for the traditional dating. Sundberg and Hahneman also recognize this fact. However, they go on to question both the "plain reading" and the common interpretation of the passage before offering an "alternative".

The text reads as follows: "Pastorem vero nuperrime temporibus nostris in urbe Roma Herma conscripsit sedente cathedra urbis Romae ecclesiae Pio episcopo fratre eius" (ll. 73-77). The Fragmentist apparently considered himself a contemporary of Pius († ca. 155). "Nuperrime" is usually taken to refer to the author. But, as a "viable" alternative[66], Sundberg suggests that the term may also serve to distinguish the Shepherd from the writings previously mentioned. The Shepherd was composed "most recently", i.e., in contrast to the clearly apostolic Revelation of John from l. 71[67]. Sundberg proposes a similar interpretation for the second half of the statement. "Temporibus nostris" does not have to mean "within our lifetime". It expresses the author's awareness of a distinction between the time of the apostles and his own post-apostolic era. That such awareness did exist can be documented from the sources[68]. Sundberg draws attention to a passage from Irenaeus in which it is argued that one should not speculate about the name of the Antichrist, since, if it were supposed to be known by the faithful, it would

---

64. HMF, p. 32.
65. Only f. 31v-75, not f. 1-31r, contain work by an eastern author; these folios mainly include the Latin version of the longer of Chrysostom's *Paraeneses ad Theodorum lapsum*.
66. SCM, pp. 9 and 11.
67. Sundberg's distinction between "very" or "most recent" is not really on point.
68. SCM, p. 9.

have been included in the Book of Revelation. About the latter, Irenaeus observes that this "was not even seen a long time ago, but almost in our own generation towards the end of the reign of Domitian" (Οὐδὲ γὰρ πρὸ πολλοῦ χρόνου ἑωράϑη, ἀλλὰ σχεδὸν ἐπὶ τῆς ἡμετέρας γενεᾶς, πρὸς τῷ τέλει τῆς Δομετιανοῦ ἀρχῆς. Latin: "neque enim ante multum temporis visum est, sed pene sub nostro saeculo, ad finem Domitiani imperii"[69]). Hahneman also qualifies Sundberg's proposal as an "alternative" which has a "precedent" in the passage from Irenaeus[70].

Sundberg and Hahneman do deserve credit for having asked whether an alternative interpretation might be possible, even though it is a question that, as they note, is not altogether new[71]. Since their reading is presented as an alternative, it follows that *in se* it is not a compelling argument against the traditional dating. Moreover, while some critics have accepted it as possible, they have been careful to qualify it as "not the most natural" interpretation[72]. But of course, if one accepts the validity of such an alternative, the traditional interpretation is inversely affected. This consideration is more than enough to necessitate a closer look at the plausibility of their proposal.

1. The authors that are quoted to illustrate the fact that in the second century a distinction was made between apostolic and post-apostolic age nowhere use (an equivalent of) the expression "temporibus nostris". Sundberg refers to Ignatius, *Eph.* 13; Polycarp, *Phil.* 3,9; and Hegesipp (Eusebius, HE 3,32,6-8 and 4,22,4)[73]. The first two would seem to be simple mistakes since no evidence relevant to his claim is to be found in these passages. In *Eph.* 11,2, Ignatius speaks of his own time as ἔσχατοι καιροί ("these are the last times"). He rather emphasizes the connection with the apostles by praying that he might "be found among the Christians of Ephesus, who have always been of one mind with the apostles in the power of Jesus Christ". In *Phil.* 9,1, Polycarp is also more interested in linking the suffering of his contemporaries Ignatius, Zosimus, and Rufus to that of Paul and the other apostles. Hegesipp speaks of the time when the Church was still "a pure and uncorrupted virgin" (3,32,7 and 4,22,4). It is said that this period ended under Traja-

69. *Adv. Haer.* 5,30,3. For the Greek, see Eusebius, HE 5,8,6.
70. HMF, pp. 34 and 36.
71. SCM, p. 8; HMF, pp. 34 n. 1 and 35 n. 5. ZAHN, *Geschichte* (n. 3), II.1, p. 54, had previously considered the alternative, proposed by Sundberg, with reference to the passage in Irenaeus. Zahn rejected it in favour of the traditional dating. Donaldson (*Critical History* [n. 16], pp. 209 and 212) opted for yet another alternative, assuming that the information was a later interpolation intended to discredit the Shepherd.
72. Cf. FERGUSON, *Canon Muratori* (n. 44), p. 678.
73. SCM, p. 9 n. 26-27. Only the last one in HMF, p. 35.

nus, when certain heretics instigated the martyrdom of Simeon (so 3,32,6 and 4,22,5: Thebouthis, an old candidate in the struggle to become James' successor). Or, as it is more generally formulated in 3,32,8, when "the sacred choir of the apostles" and "the generation of those who had been found worthy to hear through them the divine wisdom" had passed away. But Hegesipp never uses any such specific expression to characterize his own time[74], and, in 3,32,8 he remains rather vague about when exactly it was that this earliest era came to an end.

2. Hahneman favorably quotes Ferguson's warning that, in view of the state of the text, "arguments from the language employed in the Muratorian Fragment have limited value"[75]. He then applies it to the time indication given in l. 74[76]. We are in a better position with respect to the Irenaean evidence since for it we possess both the Latin translation and the original[77]. As Sundberg observes, the language of Irenaeus is similar to that of the Fragment, but it is not identical in the Latin just as it probably would not have been identical in the Greek original[78]. Sundberg reads ἐπὶ τῆς ἡμετέρας γενεᾶς as referring to the post-apostolic age in general, and Hahneman makes little of the evidence given by Ferguson to support his choice of translating the expression as "in our lifetime" (1 Clem. 5; Eusebius, HE 5,16,22)[79]. Yet, in view of Sundberg's invitation to consider an alternative meaning for "temporibus nostris" and in view of the similarity in language, one would think that this second alternative for ἐπὶ τῆς ἡμετέρας γενεᾶς would merit some serious consideration. In a sense, the problem with the passage from Irenaeus is similar to that of the Fragment. The major argument supporting Sundberg's and Hahneman's choice to read ἐπὶ τῆς ἡμετέρας γενεᾶς as "in the post-apostolic age" is that neither of them can see how Irenaeus, writing several decades after the date he gives for the composition of Revelation, can reasonably employ a phrase such as "almost in our lifetime". "It would be surprising that Irenaeus could use such language to describe a lapse of time approaching a century"[80]. Even granting the plausibility of this argument in Irenaeus's case, it still

74. Neither does Eusebius. In 3,31,6, he introduced the account about Simeon by referring to περί τε τῶν ἀποστόλων καὶ τῶν ἀποστολικῶν χρόνων, a phrase which possibly proposes a further distinction between the time of the apostles and that of their immediate successors (ed. Schwartz, GCS 9/1, p. 266).

75. FERGUSON, Canon Muratori (n. 44), p. 678.

76. HMF, p. 34.

77. See text at n. 69 above.

78. The plural "temporibus" would point to a different Greek term than γενεά. Zahn (Geschichte, II.1 [n. 3], p. 142) suggested ἐπὶ τῶν ἡμετέρων χρόνων.

79. HMF (n. 2), p. 35.

80. SCM (n. 43), p. 10.

does not follow that we can automatically apply it to the Fragmentist. The time lapse never comes close to a century regardless of which of the traditional dating suggestions one adopts. In short, it is futile to try to define what period of time is meant by οὐδὲ πρὸ πολλοῦ χρόνου, σχεδόν, or "nuperrime". Apparently, the author was not concerned with being very precise. The meaning of these terms largely depends on the point the author wants to make. Such indefinite indications are particularly amenable to hyperbolic use. In fact, this is precisely how they are used by Irenaeus (as well as by the Fragmentist). For Irenaeus, the question is not whether Revelation was composed in the time of the apostles (it obviously was). In fact, he nowhere contrasts his own time with that of the apostles. On the contrary, he links the two of them together. The expression ἐπὶ τῆς ἡμετέρας γενεᾶς is used very differently by Irenaeus from the way "temporibus nostris" would function in the Fragment according to Sundberg-Hahneman. According to Irenaeus, the name of the Antichrist is not to be found anywhere in recent literature. It is not even in the Book of Revelation (where it is hinted at; cf. *Adv. Haer.* 5,30,4), a work that was composed "almost in our lifetime". This is Irenaeus' primary point, even if he may have been "stretching the limits of 'almost'"[81] in the process.

3. In the reading proposed by Sundberg and Hahneman "nuperrime" and "temporibus nostris" are identical in meaning. According to them, they both refer to the same post-apostolic period as that in which the author lives. While it may well be plausible to maintain a distinction between the apostolic and the post-apostolic eras at the end of the second century, by the fourth century, it makes less sense. Furthermore, if this were the case, the expression "nuperrime temporibus nostris" begins to seem awkward and ambivalent, and even more than a little redundant. Sundberg observes that "the statement in the fragment is apologetic," and that "the author of the fragment is pleading a negative case against the canonicity of the Shepherd"[82]. Certainly all would agree that the Shepherd was written too late in order to belong to the apostolic era. However, if this was his point, it was unnecessary for the Fragmentist to add "nuperrime temporibus nostris". If the book was written under Pius it could obviously not be counted "among the prophets and the apostles" (ll. 79-80). Additionally, by inserting "nuperrime temporibus nostris" (not, "most/very recently, i.e., in our time", but, "most/very recently in our lifetime", as opposed to "less recently in our lifetime") the author has given a hint with respect to the time of the text's composition.

81. HMF, p. 35.
82. SCM, pp. 10-11.

4. Next, Hahneman looks to the information given by the Fragment about Hermas in order to attempt to show that its inaccurate understanding of the Shepherd provides yet another reason for rejecting the traditional date and for assigning it to the fourth century. Hahneman spends many pages to show that the date suggested for Hermas in the Fragment is unique and without corroboration from any other early source. According to him, the Fragment's data either fails to concur with, or even worse, is directly contradicted by internal evidence found in the Shepherd[83]. Some scholars have assumed that the Shepherd went through several editions, or only reached its final form over a long period of time and after receiving input from several redactors. The former of these alternatives is widely accepted. However, its acceptance is based upon literary-critical considerations and does not stem from any particular desire to make sense of the data found in the Fragment. The latter alternative remains contentious in so far as no single attempt at proving it has been widely received. Moreover, as Hahneman illustrates from the hypotheses put forward by S. Giet and W. Coleburne, there is little evidence to link any particular stage of the redaction to the time of Pius[84].

Hahneman lists four traditions regarding the Shepherd's authorship[85]. Two of these are derived from patristic sources. (a) That Clement of Rome was the author has been proposed by some since the nineteenth century. It is derived from the reference to one Clement found in *Vis.* 2,8,3[86]. (b) The marginal note in the Ethiopic version that claims it was composed by Paul the Apostle may be summarily rejected since it is probably the result of an absurd attempt to assimilate Hermas with the story of Paul-Hermes in Acts 14,12. (c) The identification of the author of the Shepherd with the Hermas mentioned by Paul in Rom 16,14 can be traced back to Origen and is repeated by Eusebius and Jerome[87]. For a number of reasons it has little to commend itself[88]. (d) That Hermas

---

83. HMF, p. 42. He lists the following: the mention of a certain Clement in *Vis.* 2,8,3, who may be Clement of Rome; the absence of a monarchical episcopacy (*Vis.* 2,8,3, in contrast with ll. 75-76 of the Fragment); the "great tribulation" of *Vis.* 1-4, which has been identified with the persecutions under Domitian or Trajan; and the silence about the Shepherd in other second-century authors (but cf. above). Cf. R.J. BAUCKHAM, *The Great Tribulation in The Shepherd of Hermas*, in *JTS* 25 (1974) 27-40. C. OSIEK, *The Second Century Through the Eyes of Hermas*, in *BTB* 20 (1990) 116-122.

84. See the discussion in HMF, pp. 44-45. Coleburne goes so far as to explicitly deny such a correlation, and none of the six authors or redactors he distinguishes can be dated that late.

85. HMF, pp. 46-48.

86. See esp. T. ZAHN, *Der Hirt des Hermas*, Gotha, Perthes, 1868, pp. 44-61 and 285-312.

87. Origen, *CommRom* 10,31; Eusebius, HE 3,6; Jerome, *De vir. ill.* 10.

88. Cf. HMF, pp. 47-51.

was the brother of Pius is found in the Fragment and in two other documents, the so-called *Liberian Catalogue*, a list of the bishops of Rome up to Liberius (352-366), and the anonymous *Carmen adversus Marcionitas*. Both of these works are of western origin and are to be dated in the fourth century (*Catalogue*) or later (*Carmen*).

It seems redundant to try to prove that the information about Hermas in the Fragment is incorrect. The arguments are well summed up by Hahneman[89]. It is also commonly agreed that this information serves (an) apologetic purpose(s). However, why an author would object to the Shepherd in precisely this fashion remains obscure. Harnack thought it had something to do with anti-Montanist polemics[90]. Hahneman surmises that the Fragmentist made up his data in order to oppose the tradition (mentioned by, and possibly originating from, Origen) which claimed an apostolic origin for the Shepherd[91]. If so, the Fragmentist would be merely another exponent of the critical assessment of the Shepherd that gradually became more widespread in the fourth century.

Hahneman argues that "it is unlikely that a contemporary witness would be so mistaken in information vital to its argument concerning the position of Hermas, which, moreover, other contemporary witnesses could or would dispute"[92]. But "contemporary" authors such as Irenaeus, Tertullian, and Clement of Alexandria, who all knew the Shepherd, provide no information about its author and, apparently, did not know a reliable tradition about its origins. Hahneman further argues that "there would be no need to deny so emphatically the apostolicity of Hermas in the Fragment, unless a tradition associating Hermas with an apostle was known"[93]. If so, one might have expected the Fragmentist to identify this tradition. His identification of Hermas differs from that of Origen, but this does not necessarily mean that he was arguing against the latter's suggestion. After all, his own proposal would probably have little effect as a critique of a tradition about Hermas and Paul that had already gained the support of Origen, Eusebius, and Jerome. Of course, weak arguments can be produced by anyone and at any time. However, what if the argument of controversy does not apply here at all? As a

89. HMF, p. 52.

90. *The Origin of the New Testament and the Most Important Consequences of the New Creation*, trans. J.R. Wilkinson (New Testament Studies, 6), London, Williams & Norgate, 1925, pp. 83-85.

91. Cf. HMF, pp. 51-52. "The purpose of linking Hermas with Pius in the Fragment appears to be to combat a supposed apostolicity for Hermas, a tradition which cannot be traced earlier than Origen" (p. 52); cf. p. 50: "Origen may be the ultimate source of the tradition".

92. HMF, p. 52.

93. HMF, p. 51.

matter of fact, there is no evidence that the Fragmentist wanted to discredit the Hermas-Paul hypothesis or any other tradition about the work's origin. He obviously has no problem with the content of the work, since he permits it to be read in private[94]. Further, he does not link it with heretics as he does with the writings that are rejected in ll. 64-65 and 81-85. The question is only whether the Shepherd can be read in church. The same question is addressed in the preceding lines with regard to the Apocalypse of Peter, but the situation is not identical. With regard to the latter composition, the Fragmentist merely notes the lack of consensus "among us" (ll. 72-73 "quam quidem ex nostris legi in ecclesia nolunt"). For the Shepherd, he concludes that it should not be read in church. He may have known that this was going on, and, if so, that may supply him with the motive for including the information on the Shepherd. But he does not say that anyone had in fact suggested this, much less that it had actually happened in his community. The Fragmentist acknowledges that the case of the Apocalypse of Peter was being debated. For the Shepherd he explains why it should not be read in church: it was written only "nuperrime temporibus nostris" under Pius and therefore cannot be reckoned with the Prophets and the Apostles.

5. In surveying the reception of the Shepherd in the early church[95], Hahneman observes that the work is generally positively regarded in the West. Irenaeus quotes it together with several undisputed books and calls it ἡ γραφή (*Adv. Haer.* 4,20,2; cf. Eusebius, HE 5,8,7). The anonymous author of a sermon *Adversus Aleatores* (probably ca. 300) even speaks of it as "scriptura divina" (c. 2)[96]. The one exception is Tertullian, who, in his Montanist phase, criticizes the work with his habitual rhetorical flourish[97]. In the East, it was frequently quoted by Clement of Alexandria and considered as "divinitus inspirata" by Origen[98]. Later, Origen did note that some had doubts about the work, but such was clearly never his own position. "What exactly occasioned this new-

---

94. On the private reading and use of Christian books, see H.Y. GAMBLE, *Books and Readders in the Early Church. A History of Early Christian Texts*, New Haven, Yale University Press, 1995, pp. 231-237 (the passage from the Fragment is mentioned on p. 235).

95. See J.R. HARRIS, *Hermas in Arcadia*, in *JBL* 21 (1887) 69-83, repr. in ID., *Hermas in Arcadia and Other Essays*, Cambridge, UP, 1896. P. HENNE, *Canonicité du Pasteur d'Hermas*, in *Revue Thomiste* 90 (1990) 81-100. C. OSIEK, *Shepherd of Hermas. A Commentary* (Hermeneia), Minneapolis, MA, Fortress, 1999, pp. 4-7.

96. Ed. Harnack, TU 5/1, p. 15.

97. *De Pudicitia* 10,12: "sed cederem tibi, si scriptura Pastoris, quae sola moechos amat, divino instrumento meruisset incidi, si non ab omni concilio ecclesiarum, etiam vestrarum, inter apocrypha et falsa iudicaretur" (ed. Dekkers, CCSL, 2, p. 1301). Cf. J.E. MORGAN WYNE, *Hermas and Tertullian*, in *Studia Patristica* 21 (1989) 154-157.

98. Clement, *Ecl. Proph.* 45; *Strom.* 1,17; 2,9; 6,6. Origen, *CommRom* 10,31.

found hesitation in Origen is not known"[99]. Hahneman speculates about possible acquaintance with the Montanist controversy in the West, but finally leaves the question open. Comments similar to those made by Origen can be found in Eusebius, who places the Shepherd among the spurious works (HE 3,25,5 νόθοι), or among those that are not universally acknowledged (HE 3,3,7, probably including the Shepherd). In the list of NT writings of the Codex Claromontanus, the Shepherd is one of four writings marked with a line and occurring at the end of the list (the other are Barnabas, Acts of Paul, and Apocalypse of Peter)[100]. If the gap of one and a half column between the text of the New Testament in the Codex Sinaiticus and its version of Barnabas and the Shepherd means anything, it could indicate hesitation on the part of the copyist. Athanasius' opinion seems to have become more conservative over the years since, in his later writings, he officially excluded the Shepherd from the canon, while continuing to regard it as being useful for catechesis[101]. Jerome likewise vacillates: in different contexts he labels it as "not canonical", "valuable", "often quoted as authoritative in the past", and "read in public in Greece"[102]. Rufinus places the Shepherd in the intermediary class of the "ecclesiastical books" of the Old and the New Testament. By this he meant that it could be read in church but could not be quoted in doctrinal matters[103]. Hahneman concludes from the evidence that, beginning with Eusebius, the Shepherd is systematically relegated to a second class status in the East. Consequently, "the statements about it in the Fragment would not be particularly remarkable if the latter was dated in the fourth century in the East"[104].

Of course, simply being "remarkable" in a particular historical context is no criterion for dating a work. However, if it is used as a criterion, it could well be that the comment of the Fragment was less remarkable in the West at the turn of the third century than it would have been in the East at the end of the fourth. The Fragment speaks positively about the content of the Shepherd, as do Irenaeus, Clement of Alexandria, and the pre-Montanist Tertullian. It does not say that the question it addresses, i.e., whether the Shepherd can be read in public, is currently under dispute. Apparently his contemporaries had not dealt with it. Perhaps the

---

99. HMF, p. 65.
100. See the text in ZAHN, *Geschichte*, II.1 (n. 3), pp. 157-159. The codex was produced in the West (Sardinia?) in the sixth century, but the catalogue probably was compiled in the fourth century in the East (HMF, p. 141).
101. *Festal Letter 39*, 7.
102. *CommKings*, prol., and esp. *De vir. ill.* 10.
103. *CommSymb* 38.
104. HMF, pp. 99-100.

judgement generated some discussion without leaving any clear traces in the West. As for the East, the attestations of the various authors generally agree. (a) They emphasize that the book is useful, if only in certain respects (Athanasius, Rufinus). (b) They also express some hesitation about reading the book, with both Athanasius and Jerome occasionally voicing Origen's "si cui placeat illum legere librum"[105]. (c) When it came to the question of how to officially "rank" the Shepherd in comparison with other normative writings, they agreed to place it in an intermediary class. Most importantly, they made this distinction clearly and explicitly[106]. (d) Finally, Jerome and Rufinus both know that the Shepherd was read publicly, a policy they never opposed, at least in principle.

If it is dated in the fourth century, the Fragment assumes a remarkable, if not a genuinely exceptional, position on all these issues. (a) It never comments on the question in what sense the book is or is not useful. (b) It expresses no hesitation with regard to private reading; as a matter of fact, this is to be encouraged. (c) The Fragment does not use "technical terminology" to characterize the various books, as would become common practice with Eusebius. The distinction between the books that "we receive" and those "we do not receive", is, at best, a primitive attempt at such a division. One can hardly speak of a "middle class" at this stage; there is simply no formal or official label for works like the Shepherd. (d) Contrary to Jerome and Rufinus, the Fragment explicitly forbids the public reading of the Shepherd and bases its decision on criteria that, apparently, were never applied in such contexts in the East.

6. The *Liberian Catalogue* and the *Carmen adversus Marcionitas* both give basically the same information on the provenance of Hermas as does the Fragment. The text of the Catalogue is slightly closer to the wording of the Fragment[107]. The Catalogue contains the list of the bishops of Rome from Peter until Liberius († 366). It is one of several documents of the so-called "Chronographer of 354"[108]. The list was probably composed in several stages. The first part (up to Urbanus, † 230) contains only the names of the bishops and the number of years of their

---

105. *CommMt* 2,53; Athanasius, *Festal Letter 39*, 11,4; Jerome, *CommHos* 7,9.

106. This is why Hahneman regards Eusebius' writings as the watershed in the evaluation of the Shepherd (see HMF, p. 70).

107. "Sub huius [Pii] episcopatu frater eius Ermas librum scripsit in quo mandatum continetur, quae [v.l. quod] ei precepit angelus, cum venit ad illum in habitu pastoris"; ed. T. MOMMSEN, *Chronica minora saec. IV, V, VI, VII* (MGH Auct. Ant., 9/1), Berlin, Weidmann, 1892, I, p. 74. *Carmen* 3,294-295: "post hunc [Hyginus] deinde Pius, Hermas cui germine frater, angelicus pastor, cui tradita verba locutus ..."; ed. K. POLLMANN, *Das Carmen adversus Marcionitas* (Hypomnemata, 96), Göttingen, Vandenhoeck & Ruprecht, 1991, p. 148.

108. The name is given by Mommsen in his edition.

episcopacy along with the names of the emperors under whose reign they took office (except for the notes on Pius and the martyrdom of Peter). For the period from Pontianus († 235) to Lucius († 254) it contains more elaborate historical notes. The next part (up to Marcus, † 336) again lacks such notes. On the other hand, there is a rather long note for Julius, the second from the last to be named († 352). This last update is probably to be placed under his successor Liberius, who, since no year of death is given, was apparently still serving his community. Lightfoot argued that the note on Pius was introduced by Hippolytus – the alleged author of the Fragment –, who had edited an older form of the initial sections of the Catalogue. The reason for this insertion is lost. Hahneman rightly wonders why Hippolytus would have bothered about Pius, while not seizing the opportunity to discredit his opponents Callistus and Zephyrinus[109]. He thinks the note on Pius was probably added in ca. 354 by the last editor, who, incidentally, was also responsible for the information that Peter and Paul suffered martyrdom on the same day, a tradition that was never made explicit before the second half of the fourth century[110]. Hahneman does not say that the editor added the information on Pius from the Fragment, though this would be a most plausible hypothesis. Even so, it still offers no proof that the Fragment would be of a date similar to the Catalogue. The reason for the note in the Catalogue remains obscure. The highly conjectural claim that its author was responding to Origen, could, if true, also be assigned to the redactor who added the section (with many notes) on the years 230-254[111]. Jerome also knows of the information about Peter and Paul, but it clearly did not originate with him. Their death had been conjoined since Clement (*1 Clem.* 5). Dionysius thought they suffered martyrdom κατὰ τὸν αὐτὸν καιρόν (HE 2,25,8). In the *Carmen*, which figures among the works of Tertullian but is undoubtedly of a later date[112], the note on Hermas also occurs in a list of bishops (from Peter to Anicetus) that is quoted to establish the date of Cerdo's and Marcion's arrival in Rome. Hahneman thinks that the poem either "directly or indirectly"[113] depends upon the Catalogue, since it agrees with it in separating Cletus and Anencletus[114].

109. His own fate is mentioned in the note on Pontianus.
110. HMF, p. 57.
111. Cf. HMF, p. 56.
112. While it has been dated as early as the mid-third and as late as the sixth century, it is now commonly placed after Nicea (HMF, pp. 59-60). Hahneman argues for 475-525 (p. 63).
113. HMF, p. 59.
114. The differences from the Catalogue (Clement after Cletus-Anencletus, and Anicetus after Pius) may be explained as corrections inserted in order to bring the list into agreement with Irenaeus (cf. Eusebius).

In other words, the *Carmen* should not be regarded an independent witness.

7. Lines 74-76 are crucial[115] to the argument in favour of the traditional dating of the Fragment, although additional support has been found in other passages, especially ll. 81-85, that provides us with names of individuals. With regard to the latter, Hahneman rightly notes that "the date of the Fragment cannot be confidently deduced from these references alone"[116]. Interpretation of this final section of the Fragment is difficult both because of suspected textual corruptions and/or *lacunae* and because no certainty can be gained regarding some of the names[117]. Hahneman reads "Miltiades" for "mitiadis" and accepts the reference to Marcion in l. 83 as genuine[118]. He considers the possibility (already suggested by Credner) that "Arsinoi" is a corruption of "Bardesanis" who is mentioned together with Marcion and/or Valentinus by both Ephraem and Theodoretus[119]. Ferguson observed that all the names that can be identified with some certainty are of second-century heretical authors[120]. Hahneman has a fourfold comment. (a) Much later authors could very well mention second-century authors. (b) The list's guiding principle may not have been that of a common date, but rather the fact that all those mentioned had authored books. (c) It would require "a sufficient period of time" for these heretical books to be known and discussed in Christian communities. (d) The list may be incomplete and may well have contained more recent authors[121]. However, the original content and length of the section remains a matter of speculation. It is obvious that the Fragment deals with books and authors; but this fact has no bearing on the question of whether or not the list also contained the names of third- or fourth-century authors. Valentinus and Marcion had been the subject of much controversy in several communities before even the earliest conceivable date of the Fragment. Furthermore, when later authors do refer to the primeval heretics, they tend to concentrate on the "important" ones (like Marcion and Valentinus). In many cases,

---

115. Hahneman calls it "the crux" (HMF, pp. 30 and 34).
116. HMF, p. 30.
117. The version of the Fragment in the Benedictine Prologues offers no help for reconstructing the original. However, it does provide evidence that the confusion was probably not due to the eighth-century copyist.
118. HMF, pp. 28-29.
119. This would go well with an eastern provenance. Cf. CREDNER, *Zur Geschichte* (n. 3), p. 91. It is more common to take the word not as a proper name, but as a corruption of "Arsinoite", a reference to Valentinus' birthplace. Cf. TREGELLES, *Canon Muratorianus* (n. 3), pp. 64-65.
120. *Canon Muratori* (n. 44), p. 681.
121. HMF, pp. 29-30.

they are not as interested in their writings as much as they are in their prototypical character as heretics. This certainly does not seem to be the case in the Fragment[122].

The information in the Fragment about the date of the Shepherd is most certainly incorrect. With good reason Hahneman can observe that "the Fragment is making a grave misstatement on a point essential to its argument for the rejection" of the Shepherd, and that "it is more reasonable to assume that the whole statement in the Fragment is in error"[123]. But there is no reason to suppose that such a statement could only be made at a later date. As to the time reference itself, Sundberg and Hahneman are most probably mistaken with their interpretation. Unfortunately it is not the only problem with the Fragment.

IV. An Anomaly in the Second Century

In a 1968 article Sundberg gave readers an overview of his understanding of how the New Testament canon was formed. He distinguished three stages: (a) Christian literature becomes Scripture; (b) parts of this corpus are brought together in closed sub-collections; and (c) canonical lists are made of all writings that have been formally accepted as canonical[124]. Hahneman takes up this outline and connects with it three distinct literary forms: the comment, the collection, and the catalogue[125]. Comments deal with the authority of certain writings as Scripture, but "there is usually no intention of completeness"[126]. Collections concentrate on certain groups of writings (the gospels, Paul's letters). They are "specific, but not final", and thus "by definition not closed"[127]. It is important to note that, on this point, Hahneman consciously departs from the Sundberg model, which, at this stage, includes "closed sub-collections"[128]. The catalogue is the final and fixed list of the writings that comprise the canon. The Fragment is "a good example" of this third category[129]. The movement has "generally" been from comment, to collection, to catalogue[130].

---

122. That the Fragmentist was most probably mistaken in his information about Marcion does not argue against the traditional date. Valentinus was known to have composed a Psalm book (so Tertullian and Origen). Cf. ZAHN, *Geschichte*, II.1 (n. 3), p. 121.
123. HMF, p. 43.
124. *Revised History* (n. 43).
125. HMF, pp. 87-90.
126. HMF, p. 87. Tertullian's *Adv. Marc.* 4,5 is quoted as a good example.
127. HMF, p. 87. He refers to the Marcionite Prologues to the Pauline letters (cf. below, n. 174).
128. Ctr. HMF, p. 89: "collections remain 'open'".
129. HMF, p. 88. It also often mentions (some of the) writings that are to be rejected.
130. HMF, p. 89.

Two further observations are worth noting here. First, Hahneman does not seem to exclude the possibility that, within this "movement", one author already works with "the concept of a fixed boundary"[131] at a time that others have not yet reached this stage. A second and equally important modification to this model made by Hahneman is the idea that this concept of "boundary" does not preclude that the status of a particular book or writing may remain "uncertain"[132]. Thus, it is possible that definite conclusions were reached regarding certain writings (or groups of writings) before they were reached for others.

Hahneman expends a lot of energy in attempting to demonstrate that the Fragment offers anachronistic and irregular evidence with respect to the earliest history of the formation of the canon. The major difficulty is that it offers too much too soon, or, in Hahneman's words, that "the Fragment, on its traditional dating, is not only an anomaly in contents and concepts, but also in form"[133]. It is "a catalogue of New Testament works"[134] from the era in which only sub-collections are attested. As it stands, this quotation is in need of clarification. "Anomaly" is the keyword in assessing the evidence. In many respects, the Fragment is a unique late-second or early-third century document. By labelling it as an anomaly, however, one contends that it cannot be explained within this historical context. It also implies that this particular context is uniform and homogeneous throughout the church, not to mention the fact that the anomalous document cannot be regarded as an indicator of a progression towards another stage. In what precise sense, then, is the Fragment an anomaly? In what way ought this notion perhaps be corrected? Hahneman compares what the Fragment has to say about various groups of writings (gospels, letters, apocalypses) with the evidence of the second and third century.

A. *The Fourfold Gospel*[135]

The Fragmentist accepts the four (soon-to-be) canonical gospels and does not speak of any others[136]. He acknowledges that there are differences between these gospels as to the "principia", but adds that this

131. HMF, p. 89.
132. HMF, p. 89, with reference to the *Apocalypse of Peter*.
133. HMF, p. 131.
134. HMF, p. 89.
135. See K.L. CARROLL, *The Creation of the Fourfold Gospel*, in *BJRL* 37 (1954-55) 68-77. EHRHARDT, *Gospels* (n. 21). R. MORGAN, *The Hermeneutical Significance of Four Gospels*, in *Interp* 33 (1979) 376-388. G.N. STANTON, *The Fourfold Gospel*, in *NTS* 43 (1997) 317-346, and in the present volume pp. 353-370. Cf. also VON CAMPENHAUSEN, *Entstehung* (n. 3), pp. 201-207. GAMBLE, *Canon* (n. 3), pp. 24-35.
136. There is no reason to suspect that the two gospels preceding the references to Luke and John (cf. ll. 2 and 9) were not the gospels of Matthew and Mark.

poses no problem for the faithful, since "by the one sovereign Spirit all things have been declared in all" (ll. 19-20). He specifically mentions the following subjects: the nativity[137], the passion, the resurrection, Jesus' conversation with his disciples, and his double parousia, the first in humility and the second in regal power and glory.

Though he realizes that it is not the whole of the issue, Hahneman goes to great lengths to show that oral tradition and "non-canonical" tradition and writings, or experiments in gospel harmonization, retained much of their influence throughout the second century and into the first decades of the third[138]. He correctly observes that one should distinguish "between acquaintance with the four gospels and the Fourfold Gospel canon"[139], and argues that this canon can only be said to have existed when the evidence for it becomes indisputable. Hahneman is critical of attempts to date the formation of the gospel canon early in the second century[140]. He also wisely refuses to argue from the so-called anti-

137. Apparently, the Fragmentist did not believe a problem existed with respect to Mk and Jn.

138. HMF, pp. 93-100. On oral tradition, see W.A. LÖHR, *Kanonsgeschichtliche Beobachtungen zum Verhältnis von mündlicher und schriftlicher Tradition im zweiten Jahrhundert*, in *ZNW* 85 (1994) 234-258. McDONALD, *Formation* (n. 3), pp. 138-142. A.D. BAUM, *Papias, der Vorzug der* Viva Vox *und die Evangelienschriften*, in *NTS* 44 (1998) 144-151.

139. HMF, p. 94.

140. HMF, p. 93 (with reference to Goodspeed and Knox). See now again T. HECKEL, *Vom Evangelium des Markus zum viergestaltigen Evangelium* (WUNT, 120), Tübingen, Mohr, 1999, p. 353 and passim (with a critique of Hahneman's dating of the Canon Muratori on pp. 339-354). Heckel reckons with "eine Entstehungszeit der Sammlung etwa zwischen 110 und 120 n.Chr". He notes, however, "Doch diese Deutung muss mit Wahrscheinlichkeiten arbeiten, die bei anderen Wertungen auch zu abweichenden Deutungen führen könnten. Dass Papias das Lk- und das Joh-Ev kennt, lässt sich m.E. zwar plausibel machen, nicht aber beweisen". But is not the lack of clear evidence fatal for the hypothesis? As for Hahneman, he almost completely overlooks the possibility that this earlier period may provide information regarding the transformation of Christian writings into Scripture and the possible implications of this process for evaluating the Fragment. Cf. the surveys in FRANK, *Sinn der Kanonbildung* (n. 3), 19-32 ("Der Zeit bis Justin"), 133-178 (Tatian, Hegesippus, Melito, Athenagoras, Theophilus). SAND, *Kanon* (n. 3), pp. 40-75. METZGER, *Canon* (n. 3), pp. 39-74 (Apostolic Fathers), 114-119 (Tatian and Theophilus), 143-148 (Justin). McDONALD, *Formation* (n. 3), pp. 142-153 and 161-164. HECKEL, *Evangelium* (above, this n.), pp. 219-265 (Papias), 286-308 (Gospel of Peter), 309-328 (Justin), and 330-334 (Marcion). Among others, see also R.M. GRANT, *Scripture and Tradition in St Ignatius of Antioch*, in *CBQ* 25 (1963) 322-325. C.H. COSGROVE, *Justin Martyr and the Emerging Christian Canon*, in *VigChr* 36 (1982) 209-232. É. JUNOD, *Choix des Écritures chrétiennes et clôture du canon*, in *LumVie* 34 (1985) 5-17. M.R. GREENWALD, *The New Testament Canon and Mishnah as Consolidations of Knowledge in the Second Century*, in *SBL SP* 1987, pp. 244-254. M. PESCE, *La trasformazione dei documenti religiosi. Dagli scritti protocristiani al canone neotestamentario*, in *VetChr* 26 (1989) 307-326. Y.-M. BLANCHARD, *Aux sources du canon, le témoignage d'Irénée* (Cogitatio fidei, 175), Paris, Cerf, 1993, pp. 21-110. F. BOVON – E. NORELLI, *Dal kerygma al canone. Lo statuto degli scritti neotestamentari nel secondo secolo*, in *Cristianesimo nella Storia* 15 (1994) 525-540. BAUM, *Papias* (n. 138).

Marcionite and Monarchian Prologues[141]. Irenaeus is the first to clearly state that "it is not possible that the Gospels can be either more or fewer in number than they are" (*Adv. Haer.* 3,11,8: "Neque autem plura numero quam haec sunt neque rursus pauciora capit esse Evangelia")[142]. He would be the "earliest promoter" of the Fourfold Gospel canon[143]. Tertullian may be another witness when he argues, against Marcion's defense of a single (i.e., "Luke-only") gospel canon, "denique nobis fidem ex apostolis Iohannes et Matthaeus insinuant, ex apostolicis Lucas et Marcus instaurant"[144]. Both Clement and Origen knew and accepted the notion of the Fourfold Gospel[145], even though they also quoted from

141. Cf. D. DE BRUYNE, *Préfaces de la Bible latine*, Namur, Godenne, 1912, ²1920. ID., *Les plus anciens prologues latins des Évangiles*, in *RBén* 40 (1928) 193-214. A. HARNACK, *Die ältesten Evangelien-Prologe und die Bildung des Neuen Testamentes*, in *Sitzungsberichte der Preussischen Akademie der Wissenschaften*, phil.-hist. Klasse, 24 (1928) 322-341. W.F. HOWARD, *The Anti-Marcionite Prologues to the Gospels*, in *ExpT* 47 (1935-36) 534-538. J. REGUL, *Die antimarcionitischen Evangelienprologe* (AGLB, 6), Freiburg, Herder, 1969, pp. 89-111, 146-148, 160-163. On the Monarchian Prologues, cf. P. CORSSEN, *Monarchianische Prologe zu den vier Evangelien* (TU 15/1), Leipzig, Hinrichs, 1896. R.G. HEARD, *The Old Gospel Prologues*, in *JTS* 6 (1955) 1-16. REGUL, *Evangelienprologe*, pp. 207-262. Cf. HMF, pp. 107-108. – The former, which have been dated ca. 160-180, are most certainly not from the same hand. They were written sometime between the end of the second (Mk) and the fourth or the fifth century (Jn) and contain no information on Mt (only Mk, Jn, and Lk, from the third or early-fourth century). The latter seem to stem from Priscillianist circles and, therefore, should be dated in the late-fourth or early-fifth century. Cf. F.L. CROSS, *The Priscillianist Prologues*, in *ExpT* 48 (1937) 188-189. A.S. JOHNSON, *The Disorder of Books. Priscillian's Canonical Defense of Apocrypha*, in *HTR* 93 (2000) 135-160.

142. οὔτε πλείονα τὸν ἀριθμὸν οὔτε ἐλάττονα ἐνδέχεται εἶναι τὰ εὐαγγέλια (ed. Rousseau-Doutreleau, SC 211, pp. 160-161 and SC 210, 114-115, with some slight differences among the various Greek witnesses).

143. HMF, p. 109. This passage from Irenaeus explains why, in 3,1,1, he had mentioned four gospels only. On Irenaeus' gospel canon, see esp. W.L. DULIÈRE, *Le Canon néotestamentaire et les écrits chrétiens approuvés par Irénée*, in *La Nouvelle Clio* 6 (1954) 199-224. VON CAMPENHAUSEN, *Entstehung* (n. 3), pp. 213-244. D. FARKASFALVY, *Theology of Scripture in St. Irenaeus*, in *RBén* 78 (1968) 319-333. FRANK, *Sinn der Kanonbildung* (n. 3), pp. 189-202. A. ZIEGENAUS, *Kanon. Von der Väterzeit bis zum Gegenwart* (Handbuch der Dogmengeschichte, I/3a.2), Freiburg–Basel–Wien, Herder, pp. 15-23. METZGER, *Canon* (n. 3), pp. 153-156. MCDONALD, *Formation* (n. 3), pp. 164-169. BLANCHARD, *Aux sources du canon* (n. 140), pp. 196-229. T.C. SKEAT, *Irenaeus and the Four-Gospel Canon*, in *NT* 34 (1992) 194-199. STANTON, *The Fourfold Gospel* (n. 135), pp. 320-322.

144. *Adv. Marc.* 4,2,2 (ed. Moreschini, SC 456, p. 68). Cf. VON CAMPENHAUSEN, *Entstehung* (n. 3), pp. 318-337, esp. 326; ZIEGENAUS, *Kanon* (n. 143), pp. 26-32.

145. Hahneman refers to *Strom.* 3,13,93,1 and *HomLk* 1,1. In discussing a quotation by Julius Cassianus (ἔφη ὁ κύριος) that there will no longer be male or female, Clement replies: πρῶτον μὲν οὖν ἐν τοῖς παραδεδομένοις ἡμῖν τέτταρσιν εὐαγγελίοις οὐκ ἔχομεν τὸ ῥητόν, ἀλλ᾽ ἐν τῷ κατ᾽ Αἰγυπτίους (ed. Stählin, GCS 15, p. 238). With this remark he also disqualifies another quotation from the same gospel mentioned in *Strom.* 3,9,63,2-3. For Origen, cf. *HomLk* 1,1: "Hoc quod ait: conati sunt, latentem habet accusationem eorum, qui absque gratia Spiritus sancti ad scribenda evangelia prosiluerunt. Matthaeus quippe et Marcus et Iohannes et Lucas non sunt conati scribere, sed Spiritu sancto pleni scripserunt evangelia", and 1,2: "Sed in his omnibus nihil aliud probamus

apocryphal writings and tradition[146]. This ambivalence may indeed indicate that the concept was not "one of long standing"[147]. But the crucial things are that they do acknowledge it, that they do occasionally use it in their argumentation, and, above all, that they do formulate it as a principle, something that they chose not to do with regard to their rather liberal use of "non-canonical" material. Hahneman refers to the much-quoted conclusion of R.P.C. Hanson on Origen's attitude to the canon: "he will accept as Christian evidence any material that he finds convincing or appealing"[148]. However, it should be noted that it is Hanson who formulates this "rule", not Origen, and that it was derived from the way Origen actually dealt with the gospel tradition. Moreover, Hahneman would have given his readers a more legitimate picture of the situation if he had extended his quote of Hanson so as to include the next sentence as well. In it Hanson observes that Origen and Clement do not know "a list of canonical works, apart from the list of four Gospels".

The concept of the Fourfold Gospel did not necessarily have to be "widely accepted" or "firmly established"[149] to be received and defended by the Fragmentist. His position may be "surprising"[150], it is not an anomaly. Hahneman finds evidence in Irenaeus and Tertullian (but not in the Fragment) that the concept was a fairly "recent development" which took shape in a polemical context[151]. Their polemics were directed against Marcion and other heretics (so Irenaeus) and, perhaps, also against others within the church[152]. This is clearly the case for

nisi quod ecclesia, id est quatuor tantum evangelia recipienda" (the Greek is also preserved; see ed. Rauer, GCS 35, pp. 4-5).

146. See VON CAMPENHAUSEN, *Entstehung* (n. 3), pp. 337-354 (Clement) and 354-376 (Origen); ZIEGENAUS, *Kanon* (n. 143), pp. 37-44 and 44-53. J. RUWET, *Clément d'Alexandrie. Canon des Écritures et apocryphes*, in *Bib* 29 (1948) 391-408. J.A. BROOKS, *Clement of Alexandria as a Witness to the Development of the New Testament Canon*, in *Second Century* 9 (1992) 41-55. A. LE BOULLUEC, *De l'usage de titres "néotestamentaires" chez Clément d'Alexandrie*, in M. TARDIEU (ed.), *La formation des canons scripturaires*, Paris, Cerf, 1992, pp. 191-202. J. RUWET, *Les "Antilegomena" dans les oeuvres d'Origène*, in *Bib* 23 (1942) 18-42. W.G. OLIVER, *Origen and the New Testament Canon*, in *RestQ* 31 (1989) 13-26. E. BAMMEL, *Die Zitate aus den Apokryphen bei Origenes*, in R.J. DALY (ed.), *Origeniana Quinta* (BETL, 105), Leuven, University Press – Peeters, 1992, pp. 131-136.

147. HMF, p. 105.

148. R.P.C. HANSON, *Origen's Doctrine of Tradition*, London, SCM, 1954, p. 143, cf. p. 137. See HMF, p. 106.

149. HMF, p. 109.

150. HMF, p. 109.

151. HMF, p. 109.

152. HMF, pp. 102-103, 104 at n. 66. See, among others, L.G. PATTERSON, *Irenaeus and the Valentinians. The Emergence of a Christian Scripture*, in *Studia Patristica* 18/3 (1991) 189-200. J.-D. DUBOIS, *L'exégèse des gnostiques et l'histoire du canon des Écritures*, in M. TARDIEU (ed.), *Les règles de l'interprétation*, Paris, Cerf, 1987, pp. 89-97.

Irenaeus, and possibly also for Tertullian. The main issue is Luke's apostolic status and, at least for Irenaeus, the authorship of the Gospel of John.

In the opening section of Book 3 of his *Adv. Haer.*, Irenaeus contends that the Gospel according to John really was the work of John, "discipulus Domini, qui et supra pectus eius recumbebat" (3,1,1). Any suspicions which might have been circulating either within or without the church regarding John's authorship was hereby emphatically rejected. For Tertullian, this was not an issue in his debate with Marcion. In fact, he seems content to simply remind his readers that both John and Matthew were apostles (*Adv. Marc.* 4,2,2).

With respect to Luke, both Irenaeus and Tertullian defend a position that Sundberg has called "dependent canonicity". In other words, that gospel's authority does not depend on Luke alone, but on his relationship to Paul. In 3,13-15, Irenaeus adds a long section in defense of both Paul's apostleship and of Luke's connection with Paul. Here, he argues against Marcion and Valentinus, as well as against those who will not recognize Paul's apostolic status (3,15,1). The problem with the former is that they, in a sense, lack sufficient respect for Luke's gospel. They excise objectionable passages and then use it to reconstruct what they think was the authentic kerygma. Irenaeus replies that it was Luke, not Marcion or Valentinus, "qui semper cum Paulo praedicavit et dilectus ab eo dictus est et cum eo evangelizavit et creditus est referre nobis evangelium, nihil aliud ab eo didicit sicut ex verbis eius ostensum est" (3,14,1). In 3,11,7, Irenaeus referred to the "solid foundations" which exist for accepting the four gospels, noting that even the heretics make use of (at least one of) them. The argument is somewhat ambivalent. The various groups he mentions use only one gospel[153], but Irenaeus nevertheless concludes that the heretics themselves witness to the truth of the Fourfold Gospel[154]. By pointing to the "firmitas circa evangelia"[155] he also implies that the Fourfold Gospel is a well-established concept. Irenaeus may be overstating his case, but he could hardly have used such an argument if he was not convinced that it had at least some validity, that it would be polemically effective, and that it would have a certain amount of appeal for his readers.

---

153. According to Irenaeus, this is the case for the Ebionites ("eo evangelio quod est secundum Matthaeum solo utentur") and for Marcion ("id quod est secundum Lucam circumcidens"). Others "prefer" Mark ("id quod secundum Marcum est praeferentes evangelium"), and the Valentinians have a particular interest in John ("eo quod est secundum Iohannem plenissime utentur").

154. "Cum ergo hi qui contradicunt nobis testimonium perhibeant et utantur his, firma et vera est nostra de illis ostensio" (ed. Rousseau-Doutreleau, SC 211, p. 160).

155. "Tanta est autem circa Evangelia haec firmitas" (p. 158).

Tertullian, although he states the matter differently, ultimately comes to the same conclusion: Luke's is an authentic gospel by virtue of its connection to Paul. To counter Marcion's preference for Luke, he does not hesitate to argue, "Lucas non apostolus, sed apostolicus, non magister, sed discipulus … posterioris apostoli sectator" (4,2,3). He makes further points by reminding his readers that Luke's gospel certainly preceded Marcion's (4,4), and that Luke is acknowledged in all the churches (4,5,2). He then repeats his initial remark on the four gospels in 4,5,1 (cf. above, on 4,2,2). He notes that, just as Mark's gospel is said to be that of Peter, it is customary to say that Luke's is that of Paul[156], since it is perfectly legitimate to "regard as those of their teachers the writings of their disciples".

The Fragment is not so openly polemical as are Irenaeus and Tertullian. It may well be that the Fragmentist (just like Origen and Clement) was not particularly interested in that aspect. On the other hand, it is remarkable that he deals with the same issues with regard to Luke and John, even if the details of his comments differ. For example, only the Fragmentist tells us (l. 4) that Paul had taken Luke with him "quasi ut iuris studiosum" (if this is in fact the correct reading). And his story about John has no parallel in any other western document of that period. He also includes in his comments on Luke (as well as on John!) an echo of the preface to Luke's gospel. Luke was not an eyewitness ("nec ipse vidit in carne"; "nec" as Mk?), but he composed his account "according to general belief" ("ex opinione", for ἐξ ἀκοῆς?, or should one prefer the conjecture "ex ordine", for Lk 1,3 καθεξῆς, cf. l. 33), "as he was able to ascertain". He composed it "in his own name" ("numeni suo"), as did John (l. 15). Unlike Luke, John was an eyewitness (l. 32 "visurem"), but his was also "an orderly account" (l. 33 "per ordinem"). Though this may give the impression that the focus has shifted from Luke's status as an evangelist to the question of his reliability[157], it should be remembered that even for the Fragmentist his reliability ultimately goes back to his companionship with Paul[158]. Because these

156. *Adv. Marc.* 4,5,3: "Nam et Lucae digestum Paulo adscribere solent" (ed. Moreschini, SC 456, p. 84).

157. A motif that is also mentioned in the comment on Acts (ll. 36-37).

158. The expression "quasi ut iuris studiosum" is difficult to interpret. Cf. ZAHN, *Geschichte*, II.1 (n. 3), pp. 25-28, on the "Doppeldoktor" Luke and arguments for amending it into "quasi itineris (sui) studiosum". METZGER, *Canon* (n. 3), p. 305 n. 2, continues to defend the text of the Fragment (as did Harnack and Ehrhardt before him) as a technical term for "an assessor or legal expert who served on the staff of a Roman official". This, however, raises the question of what relationship Paul could have had with a Roman official. More can be said in support of Lietzmann's "quasi litteris studiosum" (suggested to him by his teacher F. Bücheler; cf. his edition of the Fragment, p. 5). "Studiosus" with

views on Luke have been so frequently repeated, they probably do not offer sufficient evidence to place the Fragment in the time of Irenaeus or Tertullian. A more compelling argument can be made from the fact that the Fragment goes to so much trouble to demonstrate that the Fourth Gospel was written by John the Apostle, an issue which, as Hahneman admits, had long been settled by the time he prefers for the Fragment[159]. A further indication may be seen in the Fragmentist's combining the passages in which he discusses the status of Luke's gospel and John's authorship with a comment on the fundamental unity of the gospels. One finds the same concern in Irenaeus and Tertullian. Both of these authors express, with strikingly similar vocabulary and phrasing, the conviction that the gospels are consistent in their teaching[160]. In fact, Irenaeus and Tertullian formulate the topic almost in the form of a creed (Tertullian also refers to the "dispositio" of the gospels in 4,2,2). The Fragmentist prefers to list the various contents of the gospel story ("de nativitate …"). Yet there are some interesting agreements in wording with Irenaeus when the Fragment speaks of the "principia" of the gospels (ll. 16-17)[161], of "cum uno ac principali Spiritu declarata sint in omnibus omnia"[162], and of the "potestate regali" of the second parousia[163]. Perhaps most important is the mention of the double parousia, the last topic in the list, a topic which is certainly characteristic of second-century apologetics[164]. The best parallel is in Tertullian, *Apologeticum* 21,5, a

the dative is not exceptional (for an original τοῖς γράμμασι προσέχοντα?; so H.J. de Jonge in a private communication). This emendation would also emphasize Luke's official status and his privileged connection with Paul, while simultaneously alluding yet again to his reliability and trustworthiness.

159. HMF, p. 102: "From the beginning of the third century, the Gospel of John has been generally accepted in the churches".

160. *Adv. Haer.* 3,11,7: "et haec quidem sunt principia Evangelii, unum Deum Fabricatorem huius universitatis, eum qui et per prophetas sit adnuntiatus et qui per Moysen legis dispositionem fecerit, Patrem Domini nostri Iesu Christi adnuntiantia, et praeter hunc alterum Deum nescientia neque alterum Patrem" (ed. Rousseau-Doutreleau, SC 211, p. 158). Cf. the earlier passage 3,1,2, which follows upon his list of the four evangelists: "et omnes isti unum Deum Factorem caeli et terrae a lege et prophetis adnuntiatum, et unum Christum Filium Dei tradiderunt nobis" (p. 24). See Tertullian, *Adv. Marc.* 4,2,2 (after the quotation above, main text at n. 144): "isdem regulis exorsi, quantum ad unicum deum attinet creatorem et Christum eius, natus ex virgine, supplementum legis et prophetarum" (ed. Moreschini, SC 456, p. 68).

161. Variously translated as "elements" or "beginnings". Cf. *Adv. Haer.* 3,11,8.

162. *Adv. Haer.* 3,11,8: "quattuor principales spiritus" and "omnium Artifex Verbum qui sedit super Cherubim et continet omnia, declaratus hominibus, dedit nobis quadriforme Evangelium quod uno Spiritu continetur" (ed. Rousseau-Doutreleau, SC 211, pp. 160 and 162).

163. Cf. again 3,11,8, on the Son of God whose "dispositio" is represented by a lion, as in Rev 4,7, "efficabile eius et principale et regale significans" (p. 162).

164. Cf. Justin, *Dial.* 14; 32; 34; 40; 49; 52; 110; *1 Apol.* 52. Irenaeus, *Adv. Haer.* 4,33,1. Tertullian, *Adv. Marc.* 3,7 (= *Adv. Iud.* 14,9-10). Hippolytus, *De Antichristo* 44. *Ps-Clementine Rec.* 1,49. Victorinus, *CommRev* 1,7.

passage in which he also applies the categories of humility and glory to Christ's advent, but not to Christ himself[165].

B. Paul[166]

The section on Paul's letters (ll. 39-68) is the second largest in the Fragment behind only that dedicated to the gospels (ll. 1-34). The Fragmentist recognizes thirteen letters. He does not mention Hebrews. At the end he rejects as apocryphal a number of letters that "cannot be received in the Catholic Church" (see below). A first attempt at listing the authentic letters, which, incidentally, included additional information about the letters' number, provenance, purpose (l. 40 "quae a quo loco vel qua ex causa directe") and content, breaks off after he has mentioned only three (Cor, Gal, Rom). The author observes that it is "necessary for us to discuss these one by one" (ll. 46-47), a promise which he afterwards fails to fulfil. Instead, he continues to explain, in a decidedly bizarre way, that Paul wrote to seven churches after the model "of his predecessor John"[167]. He supposedly did this in the following order: Cor, Eph, Phil, Col, Gal, Thess, Rom. In the following lines, the list is adapted so as to include 2 Cor and 2 Thess: Paul had to write twice to these com-

---

165. "Duobus enim adventibus eius significatis, primo, qui iam expunctus est in humilitate condicionis humanae, secundo, qui concludendo saeculo imminet in sublimitate paternae potestatis acceptae <et> divinitatis exertae, primum non intellegendo secundum, quem manifestius praedicatum sperabant, unum existimaverunt" (ed. Dekkers, CCSL 2, p. 125). Cf. TREGELLES, *Canon Muratorianus* (n. 3), p. 36. ZAHN, *Geschichte* (n. 3), II.1, pp. 44-45: "in Formen, welche in der Apologetik des 2. Jahrhunderts ihre feste Ausprägung gefunden haben". M.C. ALBL, *"And Scripture Cannot Be Broken". The Form and Function of the Early Christian* Testimonia *Collections* (SNT, 96), Leiden, Brill, 1999, pp. 259-263 (on Barnabas, Justin, and Tertullian). STANTON, *Fourfold Gospel* (n. 135), pp. 322-325.

166. Cf. C. BUCK, *The Early Order of the Pauline Corpus*, in *JBL* 68 (1949) 351-357. K.L. CARROLL, *The Expansion of the Pauline Corpus*, in *JBL* 72 (1953) 230-237. C.L. MITTON, *The Formation of the Pauline Corpus of Letters*, London, Epworth, 1955. J. FINEGAN, *The Original Form of the Pauline Corpus*, in *HTR* 49 (1956) 85-103. W. SCHMITHALS, *Zur Abfassung und ältesten Sammlung der Paulinischen Hauptbriefe*, in *ZNW* 51 (1960) 225-245 (Engl. transl. in ID., *Paul and the Gnostics*, Nashville, Abingdon, 1972, pp. 239-274). K. STENDAHL, *The Apocalypse of John and the Epistles of Paul in the Muratorian Fragment*, in W. KLASSEN – G.F. SNYDER (eds.), *Current Issues in New Testament Interpretation*, London, Harper, 1962, pp. 239-245. N.A. DAHL, *Welche Ordnung* (n. 47) and ID., *The Particularity of the Pauline Epistles as a Problem in the Ancient Church*, in *Neotestamentica et Patristica*. FS O. Cullmann (SNT, 7), Leiden, Brill, 1962, pp. 261-271. P. NAUTIN, *Irénée et la canonicité des épîtres pauliniennes*, in *RHR* 182 (1972) 113-130. H.Y. GAMBLE, *The Redaction of the Pauline Letters and the Formation of the Pauline Corpus*, in *JBL* 94 (1975) 403-418. A. LINDEMANN, *Paulus im ältesten Christentum* (BHT, 58), Tübingen, Mohr, *passim*. TROBISCH, *Die Paulusbriefsammlung* (n. 28). R. PENNA, *L'origine del Corpus Paulinum*, in *CrSt* 5 (1994) 577-607.

167. At least if this is what is meant by "sequens prodecessoris sui Iohannis" (l. 49).

munities "for the sake of admonition" (l. 55 "pro correptione"). The author then returns to his comparison with Rev in order to argue that these letters were in fact intended for the universal church (ll. 55-59). In addition to the letters to the churches, Paul also wrote four letters to individuals (Phlm, Tit, 1-2 Tim), "pro affectione et dilectione". Thanks to their content, these, too, were soon accepted by the church (ll. 63-64: "in ordinatione ecclesiasticae disciplinae"). The section concludes with the aforementioned saying on gall and honey (cf. above, p. 492).

Hahneman employs several pages in order to explain, (1) that, while there is some evidence for the existence of collections of Paul's letters (without the Pastoral Epistles) in the second and early-third century, there is none for their having been made into a canon as was done in the Fragment; (2) that the Pastoral Epistles were added later in the process of expanding these collections; and (3) that there was a long standing (and diametrically opposed) difference in opinion with regard to the authenticity of Heb between the East and the West. However, amidst all these arguments, he only briefly touches on the evidence contained in the Fragment itself. He concludes that the Fragment "would be extraordinary on the traditional dating"[168], but he stops short of calling it an anomaly.

1. *Three Collections*

Hahneman discusses three early collections of Paul's letters, none of which are problem-free. The first, that of Marcion, is only indirectly preserved in the writings of his opponents (i.e., Tertullian and Epiphanius). The second, the so-called Marcionite prologues, can be reconstructed from an expanded, and much more recent, version. The third, P[46], is (most probably) incomplete.

a. Marcion. Hahneman argues that Marcion still must have thought of a collection, as opposed to a canon, since he gives no positive indication that he formally rejected certain writings[169]. This may be true, but that is certainly not how Marcion's interaction with Paul's letters was perceived at the time of the Fragment's composition. According to Tertullian, Marcion acknowledged ten letters as authentically Pauline: Gal (*Adv. Marc.* 5,2,4), 1 Cor (5,5-10), 2 Cor (5,11-12), Rom (5,13-14), 1 Thess (5,15), 2 Thess (5,16), Eph (5,17-18, which the Marcionites call "ad Laodicenses"), Col (5,19), Phil (5,20), and Phlm (5,21,1). Due to its

---

168. HMF, p. 124.
169. HMF, p. 91: "There is no direct evidence that Marcion knew or excluded other gospels". The same goes for Paul's unmentioned letters: "there is no evidence that Marcion knew them".

brevity, Phlm is said to have escaped mutilation at the hands of Marcion, a fact which left Tertullian puzzled by Marcion's inconsistency. He seemed to be inconsistent in the sense that he accepted this particular letter, while rejecting all those addressed to individuals (5,21,1). Tertullian seems to have thought that Marcion knew and consciously rejected the Pastoral Epistles[170]. It seems that Marcion's "original collection" was later expanded. Hahneman quotes evidence of various authors, ranging from Origen to the tenth-century Islamic scholar al-Nadim, in order to demonstrate that (later) Marcionites knew and made use of other New Testament writings, including (at least some of) the Pastoral Epistles[171]. This discussion is little more than a smokescreen on Hahneman's part: most of his evidence is both indirect and ambivalent[172], some of it is both late and marginal[173], and none of it deals with the expansions in terms of "canonicity" and "authenticity". As to the Fragmentist, he accepts four gospels, but never explicitly rejects others. And he offers a very incomplete list of the Catholic Epistles, but never explicitly says that he rejects those that are not mentioned. In spite of all this, Hahneman continues to maintain that he only works with the concept of a "closed canon".

b. The Marcionite Prologues. The so-called Marcionite Prologues to the letters of Paul that are found in many manuscripts of the Vulgate were intensively studied in the first decades of the twentieth century[174].

170. Of course, Tertullian would never have imagined that the Pastoral Epistles had been written to counter Marcion. So R.J. HOFFMANN, *Marcion. On the Restitution of Christianity*, Chico, CA, Scholars, 1984, pp. 281-305. Epiphanius, *Pan*. 42,12,3, follows a different order (Gal, 1-2 Cor, Rom, 1-2 Thess, Eph, Col, Phlm, Phil, Laod) while offering a comment diametrically opposed to that of Tertullian with regard to Marcion's use of Phlm ("in a completely distorted form"). He also does not speak of Marcion's silence about the Pastoral Epistles. Finally, he does not seem to regard the letter to the Laodiceans as identical with Eph, though he must have recognized some of their similarities (42,12,3 and 42,13,4; cf. also below). On the reconstruction of Marcion's text of the letters of Paul, see now U. SCHMID, *Marcion und sein Apostolos. Rekonstruktion und historische Einordnung der marcionitischen Paulusbriefausgabe* (ANTF, 25), Berlin – New York, de Gruyter, 1995, esp. pp. 35-149 (Tertullian) and 150-195 (Epiphanius).

171. Thus, John Chrysostom suggested that (later?) Marcionites based their doctrine of a twofold godhead on 2 Tim 1,18 (PG 62,615).

172. E.g., the significance of their having quoted Jn 13,34 and 15,19 as Origen attests (*Adamant*. 2,16.20; cf. also *CommMt* 15,3), or of their not rejecting Mt 23,8 as Ephraem claims (*Memra* 24,1) is not at all obvious.

173. Besides al-Nadim's *Fihrist al-'Ulum*, see also R. CASEY, *The Armenian Marcionites and the Diatessaron*, in *JBL* 57 (1938) 185-194.

174. De Bruyne argued that of the thirteen short prologues, those for 2 Cor, 2 Thess, Eph and the Pastoral Epistles, do not stem from Marcion. Harnack believed the whole series to be authentic, regarding them as the Fragmentist's source. Lagrange denied that they could be Marcionite, supporting the idea that they were paraphrases of Ambrosiaster's prologues and should, therefore, be dated in the fourth century. Bardy suggested that some of them might date from the second century while steering clear of assigning

Hahneman repeats the conclusions of N.A. Dahl[175], viz. that the actual set of thirteen prologues is the result of later expansions of a series of seven prologues (to the seven churches). These were originally composed in the middle of the second century by a non-Marcionite author, who, nevertheless, was inspired by Marcion's *Apostolikon* for the arrangement if not also for the content of his comments. Sometime in the third century, the document was translated into Latin and expanded through the addition of new prologues to other letters in order to generate a preface for an edition of a thirteen-letter Pauline corpus. In view of the many problems related to the reconstruction of the history of these prologues, it remains exceedingly difficult to decide whether they were originally conceived of as a collection or as a catalogue.

c. P[46]. It is estimated that fourteen pages (f. 98-104) are missing at the end of P[46] (ca. 200). The papyrus contains the text of nine letters in an exceptional order (Rom, Heb, 1-2 Cor, Eph, Gal, Phil, Col, 1 Thess). Most probably, the text continued with 2 Thess (and Phlm), but on no account can the missing pages be shown to have contained the rest of the corpus (2 Thess, Phlm, Past). Several solutions for this have been suggested. The first editor assumed that the papyrus may have contained only 1-2 Tim (albeit in a somewhat abbreviated form)[176]. At one point, the second editor entertained the possibility that "some additional leaves may have been attached at the end so as to take the Pastoral Epistles"[177].

them to Marcion. Cf. D. De Bruyne, *Prologues bibliques d'origine marcionite*, in *RBén* 24 (1907) 1-16. A. Harnack, *Der marcionitische Ursprung der ältesten Vulgata-Prologe zu den Paulusbriefen*, in *ZNW* 24 (1925) 204-257, and *Die Marcionitischen Prologe zu den Paulusbriefen, eine Quelle des Muratorischen Fragments*, in *ZNW* 25 (1926) 160-162. M.-J. Lagrange, *Les prologues prétendus marcionites*, in *RB* 35 (1926) 161-178. G. Bardy, art. *Marcionites (Prologes)*, in *DBS* 5 (1957) 877-881. Cf. also W. Mündle, *Die Herkunft der "Marcionitische" Prologe zu den Paulinischen Briefen*, in *ZNW* 24 (1925) 56-77. See further K.T. Schäfer, *Marius Victorinus und die Marcionitischen Prologe zu den Paulusbriefen*, in *RBén* 80 (1970) 7-16. Dahl, *Earliest Prologues* (see above, n. 47). Recently, E. Norelli has again proposed that they could have originated from a disciple of Marcion: *La tradizione ecclesiastica negli antichi prologhi latini alle epistole paoline*, in *La tradizione. Forme e modi. XVII Incontro di studiosi dell' antichità cristiana* (Studia Ephemeridis "Augustinianum", 31), Rome, Institutum Patristicum "Augustinianum", 1990, pp. 301-324. So also Kaestli, *Fragment de Muratori* (n. 46), p. 628 n. 56.

175. *Earliest Prologues* (n. 47), esp. pp. 252-262.

176. H.A. Sanders, *A Third-Century Papyrus Codex of the Epistles of St Paul*, Ann Arbor, MI, University of Michigan Press, 1935. There is no a priori reason to believe that all three Pastoral letters were always regarded as a unit. According to Jerome, Tatian accepted Tit but not 1 Tim. The missing leaves provide exactly enough space for 2 Thess, Phlm, 2 Tim, Tit. P[61] (ca. 700) contains fragments of Rom, 1 Cor, Phil, Col, 1 Thess, Tit, Phlm.

177. F. Kenyon, *The Chester Beatty Biblical Papyri. Description and Texts of the Twelve Manuscripts on Papyrus of the Greek Bible*, London, E. Walker, III, p. xi.

It has also been suggested that the omission of the Pastoral Epistles (and Phlm) was intentional and that P[46] was composed as a collection of "public letters" (with Heb)[178]. P[46] may indeed offer further evidence for a collection of Paul's letters (minus the Pastoral Epistles) at the turn of the third century, but it is at best only negative evidence[179]. Moreover, one should not forget that this is an *edition* of Paul's letters (the only one of this size and format on papyrus) and not just a list of titles or a series of prologues. In short, material (as opposed to theological or reception-history) factors may have played a role in the decision not to include the Pastoral Epistles as part of the codex.

2. *The Pastoral Epistles*

Hahneman writes: "No certain evidence of acquaintance with the Pastorals is extant before the third quarter of the second century, but from that time onwards the epistles are cited more regularly", and "Irenaeus is the earliest witness to make allusions to all the Pastorals"[180]. Shortly after this time they must have been recognized as part of the western Pauline corpus. Eusebius reports that Caius reckoned the letters of Paul to be thirteen in number, excluding only Heb[181]. It is possible, as Hahneman observes[182], that this number was inserted by Eusebius, though nothing in the passage argues against assigning it directly to Caius. Hahneman speaks of a "collection" with regard to Caius, since Eusebius deals only with the letters and not with other writings. However, Hahneman rather confusingly uses the same term for the fourth-century lists in which the number of Paul's letters is explicitly noted. Does not consistency demand that these be labelled "catalogues"[183]? In the time of Caius then the concept of an expanding corpus was apparently already known. Is it impossible for a contemporary author to bear

178. J.D. QUINN, *P[46] - The Pauline Canon?*, in *CBQ* 36 (1974) 379-385; A.T. HANSON, *The Pastoral Epistles* (NCB), Grand Rapids, MI, Eerdmans, 1982, p. 11.

179. It is possible that, following 2 Thess (and Phlm), some leaves were left blank, as is also the case in an OT manuscript from "the same find" (HMF, p. 116). That the Pastoral Epistles were known in Egypt around 200 is attested by P[32] (fragment of Tit 1,11-15; 2,3-8).

180. HMF, p. 117. There are some similarities with the Pastoral Epistles in Ignatius and Polycarp, but it is debated whether these are best explained through literary dependence. On Tertullian, see above, n. 170.

181. HE 6,20,3, repeated by Jerome, *De vir. ill.* 59. On Caius's "canon", see VON CAMPENHAUSEN, *Entstehung* (n. 3), pp. 275-282.

182. HMF, p. 118.

183. See, e.g., the so-called "Mommsen Catalogue" (!), Filastrius, the list of the Council of Carthago of 397 ("Pauli Ap. Epistolae XIII; eiusdem ad Hebraeos una"). Cf. also HMF, p. 124, for the notion of "Pauline catalogues".

witness to the same sort of movement? If the evidence of Caius is given its due significance, it largely reduces the impact of Hahneman's argument regarding the existence of earlier Pauline collections that omit the Pastoral Epistles. It would seem that they belong to another time.

3. *Hebrews*[184]

The Fragment contains two elements that are characteristic of the "western" approach to Paul's letters up to the fourth century. These are the absence of Heb and the "seven-churches pattern" (with the comparison with Rev, cf. above, pp. 495-496) as a means for explaining the number of letters addressed to various bodies of believers. In fact, the two elements are probably connected, since if Heb is included, the pattern breaks down[185]. Both are readily explainable on the traditional dating. Hahneman, on the other hand, has difficulties explaining these features within his hypothesis. Besides the Fragment, the pattern is consistently attested in the West from the first half of the third century onward[186]. Jerome is the first to mention it in the East. There is no concrete evidence that it was known to Marcion, though some have so argued[187]. Taken together, these facts could make the Fragmentist the originator both of the pattern and of the distinction he makes between "corporate" letters and letters to individuals. In any case, neither the other early witnesses nor the Fragmentist claim the distinction. If the Fragmentist was in fact the pattern's author, that scenario is perhaps less problematic than Hahneman's alternative (see above).

Until the late fourth century, the West was united with regard to its opinion of the authorship of Heb: it was not written by Paul. However, at that time, one begins to see hesitation on the part of both Jerome and Augustine. The official change occurred at some point between the first and second councils of Carthage, held in 397 and 419 respectively (see above, n. 183, and note the relevant text of the latter, viz. "Epist. Pauli

---

184. Cf. W.H.P. Hatch, *The Position of Hebrews in the Canon of the New Testament*, in *HTR* 29 (1936) 133-151. C.P. Anderson, *The Epistle to the Hebrews and the Pauline Letter Collection*, in *HTR* 59 (1966) 429-438. A detailed discussion on the reception of Heb into the corpus of Paul's letters in K.-H. Ohlig, *Die theologische Begründung des neutestamentlichen Kanons in der Alten Kirche*, Düsseldorf, Patmos, 1972, pp. 67-75. H.-F. Weiss, *Der Brief an die Hebräer* (KEK), Göttingen, Vandenhoeck & Ruprecht, 1991, pp. 115-126.

185. HMF, pp. 120 and 123.

186. HMF, p. 117 n. 97: Hippolytus (as quoted by bar Salibi, see above). Cyprian, *Test.* 1,20. Victorinus, *CommRev* 1,7 (see above, main text corresponding to nn. 34-36, and n. 164); *De fabr. mundi* 11. *Opus imperfectum in Matt.* 1. Jerome, *De vir. ill.* 5; *Ep.* 53,9. Isidorus of Sevilla, *Prooem.* 92, 94; *De num.* 38, 42.

187. Cf. HMF, p. 117 nn. 98-99 (following Goodspeed).

Ap. Numero XIV")[188]. In the East, Origen, on linguistic grounds, expressed a similar suspicion. According to Eusebius, however, it did not prevent the Alexandrian from accepting the letter (HE 6,25,11). Eusebius is also aware that the authenticity of the letter is questioned in the West (6,20,3; 3,3,5) and, on one occasion, he himself places it among the disputed works (6,13,6; diff 3,3,5; 3,25,2). Amphilochius also reports that "some" consider Heb spurious (νόθος), though he himself accepts it[189]. In the fourth and the fifth centuries one notices a tendency among some to place Heb last behind Phlm[190], or, in between the corporate letters and those written to individuals[191], in spite of the fact that it had previously been reckoned with the corporate letters[192].

Hahneman speculates that the removal of Heb from among the corporate letters "may have resulted from the introduction in the East of the western pattern of Pauline letters to seven churches"[193]. Though possible, it should be noted that most of the witnesses for the rearrangement do not mention such a pattern. Jerome, who is acquainted with it, calls Heb the "eighth epistle", "that is not generally counted with the others" (*Ep.* 53), by which he almost certainly refers to the seven corporate ones[194]. Jerome also illustrates that it was not very difficult to harmonize the eastern fourteen-letter corpus with the western pattern. Given this, it is even more remarkable that others would have made such a hash out of it. Hahneman thinks that Amphilochius' pattern of "twice seven letters", with Heb placed last coupled with the remark that it is considered spurious by some, is a somewhat unsuccessful attempt at such a harmonisation. A different, if still problematic, proposal would have been suggested by the Fragmentist. He started listing the public letters (Cor, Gal, Rom), then, coming upon Heb[195], decided to follow the western pattern. He took great care to account for 2 Cor and 2 Thess, as well as for the individual letters. This makes it still more difficult to assert that Heb was omitted due to simple carelessness, unless one were also prepared to claim that he stubbornly insisted on adhering to the old western position with regard to Heb[196]. Of course, this would make him the lone exception among fourth-century Easterners!

188. HMF, pp. 119-120.
189. *Iambi ad Seleucum*, 308-309.
190. So in Syria, "perhaps because of Western influence" (HMF, p. 122).
191. HMF, p. 123.
192. P[46]; Coptic translation of Athanasius' 39th Festal Letter. See HMF, p. 122.
193. HMF, p. 124.
194. HMF, p. 124.
195. HMF, p. 125 n. 109.
196. Both suggestions are from HMF, p. 125: "Hebrews may either have been carelessly omitted …, or else be absent from the Fragment as a result of the Western dispute about its authorship".

4. *A Canon of Paul's Letters*

The present text of the Fragment, with its incomplete list of three letters, is problematic for any hypothesis. As a matter of fact, the situation is nearly identical for both Hahneman and for those who keep to the traditional dating. In both scenarios, the "seven-churches" pattern comes across as an innovation, even for the Fragmentist himself. Nevertheless, preference should be given to the traditional position. If the Fragmentist really wanted to buck the established eastern tradition on Heb and if, as Hahneman argues, he was unfamiliar with the seven letters = seven churches pattern, one would have expected him not to have included the aforementioned comments on Cor, Gal, Rom. They would only have generated confusion, esp. given the fact that he then proceeds to employ a most unusual order that places Rom last. If, however, the innovation is placed at a time when there existed no real traditions about how Paul's letters should be organized, the Fragmentist would not have been risking an affront to the minds of his readers. He would not have been "switching" from a well-known arrangement to something completely unfamiliar.

For Hahneman, the Fragment is a "witness to a closed Pauline canon"[197]. While this is most likely correct, his argumentation proves to be less than convincing. He struggles with clearly formulating what indications should be taken as signs that a given part of the canon is closed and with what would qualify as a witness to such a development. Moreover, the Fragment does not seem to fit Hahneman's criteria. For example, take the criterion of rejection of particular letters[198]. The Fragmentist does this, but many other fourth-century catalogues never mention any apocryphal literature. Another example is in how "the collection becomes so established that it can be referred to by number only"[199]. This is indeed the case in later catalogues, even if the numbers that are given sometimes vary. The Fragmentist numbered the gospels and the seven corporate letters, but did not number the Pauline corpus.

As Hahneman understands it, the formation of the Pauline corpus was a process of "continual expansion"[200]. "The Pauline collection remained open" as long as it remained feasible to propose "additions and adjustments"[201]. There are at least two problems with this assessment. First, the notion of "continual expansion" is inadequate since the "expan-

197. HMF, p. 124.
198. HMF, p. 124.
199. HMF, p. 124.
200. HMF, p. 110; cf. p. 111: "a continually expanding Pauline collection".
201. HMF, p. 124.

sions" would have only occurred twice in the West (Pastoral Epistles
and Heb) and may have happened only once in the East (Past), where, in
any case, it was completed much earlier. A few other texts were considered as genuine by some well into the fourth century, but they are never
included among the authentic Pauline letters in catalogues of that period[202]. Second, using Hahneman's own hypothesis, it would be inappro-
priate to label the Fragment a "witness to a closed Pauline canon". By
advocating the seven-letters pattern, the Fragmentist would have been
proposing a major "adjustment" of the arrangement of the letters. This
was previously unknown in the East, to say nothing of the "heresy" he
would have committed by omitting Heb. How could any fourth-century
Easterner have possibly regarded this as an acceptable Pauline corpus?
If one accepts the traditional dating, his rejection of certain letters, his
counting of the corporate letters, his accounting for their number via the
comparison with Rev, and his inclusion in his list of the four individual
letters, are all clear indications that he wanted to offer his readers a complete Pauline corpus as he understood it, regardless of what later generations would make from his words. In short, the Fragment is "a witness
to a closed Pauline canon", but in ways quite different from those which
were commonly accepted in the East of the fourth century.

C. *Catholic Epistles*

The information contained in the Fragment regarding the Catholic
Epistles is hopelessly confusing. The text reads, "epistola sane Iude et
superscrictio Iohannis duas in catholica habentur" (ll. 68-69). It does not
mention 1-2 Peter or James, and it is unclear which of the three Johannine letters are referenced. In l. 28 the Fragmentist introduces a quotation from 1 Jn as "in epistulis suis", as if he is aware of the existence of
several but regards it as unnecessary to distinguish between them.
"Iohannis duas" seems to refer to 1-2 Jn, 1/3Jn, or 2-3 Jn. Although one
could also take the two entities referenced in ll. 68-69, i.e., the letter of
Jude and (those) of John as the "two" which are used in the church[203]. It
has been suggested that the text is corrupt and must have originally included the other letters as well. Zahn proposed an original as follows: ἡ

202. HMF, p. 110: 3 Cor; the Correspondence with Seneca; the letter to the
Laodiceans. The catalogue in the codex Claromontanus probably lists the *Acts of Paul*
among the "disputed" works.
203. See the discussion on the reference to Jn in ZAHN, *Geschichte*, II.1 (n. 3), pp. 88-
93. Cf. T.W. MANSON, *Entry into Membership of the Early Church*, in *JTS* 48 (1947) 32-
33. P. KATZ, *The Johannine Epistles in the Muratorian Canon*, in *JTS* 8 (1957) 273-274,
proposes an emendation in order to make the text refer to all three of John's letters.

μέντοι Ἰούδα ἐπιστολὴ καὶ αἱ ἐπιγεγραμμέναι Ἰωάννου δύο ... καὶ ἡ ἀποκάλυψις δὲ Ἰωάννου καὶ Πέτρου [ἐπιστολὴ μία, ἣν] μόνην ἀποδεχόμεθα. In this he attempted to make room for (at least) 1 Pet, if in a highly unusual place[204]. Lagrange even saw a way to save all seven epistles. Those of John had been mentioned already in l. 28, "de sorte qu'il n'y ait plus à revenir sur les épîtres de Jean"[205]. Thus, the text of ll. 68-69 would have read: "l'épître de Jude et deux inscrites au nom de (Pierre) sont dans l'église catholique, (et une de Jacques)"[206]. Hahneman likewise reckons with the possibility of corruption[207], but he stops short of proposing a conjecture: he leaves it open as to how the text may have originally read and as to how the corruption came about. This may seem prudent, but, obviously, it also weakens his suggestion. If one refrains from conjectures and daring reconstructions, one is left with only Jude and John. Such a combination is unparalleled throughout ancient collections or catalogues, but, it is probably less irregular at the turn of the third century in the West, a context which still has not produced any evidence showing that any one author knew and used all seven letters[208]. It would be much more remarkable in the late-fourth century, since, in that period, a seven member canon of Catholic Epistles is testified to in the West by Augustine and several African synods, and by Athanasius, Cyril of Jerusalem, Epiphanius, Gregory of Nazianze, Amphilochius (with some hesitation), and Jerome in the East[209].

For Hahneman, the Fragment is an anomaly in contents, concepts and form: "it is more than a question of just being the first"[210]. The information about the Catholic Epistles (along with a few others, e.g., the Apocalypse of Peter, the Wisdom of Solomon) remains problematic regardless of which date one is prepared to advocate. However, if one excludes this information, it appears that the writings that are mentioned are all known and, more importantly, are all accepted as both authentic

204. *Geschichte*, II.1 (n. 3), p. 143.

205. *Histoire ancienne* (n. 3), p. 74 n. 2.

206. "Comme nous enlevons d'ici la Sagesse, nous comblons la lacune par Iacobi epistula, pure conjecture, avec une ligne entière demeurée vide où nous n'osons introduire l'épître aux Hébreux" (*ibid.*).

207. HMF, p. 181: "most probably implies omissions in the Fragment".

208. HMF, p. 127, refers to the following: Irenaeus cites as Scripture 1 Pet along with both 1 and 2 Jn; Tertullian 1 Jn, 1 Pet, Jude; Novatian only 1 Jn; Cyprian 1 Jn and 1 Pet. In *Adv. Haer.* 4,16,2, Irenaeus cites Jas 2,23, but he does not identify the citation as such.

209. Some Easterners seem to have accepted only Jas, 1 Pet, and 1 Jn (John Chrysostom, Theodoretus, and the Peshitta), but, even then the Fragment is anomalous. Cf. HMF, p. 127. For the Syriac, see J.S. SIKER, *The Canonical Status of the Catholic Epistles in the Syriac New Testament*, in *JTS* 38 (1987) 311-340.

210. HMF, p. 131.

and authoritative in the late-second or early-third century. As to the concepts, the Fragment acknowledges "a closed collection of scriptures", or canon, and in some way distinguishes these writings from those that are to be disputed or rejected. However, the concept of a "closed collection" was known to Irenaeus, at least for the gospels, and also provides the most likely explanation for Tertullian's criticism of Marcion's having omitted the Pastoral Epistles from his collection of the Pauline letters (*Adv. Marc.* 5,21,1: "recusaverit").

Finally, it is stretching the evidence to claim that the Fragmentist "distinctly delineates the accepted, disputed, and rejected works"[211]. When compared with Eusebius' catalogue, which itself is perhaps not the best example in this genre, the Fragment begins to resemble "a first draft". For example, some of the rejected writings are listed in between those that were accepted. And we find a disputed book mentioned together with the Revelation of John, a text the Fragmentist most certainly regarded as authoritative. Furthermore, if some find Eusebius' terminology problematic when he distinguishes between ἀντιλεγόμενα and νόθοι[212], what are we to make of the Fragmentist's use of different (and potentially confusing) expressions (e.g., "recipere", "in honorem ecclesiae catholicae scificatae sunt", "in catholica habentur")[213]? The Fragmentist's selection of disputed or rejected writings is also remarkable. None of the "apocryphal" gospels is mentioned, none of the Apostolic Fathers (except for Hermas), nor any of the apocryphal Acts. Also absent are the five remaining Catholic Epistles. Apparently, the Fragmentist had little or no precedent for dealing with this question; and he clearly was not aware of later models.

V. A FOURTH-CENTURY CANONICAL LIST?

Hahneman finds evidence for a later dating of the Fragment in certain "peculiar" passages and by comparing the text with fourth-century catalogues. I begin with the latter. Hahneman, after correcting Sundberg's

---

211. HMF, p. 131.

212. Cf. ROBBINS, *Lexicon* (n. 50). A.D. BAUM, *Der neutestamentliche Kanon bei Eusebios* (Hist. eccl. *III,25,1-7) im Kontext seiner literaturgeschichtlichen Arbeit*, in *ETL* 73 (1997) 307-348. For Origen, cf. RUWET, *Antilegomena* (n. 145).

213. The word "canon" does not occur in the Fragment (see HMF, pp. 172-174), as is "New Testament". See METZGER, *Canon* (n. 3), pp. 289-294. W.C. VAN UNNIK, Ἡ καινὴ διαθήκη. *A Problem in the Early History of the Canon*, in *Studia Patristica* 4 (1961) 212-227; reprinted in ID., *Sparsa Collecta. The Collected Essays* II (SNT, 30), Leiden, Brill, 1980, pp. 157-171. W. KINZIG, Καινὴ διαθήκη. *The Title of the New Testament in the Second and Third Centuries*, in *JTS* 45 (1994) 519-544.

list of catalogues[214], goes on to present in some detail the contents of fifteen "undisputed catalogues" from the fourth and the early-fifth century, four other catalogues of questionable date and authenticity, and three of the most important New Testament manuscripts (Vaticanus, Sinaiticus, Alexandrinus) plus the Peshitta[215].

Hahneman contends that "there is nothing about the form of the Fragment which distinguishes it from the fifteen undisputed catalogues ... and nothing that suggests that it was earlier than the others, or that it influenced their development"[216]. These are different issues. One can hardly say that Eusebius' catalogue was of crucial importance for Jerome or Rufinus, though they both were very familiar with his work. That the Fragment does not differ from the later catalogues is simply not true. Except for Eusebius and Epiphanius, all other "later" authors offer their list of New Testament writings as part of a statement on the biblical canon and preface it with a list of accepted Old Testament writings[217].

---

214. SCM, pp. 37-38; HMF, pp. 132-133.

215. The fifteen catalogues are: Eusebius, HE 3,25,1-7; Codex Claromontanus; Cyril of Jerusalem, *Catech.* 4,36; Athanasius, *Ep. Fest.* 39; the "Mommsen Catalogue"; Epiphanius, *Pan.* 76,5; the Apostolic Canons, 85; Gregory of Nazianze, *Carm.* 12,31; the canons of the councils of Carthago; Jerome, *Ep.* 53; Augustine, *De doctr. Christ.* 2,8.12; Amphilochius, *Iambi ad Seleucum*, 289-319; Rufinus, *CommSymb* 38; Pope Innocent, *Ad Exsuper. tol.*; Syriac catalogue of St. Catherine. With regard to several of these, see P.-M. Bogaert's contribution in this volume (above, pp. 153-176). The four "disputed" (inauthentic) catalogues are the so-called Laodicene Canon; the list of books from a decree often attributed to Pope Damasus; a Roman canon list from ca. 400; and a list preserved among the writings of John Chrysostom (on these, see HMF, pp. 156-163).

Besides the discussions in the older literature (e.g., WESTCOTT, *Canon*; ZAHN, *Geschichte* [n. 3], II.1), see HMF, pp. 133-170. On Eusebius: C. SANT, *Eusebius of Caesarea's View on the Canon of the Holy Scriptures and the Texts He Used in His Works*, in *Melita Theologica* 23 (1971) 23-37. ROBBINS, *Lexicon* (n. 50). BAUM, *Eusebios* (n. 212). A.D. BAUM, *Der neutestamentliche Kanon bei Eusebios* (Hist. eccl. *III,25,1-7*) *im Kontext seiner literaturgeschichtlichen Arbeit*, in *ETL* 73 (1997) 307-348. On Athanasius: R. LORENZ, *Athanasius Ep 39*, in *ZKG* 99 (1988) 87-92. D. BRAKKE, *Canon Formation and Social Conflict in Fourth-Century Egypt. Athanasius of Alexandria's Thirty-Ninth Festal Letter*, in *HTR* 87 (1994) 205-219. On Augustine: C. MUNIER, *La tradition manuscrite de l'Abrégé d'Hippone et le canon des Écritures des églises africaines*, in *Sacris Erudiri* 21 (1972-73) 43-55. S.P. KEALY, *The Canon. An African Contribution*, in *BTB* 9 (1979) 13-26. K.-H. OHLIG, *Canon Scripturarum*, in *Augustinus Lexikon* 1 (1992) 713-724. On Amphilochius: E. ROSSIN, *Anfilochio di Iconio e il canone biblico*, in *SP* 43 (1996) 121-157. On Rufinus: M. STENZEL, *Der Bibelkanon des Rufinus von Aquileia*, in *Bib* 23 (1942) 43-61. Besides the actual catalogues, scholars have also tried to construct a particular author's "canon" by using his quotations. See, in general, F. STUHLHOFER, *Der Gebrauch der Bibel von Jesus bis Euseb. Eine statistische Untersuchung zur Kanonsgeschichte*, Wuppertal, TVG, 1988. Cf. also, W. SANDAY, *The Cheltenham List of the Canonical Books and the Writings of Cyprian*, in *Studia Biblica* 3 (1891) 217-303. B.D. EHRMAN, *The NT Canon of Didymus the Blind*, in *VigChr* 37 (1983) 1-21.

216. HMF, p. 182.

217. HMF, p. 175.

For Eusebius, the difference "may be contextual"[218], since he includes his list only after a discussion on the apostles and since he goes on to quote the OT lists of Melito and Origen later in the HE (cf. 4,26,14 and 6,25,2). Epiphanius likewise offers both lists as separate entities (OT in *Pan.* 8,6; NT in *Pan.* 76,5; two more OT lists in *De mens.* 4 and 23). Hahneman speculates that it is "perhaps probable" that the Fragment also contained an Old Testament list. However, the reference to the prophets in l. 79 provides him with little support[219].

The order of the gospels (probably Mt, Mk, Lk, and Jn) could possibly point to an eastern origin, but it offers little support for a fourth-century dating[220]. That the Fragment lists thirteen Pauline letters also proves little or nothing for Hahneman's case. More remarkable is that the Fragment does not give a total for the number of Paul's letters, a fact which would make it quite exceptional for the fourth century (cf. Eusebius, codex Claromontanus, Jerome, Syrian catalogue). It places the individual letters together as a more or less independent group (as do Claromontanus, Athanasius, Augustine, Amphilochius, and the Syrian catalogue; note that the first and the last of these do this as part of a stichometry)[221]. The Fragment's arrangement of the letters is anything but conventional. However, with the exception of the Syrian catalogue, which is very late (ca. 400) and which offers many other peculiarities (e.g., unparalleled list of Paul's letters, Catholic Epistles and Revelation absent), the real problems are limited to Col and Heb. Col is found either before (Athanasius, Amphilochius) or after Thess (Augustine), or in second to last position just before Phlm (Claromontanus). Augustine and Amphilochius have moved Heb into last place. The arrangement of the Fragment does not reflect this discussion and is absolutely unique[222]. The Syrian catalogue did at least retain the same order for the individual letters as that found in the other catalogues (1-2 Tim, Tit, Phlm; Claromontanus has Col between Tit and Phlm) and listed together the two letters to the Corinthians and the two to the Thessalonians. Nothing can be made from the truncated "list" of Catholic Epistles. Six different arrangements are attested in the later catalogues[223].

218. HMF, p. 175.

219. He does not mention the Wisdom of Solomon in this connection (see below).

220. HMF, p. 181. On the problem of the differences in the order of the gospels in various traditions, see now P.-M. BOGAERT, *Ordres anciens des évangiles et tétraévangile en un seul codex*, in *RTL* 30 (1999) 297-314.

221. HMF, p. 176.

222. Cor, Eph, Phil, Col, Gal, Thess, Rom, 2 Cor, 2 Thess, Phlm, Tit, 1-2 Tim.

223. Eusebius still hesitates about Jas, Jude, 2 Pet, 2-3 Jn. The "Mommsen Catalogue" mentions only 1-3 Jn and 1-2 Pet (accompanied by a scribe's critical comment).

The one given by Athanasius (Jas, Pet, Jn, Jude) seems to have been the most popular[224], but it was certainly not the only eastern one[225]. In the West, different arrangements are given by Augustine (Pet, Jn, Jude, Jas), Rufinus (Pet, Jas, Jude, Jn), and Pope Innocent (Jn, Pet, Jude, Jas). Jude is never placed first; the relative order Jude-Jn is found in Rufinus. Finally, the Revelation of John poses no problem for the Fragmentist since he seems to have been oblivious of the eastern discussions concerning it[226].

"The Fragment clearly lists certain spurious works" (the Shepherd and the Revelation of Peter)[227]. However, it seems that only after Eusebius such a category falls out of general use. Cyril of Jerusalem (348), who, like Eusebius, speaks of ὁμολογούμενα and ἀμφιβαλλόμενα, explicitly forbids the reading of some books[228]. Claromontanus, which singles out Barnabas, the Shepherd, the Acts of Paul, and the Apocalypse of Peter by means of a mark that seems to indicate some hesitation, is an exception. So are Athanasius and Rufinus who both frown upon the Shepherd and the Didache (Rufinus also finds the Preaching of Peter unsatisfactory). After Eusebius, it is even more exceptional to find references to rejected works. Cyril mentions the Gospel of Thomas as an example of the ψευδεπίγραφα καὶ βλαβερά. Pope Innocent is particularly interested in listing the various apocryphal Acts. Athanasius and Rufinus refer to ἀπόκρυφα but give no titles. Interestingly, even Eusebius does not mention the works the Fragment has rejected. Only much later will it again become fashionable to make long lists of writings that ought to be rejected[229].

One final observation: The Fragmentist shows an interest in accounting for both the plurality of the gospels and the particularity of the

---

224. Epiphanius, Gregory of Nazianze, Jerome, Amphilochius; note that the latter hesitates about Jude, 2 Pet, and 2-3 Jn. Cyril does not mention Jude.

225. Claromontanus: Pet, Jas, Jn, Jude; Apostolic canons and African councils: Pet, Jn, Jas, Jude.

226. Cf. STENDAHL, *Apocalypse of John* (n. 166). Hesitation about Rev is expressed by Eusebius (as well as by Origen before him) and Amphilochius. It is not mentioned by Cyril of Jerusalem, the Apostolic Canons, Gregory of Nazianze, or the Syrian Catalogue. In the Codex Claromontanus, Rev and Acts figure (without a special mark) between Barnabas and the Shepherd. See, e.g., D. STRATHMANN, *Origenes und die Apok.*, in *NKZ* 34 (1927) 228-236. A. KIRKLAND, *Did Papias Know the Apocalypse?*, in *EkklPharos* 76 (1994) 175-186 (it was not explicitly mentioned and therefore overlooked by Eusebius). F. THIELMAN, *The Place of the Apocalypse in the Canon of St Gregory Nazianzen*, in *TyndBull* 49 (1998) 155-157 (probably omitted by accident).

227. HMF, p. 181.

228. *Catech.* 33-36: "Let all the rest be put aside in a secondary rank" and "whatever books are not read in Churches, these read not even by thyself".

229. HMF, p. 180.

Pauline letters[230]. He also seems to have been intent on explicating the criteria he used for selecting the writings on his list[231]. These details distinguish the Fragment from the later catalogues in that they usually lack such elaborate comments. Once again we find little which links the Fragment with the later catalogues: if it may be characterized as an anomaly in the second century, how much more anachronistic would it appear were it to be assigned to the late fourth?

VI. PECULIARITIES

Hahneman further discusses seven "peculiarities" that, in his opinion, are difficult to explain on the traditional dating and western provenance. "In a number of these instances, however, the irregularity is removed with the supposition of a fourth-century Eastern origin for the Fragment"[232]. The passages in question are said to offer corroborative evidence for his hypothesis, especially when taking into account their "cumulative effect".

1. The first, i.e., the question of the order of the gospels, has already been mentioned. It is commonly accepted that the Fragment followed

230. Cf. H. MERKEL, *Die Widersprüche zwischen den Evangelien. Ihre polemische und apologetische Begründung in der Alten Kirche bis zu Augustin* (WUNT, 13), Tübingen, Mohr, 1971, pp. 56-62. DAHL, *Particularity* (n. 166). R.W. WALL, *The Problem of the Multiple Letter Canon of the New Testament*, in *HorizonsBT* 8 (1986) 1-31.

231. Frank (*Sinn der Kanonbildung* [n. 3], pp. 181-189) has criticized K. Aland's judgement (*NZSysT*, 1952, p. 229) that the Fragmentist did not have clear criteria in mind ("das Prinzip der Prinziplosigkeit") by arguing that the author does use the specific criteria of "historische Zuverlässigkeit", i.e., apostolicity, and universality. He further contends that these criteria were founded on the conviction that these particular writings were selected because they reflect the theological tendencies of the universal church, and that, for the author, this conviction finds its ultimate expression in the Gospel of John. However, with these latter observations he certainly goes beyond the evidence provided by the text. See the reactions by J. BEUMER, *Das Fragmentum Muratori und seine Rätsel*, in *TP* 48 (1973) 534-550, esp. pp. 546-550. H. BURKHARDT, *Motive und Massstäbe der Kanonbildung nach dem Canon Muratori*, in *TZ* 30 (1974) 207-211. For a general discussion of canonicity criteria, see H. BACHT, *Die Rolle der Tradition in der Kanonbildung*, in *Cath* 12 (1958) 16-36. E. FLESSEMAN - VAN LEER, *Prinzipien der Sammlung und Ausscheidung bei der Bildung des Kanons*, in *ZTK* 61 (1964) 404-420. OHLIG, *Begründung* (n. 184), *passim*, and, for the Fragment, esp. pp. 137-140 (the criterion of apostolicity) and 228-230 (that of catholicity). GAMBLE, *Canon* (n. 3), pp. 67-72 (they were usually not formalized). METZGER, *Canon* (n. 3), pp. 251-254. McDONALD, *Formation* (n. 3), pp. 228-249. D.G. MEADE, *Pseudonymity and Canon. An Investigation into the Relationship of Authorship and Authority in Jewish and Earliest Christian Tradition* (WUNT, 39), Tübingen, Mohr, 1986, pp. 203-207. M. EDWARDS, *Authorship and Canonicity. Some Patristic Evidence*, in C. ROWLAND et al. (eds.), *Understanding, Studying and Reading. FS J. Ashton* (JSNT SS, 153), Sheffield, Academic, 1998, pp. 174-179. A.D. BAUM, *Literarische Echtheit als Kanonkriterium in der alten Kirche*, in *ZNW* 88 (1997) 97-110.

232. HMF, p. 183.

the order Mt, Mk, Lk, Jn. This order has been attested in the East since Origen and eventually became the standard arrangement. In the fourth century it was taken over by western authors such as Jerome, Augustine, and Rufinus. However, we know that this order did not originate with Origen, who regards it as the correct chronological order for the gospels: "I have learned by tradition …"[233]. Unfortunately, Origen tells us neither the source nor the age of this tradition. Clement does not seem to have known it. This may be an indication that Origen got it from a non-Alexandrian source[234]. The order is first attested in the West well before the fourth century by an author who had come from the East. It is followed once by Irenaeus, "apparently as [a] chronological sequence"[235]. While such an order is exceptional in both the West generally and in Irenaeus particularly[236], it was not unheard of at the end of the second century. Like Irenaeus and Origen, the Fragmentist may simply have preferred the chronological order.

2. The Johannine legend. The Fragment tells "a curious legend"[237] about the origin of the Gospel of John: "cohortantibus condiscipulis et ep(iscopi)s suis dixit conieiunate mihi. odie triduo et quid cuique fuerit revelatum alterutrum nobis ennarremus eadem nocte revelatum Andreae ex apostolis ut recogniscentibus cun(c)tis Iohannis suo nomine cuncta discriberet" (ll. 10-16). A similar story is found in Clement of Alexandria (Eusebius, HE 6,14,7), Victorinus of Pettau (*CommRev* 11,1), and Jerome (*De vir. ill.* 9 and *CommMt, praef.*). Jerome's versions seem certainly to have been derived from Victorinus, especially since his "ab Asiae episcopis" makes the most sense when taken as a clarification of the latter's "episcopi"[238]. In *CommMt*, Jerome also refers to the "ecclesiastica historia" for the motif that John had been encouraged to write by "his brethren" ("a fratribus cogeretur ut scriberet"). It is not impossible that he had in mind Clement's story as told by Eusebius, taking γνώριμοι as "fratres" (Rufinus translated it as "discipuli"), though he most probably had access to at least one other source[239].

Three motifs indicate the secondary character of the Fragment's version. (a) John is "urged by his fellow disciples and bishops" ("cohortan-

233. Eusebius, HE 6,25,4-6: ὡς ἐν παραδόσει μαθὼν … (25,4).
234. HMF, p. 185. Clement gives the order Mt/Lk, Mk, Jn (cf. Eusebius, HE 6,14,5-7).
235. HMF, p. 187. *Adv. Haer.* 3,1,1; cf. Eusebius, HE 5,8,2-4.
236. Three times he follows the "Clementine" order (*Adv. Haer.* 3,9,1-11,6; 3,11,7; 4,6,1) and once he has Jn, Lk, Mt, Mk (3,11,8).
237. HMF, p. 188.
238. HMF, p. 190.
239. Hahneman acknowledges that HE is "the likely choice", but remains hesitant because the details in Jerome's version about the fast have no parallel in Eusebius (p. 189 n. 3).

tibus condiscipulis et episcopis suis"). For Hahneman, "the inclusion of *episcopi* in the Fragment suggests a later development"[240]. However, a story about how John went to the region of Ephesus in Asia Minor and appointed bishops was known to Clement[241]. In fact, if we accept the traditional dating, Victorinus' "episcopi" perhaps becomes another indication (along with his comment on Paul's corporate letters, cf. above) that he knew and used the Fragment. Victorinus, who was especially concerned to emphasize that John wrote "afterwards in reply to certain heresies"[242], may have intentionally omitted the combination of "condiscipuli" and "episcopi" due to its strangeness. Jerome made the same observation (*De vir. ill.* and *CommMt*). Yet he also knows of a second version in which John was urged by "fratres" and which he loosely combines with the former without identifying the "brethren".

(b) John invites the others to join him in a three-day fast hoping that while they fast they will each receive a revelation concerning the details of what should be written down. This seems to be another "later development". Clement knows that John was divinely inspired (πνεύματι θεοφορηθέντα), but he never mentions a fast. Jerome does, and he also seems to know that John did not fast on his own ("si indicto ieiunio in commune omnes Dominum precarentur"). The Fragment's explanation of the motif of divine inspiration by a fast cannot be regarded as new[243]. However, by itself, this fact is not enough to situate it in the fourth century.

(c) It is only in the Fragment that we read that it was Andrew's initiative that compelled John to "write down all things in his own name" and then to allow the others to review the result. Hahneman regards this motif as another interpolation and further evidence for a late date and eastern provenance[244]. It is true that stories about Andrew became particularly popular in the East[245]. However, the "acts of Andrew" is hardly a major theme of the Fragment. As Hahneman acknowledges, "the association of Andrew with John in the legend of the Muratorian Fragment may be based upon nothing more substantial than the prominence given to Andrew in the gospel of John"[246]. But while Andrew's intervention provides evidence in favour of John's authorship of the gospel, it falls

240. HMF, p. 190.
241. *Quis dives* 42; also quoted by Eusebius, cf. HE 3,23,5-6.
242. "Nam et evangelium postea conscripsit, cum essent enim Valentinus et Cerinthus et Ebion ..." (ed. Dulaey, SC 423, p. 92).
243. HMF, p. 190, who refers to the Revelation of Ezra 1,5.
244. HMF, p. 191.
245. Evidence in HMF, pp. 191-192.
246. HMF, p. 191.

short of resolving all the difficulties: e.g., apparently, the fast is broken off after only one night, contrary to John's initial intention. This may explain why, at least on this point, Victorinus and Jerome opted to follow another tradition that highlighted John's struggle with heretics in Asia Minor long after the dispersion of the other apostles. Yet again, however, even if one felt compelled to conclude that the story about Andrew must be a later interpolation, it still does not necessitate the acceptance of eastern provenance (see below, pp. 553-554).

3. The Acts of all the Apostles. The short note on the Acts contains two elements that seem more easily explicable in a fourth-century context. The title of the book is given as "Acta autem omnium apostolorum" (l. 34). It has been suggested that the insertion of the adjective "all" is a conscious attempt at anti-Marcionite polemics[247], even though such a technique is not attested elsewhere[248]. Hahneman compares it to a couple of different titles the book receives in the fourth century, i.e., "The Acts of the Twelve Apostles" (Cyril, Doctrina Addai) and "The Catholic Acts of the (Wise) Apostles" (Gregory of Nazianze, Amphilochius). This "tendency to amplify" the title would be related to anti-Manichaean polemics and to an attempt to counter their fourth-century collection of five apocryphal Acts[249]. Pope Innocent (412-417 AD) mentions several apocryphal Acts that are to be rejected. Two of these (The Acts of Peter and The Acts of John) were supposedly authored by a certain Leucianus. Much later, Photius (9th century) claims knowledge of a Manichaean collection of Acts by Leucius Charinus. Innocent's information, in addition to perhaps being incorrect, is, at best, indirect: he never explicitly labels Leucianus a Manichaean[250]. Though one must grant that the emphasis on the number twelve and on the "catholic" character of the Acts might have scored some polemical points against a collection of five apocryphal Acts, it is also obvious that any argument made from the insertion of "all" would be rather weak. The Fragment betrays concern neither for the precise, "canonical" number of apostles involved nor for the "catholicity" of the recorded "acts". Similarly "sub uno libro scripta sunt" should not be connected to a Manichaean collection of the apocryphal Acts. It would be of little help to say that Luke wrote his "in one book", since the Manichaeans also seem to have been intending to unite their Acts into one corpus (contained in one book?).

---

247. VON CAMPENHAUSEN, *Entstehung* (n. 3), p. 248 n. 214.
248. So HMF, p. 193.
249. HMF, pp. 193-194.
250. The Acts of Andrew were written by the "philosophers" Xenocharides and Leonidas.

The expression could just as easily have been inspired by Luke's opening words in Acts 1,1 (τὸν μὲν πρῶτον λόγον). After this first λόγος,
he collected in a second book "all" the "acts" of the apostles. The work
was widely known by the end of the second century. It was quoted by
Irenaeus, but only Tertullian refers to the work by its title ("Acts" or
"Acts of the Apostles"). If the Fragmentist was a contemporary of these
two, it would seem that he had little precedent on which to base a title
for the work. The manuscript reads "omniu" with a horizontal stroke
over the -u, representing final -m, as often occurs elsewhere in the
manuscript[251]. Since the canonical Acts obviously do not contain the
"acts" of "all" the apostles, it is not clear what the author of the Fragment may have meant by "omnium". Maybe he was influenced, or confused, by the immediately preceding expression "omnium mirabilium"
of l. 33 which contains a similar degree of hyperbole, unless he was inspired by the great number of occurrences of "omnes" at the beginning
of Acts referring to the group of apostles as a whole[252].

The second problem has to do with the source of the information for
Paul's journey to Spain and for Peter's martyrdom (ll. 37-39). That Luke
was the author of Acts is undisputed from Irenaeus on. However, the
question of Luke's reliability and of his being an eyewitness was obviously a fundamental issue given the wording of the gospel's prologue
and the high profile position awarded to the book's "we-sections".
Similarly, the Fragmentist may have been concerned to explain why
Luke left out some important information regarding Peter and Paul. The
Acts of Peter contain a long account of Peter's martyrdom (*Actus
Vercellenses* 30-41) and a short one about Paul's departure from Rome
for Spain (*Actus Vercellenses* 1). The Acts of Peter may have been
known (in some form) to Origen (Eusebius, HE 3,1,2), just as was most
probably the case for the author of the Didascalia. The work seems to
have originated in Asia Minor in the last decades of the second century[253]. It is also to be observed that the stories about Peter and Paul are
not directly connected with each other in the Acts. Paul's goodbye (no
information is provided about the actual journey to Spain or his missionary activity) is mentioned only to explain Simon Magus' success in
Rome (*Actus Vercellenses* 2). Peter's martyrdom follows much later and
only after his controversy with Simon. As for the Fragmentist, it is not

---

251. See, e.g., in the same line, the orthography of "autem", and in the previous, that
of "scriptorem" and "mirabilium".

252. See esp. Acts 1,14, and also 2,1.4.7.32.

253. W. SCHNEEMELCHER, *Petrusakten*, in ID., *Neutestamentliche Apokryphen*, Tübingen, Mohr, [5]1989, II, pp. 243-288, here 255.

necessary for him to have been "familiar with accounts of both"[254]. Paul's plans for a visit to Spain are mentioned in Rom 15,24.28. Hahneman points out that chapters 15 and 16 of Rom may not have been known in the West at the turn of the third century[255]. In reply it should be noted that the Fragmentist probably did not borrow his information from Rom, since there it is never said that Paul's plans were realized. The Fragmentist's "ad Spaniam" (instead of "Hispaniam") is not necessarily a transliteration of the Greek of Rom 15,24.28, but could just as easily stem from the Fragment's Latin translator. Recall too that Clement of Rome had already referred to the martyrdoms of both Peter and Paul, the latter of whom once "had reached the limits of the West" (*1 Clem.* 5,4-7)[256].

4. Laodiceans. The remaining four issues all deal with writings outside the New Testament canon. In ll. 63-68 the Fragmentist mentions an apocryphal epistle of Paul to the Laodiceans (*Laod*), another to the Alexandrians (*Alex*), and "several others" ("alia plura") that are not received in the church. It is possible to read "alia plura" as (also) referring to letters that were not ascribed to Paul (some of the Catholic Epistles?) but this is rather unlikely. The search for the epistle to the Alexandrians, which some have taken to be Heb, has thus far proven futile. A second problem is the expression "Pauli nomine fincte ad heresem marcionis" (l. 65). This could refer either to *Alex* ("fincta") or to *Alex* and *Laod* ("finctae"), or, possibly even to a separate group of Marcionite letters[257]. The meaning of "fincte ad heresem" ("in the spirit of"?) is also debated[258].

Hahneman's argument for a late date is based upon *Laod*. Two writings with this name are known to have existed. According to Tertullian, *Laod* was the title used by the Marcionites for Eph (*Adv. Marc.* 5,11,12 and 5,17,1)[259]. In Latin, there is also preserved an apocryphal epistle to

---

254. So HMF, p. 195; ctr. SCHNEEMELCHER, *Petrusakten* (n. 253), p. 245.

255. HMF, pp. 47-50.

256. Cf. H.E. LONA, *Der erste Clemensbrief* (Kommentar zu den Apostolischen Vätern, 2), Göttingen, Vandenhoeck & Ruprecht, 1998, p. 165, who analyzes the possibility of *1 Clem* having depended upon Rom and of the Fragment having depended upon *1 Clem.* "Die Notiz ist wichtig, weil hier zum ersten Mal die Überlieferung von I Clem 5,4-7 aufgenommen wird".

257. The first suggestion comes from M.R. JAMES, *The Apocryphal New Testament*, Oxford, Clarendon, 1924, pp. 478-480. The last is from J.B. LIGHTFOOT, *Saint Paul's Epistles to the Colossians and to Philemon*, London, Macmillan, 1875, p. 290 n. 1. The middle suggestion is the most common. See ZAHN, *Geschichte*, II.1 (n. 3), p. 83.

258. So ZAHN, *Geschichte*, II.1 (n. 3), p. 84: "gemäss der Irrlehre Marcions". METZGER, *Canon* (n. 3), p. 307, translates as "[both] forged in Paul's name to [further] the heresy of Marcion".

259. In some manuscripts, "to the Ephesians" is absent from 1,1. The question is of particular importance if Ephesus is given a central role in the generation of either the

the Laodiceans. It is a pastiche of about twenty verses taken from Paul's letters (esp. Phil). Its date and provenance cannot be ascertained. It is unlikely that it is a Marcionite forgery, as Harnack once maintained, since it contains nothing that is distinctively Marcionite[260]. Since the Biblical text concurs with neither the Old Latin nor the Vulgate, it has been suggested that it is a translation from a Greek original. The earliest certain evidence for the letter comes from a fifth-century author writing in the West[261]. Hahneman contends that it was commonly regarded as trustworthy in the West[262], and its frequent inclusion in Biblical manuscripts lends support to this idea. However, Filastrius of Brescia († ca. 397) notes that, although it is read by some, the/a letter to the Laodiceans is not appropriate for his audience[263]. In the East, a letter to the Laodiceans is mentioned by Epiphanius and Jerome and by a few later authors[264]. It is never quoted and is generally rejected as apocryphal. If it is identical with the Latin *Laod*, this could be another indication that it originated in the East in a relatively recent period. According to Hahneman, this data leaves us with two possibilities with respect to our document. "The Fragmentist must have been either (a) confused about Laodiceans, not realizing that the Marcionite Laodiceans was the same as the canonical Ephesians, or else (b) aware of a letter to the Laodiceans that was distinct from the canonical Ephesians. Since the Fragmentist listed two separate works, the presumption should be that he knew two different epistles"[265]. Are these really the only two possibilities? Since the Fragmentist does not quote from *Laod*, it remains possible that he had still another, now lost, letter in mind[266]. His distinction between Eph and *Laod* does not have to mean that he "*knew* two different epistles" (emphasis added). The possibility that he was confused about Marcion's *Laod* cannot be ruled out. Initially, such confusion may seem strange to those acquainted with Tertullian's comment that Marcion gave the title *Laod* to Eph (which Marcion may not have

Pauline corpus or the New Testament. See E.J. GOODSPEED, *Ephesians and the First Edition of Paul*, in *JBL* 70 (1951) 285-291. E.E. LEMCIO, *Ephesus and the New Testament Canon*, in *BJRL* 69 (1986-87) 210-234 (note the reference to the Fragment on p. 216, where we read that its date is now "under suspicion").

260. Cf. also G. QUISPEL, *De Brief aan de Laodicensen, een Marcionitische vervalsing*, in *NTT* 5 (1950) 43-46. Ctr. W. SCHNEEMELCHER, *Der Laodicenerbrief*, in *NTAp* (n. 253), II, pp. 41-44, here 43; HMF, p. 198.

261. Cf. the quotation of *Laod* v. 4 in Ps.-Augustine, *Speculum* (CSEL 12, p. 516).

262. HMF, p. 199.

263. *Diversarum haereseon liber* 89,2.

264. HMF, p. 199. Jerome, *De vir. ill.* 5. Epiphanius, *Pan.* 42,12,3.

265. HMF, p. 197.

266. HMF, p. 197: "if no other …".

known under this name). Tertullian simply states the fact: he does not employ it as an argument in his otherwise highly polemical presentation on Marcion's canon. Others may well have guessed that *Laod* was different from *Eph*. That this has happened can be shown not only from the Fragment but also from what Epiphanius says about Marcion's reception of Paul's letters. He lists both the letter to the Ephesians and "parts of" a/the letter to the Laodiceans among those accepted by the Marcionites (*Pan.* 42,9,4 and 42,12,3)[267]. *Laod* had to be rejected if one was unwilling to acknowledge that the Marcionites possessed an authentic Pauline letter now lost to the church. There is no need to assume that the Fragmentist must have been a contemporary of Epiphanius to conclude that both may have reasoned in the same way.

5. Wisdom of Solomon[268]. Much has been written on the puzzling reference to the Wisdom of Solomon found between the section dedicated to the Catholic Epistles and that on the apocalypses: "epistola sane Iude et superscrictio Iohannis duas in catholica habentur et sapientia ab amicis salomonis in honore(m) ipsius scripta apocalapse etiam Iohanis et Petri ..." (ll. 69-71). In addition to it being the only Old Testament book mentioned among a discussion of New Testament writings, there is also the problem of how to interpret the claim that Wisdom was written "ab amicis" and not by Solomon, as was common in Christian tradition well into the fourth century[269].

The original reading of this line is debated. Two emendations have been proposed. The first is relatively unimportant, since it does not substantially alter the meaning the passage would have had for the Fragmentist. It has been suggested that "ab amicis" is a mistake for an original ὑπὸ Φίλων(ος). That some regarded Philo as the author of Wisdom is also reported by Jerome[270]. Hahneman mentions the possibility that "Jerome may have seen the Fragment or derived his information from it"[271]. In his opinion, if the Fragment were to be dated in the East of the fourth century, this hypothesis becomes still more probable. But again,

---

267. See above, n. 170.

268. On Wis in the Christian Bible, see A.C. SUNDBERG, *The Old Testament Canon of the Early Church* (HTS, 20), Cambridge, MA, Harvard UP, 1964, pp. 129-169. R.M. GRANT, *The Book of Wisdom at Alexandria. Reflections on the History of the Canon and Theology* (SP, 7; TU, 92), Berlin, Akademie, 1966, pp. 462-472. É. JUNOD, *La formation et la composition de l'Ancien Testament dans l'Église grecque des quatre premiers siècles*, in S. AMSLER et al. (eds.), *Le canon de l'Ancien Testament. Sa formation et son histoire* (Le monde de la Bible, 10), Genève, Labor & Fides, 1984, pp. 105-151.

269. HMF, p. 201.

270. Cf. the preface to the Books of Solomon (ca. 392). For the emendation, see TREGELLES, *Canon Muratorianus* (n. 3), p. 55.

271. HMF, p. 201.

this does not necessarily follow (see below). Jerome may well have derived his information from the Fragment, but this does not prove that
ὑπὸ Φίλωνος ("a Philone") was the original reading. There remains the
possibility that this was simply the translator's way of trying to make
sense of ὑπὸ φίλων, for which Wis contains no evidence. Those who
defend this latter reading do so because it fits better the word order
("The Wisdom [was written] by friends of Solomon") than that of the
alternative reading ("The Wisdom of Solomon [was written] by Philo",
in which "Salomonis" should occur immediately after "sapientia")[272].
The argument becomes less compelling if one recalls that it is not the
only syntactical difficulty in the Fragment. Nevertheless, one cannot rule
out that ὑπὸ φίλων was the original reading. It may have resulted from
confusing Wis with Prov, which in 25,1 reads "the men of Hizkia
…"[273]. In the end, the difference may be not so important: in both cases
the Fragment reports the same fact, viz. that Wis was not composed by
Solomon.

The second emendation has to do with "et", for which some propose
to read "ut": Jude and Jn are received in Church in the same way as is
Wis[274]. The rather laborious description of the letters of Jude ("sane")
and Jn ("superscriptio") probably indicates that the Fragmentist is aware
that the authorship of these letters is disputed. Interestingly, he argues
that this debate is irrelevant: they are to be received just like Wis, which
is also a pseudepigraphon. Though the text may indeed be smoother if
"ut" is read for "et" (esp. since "et" follows after the main verb), one is
still faced with the issue of how far one can push such stylistic arguments. In either case, the question remains the acceptance of pseudepigrapha. The Fragment is in favour of it with respect to Jude and Jn, and
uses Wis to reinforce his argument. Still, the two solutions result in different meanings. If the text reads "ut", Wis becomes an element in a
comparison, but is not to be thought of as part of the New Testament.
With "et", Wis is equated with the Catholic Epistles and should be regarded as a New Testament book. This brings us to the second question.

Kaestli reads "ut" and therefore concludes that the Fragmentist does
not reckon Wis with the New Testament books[275]. Sundberg and Hahneman, however, read "et" and consequently think that the Fragmentist

272. Cf. KAESTLI, *Fragment de Muratori* (n. 46), p. 626.
273. There is no reason to follow Harnack in his belief that both books were mentioned in the Fragment.
274. Cf. KAESTLI, *Fragment de Muratori* (n. 46), pp. 621-624.
275. "Une telle intégration n'est d'ailleurs pas attestée par le *CM*" (*Fragment de
Muratori* [n. 46], p. 627).

considers Wis as part of the New Testament. They go so far as to find in this "et" an indication for a late date and eastern provenance. But, as always, one must ask if their evidence is compelling.

Sundberg and Hahneman sharply distinguish between the situation in the East and that in the West in the late-fourth century. In the West, Wis is in the Old Testament canon (Augustine, the Carthage synods). Apparently, however, this was not always the case. Irenaeus quoted from Wis and alluded to it without clearly indicating its status[276]. Hilary of Poitiers did not include it in his list of Old Testament books (Prol. *LibPs* 15; Sirach is also absent). Jerome and Rufinus, though reflecting eastern practice in their rejection of the book, also might have done so because they knew Wis was not normally considered as part of the western Old Testament canon. In other words, it may be that the late fourth-century divergence between the East and the West was actually a fairly recent phenomenon.

If all this is accepted, the Fragment (if fourth century) becomes a witness to an era in which the Old Testament canon was firmly and finally closed. Sundberg argues that, in the East, the extent of the OT canon was fixed by the time of Athanasius. Thus, those after Athanasius who still wanted to preserve certain Jewish writings for the church had to become, for lack of a better word, "creative". One such step was to reckon Wis as a New Testament book. Sundberg's idea of a closed canon may be too rigid. The lists drafted by fourth-century eastern authors show a considerable variety in the order in which the books of the Old Testament are listed, not to mention certain hesitations with regard to Esther[277]. Moreover, even in the East, some texts that had never belonged to the Jewish canon were eventually accepted as part of other books (Dan, Jer). Of course, it would have been more difficult for an entire book like Wis to follow this course. More relevant to their theory is the claim that several fourth-century authors did in fact try to save Wis by including it among the books of the New Testament. Sundberg and Hahneman draw particular attention to Eusebius and Epiphanius. Eusebius mentions Wis together with other New Testament writings when discussing Irenaeus' handling of Scripture (HE 5,8,1-8). Although, as Hahneman observes, it may be that "the association of Wisdom with these New Testament Scriptures appears to have been made by Eusebius, not Irenaeus"[278]. Regardless, it deserves to be noted that, in this passage, Eusebius is not

---

276. HMF, p. 204.
277. Esther was not included by Athanasius, Epiphanius (*Pan.* 8), or Gregory of Nazianze. See HMF, pp. 78-79.
278. HMF, p. 204.

compiling any New Testament canon, let alone his own personal canon, as he attempted earlier in 3,25. Furthermore, if 5,8 is invoked as an argument, it offers evidence that such an "association" had already been made before the closing of the Old Testament canon and that it could be made on the basis of a second-century author. The evidence from Epiphanius is more ambivalent than Sundberg and Hahneman would admit[279]. Epiphanius regards Wis and Sir as two books "of disputed canonicity" (*Pan.* 8,6 ἐν ἀμφιλέκτῳ), though they are not to be thought of as apocryphal (χωρὶς ἄλλων τινῶν βιβλίων ἐναποκρύφων). In *Pan.* 76,22,5, he argues that Aetius's use of the expression ἀγέννητον is found nowhere in the Old and the New Testament, or in the Wisdom of Solomon and the Wisdom of Sirach, both of which are reckoned among the "sacred scriptures" (καὶ πάσαις ἁπλῶς γραφαῖς θείαις). Both are mentioned again in *De mens.* 4 at the end of a list of OT books, along with the comment that they are useful but should not be counted with the others since they were not preserved in the ark[280]. In short, Wis and Sir do not belong to the Old Testament but neither does Epiphanius say that they are a part of the New Testament[281]. For Athanasius and Rufinus, Wis is to be reckoned with the "catechetical" or the "ecclesiastical" works, together with Sirach, Esther, Judith, Tobit, the Didache, the Shepherd (Athanasius), and also 1-2 Macc and the Preaching of Peter (Rufinus). The way the Fragmentist deals with Wis differs from that of these later authors. (a) Even if one were to accept that they intended to include Wis in their NT lists because they knew it was no longer possible to add to the OT books, one must reckon with the fact that they did not explicitly say this. The Fragmentist, on the other hand, explicitly uses this argument with regard to the Shepherd (ll. 78-80). Moreover, he uses it to exclude that particular writing both from the Old and New Testament canons. The way he formulates the argument, with "completum numero" in between "neque inter profetas" and "neque inter apostolos" (regardless of whether or not this was intentional) suggests that, for him, not only "the number of the prophets" but also that "of the apostles" is closed and complete. (b) Second, contrary to Athanasius, Rufinus, and Epiphanius, the Fragmentist mentions only one Old Testament book. And (if "et" is taken as the authentic reading) he fails to qualify this reference with respect to the books that are to be received by the church.

---

279. This argument has even impressed some of their critics (cf. Ferguson [n. 44], Henne [nn. 6, 44]; ctr Kaestli [n. 46]).

280. Another list of OT books follows in *De mens.* 23, but without the contested books.

281. See KAESTLI, *Fragment de Muratori* (n. 46), p. 621.

"In catholica habentur" would apply both to the Catholic Epistles and to Wis, with no reason for suspecting that the expression was intended to indicate an inferior status for these writings. For the Fragmentist, Wis would not belong to a separate category[282].

In summary, the association of Wis with Jude/Jn must be acknowledged as exceptional, esp. if "et" is the preferred reading. Even more remarkable is the fact that the Fragmentist, even if he did write "et", seems to have been oblivious to the way in which fourth-century authors usually positioned Wis in their lists of canonical books.

6. Revelation of Peter. If the "apocalypsis Petri" (*ApPe*), which some thought should not be read in church (ll. 71-73), is identical with the apocryphal "Revelation of Peter" (preserved only in Ethiopic and in a fragmentary Greek version), the Fragment would provide easily the earliest, not to mention the most exceptional, western attestation of this composition[283]. Hahneman observes that *ApPe*, which was probably composed in Egypt between 125-150 AD, was known almost exclusively in the East. As for western attestation, he refers to an anonymous homily of the fourth century in which *ApPe* is quoted[284]. However, it appears that the work was more widely known in the West than this, even if the data is from a later period[285]. Eusebius lists a *ApPe* among the νόθοι (HE 3,25,4-5). In HE 3,3,2 he radically rejects the work, along with the rest of the apocryphal Petrine literature, by noting that "no ecclesiastical writer of the ancient time or of our own has used their testimonies". Elsewhere in his HE, however, he reports that Clement of Alexandria reckoned it with the disputed works (6,14,1 ἀντιλεγομένας). Eusebius cannot have derived this information on Clement's use of the *ApPe* from his extant works (*Ecl. Proph.* 40,1,2; 48,1; 49). Hahneman assumes that the report reflects Eusebius' own opinion[286], although in doing so he overlooks (or forgets) that Eusebius explicitly refers to Clement's

---

282. Ctr. W. HORBURY, *The Wisdom of Solomon in the Muratorian Fragment*, in *JTS* 45 (1994) 149-159, who argues that it is not unusual in catalogues of Old and New Testament books to include disputed OT books at the end of the list. In the Fragment, however, Wis is the only OT book mentioned and it is not set apart as disputed. Even if the clause on Wis is read with the one on the apocalypses which follows, this would still not change the status of the writing as an accepted work. Note also that such a reading becomes more difficult since the conjunction "et" then becomes obsolete and the link with "apocalypse etiam" rather loose. It is unlikely that it was the writer's intention to introduce an independent clause.

283. On *ApPe*, see, e.g., C.D.G. MÜLLER, *Die Offenbarung des Petrus*, in SCHNEEMELCHER, *NTAp* (n. 253), II, pp. 562-578.

284. *Homily of the Ten Virgins*, ll. 58-59. Cf. HMF, p. 205.

285. A. HARNACK, *Die Petrusapokalypse in der abendländischen Kirche* (TU, 13), Leipzig, Hinrichs, 1895. Cf. MÜLLER, *Offenbarung* (n. 283), p. 564.

286. HMF, p. 206.

Hypotyposes, a work now extant only in a few fragments. It also seems unwise to exclude another possibility, viz. that Eusebius' confusion might result from comparing different opinions of Clement. *ApPe* continued to be disputed throughout the fourth and into the fifth century. It was even listed among the "antilegomena" in the Stichometry of Nicephorus (ca. 850)[287]. The compiler of the catalogue in the codex Claromontanus marked the work with a horizontal line before the title, just as he did for Barnabas, the Shepherd, and the Acts of Paul. Jerome, who no doubt was acquainted with Eusebius' comments, opens his *De vir. ill.* with a list of canonical and apocryphal Petrine literature. There we read that the/a "Revelation of Peter" is to be rejected and is never to be read in church. In the next century, Sozomen, while attesting that it was still being read in some Palestinian churches, does not encourage the practice[288]. Around 400, Macarius Magnes quotes (and then objects to) a passage from the *ApPe* on the judgement of heaven and earth. He never condemns the work, but from the tone of his comments as well as from the way he quickly passes from it to a quotation from Isa 35,4, it is clear that *ApPe* does not belong to his canon[289]. For Hahneman, who situates the Fragment in Palestine/Syria, its author must have been aware of this opposition to reading the *ApPe* in public. "It is in the fourth century, then, that the reservations mentioned in the Fragment would find the strongest parallel"[290]. However, if this is so, one would also expect the author to defend more forcefully the exceptional position of his community instead of expending so much more space and energy on explaining why the Shepherd should not be read in church, something he does in the following section.

7. Heretical works. The seventh and last "peculiarity" deals with the heretical authors mentioned in ll. 81-85. The passage's many difficulties make it the weakest part of the argument. Westcott's comment has been quoted by many after him: "The conclusion is hopelessly corrupt, and evidently was so in the copy from which the Fragment was derived"[291]. To this, one can also add that the twelfth-century extracts offer no help: they are equally corrupt and break off at the same point. Nevertheless,

---

287. HMF, pp. 207-208.
288. HE 7,19,9. He also mentions the *Apocalypse of Paul*, a work that was apparently still very popular in monastic circles. *ApPaul* was unknown in ancient times. It was said to have been only recently discovered under the house of Paul in Tarsus.
289. Cf. T.W. CRAFER, *The Apocriticus of Macarius Magnes*, London, SPCK, 1919, pp. xxv, 129-131. Cap. 4,6: "No one is so uneducated or so stupid as not to know that …", and 4,16: "for if we pass over the Apocalypse of Peter …".
290. HMF, p. 208.
291. *Canon* (n. 3), p. 530 n. 8.

those who have attempted to make sense of the names and titles in this section all agree that the references can in some sense be connected with the anti-Marcionite and/or anti-Montanist polemics of the late-second or early-third century.

Before turning to the issues that are discussed by Hahneman, two preliminary remarks are in order. First, it is true that "the association of Miltiades with these several heretics, however confused the passage in the Fragment, is extraordinary"[292]. A combination of a certain Arsinous (?)[293], with a Valentinus, a Miltiades (?), and a Basilides is unique, but ancient heresiography is replete with associations that are no longer clear to us or that were never intended to describe an historical situation. Second, the corrupt state of the text does not hinder Hahneman from being confident about its meaning. However, it is not at all certain whether the Fragmentist really wanted to say that Basilides was the founder of the Cataphrygians (comp. the abl. "una cum Basilide" followed by the acc.). And it is not clear whether he regarded all four heretics as the co-authors of a psalm book[294]. "Qui etiam ... una cum Basilide" could be an independent clause.

a. Miltiades. Tertullian mentions a Miltiades, together with Justin, Irenaeus and a certain Proculus, as being among those who have written against the heresies of their day (*Adv. Val.* 5). While it would be consistent with Tertullian's penchant for rhetorical irony to associate a prominent Montanist author with orthodox theologians, there is nothing in the text that mandates such a conclusion. Moreover, the evidence in Eusebius may be difficult to harmonise, but Hahneman's suggestion seems to only add to the confusion. In HE 5,28,4 the same (?) Miltiades is named second (after Justin and before Tatian and Clement, Irenaeus and Melito) in a list of contemporaneous orthodox authors. In 5,17,1-5, Eusebius quotes from an anonymous source that has reported that an opponent had attacked a certain Miltiades for criticising ecstatic prophecy. However, there is a textual problem here. Miltiades is mentioned three times in the chapter, once in the introduction, once in a quotation of the anonymous source, and a third time toward the end, where reference is made to the work of this Miltiades as an apologist. For this quo-

292. HMF, p. 211. On the spelling of the name, see above, n. 118.
293. See above, n. 119.
294. HMF, p. 211: "The last lines of the Fragment are obviously confused since Basilides 'of Asia Minor' (?) is mistakenly named as the founder of the Cataphrygians, and as someone who with Arsinous, Valentinus, and Miltiades was thought to have composed a new psalm-book for Marcion".

tation, the Syriac version and all but one of the Greek manuscripts[295] (Rufinus skipped the passage) read Alcibiades. Eusebius already quoted from the same anonymous source in the previous chapter. There the source claims that he had been ordered to write "against the heresy of those that are called the partisans of Miltiades"[296]. This Miltiades, then, would be a heretic. In HE 5,3,2-4 Eusebius once more returns to the so-called "Letter of the Martyrs of Lyon", a text which he had used extensively in 5,1-2, and reports the story of the martyr Alcibiades, who, by his extreme asceticism, caused a scandal for his companions. In the next section he is presented as the head of a faction, together with Montanus and a certain Theodotus, who is mentioned again in 5,16,14-15. Hahneman refuses to accept that there might have existed two persons with the name Miltiades, one a Montanist, the other orthodox. However, Hahneman's own interpretation makes Eusebius responsible for even more confusion. He thinks that in 5,17,1-2 Eusebius mistakenly wrote "Alcibiades" for an original "Miltiades". Eusebius also became confused at 5,16,3, but this time he wrote "Miltiades" for the "Alcibiades" of the anonymous source. Of course, it is no longer possible to find out who was responsible for the reading "Alcibiades" in 5,17,2. The reading is supported by the large majority of the manuscripts, and may have been caused by the mention of the other Montanist, Theodotus, at the end of the preceding chapter (5,16,14-15; cf. 5,3,4)[297]. Why must it have been Eusebius' mistake? The variant is found only in 5,17,2; not in 5,17,1 or 5,17,5. It is not retained in the critical editions of HE, since it makes no sense after 5,17,1[298]. Hahneman argues that the confusion in 5,17,2 is "perhaps confirmed" by that of 5,16,3[299]. However, this latter passage offers no confirmation whatsoever. There is no manuscript evidence for a variant reading. In fact, one is left with only Hahneman's conjecture that the original read "Alcibiades"[300], a proposal which reminds one of Zahn's hesitant suggestion to read "Miltiades" for "Alcibiades" in HE 5,3,4 (something not mentioned by, and, apparently, either unknown to

295. Cod. Paris. 1436, which depends upon Cod. Sinaiticus 1183, a work which is itself a copy of Cod. Laurentianus 70,20. Cf. E. Schwartz (ed. of HE), in GCS 9/3, pp. xxix-xxxiv.

296. HE 5,16,3: συγγράψαι τινὰ λόγον εἰς τὴν τῶν κατὰ Μιλτιάδην λεγομένων αἵρεσιν.

297. So HMF, p. 211.

298. Cf. Schwartz, in GCS 9/3, p. cxlv: "Durch irgend ein Versehen". Schwartz compares with similar mistakes and comments: "denkbar ist auch hier, dass ein Schreiber die ihm zur Copie übergebene Stelle einmal falsch abschrieb und Euseb sich die Mühe des Nachvergleichens gespart hat".

299. HMF, p. 210.

300. Schwartz, in GCS 9/1, p. 460; 9/3, p. cxlv.

or rejected by Hahneman). From this collection of contestables, Hahneman builds an argument for dating the Fragment later than Eusebius. The possibility of the historian having depended on the Fragment is dismissed as "unlikely". Opposed to this is the possibility that their agreement in identifying Miltiades as a heretic (in Eusebius as a Montanist) indicates that "the Fragmentist was specifically familiar with this passage in Eusebius"[301]. Further, in drawing this conclusion, Hahneman seems to have forgotton that in 5,16-17, Eusebius specifically states that for his information on anti-Montanist polemics he is dependent on an unnamed author who probably composed his work a long time ago. In fact, in 5,16,2, Eusebius says that he had mentioned him earlier. Jerome (*De vir. ill.* 39) thought the anonymous source was Rhodon, who was quoted by Eusebius in 5,13, and who, as a disciple of Tatian, takes us well into the second century. Rufinus identified the anonymous source with Apollinaris of Hierapolis, who was mentioned by Eusebius in 5,16,1 as an opponent of Montanism. The anonymous source is quoted in 5,16,3 as naming a certain Avercius Marcellus as his patron. If, as some have thought[302], this figure is Abercius, the bishop of Hierapolis († 216), it would again point to the end of the second century or the first decade of the third. Interestingly, all the authors just mentioned hail from Asia Minor[303]. Finally, the "Letter of the Martyrs of Vienne and Lyon", which Eusebius quoted extensively in 5,1-3, and from which he took the information on the "Montanist" Alcibiades, was written soon after 177 and was addressed to "the churches of Asia and Phrygia" (5,1,2). In short, the Fragmentist had several sources from which he could have got the information on Miltiades' heretical status; he did not necessarily have to have read it in Eusebius.

b. Hahneman's second argument rests on the word "catafrycum". It is a contraction of κατὰ Φρύγας. The Montanists were sometimes called "the Phrygians". The contracted form does not occur in the catalogue

301. HMF, p. 211. Montanist scholars are divided about whether Eusebius and the Fragmentist refer to the same person. Even so, they never draw anything like the kind of conclusion proposed by Hahneman. See, e.g., C. TREVETT, *Montanism. Gender, Authority and the New Prophecy*, Cambridge, UP, 1996, p. 198: "Perhaps it was the latter's [i.e., Miltiades'] writings which were rejected in ll. 81-2 of the Roman Muratorian Fragment (cf. Eusebius *HE* v.16.3)". W. TABBERNEE, *Montanist Inscriptions and Testimonia. Epigraphic Sources Illustrating the History of Montanism* (Patristic Monograph Series, 16), Macon, GA, Mercer, 1997, p. 52: "It may have been this Miltiades [i.e., the one of HE 5,16,3] whose writings are rejected as heretical by ll. 81-82 of the Muratorian Canon, but this is by no means certain".

302. Cf. P. DE LABRIOLLE, *La crise montaniste*, Paris, Leroux, 1913, pp. 581-584. TREVETT, *Montanism* (n. 301), p. 30. TABBERNEE, *Montanist Inscriptions* (n. 301), p. 53 n. 13 and 130, is less sure.

303. However, Rhodon was a disciple of Tatian in Rome (HE 5,13,1).

that is now found appended to Tertullian's *De Praescriptione Haereti-corum*. This catalogue was probably composed in Greek at the beginning of the third century. It was later translated into Latin by Victorinus of Pettau († 304). In it one reads "qui dicuntur secundum Phrygas" (7,21). From this snippet, Hahneman draws the following unwarranted conclusion: "[the fact that] the Latin contraction 'Cataphrygians' was not used until the fourth century is evidenced in the pseudo-Tertullian writing *Adversus Omnes Haereses*"[304]. A more supportable conclusion would be to say that this particular writing simply offers no evidence for it. In fact, it probably could not do so, since, as Hahneman also notes, it could be that "secundum Phrygas" is not a translation of κατὰ Φρύγας. Elsewhere in the text κατά is simply transcribed (e.g. "kata Proclum" and "kata Aeschinem"). Furthermore, it is probably incorrect to claim that the contraction is not to be found before the fourth century[305]. As for the Fragment, Hahneman takes it for granted that "catafrycum" is the translation of a contracted Greek form. He never considers the possibility that the fourth-century translator may simply have introduced it to the text. From this same period we know that Rufinus translated Eusebius' κατὰ τῆς τῶν Φρυγῶν αἱρέσεως with the contracted form "adversus Catafrygas" (HE 4,27).

c. A third issue is the expression "novum psalmorum librum marcioni(s)". Evidence for the existence of Marcionite Psalms is limited to the Fragment and to a text-critically uncertain note found in a heresy catalogue composed by Maruta, bishop of Maipherkat in Mesopotamia (ca. 400). "This circumstance would be less remarkable, of course, if the Fragment itself were a late fourth-century Eastern product from Palestine or Western Syria"[306]. The catalogue is preserved in Syriac and in an Arabic translation. The Syriac version was edited on the basis of a modern and very lacunous copy of an undated manuscript[307]. In fact, the passage on the Psalms is missing in the Syriac. It is only found in the Latin translation of the Arabic version made in the seventeenth century by the Maronite scholar Abraham Ecchellensis († 1664). The Syriac reads (in

304. So HMF, p. 212.

305. HMF, p. 212. The contracted form is well attested in the Cyprianic textual tradition, see, e.g., *Ep.* 75,7,3 ("catafrigas, -es"). Nevertheless, the most recent editor of Cyprian's letters prefers the emendation "cata Frigas", with reference to Eusebius, HE 5,16,1 and 5,18,1. Cf. ed. Diercks, CCSL 3, p. 588 (ctr. ed. Hartel, CSEL: "Cataphrygas"). The *Acts of Achatius* 4,8 (ca. 250) also read "Cataphrygas". See TABBERNEE, *Montanist Inscriptions* (n. 301), pp. 135 and 141.

306. HMF, p. 213.

307. O. BRAUN, *De Sancta Nicaena Synodo. Syrische Texte des Maruta von Maipher-kat nach einer Handschrift des Propaganda zu Rom* (Kirchengeschichtliche Studien, 4/3), Münster, Schöningh, 1898.

Braun's translation): "Statt des Petrus haben sie sich gesetzt als [Haupt] der Apostel den Marcion, [und statt der Psalmen haben sie sich gedichtet] Hymnen (*madrasche*)". Taking into account the size of the lacuna, the words within brackets were restored by the editor from Ecchellensis' text. It reads: "Marcionem principem nominabant apostolorum, Simonem Petrum e suo gradu et ordine deturbantes. Psalmos quos recitent inter preces fundendas alios a Davidis psalmis sibi effinxerint"[308]. Since this translation seems to contain an interpolation[309], yet another layer is hereby added to the search for the catalogue's original reading. Furthermore, another crucial lacuna (left open by the editor) exists at the beginning of the paragraph on the Marcionites: "Auch [haben sie corrumpirt] die Schriften, hinzugefügt und weggelassen ..."; but cf. Ecchellensis: "Idcirco sacras scripturas quibusdam in locis commutarunt addideruntque evangelio et epistolis Pauli apostoli aliquibus in locis, quaedam vero loca mutilarunt". Ecchellensis also contends that the Marcionites substituted a book of their own for the Book of Acts: "Actorum librum, qui faveret opinionibus ac dogmatibus, illumque nuncuparunt Librum propositi finis". Harnack labelled this latter title "willkürlich"[310]. The Syriac speaks of the *saka* or *Summa*, which may in fact be an appropriate title for Marcion's *Antitheses*. The information on the Psalms is not identical with that in the Fragment, the meaning of which is itself far from obvious. Was it composed for (dative) or by Marcion (genitive)[311]? In the restored Syriac version it is said that the Marcionites substituted "hymns" for the biblical Psalms[312]. The Fragmentist only knows of a "new book", not of a substitution. In short, this oblique reference, the source of which is unknown and which otherwise went unnoticed, largely no doubt due to its having been made by an author writing in faraway eastern Syria, hardly forms an argument helpful for situating the Fragment in "Palestine or Western Syria"[313].

It seems that the names in ll. 81-85 can, with some probability, be linked to historical figures who lived in the late-second or early-third century. Whether they were selected because they all had authored a book[314] is difficult to say. That it took some time before their works

---

308. G.D. MANSI (ed.), *Sacrorum conciliorum nova et amplissima collectio*, Graz, Akademische Verlagsanstalt, 1960-62, II, pp. 1058-1059. A. HARNACK, *Der Ketzer-Katalog des Bischofs Maruta von Maipherkat* (TU, 19/4), Leipzig, Hinrichs, 1899, p. 15.

309. HARNACK, *Ketzer-Katalog* (n. 308), p. 14.

310. *Ibid.*, p. 12.

311. Hahneman opts for the latter (HMF, p. 29).

312. In the Peshitta, the common word for the Psalms is *tvuhto'*.

313. For reactions against Marcion in Syriac literature up to the fourth century, see D. BUNDY, *Marcion and the Marcionites in Early Syriac Apologetics*, in *Le Muséon* 101 (1988) 21-32.

314. So HMF, p. 29.

would have been known[315] does not argue against the traditional dating, for, at that time, both the Marcionite and the Montanist controversy had captured the attention of many. It also seems best not to speculate too much with regard to what followed l. 85[316]. The little hard evidence that can be gleaned from these lines can too easily be forgotten amidst excesses of unwarranted speculation.

VII. Reception

Hahneman pays almost no attention to the issue of the Fragment's reception[317]. In his opinion, the parallel information on the seven-letters pattern in Victorinus of Pettau, which was given in order to account for the number of public letters in the Pauline corpus, does not depend on the Fragment (see above)[318]. He accepts the possibility that Jerome may have used it for his note on Wisdom, but only on the condition that the Fragment is dated in the late-fourth century (again, see above). But, in all of this, Hahneman fails to mention other evidence, somewhat later than Jerome, that is most enlightening. In 1978, J. Lemarié demonstrated that Chromatius, bishop of Aquileia (in northern Italy) from 387 to 407[319], knew and used the Fragment's material on Luke in the Prologue to his *Tractatus in Mathaeum*, written in the last decade of his life[320]. The excerpts are not identified and are not literal quotations, but the parallels remain striking. Lemarié points out that Chromatius was probably acquainted with Victorinus' lost commentaries on the gospels, just as was Fortunatianus, his predecessor in the see of Aquileia. He certainly knew Victorinus' commentary on Revelation, a work in which he could have found the comparison between John and Paul and a precedent for the seven-letter pattern. Metzger had already mentioned the parallel in Chromatius in his history of the canon[321]. More recently, Kaestli exam-

315. Again HMF, p. 29.
316. Cf. HMF, p. 30: "if the Fragment's original ending is mutilated, then further references may have followed those which have survived".
317. According to J. Moiser, *The Role of the Laity in the Formation of the New Testament Canon*, in *ScEsp* 39 (1987) 301-317, "if Sundberg is right", its influence "in the west was nil and in the east negligible" (p. 313).
318. Vallin, *La formation* (n. 49), pp. 235-236, tentatively suggests that Victorinus might be the author of the Fragment. The interest in second-century authors and controversies would be due to the use of outdated source material!
319. See the collection of studies in *Chromatius episcopus: 388-1988* (Antichità altoadriatiche, 34), Udine, Arti grafiche friulane, 1988.
320. *Saint Chromace d'Aquilée témoin du Canon de Muratori*, in *REA* 24 (1978) 101-102.
321. *Canon* (n. 3), p. 305 n. 2.

ined the material afresh and came to the conclusion that the parallels are even more extensive than previously thought and that Chromatius must have had access to the text of the Fragment itself[322].

Chromatius knew the Fragment in Latin translation. If it is to be dated in the second half of the fourth century[323], this would leave only about twenty years between its composition in Greek in Syria/Palestine and its dissemination in Latin in northern Italy. Furthermore, the Fragment it-self contains an element that points into another direction. In his note on the Shepherd, the author could have easily stopped with his comment that it had been only recently written "under Pius". The identification of Hermas as the brother of Pius is not crucial to the argument. The infor-mation is not presented as a personal opinion[324]. Rather, it looks like the Fragmentist is referring to some local tradition. The same note on Pius and Hermas is found in the Liberian Catalogue and was probably intro-duced by the final redactor in 354 during the pontificate of Liberius (see above). It is also worth noting that bishop Fortunatianus of Aquileia (†369) was on good terms with Liberius[325]. In the sixth century, the first compiler of the so-called *Liber Pontificalis* used the information on Pius in the Liberian Catalogue. This later author considers "Pastor" to be an-other name for Hermas (-es in his orthography). The confusion is found as early as Rufinus[326]. Interestingly, the compiler was acquainted with Rufinus' work[327]. While the additional information he provides about Pius' father and hometown ("Pius, natione Italus, ex patre Rufino, frater Pastoris, de civitate Aquilegia") might simply reflect more confusion[328], it could just as easily reflect the influence of a local tradition. The Fragmentist too could well have been familiar with information that had its origin in the region of Aquileia.

Should one also look at Aquileia for the origin of the legend about John and Andrew? Chromatius may have appreciated the role played by Andrew, and we know that the cult of the apostle flourished in northern

---

322. *Fragment de Muratori* (n. 46), pp. 630-634. Cf. also A. DE NICOLA, *Il prologo ai Tractatus in Matthaeum di Cromazio*, in *Chromatius episcopus* (n. 319), pp. 81-116, esp. 106 and 115. Luke is said to be "eruditissimus legis".

323. HMF, p. 216; cf. p. 217: "around 375".

324. Ctr. Origen's "puto tamen, quod Hermas iste sit scriptor libelli illius qui Pastor appellatur" (*CommRom* 10,31).

325. Cf. L. DUCHESNE, *Libère et Fortunatien*, in *Mélanges d'archéologie et d'histoire de l'École française à Rome* 28 (1908) 31-78.

326. *CommSymb* 38; cf. his translation of HE 3,3.

327. L. DUCHESNE, *Le Liber Pontificalis. Texte, introduction et commentaire*, Paris, de Boccard, 1898, repr. 1955, I, pp. lxxii and 119.

328. *Ibid.*, p. 132 n. 1: "Sans faire du Rufin historique le père du pape Pie Ier, il paraît lui avoir emprunté son nom et sa patrie".

Italy in the (late-) fourth and fifth centuries. Around 390, Chromatius pronounces a homily, "In dedicatione ecclesiae Concordiensis" (*Sermo* 26), on the occasion of the deposition of the relics of John the Baptist, Luke the evangelist, the apostle Thomas, and the apostle Andrew, the brother of Peter, in the church of Concordia ("aequales in passione, quia aequales in fidei"[329]). Chromatius even proudly announces that Aquileia will receive part of the relics of nearby Concordia: "Nos a vobis reliquias sanctorum accepimus; vos a nobis studium devotionis <et> fidei aemulationem" (26,1). The sixteenth *tractatus*, based on Mt 4,17-25, bears the title "in natale (*v.l.* natalicio) sancti Andreae"[330].

The excerpts in Chromatius are important in yet another respect. By the fourth century, Aquileia, the northern "altera Roma", had become a most important crossroads between East and West[331]. In 345, during his second exile, Athanasius lived there for a time under the protection of Fortunatianus. Rufinus was born in Concordia about the same time. He received baptism in Aquileia in 369 and, with his friend Jerome, lived there for many years in a community of ascetics before leaving for the East. Chromatius was their patron, encouraging both in their scholarly work and often mediating when they quarreled[332]. We also know that Chromatius requested from Jerome commentaries and translations of several Old Testament books. In fact, the commentaries on Habakkuk and Jonah[333], along with the translations of Proverbs and Tobit, are dedicated to him[334]. Upon his return from the East in 399, Rufinus was admitted to the presbyterium of Aquileia[335]. Chromatius urged him to translate Eusebius' *Church History* into Latin, a fact duly remembered by Rufinus in his dedication[336]. It is in Aquileia that Rufinus wrote his *Commentarius in symbolum Apostolorum*, a work that contains his list of

---

329. R. ÉTAIX - J. LEMARIÉ (eds.), *Chromatii Aquileiensis Opera* (CCSL, 9A), Turnhout, Brepols, 1974, p. 121. (26,4). Cf. C. PIETRI - L. PIETRI (eds.), *Prosopographie chrétienne du Bas-Empire. 2. Prosopographie de l'Italie chrétienne (313-604)*, I, Rome, École française, 1999, pp. 432-436, here 433.

330. Ed. Étaix – Lemarié, pp. 263-266. In the time of Petrus Chrysologus († 450), the basilica of Ravenna was dedicated to Peter's brother.

331. On the history and importance of Aquileia in the later Empire, see, e.g., P. RICHARD, art. *Aquilée*, in *DHGE* 3 (1914) 1112-1142, and the volumes on *Aquileia e l'Oriente mediterraneo* (Antichità altoadriatiche, 12), Udine, Arti grafiche friulane, 1977 (with a contribution by Y.-M. Duval on *Aquilée et la Palestine entre 370 et 420*, pp. 263-322) and on *Aquileia e l'Occidente* (Antichità altoadriatiche, 19), Udine, 1981.

332. Jerome, *Ep. adv. Rufinum* 2 (CCSL, 79, p. 75).

333. CCSL, 76A, pp. 579 and 379.

334. PL 28, c. 1241 and PL 29, c. 23. Cf. Y.-M. DUVAL, *Chromace et Jérôme*, in *Chromatius episcopus* (n. 319), pp. 151-183.

335. Palladius, *Historia Lausiaca* 46.

336. He dedicated his translation of Origen's homilies on Jonah to the same bishop.

canonical books. Jerome would soon become the eastern pier of the bridge that connected Italy with Palestine[337]. Among his acquaintances was Epiphanius of Salamis, whom he met while in Italy at the (anti-Meletian) synod of Rome in 382[338]. All four of these authors (Athanasius, Rufinus, Jerome, and Epiphanius) made their own lists of canonical books and all four lists contain one or more prominent similarities with the Fragment. Perhaps some of these similarities can be explained via their common connection with Aquileia.

In the West the Fragment's influence seems to have been very limited. Like Jerome, Augustine assigns the Wisdom of Solomon to Philo, but this fact alone is probably not enough for one to conclude that he therefore knew the Fragment[339]. There are a few (rather weak) similarities in wording with Eucherius of Lyon († ca. 450) and with the *Decretum Gelasianum* (early-sixth century)[340]. More important is the observation that in the codex Ambrosianus the text of the Fragment can be found in between the *Formulae spiritualis intelligentiae* and the *Instructiones* of Eucherius[341]. This gives an indication of how the Fragment was regarded in later times. The works of Eucherius deal with biblical "realia" and with methodology. As such, they belong to the isagogical genre, as do lists of biblical writings and expositions of the creed (see the works that are mentioned in the latter part of the codex that contains the Fragment). These are works that were used for instructing new converts. Could this fact not help to explain the rather poor quality of the text's Latin? After all, it was not uncommon for the church to attempt to speak to its less educated members on an easily accessible level[342].

---

337. Cf. H.H. HOWORTH, *The Influence of St Jerome on the Canon of the Western Church*, in *JTS* 10 (1908-09) 481-496; 11 (1909-10) 321-347; 13 (1911-12) 1-19. See also the collection of studies in Y.-M. DUVAL (ed.), *Jérôme entre l'Occident et l'Orient* (Études augustiniennes. Série Antiquité, 122), Turnhout, Brepols, 1988.

338. B. ALTANER, *Patrologie*, Freiburg, Herder, ⁸1978, p. 394.

339. He later retracted this view.

340. Koffmane-Kunitz (*Das wahre Alter* [n. 7], pp. 218-219 and 221) argued that Eucherius might have been a source for the Fragmentist, whom he then went on to identify with Gennadius (p. 222), and that the *Decretum Gelasianum* must have also known and used the Fragment. There is insufficient evidence for both of these contentions.

341. Cf. the title in the Bobbio catalogue (10th c.): "libros Eucherii de Formulis specialibus IV" (corr. "spiritualibus"). The text can be found in MURATORI, *Antiquitates Italicae*, III (n. 2), p. 819.

342. Some of Augustine's sermons were intentionally written in simple style and with unsophisticated vocabulary. With regard to homilists, canon 25 of the synod of Mainz (813) stipulated, "de officio praedicatoris ... diebus dominicis aut festivitatibus ... praedicet iuxta quod intellegere vulgus possit". This canon is quoted by J.M. HEER, *Ein Karolingischer Missions-Katechismus. Ratio de Cathecizandis Rudibus* (Biblische und Patristische Forschungen, 1), Freiburg, Herder, 1911, p. 48, in order to account for the quality of the language of the catechetical text he was studying. Heer also refers to

VIII. Conclusion

None of the arguments put forward by Sundberg and Hahneman in favour of a fourth-century, eastern origin of the Fragment are convincing. It is true that there is no "hard" evidence for the traditional dating, if, by that term, one means that the Fragmentist positively identifies himself as a contemporary of Irenaeus or Tertullian. However, there is an abundance of "circumstantial evidence". The dating on the basis of the Shepherd and the reference to Pius remain crucial. There are also the striking similarities in wording and content with other second-century, western authors (esp. the emphasis on the fundamental unity of the gospels, the motif of the double parousia, the interest in second-century heresies). There is also the fact that the Fragment often differs so markedly from later eastern catalogues (the seven-letter pattern, the absence of Heb, the incomplete list of Catholic Epistles, the lack of "technical" terminology like in Eusebius, the extensive comments on the gospels and the letters of Paul). Again, however, these differences can be reasonably explained if one accepts an earlier date. The Fragmentist's great innovation was to collect the information on the gospels, the letters, and the other writings that are "received" in (his) church into one list which that community regarded as closed (at least with respect to certain parts, e.g., the gospels, and probably also Paul's letters). This innovation is why the Fragment occupies such a significant place within the history of the development of the canon. Finally, even if it cannot be shown to have exerted a major influence, it would still be wrong to think that it has gone completely unnoticed.

"Pro captu lectoris habent sua fata libelli". The author who composed the Canon Muratori in the West at the end of the second or the beginning of the third century probably would never have imagined that his work would be mistaken for a fourth-century, eastern product. After the Fragment was composed, it seems to have been largely forgotten for many decades, until it was recovered, translated, and employed in the fourth century. After it was copied in the eighth century, it was again buried, this time for almost a thousand years. I am afraid I have to conclude that the suggestion of a fourth-century, eastern origin for the Fragment should be put to rest not for a thousand years, but for eternity.

A. Thierylaan 32   Joseph VERHEYDEN
B-3001 Leuven

Julianus Pomerius, *De vita contemplativa* 2,23 (ca. 500). Muratori quotes from Pomerius in the section immediately preceding the one dedicated to the Fragment.
* Thanks are due to Mr. Jonathan Yates for his many helpful suggestions for improving the English.

EXEGESE IM KANONISCHEN ZUSAMMENHANG
ÜBERLEGUNGEN ZUR THEOLOGISCHEN RELEVANZ
DER GESTALT DES NEUTESTAMENTLICHEN KANONS

EINLEITUNG: ZUR ABGRENZUNG DES THEMAS[1]

Die theologische Relevanz des Kanons läßt sich nur dann zureichend erfassen, wenn neben der Vielfalt seiner Einzelschriften und zusätzlich zu den überaus komplexen und langwierigen geschichtlichen Prozessen, die zu seiner Fixierung geführt haben, auch die Endgestalt der christlichen Bibel ausreichend gewürdigt wird. Natürlich kann diese Endgestalt nur als ein in sich komplexes, im wahrsten Sinne des Wortes „vielseitiges" Ganzes wahrgenommen werden. Aber genau um diese Wahrnehmung des Kanons als einer vielseitigen, komplexen Ganzheit soll es im folgenden gehen. Wir stellen uns damit bewußt auf die Ebene der Rezipienten des Kanons, nicht auf die der Beobachter der Vorgänge bei seiner Entstehung oder gar auf die seiner Autoren bzw. Redaktoren. Unsere Perspektive ist die der Adressaten des Kanons, nicht die seiner Urheber.

Nun stellt der Kanon als eine solche Einheit und Ganzheit im Gegenüber zu seinen Rezipienten nicht eine historische Gegebenheit dar, sondern ein theologisches Konstrukt. Eine „Endgestalt" des Kanons im strengen Sinne ist bekanntlich in der Alten Kirche nie offiziell fixiert worden, und die auf dem Tridentinum definierte[2] ist durch ihre Bindung an die kirchliche Überlieferung und an die Sprachgestalt der Vulgata aus reformatorischer Sicht theologisch durchaus problematisch. Freilich könnte man ebenso gegenüber der von Martin Luther gestalteten Bibel mit ihrer rechtfertigungstheologisch begründeten Zurücksetzung mancher Teile der neutestamentlichen Briefliteratur und der Johannes-Offenbarung sowie wegen ihrer primär renaissance-humanistisch begründeten

---

1. Die folgenden Ausführungen stehen im Zusammenhang mit Überlegungen zu den Aufgaben einer Theologie des Neuen Testaments im ökumenischen Horizont, wie ich sie an anderer Stelle angestellt habe, vgl. K.-W. NIEBUHR, *Jesu Wirken, Weg und Geschick. Zum Ansatz einer Theologie des Neuen Testaments ökumenischer Perspektive*, in *TLZ* 127 (2002) 3-22.

2. Vgl. H. DENZINGER & A. SCHÖNMETZER (Hgg.), *Enchiridion symbolorum, definitionum et declarationum de rebus fidei et morum*, Freiburg, Herder, [36]1976, Nr. 1501-1506; J. NEUNER & H. ROOS, *Der Glaube der Kirche in den Urkunden der Lehrverkündigung*, neu bearbeitet von K. RAHNER & K.-H. WEGER, Leipzig, Sankt-Benno-Verlag, 1980 (Lizenzausgabe der 10. Auflage des Pustet-Verlags, Regensburg), Nr. 87-92.

Ausschaltung erheblicher Teile des christlichen Alten Testaments theologische und historische Kritik anmelden[3].

Dennoch ergeben die mannigfachen Zeugnisse für eine autoritative Schriftensammlung der Kirche ausreichend klare Strukturen, die eine theologische Interpretation der Gesamtgestalt des Bibelkanons ermöglichen. Auch wenn die Grenzen der christlichen Bibel zumindest in den orthodoxen und den protestantischen Kirchen nie offiziell eindeutig definiert worden sind und auch wenn sich in der Anordnung ihrer Einzelschriften manche (kleineren) Variationen finden, vom Wortlaut im einzelnen ganz abgesehen, so bestand doch und besteht auch heute wenigstens im Blick auf das Neue Testament in allen christlichen Konfessionen hinreichende Übereinstimmung über Inhalte und Gestalt der Bibel, um sich der theologischen Aufgabe ihrer Interpretation zu stellen. Daß dies gleichzeitig eine eminent ökumenische Aufgabe ist, braucht nicht eigens betont zu werden. Gerade im Zusammenhang eines in der reformatorischen Theologie wurzelnden Schriftprinzips kann die Bibel eine kritische Funktion für die Kirche nur ausüben, wenn sie als ganze den Kirchen gegenüber als „Vorgabe der Einheit" zur Geltung gebracht wird[4].

Wir wählen also einen primär theologisch-hermeneutischen Zugang zum Kanon und fragen nach seiner Bedeutung im Kontext christlicher Lehre und Verkündigung heute. Wir verstehen diesen Zugang freilich nicht als Alternative zu verschiedenen anderen möglichen Zugängen, und wir meinen auch nicht, daß der von uns gewählte Zugang von anderen Zugangsmöglichkeiten, etwa einem primär historischen, einem ästhetisch-literaturwissenschaftlichen oder einem umfassender sozial- bzw. kulturwissenschaftlichen Zugang, isoliert werden könnte. Vielmehr sind

---

3. Exemplarisch H. GESE, *Erwägungen zur Einheit der biblischen Theologie*, ZTK 67 (1970) 417-436 (= in DERS., *Vom Sinai zum Zion. Alttestamentliche Beiträge zur biblischen Theologie* [BEvT, 64], München, Kaiser, 1990, S. 11-30, bes. 16f); s. auch N. WALTER, „*Bücher: so nicht der heiligen Schrifft gleich gehalten...*"? *Karlstadt, Luther – und die Folgen*, in A. FREUND, U. KERN, A. RADLER (Hgg.), *Tragende Tradition.* FS M. Seils, Frankfurt am Main, Lang, 1992, S. 173-197 (= in DERS., *Praeparatio Evangelica. Studien zur Umwelt, Exegese und Hermeneutik des Neuen Testaments*, herausgegeben von W. KRAUS & F. WILK [WUNT 98], Tübingen, Mohr [Siebeck], 1997, S. 341-369).

4. Hierin kann ich dem Urteil des katholischen Exegeten T. SÖDING, Art. *Kanon, biblischer K. I. Biblisch-theologisch: 3. K. der ganzen Bibel*, in LTK[3] 5 (1996) 1181f., zustimmen, der meint, eine an einer „Mitte der Schrift" oder einem „Kanon im Kanon" orientierte Kanonhermeneutik stehe in der Gefahr, „die Ganzheit der Schrift nicht mehr deutlich zu sehen u(nd) den Primat des Offenbarungs*handelns* Gottes vor den menschl(ichen) Glaubens*bezeugungen* in den bibl(ischen) Schriften zu relativieren"; vgl. auch F. HAHN, *Vielfalt und Einheit des Neuen Testaments. Zum Problem einer neutestamentlichen Theologie*, in BZ 38 (1994) 161-173.

wir überzeugt, daß die geschichtlich gewachsene Vielfalt der christlichen Bibel wesentlich ist für die Erfassung ihres Inhalts und deshalb gerade nicht theologisch eingeebnet werden darf[5]. Allerdings kann die Vielfalt des Kanons um so deutlicher hervortreten, je genauer wir seine Gesamtstruktur und die Querverbindungen zwischen seinen Teilen und Einzelschriften wahrnehmen.

Historische Differenzierung innerhalb eines kanonischen Zugangs zur Schrift ist nicht nur möglich, sondern nötig, um die Vielseitigkeit des Neuen Testaments wahrzunehmen, wahrzunehmen freilich im Zusammenhang der verschiedenen Seiten bzw. Stimmen, nicht in ihrer Isolation voneinander. Die aus der Musik übernommene Metapher der Polyphonie mag das Gemeinte verdeutlichen: Polyphonie bedeutet Mehrstimmigkeit bei Gleichzeitigkeit. Nicht jede Polyphonie klingt harmonisch, und nicht jeder nimmt Polyphonie als harmonisch wahr, selbst wenn die gehörten Stimmen dieselben sind. Es gibt aber offene und verdeckte Gesetzmäßigkeiten des Zusammenklangs, die zu erkennen bei der Wahrnehmung von Polyphonie zwar nicht unerläßlich, aber durchaus hilfreich ist. Die einzelnen Stimmen können zwar bei einer Analyse voneinander unterschieden, aber beim Erklingen der Polyphonie nie unabhängig voneinander gehört werden.

Wenn wir nach der *Gestalt* des neutestamentlichen Kanons und seiner *theologischen Relevanz* fragen, dann blenden wir im Rahmen unserer Überlegungen zwei Fragen weitgehend aus, die nämlich nach der Vorgeschichte des Kanons und die nach der Vorgeschichte der in ihn aufgenommenen Schriften. Natürlich verdankt sich die Gestalt des Kanons ganz wesentlich seiner Vorgeschichte, und natürlich hat auch die Vorgeschichte der neutestamentlichen Einzelschriften nicht unwesentlich zu ihrer Aufnahme in den Kanon beigetragen. Es gibt aber Gründe, die primär historischen Fragen hier nicht noch einmal zu besprechen. Einer liegt in begrenzter Kompetenz hinsichtlich der patristischen Spezialforschung zum Thema, ein weiterer in der unüberschaubaren, immer weiter wachsenden Forschungsliteratur zur neutestamentlichen Einleitungswissenschaft im allgemeinen und zur Kanongeschichte im besonderen.

Daß Spezialuntersuchungen zu den beiden genannten Forschungsgebieten nur relativ selten miteinander in Verbindung gebracht werden,

5. Vgl. grundsätzlich zum Verhältnis von theologischer und historisch-kritischer Exegese T. SÖDING, *Geschichtlicher Text und Heilige Schrift–Fragen zur theologischen Legitimität historisch-kritischer Exegese,* in C. DOHMEN, C. JACOB, T. SÖDING, *Neue Formen der Schriftauslegung?,* herausgegeben von T. STERNBERG (QD, 140), Freiburg–Basel–Wien, Herder, 1992, S. 75-130; U. WILCKENS, *Schriftauslegung in historisch-kritischer Forschung und geistlicher Betrachtung,* in W. PANNENBERG & T. SCHNEIDER (Hgg.), *Verbindliches Zeugnis. II: Schriftauslegung–Lehramt–Rezeption* (Dialog der Kirchen, 9), Freiburg im Breisgau, Herder; Göttingen, Vandenhoeck & Ruprecht, 1995, S. 13-71.

läßt einen übergreifenden theologischen, nicht vorrangig historisch-analytischen Zugang zu unserem Thema als sinnvoll erscheinen. Zwar gibt es aus jüngerer Zeit auch eine beachtliche Reihe von theologischen Stellungnahmen zur Kanonthematik[6]. Allerdings konzentrieren sie sich zum einen größtenteils auf das Verhältnis der beiden Testamente der christlichen Bibel zueinander, wobei der Herausbildung von autoritativen Schriftensammlungen im Frühjudentum[7] besonderes Augenmerk gilt, zum anderen auf Fragen der Schrifthermeneutik im systematisch-theologischen und ökumenischen Kontext der Gegenwart[8]. Daß mit diesen beiden Arbeitsgebieten theologisch zentrale Fragenkomplexe in Angriff genommen worden sind, soll in keiner Weise in Abrede gestellt werden. Allerdings wird auch hier nur selten die Frage nach der inneren Einheit und Ganzheit des Neuen Testament thematisiert[9].

Auf der anderen Seite steht eine Reihe von neueren Untersuchungen zur Kanongeschichte[10], die nach wie vor auf den grundlegenden Arbei-

6. Zur theologisch-hermeneutischen Problematik des Kanons vgl. W. KÜNNETH, Art. *Kanon*, in *TRE* 17 (1988) 562-570; E. KÄSEMANN (Hg.), *Das Neue Testament als Kanon. Dokumentation und kritische Analyse zur gegenwärtigen Situation*, Göttingen, Vandenhoeck & Ruprecht,1970, sowie in diesem Band T. SÖDING, *Der Kanon des Alten und Neuen Testaments. Zur Frage nach seinem theologischen Anspruch*, S. XLVII-LXXXIII.

7. Zur Herausbildung einer autoritativen Schriftensammlung im Frühjudentum vgl. J.-D. KAESTLI & O. WERMELINGER (Hgg.), *Le canon de l'Ancien Testament. Sa formation et son histoire*, Genève, Labor & Fides, 1984; R.T. BECKWITH, *Formation of the Hebrew Bible*, in M.J. MULDER (Hg.), *Mikra. Text, Translation, Reading and Interpretation of the Hebrew Bible in Ancient Judaism and Early Christianity* (CRINT, II/1), Assen–Maastricht, Van Gorcum; Philadelphia, Fortress, 1988, S. 39-86; H.P. RÜGER, *Das Werden des christlichen Alten Testaments*, in *JBT* 3 (1988) 175-189; M. HENGEL, „ *Schriftauslegung" und „Schriftwerdung" in der Zeit des Zweiten Tempels*, in M. HENGEL & H. LÖHR (Hgg.), *Schriftauslegung im antiken Judentum und im Urchristentum* (WUNT, 73), Tübingen, Mohr (Siebeck), 1994, S. 1-71; J. VAN OORSCHOT, *Altes Testament*, in U. TWO-RUSCHKA (Hg.), *Heilige Schriften. Eine Einführung*, Darmstadt, Wissenschaftliche Buchgesellschaft, 2000, S. 29-56.

8. Zur ökumenischen Diskussion vgl. den Sammelband W. PANNENBERG & T. SCHNEIDER (Hgg.), *Verbindliches Zeugnis. I: Kanon–Schrift–Tradition* (Dialog der Kirchen, 7), Freiburg im Breisgau, Herder; Göttingen, Vandenhoeck & Ruprecht, 1992.

9. Siehe aber die grundsätzlichen Stellungnahmen von P. STUHLMACHER, *Biblische Theologie des Neuen Testaments, Bd. II: Von der Paulusschule bis zur Johannesoffenbarung. Der Kanon und seine Auslegung*, Göttingen, Vandenhoeck & Ruprecht, 1999, S. 288-304, und B.S. CHILDS, *The New Testament as Canon: An Introduction*, London, SCM, 1984 (vgl. die kritische Würdigung von S. KRAUTER, *Brevard S. Childs' Programm einer Biblischen Theologie. Eine Untersuchung seiner systematisch-theologischen und methodologischen Fundamente*, in *ZTK* 96 (1999) 22-48. Zur theologischen Reflexion der Kanonbildung im Blick auf das Alte Testament einschließlich der Frage nach seiner Einheit und Ganzheit vgl. C. DOHMEN & M. OEMING, *Biblischer Kanon, warum und wozu? Eine Kanontheologie* (QD, 137), Freiburg–Basel–Wien, Herder, 1992, S. 27-90.

10. Umfassend: H. FREIHERR VON CAMPENHAUSEN, *Die Entstehung der christlichen Bibel* (BHT, 39), Tübingen, Mohr (Siebeck), 1968; B.M. METZGER, *The Canon of the New Testament*, Oxford, Clarendon, 1987; L.M. MCDONALD, *The Formation of the Chri-*

ten von Zahn, Leipoldt und Harnack aufbauen[11]. Es mag durchaus erhellend und theologisch weiterführend sein, die Zeugnisse der patristischen Literatur zur Rezeption und Interpretation der Gestalt des Kanons erneut zusammenzustellen und auszuwerten. Wir wollen uns aber in unserem Beitrag auf die Wahrnehmung der Kanon*gestalt* beschränken, wie sie als ganze den Lesern der Bibel bzw. ihren Abschreibern vor Augen stand und im Prinzip bis heute steht. Darin unterscheidet sich unser Ansatz von dem der Kanongeschichtsschreibung. Etwas überspitzt gesagt: Maßgeblich für unser Thema ist nicht das Neue Testament, um das sich die Theologen aus dogmatischen oder kirchenpolitischen Gründen gestritten haben, sondern das Neue Testament, wie es in den Gemeinden gelesen bzw. für sie produziert wurde.

In drei Arbeitsschritten wollen wir unsere Untersuchung durchführen, die vom größeren Ganzen zur jeweils kleineren Einheit fortschreiten. Zuerst blicken wir auf die Gesamtstruktur des Kanons und auf Querverbindungen zwischen seinen Teilen (I). Anschließend untersuchen wir genauer die Beziehungen zwischen der Apostelgeschichte und der neutestamentlichen Briefliteratur (II). Dann fragen wir noch einmal genauer nach Strukturmustern und Querverbindungen innerhalb der Briefkorpora (III). Abschließend überlegen wir, in welcher Weise die verschiedenen Teile des Kanons auf Jesus als seine „Mitte" bezogen sind (IV).

Daß der Schwerpunkt unserer Ausführungen bei der neutestamentlichen Briefliteratur und insbesondere bei den Katholischen Briefen liegt,

---

stian Biblical Canon, Peabody, MA, Hendrickson, 1995; Überblicke: W.G. KÜMMEL, *Einleitung in das Neue Testament,* Heidelberg, Quelle & Meyer, [20]1980, S. 420-451; W. SCHNEEMELCHER, *Haupteinleitung,* in DERS., *Neutestamentliche Apokryphen in deutscher Übersetzung, I. Band: Evangelien,* Tübingen, Mohr (Siebeck), [6]1990, S. 1-61; DERS., Art. *Bibel. III. Die Entstehung des Kanons des Neuen Testaments und der christlichen Bibel,* in TRE 6 (1980) 22-48; A.F.J. KLIJN, *Die Entstehungsgeschichte des Neuen Testaments,* in ANRW II/26.1 (1992) 64-97; K.S. FRANK, *Zur altkirchlichen Kanongeschichte,* in PANNENBERG & SCHNEIDER, *Verbindliches Zeugnis I* (s. Anm. 8), S. 128-155; D. TROBISCH, *Die Endredaktion des Neuen Testaments. Eine Untersuchung zur Entstehung der christlichen Bibel* (NTOA, 31), Freiburg (Schweiz), Universitätsverlag; Göttingen, Vandenhoeck & Ruprecht, 1996; DERS., *Die Entstehung der Paulusbriefsammlung. Studien zu den Anfängen christlicher Publizistik* (NTOA, 10), Freiburg (Schweiz), Universitätsverlag; Göttingen, Vandenhoeck & Ruprecht, 1989; zum Evangelienkanon: G.N. STANTON, *The Fourfold Gospel,* in NTS 43 (1997) 317-346; T.K. HECKEL, *Vom Evangelium des Markus zum viergestaltigen Evangelium* (WUNT, 120), Tübingen, Mohr (Siebeck), 1999; M. HENGEL, *The Four Gospels and the One Gospel of Jesus Christ. An Investigation of the Collection and Origin of the Canonical Gospels,* London, SCM, 2000.

11. T. ZAHN, *Geschichte des Neutestamentlichen Kanons,* 2 Bde. (4 Teilbde.), Erlangen–Leipzig, Deichert, 1888-1892; J. LEIPOLDT, *Geschichte des neutestamentlichen Kanons,* 2 Bde., Leipzig, Hinrichs, 1907-1908; A. VON HARNACK, *Die Entstehung des Neuen Testamentes und die wichtigsten Folgen der neuen Schöpfung,* Leipzig, Hinrichs, 1914; DERS., *Marcion: Das Evangelium vom fremden Gott: Eine Monographie zur Geschichte der Grundlegung der katholischen Kirche,* Leipzig, Hinrichs, 1921.

ergibt sich aus dem Ansatz der Fragestellung und wird im Laufe ihrer Bearbeitung noch klarer werden. Die theologisch entscheidende Struktur der christlichen Bibel besteht in der spezifischen Zuordnung ihrer beiden Teile, des Neuen und des Alten Testaments, zueinander[12]. Wenn wir diese Frage in unserem Beitrag ganz beiseite lassen, dann nur aus Gründen der Beschränkung des Themas.

I. Zur Gesamtstruktur des neutestamentlichen Kanons

Wenn wir die Gestalt des neutestamentlichen Kanons zum Ausgangspunkt unserer theologischen Überlegungen machen wollen, müssen wir zunächst bestimmen, welche Gestalt wir meinen. Für eine ökumenisch orientierte theologische Betrachtung bietet sich aus verschiedenen Gründen diejenige Gestalt des Kanons an, die Athanasius in seinem 39. Osterfestbrief beschreibt[13], obwohl sie wenigstens in zweierlei Hinsicht nicht unwesentlich von unseren heute gebräuchlichen Bibeln abweicht. Die erste Abweichung betrifft die Stellung der Katholischen Briefe zwischen Apostelgeschichte und Corpus Paulinum, die zweite die Einordnung des Hebräerbriefes in das Corpus Paulinum zwischen den 2. Thessalonicher- und den 1. Timotheusbrief. Demgegenüber steht in der Vulgata seit Hieronymus das Corpus Paulinum zwischen Apostelgeschichte und Katholischen Briefen, und der Hebräerbrief bildet den Abschluß der Paulusbriefsammlung. Leichte Variationen dieser allen modernen Bibelausgaben (abgesehen von den Lutherbibeln) zugrundeliegenden Schriftenfolge finden wir schon im Decretum Gelasianum[14] (Offenbarung *vor* den Katholischen Briefen) und hinsichtlich der Reihenfolge der Katholischen Briefe auch im Kanon des Tridentinum[15] (Petrus-

---

12. Vgl. umfassend C. Dohmen & T. Söding (Hgg.), *Eine Bibel – zwei Testamente. Positionen Biblischer Theologie* (UTB, 1893), Paderborn, Schöningh, 1995; C. Dohmen & G. Stemberger (Hgg.), *Hermeneutik der Jüdischen Bibel und des Alten Testaments*, Stuttgart, Kohlhammer, 1996; M. Sæbø (Hg.), *Hebrew Bible/Old Testament. The History of Its Interpretation, Vol. I: From the Beginnings to the Middle Ages (Until 1300)*, Göttingen, Vandenhoeck & Ruprecht, 1996; J. Trebolle Barrera, *The Jewish Bible and the Christian Bible. An Introduction to the History of the Bible.* Translated from the Spanish by W.G.E. Watson, Leiden, Brill, 1998; als exemplarischer Beitrag aus jüngster Zeit sei genannt: B. Janowski, *„Verstehst du auch, was du liest?" Reflexionen auf die Leserichtung der christlichen Bibel*, in F.-L. Hossfeld (Hg.), *Wieviel Systematik erlaubt die Schrift? Auf der Suche nach einer gesamtbiblischen Theologie* (QD, 185), Freiburg–Basel–Wien, Herder, 2001, S. 150-191.

13. Vgl. Zahn, *Geschichte des Neutestamentlichen Kanons* (s. Anm. 11), II, S. 203-212; Schneemelcher, *Haupteinleitung* (s. Anm. 10), S. 39f.

14. Vgl. Schneemelcher, *Haupteinleitung* (s. Anm. 10), S. 30-33.

15. Denzinger & Schönmetzer, *Enchiridion* (s. Anm. 2), Nr. 1503 (Neuner & Roos, *Glaube* [s. Anm. 2], Nr. 90).

briefe am Anfang). Deutlich erkennbar sind aber durchweg bestimmte Schriftengruppen, die jeweils nur en bloc verschoben, nicht aber untereinander vermischt werden. Innerhalb dieser Gruppen sind dagegen Verschiebungen durchaus möglich.

Athanasius

Tetraevangelium Apg	Kath. Briefe	Corpus Paulinum	Offenbarung
Mt Mk Lk Joh	Jak 1/2 Petr 1-3 Joh Jud	...2 Thess Hebr 1 Tim...	

Vulgata

Tetraevangelium Apg	Corpus Paulinum	Kath. Briefe	Offenbarung
Mt Mk Lk Joh	...Phlm Hebr	Jak 1/2 Petr 1-3 Joh Jud	

Decretum Gelasianum

Tetraevangelium Apg	Corpus Paulinum	Offenbarung	Kath. Briefe
Mt Mk Lk Joh	...Phlm Hebr		1/2 Petr Jak
			1-3 Joh Jud

Tridentinum

Tetraevangelium Apg	Corpus Paulinum	Kath. Briefe	Offenbarung
Mt Mk Lk Joh	...Phlm Hebr	1/2 Petr 1-3 Joh Jak Jud	

Ein Blick auf die griechischen Handschriften des Neuen Testaments bestätigt diese Gruppierung der Einzelschriften, modifiziert sie aber in einem wesentlichen Punkt: Wir finden auch hier die drei Schriftengruppen: Tetraevangelium, Corpus Paulinum und Katholische Briefe. Allerdings fassen die großen „Vollbibeln" des 4. und 5. Jahrhunderts, der Codex Sinaiticus, der Codex Vaticanus und der Codex Alexandrinus, Apostelgeschichte und Katholische Briefe zu einer Schriftengruppe zusammen, dem „Praxapostolos". Erst die Masse der byzantinischen Handschriften trennt durch Einfügung des Corpus Paulinum die Sammlung der Katholischen Briefe von der Apostelgeschichte und entspricht damit im wesentlichen der Schriftenfolge der Vulgata.

Sinaiticus

Tetraevangelium	Corpus Paulinum	Praxapostolos	Offb
Mt Mk Lk Joh	...2 Thess Hebr 1 Tim...	Apg Jak 1/2 Petr 1-3 Joh Jud	

B/A

Tetraevangelium	Praxapostolos	Corpus Paulinum	(Offb)
Mt Mk Lk Joh	Apg Jak 1/2 Petr 1-3 Joh Jud	...2 Thess Hebr (1 Tim...)	

byzantinische MSS

Tetraevangelium	Apg	Corpus Paulinum	Kath. Briefe	Offb
Mt Mk Lk Joh		...Phlm Hebr	Jak 1/2 Petr 1-3 Joh Jud	

Als erstes Ergebnis zeichnet sich ab: Die neutestamentlichen Schriften begegnen uns im Zusammenhang des Kanons durchweg in Gestalt von „Sammlungseinheiten"[16]. Als drei ursprüngliche Sammlungseinheiten lassen sich erkennen das Tetraevangelium, der Praxapostolos und das Corpus Paulinum. Dazu kommen als Einzelschriften die Johannes-Offenbarung sowie, bei Abtrennung von den Katholischen Briefen, die Apostelgeschichte. Der Hebräerbrief wird dagegen immer als Teil des Corpus Paulinum überliefert. Dieses Ergebnis entspricht dem Befund in den übrigen griechischen Handschriften. Sofern sie erkennbar Texte aus mehr als einer neutestamentlichen Schrift enthalten, folgt die Zusammenstellung der Schriften fast durchweg den Sammlungseinheiten der großen Majuskelhandschriften und weitgehend auch der Schriftenfolge innerhalb der Sammlungseinheiten. Der Befund der Bibelhandschriften wird im wesentlichen auch durch die Zeugnisse der Kirchenväter bestätigt. Zwar belegen sie zahllose Variationen der Schriftenfolge innerhalb der Sammlungseinheiten, aber so gut wie nie Vermischungen von Schriften aus unterschiedlichen Sammlungseinheiten.

Daß die Zusammenstellung der Einzelschriften zu Sammlungseinheiten nicht bloß formale Gründe hat, lehrt ein Blick auf ihre Titel in den Bibelmanuskripten[17]. Die in den Handschriften häufig belegte Kurzform der Titel der vier Evangelien (κατά + Autorenname im Akkusativ) erfordert die Ergänzung eines Obertitels für das Tetraevangelium[18]. Auch die Kurztitel der Paulusbriefe in den Handschriften (πρός + Adressatenname im Akkusativ) sind ergänzungsbedürftig und werden in vielen Handschriften auch entsprechend ergänzt. Zu der die Adressaten benennenden Wendung treten der Name des Autors und die Gattungsbezeichnung „Brief". Bei den Katholischen Briefen ist ebenfalls zum Kurztitel (Name im Genitiv) jeweils mindestens das Wort ἐπιστολή hinzuzufügen. Darüber hinaus belegen die Handschriften auch hier in der Regel weitere Charakterisierungen der Schriftengruppe bzw. der Briefautoren.

---

16. Dieses Ergebnis hat TROBISCH, *Endredaktion* (s. Anm. 10), S. 35-58, auf Grund der Untersuchung der neutestamentlichen Handschriften m.E. überzeugend nachgewiesen.

17. Vgl. dazu TROBISCH, *Endredaktion* (s. Anm. 10), S. 58-68.

18. Vgl. M. HENGEL, *Die Evangelienüberschriften* (Sitzungsberichte der Heidelberger Akademie der Wissenschaften, Philosophisch-historische Klasse, 1984/3), Heidelberg, Carl Winter, 1984, S. 8-13. Nach Hengel ist die Langform mit εὐαγγέλιον textkritisch als ursprünglich anzusehen. Sie gehe der Zusammenstellung des Vierevangelienkanons voraus. Vgl. DERS., *Gospels* (s. Anm. 10), S. 48-56; HECKEL, *Evangelium* (s. Anm. 10), S. 207-217.

Struktur der neutestamentlichen Schriftentitel

	Gattung	Autor	Adressaten	Inhalt
Tetraevangelium	εὐαγγέλιον	κατὰ N.N. (Akk.)	–	–
Corpus Paulinum	ἐπιστολή	Παύλου	πρὸς X.X. (Akk.)	–
Katholische Briefe	ἐπιστολή	N.N. (Gen.)	–	–
Apostelgeschichte	πράξεις	–	–	ἀποστόλων
Offenbarung	ἀποκάλυψις	Ἰωάννου	–	–

Wichtig ist hierbei zu sehen, daß sich die Titelformulierungen häufig nicht aus der jeweiligen Einzelschrift ableiten lassen, sondern erst aus ihrer Zusammenstellung zu Sammlungseinheiten verständlich werden. So ergibt sich die Charakterisierung des Hebräer- und des 1. Johannesbriefes als ἐπιστολή nicht unmittelbar aus ihrer literarischen Eigenart, sondern erst aus ihrem kanonischen Kontext. Auch der Titel der Apostelgeschichte entspringt schwerlich unmittelbar dem Inhalt oder der literarischen Form ihrer Darstellung[19]. Wir müssen also davon ausgehen, daß die handschriftlich belegten Titel der Einzelschriften bereits ihre Zusammenstellung zu Sammlungseinheiten voraussetzen. Damit signalisieren sie zugleich eine Rezeptionsweise neutestamentlicher Schriften, nach welcher diese nicht mehr, wie nach der ursprünglichen Intention ihrer Autoren, je für sich wahrzunehmen sind, sondern in einem spezifisch geordneten kanonischen Zusammenhang. Dieser kanonische Zusammenhang weist Strukturen auf, die theologisch aussagekräftig sind. Dies gilt ganz unabhängig davon, wo die Ursprünge und worin die historischen Ursachen für die jeweilige Gestalt des Kanons zu suchen sind.

Daß die Anordnung von Sammlungseinheiten kanonischer Schriften Ansatzpunkte zu theologischen Reflexionen bietet, zeigt ein kurzer vergleichender Blick auf die Anordnungsprinzipien der jüdischen Bibel und des christlichen Alten Testaments. Beide kanonischen Sammlungen unterscheiden sich im wesentlichen, abgesehen von der viel diskutierten Frage des Umfangs[20], durch eine charakteristische Schriftenfolge, die sowohl Zuordnungen der Schriften und Schriftengruppen untereinander ermöglicht als auch über die Grenze der Sammlung hinausweist. In der jüdischen Bibel werden alle übrigen Teile der Schrift der Tora nachgeordnet und auf sie zurückbezogen[21]. Die Schrift als ganze mit der Tora an der Spitze weist über sich hinaus auf ihre jeweils aktuelle Interpretati-

---

19. Vgl. J. JERVELL, *Die Apostelgeschichte* (KEK, 3), Göttingen, Vandenhoeck & Ruprecht, 1998, S. 56-58.
20. Vgl. nur die oben, Anm. 7, genannte Literatur.
21. Vgl. VAN OORSCHOT, *Altes Testament* (s. Anm. 7), S. 51-54.

on, die „mündliche Tora", die ihrerseits wiederum an den Wortlaut der
schriftlichen Tora gebunden bleibt.

In den christlichen Bibelhandschriften der Septuaginta[22] steht dagegen
innerhalb des Alten Testaments zwar auch der Pentateuch am Anfang.
Allerdings bildet er hier nicht mehr als Tora den hermeneutischen
Schlüssel für die folgenden Bibelteile, sondern wird den übrigen „Geschichtsbüchern" im Sinne eines heilsgeschichtlich-chronologischen
Anfangs vorangestellt. Es folgen sodann in der Regel die poetischen und
erst danach, als abschließender Teil, die prophetischen Schriften. Freilich finden sich sowohl in den Sammelhandschriften als auch in den
Kanonlisten zahlreiche Variationen der Reihenfolge der Schriften im
einzelnen. Allerdings dürfte die Umstellung des Prophetenteils an das
Ende der christlichen Sammlungen, für welche es offenbar keine jüdischen Vorbilder gab, theologisch-hermeneutische Gründe haben. Sie ist
schon in den frühesten Zeugnissen (Melito von Sardes, Origenes) zur
Gestalt des Alten Testaments belegt[23], was um so auffälliger ist, als ja
aus dem Neuen Testament durchaus die Schriftenfolge der dreigeteilten
jüdischen Bibel ablesbar war[24]. Die christliche Schriftensammlung des
Alten Testaments weist somit über die Bibel Israels hinaus auf das Neue
Testament und damit auf Christus. Auf ihn hin führt die heils-
geschichtliche Linie, an der die Reihenfolge der Teile des Alten Testaments ausgerichtet ist, und von Christus her soll das ganze Alte Testament wie in einem neuen Licht gelesen werden.

*Strukturmodell der jüdischen Bibel und des christlichen Alten Testa-
ments*

jüdische Bibel	*Altes Testament*
Tora	Geschichtsbücher
Propheten	poetische Schriften
Schriften	prophetische Schriften
„mündliche Tora"	Neues Testament

Blicken wir nun auf das Aufbauprinzip des Neuen Testaments, dann
lassen sich mindestens fünf Strukturmerkmale feststellen, die im kanoni-

22. Der durchaus uneinheitliche Befund wird differenziert dargestellt bei M. HENGEL
& R. DEINES, *Die Septuaginta als „christliche Schriftensammlung", ihre Vorgeschichte
und das Problem ihres Kanons*, in M. HENGEL & A.M. SCHWEMER (Hgg.), *Die Septuaginta zwischen Judentum und Christentum* (WUNT, 72), Tübingen, Mohr (Siebeck),
1994, S. 182-284, bes. 219-235.

23. Vgl. auch E.E. ELLIS, *The Old Testament Canon in the Early Church*, in MULDER,
Mikra (s. Anm. 7), S. 653-690, 658-661.

24. S. Lk 24,27.44; vgl. Apg 28,23; Mt 5,17; 7,12.

schen Zusammenhang theologische Bedeutung gewinnen: (1) die Korrespondenz von Tetraevangelium und Johannes-Offenbarung, (2) der Rückbezug der Apostelgeschichte auf die narrativen Jesus-Schriften, (3) die Leitfunktion der Apostelgeschichte für die Briefliteratur, (4) die Personenkontinuität zwischen den Jesus-Schriften, der Apostelgeschichte, der Briefliteratur und der Johannes-Offenbarung sowie (5) die impliziten Vorverweise aller vorangehenden Schriften und Sammlungseinheiten auf die Johannes-Offenbarung.

1. *Die Korrespondenz von Tetraevangelium und Johannes-Offenbarung*

Der Endstellung der Johannes-Offenbarung im neutestamentlichen Kanon korrespondiert die Spitzenstellung des Tetraevangeliums. Die Einrahmung von Praxapostolos und Corpus Paulinum durch Tetraevangelium und Johannes-Offenbarung führt, zumal im Zusammenhang mit dem Alten Testament, zu einer klaren heilsgeschichtlich ausgerichteten Struktur des Kanons: Der für die Kirche grund-legenden vorösterlichen Jesus-Zeit folgt die nachösterliche Apostelzeit, die schließlich hinführt zum Ausblick auf die nahe bevorstehende Wiederkunft des auferstandenen Herrn Jesus.

Textsignale am Anfang und am Schluß der kanonischen Sammlung unterstreichen diese Rahmenfunktion noch. So umspannt das Neue Testament den Zeitraum vom „Ursprung Jesu Christi, des Davidssohnes, des Abrahamssohnes" (Mt 1,1)[25] bis zum „Kommen des Herrn Jesus" (Offb 22,20)[26]. Dem texteröffnenden Hinweis der Leser auf das „Buch vom Ursprung" im ersten Satz des Neuen Testaments korrespondiert in seinem letzten Abschnitt ihre Rückbindung an die „Worte der Weissagung in diesem Buch" (Offb 22,18f).

2. *Der Rückbezug der Apostelgeschichte auf die narrativen Jesus-Schriften*

Dem Interesse der heilsgeschichtlichen Anordnung des Kanons fällt selbst die offenkundige literarische Einheit des zweiteiligen lukanischen Werkes zum Opfer, indem das Lukas-Evangelium in die Vierevangeliensammlung eingeordnet wird. Der explizite Rückbezug am Beginn

25. Von hier aus wiederum kann, wie oft gesehen wurde, eine kanonische Beziehung zum Beginn der Genesis hergestellt werden, vgl. im vorliegenden Band T. HIEKE, *Biblos Geneseos—Mt 1,1 vom Buch Genesis her gelesen*, im vorliegenden Band, S. 635-649.

26. Ausgehend vom textinternen Geltungsanspruch der Rahmenaussagen der Johannes-Offenbarung (1,1-8; 22,6-21) stellen Überlegungen zu ihrer kanonischen Rezeptionsgeschichte an: M. HASITSCHKA & K. HUBER, *Die Offenbarung des Johannes im Kanon der Bibel. Textinterner Geltungsanspruch und bewegte Geschichte der kanonischen Rezeption*, im vorliegenden Band, S. 607-618.

der Apostelgeschichte auf die Jesus-Darstellung im Lukas-Evangelium bildet nun aber die Brücke, über die Stoffe aus allen vier Evangelien, nicht nur solche des Lukas-Evangeliums, in die nachösterliche Apostelzeit transportiert werden können. Die Autorennamen der Evangelienüberschriften unterstreichen und erweitern darüber hinaus die Möglichkeiten, Beziehungen zwischen den Evangelien und der Apostelgeschichte zu entdecken bzw. herzustellen.

Durch die Schriftenfolge der kanonischen Sammlung kommt es außerdem zur unmittelbaren Aufeinanderfolge der editorischen Schlußwendungen in Joh 21 und des Prologs zur Apostelgeschichte, der wiederum den zum Lukas-Evangelium aufnimmt und fortführt. Die führende Rolle des Petrus im ersten Teil der Apostelgeschichte gerät zudem unter das Vorzeichen des Auftrags des auferstandenen Christus an ihn nach Joh 21,15-19. Die Szenen mit Petrus und Johannes in Apg 3f (vgl. auch 8,14f) rücken in das Licht ihrer Begegnung nach Joh 21,20-23[27].

Aber auch in der byzantinischen Gestalt des Kanons, wo der Praxapostolos durch das Corpus Paulinum auseinandergerissen wird, kommt es zu neuen und theologisch aufschlußreichen kanonischen Zusammenhängen. So folgt nun auf die Ankunft des gefangenen Apostels und sein ungehindertes missionarisches Wirken in Rom nach Apg 28,30f für die Leser dieser Gestalt des Kanons unmittelbar die „testamentarische" Zusammenfassung seiner Lehre im Brief des Apostels an die römische Gemeinde. Den Wortlaut der paulinischen Christusverkündigung an die Heiden, von der die Apostelgeschichte im Unterschied zu der wenigstens passagenweise wörtlich wiedergegebenen Predigt an die römischen Juden (vgl. 28,17-28) am Ende nur noch berichtet, erfahren die Leser der kanonischen Sammlung sozusagen aus des Heidenapostels eigener Feder im Römerbrief.

3. Die Leitfunktion der Apostelgeschichte für die Briefliteratur

So wie das lukanische Werk für sich betrachtet die narrative Verbindung zwischen vorösterlicher Jesus- und nachösterlicher Apostelzeit geschaffen hatte, bildet es nun auch im kanonischen Zusammenhang den narrativen Anknüpfungspunkt zur Einbeziehung aller weiteren „Apo-

---

27. TROBISCH, *Endredaktion* (s. Anm. 10), S. 125-154, findet hier Indizien für das „Editorial" einer kanonischen Ausgabe des Neuen Testaments. Soweit es um die Rekonstruktion der Leserperspektive auf das Neue Testament als ganzes geht, scheinen mir seine Ausführungen erhellend, ohne daß ich mich seiner These einer Endredaktion anschließen möchte. HECKEL, *Evangelium* (s. Anm. 10), S. 105-218, findet in Joh 21 zwar Ansätze zur Zusammenstellung der Vierevangeliensammlung. Das Verhältnis zur Apostelgeschichte berücksichtigt er dabei aber nicht.

stelschriften" und gibt Grundlinien für deren Verständnis vor. Damit erhält die Apostelgeschichte eine Scharnierfunktion für den gesamten Kanon[28]. Sie ermöglicht das Erkennen von Kontinuitätslinien über alle seine Sammlungseinheiten hinweg und damit gleichzeitig durch alle seinen Aufbau prägenden heilsgeschichtlichen Phasen hindurch. Diese Zusammenhänge werden wir im nächsten Hauptteil genauer ausführen.

4. *Die Personenkontinuität zwischen den Kanonteilen*

Aus der Lektüre der neutestamentlichen Briefe im kanonischen Zusammenhang legen sich vielfältige Rückbezüge auf die Jesus-Schriften und die Apostelgeschichte nahe. Die namentliche Identifizierung der Verfasser der Katholischen Briefe, die spätestens seit ihrer Zusammenstellung zu einer Sammlungseinheit zweifelsfrei möglich ist, legt es nahe, alle Informationen über sie in den Evangelien und der Apostelgeschichte als Leseanweisungen für ihre Briefe heranzuziehen. Auch wenn z.B. Jakobus und Judas in ihren Briefen gar nicht als leibliche Brüder Jesu erscheinen, kann ihr Verhältnis zu Jesus bei deren Lektüre doch gar nicht mehr ausgeblendet werden[29]. Dasselbe gilt entsprechend für das Petrus-Bild der Evangelien und der Apostelgeschichte, das bei der Lektüre der Petrusbriefe immer als bekannt vorausgesetzt werden muß[30].

Exemplarisch wird solche kanonische Personenkontinuität verkörpert durch Johannes[31]. Er ist im Rahmen des Kanons zu identifizieren mit dem Zebedaiden im Zwölferkreis, der als Lieblingsjünger zugleich für den Verfasser des Johannesevangeliums gehalten werden muß, in der Jerusalemer Urgemeinde zusammen mit Petrus und Jakobus eine heraus-

28. Mit Blick auf die Kanongeschichte widmet sich diesen Zusammenhängen J. SCHRÖTER, *Die Apostelgeschichte und die Entstehung des neutestamentlichen Kanons. Beobachtungen zur Kanonisierung der Apostelgeschichte und ihrer Bedeutung als kanonischer Schrift*, im vorliegenden Band, S. 395-429.

29. Vgl. T. ZAHN, *Forschungen zur Geschichte des neutestamentlichen Kanons und der altkirchlichen Literatur. VI. Teil: I. Apostel und Apostelschüler in der Provinz Asien. II. Brüder und Vettern Jesu*, Leipzig, Deichert, 1900, S. 225-363; R. BAUCKHAM, *Jude and the Relatives of Jesus in the Early Church*, Edinburgh, T & T Clark, 1990, S. 45-133; W. PRATSCHER, *Der Herrenbruder Jakobus und die Jakobustradition* (FRLANT, 139), Göttingen, Vandenhoeck & Ruprecht, 1987; J. PAINTER, *Just James. The Brother of Jesus in History and Tradition*, Edinburgh, T & T Clark, 1999.

30. Vgl. P. DSCHULNIGG, *Petrus im Neuen Testament*, Stuttgart, Katholisches Bibelwerk, 1996; P. PERKINS, *Peter. Apostle for the Whole Church*, Edinburgh, T & T Clark, 2000; C. BÖTTRICH, *Petrus. Fischer, Fels und Funktionär*, Leipzig, Evangelische Verlagsanstalt, 2001.

31. Vgl. M. HENGEL, *Die johanneische Frage. Ein Lösungsversuch. Mit einem Beitrag zur Apokalypse von* J. FREY (WUNT, 67), Tübingen, Mohr (Siebeck), 1993, S. 9-95; R.A. CULPEPPER, *John, the Son of Zebedee. The Life of a Legend*, Edinburgh, T & T Clark, 2000.

gehobene Rolle spielt, dessen Autorität als Verfasser von drei Briefen zu vernehmen ist und der schließlich als Seher die nahe Wiederkunft Christi bezeugt.

Für das Verständnis der Paulusbriefe schließlich ist im kanonischen Zusammenhang die Paulus-Darstellung der Apostelgeschichte leitend, gleichzeitig aber auch das Wissen darum, daß er im Unterschied zu den Verfassern der Katholischen Briefe keinen persönlichen Zugang zum vorösterlichen Jesus hatte.

5. Die impliziten Vorverweise auf die Johannes-Offenbarung

Alle Ausblicke in den neutestamentlichen Schriften auf das Wiederkommen des Herrn und die mit ihm zusammenhängenden endzeitlichen Geschehnisse können im kanonischen Zusammenhang als Vorverweise auf die Johannes-Offenbarung wahrgenommen werden. Natürlich ergeben sie zusammengenommen alles andere als ein eindeutiges, in sich stimmiges „apokalyptisches Gemälde". Dennoch kann es für die Rezipienten der christlichen Bibel als ganzer ja nur *ein* endzeitliches Heilsgeschehen geben, von dem die vielfältigen eschatologischen Aussagen der verschiedenen Schriften je auf ihre Weise Zeugnis geben, das aber erst in der Johannes-Offenbarung zusammenhängend und abschließend zur Sprache gebracht wird.

Besonders an diesem zuletzt benannten Gesichtspunkt wird die theologisch-hermeneutische Herausforderung deutlich, die aus einer Exegese des Neuen Testament im kanonischen Zusammenhang erwächst. Die exegetische Tradition neuzeitlicher Bibelwissenschaft, die zu immer schärferen historischen und theologischen Differenzierungen zwischen den einzelnen Schriften des Neuen Testament und innerhalb dieser noch einmal zwischen verschiedenen Überlieferungsbereichen führte, hat diese Herausforderung eher verdeckt, als daß sie sich ihr gestellt hätte. Diese forschungsgeschichtliche Entwicklung ist freilich nicht nur unumkehrbar, sondern sie hat auch zu erheblichen Erkenntnisgewinnen geführt. Die Kanonfrage ist dadurch aber nicht bewältigt, sondern eher zu einem Fundamentalproblem der Theologie des Neuen Testament geworden.

II. PRAXAPOSTOLOS UND CORPUS PAULINUM

Auch wenn wir nach den internen Beziehungen und Querverbindungen zwischen der Apostelgeschichte und den Korpora der Briefliteratur fragen, müssen wir zunächst bestimmen, von welcher Gestalt des

Kanons wir ausgehen wollen. Charakteristisch für die vorbyzantinischen Handschriften und den Kanon in der von Athanasius bezeugten Gestalt ist zum einen die Einordnung des Hebräerbriefes in die Paulusbriefsammlung zwischen den 2. Thessalonicher- und den 1. Timotheusbrief, zum anderen die Zusammenfassung von Apostelgeschichte und Katholischen Briefen zum Praxapostolos. Die Schriftenfolge der byzantinischen Handschriften und der Vulgata erweist sich demgegenüber als Ergebnis einer gezielten Rezension, wie sie ja auch für die Textgestalt des byzantinischen Texttyps vorauszusetzen ist[32].

Für die Gesamtgestalt des Kanons hat diese Umstellung erhebliche Konsequenzen. Während im vorbyzantinischen Kanon der Praxapostolos als Sammlungseinheit den Zusammenhang zwischen der narrativen Darstellung der Apostelzeit und der lehrhaften Hinterlassenschaft der Apostel hervorkehrt, betont die byzantinische Kanongestalt in erster Linie den Zusammenhang zwischen der narrativen Darstellung der *paulinischen* Mission und *seiner* brieflichen Hinterlassenschaft. Wird Paulus im vorbyzantinischen Kanon, wie es sowohl der Darstellung der Apostelgeschichte als auch seiner Selbstdarstellung entspricht, an das Ende der Reihe der „Apostel" gestellt, so gewinnt er im byzantinischen Kanon eine Leitfunktion für den Gang der Dinge in der Apostelzeit.

Allerdings wird das konturenreiche und umfassende Paulus-Bild, das durch diese Aufeinanderfolge der Paulus-Darstellung der Apostelgeschichte und der Wiedergabe der Apostelbriefe entsteht, gleichzeitig wieder eingefaßt durch die ihm vorangehenden und folgenden Kanonteile, die, um mit Paulus zu reden, den „anderen" oder „übrigen Aposteln" gewidmet sind[33]. Auch in der byzantinischen Fassung des Kanons kann also Paulus nicht ohne den urchristlichen Kontext seines Wirkens und Lehrens wahrgenommen werden. Dieser Kontext wird maßgeblich bestimmt einerseits durch die Anfänge der Jerusalemer Urgemeinde mit Petrus, Johannes und Jakobus an ihrer Spitze (Apg 1-8; 11f; 15; 21) und andererseits durch das Wirken der Jerusalemer „Säulen" (Gal 2,9) über Jerusalem hinaus durch ihre Briefe. Der Zusammenhang zwischen narrativer Darstellung der Apostelzeit und Zusammenstellung der brieflichen Hinterlassenschaft der Apostel bleibt also für beide Strukturmodelle des Kanons bestimmend, und die narrative Darstellung des Apostelwirkens geht jeweils den lehrhaften Ausführungen ihrer Briefe voraus. Die Apostel begegnen im Kanon folglich zuerst als Missionsprediger, Gemeindegründer bzw. -organisatoren und Wundertäter, erst später dann auch als Briefschreiber.

32. Vgl. TROBISCH, *Endredaktion* (s. Anm. 10), S. 40.
33. Vgl. Gal 1,19; 1 Kor 9,5.

Für die Wahrnehmung der neutestamentlichen Briefkorpora im kanonischen Zusammenhang ergeben sich daraus einige Leitfragen, die wir
im folgenden bedenken wollen: (1) Welches Leitbild für die Apostelzeit
ergibt sich aus den persönlichen Begegnungen der apostolischen Briefautoren, von denen in der Apostelgeschichte erzählt wird bzw. die in
manchen Briefen erwähnt werden? (2) Welche expliziten und impliziten
Leseanweisungen lassen die Apostelbriefe selbst erkennen? (3) Welche
Konsequenzen ergeben sich aus der narrativen Darstellung der Apostelzeit für das in den Briefen vorausgesetzte Apostelbild?

1. *Biblische Begegnungen zwischen den apostolischen Briefautoren*

Für das Bild, das die Leser des Kanons sich von den Verfassern der
Briefe machen, sind potentiell alle Stellen aussagekräftig, an denen diese
erwähnt werden, insbesondere aber solche, bei denen von mehreren
Briefautoren gleichzeitig die Rede ist. So ergibt sich, im kanonischen
Kontext gelesen, der erste Hinweis auf eine nachösterliche Begegnung
zwischen Petrus, dem Zebedaiden Johannes und den beiden Herrenbrüdern Jakobus und Judas in Jerusalem aus Apg 1,14: In einmütigem
beharrlichen Gebet sind die elf Apostel[34] beieinander mit „den Frauen
und Maria, der Mutter Jesu, und seinen Brüdern".

Die Aktivitäten von Petrus und Johannes bestimmen maßgeblich den
weiteren Erzählverlauf in Apg 2-5, wobei Petrus als Redner und Wundertäter eindeutig die Führungsrolle innehat, Johannes die des weitgehend stummen Begleiters. Paulus, der Verfolger der Gemeinde, kommt
zunächst eher unscheinbar in den Blick. Daß er auch die Jerusalemer
Apostel gewaltsam verfolgt hätte, wird geradezu vermieden zu sagen[35].
Erst bei seinem ersten Jerusalemaufenthalt nach seiner Bekehrung tritt er
in nähere Bekanntschaft mit „den Aposteln" (9,27f). Jakobus, der offenkundig auf Dauer in Jerusalem geblieben ist, wird nur beiläufig erwähnt.
Er nimmt aber jetzt offenbar eine führende Stellung innerhalb der Urgemeinde ein[36], während Petrus infolge des Martyriums des Zebedaiden
Jakobus, des Bruders des Johannes (12,2), und wegen Nachstellungen
gegen ihn selbst Jerusalem verlassen muß.

Maßgebliche Bedeutung für die Personenkonstellation zwischen den
Aposteln hat die Szene in Jerusalem nach Apg 15,1-29. Petrus und
Jakobus erscheinen hier als Wortführer der Jerusalemer Gemeinde, und
zwar namentlich herausgehoben aus dem Leitungsgremium der „Apo-

---

34. Vgl. 1,2.13.
35. Vgl. 7,58b; 8,1.3; 9,1f.
36. Vgl. in 12,17 die Wendung „Jakobus und die Brüder".

stel und Ältesten" (15,2.4.6.22.23). Paulus und Barnabas begegnen ihnen als Abgesandte und Wortführer der antiochenischen Gemeinde. Die beiden Sprecherpaare werden als einig in der Sache und gegenüber abweichenden Meinungen dargestellt. Während Petrus die gemeinsame Position der Jerusalemer und der Antiochener zur Einbeziehung der Heiden in das endzeitliche Gottesvolk ohne Beschneidung und Halten der ganzen Tora des Mose darlegt und gegenüber Widersprüchen durchsetzt, trifft Jakobus unter Berufung auf die Schrift eine dieser Position entsprechende Entscheidung. Paulus und Barnabas haben zuvor lediglich von den „Zeichen und Wundern", die Gott durch sie unter den Heiden erwirkt hat, berichtet, ohne daß ihre Ausführungen wörtlich wiedergegeben werden. Den Beschluß fassen schließlich „die Apostel und Ältesten samt der ganzen Gemeinde" (15,22). Zu denen, die Paulus und Barnabas zurück nach Antiochia begleiten, um diesen Beschluß dort bekanntzumachen und durchzusetzen, gehört auch Silas (15,22.27.32), einer der künftigen Paulus-Begleiter.

Während Petrus von jetzt an ganz von der Jerusalemer Bildfläche verschwindet und von Johannes schon seit dem Martyrium seines Bruders nicht mehr die Rede war, kommt Jakobus noch einmal in Apg 21 als Jerusalemer Gemeindeautorität in den Blick. Er verteidigt, zusammen mit „allen Ältesten", Paulus gegenüber Unterstellungen vonseiten zum Glauben gekommener gesetzestreuer Juden.

Dieses von Einvernehmen, gegenseitiger Unterstützung und Verteidigung gegen innere Abweichler und äußere Gegner geprägte Bild der Apostel in Jerusalem setzt den Maßstab für ihre Erwähnung in allen folgenden Kanonteilen. Von ihm her werden auch die späteren Begegnungen zwischen Paulus und den Jerusalemer Gemeindeautoritäten wahrgenommen, von denen im Römer- und im Galaterbrief die Rede ist. Wenn Paulus in Gal 1,17ff von seinem Besuch bei Kefas und Jakobus in Jerusalem berichtet, dann ist dies für die Leser des Kanons aufgrund von Apg 9,26-30 eine Wiederbegegnung. Auch wenn Paulus Dauer und Stellenwert dieses Besuches im Zusammenhang seiner Aussageabsicht im Galaterbrief so weit wie möglich minimiert, werden doch die Leser aufgrund ihrer Vorkenntnisse aus der Apostelgeschichte dessen Bedeutung sehr wohl einzuschätzen wissen, zumal paulinische Wendungen wie „die Apostel vor mir", „einen anderen von den Aposteln" oder „den Bruder des Herrn" ihnen das Bild von der zu jenem Zeitpunkt aktuellen Jerusalemer Personenkonstellation in Erinnerung rufen und vervollständigen.

Auch die in Gal 2,1-10 geschilderten Ereignisse in Jerusalem können die Leser der kanonischen Sammlung gar nicht anders als im Licht der

Darstellung von Apg 15 wahrnehmen, selbst wenn die Akzente beider Berichte jeweils etwas anders gesetzt sind. Folglich werden sie auch die von Paulus in Gal 2,4 erwähnten „eingedrungenen Lügenapostel" mit den pharisäischen Widersachern in der Urgemeinde nach Apg 15,5 identifizieren, und zur Begründung für die Anerkennung der beschneidungsfreien paulinischen Mission durch die Jerusalemer Gemeindeautoritäten nach Gal 2,6-10 werden sie deren Argumentationen in Apg 15,6-21 heranziehen. Die Art und Weise, wie Paulus im Galaterbrief die Jerusalemer Autoritäten namentlich nennt und tituliert[37], können sie im kanonischen Zusammenhang nur als Ehrenbezeugung verstehen, und das Ergebnis, das Jakobus und Petrus in Apg 15 begründet und verkündet haben, besiegelten für sie die Apostel nach Gal 2,9f mit Handschlag.

Der in Gal 2,11-14 von Paulus zur Sprache gebrachte Konflikt in Antiochia trägt freilich eine gewisse Spannung in das bisher entstandene harmonische Apostelbild ein, zumal hier die Protagonisten bis auf Johannes noch einmal alle namentlich genannt werden, Jakobus freilich, ohne selbst anwesend zu sein. Den im Galaterbrief offengelassenen Ausgang der Auseinandersetzung, bei der für sie Paulus immerhin doch das letzte Wort behalten hatte, werden die Leser wiederum aus ihrem durch die Apostelgeschichte bestimmten Vorwissen selbst ergänzen. Nach ihrer Darstellung jedenfalls verschwinden sowohl Petrus als auch Barnabas unmittelbar nach dem Apostelkonzil bzw. einem kurz darauf entstandenen Streit (vgl. Apg 15,39!) von der Bildfläche.

Daß der Konflikt in Antiochia die Gemeinschaft der Apostel nicht auf Dauer zerstören konnte, erfahren die Leser des Kanons zum einen aus anderen Erwähnungen des Petrus und des Jakobus bei Paulus[38], zum anderen aber vor allem aus den übrigen Apostelbriefen. Nirgends wird in ihnen ein Konflikt zwischen den Aposteln auch nur angedeutet, auch nicht im Jakobusbrief[39]. Vielmehr stehen nun die Briefe der Apostel, wie nach Gal 2,9 die Protagonisten selbst, im Kanon friedlich beieinander und reichen einander die Hände.

---

37. 2,9: „Jakobus, Kefas und Johannes, die als Säulen gelten". Vgl. dazu N. WALTER, *Die „als Säulen Geltenden" in Jerusalem—Leiter der Urgemeinde oder exemplarisch Fromme?*, in M. KARRER, W. KRAUS, O. MERK (Hgg.), *Kirche und Volk Gottes*. FS J. Roloff, Neukirchen-Vluyn, Neukirchener, 2000, S. 78-92.

38. Vgl. 1 Kor 1,12; 3,22; 9,5; 15,5.7.

39. Das gilt unabhängig davon, wie man das literarische oder traditionsgeschichtliche Verhältnis zwischen dem Jakobusbrief und (den) Paulus(briefen) beurteilt; vgl. zur Diskussion darüber zuletzt M. KONRADT, *Christliche Existenz nach dem Jakobusbrief. Eine Studie zu seiner soteriologischen und ethischen Konzeption* (StUNT, 22), Göttingen, Vandenhoeck & Ruprecht, 1998, S. 207-248. Eine Reflexion des kanonischen Zusammenhangs zwischen Paulus und Jakobus findet sich bei R.W. WALL, *Community of the Wise. The Letter of James*, Valley Forge, Trinity Press International, 1997, S. 275-306.

2. Explizite und implizite Leseanweisungen

Bei Briefen finden sich die wichtigsten Leseanweisungen gattungsbedingt im Präskript. Bei Briefsammlungen sind darüber hinaus gegebenenfalls auch Beziehungen zwischen den Präskripten verschiedener Briefe zu beachten. Sind Briefkorpora zudem noch in einen größeren literarischen Zusammenhang eingeordnet, können auch Informationen aus diesem Kontext als Leseanweisungen herangezogen werden.

Daß der Hebräerbrief als Brief des Paulus in das Corpus Paulinum eingeordnet wurde, ist Ergebnis der Berücksichtigung von verschiedenen impliziten und expliziten Leseanweisungen: Während der Hauptteil dieser Schrift am besten als Mahnrede zu charakterisieren ist, weist das Textende in 13,18-25 klare Formmerkmale eines Briefschlusses auf. Die Erwähnung „unseres Bruders Timotheus" läßt zudem im Kontext der Apostelgeschichte und der Paulusbriefsammlung an Paulus als Briefschreiber denken[40]. Das fehlende Briefpräskript ermöglicht verschiedene Einordnungen in das Corpus Paulinum. Der Länge entsprechend wäre ein Platz nach dem Römerbrief und vor den beiden nicht zu trennenden Korintherbriefen denkbar. Da keine Adressaten genannt sind, könnte der Brief aber auch als Sonderfall hinter die Gemeindebriefe und die Briefe an Einzelpersonen gerückt werden. Unter Berücksichtigung der pluralischen Adressatenanrede in der Mahnrede und im Briefschluß kommt auch seine Einordnung als letzter der Gemeindebriefe in Frage. Die Erwähnung des Timotheus im Briefschluß schafft dann eine besonders gute Verbindung zu den folgenden Timotheusbriefen. Die Zeugnisse der Kirchenväter und der griechischen Handschriften zur Stellung des Hebräerbriefes im Corpus Paulinum belegen genau diese drei aufgeführten Möglichkeiten seiner Einordnung[41].

Eindeutiger sind die Leseanweisungen, die sich aus den Präskripten der Paulusbriefe und der Katholischen Briefe ergeben. Die namentliche Nennung der Briefautoren ermöglicht ihre Einordnung in das Vorwissen der Rezipienten, das, wie wir gesehen haben, maßgeblich durch die narrativen Darstellungen der Evangelien und der Apostelgeschichte bestimmt ist. Darüber hinaus weisen die beigefügten Charakterisierungen der Briefautoren und der Adressaten eine Reihe von Querverbindungen auf, die für die zusammenhängende Lektüre der neutestamentlichen Briefkorpora von Bedeutung sind. Wir werden diese Querverbindungen im folgenden Teil näher darstellen.

40. Vgl. H.-F. WEISS, *Der Brief an die Hebräer* (KEK, 13), Göttingen, Vandenhoeck & Ruprecht, 1991, S. 746-748. Für literarisch sekundär hält den brieflichen Schluß Hebr 13,22-25 E. GRÄSSER, *An die Hebräer. 3. Teilband Hebr 10,19-13,25* (EKK, 17/3), Zürich, Benzinger; Neukirchen-Vluyn, Neukirchener, 1997, S. 409-416.

41. Vgl. TROBISCH, *Paulusbriefsammlung* (s. Anm. 10), S. 14-45.

Zur Einordnung der Briefe in das Vorwissen ihrer Leser können zusätzlich zu den Informationen der Präskripte weitere textinterne Informationen wie Namen, Situationsangaben oder autobiographische Ausführungen dienen. Für die Paulusbriefe brauchen wir die entsprechenden allseits bekannten Texte hier nicht noch einmal zusammenzustellen. Allerdings ist es für die Perspektive der kanonischen Lektüre des Corpus Paulinum von zentraler Bedeutung, daß die Pastoralbriefe implizit die mit der römischen Gefangenschaft endende Paulus-Darstellung der Apostelgeschichte fortschreiben. Der 2. Timotheusbrief thematisiert ausdrücklich den bevorstehenden Tod des Apostels (4,6-8). Für die Leser der kanonischen Sammlung knüpft er damit implizit an die Apostelgeschichte an, insbesondere an die Abschiedsrede des Paulus in Milet und seine Gefangenschaft in Rom, die auch ausdrücklich erwähnt wird[42]. Der Brief vermittelt somit das Vermächtnis des Paulus an seinen engsten Mitarbeiter und über ihn an die Leser der kanonischen Paulusbriefsammlung[43].

Unter den Katholischen Briefen lassen sich lediglich in den beiden Petrusbriefen für die Leser der kanonischen Sammlung maßgebliche situative Einordnungen erkennen. Beim 1. Petrusbrief ermöglichen die im Briefschluß genannten Silvanus und Markus sowie die Ortsangabe „Babylon" für die Absendergemeinde die Einordnung in ihr Wissen über die Apostelzeit. Silvanus und Markus sind ihnen aus der Apostelgeschichte und mehreren Paulusbriefen als Mitarbeiter des Paulus bekannt[44]. „Babylon" konnten sie als Decknamen für die Hauptstadt Rom entschlüsseln. Die Querverbindungen zum Ende des Weges des Paulus liegen damit auf der Hand.

Im 2. Petrusbrief verstärkt sich diese Parallele noch dadurch, daß hier, ähnlich wie im 2. Timotheusbrief, der bevorstehende Tod des Briefschreibers thematisiert wird (1,14f). Zudem verweist der Autor ausdrücklich nicht bloß auf seinen eigenen ersten Brief (3,1), sondern zu-

---

42. Vgl. 1,17; 4,11. Die Identifizierung des Ortes der Gefangenschaft mit Rom, die der historisch-kritischen Forschung so große Probleme bereitet, ist für die Leser der kanonischen Sammlung unproblematisch.

43. Die drei Pastoralbriefe sind wahrscheinlich gleichzeitig als Briefsammlung in der Reihenfolge 1 Tim—Tit—2 Tim entstanden, so daß der 2. Timotheusbrief als „Testament" des Apostels den Abschluß der kleinen Sammlung bildete; so mit J. ROLOFF, Art. *Pastoralbriefe*, in *TRE* 26 (1996) 50-68, bes. 57.

44. Vgl. zu Silas/Silvanus: Apg 15,22.27.32f; 16-18; 2 Kor 1,19; 1 Thess 1,1; 2 Thess 1,1, zu [Johannes] Markus: Apg 12,12.25; 13,5.13; 15,36-41; Kol 4,10; 2 Tim 4,11; Phlm 24. Zu den biblischen Querverbindungen der im 1. Petrusbrief genannten Personen zu Paulus vgl. J. HERZER, *Petrus oder Paulus? Studien über das Verhältnis des Ersten Petrusbriefes zur paulinischen Tradition* (WUNT, 103), Tübingen, Mohr (Siebeck), 1998, S. 62-73.

dem noch auf „die Apostel des Herrn und Retters" (3,2; vgl. Jud 17) und schließlich auf „unsern geliebten Bruder Paulus" und „alle seine Briefe" (3,16f). Damit steht den Lesern noch einmal die ganze Phalanx der apostolischen Größen versammelt vor Augen, die sich gegenseitig und damit gleichzeitig die Leser ihrer Schriften in der Gewißheit des Glaubens bestärken und gegenüber allen inneren und äußeren Gefährdungen zusammenschließen[45].

3. Das vorausgesetzte Apostelbild

Die Bezeichnung sämtlicher neutestamentlichen Briefautoren als Apostel ist durch die handschriftlich überlieferten Titel belegt. Während Paulus in seinen Briefen für sich selbst ein scharf konturiertes, in seiner Berufung durch den auferstandenen Christus begründetes Verständnis als Apostel vertritt, kann er darüber hinaus durchaus auch andere nachösterliche Christusverkündiger bis hin zu den Herrenbrüdern als Apostel bezeichnen bzw. in unmittelbare Nähe zu ihnen rücken[46]. Die Apostelgeschichte schränkt dagegen bekanntlich den Titel fast ganz auf unmittelbare Augenzeugen und positive Wegbegleiter des vorösterlichen Wirkens Jesu ein und kann folglich weder Paulus noch die Herrenbrüder Apostel nennen. Die Autoren des Jakobus- und des Judasbriefes bezeichnen sich auch selbst in ihren Briefen nicht als Apostel, sondern als Sklaven Jesu Christi. Wirkungsgeschichtlich betrachtet hat sich also ein einheitlicher Apostelbegriff durchgesetzt, der in den einzelnen neutestamentlichen Schriften noch keineswegs eindeutig festgelegt ist[47].

Das Apostelbild, das den Lesern des neutestamentlichen Kanons vor Augen steht, setzt sich somit zusammen aus den persönlichen Zügen verschiedener führender Gestalten der nachösterlichen Jesusbewegung, insbesondere der Jerusalemer Gemeinde, wie sie in der Apostelgeschich-

---

45. Das Paulus-Bild des 2. Petrusbriefes verdiente eine umfassende Behandlung, vgl. einstweilen A. VÖGTLE, *Petrus und Paulus nach dem Zweiten Petrusbrief*, in P.-G. MÜLLER & W. STENGER (Hgg.), *Kontinuität und Einheit*. FS F. Mussner, Freiburg–Basel–Wien, Herder, 1981, S. 223-239 (= in DERS., *Offenbarungsgeschehen und Wirkungsgeschichte. Neutestamentliche Beiträge*, Freiburg–Basel–Wien, Herder, 1985, S. 280-294). Zur Bedeutung des Briefes für eine kanonische Lektüre vgl. R.W. WALL, *The Canonical Function of 2 Peter*, in *Biblical Interpretation* 9 (2001) 64-81.

46. Vgl. 1 Kor 9,5; 15,7; Gal 1,17-19.

47. Vgl. dazu W. BAUER & M. HORNSCHUH, *Das Apostelbild in der altchristlichen Überlieferung*, in E. HENNECKE & W. SCHNEEMELCHER (Hgg.), *Neutestamentliche Apokryphen in deutscher Übersetzung. II. Band: Apostolisches, Apokalypsen und Verwandtes*, Tübingen, Mohr (Siebeck), ³1964, S. 11-52; W.A. BIENERT, *Das Apostelbild in der altchristlichen Überlieferung*, in W. SCHNEEMELCHER (Hg.), *Neutestamentliche Apokryphen in deutscher Übersetzung. II. Band: Apostolisches, Apokalypsen und Verwandtes*, Tübingen, Mohr (Siebeck), ⁶1997, S. 6-28.

te dargestellt sind, aus den literarischen Hinterlassenschaften dieser Persönlichkeiten, wie sie in den kanonischen Briefsammlungen zur Verfügung stehen, und aus ihrer gemeinsamen Benennung als Apostel. Das Leitbild von der Gemeinschaft aller Apostel wird exemplarisch in der Apostelgeschichte, insbesondere in Apg 15, entworfen und dient fortan als implizite Leseanweisung für die apostolischen Schriften. Ihre grundsätzliche Einigkeit in der Lehre und bei der Lösung von Streitfragen der Mission oder der Gemeindeorganisation bildet die Vorgabe für die theologische und kirchenpolitische Einordnung ihrer Schriften. Die polemischen Passagen ihrer Briefe können deshalb auch miteinander verbunden werden und so der Absicherung gegenüber allen denkbaren Gefährdungen der Gemeinden von innen und außen dienstbar gemacht werden.

Zweifellos erhält auf diese Weise indirekt auch das theologisch-literarische Programm der Apostelgeschichte eine Leitfunktion für die Rezeption der im Kanon versammelten Schriften und Sammlungseinheiten. Die Gestaltung der Briefkorpora unterstreicht diese Tendenz und das ihr entsprechende Apostelbild. Durch zahlreiche Querverbindungen rücken die Apostelbriefe, und mit ihnen ihre apostolischen Autoren, in immer engere Beziehung zueinander. Im 2. Petrusbrief erreicht diese Tendenz in der ausdrücklichen Zusammenstellung von „Aposteln des Herrn" (3,2)[48], „allen Paulusbriefen" (3,15f) und der eigenen Autorität des Petrus als apostolischer Briefschreiber (1,1) ihren Höhepunkt.

III. STRUKTUREN UND QUERVERBINDUNGEN IN DEN NEUTESTAMENTLICHEN BRIEFKORPORA

Sämtliche neutestamentlichen Briefautoren werden in den Titeln der Handschriften Apostel genannt, unabhängig davon, ob die Autoren in den Präskripten oder sonst irgendwo innerhalb der Briefe sich selbst so bezeichnen. Daß für die Leser der Briefkorpora damit ein einheitliches, im wesentlichen von der Apostelgeschichte geprägtes Apostelbild vorgegeben ist, haben wir gesehen. Darüber hinaus geben die Handschriftentitel und die Briefpräskripte aber noch weitere Leseanweisungen, die wir jetzt näher betrachten wollen[49].

Die Charakterisierung der Briefe des Jakobus, Petrus, Johannes und Judas als „katholisch" findet sich, ähnlich wie der Aposteltitel für Jakobus, Johannes und Judas, nur in den Handschriftentiteln. Diese verbinden also sieben Briefe der genannten Autoren miteinander und gren-

---

48. Vgl. zu dieser Übersetzung Jud 17.
49. Vgl. zum folgenden TROBISCH, *Endredaktion* (s. Anm. 10), S. 73-91.

zen sie gleichzeitig vom Corpus Paulinum ab. Aus dem Wortlaut der einzelnen Briefe hätte sich freilich eine solche Bezeichnung schwerlich ableiten lassen, und andererseits hätten auch manche der im Corpus Paulinum gesammelten Schriften durchaus Anlaß zu ihrer Benennung als „katholisch" geboten. Offensichtlich schlägt sich aber in der Zusammenstellung von sieben Apostelbriefen neben Paulus ein bewußt gewähltes Anordnungsprinzip des Kanons nieder.

Die Anordnung der Briefe innerhalb des Corpus Catholicum variiert zwar nach den Zeugnissen der Kirchenväter sehr stark, kaum aber in den Bibelhandschriften. Es wurde schon mehrfach gesehen, daß diese Reihenfolge offenbar in Abhängigkeit zur Reihenfolge der Jerusalemer „Säulen" nach Gal 2,9 steht. Das wird besonders am Codex Claromontanus deutlich, der in Gal 2,9 eine Lesart mit abweichender Reihenfolge der Personen bietet, die wiederum der Reihenfolge der Katholischen Briefe in seinem Kanonverzeichnis entspricht[50].

Blicken wir nun etwas genauer auf die Formulierung der Präskripte! Jakobus und Judas bezeichnen sich beide als Ἰησοῦ Χριστοῦ δοῦλος, eine Selbstprädikation, die sich auch in mehreren Präskripten von Paulusbriefen findet. Judas nennt sich zudem noch ἀδελφὸς δὲ Ἰακώβου. Damit ist für die Leser der Briefsammlung die Identifikation beider mit den aus den Evangelien und – für Jakobus – aus der Apostelgeschichte bekannten Herrenbrüdern eindeutig festgelegt, gleichzeitig auch zumindest für den Jakobusbrief der Abfassungsort Jerusalem, der sich zusätzlich noch aus der Adressierung des Briefes „an die zwölf Stämme in der Diaspora" nahelegt. Daß in beiden Präskripten ein ausdrücklicher Bezug auf die leibliche Verwandtschaft zu Jesus fehlt, bedeutet demgegenüber für die Leser der Briefsammlung keinen Mangel, sondern kann als Ausdruck eines bewußt gewahrten Abstands zwischen den Briefautoren und dem von ihnen als κύριος verehrten auferstanden Christus wahrgenommen werden. Apostel nennen sich beide ebenso wenig, was freilich die Abschreiber der Briefsammlung nicht daran hinderte, sie in den Titeln als solche zu bezeichnen.

Der Autor des 1. Petrusbriefes stellt sich dagegen ausdrücklich als ἀπόστολος Ἰησοῦ Χριστοῦ vor, so wie es ähnlich Paulus in den meisten seiner Briefe tut[51]. Im 2. Petrusbrief nennt sich der Autor zusätzlich noch δοῦλος, so wie Jakobus und Judas in ihren Briefen. Die auffällige Namensform des Autors im zweiten Brief (Συμεὼν Πέτρος) mag einen

50. D. LÜHRMANN, *Gal 2,9 und die katholischen Briefe. Bemerkungen zum Kanon und zur regula fidei*, in ZNW 72 (1981) 65-87.
51. Vgl. zum Präskript des 1. Petrusbriefes im Vergleich zu den Paulusbriefen HERZER, *Petrus* (s. Anm. 44), S. 22-49.

aufmerksamen Kanonleser an die Benennung des Petrus durch Jakobus beim Apostelkonzil erinnern (Apg 15,14), die einzige Stelle im Neuen Testament, an der er so genannt wird. Auch der Briefautor Petrus hat in seinen beiden Briefen keinen Anlaß, seine spezifische Beziehung zu Jesus als Mitglied des Zwölferkreises in den Präskripten zur Sprache zu bringen, obwohl sie ihren Lesern zweifellos vor Augen steht. Dagegen benennt er wie der Autor des Jakobusbriefes im ersten Brief den Aufenthaltsort seiner Adressaten mit dem Stichwort „Diaspora", identifiziert ihn freilich im Unterschied zu Jakobus geographisch präzise mit einer bestimmten kleinasiatischen Region.

Für die Johannes-Briefe lassen sich entsprechende Querverbindungen in den Präskripten nicht erkennen. Der erste hat gar keines, die beiden übrigen nennen den Autor nicht beim Namen, sondern nur mit seiner Funktion als Presbyter. Auch die Benennung der Adressaten in den beiden kurzen Johannes-Briefen ermöglicht keine genauere Orientierung der Leser. Allenfalls sehr aufmerksame unter ihnen mögen eine Verbindung hergestellt haben zwischen der metaphorischen Bezeichnung der Adressatengemeinde des 2. Johannesbriefes als „auserwählte Herrin" (2 Joh 1; vgl. 13) und der Bezeichnung der Absendergemeinde im 1. Petrusbrief als „die Miterwählte in Babylon" (1 Petr 5,13). Erst die Titel in den Handschriften[52] stellen die Verbindung zum Zebedaiden Johannes her, die sich implizit über die sprachliche und inhaltliche Nähe der Ausführungen des ersten Briefes zum Johannes-Evangelium nahelegen konnte. Und erst aufgrund dieser Verbindung kann dann das zur Verfügung stehende Wissen über den Zebedaiden Johannes auch in die Lektüre der drei Briefe eingebracht werden.

Überblicken wir die Formulierungen in den Briefpräskripten, so lassen sich folgende Querverbindungen feststellen: Die Selbstprädikation als Apostel Jesu Christi verbindet die meisten Paulusbriefe mit den Petrusbriefen, die Bezeichnung als Sklave Jesu Christi einige der Paulusbriefe mit dem Jakobus-, dem 2. Petrus- und dem Judasbrief, die Wendung an Adressaten in der Diaspora schließlich den Jakobus- mit dem 1. Petrusbrief. Zu solchen sprachlichen Verknüpfungen treten die in den Namen implizierten Verbindungen der Briefautoren, die aufgrund der Kenntnis der Apostelgeschichte und des Corpus Paulinum weiter erschlossen werden können. Schließlich ergeben sich weitere Bezüge aus expliziten Querverweisen innerhalb der Briefe, wie wir sie für den 2. Timotheusbrief und die Petrusbriefe beobachtet haben.

---

52. Vgl. zu den durchaus variierenden Formulierungen den Apparat bei NESTLE-ALAND[27].

Auch die Sammlung der Katholischen Briefe und ihre Verbindung mit dem Corpus Paulinum bietet damit günstige Ausgangspunkte für die Entdeckung kanonischer Bezüge, zumal im Zusammenhang mit der Benennung aller Briefautoren als Apostel. So wie seinerzeit Paulus und die „Säulenapostel" in Jerusalem stehen für die Leser des Kanons auch jetzt die Apostel in enger Gemeinschaft beieinander.

IV. JESUS IM KANON

Hinweise auf persönliche Begegnungen zwischen den Aposteln und Jesus finden sich in den neutestamentlichen Briefkorpora, abgesehen von den Implikationen der Namen der Briefautoren, nur in den beiden Petrusbriefen. In 1 Petr 5,1 bezeichnet sich der apostolische Briefschreiber als „Zeuge der Leiden Christi", was zumindest für die Leser des Kanons nicht anders denn als ein Hinweis auf seine Rolle im Passionsgeschehen verstanden werden kann. In 2 Petr 1,14 teilt der Autor den Adressaten mit, daß schon der Herr Jesus ihm seinen bevorstehenden Tod angekündigt habe. Wiederum wird sich den Lesern der kanonischen Sammlung dies als Hinweis auf die Begegnung des Petrus mit dem auferstandenen Jesus nach Joh 21,18f erschließen. Unmittelbar anschließend verweist Petrus die Adressaten zur Legitimation seiner Ermahnungen auf eine andere von ihm persönlich erlebte Begegnung mit Jesus, die Verklärung Jesu auf dem „heiligen Berg", bei der er „eingeweihter Zeuge seiner Größe" wurde und „die Stimme vom Himmel her" hörte, welche ihm Jesus als geliebten Gottessohn zu erkennen gab[53]. Daß vergleichbare Begegnungen mit Jesus in den übrigen apostolischen Briefen fehlen, liegt natürlich in erster Linie daran, daß sie für Paulus und die Herrenbrüder aus inneren Gründen unmöglich sind und bei den Johannes-Briefen die Identifikation mit dem Zebedaiden nur außerhalb des Brieftextes vorgenommen wird. Für Leser, die mit der Kenntnis der Evangelien und der Apostelgeschichte an die Lektüre dieser Briefe gehen, ist freilich auch in ihnen die Jesus-Geschichte stets gegenwärtig. So werden sie immer dann, wenn vom Leiden Jesu die Rede ist, die Passionsgeschichte vor Augen haben[54]. Wenn die Briefautoren von der Ankündigung der Parusie und des Endgerichts schreiben[55], werden sich die Leser der kanonischen Sammlung an Jesu Endzeitreden er-

---

53. 1,16-18; vgl. Mk 9,2-8 parr; der Wortlaut der Himmelsstimme kommt Mt 17,5 am nächsten.

54. Vgl. insbesondere 1 Kor 1,18; 11,23-25; 15,3f; Gal 3,1.13; 1 Tim 6,13; 1 Petr 1,19; 2,21-24; 3,18; 4,1.13; 5,1; 1 Joh 3,16.

55. Vgl. etwa Jak 1,12; 2,12f; 5,1-3; 2 Petr 3,4.9; 1 Joh 2,25; Jud 17.

innern. Wenn der Autor des 1. Johannesbriefes sie auf das verweist, „was wir gehört, was wir mit unseren Augen gesehen, was wir ange- schaut und was unsere Hände berührt haben"[56], dann entsteht vor den Augen der Leser ein plastisches Bild von der „Gesamterscheinung" Jesu, das sich aus all dem zusammensetzt, was sie zuvor beim Lesen ih- rer Bibel gehört, gesehen und mit ihren Händen berührt haben.

In dieser Perspektive erhalten schließlich auch die für sich genommen nur schwer zu deutenden Aussagen über die „Worte der Apostel unseres Herrn Jesus Christus" in Jud 17 bzw. „die Worte des Herrn und Hei- lands" in 2 Petr 3,2 ihren Sinn: Die Apostel treten im kanonischen Zu- sammenhang ihren Lesern nicht allein als Briefautoren gegenüber, son- dern sie werden darüber hinaus zu Vermittlern und Garanten der Jesus- Geschichte. Die von ihnen ursprünglich mündlich weitergetragene Wei- sung Jesu vermitteln sie als Briefschreiber in die Gegenwart ihrer Adres- saten. Gleichzeitig lassen sie als Zeitgenossen und Nachfolger Jesu vor den Augen der Leser des Kanons ein Gesamtbild von der Jesus-Ge- schichte, seinem Wirken, seinem Weg und seinem Geschick einschließ- lich seines österlichen Ausgangs entstehen, ein Gesamtbild, in das all das eingehen kann, was die Leser aus den apostolischen Evangelien und der Apostelgeschichte bereits vernommen haben.

V. THESEN ZUR DISKUSSION

1. Die theologische Relevanz des Neuen Testaments als Teil der christlichen Bibel erfordert die Reflexion auf die Gestalt des Kanons. Das Neue Testament muß im theologischen Sinn als Einheit und Ganz- heit wahrgenommen werden, wenn es gegenüber den Kirchen eine kriti- sche Funktion ausüben soll. Die geschichtliche Betrachtung der neute- stamentlichen Schriften und der Vorgänge, die zu ihrer Sammlung im Kanon geführt haben, darf nicht gegen die Einheit des Neuen Testa- ments ausgespielt werden; sie sollte vielmehr die Vielseitigkeit des Neu- en Testaments vor Augen führen und für die kirchliche Lehre und Ver- kündigung fruchtbar machen.

2. Zur Erschließung der Gesamtstruktur des neutestamentlichen Kanons verhilft ein Blick auf seine handschriftliche Überlieferung. Im Unterschied zu den Zeugnissen der Kirchenväterliteratur, die auf eine große Vielfalt neutestamentlicher Schriftensammlungen nach Anzahl und Anordnung der aufgenommenen bzw. ausgeschlossenen Einzel- schriften hindeuten, ergeben die großen Unzialhandschriften des 4. und

---

56. 1 Joh 1,1; vgl. 1,5; 3,11; 4,2.9.14.21; 5,6; 2 Joh 7.

5. Jahrhunderts ein erstaunlich einheitliches Bild. Offenbar besteht eine erhebliche Differenz zwischen dem Kanon, um den sich die Theologen streiten, und dem Kanon, der in ihren Gemeinden in Gebrauch steht.

3. Der in den Handschriften überlieferte Kanon besteht aus klar voneinander abgegrenzten Sammlungseinheiten: dem Tetraevangelium, dem Praxapostolos (Apostelgeschichte und Katholische Briefe), dem Corpus Paulinum und der Johannes-Offenbarung. Innerhalb der Sammlungseinheiten kann die Reihenfolge der Einzelschriften variieren, aber die Zuordnung der Einzelschriften zu den jeweiligen Sammlungseinheiten ist stabil.

4. Die Anordnung der Sammlungseinheiten in den Bibelhandschriften impliziert ein heilsgeschichtliches Programm: Der in den Evangelien beschriebenen, für die Kirche grund-legenden Jesus-Zeit folgt die nachösterliche Apostelzeit, die in der Apostelgeschichte und den apostolischen Briefen zur Sprache kommt. Sie führt schließlich hin zum Ausblick auf die nahe bevorstehende Wiederkunft des auferstandenen Herrn Jesus in der Johannes-Offenbarung.

5. Das Tetraevangelium und die apostolischen Sammlungseinheiten (Praxapostolos bzw. Corpus Paulinum) sind in der kanonischen Sammlung durch szenische Bezüge miteinander verklammert. Der Apostelgeschichte kommt dabei eine Brückenfunktion zu: Sie ermöglicht die Vermittlung der Evangelienstoffe in die Apostelzeit.

6. Für die Darstellung der apostolischen Zeit erhält die Apostelgeschichte im kanonischen Zusammenhang eine Leitfunktion. Sie ermöglicht die Einbeziehung aller apostolischen Schriften in einen einheitlichen narrativen Kontext. Durch Identifikation der Briefautoren und der in den Überschriften der Manuskripte genannten Evangelienautoren mit in der Apostelgeschichte oder in den Evangelien auftretenden Personen entsteht ein literarisch und historisch geschlossenes Sammelwerk. Die „Apostel-Lehren" werden so den „Apostel-Geschichten" ein- und untergeordnet.

7. Maßgeblich für das Bild von der Gemeinschaft der Apostel untereinander sind Schlüsselszenen aus der Apostelgeschichte, insbesondere solche, in denen mehrere Apostel einander begegnen. Sie fungieren als Modellfälle zur Lösung von Konflikten untereinander und als Musterbeispiele der Geschlossenheit der Apostel gegenüber inneren Abweichlern und äußeren Gegnern.

8. Die Apostelbriefe sind im Kanon durch textinterne Leseanweisungen und durch Personenkontinuität miteinander verbunden. Maßgebliche Bedeutung erhält die innerkanonische situative Einordnung der

beiden Briefkorpora dadurch, daß der 2. Timotheusbrief und der 2. Petrusbrief für das Corpus Paulinum bzw. das Corpus Catholicum jeweils als testamentarische Verfügungen ihrer Briefautoren gelten können.

9. Die beiden Petrusbriefe sind durch Situationsangaben, implizite Verbindungen namentlich genannter Personen und ausdrückliche Verweise unmittelbar mit dem Corpus Paulinum verknüpft, und zwar derartig, daß die Autorität des Paulus und seiner Briefe durch Petrus bestärkt werden soll. Darin schlägt sich das normative Bild ungetrübter apostolischer Gemeinschaft nieder, wie es in der Apostelgeschichte gezeichnet wird. Konflikte zwischen Aposteln, wie sie in den Paulusbriefen erkennbar sind, werden auf diese Weise „kanonisch gelöst".

10. Zwischen den Paulusbriefen und den Katholischen Briefen besteht im kanonischen Zusammenhang ein enges Netz von Querverweisen. Sie finden sich insbesondere in den Präskripten und werden in den Handschriftentiteln aufgegriffen und erweitert. Auf diese Weise wird ein einheitlicher Apostelbegriff maßgeblich, der zusammengesetzt ist aus der Aposteldarstellung in der Apostelgeschichte, dem apostolischen Selbstverständnis der Briefschreiber Paulus und Petrus und der Benennung aller neutestamentlichen Briefautoren als Apostel in den Handschriftentiteln.

11. Durch die Nennung der Autorennamen in den Handschriftentiteln und den Briefpräskripten werden Assoziationen an Erzählungen zu den betreffenden Personen in den Evangelien und der Apostelgeschichte geweckt. Das Bild der Autoren der neutestamentlichen Schriften in den Augen der Leser der kanonischen Sammlung ist dadurch erheblich plastischer, als es die textinternen Informationen über sie erwarten lassen.

12. Durch Assoziationen oder ausdrückliche Verweise auf Begegnungen der apostolischen Autoren der neutestamentlichen Schriften mit dem vorösterlichen Jesus wird die Gegenwart Jesu in die apostolische Zeit hinein und über sie hinaus in die Zeit der „apostolischen Kirche" vermittelt. Bezugnahmen auf Einzelzüge seines Wirkens, Weges und Geschicks ermöglichen im kanonischen Zusammenhang eine „Gesamtanschauung Jesu", die sich aus den narrativen Darstellungen der Evangelien, der mündlichen Verkündigung über ihn in der Apostelgeschichte und den lehrhaften Deutungen der Apostelbriefe zusammensetzt. Die Autoren aller Schriften des Kanons werden so in apostolischer Gemeinschaft zu Trägern, Vermittlern und Garanten der Erinnerung an Jesus.

Kregelstraße 10
D-04416 Markkleeberg
Deutschland

Karl-Wilhelm NIEBUHR

OFFERED PAPERS

LA CANONICITÉ DE LA FINALE LONGUE (MC 16,9-20)
VERS LA RECONNAISSANCE
D'UN DOUBLE TEXTE CANONIQUE?

Il est aujourd'hui pratiquement acquis dans le monde exégétique que Mc 16,8 constitue le dernier verset authentique du second évangile qui nous soit conservé dans l'état actuel de la tradition manuscrite. Aucune des autres finales attestée dans celle-ci ne paraît pouvoir être attribuée à Marc, tant elles diffèrent de sa manière aux plans du vocabulaire et du style. Il est certes loisible de gloser sur une éventuelle finale perdue. Mais il s'agit là d'une hypothèse fort hasardeuse motivée principalement par le refus de l'idée que Marc ait pu vouloir terminer son évangile d'une manière aussi abrupte sur le silence des femmes à qui l'annonce de la résurrection de Jésus venait d'être confiée. À la suite d'autres, j'ai montré ailleurs[1] que cette idée est tout à fait plausible et qu'elle correspond parfaitement au projet narratif de Marc, tel qu'il est mis en œuvre tout au long de son évangile.

Cependant une des autres finales, la plus longue, s'est imposée dans nos Bibles, même si c'est souvent aujourd'hui entre crochets, et sa canonicité est largement reconnue. Elle fera l'objet de mon attention dans cet article. Un bref rappel des arguments qui plaident contre son authenticité, c'est-à-dire son attribution au même auteur que l'ensemble de Mc 1,1-16,8, sera suivi d'un état de la question sur les motivations possibles de l'auteur de cette finale longue (FL). Ensuite, je rappellerai les positions sur sa canonicité dans l'Église catholique, mais aussi dans les Églises protestantes. Enfin, en fonction de la sensibilité actuelle à la perspective globale de chaque évangile, je poserai la question de la reconnaissance éventuelle d'un double texte canonique.

I. L'INAUTHENTICITÉ ET L'ANCIENNETÉ DE LA FL

La FL se trouve dans de nombreux manuscrits grecs à partir du Ve siècle (A C D K X Δ Θ Π, la plupart des manuscrits de la recension antiochienne, la famille 13 et beaucoup d'autres minuscules, plusieurs

---

1. *Un silence qui fait parler (Mc 16,8)*, in A. DENAUX (éd.), *New Testament Textual Criticism and Exegesis*. FS J. Delobel (BETL, 161), Leuven, Leuven University Press – Peeters, 2002, pp. 79-96.

lectionnaires); les manuscrits latins sauf k; les versions syriaques cureto-
nienne[2], harkléenne[3], palestinienne et peshitta; les versions bohaïrique et
fayyoumique et un manuscrit de la version sahidique; quelques manuscrits arméniens et géorgiens; on trouve des traces de la finale longue
peut-être chez Justin et Tertullien, certainement chez Tatien, Irénée (témoignage explicite), Aphraate, dans les Constitutions apostoliques, chez
Didyme, Épiphane[4].

Les défenseurs de son authenticité[5] se sont fait de plus en plus rares
au fil du temps, surtout à partir du moment où la question littéraire de
l'authenticité a été mieux distinguée de la question théologique et pastorale de la canonicité et lorsque la découverte du Sinaiticus est venue
renforcer l'absence de la FL et l'existence d'un texte court de Mc déjà
attesté par le Vaticanus. Dans la seconde moitié du XXe siècle, seul
W.R. FARMER a longuement plaidé pour l'authenticité de la FL dans son
état actuel[6]. Par ailleurs, ayant observé que Justin ne cite pas de passage
de 16,9-14, mais uniquement de 16,15-20, E. LINNEMANN a voulu reconstituer une finale originale de Mc composée d'éléments qui ont des
parallèles en Mt 28,16-17 suivis de Mc 16,15-20[7]. Mais aucune de ces
deux tentatives n'a convaincu la critique[8].

En effet, le manque de continuité entre les vv. 8 et 9, l'absence dans la
FL de nombreuses particularités linguistiques et stylistiques typiques de
Marc couplée avec la présence massive d'un vocabulaire non marcien[9]

---

2. Le manuscrit est très mutilé et ne contient de Mc que 16,17-20.

3. Elle ajoute en outre la finale courte, mais dans la marge.

4. J.K. ELLIOTT, *The Text and Language of the Endings to Mark's Gospel*, in *TZ* 27 (1971) 255-262, voir p. 255.

5. Frappés par la fragilité des témoignages textuels en faveur de la FL, les défenseurs de l'authenticité ont parfois fait preuve d'imagination comme J.D. MICHAELIS, *Einleitung in die göttlichen Schriften des Neuen Bundes*, Göttingen, Vandenhoeck & Ruprecht, [4]1788, pp. 1059-1060, qui a émis l'hypothèse d'une double édition du texte par Marc lui-même: écrite à Rome sous l'inspiration de Pierre, la première aurait été interrompue pré-maturément en 16,8, suite à l'arrestation de Pierre, tandis que Marc aurait ajouté les vv. 9-20 lors d'une seconde édition à Alexandrie (voir à ce sujet J. DEPASSE-LIVET, *Le problème de la finale de Marc: Mc 16,8. État de la question* [mémoire non publié], Leuven, 1970, pp. 23-24). Cette hypothèse a été maintes fois reprise par la suite.

6. W.R. FARMER, *The Last Twelve Verses of Mark* (SNTS MS, 25), Cambridge, Cambridge University Press, 1974.

7. E. LINNEMANN, *Der wiedergefundene Markusschluß*, in *ZTK* 66 (1969) 255-287.

8. L'ouvrage de W.R. Farmer a notamment connu une sévère revue critique de la part de J.N. BIRDSALL, in *JTS* 2 (1975) 151-160. Les erreurs méthodologiques de E. Linnemann en matière de critique textuelle ont été sévèrement dénoncées par K. ALAND, *Der wiedergefundene Markusschluß? Eine methodologische Bemerkung zur textkritischen Arbeit*, in *ZTK* 67 (1970) 3-13.

9. R. MORGENTHALER, *Statistik des neutestamentlichen Wortschatzes*, Zürich, Gotthelf, 1958, pp. 58-60, qui conclut: «Indizien für eine Echtheit finden sich praktisch keine. Hingegen sind die Unechtheitsindizien so mannigfaltig und so massiv, dass man den Schluss wird ziehen dürfen, dass Mk. 16,9-20, nach den wortstatistischen Ergebnissen

ne permettent guère d'admettre l'authenticité des vv 9-20. C'est déjà pour ces raisons que celle-ci était refusée par M.-J. LAGRANGE[10]. Elles ont été largement développées par la suite[11] et il n'est pas utile d'y revenir. La cause paraît tellement bien entendue qu'elle n'est pas traitée pour elle-même, mais seulement à travers un état de la question, dans l'ouvrage récent que J.A. KELHOFFER vient de consacrer à la FL[12].

Il est possible de déterminer le *terminus ante quem* de la FL sur base des citations anciennes d'une partie substantielle de cette finale. Le témoignage le plus clair est celui d'Irénée de Lyon qui, vers 180, cite explicitement 16,19 comme extrait de la finale de Mc: *In fine autem Euangelii ait Marcus: Et quidem Dominus Jesus, posteaquam locutus est eis, receptus est in caelos et sedit ad dexteram Dei* (Adv. Haer. III,10,6). Composé vers 170, le Diatessaron de Tatien semble bien connaître aussi l'ensemble de la FL[13]. Le *terminus ante quem* peut même remonter un peu plus haut si on reconnaît une allusion (trois mots significatifs, mais dans un ordre différent) à Mc 16,20 dans un texte de la Première apologie de Justin écrite peu après 150. Il y parle de l'essor après l'ascension du Seigneur de la parole (τοῦ λόγου) ὃν ἀπὸ Ἰερουσαλὴμ οἱ ἀπόστολοι αὐτοῦ ἐξελθόντες πανταχοῦ ἐκήρυξαν (Apol. I,45,5). Si on accepte que la FL date d'une époque où l'ensemble des évangiles néotestamentaires faisaient déjà partie d'une collection, il

beurteilt, niemals von derselben Hand geschrieben sein kann wie das übrige Markusevangelium» (p. 60, voir aussi le tableau statistique mot par mot à la p. 186). Cette conclusion a bien été mise en cause par W.R. FARMER, *The Last Twelve Verses* (n. 6), pp. 79-103. Elle a au contraire été confirmée par J.C. THOMAS, *A Reconsideration of the Ending of Mark,* in *JETS* 26 (1983) 407-419, voir pp. 410-412, après réexamen du dossier.

10. M.-J. LAGRANGE, *Évangile selon saint Marc* (ÉB), Paris, Gabalda, [6]1942, p. 463-466.

11. Voir, par exemple, B.M. METZGER, *A Textual Commentary on the Greek New Testament*, London – New York, United Bible Societies, 1971, p. 125; J.K. ELLIOTT, *The Text* (n. 4); J. HUG, *La finale de l'évangile de Marc (Mc 16,9-20)* (ÉB), Paris, Gabalda, 1978, pp. 20-32; M. GOURGUES, *À la droite de Dieu. Résurrection de Jésus et actualisation du Psaume 110:1 dans le Nouveau Testament* (ÉB), Paris, Gabalda, 1978, pp. 203-208; D.C. PARKER, *The Endings of Mark's Gospel*, in ID., *The Living Text of the Gospels*, Cambridge, Cambridge University Press, 1997, pp. 125-147, voir pp. 141-142.

12. J.A. KELHOFFER, *Miracle and Mission. The Authentification of Missionaries and Their Message in the Longer Ending of Mark* (WUNT, II/112), Tübingen, Mohr Siebeck, 2000. Pour sa part, K. ALAND, *Der Schluss des Markusevangeliums*, in M. SABBE (ed.), *L'évangile selon Marc. Tradition et rédaction* (BETL, 34), Gembloux, Duculot – Leuven, Leuven University Press, 1974, pp. 435-470, n'hésite pas à écrire: «Daß weder der kürzere noch der längere Markusschluß Anspruch auf Genuität machen können, darüber ist – von der äußeren Bezeugung einmal ganz abgesehen – eigentlich kein Wort nötig» (p. 453). Dans le même sens, M. MATJAZ, *Furcht und Gotteserfahrung. Die Bedeutung des Furchtmotivs für die Christologie des Markus* (FzB, 91), Würzburg, Echter, 1999, p. 294.

13. J. HUG, *La finale* (n. 11), p. 201; J.A. KELHOFFER, *Miracle* (n. 12), p. 170.

n'est guère possible de la faire remonter avant 120. L'hypothèse d'une datation dans une fourchette allant de 120 à 150 semble donc raisonnable[14].

II. LES MOTIVATIONS POSSIBLES DE L'AUTEUR DE LA FL

Une partie des exégètes pensent que la FL n'a pas été composée pour terminer l'évangile de Marc, mais qu'il s'agit d'un texte rédigé dans un autre but et inséré après coup à la fin de Marc. H.B. SWETE a proposé cette théorie du fragment sans s'aventurer à préciser la nature du document d'où la FL aurait été extraite[15]. De son côté, E. HELZLE souligne le caractère apologétique de ce texte et estime qu'il s'agissait primitivement d'une partie d'une sorte de catéchisme (*Lernstück*) destiné aux futurs baptisés de la communauté missionnaire[16]. Frappé par les rapports de Mc 16,14-20 avec Lc et Ac, R. PESCH pense que la FL pourrait provenir d'un texte préexistant «*als Kompilation oder Exzerpt von Ostererzählungen*»[17]. Pour M. GOURGUES, le document d'où la FL est tirée reflète sans doute une situation de crise de la mission au début du IIe s.: on y insiste sur l'importance de continuer à croire en la résurrection «sinon à cause des témoins oculaires, du moins à cause de ce qu'on a pu constater jusqu'alors de la réalité 'à l'œuvre' de la résurrection»[18]. Sans parler vraiment de fragment, J. HUG pense que la FL est «un document de la mission chrétienne en milieu hellénistique dans le deuxième tiers du second siècle», une «instruction missionnaire», dans laquelle «le mystère de Pâques n'est plus saisi comme chez Mc dans l'unité résurrection-exaltation mais déployé dans une perspective de type historisant où les différents aspects de Pâques deviennent différents moments d'une séquence»[19].

Selon une seconde hypothèse, la FL a été composée *ad hoc* pour compléter un évangile de Marc jugé incomplet. V. KRAUSS attribue l'inten-

---

14. J.A. KELHOFFER, *Miracle* (n. 12), p. 175. La datation la plus couramment citée est le deuxième tiers du IIe s.

15. H.B. SWETE, *The Gospel according to St. Mark*, London, MacMillan, 1902, p. CX.

16. E. HELZLE, *Der Schluß des Markusevangeliums (Mk 16,9-20) und das Freer-Logion (Mk 16,14 W), ihre Tendenzen und ihr gegenseitiges Verhältnis: Eine wortexegetische Untersuchung* (dissertation non publiée), Tübingen, 1959, pp. 87-90. S. LÉGASSE, *L'évangile de Marc* (LD, Com., 5), t. 2, Paris, Cerf, 1997, p. 1012, parle d'un «résumé catéchétique sur les apparitions pascales destiné à l'instruction d'une communauté».

17. R. PESCH, *Das Markusevangelium* (HTKNT, II/2), Freiburg - Basel - Wien, Herder, 1984, t. 2, p. 546.

18. M. GOURGUES, *À la droite* (n. 11), p. 208, n. 37.

19. J. HUG, *La finale* (n. 11), pp. 217, 220, 223.

tion de compléter Marc à un auteur[20] qui fait, dans le courant du premier tiers du IIe s., une compilation dans laquelle il est principalement influencé par Lc et Ac[21]. Cet auteur voulait mettre en valeur la nécessité de la mission universelle et le rôle des miracles dans la formation à la foi[22]. J.A. KELHOFFER tente, pour sa part, de démontrer que l'auteur de la FL a consciemment et volontairement imité les quatre évangiles[23]. La dépendance littéraire à l'égard des quatre évangiles paraît certaine et elle est probable envers les Actes des apôtres[24]. Il s'agirait d'une sorte de faux (*forgery*) utilisant des procédés semblables à ceux que l'on trouve dans la Lettre aux Laodicéens ou dans 5 Esdras[25]. La FL n'a pu être composée qu'à une époque où les évangiles et probablement les Actes avaient déjà été rassemblés dans une même collection et pouvaient être comparés l'un à l'autre, ce qui faisait ressortir la particularité ou plutôt la déficience de la finale de Mc[26]. Une des particularités de la FL est la promesse de miracles futurs accordée à des chrétiens anonymes (16,17 σημεῖα δὲ τοῖς πιστεύσασιν ταῦτα παρακολουθήσει), alors qu'en dehors de Jn 14,12 (et 1 Co 12,9-10) le NT ne s'intéresse qu'aux miracles réalisés par les Douze et par Paul. Il en va d'ailleurs de même dans les Actes apocryphes, sauf quelques résurrections opérées par des chrétiens sur l'ordre d'un apôtre. En revanche, les exemples de miracles attribués à des chrétiens «tout-venants» n'est pas rare chez les apologistes chrétiens des IIe et IIIe s., à commencer par Justin[27]. C'est un élément de plus en faveur de l'attribution de la FL à un chrétien du IIe s.

20. Cet auteur reste inconnu. En 1891, F.C. Conybeare a bien découvert à Edschmiadzin un manuscrit oncial arménien des évangiles datant du Xe s. et dans lequel Mc 16,8 est suivi d'un espace blanc de deux lignes portant la mention «*Ariston Eritzou*» («du prêtre Ariston») écrite de la même main, mais à l'encre rouge (fac-similé du manuscrit dans H.B. SWETE, *Mark* [n. 15], 1902, p. CX), et suivie de la FL. F.C. CONYBEARE, *Aristion, the Author of the Last Twelve Verses of Mark*, in *Expositor* iv 8 (1893) 241-254, pense pouvoir identifier cet Ariston avec Aristion, disciple du Seigneur d'après Papias (Eusèbe, *Hist. eccl.* III,39) et dater, sur cette base, la FL d'environ 100. Pour un état de la question, on peut consulter J. HUG, *La finale* (n. 11), pp. 15-16. La mention du prêtre Ariston pourrait aussi n'être qu'une conjecture du traducteur à partir de la notice d'Eusèbe (S. LÉGASSE, *Marc* [n. 16], p. 1013).

21. V. KRAUSS, «*Verkündet das Evangelium der ganzen Schöpfung!*» *Eine exegetisch-bibeltheologische Untersuchung von Mk 16,9-20* (dissertation non publiée), Wien, 1980, pp. 221-227.

22. *Ibid.*, pp. 198-203.

23. J.A. KELHOFFER, *Miracle* (n. 12), p. 121: «The influence of Matthew, Luke and John further indicate that this author did not intend for Mark 16,9-20 to be perceived as a novel composition. These allusions also point to the intentional imitation of all four of the NT Gospels». Suit une liste des parallèles entre la FL et des passages du NT (pp. 121-122).

24. *Ibid.*, pp. 123-150.

25. *Ibid.*, pp. 150-154.

26. *Ibid.*, p. 155.

27. *Ibid.*, pp. 338-339 et 476.

Plus isolée, une troisième hypothèse envisage la FL comme un texte composé pour clôturer le corpus des quatre évangiles. M. HENGEL a justement souligné que la FL est un des premiers écrits chrétiens à trahir une connaissance de tous les évangiles ainsi que des Actes des apôtres[28]. J.A. KELHOFFER souligne, pour sa part, que l'auteur de la FL a osé réviser l'évangile de Marc à l'occasion de l'émergence du canon des quatre évangiles[29]. C.A. AMPHOUX va plus loin encore. Pour lui, il ne s'agirait pas dans la FL «d'une conclusion de Marc, destinée à atténuer la fin abrupte de celui-ci, mais d'un épilogue des quatre évangiles réunis dans l'ordre Mt-Jn-Lc-Mc»[30]. Cette hypothèse s'appuie sur l'existence dès le IIe s. de deux traditions textuelles: l'une, dont le principal représentant ultérieur est le Vaticanus, atteste un texte de Mc sans la FL, tandis que l'autre, avec le Codex de Bèze, atteste la FL qui vient en finale des évangiles présentés dans l'ordre Mt-Jn-Lc-Mc[31]. P. Bogaert confirme la diffusion importante de cet ordre «dont les témoins anciens conservés sont nombreux et se retrouvent en Italie et en Égypte, en latin et en grec» et qui a résisté à l'ordre Mt-Mc-Lc-Jn (dont il n'y a pas d'attestation sûre avant Eusèbe de Césarée) «pendant un temps suffisant pour que des exemplaires nous soient parvenus»[32]. Il n'est pas exclu que la finale de Mc 16,8 ait paru encore plus abrupte lorsqu'elle venait au terme d'un codex rassemblant les quatre évangiles. Plutôt que de les laisser se terminer sur un silence apeuré, quelqu'un aurait alors pu composer une finale présentant une récapitulation des apparitions pascales présentes dans les autres évangiles et l'assortir d'un envoi en mission très univer-

28. M. HENGEL, *Die Evangelienüberschriften* (Sitzungsberichte der Heidelberger Akademie der Wissenschaften. Philosophisch-historische Klasse, Jahrgang 1984, Bericht 3), Heidelberg, Winter, 1984, p. 22: «Der sekundäre Markusschluß (16,9-20) und die ebenfalls in der 1. Hälfte des 2. Jh.s. anzusetzende *epistula apostolorum* sind so die frühesten christliche Texte, die alle Evangelien und die Apg voraussetzen». Voir aussi P. ROHRBACH, *Der Schluß des Markusevangeliums, der Vier-Evangelien-Kanon und die Kleinasiatischen Presbyter*, Berlin, Rühe, 1894, pp. 38-40.

29. J.A. KELHOFFER, *Miracle* (n. 12), p. 480.

30. C.-B. AMPHOUX, *La «finale longue de Marc»: un épilogue des quatre évangiles*, in C. FOCANT (éd.), *The Synoptic Gospels. Source Criticism and the New Literary Criticism* (BETL, 110), Leuven, Leuven University Press – Peeters, 1993, pp. 548-555, voir p. 550.

31. L'argument le plus fort de C.-B. Amphoux est la présence dans la FL de deux accords significatifs avec la tradition textuelle de D dans Lc 24 comme preuve de son rapport avec cette tradition (pp. 551-552). En revanche, l'interprétation, à partir du témoignage d'Ignace d'Antioche, des quatre signes (Mc 16,17-18) comme illustration du rôle de chacun des quatre évangiles (pp. 553-555) n'est guère convaincante.

32. P. BOGAERT, *Ordres anciens des évangiles et tétraévangile en un seul codex*, in *RTL* 30 (1999) 297-314, voir p. 307. Outre D p^{45} 032, presque tous les évangiles non vulgates (*Vercellensis, Veronensis, Codex Bezae Cantabrigiensis, Palatinus, Brixianus, Corbeiensis, Sangallensis, Monacensis*) ont l'ordre Mt-Jn-Lc-Mc. Pour plus de détails, voir le même article aux pp. 302-304.

saliste (à l'adresse de toute la création) ainsi que d'une promesse d'assistance à tous les chrétiens qui devront prendre cette mission en charge.

III. LA CANONICITÉ DE LA FL

Une partie de la tradition textuelle ancienne n'atteste donc pas la FL de Mc. Ceci est confirmé dans l'Église ancienne d'abord par Eusèbe de Césarée qui ne la lit pas dans la plupart des manuscrits de Marc qu'il connaît. En effet, à Marinus qui lui demandait comment, selon Mt (28,1), le Seigneur était ressuscité ὀψὲ σαββάτων, mais, selon Mc, πρωὶ τῇ μιᾷ τῶν σαββάτων[33], Eusèbe écrivait: «On peut répondre de deux manières: quelqu'un n'admettant pas l'authenticité de cette section, de la péricope qui contient ces mots, pourrait dire qu'elle ne se trouve *pas dans tous les exemplaires de Marc; car les exemplaires exacts* (τὰ γοῦν ἀκριβῆ τῶν ἀντιγράφων) *marquent la fin de l'histoire de Marc aux discours du jeune homme qui a apparu aux femmes…, auxquels il ajoute 'et l'ayant entendu, elles s'enfuirent et ne dirent rien à personne, car elles avaient peur'. À ce point, la fin de l'Évangile selon Marc est marquée dans presque tous les exemplaires* (ἐν ἅπασι τοῖς ἀντιγράφοις). *Ce qui suit et qui se trouve rarement* (σπανίως), *dans quelques exemplaires, mais non dans tous*, serait de trop, et surtout s'il avait quelque contradiction avec le témoignage des autres évangélistes. Voilà ce que quelqu'un pourrait dire, en écartant d'avance et en supprimant toute question superflue. Mais un autre, n'osant rejeter l'autorité de tout ce qui se trouve d'une façon quelconque dans la tradition écrite des Évangiles, dira qu'on peut lire de deux manières …»[34]. Ce témoignage négatif est confirmé par Jérôme dans sa lettre à Hédibia où il résume comme suit la première solution d'Eusèbe: *aut enim non recipimus Marci testimonium quod in raris fertur evangeliis, omnibus Graeciae libris paene hoc capitulum in fine non habentibus, praesertim cum diversa atque contraria evangelistis ceteris narrare videatur*[35]. Ce qui n'empêchera toutefois pas Jérôme de maintenir la FL dans la Vulgate.

---

33. Eusèbe semble avoir cru que la formule πρωὶ τῇ μιᾷ τῶν σαββάτων faisait partie de la finale longue, alors qu'elle se trouve en Mc 16,2, tandis qu'au v. 9 on lit ἀναστὰς δὲ πρωὶ πρώτῃ σαββάτου. Même si S.C.E. LEGG, *Evangelium secundum Marcum*, Oxford, Clarendon, 1935, ad loc., cite πρωὶ τῇ μιᾷ τῶν σαββάτων comme variante d'Eusèbe et Jérôme, il faut bien voir qu'elle n'est soutenue par aucun manuscrit connu. Une édition critique des *Quaestiones evangelicae* d'Eusèbe reste à faire et elle pourrait peut-être éclaircir ce point.

34. *Quaestiones evangelicae, Quaestio I ad Marinum* (PG 22,937-940). La traduction est celle de M.-J. LAGRANGE, *Saint Marc* (n. 10), p. 460.

35. Ep. 120,3 (PL 22,987). Sur d'autres témoignages patristiques (Hésychius de Jérusalem et Sévère d'Antioche) et médiévaux allant dans le même sens, voir J.A. KEL-

Dans le décret *De Canonicis Scripturis*, le concile de Trente donne le catalogue des livres bibliques qu'il reçoit et précise: «Si quelqu'un ne reçoit pas pour sacrés et canoniques ces mêmes livres en entier avec toutes leurs parties, tels qu'on a coutume de les lire dans l'Église catholique et tels qu'ils sont dans l'ancienne édition latine de la Vulgate (...) qu'il soit anathème»[36]. Il est intéressant de noter que, le 15 février 1546, les Pères du concile ont refusé par 24 voix contre 16 d'exposer les arguments favorables à la canonicité pour se contenter d'une simple énumération des livres saints. Dans la discussion, le 11 février, l'évêque de Fano et le général des augustins avaient proposé de «distinguer les livres authentiques et canoniques, dont notre foi dépend, des livres simplement canoniques, bons pour l'enseignement et utiles à lire dans les églises»[37]. La majorité décida que cela n'était pas nécessaire puisque la tradition n'avait pas opéré cette distinction sur laquelle Jérôme et Augustin avaient été en désaccord. Cependant, il est remarquable que la question de la FL de Mc a été explicitement posée dans les termes suivants: «Comme quelques-uns ont contesté des particules des Évangiles, à savoir le dernier chapitre de Marc, le XXIIᵉ chapitre de Luc et le VIIIᵉ de Jean, faut-il, dans le décret de réception des Évangiles, citer nommément ces parties et ordonner de les recevoir avec le reste? Ou bien, faut-il, pour assurer le même résultat, exprimer dans le décret même le nombre des chapitres des Évangiles?»[38] Le 1ᵉʳ avril, la mention du nombre des chapitres fut rejetée par 43 voix contre 3 (6 votes étant douteux) et celle des passages contestés (FL; Lc 22,43-44; Jn 7,53-8,11) par 34 voix contre 17. Le Concile préféra la formule générale citée ci-dessus[39].

HOFFER, *The Witness of Eusebius' ad Marinum and Other Christian Writings to Text-Critical Debates concerning the Original Conclusion to Mark's Gospel*, in ZNW 92 (2001) 78-112, voir pp. 97-109.

36. *Si quis autem libros ipsos integros cum omnibus suis partibus, prout in Ecclesia catholica legi consueverunt, et in veteri vulgata latina editione habentur, pro sacris et canonicis non susceperit (...); anathema sit.*

37. E. MANGENOT, art. *Canon des livres saints*, in DTC II, Paris, Letouzey et Ané, 1923, col. 1550-1605, voir col. 1596.

38. E. MANGENOT, art. *Canon* (n. 37), col. 1599. Il s'agit du deuxième de 14 «*dubia*» discutés à ce moment: *An quia de quibusdam particulis evangeliorum: Marci cap. ultimo et Lucae cap. 22. et Ioannis 8. a quibusdam est dubitatum, ideo in decreto de libris evangeliorum recipiendis sit nominatim habenda ratio harum partium, et exprimendum, ut cum aliis recipiantur, an non* (*Concilii Tridentini Acta* par la *Görresgesellschaft*, t. V, 2, ed. S. Ehses, Freiburg i. Br., Herder, 1911, p. 41).

39. Alors que l'édition de la LXX (1586-1587), pour laquelle le Vaticanus a été le manuscrit de référence partout où il était disponible, n'a pas fait de difficulté, il est frappant que l'édition du NT grec, également demandée par le Concile, s'est ensablée. S. TROMP, *De revisione textus Novi Testamenti facta Romae a Commissione Pontificia circa a. 1617 praeside S.R. Bellarmino*, in *Bib* 22 (1941) 303-306, et I.-M. VOSTÉ, *De revisione textus graeci Novi Testamenti ad votum Concilii Tridentini facta*, in *Bib* 24

Plusieurs siècles plus tard, au moment de la crise moderniste, la question fut posée de la liberté de contester l'authenticité et donc l'inspiration et la canonicité de la FL de Mc. Le décret de la Commission biblique du 12 juin 1912 répondit négativement à une question formulée de manière négative: *Utrum rationes, quibus nonnulli critici demonstrare nituntur postremos duodecim versus Evangelii Marci non esse ab ipso Marco conscriptos, sed ab aliena manu appositos, tales sint, quae ius tribuant affirmandi eos non esse ut inspiratos et canonicos recipiendos; vel saltem demonstrent versuum eorumdem Marcum non esse auctorem? Resp., Negative ad utramque partem*[40]. Au sens strict, la Commission ne s'est donc pas prononcée sur l'authenticité de la FL, mais seulement sur l'insuffisance des raisons invoquées en sa défaveur pour contester à la fois son authenticité, son inspiration et sa canonicité.

Dans le monde catholique, la canonicité de la FL est clairement reconnue et celle-ci est fréquemment utilisée dans la liturgie, y compris pour la fête de St Marc. C'est d'ailleurs la partie du second évangile qui a été la plus fréquemment citée dans les textes du Concile Vatican II. Mais cela n'exclut pas la conscience des difficultés que la FL pose au plan de la critique textuelle et de son authenticité marcienne.

Dans le monde protestant, la FL était reçue par les Réformateurs du XVIe siècle puisque le *textus receptus* fondé sur le type de texte byzantin choisi par Érasme l'incluait. Cependant depuis les travaux de K. LACHMANN (1831) et de WESTCOTT-HORT (1881), les éditions critiques s'appuient sur le texte alexandrin notamment attesté par le Vaticanus[41] et le caractère secondaire de la FL est mis en évidence dans les milieux scientifiques et chez les réformés, tandis que les évangéliques continuent d'y avoir plus naturellement recours.

IV. UN DOUBLE TEXTE CANONIQUE DE MC?

La question de l'authenticité et celles de la canonicité et de l'inspiration ont progressivement été mieux distinguées et elles le sont clairement aujourd'hui. Rejeter l'authenticité de la FL (jugement littéraire) ne

---

(1943) 304-307, cherchent une explication à cet état de fait, mais sans faire de réelle proposition. Ne serait-ce pas dû aux écarts entre le Vaticanus et la Vulgate sur des points sensibles comme la FL de Mc ou le *comma johanneum* (hypothèse suggérée par mon collègue P. Bogaert)?

40. Pontificia Commissio de Re Biblica: Reponsum IX, 26 Iunii 1912, de auctore... Evangeliorum secundum Marcum et Lucam, II, in *Enchiridion biblicum*, Roma, Pontificium Institutum Biblicum, 1927, nº 409.

41. C.-B. AMPHOUX, *Le texte grec de Marc*, in *Mélanges de science religieuse* 56/3 (1999) 5-25, voir p. 23.

revient nullement à contester sa canonicité (jugement d'Église). En s'inspirant de la proposition que l'évêque de Fano avait faite au Concile de Trente[42], on pourrait éventuellement distinguer dans les Écritures les livres authentiques et canoniques des livres ou parties simplement canoniques sans pour autant être authentiques. Il s'agirait moins d'en donner la liste que de consacrer le principe.

Pour ce qui est de la FL de Mc, ce serait éclairant à une époque où, sous l'effet des études d'histoire de la rédaction et des analyses narratives, on est plus sensible à l'unité d'ensemble de l'évangile. Or, nul n'ignore l'importance pour le sens d'un récit de sa façon de commencer et de se terminer. Comme le souligne C.-A. STEINER, «le début d'une œuvre – comme sa fin d'ailleurs – doit assister le lecteur dans son passage entre le monde réel et le monde du texte et veut programmer une réponse particulière de sa part»[43]. Autrement dit, la finale brève «ouverte, suspendue» (Mc 16,8) et la finale longue «fermée» (Mc 16,9-20) ne construisent pas le même type de lecteur. Si on se limite à la finale authentique, il apparaît que Marc provoque son lecteur à une relecture de l'évangile pour qu'il y déploie une intelligence renouvelée de l'histoire de Jésus et de l'évangile[44]. Elle le stimule à une relecture ultime et à faire un choix difficile qui revient à «naître à sa propre réponse»[45]. Ce serait honorer l'ouverture de Marc que de reconnaître en 16,8 la fin d'une première forme canonique et authentique. Cela ne devrait pas empêcher d'admettre une seconde forme incluant les vv. 9-20 canoniques, mais non authentiques.

La solution proposée est proche de celle que M. GILBERT a récemment avancée pour le Siracide. La question surgit de la constatation suivante: «Un usage actuel répandu dans l'Église est de retenir le texte court, mais il est contrebalancé par toute une ligne de la tradition ancienne, par l'usage liturgique de l'Église latine et par les Bibles catholiques actuelles qui optent pour le texte long»[46]. Opter pour un seul de ces deux tex-

---

42. Voir ci-dessus, p. 594.

43. C.-A. STEINER, *Le lien entre le prologue et le corps de l'évangile de Marc*, in D. MARGUERAT & A. CURTIS (éds.), *Intertextualités. La Bible en échos* (Le monde de la Bible, 40), Genève, Labor et Fides, 2000, pp. 161-184, voir p. 163.

44. J'ai développé ce thème dans l'article *Un silence* (n. 1), pp. 92-96.

45. C. COMBET-GALLAND, *Qui roulera la peur? Finales d'évangile et figures de lecteur (à partir du chapitre 16 de l'évangile de Marc)*, in *ETR* 65 (1990) 171-189, voir p. 188.

46. M. GILBERT, *L'Ecclésiastique: quel texte? quelle autorité?*, in *RB* 94 (1987) 233-250, voir p. 243. Le même type de question peut être posé pour de nombreux livres, à commencer bien sûr par celui de Jérémie. Par ailleurs, il existe, par exemple, deux textes catholiques officiels de Tobie, puisque dans la liturgie on utilise la Vulgate de Jérôme différente de la Néovulgate promulguée par le pape Jean-Paul II, qui est une version latine du texte grec long (observation que je dois à mon collègue P. Bogaert).

tes irait à l'encontre de la pratique ancienne ou de l'actuelle. Il est donc «plus sage de reconnaître la canonicité des deux textes»[47]. «Il y a deux états du livre de Ben Sira, et ces deux états sont l'un et l'autre canoniques, parce que l'un et l'autre sont inspirés»[48].

La reconnaissance d'un double texte canonique de Mc serait de nature à favoriser à la fois la recherche sur l'*intentio auctoris* et/ou l'*intentio operis* d'une œuvre authentique et la recherche sur le sens et la portée de fragments inauthentiques mais qui ont marqué la vie du peuple chrétien dans la tradition et sont reconnus comme canoniques pour cette raison. Elle permettrait d'éviter l'écueil de l'ambiguïté liée à la confusion plus ou moins forte des questions d'authenticité et de canonicité. En outre, elle favoriserait dans le peuple chrétien une conception des livres fondateurs de sa foi plus proche de la réalité.

Rue des Sarts, 2   Camille FOCANT
B-5380 Franc-Waret

---

47. *Ibid.*, p. 244.
48. *Ibid.*, p. 248.

HERMENEUTICAL FACTORS IN THE HARMONIZATION
OF THE GOSPELS
AND THE QUESTION OF TEXTUAL AUTHORITY

It is often taken for granted that when Tatian composed his gospel harmony, the *Diatessaron* (c. 173 CE), he intended it as a *replacement* for the "separated gospels." The four gospels appeared to yield up too many inconsistencies and in order to remedy this embarrassing situation, so it is often supposed, Tatian sought to create a refashioned narrative, a "mixed gospel", which would in theory supplant the earlier written records. Tatian's attempt to harmonize the written gospel traditions also implies, so the reasoning continues, a low view of the authority of those traditions[1].

But if, as I shall argue in this paper, the second-century harmonizing tradition is to be understood against the backdrop of ancient Jewish exegesis, in particular the genre of "rewritten scriptures", the historical evidence would seem to suggest otherwise. Given the analogies between Christian harmonization of the gospels and Jewish paraphrasing of the Hebrew Bible (henceforth HB), it would seem that Tatian's *Diatessaron*, and possibly other, earlier texts like it (the *Gospel of Peter*, the *Unknown Gospel*, the *Gospel of the Ebionites,* Justin's alleged harmony), witness not to a low view of the prior textual tradition – where there was written as opposed to oral tradition – but to a high view[2]. Whether or not Tatian

---

1. See H. GAMBLE, *The New Testamament Canon*, Philadelphia, Fortress, 1985, pp. 30-31; L.M. McDONALD, *The Formation of the Christian Canon*, Nashville, Abingdon, 1988, p. 38; T. BAARDA, *DIAPHONIA-SYMPHONIA: Factors in the Harmonization of the Gospels, Especially in the Diatessaron of Tatian*, in W.L. PETERSEN (ed.), *Gospel Traditions in the Second Century: Origins, Recensions, Text, and Transmission* (Christianity and Judaism in Antiquity, 3), Notre Dame, IN, University of Notre Dame Press, 1989, pp. 133-154, esp. 154; = T. BAARDA., *Essays on the Diatessaron*, ed. S.J. NOORDA (CBET, 11), Kampen, Kok, 1994, pp. 29-48. Cf. B.M. METZGER, *The Canon of the New Testament: Its Origin, Development, and Significance*, Oxford, Clarendon, 1987, p. 115.

2. Which of these is dependent on the canonical texts remains a matter of dispute. See, for example, the contrasting positions on the *Gospel of Peter*: J.D. CROSSAN, *Four Other Gospels: Shadows on the Contours of Canon*, Minneapolis, Winston, 1985; R.E. BROWN, *The Gospel of Peter and Canonical Gospel Priority*, in *NTS* 33 (1986-87) 321-343. Tatian's harmonizing project was, in any event, not the first of its kind. See D.A. BERTRAND, *L'Évangile des Ebionites: Une harmonie évangélique antérieure au Diatessaron*, in *NTS* 26 (1979-90) 548-563; A.J. BELLINZONI, *The Sayings of Jesus in the Writings of Justin Martyr* (SNT, 17), Leiden, Brill, 1967, 142; W.L. PETERSEN, *Tatian's Diatessaron: Its Creation, Dissemination, Significance and History in Scholarship* (VigChrSup, 25), Leiden, Brill, 1994, pp. 27-29.

and the second-century gospel harmonizers would have consciously thought of their *Vorlage* as "canonical scripture", it is my contention that their procedure implies a recognition of not only the apparent incongruity of the texts, but also, paradoxically, their authority.

Although there is no universal agreement as to precisely which documents fall into the category of "rewritten Bible", at least three texts are considered to be representative: Josephus's *Antiquities*, *Jubilees*, and the *Liber Antiquitatum Biblicarum (LAB)*[3]. Comparing these texts with Tatian's *Diatessaron*, I shall treat three issues in particular. First, what are some of the exegetical methods employed by the rewriters of scripture and how do these compare with those used by Tatian? Second, what were the authors of the rewritten texts trying to achieve and how might this compare with Tatian's goals? Third, how did the rewriters of scripture and the author of the *Diatessaron* view their (biblical) sources? In what sense, if any, did these writers see their *Vorlage*, or their own writings, as authoritative?

In the opening of his *Antiquities* Josephus claims to be setting forth the "precise details" of what is written in scripture, "neither adding nor omitting anything" (*Ant.* 1.17). Yet what follows is an account which, although generally following the narrative sequence of the HB, is hardly in keeping with what we would consider the "precise details". At points Josephus fails to mention seemingly important information; in other places he adds to the text. Many of these insertions stem not from any natural inference based on the scriptures, but from the exegetical traditions of the historian's own time. Apparently, Josephus was not averse to mixing extra-biblical and biblical sources in his own rewriting of scripture: the former served well for illuminating the latter[4].

Intending the *Antiquities* as an *apologia* for Judaism, Josephus makes it his goal to recast the story of Israel in such a way as to make it amenable to the sensibilities of his Greek audience: the narrative would also have to adhere to the highest standards of Greek historiography. For this reason, when Josephus translates the HB into the world of Hellenism, he

---

3. Another typical example of the "rewritten Bible" is the *Genesis Apocryphon*, which in the interest of brevity I have omitted from discussion. On the genre see G.W.E. NICKELSBURG, *The Bible Rewritten and Expanded*, in M.E. STONE (ed.), *Jewish Writings of the Second Temple Period* (CRINT, 2.2), Assen, Van Gorcum; Philadelphia, Fortress, 1984; P.S. ALEXANDER, *Retelling the Old Testament*, in D.A. CARSON & H.G. WILLIAMSON (eds.), *It is Written: Scripture Citing Scripture*, Cambridge, Cambridge University Press, 1988, pp. 99-121.

4. Josephus's rabbinic influence, for example, is noted by D. RUNNALS (*Moses' Ethiopian Campaign*, in *JSJ* 14 [1983] 135-56) and D.R. SCHWARTZ (*Priesthood and Priestly Descent: Josephus Antiquities 10,80*, in *JTS* 32 [1981] 129-135).

takes especial care to ensure a graceful congruence between historical cause and effect[5]. The historical task of relating the past of Israel then becomes, unavoidably, the hermeneutical task of filling in the gaps of scripture. Where there are awkward *non-sequiturs*, these are smoothed out; where the logical connection between two events is less than clear, the correlation is made explicit. In pressing home his case for the antiquity of Judaism, Josephus is careful to mediate the biblical narrative in such a way as to grant it an unimpeachable coherency.

But this "mediation" of the scriptures should not, in the case of Josephus, be understood as detracting from the authority he ascribes to them. In fact, just the opposite seems to be the case. In a well-known passage from *Contra Apion* Josephus articulates a very high view of the twenty-two books: "Although a long time has passed [since the time of Artaxerxes] no one has ventured to add, to remove or to change [the scriptures] by one syllable. Rather every Jew ... sees them as the decrees of God ... and if need be is willing to die for them" (*Cont. Ap.* 1.38-42). Of course, there is some question as to how this statement, along with Josephus's assurances of having set out the "precise details" (*Ant.* 1.17), are to be reconciled with his loose, periphrastic historiography. But none of the solutions commonly offered for this difficulty would indicate that Josephus saw scripture as anything less than authoritative[6]. Nor is there evidence that Josephus viewed his own work, however more "complete" than the HB, as superseding Torah. For Josephus and the ancient Jews in general, scripture was proven to be authoritative not in spite of but through actualization. More precisely, the urge toward harmonization and actualization arose from a profound conviction regarding the scripture's relevance and inner unity, both of which were in turn a function of the text's authority.

In *Jubilees*, as in the *Antiquities*, the representation of scripture is far from slavish. Certain biblical texts are omitted, while other traditions are inserted. Large swathes of *Jubilees* are indebted to *1 Enoch* (cf., e.g., *Jub.* 4.17-26, *1 En.* 93.1-2); there are also parallels with material from the *Temple Scroll* (*Jub.* 7.1-6) and *Third Sybilline Oracles* (*Jub.* 8.9-9.15)[7]. The author of *Jubilees* tends to economize. As a rule, where there are two biblical accounts of the same event, they are conflated (e.g., the

5. Although sometimes critical of the careless practice of Greek historiography (*Ag. Ap.* 1.23-27), Josephus is nonetheless committed to the Greek ideal of the unity of history. See V. VILLALBA, *The Historical Method of Flavius Josephus* (ALGHJ, 19), Leiden, Brill, 1986, esp. pp. xiii, 1-63.

6. See a review of options in L.H. FELDMAN, *Josephus and Modern Scholarship (1937-1980)*, Berlin, de Gruyter, 1984, pp. 122-125.

7. J.C. VANDERKAM, *Enoch Traditions in Jubilees and Other Second-Century Sources*, in *SBL SP* 1 (1978) 229-251.

second creation account in Gen 2,14-17 is omitted in *Jub.* 3.1-31)[8]. Jubilees also generally follows the narrative sequence of scripture, but the biblical ordering of events is sometimes rearranged, when such rearranging serves the logic of the narrative.

While the selection and representation of the biblical material were partially motivated by parenetic interests, a great number of deviations in *Jubilees* can be explained by the author's "profound dislike for contradictions in the biblical text"[9]. On the one hand, *Jubilees* reflects certain homiletic aims, that is, a concern with the audience as a community; on the other hand, the author's unswerving commitment to harmonization points to a hermeneutical concern with the unity of the biblical text itself. Nor in the Jewish mind are the two concerns utterly separate: a truly accurate recounting of the biblical text would mean achieving both an inner coherency and a coherency with the audience's needs. In this respect van Ruiten may be quite correct to say that *Jubilees* is an attempt "to reproduce the story of Genesis as faithfully as possible"[10], the author of the former would have likely considered his composition to be even more faithful to the story of Genesis than Genesis itself.

At the same time *Jubilees* seems to retain a complementary role vis-a-vis scripture. There is, to be sure, some sense in which the author of *Jubilees* places his rewriting of scripture on the same level as the scripture itself (*Jub.* 1.1-6). But even when texts in Second Temple Judaism were claimed as authoritative commentary, this did not imply that the commentary constituted an alternative to Torah. As James VanderKam writes: "The author [of *Jubilees*] appears to conceive of his work, not as a replacement for the parallel parts of the Torah, but as another composition alongside it"[11].

Pseudo-Philo's *LAB* shares many of the characteristics of *Antiquities* and *Jubilees*. Pseudo-Philo follows the order of his source, although some accounts are foreshortened, while others are expanded. Many of the details that Pseudo-Philo inserts are traditional. Again, there is a consistent tendency toward harmonization, a preoccupation with bringing the facts of scripture into mutual conformity[12].

8. J.T.A.G.M. VAN RUITEN, *Primaeval History Interpreted: The Rewriting of Genesis 1-11 in the Book of Jubilees* (JSJ SS, 66), Leiden, Brill, 2000, p. 368.

9. J.C. ENDRES, *Biblical Interpretation in the Book of Jubilees* (CBQ.MS, 18), Washington, DC, Catholic Biblical Association, 1987, p. 222.

10. VAN RUITEN, *History Interpreted* (n. 8), p. 375.

11. J.C. VANDERKAM, *Revealed Literature in the Second Temple Period*, in ID., *From Revelation to Canon: Studies in the Hebrew Bible and Second Temple Literature* (JSJ SS, 62), Leiden, Brill, 2000, p. 25.

12. See R. BAUCKHAM, *The Liber Antiquitatum Biblicarum of Pseudo-Philo and the Gospels as 'Midrash'*, in R.T. FRANCE & D. WENHAM (eds.), *Gospel Perspectives 3: Studies in Midrash and Historiography*, Sheffield, JSOT Press, 1983, pp. 33-75.

Despite the changes that Pseudo-Philo brings to his sacred *Vorlage*, such "improvements" do not – at least in the view of the commentators – appear to jeopardize the integrity and authority of the biblical text. *LAB* presupposes throughout not only a knowledge of the HB, but also an acknowledgment of its authoritative status. In actualizing the biblical text of scripture, a process which also entails some resolution of its difficulties, Pseudo-Philo is merely building upon the foundation of scripture, not replacing it. If in the mind of the modern reader this seems to create a difficult tension, it is one with which the first-century writer felt quite comfortable.

The tension, of course, continues beyond the first century into rabbinic Judaism. In the Mishnah there are numerous examples of the rabbis attempting to harmonize Torah. In *m. Sotah 5:3* the rabbis reconcile two apparently conflicting statements in Numbers. In *Sipre* on Numbers 42 discrepancies between Numbers and Deuteronomy are reconciled[13]. How far back these attempts toward scriptural harmonization go back is difficult to say. But the very fact that the Mishnah (not to mention the targumim) addresses concerns of this kind speaks to the relevance of harmonization in the late second-century setting.

In none of these instances are the rabbinic discussions regarding the apparent inconsistencies of the Pentateuch evidence that the rabbis questioned the authority of the Torah. Indeed, Roger Beckwith argues precisely the opposite, namely, that these attempts toward harmonization are indicators of the Torah's authority[14]:

> If the books had not been canonical, why should the rabbis have bothered to point out contradictions in them, since in uninspired books such contradictions were not surprising? It was only when a book was inspired that its apparent contradictions caused a problem, and these were the discrepancies to which the rabbis called attention and which they attempted to harmonize.

If Beckwith's argument in regard to the rabbis' appraisal of the Pentateuch is valid, the same point applies to the writings considered above. The process of bringing the biblical text into a unified narrative framework was never seen as giving rise to an *Ersatz* scripture; instead, the aim was to explain the HB as an authoritative text, to supplement it in order to eliminate its ambiguities.

It is my contention that the "rewritten Bible," as I have described it here, also provides a useful category for understanding Tatian's *Diates-*

---

13. These and further examples are compiled in R.T. BECKWITH, *The Old Testament Canon of the New Testament Church and Its Background in Early Judaism,* Grand Rapids, MI, Eerdmans, 1985, pp. 286.

14. *Ibid.*

saron. Just as the Jewish rewriters closely followed the chain of events narrated in Torah, Tatian follows – to the best of his ability – the sequence of the gospels. Again like his forerunners Tatian also includes material that may have at that time been considered apocryphal: it is widely acknowledged that the *Diatessaron* incorporates gospel material outside the tetraevangelium (for example, the *Gospel of the Ebionites*)[15].

Tatian's overriding goal, like the goal of the Jewish rewriters of scripture, is explication. This can be demonstrated with reference to Tjitze Baarda's collection of articles, *Essays on the Diatessaron*. Synthesizing Matt 10,10//Luke 9,3 ("take no ... staff") with Mark 6,8 ("take nothing ... except a staff"), Tatian appears to have combined the senses of both gospels in creative fashion: "Take only a scepter, not a stick"[16]. When recounting the words of Jesus on the cross, Tatian takes pains to include each of the four accounts, even if such inclusion necessitated some rearranging[17]. While according to Luke 4,30, Jesus avoids being thrown off a cliff by "walking right through the crowd", the author of the *Diatessaron*, perhaps fearing that his reader's imagination may fail, adds that Jesus was saved from a premature death by flying[18].

In the same volume Baarda speaks to the variety of reasons that may explain why the author of the *Diatessaron* bothered to combine four gospels into one[19]. Among these he focuses on certain philosophical or apologetic concerns which may have been of particular interest in Tatian's time (the late second century) or to Tatian personally. Although Baarda's thesis may be partially correct, it cannot explain the impetus behind gospel harmonies that seem to have pre-dated the Syriac harmony, namely, Justin's alleged harmony or the *Gospel of the Ebionites*. The historical roots of the second-century harmonizing tradition seem to go deeper than Baarda allows.

In my view, any attempt to understand Tatian's goals in composing the *Diatessaron* should not be separated from a consideration of his Jewish counterparts. In the case of the Jewish rewriters of scripture, the need does not seem to have been so much apologetic (although Josephus may

---

15. See PETERSEN, *Diatessaron* (n. 2), pp. 27-29.

16. T. BAARDA, '*A staff only, not a stick'. Disharmony of the Gospels and the Harmony of Tatian (Mt 10:9f parr.)*, in J.-M SÉVRIN (ed.), *The New Testament in Early Christianity* (BETL, 86), Leuven, University Press – Peeters, 1989, pp. 311-333; = T. BAARDA, *Essays* (n. 1), pp. 173-196.

17. T. BAARDA, *The Diatessaron of Tatian and its Influence on the Vernacular Versions. The Case of John 19:30*, in ID., *Essays* (n. 1), pp. 11-28.

18. T. BAARDA, *The Flying Jesus. Luke 4:29-30 in the Syriac Diatessaron*, in *VigChr* 40 (1986) 313-341; = ID., *Essays* (n. 1), pp. 59-86.

19. ID., *Harmonization of the Gospels* (n. 1).

be an exception to this), as hermeneutical. In other words, rather than viewing the "mixed gospel" primarily as a means of anticipating the charge of the skeptics, perhaps it is more accurate to understand it as a kind of "pure exegesis" (to adopt G. Vermes's terminology) for those who are already committed to the authority of the text in question.

This would also mean, as far as the formation of the canon is concerned, that Tatian's *Diatessaron* betokens exactly the opposite of what has been claimed. On analogy with the Jewish rewritten texts, Tatian's gospel harmony should not be understood as supplanting the authority of the written gospel traditions. On the contrary: in the Jewish tradition (to which Christianity at this stage still belongs) texts were rewritten precisely because they were regarded as authoritative[20]. This has important implications not only for the study of the second-century synoptic tradition, but for the history of canon as well. The putative harmony of Justin, the *Gospel of the Ebionites*, the *Unknown Gospel*, the *Gospel of Peter* (assuming momentarily the dependence of all of these on the written gospels), may all be witnesses to a view of the gospel text – not just the words of Jesus – as scripture.

2C Little Cloister   Nicholas PERRIN
Westminster
London SW1 3PL
England

---

20. The rewriting of sacred writings *qua* authoritative texts is also posited by Georg STEINS, *Die Chronik als kanonisches Abschlussphänomen: Studien zur Entstehung und Theologie von 1/2 Chronik* (Bonner biblische Beiträge, 93), Weinheim, Beltz, 1995, esp. pp. 507-517, in connection with Chronicles; and by C.A. EVANS, *Luke and the Rewritten Bible: Aspects of Lukan Hagiography*, in J.H. CHARLESWORTH & C.A. EVANS (eds.), *Pseudepigrapha and Early Biblical Interpretation* (JSPSup, 14), Sheffield, JSOT Press, 1993, pp. 170-201, in connection with Luke.

DIE OFFENBARUNG DES JOHANNES IM KANON DER BIBEL

TEXTINTERNER GELTUNGSANSPRUCH UND PROBLEME
DER KANONISCHEN REZEPTION

Die Offenbarung des Johannes spielt im Prozess der Kanonisierung der neutestamentlichen Schriften eine zumindest zeitweise nicht unwichtige, insgesamt sicherlich eine außergewöhnliche und nur schwer zu bewertende Rolle. Ihre Stellung im Kanon ist bis herauf in die Neuzeit immer wieder angefragt und umstritten[1]. Einerseits findet die Apokalypse bereits früh ein vergleichsweise hohes Maß an Anerkennung. Insbesondere aufgrund einer entsprechenden Notiz im Canon Muratori[2] stellt sich sogar die Frage, ob sie nicht vielleicht sogar wesentlich auf die Kanonbildung des Neuen Testaments Einfluss genommen hat und ihr eine Art kritierielle Funktion für die Gestaltwerdung des Kanon zuzuschreiben ist[3]. Auf der anderen Seite ist die Offenbarung des Johannes von Anfang an heftiger Kritik und massiver Ablehnung ausgesetzt. Am Beispiel der chiliastischen Interpretation von Offb 20,4-6 soll im zweiten Teil dieses Beitrags die bewegte Kanongeschichte der Apokalypse konkret in den Blick genommen und nach möglichen Gründen dafür gefragt werden.

1. Cf. G. MAIER, *Die Johannesoffenbarung und die Kirche* (WUNT, 25), Tübingen, Mohr (Siebeck), 1981; G. KRETSCHMAR, *Die Offenbarung des Johannes. Die Geschichte ihrer Auslegung im 1. Jahrtausend* (CTM.ST, 9), Stuttgart, Calwer Verlag 1985.
2. Die Zeilen 47-50 des Canon Muratori lauten: „... da der selige Apostel Paulus selbst, der Regel seines Vorgängers Johannes folgend [sequens prodecessoris sui Iohannis], mit Namensnennung nur an sieben Gemeinden schreibt ..."; Übersetzung nach W. SCHNEEMELCHER (ed.), *Neutestamentliche Apokryphen in deutscher Übersetzung. I. Band: Evangelien*, Tübingen, Mohr (Siebeck), 6.1990, p. 29.
3. So (in Auseinandersetzung mit J. Kunze) schon H. WINDISCH, *Der Apokalyptiker Johannes als Begründer des neutestamentlichen Kanons*, in ZNW 10 (1909) 148-174, bes. 173: „So bildet die Apokalypse durchaus den Ausgangspunkt der Kanonbildung eines NT." – Neben der Siebenzahl der Paulusbriefe in Analogie zu den sieben Sendschreiben in Offb 2-3 sind in diesem Zusammenhang die deutende Rolle von Offb 4,7 hinsichtlich der Vierzahl der Evangelien sowie die Funktion der Kanonformel Offb 22,18-19 in Bezug auf die Sammlung der neutestamentlichen Schriften insgesamt ausschlaggebend. Nach G.S. OEGEMA, *Kanon und Apokalyptik. Die Rolle der Apokalyptik im Kanonisierungsprozess der christlichen Bibel*, in J. KRAŠOVEC (ed.), *The Interpretation of the Bible. The International Symposium in Slovenia* (JSOT SS, 289), Sheffield, Academic Press, 1998, pp. 277-295, dürfte die Johannesoffenbarung eine „wichtige, wenn auch nicht bestimmende Rolle in dem Kanonisierungsprozeß" (p. 290) gespielt haben.

I. TEXTINTERNER GELTUNGSANSPRUCH DER OFFENBARUNG DES JOHANNES

A. *Der einzigartige Offenbarungsanspruch der Apokalypse*

Der unterschiedlichen kanonischen Rezeption steht ein eindeutiger Anspruch auf Autorität und Geltung im Text selbst gegenüber und geht ihr voraus. Das letzte Buch der christlichen Bibel erhebt für sich einen Offenbarungsanspruch, wie ihn in dieser Intensität sonst keine andere Schrift im Neuen Testament, ja vielleicht in der gesamten Bibel kennt. Eine Reihe von Textelementen gibt dafür den Ausschlag. Dabei ist die Tatsache an sich schon beachtenswert, dass sich diese vor allem in den rahmenden Perikopen – im Vorwort und in der briefartigen Einleitung in Offb 1,1-8 einerseits und im Buchschluss in Offb 22,6-21 andererseits – besonders konzentriert finden und damit wie eine Klammer um den eigentlichen Textkorpus herum angelegt sind. Die wesentlichen Textelemente, an denen sich dieser einzigartige Geltungsanspruch der Apokalypse textintern festmachen lässt, seien im Folgenden genannt.

Die Charakterisierung des Inhalts in Offb 1,1-3

In den programmatischen Einleitungsversen (1,1-3) wird der Inhalt des Buches auf dreifache Weise näher charakterisiert: als „Offenbarung Jesu Christi, die Gott ihm gegeben hat" (ἀποκάλυψις Ἰησοῦ Χριστοῦ ἣν ἔδωκεν αὐτῷ ὁ θεός, v. 1), als „das Wort Gottes und das Zeugnis Jesu Christi" (τὸν λόγον τοῦ θεοῦ καὶ τὴν μαρτυρίαν Ἰησοῦ Χριστοῦ, v. 2) und als „Worte der Prophetie" (τοὺς λόγους τῆς προφητείας, v. 3). Der von Johannes bezeugten Botschaft ist damit von Anfang an eine außerordentliche, ja göttliche Autorität zugesprochen, umso mehr, wenn bereits in Offb 1,1 durch den Genitivus subjectivus Ἰησοῦ Χριστοῦ und durch die angezeigte Struktur der Offenbarungsvermittlung deutlich wird, dass der eigentliche Urheber der Offenbarung Jesus Christus und deren Ursprung letztlich Gott selbst ist[4]. Dieser Aspekt begegnet mehrfach auch im weiteren Verlauf der Apokalypse, beispielsweise etwa, wenn der Auferstandene in der Vision vom Menschensohngleichen direkt einen Schreibbefehl[5] an Johannes richtet (1,11.19) und

---

4. Johannes hat demgegenüber die Funktion des Zeugen (Offb 1,2) und des Schreibers (Offb 1,11.19; 2,1.8.12.18; 3,1.7.14; 14,13; 19,9; 21,5). Cf. J. ROLOFF, *Die Offenbarung des Johannes* (ZBK.NT, 18), Zürich, Theologischer Verlag Zürich, 1984, p. 16.

5. Cf. T. SÖDING, *Die Schriftinspiration in der Theologie des Westens. Neutestamentliche Anmerkungen*, in J.D.G. DUNN, H. KLEIN, U. LUZ, V. MIHOC (eds.), *Auslegung der Bibel in orthodoxer und westlicher Perspektive. Akten des west-östlichen Neutestamentler/innen-Symposiums von Neamţ vom 4.-11. September 1998* (WUNT, 130), Tübingen, Mohr (Siebeck), 2000, pp. 169-206: „Die Schriftform ist nicht nur die Voraussetzung, die

dann selbst als der Sprecher der Sendschreiben in Offb 2 und 3 gezeichnet wird oder wenn in Offb 5 das Lamm von Gott her das Buch mit den sieben Siegeln übernimmt (5,6-7), um es in der Folge zu öffnen (Offb 6-8). Was Johannes in Form von Visionen schaut und niederschreibt, ist im Grunde also – das unterstreicht dann die korrespondierende Wendung in Offb 1,2 – Wort Gottes, Botschaft, die von Gott gegeben ist und zugleich identisch ist mit dem, wovon Jesus Christus Zeugnis gibt. Auf dieser Ebene liegt auch, wenn der Inhalt der Apokalypse in Offb 1,3 als „Worte der Prophetie" bezeichnet werden, eine Qualifizierung, die im Buchschluss erneut betont aufgegriffen wird (22,7.10.18.19). Dass sich die Apokalypse insgesamt als prophetische Schrift versteht[6], lässt sich indirekt auch ablesen an der Art und Weise ihrer starken inhaltlichen wie formalen Rezeption gerade der alttestamentlichen Prophetenbücher, insbesondere der Propheten Daniel, Ezechiel und Jesaja, in deren Linie sie sich damit wie selbstverständlich einzureihen scheint[7].

Der Seher als inspirierter Prophet

Eng verbunden mit dem Selbstverständnis der Apokalypse als prophetischer Schrift ist der Umstand, dass sich der Seher selbst als einen inspirierten Propheten stilisiert. Mehrfach ist ausdrücklich davon die Rede, dass Johannes bei seinen Visionen und Auditionen „im Geist" (ἐν

Adressaten zu erreichen, sondern garantiert auch allein, daß die ‚Offenbarung' unverfälscht verbreitet wird" (p. 198). Insofern ist die Schriftform/Buchform als ein weiteres Element für den Geltungsanspruch zu nennen.

6. Nach H. ROOSE, „*Das Zeugnis Jesu"*. *Seine Bedeutung für die Christologie, Eschatologie und Prophetie in der Offenbarung des Johannes* (TANZ, 32), Tübingen, Francke, 2000, pp. 162-188, knüpft der Seher an eine in den Adressatengemeinden beheimatete Konzeption von Prophetie an, um die Akzeptanz seiner eigenen prophetischen Botschaft zu sichern.

7. Der permanente Rückgriff auf das Alte Testament und die souveräne Verwendung, Aktualisierung und Fortschreibung alttestamentlicher Motive, Themen und Formen insgesamt unterstreichen ebenfalls das Autoritäts- und Legitimitätsbewusstsein der Offenbarung des Johannes. Darüber hinaus geht es um den Anspruch von Legitimität und Kontinuität aufgrund fundamentaler Übereinstimmung des Verfassers mit seinem „Kanon" heiliger Texte; cf. R.W. WALL, *The Apocalypse of the New Testament in Canonical Context*, in R.W. WALL & E.E. LEMCIO, *The New Testament as Canon. A Reader in Canonical Criticism* (JSNT SS, 76), Sheffield, Academic Press, 1992, pp. 274-298, pp. 289-290. – Zur Rezeption von Dan, Ez und Jes cf. G.K. BEALE, *The Use of Daniel in Jewish Apocalyptic Literature and in the Revelation of St. John*, Lanham, MD, University Press of America, 1984; J.-P. RUIZ, *Ezekiel in the Apocalypse. The Transformation of Prophetic Language in Revelation 16,17-19,10* (EHS.T, 376), Frankfurt a.M., Lang, 1989; J. FEKKES, *Isaiah and Prophetic Traditions in the Book of Revelation. Visionary Antecedents and their Development* (JSNT SS, 93), Sheffield, Academic Press, 1994. Zur Rezeption des Alten Testaments insgesamt cf. S. MOYISE, *The Old Testament in the Book of Revelation* (JSNT SS, 115), Sheffield, Academic Press, 1995; G.K. BEALE, *John's Use of the Old Testament in Revelation* (JSNT SS, 166), Sheffield, Academic Press, 1998.

πνεύματι) gewesen ist (1,10; 4,2; 17,3; 21,10; 22,6), dass er also vermittelt durch den Geist die Offenbarung empfangen hat. Diese Selbst-
stilisierung des Sehers steht dabei in der Tradition alttestamentlicher
Propheten; insbesondere Offb 1,10-11 rückt in die Nähe der Propheten-
berufungen[8]. Bei allem Selbstbewusstsein[9] und wohl auch persönlichem
Ansehen des Johannes geht es aber letztlich einzig um die Bedeutung
des Inhalts der Schrift und das absolute Gewicht ihrer Botschaft. Eine
darüber hinausgehende Legitimation durch die Autorität des Verfassers
wird nicht nur als unnötig erachtet – als Indiz dafür kann der Verzicht
auf Pseudonymität gelten –, sie wird vielmehr auch bewusst zu vermei-
den versucht, indem Johannes z.B. keine Amts- und Würdebezeich-
nungen für sich in Anspruch nimmt oder sich als Mitbruder und Mit-
knecht auf eine Stufe mit seinen Adressaten stellt[10]. Wenn überhaupt
von seiner Person her, dann lässt sich lediglich so viel sagen, dass er
aufgrund seines Schicksals, das er „wegen des Wortes Gottes und des
Zeugnisses Jesu Christi" (1,9) erduldet, Autorität für seine Botschaft beanspruchen kann[11].

Die Seligpreisung in Offb 1,3

Ein weiteres Element für den Geltungsanspruch der Apokalypse ist
die Seligpreisung in Offb 1,3, die in verkürzter Form in Offb 22,7 wieder aufgegriffen wird. In Offb 1,3 wird derjenige seliggepriesen, der die
prophetischen Worte vorliest, bzw. diejenigen, die sie hören. Das lässt
darauf schließen, dass der Seher für seine Schrift die Verlesung im Gottesdienst der christlichen Gemeinden intendiert und wohl auch fordernd
erwartet und damit auf einen sensiblen und privilegierten Ort allgemei-
ner Anerkennung von Texten als heilige Schrift kanonischen Rangs hinzielt. Wenn darüber hinaus von der Seligpreisung derer, die seine Worte
„bewahren" (τηρέω), die Rede ist (cf. Lk 11,28), dann ist dabei nicht
nur die gehorsame Befolgung des in dieser Schrift Geforderten angesprochen (cf. 3,3.8.10; 12,17; 14,12), ein paränetischer Akzent also, den
die Seligpreisung an sich bereits impliziert[12], sondern vielleicht auch der

---

8. Cf. Jes 6,1-13; Jer 1,4-10; Ez 1,1-3,15. Cf. Söding, *Die Schriftinspiration in der
Theologie des Westens* (n. 5), pp. 173.198.
9. Z.B. das betonte ἐγώ verbunden mit der einfachen Namensnennung in Offb 1,9-10;
cf. F. Bovon, *John's Self-presentation in Revelation 1:9-10*, in *CBQ* 62 (2000) 693-700.
10. Johannes tritt auch in der Auseinandersetzung mit seinen Gegnern stets hinter die
Autorität Jesu Christi zurück; so z.B. in den Sendschreiben, deren Sprecher ja eigentlich
Christus selbst ist. Cf. Roose, *„Das Zeugnis Jesu"* (n. 6), pp. 150-161.
11. *Ibid.*, p. 161.
12. Zum paränetischen Akzent von Seligpreisungen cf. H. Giesen, *Die Offenbarung
des Johannes* (RNT), Regensburg, Pustet, 1997, pp. 56.70-72.

Schutz vor drohender Verfälschung der Botschaft, die in seinem Buch niedergeschrieben ist[13].

Die Beglaubigungsformel in Offb 22,6

Die Zuverlässigkeit und die Wahrheit der Worte wird an mehreren Stellen ausdrücklich durch eine Beglaubigungsformel betont (19,9; 21,5; 22,6) und dabei textintern stets von einer Gestalt aus dem Bereich Gottes oder gar von Gott selbst (21,5) bestätigt und verbürgt. In Offb 22,6, dem Beginn des Buchschlusses, bezieht sich diese Beglaubigungsformel nicht nur auf den unmittelbaren Kontext, sondern insgesamt zurück auf das ganze Buch, dessen prophetisch inspirierter Inhalt in Gott selbst (ὁ κύριος ὁ θεὸς τῶν πνευμάτων τῶν προφητῶν) begründet und von ihm verantwortet ist (cf. 1,1-2). Damit unterstreicht der Verfasser an einer markanten Stelle im Text noch einmal „den Anspruch seines Werkes, von Gott und von Christus autorisierte prophetische Botschaft zu sein"[14].

Die Briefform

Eine nicht unwesentliche Rolle spielt der briefartige Gesamtcharakter der Apokalypse bzw. der Rückgriff auf das Briefformular paulinischer Prägung, wie er sich für Offb 1,4-8 und Offb 22,21 feststellen lässt. Auch hier geht es um die Vermittlung von Autorität und Legitimität und – damit verbunden – um die Erwartung entsprechender Beachtung und Aufmerksamkeit von Seiten der Adressaten. Gleichzeitig wird darin die unmittelbare Gegenwartsbedeutung der Botschaft angezeigt, die beispielsweise auch durch das Versiegelungsverbot in Offb 22,10 angedeutet ist. Darüber hinaus lässt sich fragen, ob mit der Verwendung der Briefform nicht ein weiterer Hinweis darauf gegeben ist, dass die Apokalypse auf eine Verlesung im Gottesdienst hinzielt[15]. Bedenkt man außerdem die symbolische Siebenzahl der Gemeinden, an die das Schreiben gerichtet ist (1,11), dann wird umso deutlicher, dass der insgesamt darin zum Ausdruck gebrachte Anspruch universal ausgerichtet ist[16].

13. Cf. Roloff, *Die Offenbarung des Johannes* (n. 4), p. 30. In Offb 1,3 wie in Offb 22,7 bezieht sich das „Bewahren" immer auf das Geschriebene (τὰ γεγραμμένα bzw. τοῦ βιβλίου τούτου).
14. Giesen, *Die Offenbarung des Johannes* (n. 12), p. 482.
15. Cf. Roose, *„Das Zeugnis Jesu"* (n. 6), p. 181-183, wonach die Gestaltung als Brief „in legitimatorischer Hinsicht wohl im Blick auf die Leiter der Gemeinden gewählt" (p. 182) ist.
16. Auch der Umstand, dass es sich wahrscheinlich um eine Art „Rundbrief" handelt (die Reihenfolge der genannten Gemeinden beschreibt einen Kreis), unterstreicht den universalen Charakter der Offenbarung des Johannes. Zur Briefform insgesamt grundlegend

Die „Kanonformel" in Offb 22,18-19

Besonderes Augenmerk verdient schließlich die so genannte Kanonformel am Ende der Offenbarung des Johannes in Offb 22,18-19, insofern sich darin ein ausgesprochenes Bewusstsein von Kanonizität mani-
festiert[17]. Johannes verbürgt sich für seine Prophetie und stellt jede
Erweiterung, aber auch jede Verkürzung des Inhalts seiner Schrift unter
entsprechende Strafandrohung. Literarisches Vorbild ist die deuteronomistische Prägung dieser schon in der Umwelt Israels weit verbreite-
ten formelhaften Wendung, wie sie etwa in Dtn 4,2 begegnet (cf. Dtn
13,1; Jer 26,2)[18]. Der Seher untermauert mit Hilfe der Kanonformel den
Offenbarungsanspruch seines ganzen Werkes, dessen herausragende
Würde und unverbrüchliche Authentizität. Weil das Buch Wort Gottes
zu sein beansprucht, steht sein Inhalt letztlich auch unter besonderem
Schutz Gottes. Im Grunde wird damit die Botschaft der Apokalypse als
sakrosankt erklärt und für sie der Anspruch auf Suffizienz bzw. Vollständigkeit[19] erhoben, eine Vollständigkeit, die sich bis hin auf die in der
Kanonformel konkret angedrohten Folgen erstreckt, insofern auch diese

---

ist die Studie von M. KARRER, *Die Johannesoffenbarung als Brief. Studien zu ihrem literarischen, historischen und theologischen Ort* (FRLANT, 140), Göttingen, Vandenhoeck
& Ruprecht, 1986.

17. Über einen rein textinternen Geltungsanspruch hinaus ist mit der Kanonformel
durch das Verbot des Wegnehmens und Hinzufügens ein Bewusstsein von Kanonizität
angezeigt, das „einen Blick auf den Übergang vom kanonischen Prozeß zur Kanonisierung" (C. DOHMEN & M. OEMING, *Biblischer Kanon – warum und wozu? Eine Kanontheologie* [QD, 137], Freiburg i.Br., Herder, 1992, p. 68) erlaubt. Selbstverständlich ist
hier noch nicht an einen Zugehörigkeitsanspruch zu einem Kanon im Sinne einer autoritativen Sammlung von Schriften zu denken, wenngleich durch die Aufnahme der Apokalypse in den Kanon und bedingt durch ihre Stellung als letzte Schrift des Neuen
Testaments die Kanonformel in Offb 22,18-19 in der Folge auch auf die ganze Sammlung bezogen und mit ihr eine Zurückweisung von Ansprüchen anderer Texte (insbesondere Apokalypsen) angezeigt werden kann. Cf. OEGEMA, *Kanon und Apokalyptik* (n. 3),
p. 290, für den die Kanonformel allerdings Indiz für die Vermutung ist, dass das Neue
Testament beim Abschluss der Johannesoffenbarung möglicherweise als Kanon bereits
feststand.

18. Cf. auch die weisheitliche Verwendung in Koh 3,14; Spr 30,6 sowie die Verwendung der Formel in äthHen 104,11-13; Arist 310f; cf. auch Mt 5,18; Irenäus, haer. IV
33,8; Eusebius, h. e. V 16,3. Zur Kanonformel cf. W.C. VAN UNNIK, *De la règle Μήτε
προσθεῖναι μήτε ἀφελεῖν dans l'histoire du canon*, in *VigChr* 3 (1949) 1-36; DOHMEN &
OEMING, *Biblischer Kanon* (n. 17), pp. 68-89. In der hellenistischen Umwelt findet die
Kanonformel vor allem im Bereich der Ästhetik breite Verwendung (cf. Aristoteles, Nik.
Eth. II 1106b). – Dass die Johannesoffenbarung diese Formel alttestamentlich-früh-
jüdischer Prägung aufgreift und damit auf das darin angezeigte Kanonverständnis zurückgreift, ist für die Frage nach ihrem (kanonischen) Geltungsanspruch an sich schon zu beachten.

19. Ein Anspruch auf Vollständigkeit ist auch für die (in ihrer Bedeutung umstrittene)
Buchrolle in Offb 5 durch die beidseitige Beschriftung angedeutet, insofern auf dieser
Buchrolle nichts mehr hinzugefügt werden kann (vgl. Ex 32,15f).

ganz im Rahmen dessen bleiben, was prophetischer Aussagegehalt der Offenbarung ist[20].

B. *Die Beweggründe für den Geltungsanspruch der Apokalypse*

Insgesamt lässt sich aus dem textinternen Befund, der freilich noch zu vertiefen und durch weitere Beobachtungen zu ergänzen wäre[21], für die Offenbarung des Johannes ein besonders außerordentlicher und universaler Geltungsanspruch ablesen. Insbesondere die in der Kanonformel angezeigte Deutlichkeit überrascht und wirft die Frage nach den Gründen für eine derartig klare Positionierung auf.

Zum einen zeigt sich darin sicherlich die tiefe Überzeugung des Sehers hinsichtlich der Wahrheit und der existenziellen Bedeutung seiner Botschaft, die er eben für absolut maßgeblich hält und wohl auch entsprechend intensiv als solche erfahren hat.

Zum zweiten wird dafür die konkrete Situation jener Gemeinden, an die sich der Verfasser direkt wendet, eine wichtige Rolle gespielt haben. Die angesprochenen Gemeinden sind – das geht vor allem aus der jeweiligen Charakterisierung in den Sendschreiben (Offb 2-3) hervor – sowohl inneren als auch äußeren Gefährdungen ausgesetzt, die in erster Linie ihre religiöse Einstellung und die ethische Haltung betreffen. Umso klarer ergeht von Johannes zusammen mit der Ermutigung zum Standhalten in der Bedrängnis der Appell zum Festhalten am ungekürzten Christusbekenntnis sowie die Warnung vor einem unangemessenen enthusiastischen Heilsbewusstsein[22].

Auf diesem Hintergrund werden jene Gruppen und deren Lehren, gegen die Johannes ausdrücklich anschreibt[23], als entsprechend einflussreich zu veranschlagen sein, so dass der Seher von vornherein mangeln-

---

20. Offb 22,18 nimmt wahrscheinlich Bezug auf die Plagenreihe in Offb 15,1 bzw. Offb 16; Offb 22,19 nimmt Bezug auf Offb 2,7 und Offb 21,1-22,5. – K. Backhaus spricht in diesem Zusammenhang von einer brisanten eschatologischen Wertigkeit des Buches; cf. K. BACKHAUS, *Die Vision vom ganz Anderen. Geschichtlicher Ort und theologische Mitte der Johannes-Offenbarung*, in K. BACKHAUS (ed.), *Theologie als Vision. Studien zur Johannes-Offenbarung* (SBS, 191), Stuttgart, Katholisches Bibelwerk, 2001, pp. 10-53, bes. p. 40: „Die Integrität des Buches sichert den Zugang zu Offenbarung und Heil."

21. Z.B. etwa die liturgische Stilisierung der Apokalypse insgesamt (Hymnen; Buchschluss …), die ebenfalls auf die gottesdienstliche Versammlung als intendierten Sitz im Leben hinzielt. Cf. BACKHAUS, *Theologie als Vision* (n. 20), p. 39; ROOSE, *„Das Zeugnis Jesu"* (n. 6), pp. 103-122 (cf. pp. 112-114 zur Funktion der Formel Maranatha).

22. Cf. BACKHAUS, *Theologie als Vision* (n. 20), pp. 16-30.52; ROOSE, *„Das Zeugnis Jesu"* (n. 6), pp. 126-137.

23. Etwa die Gruppe rund um die Prophetin Isebel (2,20). Wie bei der Lehre des Bileam (2,14) und der Lehre der Nikolaiten (2,15) wird es auch bei Isebel um eine liberale Position gegenüber der heidnischen Kultpraxis gehen sowie um falsche Prophetie. Zur Kritik des Sehers an Isebel cf. ROOSE, *„Das Zeugnis Jesu"* (n. 6), pp. 162-224.

de oder jedenfalls nicht ungeteilte Akzeptanz seiner Botschaft befürch-
ten musste und entschieden entgegenzuwirken beabsichtigte.

Möglicherweise rechnet Johannes für seine Schrift schließlich auch
mit Missverständnissen und mit über das eigentlich Gemeinte hinausgehenden Missdeutungen, wie sie dann ja auch sehr rasch in der Auslegungsgeschichte der Apokalypse zu beobachten sind[24].

So vielfältig die Beweggründe auch zu veranschlagen sein mögen, der
Anspruch, den der Verfasser der Apokalypse für sein prophetisches
Buch erhebt, setzt jedenfalls ganz auf die Autorität der Botschaft und auf
die Autorität dessen, der hinter dieser Botschaft steht. Mit der – wenn
auch keineswegs einhelligen – kanonischen Rezeption, die in erster Linie auf der Wertschätzung dieser Botschaft beruht, ist gleichzeitig die
prinzipielle Bejahung des in der Apokalypse erhobenen Anspruchs verbunden.

II. PROBLEME DER KANONISCHEN REZEPTION

Im seltsamen Kontrast zum hohen textinternen Geltungsanspruch der
Apokalypse steht die zögerliche kanonische Rezeption dieses Buches.
Bereits ein flüchtiger Blick in frühe Kanonverzeichnisse lässt dies erkennen. Neben der Gruppe von Verzeichnissen, welche die Apokalypse
enthalten[25], gibt es Listen, in denen das Buch fehlt[26], sowie Verzeichnisse, die keine klare Entscheidung treffen[27].

Insbesondere in den Kirchen des Ostens kommt es als Folge des
Kampfes gegen Chiliasmus und Montanismus, aus Angst vor falschen

---

24. Insgesamt scheint Johannes aber vorauszusetzen, dass die von ihm gebrauchten
Bilder und alttestamentlichen Bezüge allgemein verständlich sind. Nur selten finden sich
anschließende Ausdeutungen und auch der Rückgriff auf das Alte Testament erfolgt ohne
entsprechende Hinweise.

25. Zu ihnen zählen: Canon Muratori (siehe n. 2), Kanon des Origenes (Eusebius,
h. e. VI 25,3-14), Verzeichnis des Codex Claromontanus (4. Jahrhundert), der so genannte Cheltenham-Kanon (um 350), Kanon des Athanasius (367) und Kanon der dritten Synode von Karthago (397). Cf. SCHNEEMELCHER, *Neutestamentliche Apokryphen* (n. 2),
pp. 27-40; B.M. METZGER, *Der Kanon des Neuen Testaments. Entstehung, Entwicklung,
Bedeutung*, Düsseldorf, Patmos, 1993, pp. 287-297.

26. Zu nennen sind: Kanon des Cyrill von Jerusalem (um 350), Kanon der Synode
von Laodicäa (363), Kanon nach den Canones Apostolici (um 380; in den Apostolischen
Konstitutionen VIII 47), Kanon des Gregor von Nazianz (329-389). Cf. METZGER, *Der
Kanon* (n. 25).

27. Solche finden wir bei Eusebius (h. e. III 25,1-7) und im Kanon des Amphilochius
von Iconium (nach 394). Die entscheidende Stelle dort lautet: „die Offenbarung des
Johannes, Einige sagen ja, aber die meisten sagen, sie sei falsch" (METZGER, *Der Kanon*,
p. 296). Die Trullanische Synode (692) approbiert nebeneinander Kanonverzeichnisse mit
der Apokalypse und ohne sie. Cf. A. WIKENHAUSER & J. SCHMID, *Einleitung in das Neue
Testament*, Freiburg i.Br. u.a., Herder, ⁶1973, p. 646.

Propheten und aufgrund genereller Skepsis gegenüber der Prophetie zu reservierter und ablehnender Haltung gegenüber der Offenbarung des Johannes, weil die bekämpften Irrlehren sich in besonderer Weise auf dieses Buch stützen. In weiten Teilen der Ostkirche wird die Apokalypse Jahrhunderte lang nicht akzeptiert und bleibt auch vom liturgischen Gebrauch ausgeschlossen. Im Folgenden soll die Wirkungsgeschichte von Offb 20,4-6 beleuchtet werden, einer Stelle, die neben anderen Bildern der Offenbarung des Johannes (z.B. Vision vom neuen Jerusalem) sowie alttestamentlichen Aussagen (z.B. Ps 90,4) besondere Bedeutung hat in der vielfältigen und bunten Vorstellungswelt des Chiliasmus[28].

A. *Einfluss von Offb 20,4-6 auf chiliastische Vorstellungen*

Nur einige Beispiele seien erwähnt. Papias behauptet, „daß nach der Auferstehung der Toten tausend Jahre kommen werden, in denen das Reich Christi sichtbar (σωματικῶς) auf Erden bestehen werde" (Eusebius, h. e. III 39,12)[29].

Justin erwartet die „zweite Parusie" Jesu im erneuerten Jerusalem (dial. 40,4; 85,7). Dort werden – gemäß der Prophezeiung des Johannes – die an Christus Glaubenden 1000 Jahre verbringen, bevor die allgemeine und ewige Auferstehung der Toten erfolgt (dial. 81,1-4).

Irenäus bezieht Offb 20,5-6 auf „die erste Auferstehung der Gerechten" (haer. V 36,3)[30]. Diese werden „auf der Erde herrschen" (*regnabunt in terra*) und infolge der Erscheinung des Herrn wachsen und sich durch ihn daran gewöhnen, „die Herrlichkeit Gottes des Vaters zu fassen" (*assuescent capere gloriam Dei Patris*) (haer. V 35,1; cf. 35,2). Das Leben im irdischen Zwischenreich dient also zur Vorbereitung auf die Gottesschau und das endgültige Heil bei Gott. Hinsichtlich der Vorstellungen von der paradiesischen Fruchtbarkeit und vom Tierfrieden im Reich der Gerechten ist Irenäus von Papias beeinflusst (haer. V 33,3-4).

---

28. Wurzeln des Chiliasmus liegen teilweise auch im antiken Judentum, z.B. in den Vorstellungen von der wunderbaren Fruchtbarkeit der Erde (syr ApkBar 24-30) und von der Weltwoche (cf. Barn 15,3-9).

29. Eusebius wird hier und im Folgenden zitiert anhand der beiden Ausgaben: E. Schwartz, *Eusebius, Kirchengeschichte*, Leipzig, Hinrichs'sche Buchhandlung, 1914; H. Kraft, *Eusebius von Caesarea, Kirchengeschichte*, München, Kösel, 1989. – Zur Vorstellung der paradiesischen Fruchtbarkeit des tausendjährigen Reiches bei Papias cf. H.J. de Jonge, *BOTRYC BOHCEI. The Age of Kronos and the Millennium in Papias of Hierapolis*, in M.J. Vermaseren (ed.), *Studies in Hellenistic Religions* (Études préliminaires aux religions orientales dans l'Empire romain, 78), Leiden, Brill, 1979, pp. 37-49.

30. Dieses Zitat und die folgenden aus haer. V sind entnommen der Textausgabe: Irenäus von Lyon, *Gegen die Häresien V*, übersetzt und eingeleitet von N. Brox (FC, 8/5), Freiburg i.Br. – Basel – Wien, Herder, 2001.

Hippolyt betrachtet in Verbindung mit Ps 90,4 den Sabbat als Typus und Bild des tausendjährigen Herrschens der Heiligen mit Christus, „wenn er vom Himmel kommt, wie Johannes in seiner Offenbarung erzählt" (In Dan IV 23,5)[31].

Tertullian stellt sich das tausendjährige Reich der Auferstandenen als Zwischenreich hier auf Erden vor, und zwar in einem neuen Jerusalem (adv. Marc. III 24,3).

Eusebius erwähnt Gaius als einen namhaften Vertreter der Auffassung, dass der zur Zeit Trajans lebende Häretiker Kerinthos der Verfasser der Apokalypse sei, welcher auch behauptet, dass das Reich Christi auf Erden sein werde (ἐπίγειον εἶναι τὸ βασίλειον τοῦ Χριστοῦ), und zwar in Jerusalem, und dass die 1000 Jahre für die Auferstandenen wie eine freudige Hochzeitsfeier verfließen werden (h. e. III 28,1-2).

Auch Dionysios von Alexandrien vertritt die Auffassung, dass Kerinthos, der Führer der nach ihm benannten Sekte, der Verfasser der Apokalypse sei. Dieser lehre, dass das Reich Christi ein irdisches sein (ἐπίγειον ἔσεσθαι τὴν τοῦ Χριστοῦ βασιλείαν) und sinnliche Freuden schenken werde (Eusebius, h. e. III 28,3-5). Dionysios weiß auch zu berichten, dass „einige unserer Vorfahren" die Apokalypse verworfen und ganz abgelehnt haben (ἠθέτησαν καὶ ἀνεσκεύασαν πάντῃ τὸ βιβλίον) (h. e. VII 25,1-3).

Ähnlich lehrt nach Dionysios der ägyptische Bischof Nepos, gestützt auf die Apokalypse des Johannes, dass das Reich Christi auf Erden sein werde (τὴν τοῦ Χριστοῦ βασιλείαν ἐπὶ γῆς ἔσεσθαι) und dass 1000 Jahre sinnlicher Freude auf dieser Erde kommen werden (Eusebius, h. e. VII 24,1-3).

Eusebius selber ist Zeuge dafür, dass die Apokalypse in der griechischen Kirche umstritten ist. Es bestehen verschiedene Meinungen über sie und man kann sie zu den anerkannten (ὁμολογούμενα) Schriften des Neuen Testamentes zählen, aber auch zu den unechten (νόθα). Eusebius stellt jedenfalls fest, dass die einen das Buch der Offenbarung des Johannes verwerfen (ἀθετοῦσιν), andere jedoch es zu den anerkannten Schriften rechnen (ἐγκρίνουσιν τοῖς ὁμολογουμένοις) (h. e. III 25,1-4).

Als letztes Beispiel sei Viktorin von Pettau genannt. In Apocalypsin 20-21 verbindet er die Vision von der ersten Auferstehung und vom Regnum (Offb 20,4-6) mit jener vom Lamm auf dem Berg Sion (Offb 14,1-4) und der Vision vom neuen Jerusalem[32]. In De fabrica Mundi 6

---

31. HIPPOLYTE, *Commentaire sur Daniel. Texte établi et traduit* par M. LEFÈVRE (SC, 14), Paris, Cerf, 1947, p. 306.

32. De hac resurrectione ait: Et vidi agnum stantem et cum eo CXLIIII milia, id est cum Christo stantes, eos scilicet qui ex Iudeis in novissimo tempore sunt credituri per

greift er die auf Ps 90,4 gestützte Vorstellung vom tausendjährigen Weltensabbat auf[33].

Die angeführten Beispiele lassen erkennen, dass in Offb 20,4-6 manches „hineingelesen" wurde, was der Text selbst nicht enthält, z.B. die Vorstellungen vom Weltensabbat oder vom neuen Jerusalem, insbesondere aber der Gedanke eines irdischen Zwischenreiches.

B. *Hauptaussage von Offb 20,4-6*

Der Text lässt sich auch deuten ohne Zuhilfenahme der Vorstellung eines irdischen Zwischenreiches, nämlich als Bild einer schon bestehenden himmlischen Wirklichkeit. Anteil an der „ersten Auferstehung" haben die verstorbenen Christen, allen voran die Märtyrer und jene, die sich geweigert haben, das Tier anzubeten. Sie sind bereits bei Christus und herrschen mit ihm. Dies bestärkt die auf Erden lebenden Christen in der Gewissheit, dass die Macht des Bösen schon eingeschränkt ist (Offb 20,1-3: Satan ist gefesselt).

Mit dem Verbum „herrschen" (βασιλεύω) wird in Offb 20,4.6 die Tätigkeit der Auferstandenen in ihrer himmlischen Daseinsweise bei Christus bezeichnet, in Offb 5,10 das Wirken der Christen in ihrer irdischen Existenz. Das priesterliche und königliche Gottesvolk auf Erden (cf. auch Offb 1,6) weiß sich geheimnisvoll verbunden mit jenen, die schon zur Auferstehung gelangt sind[34].

C. *Kanonisierung der Apokalypse als gesamtkirchliches Zeugnis*

Die Auslegungs- und Wirkungsgeschichte der Offenbarung des Johannes ist, wie sich am Beispiel von Offb 20,4-6 zeigt, auch begleitet von Missverständnissen und Fehldeutungen. Dass dieses Buch in der West- und schließlich in der Ostkirche dennoch als kanonisch bewertet wurde, hat tiefere Bedeutung. Die Gesamtkirche bekennt sich zu diesem Buch insgesamt, auch wenn es bezüglich des Verständnisses einer Einzelstelle unterschiedliche und sogar irrtümliche Auffassungen gibt.

---

praedicationem Heliae... In hac eadem prima resurrectione et civitas futura et speciosa per hanc scripturam expressa est. Hanc primam resurrectionem et Paulus ad ecclesiam Macedoniam ita dixit (1 Thess 4,15-17) (20,1-2)... In regno ergo et in prima resurrectione exhibetur civitas sancta, quam dicit descensuram de caelo (21,1). VICTORIN DE POETOVIO, *Sur l'Apocalypse et autres écrits. Introduction, texte critique, traduction, commentaire et index* par M. DULAEY (SC, 423), Paris, Cerf, 1997, pp. 114-116.

33. Verum illud sabbatum est septimum miliarium, in quo Christus cum electis suis regnaturus est. *Ibid.*, p. 144.

34. Verbundenheit zwischen den auf Erden lebenden und noch bedrängten Gliedern des Gottesvolkes mit den schon verherrlichten zeigt sich auch in Offb 7 (Vision vom Gottesvolk in irdischer und himmlischer Existenz) und 19,1-8 (Christen in der irdischen Situation stimmen in den Lobpreis jener ein, die schon in der Vollendung sind).

SCHLUSSBEMERKUNG

Der hohe textinterne Geltungsanspruch der Offenbarung des Johannes einerseits und die seltsamen Schwierigkeiten ihrer gesamtkirchlichen kanonischen Rezeption andererseits stellen vor grundlegende hermeneutische Fragen. Sie betreffen vor allem die „intentio auctoris" und in Verbindung damit die Interpretation des Buches in dem Geist, in dem es geschrieben wurde (cf. Zweites Vatikanum, Dei Verbum 12), aber auch den „sensus operis", insofern dieses Werk nicht irgendwo am Rande steht, sondern zur singulären Gruppe der kanonischen und inspirierten Schriften zählt.

Karl-Rahner-Platz 1   Konrad HUBER
A-6020 Innsbruck   Martin HASITSCHKA

HARNACK UND OVERBECK ÜBER DIE ENTSTEHUNG
DES KANONS DES NEUEN TESTAMENTS
EIN LEIDER VERGESSENER STREIT
AUS DEM VORLETZTEN JAHRHUNDERT

In neueren Äußerungen zum neutestamentlichen Kanon wird HAR-
NACK fast immer, OVERBECK selten erwähnt. Weithin ist nicht bekannt,
daß sich beide in den 80er Jahren des 19. Jh. darüber auseinandersetzten,
welche Gesichtspunkte bei der Entstehung des ntl. Kanons eine Rolle
gespielt haben[1]. Aus diesem Streit ist m.E. auch heute noch einiges für
die historische Frage nach der Entstehung des Kanons zu lernen, wenigstens dann, wenn man sie nicht mit anderen Fragen verwechselt, wie
etwa der, wann die ntl. Schriften jeweils entstanden sind, oder der, wo
und ab wann sie in den Gemeinden öffentlich vorgelesen wurden. Im
Folgenden werde ich zunächst etwas zur Kanonsfrage im 18. und 19. Jh.
sagen (I), dann auf den Streit zwischen Overbeck und Harnack eingehen
(II) und schließlich auf dessen Nachgeschichte blicken (III).

I. DIE KANONSFRAGE IM 18. UND 19. JAHRHUNDERT

Schon 1670 betonte SPINOZA[2], es sei „zur Schrifterklärung nötig, eine
getreue Geschichte der Schrift auszuarbeiten"[3], die u.a. auch darüber
„Auskunft geben" müsse, „durch wessen Beschluß … (jedes einzelne
Buch) unter die heiligen Schriften aufgenommen wurde", und „auf welche Weise all die(se) Bücher … zu einem Ganzen vereinigt worden
sind"[4]. Dieses Programm einer „Geschichte der Schrift" griff zunächst
R. SIMON auf, dann 100 Jahre später J.S. SEMLER, der in seiner *Abhandlung von freier Untersuchung des Canons* zu dem Ergebnis kommt, der

---

1. A. HARNACK, *Das Muratorische Fragment und die Entstehung einer Sammlung
apostolisch-katholischer Schriften*, in ZKG 3 (1879) 358-408; F. OVERBECK, *Der neutestamentliche Kanon und das muratorische Fragment. Eine Überprüfung der von
A. Harnack neuerdings darüber aufgestellten Ansichten*, in DERS., *Zur Geschichte des
Kanons* (1880), Nachdruck Darmstadt, Wissenschaftliche Buchgesellschaft, 1965, pp. 71-
142 = *Franz Overbeck, Werke und Nachlaß, Bd. 2. Schriften bis 1880*, ed. E.W. Stege-
mann & R. Brändle, Stuttgart *et al.*, Metzler, 1994, pp. 379-526.
2. B. DE SPINOZA, *Tractatus theologico-politicus* (1670), in SPINOZA, *Opera. Werke*,
ed. G. Gawlick & F. Niewöhner, Bd. 1, Darmstadt, Wissenschaftliche Buchgesellschaft,
1979.
3. *Ibid.*, p. 231.
4. *Ibid.*, p. 239.

Kanon habe sich geschichtlich entwickelt und sei nicht inspiriert im herkömmlichen Sinn. Vielmehr sei „die Canonizität … (für die) Kleriker festgesetzt, daß diese keine andern Bücher zum Vorlesen und zum verbindlichen Unterricht gebrauchen dürfen"[5], und deshalb sei „die besondere Untersuchung dieser Bücher, für alle nachdenkenden Leser, was ihren eigenen Privatgebrauch betrift, frey geblieben"[6].

Im 19. Jh. stand die Diskussion über die Authentizität der einzelnen Schriften des NT im Vordergrund. Um die Geschichte des Kanons mühten sich hingegen nur wenige. Zu ihnen zählt CREDNER, der schon 1832 festhielt, der „Anstoß" zu einer „Sichtung der schriftlichen Urkunden" sei von den im Anfang des 2. Jh. „hervorbrechenden Ketzereien" ausgegangen; diese Sichtung habe dann in der 2. Hälfte des 2. Jh. die „rechtgläubige Kirche" gemacht, die als „Kanon" aufstellte: „als rein christliche Urkunden der kirchlichen Lehre können nur die apostolischen Schriften Geltung haben"[7]. Gegen diese Sicht der Entstehung des Kanons wandte sich 1888 ZAHN: „Seit mehr als hundert Jahren hat sich unter denjenigen protestantischen Theologen, welche mit dem Kirchenglauben … verfallen waren, die Vorstellung befestigt, daß der Kanon des NT's nach der Mitte des 2. Jahrhunderts entstanden sei", und zwar „im Gegensatz zu den gnostischen Parteien" und im „Kampf mit dem Montanismus"; man meine, „um 140-160 (bei Justin) gab es noch keinen Kanon …, um 180-190 hatte die Kirche einen Kanon"; „was anfangs einige Neuerer … behaupteten, versuchte man später zusammenhängender zu beweisen. Heute wird es, bald mit der überlegenen Miene des gewiegten Geschichtskenners, bald in dem marktschreierischen Ton des Demagogen, der seinem Pöbel zu imponieren weiß, als ausgemachte Thatsache allen Untersuchungen zu Grunde gelegt"[8]. Zahn verunglimpft hier andere, ohne ihre Namen zu nennen, doch zweifellos denkt er an Overbeck und Harnack[9].

---

5. J.S. SEMLER, *Abhandlung von freier Untersuchung des Canons*, 4 Bde, Halle, Hemmerde, 1771-1775, I, pp. 15f.

6. *Ibid.*, I, p. 19.

7. So K.A. CREDNER, *Ansehen und Gebrauch der neutestamentlichen Schriften in den beiden ersten Jahrhunderten*, in DERS., *Beiträge zur Einleitung in die biblischen Schriften*, Bd. 1, Halle, Verlag der Buchhandlung des Waisenhauses, 1832, pp. 1-91, bes. pp. 83-84. Im selben Verlag erschien 1838 Bd. 2 der *Beiträge*, 1847 DERS., *Zur Geschichte des Kanons*. Posthum gab G. VOLKMAR heraus: K.A. CREDNER, *Geschichte des Neutestamentlichen Kanon*, Berlin, Georg Reimer 1860.

8. T. ZAHN, *Geschichte des Neutestamentlichen Kanons. Bd. 1: Das Neue Testament vor Origenes*. 1. Hälfte, Erlangen, Deichert, 1888, 435-436.

9. Nicht umsonst reagiert darauf A. HARNACK, *Das Neue Testament um das Jahr 200. Theodor Zahn's Geschichte des neutestamentlichen Kanons … geprüft*, Freiburg, Mohr, 1889. A. JÜLICHER stellt in seiner Rezension der beiden Bücher (*TLZ* 14 [1889] 163-171) fest: „Daß der Hauptbegriff, eben der des neutestamentl. Kanons, bei Zahn bald alles, bald nichts bedeutet, daß er bald nur kirchliche Vorlesebücher … darunter versteht, bald

II. Der Streit zwischen Overbeck und Harnack über die Entstehung des Kanons

In drei Punkten stimmten Harnack und Overbeck überein: (1) Es gab zur Zeit Justins noch keinen neutestamentlichen Kanon; (2) dieser kam erst in der 2. Hälfte des 2. Jh. im Kampf gegen Gnosis und Montanismus zustande; (3) bei Irenäus und Tertullian galt für den Kanon allein das historische Prinzip der apostolischen Herkunft seiner Bestandteile. Darüber hinaus meint Harnack in 1879, das aus dem „9. Decennium" des 2. Jh. stammende muratorische Fragment repräsentiere „unzweifelhaft eine ältere Stufe der Ansichten vom neutestamentlichen Kanon" als Irenäus und Tertullian[10]. Man habe „noch ein Bewusstsein davon ... (gehabt), dass die Kirche am Kanon producire"[11]. Noch habe „das Prinzip der Apostolicität des Kanons durchaus nicht unbedingt" gegolten[12], es sei „insbesondere durch das Prinzip der Katholicität der aufzunehmenden Schriften zweifach beschränkt (worden), sofern diese sowohl auf die Katholicität ihrer ... Adresse als auf die ihres Inhalts geprüft wurden. Daher ... (habe) weder alles Apostolische als solches als kanonisch (gegolten), noch ... (sei) Nichtapostolisches streng aus dem Kanon ausgeschlossen (gewesen) ... Nur gegen gewisse Ansprüche des Montanismus ... (sei) der Kanon geschlossen (gewesen), sonst noch offen ... Noch ... (sei) ihm formelle Gleichstellung mit dem A.T. nicht zu Theil geworden..., Inspiration noch nicht zugesprochen ...".

Angesichts der „großen Dunkelheit" in vielen Fragen der Geschichte der alten Kirche gilt bei Overbeck grundsätzlich „für die Forschung als

---

inspirirte Werke von Aposteln, von trugloser Wahrheit und unverbrüchlicher Auctorität, ..., daß sonach Zahn trotz alle Gelehrsamkeit und allen Scharfsinns gar nicht im Stande ist, eine quellenmäßige Geschichte des neutestl. Kanons zu schreiben, das hat Harnack über allen Streit erhoben" (167). Harnack selbst hält 1914 (*Entstehung* [Anm. 36]) zwar fest, nach dem „landläufige(n) Urteil" habe „Zahn, der gelehrteste Kritiker, ... bewiesen, daß das N.T. bereits am Ende des apostolischen Zeitalters um das J. 100 entstanden ist; die sogenannten Kritiker aber von sehr viel geringerer Gelehrsamkeit rücken die Entstehung des N.T.s um ein Jahrhundert herunter" (145), doch dann versichert er, er wolle nicht „einen Streit wieder auf(zu)nehmen, der vor Jahrzehnten zwischen Zahn und ... (ihm) in allzu temperamentvoller Weise geführt worden ist", und er ist sich sicher, die Differenz von 100 Jahren zwischen Zahn und den anderen Kritikern würde sehr viel geringer, „wenn Zahn sich entschließen würde, als punctum saliens nicht ‚die Lektion' der einzelnen Schriften, sondern die völlige Gleichstellung einer neuen Sammlung mit dem A.T. aufzustellen" (152).

10. HARNACK, *Das Muratorische Fragment* (Anm. 1), p. 403.
11. *Ibid.*, p. 405.
12. Ab hier folge ich OVERBECKS (Anm. 1, p. 74) präziser Zusammenfassung der Thesen Harnacks.

methodischer Grundsatz ..., das Unbekannte zunächst aus dem Bekannten zu erschliessen, im vorliegenden Falle also bei den vollkommen hellen Thatsachen über den Bestand und die Geltung des neutestamentlichen Kanons, wie sie bei ... (Irenäus und Tertullian) am Ende des zweiten Jahrhunderts vorliegen, einzusetzen und von da zurückzuschliessen"[13]. Näherhin überprüft Overbeck die Thesen Harnacks in zwei Schritten. Zunächst (a) fragt er, „ob die älteste Phase der Geschichte des Kanons, welche Harnack aus dem muratorischen Fragment erschliesst, überhaupt Wahrscheinlichkeit hat", dann (b) untersucht er „die Begründung dieser Phase in der Interpretation des Fragments"[14].

(a) Overbecks „erster Einwand" ist „die Schwierigkeit, den von Harnack aus dem muratorischen Fragment herausgedeuteten Standpunkt als den dem Irenäus und Tertullian unmittelbar vorausgegangenen sich vorzustellen"[15]. Wäre Harnack im Recht, dann müßten bei Irenäus und Tertullian „Nachwirkungen" der von ihm postulierten früheren Prinzipien „nachzuweisen sein"[16]. Diesen Nachweis versuche Harnack erst gar nicht, da es auch für ihn bei Irenäus und Tertullian „kein anderes Prinzip der Zusammensetzung des Kanons (gibt) ... als das der apostolischen Herkunft seiner Bestandtheile"[17].

Als „zweites" wendet Overbeck gegen Harnack ein, es sei „ein Grundirrthum" der „Abhandlung ..., dass sie Sätze, welche implicite in der Kanonisirung der apostolischen Schriften lagen, erst als das Ergebniss einer Art von Entwickelung des Begriffs der Kanonicität betrachtet"[18]. So sei gegen Harnacks These, erst im 3. Jh. und noch nicht im 2. Jh. werde das NT dem AT gleichgestellt und wie jenes für inspiriert gehalten, zu fragen: „Allein was konnte denn die Schriften der Apostel über alle übrige christliche Litteratur erheben ... (im 2. Jh.) Anderes heissen, als sie in die Sphäre versetzen, in welcher die Schriften des A.T. und die Worte Christi sich befanden und ihnen denselben Ursprung zusprechen?"[19]. Gegen Harnacks Meinung, es habe auf der frühesten Stufe der Kanonisierung „eine Sammlung apostolischer Schriften (gegeben), welche Schriften dieses Ursprungs eventuell ausschloss, dagegen das Nichtapostolische eventuell aufnahm"[20], sei zu bedenken, daß gerade damals eine derartige Unterscheidung sehr fern gelegen habe; „denn auf dem

13. OVERBECK, *Kanon* (Anm. 1), p. 72.
14. *Ibid.*, p. 73.
15. *Ibid.*, pp. 75f.
16. *Ibid.*, p. 75.
17. *Ibid.*, pp. 74f.
18. *Ibid.*, p. 76.
19. *Ibid.*, p. 76.
20. *Ibid.*, p. 76.

Glauben an den unbedingten und einzigartigen Werth des Apostolischen beruhte überhaupt das ganze Unternehmen, es als Damm der Gnosis und dem Montanismus entgegenzusetzen"[21]. Und eben in dieser Zeit sei „die Katholicität des Kanons" nicht, wie Harnack meint, als Kriterium vom „kirchliche(n) … Selbstbewusstsein" angewendet worden, sondern sie sei bereits vorausgesetzt worden[22]. Gegen Harnacks doppeltes Prinzip der Katholizität des Inhalts und der Adresse wendet Overbeck Folgendes ein. Einmal beweise Tertullians „Traditionstheorie", daß die „*Katholicität des Inhalts* der apostolischen Schriften" ursprünglich nicht „als *zweites Prinzip* neben der(en) Apostolicität" gehandhabt wurde; wenn Tertullian die ntl. Schriften „unter den Schutz einer bestimmt umgrenzten Interpretation" durch die regula fidei stellt, so sei das „aus der Noth hervorgegangen …, eine bisher blinde Voraussetzung durch eine äusserliche Auskunft gegen Zweifel sicher zu stellen"[23]. Gegen die Bedeutung, die Harnack der *Katholizität der Adresse* zuschreibt, sprächen „die Traditionstheorie des Irenäus" und „die Geschichte der Reception der katholischen Briefe"; Irenäus konstruiere „den Begriff der Katholicität aus *Local*traditionen", das setze „schwerlich eine Zeit voraus, die sich eben erst an der ursprünglich localen Bestimmung apostolischer Schriften gestossen hätte"; die mühsame Anerkennung der „sogenannt katholischen Briefe" aber würde „unbegreiflich", wenn „*ursprünglich* die Katholicität der Bestimmung einer apostolischen Schrift ausdrücklich unter den Bedingungen ihrer Kanonisirung gezählt" worden wäre[24].

(b) An Harnacks Gebrauch des *muratorischen Fragments* kritisiert Overbeck, dieser habe die „Einzigartigkeit dieses Stücks in der altkirchlichen Litteratur"[25] und „die Dunkelheit … (seines) Ursprungs" nicht gebührend beachtet und sei bei dessen „Interpretation" keineswegs dem „allgemeinen methodischen Grundsatz" gefolgt, „sich innerhalb der Grenzen des sonst Bekannten zu halten und Neuheiten… eher auszuweichen als sie aufzusuchen"[26]. Wenn Harnack meint, in diesem Fragment werde zwischen dem alt- und neutestamentlichen Kanon unterschieden, so sei „das gelegentliche Vorkommen der Bezeichnung *scriptura* für das A.T. … und der Bezeichnung *apostoli* für die Schriften der neuen Sammlung … (nicht) ein beim Fragmentisten charakteristischer und stehender Sprachgebrauch"[27]. Auch Harnacks These, „dass dem

21. *Ibid.*, p. 79.
22. *Ibid.*, p. 79.
23. *Ibid.*, p. 81.
24. *Ibid.*, p. 83.
25. *Ibid.*, p. 96.
26. *Ibid.*, p. 99.
27. *Ibid.*, p. 99.

Fragmentisten zufolge weder das Apostolische als solches Anspruch auf
Aufnahme in den Kanon hat, noch Nichtapostolisches daraus als solches
ausgeschlossen ist"[28], lasse sich nicht halten; denn „der Abschnitt des
Fragments über die Apocalypsen ["als Apokalypsen nehmen wir nur die
des Johannes und die des Petrus an"] ... (beweise), dass für seinen Verfasser das Princip der Apostolicität des Kanons unbedingt, nämlich auch
die Kanonicität alles Apostolischen gilt"[29]. Overbeck beschließt seine
Kritik an Harnack mit den Worten: „So kann ich denn im ganzen Fragment keinen Grund entdecken, dem Verfasser andere als die gemein-
katholischen Ansichten über die Apostolicität des Kanons unterzule-
gen"[30].

Harnack erklärte 1885, Overbecks Einwürfe hätten ihn beeindruckt;
deshalb habe er „das Fragment und die ... aus ihm gezogenen Schlüsse
hier fast ganz bei Seite" gelassen[31]. Von einer Katholizität der Adresse
und des Inhalts spricht Harnack nicht mehr, wohl aber davon, daß man
„im Kampf mit Marcion und den Gnostikern"[32] „alles Apostolische
sammeln" mußte[33]. Irenäus und Tertullian hätten in der Tat „Alles, was
... als apostolisch galt, für kanonisch gehalten", das muratorische Fragment jedoch – und das richtet sich gegen Overbeck – sei nicht so eindeutig; „darin aber stimm(t)en die drei ... überein": „die apostolische
regula fidei (sei) die letzte Instanz" bei der Frage, „ob eine Schrift wirklich apostolisch ist oder nicht"[34].

III. DIE NACHGESCHICHTE DES STREITS
ZWISCHEN OVERBECK UND HARNACK

Die Nachgeschichte des Streites zwischen Overbeck und Harnack ist
verwirrend und einfach zugleich. Gegen Ende des 19. Jh. stimmten kritische Neutestamentler wie Holtzmann und Jülicher nicht Harnack oder
auch Zahn zu, sondern Overbeck[35], doch im 20. Jh. spielen die Ansich-

---

28. *Ibid.*, p. 109.
29. *Ibid.*, p. 114.
30. *Ibid.*, p. 141.
31. A. HARNACK, *Lehrbuch der Dogmengeschichte*, Bd. 1, Tübingen, Mohr, 1885, p. 379, Anm. 2.
32. *Ibid.*, p. 380.
33. *Ibid.*, p. 381.
34. *Ibid.*, p. 389, Anm. 1.
35. H.J. HOLTZMANN, *Lehrbuch der historisch-kritischen Einleitung in das Neue Testament*, Freiburg i.B., Mohr, ³1892, p. 118; A. JÜLICHER, *Einleitung in das Neue Testament*, Freiburg i.B., Leipzig, Mohr, 1894, p. 273.

ten Harnacks eine große Rolle, besonders in der Form, wie er sie 1914 noch einmal vortrug[36]. Wie 1885 betont er, man habe „das *alte* (apostolische) Gut" mit dem „Maßstab" der regula fidei „aus der Fülle der sich aufdrängenden, irreführenden Literatur" ausgeschieden, und er identifiziert es wieder wie 1879 mit den „rechtgläubigen (katholischen) Schriften". Wie stark die Sicht Harnacks bis in die jüngste Zeit wirkt, das zeigt sich bei SCHNELLE, der 1999 folgende „Kriterien der Kanonsbildung" nennt: Apostolizität, regula fidei sowie Gebrauch und Anerkennung in allen Kirchengebieten[37].

Fast vergessen aber ist Overbecks Sicht und sein Streit mit Harnack. Leider! Denn hinter diesem Streit steht die bedenkenswerte Frage, ob auch der Inhalt einer Schrift (Katholizität, regula fidei) über ihre Zugehörigkeit zum ntl. Kanon entschieden hat oder allein ihre Abfassung durch einen Apostel oder Apostelschüler. Im ersten Fall wären alle Schriften des NT von gleichem Wert und müßten entsprechend behandelt werden, im zweiten Fall wäre es möglich, die Schriften des NT unterschiedlich zu gewichten – was faktisch seit der Reformation ja auch immer wieder geschehen ist und geschieht.

Rudolf-Harbig-Weg 23   Martin RESE
D - 48149 Münster/Westf.

---

36. A. VON HARNACK, *Die Entstehung des Neuen Testaments und die wichtigsten Folgen der neuen Schöpfung*, Leipzig, Hinrichs, 1914, p. 14.

37. U. SCHNELLE, *Einleitung in das Neue Testament* (UTB, 1830), Göttingen, Vandenhoeck & Ruprecht, 1994, p. 412; [3]1999, p. 371.

CANONICAL COHERENCE
IN READING ISRAEL'S SCRIPTURES WITH A SEQUEL

Canonicity is a way of valuing time. It questions whether the present can have meaning in and of itself. In *A la recherche du temps perdu* Proust plays on a double meaning of *temps perdu* in the sense of (1) time that is squandered and (2) the past that is beyond recuperation. Memory of the past, however, halts the squandering of time in the present. This in turn involves a double evaluation of the past. On the one hand, something has happened in the past to make things go wrong for the present – the "fall" in traditional Christian theology. Human beings so participate in evil that we cannot make the present right. "The wall cannot climb itself. How bad is it? ... God's envoy is reviled as in league with Beelzebul, and the city of the great king kills the prophets and those who are sent to it"[1]. On the other hand, something has happened in the past to provide resources for the redemption of the present – redemptive history in Christian theology.

Heidegger attributed equal importance to the future, in the anticipation of death, as having the potential to give significance to time. The future liberates existence by anticipatory resoluteness. This anticipatory resoluteness leads to taking action directed toward determining what is to be[2]. Something of these perspectives of Proust and Heidegger are reflected in canonicity. That is, canonicity valorizes the past and projects a future with the potential of giving meaning to the present. In its history the church has so valorized the Bible as to attribute to it the unique capacity for determining who human beings are and what our destiny is. The valorization of the past makes the historical context of biblical texts important. But the valorization of the past and the projection of a future with potential to give meaning to the present also liberate biblical texts for new contexts[3]. In fact, only when the Bible is so liberated to speak to

---

1. D. ALLISON, *Jesus of Nazareth: Millenarian Prophet*, Minneapolis, Fortress, 1998, p. 218.

2. M. HEIDEGGER, *Being and Time*, London, SCM, 1962, pp. 349-423: "This phenomenon has the unity of a future which makes present in the process of having been" (p. 374).

3. T. OGLETREE describes this valorization of the Bible phenomenologically rather than as an issue of authority. In history biblical texts prove persuasive over and over like Hans Georg Gadamer's "classical" texts (*The Use of the Bible in Christian Ethics*, Philadelphia, Fortress, 1983, p. 2). See H. KARPP, *Schrift, Geist und Wort Gottes: Geltung und Wirkung der Bibel in der Geschichte der Kirche – von der alten Kirche bis zum Ausgang*

contemporary life, is it freed from purely antiquarian interests and valorized for the present.

Of course, the canon itself is also problematic. The development of the canon was at least partially the consequence of authoritarian power struggles[4]. So also the continuing struggle over the Bible has been at least partially the consequence of authoritarian power struggles, and thus canon has meant authoritarianism rather than valorization. Henning Graf Reventlow has shown how the battle over the authority of the Bible in eighteenth century England was in partnership with political parties. High Church Tories used the Bible to support their authority to determine internal affairs of the church independent of the monarchy. Whig ideologues advanced their biblical criticism – with immense sway on the development of modern biblical criticism – in order to repudiate the claims of Tories[5]. So canon and interpretation of canon have been parts of a process of determining who gets to tell whom what to do. But it is also the consequence of a process of valorization that is based on the church's concrete experiences of the Bible's power of persuasion[6]. To be canon means to be a part of what the past has valorized with potential for significance in the future. I side with what Karlfried Froehlich identifies as a functional rather than ontological canon[7], that is the actual function of scripture in human existence. Recognizing the function of historic valorization provides a hermeneutical perspective for biblical interpretation.

Following the order of books in the Masoretic Text, Jack Miles discerns a movement from narrative (stories about God and Israel) to speech (testimonies about God) to silence – the last ten books constituting a kind of twilight[8]. God's development comes to an end, and God's people revere an ossified deity.

---

der Reformationszeit, Darmstadt, Wissenschaftliche Buchgesellschaft, 1992, p. 1; T. FRETHEIM & K. FROEHLICH, *The Bible as the Word of God in a Postmodern Age*, Minneapolis, Fortress, 1998, p. 21.

4. See J. BARR, *Holy Scripture: Canon, Authority, Criticism*, Philadelphia, Westminster, 1983, pp. 57-58. Some of the power struggles were within Christianity. But controversy with Judaism and Islam also contributed to the development of Christian authoritarian uses of the Bible. See KARPP, *Schrift, Geist und Wort* (n. 3), pp. 64-66. J. BRIGHT attempts to rescue "authority" from "authoritarianism" (*The Authority of the Old Testament*, Nashville, Abingdon, 1967, pp. 15-58). But his argument is clearly grounded in the foundationalism of original authorial intention available through objective grammatico-historical research.

5. H. REVENTLOW, *The Authority of the Bible and the Rise of the Modern World*, Philadelphia, Fortress, 1985, pp. 328-334; BARR, *Holy Scripture* (n. 4), p. 33. With respect to similar struggles during the Middle Ages see KARPP, *Schrift, Geist und Wort* (n. 3), pp. 66-81.

6. See KARPP, *Schrift, Geist und Wort* (n. 3), p. 3.

7. FRETHEIM & FROEHLICH, *Bible as Word of God* (n. 3), p. 26.

8. J. MILES, *God: A Biography*, New York, Vintage, 1995, p. 11.

Hardly! For one thing both ancient Judaism and early Christianity grappled ardently with scripture in order to correlate their experience of God in the scriptures with the concrete realities in their own history, especially the destruction of the temple and the crucifixion of Jesus respectively. Harry Gamble makes the person of Jesus primary for early Christianity and the appeal to scripture secondary[9]. But this diachronic sequence is impossible because Jesus himself had already reflected on scripture and early Christianity came to an understanding of Jesus through its reflection on scripture. This reciprocity makes it inadequate to speak merely of Jesus as a Christian key to the Old Testament, because the Old Testament is equally a key to who Jesus is. The Jesus of early Christianity is a scripturally interpreted Jesus.

But what if the Jewish scriptures have a sequel? What if readers adopt a strategy of reading the New Testament in sequence with the books of the Masoretic Text or the Septuagint? Such a strategy raises the question of the relationship between the Old and New Testaments. The correlation between the two does not fit simple patterns (such as promise/fulfillment or type/antitype)[10]. The originals were not even written in the same language. Could Dostoyevsky's *The Brothers Karamazov* have an authorized sequel written in French[11]? But Marcion notwithstanding, the New Testament never existed independently from the Old Testament[12]. In fact, historically the New Testament was added on secondarily to the original scriptures of the early church contained in the Septuagint or the Hebrew or the Aramaic as the case may be.

There are three important ways in which the New Testament bears the character of a sequel. (1) Every book in the New Testament presupposes the characterization of God in the Old Testament, and thus none other than God fuses the two testaments[13]. (2) Virtually every book in the New

9. H. GAMBLE, *Christianity: Scripture and Canon*, in *The Holy Book in Comparative Perspective*, F. DENNY & R. TAYLOR (eds.), (Studies in Comparative Religion), Columbia, SC, University of South Carolina Press, 1985, pp. 36-62, esp. p. 37. Similarly, G. LINDBECK, *Postcritical Canonical Interpretation: Three Modes of Retrieval*, in C. SEITZ & K. GREENE-MCCREIGHT (eds.), *Theological Exegesis*. FS B. Childs, Grand Rapids, Eerdmans, 1999, pp. 26-51, esp. pp. 28-29, but see p. 30.

10. J. LEVENSON too facilely assumes the relationship between the two testaments to be promise/fulfillment; see his *The Hebrew Bible, the Old Testament, and Historical Criticism: Jews and Christians in Biblical Studies*, Louisville, Westminster John Knox, 1993, pp. 8-9.

11. Note a similar objection in R. ALTER, *The Art of Biblical Narrative*, New York: Basic Books, 1981, p. ix.

12. See H. VON CAMPENHAUSEN, *The Formation of the Christian Bible*, London, Black, 1972. On the importance of the Old Testament for the New see BARR, *Holy Scripture* (n. 4), pp. 11-14.

13. "The monotheism of the Old Testament is everywhere assumed", so B. CHILDS, *Biblical Theology of the Old and New Testaments. Theological Reflection on the Christian Bible*, Minneapolis, Fortress, 1992, p. 362. Similarly, K. KOCH, *Two Testaments –*

Testament presupposes the story of God's relationship with a chosen people from Abraham to the restoration after the exile, and this story is essential for the characterization of God[14]. The sequel presumes a continuation of the same story, and through the continuation, Israel's national story becomes universal. (3) Further, virtually every book in the New Testament quotes or alludes to the Old Testament explicitly recognizing it at times as scripture[15].

Both Jews and Christians read the Jewish scriptures with sequels, Jews with the Talmud and Christians with the New Testament. The combination of precursor and sequel is, in the words of Jon Levenson, "to some degree coherent and to some degree incoherent with *all* its recontextualizations – Jewish, Christian, and other"[16]. This creates a dialectic in which both precursor and sequel resonate back and forth with each other in a tensive interplay creating meaning beyond the independent meaning of either text. This tensive interplay is not merely a question of the retrospective of a sequel on Jewish scripture. Rather, Jewish scripture already points beyond itself in expectation of such things as an ideal Davidic king, an establishment of a new covenant, a new Exodus, and the blessing of all the nations in the Abrahamic covenant[17]. On the

One Bible. New Trends in Biblical Theology, in *Bangalore Theological Forum* 28 (1996) 38-58. Koch emphasizes the process of canonization and takes creation and monotheism, salvific history, and the election of one people of God as cases in point. With emphasis also on the traditio-historical process of canonization and on the revelation of God see H. GESE, *Tradition and Biblical Theology*, in D. KNIGHT (ed.), *Tradition and Theology in the Old Testament*, Philadelphia, Fortress, 1977, pp. 301-326. Contra Gese, CHILDS points out that the New Testament is not a redactional layer on the Old Testament; see his *Biblical Theology* (above), p. 76.

14. On narrative as a source of characterization of God see CHILDS, *Biblical Theology* (n. 13), pp. 352-354. As is well known, 1-3 John contain no quotations. 1 John presumes that readers know the story of Cain beyond the brief allusion in 3:12. *Hilasmos* (2,2; 4,10) obviously presupposes the LXX (F. BÜSCHEL, art. *hilasmos, TDNT*, vol. 3, pp. 317-318). 2 John presumes the identity of God as Father and identifies Jesus derivatively from this God (v. 3). 3 John goes no further than to introduce God with the presumption that readers know who this God is.

15. MILES has it all wrong when he says that as a new religion early Christianity had few sacred traditions to preserve (*God* [n. 8], p. 17). *Early* Christianity considered itself an old religion, that is, the continuation of the story of the God of Abraham and Sarah, and it devoted itself passionately to preserve those traditions within a new vision of reality.

16. LEVENSON, *Hebrew Bible* (n. 10), p. 16. On the perils for both Christians and Jews of reading with sequels see pp. 29-30, 39. On the other hand, R. CLEMENTS shows how early Jewish and early Christian uses of prophecy were extensions of consistent patterns of doom followed by hope which were imposed on diversity in prophecy (*Patterns in the Prophetic Canon*, in W. COATS & B. LONG [eds.], *Canon and Authority. Essays in Old Testament Religion and Theology*, Philadelphia, Fortress, 1977, pp. 42-55).

17. G. VON RAD declares that in the Old Testament "expectation keeps mounting up to vast proportions" (*Old Testament Theology. The Theology of Israel's Prophetic Traditions*, New York, Harper & Row, 1965, vol. 2, p. 321). J. DUNN speaks of a "continuity of living tradition"; see his *Levels of Canonical Authority*, in *Horizons in Biblical Theology* 4 (1982) 13-60, esp. p. 28.

Christian side, the interplay with the Old Testament gives the New Testament the character of a sequel – authorized or not – and as is the case with all sequels, the continuing story radically alters the one that terminates with the Hebrew and Aramaic texts. Readers can see the radical alteration of the story on a very explicit level in Luke 24 where the risen Jesus opens the minds of his disciples to understand scripture anew. As the interpretation of explicit texts in Acts shows, this goes so far as a modicum of rewriting the scriptures[18]. So religious traditions that have assimilated Israel's scriptures discern the character of God in scripture in quite different ways from Jack Miles.

My attempt to demonstrate the unity of the two testaments would be a gigantic falsification if I were to ignore the tensions created by adding a sequel. On the one hand, there is the problem of what Harold Bloom calls "a lie against time"[19]. In a chronologically later period, the New Testament claims a revised understanding of old texts as the meaning of those texts, a meaning that they did not have in earlier settings. On the other hand, there is the problem of tensive points of view, not the least of which is Paul's view of scripture. Paul can pose strong tensions with texts from the Old Testament (e.g. Rom 10,5). These tensions are part of what makes interpretation a constant task for Christianity. In spite of the tensions, however, there is unity is assuming continuity in the character of God. To state this in terms of the Marcionite controversy, God the creator is also God the redeemer, and for all the Christian debt to Judaism, the Old Testament ultimately is also a genuinely Christian book[20].

A modern ideological issue begs me to comment on terminology. In previous paragraphs, I use both Masoretic Text and Old Testament. In some circles the term "Old Testament" has come under strong critique with the presumption that it represents Christian triumphalism over Judaism[21]. The charge is that this terminology in itself implies that the old is antiquated and the new supersedes it.

18. R. BRAWLEY, *Text to Text Pours Forth Speech: Voices of Scripture in Luke-Acts* (Indiana Studies in Biblical Literature), Bloomington, IN, Indiana University Press, 1995. Paul "rewrites" the scriptures, e.g., 2 Cor 3:12-13; Rom 10:6-8. This position is altogether different from Marcion and the Epistle of Barnabas who take the new to be without precursor.

19. H. BLOOM, *The Anxiety of Influence: A Theory of Poetry*, Oxford, Oxford University Press, 1975, pp. 14-16, 141-148; ID., *A Map of Misreading*, Oxford, Oxford University Press, 1975, pp. 74, 84, 95-104; ID., *Poetry and Repression: Revisionism from Blake to Stevens*, New York, Yale University Press, 1976, pp. 16-20; ID., *Agon: Towards a Theory of Revisionism*, Oxford, Oxford University Press, 1982, pp. 135-137.

20. B. CHILDS, *On Reclaiming the Bible for Christian Theology*, in C. BRAATEN & R. JENSON (eds.), *Reclaiming the Bible for the Church*, Grand Rapids, Eerdmans, 1995, pp. 1-17, esp. p. 12; KARPP, *Schrift, Geist und Wort* (n. 3), pp. 22, 25.

21. L. GASTON calls the terminology Old and New Testament "misleading", indicating that "Old" means obsolete and "New" superseding (*Paul and the Torah*, Vancouver,

I do not accept the premise that the term old insinuates supersession. But for those who do, a popular alternative is "Hebrew Bible". Unfortunately, this is not without problems. (1) Small portions of Israel's scriptures are written in Aramaic. It is slightly disingenuous to call this a Hebrew Bible. (2) What is more, at times the Hebrew of the Masoretic Text is uncertain, and textual criticism of the Masoretic Text sometimes appropriates readings that derive from versions in such languages as Aramaic, Greek, Syriac, Latin, Coptic, and Ethiopic. It is slightly disingenuous to call this a Hebrew Bible. (3) Though it consists of Jewish literature, the scripture that early Christianity appropriated varies from the Jewish scriptures in such matters as sequence and what is included. Thus the composition of the Christian Old Testament is a product of Christian deliberation rather than simply Jewish determination. Most of the New Testament makes reference not to a Hebrew version but to the Greek Septuagint, some of the contents of which differ from the Masoretic Text. Thus, the Christian Old Testament is not identical to the Masoretic Text[22]. The scripture (ἡ γραφή) that the New Testament presupposes is hardly a Hebrew Bible. (4) Hebrew Bible is a contemporary construct that is dissonant for both Jews and Christians. (5) The terminology Hebrew Bible implies that the Masoretic Text is autonomous, and it does not reflect the strategy to read this portion of scripture with a sequel. It is

University of British Columbia Press, 1987, pp. 4, 151). To say that the terms are misleading depends, of course, on what one takes the terms to mean. As references to an original collection of documents to which a sequel is added, I do not take the terms to be misleading. Attempts such as Gaston's to preserve the integrity of Israel's scriptures are the opposite of earlier attempts in Germany to dissociate the two Testaments on the basis of a negative evaluation of Israel's religion including F. SCHLEIERMACHER, *The Christian Faith*, Edinburgh, Clark, 1928, pp. 60-62: "... the Old Testament is ... but the husk or wrapping of its prophecy, and ... whatever is most definitely Jewish has least value" (p. 62), and A. VON HARNACK, *Marcion: The Gospel of the Alien God*, Durham, NC, Labyrinth, 1990 (German orig. 1924), pp. 134-138: "The rejection of the Old Testament in the second century was a mistake which the great church rightly avoided; to maintain it in the sixteenth century was a fate from which the Reformation was not yet able to escape; but still to preserve it in Protestantism as a canonical document since the nineteenth century is the consequence of a religious and ecclesiastical crippling" (p. 134).

22. CHILDS, *Biblical Theology* (n. 13), p. 74; GAMBLE, *Christianity* (n. 9), p. 38; R. RENDTORFF, *Zur Bedeutung des Kanons für eine Theologie des Alten Testaments*, in H.G. GEYER, *et al.* (eds.), *"Wenn nicht jetzt, wann dann?"*. FS H.-J. Kraus, Neukirchen, Neukirchener Verlag, 1983, pp. 3-11, esp. p. 11. P. STUHLMACHER observes that the terminology "Hebrew Bible" excludes the LXX as a decisive element in the canonical process (*Der Kanon und seine Auslegung*, in C. LANDMESSER, H.-J. ECKSTEIN, H. LICHTENBERGER (eds.), *Jesus Christus als die Mitte der Schrift. Studien zur Hermeneutik des Evangeliums* [BZNT 86], Berlin, de Gruyter, 1997, pp. 263-290, esp. pp. 271-273); ID., *Die Mitte der Schrift – biblisch-theologisch betrachtet*, in K. ALAND & S. MEUER (eds.), *Wissenschaft und Kirche*. FS E. Lohse (Texte und Arbeiten zur Bibel), Bielefeld, Luther-Verlag, 1989, pp. 29-56, esp. pp. 30-32.

more than slightly disingenuous for Christians to imply that the precursor of the New Testament is autonomous and then proceed to read that precursor with a sequel. (6) The Old Testament is not merely preparatory for the New but constitutive for it[23]. *Early* Christianity never existed without scriptures but originated as a particular way of interpreting Jewish scriptures[24] that over the first two Christian centuries included binding a two-fold canon *together* – Old Testament and New Testament.

An additional issue of terminology is the use in some circles of "Christian Bible" or "Christian Scriptures" to refer to the New Testament. After the historical process of canonization, Christians have defined their Bible almost universally as the Old and New Testaments together[25]. Referring to the New Testament as the Christian Bible falsifies both the historical development of and the practical function of the canon in Christianity.

Is the terminology Old Testament after all supersessionist? True, many apologists in church history, including the Gospel of John and Hebrews, have attempted to assert the superiority of Jesus over Moses in such a way as to imply supersessionism. Similarly, the Old Testament has been falsified as embodying legalism and the New equally falsified as embodying love in a supersessionist fashion. On the other hand, it is only in our contemporary consumer society where new cars and new fashions supersede older ones that the new displaces the old. The terminology of old and new covenant derives conspicuously from the Old Testament itself, that is, Jer 31,31, a text picked up by both Paul and Hebrews and alluded to in the Lucan and Pauline Last Supper traditions. The New Testament itself values what is old – the venerable traditions of the forebears. Supersessionism is Marcionite. If there is a triumphalistic way in which the New Testament supersedes the Old, it cuts itself off from the Old like Marcion's canon.

Not only does the New Testament presuppose the characterization of God in its precursor, it also presupposes the functional canonicity of the Old Testament. In fact, historically, the Christian canon was originally the Old Testament. Some form of what we call the Masoretic Text, or the Septuagint, or the Targums as the case may be, was for the New Testament *the scripture* (ἡ γραφή)[26]. I would argue that even Hebrews is

---

23. "The Old is understood by its relation to the New, but the New is incomprehensible apart from the Old" (CHILDS, *Biblical Theology* [n. 13], p. 77). See KARPP, *Schrift, Geist und Wort* (n. 3), p. 11.

24. J. BARTON, *People of the Book? The Authority of the Bible in Christianity*, London, SPCK, 1988, p. 26.

25. See STUHLMACHER, *Mitte der Schrift* (n. 22), p. 30.

26. It is impossible to know the precise boundaries of the scriptures for the first century church. See BARR, *Holy Scripture* (n. 4), pp. 61-63.

not supersessionist in that it has to do with passing away of deficiencies but is built on interpreting christologically the way God spoke to the ancestors through the prophets (see Heb 1,1-2).

The Bible is very much a theocentric story. It is about God in relation to humanity and the world. With due regard for differences between the two Testaments, to assign to each their own distinct voices with respect to God is inadequate because the New Testament presumes the characterization of the God of the Old Testament as a part of its cultural repertoire. To reverse the perspective, the God of the Old Testament exercises a degree of control on the New Testament. Thus for example the God who is Creator is the God whose *Messiah* Jesus is. But the God whose Messiah Jesus is, is God the *Creator*. One can indeed speak of an early Christian assumption that the God of both Testaments is the same God, but only with the radically revisionary qualification that the God of the Old Testament is also the God who raised Jesus from the dead[27]. The voices of the two Testaments are indeed distinct, but they speak in a reciprocal relationship with each other so that they express more than either expresses independently of the other.

As canon, that is, as tradition valorized by the past with a vision of the future, the two-fold form of the Christian Bible reaches by extension to modern human beings. Canonicity means a presumption of coherence. The Christian canon of two Testaments means also that each Testament has its own coherence even as each is composed of plural voices – the coherence of a theocentric story before Jesus and its sequel after Jesus. This structure means also that multivocality lies underneath the presumption of unity between the two parts of the canon. Each testament speaks in its own voice even as its discrete voice interacts with another. At times, the two voices clash in contradiction. Thus canonical coherence means that voices can exercise a correcting function with respect to each other[28]. At other times, however, they reinforce, redirect, and extend each other.

5555 S. Woodlawn Avenue,   Robert L. BRAWLEY
Chicago, IL 60637
USA

---

27. See STUHLMACHER, *Mitte der Schrift* (n. 22), p. 53. In spite of the presumption in the New Testament that the God who raised Jesus is the God of the Old Testament, there are distinct emphases. See CHILDS, *Biblical Theology* (n. 13), pp. 351, 361, 363-368.
28. So DUNN, *Levels* (n. 17), p. 31.

BIBLOS GENESEOS
MT 1,1 VOM BUCH GENESIS HER GELESEN

Der zweite Kanonteil der zweieinen christlichen Bibel beginnt mit
Βίβλος γενέσεως Ἰησοῦ Χριστοῦ υἱοῦ Δαυὶδ υἱοῦ Ἀβραάμ[1]. Es besteht weitgehender Konsens darüber, dass der erste Vers des Matthäus-
evangeliums eine Überschrift und ein Metatext ist. Metatext deshalb,
weil darin nicht nur auf eine außersprachliche Wirklichkeit (die Person
Jesus), sondern auch auf etwas Sprachliches, einen Text, referiert wird:
Βίβλος[2].

I. BIBLOS GENESEOS – ÜBERSCHRIFT WOZU?

Der Konsens endet aber rasch bei der Frage, wozu Mt 1,1 genau die
„Überschrift" ist bzw. wie weit sich der Text erstreckt, auf den βίβλος
γενέσεως sich bezieht[3]. Mindestens zwei Alternativen stehen zur Wahl:
Βίβλος γενέσεως könnte sich nur auf die folgende Genealogie Jesu
und allenfalls noch auf die Kindheitsgeschichte Jesu, also seine „Abstammung" beziehen. Βίβλος γενέσεως könnte aber auch Überschrift
und Titel des ganzen Matthäusevangeliums sein, und geht man im Blick
auf den Kanon einen Schritt weiter, Titel des gesamten zweiten Kanon-
teils, also des Neuen Testaments.

In der bisherigen Forschungsdiskussion scheint dies die Hauptfrage
zu Mt 1,1 zu sein, und entsprechend gibt es Argumente und Vertreter für
beide Möglichkeiten. Diejenigen, die in Mt 1,1 eine Überschrift über die
Genealogie (bis 1,17), das erste Kapitel oder höchstens bis zum Ende
der Kindheitsgeschichten (etwa 2,23) sehen[4], führen im Wesentlichen

---

1. O. EISSFELDT, *Biblos geneseos*, in G. DELLING (ed.), *Gott und die Götter*. FS
E. Fascher, Berlin, Evangelische Verlagsanstalt, 1958, pp. 31-40; Nachdruck in R. SELL-
HEIM & F. MAASS (eds.), *Otto Eißfeldt: Kleine Schriften III*, Tübingen, Mohr (Siebeck),
1966, pp. 458-470, hat zwar den gleichen Einstieg, legt dann aber das Schwergewicht
ganz auf den alttestamentlichen Befund.
2. Vgl. dazu M. MAYORDOMO-MARIN, *Den Anfang hören. Leserorientierte Evange-
lienexegese am Beispiel von Matthäus 1-2* (FRLANT, 180), Göttingen, Vandenhoeck &
Ruprecht, 1998, p. 207.
3. Vgl. H. FRANKEMÖLLE, *Jahwe-Bund und Kirche Christi. Studien zur Form- und
Traditionsgeschichte des „Evangeliums" nach Matthäus* (NTA, 10), Münster, Aschendorff, ²1984 (¹1974), p. 360 (mit weiteren Literaturangaben).
4. Genannt seien hier unter anderem: G. SCHRENK, Art. βίβλος, βιβλίον, in *TWNT* 1
(1933) 613-620.615; M. LAMBERTZ, *Die Toledoth in Mt 1,1-17 und Lc 3,23bff.*, in

folgende Argumente an: Das Wort βίβλος könne neben einem ganzen Buch auch ein einzelnes Blatt oder Schriftstück sowie einen Teil eines Gesamtwerkes bezeichnen. Der Ausdruck γένεσις könne trotz seines weiten Bedeutungsspektrums mit „Ursprung, Abstammung, Geburt, Zeugung, Familienlinie, Generation" eingegrenzt werden. Damit ist man auf die folgende Genealogie verwiesen und kommt zu der Übersetzung „Stammbaum" für βίβλος γενέσεως (so die Einheitsübersetzung[5]). Unter der Annahme, dass Mt 1,1 in der Gestaltung von Mk 1,1 beeinflusst ist, fällt das Fehlen des Titels „Sohn Gottes" auf. Die Nennung von David und Abraham zeige, dass Mt 1,1 „streng auf die folgende Genealogie bezogen ist"[6]. Dies könne auch daran abgelesen werden, dass Mt 1,18 neu anhebe mit „Die Geburt (γένεσις) Jesu Christi aber geschah so" und damit das Wort γένεσις wiederhole[7].

Für die gegenteilige Anschauung, dass mit Mt 1,1 das ganze Evangelium überschrieben ist[8], kann ebenfalls bei den Einzelbegriffen der Wendung βίβλος γενέσεως angesetzt werden. Bei βίβλος ist zunächst an

H. KUSCH (ed.), *Festschrift Franz Dornseiff*, Leipzig, Bibliographisches Institut, 1953, pp. 201-225; W.B. TATUM, *„The Origin of Jesus Messiah" (Matt 1:1, 18a): Matthew's Use of the Infancy Traditions*, in JBL 96 (1977) 523-535; U. LUZ, *Das Evangelium nach Matthäus, Teilband 1, Mt 1-7* (EKK-NT, 1), Zürich – Einsiedeln – Köln, Benziger; Neukirchen-Vluyn, Neukirchener, 1985, p. 88; J. GNILKA, *Das Matthäusevangelium. 1. Teil*, Freiburg, Herder, 1986, p. 7 (dort weitere Literaturangaben); G.N. STANTON, *Matthew: βίβλος, εὐαγγέλιον, or βίος*, in F. VAN SEGBROECK et al. (eds.), *The Four Gospels 1992*. FS Frans Neirynck (BETL, 100), Leuven, Peeters, 1992, pp. 1187-1201; R.E. BROWN, *The Birth of the Messiah*, New York et al., Doubleday, 1993, pp. 58-59.583-586; J. NOLLAND, *What kind of Genesis do we have in Matt 1.1?*, in NTS 42 (1996) 463-471, bes. 471 (Lit.). – Eine Sonderposition vertritt E. KRENTZ, der Mt 1,1 in Analogie zu Gen 5,1-6,8 als Abschnittsüberschrift für Mt 1,1-4,16 auffasst (*The Extent of Matthew's Prologue. Toward the Structure of the First Gospel*, in JBL 83 [1964] 409-414).

5. Das Problem dieser Übersetzung ist, dass für „Stammbaum" gewöhnlich γενεαλογία (1 Tim 1,4; Tit 3,9; vgl. auch Hebr 7,3.6; 1 Chr 5,1) verwendet wird. Ferner ist zu fragen, warum Matthäus für sein erstes Kapitel (oder wie weit man immer die Reichweite von βίβλος γενέσεως ansetzen will) eine Überschrift setzt, dann aber keine weiteren Überschriften bringt. Vgl. T. ZAHN, *Das Evangelium des Matthäus*, Leipzig, Deichert, [3]1910, pp. 39-40.

6. GNILKA, *Matthäusevangelium* (n. 4), p. 7.

7. Vgl. EISSFELDT, *Biblos geneseos* (n. 1), p. 36, beziehungsweise p. 465.

8. Vgl. unter anderem: ZAHN, *Matthäus* (n. 5), pp. 39-40; H.C. WAETJEN, *The Genealogy as the Key to the Gospel According to Matthew*, in JBL 95 (1976) 205-230.215; W.D. DAVIES & D.C. ALLISON, *A Critical and Exegetical Commentary on the Gospel According to Saint Matthew*. Vol. 1, *Introduction and Commentary on Matthew I-VII* (ICC), Edinburgh, T & T Clark, 1988, pp. 149-160; B. VAN ELDEREN, *The Significance of the Structure of Matthew 1*, in J. VARDAMAN & E.M. YAMAUCHI (eds.), *Chronos, Kairos, Christos*, Winona Lake, IN, Eisenbrauns, 1989, pp. 3-14, bes. p. 7; D. DORMEYER, *Mt 1,1 als Überschrift zur Gattung und Christologie des Matthäus-Evangeliums*, in F. VAN SEGBROECK et al. (eds.), *The Four Gospels* (n. 4), pp. 1361-1381; H. FRANKEMÖLLE, *Matthäus. Kommentar 1*, Düsseldorf, Patmos, 1994, pp. 128-130; MAYORDOMO-MARIN, *Anfang* (n. 2), pp. 206-217.

die einfachere Bedeutung „Buch" zu denken, zumal, wenn der Begriff am Anfang eines solchen steht[9]. Es gibt eine Reihe von Analogien dafür, dass Werke mit βίβλος oder βιβλίον beginnen und sich dieser Begriff auf das Buch bezieht (vgl. Nah 1,1; Tob 1,1; Bar 1,1; vgl. Neh 1,1: λόγοι Νεεμια υἱοῦ Αχαλια)[10]. Ferner sei es nicht nachvollziehbar, weshalb Matthäus, der aus Mk 1,1 eine Überschrift kenne, *ohne* eine Überschrift mit einem „Stammbaum-Dokument" wie mit der Tür ins Haus falle. Schließlich sei auf Gen 11,27 und 25,19 zu verweisen, wo mit dem Begriff γενέσεις sowohl die Stammbäume als auch die Erzählungen über die Terach-Söhne Abram, Nahor und Haran sowie über den Abrahamssohn Isaak eröffnet werden[11]. Die Bedeutung von γένεσις ist damit nicht auf „Ursprung, Geburt etc." festgelegt, sondern das Spektrum kann bis „Dasein, Geschichte, Leben" reichen[12].

II. ÄNDERUNG DER FRAGERICHTUNG: VOM AUTOR ZUM LESER

Die Einzelbetrachtung der Begriffe βίβλος und γένεσις bleibt unbefriedigend und führt letztlich nicht weiter. Die Frage nach der „Reichweite" der Überschrift Mt 1,1 kann so nicht beantwortet werden – und schließlich ist das auch (trotz der intensiven Diskussion) nicht das Kernproblem. Eine derartige Untersuchungsrichtung zeigt die Zentriertheit vieler bisheriger Ansätze auf die Erhebung der Intention des (historischen) Autors. Doch selbst wenn man sicher herausfinden könnte, was genau Matthäus mit βίβλος γενέσεως meinte, hätte man damit die Wendung und die Überschrift noch nicht verstanden.

Weiterführend erscheint es daher, die Fragerichtung zu ändern und eine andere Perspektive einzunehmen: die des Lesers. Statt unmittelbar nach der Intention des *Autors* „Matthäus" zu suchen (und die mit *dem* Sinn des Textes schlechthin gleichzusetzen), soll nun nach dem Potential gefragt werden, das der *Text* seinen *Leserinnen und Lesern* an Verstehensmöglichkeiten eröffnet. Schon der metasprachliche Hinweis in Mt 1,1 auf ein Buch (βίβλος) als ein Schriftstück setzt einen Leser voraus und richtet sich an einen Leser. Dabei geht Mt 1,1 davon aus, dass dieser

9. Vgl. FRANKEMÖLLE, *Jahwe-Bund* (n. 3), pp. 362-364.
10. Siehe dazu DAVIES and ALLISON, *Matthew* (n. 8), p. 152.
11. Vgl. DORMEYER, *Mt 1,1* (n. 8), p. 1363. – Mit eben dieser Beobachtung, dass βίβλος γενέσεως in der Septuaginta sowohl eine Genealogie als auch die Geschichte eines Ahnen bezeichnen kann, wird gelegentlich argumentiert, dass Mt 1,1 sowohl Überschrift über das ganze Evangelium als auch über die unmittelbar folgende Genealogie sei (vgl. z.B. J.L. LEUBA, *Note exégétique sur Matthieu 1,1a*, in *RHPR* 22 [1942] 56-61).
12. Als Beispiele dafür führt FRANKEMÖLLE, *Jahwe-Bund* (n. 3), p. 363, u.a. Gen 6,9; 37,2; aber auch Weish 7,5; Jdt 12,18; Jak 1,23 an.

Leser einige Voraussetzungen erfüllt. Das beginnt schon bei den Namen „David" und „Abraham", die nicht erklärt werden – vielmehr wird das Wissen des Lesers über diese Personen abgerufen und zur Qualifikation der vorgestellten Hauptperson „Jesus Christus" verwendet. Es dürfte ein weiterer Konsenspunkt sein, dass Mt 1,1 (und auch die folgende Genealogie) einen hohen Verweischarakter auf den ersten Teil des christlichen Kanons, das Alte Testament, hat – und damit ist vorausgesetzt, dass der Leser seinen Bibelkanon intensiv kennt, Bezüge herstellen kann und Texte im Licht von anderen Texten lesen kann[13]. Für einen solchen Leser, der durch den Text selbst konstruiert ist, passiert bei der Lektüre von Mt 1,1 vor dem Hintergrund des Buches Genesis viel. *Das* gilt es wissenschaftlich zu reflektieren. Dabei geht es um einen „hermeneutischen Paradigmenwechsel"[14].

III. DER INTERTEXTUELLE RÜCKVERWEIS AUF GENESIS 2,4 UND 5,1

Die Genitivverbindung βίβλος γενέσεως kann zu ihrer Bedeutungsfindung nicht in ihre etymologischen Bestandteile getrennt werden. Im Rezeptionsvorgang werden immer größere syntaktische Einheiten erfasst. Damit kommt man nicht mehr hinter die von MAYORDOMO-MARIN formulierte Erkenntnis zurück, dass „βίβλος γενέσεως als Einheit ein deutlicher intertextueller Rückverweis auf die Septuagintafassung von Gen 2,4 und 5,1 ist und von dorther verstanden werden sollte"[15]. Nun

13. Der hier vorausgesetzte Leserbegriff geht – ohne literaturwissenschaftliche Theorien überstrapazieren zu wollen – in die Richtung dessen, was U. ECO unter „Modell-Leser" versteht (vgl. U. ECO, *Im Wald der Fiktionen. Sechs Streifzüge durch die Literatur*, München, dtv, ²1999, pp. 18-19).

14. Vgl. dazu programmatisch die methodischen Grundlagen in G. STEINS, *Die „Bindung Isaaks" im Kanon (Gen 22). Grundlagen und Programm einer kanonischintertextuellen Lektüre* (HBS, 20), Freiburg – Basel – Wien, Herder, 1999, pp. 84-102.86; und C. DOHMEN, *Die Bibel und ihre Auslegung*, München, Beck, 1998, pp. 99-102; vgl. DERS., *Vom vielfachen Schriftsinn. Möglichkeiten und Grenzen neuerer Zugänge zu biblischen Texten*, in T. STERNBERG (ed.), *Neue Formen der Schriftauslegung?* (QD, 140), Freiburg, Herder, 1992, pp. 13-74.36; ferner FRANKEMÖLLE, *Matthäus* (n. 8), p. 40.

15. MAYORDOMO-MARIN, *Anfang* (n. 2), p. 210. Er betont in Anm. 43, dass eine Suche in der CD-ROM-Fassung des Thesaurus Linguae Graecae keine weiteren Belege für die syntaktische Einheit βίβλος γενέσεως außerhalb der von Gen 2,4 und 5,1 beeinflussten Literatur ergeben hat. – Die Versuche, βίβλος γενέσεως als Übersetzung des rabbinischen Terminus ספר יוחסין aufzufassen, schildert und widerlegt M.D. JOHNSON, *The Purpose of the Biblical Genealogies*, Cambridge, University Press, 1969, pp. 147-149, und schließt, dass die Wendung βίβλος γενέσεως am besten als „reflection of the toledoth formula in Genesis, in either the Hebrew or Greek form, or both" anzusehen seien. – Insofern βίβλος γενέσεως als syntaktische Einheit zu werten ist, liegen die beiden Belege für γένεσις in Mt 1,1 und 1,18 auf verschiedenen Ebenen und können, ja sollten unterschiedlich übersetzt werden (mit DAVIES & ALLISON, *Matthew* [n. 8], p. 155; gegen LAMBERTZ, *Toledoth* [n. 4], p. 203, u.a.).

wurden die Bezüge zu den beiden Genesis-Stellen immer schon gesehen, ebenso die Tatsache, dass γένεσις das festgefügte Übersetzungsäquivalent zum hebräischen תולדות ist[16]. Jedoch wurden aus diesen Beobachtungen nur sehr vorsichtige Schlussfolgerungen gezogen[17], wenn man sich nicht nur auf die Nennung der Stellen beschränkte. Der Befund muss daher nochmals deutlicher aufgezeigt werden.

Die Wendung βίβλος γενέσεως begegnet in der Septuaginta in Gen 2,4 und 5,1. Dabei übersetzt βίβλος γενέσεως den hebräischen Text (HT) von 5,1: סֵפֶר תּוֹלְדֹת. In Gen 2,4 hingegen fehlt ein dem βίβλος entsprechendes Element im HT. Es ist davon auszugehen, dass bei der Übersetzung der Terminus βίβλος aus 5,1LXX in 2,4LXX eingetragen worden ist[18]. Βίβλος taucht im Buch Genesis nicht weiter auf, wohl aber γένεσις: Die Septuaginta wählt diesen Begriff als den für das Buch typischen Titel: ΓΕΝΕΣΙΣ[19]. Ab Gen 6,9 ist die pluralische Wendung αὗται αἱ γενέσεις die geprägte Übersetzungswendung für den Fachbegriff אֵלֶּה תּוֹלְדֹת[20]. Diese Wendung, die Toledot-Formel, strukturiert systematisch das Buch Genesis. Die Septuaginta übernimmt mit der stereotypen Übersetzung dieses Toledot-System.

> Die Annahme von NOLLAND, dass der hebräische Begriff תולדות nach vorne in Richtung der kommenden Generationen, der griechische Terminus γένεσις hingegen zurück in Richtung der Ursprünge weise[21], ist nicht nachvollziehbar. Mag dies noch bei Gen 2,4 einleuchten, so kann schon 5,1aLXX nicht als Rückbezug auf einen Bericht über die Ursprünge der Menschen gedeutet werden, denn unmittelbar geht eine ganze Reihe anderer Texte voraus (die Geburt von Set und Enosch, die Genealogie der Kainiten, Kain und Abel, die Sündenfallgeschichte …). Auch an den folgenden Belegstellen von αὗται αἱ γενέσεις wirken die Versuche

16. Vgl. NOLLAND, *Genesis in Matt 1.1* (n. 4), p. 468, Anm. 24.

17. Vgl. die Reaktion von NOLLAND, *Genesis in Matt 1.1* (n. 4), p. 470, auf den „link" zwischen Mt 1,1 und Gen 2,4; 5,1: „What are we left with? Actually not very much".

18. Vgl. NOLLAND, *Genesis in Matt 1.1* (n. 4), p. 467, Anm. 21; M. RÖSEL, *Übersetzung als Vollendung der Auslegung. Studien zur Genesis-Septuaginta* (BZAW, 223), Berlin – New York, de Gruyter, 1994, p. 57.

19. Dass in Mt 1,1 das aus Gen 2,4 und 5,1 LXX bekannte Demonstrativpronomen und der Artikel (αὕτη ἡ) fehlen, hebe den Überschriftcharakter von Mt 1,1 hervor und assoziiere neben Gen 2,4 und 5,1 auch den Titel des Buches Genesis in der Septuaginta. Vgl. MAYORDOMO-MARIN, *Anfang* (n. 2), p. 211. – DAVIES & ALLISON, *Matthew* (n. 8), p. 151, zeigen, dass Γένεσις bereits zur Zeit des Evangelisten als Titel des ersten Buches der Septuaginta bestanden hat. Als Belege führen sie u.a. Justin (Dial. 20,1), Origenes (Orat. 23,3; vgl. Eusebius, Hist. eccl. 6,25), Melito von Sardes (Eusebius, Hist. eccl. 4,26) sowie drei Belege bei Philo (Poster.C. §127; Abr. §1, Aet. mundi §19) an. In letzterer Stelle bemerkt Philo, dass Mose das erste der fünf Bücher mit Γένεσις überschrieben habe.

20. Zu den Stellenangaben siehe das Folgende. Ausnahmen sind Gen 31,13; 32,10 (das Land der Verwandtschaft) und 40,20 (der Geburtstag).

21. Vgl. NOLLAND, *Genesis in Matt 1.1* (n. 4), pp. 467-469.

NOLLANDS, einen primären Rückbezug auf die vorausgehenden Texte („antecedent reference") zu zeigen, sehr gezwungen. Gerade das Demonstrativpronomen (αὕτη, αὗται) markiert deutlich die Verbindung zum unmittelbar Folgenden[22]. Das Toledot-System des Buches Genesis bleibt durch die stereotype Übersetzung in der Septuaginta erhalten.

IV. DIE BESONDERHEIT DER SEPTUAGINTA-FASSUNG VON GEN 5,1

Dennoch gibt es eine Besonderheit in der Septuaginta-Fassung von Gen 5,1 zu notieren: Das Wort אָדָם in 5,1aHT wird mit dem Plural ἀνθρώπων übersetzt:

Gen 5,1 LXX	Gen 5,1 HT
a αὕτη ἡ βίβλος γενέσεως ἀνθρώπων	זֶה סֵפֶר תּוֹלְדֹת אָדָם
b ᾗ ἡμέρᾳ ἐποίησεν ὁ θεὸς τὸν Αδαμ	בְּיוֹם בְּרֹא אֱלֹהִים אָדָם
c κατ' εἰκόνα θεοῦ ἐποίησεν αὐτόν	בִּדְמוּת אֱלֹהִים עָשָׂה אֹתוֹ׃

Gen 5,2 LXX	Gen 5,2 HT
ἄρσεν καὶ θῆλυ ἐποίησεν αὐτοὺς	זָכָר וּנְקֵבָה בְּרָאָם
καὶ εὐλόγησεν αὐτούς	וַיְבָרֶךְ אֹתָם
καὶ ἐπωνόμασεν τὸ ὄνομα αὐτῶν Αδαμ	וַיִּקְרָא אֶת־שְׁמָם אָדָם
ᾗ ἡμέρᾳ ἐποίησεν αὐτούς	בְּיוֹם הִבָּרְאָם׃

Übersetzung nach LXX:	Vulgata:
5,1 Dies (ist) das Buch des Ursprungs der Menschen/Menschheit.	hic est liber generationis Adam
Am Tag, da Gott den Adam (den Menschen) machte,	in die qua creavit Deus hominem
machte er ihn wie ein Bild Gottes,	ad similitudinem Dei fecit illum
5,2 männlich und weiblich machte er sie	masculum et feminam creavit eos
und er segnete sie,	et benedixit illis
und er benannte sie mit ihrem Namen: Adam,	et vocavit nomen eorum Adam
am Tag, da er sie machte.	in die qua creati sunt.

Von der Toledot-Formel her ist אָדָם in 5,1aHT eindeutig als Eigenname aufzufassen. Vom Rückbezug auf Gen 1,27 ist אָדָם in 5,1bHT als generische Bezeichnung („der Mensch") zu interpretieren. Warum scheint die Septuaginta beides zu vertauschen? Bei genauerer Betrachtung des Kontextes wird deutlich, dass auch in der Septuaginta Αδαμ in 5,1-2 weniger als Eigenname einer Person erscheint: *Eine* Person kann nicht zugleich männlich und weiblich sein und kann nicht mit plura-

---

22. Vgl. MAYORDOMO-MARIN, *Anfang* (n. 2), p. 211.

lischen Personalpronomen (αὐτούς) angesprochen werden, ferner erhalten das männliche und das weibliche Exemplar als „*ihren* Namen" Αδαμ. Dieser Name Αδαμ ist damit in 5,1-2LXX ein Kollektivbegriff, ebenso wie ὁ Αδαμ in Gen 2-3 (also mit bestimmtem Artikel wie in 5,1bLXX: τὸν Αδαμ) „den Menschen" meint. Erst in 5,3 ist Adam klar eine männliche Person.

Mit der Änderung in den Genitiv Plural in 5,1aLXX betont die Septuaginta, dass alle Menschen, die gesamte Menschheit[23], von dem Adam abstammt, den männlichen und weiblichen Wesen, die gesegnet und gemäß dem Bild Gottes (LXX![24]) gemacht sind. Ein ursächlicher Einfluss könnte auch von Gen 2,4 her kommen, da in der Übersetzung eine Parallelität erreicht wird:

2,4: αὕτη ἡ βίβλος γενέσεως οὐρανοῦ καὶ γῆς	5,1: αὕτη ἡ βίβλος γενέσεως ἀνϑρώπων
Himmel und Erde = Weltschöpfung	Menschenschöpfung

Ferner ist zu bemerken, dass an diesen beiden Stellen der Singular γένεσις für תולדות verwendet wird, während an den anderen Belegen der Toledot-Formel der Plural steht (αὗται αἱ γενέσεις). Der Singular könnte aufgrund der Allgemeinbegriffe „Himmel und Erde" sowie „Menschheit" gewählt worden sein, während an den anderen Stellen die Nachfahren (Plural) von Einzelpersonen und ihr Geschick Inhalt der γενέσεις sind. Der Singular in 5,1LXX könnte auch die Besonderheit und das Gewicht dieses Anfangs (der Menschheit) unterstreichen (und dann auf 2,4LXX übertragen worden sein)[25].

Mit dieser Besonderheit der Septuaginta-Fassung von Gen 5,1 ist aber nicht das Toledot-System als solches in Frage gestellt.

V. DAS TOLEDOT-SYSTEM DES BUCHES GENESIS

Der Begriff תולדות, der in der Septuaginta in 2,4 und 5,1 mit (βίβλος) γενέσεως, ab 6,9 mit αἱ γενέσεις wiedergegeben wird, fungiert im Buch Genesis als Gliederungsmerkmal, so dass von einem Toledot-System gesprochen werden kann[26]. Am Anfang eines Abschnittes steht die

---

23. Vgl. FRANKEMÖLLE, *Matthäus* (n. 8), p. 130; RÖSEL, *Übersetzung* (n. 18), p. 122.

24. Nach dem HT ist bei Gen 1,26f. an eine Gottesstatue zur Repräsentation der Gottheit zu denken, während die LXX die griechische Urbild-Abbild-Spekulation impliziert. Zu צלם/דמות + Präposition vs. κατ᾽ εἰκόνα vgl. W. GROSS, *Gen 1,26.27; 9,6: Statue oder Ebenbild Gottes? Aufgabe und Würde des Menschen nach dem hebräischen und dem griechischen Wortlaut,* in *JBT* 15 (2000), pp. 11-38, speziell 35-37.

25. Vgl. J.W. WEVERS, *Notes on the Greek Text of Genesis* (SBL SCS 35), Atlanta, Scholars Press, 1993, pp. 22.68.

26. Vgl. dazu grundlegend, wenn auch in einigen Konsequenzen problematisch: S. TENGSTRÖM, *Die Toledotformel und die literarische Struktur der priesterlichen Erwei-*

Toledot-Formel „X אֵלֶּה תּוֹלְדֹת" (wobei X für einen Eigennamen steht, Ausnahme: Gen 2,4). Dieser Abschnitt enthält Genealogien und Erzählungen über die Nachkommen des X und erstreckt sich bis zur Notiz über den Tod des X bzw. bis zu einer neuen Toledot-Formel.

Die Unterscheidung KOCHS[27] in eine Epochen- und eine Generationen-Toledot ist dabei nicht unproblematisch. Als Epochen-Toledot werden diejenigen Formeln bezeichnet, auf die Erzählungen folgen (6,9: Noach; 11,27: Terach; 25,19: Isaak; 37,2: Jakob; auch 2,4: Himmel und Erde). Bei den Generationen-Toledot folgt auf die Formel eine „listenartige Aufzählung" (5,1: Adam; 11,10: Sem; 25,12: Ismael; 36,1.9: Esau; auch 10,1: Noachs Söhne). Entsprechend werden daraus fünf Themen oder Epochen abgeleitet, die das Buch Genesis gliedern sollen. Was zunächst einleuchtend klingt, wirft bei näherer Betrachtung Schwierigkeiten auf: Kann ein und dieselbe Formel zwei verschiedene Gliederungsebenen bezeichnen? Bestimmt tatsächlich der folgende Kontext (Genealogie oder Erzählung) den Rang des Einschnitts? KOCHS Versuch, die beiden Typen als Ein- und Ausleitung einer Epoche zu fassen, wirkt etwas gezwungen. Ein weiteres gravierendes Problem ist die Israel-Zentriertheit in KOCHS Epochengliederung: Die Völkertafel, die Ismael- und die Esau-Toledot gehen in dem Fünf-Epochen-Schema völlig unter. Zwar ist klar, dass das Toledot-System des Buches Genesis auf die zwölf Söhne Jakobs als Konstituenten Israels zuläuft, doch immerhin werden die Völker, Ismael und Esau nicht nur erwähnt, sondern in ihrer „geschichtlichen" Dimension ausgefaltet, wenn auch in der gerafften Form einer Genealogie. Sie haben das Gewicht eines eigenen (wenn auch vielleicht kurzen) Abschnittes. Dies ist jedenfalls plausibler als beispielsweise die Annahme, die Genealogie der „Seitenlinie Ismaels" (Gen 25,12-18) schließe die „Terachzeit" (Gen 11,27-25,18) ab. Die „Seitenlinien" werden im Erzählverlauf nicht unter-, sondern eingeordnet. Das betont KOCH auch in seinem Schlussresümee: Es geht nicht um eine Antithese Israels zu den Völkern, um eine Religion als „ganz andere" gegen die Religionen der Völker, sondern um bleibende,

terungsschicht im Pentateuch (CB OT, 17), Uppsala, CWK Gleerup, 1981; siehe auch EISSFELDT, Biblos geneseos (n. 1), passim; weitere Literaturhinweise bei T. NAUERTH, Untersuchungen zur Komposition der Jakoberzählungen (BEATAJ, 27), Frankfurt/M., Lang, 1997, p. 15, Anm. 31. In einer synchronen Lektüre erkennt auch D. CARR „patterns", also ein Toledot-System (Βίβλος γενέσεως Revisited: A Synchronic Analysis of Patterns in Genesis as Part of the Torah, in ZAW 110 [1998] 159-172.327-347. Dass das Buch Genesis in der Endkomposition durch die Toledot-Formeln strukturiert ist, hat K. KOCH herausgearbeitet: Die Toledot-Formeln als Strukturprinzip des Buches Genesis, in S. BEYERLE (ed.), Recht und Ethos im Alten Testament – Gestalt und Wirkung. FS H. Seebass, Neukirchen-Vluyn, Neukirchener, 1999, pp. 183-191. – Das Toledot-System ist Teil des umfassenderen genealogischen Systems; vgl. dazu jüngst F. CRÜSEMANN, Menschheit und Volk. Israels Selbstdefinition im genealogischen System der Genesis, in EvTh 58 (1998) 180-195, deutsche Fassung von DERS., Human Solidarity and Ethnic Identity. Israel's Self-Definition in the Genealogical System of Genesis, in M.G. BRETT (ed.), Ethnicity and the Bible, Leiden, Brill, 1996, pp. 57-76. – Das Toledot-System stelle ich in meinem Habilitationsprojekt „Die Genealogien der Genesis" ausführlicher vor und zeige dort die Folgen für die Interpretation des Buches Genesis auf.

abgestufte Beziehungen. Gerade diese Sicht macht es beispielsweise notwendig, Esau und seinen Nachkommen den Rang eines eigenen Abschnittes zuzuerkennen und ihn nicht unter die „Isaakzeit" zu subsumieren. Damit ist KOCHs Schlussfolgerung auf eine Strukturierung des Buches Genesis in fünf thematische Epochen nicht angebracht. Zu unterstreichen ist jedoch seine Beobachtung, dass die Toledot-Formeln das Strukturprinzip des Buches Genesis sind. Die Unterscheidung in Epochen- und Generationen-Toledot ist als formkritische Beschreibung gerechtfertigt. Die Typen können aber nicht für unterschiedliche Strukturebenen herangezogen werden. Vielmehr markieren die Toledot-Formeln jeweils eigenständige Abschnitte.

Toledot-Formel	Name	Nachkommen	Genealogie	Todesnotiz
Gen 2,4	Himmel und Erde			
Gen 5,1	Adam	Set bis Noach	5,3-32	
Gen 6,9	Noach	Sem, Ham, Jafet		9,29
Gen 10,1	Söhne Noachs	Völkertafel	10,1-32	
Gen 11,10	Sem	Arpachschad bis Terach	11,10-26	
Gen 11,27	Terach	Abram, Haran, Nahor	11,27	11,32/25,7-11 (Abraham)
Gen 25,12	Ismael	12 Söhne	25,12-16	25,17
Gen 25,19	Isaak	Esau und Jakob	35,22-26	35,28-29
Gen 36,1.9	Esau	„Edom"	36,1-14	(36,43)
Gen 37,2	Jakob	12 Söhne, 1 Tochter	46,8-27	49,33/50,26 (Josef)
Num 3,1	Mose und Aaron	Nadab, Abihu, Eleasar, Itamar	Num 3,2	Num 33,39
Rut 4,18	Perez	Hezron bis David	Rut 4,18-22	

Aus diesem System wird klar, dass תולדות / γενέσεις nicht nur Ursprung, Genealogie oder Geschlechterfolge meint (s.o.). Als Gliederungsmerkmal impliziert „Toledot X" die Geschichte des X und seiner Nachkommen. In manchen Fällen wird diese Geschichte mit einer Genealogie eröffnet. In diesem Sinne kann βίβλος γενέσεως auch der Titel für das gesamte Matthäusevangelium sein: „Buch der Geschichte Jesu Christi ..."[28].

Die genealogischen Konzepte der Septuaginta und des hebräischen Textes des Buches Genesis werden bei der kanonischen Lektüre von Mt 1,1 impliziert[29]. Dies gilt es zu reflektieren. In folgender synoptischer

27. Vgl. KOCH, *Toledot-Formeln* (n. 26), p. 186.
28. So die Übersetzung von FRANKEMÖLLE, *Matthäus* (n. 8), p. 128.
29. Zumindest ist dieser universale Horizont möglich. Was im einzelnen aktuellen Lesevorgang realisiert wird, ist eine andere Frage. Aber die Bibel ist – das zeigen auch

Übersicht sind die Bezüge dargestellt. Zu beachten ist dabei, dass es hier um intertextuelle Bezüge geht, nicht um entstehungsgeschichtliche Aussagen.

VI. Biblos geneseos im Buch Genesis und in Mt 1,1

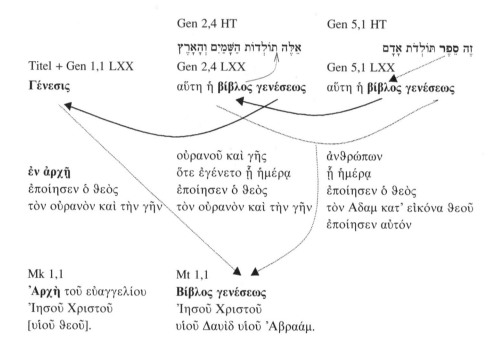

Mk 1,1
Ἀρχὴ τοῦ εὐαγγελίου
Ἰησοῦ Χριστοῦ
[υἱοῦ θεοῦ].

Mt 1,1
Βίβλος γενέσεως
Ἰησοῦ Χριστοῦ
υἱοῦ Δαυὶδ υἱοῦ Ἀβραάμ.

Joh 1,1
Ἐν ἀρχῇ ἦν ὁ λόγος,
καὶ ὁ λόγος ἦν πρὸς τὸν
θεόν, καὶ θεὸς ἦν ὁ λόγος.

Auch der Evangelienanfang von Markus könnte eine Andeutung auf den Beginn des Buches Genesis (LXX) darstellen. Deutlicher ausgeprägt ist das im Johannesevangelium, das den berühmten Buchanfang ἐν ἀρχῇ (בְּרֵאשִׁית) ausdrücklich zitiert. Der Anfang des Matthäus-Evangeliums mit dem Rückbezug auf das Buch Genesis ist also nicht ohne Analogie[30]. Ebenso sei nur kurz angedeutet, dass es für einen erzählenden Text durchaus angemessen ist, mit einer Genealogie einzusteigen[31].

diese Beobachtungen – nicht zur Einmal-Lektüre gedacht. „[M]anche Geschichten verlangen eine nie zu beendende Lektüre." (Eco, *Im Wald* [n. 13], p. 41).
    30. Vgl. Frankemölle, *Jahwe-Bund* (n. 3), pp. 361-362.
    31. Nähere Hinweise und Quellen dazu bei Nolland, *Genesis in Matt 1.1* (n. 4), p. 470.

VII. Sohn Davids, Sohn Abrahams

Die beiden Epitheta Jesu Christi in Mt 1,1, die Davids- und Abra-hamssohnschaft, haben eine ganze Reihe christologischer Implikationen, die hier nicht dargelegt werden müssen[32]. Der Blick auf das genealogische System des Buches Genesis fügt diesem Sinnpotential weitere Aspekte hinzu. Dass Jesus als „Sohn Davids" vorgestellt wird, hat neben den königlichen und messianischen Assoziationen, die geweckt werden, auch den Effekt, dass damit an die letzte Genealogie nach dem Toledot-System nahtlos angeschlossen wird. Die von Adam an *durchgehende* Linie im genealogischen System der Genesis führt von Jakob über Juda zu dessen Sohn Perez (Gen 38,29; 46,12) – und an diesen Sohn wird in Rut 4,12 bzw. 4,18 mit der Toledot Perez angeknüpft, die wiederum bis David führt (Rut 4,22). Jesus wird damit in das System Israels der genealogischen Abkunft integriert.

Als „Sohn Abrahams" hat Jesus (wie jeder Israelit/Jude) teil an Bund und Verheißung. Textlich steht Jesus damit auf der Ebene von Isaak und Ismael, die *beide* als „Sohn Abrahams" bezeichnet werden (Gen 25,12.19). Mt 1,2 macht dann aber klar, dass es um die Isaak-Linie geht, indem Gen 25,19 nahezu wörtlich übernommen wird:

Gen 25,19 καὶ αὗται αἱ γενέσεις Ἰσαακ τοῦ υἱοῦ Αβρααμ	Mt 1,1 Βίβλος γενέσεως Ἰησοῦ Χριστοῦ υἱοῦ Δαυὶδ υἱοῦ Ἀβραάμ.
Αβρααμ ἐγέννησεν τὸν Ισαακ	Mt 1,2a Ἀβραὰμ ἐγέννησεν τὸν Ἰσαάκ, …

Diese Parallelität ermöglicht auch eine Assoziation an eine Isaak-Typologie: Wie Isaak ist der Messias Jesus ein Sohn der Verheißung (vgl. Paulus in Gal 3,16 in Verbindung mit Gen 22,17; ferner Gal 4,23.29)[33]. Im Vordergrund steht jedoch die Integration Jesu in das genealogische System, die natürlich auch eine Teilhabe an Bund und Verheißung impliziert.

Eine andere (weitere) Lesemöglichkeit besteht darin, in der Bezeichnung Jesu als „Sohn Davids" die Erfüllung der Geschichte Israels und der messianischen Verheißungen zu sehen, in dem Epitheton „Sohn Abrahams" aber den über Israel weit hinausgehenden Blick auf die Völker, da Abraham im Frühjudentum als erster Proselyt oder Konvertit galt und nach Gen 12,3 Segen für alle Geschlechter des Erdbodens bringt.

---

32. Vgl. dazu einschlägig u.a. Dormeyer, *Mt 1,1* (n. 8), passim; Mayordomo-Marín, *Anfang* (n. 2), pp. 214f. – Belege in der rabbinischen Literatur, die ebenfalls Abraham und David als Angelpunkte in der Geschichte ansehen, führt Johnson, *Purpose* (n. 15), pp. 149-151, an.

33. Vgl. dazu Näheres bei R. Pesch, *»Er wird Nazoräer heißen«. Messianische Exegese in Mt 1-2*, in F. Van Segbroeck et al. (eds.), *The Four Gospels 1992*. FS Frans Neirynck (BETL, 100), Leuven, Peeters, 1992, pp. 1385-1401, bes. p. 1395.

Mt 1,1 weckt so die Spannung zwischen Partikularismus („Heil für Israel") und Universalismus („Heil für alle Völker")[34]. Sieht man in der Prädikation „Sohn Abrahams" einen Hinweis auf einen Israel übersteigenden Heilswillen Gottes, „spannt sich ein Bogen von V 1 zu 28,19f, wo am Ende des Evangeliums im Missionsbefehl die Universalität des christlichen Heils nachdrücklich zugesagt wird"[35].

VIII. WAS GESCHIEHT BEI DER KANONISCH-INTERTEXTUELLEN LEKTÜRE VON MT 1,1?

Es wird deutlich, dass der knappe Vers Mt 1,1 zentrale Aspekte und Konzepte des Buches Genesis wachruft. Wenn dies alles bei einer idealtypischen, kanonkundigen intertextuellen Lektüre[36] realisiert wird, aktiviert dies eine ganze Reihe von Sinnpotentialen.

Die Hauptfigur Jesus Christus wird vorgestellt – dies ist auch im profanen Bereich zu allen Zeiten eine Hauptaufgabe eines aussagekräftigen Titels. Zugleich geschieht diese Vorstellung mit einer deutlich „biblisch" geprägten Sprache, deren Assoziationsreichtum zum einen eine „ehrwürdig-sakrale Atmosphäre" bewirkt, zum anderen das „Alte Testament" als primären intertextuellen Bezugsrahmen auf den Plan ruft[37].

Dieser Hauptfigur Jesus wird auf subtile Weise ein ungeheures Gewicht beigemessen, indem durch den intertextuellen Bezug auf Gen 2,4; 5,1 in der *Septuaginta*-Fassung mit der Wendung βίβλος γενέσεως der Genitiv Ἰησοῦ Χριστοῦ von Mt 1,1 mit οὐρανοῦ καὶ γῆς von Gen 2,4 und ἀνθρώπων von 5,1 auf eine Ebene gestellt wird. Es geht vielleicht

34. Vgl. dazu FRANKEMÖLLE, *Matthäus* (n. 8), pp. 132-134.

35. GNILKA, *Matthäusevangelium* (n. 4), p. 7. GNILKA will Mt 1,1 zwar nicht als Überschrift über das Evangelium ansehen, meint aber doch, dass der Vers „als eine Art Resümee der matthäischen Theologie gelesen werden soll" (ebd. p. 8). – Vgl. auch VAN ELDEREN, *Significance* (n. 8), p. 7.

36. Zu Begriff, Methodik und Programm der „kanonisch-intertextuellen Lektüre" vgl. STEINS, *Bindung Isaaks* (n. 14). Hier können einige Thesen daraus nur angedeutet werden: Der „Kanon" ist in erster Linie ein literaturwissenschaftlicher (kein dogmatischer) Begriff („Kanon als Text in literarischer Hinsicht", p. 17) und bezeichnet den „letzten Kontext" in zeitlicher und sachlicher Hinsicht (p. 19), der als letzte Kontextualisierung ein besonderes Gewicht erhält und für die Auslegung der primären Kontext des Einzeltextes ist (p. 21). Der Bibelkanon ist daher der privilegierte Intertext (p. 99). Damit etabliert der Kanon eine spezifische Rezeptionsvorgabe (p. 25): „Der Kanon stellt einen Spielraum von Kontextualisierungsmöglichkeiten bereit. Er leitet an zu einer kreativen Lektüre und erfordert diese, um das Potential auszuschöpfen" (p. 26). Zudem ist in der zwei-einen christlichen Bibel für das Verhältnis von AT und NT die „doppelte Leseweise" nach dem „Konzept der doppelten Hermeneutik" (Jüdische Bibel/Altes Testament) zu beachten, vgl. C. DOHMEN & G. STEMBERGER, *Hermeneutik der Jüdischen Bibel und des Alten Testaments*, Stuttgart u.a., Kohlhammer, 1996, pp. 211-213.

37. MAYORDOMO-MARIN, *Anfang* (n. 2), p. 216.

zu weit, damit Jesus als eine eschatologische neue Schöpfung angedeutet zu sehen[38]. Aber immerhin wird damit dem Jesusgeschehen eine Bedeutung beigemessen, die den Ereignissen der Welt- und Menschenschöpfung gleichkommt[39].

Ein bisher kaum wahrgenommener Effekt von Mt 1,1 ist die Einbindung Jesu in das genealogische System und das Toledot-System des Buches Genesis. Diese Einbindung geschieht einerseits durch die von der Wendung βίβλος γενέσεως hergestellten Bezüge, andererseits durch die Epitheta „Sohn Davids", womit an die Rut-Genealogie angeknüpft wird, die wiederum über Perez und Juda an den Genesis-Genealogien hängt, und „Sohn Abrahams", womit an die Konzepte von Bund und Verheißung angeschlossen wird. Diese genealogischen Feinheiten haben auch die Leserinnen und Leser des Matthäus-Evangeliums nicht unmittelbar parat, so dass es völlig angemessen ist, das genealogische System explizit zu wiederholen. Daher folgt die Genealogie Mt 1,2-17, durch die zahlreiche weitere Bezüge zum Buch Genesis geschaffen werden. In gewisser Weise weicht der Matthäus-Text damit vom Schema ab: Anders als etwa bei der Genealogie Gen 5,1-32, die die *Nachfahren* Adams listet, werden nicht die Nachfahren, sondern die *Vorfahren* Jesu angeführt. Diese „Mischform" und „Umformung der Gattung"[40] sind erzähltechnisch und christologisch bedingt. Der Matthäus-Text muss eine gewisse „Nachhilfe" im Alten Testament geben, damit die Bezüge nicht nur angedeutet, sondern ausgedrückt werden. Das Toledot-System als solches bzw. die Bezugnahme darauf bleibt erkennbar.

Damit ist Jesus Teilhaber am Toledot-System und an der Verheißungslinie, die mit dem Segen für die Menschen (Gen 5,2!) und dann vor allem mit Abraham beginnt. *Zugleich* aber ist Jesus ein neuer Meilenstein in diesem System, ein neuer Abschnitt vom Range eines Abraham, Isaak, Jakob. Mt 1,1 hebt Jesus auf diese Ebene. Das Ergebnis der Lektüre von Mt 1,1 vor dem Hintergrund des Buches Genesis ist damit eine Spannung aus *Kontinuität* und *Diskontinuität*: An den Ursprung,

---

38. Vgl. Davies & Allison, *Matthew* (n. 8), pp. 150-151. Nolland, *Genesis in Matt 1.1* (n. 4), pp. 463.466, und Stanton, *Matthew* (n. 4), p. 1189, wenden sich zu Recht gegen diese Auffassung.

39. Nolland, *Genesis in Matt 1.1* (n. 4), p. 470, sieht ebenfalls die biblische Sprache und die Unterstreichung der Bedeutung Jesu als wesentliche Implikationen des Bezugs von Mt 1,1 auf Gen 2,4; 5,1. Gegen sein skeptisches Urteil, dass dies „not very much" sei, meine ich, dass dies schon sehr viel ist. B.T. Viviano (*The Genres of Matthew 1-2: Light from 1 Timothy 1:4*, in *RB* 97 [1990] 31-53.52) formuliert es so: Man kann vermuten, dass der Evangelist ein Signal geben wollte, dass er eine „neue Genesis" schreiben will, eine neue Epoche in der Heilsgeschichte. Ähnlich sagt das auch Frankemölle, *Jahwe-Bund* (n. 3), p. 365.

40. Vgl. Mayordomo-Marin, *Anfang* (n. 2), p. 223.

die Traditionen und die Verheißungen Israels wird voll und ganz angeknüpft, aber zugleich wird der Anfang einer neuen geschichtlichen Epoche mit Jesus Christus markiert[41]. Diese Lektüreweise erinnert an das
Wort im Munde Jesu in Mt 13,52: „Jeder Schriftgelehrte also, der ein
Jünger des Himmelreichs geworden ist, gleicht einem Hausherrn, der
aus seinem reichen Vorrat Neues und Altes hervorholt".

In der Perspektive des Kanons hat Mt 1,1 als Portal zum Matthäusevangelium wie zum gesamten Neuen Testament erhebliche Bedeutung:
Dieses Portal verweist ganz massiv auf einen *anderen* Textzusammenhang, auf den ersten Teil der christlichen Bibel, näherhin auf dessen Anfang, das Buch Genesis. Auf einen Leser, der mit „David" und „Abraham" (und den ab Mt 1,2 folgenden Namen) nichts anfangen kann,
wirkt dieses Portal abweisend und verweisend auf die erforderliche Lektüre des „ersten Bandes". Gerade ein zuerst separat auftretendes Matthäusevangelium (vor der Festigung des Kanons aus AT und NT)
braucht so einen Wächter, der den notwendigen Verstehenshintergrund
anmahnt und aufzeigt. Sind die „kanonisch" Lesenden mit dem „ersten
Band" vertraut, so ist das Portal Mt 1,1 eine Einladung: Sie können anhand von Mt 1,1-17, dem „Inhaltsverzeichnis des AT" [42], Tradition und
Verheißung Israels rekapitulieren – und erst auf dieser Basis ist „das
Buch der Geschichte Jesu Christi" zu verstehen, das jetzt nicht nur das
Matthäusevangelium, sondern das gesamte Neue Testament ist.

IX. HAT MATTHÄUS DAS ALLES SO INTENDIERT?

Damit stellt sich am Schluss der Betrachtung die Frage, ob der Autor
des Evangeliums dies alles so beabsichtigt hat. Diese Frage ist interessant und berechtigt, kann und muss im Rahmen dieses Ansatzes aber
nicht beantwortet werden. Sie ist nur dann entscheidend, wenn in der
Erhebung der Autorintention die einzige Aufgabe der Exegese gesehen
wird und diese Intention der alleinige Maßstab für die „Richtigkeit" einer Interpretation wäre. Das kann sie aus mehreren Gründen aber nicht
sein[43]. Bei antiken und biblischen Autoren ist deren Intention wenn

---

41. Ähnlich FRANKEMÖLLE, *Matthäus* (n. 8), p. 135: Christologisch ergibt sich die
These, „dass die darzustellende ‚Geschichte Jesu Christi' die in der Bibel erzählte Geschichte erfüllt und konsequent weiterführt". Oder GNILKA, *Matthäusevangelium* (n. 4),
p. 8: „E [=der Evangelist Matthäus] knüpft an das Alte an, im gewissen Sinn schreibt er
eine Fortsetzung des AT, weiß aber um den Umbruch der Zeit, der mit Jesus Christus erfolgt ist".

42. Diese Formulierung hat der Student Florian Kreuzer im Seminar „Der Kanon des
AT" an der Universität Regensburg im Wintersemester 2000/2001 angeregt, und ich grei-
fe sie dankend auf.

43. Vgl. dazu auch die Problemanzeigen bei MAYORDOMO-MARIN, *Anfang* (n. 2),
pp. 170-187.

überhaupt nur über den auszulegenden Text (und andere Texte) greifbar, damit also höchstens indirekt zugänglich. Bei modernen Autorinnen und Autoren lässt es sich problemlos nachweisen, dass eine bestimmte Interpretation oder Sichtweise nach Auskunft der Verfasser nicht direkt intendiert war, deswegen aber durchaus als „richtig" angesehen werden kann. Ebenso lehrt die Erfahrung, dass Texte immer „multidimensional" sind und durchaus Potential für mehrere „Sinne" bzw. Interpretationsmöglichkeiten bieten. Das liegt unter anderem daran, dass die Leserinnen und Leser eines Textes durch ihren Verstehenshintergrund, ihr Wissen und ihre Emotionen, zur Sinnkonstitution des Textes wesentlich mit beitragen.

Wo liegen dann die „Grenzen der Interpretation" (Umberto Eco)[44]? Will man einen Text nicht nur für das selbstkonstruierte Sinngefüge und Weltbild *benutzen*, dann muss man sich die Mühe machen, die verschiedenen Elemente eines Textes in einen einzigen Sinnzusammenhang zu bringen. Man kann dies die *intentio operis* nennen, anhand der man erkennen kann, dass bestimmte Interpretationen dem Text näher oder ferner stehen. Der Text selbst legt die Grenzen der Interpretation fest, und jede Auslegung muss sich an dem messen lassen, was der Text sagt. Aufgabe der Exegese ist damit nicht das Erheben *eines* Sinnes, von dem behauptet wird, es wäre die Intention des Autors, sondern das Aufzeigen des breiteren Sinnpotentials durch mehrfache intensive und intertextuelle Lektüre sowie der Heranziehung aller Ergebnisse historisch-kritischer Methoden, um die Grenzen der Interpretation auszuloten.

In diesem Sinne wäre zu fragen, ob es in den eben besprochenen Texten und Kontexten, v.a. Mt 1,1, Hinweise gäbe, die gegen die vorgeführte „Lektüre" sprechen. Wenn nicht, dann halte ich die vorgelegte Interpretation in Form einer wissenschaftlich reflektierten (intersubjektiv nachvollziehbaren) Lektüre für verantwortbar[45].

Sägemühle 7   Thomas HIEKE
D-91275 Auerbach-Michelfeld

---

44. Vgl. zum Folgenden DOHMEN, *Die Bibel* (n. 14), pp. 40-42.
45. Für kritische und anregende Hinweise danke ich Prof. Dr. Georg Steins, Prof. Dr. Christoph Dohmen sowie den Teilnehmern am alttestamentlichen Oberseminar in Regensburg, Dr. Tobias Nicklas, Dr. Christian Wagner und Dr. Martin Mark.

SCRIPTURE AND COMMUNITY IN DIALOGUE

Hermeneutical Reflections on the Authority of the Bible

The focus of this paper is on the hermeneutical aspects of biblical authority. While the traditional view of canon is that the biblical text is normative, the emphasis has now shifted to the canonical autonomy of the community. This new emphasis is seen in various forms of reader-response criticism and liberation theology. What is the implication of this? Where does the locus for determining canonical authority truly lie – with the text, with the community or between the two? Is the experience of the community just as important a "text" as Scripture itself? These are some of the questions which will be discussed in this contribution.

Tradition as an Ongoing Interpretation

The concept of tradition is of great importance for understanding the nature of canon. It is to be noticed that traditions are the means by which the community understands itself in relation to the past[1]. Biblical traditions remember the past for the sake of the present and the future. They are not primarily concerned with historical fact so much as they are concerned with the significance of those past events for the present, and the promise they hold for the future.

Biblical texts and traditions are in themselves interpretations. They are interpretations made *ad hoc* with a view to a concrete new time and environment. The situation changes so that a mere literal repetition of the original message, orthodox as it might be, could lead to heresy, not to faith[2].

The ongoing interpretation is marked by a *rereading* of the traditions of the past. New situations forced re-examination and recasting of tradition, providing the believing community with a dynamic and living traditional base upon which to build and in terms of which to understand its past in the light of its changing present and future.

---

1. See P. ACHTEMEIER, *The Inspiration of Scripture. Problems and Proposals*, Philadelphia, Westminster Press, 1980, pp. 124-125.

2. Cf. E. SCHWEIZER, *Scripture – Tradition – Modern Interpretation*, in ID., *Neotestamentica. Deutsche und englische Aufsätze 1951-1963*, Zürich – Stuttgart, Zwingli, 1963, pp. 203-225, esp. p. 207.

In the experience of the believing communities, some traditions were found to be of more value than others, and these traditions were included in the ongoing traditions of the community. Here the task becomes urgent how to discern between more valuable and less valuable traditions.

Searching to discern between different forms of tradition, the Faith and Order meeting in Montreal (1963) made a distinction between Tradition (with a capital "T") and traditions (with a small "t")[3]. The former designates "The Gospel itself, transmitted from generation to generation in and by the Church, Christ himself present in the life of the Church"; whereas "traditions" – and the "process of tradition" – indicate how in different Christian confessions and different cultural situations this one Tradition has been diversely understood and transmitted.

The intention behind this distinction is that Tradition should be understood not as a sum of tenets fixed once and for all and transmitted from generation to generation, but rather as *living reality*. Nevertheless it has been criticized for precisely this reductionism[4].

The "Inner Hermeneutics" of the Bible

In the last three decades, the discussions on "canonical criticism" have taken two different directions. The first direction is represented by B.S. Childs. He emphasizes the Bible's final literary form (*norma normata*)[5]. The second direction is represented by J.A. Sanders. He emphasizes the ongoing religious function (*norma normans*)[6]. For Sanders, canonical function takes precedence over canonical form, the literary shape of a particular community's Bible is subsumed under the interpreter's more important vocation of adapting Scripture's meaning to the community's ever-changing life situation.

Several factors are in favour of this second approach to canonical criticism. M. Fishbane has shown how, in the scribal activity apparent

3. *The Bible. Its Authority and Interpretation in the Ecumenical Movement*, ed. E. FLESSEMAN-VAN LEER, Geneva, World Council of Churches, 1980, p. 19. See also G. EBELING, *Die Geschichtlichkeit der Kirche und ihrer Verkündigung als theologisches Problem*, Tübingen, Mohr – Siebeck, 1954, pp. 67-68: "Die Tradition schlechthin – wir können kurz sagen: Jesus Christus – ist zu unterscheiden von den Traditionen, zu denen sich das Zeugnis von Jesus Christus gestaltet".

4. See J. ROLOFF, *Die Geschichtlichkeit der Schrift und die Bezeugung des einen Evangeliums*, in V. VAJTA (ed.), *Evangelium als Geschichte. Identität und Wandel in der Weitergabe des Evangeliums*, Göttingen, Vandenhoek & Ruprecht, 1974, pp. 126-158, esp. p. 132.

5. E.g. B.S. CHILDS, *Introduction to the Old Testament as Scripture*, Philadelphia, Fortress, 1979, ID., *The New Testament as Canon. An Introduction*, London, SCM Press, 1984.

6. E.g. J.A. SANDERS, *Torah and Canon*, Philadelphia, Fortress, 1972, ID., *Canon and Community. A Guide to Canonical Criticism*, Philadelphia, Fortress, 1984.

within the Bible itself, the process of earlier traditions taken up by later traditions began very early in ancient Israel. This intertextual phenomenon is characterized as "inner-biblical exegesis"[7]. J.E Brenneman points out that the canonical process thus began before the formal closure of the canon and continues right up to the present hour[8]. In a similar way S. Croatto understands "the hermeneutical process as *part of the very message of the Bible*". He continues:

> "That is to say, the Bible, taken as "product" of a hermeneutic process, favors us with an important reading key: that its kerygmatic meaning is bestowed only in the prolongation of the same hermeneutic process... that has constituted the Bible. Thus, to lay claim to "fixing" its meaning once and for all at the moment of its production is to deny its *open meaning*"[9].

Another representative of intertextuality as a process is the feminist scholar P. Trible. She uses the metaphor of the "Bible's journey": "The Bible is a pilgrim wandering through history to merge past and present". Composed of diverse traditions that span centuries, the Bible embraces claims and counterclaims in witness to the complexities and ambiguities of existence[10]. Trible's mode of reading is the "hermeneutics functioning within scripture". By tracing the pilgrimage of a text she finds that "A single text appears in different versions with different functions in different contexts. Through applications it confesses, challenges, comforts and condemns. What it says on one occasion, it denies on another. Thus scripture in itself yields multiple interpretations of itself"[11].

Canonizing the Interpretative Process

When speaking of the canon one usually thinks only of the content of Christian faith. However, H.-R. Weber points out that *the church has canonized also an interpretative process*[12]. The transmission *and* re-

---

7. M. FISHBANE, *Inner Biblical Exegesis. Types and Strategies of Interpretation in Ancient Israel*, in G. HARTMAN & S. BUDICK, *Midrash and Literature*, New Haven – London, Yale University Press, 1986, pp. 19-37, esp. p. 36.

8. J.E. BRENNEMAN, *Canons in Conflict. Negotiating Texts in True and False Prophecy*, New York – Oxford, Oxford University Press, 1997, p. 23.

9. S. CROATTO, *Biblical Hermeneutics. Towards a Theory of Rereading as the Production of Meaning*, Maryknoll, NY, Orbis Books, 1987, pp. 68-69. For a detailed discussion of this view see G. WEST, *Biblical Hermeneutics of Liberation. Modes of Reading the Bible in the South African Context*, Pietermaritzburg, Cluster Publications; Maryknoll, NY, Orbis Books, 1995 (second revised edition), pp. 154-171.

10. P. TRIBLE, *God and the Rhetoric of Sexuality*, Philadelphia, Fortress, 1978, p. 1.

11. TRIBLE, *God and the Rhetoric of Sexuality* (n. 10), p. 4.

12. H.-R. WEBER, *Power. Focus for a Biblical Theology*, Geneva, World Council of Churches, 1989, p. 25.

interpretation of biblical traditions of faith which can be observed in the
Bible remain normative. Therefore a theology which simply transmits
and repeats biblical affirmations without sensitivity to new contexts of
Christian obedience risks the danger of becoming unbiblical. Conversely, a theology which "reinvents" Christian faith only in response to
the challenges of its own time without being guided and corrected by
Bible study cannot claim to be biblical.

The Bible is by definition an open book, open to the ongoing process of transmission and interpretation. Just as in the course of biblical
history there were times when one or two of the traditions of faith
dominated while others receded into the background, so it happens
throughout church history and even today. The canonized interpretative
process gives freedom for a new theological thinking and new prophetic
action.

The question is often raised whether in this ongoing interpretative
process we can go *beyond* the affirmations of canonized biblical faith.
This question must be answered affirmatively[13]. We will discover new
aspects of the biblical message when we are engaged in dialogue with
our time and when we are challenged by different cultural and religious
currents. Furthermore, in the Gospel of John it is promised that the Spirit
will guide us into all the truth and that the Spirit of truth will teach us
what now we cannot yet bear and understand (John 16,12-15).

To summarize, then, the Bible reflects the life of the faithful community over a span of centuries. In the process of faithfull hearing and interpreting traditions in the light of new historical situations, the life of
the community changed, and differed, from its earlier stage.

A Closed Canon – an Open Text

In the interaction between text and community the question is where
to locate the authority, in the text itself or in the community. Basically
there are two different approaches: a "hermeneutics of trust" and a
"hermeneutics of suspicion"[14]. Many interpreters would probably say
that their attitude towards the Bible is neither wholly positive nor wholly

13. Cf. WEBER, *Power* (n. 12), p. 25. See also R.W. WALL, *Reading the New Testament in Canonical Context*, in J.B. GREEN (ed.), *Hearing the New Testament. Strategies
for Interpretation*, Grand Rapids, MI, Eerdmans, 1995, pp. 370-393, esp. p. 382. Walls
distinguishes between a conversation which is *intercanonical* (i.e., conversations between
different biblical traditions or writers) and a conversation which is *intercatholic* (i.e., conversations between the Bible and different faith traditions); the first "norms" and guides
the second.

14. Cf. F. WATSON, *Introduction. The Open Text*, in ID. (ed.), *The Open Text. New
Directions for Biblical Studies?*, London, SCM Press, 1993, pp. 1-12, esp. p. 10.

negative. Yet it proves difficult for them to be both trusting and suspicious at one and the same time.

Some proponents of the "hermeneutics of suspicion" have argued in favour of a re-writing of the Bible, that is a new edition of the Bible which is not any more an agent of sexism, racism and other forms of discrimination. This is for instance the case with some feminists and some liberation theologians[15]. On the surface it seems that this idea has support in the Bible itself. It is clear from historical-critical investigation that there is a *re-writing process within the Bible itself*. Thus, for instance, the writing of the gospels in the church of the first century clearly represents a process during which the Jesus tradition was re-edited repeatedly and even a whole Gospel book (Mark) was re-written to serve Christian communities in other geographical and cultural settings and in an advanced stage of the early church's development (cf. Luke 1,1-4).

The purpose of writing and rewriting biblical books was to adapt faith traditions and convictions to new experiences in changing historical circumstances and cultural conditions. Yet, at a certain point in time, the religious communities of Judaism and the Christian church set an end to this process by establishing a canon of books which was to be normative for them and hence unchangeable. From then onward any effort was to be *interpretation rather than revision*[16].

This means that there is no need for a new edition of the Bible. Rather, the biblical tradition must be understood in its own situation and then interpreted in today's society. What is required is not a new Bible but a new hermeneutics. The canon is closed, but the biblical texts are open for never-ending re-readings.

Scripture and Experience in a Possible Conflict

The question remains, however, where to put the emphasis in regard to authority. This problem can be illustrated by pointing to a disagreement among feminist scholars. One position is that statements which deny humanity cannot be from God. R. Ruether, for instance, argues that "Whatever denies, diminishes, or distorts the full humanity of women is, therefore, appraised as not redemptive"; "… what does promote full humanity of women is of the Holy, it does reflect true relation to the di-

---

15. E.g. C.S. BANANA, *The Case for a New Bible*, in I. MUKONYORA, J.L. COX, F.J. VERSTRAELEN (eds.), *"Rewriting" the Bible. The Real Issues*, Gweru, Mambo Press, 1993, pp. 17-32.

16. Cf. F.J. VERSTRAELEN, *The Real Issues Regarding the Bible. Summary, Findings and Conclusions*, in *"Rewriting" the Bible* (n. 15), pp. 265-289, esp. p. 269.

vine, it is the true nature of things, the authentic message of redemption and the mission of redemptive community"[17].

According to another position, the experiences of women determines what is oppressive and what is not. E. Schüssler Fiorenza, for instance, argues that "a feminist theological interpretation of the Bible cannot take as its point of departure the normative authority of the biblical archetype, but must begin with women's experience in their struggle for liberation"[18]. In this position the emphasis is on the *community as the hermeneutical centre*.

The authority of the Bible and the authority of the community should not be seen as an either-or. There is a dual process of value reinforcement between theology and experience. This is well expressed by O.C. Thomas: "The (theological) proposal orders, makes sense of, illuminates, and thus successfully interprets the experience. The experience supports, and thus gives evidence for the proposal"[19].

Towards a Mutual Critical Dialogue between Canon and Community

This brings us to a few concluding reflections on the authority of the Bible in relation to the community. The traditional way of setting the Bible and the church over against each other or one over the other in authority fails to testify appropriately to the historical complexity.

The community of faith is the proper context in which the Bible is to be understood. This in a way is not something new. Form criticism already called attention to the communities which preserved, shaped and generated the tradition. However, the active role of the community has been emphasized even more by new methods (sociological studies, contextual exegesis, etc.). Thus there is a hermeneutical circle operating within the believing community. J. Barr rightly notes:

> "The Bible takes origin from within the life of the believing communities; it is interpreted within the continuing life for these communities; the standard of its religious interpretation is the structure which these communities maintain; and it has the task of providing a challenge, a force of innovation and a source of purification, to the life of these communities"[20].

17. R. RUETHER, *Sexism and God-Talk. Toward a Feminist Theology*, Boston, Beacon Press, 1983, pp. 18 and 19.
18. E. SCHÜSSLER FIORENZA, *Bread Not Stone. The Challenge of Feminist Biblical Interpretation*, Boston, Beacon Press, 1984, p. 13.
19. O.C. THOMAS, *Theology and Experience*, in *HTR* 78 (1985) 179-201, esp. 197. For further reflections see A.-L. ERIKSSON, *Bibelns auktoritet och kvinnors erfarenhet*, in P. BLOCK (ed.), *Om Tolkning V. Bibelen som auktoritet*, Stockholm, Svenska kyrkans forskningsråd, 1998, pp. 135-147, esp. p. 144.
20. J. BARR, *The Bible as a Document of Believing Communities*, in H.D. BETZ (ed.), *The Bible as a Document of the University*, Chico, California, Scholars Press, 1981, pp. 25-47, p. 25.

Thus, there is a dialectic between "the text" of life (experience) and the text of Scripture, and this dialectic is the kernel of the interpretive enterprise[21]. The community of Christians formed and shaped the Christian canon. But the canon in turn forms and shapes the community[22]. However, if the Bible represents the self-understanding of the community that produced it, it is by no means an idealized statement of Christian propaganda. Rather, the Bible, Old and New Testaments alike, is a series of critique of the very community that produced it[23].

The relationship between the text and the interpreter can be seen as a mutual challenge. S. Schneiders notes that "for the dialogue between text and reader to be genuin, the text must maintain its identity, its 'strangeness', which both gifts and challenges the reader. It must be allowed to say what it says, regardless of whether this is comfortable or assimilable to the reader"[24]. How, then, can we remain open to the challenges of the text? At least two points must be made.

First, we all read the Bible selectively. None of us can fully overcome this problem, but we can correct wrong notions by a serious study of the biblical text and by following a method which helps us to hear the text on its own terms. This means first and foremost to be prepared to let our self-asserting reading of the text be challenged by a prophetic critical reading. The model for such a reading is given by Luke in 4,16-30[25].

Second, to counteract the absolutizing of one's own situation it is necessary to stimulate an ecumenical and cross-cultural hermeneutics of the gospel, that is a dialogue between different contextual readings of the Bible[26].

As regards the authority of the Bible it cannot be based on some hypothetical "objective reading"; rather, it grows out of a living encounter with Scripture. The experience of the community cannot be discounted.

---

21. Cf. C. ROWLAND & M. CORNER, *Liberating Exegesis. The Challenge of Liberation Theology to Biblical Studies*, London, SPCK, 1990, p. 41; see also J. NISSEN, *Scripture and Experience as the Double Source of Mission. Hermeneutical Reflections*, in T. OKURE (ed.), *To Cast Fire Upon the Earth. Bible and Mission Collaborating in Today's Multicultural Global Context*, Pietermaritzburg, Cluster Publications, 2000, pp. 178-193.

22. Cf. W. VOGELS, *The Role of the Reader in Biblical Authority*, in *Theology Digest* 47 (2000) 219-225, esp. p. 220.

23. Cf. ACHTEMEIER, *The Inspiration of Scripture* (n. 1), p. 92.

24. S.M. SCHNEIDERS, *The Revelatory Text. Interpreting the New Testament as Sacred Scripture*, San Francisco, Harper, 1991, p. 171.

25. This text reflects a conflict between two forms of reading: an *in-group exegesis* and a *prophetic-critique hermeneutics*. For a more detailed analysis see J. NISSEN, *New Testament and Mission. Historical and Hermeneutical Perspectives*, Frankfurt a. M., Peter Lang, 1999, pp. 68-69.

26. Cf. NISSEN, *Scripture and Experience* (n. 21), pp. 189-190.

It constitutes a vital part of the unending dialogue with God's living word[27].

At the same time, there is a need for re-evaluation of authority itself[28]. Authority is often seen as being something inflexible and hierarchical. True authority can never be imposed; it only works when offered, chosen and freely accepted. When applied from above, vertically, it is oppressive, but when it happens horizontally, it expands – not in an exclusive way but inclusively. The Word became words: stories, dialogues, lives, action – flesh. The early Christian community was involved in the shaping of the text itself, "living the Scriptures" by telling and living its story in changing circumstances.

The first communities ventured to write the gospel anew. Today's communities must do the same[29]. This is the presupposition for the realization of true authority. When the community ventures to write the gospel anew, the Bible will remain a living reality, a source for continuing dialogue.

Department of Biblical Studies   Johannes NISSEN
Faculty of Theology
University of Aarhus
DK 8000 Aarhus C

---

27. Cf. the ecumenical document *The Authority of Scripture in Light of New Experiences of Women*, in W.H. LAZARETH (ed.), *The Lord of Life*, Geneva, World Council of Churches, 1983, pp. 101-115, esp. p. 112.

28. *The Authority of Scripture* (n. 27), p. 113. See also SCHNEIDERS, *The Revelatory Text* (n. 24), pp. 56-57.

29. Cf. E. SCHILLEBEECKX, *Christus und die Christen. Die Geschichte einer neuen Lebenspraxis*, Freiburg im Breisgau, Herder, 1977, pp. 407-408.

SCRIPTURES AND CANON
INTERPRETATIONS OF THE BIBLE
IN CONTEMPORARY AFRICAN CHRISTIANITY

This paper briefly delves into the delicate history that gave the church the *Septuagint,* the Greek translation of the Hebrew Bible, as its *Scripture* and into the subsequent emergence of scriptures in the early church[1]. It probes the processes of the canonization of the twenty-seven books that make up the New Testament (NT). It agrees with recent opinion that the canonization of the books is a Church heritage[2]. It goes on to demonstrate how this collection that the Church acknowledges as inspired and normative for faith and morals is being interpreted in contemporary African churches and society. It concludes that for African Christians as for early Christian evangelists the Christ event attested to and witnessed in the NT books happened according to the scriptures (1 Cor 15,3). And that as the canon of scriptures was interpreted in the early church so do African Christian evangelists, pastors and trained readers today *re-read* the canonical books of the NT "with the African eyes"; that is, *reading* with different social lenses on the people; the African humanity who are struggling for the *reconstruction* of the physical and spiritual aspects of their societies.

I. SCRIPTURES

By the time Christian evangelists and writers began to compose the earliest Christian literatures, there had already existed *hai graphai*, the scriptures; namely the books of the Septuagint, the Greek literal translation of the Old Testament made at Alexandria some three centuries before Christ as the *scripture* par excellence. For them, this was the major vehicle of divine revelation. Contemporary NT literary criticism has abundantly made it clear that the Septuagint was indeed the Bible of the earliest church, in order words, the *scripture* the writers and the redactors of both Matthew and Luke even Paul had known, read and

1. P. STUHLMACHER, *Biblische Theologie des Neuen Testaments I. Grundlegung: Von Jesus zu Paulus*, Göttingen, Vandenhoeck & Ruprecht, 1992; H. HÜBNER, *Biblische Theologie des Neuen Testaments 1-3*, Göttingen, Vandenhoeck & Ruprecht, 1990-1995.
2. J. GNILKA, *Theologie des Neuen Testaments*, Freiburg–Basel–Wien, Herder, 1994.

used[3]. The evangelist of the Third Gospel tells us this quite poignantly. In the encounter between the Risen Jesus and the two disciples on the road to Emmaus, the Risen Lord interpreted and taught them the *Scriptures* "beginning with Moses and all the prophets" (Lk 24,27). When they acknowledged the power of his words, they exclaimed: "Did not our hearts burn within us while he talked to us on the road, while he opened to us the *Scriptures*" (Lk 24, 32). Such scriptures and their interpretation were the glad tidings that warmed the hearts of our "ancestors" in faith as it continues to do today in the African congregations.

In subsequent years, Paul had promoted the epistolary genre as a relevant means of consolidating the faith of Christians he had converted as well as of educating other communities in different parts of the Mediterranean world. There also developed a flurry of Christian literature on the life, words and deeds of Jesus. Many of these documents had acquired the status of *scripture* as Jesus was in their plot the embodiment of divine revelation as Son of God and the Risen Messiah. Later on, as heretics appeared on the scene and adulterated or produced variants of the books, there came a limited understanding of the term, *scripture*. During the heretical movement led by Montanus (156-157 AD) who had accentuated the role of women prophetesses in his church, there flourished a vast volume of "sacred scriptures", most of them with grotesque charismatic flair. There arose, at this juncture, the problem of collecting and selecting those books that could be considered vehicles of authentic revelation useful to encourage suffering Christians; in other words, the *scriptures* that could be read with "the eyes of the sufferers" in the light of Christ's passion, death and glorification. Therefore, persecutions and heresies became strong factors that contributed to the *collection* and *selection* of the books as *scriptures*.

II. CANON

In the light of the prevailing state of affairs where several books were claimed as *hagiographies*, many Church Fathers and other persons individually initiated informal collection of the books that were credited as containing authentic revelation. By the middle of the second century, the Pauline Corpus as well as the Four Gospels were already available in collections. The process of inclusion and exclusion that led to the collection of "the list of sacred books accepted by the church as authoritative in matters of faith and life"[4] was nevertheless gradual and unofficial

3. M. MÜLLER, *The Septuagint as the Bible of the New Testament Church*, in *SJOT* (1993) 194-207.

4. A.M. HUNTER, *Introducing the New Testament*, London, SCM Press, 1989, p. 14.

spanning through three centuries. However, some of such books became well accepted as normative ecclesiastical documents in the regions they originated from. At this stage, the idea of a New Testament *sub-canon* was beginning to emerge[5].

By the middle of the second century to about the year 190 CE, the NT canon had become almost a reality.

The indebtedness of the New Testament books to African churchmen is attested to in the long history of the process of the canonization of its *scriptures*. Apart however from Marcion, who was the first person to actually visualize the idea of the NT canon, Clement (150-215), Tertullian (160-225), Origen (185-254), Dionysius (247-260), and Athanasius (296-373) – the famous theologians who had earned a place in the roll of honour in the African Church (Alexandria) in the second half of the second century to the middle of the fourth century – had all contributed immensely to the development of the Christian canon. But it was not until the fourth century in the Greek east and the Latin west that a wide recognition of a canon of twenty-seven books was officially declared the authoritative books of the Church at a Council of Hippo Regius in Africa (393).

In spite of this historic landmark, two later African Councils in Carthage (now modern Tunis) re-affirmed in 397 and 419 the resolution reached at Hippo. In each case, St. Augustine was an authority in the decision processes that gave Christianity its authoritative books. Evidence from reliable historical records show that Augustine was a great African Church Father whose list contained the same twenty-seven books as we have them today in the New Testament. It is also the pride of contemporary African Christianity that by 405 AD, the Papacy had endorsed without question the verdict *ex Africa*.

In sum, three phases can be sketched in the history of the New Testament canon: (a) the proliferation of Christian literature considered as *scripture/s;* (b) the conscious collection of some of these writings into a closed sub-collection; and (c) the formation of the New Testament List (canon). This means that there was first, the *scriptures,* then the collection and finally, the canonization of the twenty-seven books.

III. INTERPRETATION

This section of the paper discusses how contemporary African Christians see it their duty to interpret and inculturate the teaching of the NT

5. J.W. MILLER, *The Origins of the Bible: Re-thinking Canon History*, New York, Paulist Press, 1994.

as *scripture* received and accepted by the Church on the African soil. For contemporary African Christians, the *scriptures* must be made meaningful and preached to *touch on* life rather than infantilizing the faithful. In contemporary African Christianity, there is a rich variety of methods being adopted in biblical interpretation. Some interpreters adopt the historical critical method or any of its variants to interpret the texts of the Bible and then apply their meanings to the African context in question. In recent times, there has occurred a proliferation of Independent Churches, Pentecostal and Evangelical organizations in contemporary Africa. Even in the secular media, it has been observed that the new churches "are mainly headed by young people" who are not well educated and are theologically ill-grounded in the Bible yet, most of them are known to lead large numbers of people and followers[6]. Many of these kinds of people thumb through the Bible from Genesis to Revelation without the slightest qualm on the historicity of the texts and the veracity of the preachment they make out of them, even when taken out of context[7]. But at the same time, many of the more charismatic pastors are revolutionizing Bible interpretation as "they have", as J.N.K. Mugambi eloquently observes, "appropriated the Bible in their own way, in accordance with their understanding and experience"[8]. Most of them, prosperity gospelers, find in the Bible messages that favour their preaching on the blessedness of material possessions pretending ignorance of the significance of Paul the renouncer of economic wealth and resources and Zacchaeus, the responsible steward of material goods.

In a study on the interpretation of the Bible in the African Indigenous Churches (AICs) in Malawi, H.B.P. Mijoka discovers the use of thematic and verse-by-verse approach by untrained readers of the Bible. He finds out that such readers have incipient knowledge of Biblical texts they read and manifest their own way of approaching and interpreting the texts with such devices as prayers, stories, songs, retelling, proverbs and proof-texts to make the Bible meaningful to their audience[9]. Mijoka's research focused on the interpretation of the Bible

6. K. BUHERE, *Theology of Christian Churches: Which Way Forward?* in *Kenya Times*, Nairobi, Thursday, June 7, 2001, p. 14.

7. C.U. MANUS, *The Use and Role of the Bible in Three New Religious Movements in Nigeria: Lessons for Slovenian Christian Culture*, in J. KRASOVEC (ed.), *The Interpretation of the Bible,* Sheffield, Sheffield Academic Press, 1998, pp. 1805-1825.

8. J.N.K. MUGAMBI, *Foundations for an African Approach to Biblical Hermeneutics*, in M. GETUI, *et al.* (eds.), *Interpreting the New Testament in Africa*, Nairobi, Acton Publishers, 2002, pp. 1-30, esp. p. 20

9. H.B.P. MIJOKA, *Hidden and Public Ways of Doing Contextual Bible Study in Southern Africa: South Africa and Malawi as Case Studies,* in *Religion in Malawi* 7 (1997) 41-44, esp. pp. 42-43.

in Malawi. In 1998, D.T. Adamo and I myself investigated the method
and interpretation of the Bible by three AICs in Nigeria[10]. Adamo's
findings reveal that the AICs include the Pentecostal and Evangelical
Churches that strongly hold the view that the Bible works miracles
when used in "the combination of the Word of God and African indigenous medicine for protection against all kinds of evil that may befall
humankind"[11]. They search the Bible in their own way with the purpose
of finding "greater power in Christianity"[12]. In the tradition of their
religio-cultural backgrounds, members and pastors of these churches
read the Bible to seek protection from all sorts of evil as if the Bible is
a source of hidden mystical power as was known in African Indigenous
Religions from which they were converted to Christianity. Thus Adamo
concludes that the AICs in Nigeria interpret the Bible incantationally
as potent words, use portions of it as charms and amulets and have
recourse to the whole book as a source of medicine for all sorts of protection[13]. Besides these uncritical modes of biblical interpretation among
the "untrained" church leaders and preachers in Africa, let us briefly
examine the *inculturation method* as a critical tool of analysis and interpretation.

IV. INCULTURATION HERMENEUTICS

The *inculturation hermeneutics* has begun to take pride of place
among Biblical scholars in the mainline Church-instituted Colleges and
Seminaries as well as in the secular tertiary institutions such as University Departments of Religious Studies and Theology. This is a methodology in which the academically trained interpreter employs the resources
of African social or religio-cultural contexts, that is, African view of reality and African life experience, to examine the text of a given passage
of the Bible and to derive meaning suitable to her/his context[14]. She/he

10. D.T. ADAMO, *Reading the Bible Protectively in African Indigenous Churches in
Nigeria*, SNTS Post Conference Meeting on African Hermeneutics and Theology,
Hammanskraal, South Africa, August, 7-9, 1999. MANUS, *The Use* (n. 7).
11. ADAMO, *Reading the Bible Protectively*, p. 1.
12. *Ibid.*, p. 4.
13. *Ibid.*, pp. 5-9.
14. C.U. MANUS, *Methodological Approaches in Biblical Scholarship: The Case of
West Africa,* forthcoming in E. KATONGOLE (ed.), *Readings in African Biblical Hermeneutics*, Scranton, Scranton University Press, 2002. Noteworthy among my recent studies
are: *Paul's Speech at the Areopagus (Acts 17,22-34): An African Reading*, in GETUI, *Interpreting* (n. 8), pp. 213-230. *Inculturating New Testament Christologies in Africa: The
Case of Yoruba and Igbo Grassroots Christians in Ile-Ife, Osun State, Nigeria*, in
Zeitschrift für Missionswissenschaft und Religionswissenschaft 2 (2002) 116-143.

reads the scripture with a community of ordinary readers and from the perspective of the ordinary Africans. This interpretative process requires, as J.S. Ukpong, the Nigerian biblical scholar, asserts, a "participatory and dialogic dynamics and entails, among other things, a commitment to a particular contextual starting-point and wrestling with societal issues"[15]. For most African Biblical scholars adopting this approach, the *context* in which the text is interpreted is made the *subject* of the interpretation[16]. In most regions of Africa, the term *ordinary people* refers to a social class that does not belong to the elite group. Most of them are simple-folk Christians who live their lives by the worldview provided by their traditional worldviews. Generally they live poor and are on the periphery of the society. Most members of this class inhabit the rural regions and others have migrated to the urban slums in search of daily bread. Every day, they toil and labour to keep body and soul together and to fend for their families[17].

But in spite of their low standard of living, they have a good sense of self-worth, respect for human dignity and unflinching faith in their Christian vocation. They engage in Group-Bible-sharing sessions in their churches or in house to house meetings. They find in the scriptures "inspiration, strength and courage to continue to live on and the desire to transform themselves and their society. All these aspirations, consciously or unconsciously, influence the way they read the Bible"[18]. Inculturation hermeneutics has come to be employed by academically trained readers in Africa for biblical interpretations that are dictated by the perspectives, openness and concerns of the ordinary readers, in order to prosper their ordinary readings. This method includes a lot of options. The first is the theoretical assumptions of the conceptual framework for which the text is read. Secondly, questions are raised on the text, not at all from the viewpoint of those who hold magisterial authority, positions and power over the text but actually from the point of view of the simple folk whom the text identifies as lowly, pauperized and marginalized. Thirdly, the method attempts to uplift the *voices* of this class of Christians who are only thematically oblique in the text.

15. J.S. UKPONG, *Bible Reading with a Community of Ordinary Readers*, in GETUI, *Interpreting* (n. 8), pp. 188-212, esp. p. 188; also ID., *Rereading the Bible with the African Eyes: Inculturation and Hermeneutics*, in *Journal of Theology for Southern Africa* 91 (1995) 3-14.

16. J.C. LOBA MKOLE, *New Testament in Africa: From Celebrations to Translations*, SNTS Post Conference Meeting on African Hermeneutics and Theology, Hammanskraal, 8-10 August, 1999, pp. 1-2.

17. UKPONG, *Bible Reading with a Community* (n. 15), p. 189-190.

18. *Ibid.*, p. 190.

Gerald West, a South African biblical scholar, had injected into the African biblical hermeneutics system the notions of "reading behind the text", "reading in or on the text" and "reading in front of the text"[19]. By these critical approaches, African biblical scholars' interpretative methodologies share with the historical critical method the *dictum* that the Bible is "a culture's literary property"[20] that needs to be understood in its concrete historical and social cultural contexts. As contexts determine the theologizing one does, the text being interpreted may have to be linked to a specific contemporary context. What African scholars are doing most of the time is to ensure that the meaning of a text is not only that intended by the author from his culture's worldview[21]. For some African scholars, meaning is produced in a process where the text is read with African communities who are enjoined to interact with it as it is structured in its historical and socio-cultural contexts. In this enterprise, readers are not seen as isolated individuals but as communities or individuals that are reading and exploring their Christian traditions in the light of contemporary experience.

V. A CASE EXAMPLE

I wish to illustrate my submission with my current reading of Mt 18, 15-22 in the Nigerian and Kenyan contemporary socio-political contexts. This is a text where the evangelist, Matthew, has documented a tripartite stage of conflict resolution and post-conflict reconciliation not dissimilar to African cultural approaches[22]. My interpretation involves the adoption of a conceptual framework that provides the grid through which lessons contained in the text are processed and appropriated to address contemporary ethnic crises in modern Africa. The reading is anchored on ordinary African population; specifically Nigerians and Kenyans in view of a reality which is dictated by their life experiences of incessant occurrences of ethnic, sub-ethnic and intra-ethnic conflicts that destabilize the societies and vitiate the principles and values of democratic governance in the two nations. The social political situations of

19. G.O. WEST, *Biblical Hermeneutics of Liberation: Modes of Reading the Bible in the South African Context*, Pietermaritzburg, Cluster Publications, 1995.

20. R. MORGAN & J. BARTON, *Biblical Interpretation* (The Oxford Bible Series), Oxford, University Press, 1988, p. 174.

21. *Ibid.*

22. C.U. MANUS, *Inter/Sub-Ethnic Conflicts Resolution & Reconciliation in Nigeria and Kenya: A Reading of Mt 18,15-22.* Current Research Project, Religious Studies Department, Nairobi, Kenyatta University, 2001.

the two nations provide significant aspects of the conceptual framework of my reading Mt 18, 15-22. To make the text be understood by my audience, I would neither wish to separate ethnicism nor religious fundamentalism from politics that are often the root causes of the conflicts. My research on conflict situations in both countries reveals that both Nigerians and Kenyans do not distinguish the one from the other. They see both as two sides of the same coin. In other words, for the peoples of the two countries, reality is one whole comprising ethnic, religious and political issues. In reading Mat 18,15ff as a suitable text to draw lessons for conflict resolution and reconciliation, I have to look beyond the veneer of Matthean ecclesiology to discover the text's implications on contemporary Christian Africa where religious, tribal and ethnic considerations determine the conduct of most people. In that light, Matthew's injunctions are not held as deriving from a mere pious religious narrative but as one in which theological, political and social issues can be seen together. As I interpret the text, my task, *inter alia,* is to express my findings in clear and lucid terms and not in abstract concepts typical of academic exegetes. I also take full account of the compositional nature or the narrative genre and the implications these have on the meaning one gives of the text. The triple-stage composition of the narrative and the portion on forgiveness and reconciliation are found useful to establish the meaning implicated in the text and its bearing in formulating principles for conflict resolution and reconciliation for the two peoples. Besides, the narrative plot of the *logion* requires critical attention of the African context *vis à vis* what the evangelist had penned to leaders of his community in the first century of the Common Era.

It must be understood that Mat 18,15-22 was written in the style of a communal address to a living community. *Mutatis mutandis,* I read the text to address people of both countries whose contemporary religious, ethnic and inter-ethnic relations are ever on belligerent course. The text draws the attention of my readership to the cardinal lessons of the biblical gospel and some African traditional approaches to dialogue and conflict-resolution. At the end of the reading the themes of *forgiveness, reconciliation, dialogue* and *confidence-building measures* emerge as what the texts furnish. These lessons are then clearly attuned down to earth and anchored to address the Nigerian and Kenyan peoples' contemporary social political contexts where ethnic rivalries more often than not take on political coloration and result in wanton blood letting. Indeed Mt 18,15-22 read in *pari passu* with the African narratives helps African Christians build bridges of understanding to promote forgiveness and reconciliation. From such interpretations, African Christians are shown the importance of fraternal love, the need to shun violence and to sue for peace and forgiveness.

In reality, intercultural hermeneutics progresses in four steps:

(a) exposition of the African context with the aid of a or some cultural narrative/s against which the biblical text is to be interpreted;

(b) exposition of the biblical context of the passage to be interpreted. This involves an historical critical analysis of the context of the text to show the closeness between the African context and the context of the text being interpreted[23];

(c) exposition of the biblical text in the perspectives of literary criticism[24];

(d) the hermeneutical deliverance of the text in the light of the context/s[25] that is analyzed, that is, the interpretation and articulation of the meaning of the text so that it speaks to the current situation/s[26].

This profile constitutes the essentials of the emerging critical mode of reading the Bible by trained African biblical exegetes. As observed before, there are African Christians who have no special training in reading the Bible with critical methods like the Intercultural and the Inculturational, African Feminist, African Social Critical, Black African Contextual and Africa in the Bible Hermeneutics[27]. They represent groups with latent knowledge of the unsophisticated exegetical devices and tools. Western biblical scholarship would do well to come to appreciate their contributions to biblical interpretation. As Gerald West advises: "Trained readers bring critical resources for reading the Bible. Ordinary readers bring resources from their context for reading the Bible. Together we enable the Bible to speak to us"[28]. Indeed, they are making meaning out of the Bible as a religious object that contains religious material[29]. Thus contemporary African Biblical scholarship is drawing the attention of Western scholars to come to acknowledge the existence of interpretations made within *localized* contexts as equally valid. Our plea, as Justin Ukpong insists, is that it should be understood that any tool of biblical

23. J.S. UKPONG, *Essays in Inculturation Hermeneutics: Guidelines for the Publication of Essays on Intercultural Hermeneutics in Biblical Interpretation.* Unpublished Ms., Nashville, 2001, p. 1

24. G.O. WEST, *The Relationship between the Modes of Reading The Bible and the Ordinary Reader*, in *Scriptura Supplement* 9 (1991) 87-110, esp. 88-89.

25. MANUS, *Methodological Approaches in Biblical Scholarship.*

26. On this, see my *Christ, the African King. New Testament Christology* (Studies in Intercultural History of Christianity, 82), Frankfurt/Main, Peter Lang, 1993, pp. 239-252.

27. D.T. ADAMO, *Africa and the Africans in the Old Testament,* San Francisco, Christian Universities Press, 1998.

28. G.O. WEST, *Contextual Bible Study*, Pietermaritzburg, Cluster Publications, 1993, p. 49.

29. MORGAN & BARTON, *Biblical Interpretation* (n. 20), p. 167.

interpretation emerges out of a certain social cultural context and generally bears the imprint of that context. In the global village we claim to live in, there is no longer any tool of interpretation that must be held as universal, scientific or objective. Western tools adopt the Western conceptual framework for interpretation and make the Western context the subject of the exegesis. Intercultural hermeneutics seeks to make African contexts the subject of exegesis by using African framework to flesh out its interpretation[30]. Through the interface with the African approaches, contemporary biblical scholarship stands to be enriched as pluriform methodologies will no doubt promote a global networking in biblical scholarship.

CONCLUSION

There is no doubt that the Bible is held as a significant resource book in Christian Africa today. Ample evidence abounds that the Bible is the most widely spread and vastly translated religious book in the continent, at least, in sub-Saharan Africa[31]. John S. Mbiti, Kenya's foremost biblical scholar, has drawn attention to the "sacred space" the Bible occupies in African Christianity[32]. On a thorough-going research on the subject, Mbiti has discovered that the growth, dynamism and the permanent presence of Christianity in Africa is due to the significance and the centrality accorded the Bible. David B. Barrett has noted that the translations of the Bible into the vernacular languages of Africa have made it possible to develop a Christianity truly possessed by Africans[33]. There is agreement that the rapid emergence of African Independent Churches, the Pentecostal and Charismatic movements in different parts of the continent is largely the consequence of the availability and possession of the vernacular Bible. For Mugambi, "wherever the Bible is available in local African languages, it becomes an integral part of local literature, in very much the same way it did in Europe during the Reformation"[34]. As Maluleke rightly asserts, "the Bible's significance and influence goes far

30. ADAMO, *Africa and the Africans in the Old Testament* (n. 10), p. 1.
31. *The African Bible,* Nairobi, Paulines Publications Africa, 1999.
32. J.S. MBITI, *Bible and Theology in African Christianity*, Nairobi, Oxford University Press, 1986; ID., *The Biblical Basis for Present Trends in African Theology*, in K. APIPIAH-KUBI & T. SERGIO (eds.), *African Theology en Route. Papers from the Pan-African Conference of Third World Theologians*, Maryknoll, NY, Orbis, pp. 83-94.
33. D.B. BARRETT, *World Christian Encyclopedia: A Comparative Survey of Churches and Religions in the Modern World AD 1900-2000*, Nairobi, Oxford University Press, 1982.
34. MUGAMBI, *An African Approach to Biblical Hermeneutics* (n. 8), p. 3.

beyond the confines of the 'official church' and various denominations"[35]. In Nigeria there are textbooks that help students in Secondary Schools understand the Bible[36]. In the Southern African countries, literacy training is based on regular Bible reading and memorization of passages in class. In defense of this situation, Maluleke auspiciously informs us that:

> The Bible has therefore served – and continues in many places to serve – as the most accessible basic vernacular literature text, a story-book, a compilation of novels and short stories, a book of prose and poetry, a book of spiritual devotion – i. e., the 'Word of God' – as well as a 'science' book that explains the origins of all creatures[37].

On the same issue, he further adds:

> In some parts of Africa, the dead are buried with the Bible on their chests and the Bible is buried into the concrete foundations on which new houses are to be built. In many African Independent Churches, it is the physical contact between the sick and the Bible that is believed to hasten healing[38].

As the Christians of the Apostolic era re-interpreted the LXX and accepted their contributions as the living voice of the apostolic witnesses, so, today, do African Christians hold their interpretations of the canonical books of the NT as the re-enactment of the "living voice" of the apostolic witness to which they must bear witness to Africans of the 21st century; especially as most of them consider the scripture a valid instrument of social change and transformation in their church and society[39]. This solid faith confers on the African Bible readers the will to relate the biblical gospel to the life of the individual and the community[40].

Kenyatta University   Chris Ukachukwu MANUS
Religious Studies Department
Nairobi
Kenya

35. T.S. MALULEKE, *The Bible and African Theologies*, in GETUI, *Interpreting* (n. 8), pp. 165-176, esp. 166.

36. C.U. MANUS *et al.*, *Christian Religious Knowledge for the Nigerian Secondary Schools*, Vols. 1, 2 & 3, Lagos, Nelson, 1992.

37. MALULEKE, *The Bible* (n. 35), p. 166.

38. *Ibid.*

39. J.N.K. MUGAMBI, *From Liberation to Reconstruction: African Christian Theology After the Cold War*, Nairobi, East African Educational Publishers, 1995.

40. N. ONWU, *The Current State of Biblical Studies in Africa*, in *Journal of Religious Thought* 41 (1985) 35-46; S.O. ABOGUNRIN, *Biblical Research in Africa: The Task Ahead*, in *African Journal of Biblical Studies* 1 (1986) 7-24.

INDEXES

ABBREVIATIONS

AB	Anchor Bible
ABD	*Anchor Bible Dictionary*
AGLB	Aus der Geschichte der lateinischen Bibel
ALBO	Analecta lovaniensia biblica et orientalia
ALGHJ	Arbeiten zur Literatur und Geschichte des hellenistischen Judentums
AnBib	Analecta biblica
ANRW	Aufstieg und Niedergang der römischen Welt
ANTF	Arbeiten zur neutestamentlichen Textforschung
APF	*Archiv für Papyrusforschung*
ATD	Das Alte Testament Deutsch
ATD.E	Das Alte Testament Deutsch. Ergänzungsband
ATR	*Anglican Theological Review*
BBB	Bonner biblische Beiträge
BEATAJ	Beiträge zur Erforschung des Alten Testaments und des antiken Judentums
BETL	Bibliotheca ephemeridum theologicarum lovaniensium
BEvT	Beiträge zur evangelischen Theologie
BHT	Beiträge zur historischen Theologie
Bib	*Biblica*
BibRev	*Bible Review*
Bijdragen	*Bijdragen. Tijdschrift voor filosofie en theologie*
BiOr	*Bibliotheca orientalis*
BJRL	*Bulletin of the John Rylands Library*
BKAT	Biblischer Kommentar: Altes Testament
BN	*Biblische Notizen*
BOT	De boeken van het Oude Testament
BTB	*Biblical Theology Bulletin*
BTS	Biblisch-theologische Studien
BWANT	Beiträge zur Wissenschaft vom Alten und Neuen Testament
BZ	*Biblische Zeitschrift*
BZAW	Beihefte zur *ZAW*
BZNW	Beihefte zur *ZNW*
CAT	Commentaire de l'Ancien Testament
Cath	*Catholica* (München)
CBET	Contributions to Biblical Exegesis and Theology
CB OT	Coniectanea biblica. Old Testament Series
CBQ	*Catholic Biblical Quarterly*
CBQ.MS	Catholic Biblical Quarterly Monograph Series
CC SL	Corpus christianorum. Series latina
CH	*Church History*

CoF	Cogitatio fidei
Concilium (D)	*Concilium* (Einsiedeln)
CRB	Cahiers de la *Revue biblique*
CRINT	Corpus rerum iudaicarum ad Novum Testamentum
CritRR	*Critical Review of Books in Religion*
CrSt	*Cristianesimo nella storia*
CSCO	Corpus scriptorum christianorum orientalium
CSEL	Corpus scriptorum ecclesiasticorum latinorum
CTM	Calwer theologische Monographien
DACL	*Dictionnaire d'archéologie chrétienne et liturgie*
DBAT	*Dielheimer Blätter zum Alten Testament*
DB(S)	*Dictionnaire de la Bible (Supplément)*
DHGE	*Dictionnaire d'histoire et de géographie ecclésiastiques*
DJD	*Discoveries in the Judaean Desert*
DNP	*Der Neue Pauly: Enzyklopädie der Antike*
DSD	Dead Sea Discoveries
DTC	*Dictionnaire de théologie catholique*
EB	Études bibliques
EdF	Erträge der Forschung
EHPhR	Etudes d'histoire et de philosophie religieuses
EHS.T	Europäische Hochschulschriften: Theologie
EKK	Evangelisch-katholischer Kommentar
EkklPharos	*Ekklesiastikos Pharos*
ETL	*Ephemerides theologicae lovanienses*
ETR	*Études théologiques et religieuses*
EvTh	*Evangelische Theologie*
EWNT	*Exegetisches Wörterbuch zum Neuen Testament*
ExpT	*Expository Times*
FAT	Forschungen zum Alten Testament
FRLANT	Forschungen zur Religion und Literatur des Alten und Neuen Testaments
FTS	Frankfurter theologische Studien
FzB	Forschung zur Bibel
GCS	Die griechischen christlichen Schriftsteller der ersten drei Jahrhunderte
GTA	Göttinger theologische Arbeiten
GuL	*Geist und Leben*
HAT	Handbuch zum Alten Testament
HBS	Herders biblische Studien
HDG	Handbuch der Dogmengeschichte
HK(AT)	Handkommentar (zum Alten Testament)
HNT	Handbuch zum Neuen Testament
HNT Erg	Handbuch zum Neuen Testament. Ergänzungshefte
HorizonsBT	Horizons in Biblical Theology

HSS	*Harvard Semitic Studies*
HTK(AT)	Herders theologischer Kommentar (zum Alten Testament)
HTK(NT)	Herders theologischer Kommentar (zum Neuen Testament)
HTR	*Harvard Theological Review*
HTS	Harvard Theological Studies
ICA	Initiations au christianisme ancien
ICC	International Critical Commentary
IDB	*Interpreter's Dictionary of the Bible*
IEJ	*Israel Exploration Journal*
Interp	*Interpretation. A Journal of Bible and Theology* (Richmond)
JANES	*Journal of the Ancient Near Eastern Society* (Columbia University)
JBC	*The Jerome Biblical Commentary*
JBL	*Journal of Biblical Literature*
JBT	*Jahrbuch für biblische Theologie*
JEC	*Journal of Early Christian Studies*
JEH	*Journal of Ecclesiastical History*
JETS	*Journal of the Evangelical Theological Society*
JJS	*Journal of Jewish Studies*
JSJ	*Journal for the Study of Judaism*
JSJ SS	Journal for the Study of Judaism Supplement Series
JSNT SS	Journal for the Study of the New Testament Supplement Series
JSOT	*Journal for the Study of the Old Testament*
JSOT SS	Journal for the Study of the Old Testament Supplement Series
JSPSup	Journal for the Study of the Pseudepigrapha Supplement Series
JSS	*Journal of Semitic Studies*
JTS	*The Journal of Theological Studies*
KAT	Kommentar zum Alten Testament
KAV	Kommentar zu den Apostolischen Vätern
KBANT	Kommentare und Beiträge zum Alten und Neuen Testament
KEK(NT)	Kritisch-exegetischer Kommentar (über das Neue Testament)
KT	Kaiser Taschenbücher
LD	Lectio divina
LTK	*Lexicon für Theologie und Kirche*
LTK.E	*Lexicon für Theologie und Kirche*. Ergänzungsband
LumVie	*Lumière et vie*
MGH Auct. Ant.	Monumenta Germaniae historica, Auctores antiquissimi
Mobi	Le monde de la Bible

NA	Nestle-Aland, *Novum Testamentum graece*
NHS	Nag Hammadi Studies
NICOT	New International Commentary on the Old Testament
NJBC	*The New Jerome Biblical Commentary*
NKZ	*Neue kirchliche Zeitschrift*
NT	*Novum Testamentum*
NTA	Neutestamentliche Abhandlungen
NTD	Das Neue Testament Deutsch
NTOA	Novum Testamentum et orbis antiquus
NTS	*New Testament Studies*
NTT	*Nederlands theologisch tijdschrift*
NTTS	New Testament Tools and Studies
NZSysT	*Neue Zeitschrift für systematische Theologie*
OBO	Orbis biblicus et orientalis
OLP	*Orientalia lovaniensia periodica*
OTE	Old Testament Essays
ÖTK	Ökumenische Taschenbuchkommentare
OTL	Old Testament Library
OTS	*Oudtestamentische studiën*
PG	Patrologia graeca (J. MIGNE ed.)
PL	Patrologia latina (J. MIGNE ed.)
PO	Patrologia orientalis
PTA	Papyrologische Texte und Abhandlungen
PTS	Patristische Texte und Studien
PVTG	Pseudepigrapha Veteris Testamenti graece
QD	Quaestiones disputatae
RB	*Revue biblique*
RBén	*Revue bénédictine*
REA	*Revue des études anciennes*
RestQ	*Restoration Quarterly*
RGG	*Die Religion in Geschichte und Gegenwart*
RHPR	*Revue d'histoire et de philosophie religieuses*
RHR	*Revue de l'histoire des religions*
RivBib	*Rivista biblica (italiana)*
RNT	Regensburger Neues Testament
RQ	*Revue de Qumrân*
RSPT	*Revue des sciences philosophiques et théologiques*
RSR	*Recherches de science religieuse*
RTL	*Revue théologique de Louvain*
SB	Sources bibliques
SBAB	Stuttgarter biblische Aufzatzbände
SBB	Stuttgarter biblische Beiträge
SBL DS	Society of Biblical Literature Dissertation Series
SBL EJL	Society of Biblical Literature Early Judaism and its Litera-

	ture
SBL MS	Society of Biblical Literature Monograph Series
SBL SBS	Society of Biblical Literature Sources for Biblical Studies
SBL SCS	Society of Biblical Literature Septuagint and Cognate Studies
SBL SP	Society of Biblical Literature Seminar Papers
SBL SS	Society of Biblical Literature Semeia Studies
SBS	Stuttgarter Bibelstudien
SC	Sources chrétiennes
ScEsp	*Science et Esprit*
ScotJT	*Scottish Journal of Theology*
SHAW.PH	Sitzungsberichte der Heidelberger Akademie der Wissenschaften, Philosophisch-historische Klasse
SJOT	*Scandinavian Journal of the Old Testament*
SNT	Supplements to *Novum Testamentum*
SNTA	Studiorum Novi Testamenti auxilia
SNTS.MS	Society of New Testament Studies Monograph Series
SNTU	Studien zum Neuen Testament und seiner Umwelt
SP	Studia patristica
SPB	Studia post-biblica
SQS	Sammlung ausgewählter kirchen- und dogmengeschichtlicher Quellenschriften
SSN	Studia semitica neerlandica
ST	*Studia theologica. Scandinavian Journal of Theology*
StANT	Studien zum Alten und Neuen Testament
STDJ	Studies on the Texts of the Desert of Judah
StUNT	Studien zur Umwelt des Neuen Testaments
SubBib	Subsidia biblica
SVT	Supplements to *Vetus Testamentum*
SVTP	Studia in Veteris Testamenti pseudepigrapha
TANZ	Texte und Arbeiten zum neutestamentlichen Zeitalter
TB	Theologische Bücherei
TDNT	*Theological Dictionary of the New Testament*
THK	Theologischer Handkommentar zum Neuen Testament
TLZ	*Theologische Literaturzeitung*
TM	Texte masorétique
TP	*Theologie und philosophie*
TR	*Theologische Rundschau*
Trans	*Transeuphratène*
TRE	*Theologische Realenzyklopädie*
TTZ	*Trierer theologische Zeitschrift*
TU	Texte und Untersuchungen
TvT	*Tijdschrift voor theologie*
TWAT	*Theologisches Wörterbuch zum Alten Testament*
TWNT	*Theologisches Wörterbuch zum Neuen Testament*
TyndBull	*Tyndale Bulletin*
TZ	*Theologische Zeitschrift*
UF	*Ugarit Forschungen*

UTB	Uni-Taschenbücher
UTB.W	Uni-Taschenbücher für Wissenschaft
VetChr	*Vetera christianorum*
VigChr	*Vigiliae christianae*
VigChrSup	Supplements to *Vigiliae christianae*
VT	*Vetus Testamentum*
WBC	Word Biblical Commentary
WMANT	Wissenschaftliche Monographien zum Alten und Neuen Testament
WTJ	*Westminster Theological Journal*
WUNT	Wissenschaftliche Untersuchungen zum Neuen Testament
ZAC	*Zeitschrift für antikes Christentum/Journal of Ancient Christianity*
ZAW	*Zeitschrift für die Alttestamentliche Wissenschaft*
ZBK.NT	Zürcher Bibelkommentare. Neues Testament
ZKG	*Zeitschrift für Kirchengeschichte*
ZNW	*Zeitschrift für die neutestamentliche Wissenschaft*
ZPE	*Zeitschrift für Papyrologie und Epigraphik*
ZTK	*Zeitschrift für Theologie und Kirche*
ZWT	*Zeitschrift für wissenschaftliche Theologie*

INDEX OF AUTHORS

Asterisked (*) page numbers refer to pages on which an author is mentioned in one or more footnotes.

INDEX OF REFERENCES
TO BIBLICAL, JEWISH, CHRISTIAN
AND CLASSICAL LITERATURE

BIBLE

NON-BIBLICAL REFERENCES

JEWISH LITERATURE

CHRISTIAN LITERATURE

BIBLICAL PAPYRI AND RELATED MS. FRAGMENTS

CLASSICAL LITERATURE

ISLAMIC AUTHOR

LIST OF CONTRIBUTORS

BIBLIOTHECA EPHEMERIDUM THEOLOGICARUM LOVANIENSIUM

SERIES I

* = Out of print

*1. *Miscellanea dogmatica in honorem Eximii Domini J. Bittremieux,* 1947.

*2-3. *Miscellanea moralia in honorem Eximii Domini A. Janssen,* 1948.

*4. G. PHILIPS, *La grâce des justes de l'Ancien Testament,* 1948.

*5. G. PHILIPS, *De ratione instituendi tractatum de gratia nostrae sanctificationis,* 1953.

6-7. *Recueil Lucien Cerfaux. Études d'exégèse et d'histoire religieuse,* 1954. 504 et 577 p. Cf. *infra,* n°s 18 et 71 (t. III). 25 € par tome

8. G. THILS, *Histoire doctrinale du mouvement œcuménique,* 1955. Nouvelle édition, 1963. 338 p. 4 €

*9. *Études sur l'Immaculée Conception,* 1955.

*10. J.A. O'DONOHOE, *Tridentine Seminary Legislation,* 1957.

*11. G. THILS, *Orientations de la théologie,* 1958.

*12-13. J. COPPENS, A. DESCAMPS, É. MASSAUX (ed.), *Sacra Pagina. Miscellanea Biblica Congressus Internationalis Catholici de Re Biblica,* 1959.

*14. *Adrien VI, le premier Pape de la contre-réforme,* 1959.

*15. F. CLAEYS BOUUAERT, *Les déclarations et serments imposés par la loi civile aux membres du clergé belge sous le Directoire (1795-1801),* 1960.

*16. G. THILS, *La «Théologie œcuménique». Notion-Formes-Démarches,* 1960.

17. G. THILS, *Primauté pontificale et prérogatives épiscopales. «Potestas ordinaria» au Concile du Vatican,* 1961. 103 p. 2 €

*18. *Recueil Lucien Cerfaux,* t. III, 1962. Cf. *infra,* n° 71.

*19. *Foi et réflexion philosophique. Mélanges F. Grégoire,* 1961.

*20. *Mélanges G. Ryckmans,* 1963.

21. G. THILS, *L'infaillibilité du peuple chrétien «in credendo»,* 1963. 67 p. 2 €

*22. J. FÉRIN & L. JANSSENS, *Progestogènes et morale conjugale,* 1963.

*23. *Collectanea Moralia in honorem Eximii Domini A. Janssen,* 1964.

24. H. CAZELLES (ed.), *De Mari à Qumrân. L'Ancien Testament. Son milieu. Ses écrits. Ses relectures juives* (Hommage J. Coppens, I), 1969. 158*-370 p. 23 €

*25. I. DE LA POTTERIE (ed.), *De Jésus aux évangiles. Tradition et rédaction dans les évangiles synoptiques* (Hommage J. Coppens, II), 1967.

26. G. THILS & R.E. BROWN (ed.), *Exégèse et théologie* (Hommage J. Coppens, III), 1968. 328 p. 18 €

*27. J. COPPENS (ed.), *Ecclesia a Spiritu sancto edocta. Hommage à Mgr G. Philips,* 1970. 640 p.

28. J. COPPENS (ed.), *Sacerdoce et célibat. Études historiques et théologiques,* 1971. 740 p. 18 €

29. M. DIDIER (ed.), *L'évangile selon Matthieu. Rédaction et théologie*, 1972. 432 p.   25 €
*30. J. KEMPENEERS, *Le Cardinal van Roey en son temps*, 1971.

SERIES II

31. F. NEIRYNCK, *Duality in Mark. Contributions to the Study of the Markan Redaction*, 1972. Revised edition with Supplementary Notes, 1988. 252 p.
                                                                          30 €
32. F. NEIRYNCK (ed.), *L'évangile de Luc. Problèmes littéraires et théologiques*, 1973. *L'évangile de Luc – The Gospel of Luke*. Revised and enlarged edition, 1989. x-590 p.   55 €
33. C. BREKELMANS (ed.), *Questions disputées d'Ancien Testament. Méthode et théologie*, 1974. *Continuing Questions in Old Testament Method and Theology*. Revised and enlarged edition by M. VERVENNE, 1989. 245 p.
                                                                          30 €
34. M. SABBE (ed.), *L'évangile selon Marc. Tradition et rédaction*, 1974. Nouvelle édition augmentée, 1988. 601 p.   60 €
35. B. WILLAERT (ed.), *Philosophie de la religion – Godsdienstfilosofie. Miscellanea Albert Dondeyne*, 1974. Nouvelle édition, 1987. 458 p.   60 €
36. G. PHILIPS, *L'union personnelle avec le Dieu vivant. Essai sur l'origine et le sens de la grâce créée*, 1974. Édition révisée, 1989. 299 p.   25 €
37. F. NEIRYNCK, in collaboration with T. HANSEN and F. VAN SEGBROECK, *The Minor Agreements of Matthew and Luke against Mark with a Cumulative List*, 1974. 330 p.   23 €
38. J. COPPENS, *Le messianisme et sa relève prophétique. Les anticipations vétérotestamentaires. Leur accomplissement en Jésus*, 1974. Édition révisée, 1989. XIII-265 p.   25 €
39. D. SENIOR, *The Passion Narrative according to Matthew. A Redactional Study*, 1975. New impression, 1982. 440 p.   25 €
40. J. DUPONT (ed.), *Jésus aux origines de la christologie*, 1975. Nouvelle édition augmentée, 1989. 458 p.   38 €
41. J. COPPENS (ed.), *La notion biblique de Dieu*, 1976. Réimpression, 1985. 519 p.   40 €
42. J. LINDEMANS & H. DEMEESTER (ed.), *Liber Amicorum Monseigneur W. Onclin*, 1976. XXII-396 p.   25 €
43. R.E. HOECKMAN (ed.), *Pluralisme et œcuménisme en recherches théologiques. Mélanges offerts au R.P. Dockx, O.P.*, 1976. 316 p.   25 €
44. M. DE JONGE (ed.), *L'évangile de Jean. Sources, rédaction, théologie*, 1977. Réimpression, 1987. 416 p.   38 €
45. E.J.M. VAN EIJL (ed.), *Facultas S. Theologiae Lovaniensis 1432-1797. Bijdragen tot haar geschiedenis. Contributions to its History. Contributions à son histoire*, 1977. 570 p.   43 €
46. M. DELCOR (ed.), *Qumrân. Sa piété, sa théologie et son milieu*, 1978. 432 p.   43 €
47. M. CAUDRON (ed.), *Faith and Society. Foi et société. Geloof en maatschappij. Acta Congressus Internationalis Theologici Lovaniensis 1976*, 1978. 304 p.   29 €

*48. J. KREMER (ed.), *Les Actes des Apôtres. Traditions, rédaction, théologie,* 1979. 590 p.

49. F. NEIRYNCK, avec la collaboration de J. DELOBEL, T. SNOY, G. VAN BELLE, F. VAN SEGBROECK, *Jean et les Synoptiques. Examen critique de l'exégèse de M.-É. Boismard,* 1979. XII-428 p.   25 €

50. J. COPPENS, *La relève apocalyptique du messianisme royal. I. La royauté – Le règne – Le royaume de Dieu. Cadre de la relève apocalyptique,* 1979. 325 p.   25 €

51. M. GILBERT (ed.), *La Sagesse de l'Ancien Testament,* 1979. Nouvelle édition mise à jour, 1990. 455 p.   38 €

52. B. DEHANDSCHUTTER, *Martyrium Polycarpi. Een literair-kritische studie,* 1979. 296 p.   25 €

53. J. LAMBRECHT (ed.), *L'Apocalypse johannique et l'Apocalyptique dans le Nouveau Testament,* 1980. 458 p.   35 €

54. P.-M. BOGAERT (ed.), *Le livre de Jérémie. Le prophète et son milieu. Les oracles et leur transmission,* 1981. *Nouvelle édition mise à jour,* 1997. 448 p.   45 €

55. J. COPPENS, *La relève apocalyptique du messianisme royal. III. Le Fils de l'homme néotestamentaire.* Édition posthume par F. NEIRYNCK, 1981. XIV-192 p.   20 €

56. J. VAN BAVEL & M. SCHRAMA (ed.), *Jansénius et le Jansénisme dans les Pays-Bas. Mélanges Lucien Ceyssens,* 1982. 247 p.   25 €

57. J.H. WALGRAVE, *Selected Writings – Thematische geschriften. Thomas Aquinas, J.H. Newman, Theologia Fundamentalis.* Edited by G. DE SCHRIJVER & J.J. KELLY, 1982. XLIII-425 p.   25 €

58. F. NEIRYNCK & F. VAN SEGBROECK, avec la collaboration de E. MANNING, *Ephemerides Theologicae Lovanienses 1924-1981. Tables générales. (Bibliotheca Ephemeridum Theologicarum Lovaniensium 1947-1981),* 1982. 400 p.   40 €

59. J. DELOBEL (ed.), *Logia. Les paroles de Jésus – The Sayings of Jesus. Mémorial Joseph Coppens,* 1982. 647 p.   50 €

60. F. NEIRYNCK, *Evangelica. Gospel Studies – Études d'évangile. Collected Essays.* Edited by F. VAN SEGBROECK, 1982. XIX-1036 p.   50 €

61. J. COPPENS, *La relève apocalyptique du messianisme royal. II. Le Fils d'homme vétéro- et intertestamentaire.* Édition posthume par J. LUST, 1983. XVII-272 p.   25 €

62. J.J. KELLY, *Baron Friedrich von Hügel's Philosophy of Religion,* 1983. 232 p.   38 €

63. G. DE SCHRIJVER, *Le merveilleux accord de l'homme et de Dieu. Étude de l'analogie de l'être chez Hans Urs von Balthasar,* 1983. 344 p.   38 €

64. J. GROOTAERS & J.A. SELLING, *The 1980 Synod of Bishops: «On the Role of the Family». An Exposition of the Event and an Analysis of its Texts.* Preface by Prof. emeritus L. JANSSENS, 1983. 375 p.   38 €

65. F. NEIRYNCK & F. VAN SEGBROECK, *New Testament Vocabulary. A Companion Volume to the Concordance,* 1984. XVI-494 p.   50 €

66. R.F. COLLINS, *Studies on the First Letter to the Thessalonians,* 1984. XI-415 p.   38 €

67. A. PLUMMER, *Conversations with Dr. Döllinger 1870-1890.* Edited with Introduction and Notes by R. BOUDENS, with the collaboration of L. KENIS, 1985. LIV-360 p.   45 €

68. N. Lohfink (ed.), *Das Deuteronomium. Entstehung, Gestalt und Botschaft /
Deuteronomy: Origin, Form and Message,* 1985. xi-382 p.   50 €

69. P.F. Fransen, *Hermeneutics of the Councils and Other Studies.* Collected
by H.E. Mertens & F. De Graeve, 1985. 543 p.   45 €

70. J. Dupont, *Études sur les Évangiles synoptiques.* Présentées par F.
Neirynck, 1985. 2 tomes, xxi-ix-1210 p.   70 €

71. *Recueil Lucien Cerfaux,* t. III, 1962. Nouvelle édition revue et complétée,
1985. lxxx-458 p.   40 €

72. J. Grootaers, *Primauté et collégialité. Le dossier de Gérard Philips sur
la Nota Explicativa Praevia (Lumen gentium, Chap. III).* Présenté avec
introduction historique, annotations et annexes. Préface de G. Thils,
1986. 222 p.   25 €

73. A. Vanhoye (ed.), *L'apôtre Paul. Personnalité, style et conception du
ministère,* 1986. xiii-470 p.   65 €

74. J. Lust (ed.), *Ezekiel and His Book. Textual and Literary Criticism and
their Interrelation,* 1986. x-387 p.   68 €

75. É. Massaux, *Influence de l'Évangile de saint Matthieu sur la littérature
chrétienne avant saint Irénée.* Réimpression anastatique présentée par
F. Neirynck. *Supplément: Bibliographie 1950-1985,* par B. Dehandschutter, 1986. xxvii-850 p.   63 €

76. L. Ceyssens & J.A.G. Tans, *Autour de l'Unigenitus. Recherches sur la
genèse de la Constitution,* 1987. xxvi-845 p.   63 €

77. A. Descamps, *Jésus et l'Église. Études d'exégèse et de théologie.* Préface
de Mgr A. Houssiau, 1987. xlv-641 p.   63 €

78. J. Duplacy, *Études de critique textuelle du Nouveau Testament.* Présentées
par J. Delobel, 1987. xxvii-431 p.   45 €

79. E.J.M. van Eijl (ed.), *L'image de C. Jansénius jusqu'à la fin du XVIIIᵉ
siècle,* 1987. 258 p.   32 €

80. E. Brito, *La Création selon Schelling. Universum,* 1987. xxxv-646 p.
          75 €

81. J. Vermeylen (ed.), *The Book of Isaiah – Le livre d'Isaïe. Les oracles
et leurs relectures. Unité et complexité de l'ouvrage,* 1989. x-472 p.
          68 €

82. G. Van Belle, *Johannine Bibliography 1966-1985. A Cumulative Bibliography on the Fourth Gospel,* 1988. xvii-563 p.   68 €

83. J.A. Selling (ed.), *Personalist Morals. Essays in Honor of Professor
Louis Janssens,* 1988. viii-344 p.   30 €

84. M.-É. Boismard, *Moïse ou Jésus. Essai de christologie johannique,* 1988.
xvi-241 p.   25 €

84ᴬ. M.-É. Boismard, *Moses or Jesus: An Essay in Johannine Christology.*
Translated by B.T. Viviano, 1993, xvi-144 p.   25 €

85. J.A. Dick, *The Malines Conversations Revisited,* 1989. 278 p.   38 €

86. J.-M. Sevrin (ed.), *The New Testament in Early Christianity – La réception des écrits néotestamentaires dans le christianisme primitif,* 1989.
xvi-406 p.   63 €

87. R.F. Collins (ed.), *The Thessalonian Correspondence,* 1990. xv-546 p.
          75 €

88. F. Van Segbroeck, *The Gospel of Luke. A Cumulative Bibliography
1973-1988,* 1989. 241 p.   30 €

89. G. THILS, *Primauté et infaillibilité du Pontife Romain à Vatican I et autres études d'ecclésiologie,* 1989. XI-422 p. 47 €
90. A. VERGOTE, *Explorations de l'espace théologique. Études de théologie et de philosophie de la religion,* 1990. XVI-709 p. 50 €
*91. J.C. DE MOOR, *The Rise of Yahwism: The Roots of Israelite Monotheism,* 1990. *Revised and Enlarged Edition,* 1997. XV-445 p.
92. B. BRUNING, M. LAMBERIGTS & J. VAN HOUTEM (eds.), *Collectanea Augustiniana. Mélanges T.J. van Bavel,* 1990. 2 tomes, XXXVIII-VIII-1074 p. 75 €
93. A. DE HALLEUX, *Patrologie et œcuménisme. Recueil d'études,* 1990. XVI-887 p. 75 €
94. C. BREKELMANS & J. LUST (eds.), *Pentateuchal and Deuteronomistic Studies: Papers Read at the XIIIth IOSOT Congress Leuven 1989,* 1990. 307 p. 38 €
95. D.L. DUNGAN (ed.), *The Interrelations of the Gospels. A Symposium Led by M.-É. Boismard – W.R. Farmer – F. Neirynck, Jerusalem 1984,* 1990. XXXI-672 p. 75 €
96. G.D. KILPATRICK, *The Principles and Practice of New Testament Textual Criticism. Collected Essays.* Edited by J.K. ELLIOTT, 1990. XXXVIII-489 p. 75 €
97. G. ALBERIGO (ed.), *Christian Unity. The Council of Ferrara-Florence: 1438/39 – 1989,* 1991. X-681 p. 75 €
98. M. SABBE, *Studia Neotestamentica. Collected Essays,* 1991. XVI-573 p. 50 €
99. F. NEIRYNCK, *Evangelica II: 1982-1991. Collected Essays.* Edited by F. VAN SEGBROECK, 1991. XIX-874 p. 70 €
100. F. VAN SEGBROECK, C.M. TUCKETT, G. VAN BELLE & J. VERHEYDEN (eds.), *The Four Gospels 1992. Festschrift Frans Neirynck,* 1992. 3 volumes, XVII-X-X-2668 p. 125 €

SERIES III

101. A. DENAUX (ed.), *John and the Synoptics,* 1992. XXII-696 p. 75 €
102. F. NEIRYNCK, J. VERHEYDEN, F. VAN SEGBROECK, G. VAN OYEN & R. CORSTJENS, *The Gospel of Mark. A Cumulative Bibliography: 1950-1990,* 1992. XII-717 p. 68 €
103. M. SIMON, *Un catéchisme universel pour l'Église catholique. Du Concile de Trente à nos jours,* 1992. XIV-461 p. 55 €
104. L. CEYSSENS, *Le sort de la bulle Unigenitus. Recueil d'études offert à Lucien Ceyssens à l'occasion de son 90ᵉ anniversaire.* Présenté par M. LAMBERIGTS, 1992. XXVI-641 p. 50 €
105. R.J. DALY (ed.), *Origeniana Quinta. Papers of the 5th International Origen Congress, Boston College, 14-18 August 1989,* 1992. XVII-635 p. 68 €
106. A.S. VAN DER WOUDE (ed.), *The Book of Daniel in the Light of New Findings,* 1993. XVIII-574 p. 75 €
107. J. FAMERÉE, *L'ecclésiologie d'Yves Congar avant Vatican II: Histoire et Église. Analyse et reprise critique,* 1992. 497 p. 65 €

108. C. BEGG, *Josephus' Account of the Early Divided Monarchy (AJ 8, 212-420). Rewriting the Bible*, 1993. IX-377 p.   60 €

109. J. BULCKENS & H. LOMBAERTS (eds.), *L'enseignement de la religion catholique à l'école secondaire. Enjeux pour la nouvelle Europe*, 1993. XII-264 p.   32 €

110. C. FOCANT (ed.), *The Synoptic Gospels. Source Criticism and the New Literary Criticism*, 1993. XXXIX-670 p.   75 €

111. M. LAMBERIGTS (ed.), avec la collaboration de L. KENIS, *L'augustinisme à l'ancienne Faculté de théologie de Louvain*, 1994. VII-455 p.
                    60 €

112. R. BIERINGER & J. LAMBRECHT, *Studies on 2 Corinthians*, 1994. XX-632 p.
                    75 €

113. E. BRITO, *La pneumatologie de Schleiermacher*, 1994. XII-649 p. 75 €

114. W.A.M. BEUKEN (ed.), *The Book of Job*, 1994. X-462 p.   60 €

115. J. LAMBRECHT, *Pauline Studies: Collected Essays*, 1994. XIV-465 p.
                    63 €

116. G. VAN BELLE, *The Signs Source in the Fourth Gospel: Historical Survey and Critical Evaluation of the Semeia Hypothesis*, 1994. XIV-503 p.
                    63 €

117. M. LAMBERIGTS & P. VAN DEUN (eds.), *Martyrium in Multidisciplinary Perspective. Memorial L. Reekmans*, 1995. X-435 p.   75 €

118. G. DORIVAL & A. LE BOULLUEC (eds.), *Origeniana Sexta. Origène et la Bible / Origen and the Bible. Actes du Colloquium Origenianum Sextum, Chantilly, 30 août – 3 septembre 1993*, 1995. XII-865 p.   98 €

119. É. GAZIAUX, *Morale de la foi et morale autonome. Confrontation entre P. Delhaye et J. Fuchs*, 1995. XXII-545 p.   68 €

120. T.A. SALZMAN, *Deontology and Teleology: An Investigation of the Normative Debate in Roman Catholic Moral Theology*, 1995. XVII-555 p.
                    68 €.

121. G.R. EVANS & M. GOURGUES (eds.), *Communion et Réunion. Mélanges Jean-Marie Roger Tillard*, 1995. XI-431 p.   60 €

122. H.T. FLEDDERMANN, *Mark and Q: A Study of the Overlap Texts*. With an *Assessment* by F. NEIRYNCK, 1995. XI-307 p.   45 €

123. R. BOUDENS, *Two Cardinals: John Henry Newman, Désiré-Joseph Mercier*. Edited by L. GEVERS with the collaboration of B. DOYLE, 1995. 362 p.   45 €

124. A. THOMASSET, *Paul Ricœur. Une poétique de la morale. Aux fondements d'une éthique herméneutique et narrative dans une perspective chrétienne*, 1996. XVI-706 p.   75 €

125. R. BIERINGER (ed.), *The Corinthian Correspondence*, 1996. XXVII-793 p.
                    60 €

126. M. VERVENNE (ed.), *Studies in the Book of Exodus: Redaction – Reception – Interpretation*, 1996. XI-660 p.   60 €

127. A. VANNESTE, *Nature et grâce dans la théologie occidentale. Dialogue avec H. de Lubac*, 1996. 312 p.   45 €

128. A. CURTIS & T. RÖMER (eds.), *The Book of Jeremiah and its Reception – Le livre de Jérémie et sa réception*, 1997. 331 p.   60 €

129. E. LANNE, *Tradition et Communion des Églises. Recueil d'études*, 1997. XXV-703 p.   75 €

130. A. DENAUX & J.A. DICK (eds.), *From Malines to ARCIC. The Malines Conversations Commemorated*, 1997. IX-317 p. 45 €
131. C.M. TUCKETT (ed.), *The Scriptures in the Gospels*, 1997. XXIV-721 p. 60 €
132. J. VAN RUITEN & M. VERVENNE (eds.), *Studies in the Book of Isaiah. Festschrift Willem A.M. Beuken*, 1997. XX-540 p. 75 €
133. M. VERVENNE & J. LUST (eds.), *Deuteronomy and Deuteronomic Literature. Festschrift C.H.W. Brekelmans*, 1997. XI-637 p. 75 €
134. G. VAN BELLE (ed.), *Index Generalis ETL / BETL 1982-1997*, 1999. IX-337 p. 40 €
135. G. DE SCHRIJVER, *Liberation Theologies on Shifting Grounds. A Clash of Socio-Economic and Cultural Paradigms*, 1998. XI-453 p. 53 €
136. A. SCHOORS (ed.), *Qohelet in the Context of Wisdom*, 1998. XI-528 p. 60 €
137. W.A. BIENERT & U. KÜHNEWEG (eds.), *Origeniana Septima. Origenes in den Auseinandersetzungen des 4. Jahrhunderts*, 1999. XXV-848 p. 95 €
138. É. GAZIAUX, *L'autonomie en morale: au croisement de la philosophie et de la théologie*, 1998. XVI-760 p. 75 €
139. J. GROOTAERS, *Actes et acteurs à Vatican II*, 1998. XXIV-602 p. 75 €
140. F. NEIRYNCK, J. VERHEYDEN & R. CORSTJENS, *The Gospel of Matthew and the Sayings Source Q: A Cumulative Bibliography 1950-1995*, 1998. 2 vols., VII-1000-420* p. 95 €
141. E. BRITO, *Heidegger et l'hymne du sacré*, 1999. XV-800 p. 90 €
142. J. VERHEYDEN (ed.), *The Unity of Luke-Acts*, 1999. XXV-828 p. 60 €
143. N. CALDUCH-BENAGES & J. VERMEYLEN (eds.), *Treasures of Wisdom. Studies in Ben Sira and the Book of Wisdom. Festschrift M. Gilbert*, 1999. XXVII-463 p. 75 €
144. J.-M. AUWERS & A. WÉNIN (eds.), *Lectures et relectures de la Bible. Festschrift P.-M. Bogaert*, 1999. XLII-482 p. 75 €
145. C. BEGG, *Josephus' Story of the Later Monarchy (AJ 9,1–10,185)*, 2000. X-650 p. 75 €
146. J.M. ASGEIRSSON, K. DE TROYER & M.W. MEYER (eds.), *From Quest to Q. Festschrift James M. Robinson*, 2000. XLIV-346 p. 60 €
147. T. RÖMER (ed.), *The Future of the Deuteronomistic History*, 2000. XII-265 p. 75 €
148. F.D. VANSINA, *Paul Ricœur: Bibliographie primaire et secondaire - Primary and Secondary Bibliography 1935-2000*, 2000. XXVI-544 p. 75 €
149. G.J. BROOKE & J.D. KAESTLI (eds.), *Narrativity in Biblical and Related Texts*, 2000. XXI-307 p. 75 €
150. F. NEIRYNCK, *Evangelica III: 1992-2000. Collected Essays*, 2001. XVII-666 p. 60 €
151. B. DOYLE, *The Apocalypse of Isaiah Metaphorically Speaking. A Study of the Use, Function and Significance of Metaphors in Isaiah 24-27*, 2000. XII-453 p. 75 €
152. T. MERRIGAN & J. HAERS (eds.), *The Myriad Christ. Plurality and the Quest for Unity in Contemporary Christology*, 2000. XIV-593 p. 75 €
153. M. SIMON, *Le catéchisme de Jean-Paul II. Genèse et évaluation de son commentaire du Symbole des apôtres*, 2000. XVI-688 p. 75 €

154. J. VERMEYLEN, *La loi du plus fort. Histoire de la rédaction des récits davidiques de 1 Samuel 8 à 1 Rois 2*, 2000. XIII-746 p. 80 €
155. A. WÉNIN (ed.), *Studies in the Book of Genesis. Literature, Redaction and History*, 2001. XXX-643 p. 60 €
156. F. LEDEGANG, *Mysterium Ecclesiae. Images of the Church and its Members in Origen*, 2001. XVII-848 p. 84 €
157. J.S. BOSWELL, F.P. MCHUGH & J. VERSTRAETEN (eds.), *Catholic Social Thought: Twilight of Renaissance*, 2000. XXII-307 p. 60 €
158. A. LINDEMANN (ed.), *The Sayings Source Q and the Historical Jesus*, 2001. XXII-776 p. 60 €
159. C. HEMPEL, A. LANGE & H. LICHTENBERGER (eds.), *The Wisdom Texts from Qumran and the Development of Sapiential Thought*, 2002. XII-502 p. 80 €
160. L. BOEVE & L. LEIJSSEN (eds.), *Sacramental Presence in a Postmodern Context*, 2001. XVI-382 p. 60 €
161. A. DENAUX (ed.), *New Testament Textual Criticism and Exegesis. Festschrift J. Delobel*, 2002. XVIII-391 p. 60 €
162. U. BUSSE, *Das Johannesevangelium. Bildlichkeit, Diskurs und Ritual. Mit einer Bibliographie über den Zeitraum 1986-1998*, 2002. XIII-572 p. 70 €
163. J.-M. AUWERS & H.J. DE JONGE (eds.), *The Biblical Canons*, 2003. LXXXVIII-718 p. 60 €
164. L. PERRONE (ed.), *Origeniana Octava. Origen and the Alexandrian Tradition*, 2003. Forthcoming.
165. R. BIERINGER, V. KOPERSKI & B. LATAIRE (eds.), *Resurrection in the New Testament. Festschrift J. Lambrecht*, 2002. XXXI-551 p. 70 €
166. M. LAMBERIGTS & L. KENIS (eds.), *Vatican II and Its Legacy*, 2002. XII-512 p. 65 €
167. P. DIEUDONNÉ, *La Paix clémentine. Défaite et victoire du premier jansénisme français sous le pontificat de Clément IX (1667-1669)*, 2003. XXXIX-302 p. 70 €

PRINTED ON PERMANENT PAPER • IMPRIME SUR PAPIER PERMANENT • GEDRUKT OP DUURZAAM PAPIER - ISO 9706

N.V. PEETERS S.A., WAROTSTRAAT 50, B-3020 HERENT